RULERS
AND
GOVERNMENTS
OF THE WORLD

RULERS AND GOVERNMENTS OF THE WORLD
General Editor: C. G. Allen

Volume 1
Earliest Times to 1491
Compiled by Martha Ross

Volume 2
1492 to 1929
Compiled by Bertold Spuler

Volume 3
1930 to 1975
Compiled by Bertold Spuler

RULERS
AND
GOVERNMENTS
OF THE WORLD

Volume 2
1492 to 1929

BERTOLD SPULER

BOWKER
LONDON & NEW YORK

First published 1977 in Great Britain by Bowker Publishing Company Limited, Epping, Essex and in the United States of America by R. R. Bowker Co., 1180 Avenue of the Americas, New York, NY 10036

ISBN for this volume 0 85935 009 6
ISBN for complete set of 3 volumes 0 85935 051 7
Library of Congress catalog card number 77-702-94

Translated from German by John Fletcher
Translation edited by C. G. Allen

This book is a translation of *Regenten und Regierungen der Welt*, compiled by Bertold Spuler, volume 3, *Neuere Zeit 1492-1918*, 2nd edition, published by A. G. Ploetz Verlag, Würzburg, 1963 (ISBN 3 87640 023 6; copyright A. G. Ploetz Verlag 1963) and part of volume 4, *Neueste Zeit 1917/18-1964*, 2nd edition, published by A. G. Ploetz Verlag, Würzburg, 1964 (ISBN 3 87640 024 4; copyright A. G. Ploetz Verlag 1964). The translation has been updated.

Printed in Great Britain by
Thomson Litho Ltd., East Kilbride, Scotland.

Preface

A generation of reference librarians has found in Bertold Spuler's *Regenten und Regierungen der Welt*, first published in 1953, a handy and comprehensive guide to those in power at various times in various countries and to the basic biographical facts about them. But to make full use of it one did need to be competent in German. Volumes 2 and 3 of this English version are based on the second edition of volumes 3 and 4 of *Regenten und Regierungen der Welt*, covering respectively the periods 1492 to 1918 and 1917/18 to 1964, which appeared in 1964, and on the supplements thereto. Volume 1 of the English version is entirely new, and coverage of volume 3 has been extended to the end of 1975. To have followed the German edition in breaking at 1917/18 would have produced an unduly swollen third volume, and it was decided, with some regrets, to make the break at the end of 1929. This date has no special significance, but as the irregular dating of the German original suggests, it is in fact impossible to find a date when the whole world neatly changes. As in the original, rulers and ministers whose periods of power span the break appear in both volumes.

The characteristics of this edition remain the same as those of the original, of which (volume 1 apart) it is basically a translation, reproducing in English form the abundant materials which Dr Spuler has collected over the years from archival sources, from reliable histories and reference works, from expert informants and from the press. As the introductions make clear, additions and revisions have been made, but what Dr Spuler modestly refers to as 'the arbitrary element' remains. To keep the task and the published volumes within reasonable bounds it has at all times been necessary to restrict the number of states covered and the detail given about each state. It is hoped that the selection reflects the needs of the majority of users of the work. All rulers are given for every state included. For major countries in the modern era, complete lists of cabinets are given; for other states, only the names of prime ministers.

Similarly, though new material is always coming to light and historical judgements are continually being revised, there must inevitably be a limit to the number of sources to which the editors of *Rulers and Governments of the World* can refer. It is believed, however, that the English edition will be of great value to its users just as the German editions have been. The publishers will of course be very grateful for corrections and suggestions for improvement.

The present editor gratefully acknowledges the generous help of the libraries of the Australian and Canadian High Commissions, the South African Embassy, of the School of Slavonic and East European Studies, the School of Oriental and African Studies and the Institute of Historical Research, the British Library of Political and Economic Science, the Scandinavian Library at University College London and the British Library.

C. G. Allen

Introduction to Volume 2

This volume is substantially a translation of volume 3 and parts of volume 4 of the German original. However, both the process of giving the work an English dress and the new division of the volumes have brought new perspectives and information, which have led to revisions and additions, in places considerable.

Most national states, the principal German provinces, such independent Italian cities and territories as had a single ruler or, at most, a pair, and such other autonomous duchies, principalities or other territories as seemed sufficiently interesting or important have been included. From Africa, however, only the Mediterranean states, Ethiopia, Zanzibar and South Africa are given (as in the German edition). Since the publication schedule made it difficult to assemble material for other African states in time for this volume, it will be included in volume 1. However, cross-references to the new material will be found throughout the present volume.

All states are listed under their English names, with references from variants and from the names of those states which for some reason are subsumed under another, as Florence is under Tuscany. Where necessary, the entry begins with a brief note explaining the origin of the state. The names of the successive heads of state follow, the title being given in English, unless there is no recognized equivalent. Changes of dynasty and regime are indicated, but the whole is one sequence. In the case of self-governing colonies and dominions the names of the representatives of the home country (governors, commissioners, etc.) are given. The date of accession, appointment, election or usurpation is given in the left-hand column, and unless otherwise stated the period of rule extends until the date next below. Where it can be done with reasonable consistency, the month and day are given, but for some countries and periods we have had to be content with the year alone. Uncertain dates are accompanied by a question mark, and when information is lacking, the day, month, year, or the whole date is replaced by one. Occasionally, where authorities or the criteria for establishing a date differ, two dates are given, and in some cases, as for instance when converting the years of other calendars, a pair of years. Periods of foreign domination, resulting in gaps in the sequence or the presence of rival claimants, are noted at the appropriate point.

Against the date stands the name of the head of state, with date of birth if known. The date of death of a hereditary ruler is not given unless it differs from the date of accession of his successor, nor usually his place of birth or death. Full information is given where practicable for other heads of state. Where a ruler has a broken reign or a president serves more than once, the biographical information is given the first time only. Names of monarchs are given in their English form where it is still customary to do so; but usage being variable, the form may not always be that to which any particular reader is accustomed.

A dash (——) in a name means that it has not been possible to discover the person's forename.

The lists of members of governments follow. In the simplest cases these consist of a list of prime ministers (or their equivalent in the constitution of the state concerned), with or without a list of foreign ministers. For Germany and Russia separate lists of a number of different ministers are given for the period preceding the formation of regular cabinets. In all these lists the treatment of the entries is the same as for non-hereditary heads of state. (For England see p. x below.) For a limited number of countries ministries are given and the layout is different. The covering dates of the ministry and the name by which it is known, usually that of the prime minister, are given as a heading. The left-hand column contains the names of the departments, headed by the prime minister and continuing with foreign and home affairs. The order of the remaining posts varies from country to country, even where comparable posts exist, and changes gradually over time within a single country, but is fairly consistent from one cabinet to the next. No attempt is made to indicate the order of precedence within the cabinet, if any. The names of posts are given in English translation, but the posts are not equated with English ones or with each other. Where no date is given, ministers can be taken to remain in office for the duration of the ministry; where they change, their period of office is given before the name and acting office indicated where appropriate. Where there are gaps between ministries, as happens in the Netherlands, this does not preclude the individual ministers remaining at their posts until the formation of a new ministry. Biographical details are given, as for heads of state, on first mention, and on subsequent occasions a reference is made to the name of the ministry in which the minister in question first held office.

Though in the 19th century many politicians from Central Europe and the Balkans were still referred to in English sources by English (or French) forms of their Christian names, the practice is no longer common today except for Greek names. Accordingly all names except Greek ones are given in the vernacular form. (As they had to be converted from German, it is possible that some have been incorrectly left in German form; but it must also be remembered that Hungarians and Czechs, for instance, might have German names.) In the same pragmatic spirit the transcription of names not in the Latin alphabet has been carried out somewhat loosely, with the result, one hopes, that most readers will find them in the form to which they are accustomed. Thus in Greek both eta and iota are transliterated as i, as they are by most Greeks. The Russian terminations - ий and - ый are both reduced to -y, as in Trotsky; the soft sign has been ignored or represented by y, as in the common sequence -yev-. No diacritical marks are used in the transliteration of the Arabic alphabet, nor are long vowels distinguished. Local variations of pronunciation, inconsistent with the standard transliteration, are taken account of, as are accepted conventional transcriptions. Chinese names are given in Wade–Giles transcription, these being the forms which as yet most users will meet elsewhere.

In the German edition of this work, the Christian names of statesmen of a number of European countries are given in their German form, and as it was dangerous to attempt to restore the vernacular form by rule (four different Hungarian names are represented by the German Andreas), recourse was had to vernacular reference books, so that additional biographical information was obtained in the process. This applies to Czechoslovakia, Croatia, Estonia, Finland, Hungary, Lithuania and Poland. In the case of Albania, Courland, Romania and the Ukraine new historical sources came to light and revisions of substance were carried out. The new division of volumes resulted in the addition of the Greek and Spanish foreign ministers from 1833 to 1918, and some revision of other dates was carried out at the same time. Other changes of miscellaneous origin have been the addition of biographical details for Denmark and Norway, entries for Genoa, Lucca, Mantua and Milan, considerable additions under Monaco and some revisions and additions under the Netherlands. Conversely France, though amplified in respect of biographical details, has been slimmed in places by the omission of junior ministers. So has Germany, and in view of the termination of hereditary rule and the increased centralization under the Weimar republic entries for the German Länder end at 1918.

The entry for the United Kingdom (under which England and Wales is subsumed) has been considerably altered. To avoid any premature suggestion of a prime minister and his cabinet a clear break has been made at 1721. Before that date the *de facto* chief ministers of the crown are listed against a skeleton chronology under the head of Principal Counsellors and the more important offices held by them are given, with their dates. In the same way, but in a separate list, the names and offices of certain subordinate ministers are given. From Walpole's first ministry onwards, this being the traditional beginning of the premiership, the ministries have been listed in cabinet form, but the cabinets are notional from 1721 to 1782, since there is no fixed membership. From 1782 the lists are strictly those of the official cabinet, and for this reason the names given sometimes differ from those in the German edition.

Of the Asian states the lists for Burma, Cambodia, Indo-China, Laos, Nepal, Thailand, Tibet and Viet-Nam have been considerably revised and enlarged, and some revision and addition of biographical details have taken place in the case of China, India and Turkey. The entry for Mongolia has been recast in light of recent demythologizing, and Georgia also has been thoroughly revised, with the addition of the rulers of Imereti.

The entries for New Zealand and still more for Australia, Canada and South Africa have been greatly amplified, and numerous smaller revisions and additions made to the Latin American entries.

C. G. Allen

Index of States

Afghanistan

Part of Indian Empire until the early 18th century.

HEADS OF STATE

Khans

House of Durrani

1747	*Ahmad Shah*
1773	*Timur Shah*, son
1793	*Zeman Shah*, son
1799	*Mahmud Shah*, brother (for 1st time)
1803	*Shah Shuja*, brother (for 1st time) deposed
1810	*Mahmud Shah* (for 2nd time) exiled in 1818
1818 – 1826	Various independent khanates

House of Barakzai

1826 (1835)	*Dost Mohammed Khan* (for 1st time) abdicated
1839 – 1841	*Shah Shuja* (for 2nd time)
1842	*Dost Mohammed Khan* (for 2nd time)
29 May 1863	*Sher Ali Khan*, son (for 1st time) (b. 1825; d. 21 Feb 1879)
5 May 1866	*Afzal Khan*, brother
Oct 1867	*Azam Khan*, brother (d. 12 Oct 1869)
Mar 1869	*Sher Ali Khan* (for 2nd time)
21 Feb 1879	*Yaqub Khan*, son (b. 1849; d. 15 Nov 1923)
24 Dec 1879	*Musa Khan*, son
Mar 1880	*Ayub Khan*, uncle
4 Oct 1881	*Abdur Rahman Khan*, son of Afzal Khan (b. 1845)
3 Oct 1901	*Habibullah Khan*, son (b. 3 Jul 1872)
20 Feb 1919	*Amanullah Khan*, son (for 1st time) (b. 1 Jun 1892; d. Zurich 25 Apr 1960)
14 Jan 1929	*Inayatullah Khan*, brother (b. 20 Oct 1888)
17 Jan – 17 Oct 1929 *	*Habibullah Ghazi* (Bacha-i-Saqqo) (d. 3 Nov 1929) usurper
17 Oct 1929 – 8 Nov 1933	*Nadir Shah*, great-nephew of Dost Mohammed (b. 10 Apr 1880)

* 28 Jan – 15 Jul 1929	*Ali Ahmad Khan*, pretender
28 Jan – 23 May 1929	*Amanullah Khan* (for 2nd time) abdicated

1

MEMBERS OF GOVERNMENT

Prime Ministers

14 Nov 1929 – May 1946	*Sardar Mohammed Hashim Khan* (b. Dehra Dun, India, between 1882 and 1885; d. Kabul 26 Oct 1953)

Akan (Bron) States

For Akwamu, Ashanti, Bono and Denkyera, Akan states of the 13th to 19th centuries, occupying modern Ghana and parts of Togo and the Ivory Coast, see volume 1.

Albania

From 15th century until 1912 part of the Turkish Empire.

HEADS OF STATE

President

28 Nov 1912	*Ismail Qemal*

Prince

7 Mar – 2 Sep 1914	*William I (Frederick Henry), Price of Wied* (b. 26 Mar 1876; d. 18 Apr 1945) left country but did not formally abdicate
Sept 1914 – Nov 1918 *	Occupied by France, Italy and Austria
* 2 Oct 1914 – 24 Feb 1916	*Esad Toptani* (b. 1863; d. 13 Mar 1920) occupied Tirana and proclaimed himself head of government

Councils of Regency

Apr 1920	*Aqif Pashë Elbasani, Mgr Luigj Bumçi, Mihal Turtulli, Abdi Toptani*
25 Dec 1921	*Omer Vrioni*, resigned Feb 1922, *Sotir Peci, Antoine (Ndoc) Pistulli*, resigned Feb 1922, *Refik Toptani*
Dec 1922	*Xhafer Ypi* (d. 19 Nov 1940), *Sotir Peci, Gjon Coba, Refik Toptani*

President

31 Jan 1925 – 31 Aug 1928	*Achmed Bey Zogu* (b. Burgajet 8 Oct 1895; d. Suresnes, France, 9 Apr 1961) also Prime Minister; from 1 Sept 1928, King (see below)

King

House of Mat

1 Sep 1928 – 8 Apr 1939	*Achmed Zogu* (see President) formally abdicated 2 Jan 1946

MEMBERS OF GOVERNMENT

Prime Ministers

Mar – summer 1914	*Turhan Pashë Permëti* (for 1st time)
2 Oct 1914	*Esad Toptani* (see Heads of State)
1914	*Abdullah Rushdi*
28 Dec 1918	*Turhan Pashë Permëti* (for 2nd time)
27 Mar – 20 Nov 1920	*Sulejman Delvina*
10 Dec 1920 – mid-Oct 1921	*Iljaz Bej Vrioni* (for 1st time) (b. Berat 1883; d. Paris 17 Mar 1932)
19 Oct – 6 Dec 1921	*Pandeli Evangeli* (for 1st time) (b. Korça 1859)
24-30 Dec 1921	*Xhafer Ypi* (see Councils of Regency)
30 Dec 1921 – Dec 1922	*Omer Vrioni* (see Councils of Regency)
24 Dec 1922	*Achmed Zogu* (for 1st time) (see President)
27 May – 10 Jun 1924	*Iljaz Bej Vrioni* (for 2nd time)

16 Jun – 24 Dec 1924	*Fan (Theophanes) Noli, Bishop of Valona* (b. Ibrik Tepe 6 Jan 1882; d. Fort Lauderdale, Florida, 14 Mar 1965)
6 – 31 Jan 1925	*Achmed Zogu* (for 2nd time)
9 Feb 1925 – 11 Feb 1927	*Achmed Zogu* (for 3rd time)
14 Feb – 21 Oct 1927	*Achmed Zogu* (for 4th time)
24 Oct 1927 – 10 May 1928	*Achmed Zogu* (for 5th time)
12 May – 1 Sep 1928	*Achmed Zogu* (for 6th time) from 1 Sep 1928, King
7 Sep 1928 – 12 Jan 1929	*Koço Kota* (for 1st time) (b. Korça 1889; d. 1949(?))
15 Jan 1929 – 3 Mar 1930	*Koço Kota* (for 2nd time)

Algeria

HEADS OF STATE

Military Commanders

11 Apr 1830	*Louis de Chaisne, Comte Bourmont* (b. Bourmont 2 Sep 1773; d. 27 Oct 1846)
12 Aug 1830	*Bertrand Comte Clausel* (b. Mirepoix 12 Dec 1772; d. Toulouse 21 April 1842)
21 Feb 1831	*Pierre Baron Berthezène* (b. Vendargues 1775; d. 1847)
6 Dec 1831	*(Anne Jean Marie) René Savary, Duc de Rovigo* (b. Marcq 26 Apr 1774; d. Paris 2 Jun 1833)
29 Apr 1833	(acting:) *Théophile Viorol*

Governors General (of the French Possessions in North Africa; from 1845 'of Algeria')

27 Jul 1834	*Jean Baptiste Drouet, Comte d'Erlon* (b. Reims 29 Jul 1765; d. Paris 25 Jan 1844)
8 Jul 1835	*Bertrand Comte Clausel* (see Military Commanders)

12 Feb – 12 Oct 1837	*Charles Marie Denys Comte de Danremont* (b. Chaumont 8 Feb 1793; d. Constantine 12 Oct 1837)
11 Nov (1 Dec) 1837	*Sylvain Charles Comte Valée* (b. Brienne-le-Château 1773; d. Paris 1846)
Dec 1840	*Thomas Robert Bugeaud de la Piconnerie* (from 1844: *Duc d'Isly*) (b. Limoges 15 Oct 1784; d. Paris 10 Jun 1849)
1 Sep 1845	(acting:) *Christophe Juchault de Lamoricière* (b. Nantes 5 Feb 1806; d. Prouzel 11 Sep 1865)
6 Jul 1847	(acting:) *Marie Alphonse Bedeau* (b. Vertou 10 Aug 1804; d. Vertou 28 Aug 1863)
27 Sep 1847	*Henri Eugène Philippe Louis d'Orléans, Duc d'Aumale*, 4th son of King Louis Philippe of France (b. Paris 16 Jan 1822; d. Sicily 7 May 1897)
24 Feb 1848	*Eugène Cavaignac* (b. Paris 15 Oct 1802; d. Ournes 28 Oct 1857)
29 Apr 1848	*Nicholas Théodule Changarnier* (b. Autun 26 Apr 1793; d. Paris 14 Feb 1877)
9 Sep 1848	*Baron Viala Charon* (b. Paris 29 Jul 1794; d. Paris 26 Nov 1880)
22 Oct 1850	*Alphonse Comte d' Hautpoul* (b. Versailles 4 Jan 1789; d. Paris 28 Jul 1865)
10 May 1851	*Aimable Jean Jacques Pélissier* (from 1856: *Duc de Malakoff*) (b. Maromme 6 Nov 1794; d. Algiers 22 May 1864)
11 Dec 1851 – 31 Aug 1858	*Jacques Louis César Alexandre Comte Randon* (b. Grenoble 25 Mar 1795; d. Geneva 15 Jan 1871)

Ministers for Algeria and the Colonies

24 Jun 1858	*Prince Napoleon Bonaparte*, son of King Jerome of Westphalia (b. Trieste 9 Sept 1822; d. Rome 18 Mar 1891)
21 Mar 1859	*Prosper Comte de Chasseloup-Laubat* (b. Alessandria 29 Mar 1805; d. Versailles 29 Mar 1873)
24 Nov 1860 – 22 May 1864	*Aimable Pélissier, Duc de Malakoff* (see Governors General)
1 Sep 1864	*Marie Edmé Patrice Maurice de Mac-Mahon, Duc de Magenta* (b. Sully 13 Jul 1808; d. Loiret 17 Oct 1893)
27 Jul 1870	(acting:) *Louis Baron Durieu*
23 Oct 1870	(acting:) *Jean Walsin-Esterhazy* (b. 1804)
24 Oct 1870	*Henry Gabriel Didier* (b. Fresnes 12 May 1807; d. 23 Dec 1891) Civil Governor, did not take office

Special Commissioners of the Republic

16 Nov 1870	*Charles de Bouzet*, Prefect of Oran
8 Feb 1871	*Alexis Lambert*, Prefect of Oran

Governors General

29 Mar 1871	*Louis Comte de Gueydon* (b. Granville 22 Nov 1809; d. Paris 1 Dec 1886)
10 Jun 1873	*Antoine Eugène Alfred Chanzy* (b. Nouart 18 Mar 1823; d. Chalons-sur-Marne 4 Jan 1883)
15 Mar 1870	(acting:) *Albert Grévy* (b. Mont-sous-Vaudrey 23 Aug 1824; d. Mont-sous-Vaudrey 11 Jul 1899)
26 Nov 1881	*Louis Tirman* (b. Mézières 1837; d. Château Taboureaux 1899)
18 Apr 1891	*Jules Cambon* (b. Paris 5 Apr 1845; d. Vevey 19 Sep 1935)
28 Sep 1897	*Auguste Loze* (b. Le Cateau 1850; de. Paris 1915) declined appointment
1 Oct 1897	*Louis Lépine* (b. Lyon 1846; d. Paris 1933)
26 July 1898	*Edouard Laferrière* (b. Angoulême 1813; d. Bournonne-les-Bains 1901)
3 Oct 1900	(acting:) *Célestin Charles Jonnart* (for 1st time) (b. Fléchin 27 Dec 1857; d. Paris 30 Sep 1927)
18 Jun 1901	*Paul Revoil* (b. Nîmes 1856; d. Arles 1914)
11 Apr 1903	(acting:) *Maurice Varnier*
5 May 1903	(acting:) *Célestin Charles Jonnart* (for 2nd time)
22 May 1911	*Charles Lutaud*
29 Jan 1918 – 29 Aug 1919	(acting:) *Célestin Charles Jonnart* (for 3rd time)
29 Aug 1919 – 28 Jul 1921	*Jean Baptiste Eugène Abel* (b. Toulon 12 Jan 1863; d. Toulon 30 Sep 1921)
28 Jul 1921 – 17 Apr 1925	*Théodore Steeg* (b. Libourne 19 Dec 1868; d. Paris 10 Dec 1950)
17 Apr 1925 – 12 May 1925	(acting:) *Henri Dubief*
12 May 1925 – 20 Nov 1927	*Maurice Viollette* (b. Janville 3 Sep 1870; d. Paris 9 Sep 1960)
20 Nov 1927 – 3 Oct 1930	*Pierre Louis Bordes*

Argentina

Late 16th century	Part of Spanish Empire
25 May 1810	Local junta seized power from Viceroy and set up 'United Provinces of the Río de la Plata' (including modern Argentina, Bolivia, Paraguay and Uruguay) declaring loyalty to deposed Spanish king, Ferdinand VII
1814	Paraguay seceded
1816	Uruguay invaded by and incorporated in Brazil
9 July 1816	United Provinces of the Río de la Plata declared independent but each province ruled by local juntas or caudillos without central government until 1825-6
6 Aug 1825	Independence of Bolivia

HEADS OF STATE

Presidents

5 Feb 1826 – 27 Jul 1827	*Bernardino Rivadavia* (b. Buenos Aires 20 May 1780; d. Cadiz, Spain, 2 Sep 1845)
7 Jul – Aug 1827	*Vicente López y Planes* (b. Buenos Aires 3 May 1785; d. Buenos Aires 10 Oct 1856)
1827 – 1829	Presidency in abeyance
6 Dec 1829	*Don Juan Manuel de Rosas* (for 1st time) (b. 30 Mar 1793; d. 14 Mar 1877) from 14 Jul 1827 Commandant General of the forces in the province of Buenos Aires
1832 – Aug 1835	*Juan Ramón Balcarce* (b. Buenos Aires 16 Mar 1773; d. Concepción 12 Nov 1836)
1835 – 3 Feb 1852	*Don Juan Manuel de Rosas* (for 2nd time)
23 Jun 1852 – 1860 *	*Justo José de Urquiza* (b. 1800; d. 12 Apr 1870) in opposition, from 5 Mar 1854 President
5 Mar 1860 – Sep 1861	*Santiago Derqui* (b. Cordoba 9 Jul 1810; d. Corrientes 5 Sep 1867)
* 11 Sep 1852 – 6 Jun 1860	Secession of Buenos Aires province from the rest of Argentina
Sep 1852	*Valentin Alsina*, Governor of Buenos Aires
1857	—— *Obligado*, President of Buenos Aires

14 Oct 1862 – 12 Oct 1868	*Bartolomé Mitré* (b. Buenos Aires 26 Jun 1821; d. Buenos Aires 19 Jan 1906)
1865 – Jan 1868	*Vice-President Marcos Paz* (d. Jan 1868) in charge of Government during President Mitré's absence in Paraguay
12 Oct 1868	*Domingo Faustino Sarmiento* (b. 13 Feb 1811; d. 12 Sep 1888)
12 Oct 1874	*Nicolas Avellaneda* (b. 1 Oct 1836; d. 26 Dec 1888) *Julio Argentino Roca* (for 1st time) (b. 1843; d. 19 Oct 1914)
12 Oct 1886	*Miguel Juarez Celman,* brother-in-law (b. 29 Sep 1844; d. 17 Dec 1907)
6 Aug 1890	*Carlos Pellegrini* (b. 1848; d. 17 Jun 1906)
12 Oct 1892 – Jan 1895	*Luis Saenz Peña* (b. 1823; d. 4 Jul 1907)
23 Jan 1895	*José Evaristo Uriburu* (b. 19 Nov 1831; d. 23 Oct 1914)
12 Oct 1898	*Julio Roca* (for 2nd time)
12 Oct 1904	*Manuel Quintana* (b. 1834; d. 12 Mar 1906)
12 Mar 1906	*José Figueroa Alcorta* (b. 1860; d. 1931)
12 Oct 1910	*Roque Saenz Peña,* son of Luis Saenz Peña (b. 19 Mar 1851; d. 11 Aug 1914)
Apr 1914	*Victorino de la Plaza* (b. 1839; d. 29 Sep 1919)
12 Oct 1916	*Hipólito Irigoyen* (for 1st time) (b. 13 Jul 1850; d. 3 Jul 1933)
12 Oct 1922	*Marcelo Torcuato de Alvear* (b. 4 Oct 1868; d. 23 Mar 1942)
1 Apr 1928 – 7 Sep 1930	*Hipólito Irigoyen* (for 2nd time)

MEMBERS OF GOVERNMENT

Foreign Ministers

1917	*Honorio J. Pueyrredón* (b. Buenos Aires 9 Jul 1876; d. 23 Sep 1945)
12 Oct 1922	*Angel Gallardo* (b. Buenos Aires 19 Nov 1867; d. Buenos Aires 13 May 1934)
12 Oct 1928 – 7 Sep 1930	*Horacio B. Oyhanarte* (b. Rojas 1885; d. Buenos Aires 7 Nov 1946)

Australia

1 Jan 1901	Western Australia, South Australia, New South Wales, Victoria, Tasmania and Queensland joined to form the Commonwealth of Australia within the then British Empire

Governors General

1 Jan 1901	*John Adrian Louis Hope, 7th Earl of Hopetown* (from 1902: *1st Marquis of Linlithgow*) (b. Hopetown 25 Sep 1860; d. Pau 29 Feb 1908)
17 Jul 1902	*Hallam Tennyson, 2nd Baron* (b. 11 Aug 1852; d. 2 Dec 1928)
21 Jan 1904	*Henry Stafford Northcote, 1st Baron* (b. London 18 Nov 1846; d. Ashford, Kent 29 Sep 1911)
9 Sep 1908	*William Humble Ward, 2nd Earl of Dudley* (b. London 25 May 1867; d. London 29 Jun 1932)
31 Jul 1911	*Thomas Denman, 3rd Baron* (b. 16 Nov 1874; d. Hove 24 Jun 1954)
18 May 1914	*Ronald Craufurd Munro-Ferguson* (from 1920: *1st Viscount Novar*) b. Kirkcaldy 6 Mar 1860; d. Raith 30 Mar 1934)
6 Oct 1920	*Henry William Forster, 1st Baron* (b. 31 Jan 1866; d. 15 Jan 1936)
8 Oct 1925 – 2 Oct 1930	*John Lawrence Baird* (from 1925: *1st Baron Stonehaven*; from 1938: *1st Viscount Stonehaven*) (b. 27 Jun 1874; d. 20 Aug 1941)

MEMBERS OF GOVERNMENT

1 Jan 1901 – 24 Sep 1903: Barton

Prime Minister and Foreign Affairs	*Sir Edmund Barton* (b. Sydney 8 Jan 1849; d. Medlow, Bath, 6 Jan 1920)
Attorney General	*Alfred Deakin* (b. 3 Aug 1856; d. 7 Oct 1919)
Home Affairs	1 Jan 1901 – 7 Aug 1903: *Sir William John Lyne* (b. Apslawn, Tasmania, 6 Apr 1844; d. 3 Aug 1913)
	7 Aug – 24 Sep 1903: *Sir John Forrest* (from 2 Feb 1918: *Baron Forrest*) (b. Bunbury 22 Aug 1847; d. at sea 3 Sep 1918)

Treasurer　　　　　　　*Sir George Turner* (b. Melbourne 8 Aug 1851; d. Melbourne 13 Aug 1916)

Trade and Customs　　　1 Jan 1901 – 24 Jul 1903: *Charles Cameron Kingston* (b. Adelaide 22 Oct 1850; d. Adelaide 11 May 1908) 7 Aug – 24 Sep 1903: *Sir William John Lyne* (see above)

Defence　　　　　　　　1 Jan – 10 Jan 1901: *Sir James Robert Dickson* (b. Plymouth 30 Nov 1832; d. 10 Jan 1901) 17 Jan – 7 Aug 1903: *Sir John Forrest* (see above) 7 Aug – 24 Sep 1903: *James George Drake* (b. London 26 Apr 1850; d. 1 Aug 1941)

24 Sep 1903 – 27 Apr 1904: Deakin I

Prime Minister and Foreign Affairs　　*Alfred Deakin* (for 1st time) (see Barton)

Trade and Customs　　　*Sir William John Lyne* (see Barton)

Treasurer　　　　　　　*Sir George Turner* (see Barton)

Home Affairs　　　　　*Sir John Forrest* (see Barton)

Attorney General　　　*James George Drake* (see Barton)

Defence　　　　　　　　*Austin Chapman* (b. Bowral 10 Jul 1864; d. 12 Jan 1926)

27 Apr – 18 Aug 1904: Watson

Prime Minister and Treasurer　　*John Christian Watson* (b. Valparaiso 9 Apr 1867; d. Sydney 18 Nov 1941)

Foreign Affairs　　　　*William Morris Hughes* (b. London 25 Sep 1864; d. Sydney 27 Oct 1952)

Attorney General　　　*Henry Bournes Higgins* (b. Newtownards, Ireland 3 Jan 1851; d. Drowana 13 Jan 1929)

Home Affairs　　　　　*Egerton Lee Batchelor* (b. Adelaide 10 Apr 1865; d. Warburton 8 Oct .1911)

Trade and Customs　　　*Andrew Fisher* (b. Crosshouse, Ayrshire, 29 Aug 1862; d. London 22 Oct 1928)

Defence　　　　　　　　*Anderson (Andrew) Dawson* (b. Rockhampton 16 Jul 1863; d. 20 Jul 1910)

18 Aug 1904 – 5 Jul 1905: Reid

Prime Minister and Foreign Affairs　　*George Houstoun Reid* (from 1909: *Sir*) (b. Johnstone 22 Feb 1848; d. London 12 Sep 1918)

Trade and Customs	*Allan McLean* (b. Scotland 3 Feb 1840; d. Melbourne 13 Jul 1911)
Attorney General	*Sir Josiah Henry Simon*
Treasurer	*Sir George Turner* (see Barton)
Home Affairs	*Dugald Thomson* (b. London 28 Dec 1848; d. 28 Nov 1922)
Defence	*James Whiteside McCay* (from 1918: *Sir*) (b. Ballymure, Ireland, 21 Dec 1864; d. Melbourne 1 Oct 1930)

5 Jul 1905 – 13 Nov 1908: Deakin II

Prime Minister and Foreign Affairs	*Alfred Deakin* (for 2nd time) (see Barton)
Attorney General	5 Jul 1905 – 12 Oct 1906: *Sir Isaac Alfred Isaacs* (b. Melbourne 6 Aug 1855; d. Melbourne 11 Feb 1948)
	12 Oct 1906 – 13 Nov 1908: *Sir Littleton Ernest Groom* (b. Toowoomba 22 Apr 1867; d. Canberra 6 Nov 1936)
Trade and Customs	5 Jul 1905 – 30 Jul 1907: *Sir William John Lyne* (see Barton)
	30 Jul 1907 – 13 Nov 1908: *Austin Chapman* (see Deakin I)
Treasurer	5 Jul 1905 – 30 Jul 1907: *Sir John Forrest* (see Barton)
	30 Jul 1907 – 13 Nov 1908: *Sir William John Lyne* (see Barton)
Defence	5 Jul 1905 – 24 Jan 1907: *Thomas Playford* (b. London 1837; d. Adelaide 19 Apr 1915)
	24 Jan 1907 – 13 Nov 1908: *Thomas Thomson Ewing* (b. Pitt Town, N.S.W.; d. 15 Sep 1920)
Home Affairs	5 Jul 1905 – 12 Oct 1906: *Sir Littleton Ernest Groom* (see above)
	12 Oct 1906 – 24 Jan 1907: *Thomas Thomson Ewing (see above)*
	24 Jan 1907 – 13 Nov 1908: *John Henry Keating* (b. Hobart 28 Jun 1872)

13 Nov 1908 – 2 Jun 1909: Fisher

Prime Minister and Treasurer	*Andrew Fisher* (see Watson)
Attorney General	*William Morris Hughes* (see Watson)
Foreign Affairs	*Egerton Lee Batchelor* (see Watson)
Home Affairs	*Hugh Mahon* (b. Jan 1858; d. 28 Aug 1931)
Defence	*George Foster Pearce* (b. Mount Barker, South Africa, 14 Jan 1910; d. Melbourne 24 Jun 1952)

Trade and Customs	*Frank Gwynne Tudor* (b. Williamstown 27 Jan 1866; d. 10 Jan 1922)

2 Jun 1909 – 29 Apr 1910: Deakin III

Prime Minister	*Alfred Deakin* (for 3rd time) (see Barton)
Defence	*Joseph Cook* (b. 1860; d. Sydney 30 Jul 1947)
Treasurer	*Sir John Forrest* (see Barton)
Trade and Customs	*Sir Robert Wallace Best* (b. Fitzroy 1856, d. 27 May 1946)
Foreign Affairs	*Sir Littleton Ernest Groom* (see Deakin II)
Attorney General	*Patrick McMahon Glynn* (b. Gort, Ireland, 25 Aug 1855; d. 28 Oct 1931)
Home Affairs	*George Warburton Fuller* (b. Kiama 22 Jan 1861; d. Sydney 22 Jul 1940)

29 Apr 1910 – 24 Jun 1913: Fisher II

Prime Minister and Treasurer	*Andrew Fisher* (for 2nd time) (see Watson)
Attorney General	*William Morris Hughes* (see Watson)
Foreign Affairs	29 Apr 1910 – 8 Oct 1911: *Egerton Lee Batchelor* (see Watson)
	14 Oct 1911 – 24 Jun 1913: *Josiah Thomas*
Defence	*George Foster Pearce* (see Fisher I)
Trade and Customs	*Frank Gwynne Tudor* (see Fisher I)
Home Affairs	*King O'Malley*

24 Jun 1913 – 17 Sep 1914: Cook

Prime Minister and Home Affairs	*Joseph Cook* (see Deakin III)
Treasurer	*Sir John Forrest* (see Barton)
Attorney General	*William Hill Irvine* (b. Newry 6 Jul 1858; d. 20 Aug 1943)
Defence	*Edward Davis Millen* (b. 1861; d. 14 Sep 1923)
Foreign Affairs	*Patrick McMahon Glynn* (see Deakin III)
Trade and Customs	*Sir Littleton Ernest Groom* (see Deakin II)

17 Sep 1914 – 27 Oct 1915: Fisher III

Prime Minister and Treasurer	*Andrew Fisher* (for 3rd time) (see Watson)

Attorney General	*William Morris Hughes* (see Watson)
Defence	*George Foster Pearce* (see Fisher I)
Trade and Customs	*Frank Gwynne Tudor* (see Fisher I)
Foreign Affairs	17 Sep – 9 Dec 1914: *John Andrew Arthur*
	14 Dec 1914 – 27 Oct 1915: *Hugh Mahon* (see Fisher I)
Home Affairs	*William Oliver Archibald* (d. 28 Jun 1926)
Navy (new post)	12 Jul 1915 – 27 Oct 1915: *Jens August Jenson*

27 Oct 1915 – 14 Nov 1916: Hughes I

Prime Minister and Attorney General	*William Morris Hughes* (for 1st time) (see Watson)
Defence	*George Foster Pearce* (see Fisher I)
Trade and Customs	27 Oct 1915 – 14 Sep 1916: *Frank Gwynne Tudor* (see Fisher I)
	29 Sept – 14 Nov 1916: *William Morris Hughes* (see Watson)
Foreign Affairs	*Hugh Mahon* (see Fisher I)
Navy	*Jens August Jenson* (see Fisher III)
Treasurer	27 Oct 1915 – 27 Oct 1916: *William Guy Higgs*
	27 Oct – 14 Nov 1916: no appointment made
Home Affairs	*King O'Malley* (see Fisher II)

14 Nov 1916 – 17 Feb 1917: Hughes II

Prime Minister and Attorney General	*William Morris Hughes* (for 2nd time) (see Watson)
Defence	*George Foster Pearce* (see Fisher I)
Navy	*Jens August Jenson* (see Fisher III)
Treasurer	*Alexander Poynton* (b. Castlemaine, Victoria, 8 Aug 1853)
Trade and Customs	*William Oliver Archibald* (see Fisher III)
Home Affairs	*Frederick William Bamford* (b. Dubbo, N.S.W., 11 Feb 1849)
Works and Railways (new post)	*Patrick Joseph Lynch* (b. Newcastle, Ireland, May 1867; d. 15 Jan 1944)

17 Feb 1917 – 10 Jan 1918: Hughes III

Prime Minister and Attorney General	*William Morris Hughes* (for 3rd time) (see Watson)
Navy	*Joseph Cook* (see Deakin III)
Treasurer	*Sir John Forrest* (see Barton)

Defence   *George Foster Pearce* (see Fisher I)

Works and Railways   *William Alexander Watt* (b. Kyneton 23 Nov 1871; d. 13 Sep 1946)

Home Territories   *Patrick McMahon Glynn* (see Deakin III)

10 Jan 1918 – 9 Feb 1923: Hughes IV

Prime Minister	*William Morris Hughes* (for 4th time) (see Watson)
Attorney General	10 Jan 1918 – 21 Dec 1921: *William Morris Hughes* (see Watson)
	from 21 Dec 1921: no appointment made
Foreign Affairs	from 21 Dec 1921: *William Morris Hughes* (see Watson)
Navy	10 Jan 1918 – 28 Jul 1920: *Sir Joseph Cook* (see Deakin III)
	28 Jul 1920 – 21 Dec 1921: *William Henry Laird Smith*
	from 21 Dec 1921: no appointment made
Treasurer	10 Jan – 27 Mar 1918: *Sir John Forrest* (see Barton)
	27 Mar 1918 – 15 Jun 1920: *William Alexander. Watt* (see Hughes III)
	28 Jul 1920 – 11 Nov 1921: *Sir Joseph Cook* (see Deakin III)
	21 Dec 1921 – 9 Feb 1923: *Stanley Melbourne Bruce* (b. 15 Apr 1883; d. London 25 Aug 1967)
Defence	10 Jan 1918 – 21 Dec 1921: *George Foster Pearce* (see Fisher I)
	21 Dec 1921 – 5 Feb 1923: *Walter Massey-Greene*
Works and Railways	10 Jan – 27 Mar 1918: *William Alexander Watt* (see Hughes III)
	27 Mar 1918 – 21 Dec 1921: *Sir Littleton Ernest Groom* (see Deakin II)
	21 Dec 1921 – 9 Feb 1923: *Richard Witty Foster* (b. Goodanham 20 Aug 1856; d. 5 Jan 1932)
Home and Territories	10 Jan 1918 – 3 Feb 1920: *Patrick McMahon Glynn* (see Deakin III)
	4 Feb 1920 – 21 Dec 1921: *Alexander Poynton* (see Hughes II)
	21 Dec 1921 – 9 Feb 1923: *George Foster Pearce* (see Fisher I)
Trade and Customs	10 Jan – 13 Dec 1918: *Jens August Jenson* (see Fisher III)
	13 Dec 1918 – 17 Jan 1919: *William Alexander Watt* (see Hughes III)

17 Jan 1919 – 21 Dec 1921: *Walter Massey-Greene* (see above)

21 Dec 1921 – 5 Feb 1923: *Arthur Stanislaus Rodgers*

Health (new post)   10 Mar 1921 – 5 Feb 1923: *Walter Massey-Greene* (see above)

9 Feb 1923 – 22 Oct 1929: Bruce

Prime Minister and Foreign Affairs | *Stanley Melbourne Bruce* (see Hughes IV)

Treasurer   *Earle Christmas Grafton Page* (b. Grafton, N.S.W., 8 Aug 1880)

Home and Territories   9 Feb 1923 – 18 Jun 1926: *Sir George Foster Pearce* (see Fisher I)

18 Jun 1926 – 2 Apr 1927: *Sir Thomas William Glasgow* (b. Blackmount, Queensland, 6 Jun 1876; d. 5 Jun 1955)

2 Apr 1927 – 24 Feb 1928: *Charles William Clannom Marr* (b. Petersham, N.S.W., 1880)

24 Feb – 29 Nov 1928: *Sir Neville Reginald Howse* (b. Somerset 26 Oct 1864; d. London 19 Sep 1930)

29 Nov 1928 – 22 Oct 1929: *Charles Lydiard Aubrey Abbott* (b. Sydney 4 May 1886)

Attorney General   9 Feb 1923 – 18 Dec 1925: *Sir Littleton Ernest Groom* (see Deakin II)

18 Dec 1925 – 22 Oct 1929: *John Greig Latham* (b. Ascot Vale, Victoria, 25 Aug 1877)

Industry (new post)   10 Dec 1928 – 22 Oct 1929: *John Greig Latham* (see above)

Postmaster General   *William Gerrand Gibson* (b. Gisborne 20 May 1869; d. 22 May 1955)

Trade and Customs   9 Feb 1923 – 26 May 1924: *Sir Austin Chapman* (see Deakin I)

29 May – 13 Jun 1924: *Sir Littleton Ernest Groom* (see Deakin II)

13 Jun 1924 – 7 May 1928: *Herbert Edward Pratten* (b. Bristol 7 May 1865; d. 7 May 1928)

8 May – 24 Nov 1938: *Stanley Melbourne Bruce* (see Hughes IV)

24 Nov 1928 – 22 Oct 1929: *Henry Somer Gullett* (b. Hanton, Victoria, 26 Mar 1878; d. Canberra 13 Aug 1940)

Works and Railways   9 Feb 1923 – 5 Aug 1924: *Percy Gerald Stewart* (d. 15

15

	Oct 1931)
	8 Aug 1924 – 29 Nov 1928: *William Caldwell Hill* (b. Victoria 14 Apr 1866)
	10 Dec 1928 – 22 Oct 1929: *William Gerrand Gibson* (see. above)
Defence	9 Feb 1923 – 16 Jan 1925: *Eric Kendall Bowden* (b. Parramatta 1872; d. 13 Feb 1921)
	16 Jan 1925 – 2 Apr 1927: *Sir Neville Reginald Howse* (see above)
	2 Apr 1927 – 22 Oct 1929: *Sir Thomas William Glasgow* (see above)
Health	9 Feb 1923 – 26 May 1924: *Sir Austin Chapman* (see above)
	29 May – 13 Jun 1924: *Sir Littleton Ernest Groom* (see Deakin II)
	13 Jun – 16 Jan 1925: *Herbert Edward Pratten* (see above)
	16 Jan 1925 – 2 Apr 1927: *Sir Neville Reginald Howse* (for 1st time) (see above)
	2 Apr 1927 – 24 Feb 1928: *Stanley Melbourne Bruce* (see Hughes IV)
	24 Feb 1928 – 22 Oct 1929: *Sir Neville Reginald Howse* (for 2nd time) (see above)

22 Oct 1929 – 6 Jan 1932: Scullin

Prime Minister, Foreign Affairs and Industry	*James Henry Scullin* (b. Ballarat 18 Sep 1876; d. Melbourne 28 Jan 1953)
Treasurer	22 Oct 1929 – 9 Jul 1930: *Edward Granville Theodore* (b. Port Adelaide 29 Dec 1884; d. 9 Feb 1950) 9 Jul 1930 – 29 Jan 1931: *James Henry Scullin* (see above) 29 Jan 1931 – 6 Jan 1932: *Edward Granville Theodore* (for 2nd time) (see above)
Attorney General	*Frank Brennan* (b. Sedgewick, Victoria; d. 5 Nov 1950)
Postmaster and Works and Railways	22 Oct 1929 – 4 Feb 1931: *Joseph Aloysius Lyons* (b. 15 Sep 1874; d. 7 Apr 1939)
	4 Feb 1931 – 6 Jan 1932: *Albert Ernest Green* (b. Avoca 21 Dec 1869)
Trade and Customs	22 Oct 1929 – 4 Feb 1931: *James Edward Fenton* (b. Yalloch; d. 2 Dec 1950)
	4 Feb 1931 – 6 Jan 1932: *Francis Michael Forde* (b.

	Mitchell, Queensland, 18 Jul 1890)
Home Affairs	*Arthur Blakeley*
Health	22 Oct 1929 – 3 Mar 1931: *Frank Anstey* (b. London 18 Aug 1865)
	3 Mar 1931 – 6 Jan 1932: *John McNeill*
Defence	22 Oct 1929 – 4 Feb 1931: *Albert Ernest Green* (see above)
	4 Feb – 3 Mar 1931: *John Joseph Daly* (b. 10 Nov 1891; d. 13 Apr 1942)
	3 Mar 1931 – 6 Jan 1932: *Joseph Benedict Chifley* (b. 22 Sep 1885; d. 13 Jun 1951)

Austria

HEADS OF STATE

Archdukes

House of Habsburg

19 Aug 1493 – 12 Jan 1519	*Maximilian I*, son of Emperor Frederick III (b. 22 Mar 1459) from 1486: King of the Romans; from 1490 to 1493: deputy for his father; from 19 Aug 1493: Holy Roman Emperor
28 May 1519	*Charles I*, grandson, son of Philip I of Spain (b. 24 Feb 1500; d. Estremadura 21 Sep 1558) from 23 Jan 1516 to 15 Jan 1556: King Charles I of Spain; from 26 Jun 1519 to 1 Sep 1556: Holy Roman Emperor Charles V; abdicated as Archduke 1521
21 Apr 1521	*Ferdinand I*, brother (b. 10 Mar 1503) from 28 Oct 1527 to 8 Sep 1563: King of Hungary; from 1531: King of the Romans; from 1 Sep 1556: Holy Roman Emperor
25 Jul 1564	*Maximilian II*, son (b. 31 Jul 1527) from 24 Nov 1562: King of the Romans; from 8 Sep 1563 to 25 Sep 1572: King Maximilian of Hungary; from 25 Jul 1564: Holy Roman Emperor Maximilian II
12 Oct 1576 – 20 Jan 1612	*Rudolf V*, son (b. 18 Jul 1552) from 25 Sep 1572 to 19 Nov 1608: King Rudolf of Hungary; from 12 Oct 1576: Holy Roman Emperor Rudolf II

12 Oct 1576 – 2 Nov 1618	*Maximilian III*, brother (b. 12 Oct 1558)
1576 – 13 Dec 1621	*Albert (Albrecht) II*, brother (b. 13 Nov 1559) from 1596: Stadholder of Spanish Netherlands
20 Jan 1612	*Matthias*, brother (b. 24 Feb 1557) from 19 Nov 1608 to 1 Jul 1618: King Matthias II of Hungary; from 13 Jun 1612: Holy Roman Emperor Matthias
20 Mar 1619	*Ferdinand II*, cousin, son of Archduke Charles of Steiermark (b. 9 Jul 1578) from 1 Jul 1618 to 7 Dec 1625: King of Hungary; from 20 Aug 1619: Holy Roman Emperor
15 Feb 1637 – 2 Apr 1657	*Ferdinand III*, (b. 13 Jul 1608) from 7 Dec 1625: King of Hungary; from 12 Dec 1636: King of the Romans; from 12 Feb 1637: Holy Roman Emperor
18 Jul 1658	*Leopold I*, son (b. 9 Jun 1640) from 27 Jun 1655 to 9 Dec 1687: King of Hungary; from 18 July 1658: Holy Roman Emperor
5 May 1705	*Joseph I*, son (b. 26 Jul 1678) from 9 Dec 1687: King of Hungary; from 24 Aug 1690: King of the Romans; from 5 May 1705: Holy Roman Emperor
17 Apr 1711	*Charles III*, brother (b. 1 Oct 1685) from 12 Oct 1711: Holy Roman Emperor Charles VI; from 22 May 1712: King Charles III of Hungary
20 Oct 1740	(Archduchess) *Maria Theresa*, daughter (b. 13 May 1717) from 20 Oct 1740: Queen of Hungary; married to Francis of Lorraine, subsequently Holy Roman Emperor Francis I

House of Habsburg-Lorraine

29 Nov 1780 – 20 Feb 1790	*Joseph II*, son (b. 13 Mar 1741) from 27 Mar 1764: King of the Romans; from 18 Aug 1765: Holy Roman Emperor; from 29 Nov 1780: King of Hungary
30 Sep 1790 – 1 Mar 1792	*Leopold II*, brother (b. 5 May 1747) from 18 Aug 1765 to 21 Jul 1790: Grand Duke Leopold I of Tuscany; from 20 Feb 1790: King of Hungary; from 30 Sep 1790: Holy Roman Emperor
12 Jul 1792	*Francis I*, son (b. 12 Feb 1768) from 12 Jul 1792 to 6 Aug 1806: Holy Roman Emperor Francis II; from 14 Aug 1804: Emperor of Austria

Emperors

2 Mar 1835	*Ferdinand I*, son (b. 19 Apr 1793; d. 29 Jun 1875)

	from 28 Sep 1830 to 2 Dec 1848: King Ferdinand V of Hungary
2 Dec 1848	*Francis Joseph*, nephew (b. 18 Aug 1830) from 2 Dec 1848: King of Hungary
21 Nov 1916 –11 Nov 1918	*Charles*, great-nephew (b. 17 Aug 1887; d. 1 Apr 1922) from 21 Nov 1916: King Charles IV of Hungary
Nov 1918	Republic

Presidents

16 Feb 1919	*Karl Seitz* (SPÖ) (b. Vienna 4 Sep 1869; d. 3 Feb 1950) President of the National Assembly and acting Head of State
9 Dec 1920 – 9 Dec 1928	*Michael Hainisch* (Christ Soc) (b. Gloggnitz 15 Aug 1858; d. Vienna 26 Feb 1940)
10 Dec 1928 – 13 Mar 1938	*Wilhelm Miklas* (Christ Soc) (b. Krems 15 Oct 1872; d. Vienna 15 Mar 1956)

MEMBERS OF GOVERNMENT

Ministers (Austria)

1519 – 1530	*Mercurino de Gattinara* (b. Arborio 1465; d. Innsbruck 5 Jun 1530) Chancellor
1530 – 1550	*Nicholas Perrenot* (b. Omans 1486; d. Augsburg 28 Aug 1550) Secretary of State
1550 – 1558	*Cardinal Anton Perrenot*, son (b. Besançon 20 Aug 1517; d. Madrid 21 Sep 1586)
1611 – 1618	*Cardinal Melchior Klesel* (b. Vienna Feb 1553; d. Vienna 18 Sep 1630) Head of Privy Council
1615 – 1632	*Hans Ulrich* (from 1623: *Prince) Eggenberg* (b. 1568; d. 18 Oct 1634) Lord Chamberlain and Head of Council of State
1634 – 1650	*Max, Count Trauttmannsdorff* (b. Graz 23 May 1584; d. Vienna 8 Jun – 1650) Head of Privy Council
1650 – 1657	*Johann Weikard, Prince Auersperg* (b. 11 Mar 1615; d. Laibach 13 Nov 1677)
1669 – 1674	*Václar Euseb, Count Lobkovic* (b. 30 Jan 1609; d. Raudnitz 22 Apr 1677) President of State Council
1683 – 1693	*Theodor, Count Strattmann*, Lord Chancellor
1698 – 1706	*Ferdinand Bonaventura, Count Harrach* (b. 14 Jul

	1637; d. 15 Jun 1706) Lord Chamberlain and Head of State Council
1705 - 1712	*Jan Václav, Count of Vratislav,* Chancellor of Bohemia and member of State Council
1727 - 1753	*Johann Christof, Baron Bartenstein* (b. Strassburg 1689; d. Vienna 6 Aug 1767) State Secretary
1742 - 1753	*Anton Corfiz, Count Uhlfeld* (b. 15 Jun 1699; d. Vienna 31 Dec 1760) Lord Chancellor
1753 - 1792	*Wenzel Anton, Count Kaunitz* (from 1764: *Prince*) *Kaunitz-Rittberg* (b. Vienna 2 Feb 1711; d. Vienna 27 Jun 1794) Lord Chamberlain and Chancellor
1792 - Mar 1793	*Johann Philipp, Count Cobenzl* (b. Laibach 28 May 1741; d. Vienna 30 Aug 1810) Lord Chamberlain and Chancellor, from 1779 Vice-Chancellor, Lord Chamberlain and Chancellor
1793 - 1800	*Johann Amadeus Franz von Paula Maria, Baron Thugut* (b. Linz 31 Mar 1736; d. Vienna 28 May 1818) Head of State Council
1800 - 1801	(acting:) *Ferdinand, Count* (from 1805: *Prince*) *Trauttmannsdorff* (b. 12 Jan 1749; d. 27 Aug 1827) Minister of Foreign Affairs
1801 - Dec 1805	*(Johann) Ludwig (Josef), Count Cobenzl* (b. Brussels 21 Nov 1753; d. Vienna 22 Feb 1809) Lord Chamberlain, Chancellor and Minister of Foreign Affairs
25 Dec 1805 - 4 Oct 1809	*Johann Philipp Karl, Count Stadion-Warthousen* (b. Mainz 18 Jun 1763; d. Baden bei Wien 15 May 1824) Lord Chamberlain and Chancellor
8 Oct 1809 - 13 Mar 1848	*Clemens Wenzel Lothar, Prince* (until 1813: *Count*) *Metternich-Winneburg* (from 1818: *Duke*) *Portella* (b. Coblenz 15 May 1773; d. Vienna 11 Jun 1859) until 1821: Lord Chamberlain and Minister of State, Minister of Foreign Affairs, later Lord Chamberlain and Chancellor
13 Mar 1848	*Field Marshal Alfred Candidus Ferdinand, Prince of Windisch-Grätz* (b. Brussels 11 May 1787; d. Vienna 21 Mar 1862) Authorized Head of the Goverment

20 Mar - 18 Jul 1848: Kolowrat-Libšteinsky

| Prime Minister | 20 Mar - 5 Apr 1848 (acting:) *František Antonín, Count Kolowrat-Libšteinsky* (b. Prague 31 Jan 1778; |

d. Vienna 4 Apr 1861)

19 Apr – 4 May 1848 (acting:) *Karl Ludwig, Count Ficquelmont* (b. Schloss Duss 23 Mar 1777; d. Venice 7 April 1857)

19 May – 8 Jul 1848 (acting:) *Franz, Baron Pillersdorf* (b. Vienna 1 Mar 1786; d. 22 Feb 1862)

8 – 18 Jul 1848: *Anton, Baron Doblhoff-Dier* (b. Gorz 10 Nov 1800; d. Vienna 16 Apr 1872)

Foreign Affairs	20 Mar – 4 May 1848: *Karl Ludwig, Count Ficquelmont* (see above)
	8 May – 18 Jul 1848; *Johann (Philipp), Baron Wessenberg-Ampringen* (b. Dresden 28 Nov 1773; d. Freiburg im Breisgau 1 Aug 1858)
Home Affairs	*Franz, Baron Pillersdorf* (see above)
Education	*Franz, Baron Sommaruga* (b. Vienna 18 Apr 1780; d. Heiligenstadt 2 Oct 1860)
Justice	20 Mar – 21 Apr 1848: *Ludwig, Count Taaffe* (b. Brno 25 Dec 1791; d. Vienna 21 Dec 1855)
	22 Apr – 17 Jul 1848: *Franz, Baron Sommaruga* (see above)
War	2 – 28 Apr 1848: *Peter von Zanini* (b. Stein 1786; d. Vienna 11 Sep 1855)
	28 Apr – 18 Jul 1848: *Theodor Count Baillet de Latour* (b. Linz 15 Jun 1780; d. Vienna 6 Oct 1848)
Finance	20 Mar – 1 Apr 1848: *Karl Friedrich Baron Kubeck von Kübau* (b. Iglau 28 Oct 1780; d. Hadersdorf 11 Sep 1855)
	2 Apr – 18 Jul 1848: *Philipp Baron Krauss* (b. Lvov 28 Mar 1792; d. Schönbrunn 26 Jun 1861)
Commerce	8 May – 18 Jul 1848: *Anton Baron Doblhoff-Dier* (see above)
Labour	8 May – 8 Jul 1848: *Andreas* (from 1854: *Baron*) *Baumgartner* (b. Friedberg 23 Apr 1793; d. Vienna 30 Jul 1865)

18 Jul – 21 Nov 1848: Wesenberg-Ampringen

Prime Minister	*Johann, Baron Wessenberg-Ampringen* (see Kolowrat-Libšteinsky)
Foreign Affairs	*Johann, Baron Wessenberg-Ampringen* (see Kolowrat-Libšteinsky)
Home Affairs and Education	*Anton, Baron Doblhoff-Dier* (see Kolowrat-Libšteinsky)

Justice	*Alexander Baron Bach* (b. Loosdorf 4 Jan 1813; d. Schonberg 13 Nov 1893)
War	8 Jul – 6 Oct 1848: *Theodor, Count Baillet de Latour* (see Kolowrat-Libšteinsky)
Finance	*Philipp, Baron Krauss* (see Kolowrat-Libšteinsky)
Commerce	*Theodor von Hornbostel* (b. Vienna 29 Oct 1815; d. Vienna 2 Jun 1898)
Labour	19 Jul – 22 Sep 1848: *Ernest von Schwarzer* (b. Fulnek 18 Aug 1808; d. Vienna 18 Mar 1860) 23 Sep – 20 Nov 1848: *Theodor von Hornbostel* (see above)

21 Nov 1848 – 5 Apr 1852: Schwarzenberg

Prime Minister	*Felix, Count Schwarzenberg* (b. Krumau 2 Oct 1800; d. Vienna 5 Apr 1852)
Foreign Affairs	*Felix, Count Schwarzenberg* (see above)
Secretary	21 Nov 1848 – 27 Jul 1849: *Franz Seraph, Count Stadion* (b. Vienna 27 Jul 1806; d. Vienna 8 Jun 1853)
Home Affairs	28 Jul 1849 – 5 Apr 1852: *Alexander, Baron Bach* (see Wessenberg)
Education	21 Nov 1848 – 27 Jul 1849: (acting:) *Franz Seraph, Count Stadion* (see above) 28 Jul 1849 – 5 Apr 1852: *Leo, Count Thun und Hohenstein* (b. Tetschen 7 Apr 1811; d. Vienna 17 Dec 1888)
Justice	1 Nov 1848 – 27 Jul 1849: *Alexander, Baron Bach* (see Wessenberg) 28 Jul 1849 – 22 Jan 1851: *Anton von Schmerling* (b. Vienna 23 Aug 1805; d. Vienna 23 May 1893) 23 Jan 1851 – 5 Apr 1852. *Karl* (from 1852: *Baron*) *Krauss* (b. Lvov 13 Sep 1789; d. Vienna 5 Mar 1881)
War	21 Nov 1848 – 1 Jun 1849: *Franz, Baron Cordon* (b. Vienna 4 May 1796; d. Vienna 15 Jan 1869) 2 Jun – 15 Jul 1849; *Ferencz, Count Gyulay* (b. Pest 1 Sep 1798; d. Vienna 21 Sep 1868) 16 Jul 1849 – 5 Apr 1852: *Anton, Baron Csorich z Monte Cretto* (b. Mahično 1795; d. Vienna 15 Jul 1864)
Finance	1 Nov 1848 – 20 Dec 1851: *Philipp, Baron Krauss* (see Kolowrat-Libšteinsky) 21 Dec 1851 – 5 Apr 1852: *Andreas, Baron*

Commerce

Baumgartner (see Kolowrat-Libšteinsky)
21 Nov 1848 – 23 May 1851: *Karl Ludwig* (from 19 Dec 1849: *Baron) Bruck* (b. Elberfeld 8 Oct 1798; d. Vienna 23 Apr 1860)
23 May 1851 – 5 Apr 1852: *Andreas, Baron Baumgartner* (see Kolowrat-Libšteinsky)

Agriculture and Mining

21 Nov 1848 – 5 Apr 1852: *Ferdinand Thinn* (from 1853: *Baron Thinnfeld)* (b. 24 Apr 1793; d. Feistritz 8 Apr 1868)

11 Apr 1852 – 21 Aug 1859: Buol-Schauenstein

Prime Minister

Karl Ferdinand, Count Buol-Schauenstein (b. Vienna 17 May 1797; d. Vienna 28 Oct 1865)

Foreign Affairs

11 Apr 1852 – 17 May 1859: *Karl Ferdinand, Count Buol-Schauenstein* (see above)
17 Mar – 21 Aug 1859: *Johann Bernhard, Count Rechberg und Rothenlöwen* (b. Regensburg 17 Jun 1806; d. Vienna 26 Feb 1899)

Home Affairs

Alexander, Baron Bach (see Wessenberg)

Education

Leo, Count Thun und Hohenstein (see Schwarzenberg)

Justice

11 Apr 1852 – 17 May 1857: *Karl, Baron Krauss* (see Schwarzenberg)
18 May 1857 – 17 May 1859: *Ferencz, Count Nádasdy* (b. Pest 1 Apr 1801; d. Pest 1 Nov 1883)

Police

Johann Franz, Baron Kempen von Fichtenstamm (b. Pardubitz 26 Jun 1793; d. Schwarzau 29 Nov 1863)

War

11 May 1852 – 7 Mar 1853: *Anton, Baron Csorich ẕ Monte Cretto* (see Schwarzenberg)
7 Mar 1853 – 17 May/20 Jul 1859: *Archduke William of Austria*, son of Archduke Charles (b. Vienna 21 Apr 1827; d. Vienna 29 Jul 1894)

Finance

11 Apr 1852 – 3 May 1855: *Andreas, Baron Baumgartner* (see Kolowrat-Libšteinsky)
10 May 1855 – 17 May 1859: *Karl Ludwig, Baron Bruck* (see Schwarzenberg)

Commerce and Labour

11 Apr 1852 – 6 Feb 1855: *Andreas, Baron Baumgartner* (see Kolowrat-Libšteinsky)
7 Feb 1855 – 21 Aug 1859: *Georg, Count Toggenburg* (b. Rhäzüns 24 Jan 1810; d. Bozen 8 Mar 1888) 21 Aug 1859: post abolished

Agriculture and Mining	11 Apr 1852 – 17 Jan 1853: *Ferdinand Thinn, Baron Thinnfeld* (see Schwarzenberg) 17 Jan 1853: post abolished

21 Aug 1859 – 4 Feb 1861: Rechberg and Rothenlöwen

Prime Minister	*Johann Bernhard, Count Rechberg und Rothenlöwen* (see Buol-Schauenstein)
Foreign Affairs	*Johann Bernhard, Count Rechberg und Rothenlöwen* (see Buol-Schauenstein)
Home Affairs	21 Aug – 28 Aug 1859: *Alexander, Baron Bach* (see Wessenberg) 28 Aug 1859 – 13 Dec 1860: *Agenor, Count Gołuchowski* (b. Lvov 8 Feb 1812; d. Lvov 3 Aug 1875) also Minister of State from 20 Oct 1860 15 Dec 1860 – 4 Feb 1861: *Anton von Schmerling* (see Schwarzenberg)
Education	21 Aug 1859 – 20 Oct 1860: *Leo, Count Thun und Hohenstein* (see Schwarzenberg) 20 Oct 1860 – 4 Feb 1861 (acting:) *Alexander, Baron Helfert* (b. Prague 3 Nov 1820; d. Vienna 16 Mar 1910)
Justice	17 May 1859 – 14 Oct 1860: *Ferencz, Count Nádasdy* (see Buol-Schauenstein) 20 Oct 1860 – 4 Feb 1861: *Josef* (from 1867: *Baron*) *Lasser von Zollheim* (b. Salsburg 30 Sep 1815; d. Vienna 18 Nov 1879)
War (officially from 1860)	21 Aug 1859 – Oct 1860: *Archduke William of Austria* (see Buol-Schauenstein) 20 Oct 1860 – 4 Feb 1861: *August Franz Josef Christof, Count Degenfeld-Schonburg* (b. Gross-Kanischa 10 Dec 1798; d. Altmünster 5 Dec 1876)
Finance	17 May 1859 – 22 Apr 1860: *Karl Ludwig, Baron Bruck* (see Schwarzenberg) 22 Apr 1860 – 4 Feb 1861 (acting:) *Ignaz* (from 1907: *Baron*) *Plener* (b. Vienna 21 May 1810; d. Vienna 17 Feb 1908)
Police	21 Aug – 21 Oct 1859: *Josef Alexander, Baron* (from 1888: *Count*) *Hübner* (b. Vienna 26 Nov 1811; d. Vienna 30 Jul 1892) 21 Oct 1859 – 19 Oct 1860: *Adolf, Baron Thierry* (b. Kuttenberg 1803; d. Wiesbaden 6 Nov 1867)
Hungarian Chancellor	20 Oct – 13 Dec 1860: *Miklos, Baron Vay* (b.

Alsózsolza 29 Apr 1802; d. Budapest 13 May 1894)
13 Dec 1860 – 4 Feb 1861; *Károlyi, Baron Mecséry*
(b. Tabor 18 Jan 1804; d. Graz 12 Oct 1886)

Without Portfolio   20 Oct 1860 – 4 Feb 1861; *Antal, Count Szécsen* (b. Buda 17 Oct 1819; d. Aussee 23 Aug 1896)

4 Feb 1861 – 26 Jan 1865: Rainer

Prime Minister	4 Feb 1861 – 20 Jun 1865: *Archduke Rainer of Austria*, uncle of Emperor Leopold II (b. Milan 11 Jan 1827; d. Vienna 27 Jan 1913)
Premier	*Anton von Schmerling* (see Schwarzenberg)
Foreign Affairs	4 Feb 1861 – 27 Oct 1864: *Johann Bernhard, Count Rechberg und Rothenlöwen* (see Buol-Schauenstein) 27 Oct 1864 – 27 Jun 1865: *Alexander, Count Mensdorff-Pouilly* (from 1869: *Prince Dietrichstein zu Nikilsburg*) (b. Coburg 4 Aug 1813; d. Prague 14 Feb 1871)
Home Affairs	*Josef, Baron Lasser von Zolheim* (see Rechberg und Rothenöwen)
Police	*Károly, Baron Mecséry* (see Rechberg und Rothenlöwen)
Education	From 4 Feb 1861 merged with the Prime Minister's department
Justice	13 Dec 1860 – 3 Feb 1861: *Josef, Baron Lasser von Zollheim* (see Rechberg und Rothenlöwen) 4 Feb 1861 – 18 Dec 1862: *Adolf Pratobevera, Baron Wiesborn* (b. Bielitz 12 Jun 1806; d. Vienna 16 Feb 1875) 18 Dec 1862 – 27 Jun 1865: *Franz* (from 1871: *Baron*) *Hein* (b. Olomovc 28 Jun 1808; d. Brno 18 Feb 1890)
War	4 Dec 1861 – 19 Feb 1864: *August Franz Johann Christof, Count Degenfeld-Schonburg* (see Rechberg und Rothenlöwen) 19 Feb 1864 – 27 Jun 1865: — *von Franck*
Navy	26 Jan – 29 Aug 1862: *Matthias Konstantin Capello, Count Wickenburg* (b. Düsseldorf 16 Jul 1797; d. Gleichenberg 26 Oct 1880) 30 Aug 1862 – 27 Jun 1865: *Friedrich, Baron Burger* (b. Wolsfberg 7 Jul 1804; d. Vienna 2 Oct 1873)
Finance	*Ignaz, Baron Plener* (see Rechberg und Rothenlöwen)

Commerce	4 Feb 1861 – 20 Oct 1863; *Matthias, Count Wickenburg* (see above)
	20 Oct 1863 – 26 Jun 1865 (acting:) *Josef, Bron Kalchberg* (b. Graz 27 Mar 1801; d. Graz 27 Apr 1882)
Without Portfolio	4 Feb 1861 – 18 Jul 1861: *Antal, Count Szécsen* (see Rechberg und Rothenlöwen)
	19 Jul 1861 – 26 Jun 1865: *Moritz, Count Esterházy (b. Vienna 23 Sep 1807; d. Pirna 8 Nov 1890)*
Hungarian Chancellor	18 Jul 1861 – 22 Jul 1864: *Antal, Count Forgách de Ghymes* (b. Bratislava 6 Mar 1819; d. Lučenec 2 Apr 1885)
	22 Jul 1864 – 26 Jun 1865: *Armin, Count Zichy de Vásonykeö* (b. Jakolháza 7 May 1814; d. Jakolháza 18 May 1880)

26 Jun – 27 Jul 1865: Mensdorff-Pouilly

Alexander, Count Mensdorff-Pouilly (see Rainer) caretaker Prime Minister with the same ministry

27 July 1865 – 7 Feb 1867: Belcredi ('Ministry of the Three Counts')

Prime Minister	*Richard, Count Belcredi* (b. Ingrowitz 12 Feb 1823; d. Gmunden 2 Dec 1902)
Foreign Affairs	27 Jul 1865 – 30 Oct 1866: *Alexander, Count Mensdorff-Pouilly* (see Rainer)
	30 Oct 1866 – 7 Feb 1867: *Friedrich Ferdinand, Baron* (from 5 Dec 1868: *Count*) *Beust* (b. Dresden 13 Jan 1809; d. Altenberg 23 Oct 1886)
Home Affairs and Police	*Richard, Count Belcredi* (see above)
Justice	*Emmanuel* (from 1869: *Baron*) *Komers von Lindenbach* (b. Humpoletz 20 Dec 1810; d. Žak 18 Jan 1889)
War	27 Jul 1865 – 6 Sep 1866: —— *von Franck* (see Rainer)
	Sep 1866 – 7 Feb 1867: *Franz, Baron John* (b. Bruck 20 Nov 1815; d. Vienna 25 May 1876)
Finance	27 Jul 1865 – 21 Jan 1867: *Johann, Count Larisch-Moennich* (b. Schönstein 3 May 1821; d. Lamport Hall, Northamptonshire. 3 Jun 1884)
	21 Jan – 7 Feb 1867 (acting:) *Franz Karl* (from 1866:

	Baron) Becke (b. Kollinetz 31 Oct 1818; d. Vienna 15 Jan 1870)
Commerce	27 Jul – 30 Sep 1865: *Joseph, Baron Kalchberg* (see Rainer)
	30 Sep 1865 – 7 Feb 1867: *Bernhard, Baron Wüllerstorf und Urbair* (b. Trieste 29 Jan 1816; d. Klobenstein 10 Aug 1893)
Without Portfolio	27 Jul 1865 – 30 Oct 1866: *Moritz, Count Esterházy* (see Rainer)
Hungarian Chancellor	*György Mailáth* (b. Bratislava 3 Dec 1818; d. Buda 29 March 1883)

7 Feb – 30 Dec 1867: Beust

Prime Minister	*Friedrich Ferdinand, Baron Beust* (see Belcredi) from 23 Jun 1867 Chancellor)
Deputy Prime Minister	26 Jun – 30 Jul 1867: *Eduard, Count Taaffe* (b. Vienna 24 Feb 1833; d. Schloss Ellischau 29 Nov 1895)
Foreign Affairs	*Friedrich Ferdinand, Baron* (from 5 Dec 1868: *Count) Beust* (see Belcredi)
Home Affairs	7 Feb – 30 Dec 1867: *Eduard, Count Taaffe* (see above)
Education	28 Jun – 30 Dec 1867 (acting:) *Anton* (from 1869: *Baron) Hye-Gluneck* (b. Gluneck 26 May 1807; d. Vienna 8 Dec 1894)
Justice	7 Feb – 28 Jun 1867: *Emmanuel Komers von Lindenbach* (see Belcredi)
	28 Jun – 30 Dec 1867: *Anton, Baron Hye-Gluneck* (see above)
War	*Franz, Baron John* (see Belcredi)
Finance	*Franz Karl, Baron Becke* (see Belcredi)
Commerce	7 Feb – 18 Apr 1867: *Bernhard, Baron Wüllerstorf und Urbair* (see Belcredi)
	18 Apr – 29 Dec 1867: *Franz Karl, Baron Becke* (see Belcredi)

MINISTERS FOR THE COMMON AFFAIRS OF AUSTRIA AND HUNGARY

Lord Chamberlains and Ministers for Foreign Affairs

24 Dec 1867 – 8 Nov 1871	*Friedrich Ferdinand, Baron* (from 1868: *Count) Beust* (see Belcredi)

14 Nov 1871	*Gyula, Count Andrássy* (b. Kaschau 3 Mar 1823; d. Volosca 18 Feb 1890)
8 Oct 1879 – 10 Oct 1881	*Heinrich, Baron von Haymerle* (b. Vienna 7 Dec 1828; d. Vienna 10 Oct 1881)
20 Nov 1881 – 2 May 1895	*Gustáv Zsigmond, Count Kálnoky* (b. Lettowitz 29 Dec 1832; d. Prodlitz 13 Feb 1898)
16 May 1895	*Agenor, Count Gołuchowski* (b. Lvov 25 Mar 1859; d. Lvov 28 Mar 1921)
24 Ot 1906	*Alois, Baron* (from 1909: *Count) Lexa von Aehrenthal* (b. Gross-Skal 27 Nov 1854; d. Vienna 17 Feb 1912)
17 Feb 1912	*Leopold, Count Berchtold* (b. Vienna 18 Apr 1863; d. Schloss Perznye 21 Nov 1942)
13 Jan 1915	*István, Baron* (from 1918: *Count) Burián* (for 1st time) (b. Stampfen 16 Jan 1851; d. Vienna 20 Oct 1922)
22 Dec 1916	*Ottokar* (until 1919: *Count) Czernin* (b. Dimokur 26 Sep 1872; d. Vienna 4 Apr 1932)
16 Apr 1918	*István, Count Burián* (for 2nd time)
24 Oct 1918	*Gyula, Count Andrássy* (b. Töke Terebes 30 Jun 1860; d. Budapest 11 Jun 1929)
2 – 11 Nov 1918	*Ludwig, Baron Flotow* (b. Vienna 17 Nov 1867; d. Gmunden 6 Apr 1948)

Common Finance Ministers

24 Dec 1867	*Franz Karl, Baron Becke* (see Belcredi)
15 Jan 1870	(acting:) *Friedrich Ferdinand, Baron Beust* (see Lord Chamberlains and Ministers for Foreign Affairs)
21 May 1870	*Menyhért (from 1871: Count) Lónyay* (b. Nagylónya 6 Jan 1822; d. Buda 3 Nov 1884)
Nov 1871 – Jan 1872	(acting:) *Gyula, Count Andrássy (see Lord Chamberlains and Ministers for Foreign Affairs)*
15 Jan 1872 – 11 Jun 1876	*Ludwig* (from 1865: *Baron) von Holzgethan* (b. Vienna 1 Oct 1810; d. Vienna 12 Jun 1876)
17 Jun 1876	(acting:) *Gyula, Count Andrássy* (see Lord Chamberlains and Ministers for Foreign Affairs)
14 Aug 1876	*Leopold Friedrich, Baron Hofmann* (b. Vienna 4 May 1822; d. Vienna 24 Oct 1885)
8 Apr 1880	*József Szlávy* (b. Győr 23 Nov 1818; d. Zsitvaujfalu 8 Aug 1900)
4 Jun 1882 – 13 Jul 1903	*Benjamin Kállay* (b. Nagykálló 22 Dec 1839; d. Vienna 13 Jul 1903)

14 Jul 1903	(acting:) *Agenor, Count Gołuchowski* (see Lord Chamberlains and Ministers for Foreign Affairs)
24 Jul 1903	*István, Baron Burián* (for 1st time) (see Lord Chamberlains and Ministers of Foreign Affairs)
20 Feb 1912	*Leon Biliński* (b. Zaleszczyki 15 Jun 1846; d. Vienna 14 Jun 1923)
7 Feb 1915 – 28 Oct 1916	*Ernst von Koerber* (b. Trient 6 Nov 1850; d. Baden bei Wien 5 Mar 1919)
2 Dec 1916	*Conrad, Prince of Hohenlohe-Waldenburg-Schillingsfürst* (b. Vienna 16 Dec 1863; d. Leoben 21 Dec 1918)
22 Dec 1916	*István, Baron Burián* (for 2nd time) (see Lord Chamberlains and Ministers for Foreign Affairs
16 Apr 1918	*Alexander Bernhard, Baron Spitzmüller* (b. Vienna 12 Jun 1862; d. Velden 5 Sep 1953)
4 – 11 Nov 1918	*Paul, Baron Kuh-Chrobak* (b. Vienna 11 Mar 1863; d. Meran 8 Jan 1931)

Ministers for War

24 Dec 1867	*Franz, Baron John* (see Belcredi)
18 Jan 1868	*Franz, Baron Kuhn* (b. Prossnitz 15 Jul 1817; d. Strassoldo 25 May 1896)
14 Jun 1874	*Alexander, Baron Koller* (b. Prague 3 Jun 1813; d. Baden bei Wien 29 May 1890)
20 Jun 1876	*Artur, Count Bylandt-Rheydt*, the Elder (b. Vienna 5 May 1821; d. Vienna 21 Feb 1891)
Mar 1888	*Ferdinand, Baron Bauer* (b. Lvov 7 Mar 1825: d. Vienna 26 Jul 1893)
Jul 1893	(acting:) *Rudolf, Baron Merkl* (b. Vienna 28 Mar 1831; d. Vienna 22 Jan 1910)
23 Sep 1893	*Edmund* (from 1899 *Baron*) *von Krieghammer* (b. Landshut 4 Jun 1831; d. Ischl 21 Aug 1906)
Dec 1902	*Heinrich* (from 1909 until 1919: *Baron*) *von Pitreich* (b. Laibach 10 July 1841; d. Vienna 13 Jan 1920)
Oct 1906	*Franz* (from 1908: *Baron*) *Schönaich* (b. Vienna 27 Feb 1844; d. Vienna 28 Jan 1916)
Sep 1911	*Moritz* (from 1915 until 1919: *Baron*) *Aufffenberg* (b. Troppau 22 May 1852; d. Vienna 18 May 1928)
Dec 1912	*Alexander* (from 1915 until 1919: *Baron*) *Krobatin* (b. Olomouc 12 Sep 1849; d. Vienna 28 Dec 1933)
Apr 1917 – Nov 1918	*Rudolf Stöger-Steiner* (b. Pernegg 26 Apr 1861; d. Graz 12 May 1921)

Heads of the Navy Department in the War Ministry

25 Feb 1868 – 7 Apr 1871	*Wilhelm von Tegetthoff* (b. Marburg 23 Dec 1827; d. Vienna 7 Apr 1871)
26 Apr 1871 – Nov 1883	*Friedrich, Baron Pöckh*
1883	*Maximilian Daublebsky, Baron Sterneck* (b. Klagenfurt 14 Feb 1829; d. Vienna 5 Dec 1897)
5 Dec 1897	*Hermann, Baron Spaun* (b. Vienna 9 May 1833; d. Graz 23 May 1919)
6 Oct 1904	*Rudolf, Count Montecuccoli* (b. Modena 22 Feb 1843; d. Baden bei Wien 17 May 1922)
Feb 1913 – 8 Feb 1917	*Anton Haus* (b. Tolmein 13 Jun 1851; d. Pola 8 Feb 1917)
16 Feb – 28 Apr 1917	*Karl Kailer von Kagenfels* (b. Pola 24 May 1862; d. Vienna 28 Apr 1917)
30 Apr 1917	*Maximilian Njegovan* (b. Agram 1858; d. Jul 1930)
27 Feb 1918 – Jan 1919	*Franz von Holub*

AUSTRIAN MINISTERS

30 Dec 1867 – 12 Apr 1870: Karl Auersperg ('The Citizens Ministry')

Prime Minister	30 Mar 1867 – 24 Sep 1868: *Karl, Prince Auersperg* (b. Prague 1 May 1814; d. Prague 4 Jan 1890)
	24 Sep 1868 – 15 Jan 1870 (until 17 April 1869 deputy): *Eduard, Count Taaffe* (see Beust)
	15 – 31 Jan 1870: *Ignaz von Plener* (see Rechberg und Rothenlöwen)
	1 Feb – 4 Apr 1870: *Leopold Hasner von Artha* (b. Prague 15 Mar 1818; d. Ischl 5 Jun 1891)
Deputy Prime Minister	30 Mar 1867 – 26 Ap 1868: *Eduard, Count Taaffe* (see Beust)
Home Affairs	30 Dec 1867 – 12 Apr 1870: *Karl Giskra* (b. Mährisch-Trübau 29 Jan 1820; d. Baden bei Wien 1 Apr 1879)
Education	30 Dec 1867 – 31 Jan 1870: *Leopold Hasner von Artha* (see above)
	31 Jan – 4 Apr 1870: *Karl von Stremayr* (b. Graz 30 Oct 1923; d. Pottschach 22 Jun 1904)
Justice	*Eduard Herbst* (b. Vienna 9 Dec 1820; d. 25 Jun 1892)

Defence	30 Dec 1867 – 15 Jan 1870: *Eduard, Count Taaffe* (see Beust)
	15 – 31 Jan 1870 (acting:) *Ignaz von Plener* (see Rechberg und Rothenlöwen)
	1 Feb – 11 Apr 1870): *Johannes von Wagner* (b. Klobac 19 Apr 1816; d. Sambor 28 Oct 1894)
Finance	*Rudolf Brestel* (b. Vienna 16 May 1816; d. Vienna 3 Mar 1881)
Commerce	*Ignaz von Plener* (see Rechber und Rothenlöwen)
Agriculture	30 Dec 1867 – 15 Jan 1870: *Alfred, Count Potocki* (b. Landeshut 29 Jul 1822; d. Paris 18 May 1889)
	1 Feb – 12 Apr 1870: *Anton* (from 1886: *Baron*) *Banhans* (b. Michelob 8 Nov 1925; d. Vienna 26 May 1902)
Without Portfolio	30 Dec 1867 – 15 Jan 1870: *Johann Nepomuk Berger* (b. Prossnitz 16 Sep 1816; d. Vienna 9 Dec 1870)

12 Apr 1870 – 4 Feb 1871: Potocki

Prime Minister	*Alfred, Count Potocki* (see Karl Auersperg)
Home Affairs	*Eduard, Count Taaffe* (see Beust)
Education	12 Apr – 29 Apr 1870 (acting:) *Adolf von Tschabuschnigg* (b. Klagenfurt 20 Jul 1809; d. Vienna 1 Nov 1877)
	30 Jun 1870 – 4 Feb 1871: *Karl von Stremayr* (see Karl Auersperg)
Justice	*Adolf von Tschabuschnigg* (see above)
Defence	12 Apr – 6 May 1870 (acting:) *Eduard, Count Taaffe* (see Beust)
	6 May – 28 Jun 1870: *Victor, Baron Widmann* (b. 8 Sep 1836; d. Vienna 25 Jan 1886)
	28 Jun 1870 – 4 Feb 1871: *Alfred, Count Potocki* (see Karl Auersperg)
Finance	12 Apr – 6 May 1870: *Karl, Baron Distler* (b. Hagenberg 3 Oct 1817; d. Vienna 8 Dec 1889)
	6 May 1870 – 4 Feb 1871: *Ludwig, Baron Holzgethan* (b. Vienna 1 Oct 1810; d. Vienna 11 Jun 1876)
Commerce	*Sisinio* (from 1871: *Baron*) *de Pretis* (b. Hamburg 14 Feb 1828; d. Vienna 15 Dec 1890)
Agriculture	*Alfred, Count Potocki* (see Karl Auersperg) from 6 May 1870: *Alexander, Baron Petrino*

6 Feb - 30 Oct 1871 (acting:) Hohenwart

Prime Minister	*Karl (Siegmund) Count Hohenwart* (b. Vienna 12 Feb 1824; d. Vienna 26 Apr 1899)
Home Affairs	*Karl, Count Hohenwart* (see above)
Education	*Josef Jireček* (b. Vysoké Mýto 9 Oct 1825; d. Prague 25 Nov 1888)
Justice	*Karl Habietinek* (b. Prague 2 Mar 1830; d. Vienna 21 Mar 1915)
Defence	*Heinrich, Baron Scholl* (b. Venice 27 Apr 1815; d. Görz 15 May 1879)
Finance	*Ludwig, Baron Holzgethan* (see Potocki)
Commerce	*Albert Schäffle* (b. Nürtingen 24 Feb 1831; d. Stuttgart 25 Mar 1903)
Agriculture	*Albert Schäffle* (see above)
Minister for Galicia	11 Apr - 30 Oct 1871: *Kazimierz Grocholski* (b. Rozyska 1815; d. Abbazia 10 Dec 1888)

30 Oct - 25 Nov 1871 (acting:) Holzgethan

Prime Minister	*Ludwig, Baron Holzgethan* (see Potocki)
Home Affairs	*August, Baron Wehli* (b. Prague 1 Nov 1810; d. Aussee 20 Oct 1892)
Education	*Karl Fidler* (b. Urfahr 1818; d. Vienna 20 Dec 1887)
Justice	*Georg Peter, Baron Mitis* (b. Vienna 17 Apr 1817; d. Hietzing 25 Jul 1889)
Defence	*Heinrich, Baron Scholl* (see Hohenwart)
Finance	*Ludwig, Baron Holzgethan* (see Potocki)
Commerce	*Ludwig, Baron Possinger* (b. Giab 6 Jan 1823; d. Graz 30 Jan 1905)
Agriculture	*Otto, Baron Wiedenfeld* (b. Troppau 16 Nov 1818; d. Aussee 5 Jul 1897)
Minister for Galicia	*Kazimierz Grocholski* (see Hohenwart)

25 Nov 1871 - 15 Feb 1879: Adolf Auersperg

Prime Minister	*Adolf (Wilhelm Daniel), Prince Auersperg* (b. Prague 21 Jul 1821; d. Schloss Goldegg 5 Jan 1885)
Home Affairs	25 Nov 1871 - 5 Jul 1878: *Josef, Baron Lasser* (see Rechberg und Rothenlöwen)
	5 Jul 1878 - 15 Nov 1879 (acting:) *Adolf, Prince Auersperg* (see above)
Education	*Karl von Stremayr* (see Karl Auersperg)

Justice	*Julius Glaser* (b. Postelberg 19 Mar 1831; d. Vienna 26 Dec 1885)
Defence	*Julius Josef Joachim Ludwig* (from 1877: *Baron*) *Horst* (b. Hermannstadt 12 Apr 1830; d. Graz 6 Feb 1904) initially acting, from 23 Mar 1872 confirmed as minister
Finance	25 Nov 1871 – 15 Jan 1872: *Ludwig, Baron Holzgethan* (see Potocki)
	15 Jan 1872 – 15 Feb 1879: *Sisinio, Baron de Pretis* (see Potocki)
Commerce	25 Nov 1871 – 20 May 1875: *Anton, Baron Banhans* (see Karl Auersperg)
	20 May 1875 – 15 Feb 1879: *Johann* (from 1889: *Baron*) *Chlumecky* (b. Zara 23 Mar 1834; d. Bad Aussee 11 Dec 1924)
Agriculture	25 Nov 1871 – 20 May 1875: *Johann Chlumecky* (see above)
	20 May 1875 – 15 Feb 1879: *Hieronymus, Count Colleredo-Mansfeld* (b. Przemysl 20 Jul 1842; d. Blakenberg 29 Jul 1881)
Minister for Galicia	21 Apr 1873 – 15 Feb 1879: *Florian* (from 1880: *Baron*) *Ziemiałkowski* (b. Berezowick 27 Dec 1817; d. Vienna 27 Mar 1900)
Without Portfolio	*Joseph Unger* (b. Vienna 2 Jul 1828; d. 2 May 1913)

15 Feb – 12 Aug 1879 (acting:) Stremayr

Prime Minister	*Karl von Stremayr* (see Karl Auersperg)
Home Affairs	*Eduard, Count Taaffe* (see Beust)
Education	*Karl von Stremayr* (see Karl Auersperg)
Justice	*Julius Glaser* (see Adolf Auersperg)
Defence	*Julius, Baron Horst* (see Adolf Auersperg)
Finance	*Sisinio, Baron de Pretis* (see Potocki)
Commerce	*Johann Chlumecky* (see Adolf Auersperg)
Agriculture	*Hieronymus, Count Colleredo-Mansfeld* (see Adolf Auersperg)
Minister for Galicia	*Florian, Baron Ziemiałkowski* (see Adolf Auersperg)

12 Aug 1879 – 11 Nov 1893: Taaffe

Prime Minister	*Eduard, Count Taaffe* (see Beust)
Home Affairs	*Eduard, Count Taaffe* (see Beust)
	12 Aug 1879 – 16 Feb 1880 (acting:) *Karl von*

Stremayr (see Karl Auersperg)
16 Feb 1880 – 5 Nov 1885: *Siegmund, Baron Conrad von Eybesfeld* (b. Kainberg 11 Aug 1821; d. Graz 9 Jul 1898)
5 Nov 1885 – 11 Nov 1893: *Paul* (from 1889: *Baron*) *Gautsch von Frankenthurn* (b. Vienna 26 Feb 1851; d. Vienna 20 Apr 1918)

Justice

12 Aug 1879 – 26 Jun 1880: *Karl von Stremayr* (see Karl Auersperg)
26 Jun 1880 – 14 Jan 1881: *Moritz, Baron Streit* (d. Vienna 23 Mar 1890)
14 Jan 1881 – 11 Oct 1888: *Alois* (from 1882: *Baron*) *Pražák* (b. Uherské-Hradište 21 Feb 1820; d. Vienna 30 Jan 1901)
11 Oct 1888 – 11 Nov 1893: *Friedrich, Count Schönborn* (b. Prague 11 Sep 1841; d. Vienna 21 Dec 1907)

Defence

12 Aug 1879 – 26 Jun 1880: *Julius, Baron Horst* (see Adolf Auersperg)
26 Jun 1880 – 11 Nov 1893: *Zeno, Count Welser von Welsersheimb* (b. Laibach 1 Dec 1835; d. Tab 2 Feb 1921)

Finance

12 Aug 1879 – 16 Feb 1880 (acting:) *Emil Chertek* (b. 22 Sep 1833; d. Prein 7 Oct 1922)
16 Feb – 26 Jun 1880: *Adolf, Baron Kriegs-Au* (b. Vienna 13 Dec 1819; d. Vienna 30 Oct 1884)
26 Jun 1880 – 2 Feb 1891: *Julian von Dunajewski* (b. Neu-Sandez 4 Jul 1822; d. Krakow 28 Dec 1907)
4 Feb 1891 – 11 Nov 1893: *Emil Steinbach* (b. Vienna 11 Jun 1846; d. Purkersdorf, Vienna, 26 May 1907)

Commerce

12 Aug 1879 – 26 Jun 1880: *Karl, Baron Korb von Weidenheim* (b. Prague 7 Apr 1835; d. Brno 15 Oct 1881)
26 Jun 1880 – 14 Jan 1881: *Alfred* (from 1882 *Baron*) *Kremer* (b. Vienna 13 May 1828; d. Dobling 27 Dec 1889)
14 Jan 1881 – 16 May 1886: *Felix, Baron Pino-Friedenthal* (b. Vienna 14 Oct 1826; d. Völkermarkt 14 Apr 1906)
16 Mar – 26 Jun 1886 (acting:) *Karl* (from 1882: *Baron*) *Pusswald* (b. Vienna 1820; d. Vienna 22 May 1895)

26 Jun 1886 – 11 Nov 1893: *Olivier, Marquis de Bacquehem* (b. Troppau 25 Aug 1847; d. Vienna 22 Apr 1917)

Agriculture	*Julius, Count Falkenhayn* (b. Vienna 20 Feb 1829; d. 12 Jan 1899)
Minister for Galicia	13 Aug 1879 – 11 Oct 1888: *Florian, Baron Ziemiałkowski* (see Adolf Auersperg)
	11 Oct 1888 – 12 Nov 1892: *Filip Zaleski* (b. Lvov 26 Sep 1836; d. Truskawice 21 Sep 1911)
Czech Affairs	12 Aug 1879 – 22 Dec 1891: *Alois* (from 1882: *Baron*) *Prazák* (see above)
German Affairs	22 Dec 1891 – 12 Nov 1893: no appointment made
	23 Dec 1891 – 8 Dec 1892: *Gandolf, Count Küenburg* (b. Prague 12 May 1841; d. Salzburg 2 Mar 1921)

11 Nov 1893 – 19 Jun 1895: Windisch-Grätz

Prime Minister	*Alfred (August) Prince Windisch-Grätz* (b. Prague 31 Oct 1851; d. Tachau 23 Nov 1927)
Home Affairs	*Olivier, Marquis de Bacquehem* (see Taaffe)
Education	*Stanisław Madeyski-Poraj* (b. Sieniawa 24 Apr 1841; d. Lussingrande 19 Jun 1910)
Justice	*Friedrich, Count Schönborn* (see Taaffe)
Defence	*Zeno, Count Welser von Welsersheimb* (see Taaffe)
Finance	*Ernst von Plener* (b. Eger 18 Oct 1841; d. Vienna 29 Apr 1923)
Commerce	*Gundaker, Count Wurmbrand-Stuppach* (b. Josefstadt 9 May 1838; d. Graz 26 Mar 1901)
Agriculture	*Julius, Count Falkenhayn* (see Taaffe)
Minister for Galicia	*Apollinar Jaworski* (b. 23 Jul 1825; d. Lvov 22 Oct 1904)

19 Jun – 30 Sep 1895 (acting:) Kielmansegg

Prime Minister	*Erich, Count Kielmansegg* (b. Hanover 13 Feb 1847; d. Vienna 5 Feb 1923)
Home Affairs	*Erich, Count Kielmansegg* (see above)
Education	(acting:) *Eduard Rittner* (b. Bursztyn 26 Dec 1845; d. Vienna 27 Sep 1899)
Justice	(acting:) *Karl Count Krall von Krallenberg* (b. Vienna 22 Mar 1829; d. Vienna 30 Mar 1907)
Defence	*Zeno, Count Welser von Welsersheimb* (see Taaffe)

Finance	*Eugen Böhm von Bawerk* (b. Brno 12 Feb 1851: d. Kramsach 27 Aug 1914)
Commerce	(acting:) *Heinrich von Wittek* (b. Vienna 29 Jan 1844; d. Vienna 10 Apr 1930)
Agriculture	(acting:) *Ferdinand* (from 1899: *Baron*) *Florentin von Blumfeld* (b. Marburg 3 Nov 1835; d. Vienna 13 Mar 1902)
Minister for Galicia	*Apollinar von Jaworski* (see Windisch-Grätz)

30 Sep 1895 – 30 Nov 1897: Badeni

Prime Minister	*Kazimierz Felix, Count Badeni* (b. Lvov 14 Oct 1846; d. Lvov 9 Jul 1909)
Home Affairs	*Kazimierz Felix, Count Badeni* (see above)
Education	*Paul, Baron Gautsch von Frankenthurn* (see Taaffe)
Justice	*Johann Nepomuk, Count Gleispach* (b. Görz 29 Sep 1840; d. Graz 22 Dec 1906)
Defence	*Zeno, Count Welser von Welsersheimb* (see Taaffe)
Finance	*Leon Biliński* (b. Zaleszczyki 15 Jun 1846; d. Vienna 14 Jun 1923)
Commerce	*Hugo Glanz, Baron Eicha* (b. Hermannstadt 19 Dec 1848; d. Vienna 9 Jun 1915)
Agriculture	*Johann, Count Ledebur-Wicheln* (b. Krzemusch 30 May 1842; d. Prague 14 May 1903)
Minister for Galicia	29 Sep 1895 – 17 Jan 1896 (acting:) *Leon Biliński* (see above)
	17 Jan 1896 – 28 Nov 1897: *Eduard Rittner* (see Kielmansegg)
Railways (new post)	17 Jan 1896 – 30 Nov 1897: *Emil* (from 1898: *Baron*) *Guttenberg* (b. Tamsweg 4 Jan 1841; d. Salzburg 30 Jan 1941)

30 Nov 1897 – 5 Mar 1898: Gautsch von Frankenthurn I

Prime Minister	*Paul, Baron Gautsch von Frankenthurn* (for 1st time) (see Taaffe)
Home Affairs	*Paul, Baron Gautsch von Frankenthurn* (see Taaffe)
Education	*Vinzenz, Count Baillet de Latour* (b. Graz 5 Oct 1848; d. Vienna 4 Dec 1913)
Justice	*Ignaz* (from 1909: *Baron*) *Ruber* (b. Brno 8 May 1845; d. Vienna 7 Nov 1933)
Defence	*Zeno, Count Welser von Welsersheimb* (see Taaffe)
Finance	*Eugen Böhm von Bawerk* (see Kielmansegg)

Commerce   *Ernst von Koerber* (b. Trient 6 Nov 1850; d. Gutenbrunn 5 Mar 1919)

Agriculture   *Artur, Count Bylandt-Rheydt*, the Younger (b. Prague 3 Feb 1854; d. Baden bei Wien 6 Jul 1915)

Railways   *Heinrich von Wittek* (see Kielmansegg)

Minister for Galicia   17 Dec 1897 – 5 Mar 1898: *Hermann, Baron Loebl* (b. Drohobycz 29 Dec 1835; d. Lvov 11 Mar 1907)

5 Mar 1898 – 2 Oct 1899: Thun und Hohenstein

Prime Minister   *Franz, Count Thun und Hohenstein* (b. Tetschen 2 Sep 1847; d. Tetschen 1 Nov 1916)

Home Affairs   *Franz, Count Thun und Hohenstein* (see above)

Education   *Artur, Count Bylandt-Rheydt*, the Younger (see Gautsch von Frankenthurn I)

Justice   *Ignaz, Baron Ruber* (see Gautsch von Frankenthurn I)

Defence   *Zeno, Count Welser von Welsersheimb* (see Taaffe)

Finance   *Josef Kaizl* (b. Volyn 10 Jun 1854; d. Miskowitz 19 Aug 1901)

Commerce   5 Mar – 6 Oct 1898: *Josef Baernreither* (b. Prague 12 Apr 1845; d. Teplitz 19 Sep 1925)
                  6 Oct 1898 – 23 Sep 1899: *Joseph, Baron Di Pauli von Treuheim* (b. Innsbruck 9 Mar 1844; d. Vienna 28 Jan 1905)

Agriculture   *Michael, Baron Kast von Ebelsberg* (b. Nedelischt 15 Oct 1859; d. Ebelsberg 29 Jul 1932)

Railways   *Heinrich von Wittek* (see Kielmansegg)

Commissioner for Galicia   *Adam Jędrzejowicz* (b. Zaczernie 17 Dec 1847; d. Krakow 4 May 1924)

2 Oct – 21 Dec 1898: Clary und Aldringen

Prime Minister   *Manfred, Count Clary und Aldringen* (b. Vienna 30 May 1852; d. Schloss Hernau 12 Feb 1928)

Home Affairs   *Ernst von Koerber* (see Gautsch von Frankenthurn I)

Education   (acting:) *Wilhelm August von Hartel* (b. Hof 18 May 1839; d. Vienna 14 Jan 1907)

Justice   *Eduard von Kindinger* (b. Milan 1833; d. Trieste 26 Apr 1906)

Defence   *Zeno, Count Welser von Welsersheimb* (see Taaffe)

Finance   (acting:) *Seweryn von Kniaziołucki* (b. Strzalkowa 24 Mar 1853; d. Vienna 25 Feb 1913)

Commerce	(acting:) *Franz Stibral* (b. Vienna 16 Nov 1854; d. Salzburg 3 Feb 1930)
Agriculture	*Manfred, Count Clary und Aldringen* (see above)
Railways	*Heinrich von Wittek* (see Kielmansegg)
Minister for Galicia	*Kazimierz Chłędowski* (b. Lubatówka 28 Feb 1843; d. Vienna 26 Mar 1920)

21 Dec 1899 – 18 Jan 1900: Wittek

Prime Minister	*Heinrich von Wittek* (see Kielmansegg)
Home Affairs	*Josef Stummer* (b. Bistřice 1834; d. Eger 15 Jul 1903)
Education	(acting:) *Alfred von Bernd* (b. Vienna 19 Oct 1848; d. Vienna 24 Dec 1920))
Justice	(acting:) *Ferdinand von Schrott*
Defence	*Zeno, Count Welser von Welsersheimb* (see Taaffe)
Finance	(acting:) *Adolf, Baron Jorkasch-Koch* (b. Lvov 3 Oct 1848; d. Vienna 22 Apr 1929)
Commerce	(acting:) *Franz Stibral* (see Clary und Aldringen)
Agriculture	(acting:) *Ferdinand, Baron Blumfeld* (see Kielmansegg)
Railways	*Heinrich von Wittek* (see Kielmansegg)
Minister for Galicia	*Kazimierz Chłędowski* (see Clary und Aldringen)

19 Jan 1900 – 27 Dec 1904: Koerber I

Prime Minister	*Ernst von Koerber* (for 1st time) (see Gautsch von Frankenthurn I)
Home Affairs	*Ernst von Koerber* (see Gautsch von Frankenthurn I)
Education	*Wilhelm August von Hartel* (see Clary und Aldringen)
Justice	18 Jan 1900 – 17 Nov 1902: *Alois, Baron Spens von Booden* (b. Teschen 7 Jul 1835; d. Vienna 2 Apr 1919)
	17 Nov 1902 – 31 Dec 1904: *Ernst von Koerber* (see Gautsch von Frankenthurn I)
Defence	*Zeno, Count Welser von Welsersheimb* (see Taaffe)
Finance	18 Jan 1900 – 26 Oct 1904: *Eugen Böhm von Bawerk* (see Kielmansegg)
	26 Oct – 27 Dec 1904: *Mansuet Kosel* (b. Krotoszyn 25 Aug 1856; d. Vienna 22 Aug 1919)
Commerce	*Guido, Baron Call* (b. Trieste 6 Sep 1849; d. Graz 12 May 1927)
Agriculture	18 Jan 1900 – 26 Oct 1904: *Karl, Baron Giovanelli* (b. Brescia 28 Oct 1847; d. Kaltern 6 Jun 1922)

26 Oct – 27 Dec 1904: *Ferdinand von Longueval, Count Buquoy* (b. Vienna 15 Sep 1856; d. Görz 27 Sep 1909)

Railways	*Heinrich von Wittek* (see Kielmansegg)
Minister for Galicia	*Leonhard Piętak* (b. Przemysl 24 Feb 1841; d. Vienna 25 Feb 1909)
	18 Jan 1900 – 10 Jul 1903: *Antonin Rezek* (b. Jindřichův Hradec 13 Jan 1853; d. Prague 4 Feb 1909)
Czech Affairs	26 Oct 1904 – 27 Dec 1904: *Antonin Randa* (b. Bistřice 8 Jul 1834; d. Prague 6 Oct 1914)

1 Jan 1905 – 30 April 1906: Gautsch von Frankenthurn II

Prime Minister	*Paul, Baron Gautsch von Frankenthurn* (for 2nd time) (see Taaffe)
Home Affairs	*Artur, Count Bylandt-Rheydt*, the Younger (see Gautsch von Frankenthurn I)
Education	1 Jan – 11 Sep 1905: *Wilhelm August von Hartel* (see Clary und Aldringen)
	11 Sep 1905 – 30 Apr 1906: *Richard, Baron Bienerth* (from 1915: *Count Bienerth-Schmerling*) (b. Verona 2 Mar 1863; d. Vienna 3 Jun 1918)
Justice	Franz Klein (b. Vienna 24 Apr 1854; d. Vienna 6 Apr 1926)
Defence	1 Jan – Mar 1905: *Zeno, Count Welser von Welsersheimb* (see Taaffe)
	11 Mar 1905 – 30 Apr 1906: *Franz* (from 1908: *Baron*) *Schönaich* (b. Vienna 27 Feb 1844; d. Vienna 28 Jan 1916)
Finance	*Mansuet Kosel* (see Koerber I)
Commerce	1 Jan – 11 Sep 1905: *Guido, Baron Call* (see Koerber I)
	11 Sep 1905 – 30 Apr 1906: *Leopold, Count Auersperg* (b. Buda 16 May 1855; d. Baden bei Wien Feb 1918)
Agriculture	*Ferdinand von Longueval, Count Buquoy* (see Koerber I)
Railways	1 Jan – 2 May 1905: *Heinrich von Wittek* (see Kielmansegg)
	2 May 1905 – 30 Apr 1906: *Ludwig Wrba* (b. Venice 6 Mar 1844; d. Pressbaum 20 Aug 1927)
Minister for Galicia	*Leonhard Piętak* (see Koerber I)
Czech Affairs	*Antonin Randa* (see Koerber I)

2 May – 28 May 1906: Hohenlohe-Waldenburg-Schillingsfürst

Prime Minister	*Konrad, Prince Hohenlohe-Waldenburg-Schillingsfürst* (b. Vienna 16 Dec 1863; d. Leoben 21 Dec 1918)
Home Affairs	*Konrad, Prince Hohenlohe-Waldenburg-Schillingsfürst* (see above)
Education	*Richard, Baron Bienerth* (see Gautsch von Frankenthurn II)
Justice	*Franz Klein* (see Gautsch von Frankenthurn II)
Defence	*Franz, Baron Schönaich* (see Gautsch von Frankenthurn II)
Finance	*Mansuet Kosel* (see Koerber I)
Commerce	*Leopold, Count Auersperg* (see Gautsch von Frankenthurn II)
Agriculture	*Ferdinand von Longueval, Count Buquoy* (see Koerber I)
Railways	*Ludwig Wrba* (see Gautsch von Frankenthurn II)
Minister for Galicia	*Leonhard Piętak* (see Koerber I)
Czech Affairs	*Antonin Randa* (see Koerber I)

2 Jun 1906 – 7 Nov 1908: Beck

Prime Minister	*Max Vladimir, Baron von Beck* (b. Währing 6 Sep 1854; d. Vienna 20 Jan 1943)
Home Affairs	*Richard, Baron Bienerth* (see Gautsch von Frankenthurn II)
Education	*Gustav Marchet* (b. Baden 29 May 1946; d. Schlackenwerth 27 Apr 1916)
Justice	*Franz Klein* (see Gautsch von Frankenthurn II)
Defence	2 Jun – 24 Oct 1906: *Franz, Baron Schönaich* (see Gautsch von Frankenthurn II)
	28 Oct 1906 – 1 Dec 1907: *Julius* (from 1907: *Baron*) *Latscher von Lauendorf* (b. Iglau 22 July 1846; d. Salzburg 2 Aug 1909)
	1 Dec 1907 – 7 Nov 1908: *Friedrich* (from 1912: *Baron*) *Georgi* (b. Prague 27 Jan 1852; d. Vienna 23 Jun 1926)
Finance	*Witold von Korytowski* (b. Grochowicka 8 Aug 1850; d. Poznan 11 Jun 1923)
Commerce	3 Jun 1906 – 9 Nov 1907: *Josef Fořt* (b. Key 25 Dec 1850; d. in train between Karlsruhe and Kehl, 11 May 1929)

	9 Nov 1907 – 7 Nov 1908: *Franz Fiedler* (b. Dwar 13 Dec 1858; d. Prague 28 Jan 1925)
Agriculture	2 Jun 1906 – 9 Nov 1907: *Leopold, Count Auersperg* (see Gautsch von Frankenthurn II)
	9 Nov 1907 – 7 Nov 1908: *Alfred Ebenhoch* (b. Bregenz 18 May 1855; d. Vienna 30 Jan 1912)
Railways	*Julius Derschatta* (b. Zara 12 Sep 1852; d. Vienna 3 Feb 1924)
Minister of Galicia	2 Jun 1906 – 20 Nov 1907: *Wojciech, Count Dzieduszycki* (b. Jezupol 13 Jul 1848; d. Vienna 23 Mar 1909)
	20 Nov 1907 – 7 Nov 1908: *David Abrahamowitz* (b. Targowica Polna 30 Jun 1839; d. Lvov 24 Dec 1926)
Czech Affairs	2 Jun 1906 – 9 Nov 1907: *Bedřich Pacák* (b. Belohrad 14 Sep 1846; d. Veltrusy 23 May 1914) 9 Nov 1907 – 7 Nov 1908: *Karel Prášek* (b. Řivno 4 Feb 1868; d. Košetice 13 Feb 1932)
German Affairs	2 Jun 1906 – 9 Nov 1907: *Heinrich Prade* (b. Reichenberg 5 Jun 1853; d. Vienna 22 Apr 1927)
	9 Nov 1907 – 29 Apr 1908: *Franz Peschka* (b. Abtsdorf 14 Aug 1856; d. Vienna 29 Apr 1908)
	6 May – 7 Nov 1908: *Heinrich Prade* (see above)
Public Works (new post)	21 Mar – 7 Nov 1908: *Albert Gessmann* (b. Vienna 18 Jan 1852; d. Prein 7 Jul 1920)
Without Portfolio	9 Nov 1907 – 21 May 1908: *Albert Gessmann* (see above)

15 Nov 1908 – 9 Jan 1911: Bienerth I

Prime Minister	*Richard, Baron Beinerth* (for 1st time) (see Gautsch von Frankenthurn II)
Home Affairs	*Guido, Baron Haerdtl* (b. Vienna 23 Feb 1859; d. Vienna 20 Jul 1928)
Education	15 Nov 1908 – 10 Feb 1909: *Josef Kaněra* (b. Nachod 6 Mar 1854; d. Vienna 1 Nov 1914)
	10 Feb 1909 – 9 Jan 1911: *Karl, Count Stürgkh* (b. Graz 30 Oct 1859; d. Vienna 21 Oct 1916)
Justice	14 Nov 1908 – 10 Feb 1909: *Robert Holzknecht von Hort* (b. Tischnowitz 2 Apr 1838; d. Vienna 12 Jul 1918)
	10 Feb 1909 – 9 Jan 1911: *Viktor von Hochenburger* (b. Graz 24 Jun 1857; d. Graz 9 Aug 1918)
Defence	*Friedrich Georgi* (see Beck)

Finance	15 Nov 1908 – 10 Feb 1909: *Adolf, Baron Jorkasch-Koch* (see von Wittek)
	10 Feb 1909 – 9 Jan 1911: *Leon Biliński* (see Badeni)
Commerce	15 Nov 1908 – 10 Feb 1909: *Viktor Mataja* (b. Vienna 20 Jul 1857; d. Vienna 19 Jun 1934)
	10 Feb 1909 – 9 Jan 1911: *Richard* (from 1916: *Baron*) *Weiskirchner* (b. Vienna 24 Mar 1861, d. Vienna 30 Apr 1926)
Agriculture	15 Nov 1908 – 10 Feb 1909; *Josef von Pop* (b. Brozno 27 Oct 1848; d. Vienna 20 Jul 1917)
	10 Feb – 1 Nov 1909; *Albien Bráf* (b. Trebitsch 27 Feb 1851; d. Rostok 1 Jul 1912)
	1 Nov 1909 – 10 Feb 1911; *Josef von Pop* (see above)
Railways	15 Nov 1908 – 10 Feb 1909; *Sidonius von Forster* (b. Prague 9 Jun 1860; d. Vienna 15 Jan 1922)
	10 Feb 1909 – 9 Jan 1911; *Ludwig Wrba* (see Gautsch von Frankenthurn II)
Minister for Galicia	15 Nov 1908 – 4 May 1909: *David Abrahamowitz* (see Beck)
	4 Mar 1909 – 9 Jan 1911: *Władysław Dulęba* (b. Krakow 24 Sep 1851; d. Kosow 17 Jun 1930)
Czech Affairs	15 Nov 1908 – 1 Nov 1909; *Jan Žáček* (b. Olomouc 31 May 1849; d. Brno 10 Apr 1934)
	1 Nov 1909 – 9 Jan 1911: no appointment made
German Affairs	15 Nov 1908 – 21 Feb 1910: *Gustav Schreiner* (b. Nemelkau 11 Jun 1847; d. Oberstankau 14 Jun 1922)
	21 Feb 1910 – 9 Jan 1911: no appointment made
Labour	15 Nov 1908 – 10 Feb 1909: *Maximilian, Count Wickenburg* (b. Graz 21 Mar 1857; d. Grundlsee 4 Feb 1918)
	10 Feb 1909 – 9 Jan 1911: *August Ritt* (b. Budweis 26 Aug 1852; d. Vienna 30 Mar 1934)

9 Jan – 28 Jun 1911: Bienerth II

Prime Minister	*Richard, Baron Bienerth* (for 2nd time) (see Gautsch von Frankenthurn II)
Home Affairs	*Maximilian, Count Wickenburg* (see Bienerth I)
Public Worship and Education	*Karl, Count Stürgkh* (see Bienerth I)
Justice	*Viktor von Hochenburger* (see Bienerth I)
Finance	*Robert Meyer* (b. Vienna 8 Jan 1855; d. Vienna 10 Jun 1914)

Commerce	9 Jan - 14 Jun 1911: *Richard Weiskirchner* (see Bienerth I)
	14 - 26 Jun 1911: no appointment made
Labour	*Karl Marek* (b. Passek 1850)
Railways	*Stanisław Głąbiński* (b. Skole 25 Feb 1862; d. (?) 1943)
Agriculture	*Adalbert, Baron Widmann* (b. Platsch 20 May 1968)
Defence	*Friedrich* (from 1912: *Baron*) *Georgi* (see von Beck)
Commissioner for Galicia	*Wacław* (from 1913: *Count*) *Zaleski* (b. Lvov 28 Jun 1868; d. Meran 24 Dec 1913)

28 Jun - 28 Oct 1911: Gautsch von Frankenthurn III

Prime Minister	*Paul, Baron Gautsch von Frankenthurn* (for 3rd time) (see Taaffe)
Home Affairs	*Maximilian, Count Wickenburg* (see Bienerth I)
Public Worship and Education	*Karl, Count Stürgkh* (see Bienerth I)
Justice	*Viktor von Hochenburger* (see Bienerth I)
Finance	*Robert Meyer* (see Bienerth II)
Commerce	*Viktor Mataja* (see Bienerth I)
Labour	*Karl Marek* (see Bienerth II)
Railways	*Victor Röll* (b. Czernowitz 22 May 1853; d. Vienna 12 Oct 1922)
Agriculture	*Adalbert, Baron Widmann* (see Bienerth II)
Defence	*Friedrich Georgi* (see von Beck)
Minister for Galicia	*Wacław von Zaleski* (see Bienerth II)

3 Nov 1911 - 21 Oct 1916: Stürgkh

Prime Minister	*Karl, Count Stürgkh* (see Bienerth I)
Home Affairs	3 Nov 1911 - 30 Nov 1915: *Karl, Baron Heinold von Udynski* (b. Udine 25 Aug 1862; d. Brno 29 Dec 1943)
	30 Nov 1915 - 29 Aug 1916: *Konrad, Prince Hohenlohe-Waldenburg-Schillingsfürst* (see Hohenlohe-Waldenburg-Schillingsfürst)
	29 Aug - 21 Oct 1916: *Erasmus, Baron Handel* (b. Mirskofen 1 Jun 1860; d. Salzburg 6 Jun 1928)
Education	*Max* (from 1916: *Baron*) *Hussarek von Heinlein* (b. Bratislava 3 May 1865; d. Vienna 7 Mar 1935)
Justice	*Viktor von Hochenburger* (see Bienerth I)
Finance	3 Nov - 19 Nov 1911: *Robert Meyer* (see Bienerth II)
	19 Nov 1911 - 8 Oct 1913: *Wacław von Zaleski* (see Bienerth II)

	8 Oct 1913 – 30 Nov 1915: *August, Baron Engel von Mainfelden* (b. Vienna 1 Jul 1855; d. Vienna 9 Jan 1941)
	3 Nov 1915 – 21 Oct 1916: *Karl von Leth* (b. Vienna 27 May 1861; d. Vienna 17 Nov 1930)
Commerce	3 Nov 1911 – 20 Sep 1912; *Moritz* (from 1912: *Baron*) *Roessler* (b. Vienna 13 Jul 1857; d. Vienna 12 Dec 1912)
	20 Sep 1912 – 30 Nov 1915; *Rudolf* (from 1915: *Baron*) *Schuster* (b. Budapest 12 Apr 1855; d. Vienna 31 May 1930)
	30 Nov 1915 – 21 Oct 1916: *Alexander Bernhard* (from 1917: *Baron*) *Spitzmüller* (b. Vienna 12 Jun 1862; d. Velden 5 Sep 1953)
Labour	*Otaker* (from 1915: *Baron*) *Trnka* (b. Pardubice 19 Jul 1871; d. Vienna 25 Jun 1919)
Railways	*Sidonius von Forster* (see Bienerth I)
Agriculture	3 Nov – 19 Nov 1911 (acting:) *Wacław von Zaleski* (see Bienerth II)
	19 Nov 1911 – 1 Jul 1912: *Albin Bráf* (see Bienerth I)
	1 Jul – 20 Sep 1912: *Karl, Baron Heinold von Udynski* (see above)
	21 Sep 1912 – 21 Oct 1916: *Franz, Baron Zenker* (b. Vienna 6 Aug 1856; d. Vienna 5 Mar 1925)
Defence	*Friedrich* (from 1912: *Baron*) *Georgi* (see von Beck)
Minister for Galicia	19 Nov 1911 – 26 Dec 1913: *Władisław Długosz* (b. Krakow 24 Jul 1864; d. Krakow 24 Jun 1937)
	2 Jan 1914 – 21 Oct 1916; *Zdzisław Morawski* (b. Poznan 1859)
Food (new post)	12 – 21 Oct 1916: *Oskar von Keller*

31 Oct – 13 Dec 1916: Koerber II

Prime Minister	*Ernst von Koerber* (for 2nd time) (see Gautsch von Frankenthurn I)
Home Affairs	*Erwin, Baron Schwartzenau* (b. Vienna 11 Sep 1858; d. Vienna 13 Jan 1926)
Public Worship and Education	*Max, Baron Hussarek von Heinlein* (see Stürgkh)
Justice	*Franz Klein* (see Gautsch von Frankenthurn II)
Finance	*Karl Marek* (b. Eger 1860)
Commerce	*Franz Stibral* (see Clary und Aldringen)
Labour	*Otaker, Baron Trnka* (see Stürgkh)

Railways	*Ernst Schaible* (b. Grafenegg 18 Oct 1868; d. Vienna 6 Feb 1956)
Agriculture	*Heinrich, Count Clam-Martinitz* (b. Vienna 1 Jan 1863; d. Clam 7 Mar 1832)
Defence	*Friedrich, Baron Georgi* (see von Beck)
Minister for Galicia	*Michal Bobrzyński* (b. Krakow 30 Sep 1849; d. Dupuchow 2 Jul 1935)
Food	*Oskar von Keller* (see Stürgkh)

20 Dec 1916 - 23 Jun 1917: Clam-Martinitz

Prime Minister	*Heinrich Count Clam-Martinitz* (see Koerber II)
Home Affairs	*Erasmus, Baron Handel* (see Stürgkh)
Public Worship and Education	*Max, Baron Hussarek von Heinlein* (see Stürgkh)
Justice	*Josef, Baron Schenk* (b. Tarnopol 23 Aug 1858; d. Vienna 19 Apr 1941)
Finance	*Alexander, Baron Spitzmüller* (see Stürgkh)
Commerce	*Karl Urban* (b. Prague 1 Sep 1865; d. Prague Oct 1940)
Labour	*Otakar, Baron Trnka* (see Stürgkh)
Railways	*Sidonius von Forster* (see Bienerth I)
Agriculture	20 Dec 1916 - 1 Jun 1917; *Heinrich Count Clam-Martinitz* (see Koerber II)
	1 - 23 Jun 1917: *Ernest Seidler von Feuchtenegg* (b. Schwechat 5 Jun 1862; d. Vienna 23 Jan 1931)
Defence	*Friedrich, Baron Georgi* (see von Beck)
Minister for Galicia	*Michal Bobrzyński* (see von Koerber II)
Food	20 Dec 1916 - 5 Jan 1917: *Oscar Kokstein* (b. Warasdin 24 Nov 1860; d. Vienna 1 Mar 1943)
	5 Jan - 21 Jun 1917: *Anton Höfer* (b. Bozen 1 Jan 1871; d. Vienna 22 Jul 1949)
Without Portfolio	*Josef Baernreither* (see Thun und Hohenstein)

23 Jun 1917 - 25 Jul 1918: Seidler von Feuchtenegg

Prime Minister	*Ernst Seidler von Feuchtenegg* (see Clam-Martinitz)
Home Affairs	23 Jun 1917 - 11 Jun 1918: *Friedrich Count Toggenburg* (b. Bozen 12 Jul 1866; d. Bozen 9 Mar 1956)
	11 Jun - 22 Jul 1918: *Edmund von Gayer* (b. Weisskirchen 1 Nov 1860; d. Vienna 14 Aug 1952)
Public Worship and Education	*Ludwig Alexis Cwikliński* (b. Gnesen 27 Jul 1853; d. Poznan 1943)

Justice	*Hugo von Schauer* (b. Leibnitz 1 Apr 1862; d. Voitsberg 2 Apr 1920)
Finance	*Ferdinand, Baron Wimmer* (b. Persenbeug 18 Dec 1860; d. Achental 3 Nov 1919)
Commerce	23 Jun – 30 Aug 1917: *Viktor Mataja* (see Bienerth I) 30 Aug 1917 – 22 Jul 1918: *Friedrich, Baron Wieser* (b. Vienna 10 Jul 1851; d. Vienna 23 Jul 1926)
Labour	23 Jun – 30 Aug 1917: *Emil* (from 1918: *Baron*) *Homann von Herimberg* (b. Vienna 1 Sep 1862; d. Leoben 9 Feb 1945) 30 Aug 1917 – 22 Jul 1918: *Friedrich, Baron Wieser* (see above)
Railways	*Karl, Baron Banhans* (b. Klaster Hradice 12 Jun 1861; d. Vienna 15 Jul 1942)
Agriculture	23 Jun 1917 – 30 Aug 1917: *Moritz von Ertl* (b. Vienna 14 Jan 1859; d. Vienna 1 Apr 1934) 30 Aug 1917 – 22 Jul 1918: *Ernst, Count Silva-Tarouca* (b. Čech 3 Jan 1860; d. Schwaigern 15 Aug 1936)
Defence	*Karl* (from 1918: *Baron*) *Czapp von Birkenstetten* (b. Belovar 9 Jan 1864; d. Vienna 20 Oct 1952)
Minister for Galicia	*Juljusz Twardowski* (b. Vienna 23 Jan 1874; d. Krakow 3 Jun 1945)
Food	23 Jun 1917 – 26 Feb 1918: *Anton Höfer* (see Clam-Martinitz) 26 Feb – 11 Jun 1918: *Ludwig Paul* (b. Vienna 16 Sep 1864; d. Vienna 1 Jul 1920)
Social Welfare (new post)	7 Oct 1917 – 22 Jul 1918: *Viktor Mataja* (see Bienerth I)
Health (new post)	30 Aug 1917 – 22 Jul 1918: *Ivan Horbachevsky* (b. Zarubińce 15 May 1854; d. Prague 24 May 1942)
Withot Portfolio	29 Aug 1917 – 26 May 1918: *Ivan von Žolger* (b. Devina 21 Oct 1867; d. Lassnitz 10 May 1925)

25 Jul – 27 Oct 1918: Hussarek von Heinlein

Prime Minister	*Max, Baron Hussarek von Heinlein* (see Stürgkh)
Home Affairs	*Edmund von Gayer* (see Seidler von Feuchtenegg)
Education and Public Worship	*Georg von Madeyski-Poray*
Justice	*Hugo von Schauer* (see Seidler von Feuchtenegg)
Finance	*Ferdinand, Baron Wimmer* (see Seidler von Feuchtenegg)

Commerce	*Friedrich, Baron Wieser* (see Seidler von Feuchtenegg)
Labour	*Emil Homann von Herimberg* (see Seidler von Feuchtenegg)
Railways	*Karl, Baron Banhans* (see Seidler von Feuchtenegg)
Agriculture	*Ernst, Count Silva-Tarouca* (see Seidler von Feuchtenegg)
Defence	*Karl, Baron Czapp von Birkenstetten* (see Seidler von Feuchtenegg)
Minister for Galicia	*Kazimierz Galecki* (b. Czarny Dunajec 19 Jul 1863; d. Krakow 1941)
Food	*Ludwig Paul* (see Seidler von Feuchtenegg)
Czech Affairs	*Ivan von Žolger* (see Seidler von Feuchtenegg)
Health	30 Jul – 27 Oct 1918: *Ivan Horbachevsky* (see Seidler von Feuchtenegg)
Social Welfare	*Viktro Mataja* (see Bienerth I)

27 Oci – 11 Nov 1918: Lammasch

Prime Minister	*Heinrich Lammasch* (b. Seitenstetten 21 Dec 1853; d. Salzburg 6 Jan 1920)
Home Affairs	*Edmund von Gayer* (see Seidler von Feuchtenegg)
Education and Public Worship	*Richard von Hampe* (b. Vienna 10 May 1863; d. Klosterneuburg 24 Oct 1931)
Justice	*Paul von Vittorelli* (b. Trieste 9 Mar 1851; d. Vienna 20 Apr 1932)
Finance	*Josef Redlich* (b. Goding 18 Jun 1869; d. Vienna 11 Nov 1936)
Commerce	*Friedrich, Baron Wieser* (see Seidler von Feuchtenegg)
Labour	*Emil, Baron Homann von Herimberg* (see Seidler von Feuchtenegg)
Railways	*Karl, Baron Banhans* (see Seidler von Feuchtenegg)
Agriculture	*Ernst, Count Silva-Tarouca* (see Seidler von Feuchtenegg)
Defence	*Frederick, Baron Lehne von Lensheim* (b. Vienna 8 Jan 1870; d. Grundlsee 7 Jul 1951)
Minister for Galicia	*Kazimierz Galecki* (see Hussarek von Heinlein)
Social Welfare	*Ignaz Seipel* (b. Vienna 19 Jul 1876; d. Permitz 2 Aug 1932)
Health	*Ivan Horbachevsky* (see Seidler von Feuchtenegg)
Food	*Ludwig Paul* (see Seidler von Feuchtenegg)

47

MINISTERS OF THE FEDERAL REPUBLIC OF AUSTRIA

30 Oct 1918 – 3 Mar 1919: Renner I

Chancellor	*Karl Renner* (for 1st time) (SPÖ) (b. Untertannowitz 14 Dec 1870; d. Vienna 31 Dec 1950)
Foreign Affairs	30 Oct – 11 Nov 1918: *Viktor Adler* (SPÖ) (b. Prague 24 Jun 1852; d. Vienna 11 Nov 1918)
	21 Nov 1918 – 3 Mar 1919: *Otto Bauer* (SPÖ) (b. Vienna 5 Sep 1882; d. Paris 4 Jul 1938)
Home Affairs	*Heinrich Mataja* (Christ Soc) (b. Vienna 14 Mar 1877; d. 1936)
Education	*Rafael Pacher* (German Nat) (b. 21 Jul 1857)
Justice	*Julius Roller* (German Nat)
Finance	*Otto Steinwender* (German Nat) (b. Klagenfurt 17 Feb 1847; d. Villach 20 Mar 1921)
Commerce and Industry	*Karl Urban* (German Nat) (see Clam-Martinitz)
Labour	*Johann Zerdik* (Christ Soc)
Agriculture	*Josef Stöckler* (Christ Soc)
War	*Josef Mayer* (German Agr) (b. Eger 9 Apr 1877)
Food	*Hans Löwenfeld-Russ* (b. Vienna 29 Oct 1873)
Transport	*Karl Jukel* (Christ Soc) (b. Vienna 21 Jan 1865)
Health	*Ignaz Kaup* (b. Maribor 11 Jan 1870; d. Munich 25 May 1944)
Welfare	*Ferdinand Hanusch* (SPÖ) (b. Oberdorf 9 Nov 1866; d. Vienna 28 Sep 1923)

15 Mar – 17 Oct 1919: Renner II

Chancellor	*Karl Renner* (for 2nd time) (SPÖ) (see Renner I)
Vice Chancellor	*Jodok Fink* (Christ Soc) (b. Andelsbuch 19 Feb 1853; d. Andelsbuch 1 Jul 1929)
Foreign Affairs	15 Mar – 26 Jul 1919 (acting:) *Otto Bauer* (SPÖ) (see Renner I)
	from 3 Apr 1919 (deputy:) *Franz Klein* (see Gautsch von Frankenthurn II)
	26 Jul – 17 Oct 1919: *Karl Renner* (SPÖ) (see Renner I)
Home Affairs	15 Mar – 9 May 1919: *Karl Renner* (SPÖ) (see Renner I)
	9 May – 17 Oct 1919: Matthias Eldersch (SPÖ) (b. Brno 24 Feb 1869; d. Vienna 20 Apr 1931)
Justice	*Richard Bratusch*

Finance	*Joseph Schumpeter* (b. Triesch 8 Feb 1883; d. Taconic, Conn., 8 Jan 1950)
Trade and Industry	*Johann Zerdik* (Christ Soc) (see Renner I)
Labour	*Ferdinand Hanusch* (SPÖ) (see Renner I)
Transport	*Ludwig Paul* (see Seidler von Feuchtenegg)
Agriculture and Forestry	*Josef Stöckler* (Christ Soc) (see Renner I)
Reconstructon	*Wilhelm Ellenbogen* (SPÖ) (b. Lundenburg 9 Jul 1863; d. New York 25 Feb 1951) Under-Secretary of State
War	*Julius Deutsch* (SPÖ) (b. Lackenback 2 Feb 1884; d. Vienna 17 Jan 1968)
Food	*Hans Löwenfeld-Russ* (see Renner I)
Health	9 May – 17 Oct 1919: *Julius Tandler* (SPÖ) (b. Iglau 16 Feb 1869) Under-Secretary of State

17 Oct 1919 – 11 Jun 1920: Renner III

Chancellor	*Karl Renner* (for 3rd time) (SPÖ) (see Renner I)
Vice Chancellor	*Jodok Fink* (Christ Soc) (see Renner II)
Foreign Affairs	*Karl Renner* (SPÖ) (see Renner I)
Home Affairs and Education	*Matthias Eldersch* (SPÖ) (see Renner II)
Administrative Reforms	*Michael Mayr* (Christ Soc) (b. Adlwang 10 Apr 1864; d. Waldkirchen 22 May 1922)
Finance	*Richard Reisch* (b. Vienna 7 Apr 1866; d. Vienna 17 Dec 1938)
Justice	*Rudolf Ramek* (Christ Soc) (b. Teschen 12 Apr 1881; d. Vienna 7 Jul 1941)
Labour	*Ferdinand Hanusch* (SPÖ) (see Renner I)
War	*Julius Deutsch* (SPÖ) (see Renner II)
Agriculture and Forestry	*Josef Stöckler* (Christ Soc) (see Renner I)
Trade, Industry and Building	*Johann Zerdik* (Christ Soc) (see Renner I)
Food	*Hans Löwenfeld-Russ* (SPÖ) (see Renner I)
Transport	*Ludwig Paul* (see Seidel von Feuchtenegg)

7 Jul – 20 Nov 1920: Mayr I

Head of Cabinet	*Michael Mayr* (for 1st time) (Christ Soc) (see Renner III)

Deputy Head of Cabinet	7 Jul – 22 Oct 1920: *Ferdinand Hanusch* (SPÖ) (see Renner I)
	22 Oct – 20 Nov 1920: *Eduard Heinl* (Christ Soc) (b. Vienna 9 Apr 1880; d. Vienna 10 Apr 1957)
Foreign Affairs	7 Jul – 22 Oct 1920: *Karl Renner* (SPÖ) (see Renner I)
	22 Oct – 20 Nov 1930: *Michael Mayr* (Christ Soc) (see Renner III)
Home Affairs	*Walter Breisky* (Christ Soc) (b. Berne 8 Jul 1871; d. Klosterneuburg 25 Sep 1944)
Finance	*Richard Reisch* (see Renner III)
Education	*Walter Breisky* (Christ Soc) (see above)
Justice	*Julius Roller* (Greater German Party) (see Renner I)
Labour	7 Jul – 22 Oct 1920: *Ferdinand Hanusch* (SPÖ) (see Renner I)
	22 Oct – 20 Nov 1920: *Eduard Heinl* (Christ Soc) (see above)
War	7 Jul – 22 Oct 1920: *Julius Deutsch* (SPÖ) (see Renner II)
	22 Oct – 20 Nov 1920: *Walter Breisky* (Christ Soc) (see above)
Nationalization	7 Jul – 22 Oct 1920: *Wilhelm Ellenbogen* (SPÖ) (see Renner II)
Agriculture and Forestry	until 22 Oct 1920: no appointment made
	22 Oct – 20 Nov 1920: *Alois Haueis* (Christ Soc) (b. Zams in Tirol 30 Mar 1860)
Commerce	*Eduard Heinl* (Christ Soc) (see above)
Food	9 Jul – 20 Nov 1920: *Alfred Grünberger* (b. Karlsbad 15 Oct 1875; d. Paris 24/25 Apr 1935)
Transport	*Karl Pesta*

20 Nov 1920 – 1 Jun 1921: Mayr II

Chancellor	*Michael Mayr* (for 2nd time) (Christ Soc) (see Renner III)
Vice Chancellor	*Walter Breisky* (Christ Soc) (see Mayr I)
Foreign Affairs	*Michael Mayr* (Christ Soc) (see Renner III)
Home Affairs	20 Nov 1920 – 7 Apr 1921: *Egon Glanz* (Christ Soc) (b. Vienna 29 Dec 1880; d. Vienna 16 Apr 1945)
	7 – 23 Apr 1921: *Walter Breisky* (Christ Soc) (see Mayr I)
	23 Apr – 1 Jun 1921: *Rudolf Ramek* (Christ Soc) (see Renner III)
Education	*Walter Breisky* (Christ Soc) (see Mayr I)

Finance	*Ferdinand Grimm* (b. Vienna 15 Feb 1869; d. Bad Kreuzen 8 Nov 1948)
Justice	*Rudolf Paltauf*
Commerce	*Eduard Heinl* (Christ Soc) (see Mayr I)
Food	*Alfred Grünberger* (see Mayr I)
Agriculture and Forestry	*Alois Haueis* (Christ Soc) (see Mayr I)
War	20 Nov 1920 – 7 Apr 1921: *Egon Glanz* (Christ Soc) (see above)
	7 – 28 Apr 1921: *Walter Breisky* (Christ Soc) (see Mayr I)
	28 Apr – 1 Jun 1921: *Karl Vaugoin* (Christ Soc) (b. Vienna 8 Jul 1873; d. Krems 11 Jun 1949)
Labour	*Josef Resch* (Christ Soc) (b. Vienna 8 Sep 1880)
Transport	*Karl Pesta* (see Mayr I)

21 Jun 1921 – 26 Jan 1922: Schober I

Chancellor	*Johann Schober* (for 1st time) (b. Perg 14 Nov 1874; d. Pottenbrunn 19 Aug 1932)
Vice Chancellor	*Walter Breisky* (Christ Soc) (see Mayr I)
Foreign Affairs	*Johann Schober* (see above)
Home Affairs	21 Jun 1921 – 16 Jan 1922: *Leopold Waber* (Greater German Party) (b. Unicov 17 Mar 1875)
	16 – 26 Jan 1922: *Johann Schober* (see above)
Education	*Walter Breisky* (Christ Soc) (see Mayr I)
Justice	*Rudolf Paltauf* (see Mayr II)
Finance	21 Jun – 7 Oct 1921: *Ferdinand Grimm* (see Mayr II)
	7 Oct 1921 – 26 Jan 1922: *Alfred Gürtler* (Christ Soc) (b. Gabel 30 Oct 1875; d. Graz 16 Mar 1933)
Commerce	21 Jun – 7 Oct 1921: *Alexander Angerer* (Greater German Party)
	7 Oct 1921 – 26 Jan 1922: *Alfred Grünberger* (see Mayr I)
Labour	*Franz Pauer* (b. Vienna 25 Nov 1870; d. 1936)
Agriculture and Forestry	*Leopold Hennet* (Christ Soc) (b. Gaaden 10 May 1876; d. Vienna 27 Mar 1950)
War	21 Jun – 7 Oct 1921: *Karl Vaugoin* (Christ Soc) (see Mayr II)
	7 Oct 1921 – 26 Jan 1922: *Josef Wächter*
Food	21 Jun – 7 Oct 1921: *Alfred Grünberger* (see Mayr I)
	7 Oct 1921 – 26 Jan 1922: merged with the Ministry of Commerce

Transport   *Walter Rodler* (b. 1867; d. Vienna 28 Dec 1931)

27 Jan – 24 May 1922: Schober II

Chancellor	*Johann Schober* (for 2nd time) (see Schober I)
Vice Chancellor	*Walter Breisky* (Christ Soc) (see Mayr I)
Foreign Affairs	*Leopold Hennet* (Christ Soc) (see Schober I)
Home Affairs	*Johann Schober* (see Schober I)
Education	*Walter Breisky* (Christ Soc) (see Mayr I)
Justice	*Rudolf Paltauf* (see Mayr II)
Finance	27 Jan – 10 May 1922: *Alfred Gürtler* (Christ Soc) (see Schober I)
	10 – 24 May 1922: *Johann Schober* (see Schober I)
Commerce and Food	*Alfred Grünberger* (see Mayr I)
Labour	*Franz Pauer* (see Schober I)
War	*Josef Wächter* (see Schober I)
Transport	*Walter Rodler* (see Schober I)
Agriculture and Forestry	*Leopold Hennet* (Christ Soc) (see Schober I)

31 May 1922 – 16 Apr 1923: Seipel I

Chancellor	*Ignaz Seipel* (for 1st time) (Christ Soc) (see Lammasch)
Vice Chancellor	*Felix Frank* (Greater German Party) (b. Vienna 31 Oct 1876)
Foreign Affairs	*Alfred Grünberger* (see Mayr I)
Home Affairs	*Felix Frank* (see above)
Education	*Emil Schneider* (Christ Soc) (b. Höchst in Vorarlberg 28 May 1883)
Justice	*Leopold Waber* (Greater German Party) (see Schober I)
Finance	31 May – 14 Nov 1922: *August Ségur* (b. Brno 22 Jan 1881; d. Vienna 1 Mar 1931)
	14 Nov 1922 – 16 Apr 1923: *Viktor Kienböck* (Christ Soc) (b. Vienna 18 Jan 1873; d. Vienna 24 Nov 1956)
Commerce	*Emil Kraft* (Greater German Party) (b. Graz 26 Jan 1865; d. Graz 5 Sep 1931)
Labour	*Richard Schmitz* (Christ Soc) (b. Vienna 14 Aug 1885; d. Vienna 27 Apr 1954)
War	*Karl Vaugoin* (Christ Soc) (see Mayr II)
Agriculture, Forestry and Food	*Rudolf Buchinger* (Christ Soc) (b. Staasdorf 3 Mar 1879; d. Tulln 20 Feb 1950)

Transport | *Franz Odehnal* (Christ Soc) (b. Brno 26 Dec 1870; d. Vienna 24 Dec 1928)

17 Apr – 20 Nov 1923: Seipel II

Chancellor	*Ignaz Seipel* (for 2nd time) (Christ Soc) (see Lammasch)
Vice Chancellor	*Felix Frank* (Greater German Party) (see Seipel I)
Foreign Affairs	*Alfred Grünberger* (see Mayr I)
Home Affairs	*Ignaz Seipel* (Christ Soc) (see Lammasch)
Education	*Emil Schneider* (Christ Soc) (see Seipel I)
Justice	*Felix Frank* (see Seipel I)
Finance	*Viktor Kienböck* (Christ Soc) (see Seipel I)
Commerce and Transport	*Hans Schürff* (Greater German Party) (b. Mödling 12 May 1875; d. Vienna 27 Mar 1939)
Labour	*Richard Schmitz* (Christ Soc) (see Seipel I)
War	*Karl Vaugoin* (Christ Soc) (see Mayr II)
Agriculture and Forestry	*Rudolf Buchinger* (Christ Soc) (see Seipel I)

20 Nov 1923 – 8 Nov 1924: Seipel III

Chancellor	*Ignaz Seipel* (for 3rd time) (Christ Soc) (see Lammasch)
Vice Chancellor	*Felix Frank* (Greater German Party) (see Seipel l)
Foreign Affairs	*Alfred Grünberger* (see Mayr I)
Home Affairs	*Ignaz Seipel* (Christ Soc) (see Lammasch)
Education	*Emil Schneider* (Christ Soc) (see Seipel I)
Justice	*Felix Frank* (see Seipel I)
Finance	*Viktor Kienböck* (Christ Soc) (see Seipel I)
Commerce and Transport	*Hans Schürff* (Greater German Party) (see Seipel II)
Labour	*Richard Schmitz* (Christ Soc) (see Seipel I)
War	*Karl Vaugoin* (Christ Soc) (see Mayr II)
Agriculture and Forestry	*Rudolf Buchinger* (Christ Soc) (see Seipel I)

19/20 Nov 1924 – 14 Jan 1926: Ramek I

Chancellor	*Rudolf Ramek* (for 1st time) (Christ Soc) (see Renner III)
Vice Chancellor	*Leopold Wabeer* (Greater German Party) (see Schober I)

Foreign Affairs	*Heinrich Mataja* (Christ Soc) (see Renner I)
Home Affairs	*Rudolf Ramek* (Christ Soc) (see Renner III)
Education	*Emil Schneider* (Christ Soc) (see Seipel I)
Justice	*Leopold Waber* (see Schober I)
Finance	*Jakob Ahrer* (Christ Soc) (b. 1888)
Commerce and Transport	*Hans Schürff* (Greater German Party) (see Seipel III)
Labour	*Josef Resch* (Christ Soc) (see Mayr II)
War	*Karl Vaugoin* (Christ Soc) (see Mayr II)
Agriculture and Forestry	*Rudolf Buchinger* (Christ Soc) (see Seipel I)

15 Jan – 15 Oct 1926: Ramek II

Chancellor	*Rudolf Ramek* (for 2nd time) (Christ Soc) (see Renner III)
Vice Chancellor	*Leopold Waber* (Greater German Party) (see Schober I)
Foreign Affairs	*Rudolf Ramek* (Christ Soc) (see Renner III)
Home Affairs	*Rudolf Ramek* (Christ Soc) (see Renner III)
Education	15 Jan – 16 Jun 1926: *Emil Schneider* (Christ Soc) (see Seipel I)
	16 – 25 Jun 1926: *Josef Resch* (Christ Soc) (see Mayr II)
	25 Jun – 15 Oct 1926: *Anton Rintelen* (Christ Soc) (b. Graz 15 Nov 1876; d. Graz 28 Jan 1946)
Justice	*Leopold Waber* (Greater German Party) (see Schober I)
Finance	*Josef Kollmann* (Christ Soc) (b. Gottschee 23 Oct 1868)
Commerce and Transport	*Hans Schürff* (Greater German Party) (see Seipel II)
Labour	*Josef Resch* (Christ Soc) (see Mayr II)
War	*Karl Vaugoin* (Christ Soc) (see Mayr II)
Agriculture and Forestry	*Andreas Thaler* (Christ Soc) (b. Oberau 10 Sep 1883; d. Dreizehnlinden, Brazil, 1939)

20 Oct 1926 – 18 May 1927; Seipel IV

Chancellor	*Ignaz Seipel* (for 4th time) (Christ Soc) (see Lammasch)
Vice Chancellor	*Franz Dinghofer* (Greater German Party) (b. Linz 6 Apr 1873; d. Vienna 12 Jan 1956)

Foreign Affairs	*Ignaz Seipel* (see Lammasch)
Home Affairs	*Ignaz Seipel* (see Lammasch)
Education	*Richard Schmitz* (Christ Soc) (see Seipel I)
Justice	*Franz Dinghofer* (see above)
Finance	*Viktor Kienböck* (Christ Soc) (see Seipel I)
Commerce and Transport	*Hans Schürff* (Greater German Party) (see Seipel II)
Labour	*Josef Resch* (Christ Soc) (see Mayr II)
War	*Karl Vaugoin* (Christ Soc) (see Mayr II)
Agriculture and Forestry	*Andreas Thaler* (Christ Soc) (see Ramek II)

19 May 1927 – 3 Apr 1929: Seipel V

Chancellor	*Ignaz Seipel* (for 5th time) (Christ Soc) (see Lammasch)
Vice Chancellor	*Karl Hartleb* (Country Party) (b. St. Georgen bei Neumarkt 23 Oct 1886)
Foreign Affairs	*Ignaz Seipel* (see Lammasch)
Home affairs	*Ignaz Seipel* (see Lammasch)
Education	*Richard Schmitz* (Christ Soc) (see Seipel I)
Justice	19 May 1927 – 4 Jul 1928: *Franz Dinghofer* (Greater German Party) (see Seipel IV) in charge from 19 May – 31 Aug 1927, minister thereafter
	6 Jul 1928 – 3 Apr 1929: *Franz Slama* (Greater German Party)(b. Brno 19 Jun 1885)
Finance	*Viktor Kienböck* (Christ Soc) (see Seipel I)
Commerce and Transport	*Hans Schürff* (Greater German Party) (see Seipel II)
Labour	*Josef Resch* (Christ Soc) (see Mayr II)
War	*Karl Vaugoin* (Christ Soc) (see Mayr II)
Agriculture and Forestry	*Andreas Thaler* (Christ Soc) (see Ramek II)

4 May – 25 Sep 1929: Streeruwitz

Chancellor	*Ernest Streeruwitz* (b. Mies 23 Sep 1874; d. Vienna 19 Oct 1952)
Vice Chancellor	*Vinzenz Schumy* (Country Party) (b. Saak bei Arnoldstein 28 Jul 1878)
Foreign Affairs	*Ernest Streeruwitz* (see above)
Home Affairs	*Vinzenz Schumy* (see above)

Education	*Emmerich Czermak* (Christ Soc) (b. Datschitz 18 Mar 1885)
Justice	*Franz Slama* (Greater German Party) (see Seipel V)
Finance	*Johann (Josef) Mittelberger* (Christ Soc)
Commerce and Transport	*Hans Schürff* (Greater German Party) (see Seipel II)
Labour	*Josef Resch* (Christ Soc) (see Mayr II)
War	*Karl Vaugoin* (Christ Soc) (see Mayr II)
Agriculture and Forestry	*Florian Födermayr* (Christ Soc) (b. Kronstorf bei Emms 18 Apr 1877)

26 Sep 1929 – 25 Sep 1930: Schober III

Chancellor	*Johann Schober* (for 3rd time) (Schober Group) (see Schober I)
Vice Chancellor	26 Sep 1929 – 24 Sep 1930: *Karl Vaugoin* (Christ Soc) (see Mayr II)
Foreign Affairs	*Johann Schober* (see Schober I)
Home Affairs	*Vinzenz Schumy* (Country Party) (see Streeruwitz)
Education	26 Sep – 16 Oct 1929: *Johann Schober* (see Schober I) 16 Oct 1929 – 25 Sep 1930: *Heinrich Srbik* (b. Vienna 10 Nov 1878; d. Ehrwald 16 Feb 1951)
Justice	*Franz Slama* (Greater German Party) (see Seipel V)
Finance	26 Sep – 16 Oct 1929: *Johann Schober* (see Schober I) 16 Oct 1929 – 25 Sep 1930: *Otto Juch* (Christ Soc) (b. Kirchbichl 25 Feb 1876)
Commerce and Transport	26 Sep 1929 – 17 Jun 1930: *Michael Hainisch* (Christ Soc) (b. Ane bei Gloggnitz 15 Aug 1858; d. Vienna 26 Feb 1940) 17 Jun – 22 Sep 1930: *Friedrich Schuster* (b. 1863; d. Graz 31 Aug 1932) 22 – 25 Sep 1930: no appointment made
Labour	*Theodor Innitzer* (b. Weipert 25 Dec 1875; d. Vienna 9 Oct 1955) 1932 Archbishop of Vienna, 1933 Cardinal
War	26 Sep 1929 – 24 Sep 1930: *Karl Vaugoin* (Christ Soc) (see Mayr II) 24 – 25 Sep 1930: no appointment made
Agriculture and Forestry	26 Sep 1929 – 24 Sep 1930: *Florian Födermayr* (Christ Soc) (see Streeruwitz) 24 – 25 Sep 1930: no appointment made

Austria-Hungary

See Austria and Hungary. For ministers with responsibility for both parts of the state between 24 Dec 1868 and 11 Nov 1918, see Austria.

Azerbaijan

14 Feb 1918	Azerbaijan with Georgia and Armenia forms the Autonomous and Democratic Transcaucasian Federal Republic (see Georgia)
26 May 1918	Break-up of Transcaucasian Republic; Azerbaijan independent

HEAD OF STATE

President of National Assembly

28 May 1918 – 27 Apr 1920	*Mehmet Emin Resulzade* (b. Baku 31 Jan 1884; d. Ankara 6 Mar 1955)

MEMBERS OF GOVERNMENT

Prime Ministers

28 May 1918	*Fath Ali Khan Cho'i* (Russian form: *Choinsky*) (for 1st time) (d. May(?) 1920)
17 Jun	*Fath Ali Khan Cho'i* (for 2nd time)
18 Dec 1918	*Fath Ali Khan Cho'i* (for 3rd time)
14 Apr 1919 – 27 Apr 1920	*Nasib Bey Yusofbeli* (d. May(?) 1920)
27 Apr 1920	Azerbaijan occupied by Soviet Army and incorporated in Russia.

Baden

HEADS OF STATE

Margraves and Grand Dukes

19 Apr 1527	Margravate divided into three parts, of which after the death of the Margrave *Philipp I* (b. 6 Nov 1479; d. 7 Nov 1533) the Baden-Baden and Baden-Durlach lines survived.

Baden-Baden line (Catholic, extinct 1771)

7 Nov 1533	*Bernhard III*, brother (b. 7 Dec 1474)
29 Jun 1536	*Philibert*, son (b. 22 Jan 1536)
3 Dec 1569 – 17 Jun 1588	*Philipp II*, son (b. 19 Feb 1559)
1595 – 1622	Administered from Baden-Durlach
Mar 1622	*Wilhelm I*, son of the Margrave Eduard Fortunatus von Baden (-Rodemachern) (b. 30 Jul 1593)
22 May 1697	*Ludwig Wilhelm*, grandson (b. 18 Apr 1655)
4 Jan 1707	*Ludwig Georg*, son (7 Jun 1702)
22 Oct 1761 – 21 Oct 1771	*August Wilhelm*, brother (14 Jan 1706)

Baden-Durlach line (Protestant from 1555)

7 Nov 1533	*Ernst*, brother of Philipp I (b. 17 Oct 1482; d. 6 Feb 1553)
Sep 1552	*Bernhard (IV)*, son (b. Feb 1517)
20 Jan 1553	*Karl II*, brother (b. 24 Aug 1529)
1577 – 1604	Baden-Durlach split by dynastic rivalries
23 Mar 1577 – 14 Apr 1604	*Ernst Friedrich*, son (b. 17 Oct 1560)
1577 – 17 Aug 1590	*Jakob III*, brother (b. 26 May 1562)
1577 – 12 Apr 1622	*Georg Friedrich*, brother (b. 30 Jan 1573; d. 24 Sep 1633)
24 Aug 1590 – 2 Mar 1591	*Ernst Jakob*, son of Jakob III (b. 24 Aug 1594)
12 Apr 1622	*Friedrich V*, son of Georg Friedrich (b. 6 Jul 1594)
8 Sep 1659	*Friedrich VI*, son (b. 16 Nov 1617)
31 Jan 1677	*Friedrich VII*, Magnus, son (b. 23 Sep 1647)
25 Jun 1709	*Karl III*, Wilhelm, son (b. 17 Jan 1679)
12 May 1738	*Karl Friedrich*, grandson (b. 22 Nov 1728) Elector from 8 May 1803, Duke from 5 May 1806
13 Aug 1806	Grand Duke

10 Jun 1811	*Karl*, grandson (b. 8 Jun 1786)
3 Dec 1818	*Ludwig I*, uncle (b. 9 Feb 1763)
30 Mar 1830	*Leopold*, brother (b. 29 Aug 1790)
24 Apr 1852	*Ludwig II*, son (b. 15 Aug 1824; d. 22 Jan 1858)
5 Sep 1856	*Friedrich I*, brother (b. 9 Sep 1826) Regent from 24 Apr 1852
28 Sep 1907 – 14 (22) Nov 1918	*Friedrich II*, son (b. 9 Jul 1857; d. 9 Aug 1928)
From 1918	Monarchy abolished and many functions taken over by central government of Germany

MEMBERS OF GOVERNMENT

1830 – 1838: Winter

Prime Minister	*Georg Ludwig Winter* (b. Prechtal 18 Jan 1778; d. Karlsruhe 27 Mar 1838)
Foreign Affairs and Lord Chamberlain	(1816) – Feb 1831: *Wilhelm Ludwig Leopold Reinhard, Baron Berstett* (b. Berstett 6 Jul 1769; d. Karslruhe 16 Feb 1837)
	27 Jul 1831 – Oct 1835: *Johann, Baron Türckheim* (b. Strasbourg 17 Oct 1778; d. Ragoz 30 Jul 1847)
	Oct 1835 – 27 Mar 1838: *Friedrich Landolin Karl, Baron Blittersdorf* (b. Mahlberg 10 Feb 1792; d. Frankfurt 16 Apr 1861)
Home Affairs	*Georg Ludwig Winter* (see above)
Finance (from 1828)	*Christian Friedrich von Boeckh* (b. Karlsruhe 13 Aug 1777; d. Karlsruhe 21 Dec 1855)

1838 – 1839: Nebenius I

Prime Minister	*Karl Friedrich Nebenius* (for 1st time) (b. Rhodt bei Landau 29 Sep 1785; d. 8 Jun 1857)
Foreign Affairs	*Friedrich Landolin Karl, Baron Blittersdorf* (see Winter)
Home Affairs	*Karl Friedrich Nebenius* (see above)
Finance	*Christian Friedrich von Boeckh* (see Winter)

1839 – Nov 1843: Blittersdorf

Prime Minister and Foreign Affairs	*Friedrich Landolin Karl, Baron Blittersdorf* (see Winter)

| Home Affairs | *Franz, Baron Rüdt von Collenberg-Eberstadt* (b. Ohringen 16 Nov 1789; d. 16 May 1860) |
| Finance | *Christian Friedrich von Boeckh* (see Winter) |

Nov 1843 – 28 Mar 1845: von Boeckh

Prime Minister	*Christian Friedrich von Boeckh* (see Winter)
Foreign Affairs	*Alexander von Dusch* (b. Neustadt an der Hardt 27 Jan 1789; d. Heidelberg 27 Oct 1876)
Home Affairs	Nov 1843 – 1 Nov 1844: *Franz, Baron Rüdt von Collenberg-Erberstadt* (see Blittersdorf) 1 Nov 1844 – 1845: *Erhardt* (d. 1845)
Finance	Nov 1844 – 28 Mar 1845: *Franz Anton Regenauer* (b. Bruchsal 10 Feb 1797; d. 18 Jul 1864)

Mar 1845 – 19 Dec 1846: Nebenius II

Prime Minister	*Karl Friedrich Nebenius* (for 2nd time) (see Nebenius I)
Foreign Affairs	*Alexander von Dusch* (see von Boeckh)
Finance	*Franz Anton Regenauer* (see von Boeckh)
Without Portfolio	*Johann Baptist Bekk* (b. Triberg 29 Oct 1797; d. Bruchsal 22 Mar 1855)

19 Dec 1846 – 9 Mar 1848: Bekk

Prime Minister	*Johann Baptist Bekk* (see Nebenius II)
President of the Council of State	*Karl Friedrich Nebenius* (see Nebenius I)
Foreign Affairs	*Alexander von Dusch* (see von Boeckh)
Home Affairs	*Johann Baptist Bekk* (see Nebenius II)
Finance	19 Dec 1846 – 7 Feb 1848: *Franz Anton Regenauer* (see von Boeckh)
Justice	19 Dec 1846 – 7 Feb 1848: *Christof Franz Trefurt* (b. Neckarbischofsheim 10 Feb 1790; d. Lichtental 28 Jul 1861)

9 Mar 1848 – 3/8 Jun 1849: Hoffman

Prime Minister	*Karl Georg Hoffmann* (b. Ludwigsburg 14 Oct 1796; d. 11 Sep 1865)
Foreign Affairs	*Alexander von Dusch* (see von Boeckh)
Home Affairs	*Johann Baptist Bekk* (see Nebenius II)

Finance	*Karl Georg Hoffmann* (see above)
Justice	*Franz, Baron Stengel* (b. 5 Mar 1803; d. 22 Sep 1870)
War	23 Mar 1848 – 3 Jun 1849: *Friedrich Hoffmann*, brother of Karl Georg (b. Ludwigsburg 15 Jan 1795; d. Karlsruhe 8 Dec 1879)

14 May – 30 Jun 1849: Revolutionary Executive Committee in Karslruhe and Rastatt

Chairman	*Lorenz Brentano* (b. Mannheim 4 Nov 1813; d. Chicago 17 Sep 1891)
Finance	14 May – (?) 1849: *Ahmed Gögg* (?) – 30 Jun 1849: *Florian Mordes*
War	14 – 26 May 1849: *Karl Eichfeld* 26 May – 30 Jun 1849: *Franz Sigel* (b. Sinsheim 18 Nov 1824; d. New York 21 Aug 1902)
Member	—— *Peter*

1 Jul 1849 – May 1856: Klüber

Prime Minister	*Friedrich Adolf Klüber* (b. 1791; d. 1858)
Foreign Affairs	*Ludwig, Baron* (from 1877: *Count*) *Rüdt von Collenberg-Bödigheim* (b. 20 Jun 1799; d. Bödigheim 14 Aug 1885)
Home Affairs	1 Jul 1849 – Jun 1853: *Adolf, Baron Marschall von Bieberstein* (b. Karlsruhe 10 Mar 1806; d. Unteribental 11 Sep 1891)
Finance	*Franz Anton Regenauer* (see von Boeckh)
Justice	*Anton von Stabel* (b. Stockach 9 Oct 1806; d. Karlsruhe 22 Mar 1880)
War	16 Jun 1849 – 7 Apr 1854: *Franz Xaver August, Baron Roggenbach* (b. Schopfheim 20 Feb 1798; d. 7 Jun 1854)

May 1856 – 2 Apr 1860: Stengel

Prime Minister	*Franz, Baron Stengel* (see Hoffmann)
Finance	*Franz Anton Regenauer* (see von Boeckh)
Justice	*Anton von Stabel* (see Klüber)

2 Apr 1860 – 24 Jul 1866: von Stabel

Prime Minister	*Anton von Stabel* (see Klüber)

Foreign Affairs   2 Apr 1860 – 1 May 1861 (acting:) *Anton von Stabel* (see Klüber)

1 May 1861 – 19 Oct 1865: *Franz, Baron Roggenbach* (b. Mannheim 23 Mar 1825; d. Frieburg im Breisgau 25 May 1907)

19 Oct 1865 – 23 Jul 1866: *Ludwig, Baron Edelsheim* (b. Karlsruhe 24 Oct 1823; d. Constance 23 Feb 1872)

Home Affairs   *August Lamey* (b. Karlsruhe 27 Jul 1816; d. Mannheim 14 Jan 1896)

War   *Damian Ludwig* (b. Aschaffenburg 26 Jan 1804; d. 8 Nov 1871)

Finance   2 Apr 1860 – 1862: *Vollarth Vogelmann* (b. Wertheim am Main 5 Feb 1808; d. Homburg vor der Höh 17 Jul 1871)

1862 – 30 Jun 1866: *Karl Mathy* (b. Mannheim 17 Mar 1806; d. Karlsruhe 3 Feb 1868)

Trade (new post)   1864 – 30 Jun 1866: *Karl Mathy* (see above)

27 Jul 1866 – 3 Feb 1868: Mathy

Prime Minister   *Karl Mathy* (see von Stabel)

Foreign Affairs   *Rudolf, Baron Freydorf* (b. Karlsruhe 28 Feb 1819; d. Karlsruhe 15 Nov 1882)

Home Affairs   *Julius Jolly* (b. Mannheim 21 Feb 1823; d. Karlsruhe 14 Oct 1891)

War   *Damian Ludwig* (see von Stabel)

Finance   (acting:) *Karl Mathy* (see von Stabel)

Trade   *Karl Mathy* (see von Stabel)

Without Portfolio   *August Nüsslin* (b. Mannheim 19 Mar 1812; d. 17 Oct 1887)

12 Feb 1868 – 21 Sep 1876: Jolly

Prime Minister   *Julius Jolly* (see Mathy)

Foreign Affairs   12 Feb 1868 – 1 Jul 1871: *Rudolf, Baron Freydorf* (see Mathy) from 7 Jul 1871: post abolished

Home Affairs   *Julius Jolly* (see Mathy)

War   12 Feb 1868 – 17 Dec 1871: *Gustav Friedrich von Beyer* (b. Berlin 26 Feb 1812; d. Leipzig 7 Dec 1889) from 17 Dec 1871: post abolished

Justice   19 Oct 1868 – 21 Sep 1876: *Hermann Obkircher* (b. Villingen 22 Apr 1819; d. Karlsruhe 30 Sep 1881)

Finance   *Moritz Ellstätter* (b. Karlsruhe 11 Mar 1827; d.

	Karlsruhe 14 Jun 1905)
Trade	12 Feb 1868 – 28 Oct 1872: *Gottfried, Baron Dusch* (b. Karlsruhe 18 Feb 1821; d. Nice 24 Dec 1891)
	28 Oct 1872 – 21 Sep 1876: *Friedrich Turban* (b. Bretten 5 Oct 1821; d. Karlsruhe 12 Jun 1878)
Without Portfolio	*August Nüsslin* (see Mathy)

24 Sep 1876 – Mar 1893: Turban

Prime Minister	*Friedrich Turban* (see Jolly)
Home Affairs	24 Sep 1876 – 20 Apr 1881: *Franz Ludwig von Stoesser* (b. Heidelberg 21 Jun 1824; d. Freiburg im Breisgau 26 Feb 1901)
	20 Apr 1881 – 8 Oct 1890: *Friedrich Turban* (see Jolly)
	9 Oct 1890 – Mar 1893: *August Eisenlohr* (b. Mannheim 25 Feb 1833; d. Karlsruhe 13 Mar 1916)
Justice and Lord Chamberlain	24 Sep 1876 – 20 Apr 1881: *Karl von Grimm* (b. Karslruhe 2 Feb 1830; d. Karlsruhe 6 Apr 1898)
	20 Apr 1881 – Mar 1893: *Franz Wilhelm Nokk* (b. Bruchsal 30 Nov 1832; d. Karlsruhe 13 Feb 1903)
Finance	*Moritz Ellstätter* (see Jolly)
Trade	1876 – 1881: *Friedrich Turban* (see Jolly)
Education and Public Worship	20 Apr 1881 – Mar 1893: *Franz Wilhelm Nokk* (see above)
Without Portfolio	24 Sep 1876 – 20 Apr 1881: *August Nüsslin* (see Mathy)
	17 Jun 1883 – 9 Oct 1890: *August Eisenlohr* (see above)

7 Mar 1893 – Jun 1901: Nokk

Prime Minister	*Franz Wilhelm Nokk* (see Turban)
Foreign Affairs	*Artur von Brauer* (b. Karlsruhe 17 Nov 1845; d. Baden-Baden 25 Apr 1926)
Home Affairs	7 Mar 1893 – Sep 1900: *August Eisenlohr* (see Turban)
	Sep 1900 – Jun 1901: *Karl Schenkel* (b. Schaffhausen 11 Aug 1845; d. Karlsruhe 9 Feb 1909)
Justice and Education	*Franz Wilhelm Nokk* (see Turban)
Finance	*Adolf Buchenberger* (b. Mosbach 18 May 1848; d. Karlsruhe 20 Feb 1904)
Trade	Post abolished

Jun 1901 – 8 Mar 1905: von Brauer

Prime Minister and Foreign Affairs	*Artur von Brauer* (see Nokk)
Home Affairs	*Karl Schenkel* (see Nokk)
Justice and Public Worship	*Alexander, Baron Dusch* (b. Karlsruhe 11 Sep 1851; d. Mauren 17 Sep 1923)
Finance	Jun 1901 – 20 Feb 1904: *Adolf Buchenberger* (see Nokk)
	1904 – 8 Mar 1905: *Eugen Becker* (b. Pforzheim 21 Feb 1848; d. Karlsruhe 2 Jan 1914)

8 Mar 1905 – 22 Dec 1917: Dusch

Prime Minister	*Alexander, Baron Dusch* (see von Brauer)
Foreign Affairs and Lord Chamberlain	8 Mar 1905 – 19 May 1911: *Adolf, Baron Marschall von Bieberstein* (b. Karlsruhe 11 Jan 1848; d. Freiburg im Breisgau 13 Nov 1920)
	19 May 1911 – 22 Dec 1917: *Josef Nikolaus Rheinbolt* (b. Sinzheim, Baden, 6 Dec 1860; d. Forte dei Marmi 22 Sep 1931)
Home Affairs	8 Mar 1905 – 23 Apr 1907: *Karl Schenkel* (see Nokk)
	23 Apr 1907 – 22 Dec 1917: *Heinrich, Baron Bodman* (b. Freiburg im Breisgau 21 Jan 1851; d. Freiburg im Breisgau 26 Apr 1929)
Justice	*Alexander, Baron Dusch* (see von Brauer)
Public Worship	8 Mar 1905 – 19 May 1911: *Alexander, Baron Dusch* (see von Brauer)
	19 May 1911 – 30 Jun 1915: *Franz Boehm* (b. Mannheim 25 Jul 1861; d. Karlsruhe 30 Jun 1915)
	23 Jul 1915 – 22 Dec 1917: *Wilhelm Hübsch* (b. Westheim 3 Mar 1848; d. Karlsruhe 12 Jan 1928)
Finance	8 Mar 1905 – 1906: *Eugen Becker* (see von Brauer)
	1906 – 1 Jul 1910: *Max Honsell* (b. Konstanz 10 Nov 1843; d. Karlsruhe 1 Jul 1910)
	Sep 1910 – 22 Dec 1917: *Josef Nikolaus Rheinboldt* (see above)

22 Dec 1917 – 14 Nov 1918: Bodman

Prime Minister	*Heinrich, Baron Bodman* (see Dusch)
Foreign Affairs and Lord Chamberlain	*Adalbert Düringer* (b. Mannheim 11 Jul 1855; d. Berlin 2 Sep 1924)

Home Affairs	*Heinrich, Baron Bodman* (see Dusch)
Justice	*Adalbert Düringer* (see above)
Public Worship	*Wilhelm Hübsch* (see Dusch)
Finance	*Josef Nikolaus Rhienboldt* (see Dusch)

Bambara States

For Segu and its rival offshoot kingdom Kaarta, Islamic states in Mali, 13th to 19th centuries: see volume 1.

Bavaria

HEADS OF STATE

Dukes

1 Feb 1501	*Albrecht IV*, son of Albrecht III (b. 15 Dec 1447)
18 Mar 1508	*Wilhelm IV*, Son (b. 13 Nov 1493)
6 Mar 1550	*Albrecht V*, son (b. 29 Feb 1528)
24 Oct 1579	*Wilhelm V*, son (b. 29 Sep 1548; d. 17 Feb 1626)
15 Oct 1597	*Maximilian I*, son (b. 15 Apr 1573); from 25 Feb 1623 Elector

Electors

27 Sep 1651	*Ferdinand*, son (b. 31 Oct 1636)
26 May 1679	*Maximilian II*, son (b. 11 Jul 1662) Stadholder of the Spanish Netherlands 1691 expelled from Bavaria 1704, restored 1714
26 Feb 1726	*Karl Albert*, son (b. 6 Aug 1697) from 24 Jan 1742: Holy Roman Emperor Charles VII
20 Jan 1745	*Maximilian III*, son (b. 28 Mar 1727)
30 Dec 1777	*Karl Theodor*, son of Johann Christian of Pfalz-Sulzbach (b. 11 Dec 1724) from 1742: Elector Palatine
16 Feb 1799	*Maximilian IV*, brother of Karl II of Pfalz-Birkenfeld (b. 27 May 1756) from 1 Jan 1806: King Maximilian I

Kings

1 Jan 1806	*Maximilian I*, previously Elector Maximilian IV
13 Oct 1825	*Ludwig I*, son (b. 25 Aug 1786; d. 29 Feb 1868) abdicated 20 Mar 1848
20 Mar 1848	*Maximilian II*, son (b. 28 Nov 1811)
10 Mar 1864	*Ludwig II*, son (b. 25 Aug 1845)
13 Jun 1886 – 5 Nov 1913	*Otto*, brother (b. 27 Apr 1848; d. 11 Oct 1916) of unsound mind

Prince-Regents

10 Jun 1886	*Luitpold*, brother of Maximilian II (b. 12 Mar 1821)
12 Dec 1912	*Ludwig*, son (b. 7 Jan 1845; d. 18 Oct 1921)
5 Nov 1913 – 7/8 Nov 1918	*Ludwig III*, previously Prince-Regent
From 8 Nov 1918	Monarchy abolished and many functions taken over by central government of Germany

MEMBERS OF GOVERNMENT

21 Feb 1799 – 2 Feb 1817: Montgelas

Prime Minister	*Maximilian, Count Montgelas* (b. Munich 10 Sep 1759; d. Munich 14 Jun 1838)
Justice	1806 – 2 Feb 1817: *Heinrich Alois, Count Reigersberg* (b. Würzburg 30 Jan 1770; d. 4 Nov 1856)

2 Feb 1817 – Oct 1825: Reigersberg

Prime Minister	*Heinrich Alois, Count Reigersberg* (see Montgelas)
Foreign Affairs	*Alois, Count Rechberg und Rothenlöwen* (b. Munich 18 Sep 1766; d. Schloss Donzorf 10 Mar 1849)
Home Affairs	*Karl Friedrich, Count Thürheim* (b. 6 Nov 1763; d. Munich 11 Nov 1832)
Justice	Feb 1817 – 14 Jun 1823: *Heinrich Alois, Count Reigersberg* (see Montgelas) 14 Jun 1823 – Oct 1825: *Georg Friedrich, Baron Zentner* (b. Strassheim 27 Aug 1752; d. Munich 20 Oct 1835)
Finance	*Maximilian, Baron Lerchenfeld* (b. Ingolstadt 16 Nov 1778; d. Heinersreuth 14 Aug 1843)

War	Feb 1817 – 1822: *Johann Nepomuk Josef Florian, Count Triva* (b. Munich 26 Sep 1755; d. Munich 8 Mar 1827)
	1822 – Oct 1825: *Nikolaus Hubert, Baron Maillot de la Treille* (d. Munich 28 Aug 1834)

Oct 1825 – 30 Dec 1831: Zentner

Prime Minister	*Georg Friedrich, Baron Zentner* (see Reigersberg)
Foreign Affairs	Oct 1825 – Apr 1827: *Karl Friedrich, Count Thürheim* (see Reigersberg)
	1827 – 1 Sep 1828: *George Friedrich, Baron Zentner* (see Reigersberg)
	Sep 1828 – 30 Dec 1831: *Josef Ludwig, Count Armansperg* (b. Kötzting 28 Feb 1787; d. 3 Apr 1853)
Home Affairs	Oct 1825 – 1 Sep 1828: *Josef Ludwig, Count Armansperg* (see above)
	1 Sep 1828 – 24 May 1831: *Eduard von Schenk* (b. Dusseldorf 18 Oct 1788; d. Munich 26 Apr 1841)
Justice	*Georg Friedrich, Baron Zentner* (see Reigersberg)
Finance	*Josef Ludwig, Count Armansperg* (see above)
War	Oct 1825 – 1829: *Nikolaus Hubert, Baron Maillot de la Treille* (see Reigersberg)
	1829 – 30 Dec 1831: *Johann Georg von Weinrich* (b. Mainz 11 Jan 1768; d. Munich 12 Dec 1836)

31 Dec 1831 – 25 Oct 1837: Gise

Foreign Affairs	*Friedrich August Koch, Baron Gise* (b. Regensberg 17 Mar 1783; d. 4 Dec 1860)
Home Affairs	*Ludwig Kraft Ernst, Prince Öttingen-Wallerstein* (b. Öttingen 31 Jan 1791; d. Lucerne 22 Jun 1870)
Justice	31 Dec 1831 – 21 Oct 1832: *Max Josef, Baron Zu-Rhein* (b. Würzburg, 7 Aug 1780; d. 21 Oct (?) 1832/42)
	Oct 1832 – 25 Oct 1837: *Sebastian, Baron Schenk* (b. Hillstädt 28 Sep 1774; d. Munich 16 May 1848)
Finance	1832: —— *von Mieg*
	May 1833 – 31 Dec 1834: *Maximilian, Baron Lerchenfeld* (see Reigersberg)
	1835 – 1837: —— *von Wirschinger*
War	31 Dec 1831 – 12 Dec 1836: *Johann Georg von Weinrich* (see Zentner)

1 Nov 1837 – 17 Feb 1847: von Abel

Prime Minister	*Karl von Abel* (b. Wetzler 19 Nov 1788; d. Munich 3 Sep 1859)
Foreign Affairs	1 Nov 1837 – May 1846: *Friedrich August Koch, Baron Gise* (see Gise) Spring 1846 (definitively 1 Jan 1847) – Feb 1847: *Otto Camillus Hugo, Count Bray-Steinburg* (b. Berlin 17 May 1807; d. Munich 9 Jan 1899)
Home Affairs	*Karl von Abel* (see above)
Justice	1 Nov 1837 – May 1846: *Sebastian, Baron Schrenk* (see Gise) May 1846 – 17 Feb 1847: *Karl, Baron Schrenk*, son (b. Wetterfeld 17 Aug 1806; d. Wetterfeld 10 Sep 1884)
Finance	1837 – 1840: —— *von Wirschinger* (see Gise) 1840 – 1845: *Karl, Count Seinsheim* (b. Münster 17 Feb 1784; d. Münster 29 Nov 1864)
Public Worship	1 Nov 1837 – 15 Dec 1846: *Karl von Abel* (see above) 15 Dec 1846 – Feb 1847: *Karl, Baron Schrenk* (see above)
War	1837 – 1838: *Baron Hertling* 1839 – 17 Feb 1847: *Anton, Baron Gumppenberg* (b. Praitenbrunn 10 Jan 1787; d. Munich 5 Apr 1855)

Feb – 30 Nov 1847: Zu-Rhein

Prime Minister	*Friedrich, Baron Zu-Rhein*, son of Max Josef
Foreign Affairs and Justice	*Georg Ludwig von Maurer* (b. Erpolzheim 2 Nov 1790; d. Munich 9 May 1872) administrator
Home Affairs	*Johann Baptist von Zenetti* (b. Wertingen 1785; d. Munich 5 Oct 1856) administrator
Finance	*Friedrich, Baron Zu-Rhein* (see above) administrator
Public Worship	*Hermann von Beisler* (b. Bensheim 1790; d. Munich 15 Oct 1859)

30 Nov 1847 – 11 Mar 1848: Ottingen-Wallerstein

Prime Minister, Foreign Affairs and Public Worship	*Ludwig, Prince Ottingen-Wallerstein* (see Gise)
Home Affairs	—— *von Berks*
Finance	—— *von Heres*, administrator
Justice	*Hermann von Beisler* (see Zu-Rhein) administrator

War	*Baron Hohenhausen*, administrator

12 Mar 1848 – 8 Feb 1849 (in charge until 7 Mar 1849): Bray-Steinburg I

Foreign Affairs	*Otto Camillus Hugo, Count Bray-Steinburg* (for 1st time) (see von Abel)
Home Affairs	8 Mar – 1 Dec 1848: *Gottlieb, Baron Thon-Dittmer* (b. 25 Dec 1802; d. 14 Mar 1853)
	1 – 20 Dec 1848: *Gustav, Baron Lerchenfeld* (b. 30 May 1806; d. Berchtesgaden 10 Oct 1866)
	Dec 1848 – Mar 1849: *Hermann von Beisler* (see Zu-Rhein)
Finance	8 Mar – 20 Dec 1848: *Gustav, Baron Lerchenfeld* (see above)
	Dec 1848 – Feb 1849: —— *von Weigand*
Justice	*Karl Friedrich von Heintz* (b. Kleeburg 4 Apr 1802; d. Munich 16 Aug 1868)
Public Worship	8 Mar – 1 Dec 1848: *Hermann von Beisler* (see Zu-Rhein)
	1 – 20 Dec 1848: *Gustav, Baron Lerchenfeld* (see above)
Army	—— *von Weishaupt* (d. Munich 18 Dec 1853)
War	*Georg Wilhelm von Le Suire* (b. Mengeringhausen 9 June 1787; d. Nuremberg 10 Mar 1852) administrator

7 Mar 1849 – 27 Mar 1859: Pfordten I

Prime Minister	Dec 1849 – 27 Mar 1859: *(Karl) Ludwig (Heinrich), Baron Pfordten* (for 1st time) (b. Ried im Innviertel 11 Sep 1811; d. Munich 18 Aug 1880)
Foreign Affairs and Trade	Apr 1849 – 27 Mar 1859: *Ludwig, Baron Pfordten* (see above)
Home Affairs	Mar – Jun 1849: —— *von Forster*
	9 Jun 1849 – 1852: *Theodor von Zwehl* (b. Vallendar 7 Feb 1800; d. Munich 17 Dec 1875)
	1852 – 27 Mar 1859: *August, Count Reigersberg* (b. 23 Oct 1815; d. Landhut an der Isar 16 May 1888)
Finance	7 Mar 1849 – 18 Dec 1858: *Josef von Aschenbrenner* (b. Neumarkt 29 Jun 1798; d. Munich 18 Dec 1858)
	Dec 1858 – Mar 1859: *E. von Fischer* administrator
Justice	7 Mar 1849 – 1854: *Karl Joseph* (from 1859: *Baron*) *von Kleinschrod* (b. Würzburg 10 Jul 1797; d. Munich 24 Sep 1866)

	1854 (acting:) *Joseph von Aschenbrenner* (see above)
	9 Sep 1854 – 30 Apr 1859: *Friedrich von Ringelmann* (b. Würzburg 20 Oct 1803; d. 13 Jan 1870)
Public Worship	16 Mar 1849 – 1852: *Friedrich von Ringelmann* (see above)
	1852 – 27 Mar 1859: *Theodor von Zwehl* (see above)
War	May 1849 – 1854: *Ludwig von Lüder*
	1855 – 1859: *Georg Wilhelm von Manz* (b. Dillingen 2 Apr 1804; d. Munich 5 Jan 1867)

27 Mar 1859 – Dec 1864: Schrenk

Foreign Affairs, Trade and Lord Chamberlain	*Karl, Baron Schrenk* (see von Abel)
Home Affairs	*Max von Neumayr* (b. Munich 27 Jul 1808; d. 14 Jan 1881)
Justice	1 May 1859 – 1 Aug 1864: *Karl, Baron Mulzer* (b. Wetzlar 8 Apr 1805; d. Nuremberg 23 Jan 1875)
Finance	*Benno von Pfeufer* (b. Bamberg 21 Aug 1804; d. Munich 10 Feb 1871)
War	27 Mar 1859 – 1861: *Ludwig von Lüder* (see Pfordten I)
	1861 – 1862: *Moritz von Spies* (b. Ansbach 31 Dec 1805; d. Munich 10 Oct 1862)
	1862 —— *von Hess*, administrator
	1862 – 1863 *Philipp Karl Friedrich von Liel* (b. Coblenz 10 May 1799; d. Badenweiler 7 Aug 1863)
	1863 – Dec 1864: *Eduard von Luz*
Public Worship	*Theodor von Zwehl* (see Pfordten I)

Dec 1864 – 29 Dec 1866: Pfordten II

Prime Minister and Foreign Affairs	*Ludwig, Baron Pfordten* (for 2nd time) (see Pfordten I)
Home Affairs	Dec 1864 – 1865: *Max von Neumayr* (see Schrenk)
	1865 —— *von Koch*, administrator
	1865 – 1866: —— *von Vogel*
Justice	*Eduard von Bomhard* (b. Bayreuth 2 Oct 1809; d. Munich 30 Sep 1886)
Finance	*Benno von Pfeufer* (see Schrenk)
War	*Eduard von Luz* (see Schrenk)
Trade	1864 – 1865: *Benno von Pfeufer* (see Schrenk)

1865 - 1866: *Adolf* (from 1880: *Baron*) *von Pfretzschner* (b. Wurzburg 15 Aug 1820; d. Munich 27 Apr 1901)

Public Worship   —— *von Koch* (see above)

31 Dec 1866 - 7 Mar 1870; Hohenlohe-Schillingsfürst

Prime Minister, Foreign Affairs and Lord Chamberlain	*Chlodwig (Karl Viktor), Prince Hohenlohe-Schillingsfürst* (b. Rotenburg an der Fulda 31 Mar 1819; d. Ragaz 6 Jul 1901)
Home Affairs	31 Dec 1866 - 1868: *Johann, Baron Pechmann* (b. Vilsbiburg 7 Jan 1809; d. Munich 24 Feb 1868)
	1868 - Sep 1869: *Winfried Hoermann von Hoerbach* (b. Mainz 25 Jun 1821; d. Munich 21 Oct 1896)
	26 Sep 1869 - 7 Mar 1870: *Paul von Braun* (b. Kitzingen 16 Sep 1820; d. Speyer 26 Feb 1892)
Justice	31 Dec 1866 - 27 Apr 1867: *Eduard von Bomhard* (see Pfordten II)
	Apr - Sep 1867: *E. von Fischer*, administrator
	18 Sep 1867 - 7 Mar 1870: *Johann von Lutz* (b. Münnerstadt 4 Dec 1826; d. Pöcking 3 Sep 1890)
Finance	*Adolf von Pfretzschner* (see Pfordten II)
Trade	*Gustav von Schlör* (b. Hellziehen 4 Apr 1820)
Army	*Siegmund, Baron Pranckh* (b. Altötting 5 Dec 1821; d. Munich 8 May 1888)
Public Worship	31 Dec 1866 - 26 Sep 1869: *Franz von Gresser*
	26 Sep 1869 - 7 Mar 1870: *Johann von Lutz* (see above)

7 Mar 1870 - 4 Jun 1871: Bray-Steinburg II

Prime Minister and Foreign Affairs	*Otto Camillus Hugo, Count Bray-Steinburg* (for 2nd time) (see von Abel)
Home Affairs	1870 - 1871: *Paul von Braun* (see Hohenlohe-Schillingsfürst)
Justice	*Johann von Lutz* (see Hohenlohe-Schillingsfürst)
Finance	*Adolf von Pfretzschuer* (see Pfordten II)
Trade	*Gustav von Schlör* (see Hohenlohe-Schillingsfürst)
Army	*Siegmund, Baron Pranckh* (see Hohenlohe-Schillingsfürst)
Public Worship	*Johann von Lutz* (see Hohenlohe-Schillingsfürst)

22 Jul 1871 – 2 Jun 1872: Hegnenberg-Dux

Foreign Affairs and Lord Chamberlain	*Friedrich Adam Justus, Baron Hegnenberg-Dux* (b. Schloss Hofhegnenberg 2 Sep 1810; d. 2 Jun 1872)
Home Affairs	*Sigmund* (from 1881: *Baron*) *von Pfeufer* (b. Bamberg 24 Feb 1824; d. Munich 23 Sep 1891)
Justice	*Johann Nepomuk von Fäustle* (b. Augsburg 28 Dec 1828; d. Munich 17 Apr 1887)
Finance	*Adolf, Baron Pfretzschner* (see Pfordten II)
Trade	Post abolished
War	*Siegmund, Baron Pranckh* (see Hohenlohe-Schillingsfürst)
Public Worship	*Johann von Lutz* (see Hohenlohe-Schillingsfürst)

24 Sep 1872 – 4 Mar 1880: Pfretzschner

Prime Minister and Foreign Affairs	*Adolf, Baron Pfretzschner* (see Pfordten II)
Justice	*Johann Nepomuk von Fäustle* (see Hegnenberg-Dux)
Finance	24 Sep 1872 – 26 Sep 1877: *Georg von Berr* (b. Pottenstein 7 Aug 1830; d. Munich 14 Jan 1919)
	26 Sep 1877 – 4 Mar 1880: *Emil, Baron Riedel* (b. Kurzenaltheim 6 Apr 1832; d. Munich 13 Aug 1906)
War	24 Sep 1872 – 4 Apr 1875: *Siegmund, Baron Pranckh* (see Hohenlohe-Schillingsfürst)
	4 Apr 1875 – 4 Mar 1880: *Josef Maximilian Fridolin von Maillinger* (b. Passau 4 Oct 1820; d. Bad Aibling 6 Oct 1901)
Public Worship	*Johann von Lutz* (see Hohenlohe-Schillingsfürst)

4 Mar 1880 – 31 May 1890: Lutz

Prime Minister	*Johann* (from 1884: *Baron*) *Lutz* (see Hohenlohe-Schillingsfürst)
Foreign Affairs	*Krafft, Baron Crailsheim* (b. Ansbach 15 Mar 1841; d. Munich 14 Feb 1926)
Home Affairs	4 Mar 1880 – 24 Jun 1881: *Sigmund von Pfeufer* (see Hegnenberg-Dux)
	24 Jun 1881 – 31 May 1890: *Max, Baron Feilitzsch* (b. Trogen 12 Aug 1834; d. Munich 19 Jun 1913)
Justice	4 Mar 1880 – 17 Apr 1887: *Johann Nepomuk von Fäustle* (see Hegnenberg-Dux)

	24 Apr 1887 – 31 May 1890: *Leopold, Baron Leonrod* (b. Ansbach 13 Dec 1829; d. Munich 6 Oct 1905)
Finance	*Emil, Baron Riedel* (see Pfretzschner)
War	4 Mar 1880 – 10 Apr 1885: *Josef von Maillinger* (see Pfretzschner)
	10 Apr 1885 – 6 May 1890: *Adolf von Heinleth* (b. Munich 24 Oct 1823; d. Munich 26 Feb 1895)
	6 – 31 May 1890: *Benignus von Safferling* (b. Freising 30 Sep 1825; d. Partenkirchen 4 Sep 1899)
Public Worship	*Johann, Baron Lutz* (see Hohenlohe-Schillingsfürst)

31 May 1890 – 18 Feb 1903; Crailsheim

Prime Minister and Foreign Affairs	*Krafft, Baron Crailsheim* (see Lutz)
Home Affairs	*Max, Baron Feilitzsch* (see Lutz)
Justice	31 May 1890 – 26 Nov 1902: *Leopold, Baron Leonrod* (see Lutz)
	26 Nov 1902 – 18 Feb 1903: *Ferdinand von Miltner* (b. Fürth 5 Jul 1856; d. Munich 18 Jun 1920)
Finance	*Emil, Baron Riedel* (see Pfretzschner)
War	31 May 1890 – Jun 1893: *Benignus von Safferling* (see Lutz)
	Jun 1893 – 18 Feb 1903: *Adolf, Baron Asch* (b. Munich 30 Oct 1839; d. Munich 18 Feb 1906)
Public Worship	31 May 1890 – 24 Mar 1895: *Ludwig August von Müller* (b. Dachau 19 Aug 1846; d. Munich 24 Mar 1895)
	30 Mar 1895 – 11 Jul 1902: *Robert August von Landmann* (b. Grossweingarten 12 May 1845; d. Munich 12 Mar 1926)
	7 Aug 1902 – 18 Feb 1903: *Klemens, Baron Podewils-Dürniz* (b. Laudshut an der Isar 17 Jan 1850; d. Munich 14 Mar 1922)

18 Feb 1903 – 8 Feb 1912: Podewils-Dürniz

Prime Minister and Foreign Affairs	*Klemens, Baron Podewils-Dürniz* (see Crailsheim)
Home Affairs	18 Feb 1903 – 3 Apr 1907: *Max* (from 1904: *Count*) *Feilitzsch* (see Lutz)
	3 Apr 1907 – 8 Feb 1912: *Maximilian Friedrich von*

	Brettreich (b. Bamberg 25 Dec 1858; d. at sea 21 Mar 1938)
Justice	*Ferdinand von Miltner* (see Crailsheim)
Finance	18 Feb 1903 – 30 Oct 1904: *Emil, Baron Riedel* (see Pfretzschner)
	30 Oct 1904 – 8 Feb 1912: *Hermann von Pfaff*
War	18 Feb 1903 – 4 Apr 1905: *Adolf, Baron Asch* (see Crailsheim)
	4 Apr 1905 – 8 Feb 1912: *Karl, Baron* (later: *Count*) *Horn* (b. Würzburg 16 Feb 1847; d. Munich 5 Jun 1923)
Public Worship	*Anton von Wehner* (b. Schillingsfürst 16 Nov 1850; d. Munich 10 Mar 1915)
Transport (new post)	1 Jan 1904: *Heinrich von Frauendorfer* (b. Hof bei Waldmünchen 27 Nov 1855; d. Geiselgasteig 23 Jul 1921)

10 Feb 1912 – 2 Nov 1917: Hertling

Prime Minister and Foreign Affairs	*Georg, Baron* (from 1914: *Count*) *Hertling* (b. Darmstadt 31 Aug 1843; d. Ruhpolding 4 Jan 1919)
Home Affairs	10 Feb 1912 – 7 Dec 1916: *Max, Baron Soden-Frauenhofen* (b. Ludwigsburg 7 Aug 1844; d. Munich 22 Dec 1922)
	7 Dec 1916 – 2 Nov 1917: *Maximilian von Brettreich* (see Podewils-Durniz)
Justice	*Heinrich von Thelemann* (b. Aschaffenburg 15 Dec 1851; d. Munich 2 Feb 1923)
Finance	*Georg von Breunig* (b. Dettelbach 2 Jul 1855; d. Munich 6 Jan 1933)
War	10 – 14 Feb 1912: *Karl, Count Horn* (see Podewils-Dürniz)
	14 Feb 1912 – 7 Dec 1916: *Otto Baron Kress von Kressenstein* (b. Germersheim 16 Nov 1850; d. Munich 18 Feb 1929)
	7 – 11 Dec 1916 (acting:) *Maximilian, Baron Speidel* (b. Munich 13 Sep 1856)
	11 Dec 1916 – 2 Nov 1917: *Philipp von Hellingrath* (b. Munich 22 Feb 1862)
Public Worship	*Eugen von Knilling* (b. Munich 1 Aug 1865; d. Munich 20 Oct 1927)
Transport	*Lorenz von Seidlein* (b. Bamberg 15 Nov 1856)

10 Nov 1917 - 8 Nov 1918: von Dandl

Prime Minister and Foreign Affairs	*Otto von Dandl* (b. Straubing 13 May 1868)
Home Affairs	*Maximilian von Brettreich* (see Podewils-Dürniz)
Justice	*Heinrich von Thelemann* (see Hertling)
Finance	*Georg von Breunig* (see Hertling)
War	*Philipp von Hellingrath* (see Hertling)
Public Worship	*Eugen von Knilling* (see Hertling)
Transport	*Lorenz von Seidlein* (see Hertling)

Belgium

Until 1794	Successively in Burgundian, Spanish and Austrian possession (see Netherlands)
1794 – 1814	Held by France
1815 – 1830	Part of the United Netherlands under Wilhelm I
25 Sep 1830	Separate provisional government set up
4 Oct 1830	Proclamation of independence
20 Dec 1830	Independence recognized

HEADS OF STATE

Kings

4 Jun 1831	*Leopold I*, son of Duke Francis of Coburg (b. 16 Dec 1790)
10 Dec 1865	*Leopold II*, son (b. 9 Apr 1835)
17 Dec 1909 – 17 Feb 1934	*Albert*, nephew (b. 8 Apr 1875)

MEMBERS OF GOVERNMENT

25 Sep 1830 - 24 Feb 1831: Rogier I (Provisional Government)

Prime Minister	*Charles Rogier* (for 1st time) (b. St Quintin, France, 12 Aug 1800; d. Brussels 27 May 1885)

Other Members   *Goswin Joseph Auguste, Baron Stassart* (b. Mechlin 2 Sep 1780; d. Brussels 10 Oct 1854); *(Philip) Felix (Balthasar Otto Ghislain) Comte de Mérode* (b. Maastricht 13 Apr 1791; d. Brussels 7 Feb 1857) from 26 Sep 1830: *Alexander Gendebien* (b. Mons 4 May 1789; d. 6 Dec 1869) from 28 Sep 1830: *Louis de Potter* (b. Bruges 26 Apr 1786; d. Bruges 22 Jul 1859) And 5 others

24 Feb – 21 Jul 1831: Surlet de Chokier

Regent   *Erasme Louis, Baron Surlet de Chokier* (b. Liége 27 Nov 1769; d. Singelom 7 Aug 1839)

Minister of State   *Paul Devaux* (b. Bruges 10 Apr 1801; d. Brussels 30 Jan 1880)

Jul 1831 – Oct 1832: de Brouckère (acting government)

War   Aug 1831 – Mar 1832: *Charles de Brouckère* (b. Bruges 19 Jan 1796; d. Brussels 20 Apr 1860) 15 Mar – 20 May 1832: *Felix Comte de Mérode* (see Rogier I)

Justice   *Alexander Gendebien* (see Rogier I)

Without Portfolio   12 Nov 1831 – 15 Mar 1832 and 20 May – Oct 1832: *Felix, Comte de Mérode* (see Rogier I)

20 Oct 1832 – 4 Aug 1834: Rogier II

Prime Minister   *Charles Rogier* (for 2nd time) (see Rogier I)

Foreign Affairs   *Albert Joseph Goblet, Comte d'Alviella* (b. Doornik 26 May 1790; d. Brussels 5 May 1873)

Home Affairs   *Charles Rogier* (see Rogier I)

Justice   *Joseph Lebeau* (b. Huy 2 Jan 1794; d. Huy 19 Mar 1865)

Aug 1834 – Aug 1840: de Theux de Meylandt I

Prime Minister   *Barthélemy Théodore, Comte de Theux de Meylandt* (for 1st time) (b. Schaerbeek 25 Feb 1794; d. Meylandt 21 Aug 1874)

Foreign Affairs   *Barthélemy Théodore, Comte de Theux de Meylandt* (see above)

Home Affairs   *Felix Amand de Muelenaere* (b. Pitthem 9 Feb 1794;
                      d. Pitthem 5 Aug 1862)
Justice   Dec 1838: *Anton Ernst* (b. Aubel 1796; d. Boppard
                      1841)
Public Works (new post)From Jan 1837: *Jean Baptiste, Baron Nothomb* (b.
                      Messancy 3 Jun 1805; d. Berlin 15 Sep 1881)

April 1840 - June 1841: Lebeau

Prime Minister   *Joseph Lebeau* (Clerical) (see Rogier II)
Foreign Affairs   *Joseph Lebeau* (see Rogier II)
Education and   *Charles Rogier* (see Rogier I)
  Labour

April 1841 - June 1845: Nothomb Moderate-Clerical and Liberal Coalition Cabinet

Prime Minister   *Jean Baptiste, Baron Nothomb* (see de Theux de
                      Meylandt I)
Foreign Affairs   16 Apr 1843 - Jun 1845: *Albert Joseph Goblet* (see
                      Rogier II)
Justice   16 Apr 1843 - Jun 1845: *Jules Joseph, Baron
                      d'Anethan* (b. Brussels 24 Apr 1803; d. 8 Oct 1888)
Labour   *Adolphe Dechamps* (b. Melle 17 June 1807; d.
                      Manage 19 Jul 1875)

June 1845 - Mar 1846: van de Wyer

Prime Minister   *Sylvain van de Weyer* (Liberal) (b. 19 Jan 1802; d. 27
                      May 1885)
Foreign Affairs   *Adolphe Dechamps* (clerical) (see Nothomb)
Finance   *Jules Malou* (Clerical) (b. Ypres 19 Oct 1810; d.
                      Woluwe-St. Lambert 11 Jul 1886)
Justice   *Jules Joseph, Baron d'Anethan* (clerical) (see
                      Nothomb)
Public Works   *Adolphe Dechamps* (see Nothomb)

Mar 1846 - Aug 1847: de Theux de Meylandt II

Prime Minister   *Barthélemy Théodore, Comte de Theux de Meylandt*
                      (for 2nd time) (Clerical) (see de Theux de Meylandt I)
Foreign Affairs   *Adolphe Dechamps* (see Nothomb)
Justice   *Jules Joseph, Baron d'Anethan* (Clerical) (see
                      Nothomb)

12 Aug 1847 - Aug 1852: Rogier III

Prime Minister	*Charles Rogier* (for 3rd time) (Liberal) (see Rogier I)
Home Affairs	*Charles Rogier* (see Rogier I)
Finance	Jul 1848 - Aug 1852: *Hubert Joseph Walter Frère-Orban* (Liberal) (b. Liège 24 Apr 1812; d. Brussels 2 Jan 1896)
War	12 Aug 1847 - 1850: *Pierre Emmanuel Felix* (from 1860: *Baron*) *Chazal* (b. Tarbes 1808; d. Pau 15 Jan 1892)

Sep/Oct 1852 - 30 Mar 1855: de Brouckère

Prime Minister	*Henri de Brouckère* (moderate-Liberal) (b. Bruges 1801; d. Brussels 25 Jan 1891)
Foreign Affairs	*Henri de Brouckère* (see above)

Mar 1855 - 30 Oct 1857: de Decker

Prime Minister	*Pierre Jacques François de Decker* (Moderate-Clerical) (b. Zèle 25 Jan 1812; d. Brussels 6 Jan 1891)
Foreign Affairs	*Charles, Comte Vilain XIIII* (b. Brussels 15 May 1803; d. Leuth Castle, Limburg, 16 Nov 1878)
Home Affairs	*Pierre de Decker* (see above)
Justice	*Alphonse Nothomb* (b. Luxembourg 12 Jul 1817; d. Luxembourg 15/16 May 1898)

30 Oct 1857 - 30 Dec 1867: Rogier IV

Prime Minister	*Charles Rogier* (for 4th time;) (Liberal) (see Rogier I)
Foreign Affairs	30 Oct 1857 - 28 Oct 1861; —— *de Vrière*
	28 Oct 1861 - 30 Dec 1867: *Charles Rogier* (see Rogier I)
Home Affairs	30 Oct 1857 - 28 Oct 1861: *Charles Rogier* (see Rogier I)
	28 Oct 1861 - 30 Dec 1867: *Alphonse Vandenpeereboom* (b. Ypres 1812; d. Brussels 1884)
Finance	30 Oct 1857 - June 1861 and 27 Oct 1861 - 30 Dec 1867: *Hubert Frère-Orban* (see Rogier III)
War	1859 - May 1860: *Pierre Felix, Baron Chazal* (see Rogier III)
	May 1860 - 14 Oct 1865: *Frederick Xaver Ghislain, Comte de Mérode* (b. 26 Mar 1820; d. Rome 11 Jul 1874)

	Oct 1865 – 4 Nov 1866: *Pierre Felix, Baron Chazal* (see Rogier III)
	14 Nov 1866 – 1867: *Auguste Louis Goethals* (b. Turin 1812; d. Brussels 1889)
Justice	30 Oct 1857 – 12 Nov 1865: *Victor Tesch* (b. Mertzig 10 Mar 1812; d. Mertzig 16 Jun 1892)
	Nov 1865 – 30 Dec 1867: *Jules Bara* (b. Doornik 31 Aug 1835; d. Brussels 26 Jun 1900)

2 Jan 1868 – 17 Jun 1870: Frère-Orban

Prime Minister	*Hubert Frère-Orban* (for 1st time) (Liberal) (see Rogier III)
Foreign Affairs	*Jules Edmond Vanderstichelen* (b. Ghent 18 Sep 1822; d. Brussels 19 Jul 1880)
Home Affairs	*Eudore Pirmez* (b. Marcinelle 14 Sep 1830; d. Brussels 2 Mar 1890)
Justice	*Jules Bara* (see Rogier IV)
Finance	*Hubert Frère-Orban* (see Rogier III)
War	*Bruno Jean Baptiste Renard* (b. Doornik 1804; d. Brussels 1879)

3 Jul 1870 – 1 Dec 1871: d'Anethan

Prime Minister	*Jules Joseph, Baron d'Anethan* (Clerical) (see Nothomb)
Foreign Affairs	*Jules Joseph, Baron d'Anethan* (see Nothomb)
Home Affairs and Education	*Joseph Bruno Maria Konstantin Kervyn de Lettenhove* (b. St. Michel 17 Aug 1817; d. St. Michel 2 Apr 1891)
Justice	*Prosper Cornesse* (b. Stablo 1829; d. Messancy 1889)
Finance	3 Jul – 3 Aug 1870: *Pierre Amand Tack* (b. Courtrai 18 Dec 1818; d. Courtrai 11 Apr 1910)
	3 Aug 1870 – 1 Dec 1871: *Victor Jacobs* (b. Antwerp 18 Jan 1838; d. Brussels 20 Dec 1891)

7 Dec 1871 – 21 Aug 1874: de Theux de Meylandt III

Prime Minister	*Barthélemy Théodore, Comte de Theux de Meylandt* (for 3rd time) (Clerical) (see de Theux de Meylandt I)
Foreign Affairs	*Guillaume Bernard Ferdinand Charles, Comte d'Aspremont-Lynden* (b. 15 Oct 1815; d. 6 Sep 1889)
Finance	*Jules Malou* (see van de Weyer)

War	7 Dec 1871 – Dec 1872: *Henri Louis, Baron Guillaume* (b. Amiens 1812; d. Brussels 1877)
	Dec 1872 – 21 Aug 1874: *Séraphin François Thiebauld* (b. Genappe 23 Nov 1811; d. Brussels 6 May 1879)
Public Works	Oct 1873 – 21 Aug 1874: *Auguste Marie François Beernaert* (b. Ostend 26 Jul 1829; d. Lucerne 6 Oct 1912)

Aug 1874 – 19 Jul 1878: Malou I

Prime Minister	*Jules Malou* (for 1st time) (Clerical) (see van de Weyer)
Foreign Affairs	*Guillaume, Comte d'Aspremont-Lynden* (see de Theux de Meylandt III)
Home Affairs	*Jules Malou* (see van de Weyer)
Finance	*Jules Malou* (see van de Weyer)
War	*Séraphin François Thiebauld* (see de Theux de Meylandt III)
Public Works	*Auguste Beernaert* (see de Theux de Meylandt III)

19 Jun 1878 – 16 Jun 1884: Frère-Orban

Prime Minister	*Hubert Frère-Orban* (for 2nd time) (Liberal) (see Rogier III)
Foreign Affairs	*Hubert Frère-Orban* (see Rogier III)
Home Affairs	*Gustave Rolin-Jacquemyns* (b. Ghent 31 Jan 1835; d. Brussels 8 Jan 1902)
Justice	*Jules Bara* (see Rogier IV)
Finance	*Charles Graux* (b. Brussels 1837; d. Brussels 1910)
Education (new post)	*Pieter Edward (van) Humbeeck* (b. Brussels 7 May 1829; d. 6 Jul 1890)
War	19 Jun 1878 – Dec 1880: *Bruno Jean Baptiste Renard* (see Frère-Orban I)
	Dec 1880 – 16 Jun 1884: — *de Gratry*

16 Jun – 26 Oct 1884: Malou II

Prime Minister	*Jules Malou* (for 2nd time) (Clerical) (see van de Weyer)
Foreign Affairs	—— *Moreau-Dandry*
Home Affairs	*Victor Jacobs* (see d'Anethan)
Justice and Public Worship	*Charles Frédéric Auguste, Comte Woeste* (b. Brussels 26 Feb 1837; d. 6 Apr 1922)

Finance	*Jules Malou* (see van de Weyer)
Agriculture and Commerce	*Auguste Beernaert* (see de Meylandt III)
War	—— *Ponthus*

26 Oct 1884 – 18 Mar 1894: Beernaert

Prime Minister	*Auguste Beernaert* (Moderate Clerical) (see de Theux de Meylandt III)
Foreign Affairs	26 Oct 1884 – 29 Mar 1892: *Joseph, Prince de Caraman-Chimay* (b. Menars, France, 9 Oct 1836; d. Brussels 29 Mar 1892)
	1 Nov 1892 – 18 Mar 1894: *Henri Marie Ghislain, Comte de Mérode, Marquis of Waterloo, Prince of Rubempré and Grimberghe* (b. 28 Dec 1856; d. Lausanne 13 Jul 1908)
Home Affairs	26 Oct 1884 – 24 Oct 1887: *Johann Joseph Thonissen* (b. Hasselt 21 Jan 1816; d. Louvain 17 Aug 1891)
	24 Oct 1887 – Jul 1891: —— *de Volder*
	Jul 1891 – 18 Mar 1894: *Jules Philippe Marie de Burlet* (b. Ixelles 1844; d. Brussels 1 Mar 1897)
Justice	26 Oct 1884 – Oct 1887: —— *de Volder* (see above)
	Oct 1887 – 1893: *Jules Lejeune* (b. Luxembourg 5 May 1828; d. Brussels 18 Feb 1911)
War	—— *Ponthus* (see Malou II)
Finance	*Auguste Beernaert* (see de Theux de Meylandt III)
Lord Chamberlain	1840 – 28 Dec 1887: *Julius van Praet* (b. Bruges 2 Jul 1806; d. 28 Dec 1887)
	Also ministries for Agriculture, Trade, Public Works and Railways

26 Mar 1894 – 25 Feb 1896: de Burlet

Prime Minister	*Jules de Burlet* (see Beernaert)
Foreign Affairs	26 Mar 1894 – 28 Jun 1895: *Henri Comte de Mérode* (see Beernaert)
Home Affairs	*Jules de Burlet* (see Beernaert)
Finance	*Paul* (from 1900: *Comte*) *de Smet de Nayer* (b. Ghent 13 May 1843; d. Brussels 10 Sep 1913)

26 Feb 1896 – 23 Jan 1899: de Smet de Nayer I

Prime Minister	*Paul* (from 1900: *Comte*) *de Smet de Nayer* (for 1st

	time) (Clerical) (see de Burlet)
Foreign Affairs	*Paul Louis Marie Célestin de Favereau* (b. Liège 15 Jan 1856; d. Bende 26 Sep 1922)
War and Labour	26 Feb 1896 – 1897: *Albert Nyssens* (b. Ypres 1855) 1897 – 23 Jan 1899: *Julius Vandenpeereboom* (b. Courtrai 18 Mar 1843; d. Brussels 13 Mar 1917)

24 Jan – 1 Aug 1899: Vandenpeereboom

Prime Minister	*Julius Vandenpeereboom* (Clerical) (see de Smet de Nayer I)
War	*Julius Vandenpeereboom* (see de Smet de Nayer)
Labour	*Gerhard Cooreman* (b. 25 Mar 1852; d. 2 Dec 1926)

5 Aug 1899 – 12 Apr 1907: de Smet de Nayer II

Prime Minister	*Paul, Comte de Smet de Nayer* (for 2nd time) (Clerical) (see de Burley)
Justice	*Jules van den Heuvel* (b. Ghent 16 Nov 1854; d. Brussels 22 Oct 1926)
Finance and Labour	*Paul, Comte de Smet de Nayer* (see de Burlet)
Education	*Jules de Trooz* (b. Louvain 21 Feb 1857; d. Brussels 31 Dec 1907)
War	—— *Causeband d'Alkmade*

2 May – 31 Dec 1907: de Trooz

Prime Minister	*Jules de Trooz* (Clerical) (see de Smet de Nayer II)
Foreign Affairs	*Julien Davignon* (b. St Josse ten-Noode 1854; d. Nice 14 Mar 1916)
Home Affairs	*Jules de Trooz* (see de Smet de Nayer II)
Justice	*Jules Renkin* (b. Ixelles 3 Dec 1862; d. Brussels 16 Jul 1934)
Finance	*Julien Liebaert* (b. Courtrai 22 Jun 1848; d. Brussels 17 Sep 1930)
Arts and Sciences	*Édouard Eugène François, Baron Descamps-David* (b. Beloeil 27 Aug 1847; d. 17 Jan 1933)
War	*Édouard Hellebaut* (b. 21 Feb 1842)

8 Jan 1908 – 8 Jun 1911: Schollaert

Prime Minister	*Frans Schollaert* (Clerical) (b. Wilsele 19 Aug 1851; d. 29 Jun 1917)

Foreign Affairs	*Julien Davignon* (see de Trooz)
Home Affairs	8 Jan 1908 – mid-Sep 1910: *Frans Schollaert* (see above)
	mid-Sep 1910 – 8 Jun 1911: *Paul Marie Clément Charles Vicomte Berryer* (b. Liège 4 May 1868; d. Liège 14 June 1936)
Justice	*Theóphile Charles André, Vicomte de Lantsheere* (b. Asse 4 Nov 1833; d. Brussels 21 Feb 1918)
Transport	8 Jan 1908 – mid Sep 1910: *Auguste Delbeke* (b. Courtrai 12 Aug 1853)
	mid-Sep 1910 – 8 Jun 1911: *Charles, Baron* (from 1919: *Comte*) *de Broqueville* (b. Moll 4 Dec 1860; d. 4 Sep 1940)
Finance	8 Jan – Nov 1908; *Jules Renkin* (see de Trooz)
	Nov 1908 – 8 Jun 1911: *Julien Liebaert* (see de Trooz)
Education	8 Jan 1908 – mid Sep 1910: *Édouard, Baron Descamps-David* (see de Trooz)
	mid-Sep 1910 – 8 Jun 1911: *Frans Schollaert* (see above)
Colonies (new post)	from Nov 1908: *Jules Renkin* (see de Trooz)
War	*Édouard Hellebaut* (see de Trooz)
Railways and Postal Services	*Joris Helleputte* (Young Clerical) (b. Ghent 31 Aug 1852; d. Brussels 22 Feb 1925)

14 Jun 1911 – 3 Jun 1918: de Broqueville I

Prime Minister	*Charles, Baron de Broqueville* (for 1st time) (Clerical) (see Schollaert)
Foreign Affairs	14 Jun 1911 – 21 Jan 1916: *Julien Davignon* (see de Trooz)
	21 Jan 1916 – 30 Jul 1917: *Eugène, Baron van Beyens* (b. Paris 24 Mar 1855; d. Elsene 3 Jan 1934)
	30 Jul 1917 – beginning of Jan 1918: *Charles, Baron de Broqueville* (see Schollaert)
	beginning of Jan – 3 Jun 1918: *Paul Hymans* (Liberal) (b. Brussels 23 Mar 1865; d. Nice 8 Mar 1941)
Home Affairs	14 Jun 1911 – 1915: *Paul Marie Clément Charles, Vicomte Berryer* (see Schollaert)
	1915 – 1916: *Paul Hymans* (see above)
	Jul 1917 – 3 Jun 1918: *Émile Vandervelde* (Socialist) (b. Elsene 25 Jan 1866; d. Brussels 27 Dec 1938)
Justice	*Henri, Comte Carton de Wiart* (Young Clerical) (b. Brussels 31 Jan 1869; d. Brussels 6 May 1951)

Finance	14 June 1911 – 27 Feb 1914: *Édouard Michel Levie* (Young Clerical) (b. Binche 4 Oct 1851; d. Brussels 6 Mar 1939)
	27 Feb 1914 – 3 Jun 1918: *Alois, Burgrave van de Vyvere* (b. Tielt 8 Jun 1871)
Transport	14 Jun 1911 – 12 Nov 1912: *Charles, Baron de Broqueville* (see Schollaert)
	12 Nov 1912: Transport Ministry divided into ministries for Railways, and for Shipping, Posts and Telegraphs
Arts and Education	*Prosper* (from 1925: *Vicomte*) *Poullet* (b. Louvain 5 Mar 1868; d. 3 Jul 1937)
War	14 Jun 1911 – 23 Feb 1912: *Édouard Hellebaut* (see de Trooz)
	4 Apr – 11 Nov 1912: *Auguste Edouard Michel* (b. 1855)
	12 Nov 1912 – 1916: *Charles, Baron de Broqueville* (see Schollaert)
	1916 – Jul 1917: *Émile Vandervelde* (see above)
	4 Aug 1917 – 3 Jun 1918: —— *Cennynck*
Colonies	*Jules Renkin* (see de Trooz)
Without Portfolio	4 Aug 1914 – 3 Jun 1918: *Émile Vandervelde* (Socialist) (see above)
	20 Dec 1915 – 3 Jun 1918: *Paul Hymans* (see above)
	11 Jan 1916 – 3 Jun 1918: *Julien Liebart* (see de Trooz)
	11 Jan 1916 – 3 Jun 1918: *Gerhard Cooreman* (see Vandenpeereboom)
	11 Jan 1916 – 3 Jun 1918: *Frans Schollaert* (see Schollaert)
	Also ministries for Industry and Labour and for Agriculture and Public Works.

3 Jun – 21 Nov 1918: Cooreman

Prime Minister	*Gerhard Cooreman* (see Vandenpeereboom)
Minister of State	*Charles, Baron Broqueville* (see Schollaert)
	All other Ministers continued in office

22 Nov 1918 – 17 Nov 1919: Delacroix I

Prime Minister	*Léon Delacroix* (for 1st time) (no party) (b. 27 Oct 1867; d. Baden-Baden 15 Oct 1929)
Foreign Affairs	*Paul Hymans* (Liberal) (see de Broqueville I)

Home Affairs	*Charles, Comte de Broqueville* (Catholic) (see Schollaert)
Justice	*Émile Vandervelde* (Socialist) (see de Broqueville I)
Finance	*Léon Delacroix* (see above)
Arts and Sciences	*Henri Jaspar* (Catholic) (b. Brussels 28 Jul 1870; d. 15 Feb 1939)
War	*Paul Émile Janson* (Liberal) (b. 30 May 1872; d. Weimar 4 Jul 1944)
Colonies	*Ludwig Franck* (b. Antwerp 27 Mov 1868; d. Eertbrugge-Wijnegem 31 Dec 1937)
Public Works	*Eduard Anseele* (Socialist) (b. Ghent 25 Jul 1856; d. Ghent 18 Feb 1938)

27 Nov 1919 – 3 Nov 1920: Delacroix II

Prime Minister	*Léon Delacroix* (for 2nd time) (see Delacroix I)
Foreign Affairs	*Paul Hymans* (Liberal) (see de Broqueville I)
Home Affairs	27 Nov 1919 – 2 Jun 1920: *Jules Renkin* (Catholic) (see de Trooz)
	2 June – 3 Nov 1920: *Henri Jaspar* (Catholic) (see Delacroix I)
Justice	*Émile Vandervelde* (Socialist) (see de Broqueville I)
Finance	*Léon Delacroix* (see Delacroix I)
Arts and Sciences	*Jules Destrée* (Socialist) (b. Marcinelle 21 Aug 1863; d. Brussels 3 Jan 1936)
War	27 Nov 1919 – 2 Feb 1920; *Fulgence Paul Benoît Masson* (b. Dour 16 Feb 1854; d. Mons 24 Feb 1942)
	2 Feb – 3 Nov 1920: *Paul Émile Janson* (Liberal) (see Delacroix I)
Public Works	*Eduard Anseele* (Socialist) (see Delacroix I)

18 Nov 1920 – 19 Nov 1921: Carton de Wiart

Prime Minister	*Henri, Comte Carton de Wiart* (Catholic) (see de Broqueville I)
Foreign Affairs	*Henri Jaspar* (Catholic) (see Delacroix I)
Home Affairs	*Henri, Comte Carton de Wiart* (see de Broqueville I)
Justice	*Émile Vandervelde* (Socialist) (see de Broqueville I)
Finance	*Georges Theunis* (Catholic) (b. Liège 18 Feb 1873; d. Monty-sur-Marchienne 21 Aug 1944)
Arts and Sciences	*Alois, Burgrave van de Vyvere* (Catholic) (see de Broqueville I)

War	18 Nov 1920 – 19 Oct 1921: *Albert Devèze* (b. Ypres 6 Jun 1881)
Colonies	*Ludwig Franck* (see Delacroix I)
Labour	*Eduard Anseele* (Socialist) (see Delacroix I)

Dec 1921 – 27 Feb 1924: Theunis I

Prime Minister	*George Theunis* (for 1st time) (Catholic) (see Carton de Wiart)
Foreign Affairs	*Henri Jasper* (Catholic) (see Delacroix I)
Home Affairs	*Paul Marie Clément Charles, Vicomte Berryer* (see Schollaert)
Justice	*Fulgence Paul Benoît Masson* (Liberal) (see Delacroix II)
Finance	*Georges Theunis* (Catholic) (see Carton de Wiart)
Arts and Sciences	*Eugène Hubert* (b. St Josse-ten Noode 8 May 1853; d. Liège 1 Feb 1931)
War	*Albert Devèze* (see Carton de Wiart)
	Also ministries for Commerce, Agriculture, Colonies, Railways, Industry and Labour

11 Mar 1924 – 5 Apr 1925: Theunis II

Prime Minister	*Georges Theunis* (for 2nd time) (Catholic) (see de Wiart)
Foreign Affairs	*Paul Hymans* (Liberal) (see de Broqueville I)
Home Affairs	*Prosper* (from 1925 *Vicomte*) *Poullet* (Catholic) (see de Broqueville I)
Justice	*Fulgence Paul Benoît Masson* (Liberal) (see Delacroix II)
Finance	*Georges Theunis* (Catholic) (see de Wiart)
Arts and Sciences	*Pierre Adrien Émile Louis Nolf* (Catholic) (b. Ypres 26 Jul 1873; d. Brussels 13 Sep 1953)
War	*(Pierre Jean Joseph) Forthomme* (Liberal) (b. Verviers 24 May 1877; d. Brussels 2 Dec 1959)

13 – 22 May 1925: van de Vyvere

Prime Minister	*Alois, Burgrave van de Vyvere* (Catholic) (see de Broqueville I)
Home Affairs	*Prosper, Vicomte Poullet* (Catholic) (see de Broqueville I)
Finance	*Alois, Burgrave van de Vyvere* (see de Broqueville I)

17 Jun 1925 – 6 May 1926: Poullet

Prime Minister	*Prosper, Vicomte Poullet* (Catholic) (see de Broqueville I)
Foreign Affairs	*Émile Vandervelde* (Socialist) (see de Broqueville I)
Home Affairs	17 Jun 1925 – 5 May 1926: —— *Rolin-Jacquemyns* (Liberal)
Justice	17 Jun – 7 Dec 1925: *Paul Tschoffen* (Catholic) (b. Dinant 8 May 1878; d. Liège 11 Jul 1961)
	7 Dec 1925 – 6 May 1926: *Prosper, Vicomte Poullet* (see de Broqueville I)
Finance	*Albert (Édouard) Janssen* (Catholic) (b. Antwerp 1 Apr 1883; d. Hammn-Mille 29 Mar 1966)
Arts and Sciences	*Camille Huysmans* (Socialist) (b. Bilzen 26 May 1871; d. Antwerp 25 Feb 1968)
Defence	17 Jun 1925 – 15 Jan 1962: —— *Keestens* (Liberal) (b. Ghent 27 Dec 1867; d. St Pieters-Woluwe 14 Sep 1945)

20 May 1926 – 21 Nov 1927: Jaspar I

Prime Minister	*Henri Jaspar* (for 1st time) (Catholic) (see Delacroix II)
Foreign Affairs	*Émile Vandervelde* (Socialist) (see de Broqueville I)
Home Affairs	20 May 1926 – 19 Jan 1927: *Henri Jaspar* (see Delacroix I)
	19 Jan – 21 Nov 1927: *Maurice Vauthier* (Liberal) (b. 2 Mar 1860; d. Brussels 25 Jun 1931)
Justice	*Paul Hymans* (Liberal) (see de Broqueville I)
Finance	*Paul, Baron Houtart* (Catholic)
Arts and Sciences	*Camille Huysmans* (Socialist) (see Poullet)
Defence	*Charles, Comte de Broqueville* (Catholic) (see Schollaert)
Colonies	20 May – 27 Dec 1926: *Eduard Pecher* (Catholic) (b. 1879; d. Brussels 27 Dec 1926)
	19 Jan – 21 Nov 1927: *Henri Jaspar* (see Delacroix I)
Without Portfolio	20 May – 15 Nov 1926: *Émile Francqui* (b. Brussels 25 Jun 1863; d. Overyssche 16 Nov 1935) Governor of Belgian State Bank

22 Nov 1927 – 26 Nov 1929: Jaspar II

Prime Minister	*Henri Jaspar* (for 2nd time) (Catholic) (see Delacroix I)

Foreign Affairs	*Paul Hymans* (Liberal) (see de Broqueville I)
Home Affairs	22 Nov 1927 – 20 Oct 1929: *Albert Carnoy* (b. Louvain 7 Nov 1878)
	20 Oct – 26 Nov 1929: *Hendrik Baels* (Catholic) (b. Ostend 1878; d. Knokke 14 Jun 1951)
Justice	*Paul Émile Janson* (Liberal) (see Delacroix I)
Finance	*Paul, Baron Houtart* (Catholic) (see Jaspar I)
Arts and Sciences	22 Nov 1972 – 30 Jun 1929: *Joseph Wauters* (Liberal) (b. Rosoux 8 Nov 1875; d. Ukkel 30 Jun 1929)
Defence	*Charles, Comte de Broqueville* (Catholic) (see Schollaert)
Colonies	22 Nov 1927 – 20 Oct 1929: *Henry Jaspar* (see Delacroix I)
	20 Oct – 26 Nov 1929: *Paul Tschoffen* (Catholic) (see Poullet)

4 Dec 1929 – 21 May 1931: Jaspar III

Prime Minister	*Henri Jaspar* (for 3rd time) (Catholic) (see Delacroix I)
Foreign Affairs	*Paul Hymans* (Liberal) (see de Broqueville I)
Home Affairs	*Hendrik Baels* (Catholic) (see Jaspar II)
Justice	*Paul Émile Janson* (Liberal) (see Delacroix I)
Finance	*Paul, Baron Houtart* (Catholic) (see Jaspar I)
Arts and Sciences	*Maruice Vauthier* (Liberal) (see Jaspar I)
Defence	*Charles, Comte de Broqueville* (Catholic) (see Schollaert)
Colonies	4 – 25 Dec 1929: *Paul Tschoffen* (Catholic) (see Poullet)
	25 Dec 1929 – 18 May 1931: *Henri Jaspar* (Catholic) (see Delacroix I)
	18 – 21 May 1931: *Paul Charles* (Catholic) (b. St Josse-ten-Noode 28 Apr 1885; d. St Josse-ten-Noode 6 Apr 1954)

Benin

For the Kingdom of Benin, Nigeria, between the 14th and 20th centuries, see volume 1.

Bohemia

HEADS OF STATE

Kings

All the Kings of Bohemia except Frederick, Elector Palatine, were also Kings of Hungary and in most cases Archdukes or Emperors of Austria, but not necessarily for the same period of time. The monarchy became hereditary in 1627 and Bohemia was increasingly subordinate to the central government. The date given for accession, if not that of the death of the previous ruler, is the date of coronation as King of Bohemia. Biographical details are given under Hungary

Jagiellonian Dynasty

27 May 1471	*Vladislav II*, son of King Casimir IV of Poland
3 Mar 1516 – 29 Aug 1526	*Louis II*, son

House of Habsburg

23 Oct 1526	*Ferdinand I*, brother-in-law of Louis II
1562	*Maximilian II*, son, recognized as King in 1549
1575	*Rudolf II*, son, deposed
23 May 1611	*Matthias*, brother
29 Jun 1617	*Ferdinand II*, cousin (for 1st time) deposed
26 Aug (elected)/2 Nov 1619 (crowned) – 8 Nov 1620	*Frederick* (Friedrich V, Elector Palatine) (b. 16 Aug 1596; d. 29 Nov 1632)
1620	*Ferdinand II* (for 2nd time)
27 Nov 1627	*Ferdinand III*, son
5 Aug 1646	*Ferdinand IV*, son
1654	*Leopold I*, brother
5 May 1705	*Joseph I*, son
17 Apr 1711	*Charles VI*, brother
20 Oct 1740	*Maria Theresa*, daughter, Queen
29 Nov 1780	*Joseph II*, son
9 Oct 1790	*Leopold II*, brother
9 Aug 1792	*Francis I*, son
7 Sep 1836	*Ferdinand V*, son
2 Dec 1848	*Francis Joseph*, nephew
21 Nov 1916	*Charles VII*, great nephew
28 Oct 1918	Republic (see Czechoslovakia)

Bolivia

Until 1538	Part of Inca Empire
1538	Part of Spanish Empire
25 May 1810	Part of United Provinces of the Río de la Plata (see Argentina) but territory constantly fought over
6 Aug 1825	Independence

HEADS OF STATE

Presidents

25 Aug 1825/3 Oct 1826 – Apr 1828	*Antonio José de Sucre* (b. 3 Feb 1795; d. 3 Jun 1830)
2 Aug 1828 – 1 Jan 1829	*José Miguel Velasco* (for 1st time) (d. 1859)
Mar 1829 – 1839	*Andrés Santa Cruz* (b. La Paz 1792; d. Saint-Nazaire 25 Sep 1865)
16 Jun 1839 – 1841	*José Miguel Velasco* (for 2nd time)
18 Nov 1841	*José Ballivián* (b. May 1804; d. 1852)
Dec 1847	*José Miguel Velasco* (for 3rd time)
6 Dec 1848 – Aug 1855	*Manuel Isidro Belzú* (b. 1808; d. 1865)
1855 – Sep 1857	*Jorge Córdoba* (b. 1822; d. (?) Oct 1861)
Sep 1857	*José Maria Linares* (b. 1810; d. 1861) Dictator
15 Jan 1861 – Dec 1864	*José Maria de Achá* (d. 1868)
28 Dec 1864 – 20 Jun 1871	*José Mariano Melgarejo* (b. 1818; d. 1871)
Nov 1870/20 Jun 1871 – 27 Oct 1872	*Augustín Morales* (b. 1810; d. 27 Oct 1872)
Nov 1872 – 4 Feb 1874	*Adolfo Ballivián* (b. 1831; d. 4 Feb 1874)
14 Feb 1874	*Tomás Frías* (b. 1802; d. after 1880)
4 May 1876 – 28 Dec 1876	*Hilarión Daza* (b. 1840; d. 1 Mar 1894)
19 Jan 1880	*Narciso Campero* (b. 1815; d. 12 Aug 1896) acting from 28 Dec 1879
Aug 1884 – 15 Aug 1888	*Gregorio Pacheco* (b. 1823; d. 30 Aug 1899)
1 Aug 1888 – 1 Aug 1892	*Aniceto Arce*

6 Aug 1892	*Mariano Baptista* (b. 16 Jul 1832; d. 14 Mar 1907)
Aug 1896 – Mar 1899	*Servero Fernández Alonso*
6 Aug 1899 – 4 Aug 1904	*José Manual Pando* (b. 1849 or 1851; d. Jun 1917)
6 Aug 1904	*Ismael Montes* (b. 5 Oct 1861; d. 1933)
12 Aug 1909	*Heliodoro Villazón* (b. 1849; d. 1939)
6 Aug 1913 – 6 Aug 1917	*Ismael Montes* (for 2nd time)
15 Aug 1917	*José N. Gutiérrez Guerra* (b. 5 Sep 1869; d. 1929)
12 Jul 1920	*Bautista Saavedra* (b. 1870; d. 1939)
1 Sep 1925	*José Cabina Villanueva* (b. 1874; d. La Paz 25 Mar 1955) elected but not confirmed by Congress
12 Jan 1926 – 27 Jun 1930	*Hernando Siles* (b. 5 Aug 1833; d. 26 Nov 1942)

Bosnia and Herzegovina

Late 15th century – 1878	Part of Turkish Empire
1878	Administered as a Province by Austria-Hungary

HEADS OF STATE

Provincial Governors

Jul 1878	*Joseph, Baron Philippovich von Philippsburg* (b. Gospić 28 Apr 1919; d. Prague 6 Aug 1889)
1878 – 1882	*Stefan, Baron Jovanović*, Commander-in-Chief and Governor of Hercegovina (b. Pažariste 5 Jan 1828; d. Zara 8 Dec 1885)
18 Nov 1878	*Duke William (Nicholas) of Wurtemberg* (b. Karlsruhe 20 Jul 1828; d. Meran 6 Nov 1896) Head of Provincial Government
6 Apr 1881 – 9 Aug 1882	*Hermann, Baron Dahlen von Orlaburg* (b. Kaschau 16 Jan 1828; d. Vienna 15 Nov 1887)
1882 – Dec 1903	*Johann, Baron Appel, Governor* (b. Sikirevci 11 Nov 1826; d. Gradiska 7 Sep 1906)
8 Dec 1903 – 25 Jun 1907	*Eugen, Baron Albori* (b. Cattaro 27 Nov 1838; d. Vienna 4 Sep 1915)

91

30 Jun 1907 – 7 Mar 1909	*Anton* (from 1909: *Baron*) *Winzor* (b. Joslowitz 7 Jun 1844; d. Bratislava 30 Apr 1910)
Oct 1908	Incorporated into Austria-Hungary
7 Mar 1909	*Marian, Baron Varesanin* (b. Cunsa 1 Feb 1847; d. Vienna 23 Apr 1917)
10 May 1911	*Oskar Potiorek* (b. Bleiburg 20 Nov 1853; d. Klagenfurt 18 Dec 1933) Governor
22 Dec 1914	*Stefan, Baron Sarkotić*, (b. Sinac 4 Oct 1858; d. Vienna 16 Oct 1939) Governor
Nov/Dec 1919	Became part of the Kingdom of the Serbs, Croats and Slovenes (see Yugoslavia)

Brandenburg

HEADS OF STATE

Electors (from 1618 also Dukes of Prussia)

House of Hohenzollern (since 1415)

11 Mar 1486	*Johann Cicero*, son of Elector Albrecht Achilles (b. 2 Aug 1455)
9 Jan 1499	*Joachim I, Nestor*, son (b. 21 Feb 1484)
11 Jul 1535	*Joachim II, Hektor*, son (b. 9 Jan 1505)
2 Jan 1571	*Johann Georg*, son (b. 11 Nov 1525)
8 Jan 1598	*Joachim Friedrich*, son (b. 27 Jan 1546)
18 Jul 1608	*Johann Sigismund*, son (b. 8 Nov 1572)
23 Dec 1619	*Georg Wilhelm*, son (b. 3 Nov 1595)
1 Dec 1640	*Friedrich Wilhelm*, son (b. 16 Feb 1620)
29 Apr/9 May 1688 (– 25 Feb 1713)	*Friedrich III*, son (b. 11 Jul 1657) from 18 Jan 1701 King of Prussia (q.v.)

Brazil

Early 16th century – 1822	Ruled by Portugal

HEADS OF STATE

Emperors

12 Oct 1822	*Pedro I*, son of King Juan VI of Portugal (b. 12 Oct 1798; d. 27 Nov 1834 as King Pedro IV of Portugal)
7 Apr 1831 – 15 Nov 1889	*Pedro II*, son (b. 2 Dec 1825; d. 5 Dec 1891)

Presidents

25 Sep 1890	*Manuel Deodoro da Fonseca* (b. 5 Aug 1827; d. 23 Aug 1892)
24 Nov 1891	*Floriano Peixoto* (b. 1842; d. 29 Jun 1895)
1 Mar 1894	*Prudente José de Moraes Barros* (b. 1841; d. 3 Dec 1902)
15 Nov 1898	*Manuel Ferraz de Campos Salles* (b. 15 Feb 1841; d. 28 Jun 1913)
15 Nov 1902	*Francisco de Paula Rodriguez Alves* (b. 7 Jun 1848; d. 16 Jan 1919)
15 Nov 1906	*Affonso Augusto Moreira Penna* (b. 30 Nov 1847; d. 14 Jun 1909)
14 Jun 1909	*Nilo Peçanha* (b. 2 Oct 1857; d. 31 May 1926)
15 Nov 1910	*Hermes Rodrigo da Fonseca,* nephew of Deodoro da Fonseca (b. 12 May 1855; d. 9 Sep 1923)
15 Nov 1914	*Wenceslao Braz Pereira Gomes* (b. 26 Feb 1868; d. Itajubá 15 May 1966)
15 Nov 1918	*Delfin Moreira da Costa Ribeiro* (b. 7 Nov 1868)
28 Jul 1919	*Epitacio da Silva Pessôa* (b. 23 May 1865; d. 1942)
15 Nov 1922	*Arturo da Silva Bernardes* (b. 8 Aug 1875; d. Rio de Janeiro 23 Mar 1955)
15 Nov 1926	*Washington (Luis) Pereira de Souza* (b. Rio de Janeiro 26 Oct 1870 (1869?); d. São Paulo 4 Aug 1957)

Buganda

For the kingdom of Buganda, Uganda, from the 13th to the 20th century, see volume 1.

Bulgaria

Until 1878   Turkish province

HEADS OF STATE

Princes

House of Hesse-Battenberg
29 Apr 1879 – 7 Sep   *Alexander I*, uncle of Grand Duke Ludwig II of Hesse
   1886   (b. 5 May 1857; d. 17 Nov 1893)

House of Saxe-Coburg-Gotha
7 Aug 1887   *Ferdinand*, son of August I of Saxe-Coburg-Gotha (b.
                         26 Feb 1861; d. 10 Sep 1948) from 5 Oct 1908: King

Kings

5 Oct 1908   *Ferdinand* (see Princes) abdicated 3 Oct 1918
3 Oct 1918 – 28 Aug   *Boris III*, son (b. 30 Jan 1894)
   1943

MEMBERS OF GOVERNMENT

Prime Ministers

1879	*Todor Burmov* (b. 1834; d. 23 Oct 1906)
1879	*Archbishop Kliment* (secular name: *Vasil Drumev*)(b. c. 1840; d. 10 Jul 1901)
1 Apr 1880	*Dragan Zankov* (for 1st time) (b. 1882; d. 24 Mar 1911)
Dec 1880	*Petko Karavelov* (for 1st time) (b. 1843 or 1845; d. 7 Feb 1903)
Jul 1882	*Leonid Nikolaevich Sobolev* (for 1st time) (b. 1844) Russian General
15 Mar 1883	*Leonid Nikolaevich Sobolev* (for 2nd time)
18 Sep 1883	*Dragan Zankov* (for 2nd time)
9 Aug 1884	*Petko Karavelov* (for 2nd time)
Aug 1886	*Vasil Radoslavov* (for 1st time) (b. 15 Jul 1854; d. 21 Oct 1929)

12 Jul 1887	*Konstantin Stoilov* (for 1st time) (b. 1852; d. 5 Apr 1901)
31 Aug 1887	*Stefan Stambolov* (b. 31 Jan 1854; d. 18 Jul 1895)
31 May 1894	*Konstantin Stoilov* (for 2nd time)
21 Dec 1894	*Konstantin Stoilov* (for 3rd time)
28 Jan 1899	*Dimitŭr Grekov* (b. 13 Sep 1847; d. 8 May 1901)
12 Oct 1899	*Todor Ivanchov* (b. 1858; d. 1905)
23 Jan 1901	*Racho Petrov* (for 1st time) (b. 1861; d. 22 Jan 1942)
4 Mar 1901	*Petko Karavelov* (for 3rd time)
4 Jan 1902	*Stoyan Danev* (for 1st time) (b. 7 Feb 1858; d. 29 Jul 1949)
17 Nov 1902 – 27 Mar 1903	*Stoyan Danev* (for 2nd time)
15 May 1903	*Racho Petrov* (for 2nd time)
14 Nov 1906	*Dimitŭr Petkov* (b. 1858; d. 11 Mar 1907)
16 Mar 1907	*Petŭr Gudev* (b. 1863; d. May 1932)
29 Jan 1908	*Aleksandŭr Malinov* (for 1st time) (b. 20 Apr 1867; d. 21 Mar 1938)
(?) – 29 Mar 1911	*Stoyan Danev* (for 3rd time)
29 Mar 1911	*Ivan Geshov* (b. 20 Feb 1849; d. 11 Mar 1924)
14 Jul 1913	*Stoyan Danev* (for 4th time)
18 Jul 1913	*Vasil Radoslavov* (for 2nd time)
16 Jun – 23 Nov 1918	*Aleksandŭr Malinov* (for 2nd time)
28 Nov 1918	*Todor Todorov* (b.(?) 1858; d. 5 Aug 1924)
2 Oct 1919	*Aleksandŭr Stamboliiski* (b. 12 Mar 1878; d. 15 Jun 1923)
9 Jun 1923	*Aleksandŭr Zankov* (b. 29 Jun 1879; d. Buenos Aires 17 Jul 1959)
4 Jan 1926 – 4 Sep 1928	*Andrei Lyapchev* (for 1st time) (b. 30 Nov 1866; d. Nov 1933)
13 Sep 1928 – 15 May 1930	*Andrei Lyapchev* (for 2nd time)

Bulozi (Barotse)

For the Luyana dynasty of Bulozi, Zambia, 17th to 20th centuries, see volume 1.

Bunyoro

For the kingdom of Bunyoro, Uganda, 15th (?) to 19th centuries, see volume 1.

Burma

HEADS OF STATE

Kings

1531 – 1550	*Tabinshwehti*, Ruler of Toungoo; from 1546 King of all Burma
1551 – 1581	*Bayinnaung*
by 1752	Burma split into a number of petty states, the Dutch and British East India Companies established factories
1753	*Alaungpaya* of Shwebo reunited the nation
1760	*Naundawgyi*, son
1763	*Hsinbyushin*, brother
1776	*Singu Min*, son
1781 (for 7 days)	*Maung Maung*, son
1781	*Bodawpaya*, son of Alaungpaya
1819	*Bagyidaw*, grandson
1837	*Tharrawaddy*, brother
1846 – 1852	*Pagin Min*, son
1853 – 1878	*Mindon Min*, brother
1862	Arakan and Tenasserim (annexed 1826) amalgamated with Pegu (annexed 1852) to form British Burma
1878 – 1885	*Thibaw*, son
1 Jan 1886	The whole of Burma annexed by Great Britain and administered by Chief Commissioners (from 1897 Lieutenant Governors)
1921	Government of Burma Act made Burma a governor's province under the Government of India

Governors

1923	*Sir (Spencer) Harcourt Butler* (b. 1 Aug 1869; d. 2 Mar 1938)

| 1927 – 1932 | *Sir Charles Innes* (b. 27 Oct 1874; d. 28 Jun 1959) |

Cambodia

HEADS OF STATE

Kings

1486	*Srey Sukonthor*, son of Dharmarajadhiraja
1512	*(Neay) Kan*, usurper
1516	*Ang Chan I*, brother of Srey Sukonthor
1566	*Barom Reachea I*, son
1576	*Chetta I (Satha)*, son (d. 1596)
1594	*Reamea Chung Prei*, usurper
1596	*Barom Reachea II (Chan Ponhea Ton)*, son of Chetta I, assassinated
1599	*Barom Reachea III (Ponhea Ang)*, uncle, assassinated
1600	*Chau Ponhea Nhom*, nephew, deposed
1603	*Barom Reachea IV (Soryopor)*, uncle (b. about 1570 d. (?)1620) abdicated
1618	*Chettha II*, son
1622 – (?)1628	Interregnum
(?)1628	*Ponhea To*, son (b. 1602) shot
1628 – 1642	*Outey*, brother of Chettha II, Regent, assassinated
1630	*Ponhea Nu*, son of Chettha II
1640	*Ang Non I*, son of Prince Outey, beheaded
1642	*Chan (Rama Thupdey)*, son of Chettha II, deposed
1659	*Batom Reachea (So)*, son of Prince Outey, assassinated
1672	*Chettha III*, nephew, assassinated
1673	*Ang Chei*, son of Batom Reachea
1674	*Ang Non*, usurper
1675	*Chettha IV (Ang Sor)* (for 1st time) son of Batom Reachea, abdicated
1695	*Outey I*, nephew (d. 1695)
1695	*Chettha IV* (for 2nd time) abdicated
1699	*Ang Em,* son-in-law (for 1st time) deposed
1701	*Chetta IV* (for 3rd time) abdicated
1702	*Thommo Reachea II* (for 1st time) (b. 1690) deposed

1703	*Chettha IV* (for 4th time) (d. c.1725) abdicated
1706	*Thommo Reachea II* (for 2nd time) deposed
1710	*Ang Em* (for 2nd time) (d. 1731) abdicated
1722	*Satha II (Ang Chey)*, son, depcsed
1738	*Thommo Reachea II* (for 3rd time)
1747	*Thommo Reachea III*, son, murdered
1747	*Ang Tong*, brother (for first time) deposed
1749	*Chettha V*, son of Thommo Reachea III
1755	*Ang Tong* (for 2nd time) deposed
1758	*(Preah) Outey II*, grandson (b. 1739)
1775	*Ang Non II*, brother or cousin
1779	*Ang Eng*, son (b. 1772)
1796 – 1806	Interregnum
1806	*Ang Chan II*, son of Ang Eng (b. 1791; d. (?)1834)
1837	*Ang Mey*, daughter
1841/1845	*Ang Duong*, brother (b. 1796)
1859 – 1904	*Norodom*, son (b. Ang Vody 1834)
11 Aug 1863	French protectorate established
24 Apr 1904	*Sisovath*, brother (b. Aug 1840)
9 Aug 1927 – 23 Apr 1941	*(Sisovath) Moivong*, son (b. 27 Dec 1875)

Canada

HEADS OF STATE

Governors and Governors General

29 May 1838	*John George Lambton, Earl of Durham* (b. London 12 Apr 1792; d. Cowes 28 Jul 1840) Governor of the English provinces in North America
19 Oct 1839 – 19 Sep 1841	*Charles Edward Poulett Thomson* (from 1840: *1st Baron Sydenham*) (b. Wimbledon 13 Sep 1799; d. Kingston 4 Sep 1841) Governor of Lower Canada; from 10 Feb 1841: Governor of the Province of Canada and Governor-General of British North America
24 Sep 1841	*Sir Richard Downes Jackson*

12 Jan 1842	*Sir Charles Bagot* (b. 23 Sep 1781; d. Kingston, Ontario 19 May 1843) Governor and Governor General
30 Mar 1843	*Sir Charles Theophilus Metcalfe, Bart* (from (?): *Baron Metcalfe*) (b. Calcutta 30 Jan 1785; d. Malshanger 5 Sep 1846) Governor and Governor General
26 Nov 1845	*Charles Murray Cathcart, 2nd Earl Cathcart* (b. Walton, Essex 21 Dec 1783; d. St Leonards-on-Sea 16 Jul 1859) Administrator; from 24 Apr 1846; Governor
30 Jan 1847	*James Bruce, 8th Earl of Elgin and 12th Earl of Kincardine* (b. London 20 Jul 1811; d. Dharmsala, India, 20 Nov 1863) Governor
19 Dec 1854 – 24 Oct 1861	*Sir Edmund Walker Head* (b. Maidstone 1805; d. London 28 Jan 1868) Governor and Governor General
25 Oct 1861 – 14 Nov 1868	*Charles Stanley Monck, 4th Viscount Monck* (b. Co. Tipperary 10 Oct 1819; d. 28 Nov 1894) successively Administrator of the Province of Canada; Governor of the Province of Canada and Governor General of British North America; from 1 Jul 1867: Governor-General of the Dominion of Canada, comprising Ontario, Quebec, New Brunswick and Nova Scotia
2 Jan 1869	*John Young, Baron Lisgar* (b. Bombay 31 Aug 1807; d. Bailliesborough 6 Oct 1876)
22 May 1872	*Frederick Temple Hamilton Blackwood, Earl of Dufferin* (from 1888: *Marquis of Dufferin and Ava*) (b. Florence 21 Jun 1826; d. London 12 Feb 1902)
5 Oct 1878	*John Sutherland-Campbell, Marquis of Lorne,* son-in-law of Queen Victoria (from 1900: *9th Duke of Argyll*) (b. London 6 Aug 1845; d. Cannes 2 May 1914)
18 Aug 1883	*Henry Charles Keith Petty-Fitzmaurice, 5th Marquis of Lansdowne* (b. London 14 Jan 1845; d. London 4 Jun 1927)
1 May 1888	*Frederick Arthur Stanley, Baron Stanley of Preston,* (from 1893: *16th Earl of Derby*) (b. London 15 Jan 1841; d. Holwood, Kent, 14 Jun 1908)
22 May 1893	*John Campbell Hamilton-Gordon, 7th Earl of Aberdeen* (b. 3 Mar 1847; d. Aberdeen 7 March 1934)
30 Jul 1898	*Gilbert Elliot, 4th Earl of Minto* (b. London 9 Jul 1854; d. Hawick 1 Mar 1914)
26 Sep 1904	*Albert Henry George Grey, 4th Earl Grey* (b. 28 Nov 1851; d. Howick 29 Aug 1917)
21 Mar 1911	*Arthur, Duke of Connaught,* 3rd son of Queen Vic-

	toria (b. London 1 May 1850; d. Bagshot Park 16 Jan 1942)
11 Nov 1916	*Victor Cavendish, 9th Duke of Devonshire* (b. London 31 May 1868; d. Chatsworth 26 Nov 1950)
11 Aug 1921	*Julian Byng, Baron* (from 1928: *Viscount*) *Byng of Vimy* (b. Barnet 11 Sep 1862; d. Thorpe Hall 6 Jun 1935)
2 Oct 1926 – 4 Apr 1931	*Freeman Freeman-Thomas, 1st Viscount Willingdon* (from 1931: *1st Earl of Willingdon;* from 1936: *1st Marquis*) (b. Ratton 12 Sep 1866; d. London 12 Aug 1941)

MEMBERS OF GOVERNMENT

1 Jul 1867 – 5 Nov 1873: Macdonald I (Liberal Conservative)

Prime Minister	*Sir John Alexander Macdonald* (for 1st time) (b. Glasgow 11 Jan 1815; d. Ottawa 6 Jun 1891)
Interior	*Alexander Campbell* (from 1879: *Sir*) (b. Hedon, Yorkshire, 9 Mar 1822; d. Toronto 24 May 1892)
Agriculture	1 Jul 1867 – 15 Nov 1869: *Jean Charles Chapais* (b. Rivière Ouelle 21 Dec 1811; d. Ottawa 17 Jul 1885)
	16 Nov 1869 – 24 Oct 1871: *Christopher Dunkin* (b. London 25 Sep 1812; d. Knowlton 6 Jan 1881)
	25 Oct 1871 – 5 Nov 1873: *John Henry Pope* (b. Eastern Townships 19 Dec 1824; d. Ottawa 1 Apr 1889)
Customs	1 Jul 1867 – 21 Feb 1873: *Samuel Leonard Tilley* (from 1879: *Sir*) (b. Gagetown 8 May 1818; d. Saint John 25 Jun 1896)
	22 Feb – 5 Nov 1873: *Charles Tupper* (from 1879: *Sir*; from 1888: *Bart*) (b. Amherst 2 Jul 1821; d. Bexley Heath 30 Oct 1915)
Finance	1 Jul – 7 Nov 1867: *Alexander Tilloch Galt* (from 1869: *Sir*) (b. London 6 Sep 1817; d. Montreal 19 Sep 1893)
	18 Nov 1867 – 30 Sep 1869: *John Rose* (from 1870: *Sir*; from 1872: *Bart*) (b. Turriff, Aberdeenshire, 2 Aug 1870; d. Langwell, Caithness, 24 Aug 1888)
	9 Oct 1869 – 21 Feb 1873: *Sir Francis Hincks* (b. Cork 14 Dec 1807; d. Montreal 18 Aug 1885)
	22 Feb – 7 Nov 1873: *Samuel Leonard Tilley* (see above)

Indian Affairs	22 May 1868 – 7 Dec 1869: *Hector Louis Langevin* (from 1881: *Sir*) (b. Quebec 26 Aug 1826; d. Quebec 11 Jun 1906)
	8 Dec 1869 – 6 May 1873: *Joseph Howe* (b. Halifax 13 Dec 1804; d. Halifax 1 Jun 1873)
	7 May – 13 Jun 1873 (acting:) *James Cox Aikins* (b. Toronto 30 Mar 1823; d. Toronto 6 Aug 1904)
	14 – 30 Jun 1873: *Thomas Nicholson Gibbs* (b. Terrebonne 11 Mar 1821; d. Oshawa 7 Apr 1883)
	1 Jul – 5 Nov 1873: *Alexander Campbell* (see above)
Inland Revenue	1 Jul 1867 – 14 Jul 1868: *William Pearce Howland* (from 1879: *Sir*) (b. Paulings 29 May 1811; d. Toronto 1 Jan 1907)
	15 Jul 1868 – 15 Nov 1869 (acting:) *Alexander Campbell* (see above)
	16 Nov 1869 – 1 Jul 1872: *Alexander Morris* (b. Perth, Upper Canada, 17 Mar 1826; d. Toronto 28 Oct 1889)
	2 Jul 1872 – 3 Mar 1873: *Charles Tupper* (see above)
	4 Mar – 30 Jun 1873: *John O'Connor* (b. Boston Jan 1824; d. Cobourg 3 Nov 1887)
	1 Jul – 5 Nov 1873: *Thomas Nicholson Gibbs* (see above)
Justice and Attorney General	*Sir John Alexander Macdonald* (see above)
Marine and Fisheries	*Peter Mitchell* (b. Newcastle, New Brunswick, 4 Jan 1824; d. Montreal 25 Oct 1899)
Militia and Defence	1 Jul 1867 – 20 May 1873: *Sir George Etienne Cartier* (from 1868: *Bart*) (b. St Antoine 8 Sep 1814; d. London 20 May 1873)
	21 May – 30 Jun 1873 (acting:) *Hector Louis Langevin* (see above)
	1 Jul – 4 Nov 1873: *Hugh McDonald* (b. South River 4 May 1827; d. Antigonish 28 Feb 1899)
Postmaster General	1 Jul 1867 – 30 Jun 1873: *Alexander Campbell* (see above)
	1 Jul – 5 Nov 1873: *John O'Connor* (see above)
President of the Privy Council	1 Jul – 29 Dec 1867: *Adam Johnston Fergusson Blair* (b. Perthshire 4 Nov 1815; d. Ottawa 29 Dec 1867)
	30 Jan 1868 – 15 Nov 1869: *Joseph Howe* (see above)
	16 Nov 1869 – 20 Jun 1870: *Edward Kenny* (from 1870: *Sir*) (b. County Kenny Jul 1800; d. Halifax 16 May 1891)
	21 Jun 1870 – 1 Jul 1872: *Charles Tupper* (see above)

	2 Jul 1872 – 3 Mar 1873: *John O'Connor* (see above)
	14 – 30 Jun 1873: *Hugh McDonald* (see above)
Public Works	1 Jul 1867 – 27 Sep 1869: *William McDougall* (b. York, near Toronto, 22 Jan 1822; d. Ottawa 29 May 1905)
	29 Sep 1869 – 5 Nov 1873: *Hector Louis Langevin*, acting until 7 Dec 1869 (see above)
Receiver General	4 Jul 1867 – 15 Nov 1869: *Edward Kenny* (see above)
	16 Nov 1869 – 29 Jan 1873: *Jean Charles Chapais* (see above)
.	30 Jan – 5 Nov 1873: *Théodore Robitaille* (b. Varennes, Lower Canada, 29 Jan 1834; d. New Carlisle 17 Aug 1897)
Secretary of State of Canada	1 Jul 1867 – 7 Dec 1869: *Hector Louis Langevin* (see above)
	8 Dec 1869 – 5 Nov 1873: *James Cox Aikins* (see above)
Secretary of State for the Provinces	1 Jul 1867 – 30 Apr 1868: *Adams George Archibald* (from 1885: *Sir*) (b. Truro, Nova Scotia, 18 May 1814; d. Truro 14 Dec 1892)
	16 Nov 1869 – 6 May 1873: *Joseph Howe* (see above)
	7 May – 13 Jun 1873: *James Cox Aikins* (see above)
	14 – 30 Jun 1873: *Thomas Nicholson Gibbs* (see above)

7 Nov 1873 – 8 Oct 1878: Mackenzie (Liberal)

Prime Minister	*Alexander Mackenzie* (b. Dunkeld 28 Jan 1822; d. Toronto 17 Apr 1892)
Interior and Indian Affairs	7 Nov 1873 – 6 Oct 1876: *David Laird* (b. New Glasgow 12 Mar 1833; d. Ottawa 12 Jan 1914)
	7 – 23 Oct 1876 (acting:) *Richard William Scott* (b. Prescott 24 Feb 1825; d. Ottawa 23 Apr 1913)
	24 Oct 1876 – 8 Oct 1878: *David Mills* (b. Orford 18 Mar 1831; d. Ottawa 8 May 1903)
Agriculture	7 Nov 1873 – 14 Dec 1876: *Luc Letellier de St-Just* (b. Rivière Ouelle 12 May 1820; d. Rivière Ouelle 28 Jan 1881)
	15 Dec 1876 – 25 Jan 1877 (acting:) *Isaac Burpee* (b. Sheffield, New Brunswick, 28 Nov 1825; d. New York 1 Mar 1885)
	26 Jan 1877 – 8 Oct 1878: *Charles Alphonse Pantaléon Pelletier* (b. Rivière Ouelle 22 Jan 1837; d.

	Spencerwood 29 Apr 1911)
Customs	*Isaac Burpee* (see above)
Finance	*Richard John Cartwright* (from 1879: *Sir*) (b. Kingston 14 Dec 1835; d. Kingston 24 Sep 1912)
Inland Revenue	7 Nov 1873 – 7 Jul 1874: *Télesphore Fournier* (b. St François de Montmagny 5 Aug 1824; d. Ottawa 10 May 1896)
	8 Jul 1874 – 8 Nov 1876: *Félix Geoffrion* (b. Varennes, Lower Canada, 4 Oct 1832; d. Verchères 7 Aug 1894)
	9 Nov 1876 – 7 Jun 1877: *Toussaint Antoine Rodolphe Laflamme* (b. Montreal 15 May 1827; d. Montreal 7 Dec 1893)
	8 Jun – 7 Oct 1877: *Joseph Édouard Cauchon* (b. Quebec 31 Dec 1816; d. Whitewood, near Qu'Appelle, 24 Feb 1885)
	8 Oct 1877 – 8 Oct 1878: *Wilfred Laurier* (from 1897: *Sir*) (b. St-Lin 20 Nov 1841; d. Ottawa 17 Feb 1919)
Justice and Attorney General	7 Nov 1873 – 31 May 1874: *Antoine Aimé Dorion* (from 1877: *Sir*) (b. Ste Anne de la Pérade 17 Jan 1818; d. Montreal 31 May 1891)
	1 Jun – 7 Jul 1874 (acting:) *Albert James Smith* (from 1878: *Sir*) (b. Shediac 12 Mar 1822; d. Dorchester 30 Jun 1883)
	8 Jul 1874 – 18 May 1875: *Télesphore Fournier* (see above)
	19 May 1875 – 7 Jun 1877: *Dominick Edward Blake* (b. Adelaide Township 13 Oct 1833; d. Toronto 1 Mar 1912)
	8 Jun 1877 – 8 Oct 1878: *Toussaint Antoine Rodolphe Laflamme* (see above)
Marine and Fisheries	*Albert James Smith* (see above)
Militia and Defence	7 Nov 1873 – 29 Sep 1874: *William Ross* (b. Bouladerie 20 Dec 1824; d. Ottawa 17 Mar 1912)
	30 Sep 1874 – 20 Jan 1878: *William Berrian Vail* (b. Sussex Vale 29 Dec 1823; d. Dover 10 Apr 1904)
	21 Jan – 8 Oct 1878: *Alfred Gilpin Jones* (b. Weymouth, Nova Scotia, 28 Sep 1824; d. Halifax 15 Mar 1906)
Postmaster General	7 Nov 1873 – 17 May 1875: *Donald Alexander Macdonald* (b. St Raphael 17 Feb 1817; d. Montreal 10 Jun 1896)
	19 May – 7 Oct 1875: *Télesphore Fournier* (see above)

	9 Oct 1875 – 8 Oct 1878: *Lucius Seth Huntington* (b. Compton 26 May 1827; d. New York 19 May 1886)
President of the Privy Council	20 Jan 1874 – 8 Oct 1875: *Lucius Seth Huntington* (see above)
	7 Dec 1875 – 7 Jun 1877: *Joseph Edouard Cauchon* (see above)
	8 Jun 1877 – 8 Oct 1878: *Dominick Edward Blake* (see above)
Public Works	*Alexander Mackenzie* (see above)
Receiver General	*Thomas Coffin* (b. Barrington 1817; d. Barrington 12 Jul 1890)
Secretary of State of Canada	7 Nov 1873 – 8 Jan 1874: *David Christie* (b. Edinburgh Oct 1818; d. Paris, Ontario, 15 Dec 1880)
	9 Jan 1874 – 8 Oct 1878: *Richard William Scott* (see above)
Without Portfolio	7 Nov 1873 – 13 Feb 1874: *Dominick Edward Blake* (see above)
	7 Nov 1873 – 8 Jan 1874: *Richard William Scott* (see above)

17 Oct 1878 – 6 Jun 1891: Macdonald II (Liberal Conservative)

Prime Minister	*Sir John Alexander Macdonald* (for 2nd time) (see Macdonald I)
Interior	17 Oct 1878 – 16 Oct 1883: *Sir John Alexander Macdonald* (see Macdonald I)
	17 Oct 1883 – 4 Aug 1885: *David Lewis Macpherson* (from 1884: *Sir*) (b. Castle Leathers, Inverness, 12 Sep 1818; d. mid-Atlantic 16 Aug 1896)
	5 Aug 1885 – 21 Apr 1888: *Thomas White* (b. Montreal 7 Aug 1830; d. Ottawa 21 Apr 1888)
	8 May – 24 Sep 1888 (acting:) *Sir John Alexander Macdonald* (see Macdonald I)
	25 Sep 1888 – 6 Jun 1891: *Edgar Dewdney* (b. Devonshire 5 Nov 1835; d. Victoria 8 Aug 1916)
Agriculture	17 Oct 1878 – 24 Sep 1885: *John Henry Pope* (see Macdonald I)
	25 Sep 1885 – 6 Jun 1891: *John Carling* (from 1893: *Sir*) (b. London, Ontario, 23 Jan 1828; d. London, Ontario, 6 Nov 1911)
Customs	19 Oct 1878 – 6 Jun 1891: *Mackenzie Bowell* (from 1895: *Sir*) (b. Rickinghall, Suffolk, 27 Dec 1823; d. Belleville 10 Dec 1917)

Finance and (from 20 May 1879) Receiver General	17 Oct 1878 – 10 Nov 1885: *Sir Samuel Leonard Tilley* (see Macdonald I)
	10 Dec 1885 – 26 Jan 1887: *Archibald Woodbury McLelan* (b. Londonderry, Nova Scotia, 24 Dec 1824; d. Halifax 26 Jun 1890)
	27 Jan 1887 – 22 May 1888: *Sir Charles Tupper, Bart* (see Macdonald I)
	29 May 1888 – 6 Jun 1891: *George Eulas Foster* (from 1914: *Sir*) (b. Carleton County 3 Sep 1847; d. Ottawa 30 Dec 1931)
Indian Affairs	17 Oct 1878 – 2 Oct 1887: *Sir John Alexander Macdonald* (see Macdonald I)
	3 Oct 1887 – 21 Apr 1888: *Thomas White* (see above)
	8 May – 24 Sep 1888 (acting:) *Sir John Alexander Macdonald* (see Macdonald I)
	25 Sep 1888 – 6 Jun 1891: *Edgar Dewdney* (see above)
Inland Revenue	26 Oct 1878 – 28 Oct 1880: *Louis François Georges Baby* (b. Montreal 26 Aug 1834; d. Montreal 13 May 1906)
	8 Nov 1880 – 22 May 1882: *James Cox Aikins* (see Macdonald I)
	23 May 1882 – 6 Jun 1891: *John Costigan* (b. St Nicholas 1 Feb 1835; d. Ottawa 29 Sep 1916)
Justice and Attorney General	17 Oct 1878 – 19 May 1881: *James McDonald* (b. East River 1 Jul 1828; d. Halifax 3 Oct 1912)
	20 May 1881 – 24 Sep 1885: *Sir Alexander Campbell* (see Macdonald I)
	26 Sep 1885 – 6 Jun 1891: *Sir John Sparrow David Thompson* (b. Halifax 10 Nov 1844; d. Windsor Castle 12 Dec 1894)
Marine and Fisheries	19 Oct 1878 – 9 Jul 1882: *James Colledge Pope* (b. Bedeque 11 Jun 1826; d. Summerside 18 May 1885)
	10 Jul 1882 – 9 Dec 1885: *Archibald Woodbury McLelan* (see above)
	10 Dec 1885 – 28 May 1888: *George Eulas Foster* (see above)
	1 Jun 1888 – 6 Jun 1891: *Charles Hibbert Tupper* (from 1893: *Sir*) (b. Amherst 3 Aug 1855; d. Vancouver 30 Mar 1927)
Militia and Defence	19 Oct 1878 – 15 Jan 1880: *Louis François Rodrigue Masson* (b. Terrebonne 7 Nov 1833; d. Montreal 8 Nov 1903)
	16 Jan – 7 Nov 1880: *Sir Alexander Campbell* (see

Macdonald I)

8 Nov 1880 – 6 Jun 1891: *Sir Joseph Philippe René Adolphe Caron* (b. Quebec 24 Dec 1843; d. Montreal 20 Apr 1908)

Postmaster General 19 Oct 1878 – 19 May 1879: *Hector Louis Langevin* (see Macdonald I)

20 May 1879 – 15 Jan 1880: *Sir Alexander Campbell* (see Macdonald I)

16 Jan – 7 Nov 1880: *John O'Connor* (see Macdonald I)

8 Nov 1880 – 19 May 1881: *Sir Alexander Campbell* (see Macdonald I)

20 May 1881 – 22 May 1882: *John O'Connor* (see Macdonald I)

23 May 1882 – 24 Sep 1885: *John Carling* (see above)

25 Sep 1885 – 26 Jan 1887: *Sir Alexander Campbell* (see Macdonald I)

27 Jan 1887 – 9 Jul 1889: *Archibald Woodbury McLelan* (see above)

11 Jul – 5 Aug 1888 (acting:) *John Carling* (see above)

6 Aug 1888 – 6 Jun 1891: *John Graham Haggart* (b. Perth, Ontario, 14 Nov 1836; d. Ottawa 13 Mar 1913)

President of the Privy Council 17 Oct 1878 – 15 Jan 1880: *John O'Connor* (see Macdonald I)

16 Jan – 31 Jul 1880: *Louis François Rodrigue Masson* (see above)

8 Nov 1880 – 19 May 1881: *Joseph Alfred Mousseau* (b. Berthier 18 Jul 1838; d. Montreal 30 Mar 1886)

20 May 1881 – 9 Jul 1882: *Archibald Woodbury McLelan* (see above)

17 Oct 1883 – 27 Nov 1889: *Sir John Alexander Macdonald* (see Macdonald I)

28 Nov 1889 – 30 Apr 1891: *Charles Carrol Dolby* (b. Derby, Vermont, 10 Dec 1827; d. Stanstead 10 Dec 1907)

Public Works 17 Oct 1878 – 19 May 1879: *Sir Charles Tupper* (see Macdonald I)

20 May 1879 – 6 Jun 1891: *Sir Hector Louis Langevin* (see Macdonald I)

Railways and Canals 20 May 1879 – 28 May 1884: *Sir Charles Tupper* (see Macdonald I)

29 May 1884 – 1 Apr 1889: *John Henry Pope* (see Macdonald I) acting until 24 Sep 1885

	10 Apr 1889 – 6 Jun 1891: *Sir John Alexander Macdonald* (see Macdonald I) acting until 27 Nov 1889
Receiver General	8 Nov 1878 – 19 May 1879: *Alexander Campbell* (see Macdonald I)
	20 May 1879: merged with Ministry of Finance
Secretary of State of Canada	19 Oct 1878 – 7 Nov 1880: *James Cox Aikins* (see Macdonald I)
	8 Nov 1880 – 19 May 1881: *John O'Connor* (see Macdonald I)
	20 May 1881 – 28 Jul 1882: *Joseph Alfred Mousseau* (see above)
	29 Jul 1882 – 6 Jun 1891: *Joseph Adolphe Chapleau* (from 1896: *Sir*) (b. Ste-Thérèse de Blainville 9 Nov 1840; d. Montreal 13 Jun 1898)
Without Portfolio	8 Nov 1878 – 10 Feb 1880: *Robert Duncan Wilmot* (b. Frederiction 16 Oct 1809; d. Oromocto 13 Feb 1891)
	11 Feb 1880 – 16 Oct 1883: *David Lewis Macpherson* (see above)
	2 Aug 1882 – 6 Jun 1891: *Frank Smith* (from 1894: *Sir*) (b. Richill, Co. Armagh, 13 Mar 1822; d. Toronto 17 Jan 1901)
	13 May 1887 – 6 Jun 1891: *John Joseph Caldwell Abbott* (from 1892: *Sir*) (b. St Andrews 12 Mar 1821; d. Montreal 30 Oct 1893)

16 Jun 1891 – 24 Nov 1892: Abbott (Liberal Conservative)

Prime Minister	*Sir John Joseph Caldwell Abbott* (see Macdonald II)
Interior and Indian Affairs	16 Jun 1891 – 16 Oct 1892: *Edgar Dewdney* (see Macdonald II)
	17 Oct – 24 Nov 1892: *Thomas Mayne Daly* (b. Hamilton 16 Aug 1852; d. Stratford 24 Jun 1911)
Agriculture	*John Carling* (see Macdonald II)
Customs	16 Jun 1891 – 24 Jan 1892: *Mackenzie Bowell* (see Macdonald II)
	25 Jan – 24 Nov 1892: *Joseph Adolphe Chapleau* (see Macdonald II)
Finance and Receiver General	*George Eulas Foster* (see Macdonald II)
Inland Revenue	*John Costigan* (see Macdonald II)
Justice and Attorney General	*Sir John Sparrow David Thompson* (see Macdonald II)
Marine and Fisheries	*Charles Hibbert Tupper* (see Macdonald II)

Militia and Defence	16 Jun 1891 – 24 Jan 1892: *Sir Joseph Philippe René Adolphe Caron* (see Macdonald II) 25 Jan – 24 Nov 1892: *Mackenzie Bowell* (see Macdonald II)
Postmaster General	16 Jun 1891 – 19 Jan 1892: *John Graham Haggart* (see Macdonald II) 25 Jan – 24 Nov 1892: *Sir Joseph Philippe René Adolphe Caron* (see Macdonald II)
President of the Privy Council	*Sir John Joseph Caldwell Abbott* (see Macdonald II)
Public Works	16 Jun – 11 Aug 1891: *Sir Hector Louis Langevin* (see Macdonald I) 14 Aug 1891 – 10 Jan 1892: *Frank Smith* (see Macdonald II) 11 Jan – 24 Nov 1892: *Joseph Aldéric Ouimet* (b. Ste-Rose 20 May 1848; d. Montreal 12 May 1916)
Railways and Canals	17 Jun 1891 – 10 Jan 1892 (acting:) *Mackenzie Bowell* (see Macdonald II) 11 Jan – 24 Nov 1892: *John Graham Haggart* (see Macdonald II)
Secretary of State of Canada	16 Jun 1891 – 24 Jan 1892: *Joseph Adolphe Chapleau* (see Macdonald II) 25 Jan – 24 Nov 1892: *James Colębrooke Patterson* (b. Armagh 1839; d. Ottawa 17 Feb 1929)
Without Portfolio	16 Jun – 13 Aug 1891 and 11 Jan – 24 Nov 1892: *Frank Smith* (see Macdonald II)

5 Dec 1892 – 12 Dec 1894: Thompson (Liberal Conservative)

Prime Minister	*Sir John Sparrow David Thompson* (see Macdonald II)
Interior and Indian Affairs	*Thomas Mayne Daly* (see Abbott)
Agriculture	7 Dec 1892 – 12 Dec 1894: *Auguste Réal Angers* (from 1913: *Sir*) (b. Quebec 4 Oct 1838; d. Montreal 15 Apr 1919)
Finance and Receiver General	*George Eulas Foster* (see Macdonald II)
Justice and Attorney General	*Sir John Sparrow David Thompson* (see Macdonald II)
Marine and Fisheries	*Sir Charles Hibbert Tupper* (see Macdonald II)
Militia and Defence	*James Colebrooke Patterson* (see Abbott)
Postmaster General	*Sir Joseph Philippe René Adolphe Caron* (see Macdonald II)

President of the Privy Council	7 Dec 1892 - 12 Dec 1894: *William Búllock Ives* (b. Compton 17 Nov 1841; d. Sherbrooke 15 Jul 1899)
Public Works	*Joseph Aldéric Ouimet* (see Abbott)
Railways and Canals	*John Graham Haggart* (see Macdonald II)
Secretary of State of Canada	*John Costigan* (see Macdonald II)
Trade and Commerce	*Mackenzie Bowell* (see Macdonald II)
Without Portfolio	*Sir John Carling* (see Macdonald II)
	Sir Frank Smith (see Macdonald II)

21 Dec 1894 - 27 Apr 1896: Bowell (Liberal Conservative)

Prime Minister	*Sir Mackenzie Bowell* (see Macdonald II)
Interior and Indian Affairs	*Thomas Mayne Daly* (see Abbott)
Agriculture	21 Dec 1894 - 12 Jul 1895: *Auguste Réal Angers* (see Thompson)
	13 Jul - 20 Dec 1895 (acting:) *Joseph Aldéric Ouimet* (see Abbott)
	21 Dec 1895 - 5 Jan 1896: *Walter Humphries Montague* (b. Adelaide, Ontario, 21 Nov 1858; d. Winnipeg 14 Nov 1915)
	6 - 14 Jan 1896 (acting:) *Donald Ferguson* (b. Marshfield 7 Mar 1839; d. Marshfield 4 Sep 1909)
	15 Jan - 27 Apr 1896: *Walter Humphries Montague* (see above)
Customs	24 Dec 1895 - 5 Jan 1896: *John Fisher Wood* (b. Elizabethtown 12 Oct 1852; d. Brockville 14 Mar 1899)
	6 - 14 Jan 1896 (acting:) *Sir Frank Smith* (see Macdonald II)
	15 Jan - 27 Apr 1896: *John Fisher Wood* (see above)
Finance and Receiver General	21 Dec 1894 - 5 Jan 1896: *George Eulas Foster* (see Macdonald II)
	6 - 14 Jan 1896 (acting:) *Sir Mackenzie Bowell* (see Macdonald II)
	15 Jan - 27 Apr 1896: *George Eulas Foster* (see Macdonald II)
Inland Revenue	*Edward Gawler Prior* (b. Dallaghgill, Yorkshire, 21 May 1853; d. Victoria 12 Dec 1920)
Justice and Attorney General	21 Dec 1894 - 5 Jan 1896: *Sir Charles Hibbert Tupper* (see Macdonald II)
	6 - 14 Jan 1896 (acting:) *Thomas Mayne Daly* (see Abbott)

	15 Jan – 27 Apr 1896: *Arthur Rupert Dickey* (b. Amherst 18 Aug 1854; d. Amherst 3 Jul 1900)
Marine and Fisheries	*John Costigan* (see Macdonald II)
Militia and Defence	21 Dec 1894 – 25 Mar 1895: *James Colebrooke Patterson* (see Abbott)
	26 Mar 1895 – 5 Jan 1896: *Arthur Rupert Dickey* (see above)
	6 – 14 Jan 1896 (acting:) *Sir Mackenzie Bowell* (see Macdonald II)
	15 Jan – 27 Apr 1896: *Alphonse Desjardins* (b. Terebonne 6 May 1841; d. Montreal 4 Jun 1912)
Postmaster General	*Sir Joseph Philippe René Adolphe Caron* (see Macdonald II)
President of the Privy Council	*Sir Mackenzie Bowell* (see Macdonald II)
Public Works	*Joseph Aldéric Ouimet* (see Abbott)
Railways and Canals	21 Dec 1894 – 5 Jan 1896: *John Graham Haggart* (see Macdonald II)
	6 – 14 Jan 1896 (acting:) *Joseph Aldéric Ouimet* (see Abbott)
	15 Jan – 27 Apr 1896: *John Graham Haggart* (see Macdonald II)
Secretary of State of Canada	21 Dec 1894 – 25 Mar 1895: *Arthur Rupert Dickey* (see above)
	26 Mar – 20 Dec: *Walter Humphries Montague* (see above)
	27 Dec 1895 – 5 Jan 1896 (acting:) *Joseph Aldéric Ouimet* (see Abbott)
	6 – 14 Jan 1896 (acting:) *Thomas Mayne Daly* (see Abbott)
	15 Jan – 27 Apr 1896: *Sir Charles Tupper, Bart* (see Macdonald I)
Trade and Commerce	21 Dec 1894 – 5 Jan 1896: *William Bullock Ives* (see Thompson)
	5 – 14 Jan 1896 (acting:) *John Costigan* (see Macdonald II)
	15 Jan – 27 Apr 1896: *William Bullock Ives* (see Thompson)
Without Portfolio	21 Dec 1894 – 25 Mar 1895: *Walter Humphries Montague* (see above)
	Sir Frank Smith (see Macdonald II)
	2 Jan 1895 – 27 Apr 1896: *Donald Ferguson* (see above)

26 Mar – 1 Sep 1895: *James Colebrooke Patterson* (see Abbott)

1 May – 8 Jul 1896: Tupper (Liberal Conservative)

Prime Minister	*Sir Charles Tupper, Bart* (see Macdonald I)
Interior and Indian Affairs	*Hugh John Macdonald* (from 1913: *Sir*) (b. Kingston 13 Mar 1850; d. Winnipeg 29 Mar 1929)
Agriculture	*Walter Humphries Montague* (see Bowell)
Customs	*John Fisher Wood* (see Bowell)
Finance and Receiver General	*George Eulas Foster* (see Macdonald II)
Inland Revenue	*Edward Gawler Prior* (see Bowell)
Justice and Attorney General	*Arthur Rupert Dickey* (see Bowell)
Marine and Fisheries	*John Costigan* (see Macdonald II)
Militia and Defence	*David Tisdale* (b. Charlotteville 8 Sep 1835; d. Simcoe 31 Mar 1911)
Postmaster General	*Louis Olivier Taillon* (from 1917: *Sir*) (b. Terrebonne 26 Sep 1840; d. Montreal 25 Apr 1923)
President of the Privy Council	*Auguste Réal Angers* (see Thompson)
Public Works	*Alphonse Desjardins* (see Bowell)
Railways and Canals	*John Graham Haggart* (see Macdonald II)
Secretary of State of Canada	*Sir Charles Tupper, Bart* (see Macdonald I)
Trade and Commerce	*William Bullock Ives* (see Thompson)
Without Portfolio	*Donald Ferguson* (see Bowell)
	John Jones Ross (b. Quebec 16 Aug 1832; d. Ste Anne de la Pérade 4 May 1901)
	Sir Frank Smith (see Macdonald II)

11 Jul 1896 – 6 Oct 1911: Laurier (Liberal)

Prime Minister	*Sir Wilfred Laurier* (see Mackenzie)
Interior and Indian Affairs	17 Jul – 16 Nov 1896 (acting:) *Richard William Scott* (see Mackenzie)
	17 Nov 1896 – 28 Feb 1905: *Clifford Sifton* (from 1914: *Sir*) (b. Middlesex County 10 Mar 1861; d. New York 17 Apr 1929)
	13 Mar – 7 Apr 1905 (acting:) *Sir Wilfred Laurier* (see Mackenzie)
	8 Apr 1905 – 6 Oct 1911: *Frank Oliver* (b. Ching-

	uacousy Township 14 Sep 1853; d. Ottawa 31 Mar 1933)
Agriculture	*Sydney Arthur Fisher* (b. Montreal 12 Jun 1850; d. Ottawa 9 Apr 1921)
Customs	*William Paterson* (b. Hamilton 19 Sep 1839; d. Picton 18 Mar 1914)
Finance and Receiver General	20 Jul 1896 – 6 Oct 1911: *Williams Stevens Fielding* (b. Halifax 24 Nov 1848; d. Ottawa 23 Jun 1929)
Inland Revenue	30 Jun 1897 – 21 Jun 1900 (as Minister): *Sir Henri Gustave Joly de Lotbinière* (b. Epernay 5 Dec 1829; d. Quebec 15 Nov 1908) Controller from 13 Jul 1896 but not in cabinet
	22 Jun 1900 – 18 Jan 1904: *Michel Esdras Bernier* (b. St Hyacinthe 28 Sep 1841; d. St Hyacinthe 27 Jul 1921)
	19 Jan 1904 – 5 Feb 1906: *Louis Philippe Brodeur* (b. Beloeil 21 Aug 1862; d. Quebec 1 Jan 1924)
	6 Feb 1906 – 6 Oct 1911: *William Templeman* (b. Pakenham 28 Sep 1842; d. Victoria 15 Nov 1914)
Justice and Attorney General	13 Jul 1896 – 17 Nov 1897: *Sir Oliver Mowat* (b. Kingston 22 Jul 1820; d. Toronto 19 Apr 1903)
	18 Nov 1897 – 7 Feb 1902: *David Mills* (see Mackenzie)
	11 Feb 1902 – 3 Jun 1906: *Charles Fitzpatrick* (from 1907: *Sir*) (b. Quebec 19 Dec 1853; d. Quebec 17 Jun 1942)
	4 Jun 1906 – 6 Oct 1911: *Allen Bristol Aylesworth* (from 1911: *Sir*) (b. Camden Township 27 Nov 1854; d. Toronto 13 Feb 1952)
Labour	13 Jul 1896 – 18 May 1919: functions exercised by Postmaster General
	2 Jun 1909 – 6 Oct 1911: *William Lyon Mackenzie King* (b. Berlin, Ontario, 17 Dec 1874; d. Kingsmere 22 Jul 1950)
Marine and Fisheries	13 Jul 1896 – 24 Sep 1901: *Louis Henry Davies* (from 1897: *Sir*) (b. Charlottetown 4 May 1845; d. Ottawa 1 May 1924)
	15 Jan – 10 Nov 1902: *James Sutherland* (b. Ancaster 17 Jul 1849; d. Woodstock 3 May 1905)
	11 Nov 1902 – 25 Dec 1905: *Joseph Raymond Fournier Préfontaine* (b. Longueuil 16 Sep 1850; d. Paris 25 Dec 1905)
	6 Jan – 5 Feb 1906 (acting:) *Sir Wilfred Laurier* (see Mackenzie)

	6 Feb 1906 – 10 Aug 1911: *Louis Philippe Brodeur* (see above)
	11 Aug – 6 Oct 1911: *Rodolphe Lemieux* (b. Montreal 1 Nov 1866; d. Montreal 28 Sep 1937)
Militia and Defence	*Frederick William Borden* (from 1902: *Sir*) (b. Cornwallis 14 May 1847; d. Canning 6 Jan 1917)
Mines	3 May 1907 – 6 Oct 1911: *William Templeman* (see above)
Naval Service	4 May 1910 – 10 Aug 1911: *Louis Philippe Brodeur* (see above)
	11 Aug – 6 Oct 1911: *Rodolphe Lemieux* (see above)
Postmaster General	13 Jul 1896 – 15 Oct 1905: *Sir William Mulock* (b. Bondhead 19 Jan 1844; d. Toronto 1 Oct 1944)
	16 Oct 1905 – 3 Jun 1906: *Allen Bristol Aylesworth* (see above)
	4 Jun 1906 – 10 Aug 1911: *Rodolphe Lemieux* (see above)
	19 Aug – 6 Oct 1911: *Henri Sévérin Béland* (b. Louiseville 11 Oct 1869; d. Eastview 22 Apr 1935)
President of the Privy Council	*Sir Wilfred Laurier* (see Mackenzie)
Public Works	13 Jul 1896 – 21 Oct 1902: *Joseph Israël Tarte* (b. Lanoraie 11 Jan 1848; d. Montreal 18 Dec 1907)
	11 Nov 1902 – 3 May 1905: *James Sutherland* (see above)
	22 May 1905 – 29 Aug 1907: *Charles Smith Hyman* (b. London, Ontario, 31 Aug 1854; d. London, Ontario, 8 Oct 1926)
	30 Aug 1907 – 6 Oct 1911: *William Pugsley* (b. Sussex, New Brunswick, 27 Sep 1850; d. Toronto 3 Mar 1925)
Railways and Canals	20 Jul 1896 – 20 Jul 1903: *Andrew George Blair* (b. Fredericton 7 Mar 1844; d. Fredericton 25 Jan 1907)
	21 Jul 1903 – 14 Jan 1904 (acting:) *William Stevens Fielding* (see above)
	15 Jan 1904 – 2 Apr 1907: *Henry Robert Emmerson* (b. Mangerville 25 Sep 1853; d. Dorchester 9 Jul 1914)
	9 Apr – 29 Aug 1907 (acting:) *William Stevens Fielding* (see above)
	30 Aug 1907 – 6 Oct 1911: *George Perry Graham* (b. Eganville 31 Mar 1859; d. Brockville 1 Jan 1943)
Secretary of State of Canada and (from 1 Jun	13 Jul 1896 – 8 Oct 1908: *Richard William Scott* (see Mackenzie)
	9 Oct 1908 – 6 Oct 1911: *Charles Murphy* (b. Ottawa 8

1909) External Affairs	Dec 1862; d. Ottawa 24 Nov 1935)
Trade and Commerce	*Sir Richard John Cartwright* (see Mackenzie)
Without Portfolio	13 Jul 1896 – 11 Jan 1902: *Richard Reid Dobell* (b. Liverpool 1837; d. Folkestone 11 Jan 1902)
	21 Aug 1896 – 18 Jul 1899: *Christophe Alphonse Geoffrion* (b. Varennes 23 Nov 1843; d. Dorion 18 Jul 1899)
	30 Sep 1899 – 14 Jan 1902: *James Sutherland* (see above)
	25 Feb 1902 – 5 Feb 1906: *William Templeman* (see above)
	5 Feb 1904 – 21 May 1905: *Charles Smith Hyman* (see above)

10 Oct 1911 – 12 Oct 1917: Borden I (Conservative)

Prime Minister and External Affairs	*Sir Robert Laird Borden* (for 1st time) (b. Grand Pré 26 Jun 1854; d. Ottawa 10 Jun 1937)
Interior and Indian Affairs	10 Oct 1911 – 28 Oct 1912: *Robert Rogers* (b. Lakefield 2 Mar 1864; d. Guelph 21 Jul 1936)
	29 Oct 1912 – 12 Oct 1917: *William James Roche* (b. Clandeboye 30 Nov 1859; d. Ottawa 30 Sep 1937)
Agriculture	16 Oct 1911 – 12 Oct 1917: *Martin Burrell* (b. Faringdon, Berkshire, 14 Oct 1858; d. Ottawa 20 Mar 1938)
Customs	*John Dowsley Reid* (b. Prescott 1 Jan 1859; d. Prescott 26 Aug 1929)
Finance and Receiver General	*Sir William Thomas White* (b. Bronte 13 Nov 1866; d. Toronto 11 Feb 1955)
Inland Revenue	10 Oct 1911 – 19 Oct 1914: *Wilfred Bruno Nantel* (b. St Jérôme 8 Nov 1857; d. St Jérôme 22 May 1940)
	20 Oct 1914 – 5 Oct 1915: *Pierre Édouard Blondin* (b. St François du Lac 14 Dec 1874; d. St François du Lac 29 Oct 1943)
	6 Oct 1915 – 7 Jan 1917: *Esioff Léon Patenaude* (b. St Isidore de la Prairie 12 Feb 1875; d. Montreal 7 Feb 1963)
	8 Jan – 12 Oct 1917: *Albert Sévigny* (b. Tingwick 31 Dec 1881; d. Quebec 14 May 1961)
Justice and Attorney General	*Charles Joseph Doherty* (b. Montreal 11 May 1855; d. Montreal 28 Jul 1931)
Labour	*Thomas Wilson Crothers* (b. Northport 1 Jan 1850; d. Ottawa 10 Dec 1921)

Marine and Fisheries and Naval Service	*John Douglas Hazen* (from 1918: *Sir*) (b. Oromocto 5 Jun 1860; d. Saint John 27 Dec 1937)
Militia and Defence	10 Oct 1911 – 12 Oct 1916: *Sir Samuel Hughes* (b. Darlington, Ontario, 8 Jan 1853; d. Lindsay 24 Aug 1921) 23 Nov 1916 – 12 Oct 1917: *Sir Albert Edward Kemp* (b. Clarenceville 11 Aug 1858; d. Pigeon Lake 12 Aug 1929)
Mines	10 Oct 1911 – 29 Mar 1912: *Wilfred Bruno Nantel* (see above) 30 Mar – 28 Oct 1912: *Robert Rogers* (see above) 29 Oct 1912 – 9 Feb 1913: *William James Roche* (see above) 10 Feb – 5 Oct 1915: *Louis Coderre* (b. St Ours 1 Nov 1865; d. Montreal 29 Mar 1935) 6 Oct 1915 – 7 Jan 1917: *Pierre Édouard Blondin* (see above) 8 Jan – 12 Jun 1917: *Esioff Léon Patenaude* (see above) 13 Jun – 24 Aug 1917 (acting:) *Albert Sévigny* (see above) 25 Aug – 12 Oct 1917: *Arthur Meighen* (b. Anderson 16 Jun 1874; d. Toronto 5 Aug 1960)
Overseas Military Forces	*Sir George Halsey Perley* (b. Lebanon, New Hampshire, 12 Sep 1857; d. Ottawa 4 Jan 1938)
Postmaster General	10 Oct 1911 – 19 Oct 1914: *Louis Philippe Pelletier* (b. Trois Pistoles 2 Feb 1857; d. Quebec 8 Feb 1921) 20 Oct 1914 – 29 Dec 1916: *Thomas Chase Casgrain* (b. Detroit 28 Jul 1852; d. Ottawa 29 Dec 1916) 8 Jan – 12 Oct 1917: *Pierre Édouard Blondin* (see above)
President of the Privy Council	*Sir Robert Laird Borden* (see above)
Public Works	10 Oct 1911 – 28 Oct 1912: *Frederick Debartzch Monk* (b. Montreal 6 Apr 1856; d. Montreal 15 May 1914) 29 Oct 1912 – 22 Aug 1917: *Robert Rogers* (see above) 3 – 12 Oct 1917: *Charles Colquhoun Ballantyne* (b. Colquhoun 9 Aug 1867; d. Montreal 19 Oct 1950)
Railways and Canals	*Francis Cochrane* (b. Clarenceville 18 Nov 1852; d. Ottawa 22 Sep 1919)
Secretary of State of Canada	10 Oct 1911 – 28 Oct 1912: *William James Roche* (see above)

115

	29 Oct 1912 – 5 Oct 1915: *Louis Coderre* (see above)
	6 Oct 1915 – 7 Jan 1917: *Pierre Édouard Blondin* (see above)
	8 Jan – 12 Jun 1917: *Esioff Léon Patenaude* (see above)
	13 Jun – 24 Aug 1917 (acting:) *Albert Sévigny* (see above)
	25 Aug – 12 Oct 1917: *Arthur Meighen* (see above)
Solicitor General	26 Jun 1913 – 24 Aug 1917: *Arthur Meighen* (above) in cabinet from 2 Oct 1915
	31 Aug – 3 Oct 1917 (acting:) *Arthur Meighen* (see above)
Trade and Commerce	*Sir George Eulas Foster* (see Macdonald II)
Without Portfolio	10 Oct 1911 – 30 Oct 1916: *Sir George Halsey Perley* (see above)
	10 Oct 1916 – 22 Nov 1916: *Sir Albert Edward Kemp* (see above)
	Sir James Alexander Lougheed (b. Brampton 1 Sep 1854; d. Ottawa 2 Nov 1925)

12 Oct 1917 – 10 Jul 1920: Borden II (Coalition)

Prime Minister and External Affairs	*Sir Robert Laird Borden* (Con) (for 2nd time) (see Borden I)
Interior and Indian Affairs	*Arthur Meighen* (Con) (see Borden I)
Agriculture	*Thomas Alexander Crerar* (Lib) (b. Molesworth 17 Jun 1876)
Customs	12 Oct 1917 – 17 May 1918: *Arthur Lewis Sifton* (Lib) (b. St John's 26 Oct 1859; d. Ottawa 21 Jan 1921)
Customs and Inland Revenue	18 May 1918 – 1 Sep 1919: *Arthur Lewis Sifton* (Lib) (see above)
	2 Sep – 30 Dec 1919 (acting:) *John Dowsley Reid* (con) (see Borden I)
	31 Dec 1919 – 7 Jul 1920: *Martin Burrell* (Con) (see Borden I)
Finance and Receiver General	12 Oct 1917 – 1 Aug 1919: *Sir William Thomas White* (Con) (see Borden I)
	2 Aug 1919 – 10 Jul 1920: *Sir Henry Lumley Drayton* (Con) (b. Kingston 27 Apr 1869; d. Muskoka 28 Aug 1950)
Immigration and Colonization	*James Alexander Calder* (Lib) (b. Ingersoll 17 Sep 1868; d. Ottawa 20 Jul 1956)

Inland Revenue	12 Oct 1917 – 1 Apr 1918: *Albert Sévigny* (Con) (see Borden I) 14 – 17 May 1918: *Arthur Lewis Sifton* (Lib) (see Laurier) 18 May 1918: merged with Customs without change of minister
Justice and Attorney General	*Charles Joseph Doherty* (Con) (see Borden I)
Labour	12 Oct 1917 – 6 Nov 1918: *Thomas Wilson Crothers* (Con) (see Borden I) 8 Nov 1918 – 10 Jul 1920: *Gideon Decker Robertson* (Lab) (b. Welland County 26 Aug 1874; d. Ottawa 25 Aug 1933)
Marine and Fisheries and Naval Service	13 Oct 1917 – 10 Jul 1920: *Charles Colquhoun Ballantyne* (Lib) (see Borden I)
Militia and Defence	12 Oct 1917 – 15 Jan 1920: *Sidney Chilton Mewburn* (Lib) (b. Hamilton 4 Dec 1863; d. Hamilton 11 Aug 1956) 16 – 23 Jan 1920 (acting:) *James Alexander Calder* (Lib) (see above) 24 Jan – 10 Jul 1920: *Hugh Guthrie* (Lib) (b. Guelph 13 Aug 1866; d. Ottawa 3 Nov 1939)
Mines	12 Oct 1917 – 30 Dec 1919: *Martin Burrell* (Con) (see Borden I) 31 Dec 1919 – 10 Jul 1920: *Arthur Meighen* (Con) (see Borden I)
Overseas Military Forces	*Sir Albert Edward Kemp* (Con) (see Borden I)
Postmaster General	*Pierre Édouard Blondin* (Con) (see Borden I)
President of the Privy Council	*Newton Wesley Rowell* (Lib) (b. London, Ontario, 1 Nov 1867; d. Toronto 22 Nov 1941)
Public Works	12 Oct 1917: *Charles Colquhoun Ballantyne* (Lib) (see Borden I) 13 Oct 1917 – 1 Aug 1919: *Frank Broadstreet Carvell* (Lib) (b. Bloomfield 14 Aug 1862; d. Woodstock 9 Aug 1924) 6 Aug – 2 Sep 1919 (acting:) *John Dowsley Reid* (Con) (see Borden I) 3 Sep – 30 Dec 1919: *Arthur Lewis Sifton* (Lib) (see above) 31 Dec 1919 – 10 Jul 1920 (acting:) *John Dowsley Reid* (Con) (see Borden I)

Railways and Canals	*John Dowsley Reid* (Con) (see Borden I)
Secretary of State of Canada	12 Oct 1917 – 30 Dec 1919: *Martin Burrell* (Con (see Borden I)
	31 Dec 1919 – 10 Jul 1920: *Arthur Lewis Sifton* (Lib) (see above)
Soldiers' Civil Re-establishment	*Sir James Alexander Lougheed* (Con) (see Borden I)
Solicitor General	*Hugh Guthrie* (Lib) (see above) not in cabinet from 12 Oct 1917 – 4 Jul 1919, acting from 24 – 10 Jul 1920
Trade and Commerce	*Sir George Eulas Foster* (Con) (see Macdonald II)
Without Portfolio	12 Oct 1917 – 22 Sep 1919: *Francis Cochrane* (Con) (see Borden I)
	12 Oct 1917 – 20 Feb 1918: *Sir James Alexander Lougheed* (Con) (see Borden I)
	23 Oct 1917 – 24 Feb 1920: *Alexander Kenneth Maclean* (Lib) (b. Upper North Sydney 18 Oct 1869; d. Ottawa 31 Jul 1942)
	23 Oct 1917 – 7 Nov 1918: *Gideon Decker Robertson* (Lab) (see above)

10 Jul 1920 – 29 Dec 1921: Meighen I (Coalition: 'National Liberal-Conservative Party')

Prime Minister and External Affairs	*Arthur Meighen* (for 1st time) (see Borden I)
Interior and Indian Affairs	*Sir James Alexander Lougheed* (see Borden I)
Agriculture	*Simon Fraser Tolmie* (b. Victoria 25 Jan 1867; d. Victoria 13 Oct 1937)
Customs and Inland Revenue (from 4 Jun 1921: Customs and Excise)	13 Jul 1920 – 20 Sep 1921: *Rupert Wilson Wigmore* (b. Saint John 10 May 1873; d. Saint John 3 Apr 1939)
	21 Sep – 29 Dec 1921: *John Babington Macaulay Baxter* (b. Saint John 16 Feb 1868; d. Saint John 27 Dec 1946)
Finance and Receiver General	*Sir Henry Lumley Drayton* (see Borden II)
Immigration and Colonization	10 Jul 1920 – 20 Sep 1921: *James Alexander Calder* (see Borden II)
	21 Sep – 29 Dec 1921: *John Wesley Edwards* (b. Storrington Township 25 May 1865; d. Ottawa 18 Apr 1929)
Justice and Attorney General	10 Jul 1920 – 20 Sep 1921: *Charles Joseph Doherty* (see Borden I)

	4 Oct – 29 Dec 1921: *Richard Bedford Bennett* (from 1941: *Viscount Bennett*) (b. Hopewell 3 Jul 1870; d. Mickleham 27 Jun 1947)
Labour	*Gideon Decker Robertson* (see Borden II)
Marine and Fisheries and Naval Service	*Charles Colquhoun Ballantyne* (see Borden I)
Militia and Defence	*Hugh Guthrie* (see Borden II)
Mines	*Sir James Alexander Lougheed* (see Borden I)
Postmaster General	10 Jul 1920 – 20 Sep 1921: *Pierre Édouard Blondin* (see Borden I)
	21 Sep – 29 Dec 1921: *Louis de Gonzague Belley* (b. 3 Feb 1863; d. Quebec 9 Jul 1930)
President of the Privy Council	10 Jul 1920 – 20 Sep 1921: *James Alexander Calder* (see Borden II)
	21 Sep – 29 Dec 1921: *Louis Philippe Normand* (b. Three Rivers 21 Sep 1863; d. Three Rivers 27 Jun 1928)
Public Works	10 – 12 Jul 1920 (acting:) *John Dowsley Reid* (see Borden I)
	13 Jul 1920 – 29 Dec 1921: *Fleming Blanchard McCurdy* (b. Old Barns 17 Feb 1875; d. 29 Aug 1952)
Railways and Canals	10 Jul 1920 – 20 Sep 1921: *John Dowsley Reid* (see Borden I)
	21 Sep – 29 Dec 1921: *John Alexander Stewart* (b. Renfrew 1867; d. Montreal 7 Oct 1922)
Secretary of State of Canada	10 Jul 1920 – 21 Jan 1921: *Arthur Lewis Sifton* (see Borden II)
	24 Jan – 20 Sep 1921 (acting:) *Sir Henry Lumley Drayton* (see Borden II)
	21 Sep – 29 Dec 1921: *Rodolphe Monty* (b. Montreal 30 Nov 1874; d. St Hyacinthe 1 Dec 1928)
Soldiers' Civil Re-establishment	19 Jul 1920 – 21 Sep 1921 (acting:) *Sir James Alexander Lougheed* (see Borden I)
	22 Sep – 29 Dec 1921: *Robert James Manion* (b. Pembroke 19 Nov 1881; d. Ottawa 2 Jul 1943)
Solicitor General	10 Jul 1920 – 30 Sep 1921: (acting:) *Hugh Guthrie* (see Borden II)
Trade and Commerce	10 Jul 1920 – 20 Sep 1921: *Sir George Eulas Foster* (see Macdonald II)
	21 Sep – 29 Dec 1921: *Henry Herbert Stevens* (b. Bristol 8 Dec 1878)
Without Portfolio	13 Jul 1920 – 29 Dec 1921: *Sir Albert Edward Kemp* (see Borden I)

13 Jul 1920 – 29 Dec 1921: *Edgar Keith Spinney* (b. Argyle 26 Jan 1851; d. Yarmouth 12 May 1926)
21 Sep – 29 Dec 1921: *Edmund James Bristol* (b. Napanee 4 Sep 1861; d. Toronto 14 Jul 1927)
26 Sep – 29 Dec 1921: *James Robert Wilson* (b. Almonte 16 Sep 1866; d. Saskatoon 3 Apr 1941)

29 Dec 1921 – 28 Jun 1926: King I (Liberal)

Prime Minister and External Affairs	*William Lyon Mackenzie King* (for 1st time) (see Laurier)
Interior and Indian Affairs	*Charles Stewart* (b. Strabane 26 Aug 1868; d. Ottawa 6 Dec 1946)
Agriculture	*William Richard Motherwell* (b. Perth, Ontario, 6 Jan 1860; d. Abernethy 24 May 1943)
Customs and Excise	29 Dec 1921 – 4 Sep 1925: *Jacques Bureau* (b. Three Rivers 9 Jul 1860; d. Montreal 23 Jan 1933)
5 Sep 1925 – 28 Jun 1926: *George Henri Boivin* (b. Granby 26 Dec 1882; d. Philadelphia 7 Aug 1926)
Finance and Receiver General	29. Dec 1921 – 4 Sep 1925: *William Stevens Fielding* (see Laurier)
5 Sep 1925 – 28 Jun 1926: *James Alexander Robb* (b. Huntingdon 10 Aug 1859; d. Toronto 11 Nov 1929)
Immigration and Colonization	3 Jan – 2 Feb 1922 (acting:) *Hewitt Bostock* (b. Walton Heath, Surrey, 31 May 1864; d. Monte Creek 28 Apr 1930)
20 Feb 1922 – 16 Aug 1923 (acting:) *Charles Stewart* (see above)
17 Aug 1923 – 4 Sep 1925: *James Alexander Robb* (see above)
7 Sep – 12 Nov 1925: *George Newcombe Gordon* (b. Brighton, Ontario, 15 Apr 1879; d. Peterborough, Ontario, 21 Mar 1949)
13 Nov 1925 – 28 Jun 1926 (acting:) *Charles Stewart* (see above)
Justice and Attorney General	29 Dec 1921 – 3 Jan 1924: *Sir Jean Lomer Gouin* (b. Grondines 19 Mar 1861; d. Quebec 29 Mar 1929)
4 Jan 1924 – 28 Jun 1926: *Ernest Lapointe* (b. St-Éloi 6 Oct 1876; d. Montreal 26 Nov 1941)
Labour	29 Dec 1921 – 12 Nov 1925: *James Murdock* (b. Brighton, Sussex, 15 Aug 1871; d. Guelph 15 May 1949)
13 Nov 1925 – 7 Mar 1926 (acting:) *James Horace*

	King (b. Chipman 18 Jan 1873; d. Ottawa 14 Jul 1955)
	8 Mar – 28 Jun 1926: *John Campbell Elliott* (b. Ekfrid Township 25 Jul 1872; d. London, Ontario, 20 Dec 1941)
Marine and Fisheries	29 Dec 1921 – 29 Jan 1924: *Ernest Lapointe* (see above)
	30 Jan 1924 – 28 Jun 1926: *Pierre Joseph Arthur Cardin* (b. Sorel 28 Jun 1879; d. Sorel 20 Oct 1946)
Militia and Defence and Naval Service	29 Dec 1921 – 31 Dec 1922: *George Perry Graham* (see Laurier)
	1 Jan 1923: combined to form Ministry of National Defence (see below)
Mines	*Charles Stewart* (see above)
National Defence	1 Jan 1923: replaced ministries of Militia and Defence and Naval Service (see above)
	1 Jan – 27 Apr 1923: *George Perry Graham* (see Laurier)
	28 Apr 1923 – 28 Jun 1926: *Edward Mortimer Macdonald* (b. Pictou 16 Aug 1865; d. Pictou 25 May 1940) acting until 16 Aug 1923
Postmaster General	*Charles Murphy* (see Laurier)
President of the Privy Council	*William Lyon Mackenzie King* (see Laurier)
Public Works	29 Dec 1921 – 2 Feb 1922: *Hewitt Bostock* (see above)
	2 Feb 1922 – 28 Jun 1926: *James Horace King* (see above)
Railways and Canals	29 Dec 1921 – 17 Jan 1923: *William Costello Kennedy* (b. Ottawa 27 Aug 1868; d. Florida 17 Jan 1923)
	28 Apr 1923 – 19 Feb 1926: *George Perry Graham* (see Laurier)
	1 Mar – 28 Jun 1926: *Charles Avery Dunning* (b. Croft, Leicestershire, 31 Jul 1885; d. Montreal 2 Oct 1958)
Secretary of State of Canada	29 Dec 1921 – 24 Sep 1925: *Arthur Bliss Copp* (b. Jolicure 10 Jul 1870; d. Newcastle, New Brunswick, 5 Dec 1949)
	26 Sep – 12 Nov 1925: *Walter Edward Foster* (b. St Martins 9 Apr 1873; d. Rothesay 14 Nov 1947)
	13 Nov 1925 – 23 Mar 1926 (acting:) *Charles Murphy* (see Laurier)
	24 Mar – 28 Jun 1926: *Ernest Lapointe* (see above)
Solicitor General	29 Dec 1921 – 10 Apr 1923: *Daniel Duncan McKenzie* (b. Lake Ainslie 8 Jan 1859; d. Halifax 8 Jun 1927)

121

	14 Nov 1923 – 22 May 1925: *Edward James McMurray* (b. Thorndale 4 Jun 1878)
Trade and Commerce	29 Dec 1921 – 16 Aug 1923: *James Alexander Robb* (see above)
	17 Aug 1923 – 12 Nov 1925: *Thomas Andrew Low* (b. Quebec 12 Mar 1871; d. Renfrew 9 Feb 1931)
	13 Nov 1925 – 28 Jun 1926 (acting:) *James Alexander Robb* (see above)
Without Portfolio	*Raoul Dandurand* (b. Montreal 4 Nov 1861; d. Montreal 11 Mar 1942)
	29 Dec 1921 – 16 Aug 1923: *Thomas Andrew Low* (see above)
	30 Dec 1921 – 29 Oct 1925: *John Ewen Sinclair* (b. Summerfield 24 Dec 1879; d. Summerfield 23 Dec 1949)
	12 Apr – 16 Aug 1923: *Edward Mortimer Macdonald* (see above)
	20 Sep 1924 – 29 Oct 1925: *Harold Buchanan McGiverin* (b. Hamilton 4 Aug 1870; d. Victoria 4 Feb 1931)
	9 Sep 1925 – 6 Jan 1926: *Herbert Meredith Marler* (from 1936: *Sir*) (b. Montreal 7 Mar 1876; d. Montreal 31 Jan 1940)
	16 Sep – 12 Nov 1925: *(Charles) Vincent Massey* (b. Toronto 20 Feb 1887; d. London 30 Dec 1967)
	20 Feb – 6 Apr 1926: *Goerge Perry Graham* (see Laurier)

29 Jun – 25 Sep 1926: Meighen II (Conservative)

Prime Minister and External Affairs	*Arthur Meighen* (for 2nd time) (see Borden I)
Interior and Indian Affairs	29 Jun – 12 Jul 1926 (acting:) *Henry Herbert Stevens* (see Meighen I)
	13 Jul – 25 Sep 1926: *Richard Bedford Bennett* (see Meighen I)
Agriculture	29 Jun – 12 Jul 1926 (acting:) *Henry Herbert Stevens* (see Meighen I)
	13 Jul – 25 Sep 1926: *Simon Fraser Tolmie* (see Meighen I)
Customs and Excise	*Henry Herbert Stevens* (see Meighen I) acting until 12 Jul 1926
Finance and Receiver General	29 Jun – 12 Jul 1926 (acting:) *Sir Henry Lumley Drayton* (see Borden II)

	13 Jul – 25 Sep 1926: *Richard Bedford Bennett* (see Meighen I)
Immigration and Colonization	29 Jun – 12 Jul 1926 (acting:) *Robert James Manion* (see Meighen I)
	13 Jul – 25 Sep 1926 (acting:) *Sir Henry Lumely Drayton* (see Borden II)
Justice and Attorney General	29 Jun – 12 Jul 1926 (acting:) *Hugh Guthrie* (see Borden II)
	13 Jul – 25 Sep 1926: *Esioff Léon Patenaude* (see Borden I)
Labour	29 Jun – 12 Jul 1926 (acting:) *Robert James Manion* (see Meighen I)
	13 Jul – 25 Sep 1926: *George Burpee Jones* (b. Belleisle Bay 9 Jan 1866; d. Sussex 27 Apr 1950)
Marine and Fisheries	29 Jun – 12 Jul 1926 (acting:) *William Anderson Black* (b. Windsor, Nova Scotia, 9 Oct 1847; d. Halifax 1 Sep 1934)
	13 Jul – 25 Sep 1926: *Esioff Léon Patenaude* (see Borden I)
Mines	29 Jun – 12 Jul 1926 (acting:) *Henry Herbert Stevens* (see Meighen I)
	13 Jul – 25 Sep 1926 (acting:) *Richard Bedford Bennett* (see Meighen I)
National Defence	*Hugh Guthrie* (see Borden II) acting until 12 Jul 1926
Postmaster General	*Robert James Manion* (see Meighen I) acting until 12 Jul 1926
President of the Privy Council	*Arthur Meighen* (see Borden I)
Public Works	29 Jun – 12 Jul 1926 (acting:) *Sir George Halsey Perley* (see Borden I)
	13 Jul – 25 Sep 1926: *Edmond Baird Ryckman* (b. Huntingdon 15 Apr 1866; d. Toronto 11 Jan 1934)
Railways and Canals	29 Jun – 12 Jul 1926 (acting:) *Sir Henry Lumley Drayton* (see Borden II)
	13 Jul – 25 Sep 1926: *William Anderson Black* (see above)
Secretary of State of Canada	*Sir George Halsey Perley* (see Borden I) acting until 12 Jul 1926
Solicitor General	23 Aug – 25 Sep 1926: *Guillaume André Fauteux* (b. St Benoit 20 Oct 1874; d. Montreal 10 Sep 1940)
Soldiers' Civil Re-establishment and Health	29 Jun – 12 Jul 1926 (acting:) *Robert James Manion* (see Meighen I)
	13 Jul – 22 Aug 1926 (acting:) *Raymond Ducharme*

	Morand (b. Windsor, Ontario, 30 Jan 1887; d. 2 Feb 1952)
Trade and Commerce	29 Jun – 12 Jul 1926 (acting:) *Henry Herbert Stevens* (see Meighen I)
	13 Jul – 25 Sep 1926: *James Dew Chaplin* (b. St Catherines 20 Mar 1863; d. St Catherines 23 Aug 1937)
Without Portfolio	7 – 12 Jul 1926: *Richard Bedford Bennett* (see Meighen I)
	13 Jul – 25 Sep 1926: *Sir Henry Lumley Drayton* (see Borden II)
	13 Jul – 25 Sep 1926: *Raymond Ducharme Morand* (see above)
	13 Jul – 25 Sep 1926: *John Alexander Macdonald* (b. Tracadie 12 Apr 1874; d. Cardigan 15 Nov 1948)
	13 Jul – 25 Sep 1926: *Donald Sutherland* (b. Zorra Township 8 Apr 1863; d. Ingersoll 1 Jan 1949)

25 Sep 1926 – 7 Aug 1930: King II (Liberal)

Prime Minister and External Affairs	*William Lyon Mackenzie King* (for 2nd time) (see Laurier)
Interior and Indian Affairs	*Charles Stewart* (see King I)
Agriculture	*William Richard Motherwell* (see King I)
Customs and Excise	25 Sep 1926 – 30 Mar 1927: *William Daum Euler* (b. Conestego 10 Jul 1875; d. Kitchener 15 Jul 1961)
	31 Mar 1927: superseded by Ministry of National Revenue (see below)
Finance and Receiver General	25 Sep 1926 – 11 Nov 1929: *James Alexander Robb* (see King I)
	26 Nov 1929 – 7 Aug 1930: *Charles Avery Dunning* (see King I)
Immigration and Colonization	25 Sep 1926 – 29 Dec 1929: *Robert Forke* (b. Gordon, Berwickshire, 2 Jun 1860; d. Winnipeg 2 Feb 1934)
	30 Dec 1929 – 26 Jun 1930 (acting:) *Charles Stewart* (see King I)
Justice and Attorney General	*Ernest Lapointe* (see King I)
Labour	*Peter Heenan* (b. Tullaree, Ireland, 19 Feb 1875; d. 12 May 1948)
Marine and Fisheries	*Pierre Joseph Arthur Cardin* (see King I)
Mines	*Charles Stewart* (see King I)

National Defence	1 – 7 Oct 1926 (acting:) *James Alexander Robb* (see King I)
	8 Oct 1926 – 7 Aug 1930: *James Layton Ralston* (b. Amherst 27 Sep 1881; d. Montreal 22 May 1948)
National Revenue	31 Mar 1927: supersedes Customs and Excise (see above)
	31 Mar 1927 – 7 Aug 1930: *William Daum Euler* (see above)
Pensions and National Health	11 Jun 1928: supersedes ministries of Soldiers' Civil Re-establishment and Health (see below)
	11 Jun 1928 – 18 Jun 1930: *James Horace King* (see King I)
Postmaster General	*Peter John Veniot* (b. Richibucto 4 Oct 1863; d. Bathurst 6 Jul 1936)
President of the Privy Council	*William Lyon Mackenzie King* (see Laurier)
Public Works	*John Campbell Elliott* (see King I)
Railways and Canals	25 Sep 1926 – 29 Dec: *Charles Avery Dunning* (see King I) acting from 26 Nov 1929
	30 Dec 1929 – 7 Aug 1939: *Thomas Alexander Crerar* (see Borden II)
Secretary of State of Canada	*Fernand Rinfret* (b. Montreal 28 Feb 1883; d. Los Angeles 12 Jul 1939)
Soldiers' Civil Re-Establishment and Health	26 Sep 1926 – 10 Jun 1928: *James Horace King* (see King I)
	11 Jun 1928: both ministries superseded by Pensions and National Health (see above)
Solicitor General	*Lucien Cannon* (b. Arthabaska 16 Jan 1887; d. Quebec 14 Feb 1950)
Trade and Commerce	*James Malcolm* (b. Kincardine 14 Jul 1880; d. Kincardine 6 Dec 1925)
Without Portfolio	*Raoul Dandurand* (see King I)

Central America, United Provinces of

1821	Spanish possessions in Central America declared independent

| 1822 | Annexed to Mexico |
| 1823 | Completely independent federal republic comprising Guatemala, El Salvador, Honduras, Nicaragua and Costa Rica |

HEADS OF STATE

Presidents

1825	*Marvel José Arce* (b. 1787; d. 1847)
1829	*José F. Barrundia*, provisional
1830	*Francisco Morazán* (for the 1st time) (b. 1792; d. 15 Sep 1842)
1834	*José Cecilio del Vallé* (b. Honduras; d. 2 Mar 1834) died before taking office
1834-1840	*Francisco Morazán* (for 2nd time)
1838	Secession of Nicaragua
May 1838	Secession of Costa Rica
5 Nov 1838	Secession of Honduras
13 Apr 1839	Secession of Guatemala
30 Jan 1841	El Salvador became a republic in its own name

Chile

| Early 16th century-1818 | Part of Spanish Empire |
| 1 Jan (5 Apr) 1818 | Independence |

HEADS OF STATE

Presidents

5 Apr 1818	*Bernardo O'Higgins* (b. 20 Aug 1776; d. 24 Oct 1842) Dictator
28 Jan 1823 – 2 May 1827	*Ramón Freire* (b. 1787; d. 1851)
9 May 1827 – 1831	*Francisco Antonio Pinto* (b. 1785; d. 1858)
18 Sep 1831	*Joaquín Prieto* (b. 1786; d. 1854)

18 Sep 1841	*Manuel Bulnes* (b. 1799; d. 1866)
18 Sep 1851	*Manuel Montt* (b. 1809; d. 1880)
18 Sep 1861	*José Joaquín Pérez* (b. 1800; d. 1889)
18 Sep 1871	*Federico Errázuriz Zañartu* (b. 1825; d. 1877)
18 Sep 1876	*Anibal Pinto* (b. c.1825; d. 1884)
18 Sep 1881	*Domingo Santa Maria* (b. 4 Aug 1825; d. 18 Jul 1889)
18 Sep 1886 – 19 Sep 1891	*José Manuel Balmaceda* (b. (?)1838/40; d. 19 Sep 1891)
18 Dec 1891	*Jorge Montt* (b. 1847; d. 7 Nov 1922)
18 Sep 1896 – 12 Jul 1901	*Federico Errázuriz Echaurren*, son of Federico Errázuriz Zañartu (b. 1850; d. 12 Jul 1901)
18 Aug 1901	*Germán Riesco* (b. 1854; d. 1916)
1 Jan 1905	*Rafael Rayes*
18 Sep 1906	*Pedro Montt* (b. 29 Jun 1848; d. 16 Aug 1910)
16 Aug 1910	*Elías Fernández Albano* (b. 1845; d. 6 Sep 1910)
6 Sep 1910	*Emiliano Figueroa*
18 Sep 1911	*Ramón Barros Luco* (b. 1835; d. 1919)
23 Dec 1915	*Juan Luis Sanfuentes Andonaegui* (b. 27 Dec 1858; d. 27 Jul 1930)
25 Jun 1920	*Luis Barros Borgoño* (b. 25 Mar 1858; d. 1943)
23 Dec 1920 – 12 Sep 1924 and 23 Jan – 2 Oct 1925	*Arturo Alessandri y Palma* (b. 20 Dec 1868; d. 24 Aug 1950)
23 Dec 1925	*Emilio Figueroa-Larrain* (b. 1860; d. May 1931)
9 Apr 1927 – 27 Jul 1931	*Carlos Ibáñez del Campo* (b. 2 Nov 1877; d. Santiago 28 Apr 1960)

China

HEADS OF STATE

Emperors

Ming dynasty (from 1368) (personal names, with era names in brackets)

1487	*Chu Yu-t'ang (Hung-chih)* son of Chien-shên (Ch'eng-hua)
1505	*Chu Hou-chao (Chêng-tê)* (b. 1491)
1521 – 1566	*Chu Hou-tsung (Chia-ching)* cousin (b. 1507)
1567	*Chu Tsai-kou (Lung-ch'ing)* son (b. 1537)

1572	*Chu I-chün (Wan-li)* son (b. 1563)
1620	*Chu Ch'ang-lo (T'ai-ch'ang)* son (b. 1582)
1621	*Chu Yu-chiao (T'ien-ch'i)* son (b. 1605)
1627	*Chu Yu-chien (Ch'ung-ch'en)* brother (b. Peking 6 Feb 1611)

Ching dynasty (Manchu: until 1912) (era names, with personal names in brackets)

6 Jun/30 Oct 1644 – 2 Feb 1661	*Shun-chih (Fu-lin)* (b. 15 Mar 1638) Regents: 1644 – 1650: *Dorgan* (d. 1650) 1644 – 1647 and 1650 – 1657: *Jirgalang*
1662	*K'ang-hsi (Hsüan-yeh)* son (b. Peking 4 May 1654 Regents: *Soni, Suksaha, Ebilun* and *Oboi*
1722	*Yung-chêng (Yin-chen)* son (b. Peking 13 Dec 1678)
1735 – 1795	*Ch'ien-lung (Hung-li)* son (b. 25 Sep 1711; d. Peking 7 Feb 1799)
1796	*Chia-ch'ing (Yung-yen)* son (b. Peking 13 Nov 1760)
2 Sep 1820	*Tao-kuang (Min-ning)* son (b. Peking 16 Sep 1782)
4 Feb 1850	*Hsien-fêng (Yi-chu)* son (b. 1831)
22 Aug 1861	*T'ung-chih (Tsai-ch'un)* son (b. 27 Apr 1856) Regents (from Nov 1861:) the Empresses Dowager *Tz'u-hsi* and *Tz'u-an* (d. 1881) and *Prince Kung*
13 Jan 1875	*Kuang-hsü (Tsai-t'ien)* cousin (b. 2 Aug 1872) Regents: *Tz'u-hsi* (see above) and *Tz'u-an* (see above)
14 Nov 1908	*Hsüan-T'ung (P'u-i)* (b. 11 Feb 1906; d. Peking 17 Oct 1967) abdicated 12 Feb 1912; restored 1 – 12 Jul 1917; 1932 – 1946 Emperor of Manchukuo, under Japanese control; from 4 Dec 1959 imprisoned in Fushan near Mukden Regent: *Prince Chun* (resigned 29 Oct 1911) (d. Mar 1951)
From 1912	Republic

Presidents

1 Jan 1912	(provisional:) *Sun Yat-sen (San Wen)* (b. T'suiheng 12 Nov 1866; d. Peking 12 Mar 1925) later President in the Canton Administration
15 Feb 1912 – 6 Jun 1916	*Yüan Shih-k'ai* (b. 20 Sep 1859; d. 6 Jun 1916) provisonal until 10 Oct 1913
Jun 1916	*Li Yuan-hung* (for 1st time) (b. Huangp'i 1864; d. Tientsin 3 Jun 1928) previously Vice-President
14 Aug 1917	*Feng Kuo-chang* (b. Chihli 7 Jan 1859; d. Peking 28 Dec 1919)

4 Sep 1918 – 2 Jun 1922	*Hsü Shih-ch'ang* (b. 23 Oct 1855; d. 6 Jun 1939)

Canton Administration

5 May 1921 – 12 Mar 1925	*Sun Yat-sen* (see Presidents)
11 Jun 1922 – 14 Jun 1923	*Li Yuan-hung* (for 2nd time)
5 Oct 1923 – 2 Nov 1924	*Ts'ao K'un* (b. Tientsin 12 Dec 1862; d. Tientsin 17 May 1938)
24 Nov 1924 – 20 Apr 1926	*Tuan Ch'i-jui* (b. 6 Mar 1865; d. Shanghai 2 Nov 1936)
10 Apr 1926 – 7 Jun 1927	Disorders
17 Jun 1927 – 4 Jun 1928	*Chang Tso-lin* (b. Haich'eng 1873; d. Mukden June 1928) Dictator, from 13 May 1922 Governor of Manchuria
10 Oct 1928 – 15 Dec 1931	*Chiang Kai-shek* (*Chiang Chung-Cheng*) (b. Fenghua 31 Oct 1887; d. Taipe 5 Apr 1975)

MEMBERS OF GOVERNMENT

Prime Ministers

1901 – 1903	*Jung-lu*, Chief Director, Superintendency of Political Affairs
1903 – 29 Oct 1911	*Prince Ch'ing*
14 Feb – 16 Jun 1912	*T'ang Shao-yi* (for 1st time) (b. Hsingshan 1860; d. Shanghai 30 Sep 1938)
29 Jun 1912	*Lu Cheng-hsiang* (b. Shanghai 1871; d. Bruges 15 Jan 1949)
27 Jul 1912 – end Mar 1913	(acting until 23 Sep:) *Chao Ping-chün*
22 Apr 1916 – 23 May 1917	(initially acting:) *Tuan Ch'i-jui* (for 1st time)
1 – 12 Jul 1917	*Chang-hsün* (b. 14 Dec 1854; d. Tientsin Sep 1923) chief minister
13 Jul – 22 Nov 1917	*Tuan Ch'i-jui* (for 2nd time)
11 Oct 1918	*Ch'ien Neng-hsün* (b. 1870; d. (?)1925)
13 Jun 1919	*Kung Hsin-chan*
24 Sep 1919	*Chin Yün-p'eng* (for 1st time) (b. Tsining 1877)

14 May 1920	*Sa Chen-ping* (b. Minhou, Fukien 30 Mar 1859; d. Foochow 10 Apr 1951)
9 Aug 1920 – 18 Dec 1921	*Chin Yün-p'eng* (for 2nd time)
24 Dec 1921	*Liang Shih-i* (b. Sanshui 5 May 1869; d. Shanghai 9 Apr 1933)
25 Jan 1922	*Yen Hui-ching* (*W. W. Yen*) (for 1st time) (b. Shanghai 2 Apr 1877; d. Shanghai 23 May 1950)
8 Apr 1922	*Chou Tzu-ch'i* (b. Canton 1871; d. Shanghai 20 Oct 1923)
11 Jun 1922	*Yen Hui-ch'ing* (for 2nd Time)
5 Aug 1922	*T'ang Shao-yi* (for 2nd time)
19 Sep – 19 Nov 1922	(acting from 5 Aug 1922:) *Wang Ch'ung-hui* (b. 1881; d. Taipei 15 Mar 1958)
29 Nov – 10 Dec 1922	*Wang Ta-hsieh*
4 Jan – 13 Jun 1923	*Chang Shao-ts'êng*
	Head of Administration: 12 Dec 1922 – 5 Jun 1923: *Wang Cheng-t'ing* (b. Fenghua 25 Jul 1882; d. Hong Kong 21 May 1961)
13 Jun 1923	*Kao Ling-Wei*
12 Jan 1924	*Sun Pao-ch'i* (b. Hangchow 26 Apr 1867; d. Shanghai 3 Feb 1931)
2 Jul – 14 Sep 1924	*Ku Wei-chün* (*V. K. Wellington Koo*) (for 1st time) (b. Chiating 1887)
13 Sep – 31 Oct 1924	*Yen Hui-ch'ing* (for 3rd time)
2 Nov 1924 – 1925	*General Huang Fu* (b. Paikuanchen 8 Mar 1880; d. Shanghai 6 Dec 1936)
27 Nov – 26 Dec 1925	*Tuan Ch'i-jui*, simultaneously President (see above)
26 Dec 1925	*Hsu Shih-ying* (b. Chinpu 1872; d. Taipei 13 Oct 1964)
15 Feb 1926	*Chia Teh-yao*
20 Apr 1926	*Hu Wei-te*
13 May 1926	*Yen Hui-ch'ing* (for 4th time)
22 Jun 1926	*Tu Hsi-kuei* (b. 1875)
1 Oct – 29 Nov 1926	(Head of Administration until 17 Jun 1927:) *Ku Wei-chün* (*V. K. Wellington Koo*) (for 2nd time)
18 Apr 1927	*Chiang Kai-shek* (*Chiang Chung-cheng*) (see Canton Administration)
18 Jun 1927 – 1929	*P'an Fu* (b. 1871) under President Chang Tso-lin
20 Sep 1927	Nanking Government (Committee of Five): *Hu Han-min* (b. P'anyü hsien 9 Dec 1879 d. Canton 13 Jul 1936)

Wang Ching-wei (b. Canton 5 May 1884; d. Nanking 10 Nov 1944)

Ts'ai Yuan-p'ei (b. Shanyin 11 Jan 1868; d. Hong Kong 3 Mar 1940)

T'an Yen-k'ai (for 1st time) (b. Hangchow 1879; d. Nanking 22 Sep 1930)

Li Lieh Chün (b. 1882; d. Chungking 1946)

25 Oct 1928 – 22 Sep 1930	*T'an Yen-k'ai* (for 2nd time) President of the Executive

Cologne

HEADS OF STATE

Electors and Archbishops

11 Aug/15 Sep 1480 – 20 Oct 1508	*Hermann IV*, Landgrave of Hesse
13 Nov 1508/31 Jan 1509 – (?) Aug 1515	*Philipp II* von Daun-Oberstein
26 Apr/13 Jun 1515 – 16 Apr 1546/25 Feb 1547	*Hermann V* von Wied (b. 14 Jan 1577; d. 14 Aug 1552) became Protestant and ceased to be archbishop
3 Jul 1546 – 24 Sep 1556	*Adolf III* von Schauenburg
26 Oct 1556/6 Oct 1557 – 18 Jul 1558	*Anton* von Schauenburg
26 Jul 1558/31 Jan 1560 – 2 Nov 1562	*Johann Gebhard I* von Mansfield
19 Nov 1562 – 25 Oct 1567	*Friedrich IV* von Wied (b. 1518; d. 23 Dec 1568)
23 Dec 1567/9 Dec 1573 – 13 Sep 1577	*Salentin* von Isenburg (b. 1532; d. 19 Mar 1610) died as Prince of Isenburg)

5 Dec 1577/29 Feb 1580 – 1 Apr 1583	*Gebhard II* Truchsess von Waldburg (b. 10 Nov 1547; d. 31 Oct 1601) became Protestant and ceased to be archbishop
23 May/27 Jun 1583 – 17 Feb 1612	*Ernst*, Prince of Bavaria, son of Duke Albrecht V (b. 17 Dec 1554)
12 May 1612 – 13 Sep 1650	*Ferdinand*, Prince of Bavaria, son of Duke Wilhelm V (b. 6 Oct 1577) coadjutor from 18 Dec 1596
26 Oct 1650 – 3 Jun 1688	*Maximilian Heinrich*, Prince of Bavaria, nephew (b. 18 Oct 1621) coadjutor from 17 May 1642
19 Jul 1688	*Josef Klemens*, Prince of Bavaria, brother of the Elector Maximilian II (b. 5 Dec 1671)
12 Nov 1723	*Klemens August I*, Prince of Bavaria, brother of the Elector Maximilian II (b. 16 Aug 1700)
6 Feb 1761	*Maximilian Friedrich*, Count Königseck und Rothenfels
15 Apr 1784 – 27 Jul 1801	*Maximilian Franz*, Archduke of Austria, son of the Emperor Francis I (b. 8 Dec 1756)
7 Aug 1801	*Anton Viktor*, Archduke of Austria, son of the Emperor Leopold II
1815	Incorporated in Prussia

Colombia

Early 16th century – 1819	Part of Spanish Empire

HEADS OF STATE

Presidents

6 May/23 Oct 1821 – 27 Apr 1830	*Simón Bolivar* (b. 24 Jul 1783; d. 10 Dec 1830)
5 May 1830 – Oct 1832	*Joaquin Mosquera* (b. 14 Dec 1787; d. 5 Apr 1877)
7 Oct 1832 (9 Mar 1833) – Mar 1837	*Francisco de Paula Santander* (b. 1792; d. 5 May 1842)
1 Apr 1837 – 2 May 1841	*José Ignacio de Márquez* (b. 1793; d. 1880)

18 May 1841	*Pedro Alcántara Herrán* (b. 19 Oct 1800; d. 26 Apr 1872)
1845 – 1849	*Tomás Cipriano de Mosquera* (for 1st time) (b. 20 Sep 1798; d. 7 Oct 1878)
7 Mar 1849 – 1853	*José Hilario López* (b. 1798; d. 1869)
1853	*José Maria Obando* (b. 1795; d. 1861)
Apr 1854 – Mar 1857	*Manuel Maria Mallarino* (b. 1808; d. 1872)
1 Apr 1857	*Mariano Ospina* (b. 1806; d. 1875)
13 Mar 1861 – 1 Nov 1862	*Julio Arboleda* (b. 1817; d. 1 Nov 1862)
18 Jul/29 Dec 1862	*Tomás Cipriano de Mosquera* (for 2nd time) Dictator
1 Apr 1864 – 31 Mar 1866	*Manuel Murillo Toro* (for 1st time) (b. 1 Jan 1816; d. 26 Dec 1880)
1 Apr 1866	*Tomás Cipriano de Mosquera* (for 3rd time)
23 May 1867 – Apr 1868	*Santos Acosta*
1868	*Santos Gutiérrez* (b. 1820; d. 1872)
1 Apr 1870	*Eustorgio Salgar* (b. 1831; d. 1885)
1 Apr 1872	*Manuel Murillo Toro* (for 2nd time)
1 Apr 1874	*Santiago Pérez* (b. 1830; d. Paris 1900)
1 Apr 1876	*Aquileo Parra* (b. 1825; d. 1900)
1 Apr 1878	*Julián Trujillo* (b. 1828; d. 1883)
1 Apr 1880	*Rafael Núñez* (for 1st time) (b. 25 Sep 1825; d. 18 Sep 1894)
1 Apr – Dec 1882	*Francisco Javier Zaldúa* (b. 1811; d. Dec 1882)
22 Dec 1882	*José Eusebio Otálora* (b. 1828; d. 1884)
1 Apr 1884 – 1888	*Rafael Núñez* (for 2nd time)
1888	*Carlos Holguín* (b. 1832; d. Oct 1894)
7 Aug 1892	*Rafael Núñez* (for 3rd time)
18 Sep 1894	*Miguel Antonio Caro* (b. 10 Nov 1843; d. 5 Aug 1909)
7 Aug 1898	*Manuel Antonio Sanclemente* (b. 1814; d. 1902)
31 Jul 1900	*José Manuel Marroquín* (b. 1827; d. 19 Sep 1908)
7 Aug 1904	*Rafael Reyes Prieto* (b. 1850; d. 1921)
8 Jul 1909	*Jorge Holguín* (for 1st time) (d. 2 March 1928)
3 Aug 1909	*Ramón González Valencia* (b. 1854; d. 3 Oct 1928)
7 Aug 1910	*Carlos E. Restrepo* (b. 12 Sep 1867; d. 1937)
7 Aug 1914	*José Vincente Concha* (b. 21 Apr 1867; d. 9 Dec 1929)
7 Aug 1918	*Marco Fidel Suarez* (b. 1855; d. 4 Apr 1927)
11 Nov 1921	*Jorge Holguín* (for 2nd time)
7 Aug 1922	*Pedro Nel Ospina* (b. 1867; d. 1 Jul 1927)
7 Aug 1926 – 7 Aug 1930	*Miguel Abadía Méndez* (b. 5 Jun 1867; d. 15 May 1947)

Costa Rica

| 1540 | Part of Spanish Empire |
| 1821 | Part of Mexican Empire |

HEADS OF STATE

Governors

1 Dec 1821	*Pedro Alvarado*
13 Jan 1822	*Rafael Barroeta*
1 Jan 1823	Became part of United Provinces of Central America

Presidents

1 Jan 1823	*José Santos Lombardo*
6 Sep 1824	*Agustín Gutiérrez Lizano Zabal* (for 1st time)
8 Sep 1824	*Juan Mora* (b. 12 Jul 1784; d. 16 Dec 1854)
9 Mar 1933 – 1834	*José Rafael de Gallegos* (for 1st time)
1834 – Jun 1834	*Juan José Lara*
Jun 1834	*Agustín Gutiérrez Lizano Zabal* (for 2nd time)
5 May 1835	*Braulio Carillo* (for 1st time)
17 Apr 1837 – 27 May 1838	*Manuel Aguilar*
May 1838	Seceded from United Provinces of Central America
25 Jun 1838 – 11 Apr 1842	*Braulio Carillo* (for 2nd time)
15 Jul – 14 Sep 1842	*Francisco Morazán* (b. 1792; d. 15 Sep 1842)
27 Sep 1842	*José Maria Alfaro* (for 1st time)
15 Nov 1844	*Francisco María Oreamuno* (b. 1800; d. 1856)
7 Dec 1844	*Rafael Moya* (d. 1845)
1 May 1845	*José Rafael de Gallegos* (for 2nd time)
9 Jun 1846	*José María Alfaro* (for 2nd time)
8 May 1847 – 16 Jan 1849	*José María Castro* (for 1st time) (b. 1 Sep 1816; d. 1892)
26 Jan 1849	*Juan Rafael Mora* (b. 8 Feb 1814; d. 30 Sep 1860)
14 Aug 1859 – May 1863	*José María Montalegre*
8 May 1863	*Jesús Jiménez* (b. 1823; d. 1897)
8 May 1866 – 1 Sep 1868	*José María Castro* (for 2nd time)
1 Nov 1868	*Jesús Jiménez* (for 2nd time)

28 Apr 1870	*Bruno Carranza*
8 Aug 1870	*Tomás Guadia* (for 1st time) (b. 1832; d. 7 Jul 1882)
21 Nov – 1 Dec 1873	*Salvador González*
2 Dec 1873	*Rafael Barroeta*
28 Feb 1874	*Tomás Guardia* (for 2nd time)
19 May 1876	*Aniceto Esquivel*
30 Jul – 11 Sep 1876	*Vicente Herrera*
17 Sep 1876 – 7 Jul 1882	*Tomás Guardia* (for 3rd time)
20 Jul 1882 – 12 Mar 1885	*Próspero Fernández* (b. 18 Jul 1834; d. 12 Mar 1885)
13 May 1885	*Bernardo Soto y Alfaro* (b. 12 Feb 1854; d. 1931)
Nov 1889	—— *Durán*
8 May 1890	*José Joaquím Rodríguez* (b. 1838; d. 1917)
8 May 1894	*Rafael Iglesias y Castro* (b. 1861; d. 1924)
8 May 1902	*Ascención Esquivel* (b. 1848; d. 1927)
8 May 1906	*Cleto González Víquez* (for 1st time) (b. 1858; d. 1937)
8 May 1910	*Ricardo Jiménez Oreamuno* (for 1st time) (b. 1859; d. 1945)
8 May 1912	*Cleto González Viquez* (for 2nd time)
8 May 1914 – 27 Jan 1917	*Alfredo González Flores* (b. 1877)
11 Apr 1917 – 6 May 1919	*Federico Tinoco Granados* (b. 1870; d. 1931)
7 May 1919	*Julio Acosta Garcia* (for 1st time) (b. 1876; d. 6 Jul 1954)
13 Aug 1919	*Juan Bautista Quiros*
8 May 1920	*Julio Acosta García* (for 2nd time)
8 May 1924	*Ricardo Jiménez Oreamuno* (for 2nd time)
8 May 1928 – 8 May 1932	*Cleto González Víquez* (for 3rd time)

Courland and Semigallia

HEADS OF STATE

28 Nov 1561	On the annexation of Livonia by Poland, the territory south of the Duna was made a hereditary duchy under the last Master of the Teutonic Knights, who did homage on 5 March 1562

135

Dukes

House of Kettler

28 Nov 1561 – 5 Mar 1562	*Gotthard* (b. Westphalia about 1517)
17 May 1587 – 17 Aug 1641	*Friedrich*, son (b. 1569) from 1596 to 1617 Duke of Courland only
17 May 1587 – 1616	*Wilhelm*, brother (from 1596: Duke of Semigallia) (b. 20 Jul 1574; d. 7 Apr 1640) deposed 1616
17 Aug 1641	*Jakob*, son (b. 28 Oct 1610)
1 Jan 1682	*Friedrich Kazimir*, son (b. 1650)
22 Jan 1698	*Friedrich Wilhelm*, son (b. 19 Jul 1692)
1698 – 1710	Council of Regency under the leadership of:
	1698 – 1701: *Christoph Heinrich von Puttkamer* (d. 1701)
	1701 – 1708: *Friedrich von Brackel-Kuckschen* (b. 1634; d. 1708)
	1708 – 1710: *Heinrich Christian von der Brincken-Sessilen* (d. 1729)
21 Jan 1711 – 1737	*Ferdinand*, uncle (b. 1655)

House of Biron

13 Jul 1737	*Ernst Johann* (originally *Bühren*) (b. 1 Dec 1690; d. Mitau 28 Dec 1772) exiled 1740 – 1763
24 Nov 1769 – 28 Mar 1795	*Peter*, son (b. Mitau 15 Feb 1724; d. Gellenau 13 Jan 1800)
1795	Courland absorbed by Russia

Croatia

HEADS OF STATE

Bans

Mar 1848 – 19 May 1859	*Josip, Baron* (from 1855: *Count*) *Jelačić* (b. Petrovaradin 16 Oct 1801; d. Zagreb 19 May 1859)
1859	*Peter, Count Pejačević* (b. Bratislava 20 Apr 1804; d. Vienna 15 Ap 1887)
1868 – 1872	*Levin, Baron Rauch* (b. Lužnica 6 Oct 1819; d. 25 Aug 1890)

1873	*Ivan Mažuranić* (b. Novi Vinodolski 11 Aug 1814; d. Zagreb 4 Aug 1890)
1880	*Ladislav, Count Pejačević* (b. Sopron 5 Apr 1824; d. Našice 7 Apr 1901)
1883 – 1903	*Károly, Count Khuen-Héderváry* (b. Gräfenberg 23 May 1849; d. Budapest 16 Feb 1918)
1 Jul 1903 – 26 Jun 1907	*Teodor, Count Pejačević* (b. Nasice 24 Sep 1855; d. Vienna 25 Jul 1928)
Jul 1907 – Jan 1908	*Sándor Rakodczay* (b. Bratislava 25 Sep 1848)
8 Jan 1908 – end Jan 1910	*Pavao, Baron Rauch* (b. Zagreb 20 Feb 1865; d. Martijanec 29 Nov 1933)
5 Feb 1910 – 19 Jan 1912	*Nikola Tomašić* (b. Zagreb 13 Jan 1864; d. Treščerovac 29 May 1918)
20 Jan 1912 – Jul 1913	*Slavko Cuvaj* (b. Bjelovar 26 Feb 1851; d. Vienna 31 Jan 1931)
Jul/29 Nov 1913 – 8 Jun 1917	*Ivan, Baron Skrlec*
8 Jun 1917 – 29 Oct 1918	*Antun Mihalović* (b. Feričanci 1868)
1 Dec 1918	Kingdom of the Serbs, Croats and Slovenes founded (see Yugoslavia)

Cuba

HEADS OF STATE

Presidents

10 Dec 1898	Cuba declared independent, under US military government
20 May 1902	*Tomás Estrada Palma* (b. 1836; d. 4 Nov 1908)
Sep 1906	Direct administration by the USA
28 Jan 1909	*José Miguel Gómez* (b. 6 Jul 1858; d. 13 Jun 1921)
20 May 1913	*Mario García Menocal* (b. 17 Dec 1868; d. 7 Sep 1941)
20 May 1921	*Alfredo Zayas y Alonso* (b. 1861; d. 11 Apr 1934)
20 May 1925 – 12 Aug 1933	*Gerardo Machado de Morales* (b. 29 Nov 1871; d. 28 Mar 1939)

Czechoslovakia

Independent republic proclaimed 28 Oct 1915. Previously under the rule of the Emperor of Austria who was also King of Bohemia and of Hungary. For the reigns of the Kings of Bohemia see Bohemia, for biographical details see Hungary.

HEAD OF STATE

President

28 Oct 1918 – 14 Dec 1935   *Tomáš Garrigue Masaryk* (b. Hodonín 7 Mar 1850; d. Lány Castle 14 Sep 1937)

MEMBERS OF GOVERNMENT

14 Nov 1918 – 10 Jul 1919: Kramář

Prime Minister	*Karel Kramář* (b. Vysoké 27 Dec 1860; d. Prague 26 May 1937)
Foreign Affairs	*Edvard Beneš* (National Socialist) (b. Kozlan 28 May 1884; d. Lány Castle 3 Sep 1948)
Home Affairs	*Antonín Svehla* (Czech Agrarian) (b. Hostivař 15 Apr 1873; d. Hostivař 12 Dec 1933)
Justice	*František Soukup* (Socialist) (b. Kamenná Lhota 22 Aug 1871; d. 1940)
Defence	*Václav Jaroslav Klofáč* (National Socialist) (b. Nemecký Brod 21 Sep 1868; d. 1942)
Post	*Jiří Stříbrný* (National Socialist) (b. Rokycany 14 Jan 1880; d. 1955)
Finance	*Alois Rašín* (National Democratic) (b. Nechanice 18 Oct 1867; d. Prague 18 Feb 1923)
Trade	*Adolf Stránský* (Moravian Populist) (b. Habry 8 Apr 1855; d. Brno 19 Dec 1931)
Agriculture	*Karel Prášek* (Czech Agrarian) (b. Řivno 4 Feb 1868; d. Košetice 13 Feb 1932)
Railways	*Bohdan Zahradník* (b. Hostačová 25 Jun 1864; d. Vienna 19 Feb 1926)
Social Welfare	*Lev Winter* (Czech Socialist) (b. Hroby u Tábora 26 Jan 1876; d. Gräfenberg 29 Aug 1935)
Fine Arts	—— *Klesau*
Education	*Gustav Habrman* (Socialist) (b. Česká Třebová 24 Jan 1864; d. Prague 22 Mar 1932)

Public Works	*František Staněk* (Czech Agrarian) (b. Tremles 14 Nov 1867; d. Prague 19 Jul 1936)
Health	*Vavro Jan Šrobár* (b. Lisková 9 Aug 1867; d. Olomouc 6 Dec 1950)
War	14 Nov 1918 – 4 May 1919: *Milan Rastislav Stefánik* (b. Košariská 21 Jul 1880; d. Vajnor 4 May 1919) 4 May – 10 Jul 1919: no appointment made, post abolished
Without Portfolio	14 Nov 1918 – 29 May 1919: *Mořic Hruban* (b. Brodek 30 Nov 1862)

10 Jul 1919 – 15 Apr 1920: Tusar I

Prime Minister	*Vlastimil Tusar* (for 1st time) (Socialist) (b. Prague 23 Oct 1880; d. Berlin 22 Mar 1924)
Foreign Affairs	*Edvard Beneš* (see Kramář)
Home Affairs	*Antonín Švehla* (see Kramář)
Justice	*František Veselý* (National Socialist) (b. Jicín 18 Sep 1863)
Defence	*Václav Jaroslav Klofáč* (see Kramář)
Agriculture	*Karel Prášek* (see Kramář)
Post and telegraph	*František Staněk* (see Kramář)
Finance	10 Jul – 9 Sep 1919: *Cyril Horáček* (b. Horní Počernice 7 Nov 1862; d. 1938) 9 Oct 1919 – 15 Apr 1920: *Kuneš Sonntag* (Czech Agrarian) (b. Lazce 19 Feb 1878; d. Prague 29 Mar 1931)
Trade	*Ferdinand Heidler* (Nationalist) (b. Dolní Chvatliny 8 Dec 1881; d. Prague 3 Nov 1928)
Food	10 Jul 1919 – 30 Mar 1920: *Fedor Houdek* (b. Ruzomberok 5 Jan 1867) 30 Mar – 15 Apr 1920: *Kuneš Sonntag* (see above)
Railways	10 Jul – 17 Sep 1919: *Jiří Stříbrný* (see Kramář) 17 Sep 1919 – 15 Apr 1920: *Emil Franke* (Czech Socialist) (b. Brezno Velké 3 Apr 1880)
Social Welfare	*Lev Winter* (see Kramář)
Education	*Gustav Habrman* (see Kramář)
Public Works	*Antonín Hampl* (Socialist) (b. Jaroměř 12 Apr 1874; d. Berlin 1942)
Health and Slovakian Affairs	*Vavro Jan Šrobár* (see Kramář)
Coordination	*Milan Hodža* (Czech Agrarian) (b. Sučany 1 Feb 1878; d. Clearwater, Florida, 27 Jun 1944)

25 May - 15 Sep 1920: Tusar II

Prime Minister	*Vlastimil Tusar* (for 2nd time) (see Tusar I)
Foreign Affairs	*Edvard Beneš* (see Kramář)
Home Affairs	*Antonin Švehla* (see Kramář)
Justice	*Alfred Meissner* (Czech Socialist) (b. Mladá Boleslav 10 Apr 1871; d. 1950)
Defence	25 May – 16 Mar 1920: *Vlastimil Tusar* (see Tusar I) 16 Jul – 16 Sep 1920: *Ivan Markovič* (b. Myjava 3 Jun 1888)
Post and Telegraph	*František Staněk* (see Kramář)
Finance	*Karel Engliš* (National Democratic) (b. Hrabyně 17 Aug 1880; d. 1961)
Trade	*Kuneš Sonntag* (see Tusar I)
Agriculture	25 May – 24 Jun 1920: *Karel Prášek* (see Kramář) 24 Jun – 15 Sep 1920: *Kuneš Sonntag* (see Tusar I)
Food	*Václav Johanis* (Socialist) (b. Prague 26 Feb 1872)
Railways	*Jiří Stříbrný* (see Kramář)
Social Welfare	*Lev Winter* (see Kramář)
Education	*Gustav Habrman* (see Kramář)
Public Works	*Bohuslav Vrbenský* (b. Opočnice 30 Mar 1882; d. 1944)
Health and coordination	*Vavro Jan Šrobár* (see Kramář)
Without Portfolio	(acting for Slovakian affairs:) *Ivan Dérer* (Slovak Socialist) (b. Malacký 2 Feb 1884) *Rudolf Hotowetz* (b. Říčany 12 Oct 1865)

15 Sep 1920 - 2 Sep 1921: Černý I

Prime Minister	*Johan Černý* (for 1st time) (b. Uherský Ostroh 4 March 1874; d. Uherský Ostroh 10 Apr 1957)
Foreign Affairs	*Edvard Beneš* (see Kramář)
Home Affairs	*Jan Černý* (see above)
Justice	*Augustín Popelka* (b. Brno 25 Apr 1854)
Defence	*Otakar Husák* (b. Nymburk 23 Apr 1885)
Post and Telegraph	*Maxmilián Fatka* (b. Biskupice 23 Sep 1868)
Finance	15 Sep 1920 – 22 May 1921: *Karel Engliš* (see Tusar II) 22 Mar – 2 Sep 1921: *Vladimir Hanačík* (b. Brno 23 Nov 1861)
Trade	*Rudolf Hotowetz* (see Tusar II)
Agriculture	*Vladislav Brdlík* (b. Žirovnice 26 Jul 1879)
Food	15 Sep 1920 – 24 Jan 1921: *Leopold Průša* (b.

Kamenice 18 Nov 1866; d. 22 Dec 1936)
24 Jan – 25 Apr 1921 (acting:) *Vladislav Brdlík* (see above)
25 Apr – 2 Sep 1921 (acting:) *Vladislav Prokop Procházka* (b. Litomyše 1 May 1872)

Railways	*Václav Burger* (b. Mořiny 13 Apr 1859; d. Prague 18 Jan 1923)
Social Welfare	*Josef Gruber* (b. 3 Nov 1865; d. Prague 4 May 1925)
Education	*Josef Šusta* (b. Třeboň 19 Feb 1874; d. 1945)
Public Works	21 Oct 1920 – 2 Sep 1921: *František Kovařík* (b. Prostějova 25 Sep 1865)
Health	*Vladislav Prokop Procházka* (see above)
Slovakian Affairs	*Martin Mičura* (b. Dehé Pole 17 Sep 1883)
Coordination	*Vladimír Fajnor* (b. Senice na Hané 23 Oct 1875)

26 Sep 1921 – 5 Oct 1922: Beneš

Prime Minister	*Edvard Beneš* (see Kramář)
Foreign Affairs	*Edvard Beneš* (see Kramář)
Home Affairs	*Jan Černý* (see Černý I)
Justice	*Josef Dolanský* (Czech Agrarian) (b. Jičin 7 Jan 1868)
Defence	*František Udržal* (Czech Agrarian) (b. Dolní Roveň 3 Jan 1866; d. Prague 25 Sep 1938)
Post and Telegraph	*Antonín Srba* (Socialist) (b. Nechyba 3 Jun 1879)
Finance	*Augustin Novák* (b. Kralupy 20 Sep 1872)
Trade	*Vladislav Novák* (National Democratic) (b. Prague 5 Apr 1872)
Agriculture	*Fratišek Stanek* (see Kramář)
Food	(acting:) *Antonín Srba* (see above)
Railways	*Jan Šrámek* (Czech Populist) (b. Grygova 11 Aug 1870; d. (?)21 Aug 1955)
Social Welfare	*Gustav Habrman* (see Kramář)
Education	*Vavro Jan Šcrobár* (see Kramář)
Public Works	*Alois Tučný* (National Socialist) (b. Frenštát 4 Jun 1881)
Health	*Bohuslav Vrbenský* (see Tusar II)
Coordination	*Ivan Dérer* (see Tusar II)
Slovakian Affairs	*Jozef Kállay* (b. Liptovský-Sv. Mikuláš 12 Aug 1881)

Oct 1922 – 16 Nov 1925: Švehla I

Prime Minister	*Antonín Švehla* (for 1st time) (see Kramář)
Foreign Affairs	*Edvard Beneš* (see Kramář)

141

Home Affairs	*Jan Malypetr* (Czech Populist) (b. Klobúky 20 Dec 1873; d. 21 Sep 1947)
Justice	*Josef Dolanský* (see Beneš)
Defence	*František Udržal* (see Beneš)
Post and Telegraph	7 Oct 1922 – 18 Feb 1924: *Alois Tučný* (see Beneš)
	18 Feb 1924 – 16 Nov 1925: *Emil Franke* (see Tusar I) ·
Finance	7 Sep 1922 – 18 Jan 1923: *Alois Rašín* (see Kramář)
	24 Feb 1923 – 16 Nov 1925: *Bohdan Bečka* (b. Neveklov 14 Apr 1863)
Trade	*Vadislav Novák* (see Beneš)
Agriculture	*Milan Hodža* (Czech Agrarian – Slovak wing) (see Tusar I)
Food	(acting:) Minister for Post and Telegraph
Railways	7 Oct 1922 – 15 Jul 1925: *Jiří Stříbrný* (see Kramář)
	15 Jul – 16 Nov 1925: *Emile Franke* (see Tusar I)
Social Welfare	7 Oct 1922 – 28 Mar 1925: *Gustav Habrman* (see Kramář)
	28 Mar – 16 Nov 1925: *Lev Winter* (see Kramář)
Education	7 Oct 1922 – 3 Oct 1924: *Rudolf Bechyně* (Czech Socialist) (b. Nymburk 6 Apr 1881; d. Prague 3 Jan 1948)
	3 Oct 1924 – 16 Nov 1925: *Ivan Markovič* (see Tusar II)
Public Works	*Antonín Srba* (see Beneš)
Health	*Jan Šrámek* (see Beneš)
Coordination	*Ivan Markovič* (see Tusar II)
Slovakian Affairs	*Jozef Kállay* (see Beneš)

9 Dec 1925 – 17 Mar 1926: Švehla II

Prime Minister	*Antonin Švehla* (for 2nd time) (see Kramář)
Foreign Affairs	*Edvard Beneš* (see Kramář)
Home Affairs	*František Jan Nosek* (Czech Populist) (b. Chrudim 26 Apr 1886; d. Prague 17 Apr 1935)
Justice	*Karel Viškovský* (Czech Agrarian) (b. Šušice 8 Jul 1868; d. Prague 20 Nov 1932)
Defence	*Jiří Stříbrný* (see Kramár)
Post and Telegraph	*Jan Šrámek* (see Beneš)
Finance	*Karel Engliš* (see Tusar II)
Trade	*Jan Dvořáček* (National Democratic) (b. Letovice 12 Nov 1887)
Agriculture	*Milan Hodža* (see Tusar I)
Food	*Josef Dolanský* (see Beneš)

Railways	*Rudolf Bechyně* (see Švehla I)
Social Welfare	*Lev Winter* (see Kramář)
Education	*Otakar Srdínko* (Czech Agrarian) (b. Svobodné Dvory 1 Jan 1875; d. Prague 21 Dec 1930)
Public Works	*Rudolf Mlčoch* (Czech Professional) (b. Třebčín 17 Apr 1880)
Health	*Alois Tučný* (see Beneš)
Coordination	9 Dec 1925 – 5 Jan 1926: *Lev Winter* (see Kramář) 5 Jan – 17 Mar 1926: *Ivan Dérer* (see Tusar II)
Slovakian Affairs	*Jozef Kállay* (see Beneš)

18 Mar – 12 Oct 1926: Černý II

Prime Minister	*Jan Černý* (for 2nd time) (see Černý I)
Foreign Affairs	*Edvard Beneš* (see Kramář)
Home affairs	*Jan Černý* (see Černý I)
Justice	*Jiří Haussmann* (b. Prague 11 Jun 1968; d. Prague 7 Jan 1923)
Defence	*Jan Syrový* (b. Třebíč 24 Jan 1888)
Post and Telegraph	*Maxmilián Fatka* (see Černý I)
Finance	*Karel Engliš* (see Tusar II)
Trade	*František Peroutka* (b. Kutná Hora 27 Nov 1879)
Agriculture	*Juraj Slávik* (b. Dobrovniva 28 Jan 1890)
Food	(acting:) *Jan Cerný* (see Cerný I)
Railways	*Jan Říha* (b. Tábor 26 Apr 1881)
Social Welfare	*Josef Schliessl* (b. Ždanice 30 Apr 1876)
Education	*Jan Krčmář* (b. Prague 27 Jul 1877; d. 1950)
Public Works	*Václav Roubík* (b. Prague 12 Dec 1872)
Health	(acting:) *Josef Schliessl* (see above)
Coordination	*Juraj Slávik* (see above)
Slovakian Affairs	*Jozef Kállay* (see Beneš)

12 Oct 1926 – 1 Feb 1929: Švehla III

Prime Minister	*Antonin Švehla* (for 3rd time) (see Kramář)
Foreign Affairs	*Edvard Beneš* (see Kramář)
Home Affairs	*Jan Černý* (see Černý I)
Justice	*Robert Mayr-Harting* (German Christian Socialist) (b. Vienna 13 Sep 1874)
Defence	*František Udržal* (see Beneš)
Post and Telegraph	*František Jan Nosek* (see Švehla II)
Finance	12 Oct 1926 – 26 Sep 1928: *Karel Engliš* (see Tusar II) 26 Nov 1928 – 1 Feb 1929: *Bohumil Vlasák* (b. Příbram 21 Feb 1871)

Trade	12 Oct 1926 – 28 Apr 1928: *František Peroutka* (see Černý II)
	28 Apr 1928 – 1 Feb 1929: *Vladislav Novák* (see Beneš)
Agriculture	*Otakar Srdínko* (see Švehla II)
Food	(acting:) *Jan Černý* (see Černý I)
Railways	*Josef V. Najman* (Czech Professional) (b. Bohdanecká Skála 20 Apr 1882; d. Prague 4 Dec 1937)
Social Welfare	*Jan Šrámek* (see Beneš)
Education	*Milan Hodža* (see Tusar I)
Public Works	*Franz Spina* (German League) (b. Trnávka 5 Oct 1868; d. Prague 7 Sep 1938)
Health	12 Oct 1926 – 15 Jan 1927 (acting:) *Jan Šrámek* (see Beneš)
	15 Jan 1927 – 1 Feb 1929: *Jozef Tiso* (Slovak Populist) (b. Velka Bytča 13 Oct 1887; d. Bratislava 18 Apr 1947)
Coordination	12 Oct 1926 – 15 Jan 1927 (acting:) *Milan Hodža* (see Tusar I)
	15 Jan 1927 – 1 Feb 1929: *Markus Gažík* (b. Turzovka 18 Apr 1887)
Without Portfolio	For Slovakian affairs 12 Oct 1926 – 15 Jan 1927: *Jozef Kállay* (see Beneš)

1 Feb – 28 Oct 1929: Udržal I

Prime Minister	*František Udržal* (for 1st time) (see Beneš)
Foreign Affairs	*Edvard Beneš* (see Kramář)
Home Affairs	*Jan Černý* (see Černý I)
Justice	*Robert Mayr-Harting* (see Švehla III)
Defence	1 Feb – 18 Sep 1929: *František Udržal* (see Beneš)
	18 Sep – 28 Oct 1929: *Karel Viškovský* (see Švehla II)
Post and Telegraph	*František Jan Nosek* (see Švehla II)
Finance	*Karel Engliš* (see Tusar II)
Trade	*Vladislav Novák* (see Beneš)
Agriculture	*Otakar Srdínko* (see Švehla II)
Food	(acting:) *Jan Černý* (see Černý I)
Railways	*Josef V. Najman* (see Švehla III)
Social Welfare	*Jan Šrámek* (see Beneš)
Education	1 – 20 Feb 1929: *Milan Hodža* (see Tusar I)
	20 Feb – 28 Oct 1929: *Anton Štefánek* (b. Velké Leváre 15 Apr 1877)
Public Works	*Franz Spina* (see Švehla III)
Health	1 Feb – 8 Oct 1929: *Jozef Tiso* (see Švehla III)
	8 – 28 Oct 1929 (acting:) *Jan Šrámek* (see Beneš)

Coordination	1 – 27 Feb 1929: *Markus Gažík* (see Švehla III)
	27 Feb – 8 Oct 1929: *Ludvík Labaj* (Slovak Populist)
	(b. Ružomberok)
	8 – 28 Oct 1929 (acting: *Anton Štefánek* (see above)

7 Dec 1929 – 21 Oct 1932: Udvžal II

Prime Minister	*František Udržal* (for 2nd time) (see Beneš)
Foreign Affairs	*Edvard Beneš* (see Kramář)
Home Affairs	*Juraj Slávik* (see Černý II)
Justice	*Alfréd Meissner* (se Tusar II)
Defence	*Karel Viškovský* (see Švehla II)
Post and Telegraph	*Emil Franke* (see Tusar I)
Finance	7 Dec 1929 – 16 Apr 1931; *Karel Engliš* (see Tusar II)
	16 Apr 1931 – 21 Oct 1932: *Karl Trapl* (National
	Socialist) (b. Chrudim 31 Aug 1881; d. Prague 7 Apr
	1940)
Trade	*Josef Matoušek* (National Democratic) (b. Železný
	Brod 25 May 1876)
Agriculture	*Bohumir Bradáč* (Czech Agrarian) (b. Židovice 31
	May 1881; d. Oct 1935)
Food	*Rudolf Bechyně* (see Švehla I)
Railways	7 Dec 1929 – 8 Apr 1932: *Rudolf Mlčoch* (see Švehla
	II)
	9 Apr – 21 Oct 1932: *Josef Hůla* (b. 5 Jun 1873)
Social Welfare	*Ludwig Czech* (German Socialist) (b. Lvov 14 Feb
	1870; d. Theresienstadt (?) May 1945)
Education	*Ivan Dérer* (see Tusar II)
Public Works	*Johann Dostálek* (Czech Populist) (b. Šedivec 28 Apr
	1883)
Health	*Franz Spina* (see Švehla III)
Coordination	*Jan Šrámek* (see Beneš)

Dahomey

For the kingdom of Dahomey, 17th to 19th centuries, see volume 1.

Denmark

HEADS OF STATE

Kings

House of Oldenburg (from 1448)

21 May 1481	*Johann*, son of Christian I of Denmark (b. 8 Jul 1455)
20 Feb 1513	*Christian II*, the Wicked, son (b. 2 Jul 1481; d. 25 Jan 1559)
20 Apr 1523	*Frederick I*, uncle (b. 3 Sep 1471)
10 Apr 1533	Interregnum
Apr 1536	*Christian III*, son (b. 12 Aug 1503)
1 Jan 1559	*Frederick II*, son (b. 1 Jul 1534)
4 Apr 1588	*Christian IV*, son (b. 12 Apr 1577)
28 Feb 1648	*Frederick III*, son (b. 18 Mar 1609)
9 Feb 1670	*Christian V*, son (b. 15 Apr 1646)
26 Aug 1699	*Frederick IV*, son (b. 21 Oct 1671)
12 Oct 1730	*Christian VI*, son (b. 10 Dec 1699)
6 Aug 1746	*Frederick V*, son (b. 31 Mar 1723)
14 Jan 1766	*Christian VII*, son (b. 20 Jan 1749)
13 Mar 1808	*Frederick VI*, son (b. 28 Jan 1768)
3 Dec 1839	*Christian VIII*, son (b. 18 Sep 1786)
20 Jan 1848	*Frederick VII*, son (b. 6 Oct 1808)
15 Nov 1863	*Christian IX*, fourth son of Duke William of Holstein-Beck-Glücksburg (b. 8 Apr 1818)
29 Jan 1906	*Frederick VIII*, son (b. 3 Jun 1843)
14 May 1912 – 20 Apr 1947	*Christian X*, son (b. 29 Sep 1870)

MEMBERS OF GOVERNMENT

Prime Ministers or Chief Ministers

1751	*Johann Hartwig Ernst* (from 1767: *Count*) *Bernstorff* (b. Hanover 13 May 1712; d. Hamburg 18 Feb 1772) Foreign Minister
13 Sep 1770 – 17 Jan 1772	*Johann Friedrich* (from 1771: *Count*) *Struensee* (b. Halle an der Saale 5 Aug 1737; d. Copenhagen 28 Apr 1772) Secretary of State from 1771
Jan 1772 – 1784	*Ove Hoegh-Guldberg* (b. Horsens 1 Sep 1731; d. Hald 7 Feb 1808)

1784 – 21 Jun 1797	*Andreas Peter, Count Bernstorff* (1772 – Nov 1780) (b. Hannover 28 Aug 1735; d. Copenhagen 21 June 1797) Foreign Minister
Jun 1797 – 1819	*Christian Günther, Count Bernstorff*, son (b. Copenhagen 3 Apr 1769; d. Berlin 28 Mar 1835) from 1797: State Secretary; 1800: Foreign Minister; 1818/32: Prussian Foreign Minister
1810 – 1814	*Frederik, Count Moltke* (b. Odense 1754; d. Vallø) 1836: Minister of State
1814 – 5 Oct 1818	*Joachim Godske, Count Moltke* (b. Nygaard 27 Jul 1746; d. Copenhagen 5 Oct 1818)
1824 – 1842	*Otto Joachim von Moltke* (b. Copenhagen 11 Jun 1770; d. Espe 1 Feb 1853)
1842 – 1852	*Adam Wilhelm von Moltke* (b. Einsiedelborg 25 Aug 1785; d. Copenhagen 15 Feb 1864)
27 Jan 1852	*Christian Albrecht Bluhme* (for 1st time) (b. Copenhagen 27 Dec 1794; d. Copenhagen 16 Dec 1866)
21 Apr 1853	*Anders Sandøe Orsted* (b. Rudkøbing 21 Dec 1788; d. Copenhagen 1 May 1860)
12 Dec 1854	*Peter Georg Bang* (b. Copenhagen 7 Oct 1797; d. Copenhagen 2 Apr 1861)
18 Oct 1856	*Carl Christopher Georg Andrae* (b. 14 Oct 1812; d. 2 Feb 1893)
13 May 1857	*Carl Christian Hall* (for 1st time) (b. Copenhagen 25 Feb 1812; d. Frederiksborg 14 Aug 1888)
2 Dec 1859	*Carl Edvard Rotwitt* (b. Hillerød 2 Mar 1812; d. Copenhagen 8 Feb 1860)
24 Feb 1860	*Carl Christian Hall* (for 2nd time)
Dec 1863	*Ditlev Gothard Monrad* (b. Copenhagen 24 Nov 1811; d. Nykøbing 28 Mar 1887)
11 Jul 1864	*Christian Albert Bluhme* (for 2nd time)
6 Nov 1865	*Christian Emil Krog-Juel-Vind-Fris, Count Frijsenborg* (b. Frijsenborg 8 Dec 1817; d. Boller 12 Oct 1896)
28 May 1870	*Ludwig (Hennk Carl Herman) Count Holstein* (b. Holsteinborg 18 Jul 1815; d. Copenhagen 28 April 1892)
14 Jul 1874	*Christen Andreas Fonnesbech* (b. Copenhagen 7 Jul 1817; d. Copenhagen 17 May 1880)
11 Jun 1875	*Jakob Brønnum Scavenius Estrup* (b. Sorø 16 Apr 1825; d. Kongsdal 25 Nov 1913)
7 Aug 1894	*(Kjeld Thor) Tage (Otto) Baron Reedtz-Thott* (b. Gaunø 13 Mar 1839; d. Gaunø 27 Nov 1923)

147

23 May 1897	*Hugo Egmont Hørring* (b. Copenhagen 17 Aug 1842; d. Copenhagen 13 Feb 1909)
24 Apr 1900	*Hannibal Sehested* (b. Broholm 16 Nov 1842; d. Broholm 19 Sep 1924)
24 Jul 1901	*Johan Henrik Deuntzer* (b. Copenhagen 21 May 1845; d. Chasrlottenbund 16 Nov 1918)
14 Jan 1905	*Jens Christian Christensen* (b. Paabøl 21 Nov 1856; d. Hee 19 Dec 1930)
12 Oct 1908	*Niels Thomasins Neergaard* (for 1st time) (b. Ugilt 27 Apr 1854; d. Copenhagen 2 Sep 1936)
16 Aug 1909	*Johan Ludwig (Carl Christian Tido) Count Holstein* (b. Hochberg 10 Jun 1839; d. Ledreborg 1 Mar 1912)
28 Oct 1909	*Carl Theodor Zahle* (for 1st time) (b. Roskilde 19 Jan 1866; d. Lyngby 1946)
5 Jul 1910	*Klaus Bernsten* (b. Eskildstrup 12 Jun 1844; d. Copenhagen 27 Mar 1927)
21 Jun 1913	*Carl Theodor Zahle* (for 2nd time)
30 Mar 1920	*(Karl Julius) Otto Liebe* (b. Copenhagen 24 May 1860; d. Copenhagen 21 Mar 1929)
5 Apr 1920	*Aage Friis* (b. Halskov 16 Aug 1870; d. 5 Oct 1949)
5 May 1920	*Niels Thomasius Neergaard* (for 2nd time)
9 Oct 1922	*Niels Thomasius Neergaard* (for 3rd time)
23 Apr 1924	*Thorvald August Marinus Stauning* (b. Copenhagen 26 Oct 1873; d. Copenhagen 3 May 1942)
14 Dec 1926 – 25 Apr 1929	*Thomas Madsen-Mygdal* (b. Mygdal 24 Dec 1876; d. Hellerup 1943)
30 Apr 1929 – 4 Nov 1935	*Thorvald August Marinus Stauning* (for 2nd time)

Foreign Ministers

Jun 1913 – 30 Mar 1920	*(Harald R) Erik Scavenius* (b. 13 Jun 1877; d. 22 Nov 1962)
4 May 1920	*Harald (Roger) Scavenius* (b. Gjorslev 27 May 1873; d. The Hague 22 Apr 1939)
9 Oct 1922	*Christian (Magdalus Thestrup) Cold* (b. Copenhagen 10 Jun 1863; d. 1934)
23 Apr 1924 – 3 Dec 1926	*Carl Paul Oscar, Count Moltke* (b. Görz 2 Jan 1869; d. Christiansholm 5 Sep 1935)
14 Dec 1926 – 25 Apr 1929	*Laust Jevsen Moltesen* (b. Rodhede 18 Nov 1865; d. 1950)
30 Apr 1929 – Apr 1940	*Peter R. Munch* (b. Redsted 25 Jul 1870; d. Copenhagen 12 Jan 1948)

Djenne

For the Cadis of Djenne in Mali, 11th to 19th centuries, see volume 1.

Dominican Republic

HEADS OF STATE

Presidents

1795 – 1808	Ceded by Spain to France and incorporated with Haiti
1821	Independence declared
1822 – 1843	Part of Haiti
18 Nov 1844	Dominican Republic declared independent
21 Feb/6 Nov 1844 – 1848	*Pedro Santana* (b. 1801; d. 1863)
1848 – 1849	*Manuel Jiménez*
1849	*Pedro Santana*, Dictator
1849	*Buenaventura Báez* (for 1st time) (b. 1810; d. 1884)
15 Feb 1853	*Pedro Santana* (for 2nd or 3rd time)
Jun 1856	*Manuel de Regla-Motta*
6 Oct 1856 – 12 Jun 1858	*Buenaventura Báez* (for 2nd time)
Jun 1858 – Jan 1859	*José Desiderio Valverde*
31 Jan 1859 – May 1861	*Pedro Santana* (for 3rd or 4th time)
19 May 1861 – 5 May 1856	Dominica under Spanish administration, *Pedro Santana* Governor-General
1/19 May – Nov 1865	*Pedro Antonio Pimentel*
14 Nov 1865 – 29 Jun 1866	*Buenaventura Báez* (for 3rd time)
1865 – May 1868	*José Maria Cabral*, until 1866 opposition President
May 1868 – 31 Dec 1873	*Buenaventura Báez* (for 4th time)
27 Jan 1874 – 23 Feb 1876	*Ignacio (Maria) González* (for 1st time)
29 Jun 1876	*Ulises Francisco Espaillat* (b. 1823; d. 1878)
Nov 1876	*Ignacio González* (for 2nd time)

Dec 1876 – 24 Feb 1878	*Buenaventura Báez* (for 5th time)
12 Apr 1878 – 9 Dec 1879	*Cesáreo Guillermo*
Dec 1879 – 1880	*Gregorio Luperón*
12 Oct 1880 – Jul 1884	*Fernando Arturo de Meriño* (b. 1833; d. 1906)
20 Jul 1884 – 1885	*Ulises Heureaux* (for 1st time) (b. 1845; d. 26 Jul 1899)
1885 – 1887	*Francisco Gregorio Billini* (b. 1838; d. 1898)
1887 – 26 Jul 1899	*Ulises Heureaux* (for 2nd time)
1 Aug – 31 Aug 1899	*Juan Wenceslao Figuereo*
1 Sep – 14 Nov 1899	*Horacio Vásquez* (for 1st time) (b. 1855; d. 1936)
19 Nov 1899	*Juan Isidro Jiménez* (for 1st time) (b. 1846; d. 1919)
2 May 1902 – 23 Mar 1903	*Horacio Vásquez* (for 2nd time)
27 Apr – 20 Nov 1903	*Alejandro Wos y Gil*
28 Dec 1903 – 2 Apr 1904	*Juan Isidro Jiménez* (for 2nd time)
19 Jun 1904	*Carlos Morales* (b. 23 Aug 1867; d. 1914)
12 Jan 1906 – 19 Nov 1911	*Ramón Cáceres* (b. 1868; d. 19 Nov 1911)
2 Dec 1911 – 28 Nov 1912	*Eladio Victoria*
1 Dec 1912 – 1 Mar 1913	*Archbishop Adolfo Nouel y Bobadilla* (b. 1862; d. 1937)
13 Apr 1913 – 13 Apr 1914	*José Bordas y Valdés*
27 Aug	*Ramón Báez*
5 Dec 1914 – 8 May 1916	*Juan Isidro Jiménez* (for 3rd time)
16 May 1916 – 6 Oct 1922	*Francisco Henríquez y Carvajal* (b. 1848; d. 1922)
Oct 1922	*Juan Bautista Vicini Burgos* (d. 1924)
12 Jul 1924 – 18 Feb 1930	*Horacio Vásquez* (for 3rd time)

Ecuador

1534	Part of Spanish Empire
1822 – 1830	Part of Colombia

HEADS OF STATE

Presidents

17 May 1830	*Juan José (de) Flores* (b. 19 Jul 1800; d. 1 Oct 1864)
8 Aug 1835	*Vicente Rocafuerte* (b. May 1783; d. 16 May 1847)
31 Jan 1839 – 22 Jan 1843	*Juan José (de) Flores* (for 2nd time)
31 Jan 1843 – 17 Jun 1845	*Juan José (de) Flores* (for 3rd time)
8 Dec 1845 – 10 May 1850	*Vicente Ramon Roca* (b. 2 Sep 1792; d. 23 Feb 1858)
8 Dec 1850	*Diego Noboa y Arteta* (b. 15 Apr 1789; d. 3 Nov 1870)
13 Sep 1851	*José Maria Urbina* (b. 19 May 1808; d. 4 Sep 1891)
16 Oct 1856 – 1 May 1859	*Francisco Robles* (b. 5 May 1811; d. 1 Oct 1893)
21 Aug 1859 – 25 Nov 1860	*Guillermo Franco*, democratic President
1 May 1859 – 4 Sep 1865 (Generally acknowledged: 1860/61)	*Gabriel García Moreno* (for 1st time) (b. 24 Dec 1821; d. 6 Aug 1875) first Conservative President
7 Sep 1865 – 6 Nov 1867	*Geromino Carrión* (b. 1803; d. 1873)
20 Jan 1868 – 26 Jan 1869	*Javier Espinosa* (b. 1815; d. 1870)
17 Jan 1869 – 6 Aug 1875	*Gabriel García Moreno* (for 2nd time)
9 Oct 1875 – 8 Sep 1876	*Antonio Borrero y Cortazar* (b. 1827; d. 1912)
25 Dec 1876 – 9 Jun 1883	*Ignacio de Veintemilla* (b. 31 Jul 1828; d. 21 Jul 1908)
10 Feb 1884 – 30 Jun 1888	*José Maria Plácido Caamaño* (b. 1838; d. 1901)
17 Aug 1888	*Antonio Flores* (b. 1833; d. 1912)
1 Jul 1892	*Luis Cordero* (b. 6 Apr 1833; d. 30 Jan 1912)
16 Apr 1896	*Eloy Alfaro* (for 1st time) (b. 25 Jun 1842; d. 27 Jan 1912)
1 Sep 1901 – 31 Aug 1905	*Leónidas Plaza Gutiérrez* (for 1st time) (b. 1866; d. 1932)
1 Sep 1905 – 15 Jan 1906	*Lisardo García* (b. 1842; d. 1937)

17 Jan 1906 – 14 Aug 1911	*Eloy Alfaro* (for 2nd time)
1 Sep – 22 Dec 1911	*Emilio Estrada* (d. 22 Dec 1911)
Jan – Feb 1912	—— *Fraile*
Feb – 31 Mar 1912	—— *Andrade Marin*
8 Apr 1912	*Leónidas Plaza Gutiérrez* (for 2nd time)
1 Sep 1916	*Alfredo Baquerizo Moreno* (b. 1859; d. New York 19 Mar 1951)
1 Sep 1920	*José Luis Tamayo* (d. 7 Jul 1947)
1 Sep 1924	*Gonzalo Hernández Córdoba* (d. 23 Apr 1938)
9 Jul 1925	*Francisco Gómez de la Torre* and three other associates, military junta
1 Apr 1926 – 24 Aug 1931	*Isidro Ayora* (b. 31 Aug 1879)

Egypt

1517 – 1798/1914	Under Turkish control

HEADS OF STATE

Khedives (viceroys)

1805	*Mohammed Ali* (b. Kawalla 1769; d. 2 Aug 1849)
2 Aug 1848	*Ibrahim Pasha*, (?) adopted son (b. 1786 or 1789)
10 Nov 1848	*Abbas I*, grandson of Mohammed Ali (b. 1813)
14 Jul 1854	*Said*, uncle (b. 1822)
18 Jan 1863	*Ismail*, son of Ibrahim Pasha (b. 31 Dec 1830; d. 2 Mar 1895)
26 Jun 1879	*Tawfiq*, son (b. 15 Dec 1852).
7 Jan 1892	*Abbas II*, son (b. 16 Jul 1874; d. 20 Dec 1944)

Sultans

19 Dec 1914	*Hussein Kamil*, uncle (b. 21 Nov 1853)
7 Oct 1917 – 28 Apr 1936	*Ahmed Fuad I*, brother (b. 26 Mar 1868) from 1922: King

British Residents and High Commissioners

1883	*Sir Evelyn Baring* (from 1892: *Baron*; from 1899:

	Viscount; from 1901: *Earl Cromer*) (b. Cromer Hall, Norfolk 26 Feb 1841; d. London 19 Jan 1917)
1907 – 1910	*Sir Eldon Gorst* (b. New Zealand 25 Jun 1861; d. Castle Combe, 11 Jul 1911)
1911	*Herbert Horatio Kitchener, Earl Kitchener of Khartoum* (b. Crotta House, Ireland, 24 Jun 1850; d. at sea 5 Jun 1916)
1914	*Sir Arthur Henry McMahon* (b. 28 Nov 1862; d. London 29 Dec 1949)
1916	*Sir Francis Reginald Wingate* (b. Broadfield, Renfrewshire, 25 Jun 1861; d. Jan 1953)
1919	*Edward Henry Hynman Allenby, Viscount Allenby* (b. Suffolk 23 Apr 1861; d. London 14 May 1936)
1925	*George Ambrose Lloyd, Baron Lloyd* (b. Olton Hall, Warwickshire, 19 Sep 1879; d. London 4 Feb 1941)
1929 – 1933	*Sir Percy Lyham Loraine* (b. 5 Nov 1880; d. 23 May 1961)

MEMBERS OF GOVERNMENT

Prime Ministers

Apr 1914 – 4 Apr 1919	*Hussein Rushdi Pasha* (for 1st time)
9 Apr 1919	*Hussein Rushdi Pasha* (for 2nd time)
21 May – 17 Nov 1919	*Mohammed Said Pasha* (d. 20 Jul 1928)
23 Nov 1919 – 19 May 1920	*Yusof Wahba Pasha*
21 May 1920	*Mohammed Tawfiq Nasim Pasha* (for 1st time) (d. Cairo 6 Mar 1938)
15 Mar – 10 Dec 1921	*Adli Yegen Pasha* (for 1st time) (d. Paris 22 Oct 1933)
11 Dec 1921 – 29 Nov 1922	*Abdul Khaliq Sarwat Pasha* (for 1st time) (d. Paris 22 Sept 1928)
20 Nov 1922 – 9 Feb 1923	*Mohammed Tawfiq Nasim Pasha* (for 2nd time)
15 Mar 1923 – 17 Jan 1924	*Abdul Fatah Yahya Ibrahim Pasha* (b. 1876; d. 27 Sep 1951)
28 Jan	*Said Zaghlul Pasha* (b. 1860; d. Cairo 23 Aug 1927)
24 Nov 1924	*Ahmad Ziwar Pasha* (for 1st time) (d. 21 Aug 1945)
15 Mar 1925 – 6 Jun 1926	*Ahmad Ziwar Pasha* (for 2nd time)

7 Jun 1926 – 18 Apr 1927	*Adli Yegen Pasha* (for 2nd time)
23 Apr 1927 – 4 Mar 1928	*Abdul Khaliq Sarwat Pasha* (for 2nd time)
16 Mar – 25 Jun 1928	*Mustafa an-Nahas Pasha* (b. 15 Jun 1879)
27 Jun 1928 – 2 Oct 1929	*Mohammed Mahmud Pasha* (d. Cairo 2 Feb 1941)
3 Oct – 30 Dec 1929	*Adli Yegen Pasha* (for 3rd time)

El Salvador

16th century	Part of Spanish Empire
1821	Part of Mexican Empire
1 Jul 1823	Part of United Provinces of Central America

HEADS OF STATE

Governors

13 Dec 1824	*Juan Vicente Villacorta*
6 Dec 1826	*Mariano Prado* (for 1st time)
Jan 1829 – 28 Mar 1832	*José María Cornejo*
25 Jul 1832	*Mariano Prado* (for 2nd time)
1 Jul 1933 – 23 Jun 1834	*José María San Martín y Ulloa* (for 1st time)
25 Jul	*Gregorio Salazar*
Oct 1934	*Joaquín Escolán*
Apr 1835	*Nicolas Espinosa*
13 Nov 1835	*Francisco Gómez*
Apr 1836	*Diego Vijil* (b. 1799; d. 1840)
Sep 1836	*Timóteo Menéndez*
May 1839 – 3 Sep 1840	*António J. Canas* (for 1st time) (d. 1844)
23 Sep 1840 – 7 Jan 1841	*Norberto Ramírez* (d. 1851)
30 Jan 1841	Separate republic

Presidents

7 Jan 1841 – 13 Jan 1842	*Juan Lindo* (b. c. 1795; d. after 1852)
1 Feb 1842 – 1842	*António J. Cañas* (for 2nd time)
1842	*Pedro Arce*
1842	*Escolástico Marin*
1842 – 1844	*Juan José Guzmán* (for 1st time)
5 Feb 1844	*Francisco Malespín* (d. 25 Nov 1946)
2 Feb 1845	*Juan José Guzmán* (for 2nd time)
1 Feb 1846	*F. Palacios*
20 Feb 1846	*Eugenio Aguilar*
7 Feb 1848	*Doroteo Vasconcelos* (d. after 1880)
1 Mar 1851	*J. F. Quiróz*
1 Jan 1852	*Francisco Dueñas* (for 1st time) (d. after 1875)
Feb 1854	*José María San Martín y Ulloa* (for 2nd time)
Feb 1856	*Rafael Carupo*
Jan 1858 – 1860	*Miguel Santín del Castillo*
28 Jan 1860 – 26 Oct 1863	*Gerardo Barrios* (d. 29 Aug 1864)
12 Feb 1864	*Francisco Dueñas* (for 2nd time)
15 Apr 1871 – 11 Jan 1876	*Santiago González*
12 Jan 1876	*Andrés Vallés*
19 Jul 1876 – 14 May 1885	*Rafael Zaldívar y Lazo* (b. 1834; d. 1896)
22 May 1885	*Francisco Menéndez* (d. 22 Jun 1890)
22 Jun 1890 – 16 Jun 1894	*Carlos Ezeta* (b. 1855; d. 1903)
21 Jun 1894	*Rafael Gutiérrez*
13 Nov 1898 / 1 Mar 1899	*Tomás Regolado*
1 Mar 1903 – 28 Feb 1907	*Pedro José Escalón* (b. 1847; d. 6 Sep 1923)
1 Mar 1907 – 28 Feb 1911	*Fernando Figueroa* (b. 1849; d. 1912)
1 Mar 1911 – 9 Feb 1913	*Manuel Enrique Araujo* (d. 9 Feb 1913)
11 Feb 1913 – Aug 1914	*Carlos Meléndez* (for 1st time) (b. 1861; d. 1919)
29 Aug 1914 – 28 Feb 1915	*Alfonso Quiñones Molina* (for 1st time) (b. 11 Jan 1876; d. 1950)
1 Mar 1915 – 28 Feb 1919	*Carlos Meléndez* (for 2nd time)

1 Mar 1919 – 28 Feb 1923	*Jorge Meléndez*, brother (b. 1871)
1 Mar 1923 – 28 Feb 1927	*Alfonso Quiñones Molina* (for 2nd time)
1 Mar 1927 – 28 Feb 1931	*Pio Rómeo Bosque*

Estonia

Became independent of Russia 24 February 1918

MEMBERS OF GOVERNMENT

Prime Ministers and Presidents

19 May 1919	*Otto Strandman*, (for 1st time) (b. 30 Nov 1875; d. 1941)
13 Nov 1919	*Jaan Tõnisson* (for 1st time) (b. 22 Dec 1868)
5 Jul 1920	*Jaan Tõnisson* (for 2nd time)
27 Oct 1920	*Ants Piip* (b. Tuhalaane 28 Feb 1884; d. 1 Oct 1942) deported 30 Jun 1941
1922	*Johän Kukk* (b. 13 Apr 1885; d. Dec 1945)
Aug 1923	*Konstantin Päts* (b. 23 Feb 1874; d. Ufá 18 Jan 1956) deported 1941
28 Mar – 10 Dec 1924	*Friedrich Karl Akel* (b. Pärnumaa 5 Sep 1871)
17 Dec 1924	*Jüri Jaakson* (b. Fellin 16 Jan 1870; on 21 Feb 1949 was declared dead with effect from 31 Dec 1943 by a court in Oldenburg, Federal Republic of Germany)
16 Dec 1925	*Jaan Teemant* (for 1st time) (b. Vigala 24 Sep 1872)
24 Jul 1926	*Jaan Teemant* (for 2nd time)
22 Feb – 22 Nov 1927	*Jüri Uluots* (b. 1890; d. Sweden 1945/46)
10 Dec 1927	*Jaan Tõnisson* (for 3rd time)
19 Nov 1928 – 3 Jul 1929	*August Rei* (b. Pilistvere 22 Mar 1886; d. Stockholm 29 Mar 1963)
10 Jul 1929 – 3 Feb 1931	*Otto Strandman* (for 2nd time)

Ethiopia

HEADS OF STATE

Kings and Emperors

31 Jul 1508	*David II*
2 Sep 1540	*Claudius*, son
24 Mar 1560	*Menas*, brother
31 Jan 1564	*Sarsa Dengel*, son (b. 1550)
2 Aug 1597	*Jacob*, illegitimate son (for 1st time) (b. c. 1592)
Sep 1603	*Za Dengel*, nephew of Sarsa Dengel
24 Oct 1604	*Jacob* (for 2nd time)
10 Mar 1607	*Sisinnios*, great-grandson of David II (b. 1572)
17 Sep 1632	*Fasiladas (Basilides)*, son
18 Oct 1667	*John I*, son
19 Jul 1682	*Jesus I*, son (b. c. 1662; d. 13 or 14 Oct 1706)
Mar 1706	*Takla Haimanot I*, son
14 Jul 1708	*Theophilus*, son of John I
14 Oct 1711	*Justus*, great-grandson of John I (d. 19 Feb 1716)
11 Feb 1716	*David III*, son of Jesus I (b. 1796/7)
18 May 1721	*Bakaffa*, brother
19 Sep 1730	*Jesus II*, son
26 Jun 1755	*Joas I*, brother (d. 25 May 1769) deposed 18 May
26 May 1769	*John II*, son of Jesus I (b. 1698/9)
17 Oct 1769	*Takla Haimanot II*, son (b. 1755)
15 Sep 1777	*Solomon II*
20 Jul 1779	*Takla George*, brother of Takla Haimanot II (for 1st time)
8 Feb 1784	*Jesus III*, grandson of Jesus I (d. c. 1790)
24 Apr 1788	*Ba'eda Maryam*
1788 – 26 Jul 1789	*Takla George* (for 2nd time)
about 1789 – Jan 1794	*Hezekia*, son of Jesus III
1794	*Takla George* (for 3rd time)
15 Apr 1795	*Ba'eda Maryam II*
Dec 1795 – May 1796	*Takla George* (for 4th time)
2 Jun 1796	*Solomon III* (for 1st time)
15 Jul 1797	*Jonah*
4 Jan 1798	*Takla George* (for 5th time)
20 May 1799	*Solomon III* (for 2nd time)
1799	*Demetrius* (for 1st time)
24 Mar 1800	*Takla George* (for 6th time)

Jul 1800	*Demetrius* (for 2nd time)
Jun 1801	*Egwala Seyon (Gwalu)*, son of Hezekiah
3 Jun 1818	*Joas II*, brother
3 Jun 1821	*Gigar*, son of Jesus II (b. c. 1745)
Apr 1826 – (for 3 or 4 days)	*Ba'eda Maryam III*
Apr (?) 1826 – Jun 1830	*Gigar* (for 2nd time)
18 Jun 1830	*Jesus IV*, son of Solomon II
18 Mar 1832	*Gabra Krestos*
8 Jun 1832	*Sahla Dengel* (for 1st time)
1840	*John III*, son of Takla George (b. c. 1825)
Oct 1841	*Sahla Dengel* (for 2nd time)
11 Feb 1855 – 14 Apr 1868	*Theodore II* (b. Quara 1820; d. (committed suicide) 14 Apr 1868)
1872 – 10 Apr 1868	*John IV* (d. 12 Mar 1889)
9 Mar 1889	*Menelek II*, son (d. 12 Dec 1911)
15 May 1911	*Joshua* (b. Feb 1897; d. 7 Nov 1935)
27 Sep 1916	*Woisero Judito*, daughter of Menelek II (d. 2 Apr 1930) Empress
7 Oct 1928 – 12 Sep 1974	*Haile Selassie* (b. 24 Jul 1891; d. 27 Aug 1975) deposed

Finland

Proclaimed independent of Russia 1917

HEADS OF STATE

Regents

18 May – Dec 1918	*Pehr Evind Svinhufvud* (b. Sääksmäki 15 Dec 1861; d. Luumäki 29 Feb 1944)
12 Dec 1918 – Jun 1919	*Karl Gustaf Emil, Baron Mannerheim* (b. Louhisaari 4 Jun 1867; d. Lausane 27 Jan 1951)

King Elect

24 Oct – 29 Dec 1918	*Prince Friedrich Karl of Hesse* (b. 1 May 1868; d. Kassel 28 May 1940)

Presidents

25 Jul 1919 - 28 Feb 1925	*Kaarlo Juho Ståhlberg* (b. 28 Jan 1865; d. Helsinki night of 22/23 Sep 1952)
1 Mar 1925 - 28 Feb 1931	*Lauri Kristian Relander* (b. Kurkijoki 31 May 1883; d. Helsinki 9 Feb 1942)

MEMBERS OF GOVERNMENT

Prime Ministers

27 Nov 1917 - 18/27 May 1918	*Pehr Evind Svinhufvud* (see Regents) at first in Helsinki, during civil war in Vasa
27 May	*Juho Kusti Paasikivi* (b. Tampere 27 Nov 1870; d. Helsinki 14 Dec 1956)
27 Nov 1918	*Lauri Johannes Ingman* (for 1st time) (b. Teuva 30 Jun 1868; d. Turku 25 Oct 1934)
17 Apr 1919	*Kaarlo Castrén* (b. Turtola 28 Aug 1860; d. Helsinki 19 Nov 1938)
15 Aug 1919	*Juho (Heikki) Vennola* (for 1st time) (b. Oulu 19 Jun 1872; d. Helsinki 3 Dec 1938)
14 Mar 1920 - 8 Apr 1921	*Rafael Waldemar Erich* (b. Turku 10 Jun 1879; d. Helsinki 19 Feb 1946)
9 Apr 1921	*Juho (Heikki) (Vennola* (for 2nd time)
2 Jun 1922	*Aimo Kaarlo Cajander* (for 1st time) (b. Uusikaupunki 4 Mar 1879; d. Helsinki 21 Jan 1943)
14 Nov 1922	*Kyösti Kallio* (for 1st time) (b. Ylivieska 10 Apr 1873; d. Helsinki 19 Dec 1940)
18 Jan 1924	*Aimo Kaarlo Cajander* (for 2nd time)
31 May 1924	*Lauri Johannes Ingman* (for 2nd time)
31 Mar 1925	*Antti Agaton Tulenheimo* (b. Kangasala 4 Dec 1879; d. Helsinki 3 Sep 1952)
31 Dec 1925 - 23 Nov 1926	*Kyösti Kallio* (for 2nd time)
13 Dec 1926	*Väinö Alfred Tanner* (b. Helsinki 12 Mar 1881; d. Helsinki 19 Apr 1966)
17 Dec 1927	*Juho Emil Sunila* (b. Liminka 16 Aug 1875; d. Helsinki 2 Oct 1936)
22 Dec 1928 - 6 Aug 1929	*Oskari Mantere* (b. Hansjärvi 18 Sep 1874; d. Helsinki 9 Dec 1942)
16 Aug 1929 - 2 Jul 1930	*Kyösti Kallio* (for 3rd time)

France

HEADS OF STATE

Kings

House of Valois-Orleans

30 Aug 1483	*Charles VIII*, son of King Louis IX (b. 1470)
7 Apr 1498	*Louis XII*, son of Charles, Duke of Orleans (b. 27 May 1462)

House of Angoulême

1 Jan 1515	*Francis I*, son of Charles, Count of Angoulême (b. 12 Sep 1494)
31 Mar 1547	*Henry II*, son (b. 21 Mar 1519)
12 Jul 1559	*Francis II*, son (b. 27 Jan 1543)
5 Dec 1560	*Charles IX*, brother (b. 27 Jun 1550)
30 May 1574	*Henry III*, brother (b. 14 Sep 1551))

House of Bourbon

2 Aug 1589	*Henry IV*, son of Antoine, Duke of Vendome (b. 13 Dec 1553)
14 May 1610	*Louis XIII*, the Just, son (b. 27 Sep 1601)
4 May 1643	*Louis XIV*, the Great – the Sun King, son (b. 5 Sep 1638)
1 Sep 1715	*Louis XV*, great-grandson (b. 15 Feb 1710)
10 May 1774	*Louis XVI*, grandson (b. 23 Aug 1754; d. (guillotined) 21 Jan 1793) monarchy abolished 10 Aug 1792
10 Aug 1792	All powers exercised by National Legislative Assembly

Convention

21 Sep 1792	All powers exercised by National Convention

Directorate

26 Oct 1795	Powers of head of state exercised by a Directorate of five, for members see Members of Government

First Consul

9 Nov 1799	*Napoleon Bonaparte*, son of Carlo Bonaparte of

Corsica (b. 15 Aug 1769; d. St Helena 5 May 1821)
from 18 May 1804: Emperor Napoleon I

Emperor

18 May 1804   *Napoleon I* (for 1st time) previously First Consul

King

11 Apr 1814   *Louis XVIII*, brother of Louis XVI (for 1st time) (b. 17
Nov 1755)

Emperor

1 Mar 1815   *Napoleon I* (for 2nd time)

Kings

22 Jun 1815   *Louis XVIII* (for 2nd time)
16 Sep 1924 – 2 Aug   *Charles X*, brother (b. 9 Oct 1757; d. 6 Nov 1836)
1830   abdicated 2 Aug 1830

House of Orleans
8 Aug 1830 – 24 Feb   *Louis-Philippe*, son of Louis-Philippe, Duke of
1848   Orleans (b. 6 Oct 1773; d. 26 Aug 1850) abdicated 24
Feb 1848

Heads of State

Mar – May 1848   *Philippe Joseph Benjamin Buchez* (b. Montagne-la-
Petite, Belgium, 31 March 1796; d. Rhodez 12 Aug
1865) President of National Assembly
23 – 28 Jun 1848   Military dictatorship
28 Jun – 20 Dec 1848   *Eugène Cavaignac* (b. Paris 15 Oct 1802; d. Château
d'Ournes 28 Oct 1857) Head of Executive and
Chairman of Cabinet

President

10 Dec 1848   *Louis Napoleon Bonaparte*, nephew of Napoleon
Bonaparte (Emperor Napoleon I) (b. 20 Apr 1808; d. 9
Jan 1873) from 2 Dec 1852: Emperor Napoleon III

FRANCE

Emperor

2 Dec 1852   *Napoleon III** (previously President)

Presidents

31 Aug 1871	*(Marie Joseph) Louis Adolphe Thiers* (b. Marseille 15 Apr 1797; d. Saint-Germain-en-Laye 3 Apr 1877)
24 May 1873	*Marie Edmé Patrice Maurice de Mac-Mahon, Duc de Magenta* (b. Sully 13 Jul 1808; d. Loiret 17 Oct 1893)
30 Jan 1879 – 1 Dec 1887	*(François) Jules Paul Grevy* (b. Mont-sous-Vaudrey 15 Aug 1807; d. Mont-sous-Vaudrey 9 Sep 1891)
3 Dec 1887 – 24 Jun 1894	*Marie François Sadi Carnot* (b. Limoges 11 Aug 1837; d. Lyon 24 Jun 1894)
27 Jun 1894	*Jean Paul Pierre Casimir-Périer* (b. Paris 8 Sep 1847; d. Paris 11 Mar 1907)
17 Jan 1895 – 16 Feb 1899	*François Félix Faure* (b. Paris 30 Jan 1841; d. Paris 16 Feb 1899)
18 Feb 1899	*Émile Loubet* (b. Marsanne 31 Dec 1838; d. Montélimar 20 Dec 1929)
18 Feb 1906	*(Clément) Armand Fallières* (b. Mézin 6 Nov 1841; d. Mézin 22 Jun 1931)
18 Feb 1913	*Raymond Poincaré* (b. Bar-le-Duc 20 Aug 1860; d. Paris 15 Oct 1934)
18 Feb – 16 Sep 1920	*Paul Deschanel* (b. Schaerbeck 13 Feb 1856; d. Paris 28 Apr 1922)
23 Sep 1920 – 10 Jun 1924	*Alexandre Millerand* (b. Paris 10 Feb 1859; d. Versailles 6 Apr 1943)
13 Jun 1924 – 13 Jun 1931	*Gaston Doumergue* (b. Aigues-Vives 1 Aug 1863; d. 18 Jun 1937)

MEMBERS OF GOVERNMENT

1597 – 14 May 1610: Sully

Chief Minister	*Maximilien de Béthune, Baron de Rosny, Duc de Sully* (b. Rosny 13 Dec 1560; d. Villebon 22 Dec 1641)

*The title Napoleon II was given to Napoleon I's son

1610 – 1617: Lussigny

Chief Minister
Concino Concini, Baron Lussigny, Marshal of Ancre (b. Florence; d. 24 April 1617)

1617 – 1621: Luynes

Chief Minister
Charles d'Albert, Duc de Luynes (b. Pont Saint-Esprit 5 Aug 1578; d. 15 Dec 1621)

1624 – 4 Dec 1642: Richelieu

Chief Minister
Jean Armand Duplessis, Duc de Richelieu (b. Richelieu 5 Sep 1585; d. Paris 4 Dec 1642) Cardinal

1643 – 9 Mar 1661: Mazarin

Chief Minister
Jules Mazarin (b. Rome 14 Jul 1602; d. Vincennes 9 Mar 1661) Cardinal

Finance
1653 – Sep 1661: *Nicholas Fouquet* (b. Paris 27 Jan 1615; d. Pignerlo 23 Mar (?) (1680)

1661 – 6 Sep 1683: Colbert

Chief Minister
Jean Baptiste Colbert, Marquis de Seignelay (b. Rheims 29 Aug 1619; d. Paris 6 Sep 1683) Controller-General of Finance

Foreign Affairs
1661 – Jun 1671: *Hugues de Lionne, Marquis de Berni* (b. Grenoble 11 Oct 1611; d. Paris 1 Sep 1671)
Jun 1671 – Nov 1679: *Simon Arnauld, Marquis de Pomponne* (b. 1618; d. Fontainebleau Sep 1699)
1679 – 1696: *Charles, Marquis Colbert de Croissy* (b. 1625; d. 28 Jul 1696)

Justice
1661 – (?): —— *Voysin*

War
1666 – 1691: François Michel Le Tellier, Marquis de Louvois (b. Paris 18 Jan 1641; d. Versailles 16 Jul 1691)

1699 – 1715: Torcy

Chief Minister
Jean Baptiste Colbert, Marquis de Torcy (b. Paris 14 Sep 1665; d. Paris 2 Sep 1746)

1718 - 10 Aug 1723: Dubois

Chief Minister	*Guillaume Dubois* (b. Brive-la-Gaillarde 6 Sep 1656; d. Versailles 10 Aug 1723) Cardinal
Lord Chancellor	1718 – 1720: *Marc René, Marquis d'Argenson* (b. Venice 4 Nov 1652; d. Paris 8 May 1721)
Controller General of Finance	Jan – Jul 1720: *John Law of Lauriston* (b. Edinburgh 16 Apr 1671; d. Venice 21 Mar 1729)
Minister of State	1718 – 1733: *Louis Hector, Duc de Villars* (b. Moulins 8 May 1653; d. Turin 17 Jun 1734)

22 Aug - 2 Dec 1723: Orléans

Chief Minister	*Philippe, Duc d'Orléans* (b. St Cloud 2 Aug 1674; d. Versailles 2 Dec 1723) Regent

1724 - 11 Jun 1726: Bourbon et Condé

Chief Minister	*Louis Henri, Duc de Bourbon et de Condé* (b. Versailles 18 Aug 1692; d. Chantilly 27 Jan 1740)

1726 - 29 Jan 1743: Fleury

Chief Minister	*André Hercule de Fleury* (b. Lodève 22 Jun 1653; d. Issy 29 Jan 1743) Cardinal
Foreign Affairs	1737 – 1744: *Jean Jacques Amelot de Chaillou* (b. 30 Apr 1689; d. Paris 27 May 1749)
Minister of State	1726 – 20 Mar 1728: *Camille, Comte de Tallard, Marquis de la Baume d'Hostun* (b. Dauphiné 14 Feb 1652; d. Paris 20 Mar 1728)

18 Nov 1744 - 10 Jan 1747: Argenson

Chief Minister	*René Louis de Voyer de Paulmy, Marquis d'Argenson* (b. 18 Oct 1694; d. Paris 26 Jan 1757) Foreign Affairs
War	Feb 1743 – 1 Feb 1751: *Marc Pierre, Comte d'Argenson* (b. 16 Aug 1696; d. Paris 22 Aug 1764)
Finance	6 Dec 1745 – 28 Jul 1754: *Jean Baptiste de Machault d'Arnouville* (b. Paris 13 Dec 1701; d. Paris 12 Jul 1794)
Navy	3 May 1749 – Aug 1754; *Antoine Louis Rouillé, Comte de Juoy* (b. 1689; d. Neuilly 20 Sep 1761)

1754 - 25 Jun 1757: Jouy

Chief Minister	*Antoine Louis Rouillé, Comte de Jouy* (see Argenson) Foreign Affairs
War	1751 - 26 Jan 1761: *Charles Louis Auguste Fouquet, Duc de Belle-Isle* (b. Villefranche 22 Sep 1684; d. Pignerol 26 Jan 1761)
Navy	28 Jul 1754 - 1 Feb 1757: *Jean Baptiste de Machault d'Arnouville* (see Argenson)
Intendant of Commerce	1747 - 1759: *(Jean Claude Marie) Vincent de Gournay* (b. St Malo Mar 1712; d. 27 Jun 1759)

25 Jun 1757 - 1758: Bernis

Chief Minister	*François Joachim de Pierres de Bernis* (b. St Marcel 22 May 1715; d. Rome 2 Nov 1794) Foreign Affairs
Home Affairs and Administration of Paris	1757 - 1775: *Louis Prélypeaux, Comte de St Florentin* (from 1770: *Duc de la Vrillière*) (b. 18 Apr 1705; d. Paris 27 Feb 1777)

1758 - Dec 1770: Choiseul-Amboise

Chief Minister and Foreign Affairs	*Étienne François, Duc de Choiseul-Amboise* (b. 28 Jun 1719; d. Paris 8 May 1785)
Finance	4 Mar - 21 Nov 1759: *Étienne de Silhouette* (b. Limoges 5 Jul 1709; d. Brie-sur-Marne 20 Jan 1767)
Home Affairs	1757 - 1775: *Louis Prélypeaux, Comte de St Florentin* (see Bernis)

1770 - 1774: Triumvirate (Aiguillon/Maupeou/Terray)

	Armand Vigerol-Duplessis-Richelieu, Duc d' Aiguillon (b. 31 Jul 1720; d. 1782)
Chancellor	1768 - 1774: *René Nicolas Charles Augustin de Maupeou* (b. Paris 25 Feb 1714; d. Thuit 29 Jul 1792)
Finance	23 Dec 1769 - 24 Aug 1774: *Joseph-Marie Terray* (b. Boën Dec 1715; d. Paris 17 Feb 1778)
War	*Marquis de Monteynard*

1774 - 1778: Maurepas

Chief Minister	1774 - 21 Nov 1781: *Jean Frédéric Phélippeaux,*

	Comte de Maurepas (b. Versailles 9 Jul 1701; d. Versailles 21 Nov 1781)
	1781 – 1787: *Charles Gravier, Comte de Vergennes* (b. Dijon 28 Dec 1717; d. Versialles 13 Feb 1787)
	1787 – 1788: *Étienne Charles de Loménie de Brienne* (b. Paris 9 Oct 1727; d. Sens 15/16 Feb 1794) Cardinal
Foreign Affairs	1774 – 13 Feb 1787: *Charles Gravier, Comte de Vergennes* (see above)
	1787 – 12 Jul 1789: *Armand Marc, Comte de Montmorin Saint-Hérem* (b. 1745; d. Paris 2 Sep 1792)
Finance	24 Aug 1774 – 12 May 1776: *Anne Robert Jacques Turgot, Baron de l'Aulne* (b. Paris 10 May 1727; d. Paris 20 Mar 1781)
	Jun 1777 – 12 May 1781: *Jacques Necker* (b. Geneva 30 Sep 1732; d. Coppet 9 Apr 1804)
	1781 – Mar 1783: *Jean François Joly de Fleury* (b. Paris 1718; d. Paris 1802)
	30 Mar – 3 Nov 1783: *Henri François de Paule Le Fèvre d'Ormesson, Marquis d'Amboile* (b. 8 May 1751; d. Paris 1807)
	Nov 1783 – 1787: *Charles Alexandre de Calonne* (b. Douai 20 Jan 1734; d. Paris 29 Oct 1802)
	1 May 1787 – 25 Aug 1788: *Étienne Charles de Loménie de Brienne*, Cardinal (see above)
Home Affairs	1775 – 12 May 1776: *Chrétien Guillaume de Lamoignon de Malesherbes* (b. Paris 6 Dec 1721; d. Paris 22 Apr 1794)
	May 1776 – 16 Jul 1789: *Charles Louis François de Paul de Barentin* (b. 1 Jul 1736; d. Paris 30 May 1819)
Justice	1774 – 1787: *Armand Thomas Huc de Miromesnil* (b. Orléans 1723; d. Miromesnil 1796)
	1787 – 1788: *Chrétien François de Lamoignon* (b. Paris 18 Dec 1735; d. 15 May 1789)
War	25 Oct 1775 – 1777: *Charles Louis, Comte de Saint-Germain* (b. Vertamboz 15 Apr 1707; d. Paris 15 Jan 1778)
Lord Chamberlain	1783 – 1787: *Louis Auguste Le Tonnelier, Baron de Breteuil* (b. Preuilly 1733; d. 2 Nov 1807)

Aug 1788 – 1790: Necker

Chief Minister and Finance	Aug 1788 – 11 Jul 1789: *Jacques Necker* (see Maurepas)

Chief Minister	11 – 14 Jul 1789: *Louis Auguste Le Tonnelier, Baron de Breteuil* (see Maurepas) 14 Jul 1789 – Sep 1790: *Jacques Necker* (see Maurepas)

Sep 1790 – Feb 1791: Constitutional Ministry

Chief Minister	*Armand Marc, Comte de Montmorin Saint-Hérem* (see Maurepas)

Feb 1791 – 10/12 Mar 1792: The Feuillants

Chief Minister	*Antoine de Valdec de Lessart* (b. 1742; d. Versailles 9 Sep 1792)
Foreign Affairs	Jul 1789 – 20 Nov 1791: *Armand Marc, Comte de Montmorin Saint-Hérem* (see Maurepas) 20 Nov 1791 – 10 Mar 1792: *Antoine de Valdec de Lessart* (see above)
Home Affairs	16 Jul 1789 – 1790: *François Emmanuel Guignart, Comte de Saint-Priest* (b. Grenoble 12 March 1735; d. Lyon 26 Feb 1821) Jan – 20 Nov 1791: *Antoine de Valdec de Lessart* (see above) 20 Nov 1791 – 15 Mar 1792: *Bon Claude Cahier de Gerville* (b. Bayeux 30 Nov 1751; d. 15 Feb 1796)
Finance	Feb – 14 Jul 1789: *Charles Guillaume Lambert* (for 1st time) (b. 1726; d. 1813) (acting:) Controller General 14 Jul 1789 – Sep 1790: *Jacques Necker* (see Maurepas) Sep – (?) Nov 1790: *Charles Guillaume Lambert* (Controller General) (for 2nd time) Dec 1790 – Jan 1791: *Antoine de Valdec de Lessart* (see above) 18 (?28) May 1791 – 15 Mar 1792: *Louis Hardouin Tarbé* (b. Sens 11 Aug 1753; d. Sens 7 Jul 1806)
Justice	Aug 1788 – May 1789: *Charles de Barentin* (see Maurepas) 3 Aug 1789 – 20 Nov 1790: *Jérome Marie Champion de Cicé* (b. Rennes 3 Sep 1735; d. Aix 19 Aug 1810) 20 Nov 1790 – Mar 1792; *Marguerite Louis François Duport-Dutertre* (b. Paris 6 May 1754; d. Paris 28 Nov 1793)
War	30 Nov 1788 – 12 Jul 1789: *Pierre Louis de Chastenet,*

	Comte de Peységur (b. Rabastens 30 Dec 1727; d. Oct 1807) 12 Jul – 14 Aug 1789: *Victor François, Duc de Broglie* (b. 19 Oct 1718; d. Munster 30 Mar 1804) 4 Aug 1789 – Nov 1790: *Jean Frédéric de la Tour du Pin* (b. 1727; d. 1794) 16 Nov 1790 – 6 Dec 1791: *Lebègue Duportail* (b. Pithiviers 1743; d. at sea 1802) 6 Dec 1791 – 9 Mar 1792: *Louis Comte de Narbonne-Lara* (b. Colomo 24 Aug 1755; d. Torgau 17 Nov 1813)
Navy	27 Oct 1790 – 17 May 1791: *Charles Pierre Claret, Comte de Fleurieu* (b. Lyons 1738; d. 1810) May – Oct 1791: *Antoine Jean Marie Thévenard* (b. St Malo 7 Dec 1733; d. Paris 9 Feb 1815) Oct 1791 – Mar 1792: *Antoine François Bertrand de Molleville* (b. Toulouse 1744; d. Paris 1818)

15 Mar – 13 Jun 1792: Roland (Girondist Ministry)

Chief Minister and Home Affairs	*Jean Marie Roland de la Platière* (b. Thizy 18 Feb 1734; d. Rouen 10 Nov 1793)

15 Jun – 10 Aug 1792: Coalition of Feuillants and Girondists

12 Aug 1792 – 6 Apr 1793: Executive Committee (of Girondist-Montagnard Coalition)

Leader	12 Aug – 12 Sep 1792: *Georges Danton* (b. Arcis-sur-Aube 28 Oct 1759; d. (guillotined) Paris 5 Apr 1794) 12 Sep 1792 – 25 Jan 1793: *Jean Marie Roland de la Platière* (see Roland)
Foreign Affairs	16 Jun – 10 Aug 1792: *Victor Scipion Louis Joseph de la Garde* (b. 1750; d. Paris 1829 (?)) 12 Aug 1792 – 6 Apr 1793: *Barthélemy Louis Joseph Lebrun-Tondu* (b. Noyon 1763 or 1764; d. Paris Jun 1793)
War	15 Mar/9 May – 13 Jun 1792: *Joseph Servan de Gerbey* (for 1st time) (b. Romans 1741; d. Paris 1808) 15 – 18 Jun 1792: *Charles François Dumouriez* (b. Cambrai 25 Jan 1739; d. Turville Park, Buckinghamshire, 14 Mar 1823) 12 Jul – 3 Oct 1792: *Joseph Servan de Gerbey* (for 2nd time)

18 Oct 1792 – 2 Feb 1793; *Jean Nicolas Pache* (b. Paris 1746; d. Thin-le-Moutier 18 Nov 1823)

14 – 31 Mar 1793: *Pierre Riel* (from 1808: *Comte Beurnonville*) (b. Champignolles 10 May 1752; d. 23 Apr 1821)

1 – 4 Apr 1793: *Barthélemy Louis Joseph Lebrun-Tondu* (see above)

Navy 15 Mar – 10 Jul 1792: *Jean, Baron de Lacoste* (b. Dax 1730; d. 1820)

12 Aug 1792 – Apr 1793: *Gaspard Monge* (b. Beaune 10 May 1746; d. 18 Jul 1818)

Justice 13 Apr – 3 Jul 1792: *Antoine Duranthon* (b. Mussiden 1736; d. Bordeaux 20 Dec 1793)

10 Aug – 11 Oct 1792: *Georges Danton* (see above)

9 Dec 1792 – 13 Mar 1792: *Dominique Joseph* (from 1804: *Comte*) *Garat* (b. Bayonne 9 Sep 1749; d. Ustaritz 9 Dec 1833)

Finance (Public Contributions) 23 Mar – 13 Jun 1792: 12 Aug 1792 – 2 Jun 1793: *Etienne Clavière* (b. Geneva 27 Jan 1735; d. Paris 8 Dec 1793)

6 Apr 1793 – 27 Oct 1795: Committee of Public Safety

President 10/27 Jul 1793 – 27 Jul 1794: *Maximilien Robespierre* (b. Arras 6 May 1758; d. (guillotined) Paris 28 Jul 1794)

Foreign Affairs 10 Apr – 10 Jul 1793: *Georges Danton*, Chairman (see Executive Committee)

10 Jul 1793 – 30 Mar 1794: *Marie Jean Hérault de Séchelles* (b. Paris 1760; d. Paris 5 Apr 1794) Chairman

21 Jun 1793 – 2 Apr 1794: *François Louis Michel Chemin Deforgues* (b. Vire 29 Sep 1759; d. Mainey 10 Oct 1840) Minister

Home Affairs 14 Mar – 15 Aug 1793: *Joseph Garat* (see Executive Committee)

Justice 20 Mar 1793 –(?)27 Oct 1795: *Louis Jérôme Gohier* (b. Semblançay 1746; d. Montmorency 29 May 1830)

Finance 10 Apr – 10 Jul 1793: *Joseph Cambon* (b. Montpellier 17 Jun 1754; d. Brussels 5 Feb 1820)

War 4 Apr 1793 – Apr 1794: *Jean Baptiste Noel Bouchotte* (b. Metz 25 Dec 1754; d. 8 Apr 1840)

14 Aug 1793 – 26 Oct 1795: *Lazare Nicolas Marguerite*

(from 1815: *Comte*) *Carnot* (b. Nolay 13 May 1753; d. Magdeburg 3 Aug 1823) Chairman of Military Committee

10 Jul 1793 – 4 Apr 1795: *Pierre Louis Prieur de la Marne* (b. Sommesous 1 Aug 1756; d. Brussels 31 May 1827)

Navy   Apr – Jul (?) 1793: —— *Dalbarède*

10 Jul 1793 – 26 Oct 1795: *André Jeanbon Saint-André* (b. Montaubon 25 Feb 1749; d. Mainz 10 Dec 1813) Committee Chairman

Inquisition   6 Sep 1793 – Aug 1794: *Jean Nicolas Billaud-Varennes* (b. La Rochelle 23 Apr 1765; d. Haiti 3 Jun 1819) and *Jean Marie Collot d'Herbois* (b. Paris about 1750; d. Cayenne 8 Jan 1796)

Public Security   10 Jul 1793 – 27 Jul 1794: *Georges Couthon* (b. Orcet 1756; d. Paris 28 Jul 1794)

28 Oct 1795 – 9 Nov 1799: Directorate

1795 – 1799: *Paul Jean François Nicolas, Comte de Barras* (b. Fox-Amphous 30 Jun 1755; d. Chaillot 29 Jan 1829)

1795 – 16 May 1799: *Jean François Rewbell* (b. Kolmar 8 Oct 1747; d. Kolmar(?) 23 Nov 1807)

28 Oct 1795 – Jun 1799: *Louis Marc de Larevellière-Lépeaux* (b. Montaigne 14 Aug 1753; d. Paris 27 Mar 1824)

28 Oct 1795 – 9 Nov 1799: *Charles Louis François Honoré Le Tourneur* (b. Granville 1751; d. Laeken 1817)

1795 – 4 Sep 1797: *Lazare Nicolas Marguerite* (from 1815: *Comte*) *Carnot* (see Committee of Public Safety)

1795 – 4 Sep 1797: *François, Marquis de Barthélemy* (b. Aubagne 20 Oct 1747; d. 23 Apr 1830)

4 Sep – Dec (?) 1797: *Nicolas Louis* (from 1804: Comte) *François* (b. Saffay 17 Apr 1750; d. 10 Jan 1828)

4 Sep 1797 – 18 Jun 1799: *Philippe Antoine* (from 1804(?) *Comte*) *Merlin de Douai* (b. Arleux 30 Oct 1754; d. 26 Dec 1838)

15 May – Aug 1798: *Jean Baptiste* (from 1806: *Comte*) *Treilhard* (b. Brive 3 Jan 1742; d. Paris 1 Dec 1810)

18 Jun – 9 Nov 1799: *Louis Jérôme Gohier* (see Committeee of Public Safety)

20 Jun – 9 Nov 1799: *Jean François Auguste Moulin* (b. Caen 14 Mar 1752; d. Pierrefitte 12 Mar 1810)

Jun 1799 – 9 Nov 1799: *Roger* (from 1815: *Comte*) *Ducos* (b. Dax 23 Jul 1754; d. Ulm 16 Mar 1816)

May 1799: *Emanuel Joseph* (from 1809: *Comte*) *Sieyès* (b. Fréjus 3 May 1748; d. Paris 20 Jun 1836)

3 Nov 1795 – 16 Jul 1797: *Charles Delacroix de Constant* (b. Givny-en-Argonne 15 Apr 1741; d. Bordeaux 26 Oct 1805)

Foreign Affairs Jul 1797 – Jul 1799: *Charles Maurice* (from 1807: *Duc*) *de Talleyrand-Périgord* (from 1806: *Prince of Benevento*; from 1815: *Duc de Dino*) (b. Paris 13 Feb 1754; d. Paris 17 May 1838)

Jul – Nov 1799: *Karl Friedrich* (from 1808: *Count*) *Reinhard* (b. Schondorf 2 Oct 1761; d. Paris 25 Dec 1837)

Home Affairs 3 Nov 1795 – 31 Jul 1797: *Pierre Bénézech* (b. 1749; d. Cap 13 Jun 1802)

Aug – Sep 1797: *Nicolas Louis François* (see above)

22 Jun 1798 – 25 Dec 1799: *Nicolas Marie Quinnette, Baron de Rochemont* (b. Paris 16 Sep 1762; d. Brussels 14 Jun 1821)

Justice 14 Nov 1795 – Jan 1796: *Philippe Antoine Merlin de Douai* (see above)

5 Jan – 3 Apr 1796: *Jean Joseph Victor Génissieu* (*x*?) (b. Dauphiné 1740 or Chabeuil 29 Oct 1749; d. Paris 11 Oct 1804)

3 Apr 1796 – 4 Sep 1797: *Philippe Antoine Merlin de Douai* (see above)

24 Sep 1797 – 20 Jul 1799: *Charles Joseph Mathieu Lambrechts* (b. Sint-Truiden 1753; d. Paris 1823)

Finance 4 – 7 Nov 1795: *Marc Michel Charles Gaudin* (from 1809: *Duc de Gaeta*) (b. Saint-Denis 16 Jan 1756; d. Gennevilliers 5 Nov 1841)

8 Nov 1795 – 15 Jan 1796: *Guillaume Charles Faypoult* (b. Champagne 1752; d. Paris Oct 1817)

24 Sep 1797 – 18 Jun 1799: *Dominique Vincent Ramel de Nogaret* (b. Montolien 3 Nov 1760; d. Brussels 31 Mary 1829)

18 Jun – 9 Nov 1799: *Robert Lindet* (b. Bernay 1749; d. Paris 17 Feb 1825)

War

3 Nov 1795 – 7 Feb 1796: *Jean Baptiste Annibal Aubert du Bayer* (b. Louisiana 29 Aug 1739; d. Istanbul 17 Dec 1797)

8 Feb 1796 – 18 Jul 1797: *Claude Petiet* (b. Chatillon-sur-Seine 9 Feb 1749; d. Paris 25 May 1806)

26 Jul 1797 – 1799: *Barthélemy (Louis Joseph) Schérer* (b. Delle 18 Dec 1747; d. Chauny 19 Aug 1804)

21 Feb – 2 Jul 1799: *Louis Marie Antoine Destouff* (from 1809: *Baron Millet de Mureau*) (b. Toulon 26 Jun 1756: d. Paris 6 May 1825)

2 Jul – 14 Sep 1799: *Jean Baptiste Jules Bernadotte* (later: King Charles XIV of Sweden) (b. Pau 26 Jan 1763; d. Stockholm 8 Mar 1844)

14 Sep – 9 Nov 1799: *Edmond Louis Alexis Dubois de Crancé* (b. Charleville 1726; d. Rethel 1814)

Navy

1 Nov 1795 – 1797: *Laurent Jean François Truguet* (b. Toulon 1752; d. Paris 1839)

16 Jul 1797 – 28 Apr 1798: *George René Pleville-le-Pelley* (b. Granville 1726; d. Paris 1805)

28 Apr 1798 – 6 Jul 1799: *Eustache Bruix* (b. Santo Domingo 17 Jul 1759; d. Paris 17 Mar 1805)

6 Jul – 25 Dec 1799: *Marc Antoine Bourdon de Vatry* (b. Saint-Maur-des-Fossés 24 Nov 1761; d. Paris 20(?) 22 Apr 1828)

Police

Jan – 3 Apr 1796: *Philippe Antoine Merlin de Douai* (see above)

3 Apr 1796 – 16 Jul 1797: *Charles* (from 1813: *Comte*) *Cochon de Lapparent* (b. Champdeniers 24 Jan 1750; d. Poitiers 17 Jul 1825)

16 – 26 Jul 1797: *Jean Jacques* (from 1808: *Comte*) Lenoir-Laroche (b. Grenoble 29 Apr 1749; d. Paris 17 Feb 1825)

26 Jul 1797 – 13 Feb 1798: *Louis Jérôme Gohier* (see Committee of Public Safety)

13 Feb – 16 May 1798: *Nicolas Dondeau* (b. Fontaine-Denis 1751)

16 May – 29 Oct 1798: *Marie Jean François Philibert Le Carlier* (b. Laon 20 Nov 1752; d. Paris 22 Jul 1799)

Oct (?) Nov 1798 – 23 Jun 1799: *Jean Pierre Duval* (b. Rouen 20 Feb 1754; d. Paris 15 Aug 1817)

23 Jun – 20 Jul 1799: *Claude Sébastien Louis Félix Bourguignon (-Dumolard)* (b. La Ferrière-du-Gua 18 Mar 1760; d. Paris 23 Apr 1829)

20 Jul 1799 – (?) 1802: *Joseph* (from 1805: *Comte*

Fouché (from 1806: *Duc d'Otranto*) (b. Pellerin 21
May 1759; d. Trieste 25 Dec 1820)

9 Nov 1799 – 4 Aug 1802: Consulate

Consuls   9 Nov 1799 – 18 May 1804: *Napoleon Bonaparte* (later
Emperor Napoleon I) (see Heads of State) from 4 Aug
1802: sole Consul for Life
9 Nov – 27 Dec 1799: *Emanuel Joseph Sieyès* (see
Directorate)
9 Nov – 27 Dec 1799: *Roger Ducos* (see Directorate)
27 Dec 1799/7 Feb 1800 – 4 Aug 1802: *Jean Jacques
Régis de Cambacérès* (from 1808: *Duc de Parma*) (b.
Montpellier 18 Oct 1753; d. Paris 8 Mar 1824)
27 Dec 1799/7 Feb 1800 – 4 Aug 1802: *Charles
François Lebrun* (from 1807: *Duc de Plaisance*) (b. St
Sauveur-Landelin 19 Mar 1739; d. St Mesme 16 Jun
1824)

Foreign Affairs   (see 1804 – 1814: Empire)

Home Affairs   9 Nov – Dec 1799 *(Pierre) Simon* (from 1804: *Comte*;
from 1817: *Marquis*) *Laplace* (b. Beaumont en Aug 28
Mar 1749; d. Paris 5 Mar 1827)
Dec 1799 – Nov 1800: *Lucien Bonaparte* (b. Ajaccio 21
Mar 1775; d. Viterbo 29 Jun 1840)
Nov 1800 – 8 Aug 1804: *Jean Antoine Chaptal* (from
1811: *Comte de Chanteloup*) (b. Nojaret 5 Jun 1756; d.
Paris 30 Jul 1832)

Education   1801 – 4 Aug 1802: *Antoine François* (from 1802(?):
Comte de Fourcroy) (b. 15 Jun 1755; d. 16 Dec 1809)

Finance   10 Nov 1799 – (?) 1 Apr 1814: *Marc Michel Charles
Gaudin, Duc de Gaeta* (b. St Denis 16 Jan 1756; d.
Gennevilliers 5 Nov 1841)

Justice   (?) 18 Jun 1799 – Dec 1799: *Jean Jacques Régis de
Cambacérès* (see above)
Dec 1799 – 1802: *André Joseph, Comte Abrial* (b.
Annonçay 19 Mar 1750; d. Paris 14 Nov 1828)

War   9 Nov 1799 – (?) Apr 1800: *Alexandre Berthier* (from
1806: *Duc de Neuchatel*; from 1809: *Prince de
Wagram*) (b. Versailles 20 Feb 1753; d. Bamberg 1 Jun
1815)
April – end of 1800: *Lazare Nicolas Marguerite
Carnot* (see Directorate)

Navy (and Colonies) end of 1800 – (?) 1807: *Alexandre Berthier* (see above)

Nov 1799 – 1801: *Pierre Alexandre Laurent Forfait* (b. Rouen 1752; d. Rouen 8 Nov 1807)

1801 – (?) 1814: *Denis, Duc de Decrès* (b. Chateauvillain 22 Jun 1761; d. 7 Dec 1820)

Police   see Directorate

1804 – 1814: Empire

Foreign Affairs

(?) 1799 – 8 Aug 1807: *Charles Maurice* (from 1807: *Duc) de Talleyrand-Périgord* (see Directorate)

8 Aug 1807 – 16 Apr 1811: *Jean Baptiste Nompère de Champagny* (from 1808: *Duc de Cadore*) (b. Roanne 4 Aug 1756; d. Paris 3 Jul 1834)

1811 – Nov 1813: *Hughes Bernard Maret, Duc de Bassano* (b. Dijon 1 Mar 1763; d. Paris 13 May 1839)

Nov 1813 – 31 Mar 1814: *Armand Augustin Louis de Caulaincourt, Duc de Vicenza* (b. Caulaincourt 9 Dec 1773; d. Paris 19 Feb 1927)

War

(?) End of 1800 – 1807: *Alexandre Berthier* (see Consulate)

1807 – 1814: *Henri Jacques Guillaume Clarke* (from 1808: *Duc de Feltre*) (b. Landrecies 17 Oct 1765; d. 28 Oct 1818)

Director of War Effort

1802 – 1809: *Jean François Aimé, Comte Dejean* (b. Castelnaudary 6 Oct 1749; d. Paris 12 May 1824)

1809 – 1813: *Jean Girard Lacuée, Comte Cessac* (b. La Massas 4 Nov 1752; d. Paris 14 Jun 1841)

Navy

(?) 1801 – 1814: *Denis, Duc de Decrès* (see Consulate)

Justice

25 Sep 1802 – 1813: *Claude Ambroise Régnier* (from 1809: *Duc de Massa*) (b. Blamont 6 Apr 1736; d. 24 Jun 1814)

1813 – 31 Mar 1814: *Louis Mattieu*, Comte Molé (b. Paris 24 Jan 1781; d. Champlatreux 25 Nov 1855)

Finance

Marc Michel Charles Gaudin (see Consulate)

Police

Jul 1804 – 3 Jun 1810: *Joseph* (from 1805: *Comte) Fouché* (from 1806: *Duc d'Otranto*) (see Directorate)

1810 – 1814: *Anne Jean Marie René Savary, Duc de Rovigo* (b. Mar 26 Apr 1774; d. Paris 2 Jun 1833)

Home Affairs

Aug 1804 – Aug 1807: *Jean Baptiste Nompère de Champagny* (see above)

9 Aug 1807 – 1 Oct 1809: *Emmanuel Cretet, Comte Champmol* (b. Pont-de-Beuvoisin 10 Feb 1747; d. Auteuil 28 Nov 1809)

	1 Oct 1809 – 31 Mar 1814; *Jean Pierre Bachasson Comte Montalivet* (b. Neukirch 5 Jul 1766; d. Lagrange 23 Jan 1823)
Education and Public Worship	Mar 1802 – Jul 1804: *Pierre Louis* (from 1809: *Comte*) *Roederer* (b. Metz 15 Feb 1754; d. 17 Dec 1835)
	Jul 1804 – 25 Aug 1807: *Jean Étienne Marie Portalis* (b. Le Beausset 1 Apr 1746; d. 25 Aug 1807)
	Jan 1808 – 31 Mar 1814: *Félix Julien Jean, Comte Bigot de Préameneu* (b. Rennes 26 Feb 1747; d. Paris 31 Jul 1825)
Postmaster General	1800 – 31 Mar 1814: *Marie Chamans*, (from 1804: *Comte Lavalette*) (b. Paris 1769; d. Paris 15 Feb 1830)
Minister of State	1809 – 1814: *Bernard Germain Étienne de Laville, Comte de Lacépède* (b. Agen 26 Dec 1756; d. Épinay 6 Oct 1825)
Secretary of State and Minister	1804 – 1811: *Hughes Bernard Maret* (see above)
	1811 – 1813: *Pierre Antoine Bruno, Comte Daru* (b. Montpellier 12 Jan 1767; d. Becheville 5 Sep 1829)
	1813: Minister
	21 Apr 1811 – Apr 1814: *Jean Baptiste Nompère de Champagny* (see above)

13 May 1814 – 30 Mar 1815: Blacas

Prime Minister	*Pierre Louis, Duc de Blacas d'Aulps* (b. Château Vérignon 12 Jan 1771; d. Schloss Kirchberg, Lower Austria 17 Nov 1839) continued in exile in Ghent until the end of June 1815
Foreign Affairs	13 May 1814 – 20 Mar 1815: *Charles Maurice, Duc de Talleyrand-Périgord* (see Directorate)
	François René, Vicomte de Chateaubriand (b. St Malo 4 Sep 1768; d. Paris 4 Jul 1848) in exile
Home Affairs	*François Xavier Marc Antoine, Duc de Montesquiou-Fezensac* (b. Château Marsan 13 Aug 1759; d. Château Cirey-sur-Blaise 5 Feb 1832)
Finance	*Joseph Dominique, Baron Louis* (b. 13 Nov 1755; d. Brie-sur-Marne 26 Aug 1837)
War	*Henri Jacques Guillaume Clarke, Duc de Feltre* (see Empire)
Navy	*Jacques Claude, Comte Beugnot* (b. Bar-sur-Aube 1761; d. Bagneux 24 Jun 1835)
Education	*Trophime Gérard, Marquis de Lally-Tollendal* (b. Paris 5 Mar 1751; d. 11 Mar 1830)

175

| Minister of State | *Jean Antoine Chaptal, Comte de Chanteloup* (see Consulate) |

20 Mar – End Jun 1815: Ministry of Napoleon I

Prime Minister	*Benjamin Constant de Rebeque* (b. Lausanne 23 Oct 1767; d. Paris 8 Dec 1830)
Foreign Affairs	20 Mar – 18 Jun 1815: *Armand Augustin Louis de Caulaincourt* (see Empire) 18 Jun – end of Jun 1815: *Louis Pierre Édouard* (from 1837: *Baron) Bignon* (b. Guerbaville 3 Jan 1771; d. Paris 5 Jan 1841)
Home Affairs	*Lazare, Comte Carnot* (see Directorate)
Justice	*Jean Jacques Régis de Cambacérès* (see Consulate)
Public Worship	*Félix, Comte Bigot de Préameneu* (see Empire)
Finance	*Marc Michel Charles Gaudin* (see Consulate)
War	*Louis Nicolas Davout* (from 1808: *Duke of Auerstädt*; from 1809: *Prince of Eckmühl*) (b. Annoux 10 May 1770; d. Paris 1 Jun 1823)
Navy	*Denis, Duc de Decrès* (see Consulate)
Police	*Joseph Fouché, Duc d'Otranto* (see Empire)
Post	*Marie Chamans, Comte Lavalette* (see Empire)

8 Jul – 24 Sep 1815: Caretaker Government

Foreign Affairs	*Charles Maurice, Duc de Talleyrand-Périgord* (see Directorate)
Police	*Joseph Fouché, Duc d'Otranto* (see Empire)
Finance	*Louis Emmanuel* (from 1810: *Comte) Corvetto* (b. Genoa 11 Jul 1756; d. Genoa 24 May 1821)
Justice	*Étienne Denis* (from 1821: *Baron*; from 1844: *Duc) de Pasquier* (b. Paris 22 Apr 1767; d. Paris 5 Jul 1862)

24 Sep 1815 – Dec 1818: Richelieu I

Prime Minister	*Armand du Plessis, Duc de Richelieu* (for 1st time) (b. Paris 25 Sep 1766; d. Paris 17 May 1822)
Finance	*Louis Emmanuel, Comte Corvetto* (see Caretaker Government)
Justice	24 Sep 1815 – 10 May 1816: *François, Marquis Barbe-Marbois* (b. Metz 31 Jan 1745; d. 12 Feb 1837) 1817 – Dec 1818: *Étienne Denis de Pasquier* (see Caretaker Government)

War	24 Sep 1815 – 1817: *Henri Jacques Guillaume Clarke, Duc de Feltre* (see Empire)
	1817 – Dec 1818: *Laurent Gouvion, Marquis de Saint Cyr* (b. Toul 16 Apr 1764; d. Hyères 17 Mar 1830)
Police	*Élie, Comte* (from 1820: *Duc*) *de Decazes* (b. Saint-Martin-de-Laye 28 Sep 1780; d. Decazeville 24 Oct 1860)
Navy	1817 – 1818: *Louis Matthieu, Comte Molé* (see Empire)
Education	*Pierre Paul Royer-Collard* (b. Sompuis 21 Jun 1763; d. Châteauvieux 4 Sep 1845)
Minister of State	*Emmerich Josef, Duc de Dalberg* (b. Mainz 30 May 1773; d. Herrnsheim 27 Apr 1833)
	Charles Nicolas Oudinot, Duc de Reggio (b. Bar-le-Duc 25 Apr 1767; d. Paris 13 Sep 1847)
	Louis Antoine Fauvelet de Bourrienne (b. Sens 9 Jul 1769; d. Caen 7 Feb 1834)

28 Dec 1818 – Nov 1819: Dessolles

Prime Minister	*Jean Joseph Paul Augustin, Marquis Dessolles* (b. Auch 3 Oct 1767; d. Montluchet 3 Nov 1828)
Foreign Affairs	*Jean, Marquis Dessolles* (see above)
Home Affairs	*Élie, Comte de Decazes* (see Richelieu I)
War	*Laurent Gouvion, Marquis de Saint Cyr* (see Richelieu I)
Finance	*Joseph Dominique, Baron Louis* (see Blacas)
Justice	1818 – 1820: *Pierre, Comte de Serre* (b. Pagny 1776; d. Castellamare di Stabia 1824)

16 Nov 1819 – Feb 1820: Decazes

Prime Minister	*Élie, Comte de Decazes* (see Richelieu I)
Foreign Affairs	*Étienne Denis, Baron de Pasquier* (see Caretaker Government)
War	*Marie Victor Nicolas Fay, Marquis de Latour-Maubourg* (b. La Motte-Gaulure 22 May 1768: d. Château de Lys 11 Nov 1850)
Finance	*Antoine, Comte Roy* (b. Savigny 1764; d. 1847)
Justice	*Pierre, Comte de Serre* (see Dessolles)

18 Feb 1820 – 19 Dec 1821: Richelieu II

Prime Minister	*Armand du Plessis, Duc de Richelieu* (for 2nd time) (see Richelieu I)
Foreign Affairs	*Étienne Denis, Baron de Pasquier* (see Caretaker Government)
Home Affairs	*Joseph Jérôme, Comte Siméon* (b. Aix-en-Provence 30 Sep 1749; d. Paris 19 Jan 1842)
Education	*Charles Ignance* (from 1822: *Comte*) *Peyronet* (b. Bordeaux 9 Oct 1778; d. Château de Montferrand 2 Jan 1854)
Navy	Dec 1820 – 19 Dec 1821: *Aimé Marie Gaspard, Marquis* (later: *Duc*) *de Clermont-Tonnerre* (b. Paris 27 Nov 1779; d. Château de Glisselles 8 Jan 1865)
Chamberlain	*Alexandre Jacques Bernard Law* (from 1809: *Comte Lauriston*) (b. Pondichery, India, 1 Feb 1768; d. Paris 10 Jun 1828)

19 Dec 1821 – 4 Jan 1828: Villèle

Prime Minister	*Joseph, Comte de Villèle* (b. Toulouse 14 Apr 1773; d. Toulouse 13 Mar 1854)
Foreign Affairs	24 Dec 1821 – 28 Dec 1822: *Matthieu Jean Félicité, Duc de Montmorency-Laval* (b. Paris 10 Jul 1760; d. 24 Mar 1826)
	28 Dec 1822 – 6 Jun 1824: *François René, Vicomte de Chateaubriand* (see Blacas)
	6 Jun – Oct 1824: *Joseph, Comte de Villèle* (see above)
	Oct 1824 – 4 Jan 1828: *Ange Hyacinthe Maxence, Baron Damas* (b. Paris 30 Sep 1785; d. 6 May 1862)
Home Affairs	*Jacques Joseph Guillaume Pierre, Comte de Corbière* (b. Amanlis 1767; d. Rennes 1853)
Finance	*Joseph, Comte de Villèle* (see above)
Justice	*Charles Ignace, Comte Peyronet* (see Richelieu II)
War	19 Dec 1821 – 19 Oct 1823: *Claude Victor-Perrin* (from 1807: *Duc de Belluno*) (b. Lamarche 7 Dec 1764; d. 1 Mar 1841)
	1823 – 1824: Aimé Marie Gaspard, Duc de Clermont-Tonnerre (see Richelieu II)
	1824 – Oct 1824: *Ange, Baron Damas* (see above)
	Oct 1824 – 4 Jan 1828: *Aimé Marie Gaspard, Duc de Clermont-Tonnerre* (see Richelieu II)
Navy	1821–1824: *Aimé Marie Gaspard, Duc de Clermont-Tonnerre* (see Richelieu II)

	4 Aug 1824 – 1828: *Andre Jean Christophe, Comte Chabrol* (b. Riom 16 Nov 1771; d. Chabannes 7 Aug 1836)
Public Worship	1824: *Denis, Comte Frayssinous* (b. Curières 9 May 1765; d. St Geniès 12 Dec 1841)
Chamberlain	19 Dec 1821 – 1824: *Alexandre Jacques Bernard Law, Comte Lauriston* (see Richelieu II)
	1824 – 4 Jan 1828: *Ambroise Polycarpe de la Rochefoucauld, Duc de Doudeauville* (b. Paris 2 Apr 1765; d. 1841)

4 Jan 1828 – 8 Aug 1829: Martignac

Prime Minister	*Jean Baptiste Gay, Vicomte de Martignac* (b. Bordeaux 20 Jun 1778; d. Paris 3 Apr 1832)
Foreign Affairs	4 Jan 1828 – 24 Apr 1829: *Pierre Louis Auguste Ferron, Comte de la Ferronnays* (b. St Malo 4 Dec 1777; d. Rome 17 Jan 1842)
	24 Apr – 7 Aug 1829: *Joseph Marie, Comte Portalis* (b. Aix 19 Feb 1778; d. Passy 4 Aug 1858)
Home Affairs	*Jean, Vicomte de Martignac* (see above)
Finance	*Antoine, Comte Roy* (see Decazes)
War	—— *de Caux*
Justice	4 Jan 1828 – May 1829: *Joseph, Comte Portalis* (see above)
Public Worship	14 May – 8 Aug 1829: *Pierre Alpinien Bertrand Bourdeau* (b. Rochechouart 18 Mar 1770; d. 12 Jul 1845)
	4 Jan 1828 – 3 Mar 1829: *Denis, Comte Frayssinous* (see Villèle)
	3 Mar – 8 Aug 1829: *Jean François Hyacinthe Feutrier* (b. Paris 1775; d. 1830)
Education	*Antoine François Henri Lefebvre de Vatimesnil* (b. Rouen 1789; d. 1860)
Navy	*Jean Guillaume Hyde de Neuville, Comte de Bemposta* (b. 24 Jan 1776; d. 28 May 1857)

8 Aug 1829 – 29 Jul 1830: Polignac

Prime Minister	*Jules (Auguste Armande Marie) Prince de Polignac* (b. 14 May 1780; d. Paris 29 Mar 1847)
Foreign Affairs	*Jules, Prince de Polignac* (see above)

FRANCE

Home Affairs	8 Aug – 18 Nov 1829: *François Régis, Comte de Labourdonnaye* (b. Angers 19 Mar 1767; d. Château de Mésangeau 28 Aug 1839) 18 Nov 1829 – 19 May 1830: *Guillaume Isidore Baron, Comte de Montbel* (b. Toulouse 4 Jul 1787; d. Vienna 3 Feb 1861) 19 May – 29 Jul 1830: *Charles Ignace, Comte Peyronet* (see Richelieu II)
Justice	8 Aug 1829 – 19 May 1830: *Jean Joseph Antoine Courvoisier* (b. Besançon 30 Nov 1775, d. Lyon 18 Sep 1835) 19 May – 29 Jul 1830: —— *Chautelauze*
Finance	8 Aug 1829 – 19 May 1830: *André, Comte Chabrol* (see Villèle) 19 May – 29 Jul 1830: *Guillaume Baron, Comte Montbel* (see above)
Public Worship	8 Aug – 18 Nov 1829: *Guillaume Baron, Comte Montbel* (see above) 18 Nov 1829 – 29 Jul 1830: *Martial, Comte Guernon de Ranville* (b. Caen 2 May 1787; d. Château de Ranville 30 Nov 1866)
Buildings and Public Works (new post)	19 May – 29 Jul 1830: *Guillaume Antoine Benoît, Baron Capelle* (b. Salles-Coran 9 Sep 1775; d. Montpellier Oct 1843)
War	*Louis Auguste Victor de Chaisne, Comte Bourmont* (b. Château de Bourmont 2 Sep 1773; d. 27 Oct 1846)
Navy	*Jean Guillaume Hyde de Neuville, Comte de Bemposta* (see Martignac)

29 Jul 1830: Mortemart (unable to form ministry)

Victor-Louis-Victurnien, Duc de Mortemart (b. Colmenil 12 Aug 1783; d. Paris 29 Jan 1834)

29 Jul – 8 Aug 1830: Lafayette (Caretaker Government)

Prime Minister	*Marie Jean Paul Roch Yves Gilbert Motier, Marquis de Lafayette* (b. Château de Chavagnac 6 Sep 1754; d. Paris 20 May 1834)
Foreign Affairs	*Louis Pierre Édouard* (from 1837: *Baron*) *Bignon* (see Ministry of Napoleon I)
War	*Étienne Maurice, Comte Gérard* (b. Damvilliers 4 Apr 1773; d. Paris 17 Apr 1852)

Education	*(François Pierre) Guillaume Guizot* (b. Nîmes 4 Oct 1787; d. Val-Richer 12 Sep 1874)
Finance	*Joseph Dominique, Baron Louis* (see Blacas)
Other Members	*Claude Antoine Gabriel, Duc de Choiseul-Stainville* (b. 26 Aug 1760; d. Paris 1 Dec 1838); *Jacques Laffitte* (b. Bayonne 24 Oct 1767; d. Paris 26 May 1844); *Casimir Périer* (b. Grenoble 21 Oct 1777; d. Paris 16 May 1832)

13 Aug – 3 Nov 1830: Broglie I

Prime Minister	*(Achille Charles Léonce) Victor, 3rd Duc de Broglie* (for 1st time) (b. Paris 28 Nov 1785; d. 25 Jan 1870)
Foreign Affairs	13 Aug – Sep (?) 1830: *Jean Baptiste, Comte Jourdan* (b. Limoges 29 Apr 1762; d. Paris 23 Nov 1833) Sep (?) – 3 Nov 1830: *Louis Matthieu, Comte Molé* (see Empire)
Home Affairs	*Guillaume Guizot* (see Lafayette)
Education	*Victor, 3rd Duc de Broglie* (see above)
Finance	*Joseph Dominique, Baron Louis* (see Blacas)
War	*Étienne Maurice, Comte Gérard* (see Lafayette)
Navy	*François Horace, Comte Sébastiani* (b. La Porta 11 Nov 1775; d. Paris 21 Jul 1851)

3 Nov 1830 – 13 Mar 1821: Laffitte

Prime Minister	*Jacques Laffitte* (see Lafayette)
Foreign Affairs	2 Nov – Dec 1830: *Nicholas Joseph, Marquis Maison* (b. Epinay 19 Dec 1771; d. Paris 13 Feb 1840) Dec 1830 – 13 Mar 1831: *François Horace Bastien, Comte Sébastiani* (see Broglie I)
Home Affairs	*Martha Camille Bachasson, Comte Montalivet* (b. Valence 25 Apr 1801; d. Lagrange 4 Jan 1880)
Justice	*Jacques Charles Dupont de l'Eure* (b. Neubourg 27 Feb 1767; d. Rougepierre 3 Mar 1855)
Finance	*Jacques Laffitte* (see Lafayette)
Education	*Félix Barthe* (b. Narbonne 28 Jul 1795; d. Paris 28 Jan 1863)
War	*Nicolas Jean de Dieu Soult, Duc de Dalmatie* (b. Saint-Amans-la-Bastide 29 Mar 1769; d. Saint-Amans-la-Bastide 26 Nov 1851)

13 Mar – 16 May 1832: Périer

Prime Minister	*Casimir Périer* (see Lafayette)
Foreign Affairs	*François, Comte Sébastiani* (see Broglie I)
Home Affairs	*Casimir Périer* (see Lafayette)
Justice	*Félix Barthe* (see Laffitte)
Education	*Martha Camille Bachasson, Comte Montalivet* (see Laffitte)
Finance	*Joseph Dominique, Baron Louis* (see Blacas)

11 Oct 1832 – Jul 1834: Soult I

Prime Minister	*Nicolas Soult* (for 1st time) (see Laffitte)
Foreign Affairs	*Victor, 3rd Duc de Broglie* (see Broglie I)
Home Affairs	*Louis Adolphe Thiers* (b. Marseille 15 Apr 1797; d. St Germain en Laye 3 Apr 1877)
Justice	*Felix Barthe* (see Laffitte)
Finance	*Jean Georges Humann* (b. Strasbourg 6 Aug 1780; d. Paris 25 Apr 1842)
Education	*Guillaume Guizot* (see Lafayette)
War	*Nicolas Soult* (see above)

Aug – 14 Nov 1834: Gérard

Prime Minister	*Étienne Maurice, Comte Gérard* (see Lafayette)

14 – 18 Nov 1834: Maret

Prime Minister	*Hughes Bernard Maret* (see Empire)
Navy	*Pierre Charles François, Baron Dupin* (b. Varzy 6 Oct 1784; d. Paris 18 Jan 1873)

18 Nov 1834 – 20 Feb 1835: Mortier

Prime Minister	*Édouard Adolphe Casimir Joseph Mortier* (from 1808: *Duc de Treviso*) (b. Câteau-Cambrésis 13 Feb 1768; d. Paris 28 Jul 1835)
Foreign Affairs	*Victor, 3rd Duc de Broglie* (see Broglie I)
Justice	*Jean Charles Persil* (b. Condom 1785; d. Antony 1870)
Finance	*Jean Georges Humann* (see Soult I)
Education	*Guillaume Guizot* (see Lafayette)
War	*Édouard Mortier* (see above)
Commerce	*Charles Marie Tannegui, Comte Duchâtel* (b. Paris 19

Feb 1803; d. Paris 5 Nov 1867)
Public Works   *Louis Adolphe Thiers* (see Soult I)

12 Mar 1835 – Feb 1836: Broglie II

Prime Minister and Foreign Affairs	*Victor, 3rd Duc de Broglie* (for 2nd time) (see Broglie I)
Justice	*Jean Charles Persil* (see Mortier)
Finance	*Jean Georges Humann* (see Soult I)
Education	*Guillaume Guizot* (see Lafayette)
War	*Nicolas Joseph, Marquis Maison* (see Laffitte)
Navy	*Victor Guy, Baron Duperre* (b. La Rochelle 20 Feb 1775; d. Paris 2 Nov 1846)

22 Feb – 25 Aug 1836: Thiers I

Prime Minister and Foreign Affairs	*Louis Adolphe Thiers* (for 1st time) (see Soult I)
Home Affairs	*Martha Camille Bachasson, Comte Montalivet* (see Laffitte)
Education	*Guillaume Guizot* (see Lafayette)
Justice	*Jean Charles Persil* (see Mortier)
War	*Nicolas Joseph, Marquis Maison* (see Laffitte)
Commerce	*Hippolyte Philibert Passy* (b. Garches 1793; d. Paris 1880)

7 Sep 1836 – 8 Mar 1839: Molé I

Prime Minister	*Louis Matthieu, Comte Molé* (for 1st time) (see Empire)
Foreign Affairs	7 Sep 1836 – 8 Mar 1839: *Louis Matthieu, Comte Molé* (see Empire) Mar – Apr 1839: *Napoléon Auguste Lannes, Duc de Montebello* (b. Paris 30 Jul 1801; d. Paris 19 Jul 1874)
Home Affairs	7 Sep 1836 – 15 Apr 1837: *Adrien Étienne Pierre, Comte de Gasparin* (b. 29 Jun 1783; d. 7 Sep 1862) 15 Apr 1837 – 8 Mar 1839: *Martha Camille Bachasson, Comte Montalivet* (see Laffitte)
Justice	7 Sep 1836 – 7 Mar 1837: *Jean Persil* (see Mortier) 7 Mar 1837 – 8 Mar 1839: *Felix Barthe* (see Laffitte)
Finance	7 Sep 1836 – 7 Mar 1837: *Charles, Comte Duchâtel* (see Mortier) 15 Apr 1837 – 8 Mar 1839: *Lacave-Laplagne*

Education   7 Sep 1836 – 7 Mar 1837: *Guillaume Guizot* (see Lafayette)
         15 Apr 1837 – 8 Mar 1839: *Narcisse Achille, Comte Salvandy* (b. Condom 11 Jun 1795; d. Graveron 16 Dec 1856)

12 May 1839 – 25 Jan 1840: Soult II

Prime Minister   *Nicolas Soult* (for 2nd time) (see Laffitte)
 and Foreign Affairs
Home Affairs   *Charles, Comte Duchâtel* (see Mortier)
Public Building   *Jules Armand Stanislas Dufaure* (b. Saujon 4 Dec 1798; d. Paris 28 Jun 1881)
War   *Antoine Virgile Schneider* (b. Saar-Union 1780; d. Paris 1847)

1 Mar – 22 Oct 1840: Thiers II

Prime Minister   *Louis Adolphe Thiers* (for 2nd time) (see Soult I)
Navy   *Albin Reine, Baron Roussin* (b. Dijon 21 Apr 1781; d. Paris 22 Feb 1854)

29 Oct 1840 – Sep 1847: Soult III

Prime Minister   *Nicolas Soult* (for 3rd time) (see Laffitte)
Foreign Affairs   *Guillaume Guizot* (see Lafayette)
Home Affairs   *Charles, Comte Duchâtel* (see Mortier)
Finance   29 Oct 1840 – 1842: *Jean Georges Humann* (see Soult I)
Education   29 Oct 1840 – 30 Dec 1844: *Abel François Villemain* (b. Paris 9 Jun 1790; d. Paris 8 May 1870)
         30 Dec 1844 – 1845: *Narcisse Achille, Comte Salvandy* (see Molé I)
         1845 – Sep 1847: *Victor Cousin* (b. Paris 28 Nov 1792; d. Cannes 13 Jan 1867)
War   *Nicolas Soult* (see Laffitte)
Navy   29 Oct 1840 – 1841: *Victor Guy, Baron Duperre* (see Broglie II)
         1841: *Charles Baudin* (b. Sedan 1792; d. Ischia 7 Jun 1854)
         1843 – May 1847: *Ange René Armand, Baron de Mackau* (b. Paris 19 Feb 1788; d. Paris 13 May 1855)
         May – Sep 1847: *Napoléon Auguste Lannes, Duc de*

Montebello (see Molé I)

Sep 1847 – 23 Feb 1848: Guizot

Prime Minister and Foreign Affairs	*Guillaume Guizot* (see Lafayette)
Home Affairs	*Charles, Comte Duchâtel* (see Mortier)
Education	*Victor Cousin* (see Soult III)
Navy	*Napoléon Auguste Lannes, Duc de Montebello* (see Molé I)

23 – 24 Feb: Molé II

Prime Minister	*Louis Matthieu, Comte Molé* (for 2nd time) (see Empire)
Justice	*Felix Barthe* (see Laffitte)

24 Feb 1848: Thiers III

Prime Minister	*Louis Adolphe Thiers* (for 3rd time) (see Soult I)
Deputy Prime Minister	*(Camille Hyacinthe) Odilon Barrot* (b. Villefort 19 Jul 1791; d. Bougival 6 Aug 1873)

24 Feb – 10 May 1848: Dupont (Caretaker Government)

Prime Minister	*Jacques Charles Dupont de L'Eure* (see Laffitte)
Foreign Affairs	*Alphonse (Marie Louis Prat) de Lamartine* (b. Mâcon 21 Oct 1790; d. Passy 1 Mar 1869)
Home Affairs	*Alexandre Auguste Ledru-Rollin* (b. Paris 2 Feb 1808; d. Fontenay 31 Dec 1874)
Justice	*(Isaac) Adolphe Crémieux* (b. Nîmes 30 Apr 1796; d. Passy 10 Feb 1880)
Finance	*Louis Antoine Garnier-Pagès* (b. Marseilles 16 Jul 1803; d. Paris 31 Oct 1878)
Minister without Portfolio	*(Jean Joseph) Louis Blanc* (b. Madrid 29 Oct 1811; d. Cannes 6 Dec 1882) (President of Labour Commission)
War and Navy	*Dominique François Arago* (b. Perpignan 26 Feb 1786; d. Paris 3 Oct 1853)

10 May – 24 Jun 1848: Executive Committee

Executive Committee of five persons, including:

	Dominique François Arago (see Dupont)
	Louis Antoine Garnier-Pagès (see Dupont)
	Alphonse de Lamartine (see Dupont)
	Alexandre Auguste Ledru-Rollin (see Dupont)
Foreign Affairs	*Jules Bastide* (b. Paris 22 Nov 1800; d. Paris 2 Mar 1879)
Home Affairs	*Adrien Barnabe Athanase Recurt* (b. Lannemezan 9 Jun 1798; d. Lévignac 7 Nov 1872)
Justice	10 May – 7 Jun 1848: *Adolphe Crémieux* (see Dupont)
Finance	**Charles Théodore Eugène Duclerc** (b. Bagnères-de-Bigorre 9 Nov 1813; d. Paris 21 Jul 1888)
Public Worship	*Eugène Bethmont* (b. Paris 1804; d. Paris 31 Mar 1860)
Education	*Lazare Hippolyte Carnot* (b. Saint-Omer 6 Apr 1801; d. 16 Mar 1888)
War	*Jean Baptiste Adolphe Charras* (b. Pfalzburg 7 Jan 1810; d. Basle 23 Jan 1865)

24 Jun – 10 Dec 1848: Cavaignac

Military Dictator	*Eugène Louis Cavaignac* (b. Paris 15 Oct 1802; d. Ournes 28 Oct 1857)
Foreign Affairs	28 Jun – 10 Dec 1848: *Jules Bastide* (see Executive Committee)
Home Affairs	24 Jun – 13 Oct 1848: *Adrien Recurt* (see Executive Committee)
Public Worship	13 Oct – 10 Dec 1848: *Jules Dufaure* (see Soult II)
	28 Jun – 10 Dec 1848: *Eugène Bethmont* (see Executive Committee)
War	28 Jun – 10 Dec 1848: *Christophe de Lamoricière* (b. Nantes 5 Feb 1806; d. Amiens 11 Sep 1865)

20 Dec 1848 – 31 Oct 1849: Barrot

Prime Minister	20 Dec 1848 – 31 Oct 1849: *Odilon Barrot* (see Thiers III)
Foreign Affairs	20 Dec 1848 – 2 Jun 1849: *Édouard Drouyn de l'Huys* (b. Paris 19 Nov 1805; d. Paris 1 Mar 1881)
	2 Jun – 31 Oct 1849: *Alexis Clérel de Tocqueville* (b. Verneuil 29 Jul 1805; d. Cannes 16 Apr 1859)
Home Affairs	20 Dec 1848 – 2 Jun 1849: *Léon Faucher* (b. Limoges 8 Sep 1803; d. Marseilles 14 Dec 1854)
	2 Jun – 31 Oct 1849: *Jules Dufaure* (see Soult II)

Justice	*Odilon Barrot* (see Thiers III)
Finance	*Hippolyte Philibert Passy* (see Thiers I)
War	*Joseph Marcellin Rulhière* (b. St. Dizier-la-Sauve 1787; d. 1862)
Navy	*Antoine, Comte Destutt de Tracy* (b. Paris 9 Sep 1781; d. Paray-le-Frésil 13 Mar 1864)
Agriculture and Commerce	20 – 29 Dec 1848: *Alexandre Bixio* (b. Chiavari 10 Nov 1808; d. Paris 1865)
	29 Dec 1848 – 2 Jun 1849: *Louis Joseph Buffet* (b. Mirecourt 26 Oct 1818; d. Paris 7 Jul 1898)
	2 Jun – 31 Oct 1849: *Victor, Vicomte Lanjuinais* (b. Paris 5 Nov 1802; d. Paris 2 Jan 1869)
Education	20 Dec 1848 – 14 Sep 1849: *Frédéric Alfred Pierre, Comte Falloux* (b. Angers 7 May 1811; d. Angers 6 Jan 1886)
	14 Sep – 31 Oct 1849: *Victor, Vicomte Lanjuinais* (see above)
Public Works	*Bertrand Théobald Joseph Lacrosse* (b. Brest 29 Jan 1796; d. Paris 28 Mar 1865)

31 Oct 1849 – 4 Jan 1851: Hautpoul I

Prime Minister	*Alphonse Henri, Comte d'Hautpoul* (for 1st time) (b. Versailles 4 Jan 1789; d. Paris 28 Jul 1865)
Foreign Affairs	31 Oct – Nov 1849: —— *Rayneval*
	Nov 1849 – 9 Jan 1851: *Jean Ernest Ducos, Vicomte de La Hire* (b. Bessières 1789; d. 1878)
Home Affairs	31 Oct 1849 – Mar 1850: *Victorien Ferdinand Barrot* (b. Paris 10 Jan 1806; d. Paris 12 Nov 1883)
	Mar 1850 – 4 Jan 1851: *Pierre Jules Baroche* (b. Paris 18 Nov 1802; d. Jersey 29 Oct 1870)
Justice	*Eugène Rouher* (b. Rome 30 Nov 1814; d. Paris 3 Feb 1884)
Finance	*Achille Fould* (b. Paris 17 Nov 1800; d. Tarbes 5 Oct 1867)
War	31 Oct 1849 – 2 Aug 1850: *Alphonse Henri Comte d'Hautpoul* (see above)
	2 Aug 1850 – 9 Jan 1851: *Jean Paul Adam, Baron* (later: *Comte*) *Schramm* (b. Arras 1 Dec 1789; d. La Courneuve 1884)
Navy	*Romain Joseph Desfossés* (b. Gouesnou 8 Dec 1789; d. Paris 26 Oct 1864)
Education	*Marie Louis Pierre Félix Esquiron De Parieu* (b.

187

	Aurillac 1815; d. Paris 1893)
Commerce and Agriculture	*Jean Baptiste Dumas* (b. Alais 15 Jul 1800; d. Cannes 11 Apr 1884)
Public Works	*Jean Martial Bineau* (b. Gennes 18 May 1805; d. Chatou 8 Sep 1855)

9 Jan – 10 Apr 1851: Hautpoul II

Prime Minister	9 – 18 Jan 1851: *Alphonse Henri, Comte d'Hautpoul* (for 2nd time) (see Hautpoul I)
Foreign Affairs	10 – 24 Jan 1851: *Édouard Drouyn de l'Huys* (see Barrot)
	24 Jan – 13 Apr 1851: *Alexandre Anatole François Henri Brenier, Baron de la Renaudière* (b. before 1810; d. La Lucassière 28 Mar 1885)
Home Affairs	*Charles Marius Vaisse* (b. Marseilles 8 Aug 1799; d. Lyons 29 Aug 1864)
Justice	*Paul Henri Ernest de Royer* (b. Versailles 29 Oct 1808; d. Paris 13 Dec 1877)
Finance	—— *Germigny*
Education	*Charles Joseph Barthélemy Giraud* (b. Pernes 20 Feb 1802; d. Paris 13 Apr 1881)
War	9 – 24 Jan 1851: *Auguste Michel Regnault de St Jean d'Angély* (b. Paris 29 Jul 1794; d. Nice 1 Feb 1870)
	24 Jan – 10 Apr 1851: *César Alexandre Randon* (b. Grenoble 25 Mar 1795; d. Geneva 15 Jan 1871)
Navy	*Théodore Ducos* (b. Bordeaux 20 Aug 1801; d. Paris 17 Apr 1855)
Commerce and Agriculture	*Eugène Schneider* (b. Blittersdorf 29 Mar 1805; d. Paris 27 Nov 1875)
Public Works	*Pierre Magne* (b. Périgueux 3 Dec 1806; d. Montaigne 19 Feb 1869)

10 Apr 1851 – 14 Dec 1854: Faucher

Prime Minister (from 2 Dec 1852: Chief Minister)	*Léon Faucher* (see Barrot)
Foreign Affairs	10 Apr – Oct 1851: *Pierre Jules Baroche* (see Hautpoul I)
	Oct 1851 – Jul 1852: *Louis Félix Étienne, Marquis de Turgot* (b. Falaise 1796; d. Versailles 1866)
	28 Jul 1852 – 14 Dec 1854: *Édouard Drouyn de l'Huys* (see Barrot)

Home Affairs	Apr – Oct 1851: *Léon Faucher* (see Barrot)
	Oct – Dec 1851: —— *Thorigny*
	2 Dec 1851 – Jan 1852: *Charles Auguste Louis Joseph, Duc de Morny* (b. Paris 23 Oct 1811; d. Paris 10 Mar 1865)
	Jan 1852 – Jul 1854: *Jean Gilbert Victor Fialin, Baron* (from 1863: *Duc*) *de Persigny* (b. Saint-Germain-L'Espinasse, 1 Jan 1808; d. Nice 13 Jan 1872)
Justice	Apr – Oct 1851: *Eugène Rouher* (see Hautpoul I)
	Oct – Nov 1851: —— *Corbin*
	Nov – Dec 1851: *Alfred Daviel* (b. Evreux 1800; d. Paris 1856)
	Dec 1851 – Jan 1852: *Eugène Rouher* (see Hautpoul)
	Jan 1852 – 14 Dec 1854: *Jacques Pierre Charles Abbatucci* (b. Zicavo, Corsica, 28 May 1792; d. 11 Nov 1857)
Finance	10 Apr – 14 Oct 1851: *Achille Fould* (see Hautpoul I)
	Oct – Nov 1851: —— *Blondel*
	2 Dec 1851 – Jan 1852: *Achille Fould* (see Hautpoul I)
	22 Jan 1852 – 14 Dec 1854: *Jean Martial Bineau* (see Hautpoul I)
Education	Apr – Oct 1851: —— *Courcelles*
	Oct – Dec 1851: *Charles Giraud* (see Hautpoul II)
	Dec 1851: —— *Fartoul*
War	10 Apr – 25 Oct 1851: *César Alexandre Randon* (see Hautpoul II)
	26 Oct 1851 – 29 Sep 1854: *Jacques Leroy de Saint-Arnaud* (b. Bordeaux 20 Aug 1796; d. Crimea 29 Sep 1854)
	11 Mar – 14 Dec 1854: *Jean Baptiste Philibert Vaillant* (b. Dijon 6 Oct 1790; d. Paris 4 Jun 1872)
Navy	10 Apr – 26 Oct 1851: *Justin Napoléon Samuel Prosper, Comte,* then *Marquis de Chasseloup-Laubat* (b. Alessandria, Lombardy, 29 Mar 1805; d. Versailles 29 Mar 1873)
	Oct – Dec 1851: —— *Fartoul* (see above)
	Dec 1851 – 14 Dec 1854: *Théodore Ducos* (see Hautpoul II)
Commerce	26 Oct – 22 Nov 1851: *François Xavier, Comte de Casabianca* (b. Nice 27 Jun 1796; d. Paris 5 Feb 1881)
	1853: *Pierre Magne* (see Hautpoul II)
Police	22 Jan 1852 – 10 Jan 1853: *Charlemagne Émile de Maupas* (b. Bar-sur-Aube 8 Dec 1818; d. Paris 18 Apr 1888)

Public Works

Minister of State

10 Apr 1853: post abolished
10 Apr – Oct 1851: *Pierre Magne* (see Hautpoul II)
26 Oct – 2 Dec 1851: *Bertrand Lacrosse* (see Barrot)
2 Dec 1851 – 1852: *Pierre Magne* (see Hautpoul II)
22 Jan – 2 Jul 1852: *Francoise Xavier, Comte de Casabianca* (see above)
20 Jul 1852 – (?) 23 Nov 1860: *Achille Fould* (see Hautpoul I)

3 Feb 1855 – 17 Jul 1869: Rouher

Chief Minister

Foreign Affairs

Home Affairs

3 Feb 1855 – 1859: *Eugène Rouher* (for 1st time) (see Hautpoul I)
24 Jun – 13 Oct 1863: *Auguste (Adolphe Marie) Billault* (b. Vannes 12 Nov 1805; d. Nantes 13 Oct 1863)
18 Oct 1863 – 17 Jul 1869: *Eugène Rouher* (for 2nd time) (see Hautpoul I)
3 Feb – 3 May 1855: *Édouard Drouyn de l'Huys* (see Barrot)
3 May 1855 – Oct 1860: *Alexandre Colonna, Comte* (from 1866: *Duc*) *de Walewski* (b. Walewice 4 May 1810; d.. Strasbourg 27 Sep 1868)
24 Oct 1860 – 18 Oct 1862: *Édouard Thouvenel* (b. Verdun 11 Nov 1818; d. Paris 18 Oct 1866)
18 Oct 1862 – 1 Sep 1866: *Édouard Drouyn de L'Huys* (see Barrot)
1 Sep 1866 – 17 Dec 1868: *Lionel, Marquis de Moustier* (b. Paris 23 Aug 1817; d. Paris 5 Feb 1869)
Dec 1868 – 17 Jul 1869: *Charles Jean Marie Félix, Marquis de La Valette* (b. Senlis 1806; d. Paris 1881)
Jul 1854 – Feb 1858: *Auguste Billault* (see above)
8 Feb – 15 Jun 1858: *Esprit Charles Marie Espinasse* (b. Saissac 2 Apr 1815; d. Magenta 4 Jun 1859)
Jun 1858 – May 1859: *Claude Alphonse Delangle* (b. Varzy 6 Apr 1797; d. Paris 26 Dec 1869)
May – 1 Nov 1859: *Ernest Henry Hyacinthe Arrighi di Casanova, Duc de Padua* (b. 26 Sep 1814; d. Paris 28 Mar 1888)
Nov 1859 – Feb 1860: *Auguste Billault* (see above)
24 Feb 1860 – Jun 1863: *Jean Fialin, Duc de Persigny* (see Faucher)
24 Jun 1863 – 28 Mar 1865: *Paul Boudet* (b. Laval 23

Nov 1800; d. Paris 17 Nov 1877)

Mar 1865 – Nov 1867: *Charles, Marquis de La Valette* (see above)

14 Nov 1867 – 17 Dec 1868: *Pierre Ernest Pinard* (b. Autun 1822; d. Bourg-en-Bresse Sep 1909)

Dec 1868 – 17 Jul 1869: *Jean Louis Victor Adolphe de Forcade de la Roquette* (b. 9 Apr 1820; d. 15 Aug 1874)

Police | 7 Feb 1858: post recreated

7 Feb – 14 Jun 1858: *Esprit Charles Marie Espinasse* (see above) also Home Affairs

24 Nov 1860 – 1868: *Alexandre Colonna, Comte de Walewski* (see above)

Justice | 3 Feb 1855 – Nov 1857: *Jacques Abbatucci* (see Faucher)

Nov 1857 – May 1859: *Paul de Royer* (see Hautpoul II)

Justice and Public Worship | 1859 – 1863: *Claude Alphonse Delangle* (see above)

1863 – 17 Jul 1869: *Pierre Jules Baroche* (see Hautpoul I)

Education | 1856 – Jun 1863: *Gustave Rouland* (b. Yvetot 1806; d. Paris 1878)

23 Jun 1863 – 17 Jul 1869: *Victor Duruy* (b. Paris 11 Sep 1811; d. Paris 25 Nov 1894)

Finance | 3 Feb 1855 – 1860: *Pierre Magne* (see Hautpoul II)

1860 – 1861: *Jean Louis Victor Adolphe de Forcade de la Roquette* (see above)

14 Nov 1861 – 19 Feb 1867: *Achille Fould* (see Hautpoul I)

Feb – Nov 1867: *Eugène Rouher* (see Hautpoul I)

Nov 1867 – 17 Jul 1869: *Pierre Magne* (see Hautpoul II)

War | 3 Feb 1855 – 1859: *Jean Baptiste Philibert Vaillant* (see Faucher)

1859 – 1867: *César Alexandre Randon* (see Hautpoul II)

1867 – 17 Jul 1869: *Adolphe Niel* (b. Muret 4 Oct 1802; d. 13 Aug 1869)

Navy | 3 Feb – (?) 1855: *Théodore Ducos* (see Hautpoul II)

1855 – 1860: *François Alphonse Hamelin* (b. Pont l'Evêque 2 Sep 1796; d. Paris 16 Jan 1864)

1866 – 1867: *Justin, Marquis de Chasseloup-Laubat* (see Faucher)

Jan 1867 – 17 Jul 1869: *Charles Rigault de Genouilly* (b. Rochefort 1807; d. Barcelona 1873)

Commerce, Agriculture and Public Works	1858 – 1865: *Eugène Rouher* (Hautpoul I) 23 Jul 1865 – 1867: *Armand Behic* (b. Paris 15 Jan 1809; d. Paris Mar 1891) 1867 – 1868: *Jean de Forcade de la Roquette* (see above)
Colonies (new post)	1858 – Mar 1859: *Prince Napoléon Joseph Charles Paul Bonaparte* (b. Trieste 9 Sep 1822; d. Rome 18 Mar 1891) 24 Mar 1859 – Jan 1867: *Justin, Marquis de Casseloup-Laubat* (see Faucher)
President of National Assembly	1854 – 1856; 1857 – 1865: *Charles, Duc de Morny* (see Faucher) 1866 – 1868: *Alexandre Colonna, Duc de Walewski* (see above)
Minister of State	(20 Jul 1852) – 23 Nov 1860: *Achille Fould* (see Hautpoul I) 24 Nov 1860 – 23 Jun 1863: *Alexandre Colonna, Duc de Walewski* (see above) 23 Jun – 18 Oct 1863: *Auguste Billault* (see above) 18 Oct 1863 – 17 Jul 1869: *Eugène Rouher* (see Hautpoul I)

17 Jul – 27 Dec 1869: Forçade

Prime Minister	*Jean de Forcade de la Roquette* (see Rouher)
Foreign Affairs	*Henri Godefroy Bernard Alphonse, Prince de Latour d'Auvergne-Lauraguais* (b. Paris 1823; d. Château des Angliers 1871)
Home Affairs	*Jean de Forcade de la Roquette* (see above)
Justice	*Jean Baptiste Marie Duvergier* (b. Bordeaux 25 Aug 1792; d. Bordeaux 2 Nov 1877)
Finance	*Pierre Magne* (see Hautpoul II)
War	17 Jul – 13 Aug 1869: *Adolphe Niel* (see Rouher) 21 Aug – 27 Dec 1869: *Edmond Leboeuf* (b. Paris 6 Dec 1809; d. Moncel 7 Jun 1888)
Navy	*Charles Rigault de Genouilly* (see Rouher)

2 Jan – 9 Aug 1870: Ollivier

Prime Minister	*Émile Ollivier* (b. Marseilles 2 Jul 1825: d. Saint-Gervaise-les-Bains 20 Aug 1913)
Foreign Affairs	2 Jan – 15 May 1870: *Napoléon, Comte Daru* (b. 11 Jun 1807; d. Paris 19 Feb 1890)

15 May – 9 Aug 1870: *Antoine Alfred Agénor, Duc de Gramont* (b. Paris 14 Aug 1819; d. Paris 18 Jan 1880)

Home Affairs — *Jean Pierre Eugène Napoléon Chevandier de Valdrôme* (b. St Quirin 17 Aug 1816; d. Paris 1 Dec 1878)

Education and Justice — *Émile Ollivier* (see above)

Finance — 2 Jan – 14 Apr 1870: *Louis Joseph Buffet* (see Barrot)
14 Apr – 9 Aug 1870: *Émile Alexis Segris* (b. Poitiers 4 Mar 1811; d. Switzerland 14 Sep 1880)

War — *Edmond Leboeuf* (see Forcade)

Navy — *Charles Rigault de Genouilly* (see Rouher)

9 Aug – 4 Sep 1870: Palikao

Prime Minister — *Charles Guillaume Marie Cousin-Montauban, Duc de Palikao* (b. Paris 24 Jun 1796; d. Versailles 8 Jan 1878)

Foreign Affairs — *Henri, Prince de Latour d'Auvergne* (see Forcade)

Home Affairs — *Julien Théophile Henri Chevreau* (b. Belleville 27 Apr 1823; d. Yerres 23 May 1903)

Finance — *Pierre Magne* (see Hautpoul II)

War — *Charles Cousin-Montauban, Duc de Palikao* (see above)

Public Works — *Jérôme Frédéric Paul, Baron David* (b. Rome 30 Jun 1823; d. Langon 28 Jan 1882)

Commerce — *Clément Duvernois* (b. Paris 6 Apr 1836; d. 8 Jul 1879)

4 Sep 1870: Trochu (Interim Administration of National Defence)

Prime Minister — *(Louis) Jules Trochu* (b. Palais 12 Mar 1815; d. Tours 7 Oct 1896)

Foreign Affairs — *(Gabriel Claude) Jules Favre* (b. Lyons 21 Mar 1809; d. Versailles 19 Jan 1880)

Home Affairs — *Léon Gambetta* (b. Cahors 3 Apr 1838; d. Paris 31 Dec 1882)

Other Posts — *Jules Simon* (b. Lorient 31 Dec 1814; d. Paris 8 Jun 1896)
Louis Joseph Ernest Picard (b. Paris 24 Dec 1821; d. Paris 13 May 1877)
Eugène Pelletan (b. Royan 29 Oct 1813; d. Paris 13 Dec 1884)
Adolphe Crémieux (see Dupont)
Jules Ferry (b. St-Dié 5 Apr 1832; d. Paris 17 Mar 1893)
Alexandre Glais-Bizoin (b. Quintin 9 Mar 1800; d. Lamballe 6 Nov 1877)

Victor Henri, Marquis de Rochefort-Luçay (b. Paris 31 Jan 1831; d. Aix-les-Bains 30 Jun 1913)
(François Victor) Emanuel Arago (b. Paris 6 Jun 1812; d. Paris 26 Nov 1896)
Louis Antoine Garnier-Pagès (see Dupont)

4 Sep 1870 – 18 Feb 1871: Bordeaux Administration

Home Affairs	*Jean Pierre Eugène Napoléon Chevandier de Valdrôme* (see Ollivier)
Justice	4 Sep – 7 Oct 1870: *Adolphe Crémieux* (see Dupont)
	7 Oct 1870 – 18 Feb 1871: *Emanuel Arago* (see Trochu)
Finance	*Louis Joseph Ernest Picard* (see Trochu)
	4 Sep – 7 Oct 1870: *Adolphe Charles Emmanuel Leflô* (b. Lesneven 2 Nov 1804; d. Nechoat 16 Nov 1887)
	7 Oct 1870 – 6 Feb 1871: *Léon Gambetta* (see Trochu)
Navy	4 Sep 1870: *Charles Marius Albert Dompierre d'Hornoy* (b. Hornoy 24 Feb 1816; d. Paris 1901)
	Sep 1870 – 6 Feb 1871: *Martin Fourichon* (b. Vivier 9 Jan 1890; d. Paris 23 Nov 1884)
Commerce	*Joseph Magnin* (b. Dijon 1 Jan 1824; d. Paris 22 Nov 1910)

18 Feb 1871 – 18 May 1873* Thiers IV

Prime Minister	*Louis Adolphe Thiers* (for 4th time) (see Soult I)
Deputy Premier	2 Sep 1871 – 18 May 1873: *Jules Dufaure* (see Soult II)
Foreign Affairs	18 Feb – 2 Aug 1871: *Jules Favre* (see Trochu)
	2 Aug 1871 – 18 May 1873: *Charles, Comte Remusat* (b. Paris 14 Mar 1797; d. Paris 6 Jun 1875)
Home Affairs	18 Feb – 6 Jun 1871: *Louis Joseph Ernest Picard* (see Trochu)
	6 Jun – 8 Oct 1871: *Félix Edmond Hyacinthe Lambrecht* (b. Douai 4 Apr 1819; d. Versailles 8 Oct 1871)
	12 Oct 1871 – 2 Feb 1872: *Casimir Périer* (b. Paris 20 Aug 1811; d. Paris 6 Jul 1876)
	6 Feb – 7 Dec 1872: *Victor Lefranc* (b. Garlin 2 Mar 1809; d. St Sever 13 Sep 1883)
	7 Jul 1872 – 17 May 1873: *Marc Thomas Eugène de*

*The Paris Commune 26 Mar – 29 May 1871

President of Committee of Public Safety	*Charles Delescluze* (b. Dreux 20 Oct 1809; d. Paris 28 May 1871)

Goulard (b. Versailles 24 Nov 1808; d. 4 Jul 1874)

17 – 18 May 1873: *Casimir Périer* (see above)

Justice | *Jules Dufaure* (see Soult II)

Finance | 18 – 25 Feb 1871: no appointment made

25 Feb 1871 – 3 Mar 1872: *Augustin Thomas Pouyer-Quertier* (b. Étoutteville-en-Caux 3 Sep 1830; d. Rouen 2 Apr 1891)

6 Mar – 7 Dec 1872 (acting: 6 Mar – 24 Apr) *Marc Thomas Eugène de Goulard* (see above)

7 Dec 1872 – 18 May 1873: *Léon Say* (b. Paris 6 Jun 1826; d. Paris 22 Apr 1896)

War | 18 Feb – 6 Jun 1871: *Adolphe Charles Emmanuel Leflô* (see Bordeaux Administration)

6 Jun 1871 – 18 May 1873: *Ernest Louis Octave Courtot de Cissey* (b. Paris 23 Dec 1810; d. Paris 15 Jun 1882)

Navy | *Louis Pierre Alexis Pothuau* (b. Martinique 30 Oct 1815; d. Paris 8 Oct 1882)

Education | 18 Feb 1871 – 17 May 1873; *Jules Simon* (see Trochu)

17 – 18 May 1873: no appointment made

Public Works | 18 Feb 1871 – 20 Jun 1872: *Charles Paulin Roger de Saubert, Baron de Larcy* (b. Le Vigan 20 Aug 1805; d. Pierrelette 7 Nov 1882)

20 Jun – (?) 1872 (acting:) *Pierre Edmond Teisserenc de Bort* (b. Châteauroux 4 Sep 1814; d. Paris 29 Jul 1892)

8 Dec 1872 – 18 May 1873: *Marie François Oscar Bardy de Fourtou* (b. Ribérac 3 Jan 1836; d. Paris 7 Dec 1897)

Commerce | 18 Feb 1871 – (?): *Félix Edmond Hyacinthe Lambrecht* (see above)

(?) – 6 Feb 1872: *Victor Lefranc* (see above)

6 Feb – 24 Apr 1872: *Marc Thomas Eugène de Goulard* (see above)

24 Apr 1872 – 18 May 1873: *Pierre Edmond Teisserenc de Bort* (see above)

18 – 25 May 1873: Thiers V

Prime Minister | *Louis Adolphe Thiers* (for 5th time) (see Soult I)
Foreign Affairs | *Charles, Comte Remusat* (see Thiers IV)
Home Affairs | *Casimir Périer* (see Thiers IV)
Justice | *Jules Dufaure* (see Soult II)
War | *Ernest Louis Octave Courtot de Cissey* (see Thiers IV)

Navy	*Louis Pierre Alexis Pothuau* (see Thiers IV)
Education	*William Henry Waddington* (b. Paris 11 Dec 1826; d. Paris 13 Jan 1894)
Public Worship	*Marie François Oscar Bardy de Fourtou* (see Thiers IV)
Public Works	*René Bérenger* (b. Bourg-les-Valence 22 Apr 1830: d. Allincourt 29 Aug 1915)
Commerce	*Pierre Edmond Teisserenc de Bort* (see Thiers IV)

25 May 1873 – 16 May 1874: Mac-Mahon

Prime Minister	*Marie Edmé Patrice Maurice de Mac-Mahon, Duc de Magenta* (see Presidents)
Deputy Premier	*Albert, 4th Duc de Broglie* (b. Paris 13 Jun 1821; d. Paris 19 Jan 1901)
Foreign Affairs	25 May – 26 Nov 1873: *Albert, 4th Duc de Broglie* (see above)
	26 Nov 1873 – 16 May 1874: *Louis Charles Élie Amanieu, Duc de Decazes* (b. Paris 29 May 1819; d. Château La Grave 17 Sep 1886)
Home Affairs	25 May – Nov 1873: *Charles Ernest Beule* (b. Saumur 29 Jun 1826; d. Paris 4 Jun 1874)
	26 Nov 1873 – 16 May 1874: *Albert, 4th Duc de Broglie* (see above)
Justice	*Jean Edmond Ernoul* (b. Loudun 5 Aug 1829; d. Lussac-les-Eglises 1899)
Finance	*Pierre Magne* (see Hautpoul II)
War	25 – 30 May 1873 (acting:) *Ernest Louis Octave Courtot de Cissey* (see Thiers IV)
	30 May 1873 – 16 May 1874: *François Charles du Barail* (b. Versailles 28 May 1820; d. Neuilly 30 Jan 1902)
Navy	*Charles Marius Albert Dompierre d'Hornoy* (see Bordeaux Administration)
Colonies	*Charles Marius Albert Dompierre d'Hornoy* (see Bordeaux Administration)
Education	*Anselme Polycarpe Batbie* (b. Seissan 31 May 1828; d. Paris 13 Jun 1887)
Public Worship	25 May 1873: amalgamated with Educaton
Public Works	25 May – 26 Nov 1873: *Alfred Pierrot-Deseilligny* (b. Paris 1828; d. Paris Apr 1875)
Agriculture and Commerce	25 May – 24 Nov 1873: *Marie Joseph Roullet de Labouillerie* (b. Paris 26 Mar 1822; d. Baugé 25 Dec 1894)

26 Nov 1873 – 16 May 1874; *Alfred Pierrot-Deseilligny* (see above)

22 May 1874 – 25 Feb 1875: Cissey

Prime Minister	*Ernest Louis Octave Courtot de Cissey* (see Thiers IV)
Foreign Affairs	*Louis Charles Élie Amanieu, Duc de Decazes* (see Mac-Mahon)
Home Affairs	22 May 1874 – 6 Jan 1875: *Marie François Oscar Bardy de Fourtou* (see Thiers IV) 6 Jan – 25 Feb 1875: *François Ernest Henri, Baron de Chabaud-Latour* (b. Nîmes 25 Jan 1804; d. Paris 11 Jun 1885)
Justice	*Adrien Albert Tailhaud* (b. Aubenas 14 Jul 1810; d. Aubenas 8 Oct 1889)
Finance	*Pierre Magne* (see Hautpoul II)
War	*Ernest Louis Octave Courtot de Cissey* (see Thiers IV)
Navy	*Louis Raymond de Chauvance, Marquis de Montaignac* (b. Paris 14 Mar 1811; d. Paris 9 Jun 1891)
Education	*Arthur Timothée Antoine, Vicomte de Cumont* (b. Angers 19 Apr 1818; d. St Georges-sur-Loire 1902)
Public Works	*Eugène Caillaux* (b. Orleans 10 Sep 1822; d. Paris 1896)
Commerce	*Louis Grivart* (b. Rennes 30 Jul 1829; d. 3 Aug 1901)

10 Mar 1875 – 21 Feb 1876: Buffet

Prime Minister	*Louis Joseph Buffet* (see Barrot)
Foreign Affairs	*Louis Charles Élie Amanieu, Duc de ecazes* (see Mac-Mahon)
Home Affairs	*Louis Joseph Buffet* (see Barrot)
Justice	*Jules Dufaure* (see Soult II)
Finance	*Léon Say* (see Thiers IV)
War	*Ernest Louis Octave Courtot de Cissey* (see Thiers IV)
Navy	*Louis Raymond de Chauvance, Marquis de Montaignac* (see Cissey)
Education	*Henri Alexandre Wallon* (b. Valenciennes 23 Dec 1812; d. Paris 13 Nov 1904)
Public Works	*Eugène Caillaux* (see Cissey)
Commerce and Agriculture	*Camille, Vicomte de Meaux* (b. Montbrison 10 Sep 1830; d. Château Écotay-l'Olme 4 Nov 1807)

22 Feb – 8 Mar 1876: Dufaure I

Prime Minister	*Jules Dufaure* (for 1st time) (see Soult II)

Foreign Affairs	*Louis Charles Élie Amanieu, Duc de Decazes* (see Mac-Mahon)
Home Affairs	(acting:) *Jules Dufaure* (see Soult II)
Justice	*Jules Dufaure* (see Soult II)
Finance	*Léon Say* (see Thiers IV)
War	*Ernest Louis Octave Courtot de Cissey* (see Thiers IV)
Navy	*Louis Raymond de Chauvance, Marquis de Montaignac* (see Cissey)
Education	*Henri Alexandre Wallon* (see Buffet)
Public Works	*Eugène Caillaux* (see Cissey)
Commerce and Agriculture	*Camille, Vicomte de Meaux* (see Buffet)

8' Mar – 12 Dec 1876: Dufaure II

Prime Minister	*Jules Dufaure* (for 2nd time) (see Soult II)
Foreign Affairs	*Louis Charles Élie, Duc de Decazes* (see Mac-Mahon)
Home Affairs	8 Mar – 11 May 1876: *Pierre Henri Aimable Ricard* (b. Charenton 12 Jun 1828; d. Paris 12 May 1876)
	16 May – 12 Dec 1876: *Émile Louis Gustave Deshayes de Marcère* (b. Domfront 16 Mar 1828; d. Messeil 26 Apr 1918)
Justice	*Jules Dufaure* (see Soult II)
Finance	*Léon Say* (see Thiers IV)
War	*Ernest Louis Octave Courtot de Cissey* (see Thiers IV)
Navy	*Martin Fourichon* (see Bordeaux Administration)
Education	*William Henry Waddington* (see Thiers V)
Public Worship	*Jules Dufaure* (see Soult II)
Public Works	*Albert Christophle* (b. Domfront 13 Jul 1830; d. Paris 23 Jan 1904)
Commerce	*Pierre Edmond Teisserenc de Bort* (see Thiers IV)

12 Dec 1876 – 16 May 1877: Simon

Prime Minister	*Jules Simon* (see Trochu)
Foreign Affairs	*Louis Charles Élie Amanieu, Duc de Decazes* (see Mac-Mahon)
Home Affairs	*Jules Simon* (see Trochu)
Justice	*Louis Joseph Martel* (b. St Omer 15 Sep 1813; d. Evreux 4 Mar 1892)
Finance	*Léon Say* (see Thiers IV)
War	*Ernest Louis Octave Courtot de Cissey* (see Thiers IV)
Navy	*Martin Fourichon* (see Bordeaux Administration)

Education	*William Henry Waddington* (see Thiers V)
Public Worship	*Louis Joseph Martel* (see above)
Public Works	*Louis Joseph Martel* (see above)
Commerce	*Pierre Edmond Teisserenc de Bort* (see Thiers IV)

18 May – 23 Nov 1877: Broglie

Prime Minister	*Albert, 4th Duc de Broglie* (see Mac-Mahon)
Foreign Affairs	*Louis Charles Élie Amanieu, Duc de Decazes* (see Mac-Mahon)
Home Affairs	*Marie François Oscar Bardy de Fourtou* (see Thiers IV)
Justice	*Albert, Duc de Broglie* (see Mac-Mahon)
Finance	*Eugène Caillaux* (see Cissey)
War	*Jean Auguste Berthaut* (b. Genlis 29 Mar 1817; d. Paris 24 Dec 1881)
Public Works	*Auguste Joseph Paris* (b. St Omer 12 Nov 1826; d. 1896)
Education	*Joseph Brunet* (b. Arnac-Pompadour 4 Mar 1829; d. Pierre-Buffière 6 Jan 1891)
Commerce and Agriculture	*Camille, Vicomte de Meaux* (see Buffet)

23 Nov – 3 Dec 1877: Rochebouet

Prime Minister	*Caïétan de Grimaudet de la Rochebouet* (b. Angers 16 May 1813; d. Paris 1899)
Foreign Affairs	*Gaston Robert Marie, Marquis de Banneville* (b. Paris 1818; d. Paris 1881)
Home Affairs	—— *Welche*
Justice	*François Ernest Louis Émile Lepelletier* (b. Villedieu 22 Dec 1826; d. Paris 1900)
Finance	*François Ernest Dutilleul* (b. Paris 1 Mar 1825; d. Paris 5 May 1907)
War	*Caïétan de Grimaudet de la Rochebouet* (see above)
Navy	—— *Quicquerel des Touches*
Public Works	*Charles Étienne Collignon* (b. Metz 16 May 1802; d. Paris 4 Dec, 1885)
Education	*Hervé Auguste Faye* (b. Saint Benoît-du-Sault 1 Oct 1814; d. Paris 4 Jul 1902)
Commerce	*Jules Antoine St Marie Ozenne* (b. Louviers 8 Dec 1809; d. Torcy 1 Mar 1889)

199

14 Dec 1877 – 30 Jan 1879: Dufaure III

Prime Minister	*Jules Dufaure* (for 3rd time) (see Soullt II)
Foreign Affairs	*William Henry Waddington* (see Thiers V)
Home Affairs	*Émile Deshayes de Marcère* (see Dufaure II)
Justice	*Jules Dufaure* (see Soult II)
Finance	*Léon Say* (see Thiers IV)
War	13 Dec 1877 – 13 Jan 1879: *Jean Louis Borel* (b. Faujeux 3 Apr 1819; d. Versailles 23 Feb 1884)
	13 – 30 Jan 1879: *Henri François Xavier Gresley* (b. Vassy 9 Feb 1819; d. Paris 2 May 1890)
Education	*Agénor Bardoux* (b. Bourges 15 Jan 1829; d. Paris 23 Nov 1897)
Navy	*Louis Pothuau* (see Thiers IV) ˙
Public Works	*Charles Louis de Saulces de Freycinet* (b. Foix 14 Nov 1828; d. Paris 14 May 1923)
Commerce	*Pierre Edmond Teisserence de Bort* (see Thiers IV)

4 Feb – 21 Dec 1879: Waddington

Prime Minister and Foreign Affairs	*William Henry Waddington* (see Thiers V)
	4 Feb – 3 Mar 1879: *Émile Deshayes de Marcère* (see Dufaure II)
	3 Mar 21 Dec 1879: *Edmond Charles Philippe Lepère* (b. Auxerre 1 Sep 1823; d. Auxerre 6 Sep 1885)
Justice	4 Feb – 12 Dec 1879; *Élie Le Royer* (b. Geneva 27 Jun 1816; d. Paris 22 Feb 1897)
Finance	*Léon Say* (see Thiers IV)
War	*Henri Gresley* (see Dufaure III)
Navy	*Jean Bernard Jauréguiberry* (b. Bayonne 26 Aug 1815; d. Paris 21˙Oct 1887)
Education	*Jules Ferry* (see Trochu)
Public Worship	4 Feb – 3 Mar 1879 (acting:) *Émile Deshayes de Marcère* (see Dufaure II)
	3 Mar – 21 Dec 1879: unknown
Public Works	*Charles Louis de Saulces de Freycinet* (see Dufaure III)
Commerce	4 Feb – 3 Mar 1879: *Edmond Lepère* (see above)
	4 Mar – 21 Dec 1879: *Pierre Emmanuel Tirard* (b Geneva 27 Sep 1827; d. Paris 4 Nov 1893)

29 Dec 1879 – 19 Sep 1880: Freycinet I

Prime Minister and Foreign Affairs	*Charles de Saulces de Freycinet* (for 1st time) (see Dufaure III)

Home Affairs	29 Dec 1879 – 16 May 1880: *Edmond Lepère* (see Waddington)
	16 May – 19 Sep 1880: *Jean Antoine Ernest Constans* (b. Béziers 3 May 1833; d. Paris 7 Apr 1913)
Justice	*Théodore Joseph Jules Cazot* (b. Alais 11 Feb 1821; d. 27 Nov 1912)
Finance	*Joseph Magnin* (see Bordeaux administration)
War	*Jean Joseph Farre* (b. Valence 5 May 1816; d. Paris 25 Mar 1887)
Navy	*Jean Bernard Jauréguiberry* (see Waddington)
Education	*Jules Ferry* (see Trochu)
Public Works	*Henri Auguste Varroy* (b. Vittel 25 Mar 1826; d. Épinal 23 Mar 1883)
Commerce and Agriculture	*Pierre Emmanuel Tirard* (see Waddington)
Posts (new post)	29 Dec 1879: *Louis Adolphe Cochery* (b. Paris 26 Apr 1819; d. Paris 13 Oct 1900)

22 Sep 1880 – 10 Nov 1881: Ferry I

Prime Minister	*Jules Ferry* (for 1st time) (see Trochu)
Foreign Affairs	*Jules Barthélemy Saint-Hilaire* (b. Paris 19 Aug 1805; d. Paris 24 Nov 1895)
Home Affairs	*Jean Antoine Ernest Constans* (see Freycinet I)
Justice	*Théodore Cazot* (see Freycinet I)
Finance	*Joseph Magnin* (see Bordeaux administration)
War	*Jean Joseph Farre* (see Freycinet I)
Navy	*Georges Charles Cloué* (b. 20 Aug 1817; d. Paris 25 Dec 1889)
Education	*Jules Ferry* (see Trochu)
Public Works	*(Marie François) Sadi Carnot* (b. Limoges 11 Aug 1837; d. Lyons 25 Jun 1894)
Commerce and Agriculture	*Pierre Emmanuel Tirard* (see Waddington)
Posts	*Louis Adolphe Cochery* (see Freycinet I)

4 Nov 1881 – 26 Jan 1882: Gambetta

Prime Minister and Foreign Affairs	*Léon Gambetta* (see Trochu)
Home Affairs	*Pierre Marie Waldeck-Rousseau* (b. Nantes 2 Dec 1846; d. Paris 10 Aug 1904)
Justice	*Théodore Cazot* (see Freycinet I)

Finance	*François Henri René Allain-Targé* (b. Angers 7 May 1832; d. Château de Targé 16 Jul 1902)
War	*Jean Baptiste Marie Édouard Campenon* (b. Tonnerre 4 May 1819; d. Paris 16 Mar 1891)
Navy	*Auguste Gougeard* (b. Brittany 15 Nov 1827: d. Auteuil 9 Mar 1886)
Education	*Paul Bert* (b. Auxerre 17 Oct 1833; d. Hanoi 11 Nov 1886)
Public Works	*David Raynal* (b. Paris 26 Feb 1840; d. Paris 27 Jan 1903)
Commerce	*Maurice Rouvier* (b. Aix 17 Apr 1842; d. Neuilly-sur-Seine 7 Jun 1911)
Agriculture	*Pierre Paul Devès* (b. Aurillac 3 Nov 1837)
Colonies	*Maurice Rouvier* (see above)
Posts	*Louis Adolphe Cochery* (see Freycinet I)
Fine Arts and State Manufacturing	*Antonin Proust* (b. Niort 15 Mar 1832; d. Paris 22 Mar 1905)

31 Jan – 29 Jul 1882: Freycinet II

Prime Minister and Foreign Affairs	*Charles de Saulces de Freycinet* (for 2nd time) (see Dufaure III)
Home Affairs	*René Goblet* (b. Aire sur la Lys 26 Nov 1828; d. Paris 13 Sep 1805)
Justice	*Gustave Amédée Humbert* (b. Metz 28 Jun 1822; d. Beauzelle 24 Sep 1894)
Finance	*Léon Say* (see Thiers IV)
War	*Jean Baptiste Billot* (b. Chaumeil 15 Aug 1822; d. Paris 1 Jun 1907)
Navy	*Jean Bernard Jauréguiberry* (see Waddington)
Education	*Jules Ferry* (see Trochu)
Public Works	*Henri Auguste Varroy* (see Freycinet I)
Commerce	*Pierre Emmanuel Tirard* (see Waddington)
Agriculture	*François de Mahy* (b. Saint-Pierre, Réunion, 22 Jul 1830; d. Paris 19 Nov 1906)
Posts	*Louis Adolphe Cochery* (see Freycinet I)

8 Aug 1882 – 28 Jan 1883: Duclerc

Prime Minister and Foreign Affairs	*Charles Théodore Eugène Duclerc* (see Executive Committee of 1848)
Home Affairs	*Armand Fallières* (b. Mézin 6 Nov 1841; d. Mézin 22 Jun 1931)

Justice	*Pierre Paul Devès* (see Gambetta)
Finance	*Pierre Emmanuel Tirard* (see Waddington)
War	*Jean Baptiste Billot* (see Freycinet II)
Navy	*Jean Bernard Jauréguiberry* (see Waddington)
Education	—— *Duvour*
Public Works	(acting:) *Pierre Legrand* (b. Lille 13 Mar 1834; d. Paris 1895)
	Aug 1882 – 28 Jan 1883: *(Anne) Charles Hérisson* (b. Surgy 12 Oct 1831)
Commerce	*Pierre Legrand* (see above)
Agriculture	*François de Mahy* (see Freycinet II)
Posts	*Louis Adolphe Cochery* (see Freycinet I)

29 Jan – 18 Feb 1883: Fallières I

Prime Minister	*Armand Fallières* (for 1st time) (see Duclerc)
War	*Jean Thibaudin* (b. Moulins-Engilbert 13 Nov 1822; d. Paris 19 Sep 1905)
Public Works	*(Anne) Charles Hérisson* (see Duclerc)
Posts	*Louis Adolphe Cochery* (see Freycinet I)

19 Feb 1883 – 30 Mar 1885: Ferry II

Prime Minister	*Jules Ferry* (for 2nd time) (see Trochu)
Foreign Affairs	19 Feb – 20 No 1883: *Paul Armand Challemel-Lacour* (b. Avranches 19 May 1827; d. Paris 26 Oct 1896)
	20 Nov 1883 – 30 Mar 1885: *Jules Ferry* (see Trochu)
Home Affairs	*Pierre Marie Waldeck-Rousseau* (see Gambetta)
Justice	*Félix Martin-Feuillée* (b. Rennes 25 Oct 1830)
Finance	*Pierre Emmanuel Tirard* (see Waddington)
War	19 Feb – 5 Oct 1833: *Jean Thibaudin* (see Fallières)
	9 Oct 1833 – 1885: *Jean Baptiste Campenon* (see Gambetta)
	3 Jan – 30 Mar 1885: *Jules Louis Lewal* (b. Paris 13 Dec 1823; d. Senlis 22 Jan 1908)
Navy	*Charles Brun* (b. Toulon 22 Nov 1821; d. 15 Jan 1897)
Education	19 Feb – 20 Nov 1883: *Jules Ferry* (see Trochu)
	20 Nov 1883 – 30 Mar 1885: *Armand Fallières* (see Duclerc)
Public Works	*David Raynal* (see Gambetta)
Commerce	19 Feb 1883 – 9 Oct 1884: *(Anne) Charles Hérisson* (see Duclerc)
	9 Oct 1884 – 30 Mar 1885: *Maurice Rouvier* (see Gambetta)

| Agriculture | *(Félix) Jules Méline* (b. Remiremont 28 May 1838; d. Paris 21 Dec 1925) |
| Posts | *Louis Adolphe Cochery* (see Freycinet I) |

6 Apr – 29 Dec 1885: Brisson I

Prime Minister	*Eugène Henri Brisson* (for 1st time) (b. Bourges 31 Jul 1835; d. Paris 13 Apr 1912)
Foreign Affairs	*Charles de Saulces de Freycinet* (see Dufaure III)
Home Affairs	*François Allain-Targé* (see Gambetta)
Justice	*Eugène Henri Brisson* (see above)
Finance	6 – 16 Apr 1885: *Jules Clamageran* (b. New Orleans 29 Mar 1827; d. Limours 4 Jun 1903)
	16 Apr – 29 Dec 1885: *(Marie François) Sadi Carnot* (see Ferry I)
War	**Jean Baptiste Campenon (see Gambetta)**
Navy	*Charles Eugène Galiber* (b. Castres 2 Jul 1824; d. Paris 26 Jan 1909)
Education	*René Goblet* (see Freycinet II)
Public Works	6 – 16 Apr 1885: *(Marie François) Sadi Carnot* (see Ferry I)
	16 Apr – 29 Dec 1885: *Charles Étienne Émile Demôle* (b. Charolles 22 Mar 1828; d. St. Julien-de-Civry 17 Jun 1908)
Commerce	*Charles François Hervé* (b. Paris 31 Jul 1821; d. Paris 15 May 1888)
Agriculture	**Pierre Legrand (see Duclerc)**
Posts	*Ferdinand Sarrien* (b. Bourbon-Lancy 15 Oct 1840; d. Paris 28 Nov 1915)

7 Jan – 3 Dec 1886: Freycinet III

Prime Minister and Foreign Affairs	*Charles de Saulces de Freycinet* (for 3rd time) (see Dufaure III)
Home Affairs	*Ferdinand Sarrien* (see Brisson)
Justice	*Charles Demôle* (see Brisson)
Finance	*(Marie François) Sadi Carnot* (see Ferry I)
War	*Georges Ernest Jean Marie Boulanger* (b. Rennes 2 Apr 1837; d. Brussels 30 Sep 1891)
Navy	*Thóphile Aube* (b. Toulon 22 Nov 1826; d. Toulon 3 Dec 1890)
Education, Public Worship and Fine Arts	*René Goblet* (see Freycinet II)

Public Works	7 Jan – early Nov 1886: *Charles Baihaut* (b. Paris 2 Apr 1835; d. Paris 24 Mar 1917)
	early Nov – 3 Dec 1886: *Édouard Millaud* (b. Tarascon 27 Sep 1834; d. Paris 15 May 1912)
Commerce	*Édouard Étienne Antoine Simon* (b. Paris 18 Jul 1840; d. 22 Nov 1913)
Agriculture	*Jules (Paul) Develle* (b. Bar-le-Duc 12 Apr 1845; d. Paris 1919)
Posts	*Étienne Armand Félix Granet* (b. Marseilles 29 Jul 1849)

16 Dec 1886 – 17 May 1887: Goblet

Prime Minister	*René Goblet* (see Freycinet II)
Foreign Affairs	*Émile Flourens* (b. Paris 27 Apr 1841; d. Paris 5 Jan 1920)
Home Affairs	*René Goblet* (see Freycinet II)
Justice	*Ferdinand Sarrien* (see Brisson)
Finance	*Albert Dauphin* (b. Amiens 26 Aug 1827; d. 1898)
War	*Georges Boulanger* (see Freycinet III)
Navy	*Théophile Aube* (see Freycinet III)
Education	*Marcellin Berthelot* (b. Paris 25 Oct 1827; d. Paris 18 Mar 1907)
Public Works	*Édouard Millaud* (see Freycinet III)
Commerce	*Auguste Lucien Dautresme* (b. Elbeuf 21 May 1826; d. Paris 19 Feb 1892)
Agriculture	*Jules Develle* (see Freycinet III)
Posts	*Étienne Granet* (see Freycinet III)

9 May – 19 Nov 1887: Rouvier I

Prime Minister	*Maurice Rouvier* (for 1st time) (see Gambetta)
Foreign Affairs	*Émile Flourens* (see Goblet)
Home Affairs	*Armand Fallières* (see Duclerc)
Justice	*Charles Jean Jacques Mazeau* (b. Dijon 1 Sep 1825; d. Paris 8 Feb 1905)
Finance	*Maurice Rouvier* (see Gambetta)
War	*Théophile Adrien Ferron* (b. Pré-St-Evroult 19 Sep 1830; d. Lyons 1894)
Navy	*Édouard Barbey* (b. Béziers 2 Sep 1831; d. Paris 26 Mar 1905)
Education	*(Jacques) Eugène Spuller* (b. Seurre 8 Dec 1835; d. Sombernon 23 Jul 1896)

Public Works	*Sévérien de Hérédia* (b. Havana 8 Nov 1836)
Commerce	*Auguste Lucien Dautresme* (see Goblet)
Agriculture	*François Paul Barbe* (b. Nancy 4 Feb 1836; d. Paris 31 Jul 1890)
Posts	*Maurice Rouvier* (see Gambetta)

11 Dec 1887 - 30 Mar 1889: Tirard I

Prime Minister	*Pierre Emmanuel Tirard* (for 1st time) see (Waddington)
Foreign Affairs	*Émile Flourens* (see Goblet)
Home Affairs	*Ferdinand Sarrien* (see Brisson)
Justice	*Armand Fallières* (see Duclerc)
Finance	*Pierre Emmanuel Tirard* (see Waddington)
War	*François Auguste Logeret* (b. Noyers 1 Feb 1845; d. Bourges 14 Feb 1913)
Navy	11 Dec 1887 - 5 Jan 1888: *François de Mahy* (see Freycinet II)
	5 Jan - 30 Mar 1888: *Jules François Émile Krantz* (b. Arches 29 Dec 1821; d. Toulon 26 Feb 1914)
Education	*Étienne Léopold Faye* (b. Marmande 16 Nov 1828; d. Birac 1900)
Public Works	*Émile Loubet* (b. Montélimar 31 Dec 1838; d. Montélimar 20 Dec 1929)
Commerce	*Auguste Lucien Dautresme* (see Goblet)
Agriculture	*Jules François Viette* (b. Blamont 6 May 1843; d. Paris 15 Feb 1894)

3 Apr 1888 - 14 Feb 1889: Floquet

Prime Minister	*Charles Thomas Floquet* (b. St Jean de Luz 5 Oct 1828; d. Paris 18 Jan 1896)
Foreign Affairs	*René Goblet* (see Freycinet II)
Home Affairs	*Charles Thomas Floquet* (see above)
Justice	*Jean Baptiste Ferroullat* (b. Lyons 4 May 1820; d. Montpellier 1903)
Finance	*Paul Louis Peytral* (b. Marseilles 20 Jan 1842; d. 1919)
War	*Charles de Saulces de Freycinet* (see Dufaure III)
Navy	*Jules Krantz* (see Tirard I)
Education	*Édouard Simon* (see Freycinet III)
Public Works	*Pierre Deluns-Montaud* (b. Allemand-du-Dropt 5 Jun 1845; d. Paris 9 Nov 1907)
Commerce	*Pierre Legrand* (see Duclerc)

Agriculture   *Jules François Viette* (see Tirard I)

21 Feb 1889 – 13 Mar 1890: Tirard II

Prime Minister   *Pierre Emmanuel Tirard* (for 2nd time) (see Waddington)
Foreign Affairs   22 Feb 1889 – 13 Mar 1890: *(Jacques) Eugène Spuller* (see Rouvier I)
Home Affairs   21 Feb 1889 – 2 Mar 1890: *Jean Constans* (see Freycinet I)
                      2 – 13 Mar 1890: *Léon Bourgeois* (b. Paris 29 May 1851; d. Château d'Oger 29 Sep 1925)
Justice   *Marius Thévenet* (b. Lyons 1845; d. Firminy 7 Apr 1910)
Finance   *Maurice Rouvier* (see Gambetta)
War   *Charles de Saulces de Freycinet* (see Dufaure III)
Navy   21 Feb – 13 Mar 1889: *Louis Jean Benjamin Jaurès* (b. Paris 3 Jan 1823; d. Paris 13 Mar 1889)
                      Mar – 9 Nov 1889: *Jules Krantz* (see Tirard I)
                      11 Nov 1889 – 13 Mar 1890: *Édouard Barbey* (see Rouvier I)
Education   *Armand Fallières* (see Duclerc)
Public Works   *Yvon Guyot* (b. Dinan 6 Jul 1843; d. Paris 21 Feb 1928)
Commerce   *Pierre Emmanuel Tirard* (see Waddington)
Agriculture   *Étienne Léopold Faye* (see Tirard I)

17 Mar 1890 – 20 Feb 1892: Freycinet IV

Prime Minister   *Charles de Saulces de Freycinet* (for 4th time) (see Dufaure III)
Foreign Affairs   *Alexandre Félix Joseph Ribot* (b. St Omer 7 Feb 1842; d. Paris 13 Jan 1923)
Home Affairs   *Jean Constans* (see Freycinet I)
Justice   *Armand Fallières* (see Duclerc)
Finance   *Maurice Rouvier* (see Gambetta)
War   *Charles de Saulces de Freycinet* (see Dufaure III)
Navy   *Édouard Barbey* (see Rouvier I)
Education   *Léon Bourgeois* (see Tirard II)
Public Works   *Yvon Guyot* (see Tirard II)
Commerce   *Jules Roche* (b. Serrières 22 May 1841; d. 1923)
Agriculture   *Jules Develle* (see Freycinet III)

27 Feb – 29 Nov 1892: Loubet

Prime Minister	*Émile Loubet* (see Tirard I)
Foreign Affairs	*Jules Develle* (see Freycinet III)
Home Affairs	*Émile Loubet* (see Tirard I)
Justice	*Louis Ricard* (b. Caen 17 Mar 1839)
Finance	*Maurice Rouvier* (see Gambetta)
War	*Charles de Saulces de Freycinet* (see Dufaure III)
Navy	27 Feb – Jul 1892: *Godefroy Cavaignac* (b. Paris 21 May 1853; d. Ourne 24 Sep 1905)
	Jul – 28 Nov 1892: *Auguste Laurent Burdeau* (b. Lyons 10 Sep 1851; d. Paris 12 Dec 1894)
Education	*Charles Dupuy* (b. Le Puy 5 Nov 1851; d. Ille-sur-Têt 23 Jul 1923)
Public Works	*Jules François Viette* (see Tirard I)
Commerce	—— *Serrien*

6 Dec 1892 – 10 Jan 1893: Ribot I

Prime Minister and Foreign Affairs	*Alexandre Félix Joseph Ribot* (for 1st time) (see Freycinet IV)
Home Affairs	*Emile Loubet* (see Tirard I)
Justice	*Léon Bourgeois* (see Tirard II)
Finance	6 – 13 Dec 1892: *Maurice Rouvier* (see Gambetta)
	13 Dec 1892 – 10 Jan 1893: *Pierre Emmanuel Tirard* (see Waddington)
War	*Charles de Saulces de Freycinet* (see Dufaure III)
Navy	*Auguste Laurent Burdeau* (see Loubet)
Education	*Charles Dupuy* (see Loubet)
Public Works	*Jules François Viette* (see Tirard I)
Commerce	—— *Serrien* (see Loubet)
Agriculture	*Jules Develle* (see Freycinet III)
Public Worship	6 Dec 1892: *Émile Loubet* (see Tirard I)
	Dec 1892 – 10 Jan 1893: *Charles Dupuy* (see Loubet)

13 Jan – 20 Apr 1893: Ribot II

Prime Minister	*Alexandre Félix Joseph Ribot* (for 2nd time) (see Freycinet IV)
Foreign Affairs	*Jules Develle* (see Freycinet III)
Home Affairs	*Alexandre Félix Joseph Ribot* (see Freycinet IV)
Justice	13 Jan – 30 Mar 1893: *Léon Bourgeois* (see Tirard II)
	12 – 15 Mar 1893: no appointment made

Finance	*Pierre Emmanuel Tirard* (see Waddington)
War	*Jules Léon Loizillon* (b. Paris 15 Jan 1829; d. Dammarie 1896)
Navy	*Adrien Bartholome Louis Rieunier* (b. Castelsarrasin 6 Mar 1833; d. Albi 1918)
Education	*Charles Dupuy* (see Loubet)
Public Works	*Jules François Viette* (see Tirard I)
Commerce	*Jules Siegfried* (b. Mulhouse 12 Feb 1837; d. Paris 1922)
Agriculture	*Albert Viger* (b. Jargeau 18 Oct 1843; d. 8 Jul 1926)
Public Worship	Amalgamated with Education

4 Apr – 25 Nov 1893: Dupuy I

Prime Minister	*Charles Dupuy* (for 1st time) (see Loubet)
Foreign Affairs	*Jules Develle* (see Freycinet III)
Home Affairs	*Charles Dupuy* (see Loubet)
Justice	*Pierre Eugène Gustave Guerin* (b. Carpentras 28 Jul 1849; d. Paris 29 Apr 1929)
Finance	*Paul Louis Peytral* (see Floquet)
War	*Jules Léon Loizillon* (see Ribot II)
Navy	*Adrien Rieunier* (see Ribot II)
Education, Fine Arts and Public Worship	*Raymond Poincaré* (b. Bar-le-Duc 20 Aug 1860; d. Paris 15 Oct 1934)
Public Works	*Jules François Viette* (see Tirard I)
Commerce and Colonies	*Louis Jean Jacques Terrier* (b. Annecy 8 Jul 1854; d. Paris 20 Aug 1895)
Under-Secretary of State for Colonies	*Théophile Delcassé* (b. Pamiers 1 Mar 1852; d. Nice 21 Feb 1923)
Agriculture	*Albert Viger* (see Ribot II)

3 Dec 1893 – 22 May 1894: Casimir-Périer

Prime Minister and Foreign Affairs	*Jean Paul Pierre Casimir-Périer* (b. Paris 8 Nov 1847; d. Paris 11 Feb 1907)
Home Affairs	*David Raynal* (see Gambetta)
Justice	*Henri Antoine Dubost* (b. L'Arbresle 6 Apr 1842; d. Paris 15 Apr 1921)
Finance	*Auguste Laurent Burdeau* (see Loubet)
War	*Auguste Mercier* (b. Arras 8 Dec 1833; d. Paris 3 Mar 1921)
Navy	*Auguste Alfred Lefèvre* (b. Brest 20 Dec 1828; d. Paris

209

night of 7/8 Jan 1907)

Education	*Jacques Eugène Spuller* (see Rouvier I)
Public Works	*Célestin Jonnart* (b. Fléchin 27 Dec 1857; d. Paris 30 Sep 1927)
Commerce	*Jean Antoine Marty* (b. Carcassonne 31 Jan 1838)
Under-Secretary of State for Colonies	*Théophile Delcassé* (see Dupuy I)
Agriculture	*Albert Viger* (see Ribot II)

30 May 1894 – 14 Jan 1895: Dupuy II

Prime Minister	*Charles Dupuy* (for 2nd time) (see Loubet)
Foreign Affairs	*Gabriel Hanotaux* (b. Beaurevoir 19 Nov 1853; d. Paris 11 Apr 1944)
Home Affairs	*Charles Dupuy* (see Loubet)
Finance	*Raymond Poincaré* (see Dupuy I)
War	*Auguste Mercier* (see Casimir-Périer)
Navy	*Félix Faure* (b. Paris 30 Jan 1841; d. 16 Feb 1899)
Education and Fine Arts	*Georges Leygues* (b. Villeneuve-sur-Lot 28 Nov 1858; d. St Cloud 2 Sep 1933)
Public Worship	*Charles Dupuy* (see Loubet)
Public Works	*Louis Barthou* (b.Oloron-St Marie 25 Aug 1862; d. Marseilles 9 Oct 1934)
Commerce	*Victor Christophe Gabriel Lourties* (b. Aire-sur-l'Adour 21 Jul 1844)
Colonies	*Théophile Delcassé* (see Dupuy I)
Agriculture	*Albert Viger* (see Ribot II)

27 Jan – 28 Oct 1895: Ribot III

Prime Minister	*Alexandre Félix Joseph Ribot* (for 3rd time) (see Freycinet IV)
Foreign Affairs	*Gabriel Hanotaux* (see Dupuy II)
Home Affairs	*Georges Leygues* (see Dupuy II)
Justice	*Louis Trarieux* (b. Aubeterre 30 Nov 1840; d. Paris 13 Mar 1904)
Finance	*Alexandre Félix Joseph Ribot* (see Freycinet IV)
War	27 Jan 1895: *Édouard Ferdinand Jamont* (b. St Philibert-de-Grandlieu 19 Jul 1831; d. Paris 1918)
	27 Jan – 28 Oct 1895: *Émile Auguste (François Thomas) Zurlinden* (b. Colmar 3 Nov 1837; d. Paris 1929)

Navy	*Armand Louis Charles Gustave Besnard* (b. Rambouillet 11 Oct 1833; d. Lorient 1903)
Education	*Raymond Poincaré* (see Dupuy I)
Public Works	*Louis Dupuy-Dutemps* (b. Les Cabannes 6 Jan 1847)
Commerce	*André Lebon* (b. Dieppe 26 Aug 1859)
Colonies	*Émile Chautemps* (b. Valleiry 2 May 1850; d. 10 Dec 1918)
Agriculture	*Henry Gadeau de Kerville* (b. Rouen 1858)

1 Nov 1895 – 22 Apr 1896: Bourgeois

Prime Minister	*Léon Bourgeois* (see Tirard II)
Foreign Affairs	1 Nov 1895 – 28 Mar 1896: *Marcellin Berthelot* (see Goblet)
	28 Mar – 22 Apr 1896: *Léon Bourgeois* (see Tirard II)
Home Affairs	1 Nov 1895 – 28 Mar 1896: *Léon Bourgeois* (see Tirard II)
	28 Mar – 22 Apr 1896: *Ferdinand Sarrien* (see Brisson I)
Justice	*Louis Ricard* (see Loubet)
Finance	*Paul Doumer* (b. Aurillac 22 Mar 1857; d. Paris 7 May 1932)
War	*Godefroy Cavaignac* (see Loubet)
Navy	*Édouard Simon* (see Freycinet III)
Education	*Émile Combes* (b. Rocquecombe 6 Sep 1835; d. Pons 25 May 1921)
Public Worship	*Louis Ricard* (see Loubet)
Public Works	*Jean François Édouard Guyot-Dessaigne* (b. Brioude 25 Dec 1833; d. Paris 31 Dec 1907)
Commerce	*Gustave Mesureur* (b. Marcq-en-Baroeul 2 Apr 1847; d. Paris 1925)
Colonies	*Paul Guieysse* (b. Lorient 11 May 1841; d. Paris 19 Feb 1914)
Agriculture	*Albert Viger* (see Ribot II)
Posts	*Gustave Mesureur* (see above)

29 Apr 1896 – 14 Jun 1898: Méline

Prime Minister	*Félix Jules Méline* (see Ferry II)
Foreign Affairs	*Gabriel Hanotaux* (see Dupuy II)
Home Affairs	*Louis Barthou* (see Dupuy II)
Justice	29 Apr 1896 – 30 Nov 1897: *Jean Baptiste Darlan* (b. Podensac 10 Jun 1848; d. Nérac 6 Nov 1912)

	30 Nov 1897 – 14 Jun 1898: *Victor Édouard Milliard* (b. Andelys 19 Dec 1844)
Finance	*Georges Charles Paul Cochery* (b. Paris 24 Mar 1855; d. 8 Aug 1914)
War	*Jean Baptiste Billot* (see Freycinet II)
Navy	*Armand Besnard* (see Ribot III)
Education	*Alfred Rambaud* (b. Besançon 2 Jul 1842; d. Paris 10 Nov 1905)
Public Works	*Adolphe Jean Eugène Turrel* (b. Ornaisons 28 May 1856)
Commerce	*Henry Boucher* (b. Bruyères 19 Sep 1847; d. Nancy 1 Feb 1927)
Colonies	*André Lebon* (see Ribot III)
Agriculture	*Félix Jules Méline* (see Ferry II)

27 Jun – 25 Oct 1898: Brisson II

Prime Minister	*Eugène Henri Brisson* (for 2nd time) (see Brisson I)
Foreign Affairs	*Théophile Delcassé* (see Dupuy I)
Home Affairs	*Eugène Henri Brisson* (see Brisson I)
Justice	*Ferdinand Sarrien* (see Brisson I)
Finance	*Paul Louis Peytral* (see Floquet)
War	27 Jun – 3 Sep 1898: *Godefroy Cavaignac* (see Loubet)
	3 – 17 Sep 1898: *Émile Auguste Zurlinden* (see Ribot III)
	17 Sep – 25 Oct 1898: *Charles Sulpice Jules Chanoine* (b. Dijon 18 Dec 1835; d. Baudement 29 Jan 1915)
Navy	*Édouard Simon* (see Freycinet III)
Education	*Léon Bourgeois* (see Tirard II)
Public Works	27 Jun – 17 Sep 1898: *Louis Charles Tillaye* (b. Vimoutiers 31 May 1847; d. Pau 6 May 1913)
	17 Sep – 25 Oct 1898: *Jules Godin* (b. Versailles 14 Mar 1844)
Commerce	*Pierre Adolphe Émile Maruéjouls* (b. Villefranche 4 Aug 1837; d. Villeneuve 22 Oct 1908)
Colonies	*Georges Trouillot* (b. Champagnole 7 May 1851; d. Paris 22 Nov 1916)
Agriculture	*Albert Viger* (see Ribot II)
Posts	*Gabriel Mougeot* (b. Montigny-le-Roy 10 Nov 1858; d. 1928)

31 Oct 1898 – 12 Jun 1899: Dupuy III

Prime Minister	*Charles Dupuy* (for 3rd time) (see Loubet)

Foreign Affairs	*Théophile Delcassé* (see Dupuy I)
Home Affairs	*Charles Dupuy* (see Loubet)
Justice	*Georges Lebret* (b. Étampes 7 Nov 1853)
Finance	*Paul Louis Peytral* (see Floquet)
War	31 Oct 1898 – 5 May 1899: *Charles de Saulces de Freycinet* (see Dufaure III)
	5 May – 12 Jun 1899: *Jules Krantz* (see Tirard I)
Navy	*Édouard Simon* (see Freycinet III)
Education	*Georges Leygues* (see Dupuy II)
Public Works	31 Oct 1898 – 5 May 1899: *Jules Krantz* (see Tirard I)
	5 May – 12 Jun 1899: *Clément Jean Monestier* (b. Saint-Rome 23 Nov 1855)
Commerce	*Paul Delombre* (b. Maubeuge 18 Mar 1848)
Colonies	*Florent Antoine Guillain* (b. Paris 1844; d. 21 Apr 1915)
Agriculture	*Albert Viger* (see Ribot II)
Posts	*Paul Delcombre* (see above)

22 Jun 1899 – 28 May 1902: Waldeck-Rousseau

Prime Minister	*Pierre Marie Waldeck-Rousseau* (see Gambetta)
Foreign Affairs	*Théophile Delcassé* (see Ribot II)
Home Affairs	*Pierre Marie Waldeck-Rousseau* (see Gambetta)
Justice	*Antoine Emmanuel Ernest Monis* (b. Châteauneuf 29 May 1846; d. Châteauneuf 26 May 1929)
Finance	*Joseph Caillaux* (b. Le Mans 30 Mar 1863; d. Mamers night of 21/22 Nov 1944)
War	22 Jun 1899 – 29 May 1900: *Gaston Alexandre Auguste, Marquis de Galliffet* (b. Paris 23 Jan 1830; d. Paris 8 Jan 1909)
	29 May 1900 – 28 May 1902: *Louis André* (b. Nuits 29 Mar 1838; d. Dijon 18 Mar 1913)
Navy	*Antoine de Lanessan* (b. Saint-Andre-de-Cubzac 13 Jul 1843; d. Écouen 7 Nov 1919)
Education	*Georges Leygues* (see Dupuy II)
Public Works	*Pierre Baudin* (b. Nantua 21 Aug 1863; d. Paris 1 Aug 1917)
Commerce	*Alexandre Millerand* (b. Paris 10 Feb 1859; d. Versailles 6 Apr 1943)
Colonies	*Albert Pierre Louis Decrais* (b. Bordeaux 18 Sep 1838; d. Mérignac 1915)
Agriculture	*Jean Dupuy* (b. Saint-Palais 1 Oct 1844; d. 31 Dec 1919)

213

7 Jun 1902 – 19 Jan 1905: Combes

Prime Minister	*Émile Combes* (see Bourgeois)
Foreign Affairs	*Théophile Delcassé* (see Dupuy I)
Home Affairs	*Émile Combes* (see Bourgeois)
Justice	*Ernest Vallé* (b. Avize 1845; d. Paris 1920)
Finance	*Maurice Rouvier* (see Gambetta)
War	7 Jun 1902 – 15 Nov 1904: *Louis André* (see Waldeck-Rousseau)
	15 Nov 1904 – 19 Jan 1905: *Maurice Berteaux* (b. Saint-Maur-les-Fossés 3 Jun 1852; d. Issy-les-Moulineaux 21 May 1911)
Navy	*Camille Pelletan* (b. Paris 23 Jun 1846; d. Paris 3 Jun 1915)
Education	*Joseph Chaumié* (b. Agen 17 Jul 1849; d. Clermont-Dessous 18 Jul 1919)
Public Worship	*Émile Combes* (see Bourgeois)
Public Works	*Pierre Maruéjouls* (see Brisson II)
Commerce	*Georges Trouillot* (see Brisson II)
Colonies	*Gaston Doumergue* (b. Aigues-Vives 1 Aug 1863; d. Aigues-Vives 18 Jun 1937)
Agriculture	*Gabriel Mougeot* (see Brisson II)
Under Secretary of State for Posts	*Alexandre Bérard* (b. Lyons 3 Feb 1859; d. Paris 1923)

24 Jan 1905 – 7 Mar 1906: Rouvier II

Prime Minister	*Maurice Rouvier* (for 2nd time) (see Gambetta)
Foreign Affairs	24 Jan – 6 Jun 1905: *Théophile Delcassé* (see Dupuy I)
	6 Jun 1905 – 7 Mar 1906: *Maurice Rouvier* (see Gambetta)
Home Affairs	24 Jan – 12 Nov 1905: *Eugène Étienne* (b. Oran 15 Dec 1844; d. Paris 13 May 1921)
	12 Nov 1905 – 7 Mar 1906: *Ferdinand Dubief* (b. Château-de-Varenes-les-Mâcon 14 Oct 1850; d. Paris 5 Jun 1916)
Justice	*Joseph Chaumié* (see Combes)
Finance	*Maurice Rouvier* (see Gambetta)
War	24 Jan – 10 Nov 1905: *Maurice Berteaux* (see Combes)
	12 Nov 1905 – 7 Mar 1906: *Eugène Étienne* (see above)
Navy	*Gaston Thomson* (b. Oran 29 Jan 1848; d. Bona 14 May 1932)
Education	*Jean Baptiste Bienvenu Martin* (b. Saint Bris 22 Jul 1847; d. Burgundy Dec 1943)

Public Works	*Armande Gauthier* (b. Fitou 28 Sep 1850)
Commerce	24 Jan – 12 Nov 1905: *Ferdinand Dubief* (see above)
	12 Nov 1905 – 7 Mar 1906: *Georges Trouillot* (see Brisson II)
Colonies	*Étienne Clementel* (b. Clermont-Ferrand 29 Mar 1864; d. Promptas 26 Dec 1936)
Agriculture	*Joseph Ruau* (b. Paris 5 Jun 1865)

12 Mar – 18 Oct 1906: Sarrien

Prime Minister	*Ferdinand Sarrien* (see Brisson I)
Foreign Affairs	*Léon Bourgeois* (see Tirard II)
Home Affairs	*Georges Clemenceau* (b. Mouilleron-en-Pareds 28 Sep 1841; d. Paris 24 Nov 1929)
Justice	*Ferdinand Sarrien* (see Brisson I)
Finance	*Raymond Poincaré* (see Dupuy I)
War	*Eugène Étienne* (see Rouvier II)
Navy	*Gaston Thomson* (see Rouvier II)
Education	*Aristide Briand* (b. Nantes 28 Mar 1862; d. Paris 7 Mar 1932)
Public Works	*Louis Barthou* (see Dupuy II)
Commerce	*Gaston Doumergue* (see Combes)
Colonies	*Georges Leygues* (see Dupuy II)
Agriculture	*Joseph Ruau* (see Rouvier II)

28 Oct 1906 – 20 Jul 1909: Clemenceau I

Prime Minister	*Georges Clemenceau* (for 1st time) (see Sarrien)
Foreign Affairs	*Stéphan Pichon* (b. Arnay-le-Duc 10 Jan 1857; d. Vers-en-Montagne 19 Sep 1933)
Home Affairs	*Georges Clemenceau* (see Sarrien)
Justice	23 Oct 1906 – end Dec 1907: *Jean Guyot-Dessaigne* (see Bourgeois)
	4 Jan 1908 – 20 Jul 1909: *Aristide Briand* (see Sarrien)
Finance	*Joseph Caillaux* (see Waldeck-Rousseau)
War	*Georges Picquart* (b. Strasbourg 6 Sep 1854; d. Amiens 19 Jan 1914)
Navy	23 Oct 1906 – 19 Oct 1908: *Gaston Thomson* (see Rouvier II)
	19 Oct 1909 – 20 Jul 1909: *Alfred Picard* (b. Strasbourg 1844; d. Paris 8 Mar 1913)
Education and Public Worship	23 Oct 1906 – 4 Jan 1908: *Aristide Briand* (see Sarrien)

	4 Jan 1908 – 20 Jul 1909: *Gaston Doumergue* (see Combes)
Public Works	*Louis Barthou* (see Dupuy II)
Commerce	23 Oct 1906 – 4 Jan 1908: *Gaston Doumergue* (see Combes)
	4 Jan 1908 – 20 Jul 1909: *Jean Cruppi* (b. Toulouse 22 May 1855; d. Fontainebleau 1933)
Colonies	*Raphael Milliès-Lacroix* (b. Dax 1850)
Labour and Health	New post; *René Viviani* (b. Sidi bel Abbès, Algeria, 8 Nov 1863; d. Plessis-Picquet 7 Sep 1925)
Agriculture	*Joseph Ruau* (see Rouvier II)

24 Jul 1909 – 2 Nov 1910: Briand I

Prime Minister	*Aristide Briand* (for 1st time) (see Sarrien)
Foreign Affairs	*Stéphan Pichon* (see Clemenceau I)
Home Affairs	*Aristide Briand* (see Sarrien)
Justice	*Louis Barthou* (see Dupuy II)
Finance	*Georges Cochery* (see Meline)
War	*Jean Jules Brun* (b. Marmande 24 Apr 1849; d. Paris 23 Feb 1911)
Navy	*Auguste Boué de Lapeyrère* (b. Castera-Lectourois 1852; d. Pau 17 Feb 1924)
Education	*Gaston Doumergue* (see Combes)
Public Worship	*Aristide Briand* (see Sarrien)
Public Works	*Alexandre Millerand* (see Waldeck-Rousseau)
Labour and Social Welfare	*René Viviani* (see Clemenceau)
Commerce	*Jean Dupuy* (see Waldeck-Rousseau)
Colonies	*Georges Trouillot* (see Brisson II)
Agriculture	*Joseph Ruau* (see Rouvier II)
Post	*Alexandre Millerand* (see Waldeck Rousseau)

3 Nov 1910 – 24 Feb 1911: Briand II

Prime Minister	*Aristide Briand* (for 2nd time) (see Sarrien)
Foreign Affairs	*Stéphan Pichon* (see Clemenceau I)
Home Affairs	*Aristide Briand* (see Sarrien)
Justice	—— *Girard*
Finance	*Louis Lucien Klotz* (b. Paris 11 Jan 1868; d. Paris 15 Jun 1930)
War	*Jean Jules Brun* (see Briand I)
Navy	*Auguste Boué de Lapeyrère* (see Briand I)

Education and Public Worship	*Maurice Faure* (b. Saillans 1850; d. Saillans 1919)
Public Works	*Louis Lafferre* (b. Pau 10 May 1861)
Commerce	*Jean Dupuy* (see Waldeck-Rousseau)
Transport	—— *Puech*
Industry	*Jean Morel* (b. Mandax 1854)
Agriculture	—— *Raynaud*

4 Mar – 22 Jun 1911: Monis

Prime Minister	*Antoine Emmanuel Ernest Monis* (see Waldeck-Rousseau)
Foreign Affairs	*Jean Cruppi* (see Clemenceau I)
Home Affairs	—— *Person*
Justice	*Gabriel Perrier* (b. Paris 12 Feb 1876)
Finance	*Joseph Caillaux* (see Waldeck-Rousseau)
War	*Maurice Berteaux* (see Combes)
Navy	*Théophile Delcassé* (see Dupuy I)
Education	*Théodore Steeg* (b. Libourne 19 Dec 1868; d. Paris 10 Dec 1950)
Public works	*Charles Dumont* (b. Bramans 1867; d. Meulan 23 Apr 1939)
Labour and Social Welfare	*Joseph Paul-Boncour* (b. St Aignan 4 Aug 1873)
Commerce	*Alfred Massé* (b. Pougues-les-Ernix 2 Jun 1870)
Colonies	*Adolphe Messimy* (b. Lyons 31 Jan 1869; d. Charnoz 1 Sep 1935)
Agriculture	*Jules Pams* (b. Perpignan 14 Aug 1852; d. Paris 11/12 May 1930)

27 Jun 1911 – 10 Jan 1912: Caillaux

Prime Minister	*Joseph Caillaux* (see Waldeck-Rousseau)
Foreign Affairs	27 Jun 1911 – 8 Jan 1912: *Justin de Selves* (b. Toulouse 19 Jul 1848; d. Paris night of 13/14 Jan 1934)
Home Affairs	*Joseph Caillaux* (see Waldeck-Rousseau)
Justice	*Jean Cruppi* (see Clemenceau I)
Finance	*Louis Lucien Klotz* (see Briand II)
War	*Adolphe Messimy* (see Monis)
Navy	*Théophile Delcassé* (see Dupuy I)
Education	*Théodore Steeg* (see Monis)
Public Works	*Victor Augagneur* (b. Lyons 16 May 1855; d. Paris 24 Apr 1931)

Labour and Social Welfare	*René Renoult* (b. Paris 29 Aug, 1867)
Commerce	*Maurice Couyba* (b. Dampierre-sur-Salon 1866; d. Paris 1931)
Colonies	*Albert Lebrun* (b. Mercy-le-Haut 29 Aug 1871; d. Paris 6 Mar 1850)
Agriculture	*Jules Pams* (see Monis)

14 Jan 1912 - 18 Jan 1913: Poincaré I

Prime Minister and Foreign Affairs	*Raymond Poincaré* (for 1st time) (see Dupuy I)
Home Affairs	*Théodore Steeg* (see Monis)
Justice	*Aristide Briand* (see Sarrien)
Finance	*Louis Lucien Klotz* (see Briand II)
War	14 Jan 1912 - 12 Jan 1913: *Alexandre Millerand* (see Waldeck-Rousseau)
	12 - 18 Jan 1913: *Albert Lebrun* (see Caillaux)
Navy	*Théophile Delcassé* (see Dupuy I)
Education	*Gabriel Henri Guist'hau* (b. Saint-Pierre, Réunion 22 Nov 1863; d. Nanates 27 Nov 1931)
Public Works	*Jean Dupuy* (see Waldeck-Rousseau)
Labour and Social Welfare	*Léon Bourgeois* (see Tirard II)
Commerce	*Ferdinand David* (b. Annemasse 15 Oct 1869; d. Paris 17 Jan 1935)
Colonies	14 Jan 1912 - 12 Jan 1913: *Albert Lebrun* (see Caillaux)
	12 - 18 Jan 1913: *René Besnard* (b. Artannes 12 Apr 1879; d. 12 Mar 1952)
Agriculture	*Jules Pams* (see Monis)

18 Jan - 18 Mar 1913: Briand III

Prime Minister	*Aristide Briand* (for 3rd time) (see Sarrien)
Foreign Affairs	*Célestin Jonnart* (see Casimir-Périer)
Home Affairs	*Aristide Briand* (see Sarrien)
Justice	*Louis Barthou* (see Dupuy II)
Finance	*Louis Lucien Klotz* (see Briand II)
War	*Eugène Étienne* (see Rouvier II)
Navy	*Pierre Baudin* (see Waldeck-Rousseau)
Education	*Théodore Steeg* (see Monis)

Public Works	*Jean Dupuy* (see Waldeck-Rousseau)
Labour and Social Welfare	*René Besnard* (see Poincaré I)
Commerce	*Gabriel Henri Guist'hau* (see Poincaré I)
Colonies	*Jean Morel* (see Briand II)
Agriculture	*Ferdinand David* (see Poincaré I)

24 Mar – 2 Dec 1913: Barthou

Prime Minister	*Louis Barthou* (see Dupuy II)
Foreign Affairs	*Stéphan Pichon* (see Clemenceau I)
Home Affairs	*Louis Lucien Klotz* (see Briand II)
Justice	*Antony Ratier* (b. Buzançais 29 Jun 1851; d. La Garde 10 Aug 1934)
Finance	*Charles Dumont* (see Monis)
War	*Eugène Étienne* (see Rouvier II)
Navy	*Pierre Baudin* (see Waldeck-Rousseau)
Education	*Louis Barthou* (see Dupuy II)
Public Works	*Joseph Thierry* (b. Hagenau 19 Mar 1857; d. San Sebastian 22 Sep 1918)
Labour and Social Welfare	*Henri Chéron* (b. Lisieux 11 May 1867; d. Lisieux 14 Apr 1936)
Commerce	*Alfred Massé* (see Monis)
Colonies	*Jean Morel* (see Briand II)
Agriculture	*Étienne Clementel* (see Rouvier II)

8 Dec 1913 – 4 Jun 1914: Doumergue

Prime Minister and Foreign Affairs	*Gaston Doumergue* (see Combes)
Home Affairs	*René Renoult* (see Caillaux)
Justice	*Jean Baptiste Bienvenu Martin* (see Rouvier II)
Finance	*Joseph Caillaux* (see Waldeck-Rousseau)
War	*Joseph Noulens* (b. Bordeaux 29 Mar 1864)
Navy	*Antoine Emmanuel Ernest Monis* (see Waldeck-Rousseau)
Education	*René Viviani* (see Clemenceau I)
Public Works	*Ferdinand David* (see Poincaré I)
Labour and Social Welfare	*Albert Métin* (b. Besançon 1871; d. San Francisco 15 Aug 1918)
Commerce	*Louis Malvy* (b. Figeac 1 Dec 1875; d. Paris 9 Jun 1949)
Colonies	*Albert Lebrun* (see Caillaux)

Agriculture	—— *Raynaud* (see Briand II)
Posts and Telegraphs	*Louis Malvy* (see above)

9 Jun – 26 Aug 1914: Viviani I

Prime Minister	*René Viviani* (for 1st time) (see Clemenceau I)
Foreign Affairs	9 Jun – 3 Aug 1914: *Léon Bourgeois* (see Tirard II)
	3 – 4 Aug 1914: *Théophile Delcassé* (see Dupuy I)
	4 – 26 Aug 1914: *Gaston Doumergue* (see Combes)
Home Affairs	*9 Jun – 3 Aug 1914: Victor Peytral* (b. Marseilles 19 Oct 1874)
	3 – 26 Aug 1914: *Georges Clemenceau* (see Sarrien)
Justice	*Alexandre Ribot* (see Freycinet IV)
Finance	9 Jun – 3 Aug 1914: *Étienne Clementel* (see Rouvier II)
	3 – 26 Aug 1914: *Alexandre Ribot* (see Freycinet IV)
War	9 Jun – 3 Aug 1914: *Joseph Noulens* (see Doumerque I)
	3 – 26 Aug 1914: *Édouard, Vicomte Castelnau-de-Curières* (b. St Affrique 24 Dec 1851; d. Montastruc-la-Conseillère 19 Mar 1944)
Navy	9 Jun – 1914; *Théophile Delcassé* (Dupuy I)
	3 Aug 1914: *Armand Gauthier* (see Rouvier II)
	3 – 26 Aug 1914: *Victor Augagneur* (see Caillaux)
Education	9 Jun – 3 Aug 1914: —— *Dessoyé*
	3 – 26 Aug 1914: *Albert Sarraut* (b. Bordeaux 28 Jul 1872)
Public Works	*Jean Baptiste Eugène Abel* (b. Toulon 12 Jan 1863; d. 30 Sep 1921)
Labour and Social Welfare	*Jean Dupuy* (see Waldeck-Rousseau)
Commerce	—— *Réville*
Colonies	*Maurice Maunoury* (b. Alexandria 16 Oct 1863; d. Paris 16 May 1925)
Agriculture	*Adrien Dariac* (b. Périgueux 14 Jun 1868)

27 Aug 1914 – 29 Oct 1915: Viviani II

Prime Minister	*René Viviani* (for 2nd time) (see Clemenceau I)
Foreign Affairs	27 Aug 1914 – 12 Oct 1915: *Théophile Delcassé* (see Dupuy I)
	12 – 29 Oct 1915: *René Viviani* (see Clemenceau I)
Home Affairs	*Louis Malvy* (see Doumerque)

Justice	*Aristide Briand* (see Sarrien)
Finance	*Alexandre Ribot* (see Freycinet IV)
War	*Alexandre Millerand* (see Waldeck-Rousseau)
Navy	*Victor Augagneur* (see Caillaux)
Education	*Albert Sarraut* (see Viviani I)
Public Works	*Marcel Sembat* (b. Bonnières 19 Oct 1862; d. Chamonix 5 Sep 1922)
Commerce	*Gaston Thomson* (see Rouvier II)
Colonies	*Gaston Doumergue* (see Combes)
Agriculture	*Ferdinand David* (see Poincaré I)
Without Portfolio	*Jules Guesde* (b. Paris 11 Nov 1845; d. St Mandé 28 Jul 1922)

29 Oct 1915 – 7 Dec 1916: Briand IV

Prime Minister	*Aristide Briand* (for 4th time) (see Sarrien)
Foreign Affairs	*Aristide Briand* (see Sarrien)
Home Affairs	*Louis Malvy* (see Doumergue)
Justice	*René Viviani* (see Clemenceau I)
Finance	*Alexandre Ribot* (see Freycinet IV)
War	29 Oct 1915 – 14 Mar 1916: *Joseph Gallieni* (b. St Béat 24 Jun 1849; d. Versailles 26 May 1916) 14 Mar – 7 Dec 1916: *Pierre Auguste Roques* (b. Marseillan 1857; d. St Cloud 1920)
Navy	*(Marie Jean) Lucien Lacaze* (b. Pierrefonds 1860; d. Paris 23 Mar 1955)
Education	*Paul Painlevé* (b. Paris 5 Dec 1863; d. 29 Oct 1933)
Public Works	*Marcel Sembat* (see Viviani II)
Labour and Social Affairs	*Albert Métin* (see Doumergue)
Commerce	*Étienne Clementel* (see Rouvier II)
Colonies	*Gaston Doumergue* (see Combes)
Agriculture	*Félix Jules Méline* (see Ferry II)
Blockade (new post)	1 Apr – 7 Dec 1916: *Denis Cochin* (b. Paris 1 Sep 1851; d. Paris 24 Mar 1922)
Without Portfolio	*Charles de Saulces de Freycinet* (see Dufaure III) *Léon Bourgeois* (see Tirard II) *Émile Combes* (see Bourgeois) *Jules Guesde* (see Viviani II) 29 Oct 1915 – 1 Apr 1916: *Denis Cochin* (see above)

12 Dec 1916 – 17 Mar 1917: Briand V

Foreign Affairs	*Aristide Briand* (for 5th time) (see Sarrien)

Home Affairs	*Louis Malvy* (see Doumerque)
Justice	*René Viviani* (see Clemenceau I)
Finance	*Alexandre Félix Joseph Ribot* (see Freycinet IV)
War	12 Dec 1916 – 14 Mar 1917: *Louis Hubert Lyautey* (b. Nancy 17 Nov 1854; d. Paris 27 Jul 1934)
	14 – 17 Mar 1917: *(Marie Jean) Lucien Lacaze* (see Briand IV)
Navy	*(Marie Jean) Lucien Lacaze* (see Briand IV)
Education	*René Viviani* (see Clemenceau I)
Colonies	*Gaston Doumergue* (see Combes)
Economy	*Étienne Clementel* (see Rouvier II)
Controller of Civil and Military Food Supplies	*Édouard Herriot* (b. Troyes 5 Jul 1872; d. Lyons 26 Mar 1957)
Munitions and War Materials	*Albert Thomas* (b. Champigny-sur-Marne 16 Jun 1878; d. Paris 8 May 1932)

20 Mar – 7 Sep 1917: Ribot IV

Prime Minister and Foreign Affairs	*Alexandre Felix Joseph Ribot* (for 4th time) (see Freycinet IV
Home Affairs	20 Mar – 1 Sep 1917: *Louis Malvy* (see Doumergue I)
	1 – 7 Sep 1917 (acting:) *Théodore Steeg* (see Monis)
Justice	*René Viviani* (see Clemenceau I)
Finance	*Joseph Thierry* (see Barthou)
War	*Paul Painlevé* (see Briand IV)
Navy	*Marie Jean Lacaze* (see Briand IV)
Education	*Théodore Steeg* (see Monis)
Public Works	—— *Desplas*
Labour and Social Welfare	*Léon Bourgeois* (see Tirad II)
Commerce	*Étienne Clementel* (see Rouvier II)
Colonies	*André Maginot* (b. Paris 17 Nov 1877; d. Paris 8 Jan 1932)
Agriculture	*Ferdinand David* (see Poincaré I)
Munitions	*Albert Thomas* (see Briand V)
Food	*Maurice Viollette* (b. Janville 3 Sep 1870: d. Paris 9 Sep 1960)
Under Secretary of State for Air	*Daniel Vincent* (b. Bettrechies 31 Mar 1874)

12 Sep – 13 Nov 1917: Painlevé I

Prime Minister	*Paul Painlevé* (for 1st time) (see Briand IV)

Foreign Affairs	*Alexandre Ribot* (see Freycinet IV)
Home Affairs	*Théodore Steeg* (see Monis)
Justice	*Raoul Peret* (b. Chatellerault 29 Nov 1870; d. Paris 22(?) Jul 1942)
Finance	*Louis Lucien Klotz* (see Briand II)
War	*Paul Painlevé* (see Briand IV)
Navy	*Charles Chaumet* (b. Prignac-et-Cazelles 1866; d. Paris 27 Jan 1932)
Education	*Daniel Vincent* (see Ribot IV)
Public Works	*Albert Claveille* (b. Mouleydier 1 Jan 1865; d. Paris 6 Sep 1921)
Labour and Social Welfare	*André Renard* (b. Nevers 14 Jun 1860)
Commerce	*Étienne Clementel* (see Rouvier II)
Colonies	*René Besnard* (see Poincaré I)
Agriculture	*Ferdinand David* (see Poincaré I)
Armaments	*Louis Loucheur* (b. Roubaix 12 Aug 1872; d. Paris 22 Nov 1931)
Food	*Maurice Long*
Foreign Embassies	*Henry Franklin-Bouillon* (b. Jersey 3 Sep 1870; d. Paris 13 Nov 1937)

17 Nov 1917 – 18 Jan 1920: Clemenceau II

Prime Minister	*Georges Clemenceau* (for 2nd time) (see Sarrien)
Foreign Affairs	*Stéphan Pichon* (see Clemenceau I)
Home Affairs	*Jules Pams* (see Monis)
Justice	*Buis Nail* (b. (?)1864; d. Paris 25 Dec 1920)
Finance	*Louis Lucien Klotz* (see Briand II)
War	*Georges Clemenceau* (see Sarrien)
Navy	*Georges Leygues* (see Dupuy II)
Education	17 Nov 1917 – 27 Nov 1919: *Louis Lafferre* (see Briand II)
	27 Nov 1919 – 18 Jan 1920: *Léon Berard* (b. Sauveterre-de-Béarn 6 Jan 1876; d. Paris night of 24/25 Feb 1960)
Public Works	17 Nov 1917 – (?): *Albert Claveille* (see Painlevé I)
	(?) – 27 Nov 1919: *Pierre Colliard* (b. Jons 30 Apr 1852; d. Paris 1924)
	27 Nov 1919 – 18 Jan 1920: *Paul Jourdain* (b. Altkirch 28 Oct 1878)
Commerce and Social Welfare	17 Nov 1917 – 27 Nov 1919: *Étienne Clementel* (see Rouvier II)

	27 Nov 1919 – 18 Jan 1920: *Louis Dubois* (b. Belle-Isle-en-Mer 10 Jun 1859)
Colonies	*Henry Simon* (b. La Bruguière 20 May 1874)
Agriculture	17 Nov 1917 – 19 Jul 1919: *Victor Boret* (b. Saumur 18 Aug 1872; d. Saumur 23 Mar 1952)
	19 Jul 1919 – 18 Jan 1920: *Joseph Noulens* (see Doumergue)
Posts	17 Nov 1917 – 27 Nov 1919: *Étienne Clementel* (see Rouvier II)
	27 Nov 1919 – 18 Jan 1920: *Louis Dubois* (see above)
Armaments	17 Nov 1917 – 26 Nov 1918: *Louis Loucheur* (see Painlevé I)
	26 Nov 1918: converted to Ministry for Industrial Reconstruction (see below)
Food	17 Nov 1917 – 19 Jul 1919: *Victor Boret* (see above)
	19 Jul 1919 – 18 Jan 1920: *Joseph Noulens* (see Doumergue)
Blockade and Occupied Territories	17 – 23 Nov 1917: *Célestin Jonnart* (see Casimir-Périer)
	23 Nov 1917 – 18 Jan 1920: *Albert Lebrun* (see Caillaux)
Industrial Reconstruction (new post)	26 Nov 1918 – 18 Jan 1920: *Louis Loucheur* (see Painlevé I)

19 Jan – 23 Sep 1920: Millerand

Prime Minister and Foreign Affairs	*Alexandre Millerand* (see Waldeck-Rousseau)
Home Affairs	*Théodore Steeg* (see Monis)
Justice	*Gustave L'Hopitau* (b. Crosnes 1860)
Finance	*Frédéric François-Marsal* (b. Paris 15 Mar 1874; d. Gisors night of 28/29 May 1958)
War	*André Lefèvre* (b. Paris 17 Jun 1869; d. Paris 4 Nov 1929)
Navy	*Adolphe Landry* (b. Ajaccio 29 Sep 1874; d. Paris 1956)
Education	*André Honnorat* (b. Paris 10 Dec 1868; d. 24 Jul 1950)
Public Works	*Yves Le Trocquer* (b. Pontrieux 5 Oct 1877)
Welfare (new post)	*Jules Breton* (b. Courrières 1 Apr 1872; d. Bellevue 2 Aug 1940)
Commerce	*Auguste Isaac* (b. Roubaix 6 Sep 1849)
Colonies	*Gaston Doumergue* (see Combes)

Agriculture	*Henri Ricard* (b. Le. Bouscat 3 Sep 1880)
Labour	*Paul Jourdain* (see Clemenceau II)
Pensions (new post)	*André Maginot* (see Ribot IV)
Liberated Territories	*Jean Ogier* (b. Paris 6 Jan 1862)
Industrial Recon- struction	Post abolished

24 Sep 1920 – 10 Jan 1921: Leygues

Prime Minister and Foreign Affairs	*Georges Leygues* (see Dupuy II)
Home Affairs	*Théodore Steeg* (see Monis)
Justice	*Gustave L'Hopitau* (see Millerand)
Finance	*Frédéric François-Marsal* (see Millerand)
War	24 Sep – 16 Dec 1920: *André Lefèvre* (see Millerand) 16 Dec 1920 – 12 Jan 1921: *Flaminius Raiberti* (b. Nice 1862)
Navy	*Adolphe Landry* (see Millerand)
Education	*André Honnorat* (see Millerand)
Public Works	*Yves Le Trocquer* (see Millerand)
Labour	*Paul Jourdain* (see Clemenceau II)
Welfare	*Jules Breton* (see Millerand)
Commerce	*Auguste Isaac* (see Millerand)
Colonies	*Gaston Doumergue* (see Combes)
Agriculture	*Henri Ricard* (see Millerand)
Pensions	*André Maginot* (see Ribot IV)
Liberated Territories	*Jean Ogier* (see Millerand)

16 Jan 1921 – 12 Jan 1922: Briand VI

Prime Minister and Foreign Affairs	*Aristide Briand* (for 6th time) (see Sarrien)
Home Affairs	*Alexandre Marraud* (b. Port-Sainte-Marie 8 Jan 1861)
Justice	*Laurent Bonnevay* (b. Saint-Didier-au-Mont d'Or 28 Jul 1870; d. 28 May 1957)
Finance	*Paul Doumer* (see Bourgeois)
War	*Louis Barthou* (see Dupuy II)
Navy	*Gabriel Henri Guist'hau* (see Poincaré I)
Education	*Léon Berard* (see Clemenceau II)
Public Works	*Yves Le Trocquer* (see Millerand)
Labour	*Daniel Vincent* (see Ribot IV)
Health	*Georges Leredu* (b. Metz 2 Jun 1860; d. Paris (?) 25 Jun 1943)

225

Commerce	*Lucien Dior* (b. Granville 1867)
Colonies	*Albert Sarraut* (see Viviani I)
Agriculture	*Edmond Lefèbvre du Prey* (b. St Omer 16 Oct 1866)
Pensions	*André Maginot* (see Ribot IV)
Liberated Territories	*Louis Loucheur* (see Painlevé I)

15 Jan 1922 – 26 Mar 1924: Poincaré II

Prime Minister and Foreign Affairs	*Raymond Poincaré* (for 2nd time) (see Dupuy I)
Home Affairs	*Maurice Maunoury* (see Viviani I)
Justice	15 Jan – 6 Oct 1922: *Louis Barthou* (see Dupuy II)
	6 Oct 1922 – 26 Mar 1924: *Maurice Colrat de Montrozier* (b. Sarrazac 24 Sep 1871; d. Paris 4 Mar 1954)
Finance	*Charles, Comte de Lasteyrie du Saillant* (b. Paris 27 Aug 1877)
War	*André Maginot* (Ribot IV)
Navy	*Flaminius Raiberti* (see Leygues)
Education	*Léon Berard* (see Clemenceau)
Labour	*Albert Peyronnet* (b. Brest 5 Jan 1862)
Health	*Paul Strauss* (b. Ronchamp 23 Sep 1852)
Commerce	*Lucien Dior* (see Briand VI)
Colonies	*Albert Sarraut* (see Viviani I
Minister for Alsace-Lorraine	*Louis Barthou* (see Dupuy II)
Agriculture	*Henri Chéron* (see Barthou)
Pensions	*André Maginot* (see Ribot IV)
Occupied and Liberated Territories	*Charles Reibel* (b. Vesoul 29 Dec 1882)

28 Mar – 1 Jun 1924: Poincaré III

Prime Minister and Foreign Affairs	*Raymond Poincaré* (for 3rd time) (see Dupuy I)
Home Affairs	*Justin de Selves* (see Caillaux)
Justice	*Edmond Lefèbvre du Prey* (see Briand VI)
Finance	*Frédéric François-Marsal* (see Millerand)
War	*André Maginot* (see Ribot IV)
Navy	*Maurice Bokanowski* (b. Le Havre 21 Aug 1879; d. Toul 2 Sep 1928)
Education	*Henri de Jouvenel* (b. Paris 15 Apr 1876; d. Paris 4 Oct 1935)

Public Works	*Yves Le Trocquer* (see Millerand)
Labour and Social Affairs	*Daniel Vincent* (see Ribot IV)
Commerce and Industry	*Louis Loucheur* (see Painlevé I)
Colonies	*Jean Fabry* (b. Villefranche 6 Jun 1876)
Agriculture	*Joseph Capus* (b. Marseilles 18 Aug 1867; d. 1 May 1947)
Post and Telegraph	*Louis Loucheur* (see Painlevé I)
Liberated Territories	*Louis Marin* (b. Faulx 7 Feb 1871; d. Paris 23 May 1960)

8 – 13 Jun 1924: François-Marsal

Prime Minister	*Frédéric François-Marsal* (see Millerand)
Foreign Affairs	*Edmond Lefèbvre du Prey* (see Briand VI)
Home Affairs	*Justin de Selves* (see Caillaux)
Justice	*Antony Ratier* (see Barthou)
Finance	*Frédéric François-Marsal* (see Millerand)
War	*André Maginot* (see Ribot IV)
Navy	*Désiré Ferry* (b. Metz 26 Oct 1886)
Education	*Adolphe Landry* (see Millerand)
Public Works	*Yves Le Trocquer* (see Millerand)
Labour	*Paul Jourdain* (see Clemenceau II)
Commerce	*Pierre Étienne Flandin* (b. Paris 12 Apr 1889; d. St Jean Cap Ferrat 13 Jun 1958)
Colonies	*Jean Fabry* (see Poincaré III)
Agriculture	*Joseph Capus* (see Poincaré III)
Liberated Territories	*Louis Marin* (see Poincaré III)

15 Jun 1924 – 10 Apr 1925: Herriot I

Prime Minister and Foreign Affairs	*Édouard Herriot* (for 1st time) (see Briand V)
Home Affairs	*Camille Chautemps* (b. Paris 1 Feb 1885; d. Washington 1 Jul 1963)
Justice	*René Renoult* (see Caillaux)
Finance	*Étienne Clementel* (see Rouvier II)
War	*Charles Nollet* (b. Marseilles 28 Jan 1865; d. Royat (?) 28 Jan 1941)
Navy	*Jacques Louis Dumesnil* (b. Larchant 4 Dec 1882; d. Paris 15 Jun 1956)
Education	*François-Albert* (b. (?)1877; d. Paris 22 Nov 1933)
Public Works	*Victor Peytral* (see Viviani I)

Labour and Social Welfare	*Julien Godart*
Commerce	*E. Raynaldy* (b. Rodez 23 Dec 1869)
Colonies	*Édouard Daladier* (b. Carpentras 18 Jun 1884)
Agriculture	*Henri Queuille* (b. Neuvic d'Ussel 31 Mar 1884)
Pensions	—— *Bovier-Lapierre*
Liberated Territories	*Victor Dalbiez* (b. Corneilla-de-Conflant 23 Jun 1876; d. Les Pavillons-sous-Bois 29 Apr. 1954)

17 Apr – 27 Oct 1925: Painlevé II

Prime Minister	*Paul Painlevé* (for 2nd time) (see Briand IV)
Foreign Affairs	*Aristide Briand* (see Sarrien)
Home Affairs	*Abraham Schrameck*
Justice	*Théodore Steeg* (see Monis)
Finance	*Joseph Caillaux* (see Waldeck-Rousseau)
War	*Paul Painlevé* (see Briand IV)
Navy	*Émile Borel* (b. St Affrique 1871; d. Paris 3 Feb 1956)
Education	*Anatole de Monzie* (b. Bazas 22 Nov 1876; d. Paris 11 Jan 1947)
Public Works	*Pierre Laval* (b. Châteldun 28 Jun 1883; d. Paris 15 Oct 1945)
Labour and Social Welfare	—— *Durafour* (b. St Etienne 12 Aug 1872; d. 25 Apr 1932)
Commerce	*Charles Chaumet* (see Painlevé I)
Colonies	*André Hesse* (b. Paris 22 Apr 1874)
Agriculture	*Jean Durand* (b. Castelnaudary 1865)
Pensions	*Louis Antériou* (b. La Voulte 1887; d. Paris 5 Mar 1931)

9 Oct – 22 Nov 1925: Painlevé III

Prime Minister	*Paul Painlevé* (for 3rd time) (see Briand IV)
Foreign Affairs	*Aristide Briand* (see Sarrien)
Home Affairs	*Abraham Schrameck* (see Painlevé II)
Justice	*Camille Chautemps* (see Herriot I)
Finance	*Paul Painlevé* (see Briand IV)
War	*Édouard Daladier* (see Herriot I)
Navy	*Émile Borel* (see Painlevé II)
Education	*Yvon Delbos* (b. Thonac 7 May 1885; d. Paris 15 Nov 1956)
Public Works	*Anatole de Monzie* (see Painlevé II)
Commerce	*Daniel Vincent* (see Ribot IV)
Colonies	*Léon Perrier*

Budget	*Georges Bonnet* (b. Bassillac 23 Jul 1889)
Agriculture	*Jean Durand* (see Painlevé II)
Pensions	*Louis Antériou* (see Painlevé II)

28 Nov 1925 – 6 Mar 1926: **Briand VII**

Prime Minister and Foreign Affairs	*Aristide Briand* (for 7th time) (see Sarrien)
Home Affairs	*Camille Chautemps* (see Herriot I)
Justice	*René Renoult* (see Caillaux)
Finance	28 Nov – 15 Dec 1925: *Louis Loucheur* (see Painlevé I)
	15 Dec 1925 – 6 Mar 1926: *Paul Doumer* (see Bourgeois)
War	*Paul Painlevé* (see Briand IV)
Navy	*Georges Leygues* (see Dupuy II)
Education	*Édouard Daladier* (see Herriot I)
Public Works	*Anatole de Monzie* (see Painlevé II)
Labour and Social Welfare	—— *Durafour* (see Painlevé II)
Commerce	*Daniel Vincent* (see Ribot IV)
Colonies	*Léon Perrier* (see Painlevé III)
Agriculture	*Jean Durand* (see Painlevé II)
Pensions	*Paul Jourdain* (see Clemenceau II)

10 Mar – 15 Jun 1926: **Briand VIII**

Prime Minister and Foreign Affairs	*Aristide Briand* (for 8th time) (see Sarrien)
Home Affairs	10 Mar – 8 Apr 1926: *Louis Malvy* (see Doumergue)
Justice	*Pierre Laval* (see Painlevé II)
Finance	*Raoul Peret* (see Doumergue)
War	*Paul Painlevé* (see Briand IV)
Navy	*Georges Leygues* (see Dupuy II)
Education	*Lucien Lamoureux* (b. Viplaix 16 Sep 1888)
Labour and Social Welfare	—— *Durafour* (see Painlevé II)
Commerce	*Daniel Vincent* (see Ribot IV)
Colonies	*Léon Perrier* (see Painlevé III)
Pensions	*Paul Jourdain* (see Clemenceau II)

23 Jun – 17 Jul 1926: **Briand IX**

Prime Minister and Foreign Affairs	*Aristide Briand* (for 9th time) (see Sarrien)

Home Affairs	*Jean Durand* (see Painlevé II)
Justice	*Pierre Laval* (see Painlevé II)
Finance	*Joseph Caillaux* (see Waldeck-Rousseau)
War	*Adolphe Guillaumat* (b. Bourgneuf 4 Jan 1863; d. Nantes 18 May 1940)
Navy	*Georges Leygues* (see Dupuy II)
Education	*Bertrand Nogaro* (b. La-Chapelle-la-Reine 5 Apr 1880; d. Créteil 1950)
Public Works	*Daniel Vincent* (see Ribot IV)
Labour and Social Welfare	—— *Durafour* (see Painlevé II)
Commerce	*Fernand Chapsal* (b. Limoges 10 Mar 1862; d. Paris 10 Feb 1939)
Colonies	*Léon Perrier* (see Painlevé III)
Minister for Alsace-Lorraine	*Pierre Laval* (see Painlevé II)

19 – 21 Jul 1926: Herriot II

Prime Minister and Foreign Affairs	*Édouard Herriot* (for 2nd time) (see Briand V)
Home Affairs	*Camille Chautemps* (see Herriot I)
Justice	*Maurice Colrat de Montrozier* (see Poincaré II)
Finance	*Anatole de Monzie* (see Painlevé II)
War	*Paul Painlevé* (see Briand IV)
Navy	*René Renoult* (see Caillaux)
Education	*Édouard Daladier* (see Herriot I)
Public Works	*André Hesse* (see Painlevé II)
Commerce	*Louis Loucheur* (see Painlevé I)
Colonies	*Adrien Dariac* (see Viviani I)
Agriculture	*Henri Queuille* (see Herriot I)
Pensions	*Georges Bonnet* (see Painlevé III)

23 Jul 1926 – 6 Nov 1928: Poincaré IV

Prime Minister	*Raymond Poincaré* (for 4th time) (see Dupuy I)
Foreign Affairs	*Aristide Briand* (see Sarrien)
Home Affairs	*Albert Sarraut* (see Viviani I)
Justice	*Louis Barthou* (see Dupuy II)
Finance	*Raymond Poincaré* (see Dupuy I)
War	*Paul Painlevé* (see Briand IV)
Navy	*Georges Leygues* (see Dupuy II)
Education	*Édouard Herriot* (see Briand V)

Public Works	*André Tardieu* (b. Paris 22 Sep 1876; d. Menton 15 Sep 1945)
Labour	29 Jul 1926 – 2 May 1928: *André Fallières* (b. Villeneuve 30 Sep 1875)
	2 May – 6 Nov 1928: *Louis Loucheur* (see Painlevé I)
Commerce	23 Jul 1926 – 2 Sep 1928: *Maurice Bokanowski* (see Poincaré III)
	14 Sep – 6 Nov 1928: *Henri Chéron* (see Barthou)
Colonies	*Léon Perrier* (see Painlevé III)
Minister for Alsace-Lorraine	*Louis Barthou* (see Dupuy II)
Agriculture	*Henri Queuille* (see Herriot I)
Pensions	—— *Maine*
Liberated Territories	*Raymond Poincaré* (see Dupuy I)
Air (new post)	14 Sep – 6 Nov 1928: *André Victor Laurent-Eynac* (b. Monestier 4 Oct 1886

11 Nov 1928 – 29 Jul 1929: Poincaré V

Prime Minister	*Raymond Poincaré* (for 5th time) (see Dupuy I)
Foreign Affairs	*Aristide Briand* (see Sarrien)
Home Affairs	*André Tardieu* (see Poincaré IV)
Justice	*Louis Barthou* (see Dupuy II)
Finance	*Henri Chéron* (see Barthou)
War	*Paul Painlevé* (see Briand IV)
Navy	*Georges Leygues* (see Dupuy II)
Education	*Alexandre Marraud* (see Briand VI)
Public Works	*Pierre Forgeot* (b. Anglure 10 Mar 1888)
Labour	*Louis Loucheur* (see Painlevé I)
Commerce	*Georges Bonnefous* (b. Paris 30 Nov 1867; d. Paris 26 May 1956)
Colonies	*André Maginot* (see Ribot IV)
Agriculture	*Jean Hennessy* (b. Richemont 26 Apr 1874)
Pensions	*Louis Antériou* (see Painlevé II)
Air	*André Victor Laurent-Eynac* (see Poincaré IV)

29 Jul – 22 Oct 1929: Briand X

Prime Minister and Foreign Affairs	*Aristide Briand* (for 10th time) (see Sarrien)
Home Affairs	*André Tardieu* (see Poincaré IV)
Justice	*Louis Barthou* (see Dupuy II)
Finance	*Henri Chéron* (see Barthou)

War	*Paul Painlevé* (see Briand IV)
Navy	*Georges Leygues* (see Dupuy II)
Education	*Alexandre Marraud* (see Briand VI)
Public Works	*Pierre Forgeot* (see Poincaré V)
Labour	*Louis Loucheur* (see·Painlevé I)
Commerce	*Georges Bonnefous* (see Poincaré V)
Air	*André Victor Laurent-Eynac* (see Poincaré IV)
Colonies	*André Maginot* (see Ribot IV)
Agriculture	*Jean Hennessy* (see Poincaré V)
Pensions	*Louis Antériou* (see Painlevé II)

2 Nov 1929 – 17 Feb 1930: Tardieu I

Prime Minister	*André Tardieu* (for 1st time) (see Poincaré IV)
Foreign Affairs	*Aristide Briand* (see Sarrien)
Home Affairs	*André Tardieu* (see Poincaré IV)
Justice	*Lucien Hubert* (b. Chesne-Populeux 27 Aug 1868)
Finance	*Henri Chéron* (see Barthou)
War	*André Maginot* (see Ribot IV)
Navy	*Georges Leygues* (see Dupuy II)
Education	*Alexnadre Marraud* (see Briand VI)
Public Works	*Georges Pernot* (b. Besançon 6 Nov 1879)
Labour	*Louis Loucheur* (see Painlevé I)
Commerce	*Pierre Étienne Flandin* (see François-Marsal)
Mercantile Marine (new post)	*Louis Rollin* (b. Uzerche 17 Mar 1879; d. 3 Nov 1952)
Air	*André Victor Laurent-Eynac* (see Poincaré IV)
Colonies	*François Pietri* (b. La Bastia, Corsica 8 Aug 1882)
Agriculture	*Jean Hennessy* (see Poincaré V)
Pensions	—— *Gallet*
Posts	—— *Germain-Martin*

Fulani Emirates

For Sokoto and Gwandu, twin capitals of the Fulani empire established in Nigeria and surrounding areas in the 19th century, see volume 1, Fulani Emirates.

For the Fulani emirates of Kano, Katsina, Nupe and Daura, 10th century onwards, see volume 1, Hausa States.

Fung Kingdom of Sennar

For the Fung Kingdom of Sennar, Nilotic Sudan, 16th to 17th centuries, see volume 1.

Genoa

HEADS OF STATE

Doges

1484	*Giano da Campofregoso* (for 1st time)
1488	Under Milanese rule
1499	Under French rule
1512	*Giano da Campofregoso* (for 2nd time)
1513	*Antoniotto Adorno* (for 1st time) (b. about 1479; d. 12 Sep 1528)
1513	*Ottaviano da Campofregoso*
1515	Under French rule
1522 – 1527	*Antoniotto Adorno* (for 2nd time)
1528	*Oberto Cataneo*
1531	*Battista Spinola* (b. 1472; d. 1539)
1533	*Battista Lomellini* (b. 1460; d. 1540)
1535	*Cristoforo Grimaldi-Rosso*
1537	*Giambattista Doria*
1539	*Andrea Giustiniani*
1541	*Leonardo Cataneo*
1543	*Andrea Centurione*
1545	*Giambattista Fornari*
1547	*Benedetto Gentile*
1549	*Gaspare Gimaldi-Bracelli*
1551	*Luca Spinola*
1553	*Jacopo Promontorio*
1555	*Agostino Pinello*
1557	*Pietro Giovanni Ciarega-Cybò*
1559	*Geronimo Vivaldi*

1561	*Paolo Battista Calvo*
1561	*Battista Cicala-Zoalio*
1563	*Giambattista Lercaro*
1565	*Ottaviano Gentile Oderico*
1567	*Simone Spinola*
1569	*Paolo Moneglia-Giustiniani*
1571	*Giannotto Lomellini* (b. 1519; d. 1574)
1573	*Jacopo Durazzo-Grimaldi*
1575	*Prosper Fatinanti-Centurione*
1577	*Giambattista Gentile*
1579	*Nicolò Doria*
1581	*Geronimo de' Franchi*
1583	*Geronimo Chiavari*
1585	*Ambrogio di Negro*
1587	*Davide Vacca*
1589	*Battista Negrone*
1591	*Giovanni Agostino Giustiniani*
1593	*Antonio Grimaldi-Cebá*
1595	*Matteo Senarega*
1597	*Lazzaro Grimaldi-Cebà*
1599	*Lorenzo Sauli* (d. 1601)
1601	*Agostino Doria*
1603	*Pietro de' Franchi*
1605	*Luca Grimaldi-de Castro*
1607	*Silvestro Invrea*
1607	*Gerolamo Assereto* (b. Recco 1543; d. 15 Mar 1627)
1609	*Agostino Pinello*
1611	*Alessandro Giustiniani*
1613	*Tommaso Spinola*
1615	*Bernardo Clavarezza*
1617	*Giovanni Jacopo Imperiale*
1619	*Pietro Durazzo*
1621	*Ambrogio Doria*
1623	*Giorgio Centurione*
1623	*Federigo de' Franchi*
1625	*Jacopo Lomellini* (b. 1570; d. 1652)
1627	*Gianluca Chiavari*
1629	*Andrea Spinola*
1631	*Leonardo Torre*
1633	*Gianstefano Doria*
1635	*Gianfrancesco Brignole*
1637	*Agostino Pallavicini* (b. 1577; d. 1649)
1639	*Giambattista Durazzo*

1641	Giovanni Agostino Marini
1643	Giambattista Lercaro
1645	Luca Giustiniani
1646	Giambattista Lomellini (d. 1674)
1648	Jacope de' Franchi
1650	Agostino Centurione
1652	Geronimo de' Franchi
1654	Alessandro Spinola
1656	Giulio Sauli (b. 1579; d. 1665)
1658	Giambattista Centurione
1660	Giovanni Bernardo Frugoni
1661	Antonio Invrea
1663	Stefano Mari
1665	Cesare Durazzo
1667	Cesare Gentile
1669	Francesco Garbarini
1671	Alessandro Grimaldi (b. 1621; d. 1683)
1673	Agostino Saluzzo
1675	Antonio Passano
1677	Giannettino Odone
1679	Agostino Spinola
1681	Luca Maria Invrea
1683	Francesco Maria Imperiale-Lercaro
1685	Pietro Durazzo
1687	Luca Spinola
1689	Oberto Torre
1691	Giambattista Cataneo
1693	Francesco Maria Invrea
1695	Bandinelli Negrone
1697	Francesco Maria Sauli (b. 1629; d. 1699)
1699	Geronimo Mari
1701	Federigo de' Franchi
1703	Antonio Grimaldi-Cebà (b. 1640; d. 1717)
1705	Stefano Onorio Feretto
1707	Domenico Maria Mari
1709	Vincenzo Durazzo
1711	Francesco Maria Imperiale
1713	Giannantonio Giustiniani
1715	Lorenzo Centurione
1717	Benedetto Viali
1719	Ambrogio Imperiale
1721	Cesare de' Franchi
1723	Domenico Negrone

1726	*Geronimo Veneroso*
1728	*Luca Grimaldi* (b. 1675; d. 1750)
1730	*Francesco Maria Balbi* (b. Genoa 11 Jan 1671; d. Genoa 16 Jan 1747)
1732	*Domenico Maria Spinola*
1734	*Gianstefano Durazzo*
1736	*Nicolò Cantaneo*
1738	*Costantino Balbi* (b. 13 Sep 1676; d. c. 1741)
1740	*Nicolò Spinola*
1742	*Domenico Maria Canevaro*
1744	*Lorenzo Mari*
1746	*Giovan Francesco Maria Brignole Sale* (b. Genoa 6 Jun 1695; d. Genoa 14 Feb 1760)
1748	*Cesare Cataneo*
1750	*Agostino Viali*
1752	*Stefano Lomellini*
1752	*Giambattista Grimaldi* (b. 1678; d. 1757)
1754	*Giovanni Jacopo Stefano Veneroso*
1756	*Giovanni Jacopo Grimaldi* (b. 1705; d. 1777)
1758	*Matteo Fransone*
1760	*Agostino Lomellini* (b. 1709; d. 1791)
1765	*Maria Gaetano Della Rovere*
1767	*Marcellino Durazzo*
1769	*Giambattista Negrone*
1771	*Giovanni Battista Cambiaso* (b. Genoa 19 Jul 1711; d Genoa 23 Dec 1772)
1773	*Alessandro Pietro Francesco Grimaldi* (b. 1715; d 1781)
1775	*Brizio Giustiniani*
1777	*Giuseppe Lomellini* (d. 1803)
1779	*Giacomo Maria Brignole* (for 1st time) (b. Genoa 1 Dec 1724; d. Florence 21 Dec 1801)
1781	*Marcantonio Gentile*
1783	*Giambattista Airoli*
1785	*Gian Carlo Pallavicini* (b. 1722; d. 1795)
1787	*Rafaele Ferrari*
1789	*Alerame Maria Pallavicini* (b. 1730; d. 1805)
1791	*Michelangelo Cambiaso* (b. Genoa 21 Sep 1738; d Genoa 14 Mar 1813)
1793	*Giuseppe Maria Doria*
1795	*Giacomo Maria Brignole* (for 2nd time)
1797 – 1814	Mostly under French occupation or annexation
1815	United to Kingdom of Sardinia

Georgia

During the fifteenth century the kingdom of Georgia split into three kingdoms and three (later four) principalities, viz Kartli, Kakheti, Imereti; Mingrelia, Guria, Meskheti and Abkhasia, previously part of Guria. Only the kings are listed.

HEADS OF STATE

Kings of Kartli

1478	*Constantine II*, nephew of Giorgi VIII, King of Georgia (until 1484 King also of Imereti)
1505	*David VIII*, son of Constantine III (d. 1525/26)
1524	*Giorgi IX*, brother (d. about 1540)
1535	*Luarsab I*, son of David VIII
1558	*Simon I*, son (for 1st time) (b. 1537; captured by the Turks 1600, became Muslim under the name Mahmud Khan; d. 1608/09 or 1611)
1569	*David IX* (Daud Khan) brother, installed by the Persians
1578	*Simon I* (for 2nd time)
1600	*Giorgi X*, son
1603 (1605)	*Luarsab II*, son (b. 1595; d. 1622)
1614 (1616)	*Bagrat VII*, son of David IX
1619	*Simon II*, son
1629	*Teimuraz I*, King of Kakheti (see Kings of Kakheti)
1632	*Rostom* (Khosro Mirza) brother of Bagrat VII (b. 1565)
1656 (1658)	*Wakhtang V* (Shah Nawaz I) Prince of Mukhran, adopted son
1676	*Giorgi XI* (for 1st time) (Shah Nawaz II) son (d. 1709)
1688	*Irakli I* (Nazar Ali Khan) grandson of Teimuraz I (b. 1643)
1703 – 1709	*Giorgi XI* (for 2nd time) (absent in Persia)
1703 – 1711	Prince Wakhtang, later Wakhtang VI, regent
1 Sep 1709	*Kaikhosro*, nephew of Giorgi (absent in Persia)
7 Sep 1711	*Wakhtang VI* (for 1st time) brother (b. 15 Sep 1675; d. Astrakhan 25 Mar 1737)
1714	*Iesse* (for 1st time) (Ali Quli Khan, later known as Mustafa Pasha) brother (for 1st time) (d. 1727)

1716	*Bakar* (Shah Nawaz III) son (b. 7 Apr 1699/1700; d. Moscow 25 Feb 1750) as Deputy for Wakhtang VI
1719 – 1723	*Wakhtang VI* (for 2nd time)
1724	*Iesse* (for 2nd time)
1727 – 1736	Interregnum
1736	*Archil* (Abdula-beg) son of Iesse
1737 – 1744	Interregnum
1744	*Teimuraz II* of Kakheti, son-in-law of Wakhtang VI (see Kings of Kakheti)
1762	United with Kakheti (see Kings of Kartli and Kakheti)

Kings of Kakheti

1476 (1492)	*Alexander I*, son of Giorgi I, formerly Giorgi VIII, King of Georgia
1511	*Giorgi II*, the Bad, son
1513	United with Kartli under David VIII
1520	*Levan*, son
1574	*Alexander II*, son (for 1st time) (b. 1527)
1603	*David I*, son
1603	*Alexander II* (for 2nd time)
1605	*Constantine I*, son
1605 – 1614, 1615 – 1616, 1623 – 1632, 1636 – 1648	*Teimuraz I*, son of David I (b. 1589; d. Astarabad 1663)
1614 – 1615, 1616 – 1623, 1633 – 1636	Interregna: Persian governors
1648	United with Kartli under Rostom
1656	Interregnum: Persian governor
1664	*Archil*, ex-King of Imereti (see Kings of Imereti)
1675	*Irakli I*, grandson of Teimuraz I, absent in Persia
1676 – 1703	Interregnum: Persian governors
1703	*David II (Imam Quli Khan)*, son (b. 1678)
1722	*Constantine II (Mahmud Quli Khan)* brother
1732	*Teimuraz II*, brother (for 1st time)
1736 – 1738	Interregnum: Persian governor
1738	*Teimuraz II* (for 2nd time) became King of Kartli
1744 – 1762	*Irakli II*, son (b. 1716) became King of Kartli; (see Kings of Kartli and Kakheti)

Kings of Kartli and Kakheti

1762	*Irakli II* (see Kings of Kakheti)

11 Sep 1798	*Giorgi XII*, son (b. 1750)
15 Jan – Feb 1801	*David Batonishvili*, son, regent
12 Sep 1801	Eastern Georgia absorbed by Russia

Kings of Imereti

1484	*Alexander I*, son of Bagrat VI, King of Georgia
1510	*Bagrat II*, son
1565	*Giorgi I*, son
1588	*Rostom* (for 1st time)
1589	*Bagrat III*, cousin
1590	*Rostom* (for 2nd time)
1604	*Giorgi II*, brother
1639	*Alexander II*, son
1660	*Bagrat IV* (for 1st time)
1661	*Wakhtang Bagration*, second husband of the widow of Alexander II (for 1st time)
1661	**Wameq Dadiani**, usurper
1661	*Archil*, son of Wakhtang VI, King of Kartli (for 1st time)
1663	*Dimitri Guriel*, Prince of Guria, made king by the Turks
1664	*Bagrat IV* (for 2nd time)
1668	*Wakhtang Bagration* (for 2nd time)
1668	*Bagrat IV* (for 3rd time)
1678	*Archil* (for 2nd time)
1679	*Bagrat IV* (for 4th time)
1681	*Giorgi III Guriel*, Prince of Guria
1683	*Alexander III*, son of Bagrat IV (for 1st time)
1690	*Archil* (for 3rd time)
1691	*Alexander III* (for 2nd time)
1695	*Archil* (for 4th time)
1696	*Giorgi IV Bagration*, nicknamed Gochia
1698	*Archil* (for 5th time)
1699	*Simon*, son of Alexander III
1700 – 1701	Interregnum
1701	*Mamia Guriel*, Prince of Guria (for 1st time)
1702	*Giorgi V*, son of Simon (for 1st time)
1711	*Mamia Guriel* (for 2nd time)
1711	*Giorgi V* (for 2nd time)
1713	*Mamia Guriel* (for 3rd time)
1713	*Giorgi V* (for 3rd time)
1716	*Giorgi VI Guriel*, son of Mamia

239

1716 – 1720	Interregnum
1720	*Alexander IV*, son of Giorgi V
1751	*Solomon I*, son (for 1st time)
1765	*Teimuraz*, nephew
1768	*Solomon I* (for 2nd time)
1784	*David*, uncle
1789 – 1810	*Solomon II*, nephew of Solomon I and grandson of Irakli II, King of Kartli and Kakheti
1810	Western Georgia absorbed by Russia
1918	Georgia regains independence
22 Apr 1918	Creation of the Democratic and Independent Transcaucasian Republic President: *Akaki Chkhenkeli* (b. 1876; d. Paris 3 Jan 1959)
26 May 1918	Foundation of the Democratic Republic of Georgia

President

May 1918 – Mar 1921	*Noe Zhordania* (b. Lanchkuti 15 Jan 1867; d. Paris 11 Jan 1953)

Head of Administration

May 1918 – Mar 1921	*Nicholas Chkhekidze* (b. 1865; d. Paris 13 Jun 1926)
Mar 1921	Federated with Soviet Russia

Germany

HEADS OF STATE

Holy Roman Emperors

House of Habsburg (1439 – 1740 and *1745 – 1806)*

19 Aug 1493 – 12 Jan 1519	*Maximilian I*, son of Frederick III (b. 22 Mar 1459) from 1486: King of the Romans*; from 1490 to 1493: deputy for his father; from 19 Aug 1493: Archduke of Austria
26 Jun 1519	*Charles V*, grandson, son of Philip I of Spain (b. 24

*The title of King of the Romans was given to the person expected to succeed to the title of Holy Roman Emperor.

	Feb 1500; d. Estremadura 21 Sep 1558) from 23 Jan 1516 to 15 Jan 1556: King Charles I of Spain; from 28 May 1519 to 21 Apr 1521: Archduke Charles I of Austria; abdicated as Holy Roman Emperor 1556
1 Sep 1556	*Ferdinand I*, brother (b. 10 Mar 1503) from 21 Apr 1521: Archduke of Austria; from 28 Oct 1527 to 8 Sep 1563: King of Hungary; from 1531: King of the Romans
25 Jul 1564	*Maximilian II*, son (b. 31 Jul 1527); from 24 Nov 1562: King of the Romans; from 8 Sep 1563 to 25 Sep 1572: King Maximilian of Hungary; from 25 Jul 1564: Archduke Maximilian II of Austria
12 Oct 1576 – 20 Jan 1612	*Rudolf II*, son (b. 18 Jul 1552) from 25 Sep 1572 to 19 Nov 1608: King Rudolf of Hungary; from 12 Oct 1576: Archduke Rudolf V of Austria
13 Jun 1612 – 20 Mar 1619	*Matthias*, brother (b. 24 Feb 1557) from 19 Nov 1608 to 1 Jul 1618: King Matthias II of Hungary; from 20 Jan 1612: Archduke Matthias of Austria
20 Aug 1619	*Ferdinand II*, cousin, son of Archduke Charles of Steiermark (b. 9 Jul 1578) from 1 Jul 1618 to 7 Dec 1625: King of Hungary; from 20 Aug 1619: Archduke of Austria
12 Feb 1637 – 2 Apr 1657	*Ferdinand III*, son (b. 13 Jul 1608) from 7 Dec 1625: King of Hungary; from 12 Dec 1636: King of the Romans; from 15 Feb 1637: Archduke of Austria
18 Jul 1658	*Leopold I*, son (b. 9 Jun 1640) from 27 Jun 1655 to 9 Dec 1687: King of Hungary; from 18 Jul 1658: Archduke of Austria
5 May 1705 – 17 Apr 1711	*Joseph I*, son (b. 26 Jul 1678) from 9 Dec 1687: King of Hungary; from 24 Aug 1690: King of the Romans; from 5 May 1705: Archduke of Austria
12 Oct 1711 – 20 Oct 1740	*Charles VI*, brother (b. 1 Oct 1685) from 17 Apr 1711: Archduke Charles III of Austria; from 22 May 1712: King Charles III of Hungary

House of Bavaria (Wittelsbach)

24 Jan 1742 – 20 Jan 1745	*Charles VII*, son of Elector Maximilian (Maximilian II) of Bavaria (b. 6 Aug 1697) from 26 Feb 1726: Elector of Bavaria

House of Habsburg

13 Sep 1745	*Francis I*, son of Duke Leopold Josef Hyacinth of Lorraine (b. 8 Dec 1708) from 9 Jul 1737: Grand Duke Francis II of Tuscany

241

18 Aug 1765 – 20 Feb 1790	*Joseph II*, son (b. 13 Mar 1741) from 27 Mar 1764: King of the Romans; from 29 Nov 1780: King of Hungary and Archduke of Austria
30 Sep 1790 – 1 Mar 1792	*Leopold II*, brother (b. 5 May 1747) from 20 Feb 1790: King of Hungary; from 30 Sep 1790: Archduke of Austria
12 Jul 1792 – 6 Aug 1806	*Francis II* (b. 12 Feb 1768; d. 2 Mar 1835) from 12 Jul 1792 to 14 Aug 1804: Archduke Francis of Austr. From 14 Aug 1804: Emperor Francis I of Austria; on Aug 1806 renounced the title of Holy Roman. Emperor, which lapsed

Reichsverweser (Head of the provisional central authority)

29 Jun 1848 – 20 Dec 1849	*Archduke Johann of Austria*, brother of Francis II (b. 20 Jan 1782; d. 10 May 1859) Regents: 6 – 18 Jun 1849 *Franz Raveaux* (b. Cologne 1 Apr 1810; d. Brussels 13 Sep 1851) *Heinrich Simon* (b. Breslau 29 Oct 1805; d. drowned in the Walensee, Switzerland, 16 Aug 1860) *Karl Vogt* (b. Giessen 5 Jul 1817; d. Geneva 5 May 1895)

Emperors of Germany

House of Hohenzollern (Prussia)

18 Jan 1871	*William I,* brother of Frederick William IV of Prussia (b. 22 Mar 1797) from 2 Jan 1861: King of Prussia
9 Mar 1888	*Frederick*, son (b. 18 Oct 1831) from 9 Mar 1888: King Frederick III of Prussia
15 Jun 1888 – 9 Nov 1918	*William II*, son (b. 27 Jan 1859; d. 4 Jun 1941)
From 1918	Republic

Presidents

11 Feb 1919	*Friedrich (Fritz) Ebert* (b. Heidelberg 4 Feb 1871; d. Berlin 28 Feb 1925)
28 Feb 1925	*Walter Simons* (b. Elberfeld 24 Sep 1861; d. Nowawes 14 Jul 1941) Deputy, President of the Supreme Court
12 May 1925 – 2 Aug 1934	*Paul (Anton Hans Ludwig) von Beneckendorf und Hindenburg* (b. Poznan 2 Oct 1847; d. Neudeck 2 Aug 1934)

MEMBERS OF GOVERNMENT

REICHSMINISTERIUM (PROVISIONAL CENTRAL GOVERNMENT, 1848/49)

Prime Ministers

9 Aug – 5 Sep 1848	*Charles, Prince of Leiningen*, half-brother of Queen Victoria of Great Britain (b. 12 Sep 1904; d. 13 Nov 1856)
16 Sep – 15 Dec 1848	*Anton von Schmerling* (b. Vienna 23 Aug 1805; d. Vienna 23 May 1893)
18 Dec 1848 – 21 Mar 1849	*Heinrich, Baron Gagern* (b. Bayreuth 20 Aug 1799; d. Darmstadt 22 May 1880) Commissary to 10 May 1849
17 May – 20 Dec 1849	*Maximilian Karl Friedrich Wilhelm Grävell* (b. Belgard 28 Aug 1781; d. Dresden 29 Sep 1860)

Foreign Affairs

15 Jul – 9 Aug 1848	*Anton von Schmerling* (see Prime Ministers)
8 Aug – 18 Sep 1848	*Johann Gustav Wilhelm Moritz Heckscher* (b. Hamburg 26 Dec 1797; d. Vienna 7 Apr 1865)
24 Sep – 15 Dec 1848	*Anton von Schmerling* (see Prime Ministers)
18 Dec 1848 – 21 Mar 1849	*Heinrich, Baron Gagern* (see Prime Ministers)
Mar – 20 Dec 1849	*August Giacomo Jochmus* (from 1859: *Baron*) Cotignola (b. Hamburg 27 Feb 1808; d. Bamberg 14 Sep 1881)

Home Affairs

12/15 Jul – 15 Dec 1848	*Anton von Schmerling* (see Prime Ministers)
18 Dec 1848 – 21 Mar/10 May 1849	*Heinrich, Baron Gagern* (see Prime Ministers)
17 May 1849	*Maximilian Grävell* (see Prime Ministers)
21 Dec 1849	*Johann Hermann Detmold* (b. Hanover 24 Jul 1807; d. Hanover 17 Mar 1856)

Finance

9 Aug – 5 Sep and 16 Sep 1848 – 10 May 1849	*Hermann von Beckerath* (b. Krefeld 13 Dec 1801; d. Krefeld 12 May 1870)

17 May – 20 Dec 1849	*Ernst* (from 1860: *Baron*) *von Merck* (b. Hamburg 20 Dec 1811; d. Hamburg 6 Jul 1863)

Justice

12 Jul – 5 Aug 1848	*Johann Gustav Heckscher* (see Foreign Affairs)
9 Aug 1848 – 10 May 1849	*Robert von Mohl* (b. Stuttgart 17 Aug 1799; d. Berlin 5 Nov 1875)
17 May – 20 Dec 1849	*Johann Hermann Detmold* (see Home Affairs)

Trade

9 Aug 1848 – 10 May 1849	*Arnold Duckwitz* (b. Bremen 27 Jan 1802; d. Bremen 19 Mar 1881)

War

12 Jul – 5 Aug 1848 and 18 Sep 1848 10 May 1849	*Eduard von Peucker* (b. Schmiedeberg 19 Jan 1791; d. Berlin 10 Feb 1876)
21 May – 20 Dec 1849	*August, Prince Sayn-Wittgenstein-Berleburg* (b. 6 Mar 1788; d. 6 Jan 1874)

Navy

Mar – 20 Dec 1849	*August Giacomo Jochmus*, Commissary (see Foreign Affairs)
Apr 1849 – 30 Apr 1853	*Karl Rudolf Bromme* (b. Leipzig 10 Sep 1804; d. Bremen 9 Jan 1860)

GERMAN EMPIRE

Chancellors

21 Mar 1871	*Otto (Edward Leopold), Prince Bismarck Schönhausen* (from 1890: *Duke of Lauenburg*) (b. Schönhausen 1 Apr 1815; d. Friedrichsruh 30 Jul 1898)
20 Mar 1890 – 26 Oct 1894	*Georg Leo Count Caprivi* (b. Charlottenburg 24 Feb 1831; d. Skyren am Oder 16 Feb 1899)

29 Oct 1894 – 15 Oct 1900	*Chlodwig (Karl Victor) Prince Hohenlohe-Schillingsfürst* (b. Rothenburg an der Fulda 31 Mar 1819; d. Ragaz 6 Jul 1901)
17 Oct 1900 – 10 Jul 1909	*Bernard (Heinrich Martin Karl) Prince Bülow* (b. Kleinflottbek 3 May 1849; d. Rome 28 Oct 1929)
14 Jul 1909 – 13 Jul 1917	*Theobald von Bethmann Hollweg* (b. Hohenfinow 29 Nov 1856; d. Hohenfinow 2 Jan 1921)
14 Jul – 24 Oct 1917	*Georg Michaelis* (b. Haynau 7 Sep 1857; d. Bad Saarow 24 Jul 1936)
25 Oct 1917 – 3 Oct 1918	*Georg, Count Hertling* (b. Darmstadt 31 Aug 1843; d. Ruhpolding 4 Jan 1919)
4 Oct – 9 Nov 1918	*Max(imilian) Prince of Baden* (b. Karlsruhe 10 Jul 1867; d. Constance 6 Nov 1929)

Vice Chancellors

Jul 1878 – 20 Jun 1881	*Otto, Count Stolberg-Wernigerode* (b. Gedern 30 Oct 1837; d. Wernigerode 19 Nov 1896)
Jun 1881	*Karl Heinrich von Boetticher* (b. Stettin 6 Jan 1833; d. Naumburg 6 Mar 1907)
1 Jul 1897	*Artur (Adolf) Count Posadowsky-Wehner* (b. Glogau 3 Jan 1845; d. Naumburg 23 Oct 1932)
24 Jan 1907	*Theobald von Bethmann Hollweg* (see Chancellors)
14 Jul 1908	*Klemens von Delbrück* (b. Halle 19 Jan 1856; d. Jena 18 Dec 1921)
22 May 1916	*Karl Helfferich* (b. Neustadt 22 Jul 1872; d. Bellinzana, Switzerland, 23 Apr 1924)
9 Nov 1917 – 9 Nov 1918	*Friedrich von Payer* (b. Tübingen 12 Jun 1847; d. Stuttgart 14 Jul 1931)

Foreign Affairs

1873 – 20 Oct 1879	*Berhard Ernst von Bülow* (b. Cismar 2 Aug 1915; d. Frankfurt 20 Oct 1879)
Summer 1881 – Autumn 1885	*Paul, Count Hatzfeld* (b. 8 Oct 1931; d. London 22 Nov 1901)
1886 – 20 Mar 1890	*Herbert, Prince Bismarck-Schönhausen* (b. Berlin 28 Dec 1849; d. Friedrichsruh 18 Sep 1904)
1 Apr 1890	*Adolf, Baron Marschall von Bieberstein* (b. Karlsruhe 12 Oct 1842; d. Badenweiler 24 Sep 1912)
20 Oct 1897 – 17 Oct 1900	*Bernhard (Heinrich Martin Karl) Count* (from 1905: *Prince) Bülow* (see Chancellors)
23 Oct 1900	*Oswald, Baron Richthofen* (b. Jassy 13 Oct 1847; d.

	Berlin 17 Jan 1906)
17 Jan 1906	*Heinrich Leonhard von Tschirschky und Bögendorff* (b. 15 Jul 1858; d. 15 Nov 1916)
7 Oct 1907	*Wilhelm* (from 1909: *Baron*) *Schoen* (b. Worms 3 Jun 1851; d. Berchtesgaden 24 Apr 1933)
28 Jun 1910 – 30 Dec 1912	*Alfred von Kiderlen-Wächter* (b. Stuttgart 10 Jul 1852; d. 30 Dec 1912)
11 Jan 1913 – 22 Nov 1916	*Gottlieb von Jagow* (b. Berlin 22 Jun 1863; d. Berlin 11 Jan 1935)
25 Nov 1916 – 5 Aug 1917	*Arthur Zimmermann* (b. Treuburg 5 Oct 1864; d. Berlin 7 Jun 1940)
7 Aug 1917	*Richard von Kühlmann* (b. Constantinople 17 Mar 1873; d. Ohlstedt 16 Feb 1948)
9 Jul – 3 Oct 1918	*Paul von Hintze* (b. Schwedt 13 Feb 1864; d. Meran 19 Aug 1941)
4 Oct – 13 Dec 1918	*Wilhelm Solf* (b. Berlin 5 Oct 1862; d. 6 Feb 1936)
20 Dec 1918 – 20 Jun 1919	*Ulrich (Karl Christian) Count Brockdorff-Rantzau* (b. Schleswig 29 May 1869; d. Berlin 8 Sep 1928)

Home Affairs (Until 1879 Presidents of the State Chancellery)

18 Jan 1871	*Rudolf von Delbrück* (b. Berlin 16 Apr 1817; d. 1 Feb 1903)
1 Jun 1876	*Karl von Hofmann* (b. Darmstadt 4 Nov 1827; d. 9 May 1910)
Sep 1880	*Karl Heinrich von Boetticher* (see Vice Chancellors)
1 Jul 1897	*Artur (Adolf) Count Posadowsky-Wehner* (see Vice Chancellors)
24 Jun 1970	*Theobald von Bethmann Hollweg* (see Chancellors)
14 Jul 1909	*Klemens von Delbrück* (see Vice Chancellors)
22 May 1916	*Karl Helfferich* (see Vice Chancellors)
23 Oct 1917	*Max Wallraf* (b. Cologne 18 Sep 1859; d. Berlin 6 Sep 1941)
6 Oct – 9 Nov 1918	*Karl Trimborn* (b. Cologne 2 Dec 1854; d. Bonn 25 Jul 1921)
15 Nov 1918 – 20 Jun 1919	*Hugo Preuss* (b. Berlin 28 Oct 1860; d. Berlin 9 Oct 1925)

Exchequer

1880	*Adolf (Heinrich Wilhelm) von Scholz* (b. Schweidnitz 1 Nov 1833; d. Seeheim 21 Mar 1924)
Jul 1882	*(Franz) Emil Emanuel von Burchard* (b. Königsberg 8

Aug 1836; d. Charlottenburg 25 Apr 1901)

Beginning Nov 1886   *(Karl) Rudolf von Jacobi* (b. Jeggau 8 Sep 1828; d. Zinnowitz 24 Jul 1903)

14 Sep 1888   *Hellmut, Baron Maltzahn* (b. Gültz 6 Jan 1840; d. Gültz 11 Feb 1923)

12 Aug 1893   *Arthur (Adolf) Count Posadowsky-Wehner* (see Vice Chancellors)

1 Jul 1897   *Max (Franz Guido) Baron Thielmann* (b. Berlin 4 Apr 1846; d. 4 May 1929)

22 Aug 1903   *Hermann Baron Stengel* (b. Speyer 19 Jul 1837; d. Munich 5 May 1919)

20 Feb 1908 – 14 Jul 1909   *Reinhold von Sydow* (b. Berlin 14 Jan 1851; d. Berlin 16 Jan 1943)

15 Jul 1909   *Adolf Wermuth* (b. Hanover 23 Mar 1851; d. Berlin 12 Oct 1927)

16 Mar 1912   *Hermann Kühn* (b. Schlawe 17 May 1851; d. Berlin 26 Feb 1937)

31 Jan 1915   *Karl Helfferich* (see Vice Chancellors)

22 May 1916   *Siegfried Count Roedern* (b. Marburg 27 Jul 1870; d. Sonnleitenhof 13 Apr 1954)

14 Nov 1918 – 19 Apr 1919   *Eugen Schiffer* (b. Breslau 14 Feb 1860; d. Berlin 5 Sep 1954)

30 Apr – 20 Jun 1919   *Bernhard Dernburg* (b. Darmstadt 17 Jul 1865; d. Berlin 15 Oct 1937)

Justice

Dec 1876 – 30 Oct 1879   *Heinrich von Friedberg* (b. Märkisch-Friedland 27 Jan 1813; d. Berlin 2 Jun 1895)

Oct 1879 – 31 Jan 1889   *Hermann von Schelling* (b. Erlangen 19 Apr 1824; d. Berlin 15 Nov 1908)

9 Feb 1889   *Otto von Öhlschläger* (b. East Prussia 16 May 1831; d. Charlottenburg 14 Jan 1904)

Feb 1891 – 24 Mar 1892   *Robert Bosse* (b. Quedlinburg 12 Jul 1832; d. Berlin 31 Jul 1901)

Apr 1892 – 20 Apr 1893   *Edward von Hanauer* (b. 1829; d. 30 Apr 1893)

1 Jul 1893   *Rudolf Arnold Nieberding* (b. Konitz 4 May 1838; d. Charlottenburg 10 Oct 1912)

5 Oct 1909 – 5 Aug 1917   *Hermann Lisco* (b. Berlin 30 Jan 1850; d. 7 Nov 1923)

Aug 1917 – 13 Feb 1919   *Paul (Georg Christof) von Krause* (b. 4 Apr 1852; d. 17 Dec 1923)

Postmaster General

1880 – 8 Apr 1897	*Heinrich von Stephan* (b. Stolp 7 Jan 1831; d. Berlin 8 Apr 1897)
1 Jul 1897	*Victor von Podbielski* (b. Frankfurt an der Oder 26 Feb 1844; d. Berlin 21 Jan 1916)
6 May 1901	*Reinhold Kraetke* (b. Berlin 11 Oct 1845; d. Berlin 14 Apr 1934)
5 Aug 1917 – 6 Feb 1919	*Otto Rüdlin* (b. 11 Feb 1861; d. Berlin 3 Feb 1928)

Navy

1 Jan 1872	*Albrecht von Stosch* (b. Coblenz 20 Apr 1818; d. Östrich im Rheingau 29 Feb 1896)
20 Mar 1883 – 5 Jul 1888	*(Georg) Leo, Count Caprivi* (see Chancellors)
1889 – 22 Jun 1890	*Karl Eduard Heusner* (b. Perl 8 Apr 1843; d. Weimar 27 Feb 1891)
23 Apr 1890	*Fritz von Hollmann* (b. Berlin 19 Jan 1842; d. Charlottenburg 21 Jan 1913)
18 Jun 1897	*Alfred (P. Friedrich) von Tirpitz* (b. Küstrin 19 Mar 1849; d. Ebenhausen 6 Mar 1930)
15 Mar 1916	*Eduard von Capelle* (b. Celle 10 Oct 1855; d. Wiesbaden 23 Feb 1931)
7 Oct 1918	*Paul Behnke* (b. Süsel 23 Aug 1866; d. Berlin 4 Jan 1937)
Nov 1918 – 13 Feb 1919	*Ernest (Karl August Klemens) von Mann* (b. 11 Apr 1864; d. 2 Oct 1934)

Colonies

17 May 1907 – 9 Jun 1910	*Bernhard Dernburg* (b. Darmstadt 17 Jul 1865; d. Berlin 15 Oct 1937)
Jun 1910 – 3 Nov 1911	*Friedrich von Lindequist* (b. Wostewitz 15 Sep 1862; d. Machershust Jun 1945)
20 Dec 1911 – 13 Dec 1918	*Wilhelm Solf* (see Foreign Affairs)
13 Feb – 20 Jun 1919	*Johannes Bell* (b. Essen 23 Sep 1868; d. Würgassen 21 Oct 1949)

Food

26 May 1916	*Adolf Tortilowicz von Batocki-Friebe* (b. Bledau 31 Jul 1868; d. Königsberg 22 May 1944)
5 Aug 1917 – 8 Nov	*Wilhelm von Waldow* (b. Berlin 31 Oct 1856; d. Dannenwalde 27 Jul 1937)
14 Nov 1918 – 13 Feb 1919	*Emanuel Wurm* (b. Breslau 16 Sep 1857; d. Berlin 3 May 1920)

Economic Affairs

5 Aug 1917	*Rudolf Schwander* (b. Kolmar 23 Dec 1868; d. Oberursel 24 Dec 1950)
20 Nov 1917 – 8 Nov 1918	*Hans Karl, Baron Stein* (b. Würzburg 28 Feb 1867; d. Völkershausen 25 Sep 1942)
14 Nov 1918 – 13 Feb 1919	*August Müller* (b. Wiesbaden 20 Nov 1873)

Labour

4 Oct 1918 – 13 Feb 1919	*Gustav (Adolf) Bauer* (b. Darkehmen 6 Jan 1870; d. Berlin 6 Sep 1944)

9 Nov 1918 – 13 Feb 1919: People's Representatives (overlapped with Imperial Government)

	Friedrich Ebert (Maj Soc) (see Heads of State) subsequently President
	Philipp Scheidemann (Maj Soc) (b. Kassel 26 Jul 1865 d. Copenhagen 29 Nov 1939)
	Otto Landsberg (Maj Soc) (b. Rybnik 4 Dec 1869; d. 1942)
9 Nov – 29 Dec 1918	*Hugo Haase* (USPD) (b. Allenstein 29 Sep 1863; d. Berlin 17 Nov 1919)
9 Nov – 29 Dec 1918	*Wilhelm Dittmann* (USPD) (b. Eutin 13 Nov 1874)
9 Nov – 29 Dec 1918	—— *Barth* (USPD) (b. Brandenburg 9 Jul 1868; d. Hanover 30 Nov 1946)
29 Dec 1918 – 13 Feb 1919	*Gustav Noske* (Maj Soc) (b. Brandenberg 9 Jul 1868; d. Hanover 30 Nov 1946)
	Rudolf Wissel (b. Göttingen 8 Mar 1869; d. Berlin 13 Dec 1962)

249

13 Feb – 20 Jun 1919: Scheidemann

Prime Minister	*Philipp Scheidemann* (Maj Soc) (see People's Representatives)
Deputy	13 Feb – 19 Apr 1919: *Eugen Schiffer* (Dem) (see Exchequer)
	30 Apr – 20 Jun 1919: *Bernhard Dernburg* (Dem) (see Exchequer)
Foreign Affairs	*Ulrich (Karl Christian) Count Brockdorff Rantzau* (no party) (see Foreign Affairs)
Home Affairs	*Hugo Preuss* (Dem) (see Home Affairs)
Finance	13 Feb – 19 Apr 1919: *Eugen Schiffer* (Dem) (see Exchequer)
	19 Apr – 21 Jun 1919: *Bernhard Dernburg* (Dem) (see Exchequer)
Economic Affairs	*Rudolf Wissell* (Maj Soc) (see People's Representatives)
Labour	*Gustav (Adolf) Bauer* (Maj Soc) (see Labour)
Justice	*Otto Landsberg* (Maj Soc) (see People's Representatives)
Defence	*Gustav Noske* (Maj Soc) (see People's Representatives)
Posts	*Johannes Giesberts* (Centre) (b. Straelen 3 Feb 1865; d. Berlin 11 Aug 1938)
Transport	*Johannes Bell* (Centre) (see Colonies)
Food	*Robert Schmidt* (Maj Soc) (b. Berlin 15 May 1864; d. Berlin 16 Sep 1943)
Colonies	*Johannes Bell* (Centre) (see Colonies)
Treasury	3 Apr – 20 Jun 1919: *Georg Gothein* (Dem) (b. Neumarkt 15 Aug 1857; d. Berlin 7 Apr 1940)
Without Portfolio	*Eduard David* (Maj Soc) (b. Ediger 11 Jun 1863; d. Berlin 24 Dec 1930)
	Matthias Erzberger (Centre) (b. Buttenhausen 20 Sep 1875; d. on the Kniebis 26 Aug 1921)
	13 Feb – 3 Apr 1919: *George Gothein* (Dem) (see above)

21 Jun 1919 – 26 Mar 1920: Bauer

Prime Minister	*Gustav Bauer* (Maj Soc) (see Labour)
Deputy	21 Jun – 3 Oct 1919: *Matthias Erzberger* (Centre) (see Scheidemann)
	3 Oct 1919 – 26 Mar 1920: *Eugen Schiffer* (Dem) (see Exchequer)

Foreign Affairs	*Hermann Müller* (Maj Soc) (b. Mannheim 18 May 1876; d. Berlin 20 Mar 1931)
Home Affairs	21 Jun – 3 Oct 1919: *Eduard David* (Maj Soc) (see Scheidemann)
	3 Oct 1919 – 26 Mar 1920: *Erich Friedrich Ludwig Koch* (Dem) (b. Bremerhaven 26 Feb 1875; d. Paraná, Brazil, Oct 1944)
Finance	21 Jun 1919 – 12 Mar 1920: *Matthias Erzberger* (Centre) (see Scheidemann)
	12 – 26 Mar 1920: no appointment made
Economic Affairs	21 Jun – 15 Jul 1919: *Rudolf Wissell* (Maj Soc) (see People's Representatives)
	15 Jul 1919 – 26 Mar 1920: *Rober Schmidt* (Maj Soc) (see Scheidemann)
Labour	*(Edward) Alexander Schlicke* (Maj Soc) (b. Berlin 26 Mar 1863)
Justice	21 Jun – 3 Oct 1919: no appointment made
	3 Oct 1919 – 26 Mar 1920: *Eugen Schiffer* (Dem) (see Exchequer)
Defence	21 Jun 1919 – 22 Mar 1920: *Gustav Noske* (Maj Soc) (see People's Representatives)
	22 – 26 Mar 1920: no appointment made
Posts	*Johannes Giesberts* (Centre) (see Scheidemann)
Transport	*Johannes Bell* (Centre) (see Colonies)
Food	21 Jun – 15 Sep 1919: *Robert Schmidt* (Maj Soc) (see Scheidemann)
	from 15 Sep 1919: amalgamated with Ministry of Agriculture
Colonies	21 Jun – 7 Nov 1919: *Johannes Bell* (Centre) (see Colonies)
	From 7 Nov 1919: post terminated
Treasury	21 Jun 1919 – 30 Jan 1920: *Wilhelm Mayer* (Centre) (b. 18 Nov 1874; d. 5 Mar 1923)
Reconstruction	30 Jan – 26 Mar 1920: no appointment made
	25 Oct 1919 – 26 Mar 1920: *Otto (Karl) Gessler* (Dem) (b. Ludwigsburg 6 Feb 1875; d. Lindenberg 24 Mar 1955)
Without Portfolio	*Eduard David* (Soc) (see Scheidemann)

13 – 17 Mar 1920: The 'Kapp-Putsch' Administration

Chancellor	*Wolfgang Kapp* (Pan German) (b. New York 24 Jul 1858; d. Leipzig 12 Jun 1922)

Home Affairs	*Traugott von Jagow* (b. Perleberg 18 May 1865; d. Berlin night of 14/15 Jun 1941)
Public Worship	*Gottfried Traub* (German Nat) (b. Rielinghausen 11 Jan 1869; d. Munich 22 Sep 1956)
Defence	*Walter, Baron Lüttwitz* (b. Bodland 2 Feb 1859; d. Breslau 22 Sep 1942)

27 Mar – 8 Jun 1920: Müller I

Chancellor	*Hermann Müller* (for 1st time) (Maj Soc) (see Bauer)
Vice Chancellor	*Erich Koch* (Dem) (see Bauer)
Foreign Affairs	*Adolf Köster* (Maj Soc) (b. Verden 8 Mar 1883; d. Belgrade 18 Feb 1930)
Home Affairs	*Erich Koch* (Dem) (see Bauer)
Finance	*Josef (Karl) Wirth* (Centre) (b. Freiburg 6 Sep 1879; d. Freiburg 3 Jan 1956)
Economic Affairs	*Robert Schmidt* (Maj Soc) (see Scheidemann)
Labour	*Alexander Schlicke* (Maj Soc) (see Bauer)
Justice	*Andreas Blunck* (Dem) (b. Krempe 20 Dec 1871; d. Aumühle 12 Apr 1933)
Defence	*Otto Gessler* (Dem) (see Bauer)
Transport	27 Mar – 1 May 1920: *Johannes Bell* (Centre) (see Colonies) 1 May – 8 Jun 1920: *Gustav Bauer* (Maj Soc) (see Labour)
Food (new post)	30 Mar – 8 Jun 1920: *Andreas Hermes* (Centre) (b. Cologne 16 Jul 1878; d. Krälingen 4 Jan 1964)
Treasury	27 Mar – 1 May 1920: *Gustav Bauer* (Maj Soc) (see Labour) 1 May – 8 Jun 1920: managed by the Minister of Transport
Reconstruction	No appointment made
Without Portfolio	*Eduard David* (Maj Soc) (see Scheidemann)

25 Jun 1920 – 4 May 1921: Fehrenbach

Chancellor	*Konstantin Fehrenbach* (Centre) (b. Wellendingen 11 Jan 1852; d. Freiburg 26 Mar 1926)
Vice Chancellor	*(Karl) Rudolf Heinze* (DVP) (b. Oldenburg 22 Jul 1865; d. Dresden 17 May 1928)
Foreign Affairs	*Walter Simons* (no party) (see Presidents)
Home Affairs	*Erich Koch* (Dem) (see Bauer)
Finance	*Josef Wirth* (Centre) (see Müller I)

Economic Affairs	*Ernest Scholz* (DVP) (b. Wiesbaden 3 May 1874; d. Berlin 26 Jun 1932)
Labour	*Heinrich Brauns* (Centre) (b. Cologne 3 Jan 1868; d. Lindenberg 19 Oct 1939)
Justice	*Andreas Blunck* (Dem) (see Müller I)
Defence	*Otto Gessler* (Dem) (see Bauer)
Posts	*Johannes Giesberts* (Centre) (see Scheidemann)
Transport	*Wilhelm Groener* (no party) (b. Ludwigsburg 22 Nov 1867; d. Berlin 4 May 1939)
Food	*Andreas Hermes* (Centre) (see Müller I)
Treasury	*Hans von Raumer* (DVP) (b. Dessau 10 Jan 1870)
Reconstruction	No appointment made

10 May - 22 Oct 1921: Wirth I

Chancellor	*Josef Wirth* (for 1st time) (Centre) (see Müller I)
Vice Chancellor	*Gustav Bauer* (Maj Soc) (see Labour)
Foreign Affairs	*Friedrich Rosen* (no party) (b. Leipzig 30 Aug 1856; d. Peking, China, 27 Nov 1935)
Home Affairs	*Georg Gradnauer* (Maj Soc) (b. Magdeburg 16 Nov 1866; d. Berlin (?) 20 Nov 1946)
Finance	(acting:) *Josef Wirth* (Centre) (see Müller I)
Economic Affairs	*Robert Schmidt* (Maj Soc) (see Scheidemann)
Labour	*Heinrich Brauns* (Centre) (see Fehrenbach)
Justice	*Eugen Schiffer* (Dem) (see Exchequer)
Defence	*Otto Gessler* (Dem) (see Bauer)
Posts	*Johannes Giesberts* (Centre) (see Scheidemann)
Transport	*Wilhelm Groener* (no party) (see Fehrenbach)
Food	*Andreas Hermes* (Centre) (see Müller I)
Treasury	*Gustav Bauer* (Maj Soc) (see Labour)
Reconstruction	*Walter Rathenau* (Dem) (b. Berlin 29 Sep 1867; d. 24 Jun 1922)

26 Oct 1921 - 14 Nov 1922: Wirth II

Chancellor	*Josef Wirth* (for 2nd time) (Centre) (see Müller I)
Vice Chancellor	*Gustav Bauer* (Maj Soc) (see Labour)
Foreign Affairs	26 Oct 1921 – 31 Jan 1922 (acting:) *Josef Wirth* (Centre) (see Müller I)
	31 Jan – 24 Jun 1922 (acting:) *Walter Rathenau* (Dem) (see Wirth I)
	26 Jun – 14 Nov 1922 (acting:) *Josef Wirth* (Centre) (see Müller I)

Home Affairs	*Adolf Köster* (Maj Soc) (see Müller I)
Finance	26 Oct 1921 – 10 Mar 1922 (acting:) *Andreas Hermes* (Centre) (see Müller I)
	10 Mar – 14 Nov 1922: *Andreas Hermes* (see Müller I)
Economic Affairs	*Robert Schmidt* (Maj Soc) (see Scheidemann)
Labour	*Heinrich Brauns* (Centre) (see Fehrenbach)
Justice	*Gustav (Lambert) Radbruch* (Maj Soc) (b. Lübeck 21 Nov 1878; d. Heidelberg 23 Nov 1949)
Defence	*Otto Gessler* (Dem) (see Bauer)
Posts	*Johannes Giesberts* (Centre) (see Scheidemann)
Transport	*Wilhelm Groener* (no party) (see Fehrenbach)
Food	26 Oct 1921 – 10 Mar 1922: *Andreas Hermes* (Centre) (see Müller I)
	31 Mar – 14 Nov 1922: *Anton Fehr* (Bavarian Farmers League; from 1924 German Farmers Party) (b. Lindenberg 24 Dec 1881; d. Lindenburg 2 Apr 1954)
Treasury	*Gustav Bauer* (Soc) (see Labour)
Reconstruction	No appointment made

22 Nov 1922 – 12 Aug 1923: Cuno

Chancellor	*Wilhelm Cuno* (no party) (b. Suhl 2 Jul 1876; d. Berlin 5 Jan 1933)
Vice Chancellor	No appointment made
Foreign Affairs	*Friedrich (Hans) von Rosenberg* (no party) (b. Berlin 26 Dec 1874; d. Fürstenzell 30 Jul 1937)
Home Affairs	*Rudolf Oeser* (Dem) (b. Coswig 13 Nov 1858; d. Berlin 3 Jun 1926)
Finance	*Andreas Hermes* (Centre) (see Müller I)
Economic Affairs	*Johannes Becker* (DVP) (b. Ludwigshöhe 3 Feb 1869; d. Oppenheim 17 Oct 1951)
Labour	*Heinrich Brauns* (Centre) (see Fehrenbach)
Justice	*Rudolf Heinze* (DVP) (see Fehrenbach)
Defence	*Otto Gessler* (Dem) (see Bauer)
Posts	*Karl Stingl* (Bayer VP) (b. Mitterteich 29 Jul 1864; d. Munich (?) 9 Nov 1936)
Transport	*Wilhelm Groener* (no party) (see Fehrenbach)
Food	22 – 25 Nov 1922: *Karl Müller* (Centre) (b. Süchteln 29 Jul 1884; d. Bonn 18 Apr 1964)
	1 Dec 1922 – 12 Aug 1923: *Hans Luther* (no party) (b. Berlin 10 Mar 1879; d. Düsseldorf 11 May 1962)
Treasury	22 Nov 1922 – 29 Mar 1923: *Heinrich Albert* (no party) (b. 12 Feb 1874; d. Wiesbaden 1 Nov 1960) from 1 Apr

	1923: post terminated
Reconstruction	22 Nov 1922 – 29 Mar 1923: no appointment made
	29 Mar – 12 Aug 1923: *Heinrich Albert* (see above)

13 Aug – 4 Oct 1923: Stresemann I

Chancellor	*Gustav Stresemann* (for 1st time) (DVP) (b. Berlin 10 May 1878; d. 3 Oct 1929)
Vice Chancellor	*Robert Schmidt* (SPD) (see Scheidemann)
Foreign Affairs	(acting:) *Gustav Stresemann* (DVP) (see above)
Home Affairs	*Wilhelm Sollman* (SPD) (b. Oberlind 1 Apr 1881; d. Mount Carmel, Connecticut, 6 Jan 1951)
Finance	*Rudolf Hilferding* (SPD) (b. Vienna 10 Aug 1877; d. Buchenwald (?) 1943)
Economic Affairs	*Hans von Raumer* (DVP) (see Fehrenbach)
Labour	*Heinrich Brauns* (Centre) (see Fehrenbach)
Justice	*Gustav Radbruch* (SPD) (see Wirth II)
Defence	*Otto Gessler* (Dem) (see Bauer)
Posts	*Anton Höfle* (Centre) (b. Otterbach 19 Oct 1828; d. Berlin 20 Apr 1925)
Transport	*Rudolf Oeser* (Dem) (see Cuno)
Food	*Hans Luther* (no party) (see Cuno)
Occupied Territories (new post)	24 Aug – 4 Oct 1923: *Johannes Fuchs* (Centre) (b. 30 Sep 1874; d. Cochem 9 Sep 1956)
Reconstruction	*Robert Schmidt* (SPD) (see Scheidemann)

6 Oct – 23 Nov 1923: Stresemann II

Chancellor	*Gustav Stresemann* (for 2nd time) (DVP) (see Stresemann I)
Vice Chancellor	No appointment made
Foreign Affairs	(acting:) *Gustav Stresemann* (see Stresemann I) 6 Oct
Home Affairs	– 3 Nov 1923: *Wilhelm Sollman* (SPD) (see Stresemann I)
	11 – 23 Nov 1923: *Karl Jarres* (no party) (b. Remscheid 21 Sep 1874; d. Duisburg 20 Oct 1951)
Finance	*Hans Luther* (no party) (see Cuno)
Economic Affairs	*Josef Koeth* (no party) (b. Lohr 7 Jul 1870; d. 26 (?) May 1936)
Labour	*Heinrich Brauns* (Centre) (see Fehrenbach)
Justice	6 Oct – 3 Nov 1923: *Gustav Radbruch* (SPD) (see Wirth II)
Defence	*Otto Gessler* (Dem) (see Bauer)

Posts	*Anton Höfle* (Centre) (see Stresemann I)
Transport	*Rudolf Oeser* (Dem) (see Cuno)
Food	*Gerhard (Theodor Alexander), Count Kanitz* (no party) (b. Podangen 9 Apr 1885; d. Frankfurt 13 Jun 1949)
Occupied Territories	*Johannes Fuchs* (Centre) (see Stresemann I)
Reconstruction	*Robert Schmidt* (SPD) (see Scheidemann)

30 Nov 1923 – 26 May 1924: Marx I

Chancellor	*Wilhelm Marx* (for 1st time) (Centre) (b. Cologne 15 Jan 1863; d. Bonn 5 Aug 1946)
Vice Chancellor	*Karl Jarres* (no party) (see Stresemann II)
Foreign Affairs	*Gustav Stresemann* (DVP) (see Stresemann I)
Home Affairs	*Karl Jarres* (no party) (see Stresemann II)
Finance	*Hans Luther* (no party) (see Cuno)
Economic Affairs	*Eduard Hamm* (Dem) (b. Passau 16 Oct 1879; d. Berlin 20 Jul 1944)
Labour	*Heinrich Brauns* (Centre) (see Fehrenbach)
Justice	30 Nov 1923 – 15 Apr 1924: *Erich Emminger* (Bayer VP) (b. Eichstätt 25 Jun 1880; d. Munich 30 Aug 1951) 15 Apr – 26 May 1924: *Kurt (Walter) Joël* (b. 18 Jan 1865; d. Berlin 15 Apr 1945)
Defence	*Otto Gessler* (Dem) (see Bauer)
Posts	*Anton Höfle* (Centre) (see Stresemann I)
Transport	*Rudolf Oeser* (Dem) (see Cuno)
Food	*Gerhard, Count Kanitz* (no party) (see Stresemann II)
Occupied Territories	(acting:) *Anton Höfle* (Centre) (see Stresemann I)
Reconstruction	30 Nov 1923 – 12 May 1924: no appointment made 12 May 1924: post abolished

3 Jun – 15 Dec 1924: Marx II

Chancellor	*Wilhelm Marx* (for 2nd time) (Centre) (see Marx I)
Vice Chancellor	*Karl Jarres* (no party) (see Stresemann II)
Foreign Affairs	*Gustav Stresemann* (DVP) (see Stresemann I)
Home Affairs	*Karl Jarres* (no party) (see Stresemann II)
Finance	*Hans Luther* (no party) (see Cuno)
Economic Affairs	*Eduard Hamm* (Dem) (see Marx I)
Labour	*Heinrich Brauns* (Centre) (see Fehrenbach)
Justice	(acting:) *Kurt Joël* (no party) (see Marx I)
Defence	*Otto Gessler* (Dem) (see Bauer)
Transport	3 Jun – 11 Oct 1924: *Rudolf Oeser* (Dem) (see Cuno)

11 Oct – 15 Dec 1924 (acting:) *Rudolf Krohne* (DVP)
(b. Rendsburg 6 Sep 1876; d. Berlin 17 Jun 1953)

Food	*Gerhard, Count Kanitz* (no party) (see Stresemann)
Posts	*Anton Höfle* (Centre) (see Stresemann I)
Occupied Territories	(acting:) *Anton Höfle* (Centre) (see Stresemann I)

15 Jan – 5 Dec 1925: Luther I

Chancellor	*Hans Luther* (for 1st time) (no party) (see Cuno)
Vice Chancellor	No appointment made
Foreign Affairs	*Gustav Stresemann* (DVP) (see Stresemann I)
Home Affairs	15 Jan – 23 Oct 1925: *Martin Schiele* (German Nat) (b. Gross-Schwarzlosen 17 Jan 1870; d. Suckow 16 Feb 1939)
	23 Oct – 3 Dec 1925 (acting:) *Otto Gessler* (Dem) (see Bauer)
Finance	15 Jan – 26 Oct 1925: *Otto von Schlieben* (German Nat) (b. Gross-Hinnersdorf 14 Jan 1875; d. Halle 22 Jul 1932)
	26 Oct – 5 Dec 1925 (acting:) *Hans Luther* (no party) (see Cuno)
Economic Affairs	15 Jan – 20 Oct 1925: *Albert Neuhaus* (German Nat) (b. Glasgow 9 Jul 1873)
	26 Oct – 5 Dec 1925 (acting:) *Rudolf Krohne* (DVP) (see Marx II)
Justice	15 Jan – 21 Nov 1925: *Josef Frenken* (Centre) (b. Loecken 27 Sep 1854)
	21 Nov – 5 Dec 1925 (acting:) *Hans Luther* (see Cuno)
Labour	*Heinrich Brauns* (Centre) (see Fehrenbach)
Defence	*Otto Gessler* (Dem) (see Bauer)
Posts	*Karl Stingl* (Bayer VP) (see Cuno)
Transport	*Rudolf Krohne* (DVP) (see Marx II)
Food	*Gerhard, Count Kanitz* (no party) (see Stresemann II)
Occupied Territories	15 Jan – 21 Nov 1925 (acting): *Josef Frenken* (Centre) (see above)
	21 Nov – 5 Dec 1925 (acting:) *Heinrich Brauns* (Centre) (see Fehrenbach)

20 Jan – 12 May 1926: Luther II

Chancellor	*Hans Luther* (for 2nd time) (no party; see Cuno)
Vice Chancellor	20 Jan – 12 May 1926: no appointment made
	12 – 16 May 1926: *Otto Gessler* (Dem) (see Bauer)

Foreign Affairs	*Gustav Stresemann* (DVP) (see Stresemann I)
Home Affairs	*Wilhelm Külz* (Dem) (b. Leipzig 18 Feb 1875; d. Berlin 10 Apr 1948)
Finance	*Peter Reinhold* (Dem) (b. Blasewitz 1 Dec 1887; d. Capri 1 Apr 1955)
Economic Affairs	*Julius Curtius* (DVP) (b. Duisburg 7 Feb 1877; d. Heidelberg 10 Nov 1948)
Labour	*Heinrich Brauns* (Centre) (see Fehrenbach)
Justice	*Wilhelm Marx* (Centre) (see Marx I)
Defence	*Otto Gessler* (Dem) (see Bauer)
Posts	*Karl Stingl* (Bayer VP) (see Cuno)
Transport	*Rudolf Krohne* (DVP) (see Marx II)
Food	*Heinrich Haslinde* (Centre) (b. 21 May 1881)
Occupied Territories	(acting:) *Wilhelm Marx* (Centre) (see Marx I)

16 May – 17 Dec 1926: Marx III

Chancellor	*Wilhelm Marx* (for 3rd time) (Centre) (see Marx I)
Vice Chancellor	No appointment made
Foreign Affairs	*Gustav Stresemann* (DVP) (see Stresemann I)
Home Affairs	*Wilhelm Külz* (Dem) (see Luther II)
Finance	*Peter Reinhold* (Dem) (see Luther II)
Economic Affairs	*Julius Curtius* (DVP) (see Luther II)
Labour	*Heinrich Brauns* (Centre) (see Fehrenbach)
Justice	*Johannes Bell* (Centre) (see Colonies)
Defence	*Otto Gessler* (Dem) (see Bauer)
Posts	*Karl Stingl* (Bayer VP) (see Cuno)
Transport	*Rudolf Krohne* (DVP) (see Mark II)
Food	*Heinrich Haslinde* (Centre) (see Luther II)
Occupied Territories	(acting:) *Johannes Bell* (Centre) (see Colonies)

29 Jan 1927 – 12 Jun 1928: Marx IV

Chancellor	*Wilhelm Marx* (for 4th time) (Centre) (see Marx I)
Vice Chancellor	*Oskar Hergt* (German Nat) (b. Naumburg 22 Oct 1869)
Foreign Affairs	*Gustav Stresemann* (DVP) (see Stresemann I)
Home Affairs	*Walter von Keudell* (German Nat) (b. Castellamare 17 Jul 1884)
Finance	*Heinrich (Franz) Köhler* (Centre) (b. Karlsruhe 29 Sep 1878; d. Karlsruhe 6 Feb 1949)
Economic Affairs	*Julius Curtius* (DVP) (see Luther II)
Labour	*Heinrich Brauns* (Centre) (see Fehrenbach)
Justice	*Oskar Hergt* (German Nat) (see above)

Defence	29 Jan 1927 – 19 Jan 1928: *Otto Gessler* (from 3 Dec 1926: no party) (see Bauer)
	19 Jan – 12 Jun 1928: *Wilhelm Groener* (no party) (see Fehrenbach)
Posts	*Georg Schätzel* (Bayer VP) (b. Neustadt an der Aisch 13 Jul 1874; d. Berlin 27 Nov 1934)
Transport	*Wilhelm Koch* (German Nat) (b. Dönges 3 Mar 1877; d. Wuppertal (?) 10 Mar 1950)
Food	*Martin Schiele* (German Nat) (see Luther I)
Occupied Territories	(acting:) *Wilhelm Marx* (see Marx I)

28 Jun 1928 – 27 Mar 1930: Müller II

Chancellor	*Hermann Müller* (for 2nd time) (SPD) (see Bauer)
Vice Chancellor	No appointment made
Foreign Affairs	28 Jun 1928 – 3 Oct 1929: *Gustav Stresemann* (DVP) (see Stresemann I)
	4 Oct 1929 – 27 Mar 1930 (acting until 11 Nov 1929:) *Julius Curtius* (DVP) (see Luther II)
Home Affairs	*Karl Severing* (SPD) (b. Herford 1 Jun 1875; d. Bielefeld 23 Jul 1952)
Finance	28 Jun 1928 – 21 Dec 1929: *Rudolf Hilferding* (SPD) (see Stresemann I)
	23 Dec 1929 – 27 Mar 1930: *Paul Moldenhauer* (DVP) (b. Cologne 2 Dec 1876; d. Cologne 1 Feb 1947)
Economic Affairs	28 Jun 1928 – 11 Nov 1929: *Julius Curtius* (DVP) (see Luther II)
	11 Nov – 23 Dec 1929: *Paul Moldenhauer* (DVP) (see above)
	23 Dec 1929 – 27 Mar 1930: *Robert Schmidt* (SPD) (see Scheidemann)
Labour	*Rudolf Wissel* (SPD) (see Scheidemann)
Justice	28 Jun 1928 – 13 Apr 1929: *Erich Koch* (Dem) (see Bauer)
	13 Apr 1929 – 27 Mar 1930: *Theodor von Guérard* (Centre) (b. Koblenz 29 Dec 1863; d. Ahaus 21 Jul 1943)
Defence	*Wilhelm Groener* (no party) (see Fehrenbach)
Posts	*Georg Schätzel* (Bayer VP) (see Marx IV)
Transport	28 Jun 1928 – 6 Feb 1929: *Theodor von Guérard* (Centre) (see above)
	7 Feb – 13 Apr 1929 (acting:) *Georg Schätzel* (Bayer VP) (see Marx IV)

	13 Apr 1929 – 27 Mar 1930: *Adam Stergerwald* (Centre) (b. Greussenheim 14 Dec 1874; d. Würzburg 7 Dec 1945)
Food	*Hermann (Robert) Dietrich* (Dem) (b. Oberprechtal 14 Dec 1879; d. Stuttgart 6 Mar 1954)
Occupied Territories	28 Jun 1928 – 6 Feb 1929: *Theodor von Guérard* (Centre) (see above)
	7 Feb – 13 Apr 1929 (acting:) *Karl Severing* (SPD) (see above)
	13 Apr 1929 – 27 Mar 1930: *Josef Wirth* (Centre) (see Müller I)

Greece

HEADS OF STATE

Before establishment of monarchy

1821 – 1830	War of Independence
1 Jan 1822 – Mar 1823	*Alexander Mavrokordatos* (b. Istanbul 11 Feb 1791; d. Aegina 18 Aug 1865) nominal President
13 Jan 1822	Declaration of Greek independence
1823	*Peter Mavromichalis (Petrobey)* (b. 1765; d. Athens 1848)
Dec 1823 – 1826	*George Koundouriotis* (b. Hydra 1782; d. Athens 1858), President of the Executive, at first rival
Apr 1826	Governmental Committee under *Andrew Zaimis* (d. Athens 1840)
May 1827/18 Jan 1828 – 9 Oct 1831	*John Capodistria* (b. Corfu 11 Feb 1776; d. Nauplia 9 Oct 1831) Governor
3 Feb 1830	Greece declared a kingdom by the Protocol of London
20 Feb 1830	*Leopold of Saxe-Coburg* (afterwards Leopold I of Belgium) offered the throne but renounced it in May without reigning
Dec 1831 – Apr 1832	*Agostino Capodistria*, President of the Council of the Provisional Government

1832 – 1833   Leadership in dispute

Kings

Bavarian Dynasty.

6 Feb 1833 – 24 Oct 1862	*Otho*, son of King Ludwig I of Bavaria (b. 1 Jun 1815; d. 26 Jul 1867) Regents: 18 Feb 1833 – 1 Jul 1835: *Josef Ludwig, Count Armansperg* (b. Kotzin 28 Feb 1787; d. Dengendorf 3 Apr 1853) 18 Feb 1833 – (?) 1 Jul 1835: *Karl Wilhelm von Heideck* (b. Saarelben 1788; d. 21 Feb 1861) 18 Feb 1833 – 1834: *Georg Ludwig von Maurer* 23 Oct 1862 – 30 Oct 1863: *Constantine Kanaris* (b. Psara c. 1790; d. Athens 14 Sep 1877), *Demetrios Voulgaris* (b. 1 Jan 1803; d. 11 Jan 1878) and *Benizelos Rouphos* (b. 1795; d. 1868)

Danish Dynasty

30 Mar 1863	*George I*, son of King Christian IX of Denmark (b. 24 Dec 1845)
18 Mar 1913	*Constantine I*, son (b. 2 Aug 1868; d. Palermo 11 Jan 1923)
12 Jun 1917 – 25 Oct 1920	*Alexander*, son (b. 1 Aug 1893)
5 Dec 1920 – 28 Sep 1922	*Constantine I* (for 2nd time)
28 Sep 1922	*George II*, son (b. 19 Jul 1890)
25 Mar 1924	Republic

Presidents

25 Mar 1924 – 18 Mar 1926	*Paul Koundouriotis* (for 1st time) (b. Hydra 9 Apr 1855; d. 22 Aug 1935)
11 Apr – 18 Aug 1926	*Theodore Pangalos* (b. Salamis 11 Jan 1878; d. 22 Feb 1952)
22 Aug 1926 – 10 Dec 1929	*Paul Koundouriotis* (for 2nd time)
15 Dec 1929 – Oct 1935	*Alexander Zaimïs* (b. Athens 9 Nov 1855; d. 15 Sep 1936)

MEMBERS OF GOVERNMENT

Prime Ministers

6 Feb 1833	*Spyridon Trikoupis* (b. Missolonghi 20 Apr 1788; d. Athens 24 Feb 1873)
24 Oct 1833	*Alexander Mavrokordatos* (for 1st time) (see Heads of State)
12 Jun 1834	*John Kolettis* (for 1st time) (b. Yannina 1773; d. 12 Sep 1847)
1 Jul 1835	*Josef Ludwig Count Armansperg* (b. Kötzin 28 Feb 1787; d. Dengendorf 3 Apr 1853) Arch-Chancellor
14 Feb 1837	*Ignaz von Rudhart* (b. 11 Mar 1790; d. Trieste 11 May 1838)
20 Dec 1837	*King Otho* (see Kings)
22 Feb/6 Jul 1841	*Alexander Mavrokordatos* (for 2nd time)
22 Aug 1841	*Antony G. Kriezis* (for 1st time) (b. Hydra 1796; d. 1865)
15 Sep 1843	*Andrew Metaxas* (b. Argostoli 1790; d. Athens 8 Sep 1850)
28 Feb 1844	*Constantine Kanaris* (for 1st time) (see Regents)
11 Apr 1844	*Alexander Mavrokordatos* (for 3rd time).
18 Aug 1844	*John Kolettis* (for 2nd time)
17 Sep 1847	*Kitsos Tzavelas* (b. Souli 1801; d. Missolonghi 20 Mar 1855)
19 Mar 1848	*George Koundouriotis* (b. 1782; d. 1858)
Oct 1848	*Constantine Kanaris* (for 2nd time)
12 Dec 1849	*Antony G. Kriezis* (for 2nd time)
16 May/29 Jul 1854	*Alexander Mavrokordatos* (for 4th time) (see Heads of State)
	16 May – 29 Jul 1854 (acting:) *Constantine Kanaris*
11 Oct 1855	*Demetrius Voulgaris* (for 1st time) (see Regents)
25 Nov 1857	*Athanasius A. Miaoulis* (b. Hydra 1815; d. Paris 1867)
	3 Feb – 7 Mar 1862 (acting:) *Constantine Kanaris*
7 Jun 1862	*Gennaios Kolokotronis* (b. 1803; d. Athens 1868)
22/23 Oct 1862	*Demetrius Voulgaris* (for 2nd time)
23 Feb 1863	*Zinovios Valvis* (for 1st time) (b. Missolonghi 1800; d. Missolonghi 1886)
9 Apr 1863	*D. Kyriakos*
10 May 1863	*Benizelos Rouphos* (for 1st and 2nd times) (see Kings)
6 Nov 1863	*Demetrius Voulgaris* (for 3rd time)
17 Mar 1864	*Constantine Kanaris* (for 3rd time)
28 Apr 1864	*Zinovios Valvis* (for 2nd time)

7 Aug 1864	*Constantine Kanaris* (for 4th time)
14 Mar 1865	*Alexander Koumoundouros* (for 1st time) (b. Selitsa 1814; d. 7 Mar 1883)
1 Nov 1865	*Epaminondas Deligeorgis* (for 1st time) (b. Tripolis 10 Feb 1829; d. Athens 27 May 1889)
15 Nov 1865	*Demetrius Voulgaris* (for 4th time)
18 Nov 1865	*Alexander Koumoundouros* (for 2nd time)
25 Nov 1865	*Epaminondas Deligeorgis* (for 2nd time)
7 Feb 1866	*Benizelos Rouphos* (for 3rd time)
21 Jun 1866	*Demetrius Voulgaris* (for 5th time)
30 Dec 1866	*Alexander Koumoundouros* (for 3rd time)
1 Jan 1868	*Aristides Moraïtinis* (b. Smyrna 1806; d. Athens 1875)
6 Feb 1868	*Demetrius Voulgaris* (for 6th time)
6 Feb 1869	*Thrasyvoulos A. Zaïmis* (for 1st time) (b. Kerpini 29 Oct 1829; d. Athens 8 Nov 1880)
21 Jul 1870	*Epaminondas Deligeorgis* (for 3rd time)
15 Dec 1870	*Alexander Koumoundouros* (for 4th time)
9 Nov 1871	*Thrasyvoulos A. Zaïmis* (for 2nd time)
6 Jan 1872	*Demetrius Voulgaris* (for 7th time)
20 Jul 1872	*Epaminondas Deligeorgis* (for 4th time)
21 Feb 1874	*Demetrius Voulgaris* (for 8th time)
8 May 1875	*Charilaos Trikoupis* (for 1st time) (b. Nauplia 23 Jul 1832; d. Cannes 11 Apr 1896)
27 Oct 1875	*Alexander Koumoundouros* (for 5th time)
8 Dec 1876	*Epaminondas Deligeorgis* (for 5th time)
13 Dec 1876	*Alexander Koumoundouros* (for 6th time)
10 Mar 1877	*Epaminondas Deligeorgis* (for 6th time)
31 May 1877	*Alexander Koumoundouros* (for 7th time)
7 Jun – 14 Sep 1877	*Constantine Kanaris* (for 5th time)
15 Sep 1877	Various ministers in turn
23 Jan 1878	*Alexander Koumoundouros* (for 8th time)
2 Nov 1878	*Charilaos Trikoupis* (for 2nd time)
7 Nov 1878	*Alexander Koumoundouros* (for 9th time)
22 Mar 1880	*Charilaos Trikoupis* (for 3rd time)
25 Oct 1880	*Alexander Koumoundouros* (for 10th time)
15 Mar 1882	*Charilaos Trikoupis* (for 4th time)
30 Apr 1885	*Theodore Diligiannis* (for 1st time) (b. Kalavryta 11 Apr 1826; d. 13 Jun 1905)
12 May 1886	*Zinovios Valvis* (for 3rd time)
21 May 1886	*Charilaos Trikoupis* (for 5th time)
7 Nov 1890	*Theodore Diligiannis* (for 2nd time)
2 Mar 1892	*Constantine Konstantopoulos* (b. Mantineia 1832; d. Athens 1910)

22 Jun 1892	*Charilaos Trikoupis* (for 6th time)
15 May 1893	*Sotirios Sotiropoulos* (b. Nauplia 1823; d. Athens May 1898)
11 Nov 1893	*Charilaos Trikoupis* (for 7th time)
22 Jan 1895	*Nicholas P. Diligiannis* (b. Athens 1845; d. Paris 1910)
12 Jun 1895	*Theodore Diligiannis* (for 3rd time)
30 Apr 1897	*Demetrius G. Rallis* (for 1st time) (b. Athens 1844; d. Athens 19 Aug 1921)
3 Oct 1897	*Alexander Th. Zaïmis* (for 1st time) (b. Athens 9 Nov 1855; d. 15 Sep 1936)
11 Nov 1898	*Alexander Th. Zaïmis* (for 2nd time)
14 Apr 1899	*George Theotokis* (for 1st time) (b. Corfu 22 Feb 1844; d. Athens 4 Jan 1916)
25 Nov 1901	*Alexander Th. Zaïmis* (for 3rd time)
2 Dec 1902	*Theodore Diligiannis* (for 4th time)
26 Jun 1903	*George Theotokis* (for 2nd time)
10 Jul 1903	*Demetrius G. Rallis* (for 2nd time)
18 Dec 1903	*George Theotokis* (for 3rd time)
28 Dec 1904	*Theodore Diligiannis* (for 5th time)
22 Jun 1905	*Demetrius G. Rallis* (for 3rd time)
11 Dec 1905	*George Theotokis* (for 4th time)
20 Jul 1909	*Demetrius G. Rallis* (for 4th time)
28 Aug 1909	*Kyriakoulis P. Mavromichalis* (b. Athens 1849; d. Athens 1916)
31 Jan 1910	*Stephen N. Dragoumis* (b. 1842; d. 18 Sep 1922)
19 Oct 1910	*Eleftherios K. Venizelos* (for 1st time) (b. Mournies 23 Aug 1864; d. Paris 18 Mar 1936)
10 Mar 1915	*Demetrius P. Gounaris* (b. Patras 5 Jan 1867; d. Athens 29 Nov 1922)
23 Aug 1915	*Eleftherios K. Venizelos* (for 2nd time)
7 Oct 1915	*Alexander Th. Zaïmis* (for 4th time)
7 Nov 1915	*Stephen Skouloudis* (b. Istanbul 1836; d. 20 Aug 1928)
22 Jun 1916	*Alexander Th. Zaïmis* (for 5th time)
16 Sep 1916	*Nicholas P. Kalogeropoulos* (for 1st time) (b. Chalcis 1853; d. 11 Jan 1927)
10 Oct 1916	*Spyridon Lambros* (b. Corfu 21 Apr 1851; d. Athens 23 Jul 1919)
3 May 1917	*Alexander Th. Zaïmis* (for 6th time)
27 Jun 1917	*Eleftherios Venizelos* (for 3rd time)
17 Nov 1920	*Demetrius G. Rallis* (for 5th time)
6 Feb 1921	*Nicholas Kalogeropoulos* (for 2nd time)
7 Apr 1921	*Demetrius P. Gounaris* (for 2nd time)
15 Mar 1922	*Demetrius P. Gounaris* (for 3rd time)

16 May 1922	*Nicholas Stratos* (b. 1872; d. 28 Nov 1922)
22 May 1922	*Peter E. Protopapadakis* (b. Apeiranthos Jan 1860; d. 28 Nov 1922)
10 Sep 1922	*Nicholas Triandaphyllakos* (b. Tripolis 1855; d. 1939)
29 Sep 1922	*Sotirios Krokidas* (b. Sieyon 1852; d. Perigiali 1924)
11 Oct 1922	*Alexander Th. Zaïmis* (for 7th time)
24 Nov 1922 – 17 Dec 1923	*Stylianos Gonatas* (b. Patras 1876; d. (?))
11 Jan 1924	*Eleftherios Venizelos* (for 4th time)
6 Feb 1924	*George Kaphandaris* (b. Frangista 1873; d. 29 Aug 1946)
11 Mar 1924	*Alexander Papanastasiou* (b. Tripolis 1876; d. Ekali 17 Nov 1936)
24 Jul 1924	*Themistocles Sophoulis* (b. Vathy 24 Nov 1860; d. Athens 24 Jun 1949)
7 Oct 1924	*Andreas Michalakopoulos* (b. 1876; d. 27 Mar 1938)
26 Jun 1925	*Alexander N. Chatzikyriakos* (b. Syros 1874; d. 24 Mar 1956)
3 Jan 1926	*Theodore Pangalos* (see Presidents)
19 Jul 1926	*Athanasius Eftaxias* (b. Dadi 1849; d. 1931)
23 Aug 1926	*George Kondylis* (b. 1879; d. 31 Jan 1936)
4 Dec 1926 – 12 Aug 1927	*Alexander Th. Zaïmis* (for 8th time)
8 Aug 1927 – 22 May 1928	*Alexander Th. Zaïmis* (for 9th time)
30 May – 28 Jun 1928	*Alexander Th. Zaïmis* (for 10th time)
4 Jul 1928	*Eleftherios Venizelos* (for 5th time)
Jun 1929	*Eleftherios Venizelos* (for 6th time)
6 Dec 1929 – 21 Dec 1930	*Eleftherios Venizelos* (for 7th time)

Foreign Ministers

Feb 1833	*Spyridon Trikoupis* (for 1st time) (see Prime Ministers)
4 Oct 1833	*Alexander Mavrokordatos* (for 1st time) (see Heads of State)
2 Jun 1834	*James Rizos Neroulos* (for 1st time) (b. Istanbul 1778; d. 1850)
4 Feb 1837	*Ignaz von Rudhart* (see Prime Ministers)
Dec 1837	*Constantine Zographos* (for 1st time) (b. Kalavryta 1796; d. Bellevue 9 Oct 1856)

16 Nov 1839	*Andronicus Paikos* (for 1st time) (b. Thessalonica 1776; d. Athens 1880)
20 Mar 1840	*Constantine Zographos* (for 2nd time)
28 May 1840	*Andronicus Paikos* (for 2nd time)
22 Feb 1841	*Alexander Mavrokordatos* (for 2nd time)
6 Jul 1841	*Demetrius Christidis* (b. 1795; d. 1879)
22 Aug 1841	*James Rizos Neroulos* (for 2nd time)
15 Sep 1843	*Andrew Metaxas* (see Prime Ministers)
28 Feb 1844	*Drosos Mansolas* (for 1st time) (b. 1769; d. Athens 1860)
11 Apr 1844	*Spyridon Trikoupis* (for 2nd time)
18 Aug 1844	*John Kolettis* (for 1st time) (see Prime Ministers)
14 Nov 1846	*Kitsos Tzavelas* (see Prime Ministers)
28 Dec 1846	*John Kolettis* (for 2nd time)
12 Aug 1847	*George A. Glarakis* (b. Chios 1789; d. 1855)
19 Mar 1848	*Drosos Mansolas* (for 2nd time)
14 Jun 1848	*Constantine Th. Kolokotronis* (b. 1894; d. 1849)
14 Jan 1849	*Andrew N. Londos* (for 1st time) (b. 1810; d. 1881)
13 Mar 1849	*George A. Rallis* (for 1st time) (b. Istanbul 1804; d. Bad Gastein 1883)
29 Apr 1849	*George A. Glarakis* (for 2nd time)
24 Dec 1849	*Andrew N. Londos* (for 2nd time)
4 Aug 1850	*Peter A. Diligiannis* (for 1st time) (b Istanbul 1812; d. Athens 27 Jul 1872)
5 May 1851	*Andronicus Paikos* (for 3rd time)
28 May 1854	*Pericles A. Argyropoulos* (b. Athens 3 Apr 1881)
4 Oct 1855	*N. Silivergos*
15 Dec 1855	*Michael Potlis* (b. Vienna 1812; d. Vienna 1863)
26 Feb 1856	*Alexander Rizos-Rangavis* (b. Istanbul 1809; d. Athens 1892)
11 Mar 1859	*Athanasius A. Miaoulis* (see Prime Ministers)
10 Jun 1859	*Andrew G. Koundouriotis* (for 1st time) (b. 1820; d. 1895)
24 Jan 1860	*Theodore Zaïmis* (b. Kerpini 1848; d. Athens 18 Oct 1922)
30 Apr 1860	*Andrew G. Koundouriotis* (for 2nd time)
7 Jun 1862	*N. Theocharis*
23 Jun 1862	*Efstathios Iliopoulos* (b. Pyrgos 1816; d. Athens 1881)
1 Aug 1862	*Nicholas M. Dragoumis* (b. Istanbul (?) 1809; d Athens 1879)
23 Oct 1862	*A. Diamantopoulos*
20 Feb 1863	*Paul Kalligas* (for 1st time) (b. 1814; d. 1896)
24 Feb 1863	*D. Mavrokordatos*

9 Apr 1863	*Theodore Diligiannis* (see Prime Ministers)
3 Jul 1863	*Paul Kalligas* (for 2nd time)
6 Nov 1863	*Peter A. Diligiannis* (for 2nd time)
17 Mar 1864	*Theodore Diligiannis* (for 2nd time)
28 Apr 1864	*Paul Kalligas* (for 3rd time)
28 May 1864	*Zinovios Valvis* (see Prime Ministers)
7 Aug 1864	*Theodore Diligiannis* (for 3rd time)
10 Dec 1864	*D. Boudouris* (for 1st time)
28 Mar 1865	*Peter Vraïlas Armenis* (b. Corfu 1812; d. London 1884)
14 Apr 1865	*D. Boudouris* (for 2nd time)
1 Nov 1865	*Epaminondas Deligeorgis* (see Prime Ministers)
15 Nov 1865	*Charalambos Christopoulos* (b. Andritsaina 1819; d. 1871)
18 Nov 1865	*Alexander Koumoundouros* (for 1st time) (see Prime Ministers)
25 Nov 1865	*Epaminondas Deligeorgis* (for 2nd time)
10 Dec 1865	*John Valassopoulos* (b. Bordonia 1820; d. Patras 1888)
7 Feb 1866	*Spyridon Valaoritis* (for 1st time) (b. Levkas 1819; d. Athens 1887)
21 Jun 1866	*Epaminondas Deligeorgis* (for 3rd time)
30 Dec 1866	*Charilaos Trikoupis* (for 1st time) (see Prime Ministers)
1 Jan 1868	*Aristides Moraïtinis* (see Prime Ministers)
16 Jan 1868	*Peter A. Diligiannis* (for 3rd time)
5 Feb 1869	*Theodore Diligiannis* (for 4th time)
(?) 1869	*P. Soutsos*
3 Jan 1870	*Spyridon Valaoritis* (for 2nd time)
21 Jul 1870	*Epaminondas Deligeorgis* (for 4th time)
3 Sep 1870	*M. Antonopoulos*
15 Dec 1870	*Charalambos Christopoulos* (for 2nd time)
Mar 1871	*Alexander Koumoundouros* (for 2nd time)
Apr 1871	*P. Petrakis*
Nov 1871	*Thrasyvoulos A. Zaïmis* (see Prime Ministers)
Jan 1872	*Demetrius Voulgaris* (see Regents)
0 Jul 1872	*Epaminondas Deligeorgis* (for 5th time)
1 Aug 1872	*John Spiliotakis* (b. Nauplia c. 1820; d. Athens 1899)
Nov 1872	*Epaminondas Deligeorgis* (for 6th time)
1 Feb 1874	*I. A. Diligiannis*
May 1875	*Charilaos Trikoupis* (for 2nd time)
7 Oct 1875	*Alexander A. Kontostavlos* (for 1st time) (b. Trieste 1835; d. Athens 1904)

8 Dec 1876	*Epaminondas Deligeorgis* (for 7th time)
13 Dec 1876	*Alexander A. Kontostavlos* (for 2nd time)
10 Mar 1877	*Epaminondas Deligeorgis* (for 8th time)
31 May 1877	*Alexander Koumoundouros* (for 3rd time)
7 Jun 1877	*Charilaos Trikoupis* (for 3rd time)
31 Jan 1878	*Theodore Diligiannis* (for 5th time)
8 Jun 1878	*Alexander Koumoundouros* (for 4th time)
23 Aug 1878	*Theodore Diligiannis* (for 6th time)
2 Nov 1878	*Charilaos Trikoupis* (for 4th time)
7 Nov 1878	*Theodore Diligiannis* (for 7th time)
15 Sep 1879	*Alexander Koumoundouros* (for 5th time)
22 Mar 1880	*Charilaos Trikoupis* (for 5th time)
25 Oct 1880	*Alexander Koumoundouros* (for 6th time)
18 Jul 1871	*Antony Rikakis* (b. Corfu 1824; d. Athens 1909)
15 Mar 1882	*Charilaos Trikoupis* (for 6th time)
11 Apr 1883	*Alexander A. Kontostavlos* (for 3rd time)
13 Apr 1885	*Theodore Diligiannis* (for 8th time)
12 May 1886	*Epaminondas Louriotis* (b. Yannina 1817; d. Athens 1887)
21 May 1886	*Stephen N. Dragoumis* (b. 1842; d. 1923)
5 Nov 1890	*Leonidas Deligeorgis* (b. Missolomghi 1839; d. Athens 1928)
2 Mar 1892	*George Philaretos* (b. Chalcis 1848; d. Athens 1929)
6 Mar 1892	*L. Meletopoulos*
22 Jun 1892	*Stephen N. Dragoumis* (for 2nd time)
15 May 1893	*Alexander A. Kontostavlos* (for 4th time)
11 Nov 1893	*Dionysius Stephanou* (b. 1835; d. 1916)
24 Jan 1895	*Nicholas P. Diligiannis* (b. Athens 1845; d. Paris 1910)
12 Jun 1895	*Alexander G. Skouzes* (for 1st time) (b. 1852; d. 1937)
30 Apr 1897	*Stephen Skouloudis* (for 1st time) (b. Crete 1838; d 1928)
3 Oct 1897	*Alexander Th. Zaïmis* (for 1st time) (see Prime Minister
14 Apr 1899	*A. Romanos* (for 1st time)
25 Nov 1901	*Alexander Th. Zaïmis* (for 2nd time)
6 Dec 1902	*Alexander G. Skouzes* (for 2nd time)
26 Jun 1903	*George Theotokis* (for 1st time) (see Prime Ministers
10 Jul 1903	*Demetrius G. Rallis* (for 1st time) (see Prime Ministers)
18 Dec 1903	*A. Romanos* (for 2nd time)
26 Jun 1904	*George Theotokis* (for 2nd time)
5 Sep 1904	*A. Romanos* (for 3rd time)
28 Dec 1904	*Alexander G. Skouzes* (for 3rd time)
22 Jun 1905	*Demetrius G. Rallis* (for 2nd time)

20 Dec 1905	*Alexander G. Skouzes* (for 4th time)
3 Aug 1907	*Demetrius Vokotopoulos* (b. Syros 1850; d. 1934)
Sep 1907	*Alexander G. Skouzes* (for 5th time)
4 Jul 1908	*George Baltatzis* (for 1st time) (b. Smyrna 1866; d. Athens 15 Nov 1922)
20 Jul 1909	*George Ch. Zographos* (for 1st time) (b. Istanbul 1863; d. 24 Jun 1920)
28 Aug 1909	*Kyriakoulis P. Mavromichalis* (see Prime Ministers)
31 Jan 1910	*D. Kallergis*
19 Oct 1910	*Nicholas Dimitrakopoulos* (b. Karytaina 28 Jan 1864; d. Vienna 21 Dec 1921)
31 Oct 1910	*John Gryparis* (b. Mykonos 27 Dec 1852; d. Athens 1922)
11 May 1912	*Lambros Koromilas* (b. Athens 1854; d. Washington 1923)
31 Aug 1913	*Demetrius Panas* (b. Galatz 1855; d. 1931)
4 Jan 1914	*George S. Streit* (b. Patras 1868; d. 1948)
13 Sep 1914	*Eleftherios K. Venizelos* (for 1st time) (see Prime Ministers)
10 Mar 1915	*George Ch. Zographos* (for 2nd time)
19 Jul 1915	*Demetrius P. Gounaris* (for 1st time) (see Prime Ministers)
27 Jun 1917	*Nicholas Politis* (for 1st time) (b. Corfu 7 Feb 1872; d. Cannes Feb 1942)
26 Dec 1918	*Alexander N. Diomidis* (b. Athens 1875; d. Nov 1950)
3 Dec 1919	*Nicholas Politis* (for 2nd time)
3 Nov 1920	*Miltiades M. Negrepontis* (b. Marseilles 1873; d. 1951)
7 Nov 1920	*Demetrius G. Rallis* (for 3rd time)
6 Feb 1921	*Nicholas P. Kalogeropoulos* (see Prime Ministers)
10 Feb 1921	*George Baltatzis* (for 2nd time)
5 Oct 1921	*Antony I. Kartalis* (b. 1867; d. 1923)
5 Mar 1922	*George Baltatzis* (for 3rd time)
16 May 1922	*Nicholas A. Stratos* (b. Athens 16 May 1872; d. Athens 15 Nov 1922)
22 May 1922	*George Baltatzis* (for 4th time)
Jun 1922	*Demetrius P. Gounaris* (for 2nd time)
22 Jun 1922	*George Baltatzis* (for 5th time)
1 Sep 1922	*Nicholas P. Kalogeropoulos* (for 2nd time)
9 Sep 1922	*E. Kanellopoulos*
16 Oct 1922	*Nicholas Politis* (for 3rd time)
7 Nov 1922	*Constantine Rendis* (for 1st time) (b. 1884; d. 1958)
1 Dec 1922	*Apostolos Alexandris* (for 1st time) (b. Lamia 21 Apr 1879)

31 Mar 1923	*Stylianos Gonatas* (for 1st time) (see Prime Ministers)
19 Apr 1923	*Apostolos Alexandris* (for 2nd time)
9 May 1923	*Stylianos Gonatas* (for 2nd time)
11 Jun 1923	*Apostolos Alexandris* (for 3rd time)
18 Jun 1923	*Stylianos Gonatas* (for 3rd time)
14 Jul 1923	*Apostolos Alexandris* (for 4th time)
6 Nov 1923	*Stylianos Gonatas* (for 4th time)
12 Jan 1924	*George Rousos* (for 1st time) (b. Leros 1868)
6 Feb 1924	*George Kaphandaris* (see Prime Ministers)
12 Mar 1924	*Alexander Papanastasiou* (see Prime Ministers)
29 Mar 1924	*George Rousos* (for 2nd time)
18 Jun 1924	*Constantine Rendis* (for 2nd time)
24 Jul 1924	*George Rousos* (for 3rd time)
20 Jan 1925	(acting:) *Andreas Michalakopoulos* (for 1st time) (see Prime Ministers)
29 Jun 1925	*Constantine Rendis* (for 3rd time)
21 Oct 1925 – 9 Jan (1926(?)	*Alexander N. Chatzikyriakos* (see Prime Ministers)
9 Jan (?)/ 19 Jul 1926	*Loukas Kanakaris Rouphos* (b. Patras 23 Aug 1878; d. 1949)
26 Aug 1926	*Pericles A. Argyropoulos* (for 1st time) (b. Athens 3 Apr 1881)
4 Oct 1926 – 30 Jun 1928	*Andreas Michalakopoulos* (for 2nd time)
4 Jul 1928 – Jun 1929	*Pericles A. Argyropoulos* (for 2nd time)
6 Jul 1929 – 21 May 1932	*Andreas Michalakopoulos* (for 3rd time)

Guatemala

15 Sep 1821	Declared independent of Spain but annexed by Mexico
1 Jul 1823 – 13 Apr 1839	Part of the United Provinces of Central America

HEADS OF STATE

Presidents

13 Apr 1839	*Mariano Rivera Paz* (for 1st time)

14 Dec 1841	*Venancio Lopez*
14 May 1842	*Mariano Rivera Paz* (for 2nd time)
11 Dec 1844 – 13 Oct 1848	*Rafael Carrera* (for 1st time) (b. 24 Oct 1814; d. 15 Apr 1965)
13 Oct 1848	*Juan Antonio Martínez*
28 Nov 1848	*José Bernardo Escobar*
30 Dec 1848	*Manuel Tejada*, refused post
1 Jan 1849	*Mariano Paredes* (b. c. 1800; d. 2 Dec 1856)
21 Oct 1851 – 15 Apr 1865	*Rafael Carrera* (for 2nd time)
24 May 1865 – 2 Jun 1871	*Vicente Cerna*
3 Jun 1871 – 3 Jun 1873	*Miguel Garcías Gránados* (d. 8 Sep 1878)
4 Jun 1873	*Justo Rufino Barrios* (b. 17 Jul 1835; d. 2 Apr 1885)
2 Apr 1885	*Alejandro Sinibaldi*
15 Apr 1885 – Mar 1892	*Manuel Lisandro Barillas* (b. 17 Jan 1864; d. Mexico 7 Apr 1907)
15 Mar 1892 – 8 Feb 1898	*José María Reina Barrios* (b. 24 Dec 1853; d. 8 Feb 1898)
31 Aug 1898	*Manuel Estrada Cabrera* (b. 21 Nov 1857; d. 24 Sep 1924)
8 Apr 1920	*Carlos Herrera y Luna* (b. 1856; d. 6 Jul 1930)
4 Mar 1922 – 26 Sep 1926	*José María Orellana* (b. 11 Jun 1872; d. 26 Sep 1926)
27 Sep 1926 – 13 Dec 1930	*Lázaro Chacón* (b. 27 Jun 1873; d. 1931)

Haiti

HEADS OF STATE

Presidents

May 1801	Independent Republic, following insurrection against France
May 1801 – 1802	*François Dominique Toussaint l'Ouverture* (b. 20 May 1743; d. 7 Apr 1803)
803	*Jean Jacques Dessalines* (from 8 Dec 1804: *Emperor*

271

	James I) (b. 1785; d. 17 Oct 1806)
17 Oct 1806 – 8 Oct 1820	*Henri Christophe* (b. 6 Oct 1767; d. 8 Oct 1920) President of Negro republic; from 1811: Emperor
1806	*Alexandre Pétion* (b. 2 Apr 1770; d. 29 Mar 1818) President of Mulatto republic
29 Mar 1818	*Jean Pierre Boyer* (b. 1776; d. 9 Jul 1850) united the two Republics 26 Nov 1820
1843	Divided into the Republics of Haiti and Santo Domingo (see Dominican Republic)
21 Mar 1843	*Charles Hérard* (b. 1787; d. 1850)
3 May 1844 – 15 Apr 1845	*Philippe Guerrier* (b. 1773; d. 15 Apr 1845)
16 Apr 1845 – Feb 1846	*Jean Louis Pierrot*
1 Mar 1846 – 27 Feb 1847	*Jean Baptiste Riché* (b. 1780; d. 27 Feb 1847)
1 Mar 1847 – 15 Jan 1859	*Faustin Soulouque* (from 26 Aug 1849: *Emperor Faustin I)* (b. 1782; d. 4 Aug 1867)
20 Jan 1859 – 13 Mar 1867	*Fabre Geffrard* (b. 19 Sep 1806; d. 1879)
14 May 1867 – 19 Dec 1869	*Sylvain Salnave* (d. 19 Dec 1869)
19 Mar 1870 – 13 May 1874	—— *Nissage-Saget*
11 Jun 1874 – 15 Apr 1876	*Michel Dominique*
17 Jul 1876 – 17 Jul 1879	—— *Boisrond Canal* (for 1st time)
23 Oct 1879 – 10 Aug 1888	*Étienne Félicité Salomon* (b. 1815; d. Paris 1888)
24 Aug – 19 Sep 1888	—— *Télémaque* (d. 19 Sep 1888)
23 Oct 1888 – 22 Aug 1889	*François Denis Légitime* (b. 1833; d. 1905)
9 Oct 1889 – 24 Mar 1896	*Louis Mondastin Floréal Hippolyte* (b. 1827; d. 24 Mar 1896)
31 Mar 1896 – 12 May 1902	*P. A. Tirésias Simon Sam*
9 May – Dec 1902	—— *Boisrond Canal* (for 2nd time)
21 Dec 1902 – 2 Dec 1908	*Alexis Nord* (b. 1822; d. 1 May 1910)
20 Dec 1908 – 2 Aug 1911	*Antoine Simon*

14 Aug 1911 – 8 Aug 1912	*Michel Cincinnatus Leconte* (d. 8 Aug 1912)
Aug 1912 – 2 May 1913	*Tancrède Auguste* (d. 2 May 1913)
4 May 1913 – 27 Jan 1914	*Michel Oreste* (b. 1859)
8 Feb – 29 Oct 1914	*Oreste Zamor* (d. 27 Jul 1915)
7 Nov 1914 – 23 Feb 1915	*Joseph Davilmare Théodore*
4 Mar – 26 Jul 1915	*Jean Velbrun-Guillaume* (d. 28 Jul 1915)
12 Aug 1915 – 15 May 1922	*Philippe Sudre Dartiguenave*
15 May 1922 – 23 Apr 1930	*Joseph Louis Bornó* (b. 20 Sep 1865; d. 29 Jul 1942)

Hanover

HEADS OF STATE

Dukes

11 Jan 1546	*William the Younger*, son of Ernest the Confessor, Duke of Brunswick (b. 4 Jul 1535)
20 Aug 1592	*Ernest II*, son (b. 31 Dec 1564)
2 Mar 1611	*Christian*, brother (b. 19 Nov 1566)
2 Nov 1633	*Augustus*, brother (b. 19 Nov 1568)
27 Jan 1636	*George*, brother (b. 17 Feb 1582) Duke of Calenberg and Hanover
2 Dec 1641	*Frederick*, brother (b. 24 Aug 1574) from 1 Oct 1636 – 10 Dec 1648: Duke of Celle
10 Dec 1648	*George William*, nephew (b. 16 Jan 1624) from 15 Mar 1665 – 28 Aug 1705: Duke of Celle
15 Mar 1665	*John Frederick*, brother (b. 25 Apr 1625) Duke of Calenberg and Hanover
20 Dec 1679	*Ernest Augustus I*, brother (b. 20 Nov 1679) from 1692: Elector

Electors

23 Jan 1698	*George I*, son (b. 27 Jun 1660) from 1/22 Aug 1714:

273

	King of England, through mother, Sophia, grand-daughter of James I of England
22 Jun 1727	*George II*, son (b. 10 Nov 1683) King of England
25 Oct 1760*	*George III*, grandson (b. 4 Jun 1738) from 1815: King of Hanover and England

Kings

29 Jan 1820*	*George IV*, son (b. 12 Aug 1762) King of England
26 Jun 1830*	*William*, brother (b. 21 Aug 1765) King William IV of England
20 Jun 1837	*Ernest Augustus II, Duke of Cumberland*, brother (b. 5 Jun 1771)
18 Nov 1851 – 20 Sep 1866	*George V*, son (b. 27 May 1819; d. 12 Jun 1878)
23 Aug 1866	Hanover united with Prussia

MEMBERS OF GOVERNMENT

Secretaries of State (Prime Ministers from 28 Mar 1848)

End of May 1805 – 12 Feb 1831	*Ernst Friedrich Herbert, Count Münster-Ledenburg* (b. Osnabrück 1 Mar 1766; d. 20 May 1839) in London
1815 – 1823	*Claus von der Decken* (b. Rittershausen 5 Jan 1742; d. Hanover 10 Feb 1826) Senior Minister
Feb 1831 – 20 Jun 1837	*Ludwig von Ompteda* (b. 17 Nov 1767; d. 26 Aug 1854) in London
28 Jun 1837 – Jun 1844	*Georg, Baron Schele* (b. Osnabrück 8 Nov 1771; d. Schelenburg 5 Sep 1844)
20 Mar 1848	*Alexander Levin, Count Bennigsen* (b. Zakret 21 Jul 1809; d. Banteln 27 Feb 1893)
28 Oct 1850	*Alexander, Baron Münchhausen* (b. Apelern 1813; d. Göttingen 4 Nov 1886)
22 Nov 1851 – 21 Nov 1853	*Eduard, Baron Schele* (b. Schelenburg 23 Sep 1805; d. Frankfurt am Main 13 Feb 1875)
Nov 1853 – 31 Jul 1855	*Eduard Christian von Lütcken* (b. Jork 2 Dec 1800; d. Osnabrück 25 Apr 1865)
*24 Oct 1816 – 20 Jun 1837	*Governor-General and Viceroy* *Adolphus Frederick, Duke of Cambridge*, youngest son of George III (b. 24 Feb 1774; d. 8 Jul 1850)

Aug 1855	*Eduard, Count Kielmansegg-Gülzow* (b. 15 Feb 1804; d. 6 Mar 1879)
Dec 1862	*Wilhelm, Baron Hammerstein* (b. Castorf 6 May 1801; d. Neustrelitz 1 Nov 1872)
21 Oct 1865 – 28 Jun 1866	*Georg Bacmeister* (b. Tullamore, Ireland, 15 Feb 1807; d. Göttingen 2 Aug 1890)

Hausa States

For Gobir, Kano, Katsina and Nupe, city states and trading centres in Northern Nigeria, 10th century onwards, and Daura, spiritual centre of Hausa, see volume 1.

Hawaii

Unified kingdom created by subjugation of local chieftancies between 1790 and 1810 by King Kamehameha I

HEADS OF STATE

Kings

1810	*Kamehameha I* (b. Nov 1758(?))
8 May 1819 – 14 Jul 1824	*Kamehameha II (Liholiho)*, son (b. 1797)
6 Jun 1825	*Kamehameha III (Kauikeauoli)*, brother (b. 17 Mar 1814)
	Regents:
	6 Jun 1825 – 1832: *Kaahumanu*, wife of Kamehameha I (d. 1832)
	1832 – 1833: *Kinau*, daughter of Kamehameha I
15 Dec 1854	*Kamehameha IV (Alexander Liholiho)*, nephew (b. 9 Feb 1834)
30 Nov 1863 – 11 Dec 1872	*Kamehameha V (Lot Kamehameha)*, brother (b. 11 Dec 1930)
8 Jan 1873 – 3 Feb 1874	*(William Charles) Lunalilo* (b. 31 Jan 1835) elected by legislature

12 Feb 1874 – 20 Jan 1891	*(David) Kalakaua* (b. 16 Nov 1836) elected by legislature
29 Jan 1891 – 17 Jan 1893	*(Lydia) Liliuokalani*, sister (b. 2 Sep 1838; d. 11 Nov 1917) Queen, deposed 17 Jan 1893, formally abdicated Jan 1895

President of Provisional Government

17 Jan 1893	*Sanford Ballard Dole* (b. Honolulu 23 Apr 1844; d. Honolulu 9 Jun 1926)
4 Jul 1894	Declaration of Republic

President of Republic

4 Jul 1894 – 14 Jun 1900	*Sanford Ballard Dole* (see above)
12 Aug 1898	Annexed to the United States of America
14 Jun 1900	Reconstituted as an incorporated territory of the United States of America

Hejaz and Hejaz-Nejd

See Saudi Arabia.

Hesse

(until 1866: Hesse-Darmstadt)

HEADS OF STATE

Dukes

31 Mar 1567	*Georg I*, 4th son of Philipp I of Hesse (Cassel) (b. 10 Sep 1547)
7 Feb 1596	*Ludwig V*, son (b. 24 Sep 1577)
27 Jun 1626	*Georg II*, son (b. 7 Mar 1605)
11 Jun 1661	*Ludwig VI*, son (b. 25 Jan 1630)

24 Apr 1678	*Ludwig VII*, son (b. 22 Jun 1658)
31 Aug 1678	*Ernst Ludwig*, brother (b. 15 Dec 1667)
12 Sep 1738	*Ludwig VIII*, son (b. 5 Apr 1691)
17 Oct 1768	*Ludwig IX*, son (b. 14 Apr 1753) from 14 Aug 1806: Grand Duke Ludwig I

Grand Dukes

14 Aug 1806	*Ludwig I*, previously Duke Ludwig I
6 Apr 1830	*Ludwig II*, son (b. 26 Dec 1777)
16 Jun 1848	*Ludwig III*, son (b. 9 Jun 1806)
13 Jun 1877	*Ludwig IV*, nephew (b. 12 Nov 1837)
13 Mar 1892 – Nov 1918	*Ernst Ludwig* (b. 25 Nov 1868; d. 9 Oct 1937) left the throne without formally abdicating
2 Mar 1919	Republic declared but most functions taken over by central government of Germany

MEMBERS OF GOVERNMENT

Prime Ministers

1821 – 14 Feb 1829	*Karl Ludwig Wilhelm von Grolmann* (b. Giessen 23 Jul 1775; d. Darmstadt 14 Feb 1829)
Feb 1829	*Karl Wilhelm Heinrich du Bos du Thil* (b. Braunfels 22 Apr 1777; d. Darmstadt 17 May 1859)
5 Mar 1848	*Heinrich (Wilhelm August) Baron Gagern* (b. Bayreuth 20 Aug 1799; d. Darmstedt 22 May 1880)
End May 1848	—— *Zimmermann*
Middle Jul 1848	*Heinrich Karl Jaup* (b. 27 Sep 1781; d. 5 Sep 1860)
Jun 1860	*Karl Friedrich Reinhard, Baron Dalwigk* (b. Darmstadt 19 Dec 1802; d. Darmstadt 28 Sep 1880)
6 Apr 1871	*Friedrich, Baron Lindelof* (b. 10 Jul 1794; d. 16 May 1882)
13 Sep 1872	*Karl von Hofmann* (b. Darmstadt 4 Sep 1827; d. 9 May 1910)
May 1876	*Julius Rinck*, called *Baron Starck* (b. 19 Dec 1825; d. 16 Sep 1910)
End May 1884	*Jakob Finger* (b. Monsheim 13 Jan 1825; d. Darmstadt 1 Feb 1904)
1898 – 29 Jan 1906	*Karl Rothe* (b. 2 Jul 1840; d. 29 Jan 1906)
4 Feb 1906 – 11 Nov 1918	*Christian Wilhelm Karl von Ewald* (b. 18 Jun 1852; d. Darmstadt 2 Sep 1932)

Hesse-Cassel

HEADS OF STATE

Dukes and Electors

8 Nov 1471	*Wilhelm I*, son of Ludwig III (b. 4 Jul 1466)
3 Jun 1493	*Wilhelm II*, brother (b. 29 Mar 1469)
11 Jul 1509	*Philipp I*, son (b. 13 Nov 1504)
31 Mar 1567	*Wilhelm IV*, son (b. 24 Jun 1532)
25 Aug 1592	*Moritz*, son (b. 25 May 1572; d. 15 Mar 1632)
17 Mar 1627	*Wilhelm V*, son·(b. 13 Feb 1602)
21 Sep 1637	*Wilhelm VI*, son (b. 23 May 1629)
16 Jul 1663	*Wilhelm VII*, son (b. 21 Jun 1651)
21 Sep 1670	*Karl I*, brother (b. 3 Aug 1654)
23 Mar 1730	*Friedrich I*, son (b. 28 Apr 1676) from 1720: King of Sweden
25 Mar 1751	*Wilhelm VIII*, brother (b. 10 Mar 1682)
1 Feb 1760	*Friedrich II*, son (b. 14 Aug 1720)
31 Oct 1785	*Wilhelm IX*, son (b. 3 Jun 1743) from 1 May 1805: Elector Wilhelm I
1 Nov 1808	Annexed to Kingdom of Westphalia under *Jerome Bonaparte*, brother of Napoleon I of France (b. Ajaccio 15 Nov 1784; d. Villegenis 24 Jun 1860)
21 Nov 1813	*Elector Wilhelm I*
27 Feb 1821	*Wilhelm II*, son (b. 28 Jul 1777)
20 Nov 1847 – 23 Jun/17 Aug 1866	*Friedrich Wilhelm*, son (b. 20 Aug 1802; d. Prague 6 Jan 1875) from 30 Sep 1831: co-regent for his father
17 Aug 1866	Incorporated in Prussia

MEMBERS OF GOVERNMENT

Prime Ministers

Jan 1831	*Baron Schenk von Schweinsberg*
May 1832	*Hans Daniel Ludwig Friedrich Hassenpflug* (for 1st time) (b. Hanau 26 Feb 1794; d. Marburg 10 Oct 1862) also Home Affairs and Justice
Jul 1837	—— *Hanstein*

late 1841 – early 1843	—— *Koch* (for 1st time)
1844	—— *Koch* (for 2nd time)
1847 – 5/6 Mar 1848	*Friedrich (Heinrich Ernst Leopold) Scheffer* (for 1st time) (b. Schrecksbach 21 Dec 1800; d. Engelbach 8 Aug 1879)
17 Mar 1848	*Bernhard Eberhard* (b. Schlüchtern 6 Apr 1795; d. Hanau 29 Feb 1860)
22 Feb 1850 – 16 Oct 1855	*Hans Hassenpflug* (for 2nd time)
Oct 1855 – Jul 1858	*Friedrich Scheffer* (for 2nd time)
May 1860 – 18 Jun 1866	—— *Stiernberg*

Holy Roman Emperors

See Germany

Holy See

See Papacy

Honduras

HEADS OF STATE

| 15 Sep 1821 | Declared independent of Spain but annexed by Mexico |

1823	*José Cecilio del Vallé* (b. Honduras; d. 2 Mar 1834)
1824	Member of United Provinces of Central America
5 Nov 1838	Seceded

Presidents

Sep 1839 – 30 Dec 1840	*Francisco Zelaya*
1 Jan 1841 – 31 Dec 1844	*Francisco Ferrera* (b. 1794; d. 1851)
1 Jan 1845 – Jan 1847	*Coronado Chavez*
14 Jan 1847	*Juan Lindo* (b. c. 1795; d. after 1852)
1 Mar 1852 – Oct 1855	*Trinidad Cabañas* (d. 1871)
14 Oct 1855	*Francisco Aguilar*
17 Feb 1856 – 11 Jan 1862	*Santos Guardiola* (d. 11 Jan 1862)
Jan – Oct 1862	*Victoriano Castellamios* (d. Oct 1862)
Oct 1862	*José Francisco Montes*
21 Jun 1863 – 26 Jul 1872	*José María Medina* (d. 8 Feb 1878)
Aug 1872 – 13 Jan 1874	*Carlos Arías* (d. 28 May 1890)
Feb 1874 – 8 Jun 1876	*Pariano Leiva* (for 1st time)
27 Aug 1876 – 9 May 1883	*Marcos Aurelio Soto* (b. 1846; d. Paris 1908)
30 Nov 1883	*Luis Bográn*
30 Nov 1891	*Pariano Leiva* (for 2nd time)
Apr 1893	*Domingo Vázquez*
22 Feb 1894	*Policarpo Bonilla* (b. 1859; d. 12 Sep 1926)
1 Feb 1899 – 30 Jan 1903	*Terencio Sierra* (d. 1907)
1 Feb 1903 – 11 Apr 1907	*Manuel Bonilla* (for 1st time) b. 1849; d. 21 Mar 1913
15 Aug 1907	*Miguel E. Dávila* (d. 14 Oct 1927)
28 Mar 1911	*Francisco Beltrán*
2 Feb 1912	*Manuel Bonilla* (for 2nd time)
21 Mar 1913 – 8 Sep 1919	*Francisco Bertrand*
1 Nov 1919 – 10 Mar 1924	*López Gutiérrez* (d. 10 Mar 1924)
27 – 31 Mar 1924	*Fausto Dávila* (b. 1858; d. 28 Sep 1928)
1 Apr 1924	*Vicente Tosta* (d. 1930)
1 Feb 1925	*Miguel Paz Baraona*
1 Feb 1929 – 1 Feb 1933	*Vincente Mejía Colindres* (b.1878)

Hungary

HEADS OF STATE

Kings

6 Apr 1490	*Laslo II (Vladislav II, King of Bohemia)* son of King Casimir IV of Poland (b. 1 Mar 1456)
3 Mar 1516 – 29 Aug 1526	*Louis II*, son (b. 1 Jul 1506) also King of Bohemia
2 Sep 1527 – 1538	*János Zápolya*, son of István Zápolya, in rebellion against the House of Habsburg (d. 21 Jul 1540)

House of Habsburg

28 Oct 1527	*Ferdinand I*, brother-in-law of Louis II (b. 10 Mar 1503; d. 25 Jul 1564) from 21 Apr 1521: Archduke of Austria; from 1531: King of the Romans; from 1 Sep 1556: Holy Roman Emperor
8 Sep 1563	*Maximilian*, son (b. 31 Jul 1527; d. 12 Oct 1576) from 24 Nov 1562: King of the Romans; from 25 Jul 1564: Archduke Maximilian II of Austria and Holy Roman Emperor Maximilian II
25 Sep 1572	*Rudolf*, son (b. 18 Jul 1552; d. 20 Jan 1612) from 12 Oct 1576: Archduke Rudolf V of Austria and Holy Roman Emperor Rudolf II
19 Nov 1608	*Matthias II*, brother (b. 24 Feb 1557; d. 20 Mar 1619) from 20 Jan 1612: Archduke Matthias of Austria; from 13 Jun 1612: Holy Roman Emperor Matthias
1 Jul 1618*	*Ferdinand II*, Cousin (b. 9 Jul 1578; d. 15 Feb 1637) from 20 Mar 1619: Archduke of Austria; from 20 Aug 1619: Holy Roman Emperor
7 Dec 1625	*Ferdinand III*, son of Ferdinand II (b. 13 Jul 1608; d. 2 Apr 1657) from 12 Dec 1636: King of the Romans; from 12 Feb 1637: Holy Roman Emperor; from 15 Feb 1637: Archduke of Austria
16 Jun 1647 – 9 Jul 1654	*Ferdinand IV*, son (b. 8 Sep 1633)

*25 Aug 1620 – Dec 1621	*Gábor Bethlen* (b. 1580; d. 25 Nov 1629) rival king

281

27 Jun 1655	*Leopold I*, brother (b. 9 Jun 1640; d. 5 May 1705) from 18 Jul 1658: Holy Roman Emperor
9 Dec 1687 – 17 Jun 1711	*Joseph I*, son (b. 26 Jul 1678) from 5 May 1705: Holy Roman Emperor
22 May 1712	*Charles III*, brother (b. 1 Oct 1685) from 12 Oct 1711: Holy Roman Emperor Charles VI
20 Oct 1740	*Maria Theresa*, daughter (b. 13 May 1717) Queen, from 20 Oct 1740: Archduchess of Austria
29 Nov 1780	*Joseph II*, son (b. 13 Mar (1741) from 18 Aug 1765: Holy Roman Emperor; from 29 Nov 1780: Archduke of Austria
20 Feb 1790	*Leopold II*, brother (b. 5 May 1747) from 30 Sep 1790: Holy Roman Emperor
1 Mar 1792	*Francis*, son (b. 12 Feb 1768; d. 2 Mar 1835) 12 Jul 1792 – 6 Aug 1806: Francis II, Holy Roman Emperor; 12 Jul 1792 – 14 Aug 1804: Archduke Francis of Austria; from 14 Aug 1804: Francis I, Emperor of Austria
28 Sep 1830	*Ferdinand V*, son (b. 12 Apr 1793; d. 29 Jun 1875) from 2 Mar 1835: Emperor of Austria
2 Dec 1848*	*Francis Joseph*, nephew (b. 18 Aug 1830) from 2 Dec 1848: Emperor of Austria
21 Nov 1916 – 13 Nov 1918 (5 Nov 1921)	*Charles IV* (b. 17 Aug 1887; d. 1 Apr 1922) from 21 Nov 1916: Charles I, Emperor of Austria
16 Nov 1918	Republic

Presidents

11 Jan 1919	*Mihály, Count Károlyi* (b. Budapest 4 Mar 1875; d. Venice 19 Mar 1955)
21 Mar – end of Jul 1919	*Sándor Garbai* (b. 1879; d. 1947)

Regent

7 – 24 Aug 1919	*Archduke Joseph of Austria-Hungary* (b. Alcsut 9 Aug 1872; d. Regensburg 6 Jul 1962)

*14 Apr 1849	*Lajos Kossuth* (b. Monok 19 Sep 1802; d. Turin 20 Mar 1894) Dictator
11 – 13 Aug 1849	*Arthur Görgey* (b. Toporcz 30 Jan 1818; d. Budapest 21 May 1916) Dictator

President

1 Mar 1920 – 15 Oct
1944

Miklós Horthy (b. Kenderes 18 Jun 1868; d. Estoril
near Lisbon 9 Feb 1957)

MEMBERS OF GOVERNMENT

17 Mar – 28 Sep 1848: Batthyány

Prime Minister	*Lajos, Count Batthyány* (b. Bratislava 14 Feb 1806; d. Pest 6 Oct 1849)
Lord Chamberlain	17 Mar – Aug 1848: *Pál Antal, Prince Esterházy* (b. 11 Mar 1786; d. Regensburg 21 May 1866)
Home Affairs	*Bertalan Szemere* (b. Vatta 27 Aug 1812; d. Pest 18 Jan 1869)
Finance	*Lajos Kossuth* (see Heads of State)
Public Works and Transport	*István, Count Széchenyi* (b. Vienna 21 Sep 1791; d. Döbling night of 7/8 Apr 1860)
Justice	*Ferenc Deák* (b. Sojtor 7 Nov 1803; d. Budapest 28 Jan 1876)
Agriculture, Industry and Trade	*Gábor Klauzál* (b. Pest 18 Nov 1804; d. Szegedin 3 Aug 1866)
Education	*József, Baron Eötvös* (b. Buda 13 Sep 1813; d. Pest 2 Feb 1871)
War	*Lázár Mészáros* (b. Baja 20 Feb 1796; d. Eywood, England, 6 Nov 1858)

28 Sep 1848 – 14 Apr 1849: Committee of National Defence

Chairman	*Lajos Kossuth* (see Heads of State)

14 Apr – 13 Aug 1849: Szemere

Prime Minister	*Bertalan Szemere* (see Batthyány)
Foreign Affairs	*Kázmér, Count Batthyány* (b. 4 Jun 1807; d. Paris 4 Nov 1854 (? 13 Jul 1854)) also (acting:) Trade
Finance	*Franz Duschek* (b. Radovesnice 28 Aug 1797; d. Csornkovec 17 Oct 1873)
Public Works and Transport	*László Csanyi* (b. Csanyi 1790; d. Pest 10 Oct 1849)

283

Justice	*Sebö Vukovics* (b. Fiume 1811; d. London 19 Nov 1872)
Education	*Mihály Horváth* (b. Szentes 20 Oct 1809; d. Karlsbad 19 Aug 1878)
War	14 Apr – May 1849 (acting:) *György Klapka* (b. Timişoara 7 Apr 1820; d. Budapest 17 May 1892) May – Jul 1849: *Arthur Görgey* (b. Toporcz 30 Jan 1818; d. Budapest 21 May 1916) Jul – 13 Aug 1849: *Lajos Aulich* (b. Bratislava 1792; d. Arad 6 Oct 1849)

13 Aug 1849 – Oct 1860

Hungary without constitutional self-government
May 1849 – 6 Jul 1850: Imperial Governor and Commander-in-Chief: *Julius Baron Haynau*, the Hyena of Brescia, illegitimate son of Elector Wilhelm I of Hesse-Cassel (b. Cassel 14 Oct 1786; d. Vienna 14 Mar 1853)
Sep 1851 – Oct 1860: Governor-General and Commander-in-Chief: *Archduke Albrecht of Austria*, son of Archduke Karl (b. Vienna 8 Aug 1817; d. Arco 18 Feb 1895)

For ministers with responsibility for both parts of Austria – Hungary between 24 Dec 1867 and 11 Nov 1918, see Austria

17 Feb 1867 – 14 Nov 1871: Andrássy

Prime Minister	*Gyula, Count Andrássy* (b. Kassa 3 Mar 1823; d. Volosca 18 Feb 1890)
Lord Chamberlain	20 Feb 1867 – 19 May 1871: *György, Count Festetics* (b. Vienna 23 Apr 1815; d. 12 Feb 1883) 19 May – 14 Nov 1871; *Béla, Baron Wenckheim* (b. 16 Feb 1811; d. 7 Jul 1879)
Home Affairs	20 Feb 1867 – 21 Oct 1869: *Béla, Baron Wenckheim* (see above) 21 Oct 1869 – 10 Feb 1871: *Pál Rajner* (b. 28 Feb 1823; d. Lontó 9 Sep 1879) 10 Feb – 14 Nov 1871: *Vilmos Tóth* (b. 28 Aug 1832; d. Nyitraivanka 14 Jun 1898)
Finance	20 Feb 1867 – 21 May 1870: *Menyhért Lónyay* (b. Nagylónya 6 Jan 1822; d. Budapest 3 Nov 1884)

	23 May 1870 – 14 Nov 1871: *Károly Kerkápoly* (b. Szentgál 13 May 1824; d. Budapest 29 Dec 1891)
Public Works and Transport	20 Feb 1867 – 21 Apr 1870: *Imre, Count Mikó* (b. Zabola 4 Sep 1805; d. Cluj 16 Sep 1876)
	21 Apr 1870 – 21 Jun 1871: *István Gorové* – (b. Pest 1819; d. 31 May 1881)
	21 Jun – 14 Nov 1871: *Lajos Tisza* (b. Geszt 12 Sep 1832; d. Budapest 26 Jan 1898)
Agriculture, Industry and Trade	20 Feb 1867 – 23 May 1870: *István Gorové* (see above)
	24 May 1870 – 14 Nov 1871: *József Szlávy* (b. Györ 23 Nov 1818; d. Zsitvaújfalu 8 Aug 1900)
Education	20 Feb 1867 – 2 Feb 1871: *József, Baron Eötvös* (see Batthyány)
	10 Feb – 14 Nov 1871: *Tivadar Pauler* (b. Buda 9 Apr 1816; d. Budapest 30 Apr 1886)
Justice	19 Feb 1867 – 11 Jun 1871; *Boldizsár Horvát* (b. Szombathely 1 Jan 1822; d. Budapest 28 Oct 1898)
	12 Jun – 14 Nov 1871: *István Bittó* (b. Sárosfa 3 May 1822; d. Budapest 7 Mar 1903)
Defence	*Gyula, Count Andrássy* (see above)
Croation Affairs	8 Dec 1868 – 26 Jan 1871: *Kálmán Bedekovich* (b. Vasvár Oct 1818; d. 10 Aug 1889)
	10 Feb – 14 Nov 1871: *Peter, Count Pejačević* (b. Bratislava 20 Apr 1804; d. Vienna 15 Apr 1887)

14 Nov 1871 – 4 Dec 1872: Lónyay

Prime Minister	*Menyhért* (from 1871: *Count*) *Lónyay* (see Andrássy)
Lord Chamberlain	*Béla Baron Wenckheim* (see Andrássy)
Home Affairs	*Vilmos Tóth* (see Andrássy)
Finance	*Károly Kerkápoly* (see Andrássy)
Public Works and Transport	*Lajos Tisza* (see Andrássy)
Agriculture, Industry and Trade	*József Szlávy* (see Andrássy)
Education	14 Nov 1871 – 4 Sep 1872: *Tivadar Pauler* (see Andrássy)
	4 Sep – 4 Dec 1872: *Agoston Trefort* (b. Homonna 6 Feb 1817; d. Budapest 27 Aug 1888)
Justice	14 Nov 1871 – 7 Sep 1872: *István Bittó* (see Andrássy).
	8 Sep – 4 Dec 1872: *Tivadar Pauler* (see Andrássy)
Defence	*Menyhért, Count Lónyay* (see Andrássy)
Croatian Affairs	*Peter, Count Pejačević* (see Andrássy)

4 Dec 1872 - 1 Mar 1874: Szlávy

Prime Minister	*József Szlávy* (see Andrássy)
Lord Chamberlain	*Béla, Baron Wenckheim* (see Andrássy)
Home Affairs	4 Dec 1872 – 5 Mar 1873: *Vilmos Tóth* (see Andrássy)
	5 Mar 1873 – 21 Mar 1874: *Gyula, Count Szapáry* (b. Pest 1 Nov 1832; d. Abbazia 20 Jan 1905)
Finance	4 Dec 1872 – 19 Dec 1873: *Károly Kerkápoly* (see Andrássy)
	19 Dec 1873 – 21 Mar 1874: *József Szlávy* (see Andrássy)
Public Works and Transport	4 Dec 1872 – 19 Dec 1873: *Lajos Tisza* (see Andrássy)
	19 Dec 1873 – 21 Mar 1874: *József, Count Zichy* (b. Brátislava 13 Nov 1841; d. Voderady 11 Nov 1924)
Agriculture, Industry and Trade	*József, Count Zichy* (see above)
Education	*Agoston Trefort* (see Lónyay)
Justice	*Tivadar Pauler* (see Andrássy)
Defence	5 – 15 Dec 1872: *József Szlávy* (see Andrássy)
	15 Dec 1872 – 21 Mar 1874: *Béla Szende* (b. Lugos 1823; d. Gavosdia 18 Aug 1882)
Croatian Affairs	*Peter, Count Pejačević* (see Andrássy)

21 Mar 1874 - 28 Feb 1875: Bittó

Prime Minister	*István Bittó* (see Andrássy)
Lord Chamberlain	*Béla, Baron Wenckheim* (see Andrássy)
Home Affairs	*Gyula, Count Szapáry* (see Szlávy)
Finance	*Kalmán Ghyczy* (b. Komarom 2 Feb 1808; d. Budapest 28 Feb 1888)
Public Works and Transport	*József Count Zichy* (see Szlávy)
Agriculture, Industry and Trade	*György Bartal* (b. Bratislava 20 Sep 1820; d. Fadd 25 Oct 1875)
Education	*Agoston Trefort* (see Lónyay)
Justice	*Tivadar Pauler* (see Andrássy)
Defence	*Béla Szende* (see Szlávy)
Croatian Affairs	*Peter, Count Pejačević* (see Andrassy)

2 Mar 1875 - 13 Mar 1890: Wenckheim/Tisza

Prime Minister	2 Mar – 20 Oct 1875: *Béla, Baron Wenckheim* (see Andrássy)

20 Oct 1875 – 13 Mar 1890: *Kálmán Tisza* (b. Geszt 10 Dec 1830; d. Budapest 23 Mar 1902)

Lord Chamberlain	2 Mar 1875 – 7 Jul 1879: *Béla, Baron Wenckheim* (see Andrássy)
	11 Jul – 25 Sep 1879 (acting:) *Kálmán Tisza* (see above)
	25 Sep 1879 – 13 Mar 1890: *Béla, Baron Orczy* (b. Budapest 22 Jan 1822; d. Vienna 7 Feb 1917)
Home Affairs	2 Mar 1875 – 11 Feb 1887: *Kálmán Tisza* (see above)
	11 Feb 1887 – 22 Mar 1889 (acting:) *Béla, Baron Orczy* (see above)
	22 Mar – 16 Jun 1889 (acting:) *Gábor Baross* (b. Pruzsina 6 Jul 1848; d. Budapest 8 May 1892)
	16 Jun 1889 – 15 Mar 1890: *Géza, Count Teleki* (b. Dés 28 Sep 1844; d. Budapest 27 Sep 1913)
Finance	2 Mar 1875 – 11 Oct 1878: *Kálmán Széll* (b. Gosztony 8 Jun 1845; d. Rátót 16 Aug 1915)
	11 Oct – 5 Dec 1878: *Kálmán Tisza* (see above)
	5 Dec 1878 – 11 Feb 1887: *Gyula, Count Szapáry* (see Szlávy)
	11 Feb 1887 – 9 Apr 1889: *Kálmán Tisza* (see above)
	9 Apr 1889 – 13 Mar 1890: *Sándor Wekerle* (b. Mór 14 Nov 1848; d. Budapest 26 Aug 1921)
Public Works and Transport	2 Mar 1875 – 14 Apr 1880: *Tamás Péchy* (b. Alsókázsmárk 1829; d. Alsókázsmárk 18 Nov 1897)
	14 – 24 Apr 1880: *Gyula, Count Szapáry* (see Szlávy)
	24 Apr 1880 – 9 Aug 1882: *Pál Ordódy* (b. Budapest 1822: d. 26 Aug 1885)
	9 Aug 1882 – 19 Sep 1886: *Gábor, Baron Kemény* (b. Csombord 9 Jul 1830; d. Ajnácskö 23 Oct 1888)
	19 Sep – 29 Dec 1886: *Béla, Baron Orczy* (see above)
	29 Dec 1886 – 15 Jun 1889: *Gábor Baross* (see above)
Trade	16 Jun 1889 – 13 Mar 1890: *Gábor Baross* (see above)
Agriculture, Industry and Trade	2 Mar 1875 – 21 Aug 1876: *Lajos, Baron Simonyi* (b. Ternopol 1824; d. Budapest 12 Dec 1894)
	22 Aug 1876 – 4 Dec 1878: *Ágoston Trefort* (see Lónyay)
	5 Dec 1878 – 11 Oct 1882: *Gábor, Baron Kemény* (see above)
	12 Oct 1882 – 8 Apr 1889: *Pál, Count Széchényi* (b. 6 Nov 1838; d. Budapest 28 Oct 1901)
	9 Apr – 15 Jun 1889: *Gyula, Count Szapáry* (see Szlávy)

Agriculture	16 Jun 1889 – 15 Mar 1890: *Gyula, Count Szapáry* (see Szlávy)
Education	2 Mar 1875 – 22 Aug 1888: *Agoston Trefort* (see Lónyay)
	22 Sep 1888 – 13 Mar 1890: *Albin, Count Csáky* (b. Krompach 19 Apr 1841; d. Budapest 15 Dec 1912)
Justice	2 Mar 1875 – 30 Jun 1878: *Béla Perczel* (b. Börzsöny 15 Jan 1819; d. 23 Mar 1888)
	1 Jul 1878 – 30 Apr 1886: *Tivadar Pauler* (see Andrássy)
	15 May 1886 – 22 Mar 1889: *Teofil Fabiny* (b. Pest 11 Oct 1822; d. Budapest 4 Mar 1908)
	23 Mar – 9 Apr 1889 (acting:) *Teofil von Fabiny* (see above)
	9 Apr 1889 – 13 Mar 1890: *Dezsö Szilágyi* (b. Nagy-Várad 1 Apr 1840: d. Budapest 31 Jul 1901)
Defence	2 Mar 1875 – 18 Aug 1882: *Béla Szende* (see Szlávy)
	20 Aug – 4 Oct 1882: *Béla, Baron Orczy* (see above)
	4 Oct 1882 – 26 Dec 1883: *Gedeon, Count Ráday* (b. Pécel 4 May 1841; d. Budapest 26 Dec 1883)
	2 Jan – 28 Oct 1884: *Béla, Baron Orczy* (see above)
	28 Oct 1884 – 13 Mar 1890: *Géza, Baron Fejérváry* (b. Josefstadt 15 Mar 1833; d. Vienna 25 Apr 1914)
Croatian Affairs	2 Mar 1875 – 25 Feb 1876: *Peter, Count Pejačević* (see Andrássy)
	25 Feb 1876 – 10 Aug 1889: *Kálmán Bedekovich* (see Andrássy)
	23 Aug 1889 – 13 Mar 1890: *Imre Josipovich* (b. Kurilovec 1 Sep 1834; d. Vienna 30 May 1910)

13 Mar 1890 – 17 Nov 1892: Szapáry

Prime Minister	*Gyula, Count Szapáry* (see Szlávy)
Lord Chamberlain	13 Mar – 24 Dec 1890: *Béla, Baron Orczy* (see Wenckheim/Tisza)
	24 Dec 1890 – 24 Oct 1892: *László Szögyény-Marich* (b. Vienna 12 Nov 1841; d. Csór 11 Jun 1916)
	24 Oct – 19 Nov 1892: *Géza, Baron Fejérváry* (see Wenckheim/Tisza)
Home Affairs	15 Mar 1890 – 17 Nov 1892: *Gyula, Count Szapáry* (see Szlávy)
Finance	*Sándor Wekerle* (see Wenckheim/Tisza)

Trade	13 Mar 1890 – 9 May 1892: *Gábor Baross* (see Wenckheim/Tisza)
	10 May – 16 Jul 1892: (acting: *Sándor Wekerle* (see Wenckheim/Tisza)
	16 Jul – 17 Nov 1892: *Béla Lukács* (b. Abrud 27 Apr 1847; d. Budapest 7 Jan 1901)
Agriculture	15 Mar 1890 – 17 Nov 1892: *András, Count Bethlen* (b. Cluj 1849; d. Betlen 25 Aug 1898)
Education	*Albin, Count Csáky* (see Wenckheim/Tisza)
Justice	*Dezsö Szilágyi* (see Wenckheim/Tisza)
Defence	*Géza, Baron Fejérváry* (see Wenckheim/Tisza)
Croatian Affairs	*Imre Josipovich* (see Wenckheim/Tisza)

17 Nov 1892 – 14 Jan 1895: Wekerle I

Prime Minister	*Sándor Wekerle* (for 1st time) (see Wenckheim/Tisza)
Lord Chamberlain	19 Nov 1892 – 10 Jun 1894: *Lajos, Count Tisza* (see Andrássy)
	10 Jun 1894 – 15 Jan 1895: *Gyula, Count Andrássy, the Younger* (b. Töketerebes 30 Jun 1860; d. Budapest 11 Jun 1929)
Home Affairs	19 Nov 1892 – 15 Jan 1895: *Károly Hieronymi* (b. Buda 1 Oct 1836; d. Budapest 4 May 1911)
Finance	*Sándor Wekerle* (see Wenckheim/Tisza)
Trade	17 Nov 1892 – 15 Jan 1895: *Béla Lukács* (see Szapáry)
Agriculture	17 Nov 1892 – 10 Jun 1894: *András, Count Bethlen* (see Szapáry)
	10 Jun – 16 Jul 1894 (acting:) *Géza, Baron Fejérváry* (see Wenckheim/Tisza)
	16 Jul 1894 – 14 Jan 1895: *Andor, Count Festetics* (b. Buda 17 Jan 1843; d. Böhönye 16 Aug 1930)
Education	17 Nov 1892 – 10 Jun 1894: *Albin, Count Csáky* (see Wenckheim/Tisza)
	10 Jun 1894 – 15 Jan 1895: *Loránd, Baron Eötvös* (b. Pest 27 Jul 1848; d. Budapest 8 Apr 1919)
Justice	*Dezső Szilagyi* (see Wenckheim/Tisza)
Defence	*Géza, Baron Fejérváry* (see Wenckheim/Tisza)
Croatian Affairs	*Imre Josipovich* (see Wenckheim/Tisza)

14 Jan 1895 – 26 Feb 1899: Bánffy

Prime Minister	*Dezső, Baron Bánffy* (b. Cluj 28 Oct 1843; d. Budapest 23 May 1911)

289

Lord Chamberlain	15 – 18 Jan 1895: *Géza, Baron Fejérváry* (see Wenckheim/Tisza)
	18 Jan 1895 – 20 Jan 1898: *Samu, Baron Jósika* (b. Salzburg 23 Aug 1848; d. 4 Jun 1923)
	20 Jan – 20 Dec 1898: *Dezső, Baron Bánffy* (see above)
	20 Dec 1898 – 26 Feb 1899: *Manó, Count Széchényi* (b. Sopron 30 Jul 1858; d. 30 Dec 1926)
Home Affairs	15 Jan 1895 – 26 Feb 1899: *Dezső Perczel* (b. Szekszard 18 Jan 1848; d. Bonyhad 20 May 1913)
Finance	15 Jan 1895 – 26 Feb 1899: *László Lukács* (b. Abrud 24 Nov 1850; d. Budapest 23 Feb 1932)
Trade	15 Jan 1895 – 26 Feb 1899: *Ernő* (from 1896: *Baron*) *Dániel* (b. Elemér 3 May 1843; d. Balatonfüred 23 Jul 1923)
Agriculture	14 Jan – 2 Nov 1895: *Andor, Count Festetics* (see Wekerle I)
	2 Nov 1895 – 26 Feb 1899: *Ignác Darányi* (b. Buda 15 Jan 1849; d. 27 Apr 1927)
Education	15 Jan 1895 – 26 Feb 1899: *Gyula* (from 1917: *Baron*) *Wlassics* (b. Zalaegerszeg 17 Mar 1852; d. 1937)
Justice	15 Jan 1895 – 26 Feb 1899: *Sándor Erdély* (b. Kőröskisjenő 1 Aug 1839; d. Budapest 15 May 1922)
Defence	*Géza, Baron Fejérváry* (see Wenckheim/Tisza)
Croatian Affairs	14 Jan 1895 – 10 Dec 1898: *Imre Josipovich* (see Wenckheim/Tisza)
	10 Dec 1898 – 26 Feb 1899: *Ervin Cseh* (b. Valpó 23 Mar 1838; d. Erdöd Jun 1918)

26 Feb 1899 – 27 Jun 1903: Széll

Prime Minister	*Kálmán Széll* (see Wenckheim/Tisza)
Lord Chamberlain	26 Feb 1899 – 7 Mar 1900: *Manó, Count Széchényi* (see Bánffy)
	7 – 29 Mar 1900 (acting:) *Kálmán Szell* (see Wenckheim/Tisza)
	29 Mar 1900 – 27 Jun 1903: *Gyula, Count Széchényi* (b. 11 Nov 1829; d. Budapest 13 Jan 1921)
Home Affairs	*Kálmán Szell* (acting:) (see Wenckheim/Tisza)
Finance	*László Lukács* (see Bánffy)
Trade	26 Feb 1899 – 4 Mar 1902: *Sándor Hegedűs* (b. Cluj 22 Apr 1847; d. Budapest 28 Dec 1906)
	4 Mar – 19 Apr 1902: *Nándor Horánszky* (b. Eger 15 Jan 1838; d. Budapest 19 Apr 1902)

5 May 1902 – 27 Jun 1903: *Lajos* (from 1911: *Baron*)
Láng (b. Budapest 13 Oct 1849; d. 28 Mar 1918)

Agriculture	*Ignác Darányi* (see Bánffy)
Education	*Gyula Wlassics* (see Bánffy)
Justice	*Sándor Plósz* (b. Pest 10 Jun 1846; d. Budapest 29 May 1925)
Defence	*Géza, Baron Fejérváry* (see Wenckheim/Tisza)
Croatian Affairs	*Ervin Cseh* (see Bánffy)

27 Jun – 3 Nov 1903: Khuen I

Prime Minister	*Károly, Count Khuen-Héderváry* (for 1st time) (b. Gräfenberg 23 May 1849; d. Budapest 16 Feb 1918)
Lord Chamberlain	*Károly, Count Khuen-Héderváry* (acting:) (see above)
Home Affairs	*Károly, Count Khuen-Héderváry* (acting:) (see above)
Finance	*László Lukács* (see Bánffy)
Trade	*Lajos Láng* (see Széll)
Agriculture	*Ignác Darányi* (see Bánffy)
Education	*Gyula Wlassics* (see Bánffy)
Justice	*Sándor Plósz* (see Széll)
Defence	*Dezső Kolossváry* (b. Veszprim 1856; d. 1915)
Croatian Affairs	*Nikola Tomašić* (b. Zagreb 13 Jan 1864; d. Breščerovac 29 May 1918)

3 Nov 1903 – 11 Jun 1905: Tisza I

Prime Minister	*István, Count Tisza* (for 1st time) (b. Budapest 22 Apr 1861; d. Budapest 30 Oct 1918)
Lord Chamberlain	3 Nov 1903 – 3 Mar 1904 (acting:) *István, Count Tisza* (see above)
	3 Mar 1904 – 18 Jun 1905: *Károly, Count Khuen-Héderváry* (see Khuen I)
Home Affairs	*István, Count Tisza* (see above)
Finance	*László Lukács* (see Bánffy)
Trade	*Károly Hieronymi* (see Wekerle I)
Agriculture	*Béla Tallián* (b. 1854; d. Szeged 23 Nov 1921)
Education	*Albert Berzeviczy* (b. Berzevice 7 Jun 1853; d. 1936)
Justice	*Sándor Plósz* (see Szell)
Defence	*Sándor Nyíry*
Croatian Affairs	*Ervin Cseh* (see Bánffy)

18 Jun 1905 – 8 Apr 1906: Fejérváry

Prime Minister	*Géza, Baron Fejérváry* (see Wenckheim/Tisza)

Lord Chamberlain	*Géza, Baron Fejérváry* (acting:) (see Wenckheim/Tisza)
Home Affairs	*József Kristóffy* (b. Makó 7 Sep 1857; d. 29 Mar 1928)
Finance	18 Jun 1905 – 6 Mar 1906 (acting:) *Géza, Baron Fejérváry* (see Wenckheim/Tisza)
	6 Mar – 8 Apr 1906: *Ferenc Hegedűs* (b. 1856; d. Budapest 15 Sep 1909)
Trade	*László Vörös* (b. Dombegyhaza 7 Jun 1849; d. Budapest 23 Oct 1925)
Agriculture	18 Jun – 18 Oct 1905: *Endre György* (b. Huszt 18 Mar 1848; d. Budapest 15 Jan 1927)
	18 Oct 1905 – 8 Apr 1906: *Arthur, Baron Feilitzsch* (b. Törökkanizsa 18 Feb 1859; d. Nagyernye 15 Jun 1925)
Education	18 Jun 1905 – 6 Mar 1906: *György Lukács* (b. Nagy Várad 10 Sep 1865; d. Budapest 1953)
	6 Mar – 8 Apr 1906: *Gyula Tost* (b. Bányavölgy 16 Nov 1846)
Justice	18 Jun 1905 – 2 Apr 1906: *Bertalan Lányi* (b. Hibbe 21 Mar 1851; d. 15 Feb 1921)
	2 – 8 Apr 1906: *Gusztáv Gegus* (b. Pilismarót 5 Oct 1855; d. Budapest 19 Feb 1933)
Defence	18 Jun 1905 – 6 Mar 1906: *Ferenc Bihar* (b. Debrecen 20 Dec 1847; d. Budapest 17 May 1920)
	6 Mar – 8 Apr 1906: *Béla Pap* (b. Marcali 1845; d. Waidhofen 1 Oct 1916)
Croatian Affairs	*Stjepan Kovačević* (b. Tovarnik 1841; d. Zagreb 25 Apr 1913)

8 Apr 1906 – 17 Jan 1910: Wekerle II

Prime Minister	*Sándor Wekerle* (for 2nd time:) (see Wenckheim/Tisza)
Lord Chamberlain	*Aladár, Count Zichy* (b. Nagyláng 4 Sep 1864; d. Budapest 16 Nov 1937)
Home Affairs	*Gyula, Count Andrássy*, the Younger (see Wekerle I)
Finance	*Sándor Wekerle* (see Wenckheim/Tisza)
Trade	*Ferenc Kossuth* (b. Pest 16 Nov 1841; d. Budapest 25 May 1914)
Agriculture	*Ignác Darányi* (see Bánffy)
Education	*Albert, Count Apponyi* (b. Vienna 29 May 1846; d. Geneva 7 Feb 1933)
Justice	8 Ap 1906 – 2 Feb 1907: *Géza Polónyi* (b. Zsitvakenéz

3 Apr 1848; d. Budapest 1 Feb 1920)
2 Feb 1907 - 23 Sep 1909; *Antal Günther* (b.
Székesfehérvár 23 Sep 1847; d. Budapest 25 Feb 1920)
23 Sep 1909 - 17 Jan 1910: *Sándor Wekerle* (see
Wenckheim/Tisza)

Defence

8 Apr 1906 - 14 Apr 1906 (acting:) *Sándor Wekerle*
(see Wenckheim/Tisza)
14 Apr 1906 - 17 Jan 1910: *Lajos Jekelfalussy* (b. 5
Mar 1828(?); d. Budapest 10 Oct 1899)

Croatian Affairs

8 - 23 Apr 1906 (acting:) *Sándor Wekerle* (see
Wenckheim/Tisza)
23 Apr 1906 - 17 Jan 1910: *Géza Josipovich* (b.
Jalkovec 21 Jan 1857; d. Budapest 23(?) May 1934)

17 Jan 1910 - 16 Apr 1912: Khuen II

Prime Minister	*Károly, Count Khuen-Héderváry* (for 2nd time) (see Khuen I)
Lord Chamberlain	*Károly, Count Khuen-Héderváry* (acting:) (see Khuen I)
Home Affairs	*Károly, Count Khuen-Héderváry* (see Khuen I)
Finance	*László Lukács* (see Bánffy)
Trade	17 Jan 1910 - 4 May 1911: *Károly Hieronymi* (see Wekerle I)
	5 May - 18 Oct 1911 (acting:)) *László Lukács* (see Bánffy)
	18 Oct 1911 - 22 Apr 1912: *László Beöthy* (b. Hencida 4 Jun 1860; d. after 1936)
Agriculture	*Béla Count Serényi* (b. Pest 16 Jun 1866; d. Budapest 15 Oct 1919)
Education	17 Jan - 1 Mar 1910 (acting:) *Ferenc Székely* (b. Szombathely 11 Mar 1842; d. Budapest 17 Mar 1921)
	1 Mar 1910 - 22 Apr 1912: *János, Count Zichy* (b. Nagyláng 30 May 1868; d. Budapest 6 Jan 1944)
Justice	*Ferenc Székely* (see above)
Defence	*Samu, Baron Hazai* (b. Rima-Szombat 26 Dec 1851; d. Budapest 13 Mar 1942)
Croatian Affairs	*Károly, Count Khuen-Héderváry* (acting:) (see Khuen I)

22 Apr 1912 - 5 Jun 1913: Lukács

Prime Minister	*László Lukács* (see Bánffy)

Lord Chamberlain	22 Apr 1912 – 10 Jan 1913 (acting:) *Lászlo Lukács* (see Bánffy) 10 Jan – 10 Jun 1913: *István, Baron* (from 1918: *Count*) *Burián* (b. Stomfa 16 Jan 1851; d. Vienna 20 Oct 1922)
Home Affairs	*László Lukács* (see Bánffy)
Finance	*János Teleszky* (b. Nagy Várad 15 Sep 1868; d. Budapest 13 Jun 1939)
Trade	*Lászlo Beöthy* (see Khuen II)
Agriculture	*Béla, Count Serényi* (see Khuen II)
Education	22 Apr 1912 – 26 Feb 1913: *János, Count Zichy* (see Khuen II) 26 Feb – 10 Jun 1913: *Béla Jankovich* (b. Pest 29 Apr 1865; d. Budapest 5 Aug 1939)
Justice	22 Apr 1912 – 4 Jan 1913: *Ferenc Székely* (see Khuen II) 4 Jan 1913 – 10 Jun 1913: *Jenő Balogh* (b. Devecser 14 May 1864; d. Budapest 15 Feb 1953)
Defence	*Samu, Baron Hazai* (see Khuen II)
Croatian Affairs	*Géza Josipovich* (see Wekerle II)

10 Jun 1913 – 15 Jun 1917: Tisza II

Prime Minister	*István, Count Tisza* (for 2nd time) (see Tisza I)
Lord Chamberlain	10 Jun 1913 – 13 Jan 1915: *István, Baron Burián* (see Lukács) 13 Jan 1915 – 29 May 1915 (acting:) *István, Count Tisza* (see Tisza I) 29 May 1915 – 15 Jun 1917: *Ervin, Baron Roszner* (b. Varsány 19 Dec 1852; d. Telekes 2 Oct 1928)
Home Affairs	*János Sándor* (b. Marosvásárhely 17 Nov 1860; d. Budapest 16 Jul 1922)
Finance	*János Teleszky* (see Lukács)
Trade	10 Jun – 13 Jul 1913: *László Beöthy* (see Khuen II) 13 Jul 1913 – 15 Jun 1917: *János, Baron Harkányi* (b. Taktaharkány 6 Apr 1859; d. Budapest 18 Nov 1838)
Agriculture	*Imre, Baron Ghillány* (b. Frics 28 Jul 1860; d. Sashalom 23 Sep 1922)
Education	*Béla Jankovich* (see Lukács)
Justice	*Jenő Balogh* (see Lukács)
Defence	10 Jun 1913 – 19 Feb 1917: *Samu, Baron Hazai* (see Khuen II) 19 Feb – 15 Jun 1917: *Sándor* (from 1918: Baron)

	Szurmay (b. Boksánbánya 19 Dec 1860; d. Budapest 26 Feb 1945)
Croatian Affairs	10 Jun – 21 Jul 1913 (acting:) *István, Count Tisza* (see Tisza I) 21 Jul 1913 – 22 Aug 1914: *Teodor, Count Pejacević* (b. Nasice 24 Sep 1855; d. Vienna 22 Jul 1928) 22 Aug 1914 – 16 Jan 1916 (acting:) *István, Count Tisza* (see Tisza I) 16 Jan 1916 – 15 Jun 1917: *Imre Hideghéthy* (b. 1860; d. 19 Oct 1920)

15 Jun – 20 Aug 1917: Esterházy

Prime Minister	*Móric, Count Esterházy* (b. Pusztamajk 27 Apr 1881; d. Vienna 26 Jun 1960)
Lord Chamberlain	15 Jun – 18 Aug 1917: *Tivadar, Count Batthyány* (b. Zalaszentgrót 23 Feb 1859; d. Budapest 2 Feb 1931) 18 – 20 Aug 1917: *Aladár, Count Zichy* (see Wekerle II)
Home Affairs	*Gábor Ugron* (b. Marosvásárhely 8 Jan 1880; d. Bakonybél 27 Oct 1960)
Finance	*Gusztáv Gratz* (b. Gölnicbánya 30 Mar 1875; d. Budapest 21 Nov 1946)
Trade	*Béla, Count Serényi* (see Khuen II)
Agriculture	*Béla Mezőssy* (b. Tolcsva 13 Nov 1870)
Education	*Albert, Count Apponyi* (see Wekerle II)
Justice	15 Jun – 18 Aug 1917: *Vilmos Vázsonyi* (b. Sümeg 22 Mar 1868; d. Baden bei Wien 29 May 1926) 18 – 20 Aug 1917: *Károly Grecsák* (b. Versec 16 Nov 1854; d. Budapest 17 Dec 1924)
Defence	*Sándor, Baron Szurmay* (see Tisza II)
Social Welfare and Labour	18 – 20 Aug 1917: *Tivadar, Count Batthyány* (see above)
Croatian Affairs	15 Jun – 18 Aug 1917: *Aladár, Count Zichy* (see Wekerle II) 18 – 20 Aug 1917: *Károly Unkelhäuser* (b. Vukovar 16 Jan 1866; d. before 1944)
Without Portfolio	18 – 20 Aug 1917 *Béla Földes* (b. Lugos 25 Sep 1848; d. Budapest 18 Jan 1945) Reconstruction 18 – 20 Aug 1917 *Vilmos Vázsonyi* (see above) Franchise

20 Aug 1917 – 31 Oct 1918: Wekerle III

Prime Minister	*Sándor Wekerle* (for 3rd time) (see Wenckheim/Tisza)
Lord Chamberlain	20 Aug 1917 – 23 Oct 1918: *Aladár, Count Zichy* (see Wekerle II)
	24 – 31 Oct 1918 (acting:) *Tivadar, Count Batthyány* (see Esterházy)
Home Affairs	20 Aug 1917 – 25 Jan 1918: *Gábor Ugron* (see Esterházy)
	25 Jan – 8 May 1918: *János Tóth* (b. Túrkeve 1864; d. Budapest 23 Dec 1929)
	8 May – 31 Oct 1918: *Sándor Wekerle* (see Wenckheim/Tisza)
Finance	20 Aug – 16 Sep 1917: *Gusztáv Gratz* (see Esterházy)
	16 Sep 1917 – 11 Feb 1918 (acting:) *Sándor Wekerle* (see Wenckheim/Tisza)
	11 Feb – 31 Oct 1918: *Sándor Popovics* (b. Pest 22 Oct 1862; d. Budapest 15 Apr 1935)
Trade	20 Aug 1917 – 25 Jan 1918: *Béla, Count Serényi* (see Khuen II)
	25 Jan – 31 Oct 1918: *József* (from Jul 1918: *Baron) Szterényi* (b. Lengyeltóti 5 Nov 1861; d. Budapest 6 Feb 1941)
Agriculture	20 Aug 1917 – 25 Jan 1918: *Béla Mezőssy* (see Esterházy)
	25 Jan – 11 Feb 1918 (acting:) *Sándor Wekerle* (see Wenckheim/Tisza)
	11 Feb – 31 Oct 1918: *Béla, Count Serényi* (see Khuen II)
Education	20 Aug 1917 – 8 May 1918: *Albert, Count Appony* (see Wekerle II)
	8 May – 31 Oct 1918: *János, Count Zichy* (see Khuen II)
Justice	20 Aug 1917 – 25 Jan 1918: *Károly Grecsák* (see Esterházy)
	25 Jan – 8 May 1918: *Vilmos Vázsonyi* (see Esterházy)
	8 May – 31 Oct 1918: *Gusztáv Töry* (b. Pest 24 Oct 1857; d. Budapest 31 Oct 1925)
Defence	*Sándor, Baron Szurmay* (see Tisza II)
Food	23 Aug 1917 – 25 Jan 1918: *János, Count Hadik* (b. Nadas 23 Nov 1863; d. Budapest 10 Dec 1933)
	25 Jan – 31 Oct 1918: *Ludwig, Prince Windischgrät.* (b. Krakow 20 Oct 1882)

Social Welfare and Labour	20 Aug 1917 – 25 Jan 1918: *Tivadar, Count Batthyány* (see Esterházy) Jul – 31 Oct 1918: *Ludwig, Prince Windischgrätz* (see above)
Croatian Affairs	*Károly Unkelhäuser* (see Esterházy)
Without Portfolio	20 Aug 1917 – 8 May 1918 *Béla Földes* (see Esterházy) Reconstruction 20 Aug 1917 – 25 Jan 1918 *Vilmos Vázsonyi* (see Esterházy) Franchise 25 Jan – 8 May 1918: *Móric, Count Esterházy* (see Esterházy)

30/31 Oct 1918: Hadik

Prime Minister	*János, Count Hadik* (see Wekerle III) unable to form ministry

31 Oct 1918: Károlyi I

Prime Minister	*Mihály, Count Károlyi* (for 1st time) (see Presidents)
Home Affairs	*Tivadar, Count Batthyány* (see Esterházy)
Finance	*Mihály, Count Károlyi* (acting:) (see above)
Trade	*Ernő Garami* (b. Budapest 13 Dec 1876; d. 28 May 1935)
Agriculture	*Barna Búza* (b. Tolcsva 1 Jan 1873; d. Budapest (?) May 1944)
Education	*Márton Lovászy* (b. Zenta 6 Nov 1864; d. Budapest 21 Aug 1927)
Justice	*Barna Búza* (acting:) (see above)
Defence	*Béla Linder* (b. 1876; d. Sombor Apr 1962)
Food	*Ferenc Verseghi Nagy* (b. Virovitica 17 Mar 1852; d. Räjtäkmuzsaj 8 Sep 1928)
Social Welfare and Labour	*Zsigmond Kunfi* (b. Nagykanizsa 28 Apr 1879; d. Vienna 18 Nov 1929)
Without Portfolio	*Oszkar Jászi* (b. Nagykároly 2 Mar 1875; d. Oberlin, Ohio, 13 Feb 1957)

This cabinet, formed of a moderate composition on 31 Oct 1918, gave the King its oath of office. By the next day, however, it asked to be released from its oath. By agreeing to this, the King in effect brought about the end of the monarchy.

0 Oct 1918 – 21 Jan 1919 Revolutionary government: Károlyi II

Prime Minister	*Mihály, Count Károlyi* (for 2nd time) (see Károlyi I)

Home Affairs	30 Oct – 13 Dec 1918: *Tivadar, Count Batthyány* (see Esterházy) 12 Dec 1918 – 21 Mar 1919: *Vince Nagy* (b. Szatmár 4 Mar 1886; d. New York 1 Jun 1965)
Justice	4 Nov 1918 – 21 Jan 1919: *Dénes Berinkey* (b. Csáz 17 Oct 1871; d. 1948)
Finance	*Vince Nagy* (see above)
Education	30 Oct – 26 Dec 1918: *Márton Lovászy* (see Károlyi I)
Defence	30 Oct – 9 Nov 1918: *Béla Linder* (see Károlyi I) 9 Nov – 13 Dec 1918: *Albert Bartha* (b. Cluj 12 Aug 1877; d. New York 2 Dec 1960) 13 Dec 1918 – 21 Jan 1919 (acting:) *Mihály, Count Károlyi* (see Károlyi I)
Social Welfare	*Zsigmond Kunfi* (see Károlyi I)
Trade	*Ernő Garami* (see Károlyi I)
Agriculture	*Barna Búza* (see Károlyi I)
Without Portfolio	*Oszkar Jászi* (see Károlyi I) for Minorities

18 Jan – 21 Mar 1919: Berinkey

Prime Minister	*Dénes Berinkey* (see Károlyi II)
Foreign Affairs, Justice and National Affairs	(acting:) *Dénes Berinkey* (see Károlyi II)
Home Affairs	*Vince Nagy* (see Károlyi II)
Finance	*Pál Szende* (b. 1879; d. 1935)
Education	*Zsigmond Kunfi* (see Károlyi I)
War	*Vilmos Böhm* (b. Budapest 6 Jan 1880; d. Stockholm late Oct 1949)
Social Welfare	*Gyula Peidl* (b. Ravazd 3 Apr 1873; d. Budapest 22 Jan 1943)

Also ministers for Agriculture, Food and Trade and three without portfolio

22 Mar – 24 Jun 1919: Garba (Communist government: People's Commissars)

Prime Minister	*Sándor Garbai* (b. 1879; d. 1947)
Foreign Affairs	*Béla Kun* (b. Szilágycseh 20 Feb 1886; d. Moscow 30 Nov 1939) 3 Apr – 24 Jun 1919 (in addition:) *Péter Ágoston* (b. Zsombolya 25 Mar 1874; d. Paris 6 Sep 1925) and *József Pogány* (b. Budapest 8 Nov 1886: d. USSR 1939)

Home Affairs and Nationalization	22 Mar – 24 Jun 1919: *Vilmos Böhm* (see Berinkey) 4 Apr – 24 Jun 1919 (in addition:) *Jenő Landler* (b. Gelse 23 Nov 1875; d. Cannes 25 Feb 1928) and *Béla Vágó* (b. Kecskemét 9 Aug 1881; d. USSR 1939)
Justice	4 Apr – 24 Jun 1919: *Zoltán Rónai* (b. Budapest 16 Aug 1880; d. Brussels 17 May 1940) and *István Láday* (b. Kecskemét 14 May 1873; d. Bucharest 192-)
Finance	22 Mar – 24 Jun 1919: *Jenő Varga* (b. Nagytétény 6 Nov 1879; d. Moscow 8 Oct 1964) 4 Apr – 24 Jun 1919 (in addition:) *Béla Székely* (b. Budapest 17 Jul 1889; d. USSR 10 Jan 1939) and *Gyula Lengyel* (b. Szatmárnémeti 8 Oct 1888; d. USSR 1941)
Education	22 Mar – 24 Jun 1919: *Zsigmond Kunfi* (see Károlyi I) 4 Apr – 24 Jun 1919 (in addition:) *György Lukács* (b. Budapest 13 Apr 1885; d. Budapest 4 Jun 1971) and *Sándor Szabatos* and *Tibor Szamuely* (b. Nyíregyháza 1890; d. Lichtendorf 3 Aug 1919)
War	22 Mar – 24 Jun 1919: *Tibor Szamuely* (see above) and *József Pogány* (see above) 4 Apr – 24 Jun 1919 (in addition:) *Béla Kun* (see above), *Vilmos Böhm* (see Berinkey), *Rezső Fiedler* (b. Budapest 1884; d. USSR 1939), *József Haubrich* (b. Detta 9 Nov 1883; d. USSR 1939) and *Béla Szántó* (b. Homokkomárom 1 Feb 1881; d. Budapest 1 Jun 1951)

24 Jun – 1 Aug 1919: Dovcsák (Communist government)

Prime Minister	*Antal Dovcsák* (b. 11 Mar 1879)
Foreign Affairs	*Béla Kun* (see Garbai)
Education	*György Lukács* (see Garbai)
War	*Tibor Szamuely* (see Garbai)

1 – 6 Aug 1919: Peidl

Prime Minister	*Gyula Peidl* (see Berinkey)
Foreign Affairs	*Péter Ágoston* (see Garbai)
Home Affairs	*Károly Peyer* (b. Városlőd 9 May 1881; d. New York 25 Oct 1956)
Justice	*Ernö Garami* (see Károlyi I)
Education	*Sándor Garbai* (see Garbai)
Defence	*József Haubrich* (see Garbai)

plus ministers for Agriculture, Trade and Industry, Food and Minorities

5 May – 7 Aug 1919: Andrássy (Counter-revolutionary government in Arad)

Prime Minister   5 May – 14 Jul 1919: *Gyula, Count Andrássy*, the younger (see Wekerle I)
14 Jul – 7 Aug 1919: *Dezső Abrahám* (b. 9 Jul 1875)
Foreign Affairs   *Gyula, Baron Bornemisza*
War   *Zoltán Szabó*
Plus 'personalities from Arad'

7 – 15 Aug 1919: Friedrich I (Counter-revolutionary government in Budapest)

Prime Minister	*István Friedrich* (for 1st time) (b. Malacka 1 Jul 1883; d. (?) 1958)
Foreign Affairs	*Gábor Tánczos* (b. Budapest 22 Jan 1872; d. Hajdúnánás 11 Aug 1953)
Home Affairs	*Adolf Samassa* (b. Aranyosmarót 13 Apr 1867; d. Budapest 31 Jan 1929)
Justice	*Béla Szászy* (b. Pócsmegyer 26 Nov 1865; d. Budapest 17 Jun 1931)
Finance	*János Grünn* (b. Besztercebánya 3 Jun 1864; d. Budapest 5 Mar 1932)
Education and Public Worship	*Sándor Imre* (b. Hódmezövásárhely 13 Oct 1877; d. Budapest 11 Mar 1945)
Defence	*Ferenc Schnetzer* (d. Budapest 4 Apr 1944)
Minorities	*Jakab Bleyer* (b. Cséb 25 Jan 1874; d. Budapest 5 Dec 1933)

15 – 27 Aug 1919: Friedrich II

Prime Minister	*István Friedrich* (for 2nd time) (see Friedrich I)
Foreign Affairs	*Márton Lovászy* (see Károlyi I)
Home Affairs	*Zsigmond, Baron Perényi* (b. Pest 25 Nov 1870; d. Budapest 18 Mar 1946)
Justice	*György Baloghy* (b. Derencsény 22 Oct 1861; d. Budapest 22 Oct 1931)
Finance	*János Grünn* (see Friedrich I)
Education and Public Worship	*Károly Huszár* (b. Nussdorf 10 Sep 1882; d. Budapest 29 Oct 1941)
Defence	*Ferenc Schnetzer* (see Friedrich I)
Minorities	*Jakab Bleyer* (see Friedrich I)

28 Aug – 17 Nov 1919: Friedrich III

Prime Minister   *István Friedrich* (for 3rd time) (see Friedrich I)

Foreign Affairs	28 Aug – 4 Sep 1919: *Márton Lovászy* (see Károlyi I)
	14 Sep – 17 Nov 1919: *József, Count Somssich* (b. Graz 19 Dec 1864; d. 22 Jan 1941)
Home Affairs	28 Aug – 12 Sep 1919: *István Friedrich* (see Friedrich I)
	12 Sep – 17 Nov 1919: *Ödön Beniczky* (b. Zólyom 12 Feb 1878; d. Budapest 20 Jan 1931)
Justice	28 Aug – 17 Sep 1919: *György Baloghy* (see Friedrich II)
	27 Sep – 17 Nov 1919: *Béla Zoltán* (b. Pest 31 Jan 1865; d. Budapest 30 Oct 1929)
Finance	*János Grünn* (see Friedrich I)
Education and Public Worship	*Károly Huszár* (see Friedrich II)
War	*Ferenc Schnetzer* (see Friedrich I)
Minorities	*Jakab Bleyer* (see Friedrich I)

23 Nov 1919 – 1 Mar 1920: Huszár

Prime Minister	*Károly Huszár* (see Friedrich II)
Foreign Affairs	*József, Count Somssich* (see Friedrich III)
Home Affairs	*Ödön Beniczky* (see Friedrich III)
Justice	*István Bárczy* (b. Budapest 3 Oct 1866; d. Budapest 1 Jun 1943)
Finance	*Frigyes, Baron Korányi* (b. Pest 21 Jun 1869; d. Budapest 27 Dec 1935)
Education and Public Worship	*István Haller* (b. Mezőpetri 18 Nov 1880; d. Budapest 5 Feb 1964)
Defence	*István Friedrich* (see Friedrich I)
Minorities	*Jakab Bleyer* (see Friedrich I)

15 Mar – 26 Jun 1920: Simonyi-Semadam

Prime Minister	*Sándor Simonyi Semadam* (b. Csesznek 23 Mar 1864; d. Budapest 4 Jun 1946)
Foreign Affairs	*Pál, Count Teleki* (b. Budapest 1 Nov 1879; d. Budapest night of 2/3 Apr 1941)
Home Affairs	19 Apr – 26 Jun 1920: *Mihály Dömötör* (b. Binóe 1 Oct 1875; d. Fajsz 2 Feb 1962)
Justice	*Gyula Ferdinandy* (b. Kassa 1 Jun 1873; d. Szikszó 16 Jan 1960)
Finance	*Frigyes, Baron Korányi* (see Huszár)
Education and Public Worship	*István Haller* (see Huszár)

Defence	*Karoly Soós* (b. Nagyszeben 1869; d. Steinbach Jun 1953)
Minorities	*Jakab Bleyer* (see Friedrich I)

19 Jul – 1 Dec 1920: Teleki I

Prime Minister	*Pál, Count Teleki* (for 1st time) (see Simonyi-Semadam)
Foreign Affairs	19 Jul – 24 Sep 1920 (acting:) *Pál, Count Teleki* (see Simonyi-Semadam)
	24 Sep – 1 Dec 1920: *Imre, Count Csáky* (b. Szepesmindszent 16 Feb 1882; d. Santa Cruz de Tenerife 22 May 1961)
Home Affairs	*Gyula Ferdinandy* (see Simonyi-Semadam)
Justice	*Vilmos Pál Tomcsányi* (b. Budapest 8 Feb 1880; d. Budapest 7 May 1959)
Finance	*Frigyes, Baron Korányi* (see Huszár)
Education and Public Worship	*István Haller* (see Huszár)
Defence	*István Sreter* (b. Cserhátsurány 10 Nov 1867; d. Budapest 2 Sep 1942)
Trade	(acting:) *Gyula Rubinek* (b. Ohaj 10 Sep 1865; d. Budapest 8 Jan 1922)
Minorities	*Jakab Bleyer* (see Friedrich I)

16 Dec 1920 – Apr 1921: Teleki II

Prime Minister	*Pál, Count Teleki* (for 2nd time) (see Simonyi-Semadam)
Foreign Affairs	16 Dec 1920 – 18 Jan 1921 (acting:) *Pál Count Teleki* (see Simonyi-Semadam)
	18 Jan – 7 Apr 1921: *Gusztáv Gratz* (see Esterházy)
Home Affairs	*Gyula Ferdinandy* (see Simonyi-Semadam)
Justice	*Vilmos Pál Tomcsányi* (see Teleki I)
Finance	*Lóránt Hegedűs* (b. Budapest 28 Jun 1872; d. 1943)
Education	*József Vass* (b. Sárvár 25 Apr 1877; d. Budapest 8 Sep 1930)
Defence	*Sándor Belitska* (b. Lajosfalva 1 Apr 1872; d Budapest 7 Dec 1939)

13 Apr – 14 Nov 1921: Bethlen I

Prime Minister	*István, Count Bethlen* (for 1st time) (b. Gernyeszég Oct 1874; d. in prison camp in USSR 1947)

Foreign Affairs	*Miklós, Count Bánffy* (b. Cluj 30 Dec 1873; d. Budapest 6 Jun 1950)
Home Affairs	*Gedeon, Count Ráday* (b. Budapest 18 Oct 1872; d. Iklad 22 Sep 1937)
Justice	*Vilmos Pál Tomcsányi* (see Teleki I)
Finance	*Lóránt Hegedűs* (see Teleki II)
Education and Public Worship	*József Vass* (see Teleki II)
Defence	*Sándor Belitska* (see Teleki II)

3 Dec 1921 - 19 Aug 1931: Bethlen II

Prime Minister	*István, Count Bethlen* (for 2nd time) (see Bethlen I)
Foreign Affairs	3 Dec 1921 - 1923:ᵊ *Miklós, Count* Bánffy (see Bethlen I)
	1923 - 17 Oct 1924: *Géza, Baron Daruvary* (b. Budapest 12 Jan 1866; d. Budapest 3 Aug 1934)
	13 Nov 1924 - 17 Mar 1925: *Tibor Scitovszky* (b. Nőtincs 21 Jun 1875; d. Los Angeles 12 Apr 1959)
	17 Mar 1925 - 10 Dec 1930: *Lajos Walko* (b. Budapest 30 Oct 1880; d. Visegrád 10 Jan 1954)
Home Affairs	3 Dec 1921 - 16 Jun 1922; *Kunó, Count Klebelsberg* (b. Magyarpécska 13 Nov 1875; d. Budapest 11 Oct 1932)
	16 Jun 1922 - 14 Oct 1926: *Ivan Rakovszky* (b. Budapest 5 May 1885; d. Jászapáti 9 Sep 1960)
	15 Oct 1926 - 19 Aug 1931: *Tibor Scitovszky* (see above)
Justice	3 Dec 1921 - 16 Jun 1922: *Vilmos Pál Tomcsányi* (see Teleki I)
	16 Jun 1922 - 1923: *Géza, Baron Daruvary* (see above)
	1923 - 20 Feb 1924: *Emil Nagy* (b. Kaposvár 16 Nov 1871; d. Budapest 20 Aug 1956)
	13 Mar 1924 - 4 Jan 1929: *Pál Pesthy* (b. Uzdborjád 9 Jul 1873; d. Sárszenlörine 7 May 1952)
	4 Jan 1929 - 19 Aug 1931: *Tibor Zsitvay* (b. Bratislava 10 Nov 1884)
Finance	3 Dec 1921 - 20 Feb 1924: *Tibor Kállay* (b. Budapest 6 Jan 1881; d. Budapest 24 May 1964)
	20 Feb - 24 Mar 1924 (acting:) *Lajos Walko* (see above)
	24 Mar - 15 Nov 1924: *Frigyes, Baron Korányi* (see Huszár)

	15 Nov 1924 – 1928: *János Bud* (b. Dragoinérfalva 30 May 1880; d. Budapest 7 Aug 1950)
	1928 – 19 Aug 1931: *Sándor Wekerle* (b. Budapest 26 Jun 1878; d. Budapest 23 Dec 1963)
Education	3 Dec 1921 – 16 Jun 1922: *József Vass* (see Teleki II)
	16 Jun 1922 – 19 Aug 1931: *Kunó, Count Klebelsberg* (see above)
Defence	3 Dec 1921 – 1925(?) *Sándor Belitska* (see Teleki II)
	(?)1925 – 10 Oct 1929: *Károly, Count Csáky* (b. Szepesmindszent 10 Apr 1873; d. Budapest 30 Apr 1945)
	10 Oct 1929 – 19 Aug 1931: *Gyula Gömbös* (b. Murga 26 Dec 1886; d. Munich 6 Oct 1936)

Iceland

Self-governing state in union with Denmark, 30 Nov 1918 – 17 Jun 1944.

Prime Ministers

4 Mar 1914 – Mar 1922	*Jón Magnússon* (b. 16 Jan 1859; d. 23 Jun 1926)
7 Mar 1922 – Mar 1924	*Sigurdur Eggerz* (b. 28 Feb 1875; d. 16 Nov 1945)
22 Mar 1924 – 27 Aug 1927	*Jón Thorlakson* (b. 3 Mar 1877; d. 20 Mar 1935)
28 Aug 1927 – Aug 1931	*Trygvi Thorhallson* (b. 9 Feb 1889; d. 31 Jul 1935)

Imereti

See Georgia.

India

HEADS OF STATE

Moghul Emperors

27 May 1526	*Babar*, son of Abu Said and descendant of Tamerlane (b. Farghana 14 Feb 1483)
28 Dec 1530	*Humayun*, son (for 1st time) (b. 5 Mar 1508)
17 May 1540 – 1555	Temporary suzerainty of Suri dynasty of Afghanistan
23 Jul 1555	*Humayun* (for 2nd time)
14 Feb 1556 – 26 Oct 1605	*Akbar*, son (b. Amirkot 14 Oct 1542)
1 Nov 1605	*Jahangir*, son
1627	*Davar Bakhsh*, grandson
24 Feb 1628	*Shan Jahan*, son of Jahangir (b. 5 Jan 1592; d. Agra 2 Jan 1666)
1657	*Murad Bakhsh*, son
1657	*Shah Shuja*, brother
31 Jul 1658	*Aurangzeb (Alamgir I)*, brother (b. 3 Nov 1618)
1707	*Azam Shah*, son
1707	*Kam Bakhsh*, brother
27 Apr 1707 – 28 Feb 1712	*Shah Alam I (Bahadur Shah I)*, brother (b. 27 Sep 1643)
1712	*Azim ash-Shan*
21/23 Apr 1712	*Jahandar Shah*, son of Shah Alam I (b. 9 Jun 1661; d. 13 Feb 1713)
21 Jan 1713	*Muhammad Farrukh Siyar*, nephew (b. 28 Jul 1687; d. 28 May 1719)
1 Mar 1719	*Rafi ad-Darajat*, cousin (d. 11 Jun 1719)
8 Jun 1719	*Shah Jahan II (Rafi ad-Daula)*, brother
7 Sep 1719	*Nekusiyar*, nephew of Shah Alam I
29 Sep 1719 – 23 Apr 1748	*Muhammad Shah*, grandson of Shah Alam I
1720	*Muhammad Ibrahim*, cousin, temporary rival
30 Apr 1748	*Ahmad Shah*, son of Muhammad Shah (b. 23 Dec 1725; d. 1 Jan 1775)
3 Jun 1754	*Alamgir II*, son of Jahandar Shah (b. 1688)
11 Dec 1759	*Shah Jahan III*, great-grandson of Aurangzeb
25 Dec 1759	*Shah Alam II*, son of Alamgir II (b. 25 Jun 1728)
1788	*Bidar Bakht*, son of Ahmad Shah, rival
18 Nov 1806	*Akbar Shah II*, son of Shah Alam II (b. 4 May 1759)

29 Sep 1837 – 29 Mar   *Bahadur Shah II*, son (b. 24 Oct 1775; d. 5 Nov
  1858   1862)

Governors and Governors-General

Governors of Bengal

·1765 – 1767   *Robert Clive, Baron Plassey* (b. 29 Sep 1725; d. 22 Nov
                      1774)
1767 – 1769   *Harry Verelst* (d. Boulogne 24 Oct 1785)
1769 – 1773   *John Cartier*

Governors-General of Bengal and India

1773 – 1785   *Warren Hastings* (b. 6 Dec 1732; d. 22 Aug 1818)
1785 – 1786   *Sir John Macpherson, Bart* (b. Sleat 1745; d.
                      Brompton Grove 12 Jan 1821)
1786 – 1793   *Charles Cornwallis, Earl* (from 1792: *Marquis*) *Corn-*
                      wallis (for 1st time) (b. London 31 Dec 1738; d.
                      Ghazipore 5 Oct 1805)
1793 – 1798   *John Shore, 1st Baron Teignmouth* (b. London 8 Oct
                      1751; d. London 14 Feb 1834)
1798 – 1805   *Richard Colley Wellesley, Marquis Wellesley* (b.
                      Dangan Castle 20 Jun 1760; d. Brompton 26 Sep 1842)
1805 – 5 Oct 1805   *Charles Cornwallis, Marquis Cornwallis* (for 2nd
                      time)
1805   *Sir George Hilaro Barlow* (b. 1762; d. Farnham 18 Dec
                      1846)
1807   *Gilbert Elliot, Earl of Minto* (b. 23 Apr 1751; d. 21 Jun
                      1814)
1813   *Francis Rawdon-Hastings, 2nd Earl of Moira* (from
                      1817: *Marquis of Hastings*) (b. 7 Dec 1754; d. (at sea)
                      near Naples 28 Nov 1826)
1823   *William Pitt Amherst, Earl Amherst* (b. 14 Jan 1773;
                      d. 13 Mar 1857)
1828   *Lord William Cavendish-Bentinck* (b. 14 Sep 1774; d.
                      Paris 17 Jun 1839)
1835   (acting:) *Charles Theophilus Metcalfe* (from 1845:
                      Baron Metcalfe) (b. Calcutta 30 Jan 1785; d.
                      Malshanger 5 Sep 1846)
1836   *George Eden, 2nd Baron Auckland* (from 1839: *Earl*
                      of Auckland) (b. Beckenham 25 Aug 1784; d.
                      Alresford 1 Jan 1849)
1842   *Edward Law, 2nd Baron Ellenborough* (from 1844:
                      Earl of Ellenborough) (b. 8 Sep 1790; d. 23 Dec 1871)

1844	*Henry Hardinge, 1st Viscount Hardinge* (from 1846: *of Lahore*) (b. Wrotham 30 Mar 1785; d. Tunbridge Wells 24 Sep 1856)
1848	*James Andrew Broun-Ramsay, Marquis of Dalhousie* (b. Dalhousie Castle 22 Apr 1812; d. Dalhousie Castle 19 Dec 1860)
Mar 1856	*Charles John Canning*, (b. Gloucester Lodge 14 Dec 1812; d. London 17 Jun 1862) from 1858: *Viceroy* (see below)

Viceroys

1858	*Charles John Canning* (from 1859: *Earl Canning*) previously Governor-General (see above)
1862 – 20 Nov 1863	*James Bruce, 8th Earl of Elgin and 12th Earl of Kincardine* (b. 20 Jul 1811; d. Dharmsala 20 Nov 1863)
1864	*Sir John Laird Mair Lawrence* (from 1869: *Baron Lawrence*) (b. Richmond, Yorkshire 4 Mar 1811; d. London 27 Jun 1879)
1869 – 8 Feb 1872	*Richard Southwell Bourke, 6th Earl of Mayo* (b. Dublin 21 Feb 1822; d. Port Blair 8 Feb 1872)
1872	*Thomas George Baring* (from 1876: *Earl Northbrook*) (b. 22 Jan 1826; d. 15 Nov 1904)
1876	*Edward Robert Bulwer-Lytton, 2nd Baron* (from 1880: *1st Earl*) *Lytton* (b. London 8 Nov 1831; d. Paris 24 Nov 1891)
1880	*George Frederick Samuel Robinson, Marquis of Ripon* (b. London 24 Oct 1827; d. Studley Royal 9 Jul 1909)
1884	*Frederick Temple Hamilton-Temple-Blackwood, 1st Marquis of Dufferin and Ava* (b. Florence 21 Jun 1826; d. Clandeboye 12 Feb 1902)
1888	*Henry Charles Keith Petty-Fitzmaurice, 5th Marquis of Lansdowne* (b. London 14 Jan 1845; d. Newtown Anner 13 Jun 1927)
1894	*Victor Alexander Bruce, 9th Earl of Elgin and 13th Earl of Kincardine* (b. Monklands, Montreal 16 May 1849; d. Dunfermline 18 Jan 1817)
1898	*George Nathaniel Curzon, Earl* (from 1921; *Marquis*) *Curzon of Kedleston* (b. Kedleston Hall 11 Jan 1859; d. London 20 Mar 1925)
1905	*Gilbert John Murray Kynynmond Elliot, 4th Earl of Minto* (b. London 9 Jul 1845; d. Hawick 1 Mar 1914)

1910 – 1916	*Charles Hardinge, Baron Hardinge of Penshurst* (b. London 20 Jun 1858; d. Penshurst 2 Aug 1944)
4 Apr 1916	*Frederick John Napier Thesiger* (from 1921: *Viscount Chelmsford*) (b. London 12 Aug 1868; d. London 1 Apr 1933)
1 Apr 1921 – 10 Apr 1925	*Rufus Daniel Isaacs* (from 1926: *Viscount Reading*) (b. London 10 Oct 1860; d. London 30 Dec 1935)
29 Oct 1925/ 1 Apr 1926 – 1929	*Edward Frederick Lindley Wood* (from 1925: *Baron Irwin*; from 1934: *3rd Viscount Halifax*; from 1944: *1st Earl Halifax*) (b. Powderham Castle 16 Apr 1881; d. Garrowby 23 Dec 1959)
Jun 1929 – Apr 1931	*George Joachim Goschen, 2nd Viscount Goschen* (b. 15 Oct 1866; d. 24 Jul 1952)

Indo-China

A protectorate was established over Annam and Tongking in 1883, and French Indo-China, comprising Annam, Tongking, Cochin China and Cambodia, came into being in 1887. From 1893 onwards the protectorate was extended over Laos. The appointment of governors antedates by a few years the formal protectorate. For details of native rulers see Cambodia, Laos and Viet-Nam.

HEADS OF STATE

Civil Governors

Jul 1879 – Nov 1882	*Charles Marie Le Myre de Vilers* (b. Vendôme 17 Feb 1833)
Jan 1883	—— *Thomson*
Jul 1885	*Charles Auguste Frédéric Bégin* (b. Grand-Bourg 2 Jul 1835; d. Pleumeure Bodou 27 Jul 1901)
Jun 1866 – Oct 1887	*Charles Filippini* (b. Corte 1834; d. Saigon 1887)
23 Oct – 2 Nov 1887	(acting Lieutenant-Governor:) *Noel Pardon*
3 – 15 Nov 1887	(acting Lieutenant-Governor:) —— *Piquet*, from 1889 Governor General (see below)

Governors General

Nov 1887	*Jean Antoine Ernest Constans* (b. Béziers 3 Mar 1833)
Apr 1888	—— *Richaud*
May 1889	—— *Piquet* (see above)
Apr 1891	*Jean Marie Antoine de Lanessan* (b. Saint-André-de-Cubzac 13 Jul 1843; d. Écouen 7 Nov 1919)
Oct 1894	(acting:) —— *Rodier*
Dec 1894 – Mar 1895	*Paul Armand Rousseau* (b. Tréflez 24 Aug 1835; d. Hanoi 10 Dec 1896)
1895 – 1897	(acting:) —— *Foures*
Feb 1897 – Mar 1902	*Paul Doumer* (b. Aurillac 22 Mar 1857; d. Paris 6 May 1932)
Oct 1902 – Feb 1907	*(Jean Baptiste) Paul Beau* (b. Bordeaux 1857; d. Paris 14 Feb 1927)
1907 – 1908	(acting:) —— *Bonhoure*
Sep 1908 – Jan 1910	—— *Klobukowsky*
1910 – 1911	(acting:) —— *Picquie*
Feb-Nov 1911	—— *Luce*
Nov 1911 – Jan 1914	*Albert Sarraut* (for 1st time) (b. Bordeaux 28 Jul 1872; d. Paris 25 Nov 1962)
1914 – 1915	(acting:) *Joost van Villenhoven* (b. Rotterdam 1877; d. Longpont 1918)
Mar 1915 – May 1916	—— *Roume*
1916 – 1917	(acting:) —— *Charles*
Jan 1917 – May 1919	*Albert Sarraut* (for 2nd time)
May 1919 – Feb 1920	(acting:) —— *Montguillot* (for 1st time)
Feb 1920 – Apr 1922	*Maurice Long*
Apr – Aug 1922	(acting:) *Paul Baudouin* (b. Paris 19 Dec 1894; d. Paris 11 Feb 1964)
Aug 1922 – Apr 1925	—— *Merlin*
Apr – Nov 1925	(acting:) —— *Montguillot* (for 2nd time)
Nov 1925 – Jan 1928	*Alexandre Varenne*
Jan – Aug 1928	(acting:) —— *Montguillot* (for 3rd time)
Aug 1928 – Feb 1934	*Pierre Pasquier*

Iran, formerly Persia

HEADS OF STATE

Shahs

Safavidi

11 May 1502	*Ismail*, son of Sheikh Haidar (b. 17 Jul 1487)
22/23 May 1524	*Tahmasp I*, son (b. 22 Feb 1514)
22 Aug 1576	*Ismail II*, son
11 Feb 1578	*Mohammed Khodabanda*, brother (d. 1587)
1581/2/2 Dec 1587	*Abbas I*, son (b. 27 Jan 1571)
21 Jan 1629	*Safi I*, grandson
12 May 1642 – 27 Sep 1667	*Abbas II*, son
3 Oct 1667 – 30 Jan 1694	*Sulaiman I*, son
28 Apr 1694 – 22 Oct 1722	*Husain I*, son (d. 1726 or 1729)
*31 Oct 1722 (effectively from 1719) – 2 Sep 1732	*Tahmasp II*, son of Husain I (put to death 1739/40) deposed 1731
3 Sep 1732 – Feb/Mar 1736	*Abbas III*, son (b. Jan 1732; d. 1739/40)
1749	*Sulaiman II*, puppet
1750	*Ismail III*, cousin (at Ispahan), puppet of Ali Mardan Khan (see below)
1752	*Husain II*, son of Tahmasp II, puppet

Afsharidi

8 Mar 1736 – 20 Jun 1747	*Nadir (Tahmasp Quli Khan)* (b. 22 Oct 1688)
7 Jul 1747 – 24 Sep 1748	*Adil (Ali Quli Khan)*, nephew (b. 1719/20; d. 1749)
1 Oct 1748 – 18 Dec 1749	*Shah Rukh*, grandson of Nadir Shah (for 1st time; in name only) (b. 1734; d. 1796)
8 Dec 1748 – Dec 1749	*Ibrahim*, brother of Adil Shah (b. 1733(?))
Apr/May 1750	*Shah Rukh* (for 2nd time) re-proclaimed 10 May 1755 in Khorasan; deposed 1796
*22 Oct 1722	*Mahmud*, Afghan usurper
Apr/May 1725 – 1729	*Ashraf*, son (d. 1730) recognized by Sultan 1727

Bakhtiari

about Mar 1750 — *Ali Mardan Khan* (in Central Persia); assassinated

Zand

1750 — *Karim Khan*, Wakil (in Southern Persia)

13 Mar – 18 Jun 1779 — *Mohammed Ali* and *Abu'l-Fath*, brother

22 Aug 1779 — *Sadiq*, uncle (at Shiraz)

14 Mar 1781 – 10 Jan 1785 — *Ali Murad*, from 1779 at Ispahan

17 Jan 1785 – 23 Jan 1789 — *Jafar*

7 May 1789 – 29 Jul 1796 — *Lutf Ali*, son (b. 1769)

Qajari

1750 – 1758 — *Mohammed Hasan Khan* (at Tehran) (b. 1715; d. 1758)

Feb 1779 (crowned 1796) — *Agham Mohammed*, son (b. 1732)

17 Jun 1797 — *Fath Ali*, nephew (b. 1771; d. 3 Oct 1834)

20 Oct 1834 — *Mohammed Shah*, grandson (b. 1807)

13 Sep 1848 — *Nasir ad-Din*, son (b. 17/18 Jul 1831)

3 Jun 1896 — *Muzaffar ad-Din*, son (b. 25 Mar 1853)

3 Jan 1907 — *Mohammed Ali*, son (b. 21 Jun 1872; d. 5 Apr 1925)

16 Jul 1909 – 31 Oct 1925 — *Ahmad Mirza*, son of Shah Mohammed Ali (b. 20/21 Jan 1898; d. Paris 27 Feb 1930)

House of Pehlevi

12 Dec 1925 – 16 Sep 1941 — *Mohammed Reza Khan*, son of Abbas Ali Khan (b. 16 Mar 1878; d. Johannesburg 26 Jul 1944)

MEMBERS OF GOVERNMENT

Prime Ministers

ug 1916 – 24 Jun 1920 — *Vusugh ad-Dowla*

ul 1920 — *Hasan Pirnija, Mushir ad-Dowla* (for 1st time) (b. 1872; d. 21 Nov 1935)

9 Oct 1920 – 18 Jan 1921 — *Mohammed Reza Khan* (for 1st time) (see under Heads of State)

an – 21 Feb 1921 — *Mohammed Reza Khan* (for 2nd time)

1 Feb/1 Mar – 24 May 1921 — *Said Ziya ad-Din* (b. 1888)

4 Jun – 12(?) Oct 1921	*Ahmad Qavam as-Saltana* (for 1st time) (b. Mazandaran 1876; d. Tehran 23 Jul 1955)
12(?) Oct 1921	*Ahmad Qavam as-Saltana* (for 2nd time)
20 Jan – 9 May 1922	*Mushir ad-Dowla* (for 2nd time)
10 Jun 1922 – 26 Jan 1923	*Ahmad Qavam as-Saltana* (for 3rd time)
15 Feb – 12 Jun 1923	*Mirza Hasan Khan* (for 1st time)
18 Jun – Oct 1923	*Mushir ad-Dowla* (for 3rd time)
29 Oct 1923 – 7 Jun 1924	*Mohammed Reza Khan* (for 3rd time)
14 Jun – 25 Aug 1924	*Mohammed Reza Khan* (for 4th time)
30 Aug 1924 – 31 Oct 1925	*Mohammed Reza Khan* (for 5th time)
1 Nov 1925 – 6 Jun 1926	*Mohammed Ali Khan Farughi* (d. Tehran 21 Dec 1942)
13 Jun – 2 Sep 1926	*Mirza Hasan Khan* (for 2nd time)
28 Oct 1926 – 31 Jan 1927	*Mirza Hasan Khan* (for 3rd time)
14 Feb – 28 May 1927	*Mirza Hasan Khan* (for 4th time)
2 Jun 1927 – 18 Jan 1931	*Mahdi Quli Khan Hidayat*

Iraq

Until 1921 part of Turkey.

HEAD OF STATE

King

23 Aug 1921 – 8 Sep 1933	*Faisal I*, son of King Husain ibn Ali (b. 20 May 1883)

MEMBERS OF GOVERNMENT

Prime Ministers

27 Oct 1920 – 10 Sep 1921	*Abdur Rahman al-Haidari al-Gilani* (for 1st time) (d. mid-Jun 1927)

10 Sep 1921 – 19 Aug 1922	*Abdur Rahman al-Haidari al-Gilani* (for 2nd time)
30 Aug – 17 Nov 1922	*Abdur Rahman al-Haidari al-Gilani* (for 3rd time)
18 Nov 1922 – 15 Nov 1923	*Abdul Mohsen Bey al-Sadun* (for 1st time) (d. 13 Nov 1929)
22 Nov 1923 – 3 Aug 1924	*Jafar Pasha al-Askari* (for 1st time)
4 Aug 1924 – 20 Jun 1925	*Yasin Pasha al-Hashimi* (d. 21 Jan 1937)
26 Jun 1925 – 1 Nov 1926	*Abdul Mohsen Bey al Sadun* (for 2nd time)
21 Nov 1926 – 31 Dec 1927	*Jafar Pasha al Askari* (for 2nd time)
14 Jan 1928 – 20 Jan 1929	*Abdul Mohsen Bey al Sadun* (for 3rd time)
28 Apr – 25 Aug 1929	*Tawfiq Bey as Suwaidi* (b. 1891)
19 Sep – 13 Nov 1929	*Sir Abdul Mohsen Bey al Sadun* (for 4th time)
18 Nov 1929 – 9 Mar 1930	*Naji Bey as-Suwaidi* (d. 21(?) Sep 1942)

Ireland, Republic of

Until 1922 part of United Kingdom of Great Britain and Ireland.

Governors General

5 Dec 1922 – Dec 1927	*Timothy Michael Healy* (b. 1855; d. 26 Mar 1931)
5 Dec 1927/1 Feb 1928 – Nov 1932	*James McNeill* (b. Glenarm 27 Mar 1869; d. 12 Dec 1938)

MEMBERS OF GOVERNMENT

Prime Ministers

Apr 1919 – 5 Dec 1921	*Eamon de Valera* (b. New York 14 Oct 1882; d. Dublin 29 Aug 1975)
0 Jan – 12 Aug 1922	*Arthur Griffith* (b. 31 Mar 1872; d. 12 Aug 1922)
Sep 1922 – 29 Mar 1930	*William Cosgrave* (b. Dublin 6 Jun 1880; d. Dublin 16 Nov 1965)

313

Foreign Ministers

Sep 1922 – Sep 1927	*Desmond Fitzgerald* (d. 9 Apr 1947)
12 Sep 1927 – 1932	*Patrick MacGilligan* (b. Coleraine 12 Apr 1889)

Italy

Formed in 19th century from Lombardy, Venice, Modena, Parma, Lucca, Naples, Sardinia and States of the Church.

HEADS OF STATE

Kings

17 Mar 1861	*Victor Emmanuel II*, son of King Charles Albert of Sardinia (b. 14 Mar 1820) from 23 Mar 1849: King of Sardinia
9 Jan 1878	*Humbert I*, son (b. 14 Mar 1844)
29 Jul 1900 – 9 May 1946	*Victor Emmanuel III*, son (b. 11 Nov 1869; d. 28 Dec 1947)

MEMBERS OF GOVERNMENT

17 Mar – 6 Jun 1861: Cavour

Prime Minister	*Count Camillo Benso di Cavour* (b. Turin 10 Aug 1810; d. Turin 6 Jun 1861)
Foreign, Home and Naval Affairs	*Count Camillo Benso di Cavour* (see above)
War	*Manfredo Fanti* (b. Carpi 26 Feb 1808; d. Florence 5 Apr 1865)

Jun 1861 – 2 Mar 1862: Ricasoli I

Prime Minister and Foreign Affairs	*Bettino, Count Ricasoli* (for 1st time) (b. Florence 9 Mar 1809; d. Brolio 23 Oct 1880)

Home Affairs	Jun – 1 Sep 1861: *Marco Minghetti* (b. Bologna 8 Nov 1818; d. Rome 10 Dec 1886)
	1 Sep 1861 – 2 Mar 1862: *Bettino, Count Ricasoli* (see above)
War	1 Sep 1861 – 2 Mar 1862: *Alessandro, Marquis Della Rovere* (b. Casale Monferrato 1815; d. Turin 17 Nov 1864)

4 Mar – 1 Dec 1862: Rattazzi I

Prime Minister	*Urbano Rattazzi* (for 1st time) b. Alessandria 29 Jun 1810; d. Frosinone 5 June 1873)
Foreign Affairs	4 – 31 Mar 1862 (acting:) *Urbano Rattazzi* (see above)
	31 Mar – 1 Dec 1862: *Giacomo Durando* (b. Mondovì 4 Feb 1807; d. Rome 22 Aug 1894)
Home Affairs	*Urbano Rattazzi* (see above)
War	*Agostino, Count Petitti Bagliani di Roveto* (b. Turin 13 Dec 1814; d. Rome 28 Aug 1890)
Navy	*Carlo, Count Pellione di Persano* (b. Vercelli 11 Mar 1806; d. Turin 28 Jul 1883)
Education	*Pasquale Stanislao Mancini* (b. Castel Baronia 17 Mar 1817; d. Capodimonte 26 Dec 1888)

9 Dec 1862 – 24 Mar 1863: Farini

Prime Minister	*Luigi Carlo Farini* (b. Ravenna 22 Oct 1812; d. Genoa 1 Aug 1866)
Foreign Affairs	*Giuseppe Pasolini* (b. Ravenna 8 Feb 1815; d. Ravenna 4 Dec 1876)
Home Affairs	*Ubaldino Peruzzi* (b. Florence 2 Apr 1822; d. Florence 9 Sep 1891)
War	*Alessandro, Marquis Della Rovere* (see Ricasoli I)
Finance	*Marco Minghetti* (see Ricasoli I)

4 Mar 1863 – 23 Sep 1864: Minghetti I

Prime Minister	*Marco Minghetti* (for 1st time) (see Ricasoli I)
Foreign Affairs	*Emilio* (after 1876: *Marquis*) *Visconti-Venosta* (b. Milan 22 Jan 1829; d. Rome 28 Nov 1914)
Home Affairs	*Ubaldino Peruzzi* (see Farini)
War	*Alessandro, Marquis Della Rovere* (see Ricasoli I)
Finance	*Marco Minghetti* (see Ricasoli I)

23 Sep 1864 – 17 Jun 1866: La Marmora

Prime Minister and Foreign Affairs	*Alfonso Ferrero del La Marmora* (b. Turin 17 Nov 1804; d. Florence 5 Jan 1878)
Home Affairs	23 Sep 1864 – 28 Aug 1865: *Giovanni Lanza* (b. Vignale 6 Nov 1815; d. Rome 9 Mar 1882) 2 Sep – 14 Dec 1865: —— *Natoli* 14 Dec 1865 – 17 Jun 1866: *Desiderato Chiaves* (b. Turin 2 Oct 1825; d. Turin 30 Jun 1895)
Justice	23 Sep 1864 – 10 Aug 1865: *Giuseppe Vacca* (b. Naples 6 Jul 1808; d. Naples 6 Aug 1876) 10 Aug 1865 – 17 Jun 1866: —— *Cortese*
Finance	23 Sep 1864 – 2 Jan 1866: *Quintino Sella* (b. Mosso 1826; d. Biella 14 Mar 1884) 2 Jan – 17 Jun 1866: *Antonio Scialoja* (b. San Giovanni Teduccio 31 Jul 1817; d. Procida 12/13 Oct 1877)
Education	23 Sep 1864 – 2 Jan 1866: —— *Natoli* (see above) 2 Jan – 17 Jun 1866: *Domenico Berti* (b. Cumiana 17 Dec 1820; d. Rome 21 Apr 1897)
War	23 Sep 1864 – 2 Jan 1866: *Agostino, Count Petitti Bagliani di Roveto* (se Rattazzi I) 2 Jan – 17 Jun 1866: —— *Pettinengo*

17 Jun 1866 – 4 Apr 1867: Ricasoli II

Prime Minister	*Bettino, Count Ricasoli* (for 2nd time) (see Ricasoli I)
Foreign Affairs	*Emilio Visconti-Venosta* (see Minghetti I)
Home Affairs	*Bettino, Count Ricasoli* (see Ricasoli I)
Justice	17 Jun 1866 – 17 Feb 1867: *Francesco Borgatti*
Finance	17 Jun 1866 – 17 Feb 1867: *Antonio Scialoja* (see La Marmora) 17 Feb – 4 Apr 1867: *Agostino Depretis* (b. Mezzana 31 Jan 1813; d. Stradella 29 Jul 1887)
Education	17 Jun 1866 – 17 Feb 1867: *Domenico Berti* (see La Marmora) 17 Feb – 4 Apr 1867: *Cesare Correnti* (b. Milan 3 Jun 1815; d. Meina 4 Oct 1888)
War	17 Jun – 18 Aug 1866: —— *Pettinengo* (see La Marmora) 18 Aug 1866 – 4 Apr 1867: —— *Cugia*
Navy	28 Jun – 1 Aug 1866: *Agostino Depretis* (see above) Aug 1866 – 4 Apr 1867: —— *Brochetti*

Without Portfolio	17 Jun – 18 Aug 1866: *Alfonso Ferrero del La Marmora* (see La Marmora)

11 Apr – 20 Oct 1867: Rattazzi II

Prime Minister	*Urbano Rattazzi* (for 2nd time) (see Rattazzi I)
Foreign Affairs	*Pompeo Di Campello* (b. Spoleto 15 Feb 1803; d. Spoleto 22 Jun 1884)
Home Affairs	*Urbano Rattazzi* (see Rattazzi I)
Finance	11 Apr – 3 Jul 1867: *Francesco Ferrara* (b. Palermo 7 Dec 1810; d. Venice 22 Jan 1900)
	3 Jul – 20 Oct 1867: *Urbano Rattazzi* (see Rattazzi I)

27 Oct – 22 Dec 1867: Menabrea I

Prime Minister and Foreign Affairs	*Federico Luigi, Count Menabrea* (from 1875: *Marquis of Val Dora*) (for 1st time) (b. Chambéry 4 Sep 1809; d. Chambéry 25 May 1896)
Finance	*Luigi Guglielmo, Count Cambray-Digny* (b. Florence 8 Aug 1820; d. Florence 11 Dec 1906)

8 Jan 1868 – 7 May 1869: Menabrea II

Prime Minister and Foreign Affairs	*Federico Luigi, Count Menabrea* (for 2nd time) (see Menabrea I)
Home Affairs	18 Jan – Sep 1868: *Carlo, Count Cadorna* (b. Pallanza 8 Dec 1809; d. Rome 2 Dec 1891)
	Sep 1868 – 7 May 1869: *Gerolamo, Count Cantelli* (b. Parma 1815; d. Parma 1884)
Justice	—— *de Filippo*
Finance	*Luigi Guglielmo, Count Cambray-Digny* (see Menabrea I)
Education	*Emilio Broglio* (b. Milan Feb 1814; d. Rome 20 Feb 1892)
War	*Ettore Bertolè-Viale* (b. Genoa 17 Dec 1827; d. Turin 13 Nov 1892)
Navy	*Agostino Antonio Riboty* (b. Puguet-Théniers 28 Nov 1816; d. Nice 9 Feb 1888)

3 May – 19 Nov 1869: Menabrea III

Prime Minister and Foreign Affairs	*Federico Luigi, Count Menabrea* (for 3rd time) (see Menabrea I)

Home Affairs	13 May – 19 Sep 1869: *Luigi Ferraris*
	19 Sep – 19 Nov 1869: *Antonio Di Rudinì, Marquis of Starabba* (b. Palermo 6 Apr 1839; d. Rome 7 Aug 1908)
Justice	*Antonio Mordini* (b. Barga 1 Jun 1819; d. Montecatini 14 Jul 1902)
Finance	*Luigi Guglielmo, Count Cambray-Digny* (see Menabrea I)
Education	*Angelo Bargoni* (b. Cremona 26 May 1829; d. Rome 25 Jun 1901)
War	*Ettore Bertolè-Viale* (see Menabrea II)
Navy	*Agostino Antonio Riboty* (see Menabrea II)

12 Dec 1869 – 23 Jun 1873: Lanza

Prime Minister	*Giovanni Lanza* (see La Marmora)
Foreign Affairs	*Emilio Visconti-Venosta* (see Minghetti I)
Home Affairs	*Giovanni Lanza* (see La Marmora)
Justice	*Matteo Raeli*
Finance	*Quintino Sella* (see La Marmora)
Education	12 Dec 1869 – 16 May 1872: *Cesare Correnti* (see Ricasoli II)
	May 1872 – 23 Jun 1873: *Antonio Scialoja* (see La Marmora)
War	12 Dec 1869 – 1870: *Giuseppe Govone* (b. Isola d'Asti 19 Nov 1825; d. Alba 25 Jan 1872)
	1870 – 23 Jun 1873: *Cesare Francesco Ricotti-Magnani* (b. Borga Lavezzaro 3 Jun 1822; d. Novara 5 Aug 1917)

10 Aug 1873 – 18 Mar 1876: Minghetti II

Prime Minister	*Marco Minghetti* (for 2nd time) (see Ricasoli I)
Foreign Affairs	*Emilio, Marquis Visconti-Venosta* (see Minghetti I)
Home Affairs	*Gerolamo, Count Cantelli* (see Menabrea II)
Justice	*Paolo Onorato Vigliani*
Education	10 Jul 1873 – 4 Feb 1874: *Antonio Scialoja* (see La Marmora)
	3 Oct 1874 – 18 Mar 1876: *Ruggiero Bonghi* (b. Naples 20 Mar 1828; d. Torre del Greco 20 Oct 1895)
War	*Cesare Francesco Ricotti-Magnani* (see Lanza)
Navy	*Simone Antonio Pacoret de Saint-Bon* (b. Chambéry 20 Mar 1828; d. Rome 26 Nov 1892)

25 Mar 1876 – 14 Dec 1877: Depretis I

Prime Minister	*Agostino Depretis* (for 1st time) (see Ricasoli II)
Foreign Affairs	*Luigi Amedeo Melegari* (b. Castelnuovo di Sotto 1807; d. Berne 22 May 1881)
Home Affairs	*Giovanni, Baron Nicotera* (b. Sambiase 9 Sep 1828; d. Naples 13 Jun 1894)
Justice	*Pasquale Stanislao Mancini* (see Rattazzi I)
Finance	*Agostino Depretis* (see Ricasoli II)
Education	*Michele Coppino* (b. Alba 1 Apr 1822; d. Alba 25 Aug 1901)
War	*Luigi Mezzacapo* (b. Trapani 25 Jan 1814; d. Rome 27 Jan 1886)
Navy	*Benedetto Brin* (b. Turin 17 May 1833; d. 24 May 1898)

14 Dec 1877 – 11 Mar 1878: Depretis II

Prime Minister and Foreign Affairs	*Agostino Depretis* (for 2nd time) (see Ricasoli II)
Home Affairs	*Francesco Crispi* (b. Ribera, Sicily 4 Oct 1819; d. Naples 11 Aug 1901)
Justice	*Pasquale Stanislao Mancini* (see Rattazzi I)
Finance	*Agostino Depretis* (see Ricasoli II)
Education	*Michele Coppino* (see Depretis I)
War	*Luigi Mezzacapo* (see Depretis I)
Navy	*Benedetto Brin* (see Depretis I)

23 Mar – 9 Dec 1878: Cairoli I

Prime Minister	*Benedetto Cairoli* (for 1st time) (b. Pavia 28 Jan 1825; d. Naples 8 Aug 1889)
Foreign Affairs	23 Mar – Mar 1878: (acting:) *Benedetto Cairoli* (see above) Mar – 9 Dec 1878: *Luigi, Count Corti* (b. Gambarana 24 Oct 1823; d. Rome 19 Feb 1888)
Home Affairs	*Giuseppe Zanardelli* (b. Brescia 29 Oct 1826; d. Maderno 26 Dec 1903)
Justice	*Raffaele Conforti* (b. Calvanico 4 May 1804; d. Caserta 3 Aug 1880)
Finance	*Federico Seismit-Doda* (b. Ragusa 1 Oct 1852; d. Rome 9 May 1893)

Education	*Federico De Sanctis* (b. Morra Irpino 28 Mar 1817; d. Naples 29 Dec 1883)
War	—— *Bruzzo*
Navy	23 Mar – 24 Oct 1878: —— *Brocatti (Brochetti?)* 24 Oct – 9 Dec 1878: *Benedetto Brin* (see Depretis I)

18 Dec 1878 – 3 Jul 1879: Depretis III

Prime Minister and Foreign Affairs	*Agostino Depretis* (for 3rd time) (see Ricasoli II)
Home Affairs	*Agostino Depretis* (see Ricasoli II)
Justice	*Diego Tajani*
Finance	*Agostino Magliani* (b. Lautino 23 Jul 1824; d. Rome 20 Feb 1892)
Education	*Michele Coppino* (see Depretis I)
War	*Gustavo Maze de la Rochè*
Navy	*Nicolo Ferracciu*

12 Jul – 18 Nov 1879: Cairoli II

Prime Minister and Foreign Affairs	*Benedetto Cairoli* (for 2nd time) (see Cairoli I)
Home Affairs	*Tommaso Villa* (b. Canale 29 Jan 1832; d. Turin 24 Jul 1915)
Finance	*Bernardino Grimaldi* (b. Catanzaro 1841; d. Rome 16 Mar 1897)
Education	*Francesco Paolo Perez* (b. Palermo 19 Mar 1812; d. Palermo 17 Feb 1892)
War	*Cesare Bonelli* (b. Turin 3 Jan 1821)

24 Nov 1879 – 14 May 1881: Cairoli III

Prime Minister and Foreign Affairs	*Benedetto Cairoli* (for 3rd time) (see Cairoli I)
Home Affairs	*Agostino Depretis* (see Ricasoli II)
Justice	*Tommaso Villa* (see Cairoli II)
Finance	*Agostino Magliani* (see Depretis III)
Education	24 Nov 1879 – Dec 1880: *Francesco De Sanctis* (see Cairoli I) Dec 1880 – 14 May 1881: *Guido Baccelli* (b. Rome 25 Nov 1830; d. Rome 10 Jan 1916)
War	24 Nov 1879 – (?): *Cesare Bonelli* (see Cairoli II) (?) – Mar 1881: *Bernardino Milon* (d. Mar 1881)

Mar – 14 May 1881: *Emilio Ferrero* (b. Turin 8 Dec
1839; d. Rome 7 Aug 1902)

Navy   *Ferdinando Acton* (b. Naples 1832; d. Rome 1891)

28 May 1881 – 22 May 1883: Depretis IV

Prime Minister	*Agostino Depretis* (for 4th time) (see Ricasoli II)
Foreign Affairs	*Pasquale Stanislao Mancini* (see Rattazzi I)
Home Affairs	*Agostino Depretis* (see Ricasoli II)
Justice	*Giuseppe Zanardelli* (see Cairoli I)
Finance	*Agostino Magliani* (see Depretis III)
Education	*Guido Baccelli* (see Cairoli III)
War	*Emilio Ferrero* (see Cairoli III)
Navy	*Ferdinando Acton* (see Cairoli III)

25 May 1883 – 20 Mar 1884: Depretis V

Prime Minister	*Agostino Depretis* (for 5th time) (see Ricasoli II)
Foreign Affairs	*Pasquale Stanislao Mancini* (see Rattazzi I)
Home Affairs	*Agostino Depretis* (see Ricasoli II)
Justice	—— *Savelli*
Finance	*Agostino Magliani* (see Depretis III)
Education	*Guido Baccelli* (see Cairoli III)
War	*Emilio Ferrero* (see Cairoli III)

30 Mar 1884 – 18 Jun 1885: Depretis VI

Prime Minister	*Agostino Depretis* (for 6th time) (see Ricasoli II)
Foreign Affairs	*Pasquale Stanislao Mancini* (see Rattazzi I)
Home Affairs	*Agostino Depretis* (see Ricasoli II)
Justice	*Enrico Pessina* (b. Naples 7 Oct 1828; d. Naples 24 Sep 1916)
Finance	*Agostino Magliani* (see Depretis III)
Education	*Michele Coppino* (see Depretis I)
War	30 Mar – 24 Oct 1884: *Emilio Ferrero* (see Cairoli III) 24 Oct 1884 – 18 Jun 1885: *Cesare Francesco Ricotti-Magnani* (see Lanza)
Navy	*Benedetto Brin* (see Depretis I)

1 Jul 1885 – 4 Apr 1887: Depretis VII

Prime Minister	*Agostino Depretis* (for 7th time) (see Ricasoli II)

Foreign Affairs	1 Jul – 6 Oct 1885 (acting:) *Agostino Depretis* (see Ricasoli II)
	6 Oct 1885 – 4 Apr 1887: *Carlo Felice Nicolis, Count Robilant* (b. Turin 8 Aug 1826; d. London 17 Oct 1888)
Home Affairs	*Agostino Depretis* (see Ricasoli II)
Justice	*Diego Tajani* (see Depretis III)
Finance	*Agostino Magliani* (see Depretis III)
Education	*Michele Coppino* (see Depretis I)
War	*Cesare Francesco Ricotti-Magnani* (see Lanza)
Navy	*Benedetto Brin* (see Depretis I)

4 Apr – 29 Jul 1887: Depretis VIII

Prime Minister and Foreign Affairs	*Agostino Depretis* (for 8th time) (see Ricasoli II)
Home Affairs	*Francesco Crispi* (see Depretis II)
Justice	*Giuseppe Zanardelli* (see Cairoli I)
Finance	*Bernardino Grimaldi* (see Cairoli II)
Education	*Michele Coppino* (see Depretis I)
War	*Ettore Bertolè-Viale* (see Menabrea II)
Navy	*Benedetto Brin* (see Depretis I)

8 Aug 1887 – 28 Feb 1889: Crispi I

Prime Minister, Foreign and Home Affairs	*Francesco Crispi* (for 1st time) (see Depretis II)
Justice	*Giuseppe Zanardelli* (see Cairoli I)
Finance	*Agostino Magliani* (see Depretis III)
Education	8 Aug 1887 – 17 Feb 1888: *Michele Coppino* (see Depretis I)
	17 Feb 1888 – 28 Feb 1889: *Paolo Boselli* (b. Savona 18 Jun 1838; d. Rome 10 Mar 1932)
War	*Ettore Bertolè-Viale* (see Menabrea II)
Navy	*Benedetto Brin* (see Depretis I)

9 Mar 1889 – 31 Jan 1891: Crispi II

Prime Minister and Foreign Affairs	*Francesco Crispi* (for 2nd time) (see Depretis II)
Justice	*Giuseppe Zanardelli* (see Cairoli I)
Finance	9 Mar 1889 – mid-Sep 1890: *Federico Seismit-Doda*

(see Cairoli I)
mid-Sep – 8 Dec 1890 (acting:) *Giovanni Giolitti* (b.
Mondovì 27 Oct 1842; d. Cavour 17 Jul 1928)
8 Dec 1890 – 31 Jan 1891: *Bernardino Grimaldi* (see
Cairoli II)

War	*Ettore Bertolè-Viale* (see Menabrea II)
Navy	*Benedetto Brin* (see Depretis I)

9 Feb 1891 – 5 May 1892: Rudinì I

Prime Minister and Foreign Affairs	*Antonio Di Rudinì, Marquis of Starabba* (for 1st time) (see Menabrea III)
Home Affairs	*Giovanni, Baron Nicotera* (see Depretis I)
Justice	*Luigi Ferraris*
Finance	9 Feb 1891 – 12 Apr 1892: *Giuseppe Colombo* (b. Milan 18 Dec 1836; d. Milan 1921)
	Apr – 5 May 1892: *Giovanni Cadolini* (b. Cremona 24 Apr 1830; d. Rome 8 Jun 1917)
Education	*Pasquale Villari* (b. Naples 12 Oct 1827; d. Florence 7 Dec 1917)
War	*Luigi Pelloux* (b. La Roche 1 Feb 1839; d. Bordighera 26 Oct 1924)
Navy	(acting:) *Antonio Di Rudinì* (see above)

15 May 1892 – 24 Nov 1893: Giolitti I

Prime Minister	*Giovanni Giolitti* (for 1st time) (see Crispi II)
Foreign Affairs	*Benedetto Brin* (see Depretis I)
Home Affairs	*Giovanni Giolitti* (see Crispi II)
Justice	15 May 1892 – 19 May 1893: *Teodorico Bonacci*
	24 May – 24 Nov 1893: *Lorenzo Eula*
Finance	10 May – 7 Jul 1892: *Vittorio Ellena* (b. Saluzzo 1844; d. Rome 19 Jul 1892)
	7 Aug 1892 – 24 May 1893: *Bernardino Grimaldi* (see Cairoli II)
	24 May – 24 Nov 1893: *Lazzaro Gagliardi*
Education	*Ferdinando Martini* (b. Valdinievole 30 Jul 1841; d. Monsummano 24 Apr 1928)
War	*Luigi Pelloux* (see Rudinì I)
Navy	—— *Ricotti*

10 Dec 1893 – 5 Jun 1895: Crispi III

Prime Minister	*Francesco Crispi* (for 3rd time) (see Depretis II)

Foreign Affairs	From Jan (?) 1894: *Alberto, Baron Blanc* (b. Chambéry 10 Nov 1835; d. Turin 31 May 1904)
Home Affairs	*Francesco Crispi* (see Depretis II)
Justice	*Vincenzo Calenda, Baron Tavani* (b. Nocera dei Pagani 8 Feb 1830; d. ca 1908)
Finance	10 Dec 1893 – 5 Jun 1894: *Sidney, Baron Sonnino* (b. Alexandria 11 Mar 1847; d. Rome 24 Nov 1922)
	14 Jun 1894 – 5 Jun 1895: *Paolo Boselli* (see Crispi I)
Education	*Guido Baccelli* (see Cairoli III)
War	*Stanislao Mocenni* (b. Siena 21 Mar 1837; d. c. 1908)
Navy	*Enrico Costantino Morin* (b. Genoa 15 May 1841; d. Forte dei Marmi 13 Sep 1910)

14 Jun 1895 – 5 Mar 1896: Crispi IV

Prime Minister	*Francesco Crispi* (for 4th time) (see Depretis II)
Foreign Affairs	*Alberto, Baron Blanc* (see Crispi III)
Home Affairs	*Francesco Crispi* (see Depretis II)
Finance	*Paolo Boselli* (see Crispi I)
Justice	*Vincenzo Calenda, Baron Tavani* (see Crispi III)
Education	*Guido Baccelli* (see Cairoli III)
War	*Stanislao Mocenni* (see Crispi III)
Navy	*Enrico Costantino Morin* (see Crispi III)

10 Mar – 11 Jul 1896: Rudinì II

Prime Minister	*Antonio Di Rudinì, Marquis of Starabba* (for 2nd time) (see Menabrea III)
Foreign Affairs	*Onorato Caetani, Duke of Sermoneta, Prince of Teano* (b. Rome 18 Jan 1842; d. 25 Sep 1917)
Home Affairs	*Antonio Di Rudini* (see Menabrea III)
Justice	*Alessandro, Marquis Costa* (b. Macerata 11 Jan 1845; d. Rome 30 Jan 1900)
Finance	*Ascanio Branca* (b. 1840; d. Rome 7 Feb 1903)
Education	*Emmanuele Gianturco* (b. Avigliano 20 Mar 1857; d. Rome 10 Nov 1907)
War	*Cesaro Francesco Ricotti-Magnani* (see Lanza)
Navy	*Benedetto Brin* (see Depretis I)

14 Jul 1896 – 3 Dec 1897: Rudinì III

Prime Minister	*Antonio Di Rudinì, Marquis of Starabba* (for 3rd time) (see Menabrea III)

Foreign Affairs	From 20 Jul 1896: *Emilio, Marquis Visconti-Venosta* (see Minghetti I)
Home Affairs	*Antonio Di Rudinì* (see Menabrea III)
Justice	*Alessandro, Marquis Costa* (see Rudinì II)
Finance	*Ascanio Branca* (see Rudinì II)
Education	*Emmanuele Gianturco* (see Rudinì II)
War	*Luigi Pelloux* (see Rudinì I)
Navy	*Benedetto Brin* (see Depretis I)

14 Dec 1897 - 28 May 1898: Rudinì IV

Prime Minister	*Antonio Di Rudinì, Marquis of Starabba* (for 4th time) (see Menabrea III)
Foreign Affairs	*Emilio, Marquis Visconti-Venosta* (see Minghetti I)
Home Affairs	*Antonio Di Rudinì* (see Menabrea III)
Justice	*Giuseppe Zanardelli* (see Cairoli I)
Finance	*Ascanio Branca* (see Rudinì II)
Education	*Niccolo Gallò* (b. Girgenti 10 Aug 1849; d. Rome 7 Mar 1907)
War	*Alessandro, Count San Marzano-Asinari* (b. Turin 20 Mar 1830; d. 16 Feb 1906)
Navy	14 Dec 1897 - 24 May 1898: *Benedetto Brin* (see Depretis I)

1 - 18 Jun 1898: Rudinì V

Prime Minister	*Antonio Di Rudinì, Marquis of Starabba* (for 5th time) (see Menabrea III)
Foreign Affairs	*Raffaele, Marquis Cappelli* (b. San Demetrio 23 Mar 1848; d. ca 1908)
Home Affairs	*Antonio Di Rudinì* (see Menabrea III)
Justice	*Teodorico Bonacci* (see Giolitti I)
Finance	*Ascanio Branca* (see Rudinì II)
Education	*Luigi Cremona* (b. Pavia 7 Dec 1830; d. Rome 10 Jun 1903)
War	*Alessandro, Count San Marzano-Asinari* (see Rudinì IV)
Navy	*Felice Napoleone Canevaro* (b. Lima 7 Jul 1838; d. Venice 30 Dec 1926)

29 Jun 1898 - 1 May 1899: Pelloux I

Prime Minister	*Luigi Pelloux* (for 1st time) (see Rudinì I)

Foreign Affairs	*Felice Napoleone Canevaro* (see Rudinì V)
Home Affairs	*Luigi Pelloux* (see Rudinì I)
Justice	*Camillo Finocchiaro-Aprile* (b. Palermo 28 Jan 1851; d. Rome 26 Jan 1916)
Finance	*Paulo Carcano* (b. Como 24 Jan 1843; d. Como 6 Apr 1918)
Education	*Guido Baccelli* (see Cairoli III)
War	*Alessandro, Count San Marzano-Asinari* (see Rudinì IV)
Navy	*Giuseppe Palumbo* (b. Naples 31 Oct 1840; d. Naples 16 Feb 1913)

14 May 1899 – 18 Jun 1900: Pelloux II

Prime Minister	*Luigi Pelloux* (for 2nd time) (see Rudinì I)
Foreign Affairs	*Emilio, Marquis Visconti-Venosta* (see Minghetti I)
Home Affairs	*Luigi Pelloux* (see Rudinì I)
Justice	*Adeodato, Count Bonasi* (b. San Felice sul Panaro 1838; d. Rome 23 Jul 1924)
Finance	*Pietro Carmine* (b. Camparada 13 Nov 1841)
Education	*Guido Baccelli* (see Cairoli III)
War	14 May 1899 – 8 Jan 1900: *Giuseppe Mirri* (b. Imola 1839; d. 6 Sep 1907)
	8 Jan – 7 Apr 1900 (acting:) *Luigi Pelloux* (see Rudinì I)
	7 Apr – 18 Jun 1900: *Coriolano, Count Ponza di San Marino* (b. Turin 9 Oct 1842; d. Cuneo 6 Jan 1906)
Navy	*Giovanni Bettolo* (b. Genoa 25 May 1846; d. Rome 14 Apr 1916)

24 Jun 1900 – 6 Feb 1901: Saracco

Prime Minister	*Giuseppe Saracco* (b. Bistagno 9 Oct 1821; d. Bistagno 19 Jan 1907)
Foreign Affairs	*Emilio, Marquis Visconti-Venosta* (see Minghetti I)
Home Affairs	*Giuseppe Saracco* (see above)
Justice	*Emmanuele Gianturco* (see Rudinì II)
Finance	*Bruno Chimirri* (b. Catanzaro 1845)
Education	*Niccolò Gallo* (see Rudinì IV)
War	*Coriolano, Count Ponza di San Marino* (see Pelloux II)
Navy	*Enrico Constantino Morin* (see Crispi III)

15 Feb 1901 - 12 Jun 1903: Zanardelli I

Prime Minister	*Giuseppe Zanardelli* (for 1st time) (see Cairoli I)
Foreign Affairs	15 Feb 1901 – 23 Apr 1903: *Giulio Prinetti* (b. Milan 6 May 1851; d. Rome 9 Jul 1908)
	23 Apr – 12 Jun 1903: *Enrico Costantino Morin* (see Crispi III)
Home Affairs	*Giovanni Giolitti* (see Crispi II)
Justice	*Francesco Cocco-Ortu* (b. Cagliari 20 Oct 1842)
Finance	*Leone Wollemborg* (b. Padua 4 Mar 1859; d. Loreggia 19 Aug 1932)
Education	*Nunzio Nasi* (b. Trapani 4 Apr 1850; d. Erice 17 Aug 1935)
War	15 Feb 1901 – 14 May 1902: *Coriolano, Count Ponza di San Marino* (see Pelloux II)
	14 May 1902 – 12 Jun 1903: *Giuseppe Ottolenghi* (b. Mantua 25 Dec 1838; d. Turin 2 Nov 1904)
Navy	15 Feb 1901 – 22 Apr 1903: *Enrico Costantino Morin* (see Crispi III)
	22 Apr – 12 Jun 1903: *Giovanni Bettolo* (see Pelloux II)

15 Jun - 21 Oct 1903: Zanardelli II

Prime Minister	*Giuseppe Zanardelli* (for 2nd time) (see Cairoli I)
Foreign Affairs	*Enrico Costantino Morin* (see Crispi III)
Home Affairs	(acting:) *Giuseppe Zanardelli* (see Cairoli I)
Justice	*Francesco Cocco-Ortu* (see Zanardelli I)
Finance	15 Jun – 3 Aug 1903: *Leone Wollemborg* (see Zanardelli I)
	3 Aug – 21 Oct 1903: *Paolo Carcano* (see Pelloux I)
Education	*Nunzio Nasi* (see Zanardelli I)
War	*Giuseppe Ottolenghi* (see Zanardelli I)
Navy	(acting:) *Enrico Costantino Morin* (see Crispi III)

3 Nov 1903 - 4 Mar 1905: Giolitti II

Prime Minister	*Giovanni Giolitti* (for 2nd time) (see Crispi II)
Foreign Affairs	*Tommaso Tittoni* (b. Rome 16 Nov 1855; d. Rome 7 Feb 1931)
Home Affairs	*Giovanni Giolitti* (see Crispi II)
Justice	*Scipione Ronchetti* (b. Portovaltravaglia 1846; d. Milan 1 Dec 1918)

Finance	3 – 9 Nov 1903: *Pietro Rosano* (b. Naples 25 Dec 1848; d. Naples 9 Nov 1903)
	Nov 1903 – 24 Nov 1904 (acting:) *Luigi Luzzatti* (b. 11 Mar 1841; d. Rome 29 Mar 1927)
	24 Nov 1904 – 4 Mar 1905: *Angelo Majorana* (b. Catania 4 Dec 1865; d. Catania 9 Feb 1910)
Education	*Vittorio Emmanuele Orlando* (b. Palermo 19 Mar 1860; d. Rome 1 Dec 1952)
War	*Ettore Pedotti* (b. Laveno 8 Mar 1842; d. Rome 1919)
Navy	*Carlo Mirabello* (b. Tortona 17 Nov 1847; d. Milan 24 Mar 1910)

27 Mar – 17 Dec 1905: Fortis I

Prime Minister	*Alessandro Fortis* (for 1st time) (b. Forlì 6 Nov 1842; d. Rome 4 Dec 1909)
Foreign Affairs	*Tommaso Tittoni* (see Giolitti II)
Home Affairs	*Alessandro Fortis* (see above)
Justice	*Camillo Finocchiaro-Aprile* (see Pelloux I)
Finance	*Angelo Majorana* (see Giolitti II)
Education	*Leonardo Bianchi* (b. Galdo 5 Apr 1848; d. Naples 23 Feb 1927)
War	*Ettore Pedotti* (see Giolitti II)
Navy	*Carlo Mirabello* (see Giolitti II)

27 Dec 1905 – 1 Feb 1906: Fortis II

Prime Minister	*Alessandro Fortis* (for 2nd time) (see Fortis I)
Foreign Affairs	*Antonio, Marquis Paternò Castello di San Giuliano* (b. Catania 10 Dec 1852; d. Rome 16 Oct 1914)
Home Affairs	*Alessandro Fortis* (see Fortis I)
Justice	*Camillo Finocchiaro-Aprile* (see Pelloux I)
Finance	*Guido Baccelli* (see Cairoli III)
Education	*Errico de Marinis*
War	*Luigi Majnoni d'Intignano* (b. Milan 24 Feb 1841)
Navy	*Carlo Mirabello* (see Giolitti II)

8 Feb – 17 May 1906: Sonnino I

Prime Minister	*Sidney, Baron Sonnino* (for 1st time) (see Crispi III)
Foreign Affairs	*Francesco, Count Guicciardini* (b. Florence 5 Oct 1851; d. Florence 1 Sep 1915)
Home Affairs	*Sidney, Baron Sonnino* (see Crispi III)

Justice	*Ettore Sacchi* (b. Cremona 31 May 1851; d. Rome 6 Apr 1924)
Finance	*Antonio Salandra* (b. Foggia 31 Aug 1853; d. Rome 9 Dec 1931)
Education	*Paolo Boselli* (see Crispi I)
War	*Luigi Majnoni d'Intignano* (see Fortis II)
Navy	*Carlo Mirabello* (see Giolitti II)

29 May 1906 – 2 Dec 1909: Giolitti III

Prime Minister	*Giovanni Giolitti* (for 3rd time) (see Crispi II)
Foreign Affairs	*Tommaso Tittoni* (see Giolitti II)
Home Affairs	*Giovanni Giolitti* (see Crispi II)
Justice	29 May 1906 – 7 Mar 1907: *Niccolò Gallo* (see Rudinì IV)
	Mar 1907 – 2 Dec 1909: *Vittorio Emmanuele Orlando* (see Giolitti II)
Finance	29 May – (?)1906: *Fausto Massimini* (b Brescia 1860)
	(?)1906 – 2 Dec 1909: *Pietro Lacava* (b. Corleto Perticara 26 Oct 1835; d. Rome 26 Dec 1912)
Education	1906 – (?): *Guido Fusinato* (b. Castelfranco Veneto 15 Feb 1860; d. Schio 22 Sep 1913)
	(?) – 28 Feb 1909: *Luigi Rava* (b. Ravenna 1 Dec 1860; d. Rome 12 May 1938)
War	29 May 1906 – end of Dec 1907: *Giuseppe Ettore Viganò* (b. Tradate 27 Apr 1843)
	end of Dec 1907 – 4 Apr 1909: *Severino, Baron Casana* (b. Turin 23 Oct 1842)
	4 Apr – 2 Dec 1909: *Paolo Spingardi* (b. Felizzano 2 Nov 1845; d. Rome 3 Oct 1918)
Navy	*Carlo Mirabello* (see Giolitti II)

0 Dec 1909 – 21 Mar 1910: Sonnino II

Prime Minister	*Sidney, Baron Sonnino* (for 2nd time) (see Crispi III)
Foreign Affairs	*Francesco, Count Guicciardini* (see Sonnino I)
Home Affairs	*Sidney, Baron Sonnino* (see Crispi III)
Justice	*Vittorio Scialoja* (b. Turin 24 Apr 1856; d. Rome 19 Nov 1933)
Finance	*Enrico Arlotta*
Education	*Eduardo Daneo* (b. Turin 13 Oct 1851)
War	*Paolo Spingardi* (see Giolitti III)
Navy	*Giovanni Bettolo* (see Pelloux II)

30 Mar 1910 – 20 Mar 1911: Luzzatti

Prime Minister	*Luigi Luzzatti* (see Giolitti II)
Foreign Affairs	*Antonio, Marquis Paternò Castello di San Giuliano* (see Fortis II)
Home Affairs	*Luigi Luzzatti* (see Giolitti II)
Justice	*Cesare Fani* (b. Perugia 1843)
Finance	*Luigi Facta* (b. Pinerolo 16 Sep 1861; d. Pinerolo 5 Nov 1930)
Education	*Luigi Credaro* (b. Sondrio 15 Jan 1860; d. Rome 15 Feb 1939)
War	*Paolo Spingardi* (see Giolitti III)
Navy	*Pasquale Leonardi Cattolica* (b. Naples 12 Feb 1851; d. Rome 26 Mar 1924)

27 Mar 1911 – 10 Mar 1914: Giolitti IV

Prime Minister	*Giovanni Giolitti* (for 4th time) (see Crispi II)
Foreign Affairs	*Antonio, Marquis Paternò Castello di San Giuliano* (see Fortis II)
Home Affairs	*Giovanni Giolitti* (see Crispi II)
Justice	*Camillo Finocchiaro-Aprile* (see Pelloux I)
Finance	*Luigi Facta* (see Luzzatti)
Education	*Luigi Credaro* (see Luzzatti)
War	*Paolo Spingardi* (see Giolitti III)
Navy	27 Mar 1911 – 28 Jul 1913: *Pasquale Leonardi Cattolica* (see Luzzatti)
	28 Jul 1913 – 10 Mar 1914: *Enrico Millo di Casalgiate* (b. Chiavari 12 Feb 1865; d. Rome 14 Jul 1930)

21 Mar – 31 Oct 1914: Salandra I

Prime Minister	*Antonio Salandra* (for 1st time) (see Sonnino I)
Foreign Affairs	21 Feb – 16 Oct 1914: *Antonio, Marquis Paternò Castello di San Giuliano* (see Fortis II)
Home Affairs	*Antonio Salandra* (see Sonnino I)
Justice	*Luigi Dari*
Finance	*Luigi Rava* (see Giolitti III)
Education	*Eduardo Daneo* (see Sonnino II)
War	21 Mar – 8 Oct 1914: *Domenico Grandi*
	8 – 31 Oct 1914: *Vittorio Italico Zupelli* (b. Capodistria 6 Mar 1859; d. Rome 22 Jan 1945)
Navy	21 Mar – 12 Aug 1914; *Enrico Millo di Casalgiate* (see

Giolitti IV)
12 Aug – 31 Oct 1914: *Leone, Count Viale* (d. 3 Feb 1918)

5 Nov 1914 – 12 Jun 1916: Salandra II

Prime Minister	*Antonio Salandra* (for 2nd time) (see Sonnino I)
Foreign Affairs	*Sidney, Baron Sonnino* (see Crispi III)
Home Affairs	*Antonio Salandra* (see Sonnino I)
Justice	*Vittorio Emmanuele Orlando* (see Giolitti II)
Finance	*Eduardo Daneo* (see Sonnino II)
Education	*Pasguale Grippo*
War	5 Nov 1914 – 5 Apr 1916: *Vittorio Italico Zupelli* (see Salandra I)
	4 Apr – 12 Jun 1916: *Paolo Morone* (b. Torre Annunziata 1854)
Navy	5 Nov 1914 – 24 Sep 1915: *Leone, Count Viale* (see Salandra I)
	30 Sep 1915 – 12 Jun 1916: *Camillo Corsi* (b. Rome 13 May 1860; d. Rome 17 Jul 1921)

19 Jun 1916 – 27 Oct 1917: Boselli

Prime Minister	*Paolo Boselli* (see Crispi I)
Foreign Affairs	*Sidney, Baron Sonnino* (see Crispi III)
Home Affairs	*Vittorio Emmanuele Orlando* (see Giolitti II)
Justice	*Ettore Sacchi* (see Sonnino I)
Finance	*Filippo Meda* (b. Milan 1 Jan 1869; d. Milan 31 Dec 1939)
Education	*Francesco Ruffini* (b. Turin 29 Mar 1934)
War	19 Jun 1916 – 16 Jun 1917: *Paolo Morone* (see Salandra II)
	16 Jun – 27 Oct 1917: *Gaetano Ettore Giardino* (b. Montemagno 24 Jan 1864; d. Turin 1935)
Navy	19 Jun 1916 – 16 Jun 1917: *Camillo Corsi* (see Salandra II)
	16 Jun – 27 Oct 1917: *Arturo Triangi*

0 Oct 1917 – 19 Jan 1919: Orlando I

Prime Minister	*Vittorio Emmanuele Orlando* (for 1st time) (see Giolitti II)
Foreign Affairs	*Sidney, Baron Sonnino* (see Crispi III)

Home Affairs	30 Oct 1917 – 26 Dec 1918: *Vittorio Emmanuele Orlando* (see Giolitti II)
Justice	*Ettore Sacchi* (see Sonnino I)
Finance	*Filippo Meda* (see Boselli)
Education	*Agostino Berenini* (b. Parma 22 Oct 1858; d. Rome 28 Mar 1939)
War	30 Oct 1917 – 20 Mar 1918: *Vittorio Alfieri* (b. Perugia 1863; d. Rome 19 Jul 1930)
	20 Mar 1918 – 19 Jan 1919: *Vittorio Italico Zupelli* (see Salandra I)
Navy	*Alberto Del Bono* (b. Golese 21 Sep 1856)

Plus 11 other ministers

19 Jan – 19 Jun 1919: Orlando II

Prime Minister	*Vittorio Emmanuele Orlando* (for 2nd time) (see Giolitti II)
Foreign Affairs	*Sidney, Baron Sonnino* (see Crispi III)
Home Affairs	*Vittorio Emmanuele Orlando* (see Giolitti II)
Justice	*Luigi Facta* (see Luzzatti)
Finance	*Filippo Meda* (see Boselli)
Education	*Agostino Berenini* (see Orlando I)
War	*Enrico Caviglia* (b. Finalmarina 4 May 1862; d. Finalmarina 22 Mar 1945)

23 Jun 1919 – 12 Mar 1920: Nitti I

Prime Minister	*Francesco Nitti* (for 1st time) (b. Melfi 19 Jul 1868; d. Melfi 20 Feb 1953)
Foreign Affairs	23 Jun – 3 Nov 1919: *Tommaso Tittoni* (see Giolitti II)
	3 Nov 1919 – 12 Mar 1920: *Vittorio Scialoja* (see Sonnino II)
Home Affairs	*Francesco Nitti* (see above)
Justice	*Lodovico Mortara* (b. Mantua 16 Apr 1855; d. Rome 1 Jan 1937)
Finance	*Francesco Tedesco* (b. Andretta 11 Mar 1853; d. Rome 9 May 1921)
Education	*Alfredo Baccelli* (b. Rome 10 Sep 1863; d. Rome 13 Sep 1955)
War	24 Jun 1919 – 12 Mar 1920: —— *Alberici*
Navy	*Giovanni Sechi* (b. Sassari 17 Jan 1871)

14 Mar – 12 May 1920: Nitti II

Prime Minister	*Francesco Nitti* (for 2nd time) (see Nitti I)
Foreign Affairs	*Vittorio Scialoja* (see Sonnino II)
Home Affairs	*Francesco Nitti* (see Nitti I)
Justice	*Lodovico Mortara* (see Nitti I)
Finance	*Karl Schanzer* (b. Vienna 18 Dec 1865; d. Rome 23 Oct 1953)
Education	*Andrea Torre* (b. Torchiara 5 Apr 1866)
War	*Ivanoe Bonomi* (b. Mantua 18 Oct 1873; d. Rome 20 Apr 1951)
Navy	*Giovanni Sechi* (see Nitti I)

21 May – 9 Jun 1920: Nitti III

Prime Minister	*Francesco Nitti* (for 3rd time) (see Nitti I)
Foreign Affairs	*Vittorio Scialoja* (see Sonnino II)
Home Affairs	*Francesco Nitti* (see Nitti I)
Justice	*Alfredo Calcioni*
Finance	*Cesare de Nava* (b. 1851(?) d. Milan 27 Nov 1933)
Education	*Andrea Torre* (see Nitti II)
War	*Giulio Rodinò*
Navy	*Giovanni Sechi* (see Nitti I)

16 Jun 1920 – 27 Jun 1921: Giolitti V

Prime Minister	*Giovanni Giolitti* (for 5th time) (see Crispi II)
Foreign Affairs	*Carlo, Count Sforza* (b. Montignoso 23 Sep 1872; d. Rome 4 Sep 1952)
Home Affairs	*Giovanni Giolitti* (see Crispi II)
Justice	*Luigi Fera* (b. Cosenza 12 Jun 1868)
Finance	16 Jun – 11 Jul 1920: *Francesco Tedesco* (see Nitti I)
	11 Aug 1920 – 27 Jun 1921: *Luigi Facta* (see Luzzatti)
Education	*Benedetto Croce* (b. Pescasseroli 25 Feb 1866; d. Rome 20 Nov 1952)
War	16 Jun 1920 – 1 Apr 1921: *Ivanoe Bonomi* (see Nitti II)
	1 Apr – 27 Jun 1921: *Giulio Rodinò* (see Nitti III)
Navy	*Giovanni Sechi* (see Nitti I)

Jul 1921 – 2 Feb 1922: Bonomi

Prime Minister	*Ivanoe Bonomi* (see Nitti II)

Foreign Affairs	*Pietro Paolo Tomasi, Marquis della Torretta* (b. Palermo 17 Apr 1873; d. Rome 4 Dec 1962)
Home Affairs	*Ivanoe Bonomi* (see Nitti II)
Justice	*Giulio Rodinò* (see Nitti III)
Finance	*Marcello Saleri* (b. Cuneo 28 May 1882)
Education	*Orso Mario Cornino* (b. Augusta 30 Apr 1876; d. Rome 23 Jan 1937)
War	*Luigi Gasparotto* (b. Sacile 31 May 1873; d. Roccolo di Cantello 29 Jun 1954)
Navy	*Eugenio Bergamasco* (b. Vercelli 15 Apr 1858)

25 Feb – 19 Jun 1922: Facta I

Prime Minister	*Luigi Facta* (for 1st time) (see Luzzatti)
Foreign Affairs	*Karl Schanzer* (see Nitti II)
Home Affairs	*Luigi Facta* (see Luzzatti)
Justice	*Luigi Rossi* (b. Verona 29 Apr 1867; d. Meran 29 Oct 1941)
Finance	*Giovanni Battista Bertone* (b. Mondovì 17 Dec 1874)
Education	*Antonio Anile* (b. Pizzodi Calabria 20 Nov 1869; d. Raiano d'Aquila 26 Sep 1943)
War	*Pietro Lanza Di Scalea* (b. Palermo 20 Oct 1863)
Navy	*Roberto De Vito* (b. Florence 19 Feb 1867)

1 Aug – 27 Oct 1922: Facta II

Prime Minister	*Luigi Facta* (for 2nd time) (see Luzzatti)
Foreign Affairs	*Karl Schanzer* (see Nitti II)
Home Affairs	*Luigi Facta* (see Luzzatti)
Justice	*Giulio Alessio* (b. Padua 13 May 1853; d. Padua 19 Dec 1940)
Finance	*Giovanni Battista Bertone* (see Facta I)
Education	*Antonio Anile* (see Facta I)
War	*Marcello Saleri* (see Bonomi)
Navy	*Roberto De Vito* (see Facta I)

30 Oct 1922 – 25 Jul 1943: Mussolini

Prime Minister	*Benito Mussolini* (b. Predappio 29 Jul 1883; d. Villa Belmonte 28 Apr 1945)
Foreign Affairs	30 Oct 1922 – 12 Sep 1929: *Benito Mussolini* (see above)
	12 Sep 1929 – 20 Jul 1932:*Dino* (from 1937: *Count*)

	Grandi di Mordano (b. Mordano 4 Jun 1895)
Home Affairs	30 Oct 1922 – 16 Jun 1924: *Benito Mussolini* (see above)
	16 Jun 1924 – 5/6 Nov 1926: *Luigi Federzoni* (b. Bologna 27 Sep 1878)
	5/6 Nov 1926 – 25 Jul 1943: *Benito Mussolini* (see above)
Justice	30 Oct 1922 – 5 Jan 1925: *Aldo Oviglio* (b. Rimini 7 Jul 1873; d. Ronerio 19 Aug 1942)
	5 Jan 1925 – 20 Jul 1932: *Alfredo Rocca* (b. Naples 1875; d. Rome 28 Aug 1935)
Finance	30 Oct 1922 – 8 Jul 1925: *Alberto de Stefani* (b. Verona 6 Oct 1879)
	6 Jul 1925 – 8 Jul 1928: *Giuseppe, Count Volpi di Misurata* (b. Venice 19 Nov 1877; d. Rome 16 Nov 1947)
	8 Jul 1928 – 20 Jul 1932: *Antonio Mosconi* (b. Vicenza 9 Sep 1866)
Education	30 Oct 1922 – 30 Jun 1924: *Giovanni Gentile* (b. Castelvetrano 30 May 1875; d. Florence 15 Apr 1944)
	30 Jun 1924 – 5 Jan 1925: *Alessandro, Count Casati* (b. Milan 5 Mar 1881; d. Arcore 4 Jun 1953)
	5 Jan 1925 – 9 Jul 1928: *Pietro Fedele* (b. Minturno 15 Apr 1873; d. Rome 9 Jan 1943)
	9 Jul 1928 – 12 Sep 1929: *Giuseppe Belluzzo* (b. Verona 25 Nov 1876; d. Rome 21 May 1952)
	12 Sep 1929 – 20 Jul 1932: *Giuliano Balbino* (b. Forsano 1879)
War	30 Oct 1922 – 28 Apr 1924: *Armando (Vittorio) Diaz* (b. Naples 5 Dec 1861; d. Rome 29 Feb 1928)
	2 Apr 1924 – 2 Apr 1925: *Antonio di Giorgio*
	2 Apr 1925 – 12 Sep 1929: *Benito Mussolini* (see above)
	12 Sep 1929 – 22 Jul 1933: *Pietro Gazzera* (b. Bene Vagienna 11 Dec 1879; d. Turin 30 Jun 1953)
Navy	30 Oct 1922 – 10 May 1925: *Paolo, Count Thaon di Revel* (b. Turin 10 Jun 1895; d. Rome 24 Mar 1948)
	10 May 1925 – 6 Nov 1933: *Giuseppe Sirianni* (b. Genoa 18 Apr 1874; d. Pieve Ligure 16 Aug 1955)
Airforce	26 Aug 1925 – 12 Sep 1929 (new post): *Benito Mussolini* (see above)
	12 Sep 1929 – 6 Nov 1933: *Italo Balbo* (b. Quartesana 5 Jun 1896; d. Tobruk 28 Jun 1940)

Japan

HEADS OF STATE

Emperors

1465	*Tsuchi-Mikado II*, son of Hanazono II (b. 1442)
1500	*Kashiwabara II*, son (b. 1464)
1526	*Nara II*, son (b. 1497)
1557	*Ogimachi*, son (b. 1517; d. 1593)
1586	*Yozei II*, grandson (b. 1571; d. 1617)
1611	*Mizuno II*, son (b. 1596; d. 1680)
1629	*Meisho*, daughter (b. 1623; d. 1696)
1643	*Komyo II*, brother (b. 1633)
1654	*Saiin II*, brother (b. 1637; d. 1685)
1662	*Reigen*, brother (b. 1654; d. 1732)
1685/87	*Higashiyama*, son (b. 1675)
1709	*Naka-no-Mikado*, son (b. 1702; d. 1737)
1735	*Sakuramachi I*, son (b. 1720; d. 1750)
1747 – 1762	*Momozono I*, son (b. 1741)
1763	*Sakuramachi II*, brother-in-law (b. 1740; d. 1813)
1771	*Momozono II* (b. 1758)
1779	*Kokaku* (b. 1771; d. 1840)
1816	*Ninko*, son (b. 1800)
1846	*Komei*, son (b. 1831)
13 Feb 1867 (12 Oct 1868)	*Mutsuhito (Meiji)*, son (b. 3 Nov 1852)
29 Jul 1912	*Yoshihito (Taisho)*, son (b. 31 Aug 1879)
24 Dec 1926	*Hirohito (Showa)*, son (b. 29 Apr 1901) Regent from 25 Nov 1921

SHOGUNATE

Tokugawa Family

1603	*Ieyasu* (b. 1542; d. 1616)
1605	*Hidetada*, son (b. 1579; d. 1632)
1623	*Iemitsu*, son (b. 1604)
1651	*Ietsuna*, son (b. 1641)
1680	*Tsunayoshi*, brother (b. 1646)
1709	*Ienobu*, nephew (b. 1662)

1713	*Ietsugu*, son (b. 1709)
1716	*Yoshimune* (b. 1684; d. 1756)
1745	*Ieshige*, son (b. 1711)
1761 – 1786	*Ieharu*, son (b. 1737)
1787	*Ienari*, cousin (b. 1773; d. 1841)
1838	*Ieyoshi*, son (b. 1793)
1853	*Iesada*, son (b. 1824)
1858	*Iemochi*, cousin (b. 1858)
1866 – 9 Nov 1867	*Keiki*, afterwards *Yoshinobu*, son of Nariaki Tokugawa (b. 1827; d. 1913)

MEMBERS OF GOVERNMENT

Prime Ministers

1871 – 1885	*Prince Sanjo Sanetomi* (b. 1849; d. 11 Feb 1891)
22 Dec 1885	*Marquis* (from 1907: *Prince*) *Hirobumi Ito* (for 1st time) (b. 2 Apr 1841; d. 26 Oct 1909)
30 Apr 1888	*Count Kiyotaka Kuroda* (b. 1840; d. 1900)
24 Dec 1889 – 1891	*Prince Aritomo Yamagata* (b. 1838; d. 1 Feb 1922)
6 May 1891 – 1892	*Prince Masayoshi Matsukata* (for 1st time) (b. 1840; d. 2 Jul 1924)
8 Aug 1892	*Marquis Hirobumi Ito* (for 2nd time)
18 Sep 1896	*Prince Masayoshi Matsukata* (for 2nd time)
14 Apr 1897	*Count Kiyotaka Kuroda* (for 2nd time)
8 Jun 1897	*Prince Masayoshi Matsukata* (for 3rd time)
12 Jan 1898	*Marquis Hirobumi Ito* (for 3rd time)
30 Jun 1898	*Shigenobu* (from 1916: *Marquis*) *Okuma* (for 1st time) (b. 1838; d. 9 Jan 1922)
8 Nov 1898	*Prince Aritomo Yamagata* (for 2nd time)
19 Oct 1900	*Marquis Hirobumi Ito* (for 4th time)
10 May 1901	*Kimmochi* (from 1920: *Prince*) *Saionji* (for 1st time) (b. 23 Oct 1849; d. 24 Nov 1940)
2 Jun 1901	*Taro* (from 1911: *Prince*) *Katsura* (for 1st time) (b. 1847; d. 10 Oct 1913)
7 Jan 1906	*Kimmochi Saionji* (for 2nd time)
14 Jul 1908	*Prince Taro Katsura* (for 2nd time)
30 Aug 1911	*Kimmochi Saionji* (for 3rd time)
21 Dec 1912 – 20 Feb 1913	*Prince Taro Katsura* (for 3rd time)
20 Feb 1913	*Count Gombei Yamamoto* (for 1st time) (b. 1852; d. 8 Dec 1933)

16 Apr 1914	*Shigenobu Okuma* (for 2nd time)
11 Aug 1915	*Marquis Shigenobu Okuma* (for 3rd time)
9 Oct 1916	*Count Musatake Terauchi* (b. 1849; d. 23 Oct 1919)
29 Sep 1918 – 4 Nov 1921	*Takashi Hara* (b. 1865; d. 4 Nov 1921)
4 – 13 Nov 1921	*Count Yasuya Uchida* (b. Kumamoto 1866; d. 1936)
13 Nov 1921	*Count Korekiyo Takahashi* (b. Jul 1854; d. 26 Feb 1936)
12 Jun 1922	*Baron Tamosaburo Kato* (b. 1859; d. 24 Aug 1923)
2 Sep 1923	*Count Gombei Yamamoto* (for 2nd time)
7 Jan 1924	*Baron Keigo Kiyoura* (b. 1850; d. 5(?) Nov 1942)
11 Jun 1924	*Prince Takaaki Kato* (for 1st time) (b. 3 Jan 1860; d. 27 Jan 1926)
2 Aug 1925	*Prince Takaaki Kato* (for 2nd time)
29 Jan 1926	*Baron Reijiro Wakatsuki* (b. 1866; d. Ito 21 Nov 1949)
20 Apr 1927 – 1 Jul	*Baron Gi-ichi Tanaka* (b. 1863; d. 29 Sep 1929)
3 Jul 1929 – 9 Apr 1931	*Osachi Hamaguchi* (b. Apr 1870; d. 25 Aug 1931)

Foreign Ministers

30·Sep 1918 – 1923	*Yasuya* (from 1920: *Count*) *Uchida* (see Prime Ministers)
4 – 13 Sep 1923	*Count Gombei Yamamoto* (see Prime Ministers)
13 Sep – Dec 1923	*Baron Hikokichi Ijuin* (b. 1864; d. 1924)
7 Jan – 7 Jun 1924	*Baron Keishiro Matsui* (b. Osaka 1868; d. 1946)
11 Jun 1924 – 27 Apr 1927	*Baron Kijuro Shidehara* (for 1st time)
27 Apr 1927 – 1 Jul 1929	*Baron Gi-ichi-Tanaka* (see Prime Ministers)
3 Jul 1929 – 11 Dec 1931	*Baron Kijuro Shidehara* (for 2nd time)

Jenne

See Djenne.

Jordan

Until 1921 part of Turkey. From 1921 until 1946 mandated to the UK by the League of Nations.

HEAD OF STATE

King

21 Mar 1921 – 20 Jul 1951	*Emir Abd Allah*, son of Sharif Husain of Hejaz (b. 1882; d. 1951)

MEMBERS OF GOVERNMENT

Prime Ministers

Mar – (?)1921	*Rashid Bey Tali*
1921	*Muzhir Bey ar-Raslan* (for 1st time)
1921 – Jan 1923	*Rida Pasha ar-Riqabi* (for 1st time)
7 Feb – 5 Sep 1923	*Muzhir Bey ar-Raslan* (for 2nd time)
5 Sep 1923 – 1924	*Hasan Khalid Pasha*
1924 – 1933	*Rida Pasha ar-Riqabi* (for 2nd time)

Kakheti

See Georgia.

Kanem-Bornu

For the Empire of Kanem-Bornu, West Africa, 8th to 20th centuries, see volume 1.

Kartli

See Georgia.

Kilwa

For the Sultans of Kilwa, Tanzania, 10th to 19th centuries, see volume 1.

Kongo

For the Kingdom of Kongo, Angola, 14th to 17th centuries, see volume 1.

Korea

HEADS OF STATE

Japanese Governors

29 Aug 1910 – 1916	*Count Masatake Terauchi* (b. 1849; d. 23 Oct 1919)
1916 – 1919	*Count Yoshimicho Hasegawa* (b. 1850; d. 1924)
Sep 1919 – 1927	*Count Makoto Saito* (for 1st time) (b. Oct 1858; d. 26 Feb 1936)
1927 – 1929	*Hanzo Yamanashi*
Aug 1929 – 1931	*Count Makoto Saito* (for 2nd time)

Kuwait

HEADS OF STATE

Emirs

1917 – 1921	*Sheikh Salim*, 2nd son of Sheikh Mubarak
1921 – 1950	*Sheikh Ahmad*, nephew

Laos

HEADS OF STATE

1486	*La Sène Thai*, son of Sai-Tiakaphat (b. 1463)
1496	*Som Phou*, son (b. 1488)
1501	*Visoun*, uncle
1520 – 1547	*Phothisarath I*, son (b. 1506)
1548	*Setthathirath*, son (b. 1534)
1571	*Sène Soulintha* (for 1st time) (b. 1511) Regent
1575	*Maha Oupahat*
1580	*Sène Soulintha* (for 2nd time) as King
1582	*Nakhone Noi*, son, deposed
1583 – 1591	Interregnum
1591	*Nokèo Koumane*, son of Setthathirath (b. 1571)
1596	*Thammikarath*, cousin by marriage (b. 1582) executed
1622	*Oupagnouvarat*, son (b. 1598)
1623	*Phothisarath II*, son of Sène Soulintha (b. 1552)
1627	*Mone Kèo*, brother
(?)	*Oupagnaovarath*, son
(?)	*Tone Kham*, son
(?)	*Visai*, brother
1637	*Souligna Vongsa*, son of Tone Kham (b. 1613)
1694	*Tan Thala*, son-in-law (b. before 1641) committed suicide
1700	*Nan Tharat*, usurper
1700	*Sai Ong Hué*, grandson of Tone Kham
1707	Kingdom divided

Lower Laos (capital – Vientiane)

1707	*Sai Ong Hué* (see above)
1735	*Ong Long*, son
1760	*Ong Boun*, son
1778 – 1782	Interregnum
1782	*Chao Nan*, son
1792	*Chao In*, brother
1805	*Chao Anou*, brother (d. 1835)
1828	Territory subjugated by the Thais

Upper Laos (capital – Luang Prabang)

1707	*King Kitsarath*, grandson of Souligna Vongsa
1726	*Khamane Noi*, cousin
1727	*Intha Som*, brother of King Kitsarath
1776	*Sotika Koumane*, son, abdicated
1781	*Tiao-Vong*, 3rd son of Intha Som (b. 1751)
1787 – 1791	Interregnum
1791	*Anourout*, 2nd son of Intha Som (d. 1819) abdicated
1817	*Mantha Thourath*, son (b. 1775)
1836 – 1850	*Souka Seum*, son (b. 1798)
1851 – 1869	*Tiantha-Koumane*, brother
1869/1872	*Oun Kham*, brother (b. 1811; d. 15 Dec 1895)
1887 – 1894	Interregnum
1893	French protectorate, later extended over the whole of Laos
1894	*Zakarine*, son (b. 1886)
24 Mar 1904 – 21 Aug 1959	*Sisavang Vong*, son (b. 14 Jul 1885; d. Luang Prabang 30 Oct 1959)

Latvia

Until November 1917 part of Russia.

HEADS OF STATE: Presidents

30 Nov 1917	*Voldemārs Zāmuēls* (b. 22 May 1872; d. 1948)

18 Nov 1918	*Kārlis Ulmanis* (b. 4 Sep 1877; d. 1942)
16 Apr 1919	No President
7 Sep 1922 – 14 Mar 1927	*Jānis Čakste* (b. 14 Sep 1859; d. 14 Mar 1927)
8 Apr 1927 – 9 Apr 1930	*Gustavs Zemgals* (b. 12 Aug 1871; d. 7 Jan 1939)

MEMBERS OF GOVERNMENT

Prime Ministers

18 Nov 1918	*Kārlis Ulmanis* (for 1st time) (see Presidents)
Jan 1919	*Peteris Stučka* (b. Koknese 26 Jul 1865; d. Moscow 25 Jan 1932)
28 Apr 1919	*Andrievs Niedra* (b. Tirza 8 Feb 1871; d. Riga 25 Sep 1942)
16 Jul 1919	*Kārlis Ulmanis* (for 2nd time)
17 Jun 1921	*Zigfrīds Meierovics* (b. 6 Feb 1887; d. 23 Aug 1925)
end of Jan 1923	*Jānis Pauļuks* (b. 1865; d. 1943)
25 Jan – 2 Dec 1924	*Voldemārs Zāmuēls* (see Presidents above)
16 Dec 1924	*Hugo Celmiņš* (for 1st time) (b. 1877) deported 1941)
25 Dec 1925 – 28 Apr 1926	*Kārlis Ulmanis* (for 3rd time)
4 May 1926	*Arturs Alberings* (b. 26 Dec 1876; d. 1934)
17 Dec 1926	*Marģers Skujenieks* (b. 23 Jun 1886; d. 1941(?))
21 Jan – 13 Nov 1928	*Pēteris Juraševskis* (b. 1872; d. 1945)
1 Dec 1928 – 3 Mar 1931	*Hugo Celmiņš* (for 2nd time)

Lebanon

Until 1914 autonomous government under Turkish control. Declared autonomous under French mandate from League of Nations in 1920. Reorganized as Lebanese Republic in 1926.

HEAD OF STATE

President

26 May 1926 – 28 Jan 1934	*Charles Dabbas* (b. Beirut 1885; d. Paris 23 Aug 1935)

Prime Ministers

31 May 1926 – 5 May 1927	*Auguste Pasha Adib* (b. Constantinople 1860; d. Paris 12 Jul 1936)
5 May 1927 – 6 Jan 1928	*Bishara Bey al-Khuri* (for 1st time) (b. 1890(?) d. 11 Jan 1960)
6 Jan – 9 Aug 1928	*Bishara Bey al-Khuri* (for 2nd time)
10 Aug 1928 – 8 May 1929	*Habib Pasha as-Sad* (d. Beirut 6 May 1942)
9 May – 9 Oct 1929	*Bishara Bey al-Khuri* (for 3rd time)
11 Oct 1929 – 20 Mar 1930	*Émile Eddé* (b. Beirut 1886; d. 28 Sep 1949)

Liberia

HEADS OF STATE

Presidents

1848 – 1956	*Joseph Jenkins Roberts* (for 1st time) (b. Norfolk, Virginia 15 Mar 1809; d. Monrovia 24 Feb 1876)
1856 – 1864	*Stephen A. Benson* (b. Maryland 1816)
1864 – 1868	*Daniel B. Warner* (d. 18 Apr 1875)
1868 – 1870	*James Spriggs Payne* (for 1st time)
1870 – 1871	*Edward James Roye* (b. Newark, Ohio 3 Feb 1815; d. Monrovia 12 Feb 1872)
1871 – 1872	*James S. Smith*, previously Vice-President
1872 – 1876	*Joseph Jenkins Roberts* (for 2nd time)
1876 – 1878	*James Spriggs Payne* (for 2nd time)
1878 – 1883	*Anthony William Gardner* (d. 1883)
1883 – 1884	*Alfred F. Russell*, previously Vice-President
1884 – 1892	*Hilary Richard Wright Johnson* (b. 1829)

1892 – 1896	*Joseph James Cheeseman* (b. 1844; d. 1896)
1896 – 1898	*William David Coleman* (for 1st time) (b. 1842; d. 1900) previously Vice-President
1898 – 1900	*William David Coleman* (for 2nd time)
1900 – 1902	*Garretson Wilmot Gibson* (for 1st time) (b. 1830) previously Secretary of State
1902 – 1904	*Garretson Wilmot Gibson* (for 2nd time)
1904 – 1912	*Arthur Barclay* (b. Barbados 31 Jul 1854)
1912 – 1920	*Daniel Edward Howard* (b. Buchanan, Grand Bassa County, 5 Aug 1861)
1920 – 1930	*Charles Dunbar Burgess King* (b. between 1872 and 1878; d. Monrovia 4 Sep 1961)

Liechtenstein

HEADS OF STATE

Princes

Gundakar Dynasty

11 Feb 1686	*Jacob Moritz*, son of Prince Hartmann of Liechtenstein (b. 25 Jul 1641)
21 Apr 1709	*Anton Florian*, brother (b. 4 May 1656)
1719	Vaduz and Schellenberg united with the Principality of Liechtenstein
11 Oct 1721	*Josef*, son (b. 27 May 1690)
17 Dec 1732	*Johann Nepomuk Karl*, son (b. 6 Jul 1724)
22 Dec 1748	*Josef Wenzel Lorenz*, cousin of Josef (b. 9 Aug 1696)

Franz Dynasty

10 Feb 1772	*Franz Josef I*, nephew (b. 29 Nov 1726)
11 Aug 1781	*Alois I*, son (b. 14 May 1759)
24 Mar 1805	*Johann I*, brother (for 1st time) (b. 26 Jun 1760) sovereign Prince from 12 Jul 1806
1807(?)	*Karl*, 3rd son (b. 14 Jun 1803; d. 12 Oct 1871)
1813	*Johann I* (for 2nd time)
20 Apr 1836	*Alois II*, son (b. 26 May 1796)

| 12 Nov 1858 – 11 Feb 1929 | *Johann II*, son (b. 5 Oct 1840) |
| 11 Feb 1929 – 30 Mar 1938 | *Franz von Paula*, brother (b. 28 Aug 1853; d. 25 Jul 1938) |

Prime Minister

| Aug 1928 – 20 Jul 1945 | *Dr Franz Josef Hoop* (b. 14 Dec 1895; d. 19 Oct 1959) |

Lithuania

The Grand Duchy of Lithuania was constitutionally separate from the state of Poland until the Union of Lublin in 1569, but the Grand Dukes were also Kings of Poland and are listed as such. As a result of the Third Partition of Poland, Lithuania north of the Memel, and later the districts to the south, passed to Russia, becoming independent in 1918.

HEADS OF STATE

King Elect

| 13 Jul 1918 | *Wilhelm von Urach, Duke of Wurtemberg* (b. 3 Mar 1864; d. Rapallo 24 Mar 1928) proclaimed king as Mindaugas II |
| 2 Nov 1918 | Proclamation rescinded |

Presidents

4 Apr 1919 – Dec 1922	*Antanas Smetona* (for 1st time) (b. Uželenis 10 Aug 1874; d. Cleveland, Ohio, 9 Jan 1944)
21 Dec 1922 – 7 Jun 1926	*Aleksandras Stulginskis* (b. Kutaliai 26 Feb 1885; d. Kaunas 22 Sep 1969)
7 Jun – 17 Dec 1926	*Kazys Grinius* (b. Sulemos Buda 17 Dec 1866; d. Chicago 4 Jun 1950)
17 Dec 1926 – Jun 1940	*Antanas Smetona* (for 2nd time)

MEMBERS OF GOVERNMENT

Prime Ministers

Nov 1918	*Augustinas Voldemaras* (for 1st time) (b. Dysna 16 Apr 1883; d. Moscow 16 Dec 1942)
27 Dec 1918 – 7 Mar 1919	*Mykolas Sleževičius* (for 1st time) (b. Drembliai 21 Feb 1882; d. Kaunas 11 Nov 1939)
12 Mar 1919	*Pranas Dovydaitis* (b. Runkiai 2 Dec 1886; d. 1942)
12 Apr 1919	*Mykolas Sleževičius* (for 2nd time)
7 Oct 1919 – 19 Jun 1920	*Ernestas Galvanauskas* (for 1st time) (b. Zizonys 20 Nov 1882; d. Aix-les-Bains 24 Jul 1867)
19 Jun 1920 – 30 Jun 1923	*Kazys Grinius* (see Presidents)
12 Feb 1923 – 9 Jun 1924	*Ernestas Galvanauskas* (for 2nd time)
18 Jun 1924 – 1 Feb 1925	*Antanas Tumenas* (b. Kurkliečiai 13 May 1880; d. Bachmaning 8 Feb 1946)
3 Feb – 19 Sep 1925	*Vytantas Petrulis*
25 Sep 1925 – 15 Jun 1926	*Leonas Bistras* (b. Liepnja 20 Oct 1890)
15 Jun – 18 Dec 1926	*Mykolas Sleževičius* (for 3rd time)
18 Dec 1926 – 19 Sep 1929	*Augustinas Voldemaras* (for 2nd time)
23 Sep 1929 – 8 Jun 1934	*Juozas Tubelis* (b. Ilgalankiai 18 Apr 1882; d. Kaunas 30 Sep 1939)

Luba/Lunda States

For the Luba/Lunda States (and Lunda/Kazembe), Central Africa, 17th to 19th centuries, see volume 1.

Lucca

HEADS OF STATE

24 Jun 1805	*Felice Baciochi* (b. Ajaccio 18 May 1762; d. Bologna

	27 Apr 1841) with his wife *Elise Bonaparte* (b. 3 Jan 1777; d. Monfalcone 9 Aug 1820)
3 Mar 1806	Dominion extended over the whole of Tuscany
1809	*Elise, Grand Duchess of Tuscany*
10 Dec 1813	Occupied by the British: various provisional governments and regencies
10 Jun 1817	*Maria Luisa, Duchess of Parma* (b. 6 Jul 1782; d. 13 Mar 1824) Duchess
1815/1824	*Carlo Ludovico*, son (b. 22 Dec 1799; d. 16 Apr 1883) Duke
4 Oct 1847	Ceded to Leopold II, Grand Duke of Tuscany

Luxembourg

HEADS OF STATE

Grand Dukes

16 Mar 1815	*William I*, son of William V of the Netherlands (b. 24 Aug 1772; d. 12 Dec 1843) King of the Netherlands
7 Oct 1840	*William II*, son (b. 6 Dec 1792) King of the Netherlands
17 Mar 1849	*William III*, son (b. 19 Feb 1817) King of the Netherlands
23 Nov 1890	*Adolf* (from 1839 – 1866: *Duke of Nassau*) son of Duke William of Nassau (b. 24 Jul 1817)
17 Nov 1905	*William IV*, son (b. 22 Apr 1852)
25 Feb 1912 – 14 Jan 1919	*(Grand Duchess) Marie Adelaide*, daughter (b. 14 Jun 1894; d. 24 Jan 1924)
14 Jan 1919 – 12 Nov 1964	*(Grand Duchess) Charlotte* (b. Castle Berg 23 Jan 1896) abdicated

MEMBERS OF GOVERNMENT

Prime Ministers

26 dec 1874 – 20 Feb 1885	*Felix, Baron Blochausen* (b. Birtringen 25 Mar 1834; d. 23 Nov 1915)

1885 – 1889	*Thilges*
22 Sep 1889 – 3 Mar 1915	*Paul Eyschen* (for 1st time) (b. Luxembourg **9** Sep 1841; d. 12 Oct 1915)
3 Mar – 12 Oct 1915	*Paul Eyschen* (for 2nd time)
12 – 21 Oct 1915	—— *Mongenast*
5 Nov 1915 – Jan 1916	—— *Loutsch*
22 Feb – 25 Dec 1916	—— *Thorn* (for 1st time)
4 Jan – 24 May 1917	—— *Thorn* (for 2nd time)
18 Jun 1917 – 6 Sep 1918	—— *Kauffmann*
27 Sep 1918 – 2 (20) Apr 1921	*Emil Reuter* (for 1st time)
15 Apr 1921 – 20 Jan 1925	*Emil Reuter* (for 2nd time)
19 Mar 1925 – 23 Jun 1926	—— *Prüm*
16 Jul 1926 – mid Apr 1932	*Joseph Bech* (b. 17 Feb 1887)

Mainz

HEADS OF STATE

Electors and Archbishops

20 May 1484 – 21 Dec 1504	*Bertold von Henneberg-Römhild* (b. 1442)
30 Dec 1504 – 15 Sep 1508	*Jakob von Liebenstein*
27 Sep 1508 – 9 Feb 1514	*Uriel von Gemmingen*
9 Mar 1514 – 24 Sep 1545	*Albrecht von Brandenburg*, son of Elector Johann (b. 28 Jun 1490)
20 Oct 1545 – 18 Mar 1555	*Sebastian von Heustenstamm*
18 Apr 1555 – 22 Mar 1582	*Daniel Brendel von Homburg*
20 Apr 1582 – 5 Apr 1601	*Wolfgang von Dalberg*

15 May 1601 – 10 Jan 1604	*Johann Adam von Bicken*
27 Feb 1604 – 17 Sep 1626	*Johann Schweikhard von Kronberg* (b. 15 Jul 1553)
20 Oct 1626 – 6 Jul 1629	*Georg Friedrich von Greiffenklau* (b. 8 Sep 1573)
6 Aug 1629 – 9 Oct 1647	*Anselm Kasimir Wambold von Umstadt* (b. 30 Nov 1583)
19 Nov 1647 – 12 Feb 1673	*Johann Philipp, Count Schönborn* (b. Eschbach 6 Aug 1605)
13 Feb 1673	*Lothar Friedrich, Baron Metternich*
3 Jul 1675 – 6 Dec 1678	*Damian Hartrad von der Leyen*
9 Jan – 26 Sep 1679	*Karl Heinrich, Baron Metternich*
7 Nov 1679	*Anslem Franz von Ingelheim*
30 Mar 1695 – 30 Jan 1729	*Lothar Franz, Count Schönborn* (b. 4 Oct 1655)
7 Apr 1729 – 18 Apr 1732	*Franz Ludwig*, brother of Elector Palatine Karl Philipp (b. 24 Jul 1664)
9 Jun 1732 – 20 Mar 1743	*Philipp Karl, Baron Eltz*
22 Apr 1743 – 4 Jun 1763	*Johann Friedrich Karl, Count Ostein*
5 Jul 1763 – 11 Jun 1774	*Emmerich Josef, Baron Breidbach* (b. Coblenz 12 Nov 1707)
18 Jul 1774 – 25 Jul 1802	*Friedrich Karl Josef, Baron Erthal* (b. Mainz 3 Jan 1719)
26 Jul 1802 – 23 Feb 1803	*Karl Theodor, Baron Dalberg* (b. Herrnsheim, near Worms, 8 Feb 1744; d. Regensburg 10 Feb 1817)
1803	Archiepiscopal possessions secularized, with lapse of electorate

Mantua

HEADS OF STATE

Dukes

House of Gonzaga

1484	*Gianfrancesco III*, son of Federigo I (b. 10 Aug 1466)

29 Mar 1519	*Federigo II*, son (b. 17 May 1500)
28 Jun 1540	*Francesco I*, son (b. 10 May 1533)
22 Feb 1550	*Guglielmo*, brother (b. 24 Apr 1538)
14 Aug 1587	*Vincenzo I*, son (b. 22 Sep 1562)
18 Feb 1612	*Francesco II*, son (b. 7 May 1586)
22 Dec 1612	*Ferdinando*, brother (b. 26 Apr 1587)
29 Oct 1626	*Vincenzo II*, brother (b. 8 Feb 1594)
25 Dec 1627	*Carlo I*, cousin of Guglielmo (b. 6 May 1580)
21 Sep 1637	*Carlo II*, grandson of Carlo I and of Francesco II (b. 3 Oct 1629)
14 Aug 1665 – 1707	*Ferdinando Carlo*, son (b. 31 Aug 1652; d. 5 Jul 1708)
1707	Mantua occupied by Imperial troops
5 Jul 1708	Fief reverted to the Emperor

Massina

For Massina, Islamic trading centre, Mali, 15th to 19th centuries, see volume 1.

Memel Territory

17th century — First World War	Part of Prussia
During First World War	Taken by Russia
10 Jan 1920	Administration taken over by the Allied High Command (condominium)

HEADS OF STATE

Commissioners

5 Jan 1920	*General Odry*, French

1922	—— *Petisne*, French
10 – 16 Jan 1923	Occupied by Lithuania
7 May 1923	Autonomy and parliamentary government granted by Lithuania on the basis of the Memel convention, ratified by the protecting powers on 8 May 1924 and by Lithuania on 30 Jul 1924

Lithuanian Governors

1923	*Žilinskas Žilius* (b. Domeikai 18 Oct 1870; d. Klaipeda 2 Mar 1932)
Dec 1926	—— *Zalkauskas*
7 Sep 1927 – 7 May 1932	*Antonas Merkys* (b. Bajoriai 1 Feb 1887; d. in USSR Mar 1955)

MEMBERS OF GOVERNMENT

Prime Ministers and Ministers

Jan 1920	—— *Altenberg*
Oct 1921	—— *Stepputat*
13/17 Jan 1923	*Erdmonas Simonaitis* (for 1st time) (b. Spečiai 30 Oct 1888; d. Veinheim 24 Feb 1969)
	Minister: *Martynas Reisgys* (b. Venckai 11 Dec 1886; d. Mauthausen 2 Apr 1942)
	Minister: —— *Toleikis*
15 Feb 1923 – 5 Feb 1925	*Viktoras Gailius* (b. Berštinkai 27 Aug 1893; d Pfullingen 7 Jul 1956)
5 Feb – 20 Nov 1925	*Endrias Borchetas* (b. Tilsit 26 Nov 1891; d. Matteson Illinois 25 Sep 1965)
1 Dec 1925 – 12 Jan 1926	—— *Juozapaitis*
12 Jan – 8 Nov 1926	*Erdmonas Simonaitis* (for 2nd time)
	Minister: —— *Kairies*
	Minister: —— *Stumber*
	Minister: *August Baldschus*
	Minister: —— *Scharffetter*
24 Nov 1926 – 4 Jan 1927	—— *Falkas*
	Minister: *Endrias Borchetas* (see above)
	Minister: —— *Scharffetter* (see above)
5 Jan – 5 Oct 1927	—— *Svelnys*
	Minister: —— *Czeskleba*

	Minister: *Endrias Borchertas* (see above)
	Minister: —— *Kadgiehn*
2 Dec 1927 – 28 May	—— *Vorbeck*
1930	Minister: —— *Sziegaud* (b. Trakeningken 31 May 1886)
	Minister: *Martynas Reisgys* (see above)

Mexico

HEADS OF STATE

Emperor

18 May 1822 – 20 Mar 1823	*Augustin I, Itúrbide* (b. 27 Sep 1783; d. 19 Jul 1824)
1823	Republic

Presidents

31 Mar 1823	*Manuel Felix Fernández Guadalupe Victoria* (b. 1768; d. 21 Mar 1843) with a triumvirate, President from 10 Oct 1824
7 Jan – 4 Dec 1828	*Manuel Gómez Pedraza* (for 1st time) (b. 1789; d. 1851)
7 Dec 1828 – 1 Jun 1829	*Vicente Guerrero* (b. 1783; d. 17 Feb 1831)
1 Jan 1830	*Anastasio Bustamente* (for 1st time) (b. 27 Aug 1780; d. 6 Mar 1853)
14 Aug – 24 Dec 1832	*Melchior Muzquiz*
24 Dec 1832	*Manuel Gómez Pedraza* (for 2nd time)
1 Apr 1833	*Antonio López de Santa Ana* (for 1st time) (b. 10 Jun 1797; d. 20 Jun 1876)
28 Jan 1835	*Miguel de Barragan* (b. 1789; d. 1 Mar 1836)
27 Feb 1836	*José Justo Caro*
1 Apr 1837	*Anastasio Bustamente* (for 2nd time)
5 Jul 1840 – 22 Sep 1841	(acting:) *Nicolas Bravo* (b. 1784/90; d. 1854

22 – 28 Sep 1841	(acting:) *Javier Echevierra*
10 Oct 1841	*Antonio López de Santa Ana* (for 2nd time)
20 Sep – Dec 1844	*Valentín Canalizo* (b. 1794)
15 Jan – 30 Dec 1845	*José Joaquín Herrera* (for 1st time) (b. 1792; d. 10 Feb 1854)
4 Jan 1846	*Mariano Paredes y Arrillaga* (b. 1797; d. 1849)
4 Jan – 28 Jul 1846	*José Mariano de Sales*
28 Jul 1846 – 14 Sep 1847	*Antonio López de Santa Ana* (for 3rd time) Dictator
14 Sep 1847 – 8 Jan 1848	*Pedro María Anaya* (b. 1795; d. 1854)
8 Jan – 2 Jun 1848	*Manuel de la Peña y Peña* (b. 1789)
3 Jun 1848 – 15 Jan 1851	*José Joaquín Herrera* (for 2nd time)
15 Jan 1851 – 6 Jan 1853	*Mariano Arista* (b. 1802; d. 1855)
6 Jan – 7 Feb 1853	*Juan Bautista Ceballos*
7 Feb – 17 Mar 1853	—— *Lombardini*
17 Mar 1853 – 16 Aug 1855	*Antonio Lopez de Santa Ana* (for 4th time)
16 Aug – 11 Sep 1855	*Martin Carrera* (b. 1807)
11 Sep – 4 Oct 1855	*Rómulo Diaz de la Vega* (d. 1877)
4 Oct – 12 Nov 1855	*Juan Álvarez* (b. 1790; d. 1867) Rival president
10 Dec 1855 – 21 Jan 1858	*Ignacio Comonfort* (b. 12 Mar 1812; d. 13 Nov 1863)
23 Jan – 23 Dec 1858	*Filipe Zuloaga*
31 Jan 1859 – 22 Dec 1860	*Miguel Miramón* (b. 29 Sep 1832; d. 19 Jun 1867)
4 May 1858/11 Jan 1861 – 18 Jul 1872	*(Carlos) Benito Juárez* (b. 21 Mar 1806; d. 18 Jul 1872) from 1864 – 1867 with Emperor Maximilian
10 Apr 1864 – 14 May 1867	(Emperor) *Maximilian*, brother of Emperor Francis Joseph of Austria (b. 6 Jul 1832; d. (shot) 19 Jun 1867)
19 Jul 1872 – 20 Nov 1876	*Sebastián Lerdo de Tejada* (b. 25 Apr 1825); d. Apr 1889)
6 Dec 1876 – 16 Feb 1877	*Juan N. Méndez* (b. 1820; d. 1894)
15 Feb 1877 – 1 Dec 1880	*Porfirio Diaz* (for 1st time) (b. 15 Sep 1830; d. 2 Jul 1915)
1 Dec 1880 – 1 Dec 1884	*Manuel González* (b. 18 Jun 1833; d. 11 Apr 1893)
1 Dec 1884 – 25 May 1911	*Porfirio Diaz* (for 2nd time)

26 May – 1 Nov 1911	*Francisco León de la Barra*
1 Nov 1911 – 22 Feb 1913	*Francisco Indalecio Madero* (b. Oct 1873; d. 22 Feb 1913)
18 Feb 1913 – 15 Jul 1914	*Victoriano Huerta* (b. 1854; d. 13 Jan 1916)
15 Jul – 12 Aug 1914	*Francisco Carbajal*
17 Jan – 9 Mar 1915	*Roque González Garza* (b. 1885; d. Mexico City 12 Nov 1962)
19 Oct 1915 – 6 May 1920	*Venustiano Carranza* (b. 20 Dec 1859; d. 20 May 1920)
24 May – 1 Dec 1920	*Adolfo de la Huerta* (b. 1881; d. Mexico 9 Jul 1955)
1 Dec 1920 – 1 Dec 1924	*Álvaro Obregón* (b. 1880; d. 17 Jul 1928)
1 Dec 1924 – 1 Dec 1928	*Plutarco (Elins) Calles* (b. 25 Sep 1877; d. 19 Oct 1945) Dictator from 9 May 1927
1 Dec 1928 – 5 Feb 1930	*Emilio Portes Gil* (b. 30 Oct 1891)

Milan

HEADS OF STATE

House of Sforza

26 Dec 1476	*Gian Galeazzo Maria*, son of Galeazzo Maria (b. 10 Jun 1469)
22 Oct 1494	*Ludovico, il Moro*, uncle (for 1st time) (b. Vigevano 3 Apr 1451 or 27 Jul 1452; d. Loches 27 May 1508) usurper, proclaimed Duke in 1499
6 Oct 1499	Milan conquered by the French
5 Feb 1500	*Ludovico* (for 2nd time)
10 Apr 1500	Ludovico captured by the French
15 Dec 1512	*Massimiliano*, son (b. 1493; d. 1530) exiled in 1515
5 Oct 1515	Renewed French occupation
1521	*Francesco Maria*, brother (for 1st time) (b. 1495; d. 24 Oct 1535)
26 Oct 1524	Milan re-conquered by the French
Feb 1525	Occupation by Imperial forces
Dec 1529	*Francesco Maria* (for 2nd time) as Imperial vassal
4 Oct 1535	Milan bequeathed to the Emperor
From 1717	Austrian possession

Modena, Reggio and Ferrara

HEADS OF STATE

Dukes

House of Este

18 May 1452	*Borso (d'Este)*, son of Duke Nicholas III of Ferrara (from 15 Apr 1471: *Duke of Ferrara*) (b. 24 Aug 1413)
20 Aug 1471	*Ercole I*, brother (b. 26 Oct 1431)
25 Jan 1505	*Alfonso I*, son (b. 21 Jul 1476)
31 Oct 1534	*Ercole II*, son (b. 4 Apr 1508)
3 Oct 1559	*Alfonso II*, son (b. 19 Jan 1533)
25 Oct 1597	*Cesare V* (b. 8 Oct 1562)
1598	Ferrara henceforth under direct papal rule
11 Dec 1628	*Alfonso III*, son (b. 22 Oct 1591; d. 24 May 1644) abdicated
1629	*Francesco I*, son (b. 5 Sep 1610)
13 Oct 1658	*Alfonso IV* (II), son (b. 13 Feb 1634)
16 Jul 1662	*Francesco II*, son (b. 6 Mar 1660)
7 Sep 1694	*Rinaldo*, uncle (b. 25 Apr 1655)
26 Oct 1737	*Francesco III*, son (b. 2 Jul 1698)
22 Feb 1780	*Ercole III*, son (b. 22 Nov 1727)

House of Hapsburg-Lorraine

14 Oct 1803	*Ferdinand*, son of the Holy Roman Emperor Francis I and son-in-law of Ercole III (b. 1 Jun 1745)
24 Dec 1806	*Francesco IV*, son (b. 6 Oct 1779)
21 Jan 1846 – 18 Mar 1860	*Francesco V*, son (b. 1 Jun 1819; d. 20 Nov 1875)
1860	Absorbed into Kingdom of Sardinia after referendum

Monaco

HEADS OF STATE

House of Grimaldi

Jul 1457	*Lambert*, son of Nicolas, Seignior of Antibes (b. c 1415) Seignior

Mar 1494	*Jean II*, son
Oct 1505	*Lucien*, brother
Aug 1523	*Augustin*, brother
Apr 1532	*Honoré I*, son of Lucien (b. c. 1520)
Oct 1581	*Charles II*, son
May 1589	*Hercule*, brother
Nov 1604	*Honoré II*, son, Seignior, from 1659: *Prince*
Jan 1662	*Louis I*, grandson (b. 25 Jul 1642)
Jan 1701	*Antoine*, son (b. 25 Jan 1661)
Feb 1731	*Jacques (de Goyon de Matignon et de Thorigny, Duke of Valentinois)* son-in-law (b. 21 Nov 1689; d. 23 Apr 1751) with his wife *Louise Hippolyte* (b. 10 Nov 1697; d. 29 Dec 1731) until Dec 1731
1733 – 1793	*Honoré III*, son (b. 10 Sep 1720; d. 12 May 1795)
1793 – 1814	Annexed to France
1814	*Honoré IV*, son of Honoré III (b. 17 May 1758)
16 Feb 1819	*Honoré V*, son (b. 14 May 1778)
2 Oct 1841	*Florestan*, brother (b. 10 Oct 1785)
20 Jun 1856	*Charles III*, son (b. 8 Dec 1818)
10 Sep 1889	*Albert*, son (b. 13 Nov 1848)
26 Jun 1922 – 9 May 1949	*Louis II*, son (b. 12 Jul 1870)

Mongolia

Under the control of China until 1911 when independence declared.

HEADS OF STATE

Khans

1 Dec 1911 – 20 Apr 1924	The 8th Jebtsundamba Khutuktu, from 3 Feb 1920 under Chinese suzerainty
3 Jun 1924	Republic

MEMBERS OF GOVERNMENT

Prime Ministers

Autumn 1912	*Sain Noyon Khan* (d. 1919)
31 Mar – Jul 1921	*Chagdarjav*
Jul 1921 – Jun 1922	*Bodo* (d. Sep 1922)
1922 – 1924	*Danzan* (d. Aug 1924)
1924 – 1928	*Tserendorji* (d. 1929)
1928 – 1932	*Amor* (b. 1886; d. 1939)

Foreign Ministers

Jul 1921 – Jun 1922	*Bodo* (see Prime Ministers)
1926 – (?)	*Dorlikjab*

Monomotapa

For the Empire of Monomotapa, Rhodesia, 15th century onwards, see volume 1.

Mossi/Dagomba States

For Dagomba and Wagadugn, Ghana, 13th to 20th centuries, see volume 1.

Montenegro

HEADS OF STATE

Princes

Crnojević Dynasty

1490 – 1496	Đurad, son of Ivan (for 1st time) (d. Anatolia 1503)

1496 – 1499	*Stephen II*, brother
1499	*Đurad* (for 2nd time) expelled by the Turks
1514 – 1528	*Skender Beg*, brother
1528 – 1697	Under Turkish rule

Petrović-Njegoš Dynasty

1697	*Danilo I Petrović* (b. c. 1670) Prince-Bishop
1735	*Sava Petrović*, nephew (b. c. 1700) Prince-Bishop
1767 – 1773	*Stephan (Sćepan Mali)* 'the false Tsar', usurper
1782	*Peter I Petrović*, nephew (b. Apr 1747) Prince-Bishop
30 Oct 1830	*Peter II Petrović Njegoš*, nephew (b. 13 Nov 1813) Prince-Bishop
31 Oct 1851	*Danilo II Petrović Nejegoš*, nephew (b. 25 May 1826) elevated Montenegro to a hereditary principality in 1852
13 Aug 1860 – 29 Nov/15 Dec 1918	*Nicholas I Petrović*, nephew (b. 7 Oct 1841; d. 1 Mar 1921) title changed to King on 28 Aug 1910
1918	Absorbed into Yugoslavia

Morocco

HEADS OF STATE

Sultans

House of Sad: Hasani branch

1525	*Abu'l-Abbas Ahmad al-Araj* (d. 1557)
1534 – 1548	*Abu Abd Allah Muhammad I, al-Mahdi, Muhammad al-Qa'im*, brother
557	*Abu Muhammad Abd Allah al-Ghalib*, son
570 – 1574	*Abu Abd Allah Muhammad II, al-Mutawakkil*, son
575 – 1576	*Abu Marwan Abd al-Malik I*, son of Muhammad I
578 – 1579	*Abu'l-Abbas Ahmad I, al-Mansur*, brother
603 – 1604	*Abu Abd Allah Muhammad III, Sheikh al Mamur*, son
607 – 1608	*Zaidan an-Nasir*, brother
629 – 1630	*Abu Marwan Abd al-Malik II*, son
634 – 1635	*al-Walid*, brother

359

1635 – 1636	*Muhammad IV*, brother
1654(?)	*Ahmad II, al-Abbas*, son of Abd al-Malik II

House of Sad: Filali branch

(1660) 1664 – 1665	*ar-Rashid ibn Muhammad ibn Ali*
8 Apr 1672	*Ismail as-Samin*, brother
20 Mar 1727	*Ahmad adh-Dhababi*, son
1728 – 1729	*Abd Allah*, son
1757 – 1758	*Muhammad I*, son
1789 – 1790	*Jazid*, son
1791 – 1792	*Hisham*, brother
1792 – 1793	*Sulaiman*, brother
19 Nov 1822	*Abd ar-Rahman*, nephew
28 Aug 1859	*Muhammad II*, son
25 Sep 1883	*Abu Ali al-Hasan*, son
7 Jun 1894	*Abd al-Aziz*, son (b. 24 Feb 1878; d. 3(?) Jun 1943)
5 Jan 1908	*Abd al-Hafiz*, brother (d. 4 Apr 1937)
12 Aug 1912 – 17 Nov 1927	*Yusuf*, brother (b. 1882)
17 Nov 1927 – 20 Aug 1953'	*(Sidi) Muhammad V*, son (b. Fez 10 Aug 1909; d Rabat 26 Feb 1961

French Residents

Apr 1912 – Dec 1916 and May 1917 – Oct 1925	*Louis Hubert Lyautey* (b. Nancy 17 Nov 1854; d Thorey 27 Jul 1934)
Oct 1924 – Jan 1929	*Théodore Steeg* (b. Libourne 19 Dec 1868; d. Paris 1 Dec 1950)
Jan 1929 – Aug 1933	*Lucien Saint* (b. Evreux 1867; d. 1938)

Nepal

HEADS OF STATE

Kings

1769	*Prithvi Narayan Shah*, raja of Gurkha, conquered t Katmandu valley and founded the modern state Nepal

1775	*Pratap Singh*, son
1778	*Rana Bahadur Shah*, son (b. 1776; d. 1806) assumed full power in 1794 and abdicated on 23 Mar 1799 **Regents:** 1778 *Rajendra Lakshmi*, Queen 1785 – 1794 *Bahadur Shah*, uncle (d. 1797)
23 Mar 1799	*Girban Juddha Bikram Shah*, son of Rana Bahadur **Regents:** 1799 *Rai Rajeshwari Devi* (for 1st time) Queen 1800 *Survarna Prabha* 1803 – 1804 *Raj Rajeshwari Devi* (for 2nd time) Queen 1806 – 1812 *Lalit Tripura Sundari,* Queen
Nov 1816	*Rajendra Bikram Shah*, son (b. 1814; d. 1811) deposed in 1847
1847 – 17 May 1881	*Surendra Bikram Shah*, son (b. 1829)
1 Dec 1881	*Prithvi Bir Bikram Shah*, grandson (b. 8 Aug 1875)
11 Dec 1911 – 7 Nov 1950	*Tribhuvan Bir Bikram Shah*, son (b. 30 Jun 1906)

MEMBERS OF GOVERNMENT

Prime Ministers

1800 – 1804	*Damodar Pande*
1804 – 1806	*Rana Bahadur Shah* (see Kings)
1806 – 1837	*Bhim Sen Thapa* (b. 21 Jul 1775; d. 29 Jul 1839)
8 Nov 1843 – 18 May 1845	*Mathabar Singh Thapa* (b. 2 Oct 1798; d. 18 May 1845)
7 Sep 1846	*Maharaja Jang Bahadur*, great-nephew of Bhim Sen Thapa (b. 18 Jun 1817; d. 25 Feb 1877)
7 Feb 1877	*Maharaja Rana Udip Singh*, brother (b. 25 Apr 1825)
2 Nov 1885	*Maharaja Bir Sham Sher Jang Bahadur Rana*, nephew (b. 10 Dec 1852)
Mar 1901	*Maharaja Deva Sham Sher Jang Bahadur Rana*, brother (b. 17 Jul 1862; d. 20 Feb 1914)
5 Jun 1901	*Maharaja Chandra Sham Sher Jang Bahadur Rana*, brother (b. 8 Jul 1863; d. Nov 1929)
1929 – 1931	*Maharaja Bhim Cham Sham Sher Jang Bahadur Rana*, brother (b. 1869; d. 1932)

Netherlands

HEADS OF STATE

Stadholders of Holland and, from 1747, Hereditary Stadholders of the Netherlands, Counts, and, from 1652, Princes of Nassau and Princes of Orange

House of Orange

1572	*William I*, the Silent, son of Count William I of Nassau-Dillenburg (b. 25(?) Apr 1533; d. (assassinated) 1584)
1585	*Maurice*, son (b. 14 Nov 1567)
23 Apr 1625	*Frederick Henry*, brother (b. 29 Jan or 24 Feb 1584)
14 Mar 1647 – 6 Nov 1650	*William II*, son (b. 27 May 1629)
2/4 Jul 1672 – 19 Mar 1702	*William III*, son (b. 14 Nov 1650) from 23 Feb 1689 King of England in conjunction with his wife Mary
4 May 1747	*William IV*, son of Prince John William of Nassau, of the line of the Stadholder of Friesland (b. 1 Sep 1711)
22 Oct 1751	*William V*, son (b. 8 Mar 1748; d. 9 Apr 1806)
16 May 1795	Batavian republic (under control of France)

Stadholders of Gelderland

1578 – Jul 1580	*John the Old*, brother of William I of Holland (b. Dillenburg 22 Nov 1535; d. 8 Oct 1606)
1581 – 1583	*William IV, Count van den Bergh*, brother-in-law of William I (b. 24 Dec 1537; d. 6 Nov 1586)

Stadholders of Friesland

1584	*William Louis of Nassau-Diez*, son of John the Old (b. Dillenburg 13 Mar 1560; d. Leeuwarden 13 Ju 1620)
13 Jul 1620	*Ernest Casimir*, brother (b. 22 Dec 1573)
2 Jun 1632	*Henry Casimir I*, son (b. Arnhem 31 Jan 1612)
2/12 Jul 1640	*William Frederick* (from 1654: *Prince of Nassau-Diez* brother (b. Arnhem 7 Aug 1613)
21/31 Oct 1664	*Henry Casimir II*, son (b. The Hague 18 Jan 1657)
15/25 Mar 1696	*John William*, son (b. 4 Aug 1687)
1711 – 22 Oct 1751	*William* (from 1747: *William IV*, Hereditar Stadholder of the Netherlands) (see above)

Kings

5 Jun 1806	*Louis*, brother of Napoleon I (b. Ajaccio 4 Sep 1778; d. Leghorn 25 Jul 1846)
1 Jul 1810	Annexed by France

House of Orange

16 Mar 1815	*William I*, son of William V of Holland (b. 24 Aug 1772; d. 12 Dec 1843)
7 Oct 1840	*William II*, son (b. 6 Dec 1792)
17 Mar 1849	*William III*, son (b. 19 Feb 1817)
23 Nov 1890 – 2 Sep 1948	*Wilhelmina*, daughter (b. 31 Aug 1880; d. Apeldoorn 28 Nov 1967) Queen, renounced the throne in favour of her daughter in 1948, after reigning 50 years. Regent: 23 Nov 1890 – 31 Aug 1898: *Emma*, mother of Queen Wilhelmina and widow of William III (b. Arolsen 2 Aug 1858; d. The Hague 20 Mar 1934)

Stadholders of the Burgundian, from 1504 Spanish, and from 1714 Austrian Netherlands

The territories were held by the Dukes of Burgundy, principally as Dukes of Luxembourg and of Brabant, and Counts of Flanders, Holland, Zeeland, Hainault and Artois. From 26 Nov 1504 Philip the Fair (Duke from 27 Mar 1482 to 25 Sep 1506) was King of Spain, and his successor Charles (d. 21 Sep 1558) was also German Emperor from 1519. In the earlier period the appointment of stadholders was not continuous. In 1568 Holland and Zeeland, with Friesland and Gelderland, revolted. For stadholders of these independent provinces see above.

1489 – 1494	*Albert of Saxe-Meissen* (b. 27 Jul 1433; d. 12 Sep 1500)
1505 – 1507	*Guillaume de Croy, Lord of Chièvres* (d. 1521)
1507 – 1515, 1518 – 30 Nov 1530	*Margaret*, daughter of Emperor Maximilian I (b. 10 Jan 1480
1531 – 1555	*Mary*, sister of Emperor Charles V, widow of King Louis II of Hungary (b. 17 Sep 1505; d. 18 Oct 1558)
1558 – 1559	*Emanuel Philibert, Duke of Savoy*, son of King Charles III of Savoy (b. 8 Jul 1528; d. 30 Aug 1580)
1559 – 1567	*Margaret of Parma*, illegitimate daughter of Emperor Charles V (b. 28 Dec 1522; d. 18 Jan. 1586)
1567 – 1573	*Fernando Álvarez de Toledo, Duke of Alba* (b. 29 Oct 1507; d. 11 Dec 1582)

1573 – 1576	*Luis de Requesens y Zúñiga* (b. Barcelona; d. Brussels 5 Mar 1576)
1576 – 7 Oct 1578	*Don John of Austria*, illegitimate son of Emperor Charles V (b. 24 Feb 1547)
1578 – 11 Dec 1592	*Alessandro, Duke of Parma*, son of Ottavio, Duke of Parma (b. 27 Aug 1545)
1592 – 1594	*Peter Ernst, Count Mansfeld-Heldrungen* (b. 1517; d. 1604)
1594 – 20 Feb 1595	*Ernst, Archduke of Austria*, brother of Emperor Rudolph II (b. 15 Jun 1553)
1595 – 1596	*Pedro Henríquez d'Azovedo y Toledo, Duke of Fuentes* (b. c. 1535; d. 22 Jul 1610)
1596 – 13 Jul 1621	*Albert (Albrecht), Archduke of Austria*, brother of Emperor Rudolf II (b. 13 Nov 1559)
1621 – 29 Nov 1633	*Isabella Klara Eugenie*, wife of the above (b. 12 Aug 1566)
1633 – 1641	*Ferdinand*, son of King Philip III of Spain (b. 1609)
1641 – 1644	*Francisco de Mello, Marquis de Ter*
1641 – 1647	*Emanuel de Moura-Cortereal, Marquis of Castel Rodrigo* (d. 1661)
1647 – 1656	*Leopold Wilhelm*, son of Emperor Ferdinand II (b. 6 Jan 1614; d. 20 Nov 1662)
1656 – Mar 1659	*John of Austria*, son of King Philip IV of Spain (b. 7 Apr 1629; d. 17 Sep 1679)
1659 – Sep 1664	*Luis de Benavides Carillo, Marquis Franiata* (d. 1668
1664 – Sep 1668	*Francisco de Moura-Cortereal, Marquis of Caste Rodrigo* (d. 1675)
1668 – Jul 1670	*Inigo Fernández de Valesco y Tovar, Duke of Feric*
1670 – Feb 1675	*Juan Domingo de Maro Duke of Monterrey* (d. 1716
1675 – Dec 1677	*Carlos de Aragón de Gurrea Borja y Aragón, Duke o Villahermosa* (d. 14 Aug 1692)
1678 – 1682	*Alessandero*, son of Duke Odoardo I of Parma (b 1635; d. 11 Feb 1689)
1682 – 1685	*Ottone Hernrico dal Carreto, Marquis of Grana*
1685 – 1692	*Francisco Antonio de Agurto, Marquis of Gastañag*
1692 – 1706	*Maximilian II of Bavaria*, son of Duke Ferdinand o Bavaria (b. 11 Jul 1662; d. 26 Feb 1726)
22 Mar 1701 – 7 Oct 1704	*Isidor de la Cueba, Marquis of Bedmar*, Deputy of th foregoing
1706 – 7 Mar 1714	Administration by a Council of State
1716 – Dec 1724	*Eugene, Prince of Savoy*, son of Prince Eugen Maurice of Savoy (b. 18 Oct 1663; d. 21 Apr 1736
1725 – 26 Aug 1741	*Marie Elisabeth*, daughter of Emperor Leopold I (

	13 Dec 1680)
1741 – 1744	*Friedrich August, Count Harrach-Rohrau*
1744 – 4 Jul 1780	*Marie Anna*, Daughter of Emperor Charles VI (b. 14 Sep 1718) from 7 Jan 1744 married to *Karl Alexander Emanuel*, brother of Emperor Franz I (b. 12 Dec 1712)
1781 – 1793	*Christine*, daughter of Emperor Franz I (b. 13 May 1742; d. 24 Jun 1798) from 8 Apr 1766 married to *Albert, Duke of Teschen*, son of Prince Friedrich August II of Saxony (b. 11 Jul 1738 d. 10 Feb 1822)
1793 – 1794	*Karl II*, son of Emperor Leopold II (b. 5 Sep 1771; d. 30 Apr 1847)

MEMBERS OF GOVERNMENT

Great Pensionaries

Jul 1572 – 1585	*Paulus Buys* (b. Amersfoort 1531; d. Ysselstein 4 May 1594)
Mar 1586 – 29 Aug 1618	*Johan. van Oldenbarnevelt* (b. Amersfoort 14 Sep 1547; d. The Hague 13 May 1619)
May 1619 – 1621	(acting:) *Andries de Witt* (b. Dordrecht 16 Jun 1573; d. The Hague (?) 26 Nov 1637)
2 Jan 1621 – 13 Sep 1628	*Anthonius Duyck* (b. The Hague c. 1560; d. 13 Sep 1629)
Sep 1629 – 1631	(acting:) *Jacob Cats* (for 1st time) (b. Brouwershaven 10 Nov 1577; d. The Hague 12 Sep 1660)
Apr 1631 – 1636	*Adriaan Pauw* (for 1st time) (b. Amsterdam 1 Nov 1585; d. 21 Feb 1653)
Jun 1636 – 1651	*Jacob Cats* (for 2nd time)
7 Sep 1651 – 21 Feb 1653	*Adriaan Pauw* (for 2nd time)
8 Jul 1653 – 4 Aug 1672	*Johan de Witt* (b. Dordrecht 24 Sep 1625; d. The Hague 20 Aug 1672)
4 Aug 1672 – 15 Dec 1688	*Caspar Fagel* (baptised The Hague 25 Jan 1634; d. 15 Dec 1688)
4 Dec 1688	(acting:) *Michel ten Hove*
Mar/27 May 1689 – 3 Aug 1720	*Anthonie Heinsius* (b. Delft 23 Nov 1641; d. The Hague 3 Aug 1720)
Sep 1720 – 17 Jun 1727	*Isaak van Hoornbeek* (b. Leiden 1653/56; d. 17 Jun 1727)
Jul 1727 – 1 Dec 1736	*Simon van Slingelandt* (b. Dordrecht 14 Jan 1664; d. 1 Dec 1736)

4 Apr 1737 – 1746	*Anthonie van der Heim* (b. 1693; d. 17 Jul 1746)
23 Sep 1746 – 1749	*Jacob Gilles*
12/18 Jun 1749 – 5 Nov 1772	*Pieter Steyn* (b. Haarlem 6 Oct 1706; d. 5 Nov 1772)
1 Dec 1722 – Nov 1787	*Pieter van Bleiswijk* (b. Delft 1724; d. 29 Oct 1790)
9 Nov 1787 – Jan 1795	*Laurens Pieter van de Spiegel* (b. Middelburg 19 Jan 1737; d. Lingen 7 May 1800)
1795 – 1805	Batavian Republic
29 Apr 1805 – 4 Jun 1806	*Rutger Jan* (from 1811: *Count*) *Schimmelpenninck* (b. Deventer 31 Oct 1761; d. Amsterdam 25 Mar 1825)

CABINETS*

25 Mar – 21 Nov 1848: Provisional Ministry: Schimmelpenninck

Prime Minister	*Gerrit, Count Schimmelpenninck* (b. Amsterdam 25 Feb 1794; d. Arnhem 4 Oct 1863)
Foreign Affairs	25 Mar – 17 May 1848: *Gerrit, Count Schimmelpenninck* (see above)
	17 May – 21 Nov 1848: *Arnold Adolf, Baron Bentinck of Nijenhuis* (b. Nijenhuis 17 Apr 1798; d. London 2 Mar 1868)
Home Affairs	25 Mar – 13 May 1848: *Lodewijk Caspar Luzac* (b Leiden 1 Aug 1786; d. The Hague 18 Feb 1861)
	13 May – 21 Nov 1848: *Jacob Mattaeus de Kempenaer* (b. Amsterdam 6 Jul 1793; d. Arnhem 11 Feb 1870)
Justice	*Dirk Donker Curtius* (b. Herzogenbusch 19 Oct 1792 d. Spa 17 Jul 1863)
Finance	25 Mar – 17 May 1848: *Gerrit, Count Schimmelpenninck* (see above)
	17 May – 3 Jun 1848 (acting:) *P. A. Ossewaarde*
	3 Jun – 21 Nov 1848: *Peter Philip van Bosse* (b Amsterdam 16 Dec 1809; d. The Hague 21 Feb 1879)
War	25 Mar – 22 May 1848: *Charles* (from 27 Jul 1849 *Baron*) *Nepveu* (b. Zandbergen 5 Oct 1791; d Bergendaal 6 Oct 1871)
	22 May – 21 Nov 1848: *G.H. Voet*
Navy	*Julius Constantijn Rijk* (b. Wetzlar 15 Jan 1787; d The Hague 2 May 1854)
Colonies	*Julius Constantijn Rijk* (see above)

*Up to 1945 – 46 there was strictly speaking no office of Prime Minister. The task of forming a cabinet was assigned to one or other of the departmental ministers.

Protestant Worship	25 Mar – 30 Jun 1848: *Lodewijk Caspar Luzac* (see above)
	30 Jun – 21 Nov 1848: *Schelte, Baron Heemstra* (b. Groningen 14 Nov 1807; d. St. Maartensdijk 20 Dec 1864)
Catholic Worship	*Leonardus Antonius Lightenvelt* (b. The Hague 28 Oct 1795; d. Hyères 29 Oct 1873)

21 Nov 1848 – 1 Nov 1894: de Kempenaer/Donker Curtius

Prime Minister	*Jacob Matthaeus de Kempenaer* and *Dirk Donker Curtius* (see Schimmelpenninck)
Foreign Affairs	*Leonardus A. Lightenvelt* (see Schimmelpenninck)
Home Affairs	*Jacob Mattaeus de Kempenaer* (see Schimmelpenninck)
Justice	21 Nov 1848 – 4 Jun 1849: *Dirk Donker Curtius* (see Schimmelpenninck)
	4 Jun – 25 Jul 1849: *Hendrik Ludolf Wichers* (b. Roden 21 Jun 1800; d. The Hague 4 Mar 1853)
	25 Aug – 1 Nov 1849: *Leonardus Antonius Lightenve* (see Schimmelpenninck)
Finance	*Peter Philip van Bosse* (see Schimmelpenninck)
War	*G.H. Voet* (see Schimmelpenninck)
Navy	21 Nov 1848 – 15 Sep 1849: *Julius Constantijn Rijk* (see Schimmelpenninck)
	15 Sep – 1 Nov 1849 (acting:) *Engelbertus Batavus van den Bosch* (b. Brussels 15 Sep 1789; d. Buitenzorg, Java 11 Feb 1851)
Colonies	21 Nov 1848 – 18 Jun 1849: *Guillaume Louis Baud* (b. The Hague 27 Dec 1801; d. The Hague 5 Jan 1891)
	18 Jun – 1 Nov 1849: *Engelbertus Batavus van den Bosch* (see above)
Protestant Worship	*Schelte, Baron Heemstra* (see Schimmelpenninck)
Catholic Worship	21 – 24 Nov 1848 (acting:) *Leonardus Antonius Lightenvelt* (see Schimmelpenninck)
	24 Nov 1848 – 1 Nov 1849: *Jacobus Arnoldus Mutsaers* (b. Tilburg 28 Jan 1805; d. The Hague 2 Feb 1880)

Nov 1849 – 19 Apr 1853: Thorbecke I

Prime Minister	*Johan Rudolf Thorbecke* (b. Zwolle 15 Jan 1798; d.

	The Hague 4 Jun 1872)
Foreign Affairs	1 Nov 1849 – 16 Oct 1852: *Herman van Sonsbeeck* (b. Zwolle 24 Jul 1796; d. Heino 29 Nov 1865)
	16 Oct 1852 – 19 Apr 1853: *Jacob Pieter Pompejus, Baron Zuylen* (b. Dordrecht 29 Jun 1816; d. The Hague 4 Nov 1890)
Home Affairs	*Johan Rudolf Thorbecke* (see above)
Justice	1 Nov 1849 – 15 Jul 1852: *Johan Theodoor Hendrik Nedermeijer, Count Rosenthal* (b. Culemborg 27 Mar 1792; d. The Hague 21 Jan 1857)
	15 Jul 1852 – 19 Apr 1853: *Martin Pascal Hubert Strens* (b. Roermond 28 Mar 1807; d. Maastricht 22 Jul 1875)
Finance	*Peter Philip van Bosse* (see Schimmelpenninck)
War	1 Nov 1849 – 15 Jul 1852: *Johannes Theodorus van Spengler* (b. Zwolle 4 Dec 1790; d. Gendringen 16 Nov 1856)
	15 Jul 1852 – 19 Apr 1853: *Hendrik Frederik Christoph, Baron Forstner van Dambenoy* (b. Maastricht 15 Aug 1792; d. Utrecht 23 Mar 1870)
Navy	1 Nov 1849 – 20 Apr 1851: *Engelbert Lucas*
	20 Apr – 1 Nov 1851 (acting:) *Johannes Theodorus van Spengler* (see above)
	1 Nov 1851 – 19 Apr 1853: *James Enslie* (b. Dordrecht 26 Dec 1795; d. The Hague 3 Jul 1877)
Colonies	*Charles Ferdinand Pahud* (from 1867: *de Mortanges*) (b. Amsterdam 18 Apr 1803; d. The Hague 31 Aug 1873)
Protestant Worship	1 Nov 1849 – 15 Jul 1852 (acting:) *Johan Theodoor Henrik Nedermeijer, Count Rosenthal* (see above)
	15 Aug 1852 – 19 Apr 1853 (acting:) *Peter Philip van Bosse* (see Schimmelpenninck)
Catholic Worship	1 Nov 1849 – 16 Oct 1852 (acting:) *Herman van Sonsbeeck* (see above)
	16 Oct 1852 – 19 Apr 1853 (acting:) *Martin Pascal Hubert Strens* (see above)

19 Apr 1853 – 1 Jul 1856: van Hall/Donker Curtius

Prime Minister	*Floris Adriaan* (from 1 Apr 1856: *Baron*) *van Hall* (for 1st time) (b. Amsterdam 15 May 1791; d. The Hague 29 Mar 1866) and *Dirk Donker Curtius* (for 2nd time) (see Schimmelpenninck)

Foreign Affairs	*Floris Adriaan, Baron van Hall* (see above)
Home Affairs	*Gerlach Cornelius Johannes van Reenen* (b. Amsterdam 13 Sep 1818; d. The Hague 31 May 1893)
Justice	*Dirk Donker Curtius* (see Schimmelpenninck)
Finance	19 Apr 1853 – 5 Jan 1854: *Elisa Cornelis Unico van Doorn* (b. Oosterwijk 13 Oct 1799; d. Maarn 2 Aug 1882)
	5 Jan – 30 Apr 1854 (acting:) *Floris Adriaan van Hall* (see above)
	30 Apr 1854 – 1 Jul 1856 (acting:) *Agnites Vrolik* (b. Amsterdam 28 Feb 1810; d. Amsterdam 8 Jun 1894)
War	*Hendrik Frederik Christoph, Baron Forstner van Dambenoy* (see Thorbecke I)
Navy	19 Apr 1853 – 16 Dec 1854: *James Enslie* (see Thorbecke I)
	16 Dec 1854 – 8 Feb 1855 (acting:) *Hendrik Frederik Christoph, Baron Forstner van Dambenoy* (see Thorbecke I)
	8 Feb 1855 – 1 Jul 1856: *Abraham Johannes de Smit van den Broecke* (b. Aardenburg 13 May 1801; d. Oost Souburg 1 Jan 1875)
Colonies	19 Apr 1853 – 31 Dec 1855: *Charles Ferdinand Pahud* (see Thorbecke I)
	1 Jan – 1 Jul 1856: *Pieter Mijer* (b. Batavia 3 Jun 1812; d. Scheveningen 6 Feb 1881)
Protestant Worship	19 Apr 1853 – 20 Jan 1854: *Elisa Cornelis Unico van Doorn* (see above)
	20 Jan 1854 – 1 Jul 1856: *Anthon Gerhard Alexander, Count van Rappard* (b. Utrecht 5 Oct 1790; d. Utrecht 1 Apr 1869)
Catholic Worship	19 Apr – 31 Dec 1853: *Leonardus Antonius Lightenvelt* (see Schimmelpenninck)
	1 Jan 1854 – 1 Jul 1856: *Jacobus Arnoldus Mutsaers* (see de Kempenaer/Donker Curtius)

Jul 1856 – 18 Mar 1858: van der Bruggen

Prime Minister	*Justinus Jacob Leonard van der Bruggen* (b. Nijmegen 6 Aug 1804; d. Ubbergen 2 Oct 1863)
Foreign Affairs	*Daniel Theodoor Gevers van Endegeest* (b. Rotterdam 25 Aug 1793; d. Endegeest 27 Jul 1877)
Home Affairs	1 Jul 1856 – 19 Jan 1857: *Gerrit Simons* (b. Uithoorn

369

	22 Jan 1802; d. The Hague 17 Nov 1868) 19 Jan 1857 – 18 Mar 1858: *Anthon Gerhard Alexander, Count van Rappard* (see van Hall/Donker Curtius)
Justice	*Justinus Jacob Leonard van der Bruggen* (see above)
Finance	*Agnites Vrolik* (see van Hall I)
War	1 Jul 1856 – 31 Dec 1857: *Hendrik Frederik Christoph, Baron Forstner van Dembenoy* (see Thorbecke I) 1 Jan – 18 Mar 1858: *Cornelis Theodorus van Meurs* (b. The Hague 13 Nov 1799; d. The Hague 29 Jan 1894)
Navy	1 Jul – 1 Aug 1856: *Abraham Johannes de Smit van den Broecke* (see van Hall/Donker Curtius) 1 Aug 1856 – 18 Mar 1858: *Johannes Servaas Lotsy* (b. Dordrecht 31 May 1808; d. The Hague 4 Apr 1863)
Colonies	*Pieter Mijer* (see Van Hall/Donker Curtius)
Protestant Worship	1 Jul 1856 – 19 Jan 1857: *Anthon Gerhard Alexander, Count van Rappard* (see van Hall/Donker Curtius) 19 Jan 1857 – 18 Mar 1858: *Meindert Wiardi Beckman* (b. Amsterdam 16 Jan 1793; d. The Hague 8 Apr 1863)
Catholic Worship	1 Jul – 1 Aug 1856: *Jacobus Arnoldus Mutsaers* (see de Kempenaer/Donker Curtius) 1 Aug 1856 – 18 Mar 1858: *Joannes Wilhelmus van Romunde* (b. Kampen 17 Jul 1802; d. The Hague 4 Mar 1860)

18 Mar 1858 – 23 Feb 1860: Rochussen/van Bosse

Prime Minister	*Jan Jacob Rochussen* (b. Etten 23 Oct 1797; d. The Hague 21 Jan 1871) and *Peter Philip van Bosse* (for 1st time) (see Schimmelpenninck)
Foreign Affairs	*Jan Karel* (from 14 Jan 1815: *Baron van Goltstein*) (b. Arnhem 3 Jun 1794; d. The Hague 17 Feb 1872)
Home Affairs	*Jacob George Hieronymus Tets van Goudriaan* (b. Haarlem 7 Dec 1812; d. Nijmegen 14 Mar 1885)
Justice	*Cornelis Hendrik Boudewijn Boot* (b. Arnhem 15 Sep 1813; d. The Hague 5 Nov 1892)
Finance	*Peter Philip van Bosse* (see Schimmelpenninck)
Colonies	*Jan Jacob Rochussen* (see above)
War	18 Mar 1858 – 1 Sep 1859: *Cornelis Theodorus van Meurs* (see van der Bruggen) 1 Sep 1859 – 23 Feb 1860: *Eduard August Otto de Casembroot* (b. Oud Vossemeer 20 Jun 1813; d. The Hague 28 Sep 1883)

Navy	*Johannes Servaas Lotsy* (see van der Bruggen)
Protestant Worship	18 Mar – 3 Apr 1858 (acting:) *Cornelis Hendrik Boudewijn Boot* (see above)
	3 Apr 1858 – 23 Feb 1860: *Joannes Bosscha* (b. Harderwijk 19 Mar 1797; d. Amsterdam 9 Dec 1874)
Catholic Worship	*Joannes Wilhelmus van Romunde* (see van der Bruggen)

23 Feb 1860 – 14 Mar 1861: van Hall/Heemstra

Prime Minister	*Floris Adriaan, Baron van Hall* (for 2nd time) (see van Hall/Donker Curtius) and *Schelte, Baron Heemstra* (see Schimmelpenninck)
Foreign Affairs	23 Feb – 8 Mar 1860 (acting:) *Floris Adriaan, Baron van Hall* (see van Hall/Donker Curtius)
	8 Mar 1860 – 14 Jan 1861: *Julius Philipr Jacob Adriaan, Count van Zuylen van Nijevelt* (b. Luxembourg 29 Aug 1819; d. The Hague 1 Jul 1894)
	14 Jan – 14 Mar 1861: *Louis Napoleon, Baron van der Goes van Dirxland* (b. Oostbroek 28 Jul 1806; d. The Hague 19 Mar 1895)
Home Affairs	*Schelte, Baron Heemstra* (see Schimmelpenninck)
Justice	23 Feb – 9 Mar 1860 (acting:) *Jacobus Arnoldus Mutsaers* (see de Kempenaer/Donker Curtius)
	9 Mar 1860 – 14 Mar 1861: *Michael Hendrik Godefroi* (b. Amsterdam 16 Dec 1813; d. Würzburg 25 Jun 1882)
Finance	23 Feb 1860 – 23 Feb 1861: *Floris Adriaan, Baron van Hall* (see van Hall/Donker Curtius)
	23 Feb – 14 Mar 1861 (acting:) *Johannes Servaas Lotsy* (see van der Bruggen)
War	*Eduard August Otto de Casembroot* (see Rochussen/van Bosse)
Navy	*Johannes Servaas Lotsy* (see van der Bruggen)
Colonies	23 Feb – 31 Dec 1860: *Jan Jacob Rochussen* (see Rochussen/van Bosse)
	1 – 9 Jan 1861 (acting:) *Johannes Servaas Lotsy* (see van der Bruggen)
	9 Jan – 14 Mar 1861: *Johan Pieter Cornets de Groot van Krayenburg* (b. Groningen 6 Apr 1808; d. The Hague 2 Jul 1878)
Protestant Worship	*Joannes Bosscha* (see Rochussen/van Bosse)
Catholic Worship	*Jocobus Arnoldus Mutsaers* (see de Kempenaer/Donker Curtius)

371

14 Mar 1861 - 31 Jan 1862: van Zuylen/Loudon

Prime Minister	*Julius Philipp Jacob Adriaan, Count van Zuylen van Nijevelt* (for 1st time) (see van Hall/Heemstra) and *James Loudon* (b. The Hague 8 Jun 1824; d. The Hague 31 May 1900)
Foreign Affairs	*Julius Philipp Jacob Adriaan, Count van Zuylen van Nijevelt* (see van Hall/Heemstra)
Home Affairs	*Schelte, Baron Heemstra* (see Schimmelpenninck)
Justice	*Michael Hendrik Godefroi* (see van Hall/Heemstra)
Finance	*Jacob George Hieronymus Tets van Goudriaan* (see Rochussen/van Bosse)
War	*Eduard August Otto de Casembroot* (see Rochussen/van Bosse)
Navy	*Willem Johan Cornelis, Count Huyssen van Kattendijke* (b. The Hague 22 Jan 1816; d. The Hague 6 Feb 1866)
Colonies	*James Loudon* (see above)
Protestant Worship	*Jolle Albertus Jolles* (b. Amsterdam 28 Dec 1814; d. Amsterdam 23 Dec 1882)
Catholic Worship	*Martin Pascal Hubert Strens* (see Thorbecke I)

1 Feb 1862 - 10 Feb 1866: Thorbecke II

Prime Minister	*Jan Rudolf Thorbecke* (for 2nd time) (see Thorbecke I)
Foreign Affairs	1 Feb - 13 Mar 1862 (acting:) *Anthony Jan Lucas, Baron Stratenus* (b. The Hague 22 Jul 1807; d. The Hague 18 Apr 1872)
	13 Mar 1862 - 2 Jan 1864: *Paul Thérèse van de Maesen de Sombreff* (b. Maastricht 25 Oct 1827; d. Maastricht 14 Nov 1902)
	2 Jan - 15 Mar 1864: (acting:) *Willem Johan Cornelis, Count Huyssen van Kattendijke* (see van Zuylen/Loudon)
	15 Mar 1864 - 10 Feb 1866: *Epimachus Jacobus Johannes Baptista Cremers* (b. Groningen 15 Jun 1823; d. Zurich 27 Oct 1896)
Home Affairs	*Johan Rudolf Thorbecke* (see Thorbecke I)
Justice	*Nicolaas Olivier* (b. Utrecht 1 Aug 1808; d. The Hague 12 Nov 1869)
Finance	1 Feb 1862 - 27 Nov 1865: *Gerardus Henri Betz* (b. Breda 30 Oct 1816; d. The Hague 20 May 1868)

27 Nov 1865 – 10 Feb 1866 (acting:) *Nicolaas Olivier* (see above)

War	*Johan Willem Blanken* (b. Emden 27 Jun 1806; d. Bloemendaal 25 Jun 1880)
Navy	1 Feb 1862 – 6 Feb 1866: *Willem Johan Cornelis, Count Huyssen van Kattendijke* (see van Zuylen/Loudon)
	6 – 10 Feb 1866: *Johan Willem Blanken* (see above)
Colonies	1 Feb 1862 – 3 Jan 1863: *Gerard Hendrik Uhlenbeck* (b. Colombo, Ceylon 17 Feb 1815; d. The Hague 2 May 1888)
	3 Jan – 2 Feb 1863 (acting:) *Gerardus Henri Betz* (see above)
	2 Feb 1863 – 10 Feb 1866: *Isaac Dignus Fransen van de Putte* (b. Goes 22 Mar 1822; d. The Hague 3 May 1902)
Protestant Worship	1 Feb – 1 Jul 1862: *Jolle Albertus Jolles* (see van Zuylen/Loudon)
	from 1 Jul 1862: post abolished
Catholic Worship	1 Feb – 1 Jul 1862: *K. A. Meeussen* (b. Bergen op Zoom 9 Mar 1815; d. The Hague 24 Jan 1884)
	from 1 Jul 1862: post abolished

10 Feb – 1 Jun 1866: Fransen van de Putte

Prime Minister	*Isaac Dignus Fransen van de Putte* (see Thorbecke II)
Foreign Affairs	*Epimachus Jacobus Johannes Baptista Cremers* (see Thorbecke II)
Home Affairs	*Johan Hendrik Geertsema* (b. Groningen 30 Jul 1816; d. Utrecht 15 Apr 1908)
Justice	*Carolus Joannes Picke* (b. Steenhoven 21 Apr 1831; d. Middelburg 18 Mar 1887)
Finance	*Peter Philip van Bosse* (see Schimmelpenninck)
War	*Johan Willem Blanken* (see Thorbecke II)
Navy	(acting:) *Johan Willem Blanken* (see Thorbecke II)
Colonies	*Isaac Dignus Fransen van de Putte* (see Thorbecke II)

1 Jun 1866 – 4 Jun 1868: van Zuylen/Heemskerk

Prime Minister	*Julius Philipp Jacob Adriaan, Count van Zuylen van Nijevelt* (for 2nd time) (see van Zuylen/Loudon) and *Jan Heemskerk* (b. Amsterdam 30 Jul 1818; d. The Hague 9 Oct 1897)

Foreign Affairs	*Julius Philipp Jacob Adriaan, Count van Zuylen van Nijevelt* (see van ̓Zuylen/ Loudon)
Home Affairs	*Jan Heemskerk* (see above)
Justice	1 Jun 1866 – 10 Nov 1867: *Eduard Joseph Hubert Borret* (b. 's Hertogenbosch 17 Aug 1816; d. The Hague 10 Nov 1867)
	10 Nov 1867 – 10 Jan 1868 (acting:) *Jan Heemskerk* (see above)
	4 Jan – 4 Jun 1868: *Willem Wintgens* (b. The Hague 8 Jan 1818; d. The Hague 12 Jan 1895)
Finance	*Rutger Jan, Count Schimmelpenninck van Nijenhuis* (b. Amsterdam 9 May 1821; d. The Hague 23 Apr 1893)
War	*J. A. van den Bosch*
Navy	*G. C. C. Pels Rijcken*
Colonies	1 Jun – 17 Sep 1866: *Pieter Mijer* (see van Hall/ Donker Curtius)
	17 Sep 1866 – 20 Jul 1867: *Nicolaas van Taack* (b. Amsterdam 3 Apr 1819; d. Heemstede 11 Aug 1890)
	20 Jul 1867 – 4 Apr 1868: *Johannes Jerphaas Hasselman* (b. Nederhemert 21 Oct 1815; d. Tiel 27 Mar 1895)
Protestant Worship	15 Jan – 4 Jun 1868 (post re-created): *Constantijn Theodoor, Baron* (from 1882: *Count*) *van Lynden van Sandenburg* (b. Utrecht 24 Feb 1826; d. Sandenburg 8 Nov 1885)
Catholic Worship	15 Jan – 4 Jun 1868 (post re-created): *Aloysius Franciscus Xaverius Luyben* (b. Waalwijk 20 Jan 1818; d. 's Hertogenbosch 9 Jun 1902)

4 Jun 1868 – 4 Jan 1871: van Bosse II

Prime Minister	*Peter Philip van Bosse* (for 2nd time) (see Schimmelpenninck)
Foreign Affairs	4 – 8 Jun 1868 (acting:) *J. J. van Mulken*
	8 Jun 1868 – 12 Dec 1870: *Theodorus Marinus Roest van Limburg* (b. Rotterdam 8 Jul 1806; d. Florence 3 Mar 1887)
	12 Dec 1870 – 4 Jan 1871 (acting:) *J. J. van Mulken* (see above)
Home Affairs	*Cornelis Fock* (b. Amsterdam 29 Nov 1828; d. The Hague 9 May 1910)

Justice	*Franciscus Gerardus Reinierus Hubertus van Lilaar* (b. Amersfoort 9 Nov 1823; d. The Hague 23 Apr 1889)
Finance	*Peter Philip van Bosse* (see Schimmelpenninck)
War	*J. J. van Mulken* (see above)
Navy	*L. G. Brocx*
Colonies	4 Jun 1868 – 16 Nov 1870: *Engelbertus de Waal* (b. The Hague 27 Nov 1821; d. The Hague 1 Jul 1905)
	16 Nov 1870 – 4 Jan 1871 (acting:) *L. G. Brocx* (see above)
·Protestant Worship	4 Jun – 29 Jul 1868: *Peter Philip van Bosse* (see Schimmelpenninck)
	29 Jul 1868: post abolished
Catholic Worship	4 Jun – 29 Jul 1868: *Franciscus Gerardus Reinierus Hubertus van Lilaar* (see above)
	29 Jul 1868: post abolished

4 Jan 1871 – 5 Jul 1872: Thorbecke III

Prime Minister	*Jan Rudolf Thorbecke* (for 3rd time) (see Thorbecke I)
Foreign Affairs	4 – 18 Jan 1871 (acting:) *J. J. van Mulken* (see van Bosse)
	18 Jan 1871 – 5 Jul 1872: *Joseph Louis Heinrich Alfred* (from 12 May 1874: *Baron*) *Gericke van Herwijnen* (b. Dillenburg 18 Feb 1814; d. Brussels 10 May 1899)
Home Affairs	*Johan Rudolf Thorbecke* (see Thorbecke I)
Justice	*Jolle Albertus Jolles* (see van Zuylen / Loudon)
Finance	*Pieter Blusse van Oud-Alblas* (b. Dordrecht 11 Mar 1812; d. The Hague 19 May 1887)
War	4 – 28 Jan 1871: *Gerard Petrus Booms* (b. Maastricht 29 Oct 1822; d. The Hague 23 Feb 1897)
	28 Jan – 23 Dec 1871: *A. Engelvaart*
	23 Dec 1871 – 5 Feb 1872 (acting:) *L. G. Brocx* (see van Bosse)
	5 Feb – 5 Jul 1872: *Félix Albert Théodore Delprat* (b. The Hague 12 May 1812; d. Amsterdam 7 Apr 1888)
Navy	*L. G. Brocx* (see van Bosse)
Colonies	*Peter Philip van Bosse* (see Schimmelpenninck)

5 Aug 1872 – 20 Jun 1874: de Vries / van de Putte

Prime Minister	*Gerrit de Vries* (b. Haarlem 22 Feb 1818; d. The Hague 4 Mar 1900) and *Isaac Dignus Fransen van de Putte* (see Thorbecke II)

NETHERLANDS

Foreign Affairs	*Joseph Louis Heinrich Alfred, Baron Gericke van Herwijnen* (see Thorbecke III)
Home Affairs	*Johan Hendrik Geertsema* (see van de Putte)
Justice	*Gerrit de Vries* (see above)
Finance	*Albert van Delden* (b. Deventer 20 Feb 1828; d. Deventer 8 Nov 1898)
War	6 Jul 1872 – 13 Sep 1873: *Menno David, Count, van Limburg-Stirum* (b. Wexford 30 Nov 1807; d. The Hague 22 Jul 1891)
	15 Sep – 6 Oct 1873 (acting:) *L. G. Brocx* (see van Bosse)
	6 Oct 1873 – 20 Jun 1874: *August Wilhelm Philip Weitzel* (b. The Hague 1816; d. The Hague 1896)
Navy	6 Jul 1872 – 18 Dec 1873: *L. G. Brocx* (see van Bosse)
	18 Dec 1873 – 16 May 1874: *Isaac Dignus Fransen van de Putte* (see Thorbecke II)
	16 May – 20 Jun 1874: *Willem Frederik van Erp Taalman Kip* (b. The Hague 19 Dec 1824; d. The Hague 16 Mar 1905)
Colonies	*Isaac Dignus Fransen van de Putte* (see Thorbecke II)

27 Aug 1874 – 25 Sep 1877: Heemskerk/van Lynden

Prime Minister	*Jan Heemskerk* (for 2nd time) (see van Zuylen/Heemskerk)
	Constantijn Theodoor, Baron van Lynden van Sandenburg (for 1st time) (see van Zuylen/Heemskerk)
Foreign Affairs	until 18 Oct 1877: *Pieter Joseph August Maria van der Does de Willebois* (b. 's Hertogenbosch 17 Feb 1816 d. The Hague 15 Sep 1892)
Home Affairs	*Jan Heemskerk* (see van Zuylen/Heemskerk)
Justice	*Constantijn Theodoor, Baron van Lynden van Sandenburg* (see van Zuylen/Heemskerk)
Finance	*Hendrik Jacob Baron van der Heim* (b. Middelburg 1? Jan 1824; d. Florence 13 Feb 1890)
War	27 Aug 1874 – 29 Apr 1875: *August Wilhelm Philip Weitzel* (see de Vries/van de Putte)
	29 Apr 1875 – 1 Jan 1876: *Hendrik Johanne Enderlein* (b. Alkmaar 7 Mar 1821; d. The Hague 2? Dec 1898)
	1 Jan – 1 Feb 1876 (acting:) *Willem Frederik van Erp Taalman Kip* (see de Vries/van de Putte)

	1 Feb – 11 Sep 1876: *Guillaume Jean Gérard Klerck* (b. Liège 13 Feb 1825; d. The Hague 17 Jan 1884)
11 – 30 Sep 1876	(acting:) *Willem Frederik van Erp Taalman Kip* (see de Vries/van de Putte)
	30 Sep 1876 – 25 Sep 1877: *Hendrik Johan Rudolf Beyen* (b. Ijsselstein 20 Feb 1817; d. The Hague 19 Jul 1892)
Navy	*Willem Frederik van Erp Taalman Kip* (see de Vries/van de Putte)
Colonies	27 Aug 1874 – 11 Sep 1876: *Willem, Baron van Goltstein van Oldenaller* (b. Hamburg 13 May 1831; d. Oldenaller 9 Sep 1901)
	11 Sep 1876 – 25 Sep 1877: *Fokko Alting Mees* (b. Appingedam 27 Nov 1819; d. Amsterdam 1 Jun 1900)

3 Nov 1877 – 11 Aug 1879: Kappeyne van de Coppello

Prime Minister	*Johannes Kappeyne van de Coppello* (b. The Hague 2 Oct 1822; d. The Hague 28 Jul 1895)
Foreign Affairs	*Willem, Baron van Heeckeren van Kell* (b. Ruurlo 1 Jul 1815; d. Ruurlo 10 Feb 1914)
Home Affairs	*Johannes Kappeyne van de Coppello* (see above)
Justice	*Hendrik Jan Smidt*
Finance	*Johan George Gleichman* (b. Rotterdam 19 Jul 1834; d. The Hague 30 Apr 1906)
Water, Commerce and Industry	8 Nov 1877 – 11 Jul 1879: *Joannes Pieter Roetert Tak van Poortvliet* (b. Engelen 21 Jun 1839; d. The Hague 26 Jan 1904)
War	3 Nov 1877 – 31 Dec 1878: *Johan Karel Hendrik de Roo van Alderwerelt* (b. Harderwijk 6 Aug 1832; d. The Hague 31 Dec 1878)
	31 Dec 1878 – 1 Feb 1879 (acting:) *Hendericus Octavius Wichers* (b. Winschoten 5 May 1831; d. Amsterdam 23 Jan 1889)
	1 Feb – 11 Jul 1879: *Jacobus Catharinus Cornelis den Beer Poortugael* (b. Leiden 1 Feb 1832; d. The Hague 30 Jan 1913)
Navy	*Hendericus Octavius Wichers* (see above)
Colonies	3 Nov 1877 – 21 Feb 1879: *Peter Philip van Bosse* (see Schimmelpenninck)
	26 Feb – 12 Mar 1879 (acting:) *Hendericus Octavius Wichers* (see above)
	12 Mar – 11 Jul 1879: *Otto van Rees* (b. Culemborg 4

Jan 1823; d. Arnhem 10 Mar 1892)

20 Aug 1879 – 1 Mar 1883: van Lynden

Prime Minister	*Constantijn Theodoor, Baron* (from 24 Aug 1882: *Count*) *van Lynden van Sandenburg* (for 2nd time) (see van Zuylen/ Heemskerk)
Foreign Affairs	20 Aug 1879 – 15 Sep 1881: *Constantijn Theodoor, Baron van Lynden van Sandenburg* (see van Zuylen/ Heemskerk) 15 Sep 1881 – 1 Mar 1883: *Willem Frederik Rochussen* (b. Amsterdam 18 Dec 1832; d. The Hague 17 Jul 1912)
Home Affairs	20 Aug 1879 – 10 Feb 1882: *Willem Six* (b. Utrecht 20 Aug 1829; d. The Hague 15 Feb 1908) 10 Feb 1882 – 1 Mar 1883: *Cornelis Pijnacker Hordijk* (b. Drupt 13 Apr 1847; d. Haarlem 3 Sept 1908)
Justice	*Antony Ewoud Jan Modderman* (b. Winschoten 27 Sep 1838; d. The Hague 7 Aug 1885)
Finance	20 Aug 1879 – 13 Jun 1881: *Simon Vissering* (b. Amsterdam 23 Jun 1818; d. Ellecom 21 Aug 1888) 13 Jun 1881 – 1 Mar 1883: *Constantijn Theodoor, Count van Lynden van Sandenburg* (see van Zuylen/ Heemskerk)
Water, Commerce and Industry	*Guillaume Jean Gérard Klerck* (see Heemskerk/ van Lynden)
War	*A. E. Reuther*
Navy	*Willem Frederik van Erp Taalman Kip* (see de Vries/ van de Putte)
Colonies	20 Aug 1879 – 1 Sep 1882: *Willem, Baron van Goltstein van Oldenaller* (see Heemskerk/ van Lynden) 1 Sep 1882 – 23 Feb 1883: *Willem Maurits de Brauw* (b. The Hague 24 Aug 1838; d. The Hague 18 Dec 1898) 23 Feb – 1 Mar 1883 (acting:) *Willem Frederik van Erp Taalman Kip* (see de Vries/ van de Putte)

23 Apr 1883 – 21 Apr 1888: Jan Heemskerk

Prime Minister	*Jan Heemskerk* (for 3rd time) (see van Zuylen/ Heemskerk)
Foreign Affairs	23 Apr 1883 – 1 Nov 1885: *Pieter J. A. M. van de Does*

	de Willebois (see Heemskerk/van Lynden)
	1 Nov 1885 – 21 Apr 1888: *Abraham Pieter Cornelis van Karnebeek* (b. Amsterdam 14 Sep 1836; d. The Hague 8 Oct 1925)
Home Affairs	*Jan Heemskerk* (see van Zuylen/Heemskerk)
Justice	*Marc Willem, Baron du Tour van Bellinchave* (b. Leewarden 29 Jul 1835; d. 't Hassink 26 Jul 1908)
Finance	23 Apr 1883 – 4 May 1885: *W. J. L. Grobbée*
	4 May 1885 – 21 Apr 1888: *Jacobus Cornelis Groen* (b. Tilburg 25 Feb 1822; d. 1 Sep 1902)
Water, Commerce and Industry	23 Apr 1883 – 11 Jul 1887: *Johannes Gregorius van den Bergh* (b. Wijk 23 Dec 1824; d. Maastricht 27 May 1890)
	11 Jul 1887 – 21 Apr 1888: *Jacob Cornelis Bastert* (b. Breukelen 4 Nov 1826; d. Maarseveen 29 Oct 1902)
War	*August Wilhelm Philip Weitzel* (see de Vries/van de Putte)
Navy	23 Apr 1883 – 19 Apr 1884: *Frederik Lambertus Geerling* (b. Maastricht 4 May 1815; d. The Hague 12 Jan 1894)
	19 Apr 1884 – 4 Aug 1885: *Willem Frederik van Erp Taalman Kip* (see de Vries/van de Putte)
	4 Aug 1885 – 26 Jan 1887: *Willem Lodewijk Adolphe Gericke*
	26 Jan 1887 – 21 Apr 1888: *Frederik Cornelis Trop* (b. Flushing 13 Mar 1828; d. The Hague 19 Jul 1900)
Colonies	23 Apr – 25 Nov 1883: *Francois Gerard van Bloemen Waanders* (b. Antwerp 4 Jul 1825; d. The Hague 22 Jul 1892)
	25 Nov 1883 – 27 Feb 1884 (acting:) *August Wilhelm Philip Weitzel* (see de Vries/van de Putte)
	27 Feb 1884 – 21 Apr 1888: *Jacobus Petrus Sprenger van Eyk* (b. Hilvarenbeek 1842; d. Utrecht 20 Mar 1907)

21 Apr 1888 – 21 Aug 1891: Mackay

Prime Minister	*Aeneas, Baron Mackay* (b. Nijmegen 29 Nov 1838; d. The Hague 13 Nov 1909)
Foreign Affairs	*Cornelis Hartsen* (b. Amsterdam 23 Jan 1823; d. Hilversum 11 Oct 1895)
Home Affairs	21 Apr 1888 – 24 Feb 1890: *Aeneas, Baron Mackay* (see above)

	24 Feb 1890 – 21 Aug 1891: *Alexander Frederik de Savornin Lohman* (b. Groningen 29 May 1837; d. The Hague 11 Jun 1924)
Justice	*Gustave Louis Marie Hubert Ruys de Beerenbrouck* (b. Roermond 26 Sep 1842; d. Born 6 Feb 1926)
Finance	*Karel Antonie Godin de Beaufort* (b. Utrecht 16 Jan 1850; d. Maarsbergen 7 Apr 1921)
Water, Commerce and Industry	*Jacob Petrus Havelaar* (b. Rotterdam 23 Jan 1840; d. The Hague 7 Apr 1918)
War	*Johannes Wilhelm Bergansius*
Navy	21 Apr 1888 – 31 Mar 1891: *Hendrik Dyserinck* (b. Haarlem 11 Mar 1838; d. Rheden 27 Sep 1906)
	31 Mar – 21 Aug 1891: *Gerhardus Kruys* (b. Vriezenveen 21 Aug 1838; d. The Hague 12 Dec 1902)
Colonies	21 Apr 1888 – 24 Feb 1890: *Levinus Wilhelmus Christiaan Keuchenius* (b. Batavia 21 Oct 1822; d. The Hague 17 Dec 1893)
	24 Feb 1890 – 21 Aug 1891: *Aeneas, Baron Mackay* (see above)

21 Aug 1891 – 9 May 1894: van Tienhoven

Prime Minister	*Cijsbert van Tienhoven* (b. Sleewijk 12 Feb 1841; d. Bentveld 10 Oct 1914)
Foreign Affairs	21 Aug 1891 – 21 Mar 1894: *Gijsbert van Tienhoven* (see above)
	21 Mar – 9 May 1894 (acting:) *Joannes Coenraad Jansen*
Home Affairs	*Joannes Pieter Roetert Tak van Poortvliet* (see Kappeyne van de Coppello)
Justice	*Hendrik Jan Smidt* (see Kappeyne van de Coppello)
Finance	*Nicolaas Gerard Pierson* (b. Amsterdam 7 Feb 1839 d. Heemstede 24 Dec 1909)
Water, Commerce and Industry	*Cornelis Lely* (b. Amsterdam 23 Sep 1854; d. The Hague 14 Jan 1929)
War	*August Lodewijk Willem Seyffardt*
Navy	*Joannes Coenraad Jansen* (see above)
Colonies	*Willem Karel, Baron van Dedem* (b. Vosbergen 6 Ju 1839; d. Calcutta 2 Apr 1895)

9 May 1894 – 27 Jul 1897: Roëll

Prime Minister	*Joan Roëll* (b. Haarlem 21 Jul 1844; d. The Hague 1

Jul 1914)

Foreign Affairs	*Joan Roëll (see above)*
Home Affairs	*Samuel van Houten* (b. Groningen 17 Feb 1837; d. The Hague 14 Oct 1930)
Justice	*Willem van der Kaay*
Finance	*Jacobus P. Sprenger van Eyk* (see Jan Heemskerk)
Water, Commerce and Industry	*Philip W. van der Sleyden*
War	*Clemens Diederik Hendrik Schneider*
Navy	*Herman Marinus van der Wijck* (b. Jogjakarta 26 May 1843; d. Velp 8 Dec 1932)
Colonies	*Jacob Hendrik Bergsma* (b. Utrecht 7 Sep 1838; d. The Hague 5 Feb 1915)

27 Jul 1897 – 1 Aug 1901: Pierson

Prime Minister	*Nicolas Gerhard Pierson* (see van Tienhoven)
Foreign Affairs	*Willem Hendrik de Beaufort* (b. Leusden 19 Mar 1845; d. The Hague 2 Apr 1918)
Home Affairs	*Hendrik Goeman Borgesius* (b. Slochteren 4 Jan 1847; d. Slochteren 17 Jan 1917)
Justice	*Pieter Wilhelm Adriaan Cort van der Linden* (b. The Hague 14 May 1846; d. The Hague 15 Jul 1935)
Finance	*Nicolas Gerard Pierson* (see van Tienhoven)
Water, Commerce and Industry	*Cornelis Lely* (see van Tienhoven)
War	27 – 30 Jul 1897 (acting:) *Joannes Coenraad Jansen* (see van Tienhoven) 31 Jul 1897 – 1 Apr 1901: *Kornelis Eland* 1 Apr – 1 Aug 1901: *Arthur Kool*
Navy	27 Jul – 21 Dec 1897: *Joannes Coenraad Jansen* (see van Tienhoven) 22 Dec 1897 – 12 Jan 1898 (acting:) *Kornelis Eland* (see above) 12 Jan 1898 – 1 Aug 1901: *Jacob Alexander Roell* (b. Amsterdam 8 Aug 1838; d. The Hague 10 Jul 1924)
Colonies	*Jacob Theodoor Cremer* (b. Zwolle 30 Jun 1847; d. Santpoort 14 Aug 1923)

1 Aug 1901 – 16 Aug 1905: Kuyper

Prime Minister	*Abraham Kuyper* (b. Maassluis 29 Oct 1837; d. The

	Hague 8 Nov-1920)
Foreign Affairs	1 Aug 1901 – 9 Mar 1905: *Robert Melvil Baron van Lynden* (b. Amsterdam 6 Mar 1843; d. The Hague 27 Apr 1910)
	9 Mar – 22 Apr 1905: *A. G. Ellis*
	22 Apr – 7 Aug 1905: *Willem Marcus van Weede van Beerencamp* (b. Amsterdam 11 Nov 1858; d. Vienna 23 Dec 1925)
Home Affairs	*Abraham Kuyper* (see above)
Justice	*Joannes Aloysius Loeff* (b. Baardwijk 15 Nov 1858; d. The Hague 10 Jul 1921)
Finance	*Joannes Josephus Ignatius Harte van Tecklenburg* (b. Utrecht 15 Oct 1853)
Water, Commerce and Industry	*Johannes Christiaan de Marex Oyens*
War	*Johannes Wilhelm Bergansius* (see Mackay)
Navy	1 Aug 1901 – 12 Dec 1902: *Gerhardus Kruys* (see Mackay)
	13 Dec 1902 – 15 Mar 1903 (acting:) *Johannes Wilhelm Bergansius* (see Mackay)
	16 Mar 1903 – 16 Aug 1905: *A. G. Ellis* (see above)
Colonies	1 Aug 1901 – 9 Sep 1902: *Titus Anthony Jacob van Asch van Wijck* (b. Utrecht 29 Aug 1849; d. The Hague 9 Sep 1902)
	10 – 24 Sep 1902: *Johannes Wilhelm Bergansius* (see Mackay)
	25 Sep 1902 – 16 Aug 1905: *Alexander Willem Frederik Idenburg* (b. Rotterdam 23 Jul 1861; d. The Hague 28 Feb 1935)

16 Aug 1905 – 11 Feb 1908: de Meester

Prime Minister	*Theodoor Herman de Meester* (Lib) (b. Harderwijk 16 Dec 1851; d. The Hague 27 Dec 1919)
Foreign Affairs	*Dirk Arnold Willem van Tets van Goudriaan* (b. The Hague 9 Oct 1844; d. The Hague 25 Jan 1930)
Home Affairs	*Pieter Rink* (Lib) (b. Tiel 13 Aug 1851; d. The Hague 6 Aug 1941)
Justice	*Eduard Ellis van Raalte* (Lib) (b. 1841; d. 24 Mar 1921)
Finance	*Theodoor Herman de Meester* (Lib) (see above)
Waterways and Waterworks	*Jacob Kraus* (b. Groningen 14 Oct 1861; d. The Hague 29 Aug 1951)
War	16 Aug 1905 – 7 Apr 1907: *Hendrik Peter Staal* (b.

	Zwolle 17 Jun 1845; d. The Hague 15 Oct 1920) 7 Apr 1907 – 11 Feb 1908: *Willem Frederik, Count van Rappard* (b. Amsterdam 4 Jan 1846; d. The Hague 22 May 1913)
Navy	16 Aug 1905 – 4 Aug 1907: *W. J. Cohen Stuart* 4 Aug 1907 – 11 Feb 1908: *Jan Wentholt* (b. Almelo 14 Jul 1851; d. The Hague 17 Dec 1930)
Agriculture, Industry and Trade	9 Sep 1905 – 11 Feb 1908: *Jacob Dirk Veegens*
Colonies	*Dirk Fock* (Lib) (b. Duurstede 19 Jun 1858; d. The Hague 18 Oct 1941)

12 Dec 1908 – 25 Aug 1913: Theodorus Heemskerk

Prime Minister	*Theodorus Heemskerk* (Anti-Rev) (b. Amsterdam 20 Jul 1852; d. Utrecht 12 Jun 1932)
Foreign Affairs	*René de Marees van Swinderen* (b. Groningen 6 Oct 1860; d. London 16 Jan 1955)
Home Affairs	*Theodorus Heemskerk* (Anti-Rev) (see above)
Justice	12 Dec 1908 – 11 May 1910: *Antonius Petrus Laurentius Nelissen* 11 May – 7 Jun 1910 (acting:) *Theodorus Heemskerk* (Anti-Rev) (see above) 7 Jun 1910 – 18 Jan 1913: *Edmond Robert Hubert Regout* (Cath) (b. Maastricht 4 Jun 1863; d. The Hague 18 Jan 1913) 18 Jan – 25 Aug 1913 (acting:) *Theodorus Heemskerk* (Anti-Rev) (see above)
Finance	*Maximilien Joseph Caspar Marie Kolkman* (b. 1853; d. 1924)
Waterways and Waterworks	12 Dec 1908 – 5 Jan 1909: *Jean Gustave Stanislas Bevers* (Cath) (b. Roermond 23 Sep 1852; d. The Hague 5 Jan 1909) 7 – 21 Jan 1908 (acting:) *Aritius Sybrandus Talma* (Anti-Rev) (b. Angeren 19 Feb 1864; d. Bennebroek 12 Jul 1916) 21 Jan 1909 – 25 Aug 1913: *Louis Hubert Willem Regout* (Cath) (b. Maastricht 27 Oct 1861; d. Rome 27 Oct 1915)
War	12 Dec 1908 – 27 Jul 1909: *Frederik Henri Alexander Sabron* 27 Jul 1909 – 4 Jan 1911: *Wouter Cool* (b. 26 May 1848; d. 20 Nov 1928)

	4 Jan 1911 – 25 Aug 1913: (1930) *Hendrikus Colijn* (Anti-Rev) (b. Haarlemmermeer 22 Jun 1869; d. Illmenau, Thuringia 18 Sep 1944)
Navy	12 Dec 1908 – 14 May 1912: *Jan Wentholt* (see de Meester)
	14 May 1912 – 25 Aug 1913 (acting:) *Hendrikus Colijn* (Anti-Rev) (see above)
Agriculture, Industry and Trade	*Aritius Sybrandus Talma* (Anti-rev) (see above)
Colonies	12 Dec 1908 – 19 May 1909 (acting:) *Theodorus Heemskerk* (Anti-Rev) (see above)
	19 May – 16 Aug 1909: *Alexander Willem Frederik Idenburg* (Anti-Rev) (see Kuyper)
	16 Aug 1909 – 25 Aug 1913: *Jan Hendrik de Waal Malefijt* (Anti-Rev)

29 Aug 1913 – 3 Jul 1918: van der Linden

Prime Minister	*Pieter Wilhelm Adriaan Cort van der Linden* (Lib) (see Pierson)
Foreign Affairs	29 Aug – 27 Sep 1913 (acting:) *Pieter Wilhelm Adriaan Cort van der Linden* (Lib) (see Pierson)
	27 Sep 1913 – 3 Jul 1918: *John Loudon* (b. The Hague 18 Mar 1866; d. Wassenaar 11 Nov 1955)
Home Affairs	*Pieter Wilhelm Adriaan Cort van der Linden* (Lib) (see Pierson)
Justice	*Bastiaan Ort*
Finance	29 Aug 1913 – 24 Oct 1914: *A. E. J. Bertling*
	24 Oct 1914 – 8 Feb 1916: *Marie Willem Frederik Treub* (Lib) (b. Voorschoten 30 Nov 1858; d. The Hague 24 Jul 1931)
	8 Feb 1916 – 22 Feb 1917: *Anton van Gijn* (b. Dordrecht 17 Sep 1866; d. The Hague 11 May 1933)
	22 Feb 1917 – 3 Jul 1918: *Marie Willem Frederik Treub* (Lib) (see above)
Waterways and Waterworks	*Cornelis Lely* (Lib) (see van Tienhoven)
War	29 Aug 1913 – 15 May 1917: *Nicolaas Bosboom* (b. The Hague 30 Sep 1855; d. The Hague 14 Nov 1937)
	15 May – 15 Jun 1917 (acting:) *Jean Jacques Rambonnet* (b. Wijhe 8 Mar 1864; d. 4 Aug 1943)
	15 Jun 1917 – 3 Jul 1918: *Bonifacius Cornelis de Jonge* (b. The Hague 22 Jan 1875; d. Zeist 24 Jun 1958)

Navy	29 Aug 1913 – 28 Jun 1918: *Jean Jacques Rambonnet* (see above)
	28 Jun – 3 Jul 1918 (acting:) *Bonifacius Cornelis de Jonge* (see above)
Agriculture, Industry and Trade	29 Aug 1913 – 19 Nov 1914: *Marie Willem Frederik Treub* (Lib) (see above)
	19 Nov 1914 – 3 Jul 1918: *Folkert Evert Posthuma* (b. Leeuwarden 20 May 1874; d. Ruurlo 3 Jun 1943)
Colonies	*Thomas Bastiaan Pleyte* (b. Leiden 23 Oct 1864; d. The Hague 25 Mar 1926)

9 Sep 1918 – 18 Jul 1922: de Beerenbrouck I

Prime Minister	*Charles Joseph Maria Ruys de Beerenbrouck* (Cath) (for 1st time) (b. Roermond 1 Dec 1873; d. Utrecht 17 Apr 1936)
Foreign Affairs	*Herman Adriaan van Karnebeek* (b. The Hague 21 Aug 1874; d. 29 Mar 1942)
Home Affairs	*Charles Joseph Maria Ruys de Beerenbrouck* (Cath) (see above)
Justice	*Theodorus Heemskerk* (Anti-Rev) (see Theodorus Heemskerk)
Finance	9 Sep 1918 – 28 Jul 1921: *Simon de Vries* (Anti-Rev) (b. Zaandam 9 Jan 1869; d. Wassenaar 25 Sep 1961)
	28 Jul 1921 – 18 Jul 1922: *Dirk Jan de Geer* (b. Groningen 14 Dec 1870; d. Soest 27 Nov 1960)
Water, Commerce and Industry	*Adrianus Antonie Henri Willem Konig* (Cath) (b. Maastricht 13 Feb 1867; d. The Hague 6 Feb 1944)
Education	25 Sep 1918 – 18 Jul 1922: *Johannes Theodoor de Visser* (b. Utrecht 9 Feb 1851; d. The Hague 14 Apr 1932)
Labour	25 Sep 1918 – 18 Jul 1922: *Petrus Josephus Matheus Aalberse* (Cath) (b. Leiden 27 Mar 1871; d. The Hague 5 Jul 1948)
War	9 Sep 1918 – 5 Jan 1920: *George August Alexander Alting von Geusau* (Cath) (b. Arnhem 24 Apr 1864; d. The Hague 9 Oct 1937)
	5 Jan – 31 Mar 1920 (acting:) *Charles Joseph Maria Ruys de Beerenbrouck* (Cath) (see above)
	31 Mar 1920 – 28 Jul 1921: *Willem Frederik Pop* (b. The Hague 14 Jun 1868; d. Voorburg 24 Jul 1931)
	28 Jul 1921 – 18 Jul 1922: *Jannes Johannes Cornelis*

	van Dijk (Anti-Rev) (b. Leeuwarden 11 Dec 1871; d. The Hague 1953)
Navy	9 – 16 Sep 1918 (acting:) *George August Alexander Alting von Geusau* (Cath) (see above)
	16 Sep 1918 – 20 Feb 1919: *Willem Naudin ten Cate* (b. Haarlem 15 Jul 1860; d. The Hague 18 Dec 1942)
	20 Feb – 17 Apr 1919 (acting:) *Charles Joseph Maria Ruys de Beerenbrouck* (Cath) (see above)
	17 Apr 1919 – 5 Jan 1920: *Hendrik Bijleveld* (Anti-Rev)
	5 Jan – 31 Mar 1920 (acting:) *Hendrik Albert van Ijsselsteyn* (d. The Hague 13 Feb 1941)
	31 Mar 1920 – 28 Jul 1921 (acting:) *Willem Frederik Pop* (see above)
	28 Jul 1921 – 18 Jul 1922 (acting:) *Jannes Johannes Cornelis van Dijk* (Anti-Rev) (see above)
Agriculture	9 Sep 1918 – 13 Sep 1922: *Hendrik Albert van Ijsselsteyn* (see above)
	13 – 18 Sep 1922 (acting:) *Charles Joseph Maria Ruys de Beerenbrouck* (Cath) (see above)
Colonies	9 Sep 1918 – 13 Nov 1919: *Alexander Willem Frederik Idenburg* (Anti-Rev) (see Kuyper)
	13 Nov 1919 – 18 Jul 1922: *Simon de Graaff* (b. Lisse 24 Aug 1861; d. Leiden 2 Oct 1948)

18 Sep 1922 – 30 Jun 1925: de Beerenbrouck II

Prime Minister	*Charles Joseph Maria Ruys de Beerenbrouck* (Cath) (for 2nd time) (see de Beerenbrouck I)
Foreign Affairs	*Herman Adriaan van Karnebeek* (see de Beerenbrouck I)
Home Affairs	*Charles Joseph Maria Ruys de Beerenbrouck* (Cath) (see de Beerenbrouck I)
Justice	*Theodorus Heemskerk* (Anti-Rev) (see Theodorus Heemskerk)
Finance	18 Sep 1922 – 11 Jul 1923: *Dirk Jan de Geer* (see de Beerenbrouck I)
	11 Aug 1923 – 30 Jun 1925: *Hendrikus Colijn* (Anti-Rev) (see Theodorus Heemskerk)
Waterways and Waterworks	*Gerardus Jacobus van Swaay* (Cath) (b. Loenen 22 Jun 1867; d. Delft 8 Jan 1945)
Education	*Johannes Theodoor de Visser* (see de Beerenbrouck I)

Labour (from 24 Nov 1922: Labour, Trade and Industry)	*Petrus Josephus Matheus Aalberse* (Cath) (see de Beerenbrouck I)
War	*Jannes Johannes Cornelis van Dijk* (Anti-Rev) (see de Beerenbrouck I)
Navy	*Evert Pieter Westerveld*
Agriculture	(acting:) *Charles Joseph Maria Ruys de Beerenbrouck* (Cath) (see de Beerenbrouck I) 24 Nov 1922: post abolished
Colonies	*Simon de Graaff* (see de Beerenbrouck I)

4 Aug – 15 Nov 1925: Colijn

Prime Minister	*Hendrikus Colijn* (Anti-Rev) (see Theodorus Heemskerk)
Foreign Affairs	*Herman Adriaan van Karnebeek* (see de Beerenbrouck I)
Home Affairs	*Dirk Jan de Geer* (see de Beerenbrouck I)
Justice	*Jan Schokking* (b. Amsterdam 10 May 1864; d. The Hague 15 Jul 1941)
Finance	*Hendrikus Colijn* (see Theodorus Heemskerk)
Waterways and Waterworks	*Max Charles Emile Bongaerts* (Cath) (b. Roermond 9 Jan 1875; d. (?))
Education	*Victor Henri Rutgers* (Anti-Rev) (b. 's Hertogenbosch 16 Dec 1877; d. Bochum 5 Feb 1945)
Labour, Trade and Industry	*Dionysius Adrianus Petrus Norbertus Koolen* (Cath) (b. Rijswijk 21 Jan 1871; d. The Hague 25 Mar 1945)
War	*Johan Marie Jacques Hubert Lambooy* (Cath) (b. Maastricht 12 Dec 1874; d. The Hague 20 Jun 1942)
Navy	(acting:) *Johan Marie Jacques Hubert Lambooy* (Cath) (see above)
Colonies	4 Aug – 26 Sep 1925: (acting:) *Hendrikus Colijn* (see Theodorus Heemskerk) 26 Sep – 15 Nov 1925: *Charles Joseph Ignace Marie Welter* (Cath) (b. The Hague 6 Apr 1880)

8 Mar 1926 – 2 Jul 1929: de Geer

Prime Minister	*Dirk Jan de Geer* (see de Beerenbrouck I)
Foreign Affairs	8 Mar 1926 – 1 Apr 1927: *Herman Adriaan van Karnebeek* (see de Beerenbrouck I) 1 Apr 1927 – 3 Jul 1929: *Frans Beelaerts van Blokland*

	(b. The Hague 21 Jan 1872; d. The Hague 27 Mar 1956)
Home Affairs	*Johannes Benedictus Kan* (b. Nijmegen 18 May 1873; d. The Hague 8 May 1947)
Justice	*Jan Donner* (Anti-Rev) (b. Assen 3 Feb 1891)
Finance	*Dirk Jan de Geer* (see de Beerenbrouck I)
Waterways and Waterworks	*Hendrik van der Vegte* (Anti-Rev) (b. Zwolle 15 Aug 1868; d. 29 Aug 1933)
Education	*Marius Alphonse Marie Waszink* (Cath) (d. Breda 23 Oct 1943)
Labour, Trade and Industry	*Joseph Rudolf Slotemaker de Bruïne* (b. Sliedrecht 6 May 1869; d. Wassenaar 1 May 1941)
War	8 Mar – 24 Apr 1926: *Louis Anne van Roijen* (d. Wassenaar 4 Apr 1946)
	24 Apr 1926 – 1 Sep 1928: *Johan Marie Jacques Hubert Lambooy* (Cath) (see Colijn)
Navy	8 Mar – 24 Apr 1926 (acting:) *Louis Anne van Roijen* (see above)
	24 Apr 1926 – 1 Sep 1928: *Johan Marie Jacques Hubert Lambooy* (Cath) (see Colijn)
Defence	1 Sep 1928 – 3 Jul 1929: *Johan Marie Jacques Hubert Lambooy* (Cath) (see Colijn)
Colonies	*Jacob Christiaan Koningsberger* (b. Hazerswoude 17 Jan 1867; d. Scheveningen 19 Mar 1951)

10 Aug 1929 – 25 Apr 1933: de Beerenbrouck III

Prime Minister	*Charles Joseph Maria Ruys de Beerenbrouck* (for 3rd time) (Cath) (see de Beerenbrouck I)
Foreign Affairs	10 Aug 1929 – 20 Apr 1933: *Frans Beelaerts van Blokland* (see de Geer)
Home Affairs	*Charles Joseph Maria Ruys de Beerenbrouck* (Cath) (see de Beerenbrouck I)
Justice	*Jan Donner* (Anti-Rev) (see de Geer)
Finance	*Dirk Jan de Geer* (see de Beerenbrouck I)
Waterways and Waterworks	*Paul Johan Reymer* (Cath)
Education	*Jan Terpstra* (Anti-Rev) (b. Scheemda 8 Jun 1888; d. The Hague 14 Dec 1952)
Labour	*Timotheus Josephus Verschuur* (Cath) (b. Utrecht 18 Mar 1886; d. Messenthin 1 May 1945)
Defence	*Laurentius Nicolaas Deckers* (Cath) (b. Heeze 14 Feb 1883)
Colonies	*Simon de Graaff* (see de Beerenbrouck I)

New Zealand

HEADS OF STATE

Governors

30 Jan 1840	*Sir George Gipps* (b. Ringwold 1791; d. Canterbury, Kent 28 Feb 1847)
	William Hobson (b. Waterford 26 Sep 1793; d. Auckland 10 Sep 1842) Lieutenant-Governor
3 Jan 1841	*William Hobson* (see above)
11 Sep 1842	*Willoughby Shortland* (b. Plymouth 30 Sep 1804; d. Courtlands 7 Oct 1869) Administrator
26 Dec 1843	*Robert Fitzroy* (b. Ampton Hall 5 Jul 1805; d. 30 Apr 1865)
18 Nov 1845 – 31 Dec 1853	*Sir George Grey* (for 1st time) (b. Lisbon 12 Apr 1812; d. London 20 Sep 1898)
3 Jan 1854	*Robert Henry Wynyard* (b. Windsor 24 Dec 1802; d. Bath 2 Jan 1864) Administrator
6 Sep 1855	*Thomas Gore Browne* (b. 3 Jul 1807; d. London 17 Apr 1887)
3 Oct 1861	*Sir George Grey* (see above) Administrator
4 Dec 1861	*Sir George Grey* (for 2nd time)
5 Dec 1868 – 19 Mar 1873	*Sir George Ferguson Bowen* (b. Ireland 2 Nov 1821; d. Brighton 21 Feb 1899)
14 Jun 1873	*Sir James Fergusson* (b. Edinburgh 14 Mar 1832; d. Kingston, Jamaica 14 Jan 1907)
3 Dec 1874 – 21 Feb 1879	*Sir George Augustus Constantine Phipps, 4th Marquis of Normanby* (b. Portland Place 23 Jul 1819; d. Brighton 3 Apr 1890) Administrator
27 Mar 1879 – 6 Sep 1880	*Sir Hercules Robinson* (from 1896: *Baron Rosmead*) (b. Westmeath 19 Dec 1824; d. London 28 Oct 1897)
29 Nov 1880 – 23 Jan 1882	*Sir Arthur Charles Hamilton Gordon, 1st Baron Stanmore* (b. London 26 Nov 1829; d. London 30 Jun 1912)
20 Jan 1883 – 22 Mar 1889	*Sir William Francis Drummond Jervois* (b. Bowes, Isle of Wight 10 Sep 1821; d. Bitterne 16 Aug 1897)
2 May 1889 – 24 Feb 1892	*William Hillier, 4th Earl of Onslow* (b. Bletsoe 7 Mar 1853; d. London 23 Oct 1911)
7 Jun 1892 – 6 Feb 1897	*David Boyle, 7th Earl of Glasgow* (b. Edinburgh 31 May 1833; d. Fairlie 13 Dec 1915)

10 Aug 1897	*Uchter John Mark Knox, 5th Earl of Guernsey* (b. Guernsey 11 Aug 1856; d. 1 Oct 1933)
20 Jun 1904 – 8 Jun 1910	*William Lee Plunket, 5th Baron Plunket* (b. Dublin 19 Dec 1864; d. Gloucester 24 Jan 1920)
22 Jun 1910 – 2 Dec 1912	*John Poynder Dickson-Poynder, Baron Islington* (b. Ryde 31 Oct 1866; d. London 6 Dec 1936)
19 Dec 1912 – 27 Jun 1917	*Arthur William de Brito Savile Foljambe, 5th Earl of Liverpool* (b. 27 May 1870; d. 15 May 1941)

Governors General

28 Jun 1917 – 1920	*Arthur William de Brito Savile Foljambe, 5th Earl of Liverpool* (see Governors)
21 Sep 1920	*John Rusworth Jellicoe, Viscount Jellicoe* (from 1925: *1st Earl Jellicoe*) (b. Southampton 5 Dec 1859; d. London 20 Nov 1935)
13 Dec 1924	*Sir Charles Fergusson* (b. Edinburgh 17 Jan 1865; d. Ayrshire 20 Jan 1951)
1 Dec 1929 – 12 Apr 1935	*Charles Bathurst Bledisloe* (from 1935: *1st Viscount Bledisloe*) (b. Lydney House, Gloucestershire 21 Sep 1867; d. 3 Jul 1958)

First Ministers, later Prime Ministers

7 May 1856	*Henry Sewell* (b. Newport, Isle of Wight, 14 Sep 1807; d. Cambridge 5 May 1879) Colonial Secretary
20 May 1856	*Sir William Fox* (for 1st time) (b. Westoe 20 Jan 1812; d. Auckland 23 Jun 1893)
2 Jun 1856	*Edward William Stafford* (for 1st time) (b. Edinburgh 23 Apr 1819; d. London 15 Feb 1901)
12 Jul 1861	*Sir William Fox* (for 2nd time)
6 Aug 1862	*Alfred Domett* (b. Camberwell 20 May 1811; d. 2 Nov 1887)
3 Oct 1863	*Sir Frederick Whitaker* (b. Brampton, Oxfordshire 23 Apr 1812; d. 4 Dec 1891)
24 Nov 1864	*Sir Frederick Aloysius Weld* (b. Chideock 9 May 1823; d. Chideock 20 Jul 1891)
16 Oct 1865	*Edward William Stafford* (for 2nd time)
28 Jun 1869	*Sir William Fox* (for 3rd time)
10 Sep 1872	*Edward William Stafford* (for 3rd time)
11 Oct 1872	*George Marsden Waterhouse* (b. Penzance 6 Apr 1824; d. Torquay 6 Aug 1906)
3 Mar 1873	*Sir William Fox* (for 4th time)

8 Apr 1873	*Sir Julius Vogel* (for 1st time) (b. London 25 Feb 1835; d. East Molesey 12 Mar 1899)
6 Jul 1875	*Daniel Pollen* (b. Dublin 2 Jun 1813; d. 18 May 1896)
15 Feb 1876	*Sir Julius Vogel* (for 2nd time)
1 Sep 1876	*Sir Harry Atkinson* (for 1st time) (b. Broxton 1 Jan 1831; d. Wellington 28 Jun 1892) government of doubtful legality
13 Sep 1876	*Sir Harry Atkinson* (for 2nd time) government re-formed
1877 – 1879	*Sir George Grey* (see Governors)
1879 – 1882	*Sir John Hall* (b. 1824; d. Jun 1907)
1882 – 1884	*Sir Harry Atkinson* (for 3rd time)
28 Aug 1884 – 1887	*Sir Robert Stout* (b. Lerwick, Shetlands 28 Sep 1844; d. 19 Jul 1930)
1887 – Dec 1890	*Sir Harry Atkinson* (for 4th time)
Dec 1890 – 27 Apr 1893	*John Ballance* (b. Glenavy, County Antrim 27 Mar 1839; d. Wellington 27 Apr 1893)
	Richard John Seddon (b. Eccleston, 22 Jun 1845; d. (at sea) 10 Jun 1906)
Jun 1906 – Jul 1912	*Joseph Ward* (from 1911: *Sir*) (for 1st time) (b. Emerald Hill, Melbourne 26 Apr 1856; d. Christchurch 8 Jul 1930)
10 Jul 1912 – 10 May 1925	*William Ferguson Massey* (b. Limavady, Ireland 26 Mar 1856; d. 10 May 1925)
1925 – 7 Dec 1928	*Joseph Gordon Coates* (b. Pahi, New Zealand 1878; d. Wellington 27 May 1943)
1926	(acting:) *William Downie Stuart* (b. Dunedin 29 Jul 1878; d. Dunedin 24 Sep 1949)
7 Dec 1928 – 15 May 1930	*Sir Joseph Ward* (for 2nd time)

Nicaragua

HEADS OF STATE

Presidents

15 Sep 1821	Independence from Spain
29 Mar 1823	Joined United Provinces of Central America

20 Apr 1825 – 8 Nov 1828	*Manuel Antonio de la Cerda* (d. 29 Nov 1828)
23 May 1830 – 1 Mar 1833	*Dionisio Herrera* (d. 1850)
21 Feb 1835 – 25 Jan 1837	*José Zepeda* (d. 25 Jan 1837)
Jan 1837 – Jun 1839	*José Núñez*
Jun – Jul 1839	*Patricio Rivas* (for 1st time)
Jul – Nov 1839	*Joaquín Cosio*
Nov 1839 – Sep 1840	*Tomás Valladares*
Sep 1840 – 4 Mar 1841	*Patricio Rivas* (for 2nd time)
4 Mar – 1 Apr 1841	*Pablo Buitrago* (d. 1848)
1 Apr 1841 – 4 Apr 1845	*Juan de Dios Orozco*
4 Apr 1845 – 6 Apr 1847	*José León Sandoval*
6 Apr 1847 – 1 Apr 1848	*José Guerrero*
1 Apr 1848 – 5 May 1851	*Norberto Ramírez*
5 May 1851	*Laureano Pineda*
1 Apr 1853 – 12 Mar 1855	*Frutos Chamorro* (b. 1806; d. 12 Mar 1855)
11 Jun 1854 – 2 Sep 1855	*Francisco Castellón* (d. 2 Sep 1855) Dictator
12 Mar 1855 – Oct 1856	*José Maria Estrada* (b. 1802; d. Oct 1856)
12 Jul 1856 – 1857	*William Walker* (b. 8 May 1822; d. 12 Sep 1860) adventurer, driven out in 1857
30 Oct 1855 – 24 Jun 1857	*Patricio Rivas* (for 3rd time)
24 Jun 1857 – 1 Mar 1867	*Tomás Martínez* (d. 12 Mar 1873)
1 Mar 1867 – 1 Mar 1871	*Fernando Guzmán*
1 Mar 1871 – 1 Mar 1875	*Vicente Cuadra*
1 Mar 1875 – 1 Mar 1879	*Pedro Joaquín Camorra*
1 Mar 1879 – 1 Mar 1883	*Joaquín Zavala*
1 Mar 1883 – 1 Mar 1887	*Adán Cárdenas* (b. 1836; d. 1916)

1 Mar 1887 – 30 Aug 1889	*Evaristo Carazo* (b. 1822; d. 30 Aug 1889)
30 Aug 1889 – 1 Jun 1893	*Roberto Sacaza*
1 Jun 1893 – 1 Feb 1894	Civil disorders
1 Feb 1894 – 16 Dec 1909	*José Santos Zelaya* (b. 1 Nov 1853; d. 17 May 1919)
20 Jun 1895 – 27 Aug 1898	Federal Republic formed with Honduras and San Salvador
16 Dec 1909 – 20 Aug 1910	*José Madriz*
20 Aug 1910 – 1 Jan 1911	*José Dolores Estrada*
1 Jan – 9 May 1911	*Juan José Estrada*, brother (d. 11 Jul 1947)
9 May 1911 – 31 Dec 1916	*Adolfo Diaz* (for 1st time) (b. 15 Jul 1877; d. San José 27 Jan 1964)
1 Jan – 25 Sep 1912	*Luis Mena*, rival President
1 Jan 1917 – 31 Dec 1920	*Emiliano Chamorro Vargas* (for 1st time) (b. 11 May 1871)
1 Jan 1921 – 12 Oct 1923	*Diego Manuel Chamorro* (d. 12 Oct 1923)
12 Oct 1923 – 7 Dec 1924	—— *Martínez Bartolo*
1 Jan 1925 – 14 Jan 1926	*Carlos Solórzano*
17 Jan – 12 Nov 1926	*Emiliano Chamorro Vargas* (for 2nd time)
12/15 Nov 1926 – 1 Jan 1929	*Adolfo Diaz* (for 2nd time)
4 Dec 1926 – (?)	*Juan Bautista Sacasa* (b. 21 Dec 1874; d. 1946) rival President
1 Jan 1929 – 31 Dec 1932	*José Maria Moncada* (b. 1867; d. 1945)

Norway

From 1397 until 1523 united with Denmark and Sweden following the Union of Kalmar (see Denmark). It was a Danish province between 1536 and 1814 (see Denmark), and united with Sweden from 1814 until 1905 (see Sweden).

HEAD OF STATE

King

House of Oldenburg

7 Nov 1905 – 21 Sep 1957	*Haakon VII*, brother of King Christian X of Denmark (b. 3 Aug 1872)

MEMBERS OF GOVERNMENT

Prime Ministers

1873	*Frederick Stang* (b. Stokke 4 Mar 1808; d. Vestre Baerum 8 Jun 1884)
1880	*Christian August Selmer* (b. Fredrikshold 16 Nov 1816; d. Bygdøy 1 Sep 1889)
3 Apr 1884	*Christian Homann Schweigaard* (b. Kristiania 14 Oct 1838; d. Kristiania 24 Mar 1899)
28 Apr 1884	*Johan Sverdrup* (b. Jarlsberg 30 Jul 1816; d. Kristiania 17 Feb 1892)
12 Jul 1889	*Emil Stang* (for 1st time) (b. Kristiania 14 Jun 1834; d. Kristiania 1 Mar 1907)
23 Feb 1892	*Johannes Wilhelm Christian Steen* (for 1st time) (b. Kristiania 22 Jul 1827; d. Voss 1 Apr 1906)
22 Apr 1893	*Emil Stang* (for 2nd time)
14 Oct 1895	*(George) Francis Hagerup* (for 1st time) (b. 22 Jan 1853; d. 8 Feb 1921)
12 Feb 1898	*Johannes Wilhelm Christian Steen* (for 2nd time)
21 Apr 1902	*Otto Albert Blehr* (for 1st time) (b. Stange 17 Feb 1847; d. 17 Jul 1927)
21 Oct 1903	*Francis Hagerup* (for 2nd time)
2 Mar 1905	*Peter Christian Hersleb Michelsen* (b. Bergen 15 Mar 1857; d. 29 Jun 1925)
28 Oct 1907	*Jorgen Gunnerson Lovland* (b. Lauvland 3 Feb 1848; d. Kristiania 21 Aug 1922)
13 Mar 1908	*Gunnar Knudsen* (for 1st time) (b. Stokke 19 Sep 1848; d. 1 Dec 1928)
1 Feb 1910	*Wollert Konow* (b. Bergen 24 May 1847; d. Oslo 25 Oct 1932)
19 Feb 1912	*Jens Christian Meinich Bratlie* (b. Nordreland 17 Jan 1856; d. 1939)
29 Jan 1913 – 20 Feb 1919	*Gunnar Knudsen* (for 2nd time)

20 Feb 1919	*Gunnar Knudsen* (for 3rd time)
20 Jun 1920	*Otto Bahr Halvorsen* (for 1st time) (b. Kristiania 28 May 1872; d. Kristiania 23 May 1923)
22 Jun 1921	*Otto Albert Blehr* (for 2nd time)
5 Mar 1923	*Otto Bahr Halvorsen* (for 2nd time)
23 May 1923	*Abraham Teodor Berge* (b. Bergen 20 Aug 1851; d. 1936)
25 Jun 1924	*Johan Ludwig Mowinckel* (for 1st time) (b. Bergen 22 Oct 1870; d. New York 30 Sep 1943)
3 Mar 1926 – 20 Jan 1928	*Ivar Lykke* (b. Trondheim 9 Jan 1872; d. 1949)
20 Jan – 15 Feb 1928	*Christopher Andersen Hornsrud* (b. Ovre Eiker 15 Nov 1859; d. Oslow 13 Dec 1960)
15 Feb 1928 – 9 May 1931	*Johan Ludwig Mowinckel* (for 2nd time)

Foreign Ministers

31 Jan 1913 – 19 Jun 1920	*Nils Claus Ihlen* (b. Kristiania 24 Jul 1855; d. Skedsmo 22 Mar 1925)
21 Jun 1920 – 22 Jun 1921	*Christian Fredrik Michelet* (for 1st time) (b. Kristiania 23 Jun 1863; d. Baerum 25 Jul 1927)
22 Jun 1921 – 30 May 1922	*Arnold Christopher Raestad* (b. Kristiania 15 Feb 1878; d. London 1945)
30 May 1922 – 6 Mar 1923	*Johan Ludwig Mowinckel* (for 1st time) (see Prime Ministers)
6 Mar 1923 – 25 Jun 1924	*Christian Fredrik Michelet* (for 2nd time)
31 Jul 1924 – 3 Mar 1926	*Johan Ludwig Mowinckel* (for 2nd time) (see Prime Ministers)
5 Mar 1926 – 20 Jan 1928	*Ivar Lykke* (see Prime Ministers)
28 Jan – 8 Feb 1928	*Edvard Bull* (b. Kristiania 4 Dec 1881; d. 26 Aug 1932)
15 Feb 1928 – 8 May 1931	*Johan Ludwig Mowinckel* (see Prime Ministers)

Oman

HEADS OF STATE

Imams, later Saiyids (Sultans)

Non-dynastic
c. 1492	*Ahmed bin Mohammed*
c. 1500	*Abul-Hasan bin Abdassalam*
1500/1	*Mohammed bin Ismail*
1529/30	*Barakat bin Mohammed*, son (for 1st time)
21 Apr 1560	*Abdullah bin Mohammed al-Hinai*
1560/1 – ?	*Barakat bin Mohammed* (for 2nd time)

Yaaruba
1615/16 or 1620	*Nasir bin Murshid*
1620	Portuguese expelled from most of Oman
1640/1 – 1670(?)	*Sultan bin Saif I*, cousin
1650(?)	Recovery of Muscat
1652	Recovery of Zanzibar
c. 1670 or 1680	*Balarab bin Sultan*, son
1692/3	*Saif bin Sultan I*, brother
1711/12	*Sultan bin Saif II*, son
	Saif bin Sultan II, son (for 1st time), elected but not proclaimed
	Muhanna bin Sultan, brother
1721/2	*Yaarub bin Balarab*, cousin
1722/3	*Saif bin Sultan II* (for 2nd time)
1724/5	*Mohammed bin Nasir*, usurper
c. 1727 – 1744	*Saif bin Sultan II* (for 3rd time)
	During the latter part of Saif's imamate the country was under Persian domination

Al Bu Said
1744 (1749?)	*Ahmed bin Said* (d. 1783), imam
1775	*Said bin Ahmed*, son, imam (until his death, c. 1811)
1779	*Hamad bin Said*, son, self-styled saiyid
1792	*Sultan bin Ahmed*, uncle (d. 18 Nov 1804)
1804 – 1806	*Badr bin Saif*, nephew, 'regent' (d. 31 Jul 1806)
1804 (1806)	*Salim bin Sultan*, cousin (d. 1821)
1804 (14 Sep 1806)	*Said bin Sultan*, brother (d. 19 Oct 1856), at first jointly with Salim

	On Said's death, Oman and Zanzibar were separated
1856	*Thuwaini bin Said*, son, *de facto*, confirmed as Sultan of Oman Apr 1861
1866	*Salim bin Thuwaini*, son
1868	*Azzan bin Qais*, grandson of Ahmed bin Said
1871	*Turki bin Said*, elder brother of Thuwaini
1888	*Faisal bin Turki*, son
1913 – 1932	*Taimur bin Faisal*, son (b. 1888; d. 1965), abdicated

Oyo

For the Alafin of Oyo, political leaders of the Yoruba states of Nigeria from the 14th century onwards, see Volume 1.

The Palatinate

HEADS OF STATE

Electors

Original line

12 Dec 1476	*Philipp*, the Sincere, son of Ludwig IV (b. 14 Jul 1448) returned to the throne after the death of his uncle, Friedrich I
28 Feb 1508	*Ludwig V*, the Peaceful, son (b. 2 Jul 1478)
16 Mar 1544	*Friedrich II*, the Wise, brother (b. 9 Dec 1482)
26 Feb 1556	*Otto Heinrich*, the Courageous (b. 10 Apr 1502)

Pfalz-Simmern line

12 Feb 1559	*Friedrich III*, son of Johann II (b. 14 Feb 1515) ruled in Simmern from 18 May 1557
26 Oct 1576	*Ludwig VI*, son (b. 4 Jul 1539)
22 Oct 1583	*Friedrich IV*, son (b. 5 Mar 1574)
9 Sep 1610	*Friedrich V*, son (b. 16 Aug 1596; d. 29 Nov 1632) King of Bohemia from 26 Aug 1619 until the Battle of Prague, 8 Nov 1620

23 Feb 1623 – 24 Oct 1648	The Palatinate subject to the *Elector Maximilian I of Bavaria* until the Peace of Westphalia
24 Oct 1648	*Karl I*, son of Friedrich V (b. 22 Dec 1617)
28 Aug 1680	*Karl II*, son (b. 31 Mar 1651)

Pfalz-Neuburg line

16 May 1685	*Philip Wilhelm*, son of Wolfgang Wilhelm of Pfalz-Neuburg (b. 25 Nov 1615) ruled in Neuburg from 20 Mar 1653
2 Sep 1690	*Johann Wilhelm*, son (b. 19 Apr 1658)
8 Apr 1716	*Karl Philip*, brother (b. 4 Nov 1661)

Pfalz-Sulzbach line

| 31 Dec 1742 | *Karl Theodor*, son of Johann Christian of Pfalz-Sulzbach (b. 11 Dec 1724) ruled in Sulzbach from 20 Jul 1733 and inherited Bavaria on the death of Maximilian III, 30 Dec 1777 |

Pfalz-Birkenfeld line

| 16 Feb 1799 – 13 Oct 1825 | *Maximilian IV of Bavaria* (from 1806: *King Maximilian I of Bavaria*) brother and from 1 Apr 1795 successor in Birkenfeld to Karl II |

Palestine

Until 1917 part of Turkey, and under British Mandate from 1920 to 1948.

HEADS OF STATE

Commissioners

12 May 1920 – Aug 1925	*Sir Herbert Louis Samuel* (from 1937: *1st Viscount Samuel*) (b. Liverpool 6 Nov 1870; d. 5 Feb 1963)
25 Aug 1925 – 1928	*Herbert Charles Onslow, Baron Plumer* (b. 1857; d. London 16 Jul 1932)
1928 – 1 Nov 1931	*Sir John Robert Chancellor* (b. Edinburgh 20 Oct 1870; d. 31 Jul 1952)

Panama

Until 3 November 1903 part of Colombia.

HEADS OF STATE

Presidents

17 (20) Feb 1904	*Manuel Amador Guerrero* (d. 2 May 1909)
1 Oct 1908 – 1 Mar 1910	*José Domingo de Obaldía* (b. 1845; d. 1 Mar 1910)
Mar – 5 Oct 1910	*Carlos A. Mendoza*
5 Oct 1910 – 1 Oct 1912	*Pablo Arosemena* (b. 24 Sep 1836)
1 Oct 1912 – 1 Oct 1916	*Belisario Porras* (for 1st time) (b. 28 Nov 1856; d. 28 Aug 1942)
1 Oct 1916 – 4 Jun 1918	*Dr Ramón Valdés* (d. 4 Jun 1918)
4 Jun – 12 Oct 1918	*Ciro L. Urriola*
12 Oct 1918 – 1 Oct 1924	*Belisario Porras* (for 2nd time)
1 Oct 1924 – 1 Oct 1928	*Roberto Chiari* (b. 1869; d. 1937)
1 Oct 1928 – 3 Jan 1931	*Florencio Harmodio Arosemena* (b. 17 Sep 1872; d. 1945)

Papacy

POPES

11 Aug 1492 – 18 Aug 1503	*Alexander VI* (Borgia) (b. Valencia 1 Jan 1431)
22 Sep – 18 Oct 1503	*Pius III* (Todeschini-Piccolomini), nephew of Pope Pius II (b. Siena 9 May 1439)
31 Oct 1503 – 21 Feb	*Julius II* (della Rovere), nephew of Pope Sixtus IV (b. Albissola 5 Dec 1443)
Mar 1513 – 1 Dec 1521	*Leo X* (Medici) (b. Florence 11 Dec 1475)

9 Jan 1522 – 14 Sep 1523	*Hadrian VI* (Dedel) (b. Utrecht 2 Mar 1459) last non-Italian pope
19 Nov 1523 – 25 Sep 1534	*Clement VII* (Medici) (b. Florence 26 May 1478)
13 Oct 1534 – 10 Nov 1549	*Paul III* (Farnese) (b. Canino 1468)
7 Feb 1550 – 23 Mar 1555	*Julius III* (Ciocchi del Monte) (b. Rome 10 Sep 1478)
9 Apr – 1 May 1555	*Marcellus II* (Cervini degli Spanocchi) (b. Montepulciano 6 May 1501)
23 May 1555 – 18 Aug 1559	*Paul IV* (Caraffa) (b. Capriglio, Abruzzi 1476)
25 Dec 1559 – 9 Dec 1565	*Pius IV* (Medici) (b. Milan 31 Mar 1499)
7 Jan 1566 – 1 May 1572	*Pius V* (Ghislieri) (b. Piedmont 27 Jan 1504) sanctified 1712
13 May 1572 – 10 Apr 1585	*Gregory XIII* (Buoncompagni) (b. Bologna 7 Jan 1502)
24 Apr 1585 – 27 Aug 1590	*Sixtus V* (Peretti) (b. Grottamare 1521)
15 – 27 Sep 1590	*Urban VII* (Castagna) (b. Rome 1521)
5 Dec 1590 – 16 Oct 1591	*Gregory XIV* (Sfondrato) (b. Cremona 11 Feb 1535)
29 Oct – 30 Dec 1591	*Innocent IX* (Facchinetti) (b. Bologna 22 Jul 1519)
30 Jan 1592 – 3 Mar 1605	*Clement VIII* (Aldobrandini) (b. Fano 24 Feb 1536)
1 – 27 Apr 1605	*Leo XI* (Medici) (b. Florence 1535)
16 May 1605 – 28 Jan 1621	*Paul V* (Borghese) (b. Rome 17 Sep 1552)
9 Feb 1621 – 8 Jul 1623	*Gregory XV* (Ludovisi) (b. Bologna 9 Jan 1554)
6 Aug 1623 – 29 Jul 1644	*Urban VIII* (Barberini) (b. Florence 1568)
15 Sep 1644 – 7 Jan 1655	*Innocent X* (Pamphili) (b. Rome 6 May 1575)
7 Apr 1655 – 22 May 1667	*Alexander VII* (Chigi) (b. Siena 13 Feb 1599)
20 Jun 1667 – 9 Dec 1669	*Clement IX* (Rospigliosi) (b. Pistoia, Tuscany 28 Jan 1600)
29 Apr 1670 – 22 Jul 1676	*Clement X* (Albieri) (b. Rome 13 Jul 1590)
21 Sep 1676 – 12 Aug 1689	*Innocent XI* (Odescalchi) (b. Como 16 May 1611)

6 Oct 1689 – 1 Feb 1691	*Alexander VIII* (Ottoboni) (b. Venice 22 Apr 1610)
12 Jul 1691 – 27 Sep 1700	*Innocent XII* (Pignatelli) (b. Spinazzola 13 Mar 1615)
23 Nov 1700 – 19 Mar 1721	*Clement XI* (Albani) (b. Urbino 22 Jul 1649)
8 May 1721 – 7 Mar 1724	*Innocent XIII* (de' Conti) (b. Palestrina 13 May 1655)
29 May 1724 – 21 Feb 1730	*Benedict XIII* (Orsini) (b. Gravina 2 Feb 1649)
12 Jul 1730 – 6 Feb 1740	*Clement XII* (Corsini) (b. Florence 7 Apr 1652)
16 Aug 1740 – 3 May 1758	*Benedict XIV* (Lambertini) (b. Bologna 31 Mar 1675)
6 Jul 1758 – 2 Feb 1769	*Clement XIII* (de la Torre de Rezzonico) (b. Venice 20 Dec 1693)
19 May 1769 – 22 Sep 1774	*Clement XIV* (Ganganelli) (b. S. Arcangelo in Vado 31 Oct 1705)
15 Feb 1775 – 29 Aug 1799	*Pius VI* (Braschi) (b. Cesena 27 Nov 1717)
14 Mar 1800 – 20 Aug 1823	*Pius VII* (Chiaramonti) (b. Cesena 14 Aug 1740)
28 Sep 1823 – 10 Feb 1829	*Leo XII* (della Genga) (b. Genga 22 Aug 1760)
31 Mar 1829 – 30 Nov 1830	*Pius VIII* (Castiglione) (b. Cingoli 20 Nov 1761)
2 Feb 1831 – 1 Jun 1846	*Gregory XVI* (Cappellari) (b. Venice 28 Sep 1775)
16 Jun 1846 – 7 Feb 1878	*Pius IX* (Mastai-Feretti) (b. Senigallia 13 May 1792)
20 Feb 1878 – 20 Jul 1903	*Leo XIII* (Pecci) (b. Carpineto 2 Mar 1810)
4 Aug 1903 – 20 Aug 1914	*Pius X* (Sarto) (b. Riese 2 Jun 1835) sanctified 1954
3 Sep 1914 – 22 Jan 1922	*Benedict XV* (della Chiesa) (b. Genoa 21 Nov 1854)
6 Feb 1922 – 10 Feb 1939	*Pius XI* (Ratti) (b. Desio 31 May 1857)

Cardinal Secretaries of State (from 1800)

4 Mar 1800 – 17 Jun 1806	*Ercole, Marquis Consalvi* (for 1st time) (b. Rome 8 Jun 1757; d. Rome 24 Jan 1824) (Pro-Secretary 14 Mar – 11 Aug 1800)

Jun 1806 – Feb 1808	*Filippo Casoni* (b. Sarzana 6 Mar 1733; d. Rome 9 Oct 1811)
Feb 1808 – Mar 1808	*Giulio Gabrielli* (acting:) (b. Rome 20 Jul 1748; d. Albano 26 Sep 1822)
18 Jun 1808 – 17 May 1814	*Bartolomeo Pacca* (b. Benevento 25 Dec 1756; d. Rome 19 Apr 1844)
17 May 1814 – 20 Aug 1823	*Ercole, Marquis Consalvi* (for 2nd time)
19 May 1814 – 2 Jul 1815	*Bartolomeo Pacca* (acting:) (see above)
28 Oct 1823 – Jun 1828	*Giulio Maria Della Somaglia* (b. Piacenza 29 Jul 1744; d. Rome 2 Apr 1830)
17 Jun 1828 – 10 Feb 1829	*Tommaso Bernetti* (for 1st time) (b. Fermo 1779; d. Fermo 21 Mar 1852)
31 Mar 1829 – 30 Nov 1830	*Giuseppe Albani* (b. Rome 13 Sep 1750; d. Pesaro 3 Dec 1834)
12 Feb 1831 – 20 Jan 1836	*Tommaso Bernetti* (for 2nd time)
20 Jan 1836 – 1 Jun 1846	*Luigi Lambruschini* (b. Genoa 16 May 1776; d. Rome 12 May 1854)
8 Aug 1846 – Jul 1847	*Pasquale Tommaso Gizzi* (b. Ceccano 22 Sep 1787; d. Lenola 3 Jun 1849)
Jul 1847 – Jan 1848	*Carlo Vizzardelli* (b. Veroli 21 Jun 1791; d. Rome 24 May 1851)
Jan – May 1848	*Giuseppe Bofondi* (b. Forlì 24 Oct 1795; d. Rome 2 Dec 1867)
May – Jun 1848	*Antonio Francesco Orioli* (b. Faenza 10 Dec 1778; d. Rome 20 Feb 1852) acting for *Luigi Ciacchi* (b. Pesaro 16 Aug 1788; d. Rome 17 Dec 1865) who remained resident in Ferrara and did not take up office
Jun – Dec 1848*	*Giovanni Soglia* (b. Imola 11 Oct 1779; d. Osimo 12 Aug 1856)

*Roman administrations during the revolution 1848 – 1850

10 Mar – 29 Apr 1848: Antonelli

Chief Minister   *Cardinal Giacomo Antonelli* (b. Sonnino 1 Apr 1806; d. Rome 6 Nov 1876)

Ministry comprised three clerical and six lay members.

14 Mar 1848   Proclamation of a constitution

1 May - 2 Aug 1848: Ciacchi

Secretary of State and Prime Minister	*Cardinal Luigi Ciacchi* (see above)
Home Affairs and Deputy Prime Minister	*Terenzio Mamiani della Rovere* (b. Pesaro 27 Sep 1799; d. Rome 21 May 1885)

2 Aug - 16 Sep 1848: Fabbri

Prime Minister	*Edoardo Fabbri* (b. Cesena 13 Oct 1778; d. 7 Oct 1853)

16 Sep - 15 Nov 1848: Rossi

Prime Minister and Home Affairs	*Pellegrino, Count Rossi* (b. Carrara 13 Jul 1787; d. Rome 15 Nov 1848) also Acting Minister for Police and for Finance

Nov - Dec 1848: Soglia

Secretary of State	*Cardinal Giovanni Soglia* (see above) Nominated by Pope as Prime Minister
24 Nov 1848	Pope Pius IX fled to Gaeta (returned on 12 Apr 1850)

15 Nov 1848 - 9 Feb 1849: 'State Junta'

Prime Minister (not recognized by Pope) Foreign Affairs	15 Nov – 11 Dec 1848: —— *Muzzarelli* 11 Dec 1848 – 9 Feb 1849: —— *Galletti* 15 Nov 1848 – 9 Feb 1849: *Terenzio Mamiani della Rovere* (see Ciacchi)
9 Feb 1849	Proclamation of Roman Republic

9 Feb - 19 Mar 1849: Executive Committee

Members	*Carlo Armellini* (b. Rome 1777; d. Sint-Josse-ten-Noode 12 Jun 1863) *Aurelio Saliceti* (b. Teramo 14 May 1804; d. Turin 22 Jan 1862) *Mattia Montecchi* (b. Rome 1 Jun 1816; d. London 28 Feb 1871)

29 Mar - 3 Jul 1849: Triumvirate

	Giuseppe Mazzini (b. Genoa 22 Jun 1805; d. Pisa 10 Mar 1872) *Carlo Armellini* (see Executive Committee) *Aurelio Saffi* (b. Forlì 13 Oct 1819; d. San Varano 10 Apr 1890); from 11 Feb 1849: Minister of Internal Affairs

3 Jul 1849: Triumvirate which arranged surrender

	Livio Mariani *Alessandro Callandrelli* (b. Rome 8 Oct 1805; d. 1888) *Aurelio Saliceti* (see Executive Committee)
30 Jun/3 Jul 1849	Rome occupied by French troops

7 Jul 1849 - 12 Apr 1850 Administration of three Cardinals:

	Cardinal Luigi Altieri (b. 17 Jul 1805; d. 11 Aug 1867) *Cardinal Della Genga* *Cardinal Vannicella-Casoni*

Dec 1848 – Mar 1852	*Giacomo Antonelli* (Pro-Secretary of State)
Mar 1852 – 6 Nov 1876	*Giacomo Antonelli*
18 Dec 1876 – 7 Feb 1878	*Giovanni Simeoni* (b. Palestrina 12 Jul 1816; d. Rome 14 Jan 1892)
5 Mar – 31 Jul 1878	*Alessandro Franchi* (b. Rome 25 Jun 1819; d. 31 Jul 1878)
9 Aug 1878 – 16 Dec 1880	*Lorenzo Nina* (b. Ecanati 12 May 1812; d. Rome 25 Jul 1885)
16 Dec 1880 – 28 Feb 1887	*Lodovico Jacobini* (b. Genzano 6 Jan 1832; d. Rome 28 Feb 1887)
1 Jun 1887 – 20 Jul 1903	*Mariano Rampolla, Marquis del Tindaro* (b. Polizzi 17 Aug 1843; d. Rome 17 Dec 1913)
Aug 1903 – 20 Aug 1914	*Raffaele Merry del Val* (b. London 10 Oct 1865; d. Vatican 26 Feb 1930); Pro-Secretary from Aug to Nov 1903
4 Sep – 10 Oct 1914	*Domenico Ferrata* (b. Gradoli, Montefiascone 4 Mar 1847; d. Rome 10 Oct 1914)
Oct 1914 – 7 Feb 1930	*Pietro Gasparri* (b. Ussita 5 May 1852; d. Rome 18 Nov 1934)

Paraguay

Until June 1811 part of the Spanish Empire

HEADS OF STATE

Presidents

1814 – 20 Sep 1840	*José Gasparo Tomás Rodríguez de Francia* (b. 1756/57: d. 20 Sep 1840)
1840 – Mar 1844	—— *Vidal*
14 Mar 1844 – 10 Sep 1862	*Carlos Antonio López*, nephew of José Gasparo Tomás Rodriguez de Francia (b. 4 Nov 1790; d. 10 Sep 1862) Dictator
Sep 1862 – 1 Mar 1870	*Francisco Solano López*, son (b. 24 Jul 1827; d. 1 Mar 1870) Dictator
10 Dec 1870 – 12 Dec 1871	*Cirilo Antonio Rivarola*

12 Dec 1871 – 25 Nov 1874	*Salvador Jovellanos* (b. 1833)
25 Nov 1874 – 12 Apr 1877	*Juan Bautista Gill* (d. 12 Apr 1877)
12 Apr 1877 – 25 Nov 1878	*Higinio Uriarte*
27 Nov 1878 – Sep 1880	*Cándido Barreiro* (d. Sep 1880)
Sep 1880 – 25 Nov 1881	*Adolfo Saguier*
25 Nov 1881 – 25 Nov 1886	*Bernardino Caballero* (b. 1848; d. 1912)
25 Nov 1886 – 25 Sep 1890	*Patricio Escobar*
25 Sep 1890 – Jun 1894	*Juan B. González* (d. 31 Jul 1912)
Jun – 25 Nov 1894	*Marcos Morínigo*
25 Nov 1894 – 25 Nov 1898	*Juan Bautista Egusquiza*
25 Nov 1898 – 11 Jan 1902	*Emilio Aceval* (b. 1854; d. 1931)
11 Jan – 25 Nov 1902	*Hector Carvallo*
25 Nov 1902 – 11 Aug 1904	*Juan Antonio Escurra*
18 Oct 1904 – 8 Dec 1905	*Juan Gaona* (b. 1846; d. 1912)
8 Dec 1905 – 25 Nov 1906	*Cecilio Baez* (b. 1862; d. 11 Jun 1941)
25 Nov 1906 – 4 Jul 1908	*Benigno Ferreira* (b. 1846; d. 1920)
5 Jul 1908 – 25 Nov 1910	*Emiliano González Navero* (for 1st time) (b. Caraguatay 1861; d. 18 Oct 1934)
25 Nov 1910 – 11 Jan 1911	*Manuel Gondra* (for 1st time)
19 Jan – 5 Jul 1911	*Albino Jara* (b. 1878; d. mid May 1912)
5 Jul – end of 1911	*Liberato Marcial Rojas*
1 Jan – 25 Mar 1912	*Pedro Peña* (b. 1867; d. 1943)
25 Mar – 31 Jul 1912	*Emiliano González Navero* (for 2nd time)
15 Aug 1912 – 15 Aug 1916	*Eduardo Schaerer* (b. 2 Dec 1873; d. 1941)
15 Aug 1916 – 5 Jun 1919	*Manuel Franco* (d. 5 Jun 1919)
5 Jun 1919 – 15 Aug 1920	*José P. Montero*

405

15 Aug 1920 – 1 Oct 1921	*Manuel Gondra* (for 2nd time)
31 Oct – 3 Nov 1921	*Félix Paiva*
3 Nov 1921 – 10 Apr 1923	*Eusebio Ayala* (b. 13/14 Aug 1875; d. 4 Jun 1942)
10 Apr 1923 – 12 Apr 1924	*Eligio Ayala* (for 1st time) (d. 24 Oct 1930)
12 Apr – 15 Aug 1924	*Luis Alberto Riart* (b. 1891(?) d. 1953)
15 Aug 1924 – 15 Aug 1928	*Eligio Ayala* (for 2nd time)
15 Aug 1928 – 26 Oct 1931	*José Particio Guggiari* (b. Lugano 17 Mar 1884; d. Buenos Aires 29 Oct 1957)

Parma

Incorporated in the States of the Church by Pope Julius II in 1512, becoming an independent duchy from 1545.

HEADS OF STATE

Dukes

House of Farnese

1545	*Pier-Luigi*, son of Pope Paul III (b. 19 Nov 1503)
10 Sep 1547	*Ottavio*, son (b. 9 Oct 1524) married to Margaret, natural daughter of Emperor Charles V
21 Sep 1586	*Alessandra*, son (b. 27 Aug 1545)
11 Dec 1592	*Rainuto*, son (b. 28 Mar 1569)
5 May 1622	*Odoardo I*, son (b. 28 Apr 1612)
12 Sep 1646	*Rainuto II*, son (b. 17 Sep 1630)
8 Dec 1694	*Francesco*, son (b. 19 May 1678)
26 May 1727 – 20 Jan 1731	*Antonio Francesco*, brother (b. 29 Nov 1679)
1735	Parma ceded to Austria by the Treaty of Vienna
3 Oct 1735	*Charles I* (b. 1 Oct 1685) German Emperor as Charles VI from 1711 – 1740
20 Oct 1740	*Maria Theresa*, daughter (b. 13 May 1717) married to Emperor Franz I
18 Oct 1748	*Philip*, son of King Philip V of Spain (b. 15 Mar 1720)

18 Jul 1765	*Ferdinand* (from 9 Feb 1801: *Archduke of Tuscany*) son (b. 20 Jan 1741)
9 Oct 1802 – 15 Feb 1804	*Jean Victor Moreau* (b. Morlaix 14 Feb 1763; d. Louny 2 Sep 1813) Commissioner, French general
21 Jul 1805	Ceded to France
1815	*Marie Louise*, daughter of Emperor Franz II, (b. 12 Dec 1791) 2nd wife of Emperor Napoleon I

House of Bourbon

17 Dec 1847	*Charles II*, son of Louis I of Etruria and grandson of Duke Ferdinand of Parma (b. 23 Dec 1799; d. 17 Apr 1883)
14 Mar 1849	*Charles III*, son (b. 14 Jan 1823)
27 Mar 1854 – 30 Apr 1859	*Robert*, son (b. 9 Jul 1848; d. 16 Nov 1907)
1860	Amalgamated with Sardinia
1861	Became part of the united Kingdom of Italy

Persia

See Iran

Peru

Part of the Spanish Empire from 1533 to 1821.

HEADS OF STATE

Presidents

9 Jul 1821 – 29 Aug 1822	*José de San Martin* (b. 25 Feb 1778; d. 17 Aug 1850) Protector
1823 – 25 Apr 1829	*Simón Bolívar* (b. 24 Jul 1783; d. 10 Dec 1830)
31 Aug 1829 – Dec 1833	*Augustín Gamarra* (for 1st time) (b. 1785; d. 1840)
30 Dec 1833	*Luis José Orbegozo* (b. 1795; d. 1847)

1835 – 20 Feb 1839	*Andrés Santa Cruz* (b. 1792; d. 25 Sep 1865)
24 Feb 1839 – 27 Jul 1842	*Augustín Gamarra* (for 2nd time)
28 Jul 1842 – Apr 1845	*Francisco Vidal*
8 Apr 1843 – 17 Jul 1846	*Manuel Ignacio de Vivanco* (b. 1806; d. 1873) Rival President
20 Apr 1845	*Ramón Castilla* (for 1st time) (b. 31 Aug 1797; d. 30 May 1867)
20 Apr 1851 – 5 Jan 1855	*José Rufino Echénique* (for 1st time) (b. 1808; d. 1887)
14 Jul 1855	*Ramón Castilla* (for 2nd time)
24 Oct 1862 – 3 Apr 1863	*Miguel San Ramón* (d. 3 Apr 1863)
5 Aug 1863 – 6 Feb 1865	*Juan Antonio Pezet y Rodríguez* (b. 1810; d. 24 Mar 1879)
Feb – 6 Nov 1865	*José Rufino Echénique* (for 2nd time)
8 Nov 1865	*Mariano Ignacio Prado* (for 1st time) (b. 18 Dec 1826; d. 1902) Dictator
Aug 1867 – 7 Jan 1868	*Mariano Ignacio Prado* (for 2nd time) President
Jan – 1 Aug 1868	—— *La Fuente*
2 Aug 1868	*José Balta* (b. 1816; d. 22 Jul 1872)
22 – 26 Jul 1872	*Silvestro Gutiérrez* (d. 26 Jul 1872) Dictator
2 Aug 1872	*Manuel Pardo* (b. 1834; d. 1878)
2 Aug 1876 – 17 Dec 1879	*Mariano Ignacio Prado* (for 3rd time)
23 Dec 1879 – 17 Jan 1881	*Nicolás Pierola* (for 1st time) (b. 5 Jan 1839; d. 24 Jun 1913) Dictator
12 Mar 1881 – 28 Sep 1881	*Francisco García Calderón* (b. 1834; d. 1905)
1881 – 1883	*Lisardo Montero* (b. 1832; d. 1905) President in the southern province of Arequipa
1881/20 Mar 1883 – 2/25 Dec 1885	*Miguel Iglesias* (b. 18 Aug 1822; d. 1901)
3 Jun 1886	*Andrés Avelino Cáceres* (for 1st time) (b. 10 Nov 1836; d. 10 Oct 1923)
10 Aug 1890 – 1 May 1894	*Remigio Morales Bermúdez* (d. 1 May 1894)
May 1894	*J. Borgoñr*
10 Aug 1894 – 19 Mar 1895	*Andrés ιvelino Cáceres* (for 2nd time)
21 Mar 1895	*Manuel Candamo* (for 1st time) (b. 1842; d. 7 May 1904)

8 Sep 1895	*Nicolás Pierola* (for 2nd time)
8 Sep 1899 – 8 Sep 1903	*Eduardo de Romaña* (b. 19 Mar 1847; d(?))
30 Sep 1903 – 7 May 1904	*Manuel Candamo* (for 2nd time)
23 Sep 1904	*José Pardo y Barreda* (for 1st time) (b. 24 Feb 1864; d. 4 Aug 1947)
24 Sep 1908	*Augusto Bernardino Leguía* (for 1st time) (b. 19 Feb 1864; d. 6 Feb 1932)
24 Sep 1912 – 4 Feb 1914	*Guillermo Billinghurst* (b. 1851; d. 28 Jan 1915)
15 May 1914	*Oscar Raimundo Benavides* (b. 18 May 1876; d. 2 Jul 1946)
18 Aug 1915 – 4 Jul 1919	*José Pardo y Barreda* (for 2nd time)
20 Jul 1919 – 25 Aug 1930	*Augusto Bernardino Leguía* (for 2nd time)

Philippines

Under Spanish control from the 16th century until 10 December 1898, when it was put under United States control by the Treaty of Paris, ending the Spanish American War.

HEADS OF STATE

American Governors General

Jul 1901 – Jan 1904	*William Howard Taft* (b. Cincinnati 15 Sep 1857; d. Washington 8 Mar 1930)
Feb 1904 – 1906	*Luke Edward Wright* (b. Giles County, Tennessee 29 Aug 1846; d. Memphis 17 Nov 1922)
Apr – Sep 1906	*Henry Clay Ide* (b. Barnet, Vermont 18 Sep 1844; d. St Johnsbury, Vermont 13 Jun 1921)

Sep 1906 – May 1909	*James Francis Smith* (b. San Francisco 28 Jan 1859; d. 29 Jun 1928)
Nov 1909 – Oct 1913	*William Cameron Forbes* (b. Milton, Massachusetts 21 May 1870; d. Dec 1959)
Aug 1913 – 1921	*Francis Burton Harrison* (b. New York 18 Dec 1873; d. 21 Nov 1957)
6 Oct 1921 – 7 Aug 1927	*Leonard Wood* (b. Winchester, New Hampshire 9 Oct 1860; d. Boston 7 Aug 1927)
End of 1927 – Mar 1929	*Henry Lewis Stimson* (b. New York 21 Sep 1867; d. Huntingdon, New York 20 Oct 1950)
1929 – 1932	*Dwight Filley Davis* (b. St Louis, Montana 5 Jul 1879; d. Washington 28 Nov 1945)

Poland

HEADS OF STATE

Kings

Jagellonian dynasty

7 Jun 1492	*Jan Olbracht*, son of King Casimir IV of Poland (b. 1450)
17 Jun 1501	*Alexander*, brother (b. 1461)
19 Aug 1506	*Sigismund I*, brother (b. 1 Jan 1467)
1 Apr 1548 – 14 Aug 1572	*Sigismund II*, *Augustus*, son (b. 2 Aug 1520)

Elected Kings

16 May 1573 – 18 Jul 1574	*Henry II*, brother of King Charles IX of France (House of Angoulême) elected to the throne of Poland, abdicated in 1574 in order to succeed to the throne of France as Henry III
1574	The 'Articuli Henriciani' declared Poland an elected kingship (aristocratic republic)
15 Sep 1575 – 13 Dec 1586	*Stephen Báthory*, son-in-law of Sigismund I (b. 27 Sep 1522)
9 Mar 1587	*Sigismund III*, nephew on mother's side of Sigismund II (b. 20 Jun 1566) until Feb 1599 King of Sweden

30 Apr 1632	*Ladislas VIII (IV) Sigismund*, son (b. 9 Jun 1595)
10 May 1648 – 16 Sep 1668	*John II, Casimir*, son of Sigismund III by second marriage (b. 22 May 1609; d. 16 Dec 1672)
19 Jun 1669 – 10 Nov 1673	*Michael Wiśniowiecki*, son of Jeremias Michael Wiśniowiecki (b. 18 Jun 1640)
19 May 1674 – 17 Jun 1696	*John III, Sobieski*, son of John Sobieski, Protector of Krakow (b. 9 Jun 1624)
17 Jun 1697 – 1 Feb 1733	*Augustus II*, the Strong (b. 12 May 1670) from 27 Apr 1694: Elector Frederick Augustus I of Saxony; exiled from Poland in 1703 by King Charles XII of Sweden, reinstated in 1709
12 Aug 1704 – Aug 1709	*Stanislas I, Leszczyński*, son of Rafael Leszczyński (b. 23 Oct 1677; d. 23 Feb 1766) chosen as King in 1733 but banished by the Russians, died as Duke of Lorraine
5 Oct 1733 – 5 Oct 1763	*Augustus III*, son of Augustus II (b. 17 Oct 1696) from 1 Feb 1733: Elector Frederick Augustus II of Saxony
7 Sep 1764 – 22 Nov 1795	*Stanislas II, Augustus Poniatowski*, son of Stanislas Poniatowski (b. 17 Jan 1732; d. 11/12 Feb 1798)
1795	Partition of Poland and end of the old Polish Kingdom

Grand Dukes of the Grand Duchy of Warsaw

1807 – 1812	*King Frederick Augustus I of Saxony*, grandson of Augustus III (b. 23 Dec 1750; d. 5 May 1827)
1815 – 1830/31	Kingdom of Poland became a province of the Russian Empire
1815 – 1826	*Grand Duke Constantine Pavlovich*, brother of Tsar Alexander I (b. 8 May 1779; d. Witebsk 27 Jun 1831) Viceroy and Commander-in-Chief of the Russian forces
1826 – 29 Nov 1830	*Grand Duke Constantine Pavlovich*, Military Governor (see above)
29 Nov 1830 – 25 Sep 1831	Polish revolt against Russian rule

Interim Administrations

6 Dec 1830 – 30 Jan 1831	*Adam Jerzy, Prince Czartoryski* (b. Warsaw 14 Jan 1770; d. Chateau Montfermeil, Paris 15 Jul 1861) Prime Minister

POLAND

30 Jan – 16 Aug 1831	*Adam Jerzy, Prince Czartoryski*, President of National Administration (see above)
17 Aug – 7 Sep 1831	*Jan, Count Krukowiecki* (b. 1770; d. Warsaw 1850) Dictator
7 – 25 Sep 1831	*Bonaventura Niemojewski* (b. Kalisch 1787; d. Paris 1835) Dictator
26 Feb 1832	Formal union with Russia

Russian Governors

1831 – 13 Feb 1856	*Ivan Fyodorovich Paskevich, Count Erivansky, Prince of Warsaw* (b. Poltava 19 May 1782; d. Warsaw 13 Feb 1856)
1856 – 30 May 1861	*Mikhail Dmitrievich Gorchakov* (b. 1795; d. Warsaw 30 May 1861)
Oct 1861 – Jun 1862	*Aleksei Nikolaievich* (from 1862: *Count Lüders*) (b. Podolia 26 Jan 1790; d. St Petersburg 13 Feb 1874)
8 Jun 1862 – 31 Oct 1863	*Grand Duke Constantine Nikolaevich*, brother of Tsar Alexander II (b. 21 Sep 1827; d. Pavlovsk 24 Jan 1892)
	Alexander, Count Wielopolski, Marquis Gonzaga (b. 15 Mar 1803; d. Dresden 30 Dec 1877) Head of Civil Administration and Vice President of the Privy Council until Mar 1863, Minister of Education from 1861
22 Jan 1863 – Feb/Apr 1864	Polish revolt against Russian rule

Heads of Revolutionary Government

16 Jan – Mar 1863	*Ludwig Mierosławski* (b. Namur 1814; d. Paris 22 Nov 1878) Dictator
10 – 19/21 Mar 1863	*Marian Langiewicz* (b. Krotosyn 5 Aug 1827; d. Lille 11 May 1887) Dictator
Mar/Oct 1863 – Feb/Apr 1864	*Romuald Traugutt* (d. Warsaw 8 Aug 1864) Dictator

Governors-General and Military Commandants

31 Oct 1863 – 18 Jan 1874	*Fyodor Fyodorovich Rembert, Count Berg* (b. Sagnitz Castle 27 May 1790; d. St Petersburg 18 Jan 1874)
1867/70	Territory of Poland divided between the ten Vistula governments

1874 – 1880	*Paul, Count Kotzebue* (b. 1801; d. 1880)
1880 – 1883	*General Petr Pavlovich Albedinsky* (d. 1883)
Dec 1883 – Dec 1894	*Osip Vladimirovich Gurko* (b. 28 Jul 1828; d. Zakharovo 28 Jan 1901)
1894 – end of 1896	*Pavel Andreievich, Count Shuvalov* (b. 25 Nov 1830; d. Yalta 20 Apr 1908)
1897 – 30 Nov 1900	*Aleksandr Konstantinovich, Prince Bagration-Imeretinsky* (b. 6 Oct 1827; d. Warsaw 30 Nov 1900)
May 1901 – Sep 1905	*Mikhail Ivanovich Chertkov* (b. 1829)
Sep 1905 – 1914	*Georgy Skalon* (d. 1914)
Summer 1915	Occupied by Germany and Austria
25 Aug 1915	Establishment of Polish Government at Warsaw
25 Aug 1915 – Nov 1918	*General Hans Hartwig von Beseler* (b. Greifswald 27 Apr 1850; d. Neubabelsberg 20 Dec 1921) Governor-General
1915 – 1917	*Field Marshal Karl Kuk* (b. Trieste 1 Dec 1853; d. Vienna 26 Nov 1935) Governor of Lublin military government under Austrian control
5 Nov 1916	Proclamation of the Kingdom of Poland
May 1917	*Archduke Karl Stephan of Austria* (b. 5 Sep 1860; d. Saybusch 1 Apr 1933) King designate but declined appointment
Jan – Aug 1917	Polish Council of State
12 Sep 1917	Establishment of Polish Council of Regency

Presidents

14 Nov 1918 – 9 Dec 1922	*Józef Piłsudski* (b. Zułów 4 Jul 1867; d. Warsaw 12 May 1935) appointed by Council of Regency
9 – 16 Dec 1922	*Gabriel Narutowicz* (b. Talsen, Lithuania 3 Mar 1865; d. Warsaw 16 Dec 1922)
20 Dec 1922 – 15 May 1926	*Stanisław Wojciechowski* (b. Kalisz 15 Mar 1869; d. Golabki 9 Apr 1953)
4 Jun 1926 – 18 Sep 1939	*Ignacy Mościcki* (b. Mierzanów 1 Dec 1867; d. Versoix 1 Oct 1946)

MEMBERS OF GOVERNMENT

4 Feb – 20 Nov 1917: No Prime Minister

Home Affairs	*Michal Łempicki*

POLAND

Justice	*Stanisław Bukowiecki* (b. Włonicy 27 Apr 1867)
Finance	1 Feb – 20 Apr 1917: *Stanisław Dzierzbicki* (b. Jaranów 1854; d. Krzywonoś 10 Sep 1919)
	20 Apr – 20 Nov 1917: (?)
Religion and Education	—— *Pomorski*
Army	*Józef Piłsudski* (see Presidents)

plus Ministers for Economic Affairs, Labour and the 'Political Department'

20 Nov (7 Dec) 1917 – 27 Feb 1918: Kucharzewski I

Prime Minister	*Jan Kucharzewski* (for 1st time) (b. Wysokie Mazowieckie 27 May 1876; d. New York 4 Jul 1952)
Home Affairs	*Jan Stecki* (b. Lublin 22 Mar 1871; d.(?))
Justice	*Stanisław Bukowiecki* (see above)
Finance	*Jan Kanty Steczkowski* (b. 1863; d. 4 Sep 1929)
Education and Public Worship	*Anton Ponikowski* (b. Siedlce 29 May 1878)

Plus Ministers for Food, Agriculture, Industry and Social Welfare

27 Feb – 3 Apr 1918: Ponikowski I

Prime Minister	*Anton Ponikowski* (for 1st time) (see Kucharzewski I)
Home Affairs	27 Feb – 25 Mar 1918: *Stefan Dziewulski* (b. Warsaw 1876; d. 10 Apr 1941)
Justice	*Wacław Makowski* (b. Vilnius 2 Nov 1880; d. Bucharest 28 Dec 1942)
Finance	*Anton Wieniawski* (b. Warsaw 7 Jun 1871)
Education	*Anton Ponikowski* (see Kucharzewski I)

4 Apr – 6 Sep 1918: Steczkowski

Prime Minister	*Jan Kanty Steczkowski* (see Kucharzewski I)
Home Affairs	*Jan Stecki* (see Kucharzewski I)
Justice	*Józef Higersberger* (b. Warsaw 1856; d. Warsaw 18 May 1921)
Finance	*Jan Kanty Steczkowski* (see Kucharzewski I)
Education	*Anton Ponikowski* (see Kucharzewski I)

6 Sep – 9 Oct 1918: Kucharzewski II

Prime Minister   *Jan Kucharzewski* (for 2nd time) (see Kucharzewski I)
                    Other ministers remained in office (see Steczkowski)

22 Oct – 5 Nov 1918: Świerzyński

Prime Minister   *Józef Świerzyński* (b. 1868)
Foreign Affairs   *Stanisław Głąbiński* (b. Skole 25 Feb 1862; d. USSR
                    probably 1943)
Home Affairs   *Zygmunt Chrzanowski* (b. Dziadkowskie 5 Apr 1872;
                    d. 30 Dec 1936)
Justice   *Józef Higersberger* (see Steczkowski)
Finance   *Józef Englisch* (b. Śrem 14 Jan 1874; d. Poznan 22 Dec
                    1924)
Education   *Anton Ponikowski* (see Kucharzewski I)
War   *Józef Piłsudski* (see Presidents)

5 – 11 Nov 1918: Wróblewski

Prime Minister   *Władyskaw Wróblewski* (b. Krakow 21 Mar 1875)
                    The ministries were run by senior civil servants

14 – 18 Nov 1918: Daszyński

Prime Minister   *Ignacy Daszyński* (b. Zbaraż 26 Oct 1866; d. Bystra 31
                    Oct 1936)

18 Nov 1918 – 17 Jan 1919: Moraczewski

Prime Minister   *Jedrzej Moraczewski* (b. Trzemeszno 13 Jan 1870; d.
                    Sulejówek 5 Aug 1944)
Foreign Affairs   18 – 30 Nov 1918: *Leon Wasilewski* (b. St Petersburg
                    24 Aug 1870; d. Warsaw 10 Dec 1936)
                    30 Nov 1918 – 17 Jan 1919: *Marian Seyda* (b. Poznan 7
                    Jul 1879)
Home Affairs   *Stanisław August Thugutt* (b. Łęczyca 30 Jun 1873; d.
                    Stockholm 15 Jun 1941)
Justice   —— *Supiński*
Finance   18 – 30 Nov 1918: *Władysław Byrka* (b. Sambor 4 Jun
                    1878)
                    30 Nov 1918 – 17 Jan 1919: *Józef Englisch* (see Świer-
                    zyński)

POLAND

Science and Art   *Medard Downarowicz* (b. Łochów 22 May 1878; d.
                      Warsaw 16 Oct 1934)
Army   *Józef Piłsudski* (see Presidents)
Without Portfolio   30 Nov 1918 – 17 Jan 1919: *Wojciech Korfanty* (b.
                      Sadzawka 20 Apr 1873; d. Warsaw 17 Aug 1939)

18 Jan – 5 Dec 1919: Paderewski

Prime Minister   *Ignacy Jan Paderewski* (b. Kurylowka 18 Nov 1860; d.
  and Foreign   New York 29 Jun 1941)
  Affairs
Home Affairs   *Stanisław Wojciechowski* (see Presidents)
Justice   18 Jan – 6 Nov 1919: —— *Supiński* (see Moraczewski)
                      6 Nov – 5 Dec 1919: —— *Sobolewski*
Finance   18 Jan – May 1919: *Józef Englisch* (see Świerzyński)
                      2 Aug – 5 Dec 1919: *Leon Biliński* (b. Zaleszczyki 15
                      Jun 1846; d. Vienna 15 Jun 1923)
Science and Art   18 Jan – 17 Aug 1919: *Zenon Przesmycki* (b. Radzyń
                      22 Dec 1861; d. Warsaw 17 Oct 1944)
                      17 Aug – 5 Dec 1919: —— *Łuczański*
War   18 Jan – 14 Mar 1919: *Jan Józef Wroczyński* (b.
                      Ozierany 11 Jan 1876)
                      14 Mar – 5 Dec 1919: *Zbigniew (?) Lewiński-
                      Brochowicz* (b. Kielce 16 Dec 1877)

13 Dec 1919 – 9 Jun 1920: Skulski

Prime Minister   *Leopold Skulski* (b. Zamość 15 Nov 1878)
Foreign Affairs   *Stanisław Patek* (b. Policzno 1 May 1866; d. 1945)
Home Affairs   *Stanisław Wojciechowski* (see Presidents)
Finance   *Władysław Grabski* (b. Borów 7 Jul 1874; d. Warsaw 1
                      Mar 1938)
Education   *Tadeusz Łopuszański* (b. Lvov 1874; d. Gliwice 1955)
Army   *Józef Krzysztof Leśniewski* (b. Newel 26 Sep 1867; d.
                      Warsaw 3 Oct 1921)

24 Jun – 23 Jul 1920: Grabski I

Prime Minister   *Władysław Grabski* (for 1st time) (see Skulski)
Foreign Affairs   *Eustachy Kajetan Władysław, Prince Sapieha* (b.
                      Biłka Szlachecka 2 Aug 1881; d. Nairobi 20 Feb 1963)
Home Affairs   *Józef Kuczyński* (b. Gadalei 10 Jun 1871; d. Batowicy
                      28 Jul 1931)

Justice	*Jan Morawski* (b. Odrzechow 4 Sep 1878)
Finance	*Władysław Grabski* (see Skulski)
Education	*Tadeusz Łopuszański* (see Skulski)
Army	*Józef Krzysztof Leśniewski* (see Skulski)

23 Jul 1920 – 10 Sep 1921: Witos I

Prime Minister	*Wincenty Witos* (for 1st time) (b. Wierzchosławice 22 Jan 1874; d. 31 Oct 1945)
Vice Premier	23 Jul – 20 Dec 1920: *Ignacy Daszyński* (see Daszyński)
Foreign Affairs	23 Jul 1920 – 26 May 1921: *Eustachy Kajetan Władysław, Prince Sapieha* (see Grabski I)
	13 Jun – 10 Sep 1921: *Konstantin, Count Skirmunt* (b. Mołodów 30 Aug 1866; d. 1951)
Home Affairs	23 Jul 1920 – 30 Jun 1921: *Leopold Skulski* (see Skulski)
	30 Jun – 10 Sep 1921: *Władysław Raczkiewicz* (b. Minsk 16 Jan 1885; d. Ruthin Castle 6 Jun 1947)
Justice	23 Jul 1920 – 16 Jun 1921: *Stanisław Nowodworski* (b. 1874; d. 1931)
	21 Jun – 10 Sep 1921: —— *Sobolewski* (see Paderewski)
Finance	23 Jul – 27 Nov 1920: *Władysław Grabski* (see Skulski)
	27 Nov 1920 – 10 Sep 1921: *Jan Kanty Steczkowski* (see Kucharzewski I)
Education	*Maciej Rataj* (b. Chłopy 19 Feb 1884; d. Warsaw 1940)
Army	23 Jul – 10 Aug 1920: *Józef Krzysztof Leśniewski* (see Skulski)
	10 Aug 1920 – 10 Sep 1921: *Kazimierz Sosnkowski* (b. Warsaw 19 Nov 1885)

20 Sep 1921 – 3 Mar 1922: Ponikowski II

Prime Minister	*Anton Ponikowski* (for 2nd time) (see Kucharzewski I)
Foreign Affairs	*Konstantin, Count Skirmunt* (see Witos I)
Home Affairs	*Medard Downarowicz* (see Moraczewski)
Justice	—— *Sobolewski* (see Paderewski)
Finance	*Jerzy Michalski* (b. Jarosław 18 Mar 1870)
Education	*Anton Ponikowski* (see Kucharzewski I)
Army	*Kazimierz Sosnkowski* (see Witos I)

11 Mar - 6 Jun 1922: Ponikowski III

Prime Minister	*Anton Ponikowski* (for 3rd time) (see Kucharzewski I)
	Other ministers remained in office (see Ponikowski II)

25 Jun - 8 Jul 1922: Śliwiński

Prime Minister	*Artur Śliwiński* (b. Ruszki 17 Aug 1877; d. Warsaw 16 Jan 1953)
Foreign Affairs	*Aleksander, Count Skrzyński* (b. Zagórzany 18 Mar 1882; d. Ostrowo 25 Sep 1931)

14 /19 - 29 Jul 1922: Korfanty

Prime Minister	*Wojciech Korfanty* (see Moraczewski)
Foreign Affairs	*Konstantin, Count Skirmunt* (see Witos I)
Home Affairs	—— *Weichart*
Justice	*Józef Kuczyński* (see Grabski I)
Finance	*Jerzy Michalski* (see Ponikowski II)
Education	—— *Godlewski*
War	*Kazimierz Sosnkowski* (see Witos I)

31 Jul - 17 Dec 1922: Novak

Prime Minister	*Julian Ignacy Novak* (b. Okocim 10 Mar 1856; d. Krakow 7 Nov 1946)
Foreign Affairs	31 Jul - 9 Dec 1922: *Gabriel Narutowicz* (see Presidents)
Home Affairs	*Antoni Kamieński* (b. Łódź 13 Jun 1878; d. Warsaw 1924)
Finance	*Wincenty Jastrzębski* (b. Przystan 11 Oct 1885)
War	*Kazimierz Sosnkowski* (see Witos I)

17 Dec 1922 - 26 May 1923: Sikorski

Prime Minister	*Władysław Sikorski* (b. Tuszów Narodowy 20 May 1881; d. near Gibraltar 3 Jul 1943)
Foreign Affairs	*Aleksander, Count Skrzyński* (see Śliwiński)
Home Affairs	*Władysław Sikorski* (see above)
Finance	17 Dec 1922 - 15 Jan 1923: *Wincenty Jastrzębski* (see Novak)
	15 Jan - 26 May 1923: *Władysław Grabski* (see Skulski)

Education   *Tadeusz Titus Stanisław Mikułowski* (b. Cieszanów 28 Oct 1884)

28 May - 13 Dec 1923: Witos II

Prime Minister	*Wincenty Witos* (for 2nd time) (see Witos I)
Foreign Affairs	28 May – 28 Oct 1923: *Marian Seyda* (see Moraczewski)
	28 Oct – 13 Dec 1923: *Roman Dmowski* (b. Kamionek 9 Aug 1864; d. Drozdowo 2 Jan 1939)
Home Affairs	*Władysław Kiernik* (b. Bochnia 27 Jul 1879)
Justice	*Stanisław Nowodworski* (see Witos I)
Finance	28 May – 1 Jul 1923: *Władysław Grabski* (see Skulski)
	1 Jul – 1 Oct 1923: *Hubert Ignacy Linde* (b. Stanisławow 3 Nov 1867; d. 1926)
	1 Oct – 13 Dec 1923: *Władysław Kuchcrski* (b. Krakow 23 Sep 1884; d. Krakow 27 Dec 19(4)
Education	28 May – 28 Oct 1923: *Stánisław Głabiński* (see Świerzyński)
	28 Oct – 13 Dec 1923: *Władysław Grabski* (see Skulski)
War	28 May – 14 Jun 1923: *Aleksander Osiński* (b. Pilica 27 Feb 1870)
	14 Jun – 28 Nov 1923: *Stanisław Maria, Count Szeptycki* (b. Przyłbicy 3 Nov 1867; d. Warsaw 1946)

20 Dec 1923 - 13 Nov 1925: Grabski II

Prime Minister	*Władysław Grabski* (for 2nd time) (see Skulski)
Foreign Affairs	20 Dec 1923 – 27 Jul 1924: *Maurycy Klemens, Count Zamoyski* (b. Warsaw 30 Jul 1871; d. Warsaw 5 May 1939)
	27 Jul 1924 – 13 Nov 1925: *Aleksander, Count Skrzyński* (see Śliwiński)
Home Affairs	20 Dec 1923 – 21 Mar 1924: *Władysław Sołtan* (b. Tver, Russia 7 Jul 1870)
	24 Mar – 17 Nov 1924: *Zygmunc Hübner*
	17 Nov 1924 – 8 Jun 1925: *Cyryl Ratajski* (b. Zalesie 3 Mar 1875; d. Warsaw 19 Oct 1942)
	8 Jun – 13 Nov 1925: —— *Roman*
Justice	20 Dec 1923 – 17 Nov 1924: *W. Cyganowski*
	17 Nov 1924 – 13 Nov 1925: —— *Żychliński*
Finance	*Władysław Grabski* (see Skulski)

POLAND

Education	20 Dec 1923 – 10 Dec 1924: *Bolesław Grzegorz Miklaszewski* (b. Ociescy 9 May 1871; d. Warsaw 1 Sep 1939)
	10 Dec 1924 – Mar 1925: *Jan Wiktor Tomasz Zawidzki* (b. Włuki 20 Dec 1866; d. Warsaw 14 Sep 1928)
	Mar – 13 Nov 1925: *Stanisław Grabski* (b. Borów 7 Apr 1871; d. Warsaw 7 May 1949)
Army	20 Dec 1923 – 17 Feb 1924: *Kazimierz Sosnkowski* (see Witos I)
	17 Feb 1924 – 13 Nov 1925: *Władysław Sikorski* (see Sikorski)

20 Nov 1925 – 5 May 1926: Skrzyński

Prime Minister and Foreign Affairs	*Aleksander, Count Skrzyński* (see Śliwiński)
Home Affairs	*Władysław Raczkiewicz* (see Witos I)
Justice	*Szczepan Piechocki* (b. Czekanow 2 Aug 1883)
Finance	*Jerzy Zdziechowski* (b. Rozdola 27 Aug 1880)
Education	*Stanisław Grabski* (see Grabski II)
War	*Lucjan Żeligowski* (b. Oszmiana 2 Oct 1865; d. London 9 Jul 1947)

10 – 15 May 1926: Witos III

Prime Minister	*Wincenty Witos* (for 3rd time) (see Witos I)
Foreign Affairs	(acting:) *Jan Morawski* (see Grabski I)
Home Affairs	—— *Zmolski*
Finance	*Jerzy Zdziechowski* (see Skrzyński)
Army	—— *Maczewski*

15 May – 4 Jun 1926: Bartel I

Prime Minister	*Kazimierz Bartel* (for 1st time) (b. Lvov 3 Mar 1882; d. Lvov 26 Jul 1941)
Foreign Affairs	*August Zaleski* (b. Warsaw 13 Sep 1883)
Home Affairs	*Kazimierz Młodzianowski* (b. 1880; d. 1928)
Justice	*Wacław Makowski* (see Ponikowski I)
Finance	*Gabriel Czechowicz* (b. Minsk 2 Oct 1876; d. Warsaw 22 Jan 1938)
Education	*Tadeusz Titus Stanisław Mikułowski* (see Sikorski I)
War	*Józef Piłsudski* (see Presidents)

Railways   *Kazimierz Bartel* (see above)

8 Jun - 30 Sep 1926: Bartel II

Prime Minister   *Kazimierz Bartel* (for 2nd time) (see Bartel I)
Finance   *Czesław Romuald Klarner* (b. Plonsk 7 Feb 1872; d.
                         Warsaw 23 Jun 1957)
                         Other ministers remained in office (see Bartel I)

2 Oct 1926 - 27 Jun 1928: Piłsudski

Prime Minister   *Józef Piłsudski* (see Presidents)
Foreign Affairs   *August Zaleski* (see Bartel I)
Home Affairs   *Felicjan Sławoj-Składkowski* (b. Gąbin 9 Jun 1885; d.
                         London 31 Aug 1962)
Justice   *Aleksander Michal Marian Meysztowicz* (b. Pojoście,
                         Lithuania 8 Dec 1864; d. Rome 1943)
Finance   *Gabriel Czechowicz* (see Bartel I)
Education   *Kazimierz Bartel* (see Bartel I)
Commerce   *Eugeniusz Felicjan Kwiatkowski* (b. Krakow 30 Dec
                         1888)
War   *Józef Piłsudski* (see Presidents)

27 Jun 1928 - 12 Apr 1929: Bartel III

Prime Minister   *Kazimierz Bartel* (for 3rd time) (see Bartel I)
Foreign Affairs   *August Zaleski* (see Bartel I)
Home Affairs   *Felicjan Sławoj-Składkowski* (see Piłsudski)
Justice   27 Jun - 23 Dec 1928: *Aleksander Michal Marian
                         Meysztowicz* (see Piłsudski)
                         23 Dec 1928 - 12 Apr 1929: *Stanisław Car* (b. Warsaw
                         26 Apr 1882; d. Warsaw 18 Jun 1938)
Finance   27 Jun 1928 - 8 Mar 1929: *Gabriel Czechowicz* (see
                         Bartel I)
                         8 Mar - 12 Apr 1929: *Tadeusz Grodyński* (b. 1888; d.
                         London 24 May 1958)
Education   *Kazimierz Świtalski* (b. Sanok 4 Mar 1886; d. Warsaw
                         28 Dec 1962)
Transport   *Alfons Walenty Kühn* (b. Przejmy 14 Feb 1879; d.
                         Warsaw 27 Jan 1944)
War   *Józef Piłsudski* (see Presidents)

14 Apr – 7 Dec 1929: Świtalski

Prime Minister	*Kazimierz Świtalski* (see Bartel III)
Foreign Affairs	*August Zaleski* (see Bartel I)
Home Affairs	*Felicjan Sławoj-Składkowski* (see Piłsudksi)
Justice	*Stanisław Car* (see Bartel III)
Finance	*Ignacy Matuszewski* (b. Warsaw 10 Sep 1891; d. New York 3 Aug 1946)
Education	*Sławomir Czerwiński* (b. Sompolno 24 Oct 1885; d. Warsaw 4 Aug 1931)
Commerce	*Eugeniusz Felicjan Kwiatkowski* (see Piłsudski)
Transport	*Alfons Walenty Kühn* (see Bartel III)
Posts and Telephones	*Ignacy Boerner* (b. Zduńska Wola 11 Aug 1875; d. Warsaw 12 Apr 1933)
War	*Józef Piłsudski* (see Presidents)

Portugal

HEADS OF STATE

Kings

Burgundian dynasty

28 Aug 1481	*John II*, son of King Alfonso (b. 3 May 1455)
25 Oct 1495	*Emmanuel I*, cousin (b. 3 May 1469)
13 Dec 1521	*John III*, son (b. 6 Jun 1502)
11 Jun 1557	*Sebastian*, grandson (b. 20 Jan 1554; d. 1578)
4 Aug 1578	*Henry*, son of King Emmanuel I (b. 31 Jan 1512) Cardinal
1580 – 1640	United with Spain

Habsburg

31 Jan 1580	*Philip I*, son of King Charles I of Spain and of Isabella, daughter of King Emmanuel I (b. 21 May 1527) from 1556 – 1598 as Philip II, King of Spain
13 Sep 1598	*Philip II*, son (b. 14 Apr 1578) from 1598 – 1621, as Philip III, King of Spain
30 Mar 1621	*Philip III*, son (b. 8 Apr 1605) from 1621 – 1665 as Philip IV, King of Spain

House of Braganza

1 Dec 1640	*John IV*, son of Duke Theodore II of Braganza (b. 18 Mar 1604)
6 Nov 1656	*Alfonso VI*, son (b. 12/21 Aug 1643; d. 12 Sep 1683)
23 Nov 1667	*Peter II*, brother (b. 26 Apr 1648)
9 Dec 1705	*John V*, son (b. 22 Oct 1689)
31 Jul 1750	*Joseph*, son (b. 6 Jun 1714)
24 Feb 1777 – 20 Mar 1816	*Maria I*, daughter (b. 17 Dec 1734) from 6 Jun 1760 married to *Peter III*, her uncle (b. 5 Jul 1717)
20 Mar 1816 – 10 Mar 1826	*John VI*, son (b. 13 May 1767) Regent from 1792, he lived with his mother in Brazil while Portugal was occupied by the French, 27 Nov 1807 – 3 Jul 1821
Mar 1809 – 15 Sep 1820	*Field Marshal William Carr* (from 1813: Portuguese title of *Duke of Elvas*, from 1814: *Baron*, from 1823: *Viscount Beresford*) (b. 2 Oct 1768; d. Kent 8 Jan 1854) Administrator for the absent King and Commander-in-Chief of the Portuguese army
29 Aug – 15 Sep 1820	*Antonio, Count Silveira*, Head of Junta
15 Sep 1820 – Sep 1821	*Bishop Gomes Freire de Andrade* (b. 6 Jun 1761; d. 8 Apr 1831) Acting Administrator for the absent King
10 Mar 1826	*Peter IV*, son of King John VI (b. 12 Oct 1798; d. 29 Nov 1834) from 1822 – 1831: Peter I, Emperor of Brazil, renouncing the Portuguese throne in favour of his daughter (as below)
5 May 1826	*Maria II*, daughter (b. 4 Apr 1819; d. 15 Nov 1853) **Regents:** 1826 – 28 Feb 1828: *Princess Isabella Maria*, aunt (b. 4 Jul 1801; d. Benfica 22 Apr 1876) 28 Feb – 30 Jun 1828: *Prince Michael*, brother of Peter IV and fiancé of Maria II, who declared himself King in opposition
30 Jun 1828 – 26 May 1834	*Michael*, uncle of Maria II (b. 26 Oct 1802; d. Bronnbach Castle 14 Nov 1866) rival King
23 Sep 1833 – 15 Nov 1853	*Maria II* (see above) proclaimed Queen; her father, the former King Peter IV, was Regent from 23 Aug – 24 Sep 1834, Maria II being declared of age on 20 Sep 1834

House of Saxe-Coburg-Gotha-Koháry

16 Sep 1837	*Ferdinand II*, son of Prince Ferdinand of Saxe-Coburg-Gotha-Koháry (b. 29 Oct 1816; d. 15 Dec 1885) given the title of King alongside his wife Maria II
15 Nov 1853	*Peter V*, son (b. 16 Sep 1837) until 16 Sep 1855 under the regency of his father, King Ferdinand II

PORTUGAL

11 Nov 1861	*Luís.* brother (b. 31 Oct 1838)
19 Oct 1889	*Carlos,* son (b. 28 Sep 1863; d. 1908)
1 Feb 1909 – 5 Oct 1910	*Manuel II,* son (b. 15 Nov 1889; d. London 2 Jul 1932)
5 Oct 1910	Republic

Presidents

15 Oct 1910	*Teófilo Braga* (for 1st time) (b. 24 Mar 1843; d. 29 Jan 1924)
2 Sep 1911	*Manoel d'Arriaga* (b. 8 Jul 1840; d. 6 Mar 1917)
29 May 1915	*Teófilo Braga* (for 2nd time)
7 Aug 1915	*Bernardino (Luís) Machado Guimarães* (for 1st time) (b. Rio de Janeiro 28 Mar 1851; d. Oporto 28 Apr 1944)
28 Apr 1918 – 14 Dec 1918	*Sidónio Pais* (b. 4 Mar 1858; d. 14 Dec 1918)
16 Dec 1918	(acting:) *João do Canto e Castro* (b. 19 May 1862; d. 14 Mar 1934)
5 Oct 1919	*Antonio José de Almeida* (b. 18 Jul 1866; d. 30/31 Oct 1929)
6 Aug 1923	*Manuel Texeira Gomes* (b. 27 May 1862; d. Bougie, Algeria 18 Oct 1941)
12 Dec 1925	*Bernardino (Luís) Machado Guimarães* (for 2nd time)
1 Jun 1926	*Manuel de Oliveira Gomes da Costa* (b. 14 Jan 1863; d. 17 Dec 1929) Dictator
9 Aug 1926 – 18 Apr 1951	*António Óscar Fragoso Carmona* (b. 24 Nov 1869; d. 18 Apr 1951)

HEADS OF GOVERNMENT

23 Sep 1822	Proclamation of a constitution by King John VI, rescinded in 1823 under pressure from Prince, later Regent and rival King Michael
29 Apr 1826	John VI sets up a new constitution, rescinded by Regent Michael on 13 Mar 1828
May 1834	Re-establishment of 1826 constitution
9 Sep 1836	Re-establishment of 1822 constitution, sworn by Queen Maria II on 8 Apr 1838
11 Feb 1842	Following the collapse of the liberals (Septembrists), the 1826 constitution was re-established by the conservatives (Chartists)

Prime Ministers

27 May – 25 Nov 1835	*João Carlos, Duke de Saldanha Oliveira e Daun* (for 1st time) (b. 17 Nov 1790; d. 21 Nov 1876)
25 Nov 1835 – 20 Apr 1836	*José Jorge Loureiro* (b. 23 Apr 1791; d. 1 Jun 1860)
20 Apr – 9 Sep 1836	*António José de Sousa, Manuel e Meneses Severim de Noronha, Duke of Terceira* (for 1st time) (b. 18 Mar 1792; d. 26 Apr 1860)
10 Sep – 4 Nov 1836	*José Manuel Inácio da Cunha Faro Meneses Portugal da Gama Carneiro e Sousa, Count Luminares* (b. 12 Jan 1788; d. 24 Oct 1859)
1836 – 1839	*Bernardo da Sá Nogueira, Marquis de Sá de Bandeira* (for 1st time) (b. 26 Sep 1795; d. 6 Jan 1876)
26 Sep 1839 – 1841	*José Lúcio Travassos Valdez, 1st Count Bomfim* (b. 23 Feb 1787; d. 10 Jul 1862)
19 Jan – 7 Feb 1842	*António Bernardo da Costa-Cabral, Count Thomar* (for 1st time) (b. 9 May 1803; d. 1 Sep 1889)
10 Feb 1842 – May 1846	*António José de Sousa, Duke of Terceira* (for 2nd time)
17 May 1846	*Pedro de Sousa-Holstein, Duke of Palmela* (b. 8 May 1781; d. 12 Oct 1850)
6 Oct 1846	*João Carlos, Duke de Saldanha Oliveira e Daun* (for 2nd time)
Jul 1849 – 26 Apr 1851	*António Bernardo da Costa-Cabral, Count Thomar* (for 2nd time)
15 May 1851	*João Carlos, Duke de Saldanha Oliveira e Daun* (for 3rd time)
6 Jun 1856 (14 Mar 1857)	*Nuno José Severo de Mendoça Rolim de Moura Bareto, 1st Duke of Loulé* (for 1st time) (b. 6 Nov 1804; d. 22 May 1875)
16 Mar 1859 – Apr 1860	*António José de Sousa, Duke of Terceira* (for 3rd time)
1 May – 4 Jul 1860	*Joaquim António de Aguiar* (for 1st time) (b. 24 Aug 1792; d. 26 May 1884)
4 Jul 1860	*Nuno José Severo de Mendoça Rolim de Moura Bareto, 1st Duke of Loulé* (for 2nd time)
9 Apr 1865	*Bernardo da Sá Nogueira, Marquis de Sá de Bandeira* (for 2nd time)
1 Sep 1865	*José Joaquim Gomes de Castro, 1st Count Castro* (b. 13 Dec 1794; d. 8 Oct 1878)
4 Sep 1866	*Joaquim António de Aguiar* (for 2nd time)
2 Jan 1868	*António José de Ávila, 1st Duke of Ávila* (for 1st time) (b. 8 Mar 1806; d. 3 May 1881)

PORTUGAL

14 Jul 1868	*Bernardo da Sá Nogueira, Marquis de Sá de Bandeira* (for 3rd time)
10 Aug 1869	*Nuno José da Mendoça Rolin de Moura Bareto, 2nd Duke of Loulé* (for 3rd time)
19 May 1870	*João Carlos, Duke de Saldanha Oliveira e Daun* (for 3rd time)
30 Aug 1870	*Bernardo da Sá Nogueira, Marquis de Sá de Bandeira* (for 4th time)
29 Oct 1870	*António José de Ávila, 1st Duke of Ávila* (for 2nd time)
13 Sep 1871	*António Maria de Fontes Pereira de Mello* (for 1st time) (b. 8 Sep 1819; d. 22 Jan 1887)
6 Mar 1877	*António José de Ávila, 1st Duke of Avila* (for 3rd time)
26 Jan 1878	*António Maria de Fontes Pereira de Mello* (for 2nd time)
29 May 1879	*Anselmo José Braamcamp* (b. 23 Oct 1819; d. 13 Nov 1885)
23 Mar 1881	*António Rodrigues Sampaio* (b. 25 Jul 1806; d. Sep 1882)
14 Nov 1881	*António Maria de Fontes Pereira de Mello* (for 3rd time)
16 Feb 1886	*José Luciano de Castro* (for 1st time) (b. 14 Dec 1835; d. 9 Mar 1914)
14 Jan – 15 Sep 1890	*António de Serpa Pimentel* (b. 20 Nov 1825; d. 2 Mar 1900)
11 Oct 1890	*João Crisóstomo de Abreu e Souza* (b. 1811; d. 1895)
18 Jan 1892	*José Dias Ferreira* (b. 30 Nov 1837; d. 8 Sep 1909)
22 Feb 1893	*Ernst Rudolf Hintze-Ribeiro* (for 1st time) (b. 7 Nov 1849; d. 1 Aug 1907)
5 Feb 1897	*José Luciano de Castro* (for 2nd time)
21 Jun 1900	*Ernst Rudolf Hintze-Ribeiro* (for 2nd time)
20 Oct 1904	*José Luciano de Castro* (for 3rd time)
20 Mar 1906	*Ernst Rudolf Hintze-Ribeiro* (for 3rd time)
17 May 1906	*João Franco* (b. 14 Feb 1855; d. 4 Apr 1929)
4 Feb 1908	*Francisco Joaquim Ferreira do Amaral* (b. 11 Jun 1844; d. 11 Aug 1923)
19 Dec 1908 – end of Mar 1909	*Arturo Alberto de Campos Henriques* (b. 28 Apr 1853; d. 7 Nov 1922)
2 Apr 1909	*Sebastião Tellez*
13 May 1909	*Venceslau de Soma Perreira de Lima* (b. 1858; d. 1919)
22 Dec 1909	*Francisco António da Veiga Beirão* (b. 24 Jul 1841; d. 11 Nov 1916)

26 Jun 1910	*António Teixeira de Sousa* (b. 5 May 1857; d. 5 Jun 1917)
4 Oct 1910	*Teófilo Braga* (see Presidents)
2 Sep 1911	*Joäo Pinheiro Chagas* (for 1st time) (b. 1 Sep 1863; d. 28 May 1925)
12 Nov 1911 – 4 Jun 1912	*Augusto de Vasconcellos* (b. 24 Sep 1867; d. 27 Sep 1951)
16 Jun 1912	*Duarte Leite* (b. 11 Aug 1864; d. 29 Sep 1950)
9 Jan 1913	*Afonso Costa* (for 1st time) (b. 6 Mar 1871; d. 11 May 1937)
8 Feb 1914	*Bernardino (Luís) Machado Guimarães* (for 1st time) (see Presidents)
7 Dec 1914	*Vitor Hugo de Azevedo Coutinho* (b. 12 Nov 1871; d. 27 Jun 1955)
28 Jan 1915	*Joaquim Pereira Pimenta de Castro* (b. 5 Sep 1846; d. 14 May 1918)
14 May 1915	*João Pinheiro Chagas* (for 2nd time)
19 May 1915	*Afonso Costa* (for 2nd time)
20 Jun 1915	*José de Castro* (b. 7 Apr 1868; d. 30(?) Jun 1929)
30 Nov 1915	*Afonso Costa* (for 3rd time)
16 Mar 1916	*António José d'Almeida* (see Presidents)
15 Apr 1917	*Afonso Costa* (for 4th time)
8 Dec 1917 – 14 Dec 1918	*Sidónio Pais* (see Presidents)
23 Dec 1918	*João Tamagnini Barbasa* (b. 30 Dec 1883; d. 15 Dec 1948)
25 Jan 1919	*José Relvas* (b. 5 Mar 1858; d. 31 Oct 1929)
31 Mar 1919	*Domingos Leite Pereira* (for 1st time) (b. Braga 19 Sep 1882; d. Oporto 27 Oct 1956)
1 Jul 1919 – 10 Jan 1920	*Alfredo Ernesto de Sá Cardoso* (b. 6 Jun 1864; d. 23 Apr 1950)
21 Jan – 5 Mar 1920	*Domingos Leite Pereira* (for 2nd time)
9 Mar – 6 Jun 1920	*António Maria Baptista* (b. 5 Jan 1866; d. 6 Jun 1920)
9 – 19 Jun 1920	*Garcia Giustiniano*
26 Jun – 9 Jul 1920	*António Maria da Silva* (for 1st time) (b. 1872; d. 14 Oct 1950)
17 Jul – 16 Nov 1920	*António Granjo* (for 1st time) (b. 1881; d. 19 Oct 1921)
20 – 27 Nov 1920	*Álvaro de Castro* (b. 9 Sep 1878; d. 29 Jun 1928)
4 Dec 1920 – 13 Feb 1921	*Abel Hipólito* (b. 1860; d. 12 Oct 1929)
14 Mar 1921	*Bernardino (Luís) Machado Guimarães* (for 2nd time)
24 May 1921	*Barros Gueiros*
28 Aug 1921	*António Granjo* (for 2nd time)

PORTUGAL

20 Oct 1921	*Manuel Maria Coelho* (b. 6 Mar 1857; d. 10 Jan 1943)
4 Nov 1921	*Liberato Pinto* (b. 29 Sep 1880; d. 4 Sep 1949)
20 Dec 1921	*Francisco Pinto da Cunha Leal* (b. 23 Aug 1888)
8 Feb 1922	*António Maria da Silva* (for 2nd time)
28 Jun – 19 Nov 1924	*Alfredo Rodrigues Gaspar* (b. 1865; d. 1 Dec 1938)
21 Nov 1924	*José Domingos dos Santos* (b. 15 Aug 1885; d. 16 Aug 1958)
15 Feb 1925	*Vitorino Máximo de Carvalho Guimarães* (b. 13 Nov 1876; d. 18 Oct 1957)
30 Jun – 1 Aug 1925	*António Maria da Silva* (for 3rd time)
7 Aug 1925	*João Pereira Bastos* (b. 29 Jan 1865; d. 3 Aug 1951)
17 Dec 1925 – 29 May 1926	*António Maria da Silva* (for 4th time)
30 May 1926	*José Mendes Cabeçadas* (b. 19 Aug 1883)
20 Jun 1926	*Manuel de Oliveira Gomes da Costa* (b. 14 Jan 1863; d. 17 Dec 1929)
9 Jul 1926 – 16 Apr 1928	*António Óscar Fragoso Carmona* (see Presidents)
19 Apr – 9 Nov 1928	*José Vicente Freitas* (for 1st time) (b. 22 Jan 1869; d. 6 Sep 1952)
12 Nov 1928 – 5 Jul 1929	*José Vicente Freitas* (for 2nd time)
9 Jul 1929 – 10 Jan 1930	*Arturo Ivens Ferraz* (b. 1 Dec 1870; d. 16 Jan 1933)

Foreign Ministers

17 Oct – 23 Dec 1918	—— *Monj*(?) (Moniz ?)
23 Dec 1918 – 31 Mar 1919	(acting:) *João Alberto Pereira de Azevedo Neves* (b. Angra do Heroismo 12 May 1877; d. Lisbon 14 Apr 1955)
31 Mar – 1 Jul 1919	*Zavier da Silva* (b. Lisbon 1 Nov 1879; d. 3 Apr 1955(?))
Jul 1919 – 6 Jun 1920	*João Carlos Melo Barreto* (for 1st time) (b. Lisbon 3 Jul 1873; d. Madrid 26 Jan 1935)
9 Jun – 9 Jul 1920	*Francisco António Correia* (b. Moncorvo 9 Nov 1877; d. Lisbon 8 Feb 1938)
9 Jul – 16 Nov 1920	*João Carlos Melo Barreto* (for 2nd time)
1 Dec 1920 – 23 May 1921	*Domingos Leite Pereira* (for 1st time) (see Prime Ministers)
24 May – 20 Oct 1921	*Alberto da Veiga Simões*
21 Dec 1921 – 8 Feb 1922	*Julio Dantas* (for 1st time) (b. Lagos 19 May 1876; d. Lisbon 25 May 1962)

1922 – 1923	*Domingos Leite Pereira* (for 2nd time)
(?) – Dec 1923	*Julio Dantas* (for 2nd time)
Dec 1923 – Jun 1924	*Domingos Leite Pereira* (for 3rd time)
28 Jun – 19 Nov 1924	*Vitorino Godinho* (b. Anciao 19 Jul 1878)
19 Nov 1924 – Feb 1925	*João de Barros* (b. Figueira da Foz 4 Feb 1881)
14 Feb – Dec 1925	*P. Martinus*
Dec 1925 – Jun 1926	*Vasco Borges* (d. Lisbon 19 Feb 1942)
17 Jun – 9 Jul 1926	*António Óscar Fragoso Carmona* (see Presidents)
9 Jul 1926 – 9 Nov 1928	*António Maria de Bettencourt Rodrigues* (b. Cape Verde 6 Mar 1854; d. Monte Estoril 1933)
12 Nov 1928 – 5 Jul 1929	*Manuel Carlos Quintão Meireles* (b. Cinta 14 Dec 1880; d. Lisbon 11 Mar 1962)
9 Jul – 9 Sep 1929	(acting:) *Arturo Ivens Ferraz* (see Prime Ministers)
9 Sep 1929 – 10 Jan 1930	*J. Fonseca Monteira*

Prussia

HEADS OF STATE

Dukes of the House of Hohenzollern

8 Apr 1525	*Albrecht*, third son of Friedrich, Margrave of Ansbach (b. 16 May 1490) from 1511 Grand Master of the Teutonic Knights, set up secular Duchy of Prussia in 1525
20 Mar 1568	*Albrecht Friedrich*, son (b. 29 Apr 1553) mentally ill

Regents of the House of Hohenzollern

20 Mar 1568 – 26 Apr 1603	*Georg Friedrich, Margrave of Ansbach* (b. 5 Apr 1539; d. 26 Apr 1603)
26 Apr 1603 – 18 Jul 1608	*Joachim Friedrich, Elector of Brandenburg*, (b. 27 Jan 1546)
18 Jul 1608 – 18 Aug 1618	*Johann Sigismund, Elector of Brandenburg*, son (b. 8 Nov 1572)
18 Aug 1618 – 18 Jan 1701	The Electors of Brandenburg were also Dukes of Prussia

429

PRUSSIA

Kings

18 Jan 1701	*Frederick I*, previously Elector of Brandenburg
25 Feb 1713	*Frederick William I*, son (b. 4/15 Aug 1688)
31 Apr 1740	*Frederick II*, the Great, son (b. 24 Jan 1712)
17 Aug 1786	*Frederick William II*, nephew (b. 25 Sep 1744)
16 Nov 1797	*Frederick William III*, son (b. 3 Aug 1770)
7 Jun 1840	*Frederick William IV*, son (b. 15 Oct 1795)
2 Jan 1861	*William I*, brother (b. 22 Mar 1797) Regent from 9 Oct 1858, German Emperor from 18 Jan 1871
9 Mar 1888	*Frederick III*, son (b. 18 Oct 1831) German Emperor
15 Jun 1888 – 9/28 Nov 1918	*William II*, son (b. 27 Jan 1859; d. 4 Jun 1941) German Emperor
9 Nov 1918	Republic

MEMBERS OF GOVERNMENT

Chief Ministers before the formation of departmental ministries in 1808

1619 – 1640	*Adam, Count Schwarzenberg* (b. 1583; d. Spandan 14 Mar 1641)
1653 – 1658	*Georg Friedrich, Count* (from 1682: *Prince*) *Waldeck* (b. Arolsen 31 Jan 1620; d. Arolsen 19 Nov 1692)
1658 – 4 Nov 1679	*Otto, Baron Schwerin* (b. 8 Mar 1616; d. 4 Nov 1679)
1695 – Dec 1697	*Eberhard, Baron Danckelmann* (b. Lingen 23 Nov 1643; d. Berlin 31 Mar 1722)
1697 – early 1711	*Johann Kasimir* (from 1699: *Count*) *Kolbe von Wartenberg* (b. Wetterau 6 Feb 1643; d. Frankfurt am Main 4 Jun 1712)
early 1711 – 16 Dec 1728	*Heinrich Rüdiger von Ilgen* (b. Minden c. 1650; d. Britz 6 Dec 1728)
(1723) 1728 – 18 Mar 1739	*Friedrich Wilhelm von Grumbkow* (b. Berlin 6 Oct 1678; d. Berlin 18 Mar 1739)
Jun 1749 – 3 Jan 1800	*Karl Wilhelm, Count Finck von Finckenstein* (b. 11 Feb 1714; d. 3 Jan 1800)
1749 – 20 Oct 1753	*Georg Dietlof von Arnim-Boitzenburg* (b. 9 Sep 1679 d. 20 Oct 1753) in similar capacity
1777 – 15 May 1802	*Friedrich Anton, Baron Heinitz* (b. Dröschkau 2 May 1725; d. 15 May 1802) Secretary of State and head of various departments
8 Nov 1786 – 1798	*Friedrich Wilhelm, Count Arnim* (b. Berlin 31 Dec 1739; d. Berlin 21 Jan 1801) Secretary of State

Foreign Affairs up to 1802 (there were usually several ministers at once)

1728 – May 1741	*Adrian Bernhard, Count Borck* (b. Döberitz 31 Jul 1668; d. Berlin 25(31?) May 1741)
1728 – 1730	*Friedrich Ernst, Baron Inn- und Knyphausen* (d. 1731)
1730 – 29 Jul 1760	*Heinrich, Count Podewils* (b. 3 Oct 1695; d. Magdeburg 29 Jul 1760)
27 Nov 1731 – 4 Aug 1740	*Wilhelm Heinrich von Thulemeier* (b. 6 Jan 1683; d. 4 Aug 1740)
1741 – 8 Mar 1747	*Caspar Wilhelm von Borcke* (b. Gersdorf 30 Aug 1704; d. 8 Mar 1747)
10 Mar 1747 – (24 Jun) 1748	*Axel von Mardefeld* (b. 1691/92; d. 8 Dec 1748)
Jun 1749 – 3 Jan 1800	*Karl Wilhelm, Count Finck von Finckenstein* (see Chief Ministers)
5 Apr 1763 – Jul 1791	*Ewald Friedrich, Baron* (from 1787: *Count*) *Hertzberg* (b. Lottin 2 Nov 1725; d. 27 May 1795)
May 1791 – 20 Oct 1802	*Philipp Karl* (from 1800: *Count*) *Alvensleben* (b. Hanover 16 Dec 1745; d. Berlin 21 Oct 1802)
790 – 1797	*Johann Rudolf von Bischoffwerder* (b. Ostramondra 1741; d. Potsdam 31 Oct 1803)
May 1791 – Feb 1793	*Friedrich Wilhelm, Count Schulenburg-Kehnert* (b. Kehnert 22 Nov 1742; d. Kehnert 7 Apr 1815)
792 – Apr 1804	*Christian Heinrich Kurt, Count Haugwitz* (for 1st time) (b. Peuke 11 Jun 1752; d. Venice 9 Feb 1832)
Apr 1804 – Feb 1806	*Karl August, Count* (from 1814: *Prince*) *of Hardenberg* (for 1st time) (b. Essenrode 31 May 1750; d. Genoa 26 Nov 1830)
Feb – Nov 1806	*Christian Heinrich Kurt, Count Haugwitz* (for 2nd time)
Nov 1806 – Apr 1807	*Karl Friedrich* (from 1816: *Count*) *von Beyme* (b. Königsberg 10 Jul 1765; d. Steglitz 10 Dec 1838)
Dec 1806/26 Jan 1807 – 4 May 1807	*Wilhelm von Zastrow* (b. Ruppin 22 Dec 1752; d. Schloss Bied 22 Jul 1830)
5 Apr – Jul 1807	*Karl August, Count of Hardenberg* (for 2nd time) as Prime Minister
0 Sep 1807 – 24 Nov 1808	*Heinrich (Friedrich Karl) Baron Stein* (b. Nassau an der Lahn 26 Oct 1756; d. Kappenberg 29 Jun 1831) Responsible for entire Civil administration

ord High Chancellors and Ministers of Justice

746 – 4 Oct 1755	*Samuel, Baron Cocceji* (b. Heidelberg 20 Oct 1679; d.

	4 Oct 1755) Minister of Justice from 1737
(?) – 9 Nov 1770	*Philipp Josef von Jarriges* (b. Berlin 13 Nov 1706; d. Berlin 9 Nov 1770)
1770 – 11 Dec 1779	*Karl Josef Maximilian, Baron Fürst und Kupferberg* (b. Silesia 1717; d. 20 Jan 1790)
1770 – 1789	*Karl Abraham, Baron Zedlitz* (b. Schwarzwaldau 4 Jan 1731; d. Korpsdorf 19 Mar 1793) Minister of Education from 1771 – 1788
1779 – 14 Feb 1795	*Johann Heinrich Kasimir* (from 1798: *Count*) *von Carmer* (b. Kreuznach 29 Dec 1721; d. Rützen 23 May 1801)
14 Feb 1795 – 1808	*Heinrich Julius von Goldbeck* (b. 2 Aug 1733; d. 10 Jun 1818)
25 Nov 1808 – 4 Jun 1810	*Karl Friedrich von Beyme* (see Foreign Affairs)

Presidents of the Privy Council

1817 – 26 Nov 1922	*Karl August, Prince of Hardenberg* (see Foreign Affairs)
Jun 1822 – 30 Jan 1823	*Otto Karl Friedrich von Voss* (b. Berlin 8 Jun 1755; d. Berlin 30 Jan 1823)
1827 – 21 Sep 1837	*Karl, Duke of Mecklenburg* (b. Hanover 30 Nov 1785; d. Berlin 21 Sep 1837)
2 Apr 1838 – 1844	*Karl, Baron Müffling* (b. Halle 12 Jun 1775; d. 16 Jan 1851)
1844 – 11 Sep 1847	*Gustav Adolf Rochus von Rochow* (b. Nennhausen Oct 1792; d. Aachen 11 Sep 1847)

Prime Ministers

19 Mar 1848	*Adolf Heinrich, Count Arnim-Boitzenburg* (b. Berlin 10 Apr 1803; d. Schloss Boitzenburg 8 Jan 1868)
29 Mar 1848	*Ludolf Camphausen* (b. 3 Jan 1803; d. 3 Dec 1890)
2 Sep – Oct 1848	*Ernst von Pfuel* (b. Berlin Nov 1779; d. Berlin 3 Dec 1866)
2 Nov 1848 – 6 Nov 1850	*Friedrich Wilhelm, Count of Brandenburg*, son of Frederick William II of Prussia (b. Berlin 24 Jan 1792; d. Berlin 6 Nov 1850)
19 Dec 1850	*Otto Theodor, Baron Manteuffel* (b. Lübben 3 Feb 1805; d. Krossen 26 Nov 1882)
6 Nov 1858	*Karl Anton, Prince Hohenzollern-Sigmaringen* (b. Sep 1811; d. 2 Jun 1885)

17 Mar 1862	*Adolf, Prince Hohenlohe-Ingelfingen* (b. 29 Jan 1797; d. 24 Apr 1873)
23 Nov 1862	*Otto (Eduard Leopold), Count* (from 1871: *Prince*) *Bismarck-Schönhausen* (for 1st time) (b. Schönhausen 1 Apr 1815; d. Friedrichsruh 30 Jul 1898)
1 Jan 1873	*Albrecht (Theodor Emil), Count Roon* (b. Pleushagen 30 Apr 1803; d. Berlin 23 Feb 1879)
9 Nov 1873	*Otto (Eduard Leopold), Prince Bismarck-Schönhausen* (for 2nd time)
20 Mar 1890	*(Georg) Leo, Count Caprivi* (b. Charlottenburg 24 Feb 1831; d. Skyren 6 Feb 1899)
23 Mar 1892	*Botho, Count Eulenburg* (b. Wicken 31 Jul 1831; d. Berlin 5 Nov 1912)
29 Oct 1894 – 15 Oct 1900	*Chlodwig (Karl Viktor), Prince Hohenlohe-Schillingsfürst* (b. Rothenburg an der Fulda 31 Mar 1819; d. Ragaz 6 Jul 1901)
17 Oct 1900 – 10 Jul 1909	*Bernhard (Heinrich Martin Karl), Count* (from 1905: *Prince*) *Bülow* (b. Klein-Flottbek 3 May 1849; d. Rome 28 Oct 1929)
14 Jul 1909 – 13 Jul 1917	*Theobald von Bethmann Hollweg* (b. Hohenfinow 29 Nov 1856; d. Hohenfinow 2 Jan 1921)
14 Jul – 24 Oct 1917	*Georg Michaelis* (b. Haynau 7 Sep 1857; d. Bad Saarow 24 Jul 1936)
25 Oct 1917 – 3 Oct 1918	*Georg, Count Hertling* (b. Darmstadt 31 Aug 1843; d. Ruhpolding 4 Jan 1919)
4 Oct – 9 Nov 1918	*Max(imilian) (Alexander Friedrich Wilhelm), Prince of Baden* (b. Karlsruhe 10 Jul 1867; d. Constance 6 Nov 1929)

Deputy Prime Ministers

9 Nov 1873 – 23 Mar 1878	*Otto Camphausen* (b. Hunshoven 12 Oct 1812; d, Berlin 18 May 1896)
29 May 1878 – 20 Jun 1881	*Otto, Count* (from 1890: *Prince*) *Stolberg-Wernigerode* (b. Gedern 30 Oct 1837; d. Wernigerode 19 Nov 1896)
Oct 1881 – 8 Jun 1888	*Robert von Puttkamer* (b. Frankfurt an der Oder 5 May 1828; d. Karzin 15 Mar 1900)
8 Aug 1888 – end of Jun 1897	*Karl Heinrich von Bötticher* (b. Stettin 6 Jan 1833; d. Naumburg 6 Mar 1907)
Jul 1897 – 5 May 1901	*Johannes von Miquel* (b. Neuenhaus 19 Feb 1828; d. Frankfurt am Main 8 Sep 1901)

1907 – 14 Jul 1909	*Theobald von Bethmann Hollweg* (see Prime Ministers)
16 Aug 1914 – 22 May 1916	*Klemens von Delbrück* (b. Halle 19 Jan 1856; d. Jena 18 Dec 1921)
22 May 1916 – 9 Nov 1917	*Paul (Justin) von Breitenbach* (b. Danzig 16 Apr 1850; d. Bückeburg 10 Mar 1930)
9 Nov 1917 – 9 Nov 1918	*Robert Friedberg* (b. Berlin 28 Jun 1851; d. Berlin 20 Jun 1920)

Foreign Affairs from 1808

1808 – 3 Jun 1814	*August Friedrich Ferdinand, Count Goltz* (b. Dresden 20 Jul 1765; d. 17 Jan 1832)
3 Jun 1814 – 16 Sep 1818	*Karl August, Prince of Hardenberg* (see Foreign Affairs up to 1808)
16 Sep 1818 – 1832	*Christian Günther, Count Bernstorff* (b. Copenhagen 3 Apr 1769; d. 28 Mar 1935)
1832 – 19 Apr 1837	*Friedrich (Jean Pierre Frédéric) Ancillon* (b. Berlin 30 Apr 1767; d. Berlin 19 Apr 1837)
1837 – 1841	*Heinrich Wilhelm, Baron Werther* (b. Königsberg 7 Aug 1772; d. Berlin 7 Dec 1859)
1841 – Spring 1842	*Mortimer, Count Maltzan* (b. 15 Apr 1793; d. 9 Aug 1843)
2 Apr 1842 – 1845	*Heinrich, Baron Bülow* (b. Schwerin 16 Sep 1792; d. Berlin 6 Feb 1846)
Autumn 1845 – 17 Mar 1848	*Karl Ernst Wilhelm, Baron Canitz und Dallwitz* (b. Kassel 17 Nov 1787; d. Frankfurt am Main 25 Apr 1850)
19 – 21 Mar 1848	*Adolf Heinrich, Count Arnim-Boitzenburg* (see Prime Ministers)
21 Mar – 20 Jun 1848	*Heinrich Alexander* (from 1849: *Baron) von Arnim* (b. Berlin 13 Feb 1798; d. Düsseldorf 5 Jan 1861)
20 – 27 Jun 1848	*Alexander (Gustav Adolf), Baron* (from 1879; *Count) Schleinitz* (for 1st time) (b. Blankenburg 29 Dec 1807; d. Berlin 19 Feb 1885)
End of Jun – 7 Sep 1848	*Rudolf von Auerswald* (b. Marienwerder 1 Sep 1795; d. Berlin 15 Jan 1866)
7 Sep – 2 Nov 1848	*August Hermann, Count Dönhoff* (b. Potsdam 10 Oct 1797; d. Friedrichstein 1 Apr 1874)
2 Nov – Dec 1848	*Friedrich Wilhelm, Count of Brandenburg* (for 1st time) (see Prime Ministers)
Dec 1848 – 23 Feb 1849	*Franz August Eichmann* (b. Berlin 29 Mar 1793; d. Berlin 14 Aug 1879)

24 Feb – 3 May 1849	*Heinrich Friedrich, Count Arnim-Heinrichsdorff* (b. Werbelow 23 Sep 1791; d. Berlin 28 Apr 1859)
May – Jul 1849	*Friedrich Wilhelm, Count of Brandenburg* (for 2nd time)
Jul 1849 – 26 Sep 1850	*Alexander (Gustav Adolf), Baron Schleinitz* (for 2nd time)
26 Sep – 2 Nov 1850	*Josef Maria von Radowitz* (b. Blankenburg 6 Feb 1797; d. Berlin 25 Dec 1853)
19 Dec 1850 – 5 Sep 1858	*Otto Theodor, Baron Manteuffel* (see Prime Ministers)
6 Sep 1858 – 12 Jul 1861	*Alexander (Gustav Adolf), Baron Schleinitz* (for 3rd time)
10 Oct 1861 – 8 Oct 1862	*Albrecht, Count Bernstorff* (b. Dreilützow 22 Mar 1809; d. London 26 Mar 1873)
8 Oct 1862 – 20 Mar 1890	*Otto (Eduard Leopold), Count* (from 1871: *Prince*) *Bismarck-Schönhausen* (see Prime Ministers)
20 Mar 1890 – 26 Oct 1894	*(Georg) Leo, Count Caprivi* (see Prime Ministers)
30 Oct 1894 – Oct 1897	*Adolf Hermann, Baron Marschall von Bieberstein* (b. Karlsruhe 12 Oct 1842; d. Badenweiler 24 Sep 1912)
Oct 1897 – 14 Jul 1909	*Bernhard (Heinrich Martin Karl), Count* (from 1905: *Prince*) *Bülow* (see Prime Ministers)
14 Jul 1909 – 14 Jul 1917	*Theobald von Bethmann Hollweg* (see Prime Ministers)
14 Jul – 24 Oct 1917	*Georg Michaelis* (see Prime Ministers)
25 Oct 1917 – 3 Oct 1918	*Georg, Count Hertling* (see Prime Ministers)
4 Oct – 9 Nov 1918	*Max(imilian) (Alexander Friedrich Wilhelm), Prince of Baden* (see Prime Ministers)

Home Affairs

Nov 1808 – Jun 1810	*(Friedrich Ferdinand) Alexander, Count Dohna-Schlobitten* (b. Schloss Finkenstein 29 Mar 1771; d. 21 Mar 1831)
Jun 1810 – Jun 1814	*Karl August, Count of Hardenberg* (see Foreign Affairs up to 1808)
1814 – 11 Jan 1819	*Friedrich* (from 1834: *Baron*) *von Schuckmann* (for 1st time) (b. Mölln 25 Dec 1755; d. Berlin 17 Sep 1834)
11 Jan – end of 1819	*Wilhelm, Baron Humboldt* (b. Potsdam 22 Jun 1767; d. Tegel 8 Jun 1835)
1819 – early 1834	*Friedrich von Schuckmann* (for 2nd time)

1834 – 20 Aug 1838	*Gustav, Baron Brenn* (b. 26 Sep 177(?); d. 20 Aug 1838)
1838 – 1842	*Gustav Adolf Rochus von Rochow* (see Presidents of the Privy Council)
1842 – 1845	*Adolf Heinrich, Count Arnim-Boitzenburg* (see Prime Ministers)
1845 – 19 Mar 1848	*Ernst von Bodelschwingh-Velmede* (b. Velmede 26 Sep 1794; d. Medebach 18 May 1854)
19 Mar – 14 Jul 1848	*Alfred von Auerswald* (b. Marienwerder 16 Dec 1797; d. Berlin 3 Jul 1870)
Jul – Sep 1848	*Friedrich von Kühlwetter* (b. Dusseldorf 17 Apr 1809; d. Münster 2 Dec 1882)
7 Sep – Nov 1848	*Franz August Eichmann* (see Foreign Affairs from 1808)
8 Nov 1848 – 19 Dec 1850	*Otto Theodor, Baron Manteuffel* (see Prime Ministers)
Dec 1850 – 7 Oct 1858	*Ferdinand Otto Wilhelm Henning von Westphalen* (b. Lübeck 23 Apr 1799; d. Berlin 2 Jul 1876)
Oct 1858 – 1859	*Eduard (Heinrich) von Flottwell* (b. Insterburg 23 Jul 1786; d. Berlin 24 May 1865)
3 Jul 1859 – 18 Mar 1862	*Maximilian, Count Schwerin-Putzar* (b. Boldekow 30 Dec 1804; d. Potsdam 3 May 1872)
18 Mar – 9 Dec 1862	*Gustav Wilhelm von Jagow* (b. 7 Sep 1813; d. Potsdam 1/2 Feb 1879)
9 Dec 1862 – 30 Mar 1878	*Friedrich (Albrecht), Count Eulenburg* (b. Königsberg 29 Jun 1815; d. Berlin 2 Apr 1881)
30 Mar 1878 – 27 Feb 1881	*Botho, Count Eulenburg* (for 1st time) (see Prime Ministers)
18 Jun 1881 – 8 Jun 1888	*Robert von Puttkamer* (see Deputy Prime Ministers)
2 Jul 1888 – 9 Aug 1892	*(Ernst) Ludwig Herrfurt* (b. Oberthau 6 Mar 1830; d. Berlin 14 Feb 1900)
9 Aug 1892 – 26 Oct 1894	*Botho, Count Eulenburg* (for 2nd time)
29 Oct 1894 – 8 Dec 1895	*Ernst (Matthias) von Koeller* (b. Kantreck 8 Jul 1841; d. Stettin 11 Dec 1928)
8 Dec 1895 – 2 Sep 1899	*Eberhard, Baron Recke von der Horst* (b. Berlin 2 Apr 1847; d. Münster 16 Feb 1911)
4 Sep 1899 – 6 May 1901	*Georg, Baron Rheinbaben* (b. Frankfurt an der Oder 21 Aug 1855; d. Düsseldorf 25 Mar 1921)
6 May 1901 – 20 Mar 1905	*Hans, Baron Hammerstein-Loxten* (b. Lüneburg 27 Apr 1843; d. Berlin 20 Mar 1905)
20 Mar 1905 – 24 Jun 1907	*Theobald von Bethmann Hollweg* (see Prime Ministers)

24 Jun 1907 – 18 Jun 1910	*Friedrich von Moltke* (b. Ranzau 1 May 1852; d. Klein-Bresa 10 Dec 1927)
18 Jun 1910 – 18 Apr 1914	*Johann von Dallwitz* (b. Breslau 24 Sep 1855; d. Karlsruhe 6 Aug 1919)
18 Apr 1914 – 5 Aug 1917	*Friedrich Wilhelm von Loebell* (b. Lehnin 17 Sep 1855; d. Brandenburg 21 Nov 1931)
5 Aug 1917 – 9 Nov 1918	*Bill Drews* (b. Berlin 11 Feb 1870; d. Berlin 17 Feb 1938)

Finance

Nov 1808 – Jun 1810	*Karl, Baron Stein zum Altenstein* (b. Ansbach 7 Oct 1770; d. 14 May 1840)
Jun 1810 – end of 1813	*Karl August, Count Hardenberg* (see Foreign Affairs up to 1808)
End of 1813 – 3 Nov 1817	*Ludwig Friedrich Viktor Hans* (from 1816: *Count Bülow*) (b. Essenrode 14 Jul 1774; d. Landeck 11 Aug 1825)
2 Aug 1817 – 1825	*Wilhelm Anton von Klewitz* (b. Magdeburg 1 Aug 1760; d. 26 Jul 1838)
1825 – 30 Jun 1830	*Friedrich Christian Adolf von Motz* (b. Kassel 18 Nov 1775; d. Berlin 30 Jun 1830)
1830 – 2 Nov 1834	*Karl Georg Maassen* (b. Cleves 23 Aug 1769; d. Berlin 2 Nov 1834)
1835 – 1842	*Albrecht, Count Alvensleben* (b. Halberstadt 23 Mar 1794; d. Berlin 2 May 1858)
May 1842 – 3 May 1844	*Ernst von Bodelschwingh-Velmede* (see Home Affairs)
3 May 1844 – Jul 1846	*Eduard (Heinrich) von Flottwell* (see Home Affairs)
Aug 1846 – Mar 1848	*Franz von Düesberg* (b. Borken 11 Jan 1793; d. Münster 11 Oct 1872)
29 Mar – 7 Sep 1848	*David Hansemann* (b. Finkenwerder 12 Jul 1790; d. Schlangenbad 4 Aug 1864)
7 Sep – Nov 1848	*Gustav von Bonin* (b. Heeren 23 Sep 1797; d. Berlin 2 Dec 1878)
8 Nov 1848 – 23 Feb 1849	*Ludwig Samuel Bogislaus Kühne* (b. Wanzleben 15 Feb 1786; d. Berlin 3 Apr 1864)
Feb 1849 – 1851	*Arnold von Rabe*
Jul 1851 – Nov 1858	*Karl von Bodelschwingh* (for 1st time) (b. Heyde, Westphalia 10 Dec 1800; d. Berlin 12 May 1873)
6 Nov 1858 – 18 Mar 1862	*Erasmus Robert, Baron Patow* (b. Mallechen 10 Sep 1804; d. Berlin 5 Jan 1890)
18 Mar – 1 Oct 1862	*August* (from 1863; *Baron*) *von der Heydt* (for 1st time) (b. Elberfeld 15 Feb 1801; d. Berlin 13 Jun 1874)

1 Oct 1862 – Jun 1866	*Karl von Bodelschwingh* (for 2nd time)
5 Jun 1866 – 28 Oct 1869	*August, Baron von der Heydt* (for 2nd time)
26 Oct 1869 – 23 Mar 1878	*Otto Camphausen* (see Deputy Prime Ministers)
26 Mar 1878 – 28 Jun 1879	*Artur Hobrecht* (b. Kobierczin 14 Aug 1824; d. Berlin 7 Jul 1912)
Jul 1879 – Jun 1882	*Karl Hermann Bitter* (b. Schwedt 27 Feb 1813; d. Berlin 12 Sep 1885)
Jun 1882 – 24 Jun 1890	*Adolf Heinrich Wilhelm von Scholz* (b. Schweidnitz 1 Nov 1833; d. Seeheim 21 Mar 1924)
24 Jun 1890 – 5 May 1901	*Johannes von Miquel* (see Deputy Prime Ministers)
6 May 1901 – 28 Jun 1910	*Georg, Baron Rheinbaben* (see Home Affairs)
28 Jun 1910 – 5 Aug 1917	*August Lentze* (b. Hamm 21 Oct 1860)
5 Aug 1917 – 9 Nov 1918	*Oskar Hergt* (b. Naumburg 22 Oct 1869)

War

Dec 1806 – Jul 1807	*Ernst Wilhelm Friedrich von Rüchel* (b. Ziezeneff 21 Jul 1754; d. Haselau 14 Feb 1823)
1808 – 1810	*Gerhard Johann David von Scharnhorst* (b. Bordenau 12 Nov 1755; d. Prague 28 Jun 1813)
3 Jun 1814 – 1819	*Hermann von Boyen* (for 1st time) (b. Kreuzburg 23 Jul 1771; d. 15 Feb 1848)
1819 – 1833	*Karl Georg Albrecht Ernst von Hake* (b. Flatow 18 Aug 1768; d. Naples 1835)
1833 – 1835	*Job von Witzleben* (b. Halberstadt 20 Jul 1783; d. Berlin 9 Jul 1837)
1835 – 1 Mar 1841	*Gustav von Rauch* (b. Brunswick 1 Jun 1774; d. Berlin 2 Apr 1841)
1 Mar 1841 – Oct 1847	*Hermann von Boyen* (for 2nd time)
7 Oct 1847 – 2 Apr 1848	*Ferdinand von Rohr* (b. Brandenburg 17 May 1783; d. Glogau 15 May 1851)
Apr – Jun 1848	*August, Count Kanitz* (b. Königsberg 20 Oct 1783; d. Potsdam 22 May 1852)
Jun – 7 Sep 1848	*Ludwig, Baron Roth von Schreckenstein* (b. Immendingen 16 Nov 1789; d. Münster 30 May 1858)
7 Sep – Nov 1848	*Ernst von Pfuel* (see Prime Ministers)

8 Nov 1848 – 27 Feb 1850	*(Karl) Adolf von Strotha* (b. Silesia 1786; d. Berlin 15 Feb 1870)
27 Feb 1850 – 31 Dec 1851	*August von Stockhausen* (b. Thuringia 1791 d. Berlin 31 Mar 1861)
1852 – 1854	*Eduard von Bonin* (for 1st time) (b. Stolp 7 Mar 1793; d. Koblenz 13 Mar 1865)
1854 – 6 Nov 1858	*Friedrich, Count Waldersee* (b. 21 Jul 1795; d. Potsdam 15 Jan 1864)
6 Nov 1858 – 28 Nov 1859	*Eduard von Bonin* (for 2nd time)
5 Dec 1859 – 9 Nov 1873	*Albrecht (Theodor Emil)* (from 1871: *Count Roon*) (see Prime Ministers)
9 Nov 1873 – Mar 1883	*Georg von Kameke* (b. Pasewalk 14 Jun 1817; d. Berlin 12 Oct 1893)
Mar 1883 – 8 Apr 1889	*Paul Bronsart von Schellendorf* (b. Danzig 25 Jan 1832; d. Schnettnienen 23 Apr 1891)
Apr 1889 – 4 Oct 1890	*Julius von Verdy du Vernois* (b. Freistadt 19 Jul 1832; d. Stockholm 30 Sep 1910)
4 Oct 1890 – 19 Oct 1893	*Hans Karl Georg von Kaltenborn-Stachau* (b. Magdeburg 23 Mar 1836; d. Brunswick 16 Feb 1898)
19 Oct 1893 – 14 Aug 1896	*Walter Bronsart von Schellendorf* (b. Danzig 21 Dec 1883; d. Berlin 13 Dec 1914)
14 Aug 1896 – 15 Aug 1903	*Heinrich von Gossler* (b. Weissenfels 29 Sep 1841; d. Berlin 10 Jan 1927)
15 Aug 1903 – 11 Aug 1909	*Karl von Einem*, called *von Rothmaler* (b. Herzberg 1 Jan 1853; d. Mülheim 7 Apr 1934)
2 Aug 1909 – 4 Jul 1913	*Josias von Heeringen* (b. Kassel 9 Mar 1850; d. Berlin 9 Oct 1926)
7 Jul 1913 – 21 Jan 1915	*Erich von Falkenhayn* (b. Burg Belchau 11 Sep 1861; d. Schloss Lindstedt 8 Sep 1922)
21 Jan 1915 – 29 Oct 1916	*Adolf Wild von Hohenborn* (b. Kassel 8 Jul 1860; d. Malsburg-Hohenborn 25 Oct 1925)
29 Oct 1916 – 9 Oct 1918	*Hermann von Stein* (b. Wedderstedt 13 Sep 1854; d. Lehnin 26 May 1927)
Oct – 9 Nov 1918	*Heinrich Scheüch* (b. Schlettstadt 21 Jun 1864; d. Bad Kissingen 3 Sep 1946)

Justice

4 Sep 1806	(acting:) *Karl Wilhelm, Baron Schroetter* (b. Wohnsdorf 9 Apr 1748; d. Königsberg 2 Dec 1819)
ug 1807 – 1809	*Karl Wilhelm, Baron Schroetter* (see above)

Nov 1808 – 4 Jun 1810	*Karl Friedrich von Beyme*, Lord High Chancellor (see Foreign Affairs up to 1808)
9 Jun 1810 – 18 Mar 1825	*Friedrich Leopold von Kircheissen* (b. Berlin 28 Jun 1749; d. Berlin 18 Mar 1825)
2 Dec 1817 – end of 1819	*Karl Friedrich, Count von Beyme*, revision of the laws and administration of justice in the new provinces (see Foreign Affairs up to 1808)
1825 – 29 Dec 1830	*Wilhelm Heinrich August Alexander, Count Danckelmann* (b. 10 May 1788; d. 29 Dec 1830)
1831 – 1832	(acting:) *Karl Albrecht Christof Heinrich von Kamptz* (b. Schwerin 16 Sep 1769; d. Berlin 3 Nov 1849)
Feb 1832 – 25 Sep 1844	*Heinrich Gottlob von Mühler* (b. Luisenhof 2 Jun 1780; d. Berlin 15 Jan 1857)
1832 – Mar 1842	*Karl Albrecht Christof Heinrich von Kamptz*, revision of the laws (see above)
Mar 1842 – Mar 1848	*Friedrich Karl von Savigny* (b. Frankfurt am Main 21 Feb 1779; d. Berlin 25 Oct 1861) revision of the laws
25 Sep 1844 – Mar 1848	*Karl Albrecht Alexander Uhden* (b. Berlin 9 Oct 1798 d. Berlin 31 Jan 1878)
20 Mar – Jun 1848	*(Ferdinand) Wilhelm (Ludwig) Bornemann* (b. Berlin 28 Mar 1798; d. Berlin 28 Jan 1864)
Jun – Sep 1848	*Karl Anton Maerker*
24 Sep – Nov 1848	*Gustav Wilhelm Kisker*
1848 – 1849	*Heinrich Wilhelm Rintelen* (b. Borgholz 13 Apr 1797 d. Münster 28 Oct 1869)
1849 – 1860	*Ludwig Simons* (d. Elberfeld 20 Jul 1870)
17 Dec 1860 – Mar 1862	*August Moritz Ludwig Heinrich Wilhelm von Bernuth* (b. Münster 11 Mar 1808; d. Berlin 25 Apr 1889)
17 Mar 1862 – 5 Dec 1867	*Leopold, Count Lippe-Biesterfeld-Weissenfeld* (b. See bei Börlitz 19 Mar 1815; d. Berlin 8 Dec 1889)
5 Dec 1867 – 30 Oct 1879	*Adolf Leonhardt* (b. Hanover 6 Jun 1815; d. Hanover 7 May 1880)
30 Oct 1879 – 17 Jan 1889	*Heinrich von Friedberg* (b. Märkisch-Friedland 27 Jan 1813; d. Berlin 2 Jun 1895)
31 Jan 1889 – 14 Nov 1894	*Hermann von Schelling* (b. Erlangen 19 Apr 1824 d. Berlin 15 Nov 1908)
14 Nov 1894 – 21 Nov 1905	*Karl Heinrich von Schönstedt* (b. Broich 6 Jan 1833; d. Berlin 31 Jan 1924)
21 Nov 1905 – 5 Aug 1917	*Maximilian von Beseler* (b. Rostock 22 Sep 1841 d. Berlin 24 Jul 1921)
5 Aug 1917 – 9 Nov 1918	*Peter Spahn* (b. Winkel im Rheingau 22 May 1846 d. Bad Wildungen 31 Aug 1925)

Trade (in existence from 1817 - 1825, 1835 - 1837 and from 1844)

2 Dec 1817 – 1825	*Ludwig Friedrich Viktor Hans, Count Bülow* (see Finance)
1835 – Jan 1837	*Christian von Rother* (b. Ruppersdorf 14 Nov 1778; d. Rogau 7 Nov 1849)
7 Jun 1844 – Mar 1848	*Friedrich Ludwig von Rönne* (b. Sestermühle 27 Nov 1798; d. Berlin 7 Apr 1865)
25 Jun – 21 Sep 1848	*Karl August Milde* (b. Breslau 14 Sep 1805; d. Salzbrunn 24 Aug 1861)
6 Dec 1848 – 18 Mar 1862	*August von der Heydt* (see Finance)
May – Oct 1862	*Heinrich Wilhelm von Holtzbrinck*
Dec 1862 – 13 May 1873	*Heinrich, Count Itzenplitz* (b. Gross-Behnitz 23 Feb 1799; d. Kunersdorf 15 Feb 1883)
13 May 1873 – 30 Mar 1878	*Heinrich von Achenbach* (b. Saarbrücken 23 Nov 1829; d. Potsdam 9 Jul 1899)
Mar 1878 – 14 Mar 1879	*Albert von Maybach* (b. Werne 29 Nov 1822; d. Berlin 21 Jan 1904)
13 Jul 1879 – Sep 1880	*Karl von Hofmann* (b. Darmstadt 4 Nov 1827; d. Darmstadt 9 May 1910)
16 Sep 1880 – 31 Jan 1890	*Otto (Eduard Leopold) Prince Bismarck-Schönhausen* (see Prime Ministers)
1 Feb 1890 – 27 Jun 1896	*Hans (Hermann) Baron Berlepsch* (b. Dresden 30 Mar 1843; d. Seebach 2 Jun 1926)
27 Jun 1896 – 6 May 1901	*Ludwig Brefeld* (b. Telgte 31 Mar 1837; d. Freiburg im Breisgau 13 Feb 1907)
6 May 1901 – 19 Oct 1905	*Theodor (Adolf) von Möller* (b. Kupferhammer 10 Aug 1840; d. Brackwede 6 Dec 1925)
19 Oct 1905 – 14 Jul 1909	*Klemens von Delbrück* (see Deputy Prime Ministers)
14 Jul 1909 – 5 Oct 1918	*Reinhold von Sydow* (b. Berlin 14 Jan 1851; d. Berlin 16 Jan 1943)
4 Oct 1918 – 5 Nov 1921	*Otto Fischbeck* (b. Guntershagen 28 Aug 1865; d. Berlin 23 May 1939)

Religious Affairs, Education and Health

1817 – Dec 1838/ (May 1840) (re-established)	*Karl, Baron Stein zum Altenstein* (see Finance)
4 May – 22 Oct 1840	(acting:) *Adalbert von Ladenberg* (for 1st time) (b. Ansbach 18 Feb 1798; d. Potsdam 15 Feb 1855)

22 Oct 1840 – 19 Mar 1848	*Johann Albrecht Friedrich Eichhorn* (b. Westheim 2 Mar 1779; d. Berlin 16 Jan 1856)
19 Mar – Jun 1848	*Maximilian, Count Schwerin-Putzar* (see Home Affairs)
25 Jun – 8 Jul 1848	*(Johann) Karl Rodbertus* (b. Greifswald 12 Aug 1805; d. Jagetzow 6 Dec 1875)
Jul 1848 – 19 Dec 1850	*Adalbert von Ladenberg* (for 2nd time)
19 Dec 1850 – 1858	*Karl Otto von Raumer* (b. Stargard 7 Sep 1805; d. Berlin 6 Aug 1859)
Autumn 1858 – 18 Mar 1862	*Moritz August von Bethmann Hollweg* (b. Frankfurt am Main 8 Apr 1795; d. Burg Rheineck 13 Jul 1877)
18 Mar 1862 – 17 Jan 1872	*Heinrich von Mühler* (b. Brieg 4 Nov 1813; d. Potsdam 2 Apr 1874)
22 Jan 1872 – 23 Jul 1879	*Adalbert Falk* (b. Metschkau 10 Aug 1827; d. Hamm 7 Jul 1900)
23 Jul 1879 – 17 Jun 1881	*Robert von Puttkamer* (see Deputy Prime Ministers)
17 Jun 1881 – 12 Mar 1891	*Gustav von Gossler* (b. Naumburg 13 Apr 1838; d. Danzig 29 Sep 1902)
13 Mar 1891 – 21 Mar 1892	*Robert, Count Zedlitz und Trützschler* (b. Freienwalde 8 Dec 1837; d. Charlottenburg 21 Oct 1914)
23 Mar 1892 – 4 Sep 1899	*Robert Bosse* (b. Quedlinburg 12 Jul 1832; d. Berlin 31 Jul 1901)
4 Sep 1899 – 24 Jun 1907	*Konrad von Studt* (b. Schweidnitz 5 Nov 1838; d. Berlin 29 Oct 1921)
24 Jun 1907 – 14 Jul 1909	*Ludwig Holle* (b. Schwelm 27 Jun 1855; d. Godesberg 12 Dec 1909)
14 Jul 1909 – 5 Aug 1917	*August von Trott zu Solz* (b. Imshausen 29 Dec 1855; d. Imshausen 1 Nov 1938)
5 Aug 1917 – 9 Nov 1918	*Friedrich Schmidt-Ott* (b. Potsdam 4 Jun 1860; d. Berlin 28 Apr 1956)

General Post Office

1808 – 15 Dec 1823	*Johann Friedrich von Seegebarth* (b. Berlin 3 Aug 1747; d. Berlin 15 Dec 1823)
1823 – 13 Jun 1846	*Karl Ferdinand Friedrich von Nagler* (b. Ansbach 1770; d. 13 Jun 1846) head of the postal service from 1821)
1846 – 1849	*(Justus Wilhelm) Eduard von Schaper* (b. Brunswick 30 Oct 1792; d. Potsdam 25 Feb 1868)

1849 – 3 Feb 1862	*(Gottlob) Heinrich Schmückert* (b. Greiffenberg 12 Nov 1790; d. Berlin 3 Feb 1862)
1862 – 1870	—— *Philippsborn*

Treasury

1817 – 26 Nov 1822	*Karl August, Count Hardenberg* (see Foreign Affairs up to 1808)
1822 – 14 Feb 1841	*Karl Friedrich Heinrich, Count Wylich und Lottum* (b. Berlin 5 Nov 1767; d. Berlin 14 Feb 1841)
1841 – Mar 1848	*Ludwig Gustav von Thile* (b. Dresden 11 Nov 1781; d. Frankfurt an der Oder 21 Sep 1852)

Agriculture

Jun – Sep 1848	*Rudolf Eduard Julius Gierke* (b. Stettin; d. Bromberg 1855)
8 Nov 1848 – Nov 1850	*Otto Theodor, Baron Manteuffel* (see Prime Ministers)
Nov 1850 – 1854	*Ferdinand Otto Wilhelm Henning von Westphalen* (see Home Affairs)
1854 – 5 Nov 1858	*Karl (Otto), Baron Manteuffel* (b. Lübben 9 Jul 1806; d. Berlin 28 Feb 1879)
Nov 1858 – Mar 1862	*Erdmann, Count Pückler-Limpurg* (b. Rogau 7 Apr 1792; d. 4 Nov 1869)
18 Mar – 9 Dec 1862	*Heinrich, Count Itzenplitz* (see Trade)
9 Dec 1862 – Jan 1873	*Werner von Selchow* (b. Danzig 1 Feb 1806; d. Brandenburg 23 Feb 1884)
Jan – Dec 1873	*Otto, Count Königsmarck* (b. Berln 2 Mar 1815; d. Ober-Lesnitz 2 May 1889)
8 Dec 1873 – 19 Nov 1874	*Heinrich von Achenbach* (see Trade)
19 Nov 1874 – 29 Jun 1879	*(Karl) Rudolf Friedenthal* (b. Breslau 15 Sep 1827; d. Giessmannsdorf 6 Mar 1890)
13 Jul 1879 – 17 Nov 1890	*Robert (from 1888: Baron) Lucius von Ballhausen* (b. Erfurt 20 Dec 1835; d. Klein-Ballhousen 10 Sep 1914)
17 Nov 1890 – 10 Nov 1894	*Wilhelm von Heyden-Cadow* (b. Stettin 16 Mar 1839; d. Plötz 20 Jun 1920)
10 Nov 1894 – 3 May 1901	*Ernst, Baron Hammerstein-Loxten* (b. Loxten 2 Oct 1827; d. Loxten 5 Jul 1914)
6 May 1901 – 11 Nov 1906	*Viktor von Podbielski* (b. Frankfurt an der Oder 26 Feb 1844; d. Berlin 21 Jan 1916)
22 Nov 1906 – 18 Jun 1910	*Bern(har)d von Arnim-Criewen* (b. Criewen 20 May 1850; d. Criewen 15 Dec 1939)

| 18 Jun 1910 – 5 Aug 1917 | *Klemens, Baron Schorlemer* (b. Alst 29 Sep 1856; d. Berlin 6 Jul 1922) |
| 5 Aug 1917 – 9 Nov 1918 | *Paul von Eisenhart-Rothe* (b. Lietzow 5 Apr 1857; d. Demmin 1 Mar 1923) |

Public Works

14 Mar 1879 – Jun 1891	*Albert von Maybach* (see Trade)
20 Jun 1891 – 23 Jun 1902	*Karl von Thielen* (b. Wesel 30 Jan 1832; d. Berlin 11 Jan 1906)
23 Jun 1902 – 28 Apr 1906	*Hermann von Budde* (b. Bensburg 15 Nov 1851; d. Berlin 28 Apr 1906)
May 1906 – 9 Nov 1918	*Paul (Justin) von Breitenbach* (see Deputy Prime Ministers)

Romania

The modern state of Romania was formed by the union of the principalities of Moldavia and Wallachia in 1859, Transylvania being added in 1918. The same rulers were often elected, successively or alternately, with or without overlap, in Moldavia and Wallachia: this is not noted in the lists. In accordance with current practice most rulers of the same name are distinguished by their traditional epithets, there being no general agreement on their numbering.

HEADS OF STATE

Hospodars of Moldavia

14 Apr 1457	*Stephen*, the Great, son of Bogdan II
2 Jul 1504	*Bogdan*, the One-Eyed, son
20 Apr 1517	*Stephen*, the Young (Ştefăniţă) brother (b. 1506; d. 14 Jan 1527)
after 14 Jan 1527	*Peter Rareş*, illegitimate son of Stephen the Great (for 1st time)
18 Sep 1538	*Stephen*, the Locust, grandson of Stephen the Great
Dec 1540	*Alexander Cornea*
Feb 1541	*Peter Rareş* (for 2nd time)
3 Sep 1546	*Ilias Rareş*, son

11 Jun 1551	*Stephen Rareş*, brother (d. 1 Sep 1552)
Sep 1552 (for 3 days)	*John Joldea*, brother-in-law
end of Sep 1552	*Alexander Lăpuşneanu*, pretended son of Bogdan (for 1st time) (d. 6 May 1568)
18 Nov 1561	*John Jacob Heraclid* (Despot Vodă) (d. 6 Nov 1563)
8 or 10 Aug 1563	*Stephen Tomşa* (d. May 1564)
24 Oct 1563/Mar 1564	*Alexander Lăpuşneanu* (for 2nd time)
Mar 1568	*Bogdan Lăpuşneanu*, son
Feb 1572	*John*, the Cruel (Ioan Vodă) son of Stephen the Young
14 Jun 1574 – 23 Nov 1577	*Peter*, the Lame, son of Mircea, Hospodar of Wallachia (for 1st time)
after 23 Nov 1577	*John Potcoavă*, half-brother of John the Cruel (d. 15 Jun 1578)
Jan 1578	*Peter*, the Lame (for 2nd time)
21 Nov 1579	*Iancu Sasul*, illegitimate son of Peter Rareş
after 11 Sep 1582	*Peter*, the Lame (for 3rd time)
28 Aug 1591 – Jun 1592	*Aaron*, the Tyrant, son of Alexander Lăpuşneanu (for 1st time) with *Stephen*, his son, from 27 Dec 1589 – 28 Aug 1591
Aug – Oct 1592	*Peter*, the Cossack, brother
27 Sep 1592	*Aaron*, the Tyrant (for 2nd time)
3 May 1595	*Stephen Răzvan*, son of Peter the Lame (d. Dec 1595)
Aug 1595	*Jeremias Movilă* (for 1st time)
before 6 Jun 1600	*Michael*, the Brave (b. 1557; d. 19 Aug 1601)
Sep 1600	*Jeremias Movilă* (for 2nd time)
10 Jul 1606	*Simeon Movilă*, brother
24 Sep 1607	*Michael (Mihailas) Movilă*, son (for 1st time) (d. 6 Feb 1608)
Oct 1607	*Constantine Movilă*, son of Jeremias Movila (for 1st time)
Nov 1607	*Michael Movilă* (for 2nd time)
Dec 1607	*Constantine Movilă* (for 2nd time)
after 28 Dec 1611	*Stephen II Tomşa* (for 1st time)
1 Dec 1615	*Alexander Movilă*
Jul 1616	*Radu Mihnea* (for 1st time)
after 19 Feb 1619	*Gaspar Graziani*
20 Sep 1620	*Alexander Iliaş* (for 1st time)
Oct 1621	*Stephen II Tomşa* (for 2nd time)
after 14 Aug 1623	*Radu Mihnea* (for 2nd time)
after 30 Jan 1626	*Miron Barnovschi* (for 1st time) exiled from 18 Jul 1629
Aug 1629	*Alexander Coconul*, son of Radu Mihnea
9 May 1630	*Moise Movilă* (for 1st time)

after 15 Dec 1631	*Alexander Iliaş* (for 2nd time)
Apr – 2 Jul 1633	*Miron Barnovschi* (for 2nd time)
5 Jul 1633	*Moise Movilă* (for 2nd time)
Apr 1634	*Basil Lupu,* (for 1st time) (d. 1661)
13 Apr 1653	*George Ştefan* (for 1st time) (d. 1668)
18 May 1653	*Basil Lupu* (for 2nd time)
18 Jul 1653	*George Ştefan* (for 2nd time)
13 Mar 1658	*George Ghica*
12 Nov 1659	*Constantine Şerban* (for 1st time), illegitimate son of Radu Şerban (d. 1685)
1 Dec 1659	*Stephen (Ştefăniţă) Lupu,* son of Basil Lupu (for 1st time) (b. 1643)
27 Jan 1661	*Constantine Şerban* (for 2nd time)
before 27 Feb – 29 Sep 1661	*Stephen Lupu* (for 2nd time)
after 29 Sep 1661 – 21 Sep 1665	*Eustratius Dabija*
after 21 Sep 1665	*George Duca* (for 1st time)
after 31 May 1666	*Iliaşcu,* son of Alexander Iliaş
after 18 Nov 1668	*George Duca* (for 2nd time)
20 Aug 1672	*Stephen Petriceicu* (for 1st time)
Nov 1673	*Dumitraşco Cantacuzino* (for 1st time)
Dec 1673	*Stephen Petriceicu* (for 2nd time)
after 4 Mar 1674	*Dumitraşco Cantacuzino* (for 2nd time)
before 20 Nov 1675	*Antony Rosetti (Ruset)*
after 8 Dec 1678	*George Duca* (for 3rd time)
4 Jan 1683 – Mar 1684	*Stephen Petriceicu* (for 3rd time)
8 Feb 1684	*Dumitraşco Cantacuzino* (for 3rd time)
25 Jun 1685	*Constantine Cantemir* (b. 28 Nov 1612)
29 Mar – 18 Apr 1693	*Demetrius Cantemir,* son (for 1st time) (b. 5 Nov 1673; d. 2 Sep 1723)
Apr 1693	*Constantine Duca* (for 1st time)
18 Dec 1695	*Antiochus Cantemir,* brother of Demetrius Cantemir (for 1st time)
23 Sep 1700	*Constantine Duca* (for 2nd time)
Sep 1703	*Michael Racoviţă* (for 1st time)
23 Feb 1705	*Antiochus Cantemir* (for 2nd time)
31 Jul 1707 – 28 Oct 1709	*Michael Racoviţă* (for 2nd time)
17 Nov 1709	*Nicholas Mavrocordat* (for 1st time) (b. 1670; d. 1730)
4 Dec 1710 – Jul 1711	*Demetrius Cantemir* (for 2nd time)
Jul – Nov 1711	Kaymakams appointed by Turks
7 Oct/19 Nov 1711	*Nicholas Mavrocordat* (for 2nd time)

5 Jan 1715	*Michael Racoviţă* (for 3rd time)
7 Oct 1726	*Gregory II Ghica*, grandson of Gregory I Ghica, Hospodar of Wallachia (for 1st time)
Apr 1733	*Constantine Mavrocordat*, son of Nicholas (for 1st time) (b. 1711; d. 1769)
27 Nov 1735 – 24 Sep 1741	*Gregory II Ghica* (for 2nd time)
14 Sep – Oct 1739	Russian military administration
Sep 1741	*Constantine Mavrocordat* (for 2nd time)
31 Jul 1743	*John Mavrocordat*, brother (b. 1684)
May 1747	*Gregory II Ghica* (for 3rd time)
Apr 1748	*Constantine Mavrocordat* (for 3rd time)
31 Aug 1749	*Constantine Racoviţă*, son of Michael (for 1st time)
3 Jul 1753	*Matthew Ghica*, son of Gregory II Ghica
19 Feb 1756 – Mar 1757	*Constantine Racoviţă* (for 2nd time)
Feb 1757	*Scarlat Ghica*, son of Gregory II Ghica (d. 1766)
Aug 1758	*John Callimachi* (b. c. 1690; d. 1780)
before 8 Jun 1761	*Gregory Callimachi*, son (for 1st time) (d. 8 Sep 1769)
29 Mar 1764	*Gregory III Ghica*, great-grandson of Gregory I Ghica (for 1st time)
5 Feb 1767 – 14 Jun 1679	*Gregory Callimachi* (for 2nd time)
29 Jun – 15 Dec 1769	*Constantine Mavrocordat* (for 4th time)
Sep 1769 – Oct 1774	Russian occupation
9 Oct 1774	*Gregory III Ghica* (for 2nd time)
11 Oct 1777	*Constantine Moruzi* (b. 1730; d. 1787)
9 Jun 1782	*Alexander Mavrocordat (Deli Bey)* son of John Mavrocordat
12 Jan 1785 – 14 Dec 1786	*Alexander Mavrocordat (Firaris)* cousin (b. 1754; d. 1819)
Dec 1786 – 19 Apr 1788	*Alexander Ipsilanti* (b. 1726)
May 1788 – Mar 1789	*Emanuel Giani-Ruset*
Oct 1788 – Jan 1792	Russian occupation
Mar 1792	*Alexander Moruzi*, son of Constantine Moruzi (for 1st time)
10 Jan 1793	*Michael Suţu* (for 1st time) (b. 1792; d. 1864)
5 May 1795	*Alexander Callimachi*, son of John Callimachi
18 Mar 1799	*Constantine Ipsilanti*, son of Alexander Ipsilanti (b. 1760; d. 24 Jun 1816)
10 Jul 1801	*Alexander (Alecu) Suţu* (b. 1758; d. 30 Jan 1821)
1 Oct 1802	*Alexander Moruzi* (for 2nd time)

24 Aug – 13 Oct 1806	*Scarlat Callimachi*, son of Alexander Callimachi (for 1st time)
17 Oct 1806	*Alexander Moruzi* (for 3rd time)
Nov 1806 – May 1812	Russian occupation
19 Mar 1807	*Alexander Hangerli*, pretender
5 Aug 1807 – 13 Jun 1810	*Scarlat Callimachi* (for 2nd time)
9 Sep 1812 – 2 Jul 1819	*Scarlat Callimachi* (for 3rd time)
24 Jun 1819 – 10 Apr 1821	*Michael Suţu* (for 2nd time)
May 1821 – Jul 1822	Turkish occupation
21 Jun 1822 – 5 May 1828	*John (Ioniţa) Sturdza*
May 1828 – Apr 1834	Russian occupation
Apr 1834 – Jun 1849	*Michael Sturdza* (b. 1795; d. 8 May 1884)
Jun/14 Oct 1849	*Gregory Alexander Ghica*, grandson of Gregory II Ghica (for 1st time) (b. 27 Aug 1807; d. 26 Aug 1857)
Oct 1853 – Sep 1854	Russian occupation
14 Oct 1854 – 8 Jul 1856	*Gregory Alexander Ghica* (for 2nd time)
Jul 1856 – Jan 1859	Kaymakams appointed
17 Jan 1859	*Alexander John Cuza*, Prince of Romania from 5 Feb 1859 (see below)

Princes of Transylvania

1541	Transylvania, previously part of Hungary, became an autonomous principality under Turkish suzerainty
1541 – 1551	*John Sigismund Zápolyai*, son of John Zápolyai (János Zápolya), King of Hungary (for 1st time)
1541 – 1559	*Isabella*, mother, Regent
1541 – 1551	*Cardinal Gheorghe Utiešenić Martinuzzi (György Fráter)* (b. 1482; d. 17 Dec 1551) Turkish Governor
1551 – 1556	Habsburg occupation
1556 – Mar 1571	*John Sigismund Zápolyai* (for 2nd time)
Mar – Jul 1571	*Gaspar Békés* (b. 1520(?); d. 7 Nov 1579) pretender
25 May 1571	*Stephen Báthori* (b. 27 Sep 1533; d. 21 Dec 1586) King of Poland from 1576 – 1586
1576 – 1581	*Christopher Báthori*, brother (b. 1530; d. 27 May 1581) voivode
May 1581 – Mar 1598	*Sigismund Báthori*, son of Stephen Báthori (for 1st time) (b. 1572; d. 27 Mar 1613)

1586 – 1588	*Ioan Ghyczy*, Governor
20 Aug 1598	*Sigismund Báthori* (for 2nd time)
29 Mar – 28 Oct 1599	*Cardinal Andrei Báthori* (b. 1566(?); d. 31 Oct 1599)
Nov 1599 – Sep 1600	*Michael*, the Brave (b. 1557; d. 19 Aug 1601) Hospodar of Wallachia, 1593 – 1601, and of Moldavia, May – Sep 1600
Feb 1601 – Jul 1602	*Sigismund Báthori* (for 3rd time)
1602 – 1603	*Georg Basta* (b. 1544; d. 26 Aug 1607) and others, as commissaries of the Emperor Rudolph II
May – 17 Jul 1603	*Moses Székely* (b. c. 1550)
1603 – Apr 1604	*Georg Basta* (for 2nd time) and others, commissaries
1604 – 29 Dec 1606	*Stephen Bocskay* (b. 1 Jan 1557)
1606 – Mar 1608	*Sigismund Rákóczi* (b. 1544; d. 5 Dec 1608)
15 Mar 1608 – 27 Oct 1613	*Gabriel Báthori* (b. 15 Aug 1589)
Oct 1613 – 15 Nov 1629	*Gabriel Bethlen* (b. 1580)
15 Nov 1629 – Sep 1630	*Catherine of Brandenburg*, widow
28 Sep – Nov 1630	*Stephen Bethlen* (b. 158–(?); d. 10 Jan 1648)
6 Dec 1630 – 11 Oct 1648	*George Rákóczi I* (b. 8 Jun 1593)
Oct 1648 – 1657	*George Rákóczi II*, (for 1st time) (b. 30 Jan 1621; d. 17 Jun 1660)
Feb 1652	*Francis Rákóczi* (b. 24 Feb 1645; d. 8 Jul 1676) elected but did not rule
Nov 1657 – Jan 1658	*Francis Rhédey* (b. c. 1610; d. 13 May 1667)
1658 – 17 Jun 1660	*George Rákóczi II* (for 2nd time)
17 Oct 1658 – Dec 1660	*Acatius Barcsai* (b. 1610; d. Jul 1661) Turkish nominee
11 Jan 1661 – Jan 1662	*John Kemény* (b. 14 Dec 1607) elected by Diet, accepted Austrian suzerainty
Sep 1661 – Apr 1690	*Michael Apafi I* (b. 13 Nov 1632) appointed by Turkey, acknowledged by Austria in 1686
Jun/Oct 1690 – 1699	*Imre Thököly* (b. 25 Sep 1657; d. Nicomedia 13 Sep 1705) nominated by Turkey, accepted by Diet on 21 Aug 1690
14 Dec 1691	Transylvania subordinated to the Austrian Emperor and ruled henceforward by governors
Jul 1704 – Feb 1711	*Francis Rákóczi II*, in revolt from 1703, elected by Diet in 1704

Hospodars of Wallachia

Mar 1492	*Vlad*, the Monk (for 2nd time)
15 Sep 1495 – Apr 1508	*Radu*, the Great
Apr 1508	*Mihnea*, the Bad, son of Vlad the Impaler (d. 12 Mar 1510)
Oct 1509 – Jan 1610	*Mircea*, son
Feb 1510	*Vlad,* the Young *(Vlăduţ)*, son of Vlad the Monk
23 Jan 1512	*Neagoe Basarab*
15 Sep 1521	*Theodosius*, son
Oct 1521	*Vlad (Radu Vodă)* (Dragomir the Monk)
Jan – Apr 1522	*Radu of Afumaţi* (for 1st time)
after 14 Apr 1523	*Vladislav III* (for 1st time)
8 Nov 1523	*Radu Bădica*
after 19 Jan 1524	*Radu of Afumaţi* (for 2nd time)
16 Jun 1524	*Vladislav III* (for 2nd time)
Sep 1524 – 2 Jan 1529	*Radu of Afumaţi* (for 3rd time) recognised in Dec 1524
19 Apr – Aug 1525	*Vladislav III* (for 3rd time) with the capital at Bucharest, country divided
after 2 Jan 1529	*Moses*, son
Jun 1530	*Vlad*, the Drowned, son of Vlad the Young
1530	*Drăghici Craiovescu (Gogoase)* pretender
after 18 Sep 1532	*Vlad Vintilă of Slatina*, presumed son of Radu the Great
after 12 Jun 1535 – Mar 1545	*Radu Paisie,* confirmed in Nov 1535
2 Apr 1536	*Drăghici Craiovescu*, pretender
Sep – Nov 1537	*Ivan Viezure*, pretender
May – Aug 1539	*Şerban*, pretender
May 1544	*Basarab Laiotă*, pretender
17 Mar 1545 – Feb 1554	*Mircea*, the Shepherd, son of Radu the Great (for 1st time)
16 Nov 1552 – May 1553	*Radu Ilie*, pretender
Mar 1554 – 26 Dec 1557	*Pătruşcu*, the Good, son of Radu Paisie
Jan 1558	*Mircea* (for 2nd time)
21 Sep 1559	*Peter*, the Young, his mother Chiajna acting as Regent
14 Jun 1568 – 30 Apr 1574	*Alexander Mircea*, son of Mircea (for 1st time) (b. 1509/10)
early May 1574	*Vintilă Vodă*, for 4 days
May 1574	*Alexander Mircea* (for 2nd time)
after 11 Sep 1577	*Mihnea*, the Renegade (for 1st time)

Jul 1583 – 15 Apr 1585	*Peter Cercel*, son of Pătrascu the Good
before 25 Apr 1585	*Mihnea*, the Renegade (for 2nd time)
after 31 May 1591 – Jul 1592	*Stephen*, the Deaf
Aug 1592	*Alexander*, the Bad, nephew of Peter the Cossack, Hospodar of Moldavia from Aug – Oct 1592
Sep 1593 – 19 Aug 1601	*Michael*, the Brave (b. 1557)
Nov 1599 – Sep 1600	*Nicholas Patrașcu*, son
Nov 1600 – Jul 1601	*Simeon Movilă* (for 1st time)
Sep 1601 – Mar 1602	*Radu Mihnea*, son of Mihnea the Renegade (for 1st time)
Nov 1601 – Jul 1602	*Simeon Movilă* (for 2nd time)
before 13 Aug 1602 – Jan 1611	*Radu Șerban* (for 1st time) (d. Mar 1620)
Jan – Mar 1611	Transylvanian occupation
Mar – May 1611	*Radu Mihnea* (for 2nd time)
Jun 1611	*Radu Șerban* (for 2nd time)
22 Sep 1611	*Radu Mihnea* (for 3rd time)
Sep 1616 – May 1618	*Alexander Iliaș* (for 1st time)
Jun 1618 – Jul 1620	*Gabriel Movilă*
Aug 1620	*Radu Mihnea* (for 4th time)
Aug 1623	*Alexander Coconul*, son
after 13 Nov 1627	*Alexander Iliaș* (for 2nd time)
Oct 1629 – 31 Jul 1632	*Leo Tomșa*
Aug 1632	*Radu Iliaș*, son of Alexander Iliaș
Sep 1632	*Matthew Basarab*
19 Apr 1654	*Constantine Șerban*, (see under Moldavia)
1658	*Mihnea III Radu*, pretended son of Radu Mihnea (d. 5 Apr 1660)
30 Nov 1659 – 11 Sep 1660	*George Ghica*
26 Sep 1660	*Gregory I Ghica*, son (for 1st time)
Dec 1664	*Radu Leon*
13 Mar 1669	*Antony of Popești*
Feb 1672	*Gregory I Ghica* (for 2nd time)
Nov 1673	*George Duca*
Nov 1678	*Șerban Cantacuzino* (b. 1640)
7 Nov 1688	*Constantine Brâncoveanu*
6 Apr 1714	*Stephen Cantacuzino*, nephew of Șerban Cantacuzino (d. 18 Jun 1716)
5 Jan 1716	*Nicholas Mavrocordat* (for 1st time) (b. 1670; d. 14

	Sep 1730)
2 Dec 1716	*John Mavrocordat*, brother (b. 1684)
Mar 1719 – 14 Sep 1730	*Nicholas Mavrocordat* (for 2nd time)
Sep 1730	*Constantine Mavrocordat*, son (for 1st time) (d. 15 Dec 1769)
Oct 1730	*Michael Racoviţă* (for 1st time)
24 Oct 1731	*Constantine Mavrocordat* (for 2nd time)
16 Apr 1733	*Gregory II Ghica*, grandson of Gregory I Ghica (for 1st time) (d. 3 Sep 1753)
27 Nov 1735	*Constantine Mavrocordat* (for 3rd time)
Sep 1741	*Michael Racoviţă* (for 2nd time)
Jul 1744	*Constantine Mavrocordat* (for 4th time)
Apr 1748	*Gregory II Ghica* (for 2nd time)
4 Sep 1752	*Matthew Ghica*, son
Jun 1753	*Constantine Racoviţă*, son of Michael Racoviţă (for 1st time) (d. 6 Feb 1764)
19 Feb 1756	*Constantine Mavrocordat* (for 5th time)
Aug 1758	*Scarlat Ghica*, son of Gregory II Ghica (for 1st time) (d. 13 Dec 1766)
16 Jun 1761	*Constantine Mavrocordat* (for 6th time)
20 Mar 1763	*Constantine Racoviţă* (for 2nd time)
6 Feb 1764	*Stephen Racoviţă*, son
29 Aug 1765	*Scarlat Ghica* (for 2nd time)
13 Dec 1766	*Alexander Ghica*, son
28 Oct 1768 – 16 Nov 1769	*Gregory III Ghica*, great-grandson of Gregory I Ghica
Nov 1769 – Jul 1774	Russian occupation
May 1770 – Oct 1771	*Emanuel Giani-Ruset*
26 Sep 1774	*Alexander Ipsilanti* (for 1st time) (b. c. 1762; d. Jan 1807)
16 Jan 1782	*Nicholas Caragea*
7 Jul 1783	*Michael Suţu* (for 1st time) (b. 1730(?); d. 1830)
6 Apr 1786 – 19 Jun 1790	*Nicholas Mavrogheni* (b. 1738; d. Sep 1790)
Nov 1789 – Jul 1791	Austrian occupation
Mar 1791	*Michael Suţu* (for 2nd time)
Jan 1793	*Alexander Moruzi* (for 1st time)
28 Aug 1796	*Alexander Ipsilanti* (for 2nd time)
3 Dec 1797 – 1 Mar 1799	*Constantine Hangerli* (d. 1 Mar 1799)
11 Mar 1799	*Alexander Moruzi* (for 2nd time)
20 Oct 1801 – May 1802	*Michael Suţu* (for 3rd time)

Jul – Aug 1802	*Alexander (Alecu) Suţu* (b. 1758; d. 30 Jan 1821) Kaymakam
30 Aug 1802	*Constantine Ipsilanti* (for 1st time) (b. 1760; d. 24 Jun 1816)
24 Aug – 13 Oct 1806	*Alexander Suţu* for first time as Hospodar (see above)
15 Oct 1806 – 31 May 1807	*Constantine Ipsilanti* (for 2nd time)
Nov 1806 – May 1812	Russian occupation
8 – 28 Aug 1807	*Constantine Ipsilanti* (for 3rd time)
8 Sep 1812 – 11 Oct 1818	*John Caragea* (d. 1845)
16 Nov 1818 – 31 Jan 1821	*Alexander Suţu* (for 2nd time)
Feb – Jun 1821	*Scarlat Callimachi*, did not effectively occupy the throne
Mar – May 1821	*Tudor Vladimirescu* (d. 26 May 1821) in revolt
May 1821 – Jul 1822	Turkish occupation
12 Jul 1822 – 11 May 1828	*Gregory D. Ghica*, great-great-grandson of Gregory I Ghica (d. 1844)
May 1828 – Apr 1834	Russian occupation
13 Apr 1834 – 19 Oct 1842	*Alexander Ghica*, half-brother of Gregory (b. 1 Oct 1795; d. 1862)
1 Jan 1843 – 25 Jun 1848	*George Bibescu* (b. 1804; d. 1 Jun 1873)
26 Jun 1848 – Jun 1849	Revolutionary or Kaymakam rule
28 Jun 1849 – 7 Jul 1856	*Barbu Ştirbei* (b. 1801; d. 13 Apr 1869) interrupted by Russian, Turkish and Austrian occupations
Jul 1856 – Feb 1859	Kaymakam rule
5 Feb 1859	*Alexander John Cuza* (see below)

Princes and Kings of Romania

5 Feb 1859	*Alexander John* (b. 20 Mar 1820; d. 15 May 1873) Prince (see above)
22 May 1866	*Carol I*, son of Prince Karl Anton of Hohenzollern-Sigmaringen (b. 20 Apr 1839) King from 26 Mar 1881
10 Oct 1914/20 Jul 1927	*Ferdinand I*, nephew (b. 24 Aug 1865)
20 Jul 1927	*Michael*, son of Carol II (b. 25 Oct 1921) King from 1930 – 1940

MEMBERS OF GOVERNMENT

Prime Ministers

3 Feb 1862	*Barbu Catargiu* (b. 7 Nov 1807; d. 20 Jun 1862)
1862	*Nicolae A. Kretzulescu* (for 1st time) (b. 1812; d. 9 Jul 1900)
24 Oct 1863	*Mihail Kogălniceanu* (b. Iaşi 6 Sep 1817; d. Paris 1 Jul 1891)
6 Feb 1865	*Nicolae A. Kretzulescu* (for 2nd time)
24 May 1866	*Lascăr Catargiu* (for 1st time) (b. Nov 1823; d. 11 Apr 1899)
28 Jul 1866	*Ion Ghica* (for 1st time) (b. Bucharest 1817; d. 4 May 1897)
13 Mar 1867	*Nicolae A. Kretzulescu* (for 3rd time)
26 Nov 1867	*Stefan Golescu* (b. Câmpulung 1809; d. 8 Sep 1874)
12 May 1868	*Nicolae Golescu*, brother (for 1st time) (b. Câmpulung 1810; d. 1878)
Jul 1868	*Ion C. Brătianu* (for 1st time) (b. Pitesti 14 Jun 1821; d. 16 May 1891)
28 Nov 1868	*Dimitrie Ghica* (b. 12 Jun 1816; d. 27 Feb 1897)
14 Feb 1870	*Nicolae Golescu* (for 2nd time)
20 Apr 1870	*Alexandru G. Golescu* (b. 1819; d. 1881)
2 May 1870	*Manolache Costache Epureanu* (for 1st time) (b. Bărlad 1823/24; d. 19 Sep 1880)
26 Dec 1870	*Ion Ghica* (for 2nd time)
24 Mar 1871	*Lascăr Catargiu* (for 2nd time)
17 Apr 1876	*Ion Emanuil Florescu* (for 1st time) (b. Râmnicul-Vâlcei 1819; d. Paris 22 May 1893)
6 May 1876	*Manolache Costache Epureanu* (for 2nd time)
5 Aug 1876	*Ion C. Brătianu* (for 2nd time)
22 Apr 1881	*Dimitrie C. Brătianu*, brother of Ion Brătianu (b. Pitesti 1818; d. 21 Jun 1892)
21 Jun 1881	*Ion C. Brătianu* (for 3rd time)
4 Apr 1888	*Teodor G. Rosetti* (b. Iasi 1837)
10 Apr 1889	*Lascăr Catargiu* (for 3rd time)
17 Nov 1889	*Gheorghe Manu*
5 Mar 1891	*Ion Emanuil Florescu* (for 2nd time)
29 Dec 1891	*Lascăr Catargiu* (for 4th time)
15 Oct 1895	*Dimitrie A. Sturdza* (for 1st time) (b. Miclăuseni 22 Mar 1833; d. 21 Oct 1914)
2 Dec 1896	*Petre S. Aurelian* (b. Slatina 24 Dec 1833; d. 1909)
12 Apr 1897	*Dimitrie A. Sturdza* (for 2nd time)

23 Apr 1899	*Gheorghe Grigore Cantacuzino* (b. Bucharest 1837; d. 5 Apr 1913)
20 Jul 1900	*Petre P. Carp* (for 1st time) (b. Iaşi 11 Jul 1837; d. 22 Jun 1919)
27 Feb 1901	*Dimitrie A. Sturdza* (for 3rd time)
Jan 1906	*Gheorghe Grigore Cantacuzino* (for 2nd time)
26 Mar 1907	*Dimitrie A. Sturdza* (for 4th time)
Mid Jan 1909	*Ion I. C. (Ionel) Brătianu* (for 1st time) (b. Florica 11 Sep 1864; d. 24 Nov 1927)
23 Dec 1909	*Mihai Pherekyde* (b. Bucharest 1841; d. 28 Jan 1924) Deputy
1910	*Ion I. C. (Ionel) Brătianu* (for 2nd time)
10 Jan 1911	*Petre P. Carp* (for 2nd time)
10 Apr 1912	*Titu Maiorescu* (b. Ciaiova 1 Mar 1840; d. 1 Jul 1917)
16 Jan 1914	*Ion I. C. (Ionel) Brătianu* (for 3rd time)
9 Feb – 14 Mar 1918	*Alexandru Averescu* (for 1st time) (b. 9 Mar 1859; d. 3 Oct 1938)
19 Mar 1918 – 10 Nov 1918	*Alexandru Marghiloman* (b. Buzeu 8 Feb 1854; d. 10 May 1925)
10 Nov 1918	*Constantin Coandă*
19 Dec 1918	*Ion I. C. (Ionel) Brătianu* (for 4th time)
12 Sep 1919	*Artur Văitoianu*
4 Dec 1919	*Alexandru Vaida-Voevod* (b. 27 Feb 1873; d. (?))
23 Mar 1920	*Alexandru Averescu* (for 2nd time)
17 Dec 1921	*Take Ionescu* (b. 13 Oct 1858; d. 21 Jun 1922)
17 Jan 1922	*Ion I. C. (Ionel) Brătianu* (for 5th time)
30 Mar 1926	*Alexandru Averescu* (for 3rd time)
7 Jun 1927	*Barbu Ştirbei* (b. 1870(?); d. end of Mar 1946)
22 Jun 1927	*Ion I. C. (Ionel) Brătianu* (for 6th time)
24 Nov 1927 – 2 Nov 1928	*Vintila I. C. Brătianu* (b. 28 Sep 1867; d. 22 Dec 1930)
10 Nov 1928 – 7 Jun 1930	*Iuliu Maniu* (b. 8 Jan 1873; d. Feb(?) 1948)

Foreign Ministers

3 Feb – 6 Jul 1862	*Apostol Arsache*
6 Jul – 11 Oct 1862	*Alexandru Cantacuzino*
12 Oct 1862 – 29 Aug 1863	*Ion Ghica* (for 1st time) (see Prime Ministers)
29 Aug 1863 – 14 Oct 1865	*Nicolae Rosetti-Bălănescu* (b. Iaşi 1829; d. Paris 1884)
15 – 29 Oct 1865	(acting:) *Savel Manu*

29 Oct 1865 – 23 Feb 1866	*Alexandru Papadopol-Callimachi* (b. Tecuci 1833; d. 1898)
23 Feb – 23 May 1866	(acting:) *Ion Ghica* (for 2nd time)
23 May – 27 Jul 1866	*Petre Mavrogheni* (b. 1819; d. 1887)
27 Jul 1866 – 13 Mar 1867	*Gheorghe Ştirbei* (b. 1832)
13 Mar – 29 Aug 1867	(acting:) *Ştefan Golescu* (for 1st time) (see Prime Ministers)
29 Aug – 13 Nov 1867	*Alexandru Teriakiu* (b. c. 1829; d. 1893)
25 Nov 1867 – 13 May 1868	(acting:) *Ştefan Golescu* (for 2nd time)
13 May – 28 Nov 1868	(acting:) *Nicolae Golescu* (see Prime Ministers)
28 Nov 1868 – 7 Sep 1869	(acting:) *Dimitrie Ghica* (see Prime Ministers)
7 Sep – 10 Dec 1869	(acting:) *Mihail Kogălniceanu* (see Prime Ministers)
10 Dec 1869 – 14 Feb 1870	*Nicolae Calimaki-Catargi* (for 1st time) (b. 1831)
14 Feb – 2 May 1870	(acting:) *Alexandru G. Golescu* (see Prime Ministers)
2 May – 30 Dec 1870	*Petre P. Carp* (for 1st time) (see Prime Ministers)
30 – 31 Dec 1870	(acting:) *Nicolae Gr. Racoviţă* (b. Bucharest 1838; d. Rome 1894)
1 Jan – 23 Mar 1871	*Nicolae Calimaki-Catargi* (for 2nd time)
23 Mar 1871 – 9 May 1873	*Gheorghe Costaforu* (b. 26 Oct 1821; d. 28 Nov 1876)
9 – 10 May 1873	(acting:) *Lascăr Catargiu* (for 1st time) (see Prime Ministers)
10 May 1873 – 19 Nov 1875	*Vasile Boerescu* (for 1st time) (b. Bucharest 1830; d. Paris 1883)
19 Nov 1875 – 11 Feb 1876	(acting:) *Lascăr Catargiu* (for 2nd time)
11 Feb – 16 Apr 1876	*Ioan Bălăceanu* (b. Bucharest 1825; d. 1914)
16 Apr – 9 May 1876	*Dimitrie Cornea*
9 May – 5 Aug 1876	*Mihail Kogălniceanu* (for 2nd time)
5 Aug 1876 – 6 Apr 1877	*Nicolae Ionescu* (b. 1850)
6 – 15 Apr 1877	(acting:) *Ion Câmpineanu* (for 1st time) (b. Bucharest 1 Oct 1841; d. 13 Nov 1888)
15 Apr 1877 – 7 Dec 1878	*Mihail Kogălniceanu* (for 3rd time)
7 Dec 1878 – 23 Jul 1879	*Ion Câmpineanu* (for 2nd time)
23 Jul 1879 – 22 Apr 1881	*Vasile Boerescu* (for 2nd time)

22 Apr – 21 Jun 1881	(acting:) *Dimitrie C. Brătianu* (see Prime Ministers)
21 Jun 1881 – 13 Aug 1882	*Eugeniu Stătescu* (b. 1838)
13 Aug 1882 – 14 Feb 1885	*Dimitrie A. Sturdza* (for 1st time) (see Prime Ministers)
14 Feb – 9 Nov 1885	*Ion Câmpineanu* (for 3rd time)
9 Nov – 28 Dec 1885	(acting:) *Ion C. Brătianu* (see Prime Ministers)
23 Dec 1885 – 4 Apr 1888	*Mihai Pherekyde* (see Prime Ministers)
4 Apr 1888 – 10 Apr 1889	*Petre P. Carp* (for 2nd time)
10 Apr 1889 – 5 Mar 1891	*Alexandru Lahovary* (for 1st time) (b. 1841; d. 1897)
5 Mar – 9 Dec 1891	*Constantin Esarcu* (b. Bucharest 1836; d. 1898)
9 Dec 1891 – 16 Oct 1895	*Alexandru Lahovary* (for 2nd time)
16 Oct 1895 – 3 Dec 1896	(acting:) *Dimitrie A. Sturdza* (for 2nd time)
3 Dec 1896 – 25 Mar 1897	*Constantin Stoicescu*
25 Mar – 12 Apr 1897	(acting:) *Petre S. Aurelian* (see Prime Ministers)
12 Apr 1897 – 23 Apr 1899	(acting:) *Dimitrie A. Sturdza* (for 3rd time)
23 Apr 1899 – 20 Jul 1900	*Ion N. Lahovary* (for 1st time) (b. 1848)
20 Jul 1900 – 27 Feb 1901	*Alexandru Marghiloman* (b. Buzeu 8 Feb 1854)
27 Feb 1901 – 31 Jul 1902	(acting:) *Dimitrie A. Sturdza* (for 4th time)
31 Jul 1902 – 26 Dec 1904	*Ion I. C. (Ionel) Brătianu* (for 1st time) (see Prime Ministers)
26 Dec 1904 – 4 Jan 1906	(acting:) *Dimitrie A. Sturdza* (for 5th time)
4 Jan 1906 – 22 Feb 1907	*Iacob Lahovary* (b. 16 Jan 1846)
22 Feb – 25 Mar 1907	(acting:) *Ion N. Lahovary* (for 2nd time) until 11 Mar
25 Mar 1907 – 9 Jan 1909	*Dimitrie A. Sturdza* (for 6th time)
9 Jan – 14 Nov 1909	(acting:) *Ion I. C. (Ionel) Brătianu* (for 2nd time)
14 Nov 1909 – 11 Jan 1911	*Alexandru G. Djuvara* (b. Bucharest 1858)
11 Jan 1911 – 17 Jan 1914	*Titu Maiorescu* (b. Craiova 15 Feb 1840; d. 1917)

17 Jan 1914 – 21 Dec 1916	*Emanoil Porumbaru*
21 Dec 1916 – 10 Feb 1918	*Ion I. C. (Ionel) Brătianu* (for 3rd time)
11 Feb – 19 Mar 1918	(acting:) *Alexandru Averescu* (see Prime Ministers)
19 Mar – 6 Nov 1918	*Constantin C. Arion*
6 Nov – 12 Dec 1918	*Constantin Coandă* (see Prime Ministers)
12 Dec 1918 – 27 Sep 1919	*Ion I. C. (Ionel) Brătianu* (for 4th time)
27 Sep – 15 Oct 1919	(acting:) *Artur Văitoianu* (see Prime Ministers)
15 Oct – 1 Dec 1919	*Nicolae Mişu*
1 Dec 1919 – 13 Mar 1920	*Alexandru Vaida-Voievod* (see Prime Ministers)
15 Mar – 13 Jun 1920	*Duiliu Zamfirescu* (b. Focşani 30 Oct 1858; d. 1922)
13 Jun 1920 – 17 Dec 1921	*Take Ionescu* (see Prime Ministers)
17 Dec 1921 – 18 Jan 1922	*Gheorghe Derussi*
19 Jan 1922 – 30 Mar 1926	*Ion Gh. Duca* (b. 20 Dec 1879; d. 29 Dec 1933)
30 Mar 1926 – 4 Jun 1927	*Ion Mitileneu*
5 – 22 Jun 1927	(acting:) *Barbu Ştirbei* (see Prime Ministers)
6 Jul 1927 – 30 Jul 1928	*Nicolae Titulescu* (b. Craiova 4 Oct 1883; d. Cannes 17 Mar 1941)
31 Jul – 10 Nov 1928	(acting:) *Constantin Argetoianu*
10 Nov 1928 – 18 Apr 1931	*Gheorghe Mironescu* (b. 28 Jan 1874(?))

Rwanda

For the Kingdom of Rwanda, 14th to 20th centuries, see volume 1.

Sarawak

24 Sep 1841	Independent state set up at the invitation of local

	chiefs by Sir James Brooke
1883	British protectorate established

HEADS OF STATE

Rajahs

24 Sep 1841	*Sir James Brooke* (b. Benares 1803)
11 Jun 1868	*Sir Charles Johnson Brooke*, nephew (b. Berrow 3 Jun 1829)
17/24 May 1917 – 1 Jul 1946	*Sir Charles Vyner de Windt Brooke*, son (b. London 26 Sep 1874; d. 9 May 1963)

Sardinia

HEADS OF STATE

Kings

1718/24 Aug 1720	Established under the Savoy dynasty
1718/24 Aug 1720	*Victor Amadeus II* (from 12 Jun 1675: *Duke of Savoy*) (b. 14 May 1666; d. 31 Oct 1732) abdicated in favour of his son
3 Sep 1730	*Charles Emmanuel III* son (b. Turin 27 Apr 1701)
20 Feb 1773	*Victor Amadeus III*, son (b. Turin 26 Jun 1726)
16 Oct 1796	*Charles Emmanuel IV*, son (b. 24 May 1751; d. Rome 6 Oct 1819) abdicated, a Jesuit from 1815
4 Jun 1802	*Victor Emmanuel I*, brother (b. Turin 24 Jul 1759; d. Moncalieri Castle 10 Jan 1824) abdicated
13 Mar 1821 – 27 Apr 1831	*Charles Felix*, brother (b. 6 Apr 1765)

Savoy-Carignan dynasty

27 Apr 1831	*Charles Albert*, son of Prince Charles of Savoy-Carignan (b. 29 Oct 1798; d. Oporto, Portugal 28 Jul 1849) abdicated
23 Mar 1849 – 9 Jan 1878	*Victor Emmanuel II*, son (b. 14 Mar 1820) from 17 Mar 1861: King of Italy

459

MEMBERS OF GOVERNMENT

11 May 1814 – 1817(?): Asinari I

Chairman of the Council of Regency	*Filippo Antonio Asinari, Marquis of San Marzano* (b. Turin 12 Nov 1767; d. Turin 19 Jul 1828)
Foreign Affairs	—— *Vallesa*

1817 – 1821: Asinari II

Chief Minister	*Filippo Antonio Asinari, Marquis of San Marzano* (see Asinari I)
Education	1819 – 1820: *Prospero Balbo* (b. Turin 1 Jul 1762; d. 14 Mar 1837)
Home Affairs	1820 – 1821: *Prospero Balbo* (see above)
Other Ministers	*Cesare di Saluzzo*
	—— *Brignole*

21 Mar 1835 – 5 Mar 1848: Solaro

Prime Minister	*Clemente, Count Solaro della Margherita* (b. Cuneo 21 Nov 1792; d. Turin 12 Nov 1869)
Foreign Affairs	21 Mar 1835 – 1847: *Clemente, Count Solaro della Margherita* (see above)
	1847 – 3 Apr 1848: *Ermolao Asinari, Count of San Marzano*, son of Filippo Antonio Asinari (b. Castiglione d'Asti 1800; d. Turin 15 Oct 1864)
Finance	1831 – 1834: *Prospero Bello*
	29 Aug 1844 – 5 Mar 1848: *Ottavio Thaon di Revel* (b. Turin 26 Jun 1803; d. 10 Feb 1868)
Other Ministers	*Cesare Alfieri, Marquis of Sostegno* (b. Turin 13 Aug 1799; d. Florence 16 Apr 1869)
	Luigi Cibrario

8 Mar – 26 Jul 1848: Balbo

Prime Minister	*Cesare, Count Balbo* (b. Turin 21 Nov 1789; d. 3 Jun 1853)
Foreign Affairs	*Lorenzo Pareto* (b. Genoa 6 Dec 1800; d. 19 Jun 1865)
Public Worship and Justice	*Federico, Count Sclopis di Solerano* (b. Turin 10 Jan 1789; d. 8 Mar 1878)
Education	*Carlo Boncompagni di Mombello* (from 1874: *Count*

of Lamporo) (b. Saluggia 25 Jul 1804; d. Turin 15 Dec 1880)

30 Jul – 20 Aug 1848: Casati (interim administration)

Prime Minister	*Gabrio, Count Casati* (b. Milan 2 Aug 1798; d. 16 Nov 1873)
Foreign Affairs	*Lorenzo Pareto* (see Balbo)
Finance	30 Jul – 7 Aug 1848: —— *Gioia*
	7 – 20 Aug 1848: *Ottavio Thaon di Revel* (see Solaro)
Education	30 Jul – 7 Aug 1848: *Vincenzo Gioberti* (b. Turin 5 Apr 1801; d. Paris 26 Oct 1852)
	7 – 20 Aug 1848: *Urbano Rattazzi* (b. Alessandria 29 Jun 1810; d. Frosinone 5 Jun 1873)
Public Works	30 Jul – 7 Aug 1848: *Pietro Paleocapa* (b. Nese 11 Nov 1798; d. Turin 13 Feb 1869)

20 Aug – (?)Sep 1848: Alfieri

Prime Minister	*Cesare Alfieri, Marquis of Sostegno* (see Solaro)
Finance	*Ottavio Thaon di Revel* (see Solaro)
War	*Giuseppe, Count Dabormida* (b. Verrua 21 Nov 1799; d. Buriaso di Pinerolo 10 Aug 1869)
Public Works, Agriculture and Trade	*Pietro de Rossi di Santarosa* (b. Savigliano 5 Apr 1805; d. Turin 5 Aug 1850)
Other Ministers	*Carlo Boncompagni di Mombello* (see Balbo)
	—— *Pinelli*

Sep – Oct 1848: Perrone

Prime Minister	—— *Perrone*

Oct – Dec 1848: Pinelli

Prime Minister	—— *Pinelli* (see Alfieri)

15 Dec 1848 – 21 Feb 1849: Gioberti

Prime Minister	*Vincenzo Gioberti* (see Casati)
Justice and Public Worship	*Urbano Rattazzi* (see Casati)

Feb – 27 Mar 1849: Chiodo

Prime Minister	*Agostino, Baron Chiodo* (b. Savona 1791; d. 25 Feb 1861)
Home Affairs	*Urbano Rattazzi* (see Casati)

27 Mar – 7 May 1849: Delaunay

Prime Minister and Foreign Affairs	*Claudio Gabriele Delaunay* (b. 1786; d. 21 Feb 1850)
Trade and Navy	*Pietro de Rossi di Santarosa* (see Alfieri)
Finance	—— *Nigra*
Without Portfolio	*Vincenzo Gioberti* (see Casati)

7 May 1849 – 4 Nov 1852: Azeglio

Prime Minister and Foreign Affairs	*Massimo Tapparelli, Marquis d'Azeglio* (b. Turin 24 Oct 1798; d. 15 Jan 1866)
Justice and Public Worship	*Giuseppe, Count Siccardi* (b. 1802; d. 28 Oct 1857)
War	3 Nov 1849 – 4 Nov 1852: *Alfonso, Marquis of La Marmora* (b. Turin 27 Nov 1804; d. Florence 5 Jan 1878)
Trade and Navy	30 Mar 1849 – 5 Aug 1850: *Pietro de Rossi di Santarosa* (see Alfieri)
	1850 – 4 Nov 1852: *Camillo, Count Benso di Cavour* (b. Turin 10 Aug 1810; d. 6 Jun 1861)
Public Works	*Pietro Paleocapa* (see Casati)
Finance	30 Mar 1849 – Apr 1851: —— *Nigra*
	Apr 1851 – 21 May 1852: *Camillo, Count Benso di Cavour* (see above)
Education	May – 4 Nov 1852: *Carlo Boncompagni di Mombello* (see Balbo)

4 Nov 1852 – Jul 1859: Cavour I

Prime Minister	*Camillo, Count Benso di Cavour* (for 1st time) (see Azeglio)
Home Affairs	1855(?) – Jul 1859: *Urbano Rattazzi* (see Casati)
Justice and Public Worship	4 Nov 1852 – Oct 1853: *Carlo Boncompagni di Mombello* (see Balbo)
	Oct 1853 – 1858: *Urbano Rattazzi* (see Casati)

Finance, Agriculture, Commerce and Industry	*Camillo, Count Benso di Cavour* (see Azeglio)
War and from 1856, Navy	*Alfonso, Marquis of La Marmora* (see Azeglio)
Public Works	4 Nov 1852 – 1857: *Pietro Paleocapa* (see Casati)

Jul 1859 – Jan 1860: La Marmora

Prime Minister	*Alfonso, Marquis of La Marmora* (see Azeglio)
Home Affairs, Justice and Public Worship	*Urbano Rattazzi* (see Casati)
Education	*Gabrio, Count Casati* (see Casati)
War	*Alfonso, Marquis of La Marmora* (see Azeglio)

23 Mar 1860 – 17 Mar 1861: Cavour II

Prime Minister, Foreign Affairs, Home Affairs and Navy	*Camillo, Count Benso di Cavour* (for 2nd time) (see Azeglio)
War	*Manfredo Fanti* (b. Carpi 26 Feb 1808; d. Florence 5 Apr 1865)
7 Feb 1861	Cavour appointed Italian Prime Minister

Saudi Arabia

HEADS OF STATE

Kings

Hashemite Dynasty of Nejd and Hejaz

May 1916	*Husain ibn Ali V*, cousin of King Faisal I of Iraq (b. 1856; d. 4 Jun 1931) King of Arabia
Oct 1924 – 19 Dec 1925	*Ali*, son (b. 1882 (1871?); d. 14 Feb 1935)

Wahhabi Dynasty

8 May 1926 – 9 Nov 1953	*Abdul Aziz III (ibn Saud)* (b. Riyadh 21 Oct 1882) King of Arabia 8 Jan 1926; King of Hejaz, early Apr 1926

Savoy

HEADS OF STATE

Dukes

24 Jun 1489	*Charles II*, posthumous son of Charles I (b. 24 Jun 1489)
16 Apr 1496	*Philip II*, great uncle, son of Duke Louis (b. 5 Feb 1438)
4 Nov 1497	*Philibert II*, son (b. 10 Apr 1480)
10 Sep 1504	*Charles III*, brother (b. 10 Oct 1486)
16 Sep 1533	*Emanuel Philibert*, son (b. 8 Jul 1528)
30 Aug 1580	*Charles Emmanuel I*, son (b. Chateau Rivoli 12 Jan 1562)
26 Jul 1630	*Victor Amadeus I*, son (b. 8 May 1587)
7 Oct 1637	*Francis Hyacinth*, son (b. 4 Sep 1632)
4 Oct 1638	*Charles Emmanuel II*, brother (b. 20 Jun 1634)
12 Jun 1675 – 3 Sep 1730	*Victor Amadeus II*, son (b. 14 May 1666; d. 30 Oct 1732) King of Sicily 1713-20
1718/24 Aug 1720	Savoy merged in the newly formed Kingdom of Sardinia

Saxony

26 Aug 1485	Division of duchy into eastern (Albertine) and western (Ernestine) halves

HEADS OF STATE: ERNESTINE LINE

Electors

26 Aug 1486	*Frederick III*, The Wise, son of the Elector Ernest (b. 18 Jan 1463)
5 May 1525	*John*, the Steadfast, brother (b. 30 Jun 1467)
16 Aug 1532	*John Frederick II*, the Magnanimous, son (b. 30 Jun 1503; d. 3 Mar 1554)
19 May 1547	Electorship passed to the Albertine line (the remaining rulers of the fragmented duchies of Saxe-Weimar-Eisenach, Saxe-Meiningen-Hildburghausen, Saxe-Altenburg and Saxe-Coburg-Gotha are not listed)

HEADS OF STATE: ALBERTINE LINE

Dukes

26 Aug 1485	*Albert III*, The Courageous, brother of the Elector Ernest (b. 27 Jul 1433) co-ruler with Ernest of the undivided duchy from 7 Sep 1464
12 Sep 1500	*George*, the Rich, son (b. 27 Aug 1471)
17 Apr 1539	*Henry*, the Pious, brother (b. 17 Mar 1473)
18 Aug 1541	*Maurice*, son (b. 21 Mar 1521) Elector from 19 May 1547

Electors

1 Jul 1553	*Augustus*, brother (b. 31 Jul 1526)
1 Feb 1586	*Christian I*, son (b. 25 Oct 1560)
25 Sep 1591	*Christian II*, son (b. 23 Sep 1583)
6 Jun 1611	*John George I*, brother (b. 6 Mar 1585)
Oct 1656	*John George II*, son (b. 31 Mar 1613)
2 Aug 1680	*John George III*, son (b. 20 Jun 1647)
2 Sep 1691	*John George IV*, son (b. 18 Oct 1668)
7 Apr 1694	*Frederick Augustus I*, brother (b. 12 May 1670) King Augustus II, the Strong, of Poland from 17 Jun 1697
Feb 1733	*Frederick Augustus II*, son (b. 17 Oct 1696) King Augustus III of Poland from 5 Oct 1733
Oct 1763	*Frederick Christian*, son (b. 5 Sep 1722)
7 Dec 1763	*Frederick Augustus III*, the Just, son (b. 23 Dec 1750) King Frederick Augustus I from 11 Dec 1806 17 Dec 1763 – 15 Sep 1768: *Xavier*, uncle (b. 25 Aug 1730; d. 20 Jun 1806) Administrator

SAXONY

Kings

5 May 1827	*Antony*, brother of Frederick Augustus I (b. 27 Dec 1755)
6 Jun 1836	*Frederick Augustus II*, nephew (b. 18 May 1797) co-regent for his uncle from 13 Sep 1830
9 Aug 1854	*John*, brother (b. 12 Dec 1801)
29 Oct 1873	*Albert*, son (b. 23 Apr 1828)
19 Jun 1902	*George*, brother (b. 8 Aug 1832)
15 Oct 1904	*Frederick Augustus III*, son (b. 25 May 1865; d. 18 Feb 1932)
13 Nov 1918	Republic

MEMBERS OF GOVERNMENT

14 May 1813 – Sep 1830: Einsiedel

Chief Minister, Foreign Affairs and Home Affairs	*Detlev, Count Einsiedel* (b. Wolkenburg 12 Oct 1773; d. 20 Mar 1861)

Sep 1830 – 1843: Lindenau

Chief Minister	*Bernhard August, Baron Lindenau* (b. Altenburg 11 Jun 1779; d. Altenburg 12 May 1854)
Foreign Affairs	Sep 1830 – 1835: *Johannes von Minkwitz* (b. Altenburg 1 Feb 1787; d. Dresden 18 Mar 1857)
	1835 – 1843: *Heinrich Anton von Zeschau* (b. Jessen 4 Feb 1789; d. Dresden 17 Mar 1870)
Home Affairs	*Bernhard August, Baron Lindenau* (see above)
Justice	from 1831: *Julius Traugott Jakob von Könneritz* (b. Merseburg 31 May 1792; d. Dresden 28 Oct 1866)
Finance	from 1831: *Heinrich Anton von Zeschau* (see above)
Public Worship and Education	1831 – 1836: *Johann Christian Gottlieb Müller*
	1836 – 1840: *Hans Georg von Carlowitz* (b. Grosshartmannsdorf 11 Dec 1772; d. Dresden 18 Mar 1840)
	1840 – 1843: *Eduard von Wietersheim* (b. Zerbst 10 Sep 1787; d. Neupouch 16 Apr 1865)
War	1831 – 1839: *Johann Adolf von Zezschwitz* (b. Taubenheim 1 Mar 1779; d. Königstein 3 May 1845)

1843 – 13 Mar 1848: von Könneritz

Chief Minister	*Julius Traugott Jakob von Könneritz* (see Lindenau)
Foreign Affairs	*Heinrich Anton von Zeschau* (see Lindenau)
Home Affairs	1843 – 1844: *Eduard von Nostitz und Jänckendorf* (b. Dresden 31 Mar 1791; d. Dresden 18 Feb 1858)
Justice	1843 – 1846: *Julius Traugott Jakob von Könneritz* (see Lindenau)
	1846 – 16 Mar 1848: *Albert von Carlowitz*, son of Hans Georg Carlowitz (b. Freiberg 1 Apr 1802; d. Kötzschenbroda 9 Aug 1874)
Finance	*Heinrich Anton von Zeschau* (see Lindenau)
Public Worship	*Eduard von Wietersheim* (see Lindenau)
War	1843 – (?): *Gustav von Nostitz-Wallwitz* (b. Dresden 31 Mar 1791; d. Dresden 18 Feb 1858)
	(?) – 13 Mar 1848: *Karl Friedrich Gustav von Oppell* (b. Kunersdorf 25 Nov 1795; d. Dresden 30 Apr 1870)

16 Mar 1848 – 24 Feb 1849: Braun

Prime Minister	*Alexander Karl Hermann Braun* (b. Plauen 10 May 1807; d. Plauen 24 Mar 1868)
Foreign Affairs	*Ludwig von der Pfordten* (b. Ried im Innviertel 11 Sep 1811; d. Munich 18 Aug 1880)
Justice	*Alexander Karl Hermann Braun* (see above)
Public Worship	*Ludwig von der Pfordten* (see above)
War	—— *von Holtzendorff*
Other Ministers	—— *Georgi*
	—— *Oberländer*

24 Feb – 2 May 1849: Held

Prime Minister	*Gustav Friedrich Held* (b. 29 May 1804; d. 24 Apr 1857)
Foreign Affairs	*Friedrich Ferdinand, Baron* (from 1868: *Count*) *von Beust* (b. Dresden 13 Jan 1809; d. Schloss Altenberg 24 Oct 1886)
Home Affairs	*Christian Albert Weinlig* (b. Dresden 9 Apr 1812; d. Dresden 18 Jan 1873)
Finance	*Karl Wolf von Ehrenstein* (b. Chemnitz 21 Jul 1805; d. Dresden 2 Jun 1865)
War	*Baron Buttlar*

2 May 1849 – 28 Oct 1858: Zschinsky

Prime Minister	*Ferdinand von Zschinsky* (b. Borstendorf 22 Feb 1797; d. Dresden 28 Oct 1858)
Foreign Affairs	*Friedrich Ferdinand, Baron von Beust* (see Held)
Home Affairs	2 May 1849 – Oct 1852: *Richard, Baron Friesen* (b. Thürmsdorf 9 Aug 1808; d. Dresden 25 Feb 1884)
	Oct 1852 – 28 Oct 1858: *Friedrich Ferdinand, Baron von Beust* (see Held)
Justice	*Ferdinand von Zschinsky* (see above)
Finance	end of May 1849 – 28 Oct 1858: *Johann Heinrich August von Behr* (b. Freiberg 13 Nov 1793; d. Dresden 20 Feb 1871)
Public Worship	14 May 1849 – May 1853: *Friedrich Ferdinand, Baron von Beust* (see Held)
	May 1853 – 28 Oct 1858: *Johann Paul, Baron Falkenstein* (b. Pegau 15 Jun 1801; d. Dresden 14 Jan 1882)
War	*Bernhard von Rabenhorst* (b. Leipzig 29 May 1801; d. Hoflössnitz 14 Apr 1873)
Lord Chamberlain	1851 – 28 Oct 1858: *Heinrich Anton von Zeschau* (see Lindenau)

28 Oct 1858 – 15 Aug 1866: Beust

Prime Minister, Foreign Affairs and Home Affairs	*Friedrich Ferdinand, Baron von Beust* (see Held)
Justice	28 Oct 1858 – Mar 1866: *Johann Heinrich August von Behr* (see Zschinsky)
	Mar – 15 Aug 1866: —— *Schneider* (d. 1871)
Finance	*Richard, Baron Friesen* (see Zschinsky)
Public Worship	*Johann Paul, Baron Falkenstein* (see Zschinsky)
War	*Bernhard von Rabenhorst* (see Zschinsky)
Lord Chamberlain	*Heinrich Anton von Zeschau* (see Lindenau)

Oct 1866 – 1 Oct 1871: Falkenstein

Prime Minister	*Johann Paul, Baron Falkenstein* (see Zschinsky)
Foreign Affairs	*Richard, Baron Friesen* (see Zschinsky)
Home Affairs	*Hermann von Nostitz-Wallwitz* (b. Oschatz 30 Mar 1826; d. Dresden 10 Jan 1906)
Justice	—— *Schneider* (see Beust)

Finance	*Richard, Baron Friesen* (see Zschinsky)
Public Worship	*Johann Paul, Baron Falkenstein* (see Zschinsky)
War	*(Georg Friedrich) Alfred* (from 1884: *Count*) *von Fabrice* (b. Quesnoy-sur-Deûle 23 May 1818; d. Dresden 25 Mar 1891)
Lord Chamberlain	Oct 1866 – 1869: *Heinrich Anton von Zeschau* (see Lindenau)

1 Oct 1871 – 1 Nov 1876: Friesen

Prime Minister and Foreign Affairs	*Richard, Baron Friesen* (see Zschinsky)
Home Affairs	*Hermann von Nostitz-Wallwitz* (see Falkenstein)
Justice	9 Oct 1871 – 1 Nov 1876: *Christian Wilhelm Ludwig von Abeken* (b. Dresden 21 Sep 1826; d. Dresden 15 Oct 1896)
Finance	*Richard, Baron Friesen* (see Zschinsky)
Public Worship	*Karl Friedrich Wilhelm von Gerber* (b. Ebeleben 11 Apr 1823; d. Dresden 23 Dec 1891)
War	*(Georg Friedrich) Alfred von Fabrice* (see Falkenstein)
Lord Chamberlain	*Johann Paul, Baron Falkenstein* (see Zschinsky)

1 Nov 1876 – 25 Mar 1891: Fabrice

Prime Minister	*(Georg Friedrich) Alfred, Count von Fabrice* (see Falkenstein)
Foreign Affairs	1 Nov 1876 – 4 Feb 1882: *Herman von Nostitz-Wallwitz* (see Falkenstein)
	4 Feb 1882: office abolished (?)
Home Affairs	1 Nov 1876 – Jan 1891: *Hermann von Nostitz-Wallwitz* (see Falkenstein)
	Jan – 25 Mar 1891: *Georg* (from 1916: *Count*) *von Metzsch-Reichenbach* (b. Friesen 14 Jul 1836; d. Dresden 7 Nov 1927)
Justice	1 Nov 1876 – 15 Oct 1890: *Christian Wilhelm Ludwig von Abeken* (see Friesen)
	15 Oct 1890 – 25 Mar 1891: *Heinrich Rudolf Schurig* (b. Radeberg 4 Mar 1835; d. Dresden 15 Jun 1901)
Finance	1 Nov 1876 – 20 Jan 1890: *Léonce Robert, Baron Könneritz* (b. Paris 4 Mar 1835; d. Dresden 20 Jan 1890)
	Jan 1890 – 25 Mar 1891: *Hans von Thümmel* (b. Gotha 25 May 1824; d. Dresden 12 Feb 1895)

Public Worship	*Karl Friedrich Wilhelm von Gerber* (see Friesen)
War	*(Georg Friedrich) Alfred, Count von Fabrice* (see Falkenstein)
Lord Chamberlain	1 Nov 1876 – 14 Jan 1882: *Johann Paul, Baron Falkenstein* (see Zschinsky)
	Jan 1882 – 25 Mar 1891: *Hermann von Nostitz-Wallwitz* (see Falkenstein)

25 Mar 1891 – 15 Jun 1901: Gerber

Prime Minister	25 Mar – 23 Dec 1891: *Karl Friedrich Wilhelm von Gerber* (see Friesen)
	Dec 1891 – 15 Jun 1901: *Heinrich Rudolf Schurig* (see Fabrice)
Home Affairs	*Georg von Metzsch-Reichenbach* (see Fabrice)
Justice	*Heinrich Rudolf Schurig* (see Fabrice)
Finance	25 Mar 1891 – 1895: *Hans von Thümmel* (see Fabrice)
	1895 – 15 Jun 1901: *Werner von Watzdorf* (b. Dresden 19 Dec 1836; d. Dresden 29 Feb 1904)
Public Worship	25 Mar – 23 Dec 1891: *Karl Friedrich Wilhelm von Gerber* (see Friesen)
	4 Jan 1892 – 15 Jun 1901: *Paul von Seydewitz* (b. Lauterbach 3 May 1843; d. Dresden 17 Dec 1910)
War	*Karl Paul von der Planitz* (b. Hohengrün 20 Sep 1837; d. Hosterwitz 19 Aug 1902)
Lord Chamberlain	25 Mar 1891 – Oct 1895: *Hermann von Nostitz-Wallwitz* (see Falkenstein)
	Oct 1895 – 15 Jun 1901: *Paul von Seydewitz* (see above)

Jun 1901 – 30 Apr 1906: Metzsch-Reichenbach

Prime Minister and Home Affairs	*Georg von Metzsch-Reichenbach* (see Fabrice)
Justice	Jun 1901 – 10 Feb 1902: *Konrad Wilhelm von Rüger* (b. Dresden 26 Oct 1837; d. Dresden 20 Feb 1916)
	10 Feb 1902 – 30 Apr 1906: *Viktor Alexander von Otto* (b. Grossenhain 25 Mar 1852; d. Dresden 26 Jul 1912)
Finance	Jul 1901 – 10 Feb 1902: *Werner von Watzdorf* (see Gerber)
	10 Feb 1902 – 30 Apr 1906: *Konrad Wilhelm von Rüger* (see above)

Public Worship	*Paul von Seydewitz* (see Gerber)
War	Jun 1901 – 19 Aug 1902: *Karl Paul von der Planitz* (see Gerber)
	Aug 1902 – 30 Apr 1906: *Max (Klemens Lothar), Baron Hausen* (b. Dresden 17 Dec 1846; d. Dresden 19 Mar 1922)
Lord Chamberlain	*Georg von Metzsch-Reichenbach* (see Fabrice)

30 Apr 1906 – 1 Dec 1910: Rüger

Prime Minister	*Konrad Wilhelm von Rüger* (see Metzsch-Reichenbach)
Home Affairs	30 Apr 1906 – 1 Jul 1909: *(Karl Adolf Philipp) Wilhelm, Count Hohenthal und Bergen* (b. Berlin 4 Feb 1853; d. Dresden 20 Sep 1909)
	1 Jul 1909 – 1 Dec 1910: *Christof, Count Vitzthum von Eckstädt* (b. Dresden 14 Oct 1863; d. Tiefenhartmannsdorf 30 Dec 1944)
Justice	*Viktor Alexander von Otto* (see Metzsch-Reichenbach)
Finance	*Konrad Wilhelm von Rüger* (see Metzsch-Reichenbach)
Public Worship	20 Apr 1906 – 1908: *Richard von Schlieben* (b. Nieder-Friedersdorf 23 Jul 1848)
	1908 – 1 Dec 1910: *Heinrich (Gustav) Beck* (b. Gera 11 Apr 1857; d. Dresden 3 Jan 1933)
War	*Max (Klemens Lothar), Baron Hausen* (see Metzsch-Reichenbach)
Lord Chamberlain	*Georg von Metzsch-Reichenbach* (see Fabrice)

Dec 1910 – 26 Oct 1918: Otto

Prime Minister	1 Dec 1910 – 26 Jul 1912: *Viktor Alexander von Otto* (see Metzsch-Reichenbach)
	26 Jul 1912 – 21 May 1914: *Max (Klemens Lothar), Baron Hausen* (see Metzsch-Reichenbach)
	21 May 1914 – 26 Oct 1918: *Heinrich (Gustav) Beck* (see Rüger)
Home Affairs	*Christof, Count Vitzthum von Eckstädt* (see Rüger)

Justice	1 Dec 1910 – 26 Jul 1912: *Viktor Alexander von Otto* (see Metzsch-Reichenbach) 4 Aug 1912 – 12 May 1918: *Paul Artur Nagel* (b. Dresden 14 Aug 1856; d. Dresden 12 May 1918) 13 Jun – 26 Oct 1918: *Rudolf Heinze* (b. Oldenburg 22 Jul 1865; d. Dresden 17 May 1928)
Finance	*Ernst von Seydewitz* (b. Lauterbach 15 Jan 1852; d. Dresden 22 Jan 1929)
Public Worship	*Heinrich (Gustav) Beck* (see Rüger)
War	1 Dec 1910 – 21 May 1914: *Max (Klemens Lothar), Baron Hausen* (see Metzsch-Reichenbach) 21 May – 10 Sep 1914: *Adolf von Carlowitz* (b. Riesa 25 Mar 1858; d. Dresden 9 Jul 1928) 10 Sep 1914 (definitively from 27 Oct 1915) – 26 Oct 1918: *Viktor von Wilsdorf* (b. Grosshartmannsdorf 18 Jan 1857; d. Dresden 24 Mar 1920)
Lord Chamberlain	*Georg, Count von Metzsch-Reichenbach* (see Fabrice)

26 Oct – 13 Nov 1918: Heinze

Prime Minister	*Rudolf Heinze* (see Otto)
Home Affairs	26 Oct – 1 Nov 1918: —— *Koch* 1 – 13 Nov 1918: *Alfred von Nostitz-Wallwitz* (b. Dresden 21 Dec 1870; d. Burg Bassenheim 21 Dec 1953)
Justice	*Rudolf Heinze* (see Otto)
Finance	*Otto Schröder* (d. Dresden 13 Dec 1923)
Public Worship	*Alfred von Nostitz-Wallwitz* (see above)
War	*Viktor von Wilsdorf* (see Otto)
Lord Chamberlain	*Georg, Count von Metzsch-Reichenbach* (see Fabrice)
Secretaries of State (1 – 13 Nov 1918)	*Max Held* (b. Potsdam 4 Nov 1872; d. Dresden 27 Dec 1933) *Julius Frässdorf* (b. Dresden 26 May 1857; d. Dresden 26 Mar 1932) *Oskar Günther* (b. Grimma 20 Mar 1861) *Emil (Robert) Nitzschke* (b. Hadersleben 31 Oct 1870; d. Leutzsch 24 Jul 1921)

Scotland

HEADS OF STATE

Kings

House of Stuart

11 Jun 1488	*James IV*, son of King James III (b. 17 Mar 1473)
9 Sep 1513 – 14 Dec 1542	*James V*, son (b. 10 Apr 1512)
1512 – 1524	*John Stuart, Duke of Albany*, nephew of James III (b. 1481; d. 2 Jul 1536) Regent
14 Dec 1542 – 24 Jul 1567	*Mary*, daughter of James V (b. 8 Dec 1542; d. 8 Feb 1587) Queen; until 19 Aug 1561 out of Scotland, abdicated 24 Jul 1567 and fled to England, where she was eventually beheaded
1542 – 1560	*Marie of Guise, Princess of Lorraine*, mother (d. 10 Jun 1560) Regent
24 Jul 1567 – 27 Mar 1625	*James VI*, son (b. 19 Jun 1566) became James I of England from 24 Mar 1603 Regents for the King during his minority: 1567 – 23 Jan 1570: *James Stuart, Earl of Moray*, illegitimate son of King James V (b. 1533; d. (murdered) Linlithgow 23 Jan 1570) 1570 – 1571; *Matthew Stuart, Earl Lennox*, father of Mary Stuart's second husband Lord Darnley, the father of James VI (d. 1571) 1571 – 1572: *John Erskine, 1st Earl of Mar* (d. 29 Oct 1572) 1572 – 1581: *James Douglas, 4th Earl of Morton* (d. (beheaded) Edinburgh 2 Jun 1581) with an interruption in 1578
27 Mar 1625	*Charles I*, son (b. 19 Nov 1600; d. (executed) 30 Jan 1649) also King of England
30 Jan 1649 – 1 May 1660	Commonwealth (see United Kingdom)
30 Jan 1649/1 May 1660	*Charles II*, son (b. 29 May 1630) in exile until 1660)
5 Feb 1685 – Dec 1688	*James VII*, brother (b. 14 Oct 1633; d. 16 Sep 1701) declared by Parliament to have abdicated in 1688, also King James II of England

473

11 Apr 1689 – 8 Mar 1702	*William III* (b. 14 Nov 1650) also King of England, together with his wife, *Mary II*, daughter of James VII (b. 30 Apr 1662; d. 28 Dec 1694)
8 Mar 1702 – 1 Aug 1714	*Anne*, sister of Mary II (b. 6 Feb 1665) Queen
1 May 1707	Scotland united with England and Ireland as the Kingdom of Great Britain and Ireland (see United Kingdom)

Serbia

Part of the Turkish Empire from 1459 to 1804.

HEADS OF STATE

Princes and Kings

5 Feb 1804	*George Petrović (Karađorđe)* (b. 14 Sep 1752 or 1 Jan 1763/67; d. 25 Jul 1817)
6 Nov 1817	*Milosh Obrenović* (for 1st time) (b. 18 Mar 1780)
13 Jun 1839	*Milan III*, son (b. 21 Oct 1819)
8 Jul 1839	*Michael III*, brother (for 1st time) (b. 16 Sep 1823)
27 Mar 1843	*Alexander Karageorgević*, son of George Petrović (b. 11 Oct 1806; d. 3 May 1885)
23 Dec 1858	*Milosh Obrenović* (for 2nd time)
26 Sep 1860	*Michael III* (for 2nd time)
10 Jun 1868	*Milan IV*, great-nephew of Milosh Obrenović (b. 22 Aug 1854; d. 11 Feb 1901) King from 6 Mar 1882
6 Mar 1889 – 11 Jun 1903	*Alexander I*, son (b. 14 Aug 1876) King, Dictator
15 Jun 1903 – 16 Aug 1921	*Peter I*, Karageorgević, son of Alexander Karageorgević (b. 11 Jul 1844)
1 Dec 1918	Kingdom of Serbs, Croats and Slovenes founded, known as the Kingdom of Yugoslavia from 1929

MEMBERS OF GOVERNMENT

Prime Ministers

1860 – 1861	*Philip Hristić* (b. 1819; d. Mentone 11 Feb 1905)
1862 – 15 Nov 1867	*Ilija Garašanin* (b. Garasi 28 Jan 1812; d. Belgrade 22 Jun 1874)
15 Nov 1867	*Jovan Ristić* (for 1st time) (b. Kragujevac 13 Feb 1831; d. 5 Sep 1899)
3 Dec 1867 – 1872(?)	*Milan Petronijević*
1872 – 5 May 1873	*Milivoje Petrović Blasnavac* (b. 16 May 1814; d. 5 Apr 1873) probably the illegitimate son of Prince Milosh Obrenović (see Heads of State)
1873 – 3 Dec 1874	*Jovan Marinović* (b. Sarajevo 1821; d. Villers-Sur-Mer 30 Jul 1893)
5 Dec 1874	*Aćim Čumić* (b. Trešnjevica 1 May 1836; d. Kusatak 27 Jul 1901)
3 Feb 1875	*Danilo Stevanović* (b. Timişoara 7 May 1815; d. Belgrade 20 Nov 1886)
1 Sep – 4 Oct 1875	*Jovan Ristić* (for 2nd time)
9 Oct 1875 – 19 Apr 1876	*Ljubomir Kaljević* (b. Užice 1841/2; d. Belgrade 20 Mar 1907)
5 May 1876 – 28 Feb 1877(?)	—— *Stevca*
28 Feb 1877(?)	*Jovan Ristić* (for 3rd time)
21 Oct 1881	*Milan Piroćanac* (b. Jagodina 19 Jan 1837; d. Belgrade 14 Mar 1897)
1 Oct 1883	*Nikola Hristić* (for 1st time) (b. Mitrovica 22 Aug 1818; d. Belgrade 9 Dec 1911)
18 Feb 1884	*Milutin Garašanin* (b. Belgrade 22 Feb 1843; d. Paris 6 Mar 1898)
13 Jun 1887	*Jovan Ristić* (for 4th time)
1 Jan 1888	*Sava Grujić* (for 1st time) (b. Kolar 7 Dec 1840; d. Belgrade 3 Nov 1913)
27 Apr 1888	*Sava Grujić* (for 2nd time)
28 Mar 1890	*Sava Grujić* (for 3rd time)
Feb 1891	*Nikola Pašić* (for 1st time) (b. Zaječar 1 Jan 1846; d. Belgrade 10 Dec 1926)
22 Aug 1892	*Jovan Avakumović* (for 1st time) (b. Belgrade 29 Dec 1841; d. 3 Aug 1928)
13 Apr 1893	*Lazar Dokić* (b. Belgrade 9 Oct 1845; d. Opatija 13 Dec 1893)
5 Dec 1893	*Sava Grujić* (for 4th time)

24 Jan 1894	*Đorđe Simić* (for 1st time) (b. Belgrade 28 Feb 1843; d. Zemun 12 Oct 1921)
3 Apr 1894	*Svetomir Nikolajević* (b. Raduša 9 Oct 1844; d. Belgrade 18 Apr 1922)
27 Oct 1894 – 4 Jul 1895	*Nikola Hristić* (for 2nd time)
7 Jul 1895	*Stojan Novaković* (for 1st time) (b. Sabac 13 Nov 1842; d. Nish 18 Feb 1915)
27 Dec 1896	*Đorđe Simić* (for 2nd time)
19 Oct 1897	*Vladan Dorđević* (b. Belgrade 3 Dec 1844; d. 31 Aug 1930)
27 Jul 1900	*Aleksa Jovanović* (b. Ćuprija 31 Aug 1846; d. Belgrade 6 May 1920)
2 Apr 1901	*Mihajlo Vujić* (for 1st time) (b. Belgrade 7 Nov 1853; d. Susak 14 Mar 1913)
18 May 1902	*Mihajlo Vujić* (for 2nd time)
18 Oct 1902	*Pera Velimirović* (for 1st time) (b. Sikol 28 Jan 1848; d. Belgrade 6 Jan 1922)
18 Nov 1902	*Dimitrije Cincar-Marković* (b. Sabac 9 Sep 1849; d. Belgrade 11 Jun 1903)
11 Jun 1903	*Jovan Avakumović* (for 2nd time)
11 Feb 1904	*Sava Grujić* (for 5th time)
10 Dec 1904 – 25 May 1905	*Nikola Pašić* (for 2nd time)
28 May 1905	*Ljubomir Stojanović* (for 1st time) (b. Užice 31 Aug 1861; d. 16 Jun 1930)
12 Aug 1905	*Ljubomir Stojanović* (for 2nd time)
7 Mar 1906	*Sava Grujić* (for 6th time)
28 Apr 1906 – 23 Jun 1908	*Nikola Pašić* (for 3rd time)
20 Jul 1908	*Pera Velimirović* (for 2nd time)
24 Feb 1909	*Stojan Novaković* (for 2nd time)
13 Oct 1909 – 26 Jun 1911	*Nikola Pašić* (for 4th time)
8 Jul 1911	*Milovan Milovanović* (b. Belgrade 1 Mar 1863; d. Belgrade 1 Jul 1912)
2 Jul – 8 Sep 1912	*Marko Trifković* (b. Belgrade 18 Sep 1864; d. 26 Jul 1930)
12 Sep 1912	*Nikola Pašić* (for 5th time)
5 Dec 1914	*Nikola Pašić* (for 6th time) in exile from 1915/18
23 Jun 1917	*Nikola Pašić* (for 7th time)
25 Mar – 30 Nov 1918	*Nikola Pašić* (for 8th time)

Siam

See Thailand.

Sicily and Naples

HEADS OF STATE

Kings of Naples

1458	*Ferdinando I*, illegitimate son of Alfonso I (b. 1423)
25 Jan 1494	*Alfonso II*, son (b. 1448)
19 Nov 1495	*Ferdinand II*, son (b. 27 Jul 1469)
7 Oct 1496	*Federico, Prince of Squillace*, uncle (b. 19 Apr 1452; d. 9 Nov 1504)

Kings of Sicily

1479 – 23 Jan 1516   *Ferdinando II* or *III*, cousin of Ferdinando I of Naples
Sicily and Naples were ruled by Spain between 1504 and 1713, as the Kingdom of the Two Sicilies.

1713 – 1720	*Victor Amadeus*, Duke of Savoy (see Savoy)
1720 – 1735	Austrian rule

Spanish Bourbon Rulers

3 Oct 1735	*Charles VII*, brother of King Ferdinand VI of Spain (b. 20 Jun 1716; d. 13 Dec 1788) from 10 Aug 1759 as Charles III, King of Spain
6 Oct 1759	*Ferdinand IV*, son, brother of King Charles IV of Spain (for 1st time) (b. 12 Jan 1751)
1806	House of Bourbon overthrown by Emperor Napoleon I of France
30 Mar 1806	*Joseph*, brother of Emperor Napoleon I (b. 7 Jan 1768; d. 28 Jul 1844) King of Spain from 1808
6 Jun (1 Aug) 1808	*Joachim Murat*, Marshal of Emperor Napoleon I (b. 25 Mar 1771; d. 13 Oct 1815) King

1812 (18 May 1815)	*Ferdinand IV* (for 2nd time) restored as Ferdinand I, King of the Two Sicilies
4 Jan 1825	*Francis I*, son (b. 19 Aug 1777)
8 Nov 1830	*Ferdinand II*, son (b. 12 Jan 1810)
22 May 1859 – 13 Feb 1861	*Francis II*, son (b. 16 Jan 1836; d. 27 Dec 1894)
14 Mar 1861	Sicily and Naples amalgamated with the Kingdom of Italy

Pretenders

| 13 Feb 1861 | *Francis II* (see Spanish Bourbon Rulers) |
| 27 Dec 1894 | *Alfonso*, brother (b. 28 Mar 1841) |

Songhay

For the Empire of Songhay, West Africa, 9th to 16th centuries, see volume 1.

South Africa, Republic of (Formerly the Union of South Africa)

Formed in 1910 by the union of Cape Colony, Natal, Orange Free State and Transvaal

CAPE COLONY

Governors and High Commissioners for South Africa

| Dec 1843 – Sep 1846 | *Sir Peregrine Maitland* (b. Longparish House, Hampshire, 1777; d. London 30 May 1854) |

28 Sep 1846 – 4 Aug 1847	*Sir Henry Pottinger* (b. Pottinger 3 Oct 1789; d. Malta 18 Mar 1856)
3 Feb 1848 – 7 Apr 1852	*Sir Harry George Wakelyn Smith* (b. Whittlesea, Isle of Ely, 1788; d. London 12 Oct 1860)
7 Apr 1852 – Mar 1854	*Sir George Cathcart* (b. 12 May 1794; d. Inkerman 5 Nov 1854)
1854 – 28 Oct 1861	*Sir George Grey* (b. Lisbon 12 Apr 1812; d. London 20 Sep 1898)
15 Jan 1862 – 19 Aug 1870	*Sir Philip Wodehouse* (b. Sennow Lodge, Norfolk, 26 Feb 1811; d. London 25 Oct 1887)
19 Aug 1870 – 21 Mar 1877	*Sir Henry Barkly* (b. Monteagle 1815; d. London 20 Oct 1898)
31 Mar 1877 – 15 Sep 1880	*Sir (Henry) Bartle (Edward) Frere* (b. Llanelli 29 Mar 1815; d. Wimbledon 29 May 1884)
2 Jan 1881 – 1 May 1889	*Sir Hercules George Robert Robinson* (from 1896: *1st Baron Rosmead*) (for 1st time) (b. Westmeath, Ireland, 19 Dec 1824; d. London 28 Oct 1897)
1 May 1889 – 30 May 1895	*Sir Henry Brougham Loch* (from 1895: *1st Baron*) (b. Drylaw, Midlothian, 23 May 1827; d. London 20 Jun 1900)
30 May 1895 – 21 Apr 1897	*Sir Hercules Robinson, 1st Baron Rosmead* (for 2nd time)
5 May 1897 – 6 Mar 1901	*Alfred Milner* (from 1902: *Viscount*) (b. Bonn 23 Mar 1854; d. Canterbury 13 May 1925)
6 May 1901 – 31 May 1910	*Sir Walter Hely-Hutchinson* (b. Dublin 22 Aug 1849; d. 23 Sep 1913)

Prime Ministers

1872 – 6 Feb 1878	*Sir John Charles Molteno* (b. London 5 Jun 1814; d. Claremont, South Africa, 1 Sep 1886)
1878 – 1881	*Gordon Sprigg* (from 1886: *Sir*) (for 1st time) (b. Ipswich 27 Apr 1830; d. Wynberg 4 Feb 1913)
1881 – 1884	*Sir Thomas Charles Scanlen* (b. Albany district 9 Jul 1834; d. Salisbury, Rhodesia, 15 May 1912)
1884 – 1886	*Sir Thomas Upington* (b. York 1845; d. Wynberg 10 Dec 1898)
1886 – 1890	*Sir Gordon Sprigg* (for 2nd time)
17 Jul 1890 – Jan 1896	*Cecil Rhodes* (b. Bishop's Stortford 5 Jul 1853; d. Cape Town 26 Mar 1902)
Jan 1896 – Sep 1898	*Sir Gordon Sprigg* (for 3rd time)
Sep 1898 – Oct 1900	*William Philip Schreiner* (b. Wittebergen Reserve 30 Aug 1857; d. Llandrindod Wells 28 Jun 1919)

Oct 1900 – 25 Feb 1904 *Sir Gordon Sprigg* (for 4th time)
25 Feb 1904 – 1908   *Sir Leander Starr Jameson* (b. Edinburgh 1853; d. London 25 Oct 1917)
Feb 1908 – 1910   *John Xavier Merriman* (b. Street, Somerset, 15 Mar 1841; d. Schoongezicht 2 Aug 1926)

NATAL

1839 – 1842	Boer Republic of Natal
1842 – 1910	British Colony

Governors

10 May 1843 – May 1844   *Henry Cloete* (b. Cape Town 15 Jun 1792; d. Rondebesch 26 Dec 1870)

4 Dec 1845 – 1 Aug 1849   *Martin Thomas West* (b. 1804(?); d. Pietermaritzburg 1 Aug 1849)

19 Apr 1850 – 3 Mar 1855   *Benjamin Chilley Campbell Pine* (from 1856: *Sir*) (for 1st time) (b. Tunbridge Wells 1809; d. London 27 Feb 1891)

5 Nov 1856 – 1864   *Sir John Scott* (b. Cumberland 7 Oct 1814; d. Chislehurst 29 Jun 1898)

24 May 1867 – 19 Jul 1872   *Robert William Keate* (b. London 16 Jun 1814; d. Cape Coast Castle 17 Mar 1872)

22 Jul 1873 – 1875   *Sir Benjamin Chilley Campbell Pine* (for 2nd time)

Feb – Oct 1875   *Sir Garnet Joseph Wolseley* (b. Co. Dublin 4 Jun 1833; d. Mentone 25 Mar 1913)

Apr – May 1880   *Sir William Bellairs* (b. Honfleur 28 Aug 1828; d. Clevedon 24 Jul 1913) Administrator

2 Jul 1880 – 27 Feb 1881   *Sir George Pomeroy Colley* (b. Dublin 1 Nov 1835; d. Majuba Hill 27 Feb 1881)

6 Mar 1882 – 23 Oct 1885   *Sir Henry E. Gascoyne Bulwer* (b. Heydon Hall 11 Dec 1836; d. Heydon Hall 30 Sep 1914)

18 Feb 1886 – 5 Jun 1889   *Sir Arthur Elibank Havelock* (b. Bath 7 May 1844; d. Bath 25 Jun 1908)

1 Dec 1889 – 1893   *Sir Charles Bullen Hugh Mitchell* (d. 7 Dec 1899)

23 Sep 1893 – 6 Mar 1901   *Sir Walter Hely-Hutchinson* (see Cape Colony Governors)

13 May 1901 – 7 Jun 1907   *Sir Henry Edward McCallum* (b. Yeovil 28 Oct 1852; d. Camberley 24 Nov 1919)

2 Sep 1907 – 23 Dec 1909   *Sir Matthew Nathan* (b. London 3 Jan 1862; d. West Coker 18 Apr 1939)

17 Jan – 31 May 1910   *Paul Sanford* (from 1891: *3rd Baron Methuen*) (b. Corsham Court, Wiltshire, 1 Sep 1845; d. 30 Oct 1932)

Chief Ministers

4 Jul 1893 – Mar 1897   *Sir John Robinson* (b. Hull, Yorkshire, 1839; d. Durban, Natal, 5 Nov 1903)
1905 – Nov 1906   *Charles John Smythe* (b. 21 Apr 1852; d. May 1918)
Nov 1906 – 1910   *Sir Frederick Robert Moor* (b. Pietermaritzburg 12 May 1853; d. Greystone, South Africa, 18 Mar 1927)

ORANGE FREE STATE

1842 – 1902   Independent state
1902 – 1910   British Crown Colony

Presidents

1854 – 1855   *Josias Philippus Hoffman* (b. Stellenbosch 1 Dec 1807; d. Smithfield 13 Oct 1879)
1855 – 1859   *Jacobus Nicolaas Boshof* (b. Agter-Kogmanskloof 31 Jan 1808; d. Weston 21 Apr 1881)
1860 – 1863   *Martinus Wessel Pretorius* (b. Pretoriuskloof 17 Sep 1818; d. Potchefstroom 19 May 1901)
2 Feb 1864 – 14 Jul 1888   *Johannes Henrik Brand* (b. Cape Town 6 Dec 1823; d. Cape Town 14 Jul 1888)
10 Oct 1888 – 22 Feb 1896   *Francis William Reitz* (b. Swellendam 5 Oct 1844; d. 26 Mar 1934)
22 Feb 1896 – 31 May 1902   *Martinus Theunis Stein* (b. Winburg 2 Oct 1857; d. Bloemfontein 29 Nov 1916)

Chief Minister

1907 – 1910   *Abraham Fischer* (b. Cape Town 9 Apr 1850; d. Cape Town 16 Nov 1913)

TRANSVAAL REPUBLIC

16 Dec 1856   Founded
1858   Proclamation of constitution

Presidents

5 Jan 1857 – 10 Sep 1860	*Martinus Wessel Pretorius* (for 1st time) (see Orange Free State Presidents)
9 Oct 1860 – 20 Jan 1863	*Stephanus Shoeman*, Administrator
24 Oct 1863 – 10 May 1864	*Willem Janse van Rensburg*
10 May 1864 – 16 Nov 1871	*Martinus Wessel Pretorius* (for 2nd time)
30 Jun 1872 – 12 Apr 1877	*Thomas W. Burgers*
12 Apr 1877 – 13 Dec 1880	Part of British South Africa
13 Dec 1880 – 1883	*Martinus Wessel Pretorius* (for 3rd time), *(Stephanus Johannes) Paulus Kruger* (b. Colesburg, Cape Colony, 10 Oct 1825; d. Clarens, Switzerland, 14 Jul 1904) (for 1st time) and *Petrus Jakobus (Piet) Joubert* (b. Uniondale 20 Jan 1831; d. Pretoria 27 Mar 1900) Triumvirate
16 Apr 1883 – 31 May 1902	*(Stephanus Johannes) Paulus Kruger* (for 2nd time) with *Willem Shalk-Burger* (b. 1852) deputy from 9 Oct 1900

British Governors

21 Jun 1902 – 1 Apr 1905	*Sir Alfred Viscount Milner* (see Cape Colony Governors)
2 Apr 1905 – 31 May 1910	*William Waldegrave Palmer, 2nd Earl of Selborne* (b. London 17 Oct 1859; d. 26 Feb 1942)

Chief Minister

1907 – 1910	*Louis Botha* (b. Greytown 27 Sep 1862; d. Rusthof 28 Aug 1919)

SOUTH AFRICA

Governors General

1910 – 1914	*Herbert 1st Viscount Gladstone* (b. London 7 Jan 1854; d. Dane End 6 Mar 1930)

1914 – 1920	*Sydney, 1st Earl Buxton* (b. London 25 Oct 1853; d. 15 Oct 1934)
1920	*Arthur, Duke of Connaught*, grandson of Queen Victoria (b. Windsor Castle 13 Jan 1883; d. London 12 Sep 1838)
1924 – 1931	*Alexander, Earl of Athlone* (b. London 14 Apr 1874; d. 16 Jan 1957) Prince of Teck until 1917

MEMBERS OF GOVERNMENT

31 May 1910 – 19 Dec 1912: Botha I

Prime Minister	*Louis Botha* (for 1st time) (b. Greytown 27 Sep 1862; d. Rusthof 28 Aug 1919)
Interior	31 May 1910 – 24 Jun 1912: *Jan Christiaan Smuts* (b. Bovenplaats 24 May 1870; d. Doornkloof 11 Sep 1950)
	25 Jun – 19 Dec 1912: *Abraham Fischer* (b. Cape Town 9 Apr 1850; d. Cape Town 16 Nov 1913)
Agriculture	31 May 1910 – 24 Jun 1912: *Louis Botha* (see above)
	25 Jun – 19 Dec 1912: *Jacobus Wilhelmus Sauer* (b. Burgersdorp 25 Oct 1850; d. Pretoria 24 Jul 1913)
Commerce and Industries	31 May 1910 – 22 Feb 1911: *Sir Frederick Robert Moor* (b. Pietermaritzburg 12 May 1853; d. Greystone 12 May 1927)
	23 Feb 1911 – 19 Dec 1912: *Sir George Leuchars* (b. Durban 16 Apr 1858; d. Sea Point 7 Feb 1924)
Defence	*Jan Christiaan Smuts* (see above)
Education	*François Stephanus Malan* (b. Bovlei 12 Mar 1871; d. Cape Town 31 Dec 1941)
Finance	31 May 1910 – 12 Jun 1912: *Henry Charles Hull* (b. Caledon 21 Nov 1860; d. Muizenberg 9 Oct 1932)
	13 Jun – 19 Dec 1912: *Jan Christiaan Smuts* (see above)
Justice	*James Barry Munnik Hertzog* (b. Wellington 3 Apr 1866; d. Pretoria 21 Nov 1942)
Lands	*Abraham Fischer* (see above)
Mines	31 May 1910 – 31 Jan 1912: *Jan Christiaan Smuts* (see above)
	1 Feb – 19 Dec 1912: *François Stephanus Malan* (see above)
Native Affairs	31 May 1910 – 24 Jun 1912: *Henry Burton* (b. Cape Town 2 Jun 1866; d. London 25 Dec 1935)

	25 Jun – 19 Dec 1912: *James Barry Munnik Hertzog* (see above)
Posts and Telegraphs	*Sir David Pieter de Villiers Graaff, Bart* (b. Wolfhuiskloof 30 Mar 1859; d. Cape Town 13 Apr 1931)
Public Works	31 May 1910 – 24 Jun 1912: *Sir David Pieter de Villiers Graaff, Bart* (see above)
	1 Feb – 19 Dec 1912: *Sir George Leuchars* (see above)
Railways and Harbours	31 May 1910 – 24 Jun 1912: *Jacobus Wilhelmus Sauer* (see above)
	25 Jun – 19 Dec 1912: *Henry Burton* (see above)
Without Portfolio	31 May 1910 – 7 Dec 1911: *Charles O'Grady Gubbins* (d. 7 Dec 1911)

20 Dec 1912 – 28 Aug 1919*: Botha II

Prime Minister	*Louis Botha* (for 2nd time) (see Botha I)
Interior	20 Dec 1912 – 16 Nov 1913: *Abraham Fischer* (see Botha I)
	17 Nov 1913 – (?) (acting:) *Jan Christiaan Smuts* (see Botha I)
	(?) – 2 Sep 1919: *Sir Thomas Watt* (b. Shawlands near Glasgow 20 Jan 1857; d. Tangier 11 Sep 1947) acting until 31 Jan 1916
Agriculture	20 Dec 1912 – 22 Sep 1913: *Louis Botha* (see Botha I)
	23 Sep 1913 – 2 Sep 1919: *Hercules Christian van Heerden* (b. 1862)
Defence	*Jan Christiaan Smuts* (see Botha I)
Education	*Francois Sephanus Malan* (see Botha I)
Finance	20 Dec 1912 – 23 Feb 1915: *Jan Christiaan Smuts* (see Botha I)
	24 Feb 1915 – 31 Jan 1916: *Sir David Pieter de Villiers Graaff, Bart* (see Botha I)
	1 Feb 1916 – 3 Oct 1917: *Henry Burton* (see Botha I)
	4 Oct 1917 – 2 Sep 1919: *Thomas Orr* (b. Loughgall 5 Feb 1857; d. Muizenberg 1937)
Justice	20 Dec 1912 – 24 Jul 1913: *Jacobus Wilhelmus Sauer* (see Botha I)
	23 Sep 1913 – 2 Sep 1919: *Nicolaas Jacobus de Wet* (b. Alival North 11 Sep 1873; d. Pretoria 16 Mar 1960)
Lands	20 Dec 1912 – 22 Sep 1913: *Abraham Fischer* (see Botha I)

*Unless otherwise stated individual ministers continued in office until 2 Sep 1919

	23 Sep 1913 – 22 Nov 1915: *Hendrick Schalk Theron* (b. Leeuwfontein 12 Feb 1869)
	1 Feb 1916 – 2 Sep 1919: *Hendrik Mentz* (b. Wittebergen 8 Aug 1877)
Mines and Industries	*François Stephanus Malan* (see Botha I)
Native Affairs	20 Dec 1912 – 24 Jul 1913: *Jacobus Wilhelmus Sauer* (see Botha I)
	23 Sep 1913 – 26 Aug 1919: *Louis Botha* (see Botha I)
Posts and Telegraphs	20 Dec 1912 – 31 Jan 1916: *Sir Thomas Watt* (see above)
	1 Feb 1916 – 15 May 1919: *Sir Johannes Hendricus Meiring Beck* (b. Worcester 28 Nov 1855; d. Rosebank 15 May 1919)
	16 May – 2 Sep 1919: *Thomas Orr* (see above)
Public Works	*Sir Thomas Watt* (see above)
Railways and Harbours	*Henry Burton* (see Botha I)
Without Portfolio	24 Jan – 22 Sep 1913: *Sir David Pieter de Villiers Graaff, Bart* (see Botha I)
	23 Sep 1913 – 2 Sep 1919: *Sir Jacobus Arnoldus Combrinck Graaff* (b. Villiersdorp 4 Mar 1863; d. London 5 Apr 1927)

3 Sep 1919 – 29 Jun 1924: Smuts I

Prime Minister	*Jan Christiaan Smuts* (for 1st time) (see Botha I)
Interior	3 Sep 1919 – 9 Mar 1921: *Sir Thomas Watt* (see Botha II)
	10 Mar 1921 – 29 Jun 1924: *Patrick Duncan* (b. Fortrie, Banffshire, 21 Dec 1870; d. Pretoria 17 July 1943)
Agriculture	3 Sep 1919 – 14 Apr 1920: *Hercules Christian van Heerden* (see Botha II)
	15 Apr 1920 – 9 Mar 1921: *François Stephanus Malan* (see Botha I)
	10 Mar 1921 – 29 Jun 1924: *Sir (Arthur Francis) Thomas William Smartt* (b. Trim, Co. Meath, 22 Feb 1858; d. Cape Town 17 Apr 1929)
Defence	3 Sep – 12 Nov 1919: *Jan Christiaan Smuts* (see Botha I)
	13 Nov 1919 – 29 Jun 1924: *Hendrik Mentz* (see Botha II)

485

Education	3 Sep 1919 – 9 Mar 1921: *François Stephanus Malan* (see Botha I)
	10 Mar 1921 – 29 Jun 1924: *Patrick Duncan* (see above)
Finance	3 Sep 1919 – 14 Apr 1920: *Thomas Orr* (see Botha II)
	15 Apr 1920 – 29 Jun 1924: *Henry Burton* (see Botha I)
Justice	*Nicolaas Jacobus de Wet* (see Botha II)
Lands	3 Sep 1919 – 14 Apr 1920: *Hendrik Mentz* (see Botha II)
	18 Mar 1921 – 24 Jun 1924: *Deneys Reitz* (b. Bloemfontein 2 Aug 1882; d. London 19 Oct 1944)
Mines and Industries	*François Stephanus Malan* (see Botha I)
Native Affairs	*Jan Christiaan Smuts* (see Botha I)
Posts and Telegraphs	3 Sep 1919 – 14 Apr 1920: *Thomas Orr* (see Botha II)
	15 Apr 1920 – 9 Mar 1921: *Sir Jacobus Arnoldus Combrinck Graaff* (see Botha II)
	10 Mar 1921 – 19 Jun 1924: *Sir Thomas Watt* (see Botha II)
Public Health	3 Sep 1919 – 9 Mar 1921: *Sir Thomas Watt* (see Botha II)
	10 Mar 1921 – 29 Jun 1924: *Patrick Duncan* (see above)
Public Works	3 Sep 1919 – 14 Apr 1920: *Sir Thomas Watt* (see Botha II)
	15 Apr 1920 – 9 Mar 1921: *Sir Jacobus Arnoldus Combrinck Graaff)* (see Botha II)
	10 Mar 1921 – 29 Sep 1924: *Sir Thomas Watt* (see Botha II)
Railways and Harbours	3 Sep 1919 – 9 Mar 1921: *Henry Burton* (see Botha I)
	10 Mar 1921 – 29 Jun 1924: *John William Jagger* (b. Northowram 20 Sep 1859; d. London 21 Jun 1930)
Without Portfolio	3 Sep 1919 – 14 Apr 1920: *Sir Jacobus Arnoldus Combrinck Graaff* (see Botha II)

30 Jun 1924 – 5 Nov 1928: Hertzog I

Prime Minister	*James Barry Munnik Hertzog* (for 1st time) (see Botha I)
External Affairs	6 Jun 1927 – 5 Nov 1928: *James Barry Munnik Hertzog* (see Botha I)
Interior	*Daniel François Malan* (b. Riebeek-West 22 May 1874; d. Cape Town 7 Feb 1959)

Agriculture	*Jan Christoffel Greyling Kemp* (b. 10 Jun 1872; d. Piet Retief 31 Dec 1946)
Defence	*Frederic Hugh Page Creswell* (b. Gibraltar 13 Nov 1866; d. Kuilsrivier 25 Aug 1948)
Education	*Daniel François Malan* (see above)
Finance	*Nicolaas Christiaan Havenga* (b. Blesbok 1 May 1882; d. Cape Town 13 Mar 1957)
Justice	*Tielman Johannes de Villiers Roos* (b. Cape Town 8 Mar 1879; d. Johannesburg 28 Mar 1935)
Labour	1 Aug 1924 – 11 Nov 1925: *Frederic Hugh Page Creswell* (see above)
	12 Nov 1925 – 5 Nov 1928: *Thomas Boydell* (b. Newcastle-upon-Tyne 15 Dec 1882; d. Cape Town 5 Jul 1966)
Lands	*Pieter Gert Wessel Grobler* (b. Rustenburg district 1 Feb 1873; d. Pretoria 22 Aug 1942)
Mines and Industries	*Fredrik William Beyers* (b. Paarl 15 Oct 1867; d. Muizenberg 14 Sep 1938)
Native Affairs	*James Barry Munnik Hertzog* (see Botha I)
Posts and Telegraphs	30 Jun 1924 – 11 Nov 1925: *Thomas Boydell* (see above)
	12 Nov 1925 – 5 Nov 1928: *Walter Bayley Madeley* (b. Woolwich 28 Jul 1873; d. Boksburg 12 Mar 1947)
Public Health	*Daniel François Malan* (see above)
Public Works	30 Jun 1924 – 11 Nov 1925: *Thomas Boydell* (see above)
	12 Nov 1925 – 5 Nov 1928: *Walter Bayley Madeley* (see above)
Railways and Harbours	*Charles Wynand Marais Malan* (b. Leeuwenjacht 9 Aug 1883; d. Cape Town 6 Feb 1933)

6 Nov 1928 – 30 Mar 1933: Hertzog II

Prime Minister and External Affairs	*James Barry Munnik Hertzog* (for 2nd time) (see Botha I)
Interior	*Daniel François Malan* (see Hertzog I)
Agriculture	*Jan Christoffel Greyling Kemp* (see Hertzog I)
Defence	*Frederic Hugh Page Creswell* (see Hertzog I)
Education	*Daniel François Malan* (see Hertzog I)
Finance	*Nicolaas Christiaan Havenga* (see Hertzog I)
Irrigation	*Ernest George Jansen* (b. Strathearn 7 Aug 1881; d. Pretoria 25 Nov 1959)
Justice	6 Nov 1928 – 18 Jun 1929: *Tielman Johannes de*

Villiers Roos (see Hertzog I)
19 Jun 1929 – 30 Mar 1933: *Oswald Pirow* (b. Aberdeen, Cape Province, 14 Aug 1890; d. Pretoria 11 Oct 1959)

Labour
6 Nov 1928 – 18 Jun 1929: *Thomas Boydell* (see Hertzog I)
19 Jun 1929 – 30 Mar 1933: *Frederic Hugh Page Creswell* (see Hertzog I)

Lands
Pieter Gert Wessel Grobler (see Hertzog I)

Mines and Industries
6 Nov 1928 – 29 Aug 1929: *Fredrik William Beyers* (see Hertzog I)
30 Aug 1929 – 30 Mar 1933: *Adriaan Paulus Johannes Fourie* (b. Klein Disselfontein 11 Aug 1882; d. Leydsdorp 6 Jul 1941)

Native Affairs
6 Nov 1928 – 18 Jun 1929: *James Barry Munnik Hertzog* (see Botha I)
19 Jun 1929 – 30 Mar 1933: *Ernest George Jansen* (see Above)

Posts and Telegraphs
Henry William Sampson (b. London 12 May 1872; d. Sea Point 6 Aug 1938)

Public Health
Daniel François Malan (see Hertzog I)

Public Works
Henry William Sampson (see above)

Railways and Harbours
Charles Wynand Marais Malan (see Hertzog I)

Spain

HEADS OF STATE

Kings

House of Hapsburg

11 Dec 1474/19 Jan 1479
Ferdinand (for 1st time) (b. 10 Mar 1452; d. 23 Jan 1516) from 1474: King Ferdinand V of Castile; from 1479: King Ferdinand II of Aragon, and *Isabella I* (b. 22 Apr 1451; d. 26 Nov 1504) joint rulers of Aragon and Castile

26 Nov 1504
Philip I, son of Emperor Maximilian I, son-in-law of Ferdinand V and Isabella I (b. 21 Jun 1478) and *Joan*, the Mad (b. 6 Nov 1479; d. 12 Apr 1535)

25 Sep 1506	*Ferdinand V of Castile and II of Aragon* (for 2nd time)
23 Jan 1516	*Charles I*, son of Philip I (b. 24 Feb 1500; d. Estremadura 21 Sep 1558) from 26 Jun 1519 to 1556: Holy Roman Emperor Charles V
15 Jan 1556	*Philip II*, son (b. 21 May 1527)
13 Sep 1598	*Philip III*, son (b. 14 Apr 1578)
30 Mar 1621	*Philip IV*, son (b. 8 Apr 1605)
17 Sep 1665	*Charles II*, son (b. 6(11?) Nov 1661)

House of Bourbon

1 Nov 1700	*Philip V*, grandson of King Louis XIV of France (for 1st time) (b. 19 Dec 1683)
10/6 Jan 1724	*Louis*, son (b. 25 Aug 1707)
31 Mar 1724	*Philip V* (for 2nd time)
9 Jul 1746	*Ferdinand VI*, son (b. 17 Sep 1713)
10 Mar 1759	*Charles III*, brother (b. 20 Jun 1716)
13 Dec 1788	*Charles IV*, son (b. 12 Nov 1748; d. 19 Jan 1819)
19 Mar 1808	*Ferdinand VII*, son (b. 14 Oct 1784)
1808 – 1813	*Joseph Bonaparte*, brother of Emperor Napoleon I (b. 7 Jan 1768; d. 28 Jul 1844) during French occupation
29 Sep 1833 – 30 Sep 1868	(Queen) *Isabella II*, daughter of Ferdinand VII (b. 10 Oct 1830; d. 9 Apr 1904) Regent: 4 Oct 1833 – 12 Oct 1840: *Maria Christina*, mother, daughter of King Francis I of Sicily (b. 27 Apr 1806; d. 22 Aug 1878) 1840 – 1843: *Baldomero Espartero*

Carlist Pretenders

29 Sep 1833	*Charles V*, brother of Ferdinand VII (b. 29 Mar 1788; d. 10 Mar 1855)
18 May 1845	*Charles VI*, son (b. 31 Jan 1818; d. 13/14 Jan 1861)
3 Apr 1860	*Juan*, brother (b. 15 May 1822; d. 21 Nov 1887)
3 Oct 1868	*Charles VII*, son (b. 30 Mar 1848)
18 Jul 1909 – Oct 1931	*James*, son (b. 27 Jun 1870)

President

30 Sep 1868	Republic
11 Feb 1869 – 2 Jan 1871	*Francisco Serrano y Domínguez, Duke de la Torre* (for 1st time) (b. Sep 1813; d. 26 Nov 1885) Regent, acting President until 15 Jun 1869

SPAIN

King

16 Nov 1870 – 11 Feb 1873	*Amadeus I*, son of King Victor Emmanuel II of Italy (b. 30 May 1845; d. 18 Jan 1890)

Presidents

1 Feb 1873 – 29 Dec 1874	Republic
1 Feb 1873 – 3 Jan 1874	The Prime Ministers functioned as President (see Prime Ministers)
3 Jan – 29 Dec 1874	*Francisco Serrano y Domínguez, Duke de la Torre* (for 2nd time) Chairman of the Executive

Kings

29 Dec 1874	*Alfonso XII*, son of Francisco de Asis de Borbón and Isabella II (b. 28 Nov 1857)
25 Nov 1885	*Maria de las Mercedes*, daughter (b. 11 Sep 1880; d. 17 Oct 1904)
17 May 1886 – 14 Apr 1931	*Alfonso XIII*, brother (b. 17 May 1886; d. 28 Feb 1941)
28 Nov 1885 – 17 May 1902	*Maria Christina*, daughter of Archduke Karl Ferdinand of Austria (b. 21 Jul 1858; d. 5 Feb 1929) Regent

MEMBERS OF GOVERNMENT

Prime Ministers

At first, with occasional exceptions, the Ministro de Estado (Foreign Minister) automatically presided over the Council of Ministers. From 1 Oct 1833 any minister might do so and in some cases the presiding minister would hold no portfolio. The latter was the normal case from 1880.

17 May 1754	*Ricardo Wall* (for 1st time) (b. Nantes; d. Granada 1778)
11 Aug 1759	*Ricardo Wall* (for 2nd time)
11 Oct 1763	*Jerónimo, Count Grimaldi* (b. Genoa 1706; d. 1789)
27 Feb 1777	*José Moñino, Count Floridablanca* (b. Hellin 21 Oct 1728; d. Seville 30 Dec 1808)
28 Feb 1792	*Pedro Pablo Arabaca de Bolea, Count Aranda* (b. Saragossa 21 Dec 1718; d. Epila 3 Jan 1798)

15 Nov 1792 – 1798	*Manuel de Godoy Álvarez de Faria Ríos Sánchez Zarzosa* (from 1792: *Duke of Alcudia and Sueca;* (from 1795: *Prince of the Peace and of Basano*; from 1809: *Prince of Posserano*) (for 1st time) (b. Badajoz 12 May 1767; d. Paris 1851) Chief Minister until 13 Mar 1808
28 Mar 1798	*Francisco de Saavedra* (for 1st time) (b. Seville 1746; d. Seville 1819)
13 Aug 1798	*Mariano Luis de Urquijo* (for 1st time) (b. Bilbao 8 Sep 1768; d. Paris 3 May 1817)
6 Sep 1798	*Francisco de Saavedra* (for 2nd time)
13 Dec 1800	*Pedro Ceballos* (for 1st time) (b. 1764; d. 1840)
1808 – 1814	*Mariano Luis de Urquijo* (for 2nd time) Secretary of the Council of Notables, in effect 1st Minister
19 Mar 1808	*Pedro Ceballos* (for 2nd time)
2 Jun 1808	*Eusebio Bardají y Azara* (for 1st time) (b. Graus 19 Dec 1776; d. Huete 7 Mar 1842)
13 Oct 1808	*Pedro Ceballos* (for 3rd time)
3 Jan 1809	*Martín de Garay* (b. Saragossa 1760; d. Saragossa 1823)
2 Nov 1809	*Francisco de Saavedra* (for 3rd time)
20 Mar 1810	*Eusebio Bardají y Azara* (for 2nd time)
27 May 1810	*Eusebio Bardají y Azara* (for 3rd time)
6 Feb 1812	*José García León y Pizarro* (for 1st time)
12 May 1812	*Ignacio de la Pezuela*
23 Jun 1812	*Carlos María Martínez, Marquis of Casa-Irujo* (for 1st time) (b. Cartagena 1765; d. Jan 1824)
27 Sep 1812	*Pedro Gómez Havelo, Marquis of Labrador* (b. 1775; d. Paris 1852)
11 Jul 1813	*Antonio Cano Manuel Ramírez de Arellano* (b. Chincilla 1768; d. 1836)
10 Oct 1813	*Juan O'Donajú* (b. Seville 1762; d. Mexico 1821)
17 Oct 1813	*Fernando Laserna*
2 Dec 1813	*José de Luyando* (for 1st time) (b. Mexico 1773; d. Rome 1835)
4 May 1814	*José Miguel de Carvajal y Manrique, Duke of San Carlos* (b. Lima 1771; d. Paris 1823)
5 Nov 1814	*Pedro Ceballos* (for 4th time)
30 Oct 1816	*José García León y Pizarro* (for 2nd time)
4 Sep 1818	*Carlos María Martínez, Marquis of Casa-Irujo* (for 2nd time)
2 Jun 1819	*Manuel González Salmón* (for 1st time)
2 Sep 1819	*Duke of San Fernando*

18 Mar 1820	*Juan Javat* (b. c.1765; d. after 1823)
2 Mar 1821	*Joaquín Anduaga*
5 Mar 1821	*Eusebio Bardají y Azara* (for 4th time)
23 Apr 1821	*Francisco de Paula Escudero* (b. Corella 26 Mar 1764; d. Madrid 14 Aug 1831)
8 Jan 1822	*Ramón López Pelegrín*
28 Feb 1822	*Francisco Martínez de la Rosa* (for 1st time) (b. 10 Mar 1789; d. 7 Feb 1862)
7 Jul 1822	*Santiago Usoz* (for 1st time)
11 Jul 1822	*Nicolás María Garelli*
23 Jul 1822	*Santiago Usoz* (for 2nd time)
5 Aug 1822 – 2 Mar 1823*	*Evaristo San Miguel y Valledor, Duke of San Miguel* (b. Gijon 26 Oct 1765; d. Madrid 29 May 1862)
2 Mar 1823	*Álvaro Flórez Estrada* (b. Pola de Somiedo 1769; d. 1853)
23 Apr 1823	*Manuel Vadillo*
13 May 1823	*José María Pando* (b. Lima 1787; d. Spain 1840)
27 May 1823	*José Vargas*
27 May 1823	*Victor Sáez* (for 1st time)
7 Aug 1823	*Victor Sáez* (for 2nd time)
29 Aug 1823	*Luis María de Salazar* (for 1st time) (b. Vitoria 1758; d. Madrid 1838)
4 Sep 1823	*José de Luyando* (for 2nd time)
2 Dec 1823	*Carlos María Martínez, Marquis of Casa-Irujo* (for 3rd time)
25 Dec 1823	*Narciso de Heredia, Count Ofalia* (for 1st time) (b. 1777; d. 1843)
18 Jan 1824	*Narciso de Heredia, Count Ofalia* (for 2nd time)
1 Jul 1824	*Francisco Zea Bermúdez, Count of Colombí* (for 1st time) (d. France 1834)
11 Jul 1824	*Luis María de Salazar* (for 2nd time)
25 Oct 1825	*Pedro Alcantara de Toledo, Duke of Infantado* (b. 1773; d. 1841)
19 Aug 1826	*Manuel González Salmón* (for 2nd time)
15 Oct 1830	*Manuel González Salmón* (for 3rd time)
8 Jan 1832	*Francisco Tadeo Calomarde* (b. Villel 10 Feb 1773; d. Toulouse 25 Jun 1842)
20 Jan 1832	*Manuel de Godoy, Duke of Alcudia* (for 2nd time)
1 Oct 1832	*José Cafranga*

*Beginning of 1823 – 28 Sep 1823	Revolutionary government *Rafael de Riego y Nuñez, Captain General of Aragon* (b. Santa María de Tuñas 24 Oct 1785; d. (executed) Madrid 7 Nov 1823)

1 Oct 1833	*Francisco Zea Bermúdez, Count of Colombí* (for 2nd time)
15 Jan 1834	*Francisco Martínez de la Rosa* (for 2nd time)
7 Jun 1835	*José María Queipo de Llano Ruiz de Saravia, Count Toreno* (b. Oviedo 26 Nov 1786; d. Paris 16 Sep 1843)
14 Sep 1835	*Juan Álvarez Mendizábal* (b. Cadiz 25 Feb 1790; d. Madrid Nov 1853)
15 May 1836	*Francisco Xavier Istúriz y Montero* (for 1st time) (b. 1790; d. 16 Apr 1871)
15 Aug 1836	*José María Calatrava* (b. 26 Feb 1781; d. 24 Jan 1846)
18 Aug 1837	*Eusebio Bardají y Azara* (for 5th time)
16 Dec 1837	*Narciso de Heredia, Count Ofalia* (for 3rd time)
7 Sep 1838	*Bernardino Fernández de Velasco, Duke of Frias* (b. Madrid 20 Jun 1783; d. 28 May 1851)
6 Dec 1838	*Evaristo Pérez de Castro* (d. 1848)
9 Dec 1838	*Isidro Alaix* (b. Ceuta 1790; d. 1853)
20 Jul 1840	*Antonio González y González* (for 1st time) (b. Valencia de Mombuey 1792; d. 1870)
12 Aug 1840	*Valentin Ferraz* (b. Aneiles 1793; d. Escorial 1866)
29 Aug 1840	*Modesto Cortázar*
11 Sep 1840 – 8 May 1841	*Baldomero Espartero, Duke of Vitoria* (for 1st time) (b. 27 Feb 1792; d. 9/10 Jan 1870)
21 May 1841	*Antonio González y González* (for 2nd time)
17 Jun 1842	*José Ramon Rodil y Galloso, Marquis of Rodil* (b. Santa Maria de Trobo 5 Feb 1789; d. Madrid 17 Feb 1853)
9 May 1843	*Joaquín María López* (for 1st time) (b. Villena 1798; d. Madrid 1855)
19 May 1843	*Alvaro Gómez Becera* (b. Caceres 1771; d. Madrid 1855)
20 Jul 1843	*Joaquín María López* (for 2nd time)
20 Nov 1843	*Salustiano de Olózaga* (b. Oyon 8 Jul 1805; d. Enghien 26 Sep 1873)
1 Dec 1843	*Luis González Bravo* (for 1st time) (b. 8 Jul 1811; d. 1 Sep 1871)
3 May 1844	*Ramón María Narváez, Duke of Valencia* (for 1st time) (b. Loja 4 Aug 1800; d. Madrid 23 Apr 1868)
12 Feb 1846	*Manuel de Pando Férnandez de Pineda Macea y Davila, Marquis of Miraflores* (for 1st time) (b. Madrid 1792; d. Madrid 1872)
4 Apr 1846	*Francisco Xavier Istúriz y Montero* (for 2nd time)
28 Jan 1847	*Juan Pedro Sánchez-Pleités Hurtado de Mendoza Ramírez de Avellano, Duke of Sotomayor* (b. Osuna

	1776; d. Madrid 30 Jan 1856)
28 Mar 1847	*Joaquín Francisco Pacheco y Gutiérrez Calderón* (b. Écija 22 Feb 1808; d. Madrid 8 Oct 1865)
12 Sep 1847	*Florencio García Gómez* (b. Tafalla 1783; d. 1855)
3 Oct 1847	*Ramón María Narváez, Duke of Valencia* (for 2nd time)
19 Oct 1849	*Count Cleonard*
20 Oct 1849	*Ramón María Narváez, Duke of Valencis* (for 3rd time)
10 Jan 1850	*Juan Bravo Murillo* (b. 9 Jun 1803; d. 11 Jan 1873)
14 Dec 1852	*Federico Roncali*
8 Apr 1853	*Francisco de Lersundi y Ormaechea* (b. Valencia 28 Jan 1817; d. Bayonne 17 Nov 1874)
19 Sep 1853	*Luis José Sartorius, Count San Luis* (b. Seville before 1820; d. Madrid 22 Feb 1871)
17 Jul 1854	*Fernando Fernández de Córdoba* (b. Beunos Aires 9 Sep 1807; d. Madrid 30 Oct 1883)
18 Jul 1854	*Angel de Saavedra*
19 Jul/28 Nov 1854	*Baldomero Espartero, Duke of Vitoria* (for 2nd time)
14 Jul 1856	*Leopoldo O'Donnell, Count of Lucena* (from 1860: *Duke of Tetuán*) (b. Sta Cruz, Teneriffe, 12 Jan 1809; d. Biarritz 5 Nov 1867)
12 Oct 1856	*Ramón María Narváez, Duke of Valencia* (for 4th time)
15 Oct 1857	*Francisco Armero y Peñaranda, Marquis of Nervión* (b. Fuentes de Andalucia 1804; d. Seville 1867)
14 Jan 1858	*Francisco Xavier Istúriz y Montero* (for 3rd time)
30 Jun 1858	*Leopoldo O'Donnell, Duke of Tetuán* (or 2nd time)
17 Jan 1863	*Leopoldo O'Donnell, Duke of Tetuán* (for 3rd time)
2 May 1863	*Manuel de Pando Fernández de Pinedo Macea y Davila, Marquis of Miraflores* (for 2nd time)
17 Jan 1864	*Lorenzo Arrazola* (b. Checa 1797; d. Madrid 1873)
1 Mar 1864	*Alejandro Mon* (b. Oviedo 1801; d. Oviedo 1882)
16 Sep 1964	*Ramón María Narváez, Duke of Valencia* (for 5th time)
21 Jun 1865	*Leopoldo O'Donnell, Duke of Tetuán* (for 4th time)
10 Jul 1866	*Ramón María Narváez, Duke of Valencia* (for 6th time)
23 Apr – 18 Sep 1868	*Luis González Bravo* (for 2nd time)
18 – 29 Sep 1868	*José Gutiérrez de la Concha, Marquis of Havana* (b. 4 Jun 1809; d. 5 Nov 1895)
3 Oct 1868	*Francisco Serrano y Domínguez, Duke de la Torre* (for 1st time) (see Presidents)

18 Jun 1869	*Juan Prim y Prats, Marquis de los Castillejos* (b. Reus 6 Dec 1814; d. Madrid 30 Dec 1870)
27 Dec 1870	(acting:) *Juan Bautista Topete y Corballa* (for 1st time) (b. 24 Jun 1821; d. 31 Oct 1885)
2 Jan 1871	*Francisco Serrano y Domínguez, Duke de la Torre* (for 2nd time)
24 Jul 1871	*Manuel Ruiz Zorrilla* (for 1st time) (b. Burgo de Osma 22 Mar 1833; d. Burgos 13 Jun 1895)
5 Oct 1871	*José Malcampo y Monge, Marquis of San Rafael* (b. San Fernando 1828; d. 1880)
21 Dec 1871	*Práxedes Mateo Sagasta* (for 1st time) (b. Torrecilla en Cameros 21 Jul 1827; d. Madrid 5 Jan 1903)
26 May 1872	*Juan Bautista Topete y Carballa* (for 2nd time)
4 – 12 Jun 1872	*Francisco Serrano y Domínguez, Duke de la Torre* (for 3rd time)
12 Jun 1872	*Manuel Ruiz Zorrilla* (for 2nd time)
12 Feb 1873	*Estanislao Figueras y Moracas* (b. 13 Nov 1819; d. 11 Nov 1882)
11 Jun 1873	*Francisco Pi y Margall* (b. 29 Apr 1824; d. 29 Nov 1901)
18 Jul 1873	*Nicolás Salmerón y Alonso* (b. 10 Apr 1838; d. 20 Sep 1908)
8 Sep 1873	*Emilio Castelar y Ripoll* (b. Cadiz 8 Sep 1832; d. San Pedro del Pinatar 25 May 1899)
3 Jan 1874	*Francisco Serrano y Domínguez, Duke de la Torre* (for 4th time)
26 Feb 1874	*Juan de Zabala y de la Puente, Marquis of Sierra Bullones* (b. Lima 27 Dec 1804; d. Madrid 29 Dec 1879)
29 Jun 1874	(acting:) *Práxedes Mateo Sagasta* (for 2nd time) until 3 Sep
30 Dec 1874	*Antonio Cánovas del Castillo* (for 1st time) (b. Malaga 8 Feb 1828; d. Santa Agueda 8 Aug 1897)
11 Sep 1875	*Joaquín Jovellar* (b. Palma 1819; d. Madrid 1892)
2 Dec 1875	*Antonio Cánovas del Castillo* (for 2nd time)
7 Mar 1879	*Arsenio Martínez-Campos* (b. 14 Dec 1831; d. Zarauz 23 Sep 1900)
9 Dec 1879	*Antonio Cánovas del Castillo* (for 3rd time)
8 Feb 1881	*Práxedes Mateo Sagasta* (for 3rd time)
13 Oct 1883	*José de Posada Herrera* (b. 1815; d. 7 Sep 1885)
18 Jan 1884	*Antonio Cánovas del Castillo* (for 4th time)
27 Nov 1885	*Práxedes Mateo Sagasta* (for 4th time)
5 Jul 1890	*Antonio Cánovas del Castillo* (for 5th time)

11 Dec 1892	*Práxedes Mateo Sagasta* (for 5th time)
23 Mar 1895	*Antonio Cánovas del Castillo* (for 6th time)
21 Aug 1897	*Marcelo de Azcárraga y Palmero* (for 1st time) (b. Manila 4 Sep 1832; d. Madrid 30 May 1915)
4 Oct 1897	*Práxedes Mateo Sagasta* (for 6th time)
5 Mar 1899	*Francisco Silvela y Le-Vielleuze* (for 1st time) (b. Madrid 15 Dec 1843; d. 29 May 1905)
22 Oct 1900	*Marcelo de Azcárraga y Palmero* (for 2nd time)
26 Feb 1901	*Práxedes Mateo Sagasta* (for 7th time)
6 Dec 1902	*Francisco Silvela y Le-Vielleuze* (for 2nd time)
20 Jul 1903	*Raimundo Fernández Villaverde* (for 1st time) (b. Palma 20 Jan 1848; d. 15 Jul 1905)
6 Dec 1903	*Antonio Maura y Montaner* (for 1st time) (b. Palma 2 May 1853; d. Torrelodones 14 Dec 1925)
16 Dec 1904	*Marcelo de Azcárraga y Palmero* (for 3rd time)
27 Jan 1905	*Raimundo Fernández Villaverde* (for 2nd time)
23 Jun 1905	*Eugenio Montero Ríos* (for 1st time) (b. Santiago de Compostela 13 Nov 1832; d. Madrid 12 May 1914)
31 Oct 1905	*Eugenio Montero Ríos* (for 2nd time)
1 Dec 1905	*Segismundo Moret y Prendergast* (for 1st time) (b. 2 Jul 1838; d. 28 Jan 1913)
5 Jul 1906	*José López Domínguez* (b. Marbella 29 Nov 1829; d. 17 Oct 1911)
30 Nov 1906	*Segismundo Moret y Prendergast* (for 2nd time)
4 Dec 1906 – 24 Jan 1907	*Antonio Aguilar y Correa, Marquis de la Vega de Armijo* (b. Madrid 30 Jun 1824; d. 13 Jun 1908)
24 Jan 1907	*Antonio Maura y Montaner* (for 2nd time)
21 Oct 1909	*Segismundo Moret y Prendergast* (for 3rd time)
9 Feb 1910	*José Canalejas y Méndez* (b. El Ferrol 31 Jul 1854; d. Madrid 12 Nov 1912)
12 Nov 1912	*Álvaro Figueroa y Torres, Count Romanones* (for 1st time) (b. Madrid 1 Aug 1863; d. Madrid 11 Sep 1950)
15 Nov 1912	*Manuel García Prieto, Marquis of Alhucemas* (for 1st time) (b. Astorga 5 Nov 1859; d. San Sebastian 15 Sep 1938)
27 Oct 1913	*Eduardo Dato y Iradier* (for 1st time) (b. Corunna 12 Aug 1856; d. Madrid 8 Mar 1921)
9 Dec 1915	*Álvaro Figueroa y Torres, Count Romanones* (for 2nd time)
19 Apr 1917	*Manuel García Prieto, Marquis of Alhucemas* (for 2nd time)
11 Jun 1917	*Eduardo Dato y Iradier* (for 2nd time)

3 Nov 1917	*Manuel García Prieto, Marquis of Alhucemas* (for 3rd time)
22 Mar 1918	*Antonio Maura y Montaner* (for 3rd time)
9 Nov 1918	*Manuel García Prieto, Marquis of Alhucemas* (for 4th time)
5 Dec 1918	*Álvaro Figueroa y Torres, Count Romanones* (for 3rd time)
14 Apr 1919	*Antonio Maura y Montaner* (for 4th time)
20 Jul 1919	*Joaquin Sánchez de Toca* (b. Madrid 24 Sep 1852; d. 13(?) Jul 1942)
12 Dec 1919	*Manuel Allendesalazar* (for 1st time) (b. 1856; d. 13 Mar 1923)
5 May 1920	*Eduardo Dato y Iradier* (for 3rd time)
8 Mar 1921	(acting:) *Gabino Bugallal Araujo*
13 Mar 1921	*Manuel Allendesalazar* (for 2nd time)
14 Aug 1921	*Antonio Maura y Montaner* (for 5th time)
8 Mar 1922	*José Sánchez Guerra y Martínez* (b. 30 Jun 1859; d. 26 Jan 1935)
5 Dec 1922	*Manuel García Prieto, Marquis of Alhucemas* (for 5th time)
4 – 13 Sep 1923	*Manuel García Prieto, Marquis of Alhucemas* (for 6th time)
13 Sep 1923 – 28 Jan 1930	*Miguel Primo de Rivera y Oraneja, Marquis of Estella* (from 1925: *Duke of Agadir*) (b. Jerez de la Frontera 8 Jan 1870; d. Paris 16 Mar 1930)

Foreign Ministers

From 1754 to 1833 the Foreign Minister regularly presided over the Council of Ministers and are accordingly listed under Prime Ministers.

1 Oct 1833	*Francisco Zea Bermúdez, Count of Colombí* (see Prime Ministers)
15 Jan 1834	*Francisco Martínez de la Rosa* (for 1st time) (see Prime Ministers)
7/13 Jun 1835	*José María Queipo de Llano Ruiz de Saravia, Count Toreno* (see Prime Ministers)
11 Sep 1835	*Julián Villalva*
14 Sep 1835	*Miguel Ricardo de Alva*
17 Sep 1835	*Juan Álvarez Mendizábal* (see Prime Ministers)
28 Apr 1836	*Ildefonso Díez de Ribera, Count Almodóvar* (for 1st time) (b. Granada 1777; d. Madrid 1846)
15 May 1836	*Francisco Xavier Istúriz y Montero* (for 1st time) (see Prime Ministers)

14 Aug 1836	*José María Calatrava* (see Prime Ministers)
10 Mar 1837	*Ildefonso Díez de Ribera, Count Almodóvar* (for 2nd time)
18 Aug 1837	*Eusebio Bardají y Azara* (see Prime Ministers)
16 Dec 1837	*Narciso de Heredia, Count Ofalia* (see Prime Ministers)
7 Sep 1838	*Bernardino Fernández de Velasco, Duke of Frias* (see Prime Ministers)
6 Dec 1838	*Evaristo Pérez de Castro* (see Prime Ministers)
9 Dec 1838	*Mauricio Carlos de Onis* (for 1st time)
20 Apr 1840	*Mauricio Carlos de Onis* (for 2nd time)
18 Jun 1840	*José de Castillo y Ayensa*
29 Aug 1840	*Juan Antoine y Zayas*
11 Sep 1840	*Vicente Sancho* (b. Petres 1784)
3 Oct 1840	*Joaquín María Ferrer y Cafranga* (b. Pasajes de San Pedro 1777; d. Santa Águeda 1861)
21 May 1841	*Antonio González y González* (see Prime Ministers)
17 Jun 1842	*Duke of Alcudia* (see Prime Ministers)
9 May 1843	*Manuel María Aguilar*
9 May 1843	*Joaquín de Frias* (for 1st time) (b. Cadiz 1782(?); d. Madrid 1851)
19 May 1843	*Olegario de los Cuetos*
25 Jul 1843	*Joaquín de Frias* (for 2nd time)
20 Nov 1843	*Salustiano de Olózaga* (see Prime Ministers)
1 Dec 1843	*Luis González Bravo* (see Prime Ministers)
3 May 1844	*Manuel de la Pezuela y Ceballos, Marquis of Viluma*
3 May 1844	*Alejandro Mon* (see Prime Ministers)
1 Jul 1844	*Ramon María Narváez, Duke of Valencia* (for 1st time) (see Prime Ministers)
21 Aug 1844	*Francisco Martínez de la Rosa* (for 2nd time)
12 Feb 1846	*Manuel de Pando Férnandez de Pineda Macea y Davila, Marquis of Miraflores* (for 1st time) (see Prime Ministers)
16 Mar 1846	*Ramon María Narváez, Duke of Valencia* (for 2nd time)
4 Apr 1846	*Francisco Xavier Istúriz y Montero* (for 2nd time)
28 Jan 1847	*Juan Pedro Sánchez-Pleités Hurtado de Mendoza Ramírez de Avellano, Duke of Sotomayor* (for 1st time) (see Prime Ministers)
28 Mar 1847	*Joaquín Francisco Pacheco y Gutierrez Calderón* (for 1st time) (see Prime Ministers)
1 Sep 1847	*Antonio Caballero*
12 Sep 1847	*Modesto Cortázar* (see Prime Ministers)

4 Oct 1847	*Ramon María Narváez, Duke of Valencia* (for 3rd time)
23 Oct 1847	*Juan Pedro Sánchez-Pleités Hurtado de Mendoza Ramírez de Avellano, Duke of Sotomayor* (for 2nd time)
29 Jul 1848	*Pedro José Pidal, Marquis of Pidal* (for 1st time) (b. Villaviciosa de Asturias 1800; d. Madrid 1865)
19 Oct 1849	*The Count of Colombí*, not Francisco Zea Bermúdez
20 Oct 1849	*Pedro José Pidal, Marquis of Pidal* (for 2nd time)
14 Jan 1851	*Manuel Bertrán de Lis* (for 1st time)
23 May 1851	*Manuel de Pandro Férnandez de Pineda Macea y Davila, Marquis of Miraflores* (for 2nd time)
7 Aug 1852	*Manuel Bertrán de Lis* (for 2nd time)
14 Dec 1852	*Federico Roncali* (see Prime Ministers)
14 Apr 1853	*Francisco de Lersundi y Ormaechea* (see Prime Ministers)
21 Jun 1853	*Ángel Calderón de la Barca* (b. Buenos Aires 1790; d. San Sebastian 1861)
18 Jul 1854	*Luis Mayans y Enríquez de Navarra* (b. Requena 1805; d. Madrid 1880)
30 Jul 1854	*Joaquín Francisco Pacheco y Gutierrez Calderón* (for 2nd time)
29 Nov 1854	*Claudio Antonio Luzuriaga* (b. San Sebastian 1810; d. San Sebastian 1874)
6 Jun 1855	*Juan de Zabala y de la Puente* (see Prime Ministers)
14 Jul 1856	*Nicomedes Pastor Díaz* (b. Vivero 1811; d. Madrid 1863)
12 Oct 1856	*Pedro José Pidal, Marquis of Pidal* (for 3rd time)
15 Oct 1857	(acting:) *Leopoldo Augusto de Cueto*
25 Oct 1857	*Francisco Martínez de la Rosa* (for 3rd time)
14 Jan 1858	*Francisco Xavier Istúriz y Montero* (for 3rd time)
30 Jun 1858	(acting:) *Leopoldo O'Donnell, Count of Lucena* (see Prime Ministers)
2 Jul 1858	*Saturnino Calderón Collantes* (b. Reinosa 1799; d. Paris 1864)
17 Jan 1863	*Francisco Serrano y Domínguez, Duke de la Torre* (see Prime Ministers)
2 Mar 1863	*Manuel de Pando Férnandez de Pineda Macea y Davila, Marquis of Miraflores* (for 3rd time)
17 Jan 1864	*Lorenzo Arrazola* (for 1st time) (see Prime Ministers)
1 Mar 1864	*Joaquín Francisco Pacheco y Gutierrez Calderón* (for 3rd time)
16 Sep 1864	*Alejandro Llorente y Lannas* (b. Cadiz 1814;

	d.Madrid 1901)
10 Dec 1864	*Antonio Benavides* (b. Baeza 1808; d. Villacarrillo 1884)
8 Jun 1865	*Lorenzo Arrazola* (for 2nd time)
21 Jun 1865	*Manuel Bermúdez de Castro*
10 Jul 1866	*Lorenzo Arrazola* (for 3rd time)
13 Jul 1866	*Eusebio Calonge y Fenollet* (b. Vitoria 1814; d. Madrid 1874)
23 Apr 1868	*Joaquín Roncali y Ceruti* (b. Cadiz 1811; d. Madrid 1875)
8 Oct 1868	*Juan Álvarez Lorenzana* (b. Oviedo 1818; d. Madrid 1883)
18 Jun 1869	*Manuel Silvela* (for 1st time) (b. Paris 1830; d. Madrid 1892)
1 Nov 1869	*Cristino Martos* (for 1st time) (b. Granada 1830; d. Madrid 1893)
9 Jan 1870	*Práxedes Mateo Sagasta* (for 1st time) (see Prime Ministers)
27 Dec 1870	*Juan Bautista Topete y Carballa* (see Prime Ministers)
4 Jan 1871	*Cristino Martos* (for 2nd time)
24 Jul 1871	(acting:) *Fernando Fernández de Cordova y Valcorel* (b. Buenos Aires 9 Sep 1809; d. Madrid 30 Oct 1883)
5 Oct 1871	(acting:) *José Malcampo y Monge, Marquis of San Rafael* (see Prime Ministers)
20 Nov 1871	*Bonifacio de Blas* (b. Villacastín 1827; d. Madrid 1880)
26 May 1872	*Augusto Ulloa y Castañón* (for 1st time) (b. Compostella 1823; d. Madrid 1879)
13 Jun 1872	*Cristino Martos* (for 3rd time)
11 Feb 1873	*Emilio Castellar y Ripoll* (see Prime Ministers)
11 Jun 1873	*José Muro López* (b. Valladolid 1840; d. Madrid 1907)
28 Jun 1873	*Eleuterio Maisonnave y Custayar* (b. Alicante 1840; d. Madrid 1890)
19 Jul 1873	*Santiago Soler y Plá* (b. Barcelona 1839; d. Barcelona 1888)
8 Sep 1873	*José Carvajal y Hué* (b. Malaga 1835; d. Madrid 1899)
3 Jan 1874	*Práxedes Mateo Sagasta* (for 2nd time)
13 May 1874	*Augusto Ulloa y Castañón* (for 2nd time)
31 Dec 1874	*Alejandro de Castro* (b. Corunna 1812; d. Zarauz 1881)
12 Sep 1875	*Emilio Alcalá Galiano*
14 Nov 1875	*Fernando Calderón Collantes* (b. Reinosa 1811; d. Madrid 1890)
14 Jan 1877	*Manuel Silvela* (for 2nd time)

10 Mar 1879	*Mariano Roca de Togores, Marquis of Molins* (b. Albacete 1812; d. Lequeitio 1889)
16 Mar 1879	*Carlos O'Donnell y Abréu, Duke of Tetuán* (for 1st time) (b. Valencia 1834; d. Madrid 1903)
9 Dec 1879	*Francisco de Borja Queipo de Llano y Gayoso de los Cobos, Count of Toreno* (b. Madrid 1840; d. Madrid 1890)
19 Mar 1880	*José de Elduayen* (for 1st time) (b. Madrid 1823; d. Madrid 1898)
8 Feb 1881	*Antonio Aguilar y Correa, Marquis de la Vega de Armijo* (for 1st time) (see Prime Ministers)
13 Oct 1883	*Servando Ruiz Gómez* (b. Avilés 1821; d. Vigo)
18 Jan 1884	*José de Elduayen* (for 2nd time)
27 Nov 1885	*Segismundo Moret y Prendergast* (for 1st time) (see Prime Ministers)
12 Jun 1888	*Antonio Aguilar y Correa, Marquis de la Vega de Armijo* (for 2nd time)
5 Jul 1890	*Carlos O'Donnell y Abréu, Duke of Tetuán* (for 2nd time)
11 Dec 1892	*Antonio Aguilar y Correa, Marquis de la Vega de Armijo* (for 3rd time)
6 Apr 1893	*Segismundo Moret y Prendergast* (for 2nd time)
4 Nov 1894	*Alejandro Groizard y Gómez de la Serna* (b. Madrid 1830; d. El Escorial 1919)
23 Mar 1895	*Carlos O'Donnell y Abréu, Duke of Tetuán* (for 3rd time)
4 Oct 1897	*Pio Gullón e Iglesias* (for 1st time) (b. Astorga 1835; d. Madrid 1916)
24 May 1898	*Juan Manuel Sánchez y Gutiérrez de Castro, Duke of Almodóvar del Río* (for 1st time) (b. Jerez 1859; d. Madrid 1906)
5 Mar 1899	*Francisco Silvela y Le-Vielleuze* (see Prime Ministers)
18 Apr 1900	*Ventura García Sancho, Marquis of Aguilar de Campoo* (for 1st time) (b. Mexico 1837; d. Madrid 1914)
6 Mar 1901	*Juan Manuel Sánchez y Gutiérrez de Castro, Duke of Almodóvar del Río* (for 2nd time)
6 Dec 1902	*Buenaventura Abarzura* (b. Havana 1843; d. Madrid 1910)
20 Jul 1903	*Manuel Mariátegui y Vinyals, Count of San Bernardo* (d. Madrid 28 Jan 1905)
5 Dec 1903	*Faustino Rodríguez San Pedro* (b. Gijon 1833; d. Gijon 1925)

16 Dec 1904	*Ventura García Sancho, Marquis of Aguilar de Campoo* (for 2nd time)
27 Jan 1905	*Wenceslao Ramírez de Villarrutia* (b. Havana 1850; d. Madrid 1933)
23 Jun 1905	*Felipe Sánchez Román* (b. Valladolid 1850; d. Madrid 1916)
30 Jun 1905	*Juan Pérez Caballero* (for 1st time) (b. Madrid 1861; d. San Sebastian 1951)
29 Oct 1905	*Pio Gullón e Iglesias* (for 2nd time)
1 Dec 1905	*Juan Manuel Sánchez y Gutierrez de Castro, Duke of Almodóvar del Río* (for 3rd time)
4 Jul 1906	*Pio Gullón e Iglesias* (for 3rd time)
30 Nov 1906	*Juan Pérez Caballero* (for 2nd time)
25 Jan 1907	*Manuel Allendesalazar* (see Prime Ministers)
21 Oct 1909	*Juan Pérez Caballero* (for 3rd time)
9 Feb 1910	*Manuel García Prieto, Marquis of Alhucemas* (for 1st time) (see Prime Ministers)
31 Dec 1912	*Juan Navarro Reverter* (b. Valencia 1844; d. Madrid 1924)
13 Jun 1913	*Antonio López Muñoz* (b. Huelva 1847; d. Madrid 1929)
27 Oct 1913	*Salvador Bermúdez de Castro y O'Lawlor, Marquis of Lema* (for 1st time) (b. Madrid 1863; d. Madrid 1946)
7 Dec 1915	*Miguel Villanueva Gómez* (b. Madrid 1852; d. Madrid 1931)
25 Feb 1916	(acting:) *Álvaro Figueroa y Torres, Count Romanones* (for 1st time) (see Prime Ministers)
30 Apr 1916	*Amalio Jimeno y Cabañas*
19 Apr 1917	*Juan Alvarado del Saz* (b. Las Palmas 1856; d. Madrid 1935)
11 Jun 1917	*Salvador Bermúdez de Castro y O'Lawlor, Marquis of Lema* (for 2nd time)
3 Nov 1917	*Manuel García Prieto, Marquis of Alhucemas* (for 2nd time)
10 Nov 1918	*Álvaro Figueroa y Torres, Count Romanones* (for 2nd time)
15 Apr 1919	*Manuel González Hontoria* (for 1st time) (b. Trubia 1878; d. 1955)
20 Jul 1919	*Salvador Bermúdez de Castro y O'Lawlor, Marquis of Lema* (for 3rd time)
13 Aug 1921	*Manuel González Hontoria* (for 2nd time)
8 Mar 1922	*Fernández Prida*
3 Dec 1922	*Francisco Bergamín y García* (b. 1855; d. Madrid 11

Feb 1937)

7 Dec 1922	*Santiago Alba y Bonifaz* (b. Zamora 1872; d. San Sebastian 7 Apr 1949)
13 Sep 1923	(acting:) *Espinosa de los Monteros*
3 Dec 1925	*José Yanguas y Messia, Count Santa Clara de Avedillo* (b. Linares 1890)
27 Feb 1927 – 30 Jan 1930	*Miguel Primo de Rivera y Oraneja, Marquis of Estella, Duke of Agadir* (see Prime Ministers)

States of the Church

See Papacy.

Sweden

Under the Kolmar Union, 1397 – 1523, Denmark, Norway and Sweden were almost always ruled jointly (see Denmark).

HEADS OF STATE

Regents

1470 – 1497	*Sten Sture I*, the Elder, nephew on mother's side of King Charles VIII (Knutson) of Sweden (for first time)
1501	*Sten Sture I* (for 2nd time)
13 Dec 1503	*Svante Sture*, cousin of Charles VIII
1 Jan 1512	*Erik Trolle*
1512 – 3 Feb 1520	*Sten Sture II*, the Younger, son
24 Aug 1521	*Gustav Eriksson Vasa* (b. 12 May 1496) subsequently King Gustav I

Kings

House of Vasa

7 Jun 1523	*Gustav I* (see above)

29 Sep 1560	*Erich XIV*, son (b. 13 Dec 1533; d. 26 Feb 1577)
29 Apr 1568	*John III*, brother (b. 21 Dec 1537)
21 May 1592	*Sigismund*, son (b. 20 Jun 1566; d. 30 Apr 1632) King of Poland as Sigismund III from 1587
22 Mar 1604	*Charles IX* (b. 4 Oct 1550) Regent from Feb 1599
30 Oct 1611	*Gustav II Adolf*, son (b. (1)9 Dec 1594; d. (1)6 Nov 1632)
16 Nov 1632	(Queen) *Christine*, daughter (b. 8 Dec 1626; d. Rome 19 Apr 1689) abdicated

House of Pfalz-Zweibrücken-Kleeburg

16 Jun 1654	*Charles X* (Gustav), grandson on mother's side of Charles IX (b. 8 Nov. 1622)
23 Feb 1660	*Charles XI*, son (b. 24 Nov 1655)
15 Apr 1697	*Charles XII*, son (b. 17 Jun 1682)
11 Dec 1718	(Queen) *Ulrika Eleonora*, sister (b. 23 Jan 1688; d. 24 Sep 1741) abdicated

House of Hessen-Kassel

26 Mar 1720	*Frederick I*, son of Duke Charles I of Hessen-Kassel (b. 28 Apr 1676) husband of Ulrika Eleonora from 4 Apr 1715

House of Holstein-Gottorp

5 Apr 1751	*Adolf Frederick*, son of Duke Christian August of Holstein-Gottorp (b. 14 May 1710)
12 Feb 1771	*Gustav III*, son (b. 24 Jan 1746; d. 1792)
29 Mar 1792 – 13 Mar 1809	*Gustav IV (Adolf)*, son (b. 1 Nov 1778; d. St Gallen 7 Feb 1837)
20 Jun 1809	*Charles XIII*, son of Adolf Frederick

House of Bernadotte

5 Feb 1818	*Charles XIV*, (Jean Baptiste Sebastien Bernadotte, Napoleonic general) adopted son of Charles XIII (b. 26 Jan 1764)
8 Feb 1844	*Oscar I*, son (b. 4 Jul 1799)
8 Jun 1859	*Charles XV*, son (b. 3 May 1826)
18 Sep 1872	*Oscar II*, brother (b. 21 Jan 1829)
8 Dec 1907 – 29 Oct 1950	*Gustav V*, son (b. 16 Jun 1858)

MEMBERS OF GOVERNMENT

Chief and Prime Ministers

7 Apr 1858 – 3 Jun 1870	*Ludwig Gerhard, Baron de Geer af Finspång* (for 1st time) (b. 18 Jul 1818; d. 24 Sep 1896) Minister of Justice and Chief Minister
3 Jun 1870 – 7 Mar 1874	*Axel Adlercreutz* (b. 2 Mar 1821; d. 20 May 1880) Minister of Justice and Chief Minister
7 Mar 1874	*Eduard Carleson* (b. 16 Nov 1820; d. 1 Apr 1884) Minister of Justice and Chief Minister
11 May 1875 – 19 Apr 1880	*Ludwig Gerhard, Baron de Geer af Finspång* (for 2nd time) Prime Minister from 12 Feb 1876
19 Apr 1880 – 13 Jun 1883	*Arvid, Count Posse* (b. 15 Jan 1820; d. 24 Apr 1901)
13 Jun 1883	*Karl Johan Thyselius* (b. 8 Jun 1811; d. 11 Jan 1891)
16 May 1884	*Oskar Robert Themptander* (b. 14 Feb 1844; d. 30 Jan 1897)
6 Feb 1888	*Dietrich Gillis, Baron Bildt* (b. 16 Oct 1820; d. 22 Oct 1894)
12 Oct 1889	*Gustav Samuel, Baron Åkerhjelm* (b. 24 Jun 1833; d. 2 Apr 1900)
Jul 1891	*Erich Gustav Boström* (for 1st time) (b. 11 Feb 1842; d. 21 Feb 1907)
12 Sep 1900	*Friedrich Wilhelm, Baron Otter* (b. 11 Apr 1833; d. 9 Mar 1910)
5 Jul 1902 – 13 Apr 1905	*Erich Gustav Boström* (for 2nd time)
13 Apr – 2 Aug 1905	*John Ramstedt* (b. 1852; d. 1925)
2 Aug 1905	*Christian Lundeberg* (b. 14 Jul 1842; d. 10 Nov 1911)
7 Nov 1905	*Karl Albert Staaf* (for 1st time) (b. 21 Jan 1860; d. 4 Oct 1915)
29 May 1906 – 30 Sep 1911	*Arvid Lindman* (for 1st time) (b. 19 Sep 1862; d. 8 Dec 1936)
7 Oct 1911	*Karl Albert Staaf* (for 2nd time)
17 Feb 1914	*Hjalmar von Hammarskjöld* (b. 4 Feb 1862; d. 12 Oct 1953)
29 Mar 1917	*Karl Swartz* (b. 9 Jun 1858; d. 6 Nov 1926)
19 Oct 1917 – 6 Mar 1920	*Nils Edén* (b. 25 Aug 1871; d. 16 Jun 1945)
6 Mar – 22 Oct 1920	*Hjalmar Branting* (for 1st time) (b. 23 Nov 1860; d. 24 Feb 1925)

27 Oct 1920	*Ludwig, Baron de Geer* (b. 27 Nov 1854; d. 25 Feb 1935)
23 Feb 1921	*Oskar Friedrich Sydow* (b. 12 Jul 1873; d. 19 Aug 1936)
13 Oct 1921	*Hjalmar Branting* (for 2nd time)
6 Apr 1923	*Ernst Trygger* (b. 20 Oct 1857; d. 24 Sep 1943)
18 Oct 1924	*Hjalmar Branting* (for 3rd time)
24 Jan 1925 – 2 Jun 1926	*Richard Sandler* (b. 29 Jan 1884)
6 Jun 1926 – 26 Sep 1928	*Karl Gustav Ekman* (b. 5 Oct 1872; d. 15 Jun 1945)
1 Oct 1928 – 2 Jun 1930	*Arvid Lindman* (for 2nd time)

Foreign Ministers

19 Oct 1917 – 22 Oct 1920	*Johannes Hellner* (b. Svedala 22 Apr 1866; d. 1947)
27 Oct 1920 – Jan 1921	*(Anton Magnus) Hermann, Count Wrangel* (b. Salsta 13 Aug 1857; d. Stockholm 19 Oct 1934)
13 Jan 1921 – 19 Apr 1923	*Hjalmar Branting* (see Chief and Prime Ministers)
11 Nov 1923 – 11 Oct 1924	*Erik, Baron Marks von Würtemberg* (b. Björnlunda 11 May 1861; d. Saltsjöbaden 5 Mar 1937)
18 Oct 1924 – 7 Jun 1926	*Östen Undén* (b. Karlstad 25 Aug 1886)
7 Jun 1926 – 26 Sep 1928	*(Jonas) Eliel Löfgren* (b. Piteå 15 Mar 1872; d. Stockholm 8 Apr 1940)
1 Oct 1928 – 2 Jun 1930	*Ernst Trygger* (see Chief and Prime Ministers)

Switzerland

HEADS OF STATE

Presidents

| 16 Nov 1848 – 31 Dec 1849 | *Jonas Furrer* (for 1st time) (b. Winterthur 1805; d. Ragaz 25 Jul 1861) |

1850	*Charles Henri Druey* (b. Pfauen 12 Apr 1799; d. Berne 29 Mar 1855)
1851	*Josef Munzinger* (b. 1791; d. 1855)
1852	*Jonas Furrer* (for 2nd time)
1853	*Wilhelm Naeff* (b. St Gall 1802; d. Berne 21 Jan 1881)
1854	*Friedrich Frey-Hérosé* (for 1st time) (b. Lindau 12 Oct 1801; d. 22 Sep 1873)
1855	*Jonas Furrer* (for 3rd time)
1856	*Jakob Stämpfli* (for 1st time) (b. Janzenhausen 23 Feb 1820; d. Berne 15 May 1879)
1857	*Constant Fornerod* (for 1st time) (b. 1819; d. 1899)
1858	*Jonas Furrer* (for 4th time)
1859	*Jakob Stämpfli* (for 2nd time)
1860	*Friedrich Frey-Hérosé* (for 2nd time)
1861	*Josef Martin Knusel* (for 1st time) (b. Lucerne 16 Nov 1813; d. Lucerne 14 Jan 1889)
1862	*Jakob Stämpfli* (for 3rd time)
1863	*Constant Fornerod* (for 2nd time)
1864	*Jakob Dubs* (for 1st time) (b. Affoltern 26 Jul 1822; d. Lausanne 13 Jan 1879)
1865	*Karl Schenk* (for 1st time) (b. Berne 1 Dec 1823; d. Berne 18 Jul 1895)
1866	*Josef Martin Knusel* (for 2nd time)
1867	*Constant Fornerod* (for 3rd time)
1868	*Jakob Dubs* (for 2nd time)
1869	*Emil Welti* (for 1st time) (b. Zurzach 23 Apr 1825; d. Berne 24 Feb 1899)
1870	*Jakob Dubs* (for 3rd time)
1871	*Karl Schenk* (for 2nd time)
1872	*Emil Welti* (for 2nd time)
1873	*Paul Cérésole* (b. 16 Sep 1832; d. 7 Jan 1905)
1874	*Karl Schenk* (for 3rd time)
1875	*Johann Jakob Scherer*
1876	*Emil Welti* (for 3rd time)
1877	*Joachim Heer* (b. 25 Sep 1825; d. Glarus 1 Mar 1879)
1878	*Karl Schenk* (for 4th time)
1879	*Bernhard Hammer* (for 1st time) (b. Olten 3 Mar 1822; d. Solothurn 6 Apr 1907)
1880	*Emil Welti* (for 4th time)
1881	*Numa Droz* (for 1st time) (b. La Chaux-de-Fonds 27 Jan 1844; d. Berne 15 Dec 1899)
1882	*Simon Bavier* (b. Chur 16 Sep 1825; d. Basle 28 Jan 1896)

1883	*Louis Ruchonnet* (for 1st time) (b. Lausanne 28 Apr 1834; d. Berne 14 Sep 1893)
1884	*Emil Welti* (for 5th time)
1885	*Karl Schenk* (for 5th time)
1886	*Adolf Deucher* (for 1st time) (b. Stechborn 15 Feb 1831; d. Berne 10 Jul 1912)
1887	*Numa Droz* (for 2nd time)
1888	*Wilhelm Friedrich Hertenstein* (b. Kyburg 5 Mar 1825; d. Berne 27 Nov 1888)
1889	*Bernhard Hammer* (for 2nd time)
1890	*Louis Ruchonnet* (for 2nd time)
1891	*Emil Welti* (for 6th time)
1892	*Walter Hauser* (for 1st time) (b. Wadenswil 1 May 1837; d. Berne 22 Oct 1902)
1893	*Karl Schenk* (for 6th time)
1894	*Emil Frey* (b. Arlesheim 24 Oct 1838; d. Arlesheim 24 Dec 1929)
1895	*Josef Zemp* (for 1st time) (b. Entlebuch 2 Sep 1834; d. 8 Dec 1908)
1896	*Adrien Lachenal* (b. Geneva 19 May 1849; d. 29 Jun 1918)
1897	*Adolf Deucher* (for 2nd time)
1898	*Eugène Ruffy* (b. Les Bannerettes 2 Aug 1854; d. Lausanne 25 Oct 1919)
1899	*Eduard Müller* (for 1st time) (b. Dresden 12 Nov 1848; d. Berne 9 Nov 1919)
1900	*Walter Hauser* (for 2nd time)
1901	*Ernst Brenner* (for 1st time) (b. 1856; d. 1911)
1902	*Josef Zemp* (for 2nd time)
1903	*Adolf Deucher* (for 3rd time)
1904	*Robert Comtesse* (for 1st time) (b. La Sagne 14 Aug 1847; d. La Tour de Peilz 17 Nov 1922)
1905	*Marc Ruchet* (for 1st time) (b. St Saphorin 14 Sep 1853; d. Berne 23 Jul 1912)
1906	*Ludwig Forrer* (for 1st time) (b. Islikon 9 Feb 1845; d. Berne 28 Sep 1921)
1907	*Eduard Müller* (for 2nd time)
1908	*Ernst Brenner* (for 2nd time)
1909	*Adolf Deucher* (for 4th time)
1910	*Robert Comtesse* (for 2nd time)
1911	*Marc Ruchet* (for 2nd time)
1912	*Ludwig Forrer* (for 2nd time)
1913	*Eduard Müller* (for 3rd time)

1914	*Artur Hoffmann* (b. St Gall 8 Jun 1857; d. 23 Jul 1927)
1915	*Giuseppe Motta* (for 1st time) (b. Airolo 17 Dec 1871; d. Berne 23 Jan 1940)
1916	*Camille Decoppet* (b. Suzévaz 4 Jun 1862; d. Berne 14 Jan 1925)
1917	*Edmund Schulthess* (for 1st time) (b. Villnachern 2 Mar 1868; d. Berne 22 Apr 1944)
1918	*Felix Calonder* (b. Schuls 7 Oct 1863; d. Chur 14 Jun 1952)
1919	*Gustave Ador* (b. Geneva 23 Dec 1845; d. Cologny 31 Mar 1928)
1920	*Giuseppe Motta* (for 2nd time)
1921	*Edmund Schulthess* (for 2nd time)
1922	*Robert Haab* (for 1st time) (b. Wädenswil 8 Aug 1865; d. Zurich 16 Oct 1939)
1923	*Karl Scheurer* (b. Sumiswald 27 Sep 1872; d. Berne 14 Nov 1929)
1924	*Ernest Louis Chuard* (b. Corcelles 31 Jul 1857; d. Lausanne 11 Nov 1942)
1925	*Jean-Marie Musy* (b. Albeuve 10 Apr 1876)
1926	*Heinrich Häberlin* (b. Weinfelden 6 Sep 1868)
1927	*Giuseppe Motta* (for 3rd time)
1928	*Edmund Schulthess* (for 3rd time)
1929	*Robert Haab* (for 2nd time)

Syria

Part of the Turkish Empire until 1920. Under French mandate from the League of Nations from 25 Apr 1920 to 27 Sep 1941.

HEADS OF STATE

Commissioners

1918 – 1919	*Georges Picot*
21 Nov 1919	*Henri Joseph Eugène Gouraud* (b. Paris 1867; d. 16 Sep 1946) Commander-in-Chief until 1922
20 Apr 1923 – Dec 1924	*Maxime Weygand* (b. Brussels 18 Jan 1867; d. 1965)

2 Jan 1925	*Maurice Sarrail* (b. Carcassonne 6 Apr 1856; d. Paris 23 Mar 1929)
6 Nov 1925 – 17 Jun 1926	*Henri de Jouvenel* (b. Paris 15 Apr 1876; d. Paris 4 Oct 1935)
12 Oct 1926 – 12 Oct 1931	*Henri Ponsot* (b. Bologna 2 Mar 1877)

Prime Ministers

Oct 1918 – 14 Dec 1919	*Ali Rida Pasha ar-Rikabi* (for 1st time) Head of Administration
14 – (?) Dec 1919	*Abd al-Hamid Pasha*
Dec 1919 – Apr 1920	*Ali Rida Pasha ar-Rikabi* (for 2nd time)
3 May – Jun 1920	*Hashim Bey al-Atasi*
26 Jun – 20 Aug 1920	*Ala ad-Din ar-Rubi* (d. 21 Aug 1926)
1 Jan – 21 Dec 1925	*Subhi Bey Barakat*
29 Dec 1925 – 6 Jan 1926	(acting:) *Taj ad-Din al-Hasani* (for 1st time) (d. Damascus 18 Jan 1943)
27 Apr – 10 Dec 1926	*Ahmad Nami Bey* (for 1st time) (b. Beirut 1878)
10 Dec 1926 – 9 Feb 1928	*Ahmad Nami Bey* (for 2nd time)
15 Feb 1928 - 19 Nov 1931	*Taj ad-Din al-Hasani* (for 2nd time)

Texas

| Until 1836 | Part of Mexico |
| 2 Mar 1836 | Declaration of independence |

HEADS OF STATE

Presidents

| Mar 1836 | *David Gouverneur Burnet* (b. Newark, New Jersey, 4 Apr 1788; d. Galveston 5 Dec 1870) provisional |
| 22 Oct 1836 | *Samuel Houston* (for first time) (b. Lexington, Virginia, 2 Mar 1793; d. Huntsville, Tennessee, 26 Jul 1863) |

Dec 1838	*Mirabeau Buonaparte Lamar* (b. Louisville, Georgia, 16 Aug 1798; d. Richmond, Virginia, 19 Dec 1859)
Dec 1841	*Samuel Houston* (for 2nd time)
Dec 1844	*Anson Jones* (b. Great Barrington, Massachusetts, 20 Jan 1798; d. (suicide) Houston 9 Jan 1858)
29 Dec 1845	Texas incorporated in the United States of America

Thailand

Named Siam until 24 Jun 1939

HEADS OF STATE

Kings

Ayuthia Dynasty

1491	*Rama Thibodi II*, brother of Boromoraja III
1529	*Boromoraja IV*, son
1534	*Ratsada*, son
1534	*Phrajai*, half-brother of Boromoraja IV
1546	*Keo*, son
1548	*Khun Worawongsa*, usurper
1548/49	*Maha-Chakraphat*, brother of Phrajai
1569	*Mahin(thara-Thirat)*, son
1569	*Maha Thammaraja, Prince of Sukhothai*
1590	*Naresuen*, son
1605	*Eka-Thotsarot*, brother
1610	*Song-Tham*, alias *Intharaja*, son
1628	*Jettha*, son
1630	*Athityawong*, brother
1630	*Prasat-Thong*, usurper
1656	*Chao-Fa-Jai*, son
1656	*Sri Suthammaraja*, uncle
1657	*Narai*, brother of Chao-Fa-Jai
1688	*Phra-Phetraja*, usurper
1703	*Phrachao Sua*, son
1709	*Puhmintharaxa (Thai Sia)*, son
1737	*Boromokot (Maha Thammaraja II)*, brother

1758	*Uthumphon*, son
1758 – 1767	*Boromoraja V (Ekathat)*, brother
1767	Sacking of Ayuthia by Burmese

Bangkok Dynasty (named the Ramadhibadi Dynasty from 1916)

1767	*Phya Taksin*, Chinese general
1782	*Rama I (Chakni)* Siamese general, founder of the dynasty
1809	*Rama II*, son
1824	*Rama III (Phra Nang Klao)*, son
1851	*Rama IV (Maha Mongkut or Phra Chom Klao)*, half-brother (b. 18 Oct 1804)
1 Oct 1868	*Chulalongkorn, Rama V*, son (b. 20 Sep 1853)
23 Oct 1910	*Rama VI (Maha Vajiravudh)*, son (b. 1 Jan 1881)
26 Nov 1925 – 2 Mar 1935	*Rama VII (Prajadhipok)*, brother (b. 8 Nov 1893; d. 30 May 1941)

Tibet

HEADS OF STATE

Originally ruled by indigenous kings, Tibet came under the sway of the Mongols in 1642. The Mongol kings were for the most part absentees and actual authority was in the hands of the Dalai Lama (Gyalpa Rimpoche), who had been recognized from the 15th century as an incarnation of Buddha. About 1650 the then Dalai Lama recognized his former teacher, the abbot of Tashi-lumpo, as an incarnation of the Dhyani-Buddha Amitabha (Opagmé). The functions of the Tashi Lama (Panchen Rimpoche) are spiritual, but some of them have from time to time exercised temporal authority. During the minority of the Dalai Lama authority is exercised by the Regent.

Kings

1481	*Dönyö Dorje*
1522(?)	*Ngawang Namgye*
1550(?)	*Töndup Tseten*
1565	*Karma Tseten*
fl. 1582	*Lhawang Dorje*
fl. 1603	*Phüntso Namgye*
1623 – 1642	*Karma Tsen-Kyong*

Titular Kings

1642	*Gusri*
1655	*Daya Khan*
1668	*Tenzin Dalai Khan*
1697	*Lhabzang Khan* (d. 1717)
1720	Chinese overlordship
1728	*Phola Sonam Tobgye*, leader of the Tibetan Council, given title of King in 1740
1747	*Gyurmé Namgyal*, son (d. 1750)
1750	Kingship abolished

Dalai Lamas

1475 – 1542	*Gedun Gyatso*
1543 – 1588	*Sonam Gyatso*
1589 – 1617	*Yönten Gyatso*
1617 – 1682	*Ngawang Lobsang Gyatso*
1683 – 1706	*Tsang-yang Gyatso*
1708 – 1757	*Kezang Gyatso*
1758 – 1804	*Jampel Gyatso*
1806 – 1815	*Luntok Gyatso*
1816 – 1837	*Tshultrin Gyatso*
1838 – 1856	*Khedrup Gyatso*
1856 – 1875	*Trinle Gyatso*
1876 – Dec 1933	*Thupten Gyatso* (b. 1875) assumed power in 1895, went into exile in India in 1904, 1908 and 1910-13

Panchen Lamas

c. 1650 – 1662	*Chökyi Gyaltsen I* (b. 1569)
1663 – 1737	*Lobzand Yishe*
1738 – 1780	*Lobzang Palden Yishe*
1781 – 1854	*Tempé Nyima*
1855 – 1882	*Chökyi Trapka*
1883 – 1937	*Chökyi Gyaltsen II*

Regents

1679 – 1720	*Sangye Gyatso*
1720 – 1750	None appointed (see Titular Kings)
1757	*Demo Rimpoche I*
1777 – 1784	*Tsomoling Nomenkhan I*

1791	*Tatsa Rimpoche I*
1810	*Demo Rimpoche II*
1819	*Tsomoling Nomenkhan II*
1844	*Tempé Nyima*, for 8 months
1845	*Reting Hutuktu I*
1862	*Shatra Lönchen*
1864	*Ganden Tripa Lobzang*
1864	*Khenrab Wangchuk*
1875	*Tatsa Rimpoche II*
1895	*Ganden Tripa Lobzang Gyantsen*
1895 – 1913	*Ganden Tripa Tsomoling Rimpoche*

Timbuctu

For Timbuctu, Mali, 16th century onwards, see volume 1.

Trier

HEADS OF STATE

Electors and Archbishops

21 Jun 1456 – 9 Feb 1503	*Johann II*, son of Duke Jakob I of Baden (b. 1439)
3 Mar 1503 – 27 Apr 1511	*Jakob II*, son of Duke Christof I of Baden (b. 6 Jun 1471)
14 May 1511 – 13 Mar 1531	*Richard Greiffenklau zu Vollraths* (b. 1467)
27 Mar 1531 – 22 Jul 1540	*Johann III von Metzenhausen* (b. 1492)
9 Aug 1540 – 23 Mar 1547	*Johann IV Ludwig von Hagen*
20 Apr 1547 – 18 Feb 1556	*Johann V, Count Isenburg*
25 Apr 1556 – 9 Feb 1567	*Johann VI von der Leyen*

7 Apr 1567 – 4 Jun 1581	*Jakob III, Baron Eltz*
31 Jul 1581 – 1 May 1599	*Johann VII von Schönenberg*
8 May 1599 – 7 Sep 1623	*Lothar, Baron Metternich* (b. 1549)
25 Sep 1623 – 7 Feb 1652	*Philipp Christof von Sötern* (b. 11 Dec 1567)
12 Mar 1652 – 1 Jun 1676	*Karl Kaspar von der Leyen* (b. 18 Dec 1618)
9 Jun 1676 – 6 Jan 1711	*Johann VIII, Hugo, Baron Orsbeck* (b. 1634)
6 Jan 1711 – 4 Dec 1715	*Karl Josef Ignaz*, son of Duke Charles V of Lorraine (b. 24 Nov 1680)
20 Feb 1716 – 7 Apr 1729	*Franz Ludwig*, son of Wilhelm, Count Palatine (b. 24 Jul 1664; d. 18 or 19 Apr 1732) also Elector of Mainz
2 May 1729 – 18 Jan 1756	*Franz Georg, Count Schönborn* (b. 15 Jun 1682)
18 Feb 1756 – 12 Jan 1768	*Johann IX, Philip von Walderdorf*
10 Feb 1768 – 25 Apr 1802	*Klemens Wenzeslaus*, son of Elector Friedrich August II of Saxony (b. 28 Sep 1739; d. 27 Jul 1812)
1802	Electorate abolished

Tukulor Empire

For the Tukulor Empire, West Africa, 18th to 19th centuries, see volume 1.

Tunisia

HEADS OF STATE

Beys

9 Jul 1705	*Husain I, ibn Ali at-Turki* (d. 25 May 1739)

Sep/Oct 1735	*Ali I, (Ali Pasha)* nephew
1756/57	*Muhammad I*, son of Husain I
Mar 1759	*Ali II (Ali Bey)*, brother
Feb/Apr 1782	*Hammuda*, son
Sep/Oct 1814	*Uthman*, brother
20 Dec 1814	*Mahmud*, son of Muhammad I
Mar 1824	*Husain II*, son
1835/36	*Mustafa*, brother
1837/38	*Ahmad I*, son
29 May 1855	*Muhammad II*, son of Husain II
23 Sep 1859	*Muhammad III, as-Sadiq*, brother (b. 1816)
28 Oct 1882	*Ali III, Muddat*, brother (b. 1817)
11 Jun 1902	*Muhammad IV, al-Haddjji*, son
11 May 1906	*Muhammad V, an-Nasir*, son of Muhammad II
10 Jul 1922	*Muhammad VI, al-Habib*, brother(?) (b. 13 Aug 1858)
11 Feb 1929 – 19 Jul 1942	*Ahmad II*

French Governors

13 May 1881	*Théodore Justin Dominique Roustan* (b. Aix 29 May 1834)
18 Feb 1881	*Paul Cambon* (b. Paris 20 Jan 1843; d. Paris 29 May 1924)
Nov 1886	*Justin Massicault* (b. Ouzouer-les-Bordelins 1838; d. Tunis 5 Nov 1892)
Nov 1892	*Maurice Rouvier* (b. Aix 17 Apr 1842; d. Neuilly-sur-Seine 7 Jun 1911)
14 Nov 1894	*René Millet* (b. 14 Sep 1849; d.(?))
Mar 1901	*Stéphan Pichon* (b. Arnay-le-Duc 10 Aug 1857; d. Lons-le-Saunier 18 Sep 1933)
Dec 1906	*Gabriel Alapetite* (b. Clamecy 5 Jan 1854; d. Paris 1932)
Oct 1918 – Jan 1921	*Pierre Étienne Flandin* (b. Paris 12 Apr 1889; d. St Jean-Cap-Ferrat 13 Jun 1958)
Jan 1921	*Lucien Saint* (b. Évreux 1867; d. 1938)
Jan 1929 – Jul 1933	*François Manceron* (b. 1872; d. 1937)

Turkey

HEADS OF STATE

Sultans

House of Osman

3 May 1481	*Bayezid II*, son of Mehmed II, the Conqueror (b. Jan 1448)
24 Apr 1512	*Selim I*, son (b. 1470)
22 Sep 1520	*Süleyman I*, son (b. 6 Nov 1494)
7 Sep 1566	*Selim II*, son (b. 28 May 1524)
15 Dec 1574	*Murad III*, son (b. 4 Jul 1546)
16 Jan 1595	*Mehmed III*, son (b. 26 May 1566)
21 Dec 1603	*Ahmed I*, son (b. 18 Apr 1590)
22 Nov 1617	*Mustafa I*, brother (for 1st time) (b. 1592; d. 1638)
26 Feb 1618	*Osman II*, son of Ahmed I (b. 3 Nov 1603)
19 May 1622	*Mustafa I* (for 2nd time)
10 Sep 1623	*Murad IV*, brother (b. 29 Aug 1612)
9 Feb 1640	*Ibrahim*, brother (b. 4 Nov 1615; d. 18 Aug 1648)
8 Aug 1648	*Mehmed IV*, son (b. 2 Jan 1642; d. 6 Jan 1693)
9 Nov 1687	*Süleyman II*, brother (b. 15 Apr 1642)
23 Jun 1691	*Ahmed II*, brother (b. 25 Feb 1643)
6 Feb 1695	*Mustafa II*, nephew (b. 5 Jun 1664; d. 29 Dec 1703)
22 Aug 1703	*Ahmed III*, brother (b. 31 Dec 1673; d. 1 Jul 1736)
1 Oct 1730	*Mahmud I*, son of Mustafa II (b. 2 Aug 1696)
14 Dec 1754	*Osman III*, brother (b. 2 Jan 1699)
30 Oct 1757	*Mustafa III*, son of Ahmed III (b. 28 Jan 1717)
21 Jan 1774	*Abdülhamid I*, brother (b. 20 Mar 1725)
7 Apr 1789	*Selim III*, nephew (b. 23/24 Dec 1761; d. 28 Jul 1808)
29 May 1807	*Mustafa IV*, son of Abdülhamid I (b. 8 Sep 1779; d. 16 Nov 1808)
28 Jul 1808	*Mahmud II*, brother (b. 20 Jul 1785)
1 Jul 1839	*Abdülmejid I*, son (b. 23 Apr 1823)
25 Jun 1861	*Abdülaziz*, brother (b. 9 Feb 1830; d. 4 Jun 1876)
30 May 1876	*Murad V*, son of Abdülmejid I (b. 21 Sep 1840; d. 29 Aug 1904)
31 Aug 1876	*Abdülhamid II*, brother (b. 21 Sep 1842; d. 10 Feb 1918)
27 Apr 1909	*Mehmed V*, brother (b. 3 Nov 1844)

3 Jul 1918	*Mehmed VI*, brother (b. 2 Feb 1861; d. San Remo 16 May 1926) became Caliph on 2 Nov 1922
19 Nov 1922 – 3 Mar 1924	*Abdülmejid II*, son of Abdülaziz (b. 29 May 1868; d. Paris 24 Aug 1944) Caliph only
29 Oct 1923	Republic

Presidents

30 Oct 1923 – 10 Nov 1938	*Mustafa Kemal Pasha* (from 26 Nov 1934; *Kemal Atatürk*) (b. Salonika 1881; d. Istanbul 10 Nov 1938)

MEMBERS OF GOVERNMENT

Grand Viziers and Chief Ministers

1483/84 – Mar 1497	*Dervish Davud Pasha* (d. Oct 1499)
8 Mar 1497 – 1497/98	*Hersek-zade Ahmed Pasha* (for 1st time) (b. Hercey-Novi 1456 or 1459; d. Bursa 1516)
1497/98 – 1499/1500	*Ibrahim ibn Khalil Chandarlı* (b. 1429/30; d. Lepanto 1499/1500)
1499/1500 – 1501/02	*Ahmed Mesih Pasha* (d. 1501/02)
1501/02 – 1503/04	*Hadım Ali* (for 1st time) (d. between Sivas and Kayseri Jul/Aug 1511)
1503/ – 1506/07	*Hersek-zade Ahmed Pasha* (for 2nd time)
1506/07 – 1511	*Hadım Ali* (for 2nd time)
1511	*Hersek-zade Ahmed Pasha* (for 3rd time)
1511 – 1512/13	*Koja Mustafa* (d. Bursa 1512/13)
1512/13 – Oct/Nov 1514	*Hersek-zade Ahmed Pasha* (for 4th time)
Oct/Nov 1514 – 26 Jan 1517	*Hadım Sinan* (d. 26 Jan 1517)
Jan/Feb 1517 – (?)1517	*Yunus Pasha* (d. 1517)
1517 – 1520	*Mustafa Pasha*
1520 – 27 Jun 1523	*Mehmed Piri Pasha*
27 Jun 1523 – 15 Mar 1536	*Ibrahim Pasha* (b. Parga(?), Epirus, 1493(?); d. 15 Mar 1536)
Mar 1536 – 13 Jul 1539	*Ayas Pasha* (b. Valona; d. 13 Jul 1539)
Jul 1539 – 8 May 1541	*Lütfi Pasha* (d. Demotica 1563(?))
May 1541 – 1544	*Hadım Süleyman* (d. Malkara 1548)

1544 – Oct/Nov 1553	*Rüstem Pasha* (for 1st time) (d. 18 Jul 1561)
Oct/Nov 1553 – 28 Sep 1555	*Kara Ahmed Arnavut* (d. 28 Sep 1555)
Sep/Oct 1555 – 18 1561	*Rüstem Pasha* (for 2nd time)
Jul 1561 – 27 Jun 1565	*Semiz Ali Pasha* (d. Brazza 27 Jun 1565)
Jul 1565 – 1576 1576	*Tavil Mehmed Sokollu Pasha* (for 1st time) (b. Rudo, Bosnia, 1505; d. 12 Oct 1579) *Jighala-zade Yusuf Sinan Pasha* (for 1st time) (b. 1547; d. Nov/Dec 1605)
1576 – 12 Oct 1579	*Tavil Mehmed Sokollu Pasha* (for 2nd time)
Oct 1579 – May/Jun 1580	*Ahmed Pasha*, son-in-law of Rüstem Pasha (d. May/Jun 1580)
May/Jun 1580 – 15 Jan 1583*	*Koja Sinan Pasha* (for 1st time) (b. 1508; d. Istanbul 4 Apr 1596)
Jan 1583 – 28 Jul 1584	*Siyavush Pasha* (for 1st time) (d. Uskudar 1601)
Aug 1584 – 29 Oct 1585	*Osman Özdemir-oghlu* (b. Egypt 1526; d. Tabriz 29 Oct 1585)
Nov 1585 – 15 Apr 1586	*Hadım Mesih* (d. 1588)
Apr 1586 – 3 Apr 1589	*Siyavush Pasha* (for 2nd time)
Apr 1589 – 2 Aug 1591	*Koja Sinan Pasha* (for 2nd time)
Aug 1591 – 23 Mar 1592	*Ferhad Pasha* (for 1st time) (d. Istanbul Oct 1595)
Mar 1592 – 29 Jan 1593	*Siyavush Pasha* (for 3rd time)
Feb 1593 – 16 Feb 1595	*Koja Sinan Pasha* (for 3rd time)
Feb – 7 Jul 1595	*Ferhad Pasha* (for 2nd time)
Jul – 21 Oct 1595	*Koja Sinan Pasha* (for 4th time)
Oct 1595	*Lala Mehmed Pasha* (b. Saruhan; d. late Oct 1595)
Oct 1595 – 4 Apr 1596	*Sinan Pasha* (for 5th time)
5 Apr – 27 Oct 1596	*Damad Ibrahim Pasha* (for 1st time) (d. Semlin, on the Danube, 10 Jul 1601)
Oct – Nov/Dec 1596	*Jighala-zade Yusuf Sinan Pasha* (for 2nd time)
9 Dec 1596 – 3 Oct 1597	*Damad Ibrahim Pasha* (for 2nd time)
Oct 1597 – 8 Apr 1598	*Hadım Hasan Pasha* (d. 8 Apr 1598)
Apr – 8 Dec 1598	*Jerrah Mehmed Pasha* (d. 1604)
8 Jan 1599 – 10 Jul 1601	*Damad Ibrahim Pasha* (for 3rd time)
Jul 1601 – 5 Oct 1603	*Yemishchi, Hasan Pasha* (d. 16 Oct 1603)

*dates henceforward are according to the Gregorian calendar

Oct 1603 – 26 Jul 1604	*Yavuz Ali Pasha* (d. Belgrade 26 Jul 1604)
end of Jul 1604 – 24 May (22 Jun(?)) 1606	*Lala Mehmed Pasha II*, (d. Uskudar 24 May (22 Jun?) 1606)
Jun – 6 Dec 1606	*Dervish Pasha* (d. Istanbul 9 Dec 1606)
11 Dec 1606 – 6 Aug 1611	*Murad Pasha* (d. Istanbul 6 Aug 1611)
Aug 1611 – 17 Oct 1614	*Nasuh Pasha* (b. Komotini, Thrace; d. (executed) 17 Oct 1614)
17 Oct 1614 – Jan 1617	*Damad Öküz Mehmed Pasha* (for 1st time) (d. Aleppo 1620)
Jan 1617 – 18 Jan 1619	*Kayserili Khalil Pasha* (for 1st time) (b. Zeytun or Ruzvan 1560; d. 1629)
18 Jan – 23 Dec 1619	*Damad Öküz Mehmed Pasha* (for 2nd time)
Dec 1619 – 8 Mar 1621	*Chelebi Güzelje Ali Pasha* (b. Kos 1580; d. 8 Mar 1621)
Mar – 17 Sep 1621	*Hüseyin Pasha*
17 Sep 1621 – 19 May 1622	*Dilaver Pasha* (d. Istanbul 19 May 1622)
May – 20 Jun 1622	*Kara Davud Pasha*, brother-in-law of Sultan Mustafa I (d. Istanbul 9 Jan 1623)
Jun – 7 Jul 1622	*Merre Hüseyin Pasha* (for 1st time) (d. 1623)
Jul – 21 Sep 1622	*Lefkeli Mustafa Pasha* (b. Lefke; d. 1648)
Sep 1622 – 5 Feb 1623	*Gürjü Hadım Mehmed Pasha* (b. 1557; d. Jul/Aug 1626)
Feb – Sep 1623	*Merre Hüseyin Pasha* (for 2nd time)
Sep 1623 – 3 Apr 1624	*Kemankesh Kara Ali Pasha* (b. Hamıd eli; d. 3 Apr 1624)
3 Apr 1624 – 28 Jan 1625	*Cherkes Mehmed Pasha* (d. Tokat 28 Jan 1625)
Jan 1625 – 1 Dec 1626	*Hafiz Ahmed Pasha* (for 1st time) (b. Plovdiv 1564; d. 10 Feb 1632)
Dec 1626 – 6 Apr 1628	*Kayserili Khalil Pasha* (for 2nd time)
6 Apr 1628 – 25 Oct 1631	*Khüsrev Pasha* (d. Tokat Feb 1632)
25 Oct 1631 – 10 Feb 1632	*Hafiz Ahmed Pasha* (for 2nd time)
Feb – 10 May 1632	*Rejeb Pasha* (d. 10 May 1632)
May 1632 – 2 Feb 1637	*Tabanı-yassı Mehmed Pasha* (b. 1589; d. Istanbul 1639)
Feb 1637 – 17 Aug 1638	*Bayram Pasha* (b. Istanbul; d. Edessa 17 Aug 1638)
Aug – 24 Dec 1638	*Tayyar Mehmed Pasha* (b. Istanbul; d. Baghdad 24 Dec 1638)

24 Dec 1638 – 22 Feb 1644	*Kemankesh Kara Mustafa Pasha* (d. Istanbul 22 Feb 1644)
10 Mar 1644 – 17 Dec 1645	*Sultan-zade Mehmed Pasha* (b. Istanbul 1602/03; d. Chania Jul 1646)
Dec 1645 – 18 Sep 1647	*Salih Pasha* (d. Istanbul 18 Sep 1647)
Sep 1647 – 7 Aug 1648	*Ahmed Hezarpare* (b. Istanbul; d. 7 Aug 1648)
Aug 1648 – 19 May 1649	*Sofu Mehmed Pasha* (d. 21 May 1649)
19 May 1649 – 5 Aug 1650	*Murad Pasha* (for 1st time) (d. Hama, Syria, late 1655)
6 Aug 1650 – 23 Aug 1651	*Melek Ahmed Pasha* (b. 1604; d. 1662)
Aug – 30 Oct 1651	*Siyavush Pasha* (for 1st time) (d. 25 Apr 1656)
30 Oct 1651 – 30 Jun 1652	*Gürjü Mehmed Pasha II* (d. Istanbul 1664 (7 Apr 1666?))
Jun 1652 – 11 Feb 1653	*Tarhonju Ahmed Pasha* (b. Mat, Albania; d. (executed) Istanbul 11 Feb 1653)
11 Feb 1653 – 29 Oct 1654	*Dervish Mehmed Pasha* (b. c.1585; d. 13 Jan 1655)
Nov 1654 – 11 May 1655	*Damad Ibshir Mustafa* (b. 1607; d. 11 May 1655)
May – 19 Aug 1655	*Murad Pasha* (for 2nd time)
Aug 1655 – 27 Feb 1656	*Süleyman Pasha* (for 1st time)
27 Feb – 6 Mar 1656	*Deli Hüseyin Pasha* (b. Bursa; d. 1659)
6 Mar 1656	*Surnazen Mehmed Pasha* (d. Erzerum 1657)
6 Mar – 25 Apr 1656	*Siyavush Pasha* (for 2nd time)
Apr – 15 Sep 1656	*Boyunu-ighri Mehmed Pasha* (b. Samsun 1578; d. Istanbul 1662)
Sep 1656 – 31 Oct 1661	*Mehmed Köprülü* (b. between 1575 and 1596; d. Adrianople 31 Oct 1661)
Nov 1661 – 3 Nov 1676	*Ahmed Fazil Köprülü*, son (b. Vezirköprü 1635; d. Ergene Köprüsü 3 Nov 1676)
5 Nov 1676 – 25 Dec 1683	*Kara Mustafa Pasha* (b. Marınca 1634/35; d. Belgrade 25 Dec 1683)
26 Dec 1683 – 17 Dec 1685	*Kara Ibrahim Pasha* (b. Handevrek 1621; d. Rhodes May 1687)
Dec 1685 – Sep/Oct 1687	*Süleyman Pasha* (for 2nd time)
4 Oct 1687 – 23 Feb 1688	*Abaza Siyavush Pasha* (d. 24 Feb 1688)

23 Feb – 2 May 1688	*Nishanjı Ismail Pasha* (b. Ayash 1619(?); d. Apr/ May 1690)
30 May 1688 – 7 Nov 1689	*Mustafa Pasha* (b. Rodosto; d. Malkara, end of 1689)
10 Nov 1689 – 19 Aug 1691	*Fazıl Mustafa Pasha Köprülü*, brother of Ahmed Fazıl Köprülü (b. Vezirköprü 1637; d. Slankamen 19 Aug 1691)
24 Aug 1691 – 21 Mar 1692	*Arabajı Ali Pasha* (b. Ohri 1620/22; d. Rhodes 21 Apr 1693)
23 Mar 1692 – 17 Mar 1693	*Haji Ali Pasha* (b. Merzifon 1640; d. Crete 1698)
14 Mar 1693 – Mar 1694	*Biyikli Mustafa Pasha* (b. Bozok; d. 1698)
13 Mar 1694 – 22 Apr 1695	*Ali Pasha Sürmeli* (b. Demotica c. 1645; d. 18 May 1695)
3 May 1695 – 11 Sep 1697	*Elmas Mehmed Pasha* (b. Sinope 1662; d. Zenta 11 Sep 1697)
17 Sep 1697 – 5 Sep 1702	*Amujezade Hüseyin Pasha Köprülü*, cousin of Fazıl Mustafa Pasha Köprülü (b. 1644; d. 5 Sep 1702)
Sep 1702 – 24 Jan 1703	*Daltaban Mustafa Pasha* (b. Bitolj; d. 24 Jan 1703)
25 Jan – 22 Aug 1703	*Rami Mehmed Pasha* (b. Istanbul 1654; d. Rhodes 1706)
22 Aug – 16 Nov 1703	*Nishanjı Kavanoz Ahmed Pasha* (d. Inebahti 1705)
18 Nov 1703 – 28 Sep 1704	*Damad Hasan Pasha* (b. Peloponnese 1655; d. Rakka on Euphrates 1713)
Oct – 25 Dec 1704	*Kalaylıkoz Ahmed Pasha* (b. Kayseri 1645; d. 1715)
25 Dec 1704 – 3 May 1706	*Baltajı Mehmed Pasha* (for 1st time) (b. Osmanık 1660; d. Lemnos 1712/13)
3 May 1706 – 15 Jun 1710	*Chorlulu Ali Pasha* (b. Chorlu 1670; d. Lesbos between 11 Dec 1711 and 9 Jan 1712)
16 Jun – 17 Aug 1710	*Numan Pasha Köprülü* (b. Istanbul 1670; d. Crete 6 Feb 1719)
18 Aug 1710 – 20 Nov 1711	*Baltajı Mehmed Pasha* (for 2nd time)
20 Nov 1711 – 11 Nov 1712	*Yusuf Pasha* (d. Rhodes 1714)
12 Nov 1712 – 6 Apr 1713	*Süleyman Pasha* (for 3rd time)
6 – 7 Apr 1713	*Ibrahim Hoca*
27 Apr 1713 – 5 Aug 1716	*Shehit Damad Ali Pasha Silâhtar* (b. Iznik 1667; d. Peterwardein 5 Aug 1716)
21 Aug 1716 – Oct 1717	*Khalil Pasha* (b. Elbasan 1655; d. 1733)

Oct 1717 – 9 May 1718	*Nishanjı Mehmed Pasha* (b. Kayseri 1670; d. Hejaz 1728)
9 May 1718 – 16 Oct 1730	*Damad Ibrahim Pasha* (b. Nevshehir; d. Istanbul 31 Oct 1730)
16 Oct 1730 – 23 Jan 1731	*Silâhtar Mehmed Pasha* (b. Istanbul; d. Aleppo 1737)
23 Jan – 11 Sep 1731	*Ibrahim Pasha Kabakulak* (b. Karahisar; d. Crete 1742)
21 Sep 1731 – 12 Mar 1732	*Topal Osman Pasha* (b. Peloponnese; d. 1732/33)
12 Mar 1732 – 14 Jul 1735	*Hekimzade Ali Âli* (afterwards Pasha) son of a Venetian convert (for 1st time) (b. 4 Jun 1689; d. Kütahya 14 Aug 1758)
14 Jul – 25 Dec 1735	*Gürjü Ismail Pasha*
10 Jan 1736 – 5 Aug 1737	*Silâhtar es-Seyyid Mehmed Pasha* (b. Demotica; d. Jeddah 1756)
22 Aug – 19 Dec 1737	*Muhsinzade Abdullah Chelebi* (b. Aleppo 1660; d. Trikala 1749)
3 Dec 1737 – 23 Mar 1739	*Yeghen Mehmed Pasha* (d. Erivan Aug 1745)
17 Mar 1739 – 23 Jun 1740	*Hajı Ivaz-zade Mehmed Pasha* (b. Jagodina 1675; d. Inebahti 1743)
22 Jul 1740 – 7 Apr 1742	*Hajı Ahmed Pasha*
21 Apr – 4 Oct 1742	*Hekimzade Ali Pasha* (for 2nd time)
4 Oct 1742 – 10 Aug 1746	*Hasan Pasha es-Said* (b. Kabali 1679; d. Amida 1748)
11 Aug 1746 – 24 Aug 1747	*Hajı Mehmed Pasha Tiryaka* (b. Istanbul 1680; d. Crete Jul 1751)
24 Aug 1747 – 2 Jan 1750	*es-Seyyid Abdullah Pasha* (d. Aleppo 1761)
9 Jan 1750 – 1 Jul 1752	*Divittar Mehmed Pasha*
1 Jul 1752 – 16 Feb 1755	*Köse Bahir Mustafa Pasha* (for 1st time)
16 Feb – 19 May 1755	*Hekimzade Ali Pasha* (for 3rd time)
19 May – 24 Aug 1755	*Naili Abdullah Pasha* (b. Istanbul 1698; d. Mecca 1758)
24 Aug – 23 Oct 1755	*Nishanjı Bıyıklı Ali Pasha* (b. Istanbul; d. 23 Oct 1755)
25 Oct 1755 – 1 Apr 1756	*Mehmed Said Pasha*
30 Apr – 3 Dec 1756	*Köse Bahir Mustafa Pasha* (for 2nd time)
12 Jan 1757 – 8 Apr 1763	*Koja Mehmed Ragıp Pasha* (b. Istanbul 1698; d. 8 Apr 1763)

11 Apr – 2 Oct(?) 1763	*Hamza Hamid Pasha* (b. Istanbul 1700; d. Arafa near Mecca Mar/Apr 1770)
29 Sep 1763 – 30 Mar 1765	*Köse Bahir Mustafa Pasha* (for 3rd time)
30 Mar 1765 – 7 Aug 1768	*Muhsinzade Mehmed Pasha* (for 1st time) (b. Istanbul 1706; d. 6 Aug 1773)
7 Aug – 20 Oct 1768	*Silâhtar Hamza Mahir Pasha* (b. Develi Karahisar 1727; d. Gallipoli Nov 1768)
Oct 1768 – 12 Aug 1769	*Yaghlıkchı-zade Nishani Mehmed Emin* (b. 1723; d. Adrianople 12 Aug 1769)
12 Aug – 12 Dec 1769	*Moldovani Ali Pasha*
13 Dec 1769 – 25 Dec 1770	*Ivaz-zade Khalil Pasha* (b. 1724; d. Nallihan 1777)
25 Dec 1770 – 11 Dec 1771	*Silâhtar Mehmed Pasha* (b. Istanbul 1710; d. Crete 1771)
Dec 1771 – 6 Aug 1773	*Muhsinzade Mehmed Pasha* (for 2nd time)
11 Aug 1773 – 7 Jul 1775	*Izzet Mehmed Pasha* (for 1st time) (b. Carsamba 1732; d. Belgrade 1783)
7 Jul 1775 – 5 Jan 1777	*Dervish Mehmed Pasha* (b. Istanbul 1729/30; d. Chios 1777)
5 Jan 1777 – 1 Sep 1778	*Darendeli Mehmed Pasha* (b. 1716; d. 1784)
1 Sep 1778 – 22 Aug 1779	*Kalafat Mehmed Pasha* (b. Sofia; d. 1792)
22 Aug 1779 – 20 Feb 1781	*Silâhtar es-Seyyid Mehmed Pasha* (b. Nigde 1735; d. Istanbul 20 Feb 1781)
20 Feb 1781 – 25 Aug 1782	*Izzet Mehmed Pasha* (for 2nd time)
25 Aug – 31 Dec 1782	*Yeghen Hajı Mehmed Pasha* (b. 1726; d. Constanza, Romania, 1786)
31 Dec 1782 – 30 Apr 1785	*Khalil Hamid Pasha* (b. 1736; d. Tenedos 1785)
30 Apr 1785 – 25 Jan 1786	*Shahin Ali Pasha* (d. Gallipoli 1789)
25 Jan 1786 – 28 May 1789	*Koja Yusuf Pasha* (for 1st time) (d. Medina 1800)
20 May 1789 – 2 Jan 1790	*Kethüda Cherkes Hasan Pasha* (d. Yenishehir 1810)
1 Jan – 30 Mar 1790	*Gazi Hasan Pasha Jezayirli* (b. Tekfurdağı 1713; d. Bulgaria 30 Mar 1790)
16 Apr 1790 – 12 Feb 1791	*Ruschuklu Jezayirli Hasan Sherif Pasha* (d. Shumen, Bulgaria, 12/13 Feb 1791)
Feb 1791 – 1791/2	*Koja Yusuf Pasha* (for 2nd time)

1791/92 – 21 Oct 1794	*Damad Melik Mehmed Pasha* (b. 1719; d. 1801)
21 Oct 1794 – 23 Oct 1798	*Izzet Mehmed Pasha* (b. Safranbolu 1743; d. Manisa 1812)
23 Oct 1798 – 24 Jun 1805	*Yusuf Ziya Pasha* (for 1st time) (d. Samos 1818)
24 Sep 1805 – 13 Oct 1806	*Hafiz Ismail Pasha*
13 Oct 1806 – 3 Jun 1807	*Hilmi Ibrahim Pasha*
3 Jun 1807 – 29 Jul 1808	*Chelebi Mustafa Pasha* (b. Istanbul; d. Samos 1810)
29 Jul – 15 Nov 1808	*Mustafa Pasha Bayraktar* (b. Chotin 1755/56; d. Istanbul 15/16 Nov 1808)
16 Nov – end of Dec 1808	*Memish Pasha* (d. Samos 1809)
End of Dec 1808 – Feb/ Mar 1809	*Charhajı Ali Pasha* (b. Konya; d. Tokat 1823)
Feb/Mar 1809 – Jan/ Feb 1811	*Yusuf Ziya Pasha* (for 2nd time)
Jan/Feb 1811 – Jun/ Jul 1812	*Ahmed Pasha*
Jun/Jul 1812 – 30 Mar 1815	*Hurshid Ahmed Pasha* (d. Yenishehir 1822)
30 Mar 1815 – 6 Jan 1818	*Mehmed Emin Rauf Pasha* (for 1st time) (b. Istanbul 1780; d. 1859)
6 Jan 1818 – 5 Jan 1820	*Dervish Mehmed Pasha* (b. Anapolis 1765; d. Yanbu, Arabia, Oct 1837)
Jan 1820 – 21 Apr 1821	*Seyyid Ali Pasha*
21 – 30 Apr 1821	*Benderli Ali Pasha*
30 Apr 1821 – 11 Nov 1822	*Hajı Salih Pasha*
11 Nov 1822 – 4 Mar 1823	*Hamdullah Abdullah Pasha* (b. Istanbul; d. Izmit 1823)
4 Mar – Dec 1823	*Silâhtar Ali Pasha*
Dec 1823 – 15 Sep 1824	*Galib Mehmed Said Pasha* (b. Istanbul 1763/64; d. Balikesir 1829)
15 Sep 1824 – 26 Oct 1828	*Benderli Selim Mehmed Pasha* (b. Chotin 1771; d. Damascus 1831)
26 Oct 1828 – Jan 1829	*Izzet Mehmed Pasha* (for 1st time)
Jan 1829 – 17 Feb 1833	*Reshid Mehmed Pasha* (d. Diarbekir 1836)
17 Feb 1833 – 8 Jul 1839	*Mehmed Emin Rauf Pasha* (for 2nd time)

8 Jul 1839 – 29 May 1841	*Mehmed Khüsrev Pasha* (b. c. 1756; d. Mürgün 3 Mar 1855)
29 May – 7 Oct 1841	*Mehmed Emin Rauf Pasha* (for 3rd time)
7 Oct 1841 – 3 Sep 1842	*Izzet Mehmed Pasha* (for 2nd time)
3 Sep 1842 – 31 Jul 1846	*Mehmed Emin Rauf Pasha* (for 4th time)
31 Jul 1846 – 28 Apr 1848	*Mustafa Reshid Pasha* (for 1st time) (b. Istanbul 13 Mar 1880; d. 7 Jan 1858)
28 Apr – 13 Aug 1848	*Ibrahim Sarım Pasha* (b. 1801; d. 1853)
13 Aug 1848 – 27 Jan 1852	*Mustafa Reshid Pasha* (for 2nd time)
27 Jan – 7 Mar 1852	*Mehmed Emin Rauf Pasha* (for 5th time)
7 Mar – 7 Aug 1852	*Mustafa Reshid Pasha* (for 3rd time)
7 Aug – 4 Oct 1852	*Mehmed Emin Ali Pasha* (for 1st time) (b. Istanbul 5 Mar 1815; d. Istanbul 7 Sep 1871)
4 Oct 1852 – 14 May 1853	*Demad Mehmed Ali Pasha* (b. Hemsin 1813; d. Istanbul 1868)
14 May 1853 – 30 May 1854	*Mustafa Naili Pasha* (b. Polyan 1788; d. 1871)
30 May – 24 Nov 1854	*Kıbrıslı Mehmed Pasha* (for 1st time) (b. Cyprus 1813; d. 1865)
24 Nov 1853 – 4 May 1855	*Mustafa Reshid Pasha* (for 4th time)
4 May 1855 – 1 Dec 1856	*Mehmed Emin Ali Pasha* (for 2nd time)
1 Dec 1856 – 2 Aug 1857	*Mustafa Reshid Pasha* (for 5th time)
2 Aug – 23 Oct 1857	*Mustafa Naili Pasha* (for 2nd time)
23 Oct 1857 – 7 Jan 1858	*Mustafa Reshid Pasha* (for 6th time)
11 Jan 1858 – 8 Oct 1859	*Mustafa Emin Ali Pasha* (for 3rd time)
8 Oct – 24 Dec 1859	*Kıbrıslı Mehmed Pasha* (for 2nd time)
24 Dec 1859 – 27 May 1860	*Müterjim Mehmed Rüshtü Pasha* (for 1st time) (b. Ayanjık 1811; d. Manisa 1882)
27 May 1860 – 6 Aug 1861	*Kıbrıslı Mehmed Pasha* (for 3rd time)
6 Aug – 22 Nov 1861	*Mehmed Emin Ali Pasha* (for 4th time)
22 Nov 1861 – 6 Jan 1863	*Kecheji-zade Mehmed Fuad Pasha* (for 1st time) (b. Istanbul 17 Jan 1814; d. Nice 12 Feb 1869)
6 Jan – 3 Jun 1863	*Yusuf Kâmil Pasha* (b. Arapkır 1808; d. 1876)
3 Jun 1863 – 5 Jun 1866	*Kecheji-zade Mehmed Fuad Pasha* (for 2nd time)

Jun 1866 – Feb 1867	*Müterjim Mehmed Rüshtü Pasha* (for 2nd time)
11 Feb 1867 – 7 Sep 1871	*Mehmed Emin Ali Pasha* (for 5th time)
Sep 1871 – 31 Jul 1872	*Mahmud Nedim Pasha* (for 1st time) (b. 1818; d. 1883)
31 Jul – 19 Oct 1872	*Midhat Pasha* (for 1st time) (b. Apr/May 1822; d. Taif, Arabia, 8 May 1884)
Oct 1872 – Feb 1873	*Müterjim Mehmed Rüshtü Pasha* (for 3rd time)
15 Feb – May 1873	*Mehmed Esad Pasha* (for 1st time) (b. Samos 1828; d. Smyrna 1875)
May 1873 – 14 Feb 1874	*Shirvani-Zade Mehmed Rüshtü Pasha* (b. Amasia 1828; d. Taif, Arabia, 1874)
14 Feb 1874 – 25 Apr 1875	*Hüseyin Avni Pasha* (b. Gelendost 1820; d. Istanbul 15/16 Jun 1876)
Apr – Aug 1875	*Mehmed Esad Pasha* (for 2nd time)
21 Aug 1875 – 13 Apr 1876	*Mahmud Nedim Pasha* (for 2nd time)
Apr – 19 Dec 1876	*Müterjim Mehmed Rüshtü Pasha* (for 4th time)
19 Dec 1876 – 5 Feb 1877	*Midhat Pasha* (for 2nd time)
5 Feb 1877 – 11 Jan 1878	*Ibrahim Edhem Pasha* (b. Chios 1813/1818; d. Istanbul 21 Mar 1893)
Jan 1878 – May 1882	Grand Viziers officially known by the title of 'Chief Ministers'
11 Jan – 4 Feb 1878	*Ahmed Hamdi Pasha* (b. Istanbul 1826; d. Beirut 1885)
4 Feb – 18 Apr 1878	*Ahmed Vefik Pasha* (for 1st time) (b. 1823; d. 2 Apr 1891)
18 Apr – end of May 1878	*Mehmed Sadik Pasha* (b. Bayındır 1825; d. Lemnos 1901)
end of May – early Jun 1878	*Müterjim Mehmed Rüshtü Pasha* (for 5th time)
early Jun 1878 – Oct 1878	*Mehmed Esad Saffet Pasha* (b. Istanbul 1814; d. 1883)
Oct 1878 – 28 Jul 1879	*Hayreddin Pasha* (b. 1819(?); d. Istanbul 1889)
28 Jul – end of Sep 1879	*Arifi Pasha* (b. Istanbul 1830; d. Istanbul 6 Dec 1895)
1 Oct 1879 – Jun 1880	*Küchük Mehmed Said Pasha* (for 1st time) (b. Erzerum 1838; d. Istanbul 1 Mar 1914)
Sep 1880 – 2 May 1882	*Küchük Mehmed Said Pasha* (for 2nd time)
Jun – Nov 1882	*Küchük Mehmed Said Pasha* (for 3rd time)
30 Nov – 2 Dec 1882	*Ahmed Vefik Pasha* (for 2nd time)
2 Dec 1882 – 25 Sep 1885	*Küchük Mehmed Said Pasha* (for 4th time)

Sep 1885 – Sep 1891	*Kıbrıslı Mehmed Kâmil Pasha* (b. Nicosia 1832; d. Larnica 14 Nov 1913)
Sep 1891 – Jun 1895	*Ahmed Jevad Pasha* (b. Damascus 1851; d. Damascus 10 Aug 1900)
9 Jun – 3 Oct 1895	*Küchük Mehmed Said Pasha* (for 5th time)
Oct – Nov 1895	*Kıbrıslı Mehmed Kâmil Pasha* (for 2nd time)
Nov 1895 – 9 Nov 1901	*Khalil Rifat Pasha* (b. Siroz 1820; d. 9 Nov 1901)
13 Nov 1901 – 15 Jan 1903	*Küchük Mehmed Said Pasha* (for 6th time)
Jan 1903 – Jul 1908	*Mehmed Ferid Pasha* (b. Jannina (or Valona?) 1852; d. San Remo 9 Dec 1914)
22 Jul – 6 Aug 1908	*Küchük Mehmed said Pasha* (for 7th time)
Aug 1908 – Feb 1909	*Kıbrıslı Mehmed Kâmil Pasha* (for 3rd time)
31 Mar – May 1909	*Ahmed Tevfik Pasha* (from 1934: *Okday*) (b. Istanbul 11 Feb 1843 (1845?); d. Istanbul 1936)
May 1909 – Jan 1910	*Hüseyin Hilmi Pasha* (b. Lesbos 1855; d. Vienna 1921)
12 Jan 1910 – 29 Sep 1911	*Ibrahim Hakkı Pasha* (b. Istanbul 12 Apr 1863; d. Berlin 30 Jul 1918)
4 Oct – 30 Dec 1911	*Küchük Mehmed Said Pasha* (for 8th time)
31 Dec 1911 – 17 Jul 1912	*Küchük Mehmed Said Pasha* (for 9th time)
22 Jul – 29 Oct 1912	*Gazi Ahmed Muhtar Pasha* (b. Bursa 1 Nov 1839; d. Istanbul 21 Jan 1918)
Oct 1912 – 23 Jan 1913	*Kıbrıslı Mehmed Kâmil Pasha* (for 4th time)
23 Jan – 14 Jun 1913	*Mahmud Sefket Pasha* (b. Baghdad 1856; d. Istanbul 14 Jun 1913)
Jun 1913 – Feb 1917	*Said Halim Pasha* (b. Cairo 1863; d. Rome 7 Dec 1921)
Feb 1917 – Oct 1918	*Mehmed Talât Pasha* (b. Karıcaali Jul 1872 (1874?); d. Berlin 15 Mar 1921)
Oct – Nov 1918	*Ahmed Izzed Pasha* (from 1934: *Furgaç*) (b. Naslić 1864; d. Istanbul 31 Mar 1937)
Nov 1918 – 10 Mar 1919	*Ahmed Tevfik Pasha* (for 2nd time)
10 Mar – 22 May 1919	*Damad (Adil) Ferid Pasha* (for 1st time) (b. Istanbul 1853; d. Nice 6 Oct 1923)
22 May – 21 Jul 1919	*Damad (Adil) Ferid Pasha* (for 2nd time)
21 Jul – 4 Oct 1919	*Damad (Adil) Ferid Pasha* (for 3rd time)
6 Oct 1919 – 2 Mar 1920	*Ali Rıza Pasha* (b. Istanbul 1859; d. Istanbul 31 Oct 1932)
8 Mar – 2 Apr 1920	*Salih Pasha*, later *Salih Hulûsi Kezrak* (b. Istanbul 1864; d. 24 Oct 1939)
5 Apr – 2 Aug 1920	*Damad (Adil) Ferid Pasha* (for 4th time)
4 Aug – 18 Oct 1920	*Damad (Adil) Ferid Pasha* (for 5th time)

21 Oct 1920 – 17 Nov   *Ahmed Tevfik Pasha* (for 3rd 5ime)
     1922

National Governments in Anakara

24 Jan 1921 – 12 Jul 1922	*Fevzi Pasha* (from 1934: *Fevzi Çakmak*) (b. Istanbul 1876; d. 10 Apr 1950)
12 Jul 1922 – 14 Aug 1923	*Hüseyin Rauf Bey* (from 1934: *Orbay*) (b. Istanbul 1881)
14 aug – 30 Oct 1923	*Ali Fethi Bey* (from 1934: *Fethi Okyar*) (for 1st time) (b. Prilep, Macedonia, 1880; d. Istanbul 7 May 1943)

30 Oct 1923 – 5 Mar 1924: Ismet I

Prime Minister	*Mustafa Ismet Pasha* (from 1934: *Ismet Inönü*) (for 1st time) (b. Smyrna 25 Sep 1884; d. 26 Dec 1973)
Foreign Affairs	*Mustafa Ismet Pasha* (see above)
Home Affairs	*Ahmed Ferid Bey* (from 1934: *Ahmet Ferit Tek*) (b. Bursa 1877)
Justice	*Seyyid Bey* (d. 1924)
Defence	*Kâzim Pasha* (from 1934: *Kâzim Özalp*) (b. Veles 1880)
Finance	30 Oct – 31 Dec 1923: *Hasan Fehmi Bey* (from 1934: *Ataç*) (d. 17 Sep 1961)
	2 Jan – 5 Mar 1924: *Mustafa Abdülhalik Bey* (from 1934: *Abdülhalik Renda*) (b. Yanya 1881; d. Istanbul 30 Sep 1957)
Education	*Mustafa Nejati Bey* (b. 1894; d. Ankara Jan 1929)
Public Works	30 Oct 1923 – 13 Jan 1924: *Ahmed Muhtar*
	13 Jan – 5 Mar 1924: *Süleyman Sırrı Bey* (d. Ankara 14 Dec 1925)
Commerce	*Hasan Hüsnü Bey* (from 1934: *Hasan Saka*) (b. Trebizond 1886; d. Istanbul 29 Jul 1960)
Health	*Refik Bey* (from 1934: *Refik Saydam*) (b. Istanbul 1881; d. Istanbul 8 Jul 1942)

7 Mar – 21 Nov 1924: Ismet II

Prime Minister	*Mustafa Ismet Pasha* (for 2nd time) (see Ismet I)
Foreign Affairs	*Mustafa Ismet Pasha* (see Ismet I)
Home Affairs	8 Mar – 14 May 1924: *Ahmed Ferid Bey* (see Ismet I)
	14 May – 21 Nov 1924: *Rejep Bey* (from 1934: *Recep Peker*) (b. Istanbul 1888; d. Istanbul 2 Apr 1950)
Justice	*Mustafa Nejati Bey* (see Ismet I)

Defence	*Kâzım Pasha* (see Ismet I)
Finance	*Mustafa Abdülhalik Bey* (see Ismet I)
Education	*Hüseyin Vasıf Bey* (from 1934: *Çınar*) (b. Smyrna 1895; d. Moscow 2 Jun 1935)
Public Works	*Süleyman Sırrı Bey* (see Ismet I)
Commerce	Post abolished
Agriculture	7 Mar – 10 Sep 1924: *Zekâi Bey* (from 1934: *Apaydın*) 10 Sep – 21 Nov 1924: *Shükrü Kaya Bey* (from 1934: *Şükrü Kaya*) (b. Istanköy 1884; d. Istanbul 1959)
Trade	*Hasan Hüsnü Bey* (see Ismet I)
Health	*Refik Bey* (see Ismet I)

21 Nov 1924 – 3 Mar 1925: Fethi

Prime Minister	*Ali Fethi Bey* (for 2nd time) (see National Governments in Ankara)
Foreign Affairs	*Shükrü Kaya Bey* (see Ismet II)
Home Affairs	21 Nov 1924 – 5 Jan 1925: *Rejep Bey* (see Ismet II) 6 Jan – 3 Mar 1925: *Jemil Bey*
Justice	*Mahmud Esad Bey* (from 1934: *Bozkurt*) (b. Karaferria 1874; d. 21 Dec 1943)
Defence	*Ali Fethi Bey* (see National Governments in Ankara)
Navy (new post)	29 Dec 1924 – 3 Mar 1925: *Ihsan Bey*
Finance	2 Jan – 3 Mar 1925: *Mustafa Abdülhalik Bey* (see Ismet I)
Education	*Sarajoghlu Shükrü Bey* (from 1934: *Şükrü Saracoglu*) (b. Ödemish 1887; d. Istanbul 27 Dec 1953)
Public Works	*Feyzi*
Agriculture	*Hasan Fehmi Bey* (see Ismet I)
Trade	*Ali Jenani Bey*
Health	*Mazhar Bey*

3 Mar 1925 – 2 Nov 1927: Ismet III

Prime Minister	*Mustafa Ismet Pasha* (for 3rd time) (see Ismet I)
Foreign Affairs	*Tevfik Rüshtü Bey* (from 1934: *Tevfik Rüştü Aras*) (b. Canakkale 1883)
Home Affairs	*Jemil Bey* (see Fethi)
Justice	*Mahmud Esad Bey* (see Fethi)
Education	3 Mar – 4 Nov 1925: *Hamdullah Suphi Bey* (from 1935: *Tanrıöver*) (b. 1886) 4 Nov 1925 – 2 Nov 1927: *Mustafa Nejati Bey* (see Ismet I)
Defence	*Rejep Bey* (see Ismet II)

Navy	*Ihsan Bey* (see Fethi)
Finance	3 Mar 1925 – 14 Jul 1926: *Hasan Hüsnü Bey* (see Ismet I)
	14 Jul 1926 – 1 Nov 1927: *Mustafa Abdülhalik Bey* (see Ismet I)
Public Works	3 Mar – 14 Dec 1925: *Süleyman Sırrı Bey* (see Ismet I)
	15 Jan 1926 – 1 Nov 1927: *Behich Bey* (from 1934: *Behiç Erkin*) (b. 1876)
Health	*Refik Bey* (see Ismet I)
Trade	3 Mar 1925 – 17 May 1926: *Ali Jenani Bey* (see Fethi)
	17 May 1926 – 1 Nov 1927: *Mustafa Rahmi Bey* (from 1934: *Köken*)
Agriculture	*Mehmed Sabri Bey*

3 Nov 1927 – 25 Sep 1930: Ismet IV

Prime Minister	*Mustafa Ismet Pasha* (for 4th time) (see Ismet I)
Foreign Affairs	*Tevfik Rüshtü Bey* (see Ismet III)
Home Affairs	*Shükrü Kaya Bey* (see Ismet II)
Justice	3 Nov 1927 – 22 Sep 1930: *Mahmud Esad Bey* (see Fethi)
Defence	*Mustafa Abdülhalik Bey* (see Ismet I)
Finance	*Sarajoghlu Shükrü Bey* (see Fethi)
Education	3 Nov 1927 – 1 Jan 1929: *Mustafa Nejati Bey* (see Ismet I)
	27 Feb – 7 Apr 1929: *Hüseyin Vasıf Bey* (see Ismet II)
	10 Apr – 2 Sep 1930: *Jemal Hüsnü Bey*
	16 – 25 Sep 1930: *Mahmud Esad Bey* (see Fethi)
Public Works	3 Nov 1927 – 11 Oct 1928: *Behich Bey* (see Ismet III)
	11 Oct 1928 – 22 Sep 1930: *Rejep Bey* (see Ismet II)
Agriculture	1 Nov 1927 – 16 Jan 1928: *Mustafa Rahmi Bey* (see Ismet III)
	16 Jan 1928: absorbed into the re-established Commerce ministry
Commerce	16 Jan 1928: re-established
	16 Jan 1928 – 28 May 1929: *Mustafa Rahmi Bey* (see Ismet III)
	29 May 1929 – 25 Sep 1930: *Shakir Bey* (from 1934: *Şakir Kesebir*) (b. Veles 1889)
Health	*Refik Bey* (see Işmet I)
Trade	3 Nov 1927 – 16 Jan 1928: *Mustafa Rahmi Bey* (see Ismet III)
	16 Jan 1928: combined with the Commerce ministry

Tuscany

Earlier Florence

HEADS OF STATE

Persons paramount in the Republic of Florence

House of Medici

8 Apr 1492	*Piero II*, son of Lorenzo I, the Magnificent (b. 15 Feb 1471; d. 28 Dec 1503)
1494	Medici exiled

1494 – 1498	*Girolamo Savonarola* (b. Ferrara 21 Sep 1452; d. Florence 23 May 1498)
22 Sep/1 Nov 1502 – 1 Sep 1512	*Piero Soderini* (b. Florence 18 May 1452; d. Rome 13 Jun 1522) life gonfalonier

House of Medici

Sep 1512 – 1513	*Giovanni* (b. 1475; d. 1521) from 9 Mar 1513: Pope Leo X
1513 – 4 May 1519	*Lorenzo II*, son of Piero II (b. 9 Sep 1492)
1521 – 1527	*Alessandro*, illegitimate son of Giulio de' Medici (Pope Clement VII) who was nephew of Lorenzo I (for 1st time) (b. 1510; d. 5 Jan 1537) banished from 1527 to 12 Aug 1530; and *Ippolito*, illegitimate son of Giuliano, Duc de Nemours, who was son of Lorenzo I
1531 – 5 Jan 1537	*Alessandro* (for 2nd time) from 1532: Duke of Florence
28 Feb 1537	*Cosimo I*, son of Giovanni de' Medici (b. 11 Jun 1519) from Aug 1569: Grand Duke of Tuscany

Grand Dukes of Tuscany

Aug 1569	*Cosimo I*, previously Duke of Florence
21 Apr 1574	*Francesco Maria*, son (b. 25 Mar 1541)
19 Oct 1587	*Ferdinando I*, brother (b. 30 Jul 1549)
14 Feb 1609	*Cosimo II*, son (b. 12 May 1590)
28 Feb 1621	*Ferdinando II*, son (b. 14 Jul 1610)
23 May 1670	*Cosimo III*, son (b. 14 Aug 1642)
31 Oct 1723	*Gian Gastone*, son (b. 26 May 1671)

House of Lorraine-Habsburg

9 Jul 1737	*Francis II*, son of Duke Leopold Joseph Hyacinth of Lorraine (b. 8 Dec 1708) from 13 Sep 1745: Holy Roman Emperor Francis I; married to Maria Theresa, Archduchess of Austria
18 Aug 1765	*Leopold I*, son (b. 5 May 1747; d. 1 Mar 1792) from 20 Feb 1790: King Leopold II of Hungary; from 30 Sep 1790: Archduke Leopold II of Austria and Holy Roman Emperor Leopold II
21 Jul 1790	*Ferdinand III*, son (for 1st time) (b. 6 May 1769) Elector of Salzburg from 27 Apr 1803 to 26 Dec 1805 and Grand Duke of Würzburg from 25 Sep 1806 to 30 May 1814
1801	*Louis of Bourbon-Parma*, King of Etruria
1808	Annexed to France
1809	*Elisa Baciocchi* (b. 3 Jan 1777; d. Monfalcone 9 Aug 1820) Grand Duchess
1814	*Ferdinand III* (for 2nd time)
21 Jul 1824	*Leopold II*, son (b. 3 Oct 1797; d. 29 Jan 1870)
21 Jul – 16 Aug 1859	*Ferdinand IV*, son (b. 10 Jun 1835; d. 17 Jan 1908)
1860	Tuscany united with Sardinia

MEMBERS OF GOVERNMENT

Prime Ministers

1815 – 13 Apr 1844	*Vittorio, Count Fossombroni* (b. Arezzo 15 Nov 1754; d. Florence 13 Apr 1844)
Apr 1844 – 25 Oct 1845	*Prince Neri (III) Corsini* (b. 1771; d. 25 Oct 1845)
Sep 1847 – Jun 1848	*Prince Neri (IV) Corsini, Marquis of Lajatico*, nephew (b. 1805; d. London 1 Dec 1859)
2 Jun – 30 Jul 1848	*Cosimo, Marquis Ridolfi* (b. Florence 28 Nov 1794; d. Florence 5 Mar 1865)
17 Aug – 27 Oct 1848	*Gino, Marquis Capponi* (for 1st time) (b. Florence 14 Sep 1792; d. 3 Feb 1876)
27 Oct 1848 – 21 Feb 1849	*Francesco Domenico Guerrazzi* (for 1st time) (b. Leghorn 12 Aug 1804; d. Fitto di Cecina 23 Sep 1873)
21 Feb – 27 Mar 1849	*Giuseppe Montanelli* (b. Fucchino 21 Jan 1813; d. 17 Jul 1862) Head of triumvirate
27 Mar – 12 Apr 1849	*Francesco Domenico Guerrazzi* (for 2nd time) Dictator

11 Mar – Apr 1849	*Gino, Marquis Capponi* (for 2nd time) acting on behalf of the Grand Duke
Apr – 24 May 1849	—— *Serristori* nominated Commissioner by the Grand Duke
24 May 1849 – 27 Apr 1859	*Giovanni Baldasseroni* (b. Leghorn 1790; d. Florence 19 Oct 1876)
27 Apr – 8 May 1859	*Ubaldino Peruzzi* (b. Florence 2 Apr 1822; d. 9 Sep 1891)
8 May 1859	*Carlo Boncompagni di Mombello* (from 1878: *Count of Lamporo*) (b. Saluggia, Turin, 25 Jul 1804; d. Turin 15 Dec 1880) Sardinian Commissioner-general
8 May – 1 Aug 1859	*Bettino Ricasoli, Count Brolio* (b. Florence 9 Mar 1809; d. Brolio 23 Oct 1880)
1 Aug 1859 – 22 Mar 1860	*Bettino Ricasoli, Count Brolio*, Commissioner-general (see above)
22 Mar 1860	Incorporated in the Italian state
22 Mar – 31 Dec 1860	*Bettino Ricasoli, Count Brolio*, Governor-general (see above)
22 Mar – 31 Dec 1860	*Prince Eugene Emmanuel of Savoy* (b. Paris 14 Apr 1816; d. Turin 15 Dec 1888) Italian governor and commander-in-chief
1 Jan 1861	Became an integral part of the Kingdom of Italy

Ukraine

HEADS OF STATE

Hetmans

1648 – 25 Aug 1657	*Bohdan Khmelnytsky* (b. Chyhyryn(?) 1593; d. 26 Aug 1657)
Aug – Sep 1657	*Yury Khmelnytsky*, son (for 1st time) (b. Subbotov c. 1641; d. Kamyanets-Podilsky 1685) became a monk under the name of Gideon in 1663
Sep 1657 – 1659	*Ivan Vyhovsky* (b. 1664)
1659 – 1663	*Yury Khmelnytsky* (for 2nd time)
1663 – autumn 1665(?)	*Pavlo Teterya* (d. 1667) Hetman on the Right Bank
17 Jun 1663 – 17 Jul 1668	*Ivan Bryukhovetsky* (b. 7 Jun 1623; d. Dikanka 17 Jul 1668) Hetman on the Left Bank

Oct – end of 1665	*Stepan Opara*, Right Bank
1666 – 29 Sep 1676	*Petro Doroshenko* (b. 1627; d. Yaropoltse 19 Nov 1698) Right Bank
1668 – 28 Jun 1672	*Demyan Mnohohrishny* (d. Selenga 1698) Left Bank
2 Sep 1670 – 27 Mar 1674	*Mykhailo Khanenko* (b. 1620; d. 1680) Right Bank
28 Jun 1672 – Jul 1687	*Ivan Samoilovych* (d. Yeniseisk 1690) Left Bank
1674 – 1679	*Ostap Hohol* (d. 1679) Right Bank
1677 – 1681	*Yury Khmelnytsky* (for 3rd time) Prince of Ukraine, under Turkish suzerainty
1683 – 1684	*Stepan Kunytsky*, Right Bank
1684 – 1689	*Andriy Mohyla*, Right Bank
1687 – 8 Jul 1709	*Ivan Mazepa* (b. Kiev 20 Mar 1632(?); d. Bendery 2 Oct 1709) Hetman of the Left Bank until 1704, the Right Bank being under Polish control, from 1704 *de facto*, from 1708 *de jure* Hetman of the whole
1689 – 1692	*Hryshko*, Right Bank
1692 – 1704	*Samoil Ivanovych*, Right Bank
1708 – 1722	*Ivan Skoropadsky* (d. 1722) Left Bank
1710 – 1714	*Pylyp Orlyk* (b. 11 Oct 1672; d. 24 May 1742) Right Bank
1722 – Dec 1724	(acting:) *Pavlo Polubotok* (b. c. 1660; d. Dec 1724) Left Bank
12 Oct 1727 – 28 Jan 1734	*Danylo Apostol* (b. 14 Dec 1654; d. 28 Jan 1734) Left Bank
1734	*Prince Shakhovskoi*, in charge of Governing Council
1747/1750 – 1764	*Kyrylo Rozumovsky* (b. 29 Mar 1728; d. 21 Jan 1803)
1674	Hetmanate abolished
1917/18	Ukrainian Peoples' Republic established in Kiev

Presidents

Apr 1918 – Dec 1918	*Pavilo Skoropadsky* (b. Wiesbaden 15 May 1873; d. Murnau 26 Apr 1945)
Feb – Dec 1919	*Simon Petlyura* (for 1st time) (b. Poltava 5 May 1879; d. Paris 25 May 1926)
May – Aug 1920	*Alexander Shulhyn* (b. Sochvyno 30 Jul 1889; d. Paris 4 Mar 1960) Prime Minister and Foreign Minister
28 Dec 1920	Incorporation of the Ukraine in the USSR
1920 – 25 May 1926	*Simon Petlyura* (for 2nd time) President in exile
1926 – 17 Jan 1954	*Andreas Livytsky* (b. Liplava 8 Apr 1879; d. Karlsruhe 17 Jan 1954) President in exile

Union of Soviet Socialist Republics

Formerly Russia.

HEADS OF STATE

Grand Dukes of Moscow

27 Mar 1462	*Ivan III*, son of Vassily III (b. 22 Jan 1440)
27 Oct 1505	*Vassily IV*, son (b. 25 Mar 1479)
3 Dec 1533	*Ivan IV*, the Terrible, son (b. 25 Aug 1530) from 16 Jan 1547: Tsar
	Regent:
	3 Dec 1533 – 3 Apr 1538: *Yelena*, mother
	1538 – 1547: Regency disputed between Belsky and Shuisky families

Tsars

16 Jan 1547	*Ivan IV*, previously Grand Duke
17 Mar 1584	*Fyodor I*, son (b. 11 May 1557)
7 Jan 1598	*Boris Fyodorovich Godunov*, brother-in-law (b. 1552)
13 Apr 1605	*Fyodor II*, son (b. 1589) deposed and murdered
10 Jun 1605	*'First False Dmitry'* (an imposter, real name possibly *Gregory Otrepiev*, who claimed to be Dmitry, son of Ivan IV, who actually died in 1591) deposed and murdered
17 May 1606 – 17 Jul 1610*	*Vassily V Ivanovich Shuisky* (b. 1552; d. 22 Sep 1612) deposed
17 Jul 1610 – 21 Feb 1613	Interregnum, Moscow occupied by Poland from Sep 1610 to Nov 1612

House of Romanov

21 Feb 1613	*Michael III*, son of Fyodor Nikitich Romanov (b. 12 Jul 1591)
*Aug 1607 – 11 Dec 1610	*'Second False Dmitry'*, also known as 'The Felon of Tushino', real name unknown; pretended that he was the First False Dmitry and had escaped death in 1606; established court as rival Tsar and received widespread support, murdered

12 Jul 1645	*Alexis*, son (b. 10 Mar 1629)
8 Feb 1676	*Fyodor III*, son (b. 30 May 1661)
27 Apr 1682	*Peter I*, the Great, half-brother (b. 30 May 1672) from

2 Nov 1721: Emperor
Regents:
Apr – May 1682: *Natalie Naryshkina*, mother
May 1682 – 1689: *Sofia Aleksyeevna*, sister of Fyodor III
Co-ruler, in name only:
26 May 1682 – 29 Jan 1696: *Ivan V*, brother of Fyodor III (b. 27 Aug 1666)

Emperors and Empresses

2 Nov 1721	*Peter I*, previously Tsar
8 Feb 1725	*Catherine I (Marta Skowronska)*, second wife (b. 1684)
17 May 1727	*Peter II*, grandson of Peter I (b. 25 Oct 1715)
28 Jan 1730	*Anna*, daughter of Ivan V (b. 25 Jan 1693)
28 Oct 1740	*Ivan VI*, son of Prince Anton Ulrich of Brunswick and great-nephew of Empress Anna (b. 23 Aug 1740; d. 5 Jul 1764) deposed

Regents:
28 Oct – Nov 1740: *Ernest Johann Biron, Duke of Courland*
Nov 1740 – 5 Dec 1741: *Anna*, mother of Ivan VI and neice of Peter I

5 Dec 1741	*Elizabeth*, daughter of Peter I (b. 29 Dec 1709)

House of Romanov-Holstein-Gottorp

5 Jan 1762	*Peter III (Karl Peter Ulrich, Duke of Holstein-Gottorp)* nephew (b. 21 Feb 1728; d. 17 Jul 1762) formally abdicated 10 Jul 1762
9 Jul 1762	*Catherine II*, the Great, wife of Peter III and daughter of Duke Christian August of Anhalt-Zerbst (b. 2 May 1729)
17 Nov 1796	*Paul*, son (b. 1 Oct 1754) assassinated
24 May 1801	*Alexander I*, son (b. 23 Dec 1777)
1 Dec 1825	*Nicholas I*, brother (b. 6 Jul 1796)
2 Mar 1855	*Alexander II*, son (b. 29 Apr 1818)
13 Mar 1881	*Alexander III*, son (b. 10 Mar 1845)
1 Sep 1894 – 15 Mar 1917	*Nicholas II*, son (b. 18 May 1868; d. (presumed shot) 17 Jul 1918)
15 Mar 1917	Formation of the Russian Socialist Federative Soviet

	Republic, followed by separate republics in other parts of the Russian Empire
1920 – 1921	Other republics linked by treaty with the RSFSR
6 Jul 1923	Constitution of the Union of Soviet Socialist Republics

Pretenders

15 Mar 1917 – 13 Jan 1918	*Michael IV*, brother of Nicholas II (b. 22 Nov 1878; d. 1918)
31 Aug 1924	*Kyrill V* (b. 12 Oct 1876; d. Paris)
12 Oct 1938	*Vladimir*, son (b. 30 Aug 1917)

Presidents (Chairmen of the Presidium of the Supreme Soviet)

7 – (?)Nov 1917	*Lev Borisovich Kamenev* (b. Tylis 22 Jul 1883; d. Moscow 25 Aug 1936)
(?)Nov 1917 – Mar 1919	*Yakov Mikhailovich Sverdlov* (b. Nizhny Novgorod 3 Jun 1885; d. Moscow 16 Mar 1919)
Mar 1919 (1923) – 19 March 1946	*Mikhail Ivanovich Kalinin* (b. Vershnaya Troitsa 7 Nov 1875; d. Moscow 3 Jun 1946)

MEMBERS OF GOVERNMENT

Chairmen of the Council of Ministers

1812 – 1816	*Count* (from 1814: *Prince*) *Nikolai Ivanovich Saltykov* (b. 1736; d. 1816)
1816 – 1827	*Prince Pyotr Vasilyevich Lopukhin* (b. 1753; d. 1827)
1827 – 1832	*Count Viktor Pavlovich Kochubei* (b. Ukraine 22 Nov 1768; d St Petersburg 15 Jun 1834)
1834 – 1838	*Count Nikolai Nikolaevich Novosiltsev* (b. 1761; d. St Petersburg 20 Apr 1838)
1838 – 1847	*Count* (from 1839: *Prince*) *Ilarion Vasilyevich Vasilchikov* (b. 1777; d. 1847)
1847 – 1848	*Count Vasily Vasilyevich Levashov* (b. 21 Oct 1783; d. 5 Oct 1848)
1848 – 1856	*Prince Aleksandr Ivanovich Chernyshev* (b. 10 Jan 1787; d. Castellamare, Southern Italy, 20 Jul 1857)
1856 – Jan 1861	*Aleksyei Fyodorovich Orlov* (from 1856: *Prince*) (b. Moscow 19 Oct 1786; d. St Petersburg 21 May 1861)

Jan 1861 – 2 Mar 1864	*Dmitry Nikolaevich, Count Bludov* (b. Shuya 16 Apr 1785; d. St Petersburg 2 Mar 1864)
7 Mar 1864 – 13 Jan 1865	*Prince Pavel Pavlovich Gagarin* (b. Moscow 15 Mar 1789; d. St. Petersburg 4 Mar 1872)
1872 – 1877	*Pavel Nikolaevich Ignatyev* (from 1877: *Count*) (b. 18 Jun 1797; d. St Petersburg 1 Jan 1880)
1877 – 16 Oct 1881	*Count Pyotr Aleksandrovich Valuev* (b. Moscow 4 Oct 1814; d. St Petersburg 18 Feb 1890)
1881 – beginning of 1887	*Mikhail* (from 1890: *Count*) *Reutern* (b. Poryechye 24 Sep 1820; d. Tsarskoe Selo 23 Aug 1890)
Beginning of 1887 – 15 Jun 1895	*Nikolai Khristianovich Bunge* (b. Kiev 23 Nov 1823; d. St Petersburg 15 Jun 1895)
1895 – 11 Jun 1903	*Ivan Nikolaevich Durnovo* (b. Chernigov 13 Mar 1834; d. on a train between Königsberg and Marienburg 11 Jun 1903)
29 Aug 1903 – 30 Oct 1905	*Sergyei Yulyevich* (from 1905: *Count*) *Witte* (b. Tiflis 29 Jul 1894; d. St Petersburg 13 Mar 1915)

Ministers for Foreign Affairs

1800 – 1802	*Peter Ludwig, Count von der Pahlen* (b. Palms, Estonia 28 Jun 1745; d. Mitau 25 Feb 1826)
20 Sep 1802 – 1804	*Count Aleksandr Romanovich Vorontsov* (b. 15 Sep 1741; d. Moscow 14 Dec 1805)
1804 – 1807	*Adam Jerzy, Prince Czartoryski* (b. Warsaw 14 Jan 1770; d. Chateau Montfermeil, Paris, 15 Jul 1861)
1807 – 1814	*Count Nikolai Petrovich Rumyanzev* (b. 1754; d. 15 Jan 1826)
1815 – 1816	(acting:) *Ivan Andreevich Weidemeyer* (b. 3 Dec 1752; d. St Petersburg 13 Mar 1820)
1816 – 1817	*Giovanni Antonio, Count Capodistria* (b. Corfù 11 Feb 1776; d. Nauplia 9 Oct 1831)
1817 – 1856	*Karl Robert, Count Nesselrode* (b. Lisbon 14 Dec 1780; d. St Petersburg 23 Mar 1862) Vice-Chancellor from 1828 Chancellor in 1845
15 Apr 1856 – 3 Apr 1882	*Prince Aleksandr Mikhailovich Gorchakov* (b. Haapsalu 15 Jun 1798; d. Baden-Baden 11 Mar 1883) Vice-Chancellor from 1862, Chancellor in 1867
Apr 1882 – 26 Jan 1895	*Nikolai Karlovich von Giers* (b. Radziwillov 9 May 1820; d. St Petersburg 26 Jan 1895) Deputy: Summer 1892, Jan – Mar 1895, Aug/Sep 1896: *Nikolai Pavlovich Shishkin* (b. 1830; d. 24 Nov 1902)

Mar 1895 – 31 Aug 1896	*Aleksei Borisovich, Prince Lobanov-Rostovsky* (b. Voronezh Province 30 Dec 1824; d. Shepetovka 31 Aug 1896)
Sep 1896 – 21 Jun 1900	*Count Mikhail Nikolaevich Muravyov* (b. St Petersburg 19 Apr 1845; d. St Petersburg 21 Jun 1900)
(Jun 1900) Jan 1901 – (1906)	*Vladimir Nikolaevich, Count Lamzdorf* (b. 6 Jan 1845; d. San Remo 19 Mar 1907)

Ministers for Home Affairs

1803 – 1807	*Count Viktor Pavlovich Kochubei* (for 1st time) (see Chairmen of the Council of Ministers)
1807 – 1811	*Aleksei Borisovich Kurakin* (b. 1755; d. 1829)
1811 – 5 Aug 1819	*Opsi Petrovich Kozodavlev* (b. 9 Apr 1754; d. 5 Aug 1819)
1819 – 1823/25	*Count Viktor Pavlovich Kochubei* (for 2nd time)
1823/25 – 1827	*Vasily Sergyeevich Lanskoi* (b. 1754; d. 1831)
1828 – 1831	*Arseny Andreevich* (from 1830: *Count*) *Zakrevski* (b. Bernikov 24 Sep 1786; d. Florence 23 Jan 1865)
1832 – 1839	*Dmitry Nikolaevich* (from 1842: *Count*) *Bludov* (see Chairmen of the Council of Ministers)
1839 – 1841/42	*Count Aleksandr Grigoryevich Stroganov* (b. 1795; d. 1891)
1841/42 – 1852	*Lev Aleksyeevich* (from 1849: *Count*) *Perovsky* (b. 20 Sep 1792; d. St Petersburg 21 Nov 1856)
1852 – 1855	*Dmitry Gavrilovich Bibikov* (b. 29 Mar 1791; d. St Petersburg 6 Mar 1870)
1855 – Apr 1861	*Sergyei Stepanovich* (from 1861: *Count*) *Lanskoi* (b. 3 Jan 1788; d. St Petersburg 7 Feb 1862)
1861 – 1868	*Pyotr Aleksandrovich* (from 1880: *Count*) *Valuev* (see Chairmen of the Council of Ministers)
1868 – end of 1877	*Aleksandr Egorovich Timashov* (b. 15 Apr 1818; d. St Petersburg 1 Feb 1893)
1878 – Aug 1880	*Lev Savych Makov* (b. 1830; d. 1883)
1880 – Mar 1881	*Count Mikhail Tarielovich Loris-Melikov* (b. Tiflis 2 Nov 1825; d. Nice 24 Dec 1888)
1 May 1881 – 11 Jun 1882	*Count Nikolai Pavlovich Ignatyev* (b. St Petersburg 29 Jan 1832; d. Krupodernitsa 3 Jul 1908)
Jun 1882 – 18 May 1889	*Count Dmitry Andreevich Tolstoi* (b. 14 Mar 1823; d. 18 May 1889)
18 May 1889 – Apr 1895	*Ivan Nikolaevich Durnovo* (see Chairmen of the Council of Ministers)

Apr 1895 – Nov 1899	*Ivan Longinovich Goremykin* (b. Novgorod 8 Nov 1839; d. in the Caucasus 24 Dec 1917)
1900 – 15 Apr 1902	*Dmitry Sergyeevich Sipyagin* (b. 20 Mar 1853; d. St Petersburg 15 Apr 1902)
1902 – 28 Jul 1904	*Vyacheslav Konstantinovich von Plehwe* (b. Meshchovsk 20 Apr 1846; d. St Petersburg 28 Jul 1904)
8 Sep 1904 – 30 Jan 1905	*Prince Pyotr Danilovich Svyatopolk Mirsky* (b. 30 Aug 1857; d. 1914)
2 Feb – 30 Oct 1905	*Aleksandr Grigoryevich Bulygin* (b. 1851; d. 1919)

Finance Ministers

1802 – 1806	*Count Aleksyei Ivanovich Vasilyev* (b. 11 Mar 1742; d. St Petersburg 27 Aug 1807)
1807 – 1810	*Fyodor Aleksandrovich Golubtsov* (b. 3 Jan 1759; d. Volgovo 18 Mar 1829)
1810 – 1823	*Dmitry Aleksandrovich Guryev* (from 1819: *Count*) (b. 1751; d. St Petersburg 12 Oct 1825)
1823 – 1844	*Georg (E. F.) Cancrin* (from 1829: *Count*) (b. Hanau 8 Dec 1764; d. St Petersburg 22 Sep 1845)
1844 – 1852	*Count Fyodor Pavlovich Vronchenko* (b. 1779; d. St Petersburg 18 Apr 1852)
1852 – 1858	*Peter von Brock* (b. 1 Sep 1805; d. 9 Feb 1875)
1858 – 1862	*Aleksandr Maximovich Knyazhevich* (b. 22 Oct 1792; d. St Petersburg 14 Mar 1872)
1862 – 1878	*Mikhail Reutern* (see Chairmen of the Council of Ministers)
Jul 1878 – end of 1880	*Samuel Greigh* (b. Nikolaev 21 Dec 1827; d. Berlin 22 Mar 1887)
1880 – Feb 1881	*Aleksandr Aggeevich Abaza* (b. 6 Aug 1821; d. St Petersburg 6 Feb 1895)
Mar 1881 – Jan 1887	*Nikolai Khristianovich Bunge* (see Chairmen of the Council of Ministers)
Jan 1887 – 15 Sep 1892	*Ivan Aleksyeevich Vyshnegradsky* (b. 1 Jan 1832; d. St Petersburg 6 Apr 1895)
Sep 1892 – 29 Aug 1903	*Sergyei Yulyevich Witte* (see Chairmen of the Council of Ministers)
31 Aug 1903 – 17 Feb 1904	*Eduard Pleske* (b. 6 Nov 1852; d. St Petersburg 9 May 1904)
10 Apr 1904 – 6 Nov 1905	*Vladimir Nikolaevich Kokovtsev* (b. 18 Apr 1853; d. France 29 Jan 1943)

Ministers of Justice

1802 – 1803	*Gavriil Romanovich Derzhavin* (b. Kazan government 13 Jul 1743; d. Swanka 21 Jul 1816)
1803 – 1810	*Prince Pyotr Vasilyevich Lopukhin* (see Chairmen of the Council of Ministers)
1810 – 1814	*Ivan Ivanovich Dmitriev* (b. Simbirsk government 20 Sep 1760; d. Moscow 15 Oct 1837)
1814 – 1817	*Dmitry Prokofyevich Troshchinsky* (b. 1754; d. 1829)
1817 – 1827	*Prince Dmitry Ivanovich Lobanov-Rostovsky* (1 Oct 1758; d. St Petersburg 7 Aug 1838)
1829 – 1839	*Dmitry Nikolaevich Dashkov* (b. 5 Jan 1789; d. St Petersburg 8 Dec 1839)
1839 – 1841	*Dmitry Nikolaevich Bludov* (see Chairman of the Council of Ministers)
1841 – 1862	*Count Viktor Nikitych Panin* (b. 9 Apr 1801; d. Nice 24 Apr 1874)
1862 – 28 Apr 1867	*Dmitry Nikolaevich Zamyatin* (b. Novgorod Province 1805; d. 1881)
1867	*Prince D. N. Urusov*
Autumn 1867 – 1878	*Count Konstantin Ivanovich von der Pahlen* (b. 1833; d. (?))
1878 – 18 Nov 1885	*Dmitry Nikolaevich Nabokov* (30 Jun 1826; d. St Petersburg 28 Mar 1904)
18 Nov 1885 – 13 Jan 1894	*Nikolai Avksentyevich Manasein* (b. Kazan Government 1 Dec 1834; d. St Petersburg 28 Sep 1895)
13 Jan 1894 – Jan 1905	*Nikolai Valerianovich Muranyov* (b. 9 Oct 1850; d. Rome 14 Dec 1908)
Jan 1905 – May 1906	*Mikhail Grigoryevich Akimov* (b. 20 Nov 1847; d. 1911)

Ministers of Education

1802 – 1810	*Count Pyotr Vasilyevich Zavadovski* (b. 1739; d. St Petersburg 22 Jan 1812)
1810 – 1814	*Count Aleksyei Kirillovich Razumovsky* (b. 23 Sep 1748; d. 17 Apr 1822)
1814 – 1824	*Prince Aleksandr Nikolaevich Golitsyn* (b. 1773/74; d. Gaspa-Aleksandriya 4 Dec 1844)
17 May 1824 – 7 May 1828	*Aleksandr Semyonovich Shishkov* (b. 20 Mar 1754; d. St Petersburg 21 Apr 1841)
1828 – 1833	*Prince Karl Lieven* (b. Kiev 12 Feb 1767; d. Senten 12 Jan 1845)

1833 – 1848	*Sergyei Semyonovich* (from 1846: *Count*) *Urarov* (b. Moscow 5 Sep 1786; d. Moscow 16 Sep 1855)
1850 – 1853	*Prince Platon Aleksandrovich Shirinsky-Shikhmatov* (b. 29 Nov 1790; d. St Petersburg 17 May 1853)
1853/54 – 1858	*Avraam Sergyeevich Norov* (b. 2(12?) Oct 1795; d. St Petersburg 4 Feb 1869)
Mar 1858 – Jun 1861	*Evgraf Petrovich Kovalevsky* (b. 21 Dec 1790; d. St Petersburg 30 Mar 1867)
1861	*Count Evfimy Vasilyevich Putyatin* (b. 20 Nov 1803; d. Paris 28 Oct 1883)
6 Jan 1862 – 26 Apr 1866	*Alekandr Vasilyevich Golovnin* (b. St Petersburg 6 Apr 1821; d. St Petersburg 15 Nov 1886)
1866 – 1880	*Count Dmitry Andreevich Tolstoi* (see Ministers for Home Affairs)
6 May 1880 – Apr 1881	*Andrei Aleksandrovich Saburov* (b. 17 Aug 1837; d.(?))
5 Apr 1881 – Mar 1882	*Baron Alexander Nicolay* (b. Copenhagen 9 Mar 1821; d. Tiflis 15 Jul 1899)
1882 – 10 Jan 1898	*Ivan Davydovich Delyanov* (b. Moscow 12 Dec 1818; d. St Petersburg 10 Jan 1898)
1898 – 15 Mar 1901	*Nikolai Pavlovich Bogolyepov* (b. Serpuchov 9 Dec 1846; d. St Petersburg 15 Mar 1901)
7 Apr 1901 – 24 Apr 1902	*Pyotr Semyonovich Vannovsky* (b. 6 Dec 1822; d. St Petersburg 29 Feb 1904)
1902 – 1904	*Grigory Eduardovich von Sänger* (b. Novgorod 25 Mar 1853; d. (?))
23 Apr 1904 – 29 Oct 1905	*Vladimir Gavrilovich Glazov* (b. 12 Sep 1848; d. 1916)

Ministers of War

Oct 1802 – 1808	*Sergyei Kozmych Vyazminitinov* (from 1816: *Count*) (b. 18 Oct 1744; d. St Petersburg 27 Oct 1819)
1808 – 1810	*Count Aleksyei Andreevich Arakcheev* (b. Novgorod government 4 Oct 1769; d. Gruzino 3 May 1834)
1810 – 1812	(acting:) *Prince Michael Barclay de Tolly* (b. Luhde-Grosshoff 27 Dec 1761; d. Insterburg 26 May 1818)
1812 – 1815	*Andrei Ivanovich Gorchakov* (b. 1768; d. Moscow 27 Feb 1855)
1815 – 1819	*Pyotr Petrovich Konovitsyn* (b. 1766; d. 1822)
1819 – 1823	*Peter Baron Möller-Zakomelsky* (b. St Petersburg 1756; d. 21 Jun 1823)
1823/24 – 1827	*Aleksandr Ivanovich Tatishchev* (b. 19 Aug 1763; d. St

543

	Petersburg 29 Jun 1833)
1828 - 1852	*Count* (from 1841: *Prince*) *Aleksandr Ivanovich Chernyshev* (see Chairmen of the Council of Ministers)
Apr 1853 - Apr 1856	*Prince Vasily Andreevich Dolgorukov* (b. 1804; d. St Petersburg 18 Jan 1868)
1856 - 1861	*Nikolai Onufrievich Suchozanet* (b. 1794; d. 1871)
1861 - Mar 1881	*Dmitry Aleksyeevich Milyutin* (from 1878: *Count*) (b. Moscow 10 Jul 1816; d. Yalta 7 Feb 1912)
1881 - 1898	*Pyotr Semyonovich Vannovsky* (see Ministers of Education)
1898 - 1904	*Aleksyei Nikolaevich Kuropatkin* (b. 29 Mar 1848; d. Shamchurin 23 Jan 1925)
1904 - 4 Jul 1905	*Viktor Viktorovich Zakharov* (b. 1848; d. Saratov 5 Dec 1905)
4 Jul 1905 (-1909)	*Aleksandr Fyodorovich Rödiger* (b. 12 Jan 1854; d. Sevastopol 8 Feb 1920)

Ministers for the Navy

1802 - 1809	*Pavel Vasilyevich Chichagov* (b. 1762/65; d. 10 Sep 1849)
1809 - 1827	*Jean Francois Prévost de Sansac, Marquis de Traversay* (b. 1754; d. 31 May 1830)
1827 - 1836	*Berend Otto von Moller* (b. Mustel 19 Feb 1764; d. St Petersburg 17 Oct 1848)
1836 - 1853	*Prince Aleksandr Sergyeevich Menshikov* (b. 11 Sep 1787; d. St Petersburg 2 May 1869)
Mar 1855 - 1857	*Ferdinand Baron von Wrangel* (b. Livonia 9 Jan 1795; d. Dorpat 6 Jun 1870)
1857 - 1860	*Nikolai Fyodorovich Metlin* (b. 9 Aug 1804; d. St Petersburg 27 Oct 1884)
1860/62 - 1876	*Nikolai Karlovich Krabbe* (b. Georgia 1 Sep 1814; d. St Petersburg 15 Jan 1876)
1876 - 1880	*Stepan Stepanovich Lesovsky* (b. 1817; d. St Petersburg 9 Mar 1884)
1881	*Aleksyei Aleksyeevich Peshchurov* (b. 1834; d. St Petersburg 9 Oct 1891)
1882 - 1888	*Ivan Aleksyeevich Shestakov* (b. 1820; d. 1888)
1888 - 1895/96	*Nikolai Matveevich Chikhachov* (b. Tver government 29 Apr 1830)
1896 - 1903	*Pavel Petrovich Tyrtov* (b. 15 Jul 1836; d. St Petersburg 17 Mar 1903)

1903 – 1905   *Theodor Avellan* (b. Lovisa, Finland, 12 Sep 1839; d. St Petersburg 30 Nov 1916)

Ministers of Agriculture

1837 – 1856   *Pavel Dmitrievich Kisilyov* (from 1839: *Count*) (b. 1788; d. Paris 26 Nov 1872)
1856 – 1857   *Vasily Aleksandrovich Sheremetev* (b. 31 Aug 1795; d. St Petersburg 23 Apr 1862)
1857 – 1862   *Mikhail Nikolaevich Muravyov* (from 1865: *Count*) (b. 7 Oct 1796; d. Luga 10 Sep 1866)
1862 – 1872   *Aleksandr Aleksandrovich Zelenoi* (b. 1818(?); d. 21 Mar 1880)
1872 – 1879   *Count Pyotr Aleksandrovich Valuev* (see Chairmen of the Council of Ministers)
1879 – 1881   (acting:) *Prince Andrei Aleksandrovich Lieven* (b. Simferopol 21 Jun 1839; d. St Petersburg 15 Mar 1913)
Mar – 1 May 1881   *Count Nikolai Pavlovich Ignatyev* (see Ministers for Home Affairs)
May 1881 – 17 Jan 1893   *Mikhail Nikolaevich Ostrovsky* (b. Moscow 11 Apr 1827; d. St Petersburg 7 Aug 1901)
9 Apr 1893 – 1905   *Aleksyei Sergyeevich Ermolov* (b. 24 Nov 1847; d. St Petersburg 18 Jan 1917)

Ministers of Transport
1801 – 1809   *Count Nikolai Petrovich Rumyantsev* (b. 1754; d. 1826)
1809 – 1812   *Prince Georg von Oldenburg*, son of Grand Duke Peter (b. Rastatt 9 May 1784; d. Tver 27 Dec 1812)
1812 – 1818   *Frants-Pavel Pavlovich Devolant*, originally *Sainte de Wollant* (b. Brabant 1 Oct 1752; d. St Petersburg 12 Dec 1818)
1819 – 1822   *Augustin A. Béthencourt y de Molina* (b. Teneriffe 2 Feb 1758; d. St Petersburg 26 Jul 1824)
1822 – 16 Jul 1833   *Duke Alexander of Wurtemberg* (b. Mömpelgard 5 May 1771; d. 16 Jul 1833)
1833 – 5 May 1842   *Count Karl Friedrich Toll* (b. Keskefer 19 Apr 1777; d. St Petersburg 5 May 1842)
end of 1842 – Oct 1855   *Count Pyotr Andreevich Kleinmichel* (b. 11 Dec 1793; d. St Petersburg 15 Feb 1869)
1855 – 1862   *Konstantin Vladimirovich Chevkin* (b. 1802; d. 15 Nov 1875)

1862 – 1868	*Pavel Petrovich Melnikov* (b. 1804; d. 1880)
1868 – 1871	*Count Vladimir Aleksyeevich Bobrinsky* (b. 1824)
1871 – 1874	*Count Aleksyei Pavlovich Bobrinsky* (b. 1826; d. 1894)
1874 – end of 1888	*Konstantin Nikolaevich Posyet* (b. 21 Jan 1820; d. St Petersburg 8 May 1899)
19 Nov 1888 – 10 Apr 1889	*Hermann Paucker* (b. Mitau 24 Oct 1822; d. St Petersburg 10 Apr 1889)
1889 – Feb 1892	*Adolf von Hübbenet* (b. 12 Sep 1830; d. Paris 6 Apr 1901)
1892	*Sergyei Yulyevich Witte* (see Chairmen of the Council of Ministers)
1892 – 1894/95	*Apollon Konstantinovich Krivoshein* (b. 1833; d.(?))
Jan 1895 – Oct 1905	*Prince Mikhail Ivanovich Khilkov* (b. 1843 (1834?); d. 1909)

Tsar's household

3 Sep 1826 – 8 Sep 1852	*Prince Pyotr Mikhailovich Volkonsky* (b. 7 May 1776; d. Peterhof 8 Sep 1852)
1852 – 1870	*Count Vladimir Fyodorovich Adlerberg* (b. St Petersburg 18 Nov 1790; d. Moscow 20 Mar 1884)
1870 – 1881	*Count Aleksandr Vladimirovich Adlerberg* (b. 13 May 1818; d. Munich 4 Oct 1888)
1881 – 1897	*Count Illarion Ivanovich Vorontsov-Dashkov* (b. 8 Jun 1837; d. Alupka 27 Jan 1916)
17 Apr 1898 – 1917	*Baron Voldemar Adolf Andreas* (from 1913: *Count*) *Fredericksz* (b. St Petersburg 28 Nov 1838; d. Grankulla, Finland, 1 Jul 1927)

Combined Ministries (operational from 1905)

30 Oct 1905 – 5 May 1906: Witte

Prime Minister	*Count Sergyei Yulyevich Witte* (see Chairmen of the Council of Ministers)
Foreign Affairs	*Count Vladimir Nikolaevich Lamzdorf* (see Ministers for Foreign Affairs)
Home Affairs	*Pyotr Nikolaevich Durnovo* (b. Moscow Province 1845; d. Petrograd 25 Sep 1915)
Finance	*Ivan Pavlovich Shipov* (b. 1865; d.(?))
Justice	*Mikhail Grigoryevich Akimov* (see Ministers of Justice)

Education	*Count Ivan Ivanovich Tolstoi* (b. 30 May 1858)
War	*Aleksandr Fyodorovich Rödiger* (see Ministers of War)
Navy	*Aleksyei Aleksyeevich Birilev* (b. 28 Mar 1844; d. 1915)
Agriculture	30 Oct 1905 – 12 Mar 1906: *Nikolai Nikolaevich Kutler* (b. 1859; d. 1924)
	12 Mar – 5 May 1906: *Aleksyei Petrovich Nikolsky* (b. 1851)
Transport	*Klavdy Semyonovich Nemeshaev* (b. 1849)
Commerce and Industry	9 Nov 1905 – Feb 1906: *Vasily Ivanovich Timiryazev* (b. 1844/49; d. St Petersburg 1 Oct 1919)
	3 Mar – 5 May 1906 (acting:) *Mikhail Mikhailovich Fyodorov* (b. 1858)
Auditor General	*Dmitry Aleksandrovich Filosofov* (b. 1861; d. 19 Dec 1907)

8 May – 23 Jul 1906: Goremykin I

Prime Minister	*Ivan Longinovich Goremykin* (for 1st time) (see Ministers for Home affairs)
Foreign Affairs	*Aleksandr Petrovich Izvolsky* (b. Moscow 18 May 1856; d. Paris 16/17 Aug 1919)
Home Affairs	*Pyot Arkadyevich Stolypin* (b. 14 Apr 1862; d. Kiev 18 Sep 1911)
Finance	*Vladimir Nikolaevich Kokovtsev* (see Finance Ministers)
Justice	*Ivan Grigoryevich Shcheglovitov* (b. 1861; d. 7 Sep 1918)
Education	*Pyot Mikhailovich von Kauffmann* (b. Tiflis 19 Jun 1857; d. Paris 6 Mar 1926)
War	*Aleksander Fyodorovich Rödiger* (see Ministers of War)
Navy	*Aleksei Aleksyeevich Birilev* (see Witte)
Agriculture	*Aleksander Semyonovich Stishinsky* (b. 1857)
Transport	*Nikolaus Schaffhausen-Schönberg-Eck-Schaufuss* (b. 19 Dec 1846; d. 12 Dec 1911)
Commerce and Industry	*Aleksandr Aleksandrovich Stoff*
Auditor General	*Peter von Schwanebach* (b. 2 Feb 1848; d. Magdeburg 14 Sep 1908)

23 Jul 1906 – 18 Sep 1911: Stolypin

Prime Minister	*Pyot Arkadyevich Stolypin* (see Goremykin II)
Foreign Affairs	23 Jun 1906 – 28 Sep 1910: *Aleksandr Petrovich Izvolsky* (see Goremykin I)
	28 Sep 1910 – 18 Sep 1911: *Sergyei Dmitrievich Sazonov* (b. Ryazan 29 Jul 1861; d. Nice 25 Dec 1927)
Home Affairs	*Pyot Arkadyevich Stolypin* (see Goremykin I)
Finance	*Vladimir Nikolaevich Kokovtsev* (see Finance Ministers)
Justice	*Ivan Grigoryevich Shcheglovitov* (see Goremykin I)
Education	23 Jul 1906 – 1908: *Pyot Mikhailovich von Kauffmann* (see Goremykin I)
	1908 – 10 Jun 1910: *Alexander Schwarz* (b. Tula 16 Jan 1848; d. St Petersburg 18 Jan 1915)
	10 Jun – 11 Oct 1910 (acting:) —— *Prush-Arkhuko*
	11 Oct 1910 – 18 Sep 1911: *Lev Aristidovich Casso* (b. Paris 20 Jun 1865; d. St. Petersburg 9 Dec 1914)
War	23 Jul 1906 – 1909: *Aleksandr Fyodorovich Rödiger* (see Ministers of War)
	1909 – 18 Sep 1911: *Vladimir Aleksandrovich Sukhomlinov* (b. 16 Aug 1848; d. Berlin 1 Feb 1926)
Navy	23 Jul 1906 – 23 Jan 1907: *Aleksyei Aleksyeevich Birilev* (see Witte)
	(?) – 1 Apr 1911: *Stepan Arkadyevich Voevodski* (b. 1859)
	1 Apr – 18 Sep 1911: *Ivan Konstantinovich Grigorovich* (b. 7 Feb 1853; d. Mentone 3 Mar 1930)
Agriculture	23 Jul 1906 – Apr 1907: *Aleksandr Semyonovich Stishinsky* (see Goremykin I)
	Apr 1907 – (?): *Prince Boris Aleksandrovich Vasilchikov* (b. 1863)
	(?) – 18 Sep 1911: *Aleksandr Vasilyevich Krivoshein* (b. Warsaw 31 Jul 1857; d. Berlin 28 Oct 1921)
Transport	1909 – 18 Sep 1911: *Sergyei Vasilyevich Rukhlov*
Commerce and Industry	23 Jul 1906 – 1907: *Dmitry Aleksandrovich Filosofov* (see Witte)
	8 Feb 1908 – 27 Jan 1909: *Ivan Pavlovich Shipov* (see Witte)
	27 Jan – 18 Nov 1909: *Vasily Ivanovich Timiryazev* (see Witte)
	18 Nov 1909 – 18 Sep 1911: *Sergyei Ivanovich Timashov* (b. 13 Oct 1858; d.(?))

23 Sep 1911 - 11 Feb 1914: Kokovtsev

Prime Minister	*Vladimir Nikolaevich Kokovtsev* (see Finance Ministers)
Foreign Affairs	*Sergyei Dmitrievich Sazonov* (see Stolypin)
Home Affairs	23 Sep 1911 – 26 Dec 1912: *Aleksandr Aleksandrovich Makarov* (b. 1857; d. 1919)
	26 Dec 1912 – 11 Feb 1914: *Nikolai Aleksyeevich Maklakov* (b. 21 Sep 1871; d. 7 Sep 1918)
Finance	*Vladimir Nikolaevich Kokovtsev* (see Foreign Ministers)
Justice	*Ivan Grigoryevich Shcheglovitov* (see Goremykin I)
Education	*Lev Aristidovich Casso* (see Stolypin)
War	*Vladimir Aleksandrovich Sukhomlinov* (see Stolypin)
Navy	*Ivan Konstantinovich Grigorovich* (see Stolypin)
Agriculture	*Aleksandr Vasilyevich Krivoshein* (see Stolypin)
Transport	*Sergyei Vasilyevich Rukhlov* (see Stolypin)
Commerce and Industry	*Sergyei Ivanovich Timashov* (see Stolypin)

11 Feb 1914 - 2 Feb 1916: Goremykin II

Prime Minister	*Ivan Longinovich Goremykin* (for 2nd time) (see Ministers for Home Affairs)
Foreign Affairs	*Sergyei Dmitrievich Sazonov* (see Stolypin)
Home Affairs	11 Feb 1914 – 19 Jun 1915: *Nikolai Aleksyeevich Maklakov* (see Kokovtsev)
	19 Jun – 10 Oct 1915: *Prince Nikolai Borisovich Shcherbatov* (b. 3 Feb 1868)
	10 Oct 1915 – 2 Feb 1916: *Aleksyei Nikolaevich Khvostov* (b. 1872; d. 1918)
Finance	12 Feb (11 May) 1914 – 2 Feb 1916: *Pyotr Lvovich Bark* (b. Ekaterinberg 1 May 1869; d. Nice 17 Jan 1937)
Justice	12 Feb – 1 Sep 1914: *Ivan Gregoryevich Shcheglovitov* (see Goremykin I)
	1 Sep 1914 – 2 Feb 1916: *Anatoly Fyodorovich Koni* (b. St Petersburg 9 Feb 1844; d. Leningrad 17 Sep 1927)
Education	12 Feb – 1 Sep 1914: *Lev Aristidovich Casso* (see Stolypin)
	1 Sep 1914 – 23 Jan 1915 (acting:) *Vladimir Dmitrievich Kuzmin-Karavaev* (b. 1859) 23 Jan 1915 –

	2 Feb 1916: *Count Pavel Nikolaevich Ignatyev* (b. 12 Jul 1870; d. 1926)
War	12 Feb 1914 – 27 Jun 1915: *Vladimir Aleksandrovich Sukhomlinov* (see Stolypin)
	27 Jun 1915 – 2 Feb 1916: *Aleksandr Andreevich Polivanov* (b. 16 Mar 1855; d. Riga 25 Sep 1920)
Navy	*Ivan Konstantinovich Grigorovich* (see Stolypin)
Agriculture	12 Feb 1914 – 9 Nov 1915: *Aleksandr Vasilyevich Krivoshein* (see Stolypin)
	27 Nov 1915 – 2 Feb 1916: —— *Naumov*
Transport	12 Feb 1914 – 14 Nov 1915: *Sergyei Vasilyevich Rukhlov* (see Stolypin)
	14 Nov 1915 – 2 Feb 1916: *Aleksandr Fyodorovich Trepov* (b. 1862/63; d. Nice 10 Nov 1928)
Commerce and Industry	12 Feb 1914 – 3 Mar 1915: *Sergyei Ivanovich Timashov* (see Stolypin)
	3 Mar 1915 – 2 Feb 1916: *Prince Dmitry Ivanovich Shakhovsky* (b. 1861)

2 Feb – 23 Nov 1916: Stürmer

Prime Minister	*Boris Vladimirovich Stürmer* (from 1916: *B. V. Panin*) (b. 28 Jul 1848; d. St Petersburg 3 Sep 1917)
Foreign Affairs	2 Feb – 23 Jul 1916: *Sergyei Dmitrievich Sazonov* (see Stolypin)
	23 Jul – 23 Nov 1916: *Boris Vladimirovich Stürmer* (see above)
Home Affairs	2 Feb – 19 Mar 1916: *Aleksyei Nikolaevich Khvostov* (see Goremykin II)
	19 Mar – 23 Jul 1916: *B. V. Stürmer* (see above)
	23 Jul – end of Sep 1916: *Aleksyei Nikolaevich Khvostov* (see Goremykin II)
	Sep – 23 Nov 1916: *Aleksandr Dmitrievich Protopopov* (b. 1865; d. 15 Mar 1917 or 7 Sep 1918(?))
Finance	*Pyotr Lvovich Bark* (see Goremykin II)
Justice	23 Jul – 23 Nov 1916: *Aleksandr Aleksandrovich Makarov* (see Kokovtsev)
Education	*Count Pavel Nikolaevich Ignatyev* (see Goremykin II)
War	2 Feb – 29 Mar 1916: *Aleksandr Andreevich Polivanov* (see Goremykin II)
	29 Mar – 23 Nov 1916: *Dmitry Savelyevich Shuvayev*
Munitions	23 Apr – 23 Nov 1916: *Nikolai Pavlovich Garin* (b. 24 Feb 1861)

Agriculture	2 Feb – 4 Jul 1916: —— *Naumov* (see Goremykin II)
	4 Jul – 23 Nov 1916: *Count Vladimir Aleksyevevich*
	Bobrinsky (b. 1868)
Transport	*Aleksandr Fyodorovich Trepov* (see Goremykin II)

23 Nov 1916 – 9 Jan 1917: Trepov

Prime Minister	*Aleksandr Fyodorovich Trepov* (see Goremykin II)
Foreign Affairs	14 Dec 1916 – 9 Jan 1917: *Nikolai Nikolaevich*
	Pokrovsky (b. 27 Jan 1850; d. Kanen 12 Dec 1930)
Home Affairs	*Aleksandr Dmitrievich Protopopov* (see Stürmer)
Justice	23 Nov 1916 – 3 Jan 1917: *Aleksandr Aleksandrovich*
	Makarov (see Kokovtsev)
	3 – 9 Jan 1917 (acting:) *Nikolai Aleksandrovich*
	Dobrovolsky (b. 22 Mar 1854; d. 1918)
Education	*Count Pavel Nikolaevich Ignatyev* (see Goremykin II)
War	*Dmitry Savelyevich Shuvayev* (see Stürmer)
Agriculture	29 Nov 1916 – 9 Jan 1917 (acting:) *Aleksandr*
	Aleksandrovich Rittikh (b. 9 Oct 1868)
Transport	*Aleksandr Fyodorovich Trepov* (see Goremykin II)

9 Jan – 15 Mar 1917: Golitsyn

Prime Minister	*Prince Nikolai Dmitrievich Golitsyn* (b. Moscow 12
	Apr 1850; d. Leningrad 3 Jul 1925)
Foreign Affairs	*Nikolai Nikolaevich Pokrovsky* (see Trepov)
Home Affairs	*Aleksandr Dmitrievich Protopopov* (see Stürmer)
Education	(acting:) —— *Kulchitsky*
War	18 Jan – 15 Mar 1917: *Mikhail Aleksyeevich Byelyaev*
	(b. 1863; D.(?))
Transport	*Eduard Bronislavovich* (?) *Voinovsky-Krieger* (d.
	1933)

14/15 Mar – 18 May 1917: Lvov I

Prime Minister	*Prince Georgy Evgenyevich Lvov* (for 1st time) (b.
	Aleksin 22 Oct 1861; d. Paris 8 Mar 1925)
Foreign Affairs	*Pavel Nikolaevich Milyukov* (b. St Petersburg 27 Jan
	1859; d. Aix-les-Bains 31 Mar 1943)
Home Affairs	*Prince Georgy Evgenyevich Lvov* (see above)
Finance	*Mikhail Ivanovich Tereshchenko*
Justice	*Aleksandr Fyodorovich Kerensky* (Soc) (b. Volsk 4
	May 1881; d. Simbirsk 11 Jun 1970)

Education	*Aleksandr Apollonovich Manuilov* (b. 28 Feb 1861; d. 20 Jul 1929)
War and (acting:) Navy	15 Mar – 12 May 1917: *Aleksandr Ivanovich Guchkov* (b. Moscow 1862; d. Paris 17 Feb 1936) 12 – 18 May 1917: *Aleksy Aleksyeevich Manikovski* (b. 23 Mar 1865; d. Jan 1920)
Agriculture	*Andrei Ivanovich Shingaryov* (b. 1869; d. St Petersburg 20 Jan 1918)
Transport	*Nikolai Vissarionovich Nekrasov* (b. 1 Nov 1879; d. 7 May 1940)
Commerce and Industry	*Aleksandr Ivanovich Konovalov* (b. 1875)
Auditor General	—— *Godnev*

8 May – 21 Jul 1917: Lvov II

Prime Minister	*Prince Georgy Evgenyevich Lvov* (for 2nd time) (see Lvov I)
Foreign Affairs	*Mikhail Ivanovich Tereshchenko* (see Lvov I)
Home Affairs	*Prince Georgy Evgenyevich Lvov* (see Lvov I)
Finance	18 May – 16 Jul 1917: *Andrei Ivanovich Shingaryov* (see Lvov I)
Justice	18 May – 18 Jul 1917: —— *Pereverzev*
Education	18 May – 16 Jul 1917: *Aleksandr Apollonovich Manuilov* (see Lvov I) 16 – 21 Jul 1917: —— *Charnovsky* (Soc)
War and Navy	*Aleksandr Fyodorovich Kerensky* (Soc) (see Lvov I)
Agriculture	*Viktor Mikhailovich Chernev* (Soc Rev) (b. 1873; d. New York 15 Apr 1952)
Transport	18 May – 17 Jul 1917: *Nikolai Vissarionovich Nekrasov* (see Lvov I)
Commerce and Industry	18 May – 16 Jul 1917: *Aleksandr Ivanovich Konovalov* (see Lvov I) 16 – 21 Jul 1917: *Sergyei N. Prokopovich* (Soc) (b. 1871; d. Geneva 4 Apr 1955)
Labour	—— *Skobelev* (Soc)
Food	18 May – Jun 1917: *Georgy Valentinovich Plekhanov* (Soc) (b. 1857; d. Terijoki, Finland, 30 May 1918) Jun – 21 Jul 1917: *Aleksei Vasilyevich Peshekhonev* (b. 2 Feb 1867; d. Riga 3 Apr 1933)
Posts and Telegraphs	*Irakly Georgievich Tsereteli* (Georgian) (Soc) (b. 1882; d. New York 21/22 May 1959)

Public Assistance	*Prince Dmitry Ivanovich Shakhovsky* (see Goremykin II)
Constituent Assembly	*David Davidovich Grimm* (b. St Petersburg 1864)
Auditor General	—— *Godnev* (see Lvov I)

21 Jul – 6 Aug 1917: Kerensky I

Prime Minister	*Aleksandr Fyodorovich Kerensky* (Soc) (see Lvov I)
Foreign Affairs	*Mikhail Ivanovich Tereshchenko* (Prog) (see Lvov I)
Home Affairs	*Irakly Georgievich Tsereteli* (Soc) (see Lvov II)
Posts and Telegraphs	*Ivan Nikolaevich Efremov* (Rad Dem) (b. 1866; d.(?))
War	—— *Skobelev* (Soc) (see Lvov II)
Navy	*Aleksandr Fyodorovich Kerensky* (Soc) (see Lvov I)
Agriculture	21 Jul – 3 Aug 1917: *Viktor Mikhailovich Chernev* (Soc Rev) (see Lvov II)
Food	*Aleksei Vasilyevich Peshekonev* (Peoples Soc) (see Lvov II)
Public Assistance	—— *Darishnikov*
Auditor General	—— *Godnev* (see Lvov I)

6 Aug – 9 Oct 1917: Kerensky II

Prime Minister	*Aleksandr Fyodorovich Kerensky* (for 2nd time) (see Lvov I)
Foreign Affairs	*Mikhail Ivanovich Tereshchenko* (Prog) (see Lvov I)
Home Affairs	6 Aug – 19 Sep 1917: *Nikolai Dmitrievich Avksentyev* (b. 1878; d. 1943)
	27 Sep – 9 Oct 1917: —— *Nikitin*
Finance	6 Aug – 14 Sep 1917: *Nikolai Vissarionovich Nekrasov* (see Lvov I)
	27 Sep – 9 Oct 1917: *Mikhail Vladimirovich Bernatsky* (b. 1876; d. Paris 17 Jul 1943)
Justice	6 Aug – 19 Sep 1917: *Aleksandr Sergyeevich Zarudny* (b. 1863)
Education	6 Aug – 1917: —— *Oldenburg* (Cadet)
	(?) – 27 Sep 1917: *Georgy Kartashov* (b. Ekaterinberg 1875; d. Menton, France, 10 Sep 1960)
	27 Sep – 9 Oct 1917: —— *Salaskin*
War	6 Aug – Sep 1917: *Aleksandr Fyodorovich Kerensky* (see Lvov I)
	Sep – 9 Oct 1917: *Aleksandr Ivanovich Verkhovsky* (b. St Petersburg 9 Dec 1886; d. 19 Aug 1938)

Navy	6 Aug – Sep 1917: *Aleksandr Fyodorovich Kerensky* (see Lvov I)
	Sep – 9 Oct 1917: *Dmitry Nikolaevich Verderevsky* (b. St Petersburg 1873; d. Paris 1946)
Agriculture	6 Aug – 13 Sep 1917: *Viktor Mikhailovich Chernev* (see Lvov II)
Food	*Aleksei Vasilyevich Peshekhonev* (see Lvov II)
Public Assistance	*Ivan Nikolaevich Efremov* (see Kerensky I)
Labour	6 Aug – 19 Sep 1917: —— *Skobelev* (see Lvov II)
Commerce and Industry	*Sergyei N. Prokopovich* (see Lvov II)
Posts and Telegraphs	—— *Nikitin* (see above)
Transport	—— *Leverovsky* (Siverovsky?)
Public Works	*Konstantin Konstantinovich Yurenev* (b. 1888)
Auditor General	*Fyodor Fyodorovich Kokoshkin* (Cadet) (b. 1872; d. St Petersburg 20 Jan 1918)

9 Oct – 7/8 Nov 1917: Kerensky III

Prime Minister	*Aleksandr Fyodorovich Kerensky* (for 3rd time) (Soc) (see Lvov I)
Foreign Affairs	*Mikhail Ivanovich Tereshchenko* (Ind) (see Lvov I)
Home Affairs	—— *Nikitin* (Ind) (see Kerensky II)
Finance	*Mikhail Vladimirovich Bernatsky* (Ind) (see Kerensky II)
Justice	—— *Malyantovich* (Soc)
War	*Aleksandr Ivanovich Verkhovsky* (Ind) (see Kerensky II)
Navy	*Dmitry Nikolaevich Verderevsky* (see Kerensky II)
Agriculture	18 Oct – 7/8 Nov 1917: *Pyotr Pavlovich Maslov* (Soc Rev) (b. 1867)
Food	*Sergyei N. Prokopovich* (Soc) (see Lvov II)
Transport	—— *Siverovsky* (Soc Rev) (see Kerensky II)
Commerce	*Aleksandr Ivanovich Konovalov* (Cadet) (see Lvov I)
Labour	*Kuzma Antonovich Gvozdyov* (Soc) (b. 1883)
Public Assistance	*Nikolai Mikhailovich Kishkin* (Cadet) (b. 1864; d. 1930)
Education	*Georgy Kartashov* (Cadet) (see Kerensky II)
Auditor General	—— *Smirnov* (Cadet)

Chairmen of the Council of People's Commissars

8 Nov 1917 – 21 Jan 1924	*Vladimir Ilyich Lenin,* original name *Ulyanov* (b. Simbirsk 10 Apr 1870; d. Gorky 21 Jan 1924)
2 Feb 1924 – 19 Dec 1930	*Aleksei Ivanovich Rykov* (b. Saratov 13 Feb 1881; d. Moscow 14/15 Mar 1938)

Commissars and Ministers of Foreign Affairs

8 Nov 1917 – 9 Mar 1918	*Lev Davidovich Trotsky,* original name *Leib Bronstein* (b. Yanovka 25 Oct 1879 or 1877; d. (assassinated) Mexico City, Mexico, 21 Aug 1940)
9 Mar – Apr 1918	*Adolf Abramovich Joffe* (b. Simferopol 22 Oct 1883; d. Moscow 17 Nov 1927)
Apr – (?) 1918	*Karl Berngardovich Radek,* original name *Sobelsohn* (b. Lvov 1885; d. 1939)
1918 – 5 Feb 1930	*Georgy Vasilyevich Chicherin* (b. Kagaul 1872; d. Moscow 7 Jul 1936)

Commissars and Ministers for Internal Affairs

8 Nov 1917 – Feb 1918	*Aleksei Ivanovich Rykov* (see Chairmen of the Council of People's Commissars)
Summer 1920 – 14 Apr 1921	*Feliks Edmundovich Dzerzhinsky (Dzierzyński)* (b. Vilnius 11 Sep 1877; d. Moscow 20 Jul 1926)
25 Apr 1921 – 24 Feb 1924	*Feliks Edmundovich Dzerzhinsky* Head of Cheka (see above)
1923 – 1928	*Aleksandr Georgievich Beloborodov* (b. Alexandrovski Savod 26 Oct 1891; d. 9 Feb 1938)
1928 – 10 May 1934	*Vyacheslav Rudolfovich Menshinsky* (b. 1880; d. Moscow 10 May 1934)

Commissars and Ministers for Defence

8 Nov 1917	Committee of three persons
15 Mar 1918 – 27 Nov 1924	*Lev Davidovich Trotsky* (see Commissars and Ministers of Foreign Affairs)
22 Feb 1924 – Jan 1926	*Lev Borisovich Kamenev* (b. Tiflis or Moscow 22 Jul 1883; d. Moscow 25 Aug 1936) Chairman of the Committee for Labour and Defence
27 Nov 1924 – 31 Oct 1925	*Mikhail Vasilyevich Frunze* (b. Tashkent 1885; d. Moscow 31 Oct 1925) confirmed on 29 Jan 1925

7 Nov 1925 – 8 May 1940	*Kliment Efremovich Voroshilov* (b. Verkhnee, later Dnepropetrovsk, 4 Sep 1881; d. Moscow 2 Dec 1969)

Commissars and Ministers of Finance

8 Nov 1917 – 25 Mar	*I. Shvartsev*, pseudonym *Stepanov*
25 Mar 1918 – 25 Apr 1921	*Isidor Emmanuilovich Gukovsky* (b. 1871; d. 25 Apr 1921)
25 Apr 1921 – 1923(?)	*Nikolai Nikolaevich Krestinsky* (b. Mogilyov 26 Oct 1883; d. Moscow 14/15 Mar 1938)
1921/23 – mid Jan 1926	*Grigory Yakovlevich Sokolnikov* (b. Romny 15 Aug 1888)
mid Jan 1926 – end of 1929	*Nikolai Pavlovich Brukhanov* (b. Simbirsk 1878; d. in prison 1938)

Commissars and Ministers of Justice

8 Nov 1917 – 25 Mar 1918	*G. I. Oppokov*
25 Mar – 14 Sep 1918	*Pyotr Ananyevich Krasikov* (b. Krasnoyarsk 14 Oct 1870; d. Zheleznovodsk 20 Aug 1939)
14 Sep 1918 – 16 Jan 1928	*Dmitry Ivanovich Kursky* (b. Kiev 22 Oct 1874; d. Moscow 20 Dec 1932)

Commissars and Ministers of Education

8 Nov 1917 – 10 Aug 1930	*Anatoly Vasilyevich Lunacharsky* (b. Poltava 1866; d. Menton, France, 27 Dec 1933)

Commissars for Internal and Foreign Trade

8 – 17 Nov 1917	*Viktor Pavlovich Nogin*, pseudonym *Makar* (b. 1878; d. 1924)
1918 – 1919	*Leonid Borisovich Krasin* (for 1st time) (b. Turgan 15 Jul 1870; d. London 24 Nov 1926)
2 Feb – Dec 1924	*Leonid Borisovich Krasin* (for 2nd time) Foreign trade
Dec 1924 – Jan 1926	—— *Sheinmann*, Internal trade
18 Nov 1925	Commissariats for Foreign and Internal Trade amalgamated, separated again on 24 Nov 1930
Jan 1926 – 12 Nov 1927	*Lev Borisovich Kamenev*, Foreign and Internal Trade (see Commissars and Ministers for Defence)
Nov 1927 – 14 Jun 1937	*Aaron Rosenholz* (d. Moscow 14/15 Mar 1938)

Commissars for Transport

1919 – 16 Dec 1920	*Leonid Borisovich Krasin* (see Commissars for Internal and foreign Trade)
16 Dec 1920 – 1921	*A. I. Emshanov*
1921 – 9 May 1921	*Grigory Evseevich Zinovyev* (b. Elizavetgrad Sep 1883; d. Moscow 25 Aug 1936)
May 1921 – 1924	*Feliks Edmundovich Dzerzhinsky* (see Commissars and Ministers for Internal Affairs)
2 Feb 1924 – 1930	*Ian Ernestovich Rudzutak* (b. 1887; d. 1938)

Chairman of the State Planning Committee

Mar 1920 – 6 Nov 1930	*Gleb Maksimilianovich Krzhyzhanovsky* (b. 1872; d. Moscow 31(?) Mar 1959)

Secretary of the Central Committee of the Communist Party

1922 – Mar 1939	*Iosif Vissarionovich Stalin,* original name *Djugashvili* (b. Gori, Georgia, 21 Dec 1879; d. Moscow 5 Mar 1953)

United Kingdom

England until 1707. Dates before 14 Sep 1752 are given according to the Julian calendar but the year begins at all times on 1 Jan ('new style').

HEADS OF STATE

Kings and Queens

House of Tudor

22 Aug 1485	*Henry VII,* son of Edmund, Earl of Richmond (b. 28 Jan 1457)
22 Apr 1509	*Henry VIII,* son (b. 28 Jun 1491)
28 Jan 1547	*Edward VI,* son (b. 12 Oct 1537)
6 Jul 1553	*Jane* (*Lady Jane Grey,* afterwards *Dudley*) cousin (b. Bradgate Oct 1537; d. (executed) 12 Feb 1554) deposed 19 Jul 1553

19 Jul 1553	*Mary I*, daughter of Henry VIII (b. 18 Feb 1516)
17 Nov 1558	*Elizabeth I*, daughter of Henry VIII (b. 7 Sep 1533)

House of Stuart

24 Mar 1603	*James I*, son of Mary, Queen of Scotland and great-grandson of Henry VII (b. 19 Jun 1566) from 24 Jul 1567: King James VI of Scotland
27 Mar 1625 – 30 Jan 1649	*Charles I*, son (b. 19 Nov 1600; d. (executed) 30 Jan 1649)
30 Jan 1649 – 12 Dec 1653	All powers exercised by Parliament, which abolished the monarchy on 7 Feb 1649

Lord Protectors

16 Dec 1653	*Oliver Cromwell* (b. 25 Apr 1599)
3 Sep 1658 – 29 Apr 1659	*Richard Cromwell*, son (b. 4 Oct 1626; d. 12 Jul 1712) resigned
1 May 1660	Parliament resolved to restore the monarchy

Kings and Queens

1 May 1660	*Charles II*, son of Charles I (b. 29 May 1630) king in exile from 30 Jan 1649; returned to England 29 May 1660
16 Feb 1685 – Dec 1688	*James II*, brother (b. 14 Oct 1633; d. 16 Sep 1701) left England 23 Dec 1688 and declared by Parliament to have abdicated
13 Feb 1689	*William III* of Orange, Stadholder of Holland (b. 4 Nov 1650) and his wife, *Mary II*, daughter of James II (b. 30 Apr 1662; d. 28 Dec 1694)
8 Mar 1702 – 1 Aug 1714	*Anne*, sister of Mary II (b. 6 Feb 1665) also Queen of Scotland
1 May 1707	Union of England and Scotland to form Great Britain

House of Hanover

1 Aug 1714	*George I*, Elector of Hanover, great-grandson of James I (b. 28 Mar 1660)
11 Jun 1727	*George II*, son (b. 30 Oct 1683) Elector of Hanover
25 Oct 1760	*George III*, grandson (b. 4 Jun 1738) Elector (from 1815: King) of Hanover; incurably ill from 1811, the Prince of Wales (later King George IV) acting as Regent
29 Jan 1820	*George IV*, son (b. 12 Aug 1762) King of Hanover
26 Jun 1830	*William IV*, brother (b. 21 Aug 1765) King of Hanover

20 Jun 1837   *Victoria*, niece, daughter of Edward, Duke of Kent (b. 24 May 1819)

House of Saxe-Coburg-Gotha (from 17 Jul 1917: House of Windsor)
22 Jan 1901   *Edward VII*, son (b. 9 Nov 1841)
6 May 1910 – 20 Jan *George V*, son (b. 3 Jun 1865)
    1936

MEMBERS OF GOVERNMENT

Officers of state up to April 1721

Principal Counsellors
Here are listed those who through the control of information, advice and to some extent patronage were pre-eminent as ministers of the sovereign. They were usually ennobled and might hold a variety of offices or none. (The term Prime Minister was first used, satirically, towards the end of the 17th century.) The dates in the left-hand column are intended merely to give a chronological framework.

1486   *John Morton*, Archbishop of Canterbury (b. Bere Regis or Milborne St Andrew about 1420; d. Knowle 15 Sep 1500) Lord Chancellor 1486 – 1500
1500   *Richard Fox(e)*, successively Bishop of Exeter, Durham and Winchester (b. Ropesley 1447 or 1448; d. (?) Winchester 5 Oct 1528) Secretary of State 1485 – 1487; Lord Privy Seal 1487 – 1516
              William Warham, Archbishop of Canterbury (b. about 1450; d. Hackington 22 Aug 1532) Lord Keeper of the Seals 1502, Lord Chancellor 1504 – 1515
              Thomas Howard, Earl of Surrey (from 1514: *1st Duke of Norfolk*) (b. 1443; d. Framlingham 21 May 1524) Lord Treasurer 1501 – 1522
1525   *Cardinal Thomas Wolsey* (b. Ipswich 1471 or 1474/5; d. Leicester 29 Nov 1530) Lord Chancellor 1515 – 1529
              Sir Thomas More (b. London 7 Feb 1478; d. (executed) London, 6 Jul 1535) Lord Chancellor 1529 – 1532
              Thomas Cromwell (from 1539: *Earl of Essex*) (b. Putney 1485 or 1490; d. 28 Jul 1540) Secretary of State 1534 – 1540; Lord Privy Seal 1536 – 1540
              Edward Seymour, Duke of Somerset (b. 1506; d. 22 Jan 1552) Protector 1547 – 1549

559

John Dudley, Duke of Northumberland (b. 1502; d. London 22 Aug 1553) Protector 1549 – 1553

1550

Stephen Gardiner, Bishop of Winchester (b. c. 1485; d. London 12 Nov 1555) Lord Chancellor 1553 – 1555

William Cecil (from 1571: *Baron Burghley*) (b. Bourn, Lincolnshire, 13 Sep 1520; d. London 4 Aug 1598) Secretary of State 1558 – 1572; Lord High Treasurer 1572 – 1598

Sir Francis Walsingham (b. c. 1530; d. London 6 Apr 1590) Secretary of State 1573 – 1590

Robert Cecil (from 1603: *Baron Cecil;* from 1604: *Viscount Cranborne:* from 1605: *Earl of Salisbury*) (b. (?) 1563; d. Marlborough 24 May 1612) Secretary of State 1596 – 1612; Lord Privy Seal 1597 – 1608; Lord Treasurer 1608 – 1612

Robert Carr, Earl of Somerset (b. 1590; d. Jul 1645) acting Secretary of State 1613 – 1616; acting Keeper of the Privy Seal 1614 – 1616

1625

George Villiers, Duke of Buckingham (b. Brooksby 20 Aug 1592; d. Portsmouth 23 Aug 1628) Gentleman of the Bedchamber 1614; Lord High Admiral 1619 – 1628

Richard Weston, Baron Weston (from 1633: *Earl of Portland*) (christened Chicheley 1 Mar 1577; d. 13 Mar 1635) Lord Treasurer 1628 – 1635; First Lord of the Admiralty 1628 – 1636

1650

Civil War and Commonwealth 1642 – 1660: offices mostly in commission

Edward Hyde, father-in-law of James II (from 1661: *Earl of Clarendon*) (b. Dinton, Wiltshire, 18 Feb 1609; d. Rouen 9 Sep 1674) Lord Chancellor 1658 – 1667

The five who follow formed the 'Cabal', but were not a united ministry in the modern sense:

Thomas Clifford (from 1672: *1st Earl of Chudleigh*) (b. Exeter 1 Aug 1630; d. Tunbridge Wells Sep 1673) a Lord of the Treasury 1667 – 1673; Lord Treasurer 1672 – 1673

Henry Bennet (from 1663: *Baron;* from 1672: *Earl of Arlington*) (b. Arlington 1618; d. Suffolk 28 Jul 1685) Secretary of State for the South* 1662 – 1674

---

*'South' and 'North' refer to the foreign responsibilities of the secretaries, but both were concerned also with Home Affairs and either took over the other's responsibilities in his absence.

George Villiers, 2nd Duke of Buckingham (b. London 30 Jan 1628; d. Kirby 16 Apr 1688) Privy Councillor 1660 – Feb 1667; Sep 1667 – 1674

Anthony Ashley Cooper (from 1661: *Baron Ashley;* from 1672: *1st Earl of Shaftesbury*) (b. Dorset 22 Jul 1621; d. Amsterdam 21 Jan 1683) a Lord of the Treasury 1667 – 1672; Lord Chancellor 1672 – 1673

John Maitland, 2nd Earl (from 1672: *1st Duke) of Lauderdale* (b. Lethington 24 May 1610; d. Tunbridge Wells 20(?)24 Aug 1682) Secretary for Scotland 1660 – 1680

1675

Thomas Osborne, Earl of Danby (from 1689: *Marquis of Carmarthen;* from 1694: *Duke of Leeds*) (b. 1631; d. Easton 26 Jul 1712) Lord Treasurer 1673 – 1679; President of the Council 1689 – 1699

Sidney Godolphin (from 1684: *Baron Godolphin;* from 1706: *Earl of Godolphin*) (christened 15 Jun 1645; d. London 15 Sep 1712) a Lord of the Treasury 1679 – 1684, 1684 – 1696, 1700 – 1701; Secretary of State for the North 1684 – 1688; Lord Treasurer 1702 – 1710

Robert Spencer, 2nd Earl of Sunderland (b. Paris 4 Aug 1640; d. Althorp 28 Sep 1702) Secretary of State 1679 – 1681, 1683 – 1688 (for the North 1679 – 1680, for the South 1680 – 1681, for the North 1683 – 1684, for the South 1684 – 1688); President of the Council 1686 – 1689; Lord Chamberlain Apr – Dec 1697

Sir George Savile (from 1682: *Marquis of Halifax*) (b. Thornhill 16 Nov 1633; d. London 5 Apr 1695) Lord Privy Seal 1682 – 1685, 1689 – 1690; President of the Council 1685 – 1686

Lawrence Hyde (from 1681 *Earl of Rochester*), uncle of Queen Anne (b. Mar 1641; d. night of 1/2 May 1711) 1st Lord of the Treasury 1679 – 1689; Lord Lieutenant of Ireland 1700 – 1703; President of the Council 1710 – 1711

Thomas Osborne (see above)

Daniel Finch, 7th Earl of Winchilsea and 2nd Earl of Nottingham (b. 1647; d. 1 Jan 1730) Secretary of State for the North 1689 – 1693; for the South 1702 – 1704; Lord President of the Council 1714 – 1716

1700

Sidney Godolphin (see above)

John Churchill, Duke of Marlborough (from 1710:

Prince of Mindelheim) (b. Ashe May/Jun 1650; d. Blenheim 16 Jun 1722) Commander-in-Chief 1701; Captain General of the Forces 1702 – 1711, 1714 – 1721

Henry St John (from 1713: *Viscount Bolingbroke*) (b. Battersea 10 Oct 1678; d. 12 Dec 1751) Secretary at War 1704 – 1708; Secretary of State 1710 – 1714 (for the North 1710 – 1713, for the South 1713 – 1714)

Robert Harley (from 1710: *Earl of Oxford*) (b. London 5 Dec 1661; d. London 21 May 1724) Secretary of State for the North 1704 – 1707; 2nd Lord of Treasury and Chancellor of the Exchequer 1710 – 1711; Lord Treasurer 1711 – 1714

Charles Townshend, 2nd Viscount Townshend (b. 1674; d. Raynham 21 Jun 1738) Secretary of State for the North 1714 – 1716; Lord Lieutenant of Ireland 1716 – 1717; Lord President of the Council 1720 – 1721; and see Governments from 1721

Robert Walpole (from 1725: *Sir Robert Walpole*; from 1742: *Earl of Orford*) (b. Houghton 26 Aug 1676; d. London 29 Mar 1745) Secretary at War 1708 – 1711; Treasurer of the Navy 1709 – 1711; Paymaster General 1714 – 1715; 1st Lord of the Treasury and Chancellor of the Exchequer 1715 – 1717; and see Governments from 1721

James Stanhope (from 1717: *Viscount Stanhope of Mahon;* from 1718: *1st Earl Stanhope*) (b. Paris 1673; d. London 4/5 Feb 1721) Secretary of State 1714 – 1717 (for the South 1714 – 1716; for the North 1716 – 1717); First Lord of the Treasury and Chancellor of the Exchequer 1717 – 1718

Charles Spencer, 3rd Earl of Sunderland (b. c. 1674; d. 19 Apr 1722) Secretary of State for the South 1706 – 1710; Lord Privy Seal 1715 – 1716; Secretary of State for the North 1717 – 1718; Lord President of the Council 1717 – 1719; 1st Lord of the Treasury 1718 – Apr 1721

Other Offices of State

Only the more important officials are listed here. Fuller lists will be found in the various volumes of the *Oxford History of England*

1600   *Charles Howard* (from 1573: *2nd Baron Howard of Effingham;* from 1596: *Earl of Nottingham*) (b. 1536;

d. Haling 14 Dec 1624) Lord High Admiral 1585 – 1619

Henry Howard, Earl of Northampton (b. Shottesham 25 Feb 1540; d. London 15 Jun 1614) Lord Privy Seal 1608 – 1614; 1st Lord of the Treasury 1612 – 1614

Thomas Howard, Earl of Suffolk (b. 24 Aug 1561; d. London 28 May 1626) Lord Treasurer 1614 – 1618

Sir Francis Bacon (from 1618: *Baron Verulam;* from 1621: *Viscount St Albans*) (b. London 22 Jan 1561; d. London 9 Apr 1626) Lord Keeper of the Great Seal 1617 – 1618; Lord Chancellor 1618 – 1621

Lionel Cranfield (from 1622: *Earl of Middlesex*) (christened 13 Mar 1575; d. 6 Aug 1645) Lord Treasurer 1621 – 1624

Sir John Coke (b. 5 Mar 1563; d. Tottenham 8 Sep 1644) Secretary of State 1625 – 1640

1625

Thomas Wentworth (from 1640: *Earl of Strafford*) (b. London 13 Apr 1593; d. (executed) London 12 May 1641) President of the Council of the North 1628 – 1640; Lord Deputy in Ireland 1632 – 1640

Sir Francis Windebank (b. 1582; d. Paris 1 Sep 1646) Secretary of State 1632 – 1641

Edward Nicholas (b. Winterborne Earls 4 Apr 1593; d. East Horsley 1 Sep 1669) Secretary of State 1641 – (?), 1661 – 1662

1642 – 1660 Civil War and Commonwealth: most offices in commission

Thomas Wriothesley, 4th Earl of Southampton (b. 1607; d. London 16 May 1667) Lord Treasurer 1660 – 1667

George Monck, 1st Duke of Albemarle (b. Potheridge 6 Dec 1608; d. New Hall, Essex, 3 Jan 1670) Captain General 1660 – 1670; a Lord of the Treasury 1660 – 1667; First Lord of the Treasury 1667 – 1670

Sir Heneage Finch (from 1674: *Baron Finch of Daventry;* from 1681: *1st Earl of Nottingham*) (b. (?)Eastwell 23 Dec 1621; d. 18 Dec 1682) Lord Keeper of the Great Seal 1673 – 1675; Lord Chancellor 1675 – 1682

1675 *Arthur Capel, Earl of Essex* (b. Jan 1631; d. London Jul 1683) 1st Lord of the Treasury 1679

Sir George Jeffreys, Lord Jeffreys (b. Wrexham 1648; d. London 19 Apr 1689) Lord Chancellor 1685 – 1689

563

Charles Talbot, 12th Earl (from 1694: *1st Duke*) *of Shrewsbury* (b. 24 Jul 1660; d. Isleworth 1 Feb 1718) Secretary of State for the South 1689 – 1690, for the North 1693 – 1695, for the South 1695 – 1698; Lord Chamberlain 1710; Lord Treasurer Aug – Oct 1714

Charles Montagu (from 1714: *Earl*) *of Halifax* (b. Horton 16 Apr 1661; d. London 19 May 1715) a Lord of the Treasury 1691 – 1699; 1st Lord of the Treasury 1714 – 1715

Sir John Somers (from 1697: *Lord*) *Somers* (b. Claines 4 Mar 1651; d. North Mimms 26 Apr 1716) Lord Keeper of the Great Seal 1693 – 1697; Lord Chancellor 1697 – 1700; President of the Council 1708 – 1710

1700

Charles Howard, 3rd Earl of Carlisle (b. 1674; d. Bath 1 May 1738) a Lord of the Treasury 1701 – 1702; 1st Lord of the Treasury May – Oct 1715

John Sheffield (from 1694: *Marquis of Normanby; from 1703: Duke of Buckinghamshire*) (b. London 7 Apr 1648; d. London 24 Feb 1721) Lord Privy Seal 1702 – 1705; Lord President of the Council 1711 – 1714

William Cowper, 1st Earl Cowper (d. Hertingfordbury 10 Oct 1723) Lord Keeper of the Great Seal 1705 – 1707; Lord Chancellor 1707 – 1710, 1714 – 1718

Of importance in the counsels of George I, though having no status in English constitutional law, were:

Andreas Gottlieb, Baron Bernstorff (b. Ratzeburg 2 Mar 1649; d. 6 Jul 1726), *Johann Casper, Count Bothmer* (b. 31 Mar 1656; d. London 1732) and *Jean Robethon*, secretary to the King

Governments from 1721

From this point ministers are listed by administrations. From 1782 the lists are lists of cabinets, the absence of a particular office indicating that it was not of cabinet rank. Lists before 1782 are analogous, but in so far as there was no fixed cabinet membership, arbitrary. The title of Prime Minister became official in 1905: before this the leader of the government, usually First Lord of the Treasury (invariably so since 1902), is put first against his proper office, and the term Prime Minister is used only when the leader of the government changed his office in the course of the administration.

24 Apr 1721 – 2 Jul 1743: Walpole/Wilmington

First Lord of the Treasury	24 Apr 1721 – 11 Feb 1742: *Sir Robert Walpole* (see Principal Counsellors)*
	11 Feb 1742 – 2 Jul 1743: *Spencer Compton, 1st Earl of Wilmington* (b. (?) 1673; d. 2 Aug 1743)
Secretary of State (North)	6 Feb 1721 – 16 May 1730: *Charles Townshend, 2nd Viscount Townshend* (see Principal Counsellors)
	16 May 1730 – 12 Feb 1742: *William Stanhope, 1st Viscount Harrington* (d. 1756)
	12 Feb 1742 – 24 Nov 1744: *John Carteret, Baron Carteret* (from 1744: *Earl Granville*) (b. 22 Apr 1690; d. Bath 2 Jan 1763)
Secretary of State (South)	4 Mar 1721 – 4 Apr 1724: *John Carteret, Baron Carteret* (from 1744: *Earl Granville*) (see Secretary of State (North)
	4 Apr 1724 – 10 Feb 1746: *Thomas Pelham-Holles, Duke of Newcastle-upon-Tyne and Newcastle-under-Lyme* (b. 21 Jul 1694; d. London 17 Nov 1768)
Lord Chancellor	May 1718 – Jan 1725: *Thomas Parker, 1st Earl of Macclesfield* (b. Leek 23 Jul 1666; d. London 28 Apr 1732)
	June 1725 – Nov 1733: *Peter King, Lord King* (b. Exeter 1669; d. Ockham 22 Jul 1734)
	1733 – 14 Feb 1737: *Charles Talbot, 1st Baron Talbot* (b. Chippenham 21 Dec 1685; d. London 14 Feb 1737)
	Feb 1737 – Nov 1746: *Philip Yorke, Baron* (from 2 Apr 1754: *1st Earl of*) *Hardwicke* (b. Dover 1 Dec 1690; d. London 6 Mar 1764)
Lord President	Apr 1721 – Mar 1725: *Henry Carleton*
	Mar 1725 – Jun 1729: *William Cavendish, 2nd Duke of Devonshire* (b.1672; d. 4 Jun 1729)
	May – Jun 1730: *Thomas Trevor, Baron Trevor* (christened 6 Mar 1658; d. Peckham 19 Jun 1730)
	Dec 1730 – Feb 1742: *Spencer Compton, 1st Earl Wilmington* (see above)
Lord Privy Seal	Jun 1720 – Mar 1726: *Evelyn Pierrepont, 1st Duke of Kingston* (b. Dean (?) 1665; d. London 5 Mar 1726)
	Mar 1726 – May 1730: *Thomas Trevor, Baron Trevor* (see above)

*George II on his accession, 22 June 1724, regarded Sir Spencer Compton as in charge of government, but he formed no ministry and Walpole resumed.

May – Dec 1730: *Spencer Compton, 1st Earl of Wilmington* (see above)

3 Jun 1731 – May 1733: *William Cavendish, 3rd Duke of Devonshire* (b. 1698; d. 5 Dec 1755)

May 1733 – 14 May 1735: *Henry Lowther, 3rd Viscount Lonsdale* (d. 6 Mar 1751)

Feb 1742 – Dec 1743: *John Leveson-Gower* (from 1746: *Earl Gower*) (d. 25 Dec 1754)

14 May 1735 – 25 Apr 1740: *Francis Godolphin, 2nd Earl Godolphin* (b. London 3 Sep 1678; d. 17 Jan 1766)

1 May 1740 – Feb 1742: *John Hervey, Baron Hervey of Ickworth* (b. 15 Oct 1696; d. 5 Aut 1743)

Lord Chamberlain	1717 – 1724: *Thomas Pelham-Holles* (see above)
	1724 – 1757: *Charles Fitzroy, 2nd Duke of Grafton* (b. 1683; d. 1757)
First Lord of the Admiralty	1717 – 1727: *James Berkeley, 3rd Earl of Berkeley* (b. 1680; d. Aubigny 17 Aug 1736)
	Daniel Finch, 8th Earl of Winchilsea and 3rd Earl of Nottingham (see above)
Chancellor of the Exchequer	24 Apr 1721 – 11 Feb 1742: *Sir Robert Walpole*, simultaneously First Lord of the Treasury (see above)
	11 Feb 1742 – Dec 1743: *Samuel Sandys* (from 1743: *1st Baron Sandys*) (b. (?)1695; d. 21 Apr 1770)
	1727 – 17 Jan 1733; *George Byng, Viscount Torrington* (b. Wrotham 27 Jan 1663; d. London 17 Jan 1733)
	1733 – Feb 1742: *Sir Charles Wager* (b. 1666; d. 24 May 1743)

26 Jul 1743 – 6 Mar 1754: Pelham

First Lord of the Treasury and Chancellor of the Exchequer	26 Jul 1743 – 9 Feb 1746: *Henry Pelham* (b. 1695/6; d. London 6 Mar 1754)
	10 – 12 Feb 1746: *William Pulteney, Earl of Bath* (b. London 22 Mar 1684; d. London 7 Jul 1764)
	13 Feb 1746 – 6 Mar 1754: *Henry Pelham* (see above)
Secretary of State (North)	12 Feb 1742 – 24 Nov 1744: *John Carteret, Baron Carteret* (from 1744: *Earl Granville*) (see Walpole/Wilmington)
	24 Nov 1744 – 10 Feb 1746: *William Stanhope, 1st Viscount Harrington* (see Walpole/Wilmington)

10 – 14 Feb 1746: *John Carteret, Earl Granville* (see Walpole/Wilmington)

14 Feb – 28 Oct 1746: *William Stanhope, 1st Viscount Harrington* (see Walpole/Wilmington)

29 Oct 1746 – 6 Feb 1748: *Philip Dormer Stanhope, 4th Earl of Chesterfield* (b. London 22 Sep 1694; d. 24 Mar 1773)

Feb 1748 – Mar 1754: *Thomas Pelham-Holles, Duke of Newcastle* (see Walpole/Wilmington)

Secretary of State (South)

Feb 1742 – 10 Feb 1746: *Thomas Pelham-Holles, Duke of Newcastle* (see Walpole/Wilmington)

10 – 14 Feb 1746: *John Carteret, Earl Granville* (see above)

14 Feb 1746 – Feb 1748: *Thomas Pelham-Holles, Duke of Newcastle* (see Walpole/Wilmington)

Feb 1748 – 13 Jun 1751: *John Russell, 4th Duke of Bedford* (b. 30 Sep 1710; d. 15 Jan 1771)

21 Jun 1751 – (?) 12 Mar 1754: *Robert d'Arcy, 5th Earl of Holdernesse* (b. Jun 1718; d. 16 May 1778)

Admiralty

10 – 12 Feb 1746: *Daniel Finch, 8th Earl of Winchilsea and 3rd Earl of Nottingham* (see Walpole/Wilmington)

13 Feb 1746 – 1748: *John Russell, 4th Duke of Bedford* (see above)

1748 – 1751: *John Montagu, 3rd Earl of Sandwich* (b. 3 Nov 1718: d. London 30 Apr 1792)

First Lord of the Admiralty

Feb 1742 – Nov 1744: *Daniel Finch, 8th Earl of Winchilsea and 3rd Earl of Nottingham* (see Walpole/Wilmington)

Nov 1744 – 10 Feb 1746: *John Russell, 4th Duke of Bedford* (see above)

1751 – 1756: *George Anson, Baron Anson of Soberton* (b. Shugborough 23 Apr 1697; d. Moor Park, Hertfordshire, 6 Jun 1762)

Lord Chancellor

Feb 1737 – Nov 1756: *Philip Yorke, Baron* (from 2 Apr 1754: *1st Earl of*) *Hardwicke* (see Walpole/Wilmington)

Lord President

Feb 1742 – Nov 1744: *William Stanhope, 1st Viscount Harrington* (see Walpole/Wilmington)

3 Jan 1745 – Jun 1751: *Lionel Cranfield-Sackfield, 1st Duke of Dorset* (b. 18 Jan 1688; d. Knole 9 Oct 1765)

June 1751 – 2 Jan 1763: *John Carteret, Earl Granville* (see Walpole/Wilmington)

Lord Privy Seal	Dec 1743 – Nov 1744: *George Cholmondeley, 3rd Earl Cholmondeley* (b. 1702/3; d. 1770) 26 Dec 1744 – 10 Feb 1746: *John Leveson-Gower* (see Walpole/Wilmington) 10 – 12 Feb 1746: *Henry Howard, 4th Earl of Carlisle* (b. 1694; d. 4 Sep 1758) 13 Feb 1746 – Jan 1755: *John Leveson-Gower, Earl Gower* (see Walpole/Wilmington)
Lord Chamberlain	1724 – 1757: *Charles Fitzroy, 2nd Duke of Grafton* (see Walpole/Wilmington)

16 Mar 1754 – Nov 1756: Newcastle I

First Lord of the Treasury	*Thomas Pelham-Holles, Duke of Newcastle* (for 1st time) (see Walpole/Wilmington)
Secretary of State (North)	Mar 1754 – 9 Jun 1757, 29 Jun 1757 – 12 Mar 1761: *Robert d'Arcy, 5th Earl of Holdernesse* (see Pelham) 14 Nov 1755 – 13 Nov 1756: *Henry Fox, 1st Baron Holland*
Secretary of State (South)	24 Mar 1754 – Oct 1755: *Sir Thomas Robinson* (from 1761: *1st Baron Grantham*) (b. 1695; d. London 30 Sep 1770)
Lord Chancellor	Feb 1737 – Nov 1756: *Philip Yorke, 1st Earl of Hardwicke* (see Walpole/Wilmington)
Lord President	Jun 1751 – 2 Jan 1763: *John Carteret, Earl Granville* (see Pelham)
Lord Privy Seal	13 Feb 1746 – 25 Dec 1754: *John Leveson-Gower, 1st Earl Gower* (see Walpole/Wilmington) Jan – Dec 1755: *Charles, 3rd Duke of Marlborough* 22 Dec 1755 – Jun 1757: *Granville Leveson-Gower, 2nd Earl Gower* (from 1786: *1st Marquis of Stafford*) (b. 4 Aug 1721; d. Trentham Hall 23 Oct 1803)
Lord Chamberlain	1724 – 1757: *Charles Fitzroy, 2nd Duke of Grafton* (see Walpole/Wilmington)
First Lord of the Admiralty	1751 – 1756: *George Anson, Baron Anson of Soberton* (see Pelham)
Chancellor of the Exchequer	Apr 1754 – Nov 1755: *Henry Bilson Legge* (b. 29 May 1708; d. Tunbridge Wells 23 Aug 1764) Nov 1755 – Nov 1756: *George Lyttleton, 1st Baron Lyttelton* (b. 17 Jan 1709; d. Hagley 22 Aug 1773)

15 Nov 1756 – Jun 1757: Chatham I

Secretary of State (South)	15 Nov/6 Dec 1756 – 6 Apr 1757: *William Pitt,* 'the Elder' (from 1766: *1st Earl of Chatham*) (for 1st time) (b. Boconnock 15 Nov 1708; d. Hayes 11 May 1778)
First Lord of the Treasury	*William Cavendish, 4th Duke of Devonshire* (b. 1720; d. Spa, Belgium, 3 Oct 1764) in charge from 6 Apr 1757
Secretary of State	*Robert d'Arcy, 5th Earl of Holdernesse* (North) Mar 1754 – 6 Apr 1757; (both) 6 Apr – 9 Jun 1757; (North) 29 Jun 1757 – 12 Mar 1761 (see Pelham)
Lord President	Jun 1751 – 2 Jan 1763: *John Carteret, Earl Granville* (see Pelham)
Lord Privy Seal	22 Dec 1755 – Jun 1757: *Granville Leveson-Gower, 2nd Earl Gower* (see Newcastle)
Lord Chamberlain	1724 – 1757: *Charles Fitzroy, 2nd Duke of Grafton* (see Walpole/Wilmington)
First Lord of the Admiralty	19 Dec 1756 – 5 Apr 1757: *Richard Grenville, Viscount Temple* (b. 26 Sep 1711; d. Stowe 11 Sep 1779) 5 Apr – 29 Jun 1757: *Daniel Finch, 8th Earl of Winchilsea and 3rd Earl of Nottingham* (see Walpole/Wilmington)
Chancellor of the Exchequer	15 Nov 1756 – Apr 1757: *Henry Bilson Legge* (see Newcastle) Apr – Jul 1757: *William Murray, 1st Earl of Mansfield* (b. Scone 2 Mar 1705; d. Highgate 20 Mar 1793)

Jun 1757 – May 1762: Newcastle II

First Lord of the Treasury	Jun 1757, for 4 days: *James Waldegrave, 1st Earl Waldegrave* (b. 14 Mar 1715; d. 28 Apr 1763) 29 Jun 1757 – May 1762: *Thomas Pelham-Holles, Duke of Newcastle* (for 2nd time) (see Walpole/Wilmington)
Secretary of State (North)	29 Jun 1757 – 12 Mar 1761: *Robert d'Arcy, 5th Earl of Holdernesse* (see Pelham) 25 Mar 1761 – Mar 1762: *John Stuart, Earl of Bute* (b. Edinburgh 25 May 1713; d. 10 Mar 1792)
Secretary of State (South)	27 Jun 1757 – 5 Oct 1761: *William Pitt* (from 1766: *1st Earl of Chatham*) (see Chatham I) 9 Oct 1761 – 21 Aug 1763: *Charles Wyndham, 2nd Viscount Egremont* (b. London 19 Aug 1710; d. London 21 Aug 1763)
Lord Privy Seal	Jun 1757 – Nov 1761: *Richard Grenville, Viscount*

	Temple (see Chatham I)
	25 Nov 1761 – Apr 1763: *John Russell, 4th Duke of Bedford* (see Pelham)
Lord Chancellor	16 Jan 1761 – 30 Jul 1766: *Robert Henley, Baron Grainge* (from 1764: *1st Earl of Northington*) (b. 1708(?); d. 14 Jun 1772) from Jun 1757 to Jan 1761: Lord Keeper of the Great Seal
Lord President	Jun 1751 – 2 Jan 1763: *John Carteret, Earl Granville* (see Walpole/Wilmington)
First Lord of the Admiralty	Jul 1757 – 6 Jun 1762: *George Anson, Baron Anson of Soberton* (see Pelham)
Lord Chamberlain	*William Cavendish, 4th Duke of Devonshire* (see Chatham I)
Chancellor of the Exchequer	Jul 1757 – Mar 1761: *Henry Bilson Legge* (see Newcastle I)
	Mar 1761 – May 1762: *William Wildman, 2nd Viscount Barrington* (b. 15 Jan 1717; d. Becket 1 Feb 1783)
Treasurer of the Navy	*George Grenville* (b. 14 Oct 1712; d. London 13 Nov 1770)

26 May 1762 – 8 Apr 1763: Bute

First Lord of the Treasury	*John Stuart, Earl of Bute* (see Newcastle II)
Secretary of State (North)	5 Jun – 9(?) Oct 1762: *George Grenville* (see Newcastle II)
	14 Oct 1762 – Sep 1763: *George Montagu Dunk, 2nd Earl of Halifax* (b. 5 Oct 1716; d. 8 Jun 1771)
Secretary of State (South)	9 Oct 1761 – 21 Aug 1763: *Charles Wyndham, 2nd Viscount Egremont* (see Newcastle II)
Lord Chancellor	17 Jan 1761 – 30 Jul 1766: *Robert Henley, Baron Grainge* (see Newcastle II)
Lord President	Jun 1751 – 2 Jan 1763: *John Carteret, Earl Granville* (see Pelham)
Lord Privy Seal	25 Nov 1761 – Apr 1763: *John Russell, 4th Duke of Bedford* (see Pelham)
First Lord of the Admiralty	Jul 1757 – 6 Jun 1762: *George Anson, Baron Anson of Soberton* (see Pelham)
	19 Jun – Oct 1762: *George Montagu Dunk, 2nd Earl of Halifax* (see above)
	18 Oct 1762 – Apr 1763: *George Grenville* (see Newcastle II)

Chancellor of the Exchequer	*Sir Francis Dashwood*, (from 1762/3: *15th Baron le Despenser*) (b. Dec 1708; d. 11 Dec 1781)

16 Apr 1763 - Jul 1765: Grenville

First Lord of the Treasury and Chancellor of the Exchequer	*George Grenville* (see Newcastle II)
Secretary of State (North)	14 Oct 1762 - Sep 1763: *George Montagu Dunk, 2nd Earl of Halifax* (see Bute) 9 Sep 1763 - Jul 1765: *John Montagu, 3rd Earl of Sandwich* (see Pelham)
Secretary of State (South)	9 Oct 1761 - 23 Aug 1763: *Charles Wyndham, 2nd Viscount Egremont* (see Newcastle II) Sep 1763 - 10 Jul 1765: *George Montagu Dunk, 2nd Earl of Halifax* (see Bute)
Lord Chancellor	17 Jan 1761 - 30 Jul 1766: *Robert Henley, 1st Earl of Northington* (see Newcastle II)
Lord President	Sep 1763 - Jul 1765: *John Russell 4th Duke of Bedford* (see Pelham)
Lord Privy Seal	*George Spencer, 4th Duke of Marlborough* (b. 26 Jan 1739; d. Blenheim 29 Jan 1817)
First Lord of the Admiralty	20 Apr - 9 Sep 1763: *John Montagu, 3rd Earl of Sandwich* (see Pelham) 16 Sep 1763 - 15 Sep 1766: *John Perceval, 2nd Earl of Egmont* (b. London 24 Feb 1711; d. 4 Dec 1770)

13 Jul 1765 - Jul 1766: Rockingham I

First Lord of the Treasury	*Charles Watson Wentworth, 2nd Marquis of Rockingham* (for 1st time) (b. 13 May 1730; d. London 1 Jul 1782)
Secretary of State (North)	11 Jul 1765 - 14 May 1766: *Augustus Henry Fitzroy, 3rd Duke of Grafton* (b. 1 Oct 1735; d. Euston Hall 14 Mar 1811) May 1766 - 20 Jan 1768: *Henry Seymour Conway* (b. 1721; d. Park Place 9 Jul 1795)
Secretary of State (South)	10 Jul 1765 - May 1766: *Henry Seymour Conway* (see above) 23 May - 29 Jul 1766: *Charles Lennox, 3rd Duke of Richmond* (b. London 22 Feb 1735; d. Goodwood 29 Dec 1806)

Lord Chancellor	17 Jan 1761 – Jul 1766: *Robert Henley, 1st Earl of Northington* (see Newcastle II)
Lord President	*Daniel Finch, 8th Earl of Winchilsea and 3rd Earl of Nottingham* (see Walpole/Wilmington)
Lord Privy Seal	25 Aug 1765 – 30 Jul 1766: *Thomas Pelham-Holles, Duke of Newcastle* (see Walpole/Wilmington)
First Lord of the Admiralty	16 Sep 1763 – 15 Sep 1766: *John Perceval, 2nd Earl of Egmont* (see George Grenville)
Chancellor of the Exchequer	*William Dowdeswell* (b. 1721; d. Nice 6 Feb 1775)
Secretary at War	*William Wildman, 2nd Viscount Barrington* (see Newcastle II)

30 Jul 1766 – 28 Jan 1770: Chatham II/Grafton

Lord Privy Seal	30 Jul 1766 – Oct 1768: *William Pitt, 1st Earl of Chatham* (for 2nd time) (see Chatham I)
First Lord of the Treasury	*Augustus Henry Fitzroy, 3rd Duke of Grafton* (see Rockingham I) in charge from Oct 1768
Secretary of State (North)	May 1766 – 20 Jan 1768: *Henry Seymour Conway* (see Rockingham I)
	20 Jan – Oct 1768: *Thomas Thynne, 3rd Viscount Weymouth* (from 25 Aug 1789: *Marquis of Bath*) (b. 13 Sep 1734; d. London 19 Nov 1796)
	21 Oct 1768 – Dec 1770: *William Henry Zuylestein, 4th Earl of Rochford* (b. St Osyth 17 Sep 1717; d. St Osyth 28 Sep 1781)
Secretary of State (South)	30 Jul 1766 – 19 or 20 Oct 1768: *William Petty-Fitzmaurice, 2nd Earl of Shelburne* (from 1784: *Marquis of Lansdowne*) (b. Dublin 20 May 1737; d. London 7 May 1805)
	21 Oct 1768 – between 12 and 17 Dec 1770: *Thomas Thynne, 3rd Viscount Weymouth* (see above)
Secretary of State (Colonies)	21 Jan 1768 – Aug 1772: *Wills Hill, 2nd Viscount Hillsborough* (from 1772: *3rd Earl of Hillsborough; from 1789: Marquis of Downshire*) (b. Fairford, Gloucestershire, 30 May 1718; d. 7 Oct 1793)
Lord Chancellor	30 Jun 1766 – mid-Jan 1770: *Charles Pratt, Baron* (from 1786; *Earl*) *Camden* (b. 1713; d. 1793)
	17 – 20 Jan 1770: *Charles Yorke* (b. London 30 Dec 1722; d. London 20 Jan 1770)
Lord President	30 Jul 1766 – Dec 1767: *Robert Henley, 1st Earl of Northington* (see Newcastle II)

	23 Dec 1767 – Nov 1779: *Granville Leveson-Gower; 2nd Earl Gower* (see Newcastle I)
Lord Privy Seal	30 Jul 1766 – Oct 1768 (see above)
	2 Nov 1768 – Feb 1770: *George William Hervey, 2nd Earl of Bristol* (b. 31 Aug 1721; d. 18 or 20 Mar 1775)
First Lord of Admiralty	15 Sep – Nov 1766: *Sir Charles Saunders* (b. (?)1713; d. London 7 Dec 1775)
	11 Dec 1766 – Jan 1771: *Edward Hawke, Baron Hawke* (b. London 1705; d. Sunbury 17 Oct 1781)
Chancellor of the Exchequer	2 Aug 1766 – 4 Sep 1767: *Charles Townshend* (b. 25 Aug 1725; d. 24 Sep 1767)
	12 Sep – 30 Nov 1767: *William Murray, 1st Earl of Mansfield* (see Chatham I)
	1 Dec 1767 – 1770: *Frederick, Lord North* (from 1790: *2nd Earl of Guildford*) (b. London 13 Apr 1733; d. 5 Aug 1792)
Secretary at War	*William Wildman, 2nd Viscount Barrington* (see Newcastle II)

28 Jan 1770 – 19 Mar 1782: North

First Lord of the Treasury and Chancellor of the Exchequer	*Frederick, Lord North* (see Chatham II/ Grafton)
Secretary of State (North)	21 Oct 1768 – Dec 1770: *William Henry Zuylestein, 4th Earl of Rochford* (see Chatham II/ Grafton)
	19 Dec 1770 – 12 Jan 1771: *John Montagu, 3rd Earl of Sandwich* (see Pelham)
	22 Jan – 6 Jun 1771: *George Montagu Dunk, 2nd Earl of Halifax* (see Bute)
	12 Jun 1771 – 6 Mar 1779: *Henry Howard, 12th Earl of Suffolk* (b. 16 May 1739; d. 6 Mar 1779)
	27 Oct 1779 – Mar 1782: *David Murray, Viscount Stormont* (from 1793: *2nd Earl of Mansfield*) (b. 9 Oct 1727; d. Brighton 1 Sep 1796)
Secretary of State (South)	21 Oct 1768 – between 12 and 17 Dec 1770: *Thomas Thynne, 3rd Viscount Weymouth* (from 25 Aug 1789: *Marquis of Bath*) (see Chatham II/ Grafton)
	Dec 1770 – 9 Nov 1775: *William Henry Zuylestein, 4th Earl of Rochford* (see Chatham II/ Grafton)

	10 Nov 1775 – 24 Nov 1779 (both departments: 6 Mar – 27 Oct 1779): *William Thynne, 3rd Viscount Weymouth* (see Chatham II/ Grafton)
	25 Nov 1779 – Mar 1782: *Wills Hill, Earl of Hillsborough* (see Chatham II/ Grafton)
Secretary of State (Colonies)	21 Jan 1768 – Aug 1772: *Wills Hill, Earl of Hillsborough* (see Chatham II/ Grafton)
	15 Aug 1772 – Nov 1775: *William Legge, 2nd Earl of Dartmouth* (b. 20 Jun 1731; d. Blackheath 15 Jul 1801)
	10 Nov 1775 – Feb 1782: *Lord George Germain* (formerly *Sackville*) (from 1782: *1st Viscount Sackville*) (b. 26 Jan 1716; d. Stoneland Lodge, Sussex, 26 Aug 1785)
	11 Feb – Mar 1782: *Welbore Ellis* (from 1794: *1st Baron Mendip*) (b. Kildare 15 Dec 1713; d. London 2 Feb 1802)
Lord Chancellor	23 Jan 1771 – 1778; *Henry Bathurst* (from 1771: *Baron Apsley*; from 1775: *2nd Earl Bathurst*) (b. 2 May 1714; d. 6 Aug 1794)
	2 Jun 1778 – 9 Apr 1783: *Edward Thurlow, 1st Baron Thurlow* (b. Bracon Ash 9 Dec 1731; d. Brighton 12 Sep 1806)
Lord President	23 Dec 1767 – Nov 1779: *Granville Leveson-Gower, Earl Gower* (Newcastle I)
	24 Nov 1779 – 27 Mar 1782: *Henry Bathurst, 2nd Earl Bathurst* (see above)
Lord Privy Seal	26 Feb 1770 – Jan 1771: *George Montagu Dunk, 2nd Earl of Halifax* (see Bute)
	12 Jan – 1 Jun 1771: *Henry Howard, 12th Earl of Suffolk* (see above)
	1 Jun 1771 – Oct 1775: *Augustus Henry Fitzroy, 3rd Duke of Grafton* (see Rockingham I)
	4 Nov 1775 – 19 Mar 1782: *William Legge, 2nd Earl of Dartmouth*, not in cabinet (see above)
First Lord of the Admiralty	11 Dec 1766 – Jan 1771: *Edward Hawke, Baron Hawke* (see Chatham II/ Grafton)
	1771 – Mar 1782: *John Montagu, 3rd Earl of Sandwich* (see Pelham)
Secretary at War	Jan 1770 – 16 Dec 1778: *William Wildman, 2nd Viscount Barrington* (see Newcastle II)
	7 Dec 1778 – 19 Mar 1782: *Charles Jenkinson, Baron Hawkesbury* (from 1796: *Earl of Liverpool*) (b. Winchester 26 Apr 1727; d. London 17 Dec 1808)

27 Mar – 1 Jul 1782: Rockingham II

First Lord of the Treasury	*Charles Watson Wentworth, 2nd Marquis of Rockingham* (for 2nd time) (see Rockingham I)
Foreign Affairs	*Charles James Fox* (b. London 24 Jan 1749; d. Chiswick 13 Sep 1806)
Home and Colonial Affairs	*William Petty-Fitzmaurice, 2nd Earl of Shelburne* (from 1784: *Marquis of Lansdowne*) (b. Dublin 20 May 1737; d. London 7 May 1805)
Lord Chancellor	*Edward Thurlow, 1st Baron Thurlow* (see North)*
Lord President	*Charles Pratt, Baron Camden* (see Chatham II/Grafton)
Lord Privy Seal	*Augustus Henry Fitzroy, 3rd Duke of Grafton* (see Rockingham I)
First Lord of the Admiralty	*Augustus Keppel, 1st Viscount Keppel* (b. 25 Apr 1725; d. 2 Oct 1786)
Commander in Chief	*Henry Seymour Conway* (see Rockingham I)
Master General of the Ordnance	*Charles Lennox, 3rd Duke of Richmond* (see Rockingham I)
Chancellor of the Exchequer	*Lord John Cavendish* (b. 22 Oct 1732; d. Twickenham 18 Dec 1796)
Chancellor of the Duchy of Lancaster	*John Dunning, 1st Baron Ashburton* (b. Ashburton 18 Oct 1731; d. Exmouth 18 Aug 1783)

4 Jul 1782 – 2 Apr 1783: Shelburne

First Lord of the Treasury	*William Petty-Fitzmaurice, 2nd Earl of Shelburne* (see Chatham II/Grafton)
Foreign Affairs	*Thomas Robinson, 2nd Baron Grantham* (b. Vienna 30 Nov 1738; d. Putney Heath 20 Jul 1786)
Home Affairs	*Thomas Townshend* (from 1783: *1st Viscount Sydney*) (b. 24 Feb 1733; d. Chislehurst 30 Jun 1800)
Lord Chancellor	*Edward Thurlow, 1st Baron Thurlow* (see North)
Lord President	*Charles Pratt, Earl Camden* (see Chatham II/Grafton)
Lord Privy Seal	*Augustus Henry Fitzroy, 3rd Duke of Grafton* (see Rockingham I)
First Lord of the Admiralty	*Augustus Keppel, 1st Viscount Keppel* (see Rockingham II)
Commander in Chief	*Henry Seymour Conway* (see Rockingham I)
Master General of the Ordnance	*Charles Lennox, 3rd Duke of Richmond* (see Rockingham I)

Chancellor of the Exchequer	*William Pitt*, 'the Younger', second son of the Earl of Chatham (b. Hayes, Kent, 28 May 1759; d. Putney 23 Jan 1806)
Chancellor of the Duchy of Lancaster	*John Dunning, 1st Baron Ashburton* (see Rockingham II)

2 Apr – Dec 1783: Portland I

First Lord of the Treasury	*William Henry Cavendish-Bentinck, 3rd Duke of Portland* (for 1st time) (b. 14 Apr 1738; d. Bulstrode 30 Nov 1809) in nominal charge
Foreign Affairs	*Charles James Fox* (see Rockingham II)
Home Affairs	*Frederick, Lord North* (see Chatham II/Grafton)
Lord President	*David Murray, Viscount Stormont* (see North)
Lord Privy Seal	*Frederick Howard, 5th Earl of Carlisle* (b. 28 May 1748; d. Castle Howard 4 Sep 1825)
First Lord of the Admiralty	*Augustus Keppel, 1st Viscount Keppel* (see Rockingham II)
Chancellor of the Exchequer	*Lord John Cavendish* (see Rockingham II)

19 Dec 1783 – 14 Mar 1801: Pitt I

First Lord of the Treasury and Chancellor of the Exchequer	*William Pitt* (for 1st time) (see Shelburne)
Foreign Affairs	19 – 23 Dec 1783: *George Nugent-Temple-Grenville, 2nd Earl Temple* (from 1784: *Marquis of Buckingham*) (b. 17 Jan 1753; d. Stowe 11 Feb 1813)
	23 Dec 1783 – Apr 1791: *Francis Osborne, Marquis of Carmarthen* (from 1789: *5th Duke of Leeds*) (b. 29 Jan 1751; d. London 31 Jan 1799)
	Apr 1791 – Mar 1801: *William Wyndham Grenville* (b. 25 Oct 1759; d. Dropmore 12 Jan 1834)
Home Affairs	19 – 23 Dec 1783: *Earl Temple* (see above)
	23 Dec 1783 – Jun 1789: *Thomas Townshend, 1st Viscount Sydney* (see Shelburne)
	Jun 1789 – Apr 1791: *William Wyndham Grenville* (see above)
	Apr/Jun 1791 – Jul 1794: *Henry Dundas* (from 1802: *1st Viscount Melville*) (b. 28 Apr 1742; d. Edinburgh 28 May 1811)

	Jul 1794 – Mar 1801: *William Henry Cavendish-Bentinck, 3rd Duke of Portland* (see Portland I)
Secretary of War	Jul 1794 – Mar 1801: *Henry Dundas* (see above)
Lord Chancellor	19 Dec 1783 – Jun 1792: *Edward Thurlow, 1st Baron Thurlow* (see North)
	1792 – Mar 1801: *Alexander Wedderburn, 1st Baron Loughborough* (from 1801: *1st Earl of Rosslyn*) (b. Edinburgh 13 Feb 1733; d. Windsor 2 Jan 1805)
Lord President	19 Dec 1783 – Nov 1784: *Granville Leveson-Gower, 2nd Earl Gower* (see Newcastle I)
	Nov 1784 – Jul 1794: *Charles Pratt, Baron* (from 1786: *Earl of Camden*) (see Chatham II/Grafton)
	Jul – Dec 1794: *William Wentworth, 4th Earl Fitzwilliam* (b. 30 May 1748; d. 8 Feb 1833)
	Dec 1794 – Sep 1796: *David Murray, 2nd Earl of Mansfield* (see North)
	Sep 1796 – Mar 1801: *John Pitt, 2nd Earl of Chatham* (b. 10 Sep 1756; d. London 24 Sep 1835)
Lord Privy Seal	13 Jan – 11 Feb 1784: *Charles Manners, 4th Duke of Rutland* (b. 15 Mar 1754; d. Dublin 24 Oct 1787)
	Nov 1784 – Jul 1794: *Granville Leveson-Gower, 2nd Earl Gower* (see Newcastle I)
	Jul – Dec 1794: *George John Spencer, 2nd Earl Spencer* (b. Wimbledon 1 Sep 1758; d. Althorp 10 Nov 1834)
	Dec 1794 – Sep 1796: *John Pitt, 2nd Earl of Chatham* (see above)
	Feb 1798 – Mar 1801: *John Fane, 10th Earl of Westmorland* (b. 1 Jun 1759; d. 15 Dec 1841)
First Lord of the Admiralty	31 Dec 1783 – 16 Jul 1788: *Richard Howe, 1st Earl Howe* (b. London 8 Mar 1726; d. 5 Aug 1799)
	16 Jul 1788 – Dec 1794: *John Pitt, 2nd Earl of Chatham* (see above)
	Dec 1794 – Mar 1801: *George John Spencer, 2nd Earl Spencer* (see above)
Master General of the Ordnance	13 Jan 1784 – Feb 1795: *Charles Lennox, 3rd Duke of Richmond* (see Rockingham I)
	Feb 1795 – Mar 1801: *Charles Cornwallis, Marquis Cornwallis* (b. 31 Dec 1738; d. 5 Oct 1805) left cabinet Jun 1798
Commander in Chief	(Member of cabinet Jan 1793 – Feb 1795:) *Jeffrey Amherst, Baron Amherst* (b. Riverhead 27 Jan 1717; d. Montreal, Kent, 3 Aug 1797)

Trade	1786 – Mar 1801 (joined cabinet 1791:) *Charles Jenkinson, Baron Hawkesbury* (from 1796: *Earl of Liverpool*) (see North)
Chancellor of the Duchy of Lancaster	Jul 1794 – Sep 1801: *Charles Jenkinson, Baron Hawkesbury* (see North)
Secretary at War	Jul 1794 – Sep 1801: *William Windham* (b. London 3 May 1750; d. 4 Jun 1810)
Without Portfolio	Jul – Dec 1794: *David Murray, 2nd Earl of Mansfield* (see North)
	Jun 1798 – Sep 1801: *John Jeffreys Pratt, 2nd Earl Camden* (from 1812: *1st Marquis*) (11 Feb 1759; d. Wilderness, Kent, 8 Oct 1840)

17 Sep 1801 – Apr 1804: Addington

First Lord of the Treasury and Chancellor of the Exchequer	*Henry Addington* (from 1805: *Viscount Sidmouth*) (b. London 30 May 1757; d. 15 Feb 1844)
Foreign Affairs	*Robert Banks Jenkinson, Lord Hawkesbury* (from 1808: *2nd Earl of Liverpool*) (b. 7 Jun 1770; d. 4 Dec 1828)
Home Affairs	Mar – Jul 1801: *William Henry Cavendish-Bentinck, 3rd Duke of Portland* (see Portland I)
	Jul 1801 – Aug 1803: *Thomas Pelham* (from 1805: *2nd Earl of Chichester*) (b. London 28 Apr 1756; d. 4 Jul 1826)
	Aug 1803 – Apr 1804: *Charles Philip Yorke* (b. 12 Mar 1764; d. London 13 Mar 1834)
War and Colonies	*Robert Hobart, Lord Hobart* (from 1804: *4th Earl of Buckinghamshire*) (b. 6 May 1760; d. London 4 Feb 1816)
Lord Chancellor	*John Scott, Earl of Eldon* (b. Newcastle-upon-Tyne 4 Jun 1751; d. London 13 Jan 1838)
Lord President	Mar – Jul 1801: *John Pitt, 2nd Earl of Chatham* (see Pitt I)
	Jul 1801 – Mar 1804: *William Henry Cavendish-Bentinck 3rd Duke of Portland* (see Portland I)
Lord Privy Seal	*John Fane, 10th Earl of Westmorland* (see Pitt I)
First Lord of the Admiralty	*John Jervis, Earl of Saint Vincent* (b. Meaford 9 Jan 1735; d. 14 Mar 1823)

Master General of the Ordnance	Jul 1801 – Apr 1804: *John Pitt, 2nd Earl of Chatham* (see Pitt I)
Duchy of Lancaster	Mar 1801 – Apr 1804: *Charles Jenkinson, Earl of Liverpool* (see North)
Trade	*Charles Jenkinson, Earl of Liverpool* (see North)
Board of Control (for India)	Oct 1802 – Apr 1804: *Henry Robert Stewart, Viscount Castlereagh* (from 1821: *Marquis of Londonderry*) (b. Mount Stewart 18 Jun 1769; d. North Cray 12 Aug 1822)

10 May 1804 – 23 Jan 1806: Pitt II

First Lord of the Treasury and Chancellor of the Exchequer	*William Pitt* (for 2nd time) (see Shelburne)
Foreign Affairs	May 1804 – Jan 1805: *Dudley Ryder, 1st Earl of Harrowby* (b. London 22 Dec 1762; d. Sandon 26 Dec 1847) Jan 1805 – Jan 1806: *Henry Phipps, Baron Mulgrave* (from 1812: *1st Earl of Mulgrave*) (b. 14 Feb 1756; d. Yorkshire 7 Apr 1831)
Home Affairs	*Robert Banks Jenkinson, Lord Hawkesbury* (see Addington)
War and Colonies	May 1804 – Jun/Jul 1805: *John Jeffreys Pratt, 2nd Earl Camden* (see Pitt I) Jun/Jul 1805 – Jan 1806: *Henry Robert Stewart, Viscount Castlereagh* (see Addington)
Lord Chancellor	*John Scott, Earl of Eldon* (see Addington)
Lord President	May 1804 – Jan 1805: *William Henry Cavendish-Bentinck, 3rd Duke of Portland* (see Portland I) Jan – Jun/Jul 1805: *Henry Addington, Viscount Sidmouth* (see Addington) Jun/Jul 1805 – Jan 1806: *John Jeffreys Pratt, 2nd Earl Camden* (see Pitt I)
Lord Privy Seal	*John Fane, 10th Earl of Westmorland* (see Pitt I)
First Lord of the Admiralty	May 1804 – May 1805: *Henry Dundas, 1st Viscount Melville* (see Pitt I) May 1805 – Jan 1806: *Charles Middleton, 1st Baron Barnham* (b. Leith 14 Oct 1726; d. 17 Jun 1813)
Master General of the Ordnance	*John Pitt, 2nd Earl of Chatham* (see Pitt I)

Trade	*James Graham, 3rd Duke of Montrose* (b. 8 Sep 1755; d. London 30 Dec 1836)
Board of Control (for India)	*Henry Robert Stewart, Viscount Castlereagh* (see Addington)
Chancellor of the Duchy of Lancaster	May 1804 – Jan 1805: *Henry Phipps, Baron Mulgrave* (see above)
	Jan – Jun/Jul 1805: *Robert Hobart, 4th Earl of Buckinghamshire* (see Addington)
	Jun/Jul 1805 – Jan 1806: *Dudley Ryder, 1st Earl of Harrowby* (see above)
Without Portfolio	Jan 1805 – Jan 1806: *William Henry Cavendish-Bentinck, 3rd Duke of Portland* (see Portland I)
	Jan – Jun/Jul 1805: *Dudley Ryder, 1st Earl of Harrowby* (see above)

11 Feb 1806 – Mar 1807: Grenville

First Lord of the Treasury	*William Wyndham Grenville, 1st Baron Grenville* (see Pitt I)
Foreign Affairs	Feb – 13 Sep 1806: *Charles James Fox* (see Rockingham II)
	Sep 1806 – Mar 1807: *Charles Grey, Viscount Howick* (from 1807: *2nd Earl Grey*) (b. Fallodon 13 Jun 1764; d. 17 Jul 1845)
Home Affairs	*George John Spencer, 2nd Earl Spencer* (see Pitt I)
Chancellor of the Exchequer	*Lord Henry Petty* (afterwards *Petty-Fitzmaurice*) (from 1809: *3rd Marquis of Lansdowne*) (b. London 2 Jul 1780; d. Bowood 31 Jan 1863)
War and Colonies	*William Windham* (see Pitt I)
Lord Chancellor	*Thomas Erskine* (from 1806: *1st Baron Erskine*) (b. Edinburgh 10 Jan (?)1750; d. Almondell 17 Nov 1823)
Lord President	Feb – Sep/Oct 1806: *William Wentworth, 4th Earl Fitzwilliam* (see Pitt I)
	Sep/Oct 1806 – Mar 1807: *Henry Addington, 1st Viscount Sidmouth* (see Addington)
Lord Privy Seal	Feb – Sep/Oct 1806: *Henry Addington, 1st Viscount Sidmouth* (see Addington)
	Sep/Oct 1806 – Mar 1807: *Henry Richard Vassal Fox, 3rd Baron Holland* (b. Winterslow House 21 Nov 1773; d. London 22 Oct 1840)
First Lord of the Admiralty	Feb – Sep/Oct 1806: *Charles Grey* (from Apr 1806: *Viscount Howick;* from 1807: *2nd Earl Grey*) (see above)

	Sep/Oct 1806 – Mar 1807: *Thomas Grenville* (b. 31 Dec 1755; d. London 17 Dec 1846)
Master General of the Ordnance	*Francis Rawdon-Hastings, 2nd Earl of Moira* (from 1817: *1st Marquis of Hastings*) (b. 7 Dec 1754; d. Naples 28 Nov 1826)
Lord Chief Justice of the King's Bench	*Edward Law, 1st Baron Ellenborough* (b. Great Salkeld 16 Nov 1750; d. London 13 Dec 1818)
Board of Control (for India)	Jul – Sep/Oct 1806: *Thomas Grenville* (see above)
Without Portfolio	Sep/Oct 1806 – Mar 1807: *William Wentworth, 4th Earl Fitzwilliam* (see Pitt I)

31 Mar 1807 – 30 Sep 1809: Portland II

First Lord of the Treasury	*William Henry Cavendish-Bentinck, 3rd Duke of Portland* (for 2nd time) (see Portland I)
Foreign Affairs	*George Canning* (b. London 11 Apr 1770; d. Chiswick 8 Aug 1827)
Home Affairs	*Robert Banks Jenkinson, Lord Hawkesbury*, (from 1808: *2nd Earl of Liverpool*) (see Addington)
Chancellor of the Exchequer	*Spencer Perceval* (b. London 1 Nov 1762; d. (assassinated) 11 May 1812)
War and Colonies	*Henry Robert Stewart, Viscount Castlereagh* (see Addington)
Lord Chancellor	*John Scott, Earl of Eldon* (see Addington)
Lord President	*John Jeffreys Pratt, 2nd Earl Camden* (see Pitt I)
Lord Privy Seal	*John Fane, 10th Earl of Westmorland* (see Pitt I)
First Lord of the Admiralty	*Henry Phipps, Baron Mulgrave* (see Pitt II)
Master General of the Ordnance	*John Pitt, 2nd Earl of Chatham* (see Pitt I)
Trade	*Henry Bathurst, 3rd Earl Bathurst* (b. 22 May 1762; d. 27 Jul 1834)
Board of Control (for India)	Jul – Sep 1809: *Dudley Ryder, 1st Earl of Harrowby* (see Pitt II)
Duchy of Lancaster	*Spencer Perceval* (see above)
Secretary at War	Jun – Sep 1809: *Lord Granville Leveson-Gower* (from 1815: *Viscount*; from 1833: *Earl Granville*) (b. 12 Oct 1773; d. London 8 Jan 1846)

4 Oct 1809 – 11 May 1812: Perceval

First Lord of the Treasury and Chancellor of the Exchequer	*Spencer Perceval* (see Portland II)
Foreign Affairs	Oct – Dec 1809: *Henry Bathurst, 3rd Earl Bathurst* (see Portland II)
	Dec 1809 – Mar/Apr 1812: *Richard Colley Wellesley, Marquis Wellesley* (b. Dublin 20 Jun 1760; d. Brompton 26 Sep 1842)
	Mar/Apr – May 1812: *Henry Robert Stewart, Viscount Castlereagh* (see Addington)
Home Affairs	*Richard Ryder* (b. 5 Jul 1766; d. Westbrook Hay 18 Sep 1832)
War and Colonies	*Robert Banks Jenkinson, 2nd Earl of Liverpool* (see Addington)
Lord Chancellor	*John Scott, Earl of Eldon* (see Addington)
Lord President	Oct 1809 – Mar/Apr 1812: *John Jeffreys Pratt, 2nd Earl Camden* (see Pitt I)
	Mar/Apr – May 1812: *Henry Addington, 1st Viscount Sidmouth* (see Addington)
Lord Privy Seal	*John Fane, 10th Earl of Westmorland* (see Pitt I)
First Lord of the Admiralty	Dec 1809 – Apr 1810: *Henry Phipps, Baron Mulgrave* (see Pitt II)
	Apr 1810 – Mar/Apr 1812: *Charles Philip Yorke* (see Addington)
	Mar/Apr – May 1812: *Robert Saunders Dundas, 2nd Viscount Melville* (b. 14 Mar 1771; d. Melville Castle 10 Jun 1841)
Master General of the Ordnance	Dec 1809 – Apr 1810: *John Pitt, 2nd Earl of Chatham* (see Pitt I)
	Apr 1810 – May 1812: *Henry Phipps, Baron Mulgrave* (see Pitt II)
Trade	*Henry Bathurst, 3rd Earl Bathurst* (see Portland II)
Board of Control (for India)	Dec 1809 – Mar/Apr 1812: *Robert Saunders Dundas*, (from 1811: *2nd Viscount Melville*) (see above)
	Mar/Apr – May 1812: *Robert Hobart, 4th Earl of Buckinghamshire* (see Addington)
Without Portfolio	4 – 30 Oct 1809: *William Henry Cavendish-Bentinck, 3rd Duke of Portland* (see Portland I)
	Nov 1809 – May 1812: *Dudley Ryder, 1st Earl of Harrowby* (see Pitt II)

Mar/Apr - May 1812: *John Jeffreys Pratt, 2nd Earl Camden* (see Pitt I)

Duchy of Lancaster
Spencer Perceval (see Portland II)

9 Jun 1812 - Feb 1827: Liverpool

First Lord of the Treasury	*Robert Banks Jenkinson, 2nd Earl of Liverpool* (see Addington)
Foreign Affairs	May 1812 - 12 Aug 1822: *Henry Robert Stewart, Viscount Castlereagh*, (from 1821: *Marquis of Londonderry*) (see Addington)
	Sep 1822 - Feb 1827: *George Canning* (see Portland II)
Home Affairs	May 1812 - Jan 1822: *Henry Addington, 1st Viscount Sidmouth* (see Addington)
	Jan 1822 - Feb 1827: *Sir Robert Peel* (b. 5 Feb 1788; d. London 2 Jul 1850)
Chancellor of the Excehquer	20 May 1812 - Dec 1822: *Nicholas Vansittart* (from 1823: *Baron Bexley*) (b. London 29 Apr 1766; d. Foots Cray, Kent, 8 Feb 1851)
	31 Jan 1823 - Feb 1827: *Frederick John Robinson* (from 1827: *1st Viscount Goderich;* from 1833: *Earl of Ripon*) (b. London 30 Oct 1782; d. Putney Heath 28 Jan 1859)
War and Colonies	*Henry Bathurst, 3rd Earl Bathurst* (see Portland II)
Lord Chancellor	*John Scott, Earl of Eldon* (see Addington)
Lord President	*Dudley Ryder, 1st Earl of Harrowby* (see Pitt II)
Lord Privy Seal	*John Fane, 10th Earl of Westmorland* (see Pitt I)
First Lord of the Admiralty	*Robert Saunders Dundas, 2nd Viscount Melville* (see Perceval)
Master General of the Ordnance	Jun 1812 - Jan 1819: *Henry Phipps, Baron Mulgrave,* (from Sep 1812: *1st Earl of Mulgrave*) (see Pitt II)
	Jan 1819 - Feb 1827: *Arthur Wellesley, Duke of Wellington* (b. Dangan Castle 29 or 30 Apr 1769; d. Walmer Castle 14 Apr 1852)
Trade	Jun - Sep 1812: *Henry Bathurst, 3rd Earl Bathurst* (see Portland II)
	Jan 1818 - Jan 1823: *Frederick John Robinson* (see above)
	Jan/Oct 1823 - Feb 1827 (joined cabinet Oct 1823:) *William Huskisson* (b. Birch Moreton Court, Warwickshire, 11 Mar 1770; d. Eccles 15 Sep 1830)

Board of Control (for India)	Jun 1812 – Jun 1816: *Robert Hobart, 4th Earl of Buckinghamshire* (see Addington) Jun 1816 – Jan 1821: *George Canning* (see Portland II) Jan 1821 – Feb 1822: *Charles Bragge Bathurst* (d. 13 Aug 1831) Feb 1822 – Feb 1827: *Charles Watkin Williams Wynn* (b. 9 Oct 1775; d. London 2 Sep 1850)
Duchy of Lancaster	Jun 1812 – Feb 1823: *Charles Bragge Bathurst* (see above) Feb 1823 – Feb 1827: *Nicholas Vansittart, Baron Bexley* (see above)
Master of the Mint	Sep 1814 – Aug 1823: *William Wellesley Pole* (from 1821: *Lord Maryborough;* from 1842: *Marquis Wellesley*) (b. Dangan Castle 20 May 1763; d. London 22 Feb 1845)
Treasurer of the Navy	Jan 1818 – Jan 1823: *Frederick John Robinson* (see above) Jan 1823 – Feb 1827 (joined cabinet Oct 1823:) *William Huskisson* (see above)
Without Portfolio	Jun – Dec 1812: *John Jeffreys Pratt, 2nd Earl Camden* (see Pitt I) Jan 1819 – May 1820: *Henry Phipps, 1st Earl of Mulgrave* (see Pitt II) Jan 1822 – 1824: *Henry Addington, 1st Viscount Sidmouth* (see Addington)

10 Apr – 8 Aug 1827: Canning

First Lord of the Treasury and Chancellor of the Exchequer	*George Canning* (see Portland II)
Foreign Affairs	*John William Ward, 4th Viscount Dudley and Ward* (from 1827: *1st Earl of Dudley*) (b. 9 Aug 1781; d. Norwood 6 Mar 1833)
Home Affairs	May – Jul 1827: *William Sturges Bourne* (b. 7 Nov 1769; d. Testwood House, Hampshire, 1 Feb 1845) Jul – Aug 1827: *Henry Petty Fitzmaurice, 3rd Marquis of Lansdowne* (see William Grenville)
War and Colonies	*Frederick John Robinson, 1st Viscount Goderich* (see Liverpool)
Lord Chancellor	*John Singleton Copley, Baron Lyndhurst* (b. Boston, Massachusetts, 21 May 1772; d. 12 Oct 1863)

Lord President	*Dudley Ryder, 1st Earl of Harrowby* (see Pitt II)
Lord Privy Seal	May – Jul 1827: *William Henry Cavendish-Bentinck-Scott, 4th Duke of Portland* (b. 24 Jun 1795; d. 27 Mar 1854)
	Jul – Aug 1827: *George Howard, 6th Earl of Carlisle* (b. London 17 Sep 1773; d. Castle Howard 7 Oct 1848)
Master General of the Ordnance	*Henry William Paget, 1st Marquis of Anglesey* (b. London 17 May 1768; d. 29 Apr 1854)
Trade and Treasurer of the Navy	*William Huskisson* (see Liverpool)
Board of Control (for India)	*Charles Watkin Williams Wynn* (see Liverpool)
Duchy of Lancaster	*Nicholas Vansittart, Baron Bexley* (see Liverpool)
Secretary at War	*Henry John Temple, Viscount Palmerston* (b. Broadlands, Hampshire, 20 Oct 1784; d. Brocket Hill 18 Oct 1865)
Master of the Mint	*George Tierney* (b. Gibraltar 20 Mar 1761; d. London 25 Jan 1830)
Woods and Forests	May – Jul 1827: *George Howard, 6th Earl of Carlisle* (see above)
	Jul – Aug 1827: *William Sturges Bourne* (see above)
Without Portfolio	May – Jul, 1827: *Henry Petty Fitzmaurice, 3rd Marquis of Lansdowne* (see William Grenville)
	Jul – Aug 1827: *William Henry Cavendish-Bentinck-Scott, 4th Duke of Portland* (see above)

31 Aug 1827 – Jan 1828: Goderich

First Lord of the Treasury	*Frederick John Robinson, 1st Viscount Goderich* (see Liverpool)
Foreign Affairs	*John William Ward, 4th Viscount Dudley and Ward,* (from 1827: *1st Earl of Dudley*) (see Canning)
Home Affairs	*Henry Petty Fitzmaurice, 3rd Marquis of Lansdowne* (see William Grenville)
Chancellor of the Exchequer	*John Charles Herries* (b. (?)Nov 1778; d. St Julians, near Sevenoaks, 24 Apr 1855)
War and Colonies	*William Huskisson* (see Liverpool)
Lord Chancellor	*John Singleton Copley, Baron Lyndhurst* (see Canning)
Lord President	*William Henry Cavendish-Bentinck-Scott, 4th Duke of Portland* (see Canning)
Lord Privy Seal	*George Howard, 6th Earl of Carlisle* (see Canning)

Master General of the Ordnance	*William Henry Paget, 1st Marquis of Anglesey* (see Canning)
Trade and Treasurer of the Navy	*Charles Grant* (from 1835: *Baron Glenelg*) (b. Kidderpore 26 Oct 1778; d. Cannes 23 Apr 1866)
Board of Control (for India)	*Charles Watkin Williams Wynn* (see Liverpool)
Duchy of Lancaster	*Nicholas Vansittart, Baron Bexley* (see Liverpool)
Secretary at War	*Henry John Temple, Viscount Palmerston* (see Canning)
Master of the Mint	*George Tierney* (see Canning)
Woods and Forests	*William Sturges Bourne* (see Canning)

22 Jan 1828 – Nov 1830: Wellington I

First Lord of the Treasury	*Arthur Wellesley, Duke of Wellington* (for 1st time) (see Liverpool)
Foreign Affairs	Jan – May/Jun 1828: *John William Ward, 1st Earl of Dudley* (see Canning)
	May/Jun 1828 – Nov 1830: *George Hamilton-Gordon, 4th Earl of Aberdeen*, (b. Edinburgh 28 Jan 1784; d. London 14 Dec 1860)
Home Affairs	*Sir Robert Peel* (see Liverpool)
Chancellor of the Exchequer	*Henry Goulburn* (b. London 19 Mar 1784; d. Betchworth House, near Dorking, 12 Jan 1856)
War and Colonies	Jan – May/Jun 1828: *William Huskisson* (see Liverpool)
	May/Jun 1828 – Nov 1830: *Sir George Murray* (b. Ochtertyre 6 Feb 1772; d. London 28 Jul 1846)
Lord Chancellor	*John Singleton Copley, Baron Lyndhurst* (see Canning)
Lord President	*Henry Bathurst, 3rd Earl Bathurst* (see Portland II)
Lord Privy Seal	Jan – Sep 1828: *Edward Law, 2nd Baron Ellenborough* (from 1844: *Earl of Ellenborough*) (b. 8 Sep 1790; d. London 22 Dec 1871)
	Sep 1828 – Nov 1830: *James St Clair Erskine, Earl of Rosslyn* (b. 1762; d. Dysart House 18 Jan 1837)
First Lord of the Admiralty	Sep 1828 – Nov 1830: *Robert Saunders Dundas, 2nd Viscount Melville* (see Perceval)
	The Duke of Clarence, Lord High Admiral from Apr 1827 to Sep 1828, did not sit in the cabinet

Trade and Treasurer of the Navy	Jan – May/Jun 1828: *Charles Grant* (see Goderich) May/Jun 1828 – Feb 1830: *William Vesey Fitzgerald* (from 1832: *Baron Fitzgerald and Vesey*) (b. 1783; d. London 11 May 1843)
Board of Control (for India)	Jan – Sep 1828: *Robert Saunders Dundas, 2nd Viscount Melville* (see Perceval) Sep 1828 – Nov 1830: *Edward Law, 2nd Baron Ellenborough* (see above)
Master of the Mint	*John Charles Herries* (see Goderich)
Duchy of Lancaster	Jan – May/Jun 1828: *George Hamilton-Gordon, 4th Earl of Aberdeen* (see above) successor not in cabinet
Secretary at War	Jan – May/Jun. 1828: *Henry John Temple, Viscount Palmerston* (see Canning) successor not in cabinet

16 Nov 1830 – Jul 1834: Grey (Whig)

Prime Minister	*Charles, 2nd Earl Grey* (see William Grenville)
Foreign Affairs	*Henry John Temple, Viscount Palmerston* (see Canning)
Home Affairs	*William Lamb, Viscount Melbourne* (b. 15 Mar 1779; d. 24 Nov 1848)
Chancellor of the Exchequer	*John Charles Spencer, Viscount Althorp* (from 10 Nov 1834: *3rd Earl Spencer*) (b. 30 May 1782; d. Wiseton Hall, Yorkshire, 1 Oct 1845)
War and Colonies	Nov 1830 – Mar 1833: *Frederick John Robinson, 1st Viscount Goderich* (see Liverpool) Mar 1833 – May/Jun 1834: *Edward (George) Geoffrey (Smith) Stanley* (from 1844: *Lord Stanley;* from 1851: *14th Earl of Derby*) (b. Knowsley Park, Lancashire, 29 Mar 1799; d. Knowsley Park 23 Oct 1869) May/Jun – Jul 1834: *Thomas Spring Rice* (from 1839: *1st Baron Monteagle of Brandon*) (b. Limerick 8 Feb 1790; d. Limerick 7 Feb 1866)
Lord Chancellor	*Henry Brougham, Baron Brougham and Vaux* (b. Edinburgh 19 Sep 1778; d. Cannes 7 May 1868)
Lord President	*Henry Petty Fitzmaurice, 3rd Marquis of Lansdowne* (see William Grenville)
Lord Privy Seal	Nov 1830 – Apr 1833: *John George Lambton, Baron Durham* (from 1833: *1st Earl of Durham*) (b. London 12 Apr 1792; d. Cowes 28 Jul 1840) Apr 1833 – May/Jun 1834: *Frederick John Robinson,*

Earl of Ripon (see Liverpool)

May/Jun – Jul 1834: *George Howard, 6th Earl of Carlisle* (see Canning)

First Lord of the Admiralty	Nov 1830 – May/Jun 1834: *Sir James Robert George Graham* (b. 1 Jun 1792; d. Netherby 25 Oct 1861) May/Jun – Jul 1834: *George Eden, 2nd Baron Auckland* (from 1839: *Earl of Auckland* (b. Beckenham 25 Aug 1784; d. Alesford 1 Jan 1849)
Trade and Treasurer of the Navy	May/Jun – Jul 1834: *James Abercromby* (from 1839: *Baron Dunfermline*) (b. 7 Nov 1776; d. Colinton House, Midlothian, 17 Apr 1858)
Board of Control (for India)	*Charles Grant* (see Goderich)
Master of the Mint	May/Jun – Jul 1834: *James Abercromby* (see above)
Duchy of Lancaster	*Henry Richard Vassal Fox, 3rd Baron Holland* (see William Grenville)
Secretary at War	Apr 1833 – Jul 1834 (admitted to cabinet May/Jun 1834:) *Edward Ellice* (b. 1781; d. Ardochy 17 Sep 1863)
Postmaster-General	Nov 1830 – May/Jun 1834: *Charles Gordon-Lennox, 5th Duke of Richmond* (b. 3 Aug 1791; d. London 21 Oct 1860)
Paymaster-General	*Lord John Russell* (from 1861: *1st Earl Russell*) (b. London 18 Aug 1792; d. Pembroke Lodge, Richmond 28 May 1878)

9 Jul – 14 Nov 1834: Melbourne I (Whig)

First Lord of the Treasury	*William Lamb, Viscount Melbourne* (for 1st time) (see Grey)
Foreign Affairs	*Henry John Temple, Viscount Palmerston* (see Canning)
Home Affairs	*John William Ponsonby, Viscount Duncannon* (from 1844: *4th Earl of Bessborough*) (b. 31 Aug 1781; d. Dublin 16 May 1847)
Chancellor of the Exchequer	*John Charles Spencer, Viscount Althorp* (see Grey)
War and Colonies	*Thomas Spring Rice* (see Grey)
Lord Chancellor	*Henry Brougham, Baron Brougham and Vaux* (see Grey)
Lord President	*Henry Petty Fitzmaurice, 3rd Marquis of Lansdowne* (see William Grenville)

Lord Privy Seal	*Constantine Henry Phipps, 2nd Earl of Mulgrave* (from 1838: *Marquis of Normanby*) (b. 15 May 1797; d. London 28 Jul 1863)
First Lord of the Admiralty	*George Eden, 2nd Baron Auckland* (see Grey)
Trade and Treasurer of the Navy	*Charles Edward Poulett Thomson* (from 1840: *Baron Sydenham*) (b. Wimbledon 13 Sep 1799; d. Kingston-on-Thames 19 Sep 1841)
Board of Control (for India)	*Charles Grant* (see Goderich)
Master of the Mint	*James Abercromby* (see Grey)
Duchy of Cornwall	*Henry Richard Vassal Fox, 3rd Baron Holland* (see William Grenville)
Secretary at War	*Edward Ellice* (see Grey)
Woods and Forests	*Sir John Camm Hobhouse* (from 1851: *Baron Broughton de Gyfford*) (b. London 27 Jun 1786; d. London 3 Jun 1869)
Paymaster-General	*Lord John Russell* (see Grey)

14 Nov – 10 Dec 1834: Wellington II (provisional administration)

Treasury, Foreign Affairs, Home Affairs and War and Colonies	*Arthur Wellesley, Duke of Wellington* (for 2nd time) (see Liverpool)
Chancellor of the Exchequer	*Thomas Denman, Baron Denman* (b. London 23 Feb 1779; d. 22 Sep 1854)
Lord Chancellor	*John Singleton Copley, Baron Lyndhurst* (see Canning)

10 Dec 1834 – Apr 1835 Peel I (Tory)

First Lord of Treasury and Chancellor of the Exchequer	*Sir Robert Peel* (for 1st time) (see Liverpool)
Foreign Affairs	*Arthur Wellesley, Duke of Wellington* (see Liverpool)
Home Affairs	*Henry Goulburn* (see Wellington I)
War and Colonies	*George Hamilton-Gordon, 4th Earl of Aberdeen* (see Wellington I)

Lord Chancellor	*John Singleton Copley, Baron Lyndhurst* (see Canning)
Lord President	*James St Clair Erskine, Earl of Rosslyn* (see Wellington I)
Lord Privy Seal	*James Archibald Stuart-Wortley-Mackenzie, 1st Baron Wharncliffe* (b. 6 Oct 1776; d. London 19 Dec 1845)
First Lord of the Admiralty	*Thomas Philip de Grey, 2nd Earl de Grey* (b. 8 Dec 1781; d. London 14 Nov 1859)
Trade and Master of the Mint	*Alexander Baring* (from 1835: *1st Baron Ashburton*) (b. 27 Oct 1774; d. Longleat 12 May 1848)
Board of Control (for India)	*Edward Law, 2nd Baron Ellenborough* (see Wellington I)
Secretary at War	*John Charles Herries* (see Goderich)
Paymaster-General	*Sir Edward Knatchbull* (b. 20 Dec 1781; d. 24 May 1849)

18 Apr 1835 – 31 Aug 1841: Melbourne II (Whig)*

First Lord of the Treasury	*William Lamb, Viscount Melbourne* (for 2nd time) (see Grey)
Foreign Affairs	*Henry John Temple, Viscount Palmerston* (see Canning)
Home Affairs	Apr 1835 – Sep 1839: *Lord John Russell* (see Grey) Sep 1839 – Aug 1841: *Constantine Henry Phipps, Marquis of Normanby* (see Melbourne I)
Chancellor of the Exchequer	Apr 1835 – Aug 1839: *Thomas Spring Rice, 1st Baron Monteagle of Brandon* (see Grey) Aug 1839 – Aug 1841: *Sir Francis Thornhill Baring* (from 1866: *1st Baron Northbrook*) (b. Calcutta 20 Apr 1796; d. Stratton Park 6 Sep 1866)
War and Colonies	Apr 1835 – Feb 1839: *Charles Grant, Baron Glenelg* (see Goderich) Feb – Sep 1839: *Constantine Henry Phipps, Marquis of Normanby* (see Melbourne I) Sep 1839 – Aug 1841: *Lord John Russell* (see Grey)
Lord Chancellor	*Charles Christopher Pepys, 1st Earl of Cottenham* (b. London 29 Apr 1781; d. Pietra Santa 29 Apr 1851
Lord President	*Henry Petty Fitzmaurice, 3rd Marquis of Lansdowne* (see William Grenville)

*On 7 May 1839 Lord Melbourne resigned but, no alternative government being formed, he resumed office a few days later.

Lord Privy Seal	Apr 1835 – Jan 1840: *John William Ponsonby, Viscount Duncannon* (see Melbourne I)
	Jan 1840 – Aug 1841: *George William Frederick Villiers, 4th Earl of Clarendon* (b. London 12 Jan 1800; d. London 27 Jun 1870)
First Lord of Admiralty	Apr – Sep 1835: *George Eden, 2nd Baron Auckland* (see Grey)
	Sep 1835 – Aug 1841: *Gilbert Elliot, 2nd Earl of Minto* (b. Lyons 16 Nov 1782; d. 31 Jul 1859)
Trade	Apr 1835 – Aug 1839: *Charles Edward Poulett Thomson* (see Melbourne I)
	Aug 1839 – Aug 1841: *Henry Labouchere* (from 1859: *Baron Taunton*) (b. London 15 Aug 1798; d. 13 Jul 1869)
Board of Control (for India)	*Sir John Cam Hobhouse* (see Melbourne I)
Duchy of Lancaster	Apr 1835 – Oct 1840: *Henry Richard Vassal Fox, 3rd Baron Holland* (see William Grenville)
	Oct 1840 – Jan 1841 (acting:) *George William Frederick Villiers, 4th Earl of Clarendon* (see above)
	Jan – Aug 1841: *Sir George Grey* (b. Gibraltar 17 May 1799; d. Fallodon 10 Sep 1882)
Secretary at War	Apr 1835 – Sep 1839: *Henry Grey, Viscount Howick* (from 1845: *3rd Earl Grey*) (b. Howick, Northumberland, 28 Dec 1802; d. 9 Oct 1894)
	Sep 1839 – 31 Aug 1841: *Thomas Babington Macaulay* (from 1857: *Baron Macaulay*) (b. Rothley-Temple, Leicestershire, 25 Oct 1800; d. Kensington 28 Dec 1859)
Woods and Forests	*John William Ponsonby, Viscount Duncannon* (see Melbourne I)
Chief Secretary	Feb 1839 – Aug 1841: *George William Frederick Howard, Lord Morpeth* (from 1848: *7th Earl of Carlisle*) (b. 18 Apr 1802; d. Castle Howard 5 Dec 1864)

1 Sep 1841 – 29 Jun 1846: Peel II (Liberal-Conservative: Peelite)

First Lord of the Treasury	*Sir Robert Peel* (for 2nd time) (see Liverpool)
Foreign Affairs	*George Hamilton Gordon, 4th Earl of Aberdeen* (see Wellington I)
Home Affairs	*Sir James Graham* (see Grey)

Chancellor of the Exchequer	*Henry Goulburn* (see Wellington I)
War and Colonies	Sep 1841 – Dec 1845: *Edward Geoffrey Stanley,* (from 1844: *Lord Stanley*) (see Grey) Dec 1845 – Jun 1846: *William Ewart Gladstone* (b. Liverpool 29 Dec 1809; d. Hawarden 19 May 1898)
Lord Chancellor	*John Singleton Copley, Baron Lyndhurst* (see Canning)
Lord President	Sep 1841 – 19 Dec 1845: *James Archibald Stuart-Wortley-Mackenzie, 1st Baron Wharncliffe* (see Peel I) Jan – Jan 1846: *Walter Francis Montague-Douglas-Scott, 2nd Duke of Buccleuch and Queensbury* (b. Dalkeith 25 Nov 1806; d. Bowhill, Selkirkshire, 16 Apr 1884)
Lord Privy Seal	1 Sep 1841 – 1842: *Richard Plantagenet Temple-Nugent-Brydges-Chandos-Grenville, 2nd Duke of Buckingham* (b. London 11 Feb 1797; d. London 29 Jul 1861) Jan 1842 – Jan 1846: *2nd Duke of Buccleugh* (see above) Jan – Jun 1846: *Thomas Hamilton, 9th Earl of Haddington* (b. Edinburgh 21 Jun 1780; d. Tynninghame House 1 Dec 1858)
First Lord of the Admiralty	Sep 1841 – Jan 1846: *Thomas Hamilton, 9th Earl of Haddington* (see above) Jan – Jun 1846: *Edward Law, 2nd Baron Ellenborough* (from 1844: *Earl of Ellenborough*) (see Wellington I)
Trade	Sep 1841 – May 1843: *Frederick John Robinson, Earl of Ripon* (see Liverpool) May 1843 – Jan 1845: *William Ewart Gladstone* (see above) Dec 1845 – Jun 1846: *James Andrew Broun-Ramsay, 10th Earl of Dalhousie* (from 1849: *1st Marquis of Dalhousie*) (b. Dalhousie Castle 22 Apr 1812; d. Dalhousie Castle, Perthshire, 19 Dec 1860)
Board of Control (for India)	Sep – Oct 1841: *Edward Law, 2nd Baron Ellenborough* (see Wellington I) Oct 1841 – May 1843: *William Vesey-Fitzgerald, Baron Fitzgerald and Vesey* (see Wellington I) May 1843 – Jun 1846: *Frederick John Robinson, Earl of Ripon* (see Liverpool)

Duchy of Lancaster	May 1844 – Jun 1846: *Lord Granville Charles Henry Somerset* (b. 22 Dec 1792; d. 23 Feb 1848)
Secretary at War	Sep 1841 – May 1844: *Sir Henry Hardinge* (from 1846: *Viscount Hardinge*) (b. Wrotham 30 Mar 1785; d. South Park, Kent, 24 Sep 1846)
	May 1845 – Jun 1846: *Sidney Herbert* (from 1860: *1st Baron Herbert of Lea*) (b. Richmond, Surrey, 16 Sep 1810; d. Salisbury 2 Aug 1861)
Woods and Forests	Jan 1845 – Feb 1846: *Henry Pelham Fiennes Pelham Clinton, Earl of Lincoln* (from 1851: *5th Duke of Newcastle*) (b. London 22 May 1811; d. Clumber 18 Oct 1864)
Without Portfolio	*Arthur Wellesley, Duke of Wellington* (see Liverpool)

6 Jul 1846 – 20 Feb 1852: Russell I (Whig)

First Lord of the Treasury	*Lord John Russell* (for 1st time) (see Grey)
Foreign Affairs	Jul 1846 – Dec 1851: *Henry John Temple, Viscount Palmerston* (see Canning)
	26 Dec 1851 – 20 Feb 1852: *Granville George Leveson-Gower, Earl Granville* (b. London 11 May 1815; d. London 31 Mar 1891)
Home Affairs	*Sir George Grey* (see Wellington II)
Chancellor of the Exchequer	*Charles Wood* (from 1866: *Viscount Halifax*) (b. Barnsley 20 Dec 1800; d. Hickleton 8 Aug 1885)
War and Colonies	*Henry Grey, 3rd Earl Grey* (see Melbourne II)
Lord Chancellor	Jul 1846 – Jun 1850: *Charles Christopher Pepys, 1st Earl of Cottenham* (see Wellington II)
	Jul 1850 – Feb 1852: *Thomas Wilde, 1st Baron Truro* (b. London 7 Jul 1782; d. London 11 Nov 1855)
Lord President	*Henry Petty Fitzmaurice, 3rd Marquis of Lansdowne* (see William Grenville)
Lord Privy Seal	*Gilbert Elliot, 2nd Earl of Minto* (see Melbourne II)
First Lord of the Admiralty	Jul 1846 – 1 Jan 1849: *George Eden, Earl of Auckland* (see Grey)
	Jan 1849 – Feb 1852: *Sir Francis Thornhill Baring* (see Wellington II)
Trade	Jul 1846 – May 1849: *George William Frederick Villiers, 4th Earl of Clarendon* (see Wellington II)
	May 1847 – Feb 1852: *Henry Labouchere* (see Wellington II)

Board of Control
(for India)

Jul 1846 – Jan 1852: *Sir John Cam Hobhouse* (from 1851: *Baron Broughton*) (see Melbourne I)
Jan – Feb 1852: *Fox Maule* (from 1861: *Maule-Ramsay*) (from 1852: *2nd Baron Panmure;* from 1860: *11th Earl of Dalhousie*) (b. Brechin Castle, Forfarshire, 22 Apr 1801; d. 6 Jul 1874)

Chancellor of the
Duchy of
Lancaster

Jul 1846 – Mar 1850: *John Campbell, Baron Campbell* (b. Springfield, Fife, 15 Sep 1779; d. London 22 Jun 1861)
Mar 1850 – 20 Feb 1852: *George Howard, 7th Earl of Carlisle* (see Melbourne II)

Secretary at War

Oct 1851 – Jan 1852: *Fox Maule* (see above)

Woods and Forests

Jul 1846 – Mar 1850: *George Howard, 7th Earl of Carlisle* (see Melbourne II)

Postmaster-
General

Ulick John Browne, 1st Marquis of Clanricarde (b. 20 Dec 1802; d. 10 Apr 1874)

Paymaster-
General

Jul 1846 – Aug 1847: *Thomas Babington Macaulay* (see Melbourne II)
Oct – Dec 1851: *Earl Granville* (see above)

Public Works

Oct 1851 – Feb 1852: *Edward Adolphus Seymour, Lord Seymour* (from 1855: *12th Duke of Somerset*) (b. 20 Dec 1804; d. Torquay 28 Nov 1885)

Chief Secretary
for Ireland

Jul 1846 – May 1847: *Henry Labouchere* (see Wellington II)

Feb – 16 Dec 1852: Derby I (Tory)

First Lord of the
Treasury

Edward Geoffrey Stanley, 14th Earl of Derby (for 1st time) (see Grey)

Foreign Affairs

James Howard Harris, 3rd Earl of Malmesbury (b. 25 Mar 1807; d. 17 May 1889)

Home Affairs

Spencer Horatio Walpole (b. Stagbury, Surrey, 11 Sep 1806; d. Ealing 22 May 1898)

Chancellor of the
Exchequer

Benjamin Disraeli (from 1876: *Earl Beaconsfield*) (b. London 21 Dec 1804; d. 19 Apr 1881)

War and Colonies

John Somerset Pakington (from 1874: *1st Baron Hampton*) (b. Powick Court, Worcester, 20 Feb 1799; d. London 9 Apr 1880)

Lord Chancellor

Edward Burtenshaw Sugden, Baron St Leonards (b. 12 Feb 1781; d. Thames Ditton 29 Jan 1875)

Lord President

William Lowther, 2nd Earl of Lonsdale (b. Uffington 21 Jul 1787; d. London 4 Mar 1872)

Lord Privy Seal

James William Brownlow Gascoyne-Cecil, 2nd

	Marquis of Salisbury (b. 17 Apr 1791; d. 12 Apr 1868)
First Lord of the Admiralty	*Algernon Percy, 4th Duke of Northumberland* (b. Beckenham, Kent, 15 Dec 1792; d. Alnwick 12 Feb 1865)
Trade	*Joseph Warner Henley* (b. Putney 1793; d. 9 Dec 1884)
Board of Control (for India)	*John Charles Herries* (see Goderich)
Postmaster-General	*Charles Philip Yorke, 4th Earl of Hardwicke* (b. Southampton 1799; d. Southampton 17 Sep 1783)
Public Works	*Lord James Manners* (from 1888: *7th Duke of Rutland*) (b. Belvoir Castle, Leicestershire, 13 Dec 1818; d. 4 Aug 1906)

28 Dec 1852 – 31 Jan 1855: Aberdeen (Coalition)

First Lord of the Treasury	*George Hamilton-Gordon, 4th Earl of Aberdeen* (see Wellington I)
Foreign Affairs	Dec 1852 – Feb 1853: *Lord John Russell* (see Grey)
	Feb 1853 – Jan 1855: *George Villiers, 4th Earl of Clarendon* (see Wellington II)
Home Affairs	*Henry John Temple, Viscount Palmerston* (see Canning)
Chancellor of the Exchequer	*William Ewart Gladstone* (see Peel II)
War and Colonies	*Henry Clinton, 5th Duke of Newcastle* (see Peel II) from Jun 1854 Secretary for War
Colonies (new post)	Jun 1854 – Jan 1855 *Sir George Grey* (see Wellington II)
Lord Chancellor	*Robert Monsey Rolfe, Baron Cranworth* (b. Cranworth 18 Dec 1790; d. London 26 Jul 1868)
Lord President	Dec 1852 – Jun 1854: *Granville George Leveson-Gower, Earl Granville* (see Russell I)
	Jun 1854 – 24 Jan 1855: *Lord John Russell* (see Grey)
Lord Privy Seal	*George Douglas Campbell, 8th Duke of Argyll* (b. Ardencaple Castle, Dunbartonshire, 30 Apr 1823; d. London 24 Apr 1900)
First Lord of the Admiralty	*Sir James Graham* (see Grey)
Board of Control (for India)	*Charles Wood* (see Russell I)
Secretary at War	*Sidney Herbert* (see Peel II)
Public Works	*Sir William Molesworth* (b. London 23 May 1810; d. London 22 Oct 1855)

Without Portfolio — *Henry Petty-Fitzmaurice, 3rd Marquis of Lansdowne* (see William Grenville)
Feb 1853 – Jun 1854: *Lord John Russell* (see Grey)

4/10 Feb 1855 – 20 Feb 1858: Palmerston I (Whig)

First Lord of the Treasury — *Henry John Temple, Viscount Palmerston* (for 1st time) (see Canning)

Foreign Affairs — *George Villiers, 4th Earl of Clarendon* (see Melbourne II)

Home Affairs — *Sir George Grey* (see Wellington II)

Chancellor of the Exchequer — 4 – 22 Feb 1855: *William Ewart Gladstone* (see Peel II)
5 Mar 1855 – Feb 1858: *Sir George Cornewall Lewis* (b. London 21 Oct 1806; d. Hampton Court, Radnorshire, 13 Apr 1863)

War — *Fox Maule, 2nd Baron Panmure* (see Russell I)

Colonies — 4 – 22 Feb 1855: *Sidney Herbert* (see Peel II)
1 Mar – Jul 1855: *Lord John Russell* (see Grey)
Jul – 22 Oct 1855: *Sir William Molesworth* (see Aberdeen)
Oct 1855 – Feb 1858: *Henry Labouchere* (see Wellington II)

Lord Chancellor — *Robert Monsey Rolfe, Baron Cranworth* (see Aberdeen)

Lord President — *Granville George Leveson-Gower, Earl Granville* (see Russell I)

Lord Privy Seal — Feb – Dec 1855: *George Campbell, 8th Duke of Argyll* (see Aberdeen)
Dec 1855 – Dec 1857: *Dudley Ryder, 2nd Earl of Harrowby* (b. London 18 May 1798; d. Sandon 19 Nov 1882)
Dec 1857 – Feb 1858: *Ulick John Browne, 1st Marquis of Clanricarde* (see Russell I)

First Lord of the Admiralty — (1852) – 22 Feb 1855: *Sir James Graham* (see Grey)
3 Mar 1855 – Feb 1858: *Charles Wood* (from 1866: *Viscount Halifax*) (see Russell I)

Trade — Mar 1855 – Feb 1858: *Edward John Stanley, 2nd Baron Stanley of Alderley* (b. Alderley 13 Nov 1802; d. London 16 Jun 1869)

Board of Control (for India) — 4 Feb – 3 Mar 1855: *Charles Wood* (from 1866: *Viscount Halifax*) (see Russell I)
3 Mar 1855 – Feb 1858: *Robert Vernon Smith* (from 1859: *Baron Lyveden*) (b. 23 Feb 1800; d. 10 Nov 1873)

Duchy of Lancaster	Mar – Dec 1855: *Dudley Ryder, 2nd Earl of Harrowby* (see above)
	Dec 1855 – Feb 1858: *Matthew Talbot Baines* (b. 17 Feb 1799; d. 22 Jan 1860)
Postmaster-General	Feb – Jul 1855: *Charles John Canning, Viscount Canning* (from 1859: *Earl Canning*) (b. 14 Dec 1812; d. 17 Jun 1862)
	Nov 1855 – Feb 1858: *George Campbell, 8th Duke of Argyll* (see Aberdeen)
Public Works	Feb – Jul 1855: *Sir William Molesworth* (see Aberdeen)
Without Portfolio	*Henry Petty-Fitzmaurice, 3rd Marquis of Lansdowne* (see William Grenville)

25 Feb 1858 – Jun 1859: Derby II (Tory)

First Lord of the Treasury	*Edward Geoffrey Stanley, 14th Earl of Derby* (for 2nd time) (see Grey)
Foreign Affairs	*James Howard Harris, 3rd Earl of Malmesbury* (see Derby I)
Home Affairs	Feb 1858 – Feb 1859: *Spencer Horatio Walpole* (see Derby I)
	Feb – Jun 1859: *Thomas Henry Sotheron-Estcourt* (b. 4 Apr 1801; d. 6 Jan 1876
Chancellor of the Exchequer	*Benjamin Disraeli* (see Derby I)
War	*Jonathan Peel* (b. Bury 12 Oct 1799; d. Twickenham 13 Feb 1879)
Colonies	Feb – May 1858: *Edward Henry Stanley, Lord Stanley* (from 1869: *15th Earl of Derby*) (b. Knowlsley 21 Jul 1826; d. 21 Apr 1893)
	May 1858 – Jun 1859: *Edward George Earle Lytton Bulwer-Lytton* (from 1866: *1st Baron Lytton*) (b. London 25 May 1803; d. Torquay 18 Jan 1873)
Lord Chancellor	*Frederick Thesiger, 1st Baron Chelmsford* (b. London 15 Jul 1794; d. London 5 Oct 1878)
Lord President	*James William Brownlow Gascoyne-Cecil, 2nd Marquis of Salisbury* (see Derby I)
Lord Privy Seal	*Charles Philip Yorke, 4th Earl of Hardwicke* (see Derby I)
First Lord of the Admiralty	*John Somerset Pakington* (see Derby I)

Trade	Feb 1858 – Feb 1859: *Joseph Walter Henley* (see Derby I)
	Feb – Jun 1859: *Richard John Hely-Hutchinson, 4th Earl of Donoughmore* (b. 4 Apr 1823; d. 22 Feb 1866)
President of the Board of Control (from Aug 1858: Secretary of State for India	Feb – May 1858: *Edward Law, Earl Ellenborough* (see Wellington I)
	May 1858 – Jun 1859: *Edward Henry Stanley, Lord Stanley* (see above)
Public Works	*Lord John James Manners* (see Derby I)

18 Jun 1859 – 26 Jun 1866: Palmerston II/Russell II (Whig)

First Lord of the Treasury	18 Jun 1859 – 18 Oct 1865: *Henry John Temple, Viscount Palmerston* (for 2nd time) (see Canning)
	30 Oct 1865 – 26 Jun 1866: *John Russell, 1st Earl Russell* (for 2nd time) (see Grey)
Foreign Affairs	18 Jun 1859 – 30 Oct 1865: *Lord John Russell* (from 1861: *1st Earl Russell*) (see Grey)
	30 Oct 1865 – 26 Jun 1866: *George Villiers, 4th Earl of Clarendon* (see Wellington II)
Home Affairs	Jun 1859 – Jul 1861: *Sir George Cornewall Lewis* (see Palmerston I)
	Jul 1861 – Jun 1866: *Sir George Grey* (see Wellington II)
Chancellor of the Exchequer	*William Ewart Gladstone* (see Peel II)
War	Jun 1859 – Jul 1861: *Sidney Herbert*, (from 1869 *Baron Herbert of Lea*) (see Peel II)
	Jul 1861 – 13 Apr 1863: *Sir George Cornewall Lewis* (see Palmerston I)
	Apr 1863 – Feb 1866: *George Frederick Samuel Robinson, 2nd Earl de Grey and Ripon* (from 1871: *Marquis of Ripon*) (b. London 24 Oct 1827; d. Ripon 4 Dec 1909)
	8 Feb – 26 Jun 1866: *Spencer Cavendish, Marquis of Hartington* (from 1891: *8th Duke of Devonshire*) (b. Hoker Hall 23 Jul 1833; d. Cannes 24 Mar 1908)
Colonies	Jun 1859 – Apr 1864: *Henry Clinton, 5th Duke of Newcastle* (see Peel II)
	Apr 1864 – Jun 1866: *Edward Cardwell* (from 1874:

	Viscount Cardwell) (b. Liverpool 24 Jul 1813; d. Torquay 15 Feb 1866)
Lord Chancellor	Jun 1859 – 22 Jun 1861: *John Campbell, Baron Campbell* (see Russell I)
	Jun 1861 – 5 Jul 1865: *Richard Bethell, 1st Baron Westbury* (b. 30 Jun 1800; d. 20 Jul 1873)
	Jul 1865 – Jun 1866: *Robert Monsey Rolfe, Baron Cranworth* (see Aberdeen)
Lord President	*Granville George Leveson-Gower, Earl Granville* (see Russell I)
Lord Privy Seal	*George Campbell, 8th Duke of Argyll* (see Aberdeen)
First Lord of the Admiralty	*Edward Adolphus Seymour, 12th Duke of Somerset* (see Russell I)
Trade	Jul 1859 – Jun 1866: *Thomas Milner-Gibson* (b. Port-of-spain 3 Sep 1806; d. Algiers 25 Feb 1885)
Secretary of State for India	Jun 1859 – Feb 1866: *Charles Wood* (from 1866: *Viscount Halifax*) (see Russell I)
	Feb – Jun 1866: *George Frederick Samuel Robinson, 2nd Earl de Grey and Ripon* (see above)
Duchy of Lancaster	1859 – 1861: *Sir George Grey* (see Wellington II)
	1861 – Mar 1864: *Edward Cardwell* (see above)
	Jan – Jun 1866: *George Joachim Goschen* (from 1900: *Viscount, Goschen*) (b. London 10 Aug 1831; d. 7 Feb 1907)
Postmaster-General	Jan 1859 – Mar 1860: *James Bruce, 8th Earl of Elgin and 12th Earl of Kincardine* (b. 20 Jul 1811; d. Dharmsala 20 Nov 1863)
	Mar 1860 – Jun 1866: *Edward John Stanley, 2nd Baron Stanley of Alderley* (see Palmerston I)
Chief Secretary for Ireland	*Edward Cardwell* (see above)
Poor Law Board	Jun – Jul 1859: *Thomas Milner-Gibson* (see above)
	Jul 1859 – Jun 1866: *Charles Pelham Villiers* (b. London 3 Jan 1802; d. London 16 Jan 1898)

6 Jul 1866 – 3 Dec 1868: Derby III/Disraeli I (Tory)

First Lord of the Treasury	6 Jul 1866 – 25 Feb 1868: *Edward Geoffrey Stanley, 14th Earl of Derby* (for 3rd time) (see Grey)
	25 Feb – 3 Dec 1868: *Benjamin Disraeli* (for 1st time) (see Derby I)
Foreign Affairs	*Edward Henry Stanley, Lord Stanley* (see Derby II)

Home Affairs	25 Jun 1866 – 17 May 1867: *Spencer Walpole* (see Derby I)
	17 May 1867 – 3 Dec 1868: *Gathorne Hardy* (from 1878: *Gathorne Gathorne-Hardy, Viscount Cranbrook;* from 1892: *Earl Cranbrook*) (b. Bradford 1 Oct 1814; d. London 30 Oct 1906)
Chancellor of the Exchequer	6 Jul 1866 – 27 Feb 1868: *Benjamin Disraeli* (see Derby I)
	27 Feb – 3 Dec 1868: *George Ward Hunt* (b. Buckhurst, Berkshire, 30 Jul 1825; d. Bad Homburg 29 Jul 1877)
	6 Jul 1866 – 2 Mar 1867: *Jonathan Peel* (see Derby II)
	8 Mar 1867 – 3 Dec 1868: *John Somerset Pakington* (see Derby I)
Colonies	25 Jun 1866 – 2 Mar 1867: *Henry Howard Molyneux Herbert, 4th Earl of Carnarvon* (b. London 24 Jun 1831; d. London 28 Jun 1890)
	Mar 1867 – 3 Dec 1868: *Richard Plantagenet Campbell Temple-Nugent-Brydges-Chandos-Grenville, 3rd Duke of Buckingham* (b. 10 Sep 1823; d. London 23 Mar 1889)
Lord Chancellor	*Frederick Thesiger, 1st Baron Chelmsford* (see Derby II)
Lord President	6 Jul 1866 – Mar 1867: *3rd Duke of Buckingham* (see above)
	8 Mar 1867 – 3 Dec 1868: *John Winston Spencer-Churchill, 7th Duke of Marlborough* (b. Garboldisham Hall, Norfolk, 1822; d. London 5 Jul 1883)
Lord Privy Seal	*James Howard Harris, 3rd Earl of Malmesbury* (see Derby I)
First Lord of the Admiralty	12 Jul 1866 – 8 Mar 1867 *John Somerset Pakington* (see Derby I)
	8 Mar 1867 – 3 Dec 1868: *Henry Thomas Lowry-Corry* (b. Dublin 9 Mar 1803; d. Bournemouth 6 May 1873)
Trade	6 Jul 1866 – 8 Mar 1867: *Sir Stafford Henry Northcote* (from 1885: *Earl of Iddesleigh*) (b. London 27 Oct 1818; d. London 12 Jun 1887)
	8 Mar 1867 – 3 Dec 1868: *Charles Gordon-Lennox, 6th Duke of Richmond* (b. London 27 Feb 1818; d. Gordon Castle 27 Sep 1893)
India	25 Jun 1866 – 2 Mar 1867: *Robert Arthur Talbot Gascoigne Cecil, Viscount Cranborne* (from 1868: *3rd Marquis of Salisbury*) (b. Hatfield 3 Feb 1830; d. 22 Aug 1903)

8 Mar 1867 – 3 Dec 1868: *Sir Stafford Northcote* (see above)

Chief Secretary for Ireland — 6 Jul 1866 – Feb 1868: *Richard Southwell Bourke, Lord Naas* (from 1867: *6th Earl of Mayo*) (b. Dublin 21 Feb 1822; d. (assassinated) Port Blair 8 Feb 1872)

Public Works — 6 Jul 1866 – 3 Dec 1868: *Lord John James Manners* (see Derby I)

Poor Law Board — 12 Jul 1866 – May 1867: *Gathorne Hardy* (see above)

Without Portfolio — May 1867 – Dec 1868: *Spencer Walpole* (see Derby I)

9 Dec 1868 – 16 Feb 1874: Gladstone I (Whig)

First Lord of the Treasury — *William Ewart Gladstone* (for 1st time) (see Peel I)

Foreign Affairs — 9 Dec 1868 – 27 Jun 1870: *George Villiers, 4th Earl of Clarendon* (see Wellington II)
Jun 1870 – 16 Feb 1874: *Granville George Leveson-Gower, Earl Granville* (see Russell I)

Home Affairs — 9 Dec 1868 – 1873: *Henry Austin Bruce* (from 1873: *1st Baron Aberdare*) (b. 16 Apr 1815; d. 25 Feb 1895)
1873 – 16 Feb 1874: *Robert Lowe* (from 1880: *Viscount Sherbrooke*) (b. Bingham 4 Dec 1811; d. Warlingham 27 Jul 1892)

Chancellor of the Exchequer — 9 Dec 1868 – 1873: *Robert Lowe* (see above)

War — *Edward Cardwell* (see Palmerston II/Russell II)

Colonies — 9 Dec 1868 – 1870: *Granville George Leveson-Gower, Earl Granville* (see Russell I)
1870 – 16 Feb 1874: *John Wodehouse, Earl of Kimberley* (b. 7 Jan 1826; d. London 8 Apr 1902)

Lord Chancellor — 9 Dec 1868 – Sep 1872: *William Page Wood, Baron Hatherley* (b. London 29 Nov 1801; d. 10 Jul 1881)
Sep 1872 – 16 Feb 1874: *Roundell Palmer, Baron Selborne* (from 1881: *1st Earl of Selborne*) (b. Oxford 27 Nov 1812; d. Blackmoore 4 May 1895)

Lord President — Dec 1868 – Aug 1873: *George Robinson, 2nd Earl de Grey* (from 1871: *Marquis of Ripon*) (see Palmerston II/Russell II)
Aug 1873 – Feb 1874: *Henry Austin Bruce, 1st Baron Aberdare* (see above)

Lord Privy Seal — 9 Dec 1868 – 1870: *John Wodehouse, Earl of Kimberley* (see above)
1870 – 16 Feb 1874: *Charles Wood, Viscount Halifax* (see Russell I)

First Lord of the Admiralty	9 Dec 1868 – 7 Mar 1871: *Hugh Culling Eardley Childers* (b. 25 Jun 1827; d. 29 Jan 1896)
	7 Mar 1871 – 16 Feb 1874: *George Joachim Goschen* (see Palmerston II/Russell II)
	9 Dec 1868 – 20 Dec 1870: *John Bright* (b. Greenbank 16 Nov 1811; d. One Ash 27 Mar 1889)
	14 Jan 1871 – 16 Feb 1874: *Chichester Samuel Parkinson Fortescue* (from 1874: *Baron Carlingford*) (b. 18 Jan 1823; d. Marseilles 30 Jan 1898)
India	*George Campbell, 8th Duke of Argyll* (see Aberdeen)
Duchy of Lancaster	Aug 1872 – Sep 1873: *Hugh Culling Eardley Childers* (see above)
	Sep 1873 – Feb 1874: *John Bright* (see above)
Postmaster-General	9 Dec 1868 – Dec 1870: *Spencer Cavendish, Marquis of Hartington* (see Palmerston II/Russell II)
Chief Secretary for Ireland	Dec 1868 – Dec 1870: *Chichester Fortescue* (see above)
	Dec 1870 – Feb 1874: *Spencer Cavendish, Marquis of Hartington* (see Palmerston II/Russell II)
Poor Law Board	Dec 1868 – Mar 1871: *George Joachim Goschen* (see Palmerston II/Russell II)
	Mar 1871 – Feb 1874: *James Stansfeld* (b. Halifax 5 Oct 1820; d. Rotherfield 17 Feb 1898)
Vice-President of the Council (Education)	(Entered cabinet Jul 1870: *William Edward Forster* (b. Bradpole 11 Jul 1818; d. London 5 Apr 1886)

20 Feb 1874 – 18 Apr 1880: Disraeli II (Tory)

First Lord of the Treasury	*Benjamin Disraeli* (from 1876: *Earl of Beaconsfield*) (for 2nd time) (see Derby I)
Foreign Affairs	20 Feb 1874 – 27 Mar 1878: *Edward Henry Stanley, 15th Earl of Derby* (see Derby II)
	30 Mar 1878 – 18 Apr 1880: *Robert Cecil, 3rd Marquis of Salisbury* (see Derby/Disraeli I)
Home Affairs	*Sir Richard Assheton Cross* (from 1886: *1st Viscount Cross*) (b. Red-Scar 20 May 1823; d. Broughton-in-Furness 8 Jan 1914)
Chancellor of the Exchequer	*Sir Stafford Henry Northcote* (see Derby III/Disraeli I)
War	20 Feb 1874 – Apr 1878: *Gathorne Hardy* (see Derby III/Disraeli I)
	30 Mar 1878 – 18 Apr 1880: *Frederick Arthur Stanley* (from 1886: *Baron Stanley;* from 1893: *16th Earl of*

	Derby) (b. London 15 Jan 1841; d. Holwood, Kent 14 Jun 1908)
Colonies	20 Feb 1874 – 27 Jan 1878: *Henry Herbert, 4th Earl of Carnarvon* (see Derby III/Disraeli I)
	1 Feb 1878 – 18 Ar 1880: *Sir Michael Hicks-Beach* (from 1915: *Earl of St Aldwyn*) (b. London 23 Oct 1837; d. London 30 Apr 1916)
Lord Chancellor	*Hugh MacCalmont Cairns, Baron Cairns* (from 1878: *Earl Cairns*) (b. Cultra Dec 1819; d. 2 Apr 1885)
Lord President	*Charles Gordon-Lennox, 6th Duke of Richmond* (see Derby III/Disraeli I)
Lord Privy Seal	20 Feb 1874 – Aug 1876: *James Howard Harris, 3rd Earl of Malmesbury* (see Derby I)
	Aug 1876 – Feb 1878: *Benjamin Disraeli, Earl of Beaconsfield* (see Derby I)
	Feb 1878 – 18 Apr 1880: *Algernon Percy, 6th Duke of Northumberland* (b. 29 May 1810; d. London 2 Jan 1899)
First Lord of the Admiralty	20 Feb 1874 – 29 Jul 1877: *George Ward Hunt* (see Derby III/Disraeli I)
	1877 – 18 Apr 1880: *William Henry Smith* (b. London 24 Jun 1825; d. Dover 6 Oct 1891)
Trade	Apr 1878 – 18 Apr 1880: *Dudley Francis Stuart Ryder* (from 1882: *3rd Earl of Harrowby*) (b. Brighton 16 Jan 1831; d. Sandon Hall, Staffordshire, 26 Mar 1900)
India	20 Feb 1874 – Apr 1878: *Robert Cecil, 3rd Marquis of Salisbury* (see Derby III/Disraeli I)
	30 Mar 1878 – 18 Apr 1880: *Gathorne Hardy* (see Derby III/Disraeli I)
Postmaster-General	*Lord John James Manners* (see Derby I)
Chief Secretary for Ireland	Aug 76 – Jan 78: *Sir Michael Hicks-Beach* (see above)

28 Apr 1880 – 9 Jun 1885: Gladstone II (Lib)

First Lord of the Treasury	*William Ewart Gladstone* (for 2nd time) (see Peel II)
Foreign Affairs	*Granville George Leveson-Gower, Earl Granville* (see Russell I)
Home Affairs	*Sir William Vernon Harcourt* (b. York 24 Oct 1827; d. Nureham 1 Oct 1904)

Chancellor of the Exchequer	28 Apr 1880 – 16 Dec 1882: *William Ewart Gladstone* (see Peel II)
	Dec 1882 – 9 Jun 1885: *Hugh Culling Eardley Childers* (see Gladstone I)
War	28 Apr 1880 – 16 Dec 1882: *Hugh Culling Eardley Childers* (see Gladstone I)
	16 Dec 1882 – 9 Jun 1885: *Spencer Cavendish, Marquis of Hartington* (see Palmerston II/ Russell II)
Colonies	28 Apr 1880 – 16 Dec 1882: *John Wodehouse, Earl of Kimberley* (see Gladstone I)
	16 Dec 1882 – 9 Jun 1885: *Edward Henry Stanley, 15th Earl of Derby* (see Derby II)
Lord Chancellor	*Roundell Palmer, Baron Selborne* (from 1881: *1st Earl Selborne*) (see Gladstone I)
Lord President	28 Jun 1880 – Mar 1883: *John Poyntz Spencer, 5th Earl Spencer* (b. London 27 Oct 1835; d. Althorp, Northamptonshire, 13 Aug 1910)
	Mar 1883 – 9 Jun 1885: *Chichester Fortescue, Baron Carlingford* (see Gladstone I)
Lord Privy Seal	28 Apr 1880 – 7 Apr 1881: *George Campbell, 8th Duke of Argyll* (see Aberdeen)
	7 Apr 1881 – Mar 1885: *Chichester Fortescue, Baron Carlingford* (see Gladstone I)
	Mar – Jun 1885: *Archibald Philip Primrose, 5th Earl of Rosebery* (b. London 7 Mar 1847; d. Epsom 20 May 1929)
First Lord of the Admiralty	*Thomas George Baring, 1st Earl Northbrook* (b. London 22 Jan 1826; d. 15 Nov 1904)
Trade	*Joseph Chamberlain* (b. London 8 Jul 1836; d. 2 Jul 1914)
Secretary of State for India	28 Apr 1880 – 16 Dec 1882: *Spencer Cavendish, Marquis of Hartington* (see Palmerston II/ Russell II)
	16 Dec 1882 – 9 Jun 1885: *John Wodehouse, Earl of Kimberley* (see Gladstone I)
Chancellor of the Duchy of Lancaster	28 Apr 1880 – 15 Jul 1882: *John Bright* (see Gladstone I)
	Jul – Dec 1882: *John Wodehouse, Earl of Kimberley* (see Gladstone I)
	Dec 1882 – Oct 1884: *John George Dodson* (from 1884: *1st Baron Monk-Bretton*) (b. London 18 Oct 1825; d. London 25 May 1897)
	Nov 1884 – 9 Jun 1885: *Sir George Otto Trevelyan* (b. Rothley Temple, Leicestershire, 20 Jul 1838; d. Wallington 17 Aug 1928)

Postmaster-General	(Entered cabinet Feb 1885:) *George John Shaw-Lefevre* (from 1906: *1st Baron Eversley*) (b. London 12 Jun 1851; d. Abbotsworthy 19 Apr 1928)
Local Government	28 Apr 1880 – 8 Dec 1882: *John George Dodson* (see above)
	8 Dec 1882 – 9 Jun 1885: *Sir Charles Wentworth Dilke* (b. London 4 Sep 1843; d. London 26 Jan 1911)
Chief Secretary for Ireland	28 Apr 1880 – 4 May 1882: *William Edward Forster* (see Gladstone I)
Viceroy of Ireland	Apr 1882 – Jun 1885: *John Poyntz Spencer, 5th Earl Spencer* (see above)

24 Jun 1885 – 26 Jan 1886: Salisbury I (Cons)

Foreign Affairs	*Robert Cecil, 3rd Marquis of Salisbury* (for 1st time) (see Derby III/Disraeli I)
Home Affairs	*Sir Richard Assheton Cross* (see Disraeli II)
First Lord of the Treasury	*Stafford Northcote, Earl of Iddesleigh* (see Derby III/Disraeli I)
Chancellor of the Exchequer	*Sir Michael Hicks-Beach* (see Disraeli II)
War	*William Henry Smith* (see Disraeli II)
Colonies	*Frederick Arthur Stanley* (see Disraeli II)
Lord Chancellor	*Hardinge Stanley Giffard, Baron Halsbury* (from 1898: *Earl of Halsbury*) (b. London 3 Sep 1823; d. London 11 Dec 1921)
Lord President	*Gathorne Gathorne-Hardy, Viscount Cranbrook* (see Derby III/Disraeli I)
Lord Privy Seal	*Dudley Ryder, 3rd Earl of Harrowby* (see Disraeli II)
First Lord of the Admiralty	*Lord George Hamilton* (b. Brighton 17 Dec 1845; d. London 22 Sep 1927)
Trade	Jun – Aug 1885: *Charles Gordon-Lennox, 6th Duke of Richmond* (see Derby III/Disraeli I)
	Edward Stanhope (b. London 24 Sep 1840; d. London 21 Dec 1893)
India	*Lord Randolph Churchill* (b. Blenheim Palace 13 Feb 1849; d. London 24 Jan 1895)
Postmaster-General	*Lord John James Manners* (see Derby I)
Vice-President of the Council (Education)	Jun – Aug 1885: *Edward Stanhope* (see above)

Chief Secretary for Ireland	Jan 1886: *William Henry Smith* (see Disraeli II)
Viceroy of Ireland	*Henry Herbert, 4th Earl of Caernarvon* (see Derby III/Disraeli I)
Lord Chancellor for Ireland	*Edward Gibson, 1st Lord Ashbourne* (b. Dublin 4 Sep 1837; d. London 22 May 1913)
Secretary for Scotland	Aug 1885 – Jan 1886: *Charles Gordon-Lennox, 6th Duke of Richmond* (see Derby III/Disraeli I)

3 Feb – 20 Jul 1886: Gladstone III (Lib)

First Lord of the Treasury	*William Ewart Gladstone* (for 3rd time) (see Peel II)
Foreign Affairs	*Archibald Philip Primrose, 5th Earl of Rosebery* (see Gladstone II)
Home Affairs	*Hugh Culling Eardley Childers* (see Gladstone I)
Chancellor of the Exchequer	*Sir William Vernon Harcourt* (see Gladstone II)
War	*Sir Henry Campbell-Bannerman* (b. Kelvinside 7 Sep 1836; d. London 22 Apr 1908)
Colonies	*Granville George Leveson-Gower, Earl Granville* (see Russell I)
Lord Chancellor	*Farrer Herschell, Baron Herschell* (b. Brampton, Hampshire, 2 Nov 1837; d. Washington 1 Mar 1899)
Lord President	*John Poyntz Spencer, 5th Earl Spencer* (see Gladstone II)
Lord Privy Seal	*William Ewart Gladstone* (see Peel II)
First Lord of the Admiralty	*George Frederick Samuel Robinson, Marquis of Ripon* (see Palmerston II/Russell II)
Trade	*Anthony John Mundella* (b. Leicester 28 Mar 1825; d. London 24 Jul 1897)
India	*John Wodehouse, Earl of Kimberley* (see Gladstone I)
Local Government	Feb – Apr 1886: *Joseph Chamberlain* (see Gladstone II)
	Apr – Jul 1886: *James Stansfeld* (see Gladstone I)
Secretary of State for Ireland	*John Morley* (from 1908: *Viscount Morley*) (b. Blackburn 24 Dec 1838: d. Wimbledon 23 Sep 1923)
Secretary for Scotland	Feb – Apr 1866: *Sir George Otto Trevelyan* (see Gladstone II)

3 Aug 1886 – 11 Aug 1892: Salisbury II (Cons)

Prime Minister	*Robert Cecil, 3rd Marquis of Salisbury* (for 2nd time) (see Derby III/Disraeli I)
Foreign Affairs	3 Aug 1886 – 12 Jan 1887: *Sir Stafford Henry Northcote, Earl of Iddesleigh* (see Derby III/Disraeli I) Jan 1887 – 11 Aug 1892: *Robert Cecil, 3rd Marquis of Salisbury* (see Derby III/Disraeli I)
Home Affairs	*Henry Matthews* (from 1895: *Viscount Llandaff*) (b. Ceylon 13 Jan 1826; d. London 3 Apr 1913)
First Lord of the Treasury	Aug 1886 – Jan 1887: *Lord Salisbury* (see Derby III/Disraeli I) Jan 1887 – 6 Oct 1891: *William Henry Smith* (see Disraeli II) 20 Oct 1891 – 11 Aug 1892: *Sir Arthur James Balfour* (from 1922: *1st Earl Balfour*) (b. Wittinghame 25 Jul 1848; d. Woking 19 Mar 1930)
Chancellor of the Exchequer	3 Aug – 23 Dec 1886: *Lord Randolph Churchill* (see Salisbury I) Jan 1887 – 11 Aug 1892: *George Joachim Goschen* (see Palmerston II/Rusell II)
War	3 Aug 1886 – early Jan 1887: *William Henry Smith* (see Disraeli II) Jan 1887 – 11 Aug 1892: *Edward Stanhope* (see Salisbury I)
Colonies	3 Aug 1886 – Jan 1887: *Edward Stanhope* (see Salisbury I) Jan 1887 – 11 Aug 1892: *Sir Henry Thurston Holland* (from 1888: *Baron Knutsford*; from 1895: *Viscount Knutsford*) (b. 3 Aug 1825; d. 29 Jan 1914)
Lord Chancellor	*Hardinge Giffard, Baron Halsbury* (see Salisbury I)
Lord President	*Gathorne Gathorne-Hardy, Viscount Cranbrook* (from 1892: *Earl Cranbrook*) (see Derby III/Disraeli I)
Lord Privy Seal	May 1887 – Aug 1892: *George Henry Cadogan, 5th Earl Cadogan* (b. Durham 12 May 1840; d. London 6 Mar 1915)
First Lord of the Admiralty	*Lord George Hamilton* (see Salisbury I)
Trade	3 Aug 1886 – Feb 1888: *Frederick Arthur Stanley, Baron Stanley* (see Disraeli II) Feb 1888 – Aug 1892: *Sir Michael Hicks-Beach* (see Disraeli II)
Secretary of State for India	*Sir Richard Assheton, 1st Viscount Cross* (see Disraeli II)

Chancellor of the Duchy of Lancaster	*Lord John James Manners*, (from 1888: *7th Duke of Rutland*) (see Derby I)
Local Government	May 1887 – Aug 1892: *Charles Thomson Ritchie* (b. Dundee 19 Nov 1838; d. Biarritz 9 Jan 1906)
Chief Secretary for Ireland	3 Aug 1886 – 5 Mar 1887: *Sir Michael Hicks-Beach* (see Disraeli II) 5 Mar 1887 – 20 Dec 1891: *Sir Arthur James Balfour* (see above) Oct 1891 – Aug 1892: *William Lawies Jackson* (from 1902: *Baron Allerton*) (b. Otley 16 Feb 1840; d. London 4 Apr 1917)
Lord Chancellor for Ireland	*Edward Gibson, 1st Lord Ashbourne* (see Salisbury I)
Secretary for Scotland	Nov 1886 – Mar 1887: *Sir Arthur James Balfour* (see above)
Without Portfolio	Mar 1887 – Aug 1892: *Sir Michael Hicks-Beach* (see Disraeli II)

16 Aug 1892 – 3 Mar 1894: Gladstone IV (Lib)

First Lord of the Treasury	*William Ewart Gladstone* (for 4th time) (see Peel II)
Foreign Affairs	*Archibald Philip Primrose, 5th Earl of Rosebery* (see Glasdstone II)
Home Affairs	*Herbert Henry Asquith* (from 1925: *Earl of Oxford and Asquith*) (b. Morley 12 Sep 1852; d. Oxford 15 Feb 1928)
Chancellor of the Exchequer	*Sir William Vernon Harcourt* (see Gladstone II)
War	*Sir Henry Campbell-Bannerman* (see Gladstone III)
Colonies	*George Robinson, Marquis of Ripon* (see Palmerston II/ Russell II)
Lord Chancellor	*Farrer Herschell, Baron Herschell* (see Gladstone III)
Lord President	*John Wodehouse, Earl of Kimberley* (see Gladstone I)
Lord Privy Seal	*William Ewart Gladstone* (see Peel II)
First Lord of the Admiralty	*John Poyntz Spencer, 5th Earl Spencer* (see Gladstone II)
Trade	*Anthony John Mundella* (see Gladstone III)
India	*John Wodehouse, Earl of Kimberley* (see Gladstone I)
Chancellor of the Duchy of Lancaster	*James Bryce* (from 1914: *Viscount Bryce*) (b. Belfast 10 May 1838; d. London 22 Jan 1922)

Postmaster-General	*Arnold Morley* (b. London 18 Feb 1849; d. 16 Jan 1916)
Local Government	*Sir Henry Hartley Fowler* (from 1908: *Viscount Wolverhampton*) (b. Sunderland 16 May 1830; d. Woodthorne 25 Feb 1911)
Vice-President (Education)	*Sir Arthur Herbert Dyke Acland* (b. Holnicote 13 Oct 1847; d. London 9 Oct 1926)
Chief Secretary for Ireland	*John Morley* (see Gladstone III)
Public Works	*George John Shaw-Lefevre* (see Gladstone II)
Secretary for Scotland	*Sir George Otto Trevelyan* (see Gladstone II)

6 Mar 1894 – 24 Jun 1895: Rosebery (Lib)

First Lord of the Treasury	*Archibald Philip Primrose, 5th Earl of Rosebery* (see Gladstone II)
Foreign Affairs	*John Wodehouse, Earl of Kimberley* (see Gladstone I)
Home Affairs	*Herbert Henry Asquith* (see Gladstone IV)
Chancellor of the Exchequer	*Sir William Vernon Harcourt* (see Gladstone II)
War	*Sir Henry Campbell-Bannerman* (see Gladstone III)
Colonies	*George Robinson, Marquis of Ripon* (see Palmerston II/Russell II)
Lord Chancellor	*Farrer Herschell, Baron Herschell* (see Gladstone III)
Lord President	*Archibald Philip Primrose, 5th Earl of Rosebery* (see Gladstone II)
Lord Privy Seal	6 Mar – May 1894: *Charles Marjoribanks, Baron Tweedmouth* (b. London 8 Apr 1849; d. Dublin 15 Sep 1909)
First Lord of the Admiralty	*John Poyntz Spencer, 5th Earl Spencer* (see Gladstone II)
Trade	6 Mar – May 1894: *Anthony John Mundella* (see Gladstone III)
	May 1894 – 24 Jun 1895: *James Bryce* (see Gladstone IV)
India	*Sir Henry Hartley Fowler* (see Gladstone IV)
Chancellor of the Duchy of Lancaster	*Charles Marjoribanks, Baron Tweedmouth* (see above)
Postmaster-General	*Arnold Morley* (see Gladstone IV)
Local Government	*George John Shaw-Lefevre* (see Gladstone II)

Vice-President (Education)	*Sir Arthur Herbert Dyke Acland,* (see Gladstone IV)
Chief Secretary for Ireland	*John Morley* (see Gladstone III)
Secretary for Scotland	*Sir George Otto Trevelyan* (see Gladstone II)

28 Jun 1895 – 11 Jul 1902: Salisbury III (Cons)

Prime Minister	*Robert Cecil, 3rd Marquis of Salisbury* (for 3rd time) (see Derby III/ Disraeli I)
Foreign Affairs	28 Jun 1895 – 1 Nov 1900: *Robert Cecil, 3rd Marquis of Salisbury* (see Derby III/ Disraeli I)
	1 Nov 1900 – 11 Jul 1902: *Henry Charles Keith Petty-Fitzmaurice, 5th Marquis of Lansdowne* (b. London 14 Jan 1845; d. London 13 Jun 1927)
Home Affairs	28 Jun 1895 – 1 Nov 1900: *Matthew White Ridley* (from 1900: *Viscount Ridley*) (b. London 25 Jul 1842; d. Blagdon 27 Nov 1904)
	1 Nov 1900 – 11 Jul 1902: *Charles Thomson Ritchie* (see Salisbury II)
First Lord of Treasury	*Sir Arthur James Balfour* (see Salisbury II)
Chancellor of the Exchequer	*Sir Michael Hicks-Beach* (see Disraeli II)
War	28 Jun 1895 – 1 Nov 1900: *Henry Petty-Fitzmaurice, 5th Marquis of Lansdowne* (see above)
	1 Nov 1900 – 11 Jul 1902: *William St John Fremantle Brodrick* (from 1920: *Earl Middleton*) (b. London 14 Dec 1856; d. Peper Harow 13 Feb 1942)
Colonies	*Joseph Chamberlain* (see Gladstone II)
Lord Chancellor	*Hardinge Giffard, Baron Halsbury* (from 1898: *Earl of Halsbury* (see Salisbury I)
Lord President	*Spencer Cavendish, 8th Duke of Devonshire* (see Palmerston II/ Russell II)
Lord Privy Seal	28 Jun 1895 – 1 Nov 1900: *Sir Richard Assheton, 1st Viscount Cross* (see Disraeli II)
	1 Nov 1900 – 11 Jul 1902: *Robert Cecil, 3rd Marquis of Salisbury* (see Derby III/ Disraeli I)
First Lord of the Admiralty	28 Jun 1895 – 1 Nov 1900: *George Joachim Goschen* (see Palmerston II/ Russell II)
	1 Nov 1900 – 11 Nov 1902: *William Waldegrave*

	Palmer, 2nd Earl of Selborne (b. London 17 Oct 1859; d. London 26 Feb 1942)
Trade	28 Jun 1895 – 1 Nov 1900: *Charles Thomson Ritchie* (see Salisbury II)
	1 Nov 1900 – 11 Jul 1902: *Gerald William Balfour* (from 1930: *2nd Earl Balfour*) (b. Edinburgh 9 Apr 1853; d. Whittinghame 14 Jan 1945)
India	*Lord George Hamilton* (see Salisbury I)
Duchy of Lancaster	*Henry James, Baron James of Hereford* (b. Hereford 30 Oct 1828; d. Kingswood Warren 18 Aug 1911)
Postmaster-General	1 Nov 1900 – 11 Jul 1902: *Charles Stewart Vane--Tempest-Stewart, 6th Marquis of Londonderry* (b. London 16 Jul 1852; d. London 8 Feb 1915)
Local Government	28 Jun 1895 – 1 Nov 1900: *Henry Chaplin, 1st Viscount Chaplin* (b. Stamford, Lincolnshire, 22 Dec 1840; d. London 29 May 1923)
	1 Nov 1900 – 11 Jul 1902: *Walter Hume Long* (from 1921: *1st Viscount Long*) (b. Bath 13 Jul 1854; d. Rood Ashton, Wiltshire, 26 Sep 1924)
Viceroy of Ireland	*George Henry Cadogan, 5th Earl of Cadogan* (see Salisbury II)
Lord Chancellor for Ireland	*Edward Gibson, 1st Baron Ashbourne* (see Salisbury I)
Secretary for Scotland	*Alexander Hugh Bruce, 6th Baron Balfour of Burleigh* (b. Kennet, Alloa, 13 Jan 1849; d. London 6 Jul 1921)
Public Works	*Aretas Akers-Douglas* (from 1911: *Viscount Chilston*) (b. St Leonards-on-Sea 21 Oct 1851; d. London 15 Jan 1926)
Agriculture	28 Jun 1895 – 1 Nov 1900: *Walter Hume Long* (see above)
	1 Nov 1900 – 11 Jul 1902: *Robert William Hanbury* (b. Tamworth 24 Feb 1845; d. London 28 Apr 1903)

12 Jul 1902 – 4 Dec 1905: Balfour (Cons)

First Lord of the Treasury	*Sir Arthur James Balfour* (see Salisbury II)
Foreign Affairs	*Henry Petty-Fitzmaurice, 5th Marquis of Lansdowne* (see Salisbury III)
Home Affairs	12 Jul – Aug 1902: *Charles Thomson Ritchie* (see Salisbury III)
	Aug 1902 – 4 Dec 1905: *Aretas Akers-Douglas* (see Salisbury III)

Chancellor of the Exchequer	12 Jul – Aug 1902: *Sir Michael Hicks-Beach* (see Disraeli II) Aug 1902 – 15 Sep 1903: *Charles Thomson Ritchie* (see Salisbury II) 5 Oct 1903 – 4 Dec 1905: *(Joseph) Austen Chamberlain* (from 1925: *Sir*) (b. Birmingham 16 Oct 1863; d. London 16 Mar 1937)
War	12 Jul 1902 – 15 Sep 1903: *William St John Fremantle Brodrick* (see Salisbury III) 5 Oct 1903 – 4 Dec 1905: *Hugh Oakeley Arnold-Forster* (b. Dawlish 14 Aug 1855; d. London 12 Mar 1909)
Colonies	12 Jul 1902 – 15 Sep 1903: *Joseph Chamberlain* (see Gladstone II) 5 Oct 1903 – 4 Dec 1905: *Alfred Lyttleton* (b. London 7 Feb 1857; d. 5 Jul 1913)
Lord Chancellor	5 Oct 1903 – 4 Dec 1905: *Hardinge Stanley Giffard, Earl of Halsbury* (see Salisbury I)
Lord President	12 Jul 1902 – 15 Sep 1903: *Spencer Cavendish, 8th Duke of Devonshire* (see Palmerston II/Russell II) 5 Oct 1903 – 4 Dec 1905: *Charles Stewart Vane-Tempest-Stewart, 6th Marquis of Londonderry* (see Salisbury III)
Lord Privy Seal	12 Jul 1902 – 15 Sep 1903: *Charles Stewart Vane-Tempest-Stewart, 6th Marquis of Londonderry* (see Salisbury III) 11 Oct 1903 – 4 Dec 1905: *James Edward Hubert Cecil, 4th Marquis of Salisbury* (b. London 23 Oct 1861; d. 4 Apr 1947)
First Lord of the Admiralty	12 Jul 1902 – Mar 1905: *William Waldegrave Palmer, 2nd Earl of Selborne* (see Salisbury III) Mar – Dec 1905: *Frederick Archibald Vaughan Campbell, 3rd Earl Cawdor* (b. Windsor 13 Feb 1847; d. Stackpole Court 8 Feb 1911)
Trade	12 Jul 1902 – Mar 1905: *Gerald William Balfour* (see Salisbury III) Mar – Dec 1905: *4th Marquis of Salisbury* (see above)
India	12 Jul 1902 – 15 Sep 1903: *Lord George Hamilton* (see Salisbury I) 5 Oct 1903 – 4 Dec 1905: *William St John Fremantle Brodrick* (see Salisbury III)
Duchy of Cornwall	12 Jul – Aug 1902: *Henry James, Baron James of Hereford* (see Salisbury III)

	Aug 1902 – 4 Dec 1905: *Sir William Hood Walrond*, (from 1905: *1st Baron Waleran* (b. 26 Feb 1849; d. London 17 May 1925)
Post	12 Jul – Aug 1902: *Charles Stewart Vane-Tempest-Stewart, 6th Marquis of Londonderry* (see Salisbury III)
	Early Aug 1902 – 15 Sep 1903: *(Joseph) Austen Chamberlain* (see above)
	5 Oct 1903 – 4 Dec 1905: *Edward, Lord Stanley* (from 1908: *17th Earl of Derby*) (b. London 4 Apr 1865; d. Prescott, Lancashire, (?)4 Feb 1948)
Local Government	*Walter Hume Long* (see Salisbury III)
	Mar – Dec 1905: *Gerald William Balfour* (see Salisbury III)
Education	*Charles Stewart Vane-Tempest-Stewart, 6th Marquis of Londonderry* (see Salisbury III)
Chief Secretary for Ireland	12 Jul 1902 – early Mar 1905: *George Wyndham* (b. London 29 Aug 1863; d. Paris 8 Jun 1913)
	Early Mar – 4 Dec 1905: *Walter Hume Long* (see Salisbury III)
Lord Chancellor for Ireland	*Edward Gibson, 1st Lord Ashbourne* (see Salisbury I)
Secretary for State for Scotland	12 Jul 1902 – 21 Sep 1903: *Alexander Hugh Bruce, 6th Baron Balfour of Burleigh* (see Salisbury III)
	5 Oct 1903 – 4 Dec 1905: *Andrew Graham-Murray* (from 1905: *Earl Dunedin*) (b. Edinburgh 21 Nov 1849; d. Edinburgh 21 Aug 1942)
Public Works	*Robert George Windsor-Clive, 14th Baron Windsor* (from 1905: *1st Earl of Plymouth*) (b. London 27 Aug 1857; d. 6 Mar 1923)
Agriculture	12 Jul 1902 – May 1903: *Robert William Hanbury* (see Salisbury III)
	May 1903 – Mar 1905: *William Hillier, 4th Earl of Onslow* (b. Bletsoe, Bedfordshire, 7 Mar 1853; d. London 23 Oct 1911)
	Mar – Dec 1905: *Ailwyn Edward Fellows* (from 1921: *Baron Ailwyn*) (b. 10 Nov 1855; d. 23 Sep 1924)

10 Dec 1905 – 6 Apr 1908: Campbell-Bannerman (Lib)

Prime Minister	*Sir Henry Campbell-Bannerman* (see Gladstone III)
Foreign Affairs	*Sir Edward Grey* (from 1916: *Viscount*) *Grey of*

	Fallodon (b. Fallodon 25 Apr 1862; d. Fallodon 7 Sep 1933)
Home Affairs	*Herbert John Gladstone* (from 1910: *1st Viscount Gladstone*) (b. London 7 Jan 1854; d. Hertfordshire 6 Mar 1930)
Chancellor of the Exchequer	*Herbert Henry Asquith* (see Gladstone IV)
War	*Richard Burdon Haldane* (from 1911: *Viscount Haldane*) (b. Cloan, Scotland, 30 Jul 1856; d. Cloan, Scotland, 19 Aug 1928)
Colonies	*Victor Alexander Bruce, 9th Earl of Elgin and 13th Earl of Kincardine* (b. Montreal 16 May 1849; d. Dunfermline 18 Jan 1917)
Lord Chancellor	*Sir Robert Reid* (from 1906: *Baron Loreburn;* from 1911: *Earl Loreburn*) (b. Corfu 3 Apr 1846; d. London 1 Dec 1923)
Lord President	*Robert Crewe-Milnes, Baron Houghton* (from 1911: *Earl of Crewe*) (b. London 12 Jan 1858; d. Leatherhead, Surrey, 20 Jun 1945)
Lord Privy Seal	*George Robinson, Marquis of Ripon* (see Palmerston II/Russell II)
First Lord of the Admiralty	*Charles Marjoribanks, Baron Tweedmouth* (see Rosebery)
Trade	*David Lloyd George* (from 1944: *1st Earl Lloyd George*) (b. Manchester 17 Jan 1863; d. Llanystumdwy 26 Mar 1945)
India	*John Morley, Viscount Morley* (see Gladstone III)
Chancellor of the Duchy of Lancaster	*Sir Henry Hartley Fowler* (from 1908: *Viscount Wolverhampton*) (see Gladstone IV)
Postmaster-General	*Sydney Charles Buxton, Viscount Buxton* (b. London 25 Oct 1853; d. London 15 Oct 1934)
Local Government	*John Burns* (Lab) (b. London 10 Oct 1858; d. 24 Jan 1943)
Education	Dec 1905 – Jan 1907: *Augustine Birrell* (b. Liverpool 19 Jan 1850; d. Chelsea 20 Nov 1933)
	Jan 1907 – Apr 1908: *Reginald McKenna* (b. London 6 Jul 1863; d. London 6 Sep 1943)
Chief Secretary for Ireland	Dec 1905 – Jan 1907: *James Bryce* (see Gladstone IV)
	Jan 1907 – Apr 1908; *Augustine Birrell* (see above)
Secretary for Scotland	*Sir John Sinclair* (from 1909: *Baron Pentland*) (b. Edinburgh 7 Jul 1860; d. Hampstead 11 Jan 1925)

Public Works	Mar 1907 – Apr 1908: *Lewis Vernon Harcourt* (from 1916: *1st Viscount Harcourt*) (b. London 1 Feb 1863; d. London 24 Feb 1922)
Agriculture	*Charles Robert Wynn-Carrington, 4th Earl Carrington* (b. London 16 May 1843; d. High Wycombe 11 Nov 1929)

6 Apr 1908 – 26 May 1915: Asquith I (Lib)

Prime Minister	*Herbert Henry Asquith* (for 1st time) (see Gladstone IV)
Foreign Affairs	*Sir Edward Grey* (see Campbell-Bannerman)
Home Affairs	6 Apr 1908 – 21 Dec 1909: *Herbert John Gladstone* (see Campbell-Bannerman)
	Feb 1910 – Oct 1911: *Winston (Leonard Spencer) Churchill* (from 1953: *Sir*) (b. Blenheim Palace 30 Nov 1874; d. London 24 Jan 1965)
	23 Oct 1911 – 26 May 1915: *Reginald McKenna* (see Campbell-Bannerman)
Chancellor of the Exchequer	*David Lloyd George* (see Campbell-Bannerman)
War	6 Apr 1908 – Jan 1912: *Richard Burdon Haldane, Viscount Haldane* (see Campbell-Bannerman)
	Jun 1912 – 30 Mar 1914: *John Edward Bernard Seeley* (from 1933: *Baron Mottistone*) (b. Nottingham 31 May 1868; d. London 7 Nov 1947)
	30 Mar – 6 Aug 1914: *Herbert Henry Asquith* (see Gladstone IV)
	6 Aug 1914 – 26 May 1915: *Herbert (Horatio) Kitchener, Earl Kitchener of Khartoum* (b. Crotta House, Ireland, 24 Jun 1850; d. (drowned at sea) 5 Jun 1916)
Colonies	6 Apr 1908 – 3 Nov 1910: *Robert Crewe-Milnes, Earl of Crewe* (see Campbell-Bannerman)
	3 Nov 1910 – 26 May 1915: *Lewis Vernon Harcourt* (see Campbell-Bannerman)
Lord Chancellor	6 Apr 1908 – Jun 1912: *Sir Robert Reid, Baron* (from 1911: *Earl*) *Loreburn* (see Campbell-Bannerman)
	Jun 1912 – 26 May 1915: *Richard Burdon Haldane, Viscount Haldane* (see Campbell-Bannerman)
Lord President	6 Apr 1908 – Sep 1908: *Charles Marjoribanks, Baron Tweedmouth* (see Rosebery)

	Sep 1908 – Jun 1910: *Henry Fowler, Viscount Wolverhampton* (see Gladstone IV)
	Jun – 3 Nov 1910: *William Lygon, 7th Earl Beauchamp* (b. London 20 Feb 1872; d. New York 15 Nov 1938)
	3 Nov 1910 – 6 Aug 1914: *John Morley, Viscount Morley* (see Gladstone III)
	6 Aug 1914 – 23 May 1915: *William Lygon, 7th Earl Beauchamp* (see above)
Lord Privy Seal	6 Apr 1908 – Oct 1908: *George Robinson, Marquis of Ripon* (see Palmerston II/ Russell II)
	Oct 1908 – 23 Oct 1911: *Robert Crewe-Milnes, Earl of Crewe* (see Campbell-Bannerman)
	23 Oct 1911 – 13 Feb 1912: *Charles Wynn-Carrington, 4th Earl Carrington* (see Campbell-Bannerman)
	14 Feb 1912 – 26 May 1915: *Robert Crewe-Milnes, Earl of Crewe* (see Campbell-Bannerman)
First Lord of the Admiralty	6 Apr 1908 – 23 Oct 1911: *Reginald McKenna* (see Campbell-Bannerman)
	23 Oct 1911 – 26 May 1915: *Winston Churchill* (see above)
Trade	6 Apr 1908 – Feb 1910: *Winston Churchill* (see above)
	Feb 1910 – 11 Feb 1914: *Sydney Buxton, Viscount Buxton* (see Campbell-Bannerman)
	11 Feb – 6 Aug 1914: *John Burns* (see Campbell-Bannerman)
	6 Aug 1914 – 26 May 1915: *Walter Runciman* (from 1937: *1st Viscount Runciman*) (b. South Shields 19 Nov 1870; d. Doxford 14 Nov 1949)
India	6 Apr 1908 – 3 Nov 1910: *John Morley, Viscount Morley* (see Gladstone III)
	3 Nov 1910 – 26 May 1915: *Robert Crewe-Milnes, Earl of Crewe* (see Campbell-Bannerman)
Duchy of Lancaster	6 Apr – Sep 1908: *Sir Henry Hartley Fowler, Viscount Wolverhampton* (see Gladstone IV)
	Sep 1908 – Jun 1909: *Edmond George Petty-Fitzmaurice, 1st Baron Fitzmaurice* (b. London 19 Jun 1846; d. Bradford-on-Avon 21 Jun 1935)
	Jun 1909 – Feb 1910: *Sir Herbert Louis Samuel* (from 1937: *1st Viscount Samuel*) (b. Liverpool 6 Nov 1870; d. 5 Feb 1963)
	Feb 1910 – Oct 1911: *Joseph Albert Pease* (from 1916: *Baron Gainford*) (b. Darlington 17 Jan 1860; d.

Headlam Hall 15 Feb 1943)
23 Oct 1911 – 11 Feb 1914: *Sir Charles Edward Henry Hobhouse* (b. Sussex 30 Jun 1862; d. 26 Jun 1941)
11 Feb 1914 – 4 Feb 1915: *Charles Frederick Gurney Masterman* (b. Wimbledon 25 Oct 1874; d. London 7 Nov 1792)
4 Feb – 26 May 1915: *Edwin Samuel Montagu* (b. Clifton 6 Feb 1879; d. London 15 Nov 1924)

Postmaster-General
6 Apr 1908 – Feb 1910: *Sydney Buxton, Viscount Buxton* (see Campbell-Bannerman)
Feb 1910 – 11 Feb 1914: *Sir Herbert Samuel* (see above)
11 Feb 1914 – 26 May 1915: *Sir Charles Hobhouse* (see above)

Local Government
6 Apr 1908 – 11 Feb 1914: *John Burns* (see Campbell-Bannerman)
11 Feb 1914 – 26 May 1915: *Sir Herbert Samuel* (see above)

Education
6 Apr 1908 – 23 Oct 1911: *Walter Runciman* (see above)
23 Oct 1911 – 26 May 1915: *Joseph Albert Pease* (see above)

Chief Secretary for Ireland
Augustine Birrell (see Campbell-Bannerman)

Secretary for Scotland
6 Apr 1908 – 14 Feb 1912: *Sir John Sinclair*, (from 1909: *Baron Pentland*) (see Campbell-Bannerman)
14 Feb 1912 – 26 May 1915: *Thomas MacKinnon Wood* (b. London 26 Jan 1855; d. London 26 Mar 1927)

Public Works
6 Apr 1908 – 3 Nov 1910: *Lewis Vernon Harcourt* (see Campbell-Bannerman)
3 Nov 1910 – 26 May 1915: *William Lygon, 7th Earl Beauchamp* (see above)

Agriculture
6 Apr 1908 – 23 Oct 1911: *Charles Wynn-Carrington, 4th Earl Carrington* (see Campbell-Bannerman)
23 Oct 1911 – 6 Aug 1914: *Walter Runciman* (see above)
6 Aug 1914 – 26 May 1915: *Auberon Thomas Herbert, 8th Baron Lucas* (b. 25 May 1876; d. France (?)4 Nov 1916)

Attorney-General
Jun 1912 – 26 May 1915: *Sir Rufus Daniel Isaacs* (from 1914: *Marquis of Reading*) (b. London 10 Oct 1860; d. London 30 Dec 1935)

617

26 May 1915 – 5 Dec 1916: Asquith II (Coalition)

Prime Minister	*Herbert Henry Asquith* (for 2nd time) (see Gladstone IV)
Foreign Affairs	*Sir Edward Grey* (see Campbell-Bannerman)
Home Affairs	26 May 1915 – 3 Jan 1916: *Sir John Allsebrook Simon* (from 1940: *Viscount Simon*) (b. Manchester 28 Feb 1873; d. London 11 Jan 1954)
	10 Jan – 5 Dec 1916: *Sir Herbert Samuel* (see Asquith I)
Chancellor of the Exchequer	*Reginald MacKenna* (see Campbell-Bannerman)
War	26 May 1915 – 5 Jun 1916: *Herbert (Horatio) Kitchener, Earl Kitchener of Khartoum* (see Asquith I)
	7 Jul – 5 Dec 1916: *David Lloyd George* (see Campbell-Bannerman)
Colonies	*Andrew Bonar Law* (Cons) (b. New Brunswick 16 Sep 1859; d. London 30 Oct 1923)
Lord Chancellor	*Sir Stanley Owen Buckmaster, 1st Baron Buckmaster* (b. Chaddington, Buckinghamshire, 9 Jan 1861; d. London 5 Dec 1934)
Lord President	*Robert Crewe-Milnes, Earl of Crewe* (see Campbell-Bannerman)
Lord Privy Seal	*George Nathaniel Curzon, Earl* (from 1921: *Marquis*) *Curzon of Kedleston* (Cons) (b. Kedleston 11 Jan 1859; d. London 20 Mar 1925)
First Lord of the Admiralty	*Sir Arthur James Balfour* (Cons) (see Salisbury II)
Trade	*Walter Runciman* (see Asquith I)
India	*(Joseph) Austen Chamberlain* (Cons) (see Balfour)
Chancellor of the Duchy of Lancaster	26 May – 19 Sep 1915: *Winston Churchill* (see Asquith I)
	26 Nov 1915 – 10 Jan 1916: *Herbert Samuel* (see Asquith I)
	10 Jan – 10 Jul 1916: *Edwin Samuel Montagu* (see Asquith I)
	10 Jul – 5 Dec 1916: *Thomas MacKinnon Wood* (see Asquith I)
Local Government	*Walter Hume Long* (see Salisbury III)
Paymaster-General	Aug – 5 Dec 1916: *Arthur Henderson* (Lab) (b. Glasgow 1 Aug 1863; d. London 20 Oct 1935)

Education	26 May 1915 – 18 Aug 1916: *Arthur Henderson* (see above) 18 Aug – 5 Dec 1916: *Robert Crewe-Milnes, Earl of Crewe* (see Campbell-Bannerman)
Chief Secretary for Ireland	20 May 1915 – 1916: *Augustine Birrell* (see Campbell-Bannerman) Jul – Dec 1916: *Henry Edward Duke* (from 1925: *1st Baron Merrivale*) (b. Walkhampton, Devonshire, 5 Nov 1855; d. London 20 May 1939)
Secretary for Scotland	26 May 1915 – 10 Jul 1916: *Thomas MacKinnon Wood* (see Asquith I) 10 Jul – 5 Dec 1916: *Harold John Tennant* (b. Inverleithen 18 Nov 1865; d. 9 Nov 1935)
Public Works	*Lewis Vernon Harcourt* (see Cambpell-Bannerman)
Agriculture	26 May 1915 – 25 Jun 1916: *William Waldegrave Palmer, Earl of Selborne* (see Salisbury III) 11 Jul – 5 Dec 1916 *David Alexander Edward Lindsay, 27th Earl of Crawford and 10th Earl of Balcarres* (b. Aberdeen 10 Oct 1871; d. Wigan 8 Mar 1940)
Attorney-General	26 May – 19 Oct 1915: *Sir Edward Carson* (b. Dublin 9 Feb 1854; d. Cleve Court, Kent, 22 Oct 1935) Nov 1915 – 5 Dec 1916: *Sir Frederick Edwin Smith* (from 1919: *1st Baron Birkenhead;* from 1922: *1st Earl of Birkenhead*) (b. Birkenhead 12 Jul 1872; d. London 30 Sep 1930)
Munitions	26 May 1915 – 7 Jul 1916: *David Lloyd George* (see Campbell-Bannerman) 10 Jul – 5 Dec 1916: *Edwin Samuel Montagu* (see Asquith I)
Blockade	Jan – Dec 1916 *Lord Robert Cecil* (from 1923: *Viscount Cecil of Chelwood*) (b. 14 Sep 1864; d. Tunbridge Wells 24 Nov 1958)
Under Secretary for Foreign Affairs	Jul 1915 – 5 Dec 1916: *Lord Robert Cecil* (see above)
Without Portfolio	*Henry Petty-Fitzmaurice, 5th Marquis of Lansdowne* (see Salisbury III)

10 Dec 1916 – 10 Jan 1919: Lloyd George I (Lib) War Cabinet

Prime Minister	*David Lloyd George* (for 1st time) (see Campbell-Bannerman)

Lord President	*George Nathaniel Curzon, Earl Curzon of Kedleston* (see Asquith II)
Chancellor of the Exchequer	*Andrew Bonar Law* (see Asquith II)
Without Portfolio	10 Dec 1916 – 10 Aug 1917: *Arthur Henderson* (see Asquith II)

10 Dec 1916 – 18 Apr 1918: *Alfred Milner, Viscount Milner* (b. Bonn 23 Mar 1854; d. Canterbury 13 May 1925)

Jun 1917 – 10 Jan 1919: *Jan Christiaan Smuts* (b. Bovenplaats 24 May 1870; d. Doornkloof 11 Sep 1950)

17 Jul 1917 – 10 Jan 1919: *Christopher Addison* (from 1937: *1st Baron;* from 1945: *1st Viscount Addison*) (b. Hogsthorpe 19 Jun 1869; d. West Wycombe 11 Dec 1951)

17 Jul 1917 – 22 Jan 1918: *Sir Edward Carson* (see Asquith II)

17 Aug 1917 – 10 Jan 1919: *George Nicoll Barnes* (b. Lochee 2 Jan 1859; d. London 21 Apr 1940)

18 Apr 1918 – 10 Jan 1919: *(Joseph) Austen Chamberlain* (see Balfour)

The war cabinet continued to function in theory until October 1919, when the ministers appointed on 10 January 1919 (or their later replacements) began to operate as a cabinet.

10 Jan/Oct 1919 – 19 Oct 1922: Lloyd George II (Coalition of Liberals and Conservatives)

Prime Minister	*David Lloyd George* (Lib) (for 2nd time) (see Campbell-Bannerman)
Foreign Affairs	10 Jan – 24 Oct 1919: *Sir Arthur James Balfour* (see Salisbury II)
	24 Oct 1919 – 19 Oct 1922: *George Nathaniel Curzon, Earl Curzon of Kedleston* (from 1921: *Marquis Curzon of Kedleston*) (see Asquith II)
Home Affairs	*Edward Shortt* (b. Newcastle-upon-Tyne 10 Mar 1862; d. London 10 Nov 1935)
Chancellor of the Exchequer	10 Jan 1919 – 1 Apr 1921: *(Joseph) Austen Chamberlain* (see Balfour)
	1 Apr 1921 – 19 Oct 1922: *Sir Robert Stevenson Horne* (from 1937: *1st Viscount Horne*) (b. Glamannan, Stirlingshire, 28 Feb 1871; d. Farnham, Surrey, 3 Sep 1940)

War and Air	10 Jan 1919 – 13 Feb 1921: *Winston Churchill* (see Asquith I)
War	13 Feb 1921 – 19 Oct 1922: *Sir Laming Worthington-Evans* (b. Broadstairs 23 Aug 1868; d. London 13 Feb 1931)
Colonies	10 Jan 1919 – 7 Jan 1921: *Alfred Milner, Viscount Milner* (see Lloyd George I)
	13 Feb 1921 – 19 Oct 1922: *Winston Churchill* (see Asquith I)
Lord Chancellor	*Sir Frederick Edwin Smith, 1st Baron Birkenhead* (from 1922: *1st Earl of Birkenhead*) (see Asquith II)
Lord President	10 Jan – 24 Oct 1919: *George Nathaniel Curzon, Earl Curzon of Kedleston* (see Asquith II)
	24 Oct 1919 – 19 Oct 1922: *Sir Arthur James Balfour* (see Salisbury II)
Lord Privy Seal	10 Jan 1919 – 17 Mar 1921: *Andrew Bonar Law* (see Asquith II)
	17 Mar 1921 – 19 Oct 1922: *(Joseph) Austen Chamberlain* (see Balfour)
First Lord of the Admiralty	10 Jan 1919 – 13 Feb 1921: *Walter Hume Long* (see Salisbury III)
	13 Feb 1921 – 19 Oct 1922: *Arthur Hamilton Lee, Baron Lee* (from 1922: *Viscount Lee of Fareham*) (b. Bridport 8 Nov 1868; d. London 21 Jun 1947)
Trade	10 Jan – 26 May 1919: *Sir Alfred Stanley* (from 1920: *Baron Ashfield*) (b. Derby 8 Nov 1874; d. London 4 Nov 1948)
	26 May 1919 – 20 Mar 1920: *Sir Auckland Campbell Geddes* (b. Edinburgh 21 Jun 1879; d. Chichester 8 Jan 1954)
	20 Mar 1920 – 1 Apr 1921: *Sir Robert Stevenson Horne* (see above)
	1 Apr 1921 – 19 Oct 1922: *Stanley Baldwin* (from 1937: *Earl Baldwin of Bewdley*) (b. Bewdley 3 Aug 1867; d. Stourport-on-Severn 14 Dec 1947)
India	10 Jan 1919 – 9 Mar 1922: *Edwin Samuel Montagu* (see Asquith I)
	18 Mar – 19 Oct 1922: *William Robert Wellesley Peel, Viscount* (from 1929: *Earl*) *Peel* (b. London 7 Jan 1867; d. Petersfield 28 Sep 1937)
Local Government	10 Jan – 1 Jul 1919: *Christopher Addison* (see Lloyd George I)
	from 1 Jul 1919: post abolished

Education	*Herbert Albert Laurens Fisher* (b. London 21 Mar 1865; d. London 18 Apr 1940)
Chief Secretary for Ireland	10 Jan 1919 – 2 Apr 1920: *Sir (James) Ian Macpherson* (from 1936: *Baron Strathcarron*) (b. Newtonmore 14 May 1880; d. London 14 Aug 1937)
	2 Apr 1920 – 19 Oct 1922: *Sir Hamar Greenwood* (from 1929: *Baron;* from 1937: *Viscount Greenwood*) (b. Whitby, Ontario, 7 Feb 1870; d. London 10 Sep 1948)
Viceroy of Ireland	10 Jan 1919 – 1 Apr 1921: *Sir John Pinkstone Denton French, Earl of Ypres* (b. Ripple Vale, Kent, 28 Nov 1852; d. Deal 22 May 1925)
	1 Apr 1921 – 19 Oct 1922: *Edmund Bernard Talbot* (earlier and later: *Fitzalan-Howard*) *1st Viscount Fitzalan of Derwent* (b. 1 Jun 1855; d. 18 May 1947)
Secretary for Scotland	*Robert Munro* (see Lloyd George I)
Public Works	1 Apr 1921 (joined cabinet Apr 1922) – 19 Oct 1922: *David Alexander Edward Lindsay, 27th Earl of Crawford and 10th Earl of Balcarres* (see Asquith II)
Agriculture	10 Jan – Aug 1919: *Rowland Edmund Prothero, Baron Ernle* (b. Clifton-on-Teme 6 Sep 1851; d. Ginge Manor 1 Jul 1937)
	Aug 1919 – 13 Feb 1921: *Arthur Hamilton Lee* (see above)
	13 Feb 1921 – 19 Oct 1922: *Sir Arthur Griffith-Boscawen* (b. Wrexham 18 Oct 1865; d. 1 Jun 1946)
Attorney-General	Nov 1921 – Mar 1922: *Sir Gordon Hewart* (from 1922: *Baron Hewart*) (b. Bury 7 Jan 1870; d. Totteridge, Hertfordshire, 5 May 1943)
Munitions (later Supply)	*Andrew Weir, Baron Iverforth* (b. 24 Apr 1865; d. 17 Oct 1955)
Labour	10 Jan 1919 – 20 Mar 1920: *Sir Robert Stevenson Horne* (see above)
	20 Mar 1920 – 19 Oct 1922: *Thomas James Macnamara* (b. Montreal 23 Aug 1861; d. London 4 Dec 1931)
Health (new post)	24 Jun 1919 – 1 Apr 1921: *Christopher Addison* (see Lloyd George I)
	1 Apr 1921 – 19 Oct 1922: *Sir Alfred Morris Mond* (from 1928: *Baron Melchett*) (b. Farnworth 23 Oct 1868; d. London 27 Dec 1930)
Transport	Aug 1919 – Nov 1921: *Sir Eric Campbell Geddes* (b.

Agra 26 Sep 1875; d. Hassocks 22 Jun 1937)

Without Portfolio   10 – 29 Jan 1919: *George Nicoll Barnes* (see Lloyd George I)
10 Jan – 28 Oct 1919: *Sir Eric Campbell Geddes* (see above)
2 Apr 1920 – 3 Feb 1921: *Sir Laming Worthington-Evans* (see above)
1 Apr 1921 – 19 Oct 1922: *Christopher Addison* (see Lloyd George I)

24 Oct 1922 – 22 Jan 1924: Bonar Law/Baldwin I (Cons)

Prime Minister	24 Oct 1922 – 20 May 1923: *Andrew Bonar Law* (see Asquith II) 27 May 1923 – 22 Jan 1924: *Stanley Baldwin* (for 1st time) (see Lloyd George II)
Foreign Affairs	*George Nathaniel Curzon, Marquis Curzon of Kedleston* (see Asquith II)
Home Affairs	*William Clive Bridgeman* (from 1929: *Viscount Bridgeman*) (b. 31 Dec 1864; d. 14 Aug 1935)
Chancellor of the Exchequer	24 Oct 1922 – 28 Aug 1923: *Stanley Baldwin* (see Lloyd George II) 28 Aug 1923 – 22 Jan 1924: *Neville Chamberlain* (b. Birmingham 18 Mar 1869; d. Heckfield 9 Nov 1940)
War	*Edward Stanley, 17th Earl of Derby* (see Balfour)
Colonies	*Victor Cavendish, 9th Duke of Devonshire* (b. London 31 May 1868; d. Chatsworth 6 May 1938)
Lord Chancellor	*George Cave, 1st Earl Cave* (b. London 23 Feb 1856; d. Burnham-on-Sea 29 Mar 1928)
Lord President	*James Edward Hubert Cecil, 4th Marquis of Salisbury* (see Balfour)
Lord Privy Seal	27 May 1923 – 22 Jan 1924: *Lord Robert Cecil* (see Asquith II)
First Lord of the Admiralty	*Leopold Charles Maurice Stennet Amery* (b. Gorachpur, India, 22 Nov 1873; d. London 16 Sep 1955)
Trade	*Philip Lloyd Graeme* (from Nov 1924: *Sir Philip Cunliffe-Lister;* from 1935: *1st Viscount;* from 1955: *1st Earl Swinton*) (b. 1 May 1884; d. 1972)
India	*William Robert Wellesley Peel, Viscount Peel* (see Lloyd George II)
Chancellor of the Duchy of Lancaster	22 Oct 1922 – 27 May 1923: *James Edward Hubert Cecil, 4th Marquis of Salisbury* (see Balfour)

Postmaster- General	27 May 1923 – 22 Jan 1924: *Sir Laming Worthington-Evans* (see Lloyd George II)
Education	*Edward Frederick Lindley Wood* (from 1925: *Baron Irwin;* from 1934: *3rd Viscount;* from 1944: *1st Earl Halifax*) (b. Powderham Castle 16 Apr 1881; d. Garrowby Hall 23 Dec 1959)
Secretary for Scotland	*Ronald Craufurd Munro-Ferguson, 1st Viscount Novar* (b. Kirkcaldy 6 Mar 1860; d. Raith 30 Nov 1934)
Agriculture	*Sir Robert Arthur Sanders* (b. 20 Jun 1867)
Labour	*Sir Anderson Montague-Barlow* (b. 28 Feb 1868; d. 31 May 1951)
Health	24 Oct 1922 – 7 Mar 1923: *Sir Arthur Griffith-Boscawen* (see Lloyd George II) 7 Mar 1923 – 28 Aug 1923: *Neville Chamberlain* (see above) 28 Aug 1923 – 22 Jan 1924: *Sir William Joynson-Hicks* (from 1929: *Viscount Brentford*) (b. Canonbury, Kent, 23 Jun 1865; d. London 8 Jun 1932)
Air	27 May 1923 – 22 Jan 1924: *Sir Samuel John Gurney Hoare* (from 1944: *1st Viscount Templewood*) (b. Cromer 24 Feb 1880; d. London 7 May 1959)

23 Jan – 4 Nov 1924: Macdonald I (Lab)

Prime Minister	*James Ramsay Macdonald* (for 1st time) (b. Lossiemouth 12 Oct 1866; d. on journey from England to South America 9 Nov 1937)
Foreign Affairs	*James Ramsay Macdonald* (see above)
Home Affairs	*Arthur Henderson* (see Asquith II)
Chancellor of the Exchequer	*Philip Snowden* (from 1931: *Viscount Snowden*) (b. Cowling, Yorkshire, 18 Jul 1864; d. Frensham, Surrey, 15 May 1937)
War	*Stephen Walsh* (b. Liverpool 26 Aug 1859; d. London 16 Mar 1929)
Colonies	*James Henry Thomas* (b. Newport 3 Oct 1874; d. London 21 Jan 1949)
Lord Chancellor	*Richard Burdon Haldane, Viscount Haldane* (see Campbell-Bannerman)
Lord President	*Charles Alfred Cripps, Baron Parmoor* (b. West Ilshey, Berkshire, 3 Oct 1852; d. Henley-on-Thames 30 Jun 1941)

Lord Privy Seal	*John Robert Clynes* (b. Oldham 27 Mar 1869; d. London 23 Oct 1949)
First Lord of the Admiralty	*Frederick John Napier Thesiger, Viscount Chelmsford* (b. London 12 Aug 1868; d. London 1 Apr 1933)
Trade	*Sidney James Webb* (from 1929: *Baron Passfield*) (b. London 13 Jul 1859; d. Liphook 13 Oct 1947)
India	*Sir Sydney Haldane Olivier, Baron Olivier* (b. Colchester 16 Apr 1859; d. Bognor Regis 15 Feb 1943)
Chancellor of the Duchy of Lancaster	*Josiah Clement Wedgwood* (from 1942: *1st Baron Wedgwood*) (b. Barlaston 16 Mar 1872; d. London 26 Jul 1943)
Postmaster-General	*Vernon Hartshorn* (b. Monmouthshire 16 Mar 1872; d. Maesteg 13 Mar 1931)
Education	*Sir Charles Philips Trevelyan* (b. London 28 Oct 1870; d. London 24 Jan 1958)
Secretary for Scotland	*William Adamson* (b. 2 Apr 1863; d. 26 Feb 1936)
Public Works	*Frederick William Jowett* (b. Bradford 1864; d. 1 Feb 1944)
Agriculture	*Noel Edward Noel-Buxton* (from 1930: *Baron Buxton*) (b. London 9 Jan 1869; d. London 12 Sep 1948)
Labour	*Thomas Shaw* (b. Colne, Lancashire, 9 Apr 1872; d. London 26 Sep 1938)
Health	*John Wheatley* (b. Waterford 24 May 1869; d. Glasgow 13 May 1930)
Air	*Christopher Birdwood Thomson, 1st Baron Thomson* (b. Nasik, India, 13 Apr 1875; d. in Airship R101 disaster 5 Oct 1930)

6 Nov 1924 – 4 Jun 1929: Baldwin II (Cons)

Prime Minister	*Stanley Baldwin* (for 2nd time) (see Lloyd George II)
Foreign Affairs	*(Joseph) Austen Chamberlain* (see Lloyd George I)
Home Affairs	*Sir William Joynson-Hicks* (see Bonar Law Baldwin I)
Chancellor of the Exchequer	*Winston Churchill* (see Asquith I)
War	*Sir Laming Worthington-Evans* (see Lloyd George II)
Colonies (from Jun 1925: Colonies and Dominions)	*Leopold Stennett Amery* (see Bonar Law/Baldwin I)

Lord Chancellor	6 Nov 1924 – Mar 1928: *George Cave, 1st Earl Cave* (see Bonar Law Baldwin I)
	Mar 1928 – 4 Jun 1929: *Sir Douglas McGarel Hogg, 1st Baron* (from 1929: *1st Viscount*) *Hailsham* (b. London 28 Feb 1872; d. Carter's Place, Sussex, 16 Aug 1950)
Lord President	6 Nov 1924 – 20 Mar 1925: *George Nathaniel Curzon, Marquis Curzon of Kedleston* (see Asquith II)
	28 Apr 1925 – 4 Jun 1929: *Arthur James Balfour, 1st Earl Balfour* (see Salisbury II)
Lord Privy Seal	*James Edward Hubert Cecil, 4th Marquis of Salisbury* (see Balfour)
First Lord of the Admiralty	*William Clive Bridgeman* (from 1929: *Viscount Bridgeman*) (see Bonar Law/Baldwin I)
Trade	*Sir Philip Cunliffe-Lister* (see Bonar Law/Baldwin I)
India	6 Nov 1924 – 19 Oct 1925: *Frederick Edwin Smith, 1st Earl of Birkenhead* (see Lloyd George II)
	19 Oct 1928 – 4 Jun 1929: *William Robert Wellesley Peel, Viscount* (from 1929: *Earl*) *Peel* (see Lloyd George II)
Chancellor of the Duchy of Lancaster	10 Nov 1924 – 29 Aug 1927: *Robert Cecil, Viscount Cecil of Chelwood* (see Asquith II)
	20 Oct 1927 – 4 Jun 1929: *Ronald John McNeill, Baron Cushendun* (b. Torquay, Ulster, 3 Apr 1861; d. London 12 Oct 1934)
Education	*Lord Eustace (Sutherland Campbell) Percy* (from 1953: *1st Baron Percy of Newcastle*) (b. 21 Mar 1887; d. London 3 Apr 1958)
Secretary for Scotland	*Sir John Gilmour* (b. Fife 27 May 1876; d. London 30 Mar 1940)
Public Works	10 Nov 1924 – Oct 1928: *William Robert Wellesley Peel, Viscount Peel* (see Lloyd George I)
Agriculture and Fishieries	6 Nov 1924 – Nov 1925: *Edward Frederick Lindley Wood* (see Bonar Law/Baldwin I)
	Nov 1925 – 4 Jun 1929: *Walter Edward Guinness* (from 1932: *1st Baron Moyne*) (b. Dublin 29 Mar 1880, d. Cairo 6 Nov 1944)
Attorney-General	6 Nov 1924 – Mar 1928: *Sir Douglas McGarel Hogg* (see above)
Labour	*Sir Arthur Herbert Drummond Ramsay Steel-Maitland* (b. India 5 Aug 1876; d. Rye 30 Mar 1935)
Health	*Neville Chamberlain* (see Bonar Law/Baldwin I)

Air	*Sir Samuel Hoare* (see Bonar Law/Baldwin I)

8 Jun 1929 – 24 Aug 1931: Macdonald II (Lab)

Prime Minister	*James Ramsay Macdonald* (for 2nd time) (see Macdonald I)
Foreign Affairs	*Arthur Henderson* (see Asquith II)
Home Affairs	*John Robert Clynes* (see Macdonald I)
Chancellor of the Exchequer	*Philip Snowden* (see Macdonald I)
War	*Thomas Shaw* (see Macdonald I)
Colonies	*Sidney James Webb, Baron Passfield* (see Macdonald I)
Dominions	8 Jun 1929 – 6 Jun 1930: the Colonial Secretary
Lord Chancellor	*John Sankey, Baron* (from 1932: *Viscount*) *Sankey* (b. Moreton 26 Oct 1866; d. London 6 Feb 1948)
Lord President	*Charles Alfred Cripps, Baron Parmoor* (see Macdonald I)
First Lord of the Admiralty	*Sir Albert Victor Alexander* (from 1950: *Viscount;* from 1963: *Earl Alexander of Hillsborough*) (b. Weston-Super-Mare 1 May 1885; d. 11 Jan 1965)
Lord Privy Seal (Unemployment)	8 Jun 1929 – 6 Jun 1930: *James Henry Thomas* (see Macdonald I)
Trade	*William Graham* (b. Peebles 29 Jul 1887; d. London 8 Jan 1932)
India	*William Wedgwood Benn* (from 1942: *Viscount Stansgate*) (b. 10 May 1877; d. London 17 Nov 1960)
Education	8 Jun 1929 – 2 Mar 1931: *Sir Charles Philips Trevelyan* (see Macdonald I)
Secretary for Scotland	*William Adamson* (see Macdonald I)
Public Works	*George Lansbury* (b. Lowestoft 21 Feb 1859; d. London 7 May 1940)
Agriculture	8 Jun 1929 – 6 Jun 1930: *Noel Edward Noel-Buxton* (from 1930: *Baron Buxton*) (see Macdonald I)
Labour	*Margaret Grace Bondfield* (b. Chard 17 Mar 1873; d. Sanderstead, Surrey, 16 Jun 1953)
Health	*Arthur Greenwood* (b. Hunslet, Leeds, 8 Feb 1880; d. London 9 Jun 1954)
Air	8 Jun 1929 – 15 Oct 1930: *Christopher Birdwood Thomson, 1st Baron Thomson* (see Macdonald I)

United States of America

HEADS OF STATE

Presidents (also Heads of Government)

1 Jan 1789	*George Washington* (b. Westmoreland County, Va, 22 Feb 1732; d. Mount Vernon, Md, 14 Dec 1799)
4 Mar 1797	*John Adams* (b. Braintree (later Quincy), Mass, 19 Oct 1735; d. Quincy, Mass, 4 Jul 1826)
4 Mar 1801	*Thomas Jefferson* (b. Shadwell, Va, 2 Apr 1743; d. Monticello, Va, 4 Jul 1826)
4 Mar 1809	*James Madison* (b. Port Conway, Va, 16 Mar 1751; d. Montpellier, Va, 28 Jun 1836)
4 Mar 1817	*James Monroe* (b. Westmoreland County, Va, 28 Apr 1758; d. New York 4 Jul 1831)
4 Mar 1925	*John Quincy Adams*, son of John Adams (b. Braintree, Mass, 11 Jul 1767; d. Washington 17 Feb 1848)
4 Mar 1829	*Andrew Jackson* (b. Waxhaw, SC, 15 Mar 1767; d. Hermitage, Tenn, 8 Jun 1845)
4 Mar 1837	*Martin van Buren* (b. Kinderhook, NY, 5 Dec 1782; d. Lindenwald, NY, 24 Jul 1862)
4 Mar 1841	*William Henry Harrison* (b. Berkeley, Va, 9 Feb 1773; d. Washington 4 Apr 1841)
4 Apr 1841	*John Tyler* (b. Charles City County, Va, 29 Mar 1790; d. Richmond, Va, 18 Jan 1862)
4 Mar 1845	*James Knox Polk* (b. Mecklenburg County, NC, 2 Nov 1795; d. Washington 15 Jun 1849)
4 Mar 1849	*Zachary Taylor* (b. Orange County, Va, 24 Nov 1784; d. Washington 9 Jul 1850)
9 Jul 1850	*Millard Fillmore* (b. Summer Hill, NY, 7 Jan 1800; d. Buffalo, NY, 8 Mar 1874)
4 Mar 1853	*Franklin Pierce* (b. Hilsborough, NH, 23 Nov 1804; d. Concord, NH, 8 Oct 1869)
4 Mar 1857	*James Buchanan* (b. Mercersburg, Pa, 22 Apr 1791; d. Lancaster, Pa, 1 Jun 1868)
4 Mar 1861	*Abraham Lincoln* (b. Hodgens Mill, Ky, 12 Feb 1809; d. Washington 14 Apr 1865)
14 Apr 1865	*Andrew Johnson* (b. Raleigh, NC, 29 Dec 1808; d. Carter Station, Tenn, 31 Jul 1875)
4 Mar 1869	*Ulysses S. Grant* (b. Point Pleasant, Ohio, 27 Apr 1822; d. Mount McGregor, NY, 23 Jul 1885)

4 Mar 1877	*Rutherford Birchard Hayes* (b. Delaware, Ohio, 4 Oct 1822; d. Fremont, Ohio, 16 Jan 1893)
4 Mar 1881	*James Abraham Garfield* (b. Cuyahoga County, Ohio, 19 Nov 1831; d. Washington 19 Sep 1881)
19 Sep 1881	*Chester Allan Arthur* (b. Fairfield, Vt, 5 Oct 1830; d. New York 18 Nov 1886)
4 Mar 1885	*Stephen Grover Cleveland* (for 1st time) (b. Caldwell, NJ, 18 Mar 1837; d. Princeton, NJ, 24 Jun 1908)
4 Mar 1889	*Benjamin Harrison*, grandson of William Henry Harrison (b. Cincinnati, Ohio, 20 Aug 1833; d. Indianapolis, Ind, 13 Mar 1901)
4 Mar 1893	*Stephen Grover Cleveland* (for 2nd time)
4 Mar 1897	*William McKinley* (b. Niles, Ohio, 29 Jan 1843; d. Buffalo, NY, 14 Sep 1901)
14 Sep 1901	*Theodore Roosevelt* (b. New York 27 Oct 1858; d. Washington 4 Jan 1919)
4 Mar 1909	*William Howard Taft* (b. Cincinnati, Ohio, 15 Sep 1857; d. Washington 8 Mar 1930)
4 Mar 1913	*Thomas Woodrow Wilson* (b. Staunton, Va, 28 Dec 1856; d. Washington 3 Feb 1924)
4 Mar 1921	*Warren Gamaliel Harding* (b. Caledonia, Ohio, 2 Nov 1865; d. San Francisco, Cal, 2 Aug 1923)
3 Aug 1923	*Calvin Coolidge* (b. Plymouth, Vt, 4 Jul 1872; d. Northampton, Mass, 5 Jan 1933)
4 Mar 1929	*Herbert Clark Hoover* (b. West Branch, Iowa, 10 Aug 1874; d. New York 20 Oct 1964)

ADMINISTRATIONS

Presidents, Vice-Presidents and Secretaries of State

1 Feb/30 Apr 1789 – 3 Nov 1797: Washington

President	*George Washington* (see Heads of State)
Vice-President	*John Adams* (see Heads of State)
Secretary of State	26 Sep 1789 – 1 Jan 1794: *Thomas Jefferson* (see Heads of State)
	2 Jan 1794 – 9 Dec 1795: *Edmund Randolph* (b. Williamsburg, Va, 10 Aug 1753; d. 12 Sep 1813)
	10 Dec 1795 – 3 Mar 1797: *Timothy Pickering* (b. Salem, Mass, 17 Jul 1745; d. 29 Jan 1829)
Secretary for the Treasury	11 Sep 1789 – 1 Feb 1795: *Alexander Hamilton* (b. Nevis, Leeward Islands 11 Jan 1757; d. Weehawken on

Hudson 12 Jul 1804)

	2 Feb 1795 – 3 Nov 1797: *Oliver Wolcott* (b. Litchfield 11 Jan 1760; d. New York 1 Apr 1833)
War	12 Sep 1789 – 1 Jan 1795: *Henry Knox* (b. Boston, Mass, 25 Jul 1750; d. 25 Oct 1806)
	2 Jan 1795 – 26 Jan 1796: *Timothy Pickering* (see above)
	27 Jan 1796 – 3 Mar 1797: *James McHenry* (b. Ballymena, Ireland 16 Nov 1753; d. 3 May 1816)
Attorney-General	26 Sep 1789 – 26 Jan 1794: *Edmund Randolph* (see above)
	27 Jan 1794 – 9 Dec 1795: *William Bradford* (b. Philadelphia 14 Sep 1755; d. 23 Aug 1795)
	10 Dec 1795 – 3 Mar 1797: *Charles Lee* (b. 1785; d. Warrenton, Fauquier County, Va, 24 Jun 1815)
Postmaster-General	26 Sep 1789 – 11 Aug 1791: *Samuel Osgood* (b. Andover, Mass, 3 Feb 1747/48; d. 12 Aug 1813)
	12 Aug 1791 – 24 Feb 1795: *Timothy Pickering* (see above)
	25 Feb 1795 – 3 Mar 1797: *Joseph Habersham* (b. Savannah 28 Jul 1751; d. Savannah 17 Nov 1815)

4 Mar 1797 – 3 Mar 1801: Adams

President	*John Adams* (see Heads of State)
Vice-President	*Thomas Jefferson* (see Heads of State)
Secretary of State	4 Mar 1797 – 12 May 1800: *Timothy Pickering* (see Washington)
	13 May 1800 – 3 Mar 1801: *John Marshall* (b. Germantown, Va, 24 Sep 1755; d. Philadelphia, Pa, 6 Jul 1835)
Treasury	4 Mar 1797 – 31 Dec 1801: *Oliver Wolcott* (see Washington)
	1 Jan – 3 Mar 1801: *Samuel Dexter* (b. Boston, Mass, 14 May 1761; d. Athens, NY, 4 May 1816)
War	4 Mar 1797 – 12 May 1800: *James McHenry* (see Washington)
	13 May 1800 – 2 Feb 1801: *Samuel Dexter* (see above)
	3 Feb – 3 Mar 1801: *Roger Griswold* (b. Lyme, Conn, 21 May 1762; d. 25 Oct 1812)
Navy	3 – 20 May 1798: *George Cabot* (b. Salem, Mass, 16 Jan 1752; d. 18 Apr 1823)

	21 May 1798 – 3 Mar 1801: *Benjamin Stoddert* (b. Charles County, Md, 1751; d. 17 Dec 1813)
Attorney-General	4 Mar 1797 – 19 Feb 1801: *Charles Lee* (see Washington)
	20 Feb – 3 Mar 1801: *Theophilus Parsons* (b. Byfield, Mass, 24 Feb 1750; d. Boston, Mass, 30 Oct 1813)
Postmaster-General	4 Mar 1797 – 3 Mar 1801: *Joseph Habersham* (see Washington)

4 Mar 1801 – 3 Mar 1809: Jefferson (Dem)

President	*Thomas Jefferson* (see Heads of State)
Vice-President	4 Mar 1801 – 3 Mar 1805: *Aaron Burr* (b. Newark, NY, 6 Feb 1756; d. Port Richmond, Staten Island, 14 Sep 1836)
	4 Mar 1805 – 3 Mar 1809: *George Clinton* (b. Little Britain, NY, 26 Jul 1739; d. 20 Apr 1812)
Secretary of State	5 Mar 1801 – 3 Mar 1809: *James Madison* (see Heads of State)
Treasury	4 Mar – 13 May 1801: *Samuel Dexter* (see Adams)
	14 May 1801 – 3 Mar 1809: *Albert Gallatin* (b. Geneva 29 Jan 1761; d. Astoria, Long Island, 12 Aug 1849)
War	5 Mar 1801 – 3 Mar 1809: *Henry Dearborn* (b. Hampton, NH, 23 Feb 1751; d. Roxbury, Mass, 6 Jun 1829)
Navy	4 Mar – 14 Jul 1801: *Benjamin Stoddert* (see Adams)
	15 Jul 1801 – 2 Mar 1805: *Robert Smith* (b. Lancaster, Pa, 3 Nov 1757; d. Baltimore 26 Nov 1842)
	3 Mar 1805 – 15 Apr 1808: *Jacob Crowninshield* (b. Salem, Mass, 31 May 1770; d. 15 Apr 1808)
Attorney-General	5 Mar 1801 – 2 Mar 1805: *Levi Lincoln* (b. Hingham, Mass, 15 May 1749; d. Worcester, Mass, 14 May 1820)
	3 Mar – 6 Aug 1805: *Robert Smith* (see above)
	7 Aug 1805 – 19 Jan 1807: *John Breckinridge* (b. Staunton, Va, 2 Dec 1760; d. 14 Dec 1806)
	20 Jan 1807 – 3 Mar 1817: *Caesar Augustus Rodney* (b. Dover 4 Jan 1772; d. Buenos Aires 10 Jan 1824)
Postmaster-General	4 Mar – 27 Nov 1801: *Joseph Habersham* (see Washington)
	28 Nov 1801 – 3 Mar 1817: *Gideon Granger* (b. Suffield, Conn, 19 Jul 1767; d. Conandaigua 31 Dec 1822)

631

4 Mar 1809 – 3 Mar 1817: Madison (Dem)

President	*James Madison* (see Heads of State)
Vice-President	4 Mar 1809 – 3 Mar 1813: *George Clinton* (see Jefferson)
	4 Mar 1813 – 3 Mar 1817: *Elbridge Gerry* (b. Marblehead, Mass, 17 Jul 1744; d. Cambridge, Mass, 23 Nov 1814)
Secretary of State	6 Mar 1809 – 1 Apr 1811: *Robert Smith* (see Jefferson)
	2 Apr 1811 – 3 Mar 1817: *James Monroe* (see Heads of State)
Treasury	4 Mar 1809 – 8 Feb 1814: *Albert Gallatin* (see Jefferson)
	9 Feb – 5 Oct 1814: *George Washington Campbell* (b. Tongue, Scotland, 8 Feb 1769; d. 17 Feb 1848)
	6 Oct 1814 – 21 Oct 1816: *Alexander James Dallas* (b. Jamaica, NY, 21 Jun 1759; d. Trenton, NJ, 16 Jan 1817)
	22 Oct 1816 – 3 Mar 1817: *William Harris Crawford* (b. Amherst County, Va, 24 Feb 1772; d. 15 Sep 1834)
War	7 Mar 1809 – 12 Jan 1813: *William Eustis* (b. Cambridge, Mass, 10 Jun 1753; d. Boston, Mass, 6 Feb 1825)
	13 Jan 1813 – 26 Sep 1814: *James Armstrong* (b. New Jersey 20 Apr 1755; d. Armstrong's Station, Ohio, 4 Feb 1816)
	27 Sep 1814 – 31 Jul 1815: *James Monroe* (see Heads of State)
	1 Aug 1815 – 3 Mar 1817: *William Harris Crawford* (see above)
Navy	7 Mar 1809 – 11 Jan 1813: *Paul Hamilton* (b. 16 Oct 1762; d. 30 Jun 1816)
	12 Jan 1813 – 18 Dec 1814: *William Jones* (b. Philadelphia, Pa, 1760; d. Bethlehem, Pa, 6 Sep 1831)
	19 Dec 1814 – 3 Mar 1817: *Benjamin William Crowninshield* (b. Salem, Mass, 27 Dec 1772; d. Boston, Mass, 3 Feb 1851)
Attorney-General	4 Mar 1809 – 10 Dec 1811: *Caesar Augustus Rodney* (see Jefferson)
	11 Dec 1811 – 9 Feb 1814: *William Pinkney* (b. Annapolis, Md, 17 Mar 1764; d. Washington 25 Feb 1822)
	10 Feb 1814 – 3 Mar 1817: *Richard Rush* (b.

Philadelphia, Pa, 29 Aug 1780; d. Philadelphia, Pa, 30
Jul 1859)

Postmaster-General
4 Mar 1809 – 16 Mar 1814: *Gideon Granger* (see Jefferson)
17 Mar 1814 – 3 Mar 1817: *Return Jonathan Meigs* (b. Middletown, Conn, 17 Nov 1764; d. Marietta, Ga, 29 Mar 1824)

4 Mar 1817 – 3 Mar 1825: Monroe

President
James Monroe (see Heads of State)

Vice-Preisdent
Daniel D. Tompkins (b. Scarsdale, NY, 21 Jun 1744; d. Staten Island, NY, 11 Jun 1825)

Secretary of State
5 Mar 1817 – 3 Mar 1825: *John Quincy Adams* (see Heads of State) .

Treasury
William Harris Crawford (see Madison)

War
7 Apr – 7 Oct 1817: *George Graham*
8 Oct 1817 – 3 Mar 1825: *John Caldwell Calhoun* (b. Calhoun Settlement, SC, 18 Mar 1782; d. 31 Mar 1850)

Navy
4 Mar 1817 – 8 Nov 1818: *Benjamin William Crowninshield* (see Madison)
9 Nov 1818 – 31 Aug 1823: *Smith Thompson* (b. Amenia, NY, 17 Jan 1768; d. Poughkeepsie, NY, 18 Dec 1843)
1 – 15 Sep 1823: *John Rogers*
16 Sep 1823 – 3 Mar 1825: *Samuel Lewis Southard* (b. Basking Ridge, NJ, 9 Jun 1787; d. Fredericksburg, Va, 26 Jun 1842)

Attorney-General
4 Mar – 12 Nov 1817: *Richard Rush* (see Madison)
13 Nov 1817 – 3 Mar 1825: *William Wirt* (b. Bladensburg, Md, 8 Nov 1772; d. Washington 18 Feb 1834

Postmaster-General
4 Mar 1817 – 25 Jun 1823: *Return Jonathan Meigs* (see Madison)
26 Jun 1823 – 3 Mar 1825: *John McLean* (b. Morris County, NJ, 11 Mar 1785; d. 4 Apr 1861)

4 Mar 1825 – 3 Mar 1829: Adams

President
John Quincy Adams (see Heads of State)

Vice-President
John Caldwell Calhoun (see Monroe)

Secretary of State
7 Mar 1825 – 3 Mar 1829: *Henry Clay* (b. Hanover County, Va, 12 Apr 1777; d. Washington 29 Jun 1852)

Treasurer	7 Mar 1825 – 3 Mar 1829: *Richard Rush* (see Madison)
War	7 Mar 1825 – 27 May 1828: *James Barbour* (b. Barboursville, Va, 10 Jun 1755; d. Barboursville, Va, 7 Jun 1842)
	28 May 1828 – 3 Mar 1829: *Peter Buell Porter* (b. Salisbury, Conn, 14 Aug 1773; d. Niagara Falls 20 Mar 1844)
Navy	*Samuel Lewis Southard* (see Monroe)
Attorney-General	*William Wirt* (see Monroe)
Postmaster-General	*John McLean* (see Monroe)

4 Mar 1829 – 3 Mar 1837: Jackson (Dem)

President	*Andrew Jackson* (see Heads of State)
Vice-President	4 Mar 1829 – 28 Dec 1832: *John Caldwell Calhoun*, resigned (see Monroe)
	4 Mar 1833 – 3 Mar 1837: *Martin van Buren* (see Heads of State)
Secretary of State	6 Mar 1829 – 23 May 1831: *Martin van Buren* (see Heads of State)
	24 May 1831 – 28 May 1833: *Edward Livingston* (b. Clermont, NY, 28 May 1764; d. Montgomery Place 23 May 1836)
	29 May 1833 – 26 Jun 1834: *Louis McLean*
	27 Jun 1834 – 3 Mar 1837: *John Forsyth* (b. Fredericksburg, Va, 22 Oct 1780; d. 21 Oct 1841)
Treasury	6 Mar 1829 – 7 Aug 1831: *Samuel Delucenna Ingham* (b. New Hope, Pa, 16 Sep 1779; d. Trenton 5 Jun 1860)
	8 Aug 1831 – 28 May 1833: *Louis McLean* (see above)
	29 May – 22 Sep 1833: *William John Duane* (b. Clonmel, Ireland, 9 May 1780; d. 26 Sep 1865)
	23 Sep 1833 – 26 Jun 1834: *Roger Brooke Taney* (b. Calvert County, Md, 17 Mar 1777; d. Washington 12 Oct 1864)
	27 Jun 1834 – 3 Mar 1837: *Levi Woodbury* (b. Francestown, NH, 22 Dec 1789; d. Portsmouth, NH, 4 Sep 1851)
War	9 Mar 1829 – 3 Jul 1831: *John Henry Eaton* (b. Halifax, NC, 18 Jun 1790; d. Washington 17 Nov 1856)
	1 Aug 1831 – 2 Mar 1837: *Lewis Cass* (b. Exeter, NH, 9 Oct 1782; d. 17 Jun 1866)

	3 Mar 1837: *Benjamin Franklin Butler* (b. Kinderhook Landing, NY, 14 Dec 1795; d. Paris 8 Nov 1858)
Navy	9 Mar 1829 – 22 May 1831: *John Branch* (b. Halifax, NC, 4 Nov 1782; d. 4 Jan 1863)
	23 May 1831 – 29 Jun 1834: *Levi Woodbury* (see above)
	30 Jun 1834 – 3 Mar 1837: *Mahlon Dickerson* (b. Hanover Neck or Morris Plains, NJ, 17 Apr 1770; d. Ferromonte 5 Oct 1853)
Attorney-General	9 Mar 1829 – 19 Jul 1831: *John Macpherson Berrien* (b. New Jersey 23 Aug 1781; d. Washington 1 Jan 1856)
	20 Jul 1831 – 14 Nov 1833: *Roger Brooke Taney* (see above)
	15 Nov 1833 – 3 Mar 1837: *Benjamin Franklin Butler* (see above)
Postmaster-General (also member of Cabinet)	9 Mar 1829 – 30 Apr 1835: *William Taylor Barry* (b. Lunenburg, Va, 5 Feb 1785; d. Liverpool 30 Aug 1835)
	1 May 1835 – 3 Mar 1837: *Amos Kendall* (b. Dunstable, Mass, 16 Aug 1789; d. 12 Nov 1869)

4 Mar 1837 – 3 Mar 1841: van Buren (Dem)

President	*Martin van Buren* (see Heads of State)
Vice-President	*Richard Mentor Johnson* (b. Louisville, Ky, 1780; d. 19 Nov 1850)
Secretary of State	*John Forsyth* (see Jackson)
Treasury	*Levi Woodbury* (see Jackson)
War	7 Mar 1837 – 3 Mar 1841: *Joel Roberts Poinsett* (b. Charleston, SC, 2 Mar 1779; d. near Statesburg, SC, 12 Dec 1851)
Navy	4 Mar 1837 – 24 Jun 1838: *Mahlon Dickerson* (see Jackson)
	25 Jun 1838 – 3 Mar 1841: *James Kirke Paulding* (b. Great Nine Partners, NY, 22 Aug 1768; d. Hyde Park, NY, 6 Apr 1860)
Attorney-General	4 Mar 1837 – 4 Jul 1838: *Benjamin Franklin Butler* (see Jackson)
	5 Jul 1838 – 10 Jan 1840: *Felix Grundy* (b. 11 Sep 1777; d. 19 Dec 1840)
	11 Jan 1840 – 3 Mar 1841: *Henry Dilworth Gilpin* (b.

Postmaster- General	Lancaster, England, 14 Apr 1801; d. 29 Jan 1860) 4 Mar 1837 – 18 May 1840: *Amos Kendall* (see Jackson) 19 May 1840 – 3 Mar 1841: *John Milton Niles* (b. Windsor, Conn, 20 Aug 1787; d. Hartford, Conn, 31 May 1856)

4 Mar 1841 – 3 Mar 1845: Harrison/Tyler (Whig)

President	4 Mar – 3 Apr 1841 *William Henry Harrison* (see Heads of State) 4 Apr 1841 – 3 Mar 1845: *John Tyler* (see Heads of State)
Vice-President	4 Mar – 3 Apr 1841: *John Tyler* (see Heads of State)
Secretary of State	5 Mar 1841 – 8 May 1843: *Daniel Webster* (b. Salisbury (later Franklin), NH, 18 Jan 1782; d. Marshfield, Mass, 24 Oct 1852) 9 May – 23 Jul 1843: *Hugh Swinton Legare* (b. Charleston, SC, 2 Jan 1797; d. 20 Jun 1843) 24 Jul 1843 – 5 Mar 1844: *Abel Parker Upshur* (b. Northampton County, Va, 17 Jun 1791; d. 28 Feb 1844) 6 Mar 1844 – 3 Mar 1845: *John Caldwell Calhoun* (see Monroe)
Treasury	5 Mar – 12 Sep 1841: *Thomas Ewing* (b. West Liberty, Va, 28 Dec 1789; d. 26 Oct 1871) 13 Sep 1841 – 2 Mar 1843: *Walter Forward* (b. Old Granby, later East Granby, Conn, 24 Jan 1786; d. 24 Nov 1852) 3 Mar 1843 – 14 Jun 1844: *John Canfield Spencer* (b. Hudson, NY, 8 Jan 1788; d. 17 May 1858) 15 Jun 1844 – 3 Mar 1845: *George Mortimer Bibb* (b. Prince Edward County, Va, 30 Oct 1776; d. 14 Apr 1859)
War	5 Mar – 12 Sep 1841: *John Bell* (b. Nashville, Tenn, 15 Feb 1797; d. Stewart County, 10 Sep 1869) 13 Sep – 11 Oct 1841: *John McLean* (see Monroe) 12 Oct 1841 – 7 Mar 1843: *John Canfield Spencer* (see above) 8 Mar 1843 – 14 Feb 1844: *James Madison Porter* (b. Norristown, Pa, 6 Jan 1793; d. 11 Nov 1862) 15 Feb 1844 – 3 Mar 1845: *William Wilkins* (b. Carlisle, Pa, 20 Dec 1779; d. 23 Jun 1865)

Navy	5 Mar – 12 Sep 1841: *George Edmund Badger* (b. New Bern, NC, 17 Apr 1795; d. 11 May 1866) 13 Sep 1841 – 14 Feb 1843: *Abel Parker Upshur* (see above) 27 Jul 1843 – 14 Feb 1844: *David Henshaw* (b. Leicester, Mass, 2 Apr 1791;.d. 11 Nov 1852) 15 Feb – 13 Mar 1844: *Thomas Walker Gilmer* (b. Gilmerton, Va, 6 Apr 1802; d. Washington 28 Feb 1844) 14 Mar 1844 – 3 Mar 1845: *John Young Mason* (b. Greensville County, Va, 18 Apr 1799; d. Paris 3 Oct 1859)
Attorney-General	5 Mar – 12 Sep 1841: *John Jordan Crittenden* (b. Versailles, Ky, 10 Sep 1787; d. Frankfort, Ky, 26 Jul 1863) 13 Sep 1841 – 30 Jun 1843: *Hugh Swinton Legare* (see above) 1 Jul 1843 – 3 Mar 1845: *John Nelson* (b. Frederickstown, Md, 1 Jun 1791; d. Baltimore, Md, 28 Jan 1860)
Postmaster- General	6 Mar – 12 Sep 1841: *Francis Granger* (b. Suffield, Conn, 1 Dec 1792; d. Conandaigua 28 Aug 1868) 13 Sep 1841 – 3 Mar 1845: *Charles Anderson Wickliffe* (b. Springfield, Ky, 8 Jun 1788; d. 31 Oct 1869)

4 Mar 1845 – 3 Mar 1849: Polk (Dem)

President	*James Knox Polk* (see Heads of State)
Vice-President	*George Mifflin Dallas* (b. Philadelphia, Pa, 10 Jul 1792; d. 31 Oct 1864)
Secretary of State	6 Mar 1845 – 3 Mar 1849: *James Buchanan* (see Heads of State)
Treasury	6 Mar 1845 – 3 Mar 1849: *Robert John Walker* (b. Northumberland, Pa, 19 Jun 1801; d. Washington 11 Nov 1869)
War	6 Mar 1845 – 3 Mar 1849: *William Learned Marcy* (b. Sturbridge (later Southbridge) Mass, 12 Dec 1786; d. 4 Jul 1857)
Navy	10 Mar 1845 – 8 Sep 1846: *George Bancroft* (b. Worcester, Mass, 3 Oct 1800; d. Washington 17 Jan 1891) 9 Sep 1846 – 3 Mar 1849: *John Young Mason* (see Harrison/Tyler)

Attorney-General	5 Mar 1845 – 16 Oct 1846: *John Young Mason* (see Harrison/Tyler) 17 Oct 1846 – 3 Mar 1849: *Nathan Clifford* (b. Rumney, NH, 18 Aug 1803; d. 25 Jul 1881)
Postmaster-General	6 Mar 1845 – 3 Mar 1849: *Cave Johnson* (b. Springfield, Tenn, 11 Jan 1793; d. Clarksville 23 Nov 1866)

4 Mar 1849 – 3 Mar 1853: Taylor/Fillmore (Whig)

President	4 Mar 1849 – 8 Jul 1850: *Zachary Taylor* (see Heads of State) 9 Jul 1850 – 3 Mar 1853: *Millard Fillmore* (see Heads of State)
Vice-President	4 Mar 1849 – 9 Jul 1850: *Millard Fillmore* (see Heads of State)
Secretary of State	7 Mar 1849 – 5 Dec 1850: *John Middleton Clayton* (b. Dagsborough, Del, 24 Jul 1796; d. 9 Nov 1856) 6 Dec 1850 – 3 Mar 1853: *Daniel Webster* (see Harrison/Tyler)
Treasury	8 Mar 1849 – 22 Jul 1850: *William Morris Meredith* (b. Philadelphia, Pa, 8 Jun 1799; d. Philadephia, Pa, 17 Aug 1873) 23 Jul 1850 – 3 Mar 1853: *Thomas Corwin* (b. Bourbon County, Ky, 29 Jul 1799: d. Washington 18 Dec 1865)
War	8 Mar 1849 – 22 Jul 1850: *George Walker Crawford* (b. Augusta, Ga, 22 Dec 1798; d. 22 Jul 1872) 23 Jul – 14 Aug 1850 (acting:) *Winfield Scott* (b. Petersburg, Va, 13 Jun 1786; d. West Point 29 May 1866) 15 Aug 1850 – 3 Mar 1853: *Charles Magill Conrad* (b. Winchester, Va, 24 Dec 1804; d. 11 Feb 1878)
Navy	8 Mar 1849 – 21 Jul 1850: *William Ballard Preston* (b. Smithfield, Va, 29 Nov 1805; d. 16 Nov 1862) 22 Jul 1850 – 21 Jul 1852: *William Alexander Graham* (b. Vesuvius Furnace, NC, 5 Sep 1804; d. Saratoga Springs, NY, 11 Jul 1875) 22 Jul 1852 – 3 Mar 1853: *John Pendleton Kennedy* (b. Baltimore, Md, 25 Oct 1795; d. Newport, RI, 18 Aug 1870)
Interior	8 Mar 1849 – 11 Sep 1850: *Thomas Ewing* (see Harrison/Tyler) 12 Sep 1850 – 3 Mar 1853: *Alexander Hugh Holmes*

Stuart (b. Staunton, Va, 2 Apr 1807; d. 13 Feb 1891)

Attorney-General	8 Mar 1849 – 21 Jul 1850: *Reverdy Johnson*
	22 Jul 1850 – 3 Mar 1853: *John Jordan Crittenden* (see Harrison/Tyler)
Postmaster-General	8 Mar 1849 – 22 Jul 1850: *Jacob Collamer* (b. Troy, NY, 8 Jan 1791; d. Woodstock, NY 9 Nov 1865)
	23 Jul 1850 – 30 Aug 1852: *Nathan Kelsey Hall* (b. Skaneateles, NY, 28 Mar 1810; d. 2 Mar 1874)
	31 Aug 1852 – 3 Mar 1853: *Samuel Dickinson Hubbard* (b. Middletown, Conn, 10 Aug 1799; d. Middletown, Cann 8 Oct 1855)

4 Mar 1853 – 3 Mar 1857: Pierce (Dem)

President	*Franklin Pierce* (see Heads of State)
Vice-President	4 Mar – 18 Apr 1853: *William Rufus Devane King* (b. Sampson County, NC, 7 Apr 1786; d. 18 Apr 1853)
Secretary of State	7 Mar 1853 – 3 Mar 1857: *William Learned March* (see Polk)
Treasury	7 Mar 1853 – 3 Mar 1857: *James Guthrie* (b. Bardstown, Ky, 5 Dec 1792; d. 13 Mar 1869)
War	7 Mar 1853 – 3 Mar 1857: *Jefferson Davis* (b. Christian (later Todd) County, Ky, 3 Jun 1808; d. New Orleans, La, 6 Dec 1889)
Navy	7 Mar 1853 – 3 Mar 1857: *James Cochran Dobbin* (b. Fayetteville, NC, 17 Jan 1814; d. 4 Aug 1857)
Interior	7 Mar 1853 – 3 Mar 1857: *Robert McClelland* (b. Greencastle, Pa, 1 Aug 1807; d. 30 Aug 1880)
Attorney-General	7 Mar 1853 – 3 Mar 1857: *Caleb Cushing* (b. Salisbury, Mass, 17 Jan 1800; d. 2 Jan 1879)
Postmaster-General	7 Mar 1853 – 3 Mar 1857: *James Campbell* (b. Southwark, Pa, 1 Sep 1812; d. 27 Jan 1893)

4 Mar 1857 – 3 Mar 1861: Buchanan (Dem)

President	*James Buchanan* (Dem) (see Heads of State)
Vice-President	*John Cabell Breckinridge* (b. near Lexington, Ky, 15 Jan 1821; d. Lexington, Ky, 17 May 1875)
Secretary of State	6 Mar 1857 – 16 Dec 1860: *Lewis Cass* (see Jackson)
	17 Dec 1860 – 3 Mar 1861: *Jeremiah Sullivan Black* (b. Stony Creek, Pa, 10 Jan 1810; d. 19 Aug 1883)
Treasury	6 Mar 1857 – 11 Dec 1860: *Howell Cobb* (b. Georgia 7 Sep 1815; d. New York 9 Oct 1868)
	12 Dec 1860 – 10 Jan 1861: *Philipp Francis Thomas* (b.

Easton, Md, 12 Sep 1810; d. 2 Oct 1890)

11 Jan – 3 Mar 1861: *John Adams Dix* (b. Boscawen, NH, 24 Jul 1798; d. New York 21 Apr 1879)

War
6 Mar 1857 – 17 Jan 1861: *John Buchanan Floyd* (b. Smithfield, Va, 1 Jun 1806; d. near Abingdon, Va, 26 Aug 1863)

18 Jan – 3 Mar 1861: *Joseph Holt* (b. Breckinridge County, Ky, 6 Jan 1807; d. 1 Aug 1894)

Navy
6 Mar 1857 – 3 Mar 1861: *Isaac Toucey* (b. Newton, Conn, 15 Nov 1792; d. Hartford, Conn, 20 Jul 1869)

Interior
6 Mar 1857 – 3 Mar 1861: *Jacob Thompson* (b. Leasburg, NY, 15 Mar 1810; d. Mephis, Tenn, 24 Mar 1885)

Attorney-General
6 Mar 1857 – 3 Mar 1861: *Edwin McMasters Stanton* (b. Steubenville, Ohio, 19 Dec 1814; d. 24 Dec 1869)

Postmaster-General
6 Mar 1857 – 13 Mar 1859: *Aaron Venable Brown* (b. Brunswick County, Va, 15 Aug 1795; d. 8 May 1859)

14 Mar 1859 – 11 Feb 1861: *Joseph Holt* (see above)

12 Feb – 3 Mar 1861: *Horatio King* (b. Paris, Me, 21 Jun 1811; d. Washington 20 May 1897)

4 Mar 1861 – 3 Mar 1869: Lincoln/Johnson (Rep)

President
4 Mar 1861 – 13 Apr 1865: *Abraham Lincoln* (see Heads of State)

14 Apr 1865 – 3 Apr 1869: *Andrew Johnson* (see Heads of State)

Vice-President
4 Mar 1861 – 3 Mar 1865: *Hannibal Hamlin* (b. Paris, Me, 27 Aug 1809; d. 4 Jul 1891)

4 Mar – 14 Apr 1865: *Andrew Johnson* (Heads of State)

Secretary of State
5 Mar 1861 – 3 Mar 1860: *William Henry Seward* (b. Florida, NY, 16 Mar 1801; d. Auburn 10 Oct 1872)

Treasury
5 Mar 1861 – 30 Jun 1864: *Salmon Portland Chase* (b. Cornish, NH, 13 Jan 1808; d. New York 7 May 1873)

1 Jul 1864 – 6 Mar 1865: *William Pitt Fessenden* (b. Boscawen, NH, 16 Oct 1806; d. 8 Sep 1869)

7 Mar 1865 – 3 Mar 1869: *Hugh McCulloch* (b. Kennebunk, Me, 7 Dec 1808; d. Holly Hill, Md, 24 May 1895)

War
5 Mar 1861 – 14 Jan 1862: *Simon Cameron* (b. Lancaster County, Pa, 8 Mar 1799; d. Donegal Springs 26 Jun 1889)

15 Jan 1862 – 11 Aug 1867: *Edwin McMasters Stanton* (see Buchanan)

12 Aug 1867 – 13 Jan 1868 (acting:) *Ulysses S. Grant* (see Heads of State)

14 Jan – 27 May 1868: *Edwin McMasters Stanton* (see Buchanan)

28 May 1868 – 3 Mar 1869: *John McAllister Schofield* (b. Gerry, NY, 29 Sep 1831; d. St Augustine, Fl, 4 Mar 1906)

Navy	5 Mar 1861 – 3 Mar 1869: *Gideon Welles* (b. Glastonbury, Conn, 1 Jul 1802; d. 11 Feb 1878)
Interior	5 Mar 1861 – 7 Jan 1863: *Caleb Blood Smith* (b. Boston, Mass, 16 Apr 1808; d. Indianapolis 7 Jan 1864)
	8 Jan 1863 – 14 May 1865: *John Palmer Usher* (b. Brookfield, NY, 9 Jan 1816; d. Philadelphia, Pa, 13 Apr 1889)
	15 May 1865 – 26 Jul 1866: *James Harlan* (b. Clark County, Ill, 26 Aug 1820; d. 5 Oct 1899)
	27 Jul 1866 – 3 Mar 1869: *Orville Hickman Browning* (b. Harrison County, Ky, 10 Feb 1806; d. 10 Aug 1881)
Attorney-General	5 Mar 1861 – 21 Jan 1863: *Edward Bates* (b. Belmont, Goochland County, Va, 4 Sep 1793; d. 25 Mar 1869)
	22 Jun 1863 – 1 Dec 1864: *Titian James Coffey* (b. Huntingdon, Pa, 5 Dec 1824; d. Washington 11 Jan 1867)
	2 Dec 1864 – 22 Jul 1866: *James Speed* (b. Jefferson County, Va, 11 Mar 1812; d. The Poplars 25 Jun 1887)
	23 Jul 1866 – 16 Jul 1868: *Henry Stanbery* (b. New York 20 Feb 1803; d. New York 26 Jun 1881)
	17 Jul 1868 – 3 Mar 1869: *William Maxwell Evarts* (b. Boston, Mass, 6 Feb 1818; d. New York 28 Feb 1901)
Postmaster-General	5 Mar 1861 – 23 Sep 1864: *Montgomery Blair* (b. Franklin County, Ky, 10 May 1813; d. 27 Jul 1883)
	24 Sep 1864 – 24 Jul 1866: *William Dennison* (b. Cincinnati, Ohio, 23 Nov 1815; d. Columbus, Ohio, 15 Jun 1882)
	25 Jul 1866 – 3 Mar 1869: *Alexander Williams Randall* (b. Ames, NY, 31 Oct 1819; d. 26 Jul 1872)

Southern States: 18 Feb 1861 – Apr 1865: Davis

President	*Jefferson Davis* (see Pierce)

Vice-President   *Alexander Hamilton Stephens* (b. Wilkes County, Ga, 11 Feb 1812; d. 4 Mar 1883)

4 Mar 1869 – 3 Mar 1877: Grant (Rep)

President   *Ulysses S. Grant* (see Heads of State)
Vice-President   4 Mar 1869 – 3 Mar 1873: *Schuyler Colfax* (b. New York 23 Mar 1823; d. Mankato, Minn, 13 Jan 1885)
                      4 Mar 1873 – 22 Nov 1875: *Henry Wilson* (b. Farmington, NH, 16 Feb 1812; d. Washington 22 Nov 1875)
Secretary of   5 – 10 Mar 1869: *Elihu Benjamin Washburne* (b.
State   Livermore, Me, 23 Sep 1816; d. 23 Oct 1887)
                      11 Mar 1869 – 3 Mar 1877: *Hamilton Fish* (b. New York 3 Aug 1808; d. 6 Sep 1893)
Treasury   11 Mar 1869 – 16 Mar 1873: *George Sewall Boutwell* (b. Brookline, Mass, 28 Jan 1818; d. 27 Feb 1905)
                      17 Mar 1873 – 1 Jan 1874: *William Adams Richardson* (b. Tyngsborough, Mass, 2 Nov 1821; d. 19 Oct 1896)
                      2 Jun 1874 – 20 Jun 1876: *Benjamin Helm Bristow* (b. Elkton, Ky, 20 Jun 1832; d. New York 22 Jun 1896)
                      21 Jun 1876 – 3 Mar 1877: *Lot Myrick Morrill* (b. Belgrade, Me, 3 May 1812; d. Portland, Me, 10 Jan 1883)
War   11 Mar – 8 Sep 1869: *John Aaron Rawlins* (b. Galena, Ill, 13 Feb 1831; d. 6 Sep 1869)
                      9 Sep – 24 Oct 1869: *William Tecumseh Sherman* (b. Lancaster, Ohio, 8 Feb 1820; d. New York 14 Feb 1891)
                      25 Oct 1869 – 7 Mar 1876: *William Worth Belknap* (b. Newburgh, NY, 22 Sep 1829; d. Washington 13 Oct 1890)
                      8 Mar – 21 May 1876: *Alphonso Taft* (b. Townshend, Vt, 5 Nov 1810; d. California 21 May 1891)
                      22 May 1876 – 3 Mar 1877: *James Donald Cameron* (b. Middletown, Pa, 14 May 1833; d. 30 Aug 1918)
Navy   5 Mar – 24 Jun 1869: *Adolph Edward Borie* (b. Philadelphia, Pa, 25 Nov 1809; d. Philadelphia, Pa, 5 Feb 1880)
                      25 Jun 1869 – 3 Mar 1887: *George Maxwell Robeson* (b. Oxford Furnace, NJ, 16 Mar 1829; d. Trenton NJ, 27 Sep 1897)
Interior   5 Mar 1869 – 31 Oct 1870: *Jacob Dolson Cox* (b.

Montreal 27 Oct 1828; d. 8 Aug 1900)
1 Nov 1870 – 18 Oct 1875: *Columbus Delano* (b.
Shoreham, Vt, 5 Jun 1809; d. 23 Oct 1869)
19 Oct 1875 – 3 Mar 1869: *Zachariah Chandler* (b.
Bedford, NH, 10 Dec 1813; d. 1 Nov 1879)

Attorney-General 5 Mar 1869 – 22 Nov 1870: *Ebenezer Rockwood Hoar*
(b. Concord, Mass, 21 Feb 1816; d. 31 Jan 1895)
23 Nov 1870 – 13 Dec 1871: *Amos Tappan Akerman*
(b. Portsmouth, NH, 23 Feb 1821; d. Cartersville, Ga,
29 Dec 1880)
14 Dec 1871 – 25 Apr 1875: *George Henry Williams* (b.
New Lebanon, NY, 26 Mar 1820; d. 4 Apr 1910)
26 Apr 1875 – 21 May 1876: *Edwards Pierrepont* (b.
New Haven, Conn, 4 Mar 1817; d. New York 6 Mar
1892)
22 May 1876 – 3 Mar 1877: *Alphonso Taft* (see above)

Postmaster- 5 Mar 1869 – 23 Aug 1874: *John Angel James Creswell*
General (b. Post Deposit, Md, 18 Nov 1828; d. Elkton, Md,
23 Dec 1891)
24 Aug 1874 – 11 Jul 1876: *Marshall Jewell* (b.
Winchester, NH, 20 Oct 1825; d. 10 Feb 1883)
12 Jul 1876 – 3 Mar 1877: *James Noble Tyner* (b.
Brookville, Ind, 17 Jan 1826; d. 1904)

4 Mar 1877 – 3 Mar 1881: Hayes (Rep)

President *Rutherford Birchard Hayes* (see Heads of State)
Vice-President *William Almon Wheeler* (b. Malone, NY, 30 Jun 1819;
d. 4 Jun 1887)
Secretary of 12 Mar 1877 – 3 Mar 1881: *William Maxwell Evarts* (see
State Lincoln/ Johnson)
Treasury 8 Mar 1877 – 3 Mar 1881: *John Sherman* (b.
Lancaster, Ohio, 10 May 1823; d. Washington 22 Oct
1900)
War 12 Mar 1877 – 11 Dec 1879: *George Washington
McCrary* (b. Evansville, Ind, 29 Aug 1835; d. Kansas
City, Mo, 23 Jun 1890)
12 Dec 1879 – 3 Mar 1881: *Alexander Ramsey* (b.
Harrisburg, Pa, 8 Sep 1815; d. 22 Apr 1903)
Navy 12 Mar 1877 – 5 Jan 1881: *Richard Wigginton
Thompson* (b. Culpeper County, Va, 9 Jun 1809; d.
Terre Haute, Ind, 9 Feb 1900)
6 Jan 1881 – 3 Mar 1881: *Nathan Goff* (b. Clarksburg,

	Va, 9 Feb 1843; d. 24 Aug 1920)
Interior	12 Mar 1877 – 3 Mar 1881: *Carl Schurz* (b. Liblar, Germany, 2 Mar 1829; d. New York 14 May 1906)
Attorney-General	12 Mar 1877 – 3 Mar 1881: *Charles Devens* (b. Charleston, Mass, 4 Apr 1820; d. 7 Jan 1891)
Postmaster-General	12 Mar 1877 – 24 Aug 1880: *David McKendree Key* (b. Greene County, Tenn, 27 Jan 1824; d. Chattanooga, Tenn, 3 Feb 1900)
	25 Aug 1880 – 3 Mar 1881: *Horace Maynard* (b. Westboro, Mass, 30 Aug 1814; d. 3 May 1882)

4 Mar 1881 – 3 Mar 1885: Garfield/Arthur (Rep)

President	4 Mar – 18 Sep 1881: *James Abraham Garfield* (see Heads of State)
	19 Sep 1881 – 3 Mar 1885: *Chester Allan Arthur*
Vice-President	4 Mar – 18 Sep 1881: *Chester Allan Arthur* (see Heads of State)
Secretary of State	5 Mar – 11 Dec 1881: *James Gillespie Blaine* (b. West Brownsville, Pa, 31 Jan 1830; d. Washington 27 Jan 1893)
	12 Dec 1881 – 3 Mar 1885: *Frederick Theodore Frelinghuysen* (b. Millstone, NJ, 4 Aug 1817; d. Newark 20 May 1885)
Treasury	5 Mar – 26 Oct 1881: *William H. Windom* (b. Belmont County, Ohio, 10 May 1827; d. 29 Jan 1891)
	27 Oct 1881 – 3 Mar 1885: *Charles James Folger* (b. Nantucket Island 16 Apr 1818; d. 4 Sep 1884)
War	5 Mar 1881 – 3 Mar 1885: *Robert Todd Lincoln*, son of Abraham Lincoln (b. Springfield, Ill, 1 Aug 1843; d. Washington 26 Jul 1926)
Navy	5 Mar 1881 – 11 Apr 1882: *William Henry Hunt* (b. Charleston, SC, 12 Jun 1823; d. St Petersburg 27 Feb 1884)
	12 Apr 1882 – 3 Mar 1885: *William Eaton Chandler* (b. Concord, NH, 28 Dec 1835; d. 30 Nov 1917)
Interior	5 Mar 1811 – 5 Jun 1882: *Samuel Jordan Kirkwood* (b. Harford County, Md, 20 Dec 1813; d. Iowa City, Iowa, 1 Sep 1894)
	6 Jun 1882 – 3 Mar 1887: *Henry Moore Teller* (b. Allegany County, NY, 23 May 1830; d. Denver, Col, 23 Feb 1914)
Attorney-General	5 Mar – 15 Dec 1881: *Isaac Wayne MacVeagh* (b.

Phoenixville, Pa, 19 Apr 1833; d. 11 Jan 1917)
16 Dec 1881 – 3 Mar 1885: *Benjamin Harris Brewster*
(b. Salem County, NJ, 13 Oct 1816; d. 4 Apr 1888)

Postmaster- General	5 Mar – 19 Dec 1881: *Thomas Lemuel James* (b. Utica, NY, 29 Mar 1831; d. 11 Sep 1916) 20 Dec 1881 – 2 Apr 1883: *Timothy Otis Howe* (b. Livermore, Me, 24 Feb 1816; d. Kenosha 25 Mar 1883) 3 Apr 1883 – 13 Oct 1884: *Walter Quintin Gresham* (b. Lanesville, Ind, 17 Mar 1832; d. 28 May 1895) 14 Oct 1884 – 3 Mar 1885: *Frank Hatton* (b. Cambridge, Ohio, 28 Apr 1846; d. Washington 30 Apr 1894)

4 Mar 1885 – 3 Mar 1889: Grover Cleveland I (Dem)

President	*Stephen Grover Cleveland* (for 1st time) (see Heads of State)
Vice-President	*Thomas Andrews Hendricks* (b. Zanesville, Ohio, 7 Sep 1819; d. Indianapolis 25 Nov 1885)
Secretary of State	6 Mar 1885 – 3 Mar 1889: *Thomas Francis Bayard* (b. Wilmington, Del, 29 Oct 1828; d. Dedham, Mass, 28 Sep 1898)
Treasury	6 Mar 1885 – 31 Mar 1887: *Daniel Manning* (b. Albany, NY, 16 May 1831; d. New York 24 Dec 1887) 1 Apr 1887 – 3 Mar 1889: *Charles Stebbins Fairchild* (b. Cazenovia, NY, 30 Apr 1842; d. 24 Nov 1924)
War	6 Mar 1885 – 3 Mar 1889: *William Crowninshild Endicott* (b. Salem, Mass, 19 Nov 1826; d. Boston, Mass, 6 May 1900)
Navy	6 Mar 1885 – 3 Mar 1889: *William Colins Whitney* (b. Conway, Mass, 5 Jul 1841; d. Lexington, Ky, 2 Feb 1904)
Interior	6 Mar 1885 – 15 Jan 1888: *Lucius Quinctius Cincinnatus Lamar* (b. Putnam County, Ga, 17 Sep 1825; d. Macon, Ga, 23 Jan 1893) 16 Jan 1888 – 3 Mar 1889: *William Freeman Vilas* (b. Chelsea, NY, 9 Jul 1840; d. Madison, Wis, 27 Aug 1908)
Agriculture (new post)	11 Feb 1889 – 3 Mar 1889: *Norman Jay Colman* (b. Richfield Springs, NY, 16 May 1827; d. 3 Nov 1911)
Attorney-General	6 Mar 1885 – 3 Mar 1889: *Augustus Hill Garland* (b. Tipton County, Tenn, 11 Jun 1832; d. Washington 26 Jan 1899)

| Postmaster-General | 6 Mar 1885 – 15 Jan 1888: *William Freeman Vilas* (see above) |
| | 16 Jan 1888 – 3 Mar 1889: *Donald McDonald Dickinson* (b. Port Ontario, Oswego County, NY, 17 Jan 1846; d. Trenton, Mich, 15 Oct 1917) |

4 Mar 1889 – 3 Mar 1893: Harrison (Rep)

President	*Benjamin Harrison* (see Heads of State)
Vice-President	*Levi Parsons Morton* (b. Shoreham, Vt, 16 Mar 1824; d. 16 May 1920)
Secretary of State	7 Mar 1889 – 28 Jun 1892: *James Gillespie Blaine* (see Garfield/Arthur)
	29 Jun 1892 – 22 Feb 1893: *John Watson Foster* (b. Pike County, Ind, 2 Mar 1836; d. 15 Nov 1917)
	23 Feb – 3 Mar 1893: *W. F. Wharton*
Treasury	7 Mar 1889 – 20 Feb 1891: *William H. Windom* (see Garfield/Arthur)
	21 Feb 1891 – 3 Mar 1893: *Charles Foster* (b. Fostoria, Ohio, 12 Apr 1828; d. 9 Jan 1904)
War	7 Mar 1889 – 3 Mar 1893: *Redfield Proctor* (b. Proctorsville, Vt, 1 Jun 1831; d. Washington 4 Mar 1908)
Navy	7 Mar 1889 – 3 Mar 1893: *Benjamin Franklin Tracy* (b. Oswego, NY, 26 Apr 1830; d. 6 Aug 1915)
Interior	7 Mar 1889 – 3 Mar 1893: *John Willock Noble* (b. Lancaster, Ohio, 26 Oct 1831; d. St Louis, Mo, 22 Mar 1912)
Agriculture	7 Mar 1889 – 3 Mar 1893: *Jeremiah MacClean Rusk* (b. Morgan County, Ohio, 17 Jun 1830; d. 21 Nov 1893)
Attorney-General	7 Mar 1889 – 3 Mar 1893: *H. H. Miller*
Postmaster-General	7 Mar 1889 – 3 Mar 1893: *John Wanamaker* (b. Philadelphia, Pa, 11 Jul 1838; d. Lindenhurst, Pa, 12 Dec 1922)

4 Mar 1893 – 3 Mar 1897: Grover Cleveland II (Dem)

| President | *Stephen Grover Cleveland* (for 2nd time) (see Heads of State) |
| Vice-President | *Adlai Ewing Stevenson* (b. Christian County, Ky, 23 Oct 1835; d. Chicago, Ill, 14 Jun 1914) |

Secretary of State	6 Mar 1893 – 9 Jan 1895: *Walter Quintin Gresham* (see Garfield/Arthur)
	10 Jun 1895 – 3 Mar 1897: *Richard Olney* (b. Oxford, Mass, 15 Sep 1835; d. 8 Apr 1917)
Treasury	6 Mar 1893 – 3 Mar 1897: *John Griffin Carlish* (b. Campbell (later Kenton) County, Ky, 5 Sep 1835; d. 31 Jul 1910)
War	6 Mar 1893 – 3 Mar 1897: *Daniel Scott Lamont* (b. Cortland County, NY, 9 Feb 1851; d. Millbrook, NY, 23 Jul 1905)
Navy	6 Mar 1893 – 3 Mar 1897: *Hilary Abner Herbert* (b. Laurensville (later Laurens) SC, 12 Mar 1834; d. Tampa, Fl, 6 Mar 1919)
Interior	6 Mar 1893 – 3 Mar 1897: *Hoke Smith* (b. Newton, NC, 2 Sep 1855; d. Atlanta 27 Nov 1931)
Attorney-General	6 Mar 1893 – 7 Apr 1895: *Richard Olney* (see above)
	8 Apr 1895 – 3 Mar 1897: *Judson Harmon* (b. Newtown, Ohio, 3 Feb 1846; d. Cincinnati, Ohio, 22 Feb 1927)
Postmaster-General	6 Mar 1893 – Mar 1895: *Wilson Shannon Bissell* (b. Oneida County NY, 31 Dec 1847; d. Oct 1903)
	Mar 1895 – 3 Mar 1897: *William Lyne Wilson* (b. Middleway, Va, 3 May 1843; d. 17 Oct 1900)
Agriculture	6 Mar 1893: *Julius Sterling Morton* (b. Adams, NY, 22 Apr 1832; d. Lake Forest, Ill, 27 Apr 1902)

4 Mar 1897 – 3 Mar 1909: McKinley/Roosevelt (Rep)

President	4 Mar 1897 – 13 Sep 1901 *William McKinley* (see Heads of State)
	14 Sep 1901 – 3 Mar 1909: *Theodore Roosevelt*
Vice-President	4 Mar 1897 – 21 Nov 1899: *Garret Augustus Hobart* (b. Long Branch, NJ, 3 Jun 1844; d. Paterson 21 Nov 1899)
	4 Mar – 14 Sep 1901: *Theodore Roosevelt* (see Heads of State)
	4 Mar 1905 – 3 Mar 1909: *Charles Warren Fairbanks* (b. Unionville Center 11 May 1852; d. Indianapolis 4 Apr 1918)
Secretary of State	4 Mar 1897 – Apr 1898: *John Sherman* (see Hayes)
	Apr – 31 Aug 1898: *William Rufus Day* (b. Ravenna, Ohio, 17 Apr 1849; d. 9 Jul 1923)
	1 Sep 1898 – 1905: *John Milton Hay* (b. Ravenna, Ohio, 17 Apr 1849; d. 9 Jul 1923)

1 Sep 1898 – 1905: *John Milton Hay* (b. Salem, Ind, 8 Oct 1838; d. New Hampshire 1 Jul 1905)

1905 – 26 Jan 1909: *Elihu Root* (b. Clinton 15 Feb 1845; d. New York 4 Feb 1937)

27 Jan – 3 Mar 1909: *Robert Bacon* (b. Jamaica Plain, Mass, 5 Jul 1860; d. 29 May 1919)

Treasury

Mar 1897 – Jan 1902: *Lyman Judson Gage* (b. Deruyter, NY, 28 Jun 1836; d. Point Loma, Cal, 26 Jan 1927)

Jan 1902 – Mar 1907: *Leslie Mortier Shaw* (b. Morristown, Vt, 2 Nov 1848; d. Washington 28 Mar 1932)

Mar 1907 – 3 Mar 1909: *George Bruce Cortelyou* (b. New York 26 Jul 1862; d. 23 Oct 1940)

War

Mar 1897 – 1899: *Russel Alexander Alger* (b. Lafayette, Ohio, 27 Feb 1836; d. 1907) 1899 – 31 Jan 1904: *Elihu Root* (see above)

1 Feb 1904 – Jun 1908: *William Howard Taft* (see Heads of State)

Jun 1908 – 3 Mar 1909: *Luke Edward Wright* (b. Giles County, Tenn, 29 Aug 1846; d. 17 Nov 1922)

Navy

Mar 1897 – 30 Apr 1902: *John Davis Long* (b. Buckfield, Me, 27 Oct 1838; d. Hingham 28 Aug 1915)

1 May 1902 – 30 Jun 1904: *William Henry Moody* (b. Newbury, Mass, 23 Dec 1853; d. Haverhill, Mass, 2 Jul 1917)

1 Jul 1904 – Mar 1905: *Paul Morton* (b. Detroit, Mich, 2 May 1857; d. 19 Jan 1911)

Mar 1905 – 16 Dec 1906: *Charles Joseph Bonaparte* (b. Baltimore, Md, 9 Jun 1851; d. near Baltimore, Md, 28 Jun 1921)

17 Dec 1906 – 30 Nov 1908: *Victor Howard Metcalf* (b. Utica, NY, 10 Oct 1853; d. 20 Feb 1936)

1 Dec 1908 – 3 Mar 1909: *Truman Handy Newberry* (b. Detroit, Mich, 5 Nov 1864; d. Detroit, Mich, 3 Oct 1945)

Interior

Mar 1897 – Dec 1898: *Cornelius Newton Bliss* (b. Fall River 26 Jan 1833; d. 9 Oct 1911)

Dec 1898 – 3 Mar 1907: *Ethan Allen Hitchcock* (b. Mobile, Ala, 19 Sep 1835; d. Washington 9 Apr 1909)

4 Mar 1907 – 3 Mar 1909: *James Rudolph Garfield* (b. Hilram, Ohio, 17 Oct 1865; d. Cleveland, Ohio, 24 Mar 1950)

Attorney-General	Mar 1897 – 1898: *Joseph McKenna* (b. Philadelphia, Pa, 10 Aug 1843; d. Washington 21 Nov 1926)
	1898 – 8 Apr 1901: *John William Griggs* (b. Newton, NJ, 10 Jul 1849; d. 28 Nov 1927)
	9 Apr 1901 – 9 Jun 1904: *Philander Chase Knox* (b. Brownsville, Pa, 6 May 1853; d. 12 Oct 1921)
	10 Jun 1904 – Dec 1906: *William H. Moody* (see above)
	Dec 1906 – 3 Mar 1909: *Charles Bonaparte* (see above)
Postmaster-General	Mar 1897: *James Albert Gary* (b. Uncasville, Conn, 22 Oct 1833; d. Baltimore, Md, 31 Oct 1920)
	21 Mar 1898 – 14 Jan 1902: *Charles Emory Smith* (b. Mansfield, Conn, 18 Feb 1842; d. Philadelphia, Pa, 19 Jan 1908)
	15 Jan 1902 – 1904: *Henry Clay Payne* (b. Ashfield, Mass, 23 Nov 1843; d. Washington 4 Oct 1904)
	1904 – 6 Mar 1905: *Robert John Wynne* (b. New York 18 Nov 1851; d. 11 Mar 1922)
	7 Mar 1905 – 4 Mar 1907: *G. B. Cortelyou* (see above)
	5 May 1907 – 3 Mar 1909: *George von Lengerke Meyer* (b. Beacon Hill 24 Jun 1858; d. 9 Mar 1918)
Agriculture	Mar 1897 – 3 Mar 1909: *James Wilson* (b. Ayrshire, Scotland, 16 Aug 1836; d. 26 Aug 1920)
Trade and labour	16 Feb 1903 – 30 Jun 1904: *G. B. Cortelyou* (see above)
	1 Jul 1904 – 11 Dec 1906: *V. H. Metcalf* (see above)
	12 Dec 1906 – 3 Mar 1909: *Oscar Salomon Straus* (b. Otterberg, Germany 23 Dec 1850; d. New York 3 May 1926)

4 Mar 1909 – 3 Mar 1913: Taft (Rep)

President	*William Howard Taft* (Rep) (see Heads of State)
Vice-President	4 Mar 1909 – 30 Oct 1912: *James Schoolcraft Sherman* (b. Utica, NY, 24 Oct 1855; d. Washington 30 Oct 1912)
Secretary of State	*Philander Chase Knox* (see MacKinley Roosevelt)
Treasury	*Franklin MacVeagh* (b. Phoenixville, Pa, 22 Nov 1837; d. 6 Jul 1934)
War	Mar 1909 – May 1911: *Jacob McGavock Dickinson* (b. Columbus, Mass, 30 Jan 1851; d. 13 Dec 1928)
	May 1911 – 3 Mar 1913: *Henry Lewis Stimson* (b. New York 21 Sep 1867; d. 20 Oct 1950)
Navy	*George von Lengerke Meyer* (see McKinley/Roosevelt)

Interior	Mar 1909 – 12 Mar 1911: *Richard Achilles Ballinger* (b. Boonesboro (later Boone) Iowa, 9 Jul 1858; d. Seattle, Wash, 6 Jun 1922)
	13 Mar 1911 – 3 Mar 1913: *Walter Lowrie Fisher* (b. Wheeling, Va, 4 Jul 1862; d. Winnetka 9 Nov 1935)
Attorney-General	*George Woodward Wickersham* (b. Pittsburg, Pa, 19 Sep 1858; d. 25 Jan 1936)
Postmaster-General	*Frank Harris Hitchcock* (b. Amherst, Ohio, 5 Oct 1869; d. Tucson 5 Aug 1935)
Agriculture	*James Wilson* see McKinley/Roosevelt)
Trade and Labour	*Charles Nagel* (b. Colorado County, Tex, 9 Aug 1849; d. Saint Louis, Mo, 5 Jan 1940)

4 Mar 1913 – 3 Mar 1921: Woodrow Wilson (Dem)

President	*Thomas Woodrow Wilson* (Dem) (see Heads of State)
Vice-President	*Thomas Riley Marshall* (b. North Manchester, Ind, 14 Mar 1854; d. Washington 1 Jun 1925)
Secretary of State	4 Mar 1913 – 9 Jun 1915: *William Jennings Bryan* (b. Salem, Ill, 19 Mar 1860; d. Dayton, Tenn, 26 Jul 1925)
	24 Jun 1915 – 3 Mar 1921: *Robert Lansing* (b. Watertown, NY, 17 Oct 1864; d. Washington 30 Oct 1928)
Treasury	6 Mar 1913 – 16 Dec 1918: *William Gibbs McAdoo* (b. Marietta, Ga, 31 Oct 1863; d. Washington 1 Feb 1941)
	Feb 1920 – 3 Mar 1921: *David Franklin Houston* (b. Monroe, NC, 17 Feb 1866; d. 2 Sep 1940)
War	5 Mar 1913 – 15 Feb 1916: *Lindley Miller Garrison* (b. 28 Nov 1864; d. 19 Oct 1932)
	7 Mar 1916 – 3 Mar 1921: *Newton Diehl Baker* (b. Martinsburg, W Va, 3 Dec 1871; d. Cleveland, Ohio, 25 Dec 1937)
Navy	*Josephus Daniels* (b. Washington, NC, 18 May 1862; d. Raleigh, NC, 15 Jan 1948)
Interior	*Franklin Knight Lane* (b. Charlottetown, Prince Edward Island, Canada, 15 Jul 1864; d. Rochester, Minn, 18 May 1921)
Attorney-General	Mar 1913 – Aug 1914: *James Clark McReynolds* (b. Elkton, Ky, 3 Feb 1862; d. 24 Aug 1946)
	Aug 1914 – 3 Mar 1921: *Thomas Watt Gregory* (b. Crawfordsville, Mass, 6 Nov 1861; d. New York 26 Feb 1933)
Postmaster-General	*Albert Sidney Burleson* (b. San Marcos, Tex, 7 Jun

	1863; d. Austin, Tex, 24 Nov 1937)
Agriculture	Mar 1913 – Jan 1920: *David Franklin Houston* (see above)
	Jan 1920 – 3 Mar 1921: *Edwin Thomas Meredith* (b. Avoca, Iowa, 23 Dec 1876; d. 17 Jun 1928)
Trade	Mar 1913 – 1 Nov 1919: *William Cox Redfield* (b. Albany, NY, 18 Jun 1858; d. New York 13 Jun 1932)
Labour	*William Bauchop Wilson* (b. Blantyre, Scotland, 2 Apr 1862; d. Savannah, Ga, 25 May 1934)

4 Mar 1921 – 4 Mar 1929: Harding/Coolidge (Rep)

President	4 Mar 1921 – 2 Aug 1923: *Warren Gamaliel Harding* (see Heads of State)
	2 Aug 1923 – 3 Mar 1929: *Calvin Coolidge* (see Heads of State)
Vice-President	4 Mar 1921 – 2 Aug 1923: *Calvin Coolidge* (see Heads of State)
	4 Mar 1925 – 3 Mar 1929: *Charles Gates Dawes* (b. Marietta, Ohio, 27 Aug 1865; d. Chicago, Ill, 23 Apr 1951)
Secretary of State	4 Mar 1921 – 9 Jan 1925: *Charles Evans Hughes* (b. Glens Falls, NY, 11 Apr 1862; d. Osterville, Mass, 27 Aug 1948)
	10 Jan 1925 – 3 Mar 1929: *Frank Billings Kellogg* (b. Potsdam, NY, 22 Dec 1856; d. St Paul, Minn, 21 Dec 1937)
Treasury	*Andrew William Mellon* (b. Pittsburgh, Pa, 24 Mar 1854; d. Southampton, NY, 26 Aug 1937)
War	4 Mar 1921 – 13 Oct 1925: *John Wingate Weeks* (b. Lancaster, NH, 11 Apr 1860; d. 12 Jul 1926)
	14 Oct 1925 – 3 Mar 1929: *Dwight Filley Davis* (b. St Louis 5 Jul 1879; d. Washington 28 Nov 1945)
Navy	4 Mar 1921 – 18 Mar 1924: *Edwin C. Denby* (b. Evansville, Ind, 18 Feb 1870; d. Detroit, Mich, 8 Feb 1929)
	19 Mar 1924 – 3 Mar 1929: *Curtis Dwight Wilbur* (b. Boonesboro (later Boone) Iowa, 10 May 1867; d. Palo Alto, Cal, 8 Sep 1954)
Interior	4 Mar 1921 – 4 Mar 1923: *Albert Bacon Fall* (b. Frankfort, Ky, 26 Nov 1861; d. 30 Nov 1944)
	5 Mar 1923 – 3 Jul 1928: *Hubert Work* (b. Marion Center, Pa, 3 Jul 1860; d. 14 Dec 1942)

21 Jan 1929 – 3 Mar 1929: *Roy Owen West* (b. Georgetown, Ill, 27 Oct 1868; d. Chicago, Ill, 29 Nov 1958)

Attorney-General   4 Mar 1921 – 6 Apr 1924: *Harry Micajah Daugherty* (b. Washington, Ohio, 26 Jan 1860; d. Columbus, Ohio, 12 Oct 1941)

7 Apr 1924 – 1 Mar 1925: *Harlan Fiske Stone* (b. Chesterfield, NH, 11 Oct 1872; d. Washington 22 Apr 1946)

2 Mar 1925 – 3 Mar 1929: *George F. Shafer* (b. Mandan, ND, 23 Nov 1888; d. Bismark, ND, 13 Aug 1948)

Postmaster-   5 Mar 1921 – 3 Mar 1922: *Will Harrison Hays* (b.
General   Sullivan, Ind, 5 Nov 1879; d. 7 Mar 1954)

4 Mar 1922 – 3 Mar 1929: *Walter Folger Brown* (b. Massillon, Ohio, 31 May 1869; d. Toledo, Ohio, 26 Jan 1961)

Agriculture   4 Mar 1921 – 21 Nov 1924: *Henry Cantwell Wallace* (b. Rock Island, Ill, 11 May 1866; d. Washington 25 Oct 1924)

22 Nov 1924 – 13 Feb 1925: *Howard Mason Gore* (b. Clarksburg, W Va, 12 Oct 1887; d. 20 Jun 1947)

14 Feb 1925 – 3 Mar 1929: *William M. Jardine* (b. Oneida County, Idaho, 16 Jan 1879; d. 17 Jan 1955)

Trade   4 Mar 1921 – 20 Aug 1928: *Herbert Clark Hoover* (see Heads of State)

21 Aug 1928 – 3 Mar 1929: *William Fairfield Whiting* (b. Holyoke, Mass, 20 Jul 1864; d. 31 Aug 1936)

Labour   4 Mar 1921 – 16 Mar 1925: *James John Davis* (b. Tredegar, South Wales, 27 Oct 1873; d. Washington 22 Nov 1947)

17 Mar 1925 – 3 Mar 1929: *John Garibaldi Sargent* (b. Ludlow, Vt, 13 Oct 1860; d. 5 Mar 1939)

4 Mar 1929 – 3 Mar 1933: Hoover (Rep)

President   *Herbert Clark Hoover* (see Heads of State)
Vice-President   *Charles Curtis* (b. Topeka, Ka, 25 Jan 1860; d. Washington 8 Feb 1936)
Secretary of   *Henry Lewis Stimson* (see Taft)
  State
Treasury   *Andrew William Mellon* (see Harding/Coolidge)
War   4 Mar – 6 Dec 1929: *James William Good* (b. Cedar

	Rapids, Iowa, 24 Sep 1866; d. Washington 18 Nov 1929)
	7 Dec 1929 – 3 Mar 1933: *Patrick Jay Hurley* (b. Choctaw, Okl, 8 Jan 1883)
Navy	*Charles Francis Adams* (b. Quincy, Mass, 2 Aug 1866; d. Boston 10 Jun 1954)
Interior	*Ray Lyman Wilbur* (b. Boone, Iowa, 13 Apr 1875; d. Stanford, Cal, 26 Jun 1949)
Attorney-General	*William DeWitt Mitchell* (b. Winona, Mass, 9 Sep 1874; d. Syosset, NY, 24 Aug 1955)
Postmaster-General	*Walter Folger Brown* (see Harding/Coolidge)
Agriculture	*Arthur M. Hyde* (b. Princeton, Mo, 12 Jul 1877; d. 17 Oct 1947)
Trade	*Robert Patterson Lamont* (b. Detroit, Mich, 1 Dec 1867; d. 19 Feb 1948)
Labour	*James John Davis* (see Harding/Coolidge)

Urbino

HEADS OF STATE

Dukes

10 Sep 1482	*Guidobaldo*, son of Federigo da Montefeltro
Jun – Nov 1502	conquered by Cesare Borgia
1508 – 18 Aug 1516	*Francesco Maria I della Rovere* (for 1st time) nephew and adopted son (b. 1490; d. Pesaro 20 Oct 1538)
18 Aug 1516	*Lorenzo de' Medici* (for 1st time) (b. 9 Sep 1492; d. 4 May 1519) made Duke of Urbino by Pope Leo X
Feb 1517	*Francesco Maria I della Rovere* (for 2nd time)
Sep 1517	*Lorenzo de' Medici* (for 2nd time)
4 May 1519	*Catarina de' Medici*, daughter (b. 13 Apr 1519; d. 5 Jan 1589) Queen of France 1547 – 1559
Dec 1521	*Francesco Maria I della Rovere* (for 3rd time)
20 Oct 1538	*Guidobaldo II*, son (b. 1514; d. 1574)
1574	*Francesco Maria II*, son (b. 20 Feb 1549; d. 28 Oct 1631)
1621	*Federico Ubaldo*, son (b. 1605; d. 1623)

1623	*Francesco Maria II* (for 2nd time)
28 Oct 1631	Duchy reverts to the Papacy

Uruguay

HEADS OF STATE

Presidents

25 Aug 1825	Independence
18 Jul/6 Nov 1830 – 1 Mar 1835	*Fructuoso Rivera* (for 1st time) (b. 1778; d. 13 Jan 1854)
1 Mar – Oct 1838	*Manuel Oribe* (d. 12 Nov 1857)
Oct 1838	*Fructuoso Rivera* (for 2nd time) Civil War
1843	*Joaquín Suárez*
1 Mar 1852 – 24 Sep 1853	*Juan Francisco Giro* (d. 1860)
12 Mar 1854 – 9 Sep 1855	*Venancio Flores* (for 1st time) (b. 1809; d. 19 Feb 1868)
Sep 1855	*Manuel Bustamente*
1 Mar 1856	*Gabriel António Pereira*
1 Mar 1860	*Bernardo Prudencio Berro* (b. c. 1800; d. 1868)
1 Mar 1864 – 15 Feb 1865	*Atanasio Cruz Aguirre* (b. 1804; d. 1875)
20 Feb 1865	*Venancio Flores* (for 2nd time)
1 Mar 1866	*Francisco A. Vidal* (for 1st time) (d. 10 May 1889)
19 – 22 Feb 1868	*Manuel Flores*, brother of Venancio Flores (d. 22 Feb 1868)
Feb 1868	*Lorenzo Batlle*
1 Mar 1872	*José L. Gomensoro* (d. 1879)
1 Mar 1873 – 18 Jan 1875	*José Pedro Ellaury* (b. 1834; d. 1894)
22 Jan 1875	*Pedro Varela* (d. 24 Oct 1879)
10 Mar 1876	*Lorenzo Latorre* (d. 1889)
13 Mar 1880	*Francisco A. Vidal* (for 2nd time)
1 Mar 1882	*Máximo Santos* (b. 1836; d. 10 May 1889)
18 Nov 1886	*Máximo Tajes* (b. 1852; d. 1912)
1 Mar 1890 – Mar 1894	*Julio Herrera y Obes* (b. 1842; d. 1912)
21 Mar 1894 – 23 Aug 1897	*Juan Idiarte Borda* (d. 23 Aug 1897)

25 Aug 1897	*Juan Lindolfo Cuestas* (b. 1837; d. Paris 1905)
1 Mar 1903	*José Batlle y Ordoñez* (for 1st time) (b. 1856; d. 20 Oct 1929)
1 Mar 1907	*Claudio Williman* (b. 2 Sep 1863; d. 9 Feb 1934)
1 Mar 1911	*José Batlle y Ordoñez* (for 2nd time)
1 Mar 1915	*Feliciano Viera* (b. 1872; d. 1927)
5 Mar 1919	*Baltasar Brum* (b. 1883; d. 31 Mar 1933)
1 Mar 1923	*José Serrato* (b. 30 Sep 1868; d. 7 Sep 1960)
1 Mar 1927 – 1 Mar 1931	*Juan Campisteguy* (b. 1859; d. Sep 1937)

Venezuela

HEADS OF STATE

Presidents

19 Jun 1810/5 Jul 1811	Independence
1819 – 17 Nov 1831	United with Colombia
18 Apr 1831 – Feb 1835	*José Antonio Páez* (for 1st time) (b. 13 Jun 1790; d. 6 May 1873)
9 Feb 1835 – 29 Apr 1836	*José María Vargas* (b. 2 Mar 1786; d. New York 13 Jul 1854)
Apr 1836 – Jan 1837	*Andrés Narvarte* (b. 1781; d. 1853)
20 Jan – May 1837	—— *Carreño*
11 May 1837	*Carlos Soublette* (for 1st time) (b. 1795; d. 11 Feb 1870)
1838 – Jan 1843	*José Antonio Páez* (for 2nd time)
28 Jan 1843	*Carlos Soublette* (for 2nd time) .
1846 – Jan 1847	*José Antonio Páez* (for 3rd time) Dictator
23 Jan 1847	*José Tadeo Monagas* (for 1st time) (b. 28 Oct 1784; d. 18 Nov 1868)
1851 – 5 Mar 1858	*José Gregorio Monagas,* brother (b. 1795; d. 1858)
15 Mar 1858 – 24 Jul 1859	*Juliano Castro*
12 Aug 1859	*Pedro Gual* (b. 1784; d. 1862)
Apr 1860 – Mar 1861	*Manuel Felipe Tovar* (b. 1803; d. Paris 21 Feb 1866)
8 Sep 1861 – 22 May 1863	*José Antonio Páez* (for 4th and 5th time)

17 Jun 1863 – 2 May 1868	*Juan Crisóstomo Falcón* (b. 1820; d. 29 Apr 1870)
Jul – 18 Nov 1868	*José Tadeo Monagas* (for 2nd time)
Feb 1869	*José Ruperto Monagas*, son
Jun 1870	*Antonio Guzmán Blanco* (for 1st time) (b. 28 Feb 1829; d. 28 Jul 1899)
20 Feb 1877	*Francisco Linares Alcántara*
May 1879	*Antonio Guzmán Blanco* (for 2nd time)
20 Feb 1884	*Joaquín Crespo* (for 1st time) (b. 1841; d. 1898)
20 Feb/14 May 1886	*Antonio Guzmán Blanco* (for 3rd time)
Aug 1887 – Oct 1889	*Hermógenes López* (b. 1828; d. 1903)
29 Jun 1888	*Juan Pablo Rojas Paúl* (b. 1829; d. 1905) as Deputy
20 Feb 1890 – 17 Jun 1892	*Raimundo Andueza Palacio* (b. 1851; d. 1900)
13 Jun	—— *Villegas*
7 Oct 1892	*Joaquín Crespo* (for 2nd time) until 19 Apr 1894 Dictator
1 Mar 1898 – 20 Oct 1899	*Ignacio Andrade* (b. 1839; d. 1925)
23 Oct 1899 – Dec 1908	*Cipriano Castro* (b. 12 Oct 1858; d. 5 Dec 1924)
19 Dec 1908 – 30 May 1929	*Juan Vicente Gómez* (for 1st time) (b. 24 Jul 1857; d. 18 Dec 1935)
19 Apr 1914 – 24 Jun 1922	*Victorino Márquez Bustillos* Deputy
30 May 1929 – 13 Jul 1931	*Juan Bautista Pérez* (b. 21 Dec 1869; d. 1952)

Venice

HEADS OF STATE

Doges

28 Aug 1486 – 20 Sep 1501	*Agostino Barbarigo*
2 Nov 1501 – 22 Jun 1521	*Leonardo Loredano*
6 Jul 1521 – 7 May 1523	*Antonio Grimani*

20 May 1523 – 23 (?17)   *Andrea Gritti*
   Dec 1538
19 Jan 1539 – 11 Nov   *Pietro Lando*
   1545
24 Nov 1545 – 23 May   *Francesco Donato*
   1553
4 Jun 1553 – 31 May   *Marc Antonio Trevisan*
   1554
11 Jun 1554 – 2 Jun   *Francesco Venier*
   1556
14 Jun 1556 – 17 Aug   *Lorenzo Priuli*
   1559
1 Sep 1559 – 4 Nov   *Girolamo Priuli*, brother
   1567
26 Nov 1567 – 5 May   *Pietro Loredano*
   1570
11 May 1570 – 4 Jun   *Aloise Mocenigo I*
   (30 May) 1577
11 Jun 1577 – 3 Mar   *Sebastiano Venier*
   1578
18 Mar 1578 – 30 Jul   *Niccolò da Ponte* (b. 1490)
   1585
18 Aug 1585 – 4 Apr   *Pasquale Cicogna*
   1595
26 Apr 1595 – 25 Dec   *Marino Grimani*
   1605
10 Jan 1606 – 16 Jul   *Leonardo Donato*
   1612
24 Jul 1612 – 29 Oct   *Marc Antonio Memmo*
   1615
2 Dec 1615 – 16 Mar   *Giovanni Bembo*
   1618
5 Apr – 9 May 1618   *Niccolò Donato*
17 May 1618 – 12 Aug   *Antonio Priuli*
   1623
8 Sep 1623 – 6 Dec   *Francesco Contarini*
   1624
4 Jan 1625 – 23 Dec   *Giovanni Cornaro*
   1629
18 Jan 1630 – 2 Apr   *Niccolo Contarini*
   1631
10 Apr 1631 – 3 Jan   *Francesco Erizzo*
   1646

20 Jan 1646 – 27 Feb 1655	*Francesco Molino*
27 Mar 1655 – 1 May 1656	*Carlo Contarini*
17 May – 5 Jun 1656	*Francesco Cornaro*
15 Jun 1656 – 29 Mar 1658	*Bertuccio Valier*
8 Apr 1658 – 30 Sep 1659	*Giovanni Pesaro*
16 Oct 1659 – 26 Jan 1675	*Domenico Contarini II*
6 Feb 1675 – 14 Aug 1676	*Niccolò Sagredo*
26 Aug 1676 – 15 Jan 1684	*Aloise Contarini II*
26 Jan 1684 – 23 Mar 1688	*Marc Antonio Giustinian*
3 Apr 1688 – 6 Jan 1694	*Francesco Morosini* (b. 1618)
25 Feb 1694 – 5 Jul 1700	*Silvestro Valier*
16 Jul 1700 – 6 May 1709	*Aloise Mocenigo II*
22 May 1709 – 12 Aug 1722	*Giovanni Corner*
24 Aug 1722 – 21 May 1732	*Aloise Mocenigo III (Sebastiano)*
2 Jun 1732 – 5 Jan 1735	*Carol Ruzzini*
17 Jan 1735 – 17 Jun 1741	*Aloise Pisani*
30 Jun 1741 – 7 Mar 1752	*Pietro Grimani*
18 Mar 1752 – 19 May 1762	*Francesco Loredano*
31 May 1762 – 31 Mar 1763	*Marco Foscarini*
19 Apr 1763 – 31 Dec 1778	*Aloise Mocenigo IV*
14 Jan 1779 – 13 (18) Feb 1789	*Paolo Renier*
9 Mar 1789 – 12 May 1797	*Luigi Manin* (d. 23 Oct 1802)

1797 – 1805 and from 1814	Under Austrian rule

Revolutionary Government 1848 – 1849

23 Mar 1848	Proclamation of Venetian Republic
Chief Executive	23 Mar – 3 Jul 1848: *Daniele Manin* (b. Venice 13 Mar 1804; d. Paris 22 Sep 1857) not related to Luigi Manin
and	*Niccolò Tommaseo* (b. Sibenik 9 Oct 1802; d. Florence 1 May 1874)
3 Jul 1848	Union with Piedmont
Prime Minister	—— *Castelli*
10 Aug 1848	Re-establishment of Republic
Chief Executives	*Daniele Manin* and *Niccolò Tommaseo*, later ambassador in Paris
13 Aug 1848	Establishment of a Dictatorship by the following triumvirate:
Civil leader	*Daniele Manin* (see above)
Army	*Giovanni Battista Cavedalis* (b. Spilimbergo 19 Mar 1794; d. 16 Jul 1858)
Navy	—— *Graziani*
15 Feb 1849	Abolition of Dictatorship, establishment of responsible government
President	5 Mar – 22 Aug 1849: *Daniele Manin* (see above)
22 Aug 1849	Venice surrenders to Austria
4 Nov 1866	Venice becomes part of Italy

Viet-Nam (Annam, Tongking and Cochin China)

Until 1945 Empire or Kingdom, usually known as Annam, under French Protection 1883 – 1945.

HEADS OF STATE

Emperors or Kings

1 Jun 1802	Nguyen Anh, King of Annam, having established

	authority over Tongking as well as Cochin China, is recognized as Emperor under the name *Gia Long*
1820	*Minh Mang*, son
Jan 1841	*Thieu Tri*, son
1848 – 1883	*Tu-Duc*, son (b. 1830; d. 17 Jul 1883)
1862	Partial cession of Cochin China to France
1867	Partial cession of Cambodia, hitherto tributary
1883	French protectorate established over Annam and Tongking
27 Jul 1883	*(Nguyen) Duc Duc*, nephew of Tu-Duc
30 Jul 1883	*(Nguyen) Hiep-Hoa*
Nov 1883	*Kien-Phuc*, nephew (b. 1868)
1 Aug 1884	*Ham-Nghi*
Jul 1885 – 31 Jan 1889	*Dong-Khanh*, brother
1887	French Indo-China established, comprising Annam, Tongking, Cochin China and Cambodia (for Governors General see Indo-China)
31 Jan 1889	*Thanh-Thai* (b. (?) 1878; d. Saigon 20 Mar 1954)
5 Mar 1907	*Duy-Tan*
May 1916	*Khai-Dinh*
6 Nov 1925 – 28 Aug 1945	*Bao Dai* (b. Hue 22 Oct 1913) from 1949 to 1955 Head of State of Viet Nam

Wurtemberg

HEADS OF STATE

Dukes

3 Nov 1457	*Eberhard I*, son of Count Ludwig I of Urach (b. 11 Dec 1445) Count; from 21 Dec 1495: Duke
24 Feb 1496	*Eberhard II*, nephew (b. 1 Feb 1447; deposed 1498; d. 17 Feb 1504)
11 Jun 1498	*Ulrich (VI)*, nephew (b. 8 Feb 1487; expelled by the Swabian League 1519, restored 1534)
6 Nov 1559	*Christof*, son (b. 12 May 1515)
26 Dec 1568	*Ludwig (III)*, son (b. 1 Jan 1554)
18 Aug 1593	*Friedrich I*, son of Count Georg of Wurtemberg-Montbéliard (b. 19 Aug 1557)
29 Jan 1608	*Johann Friedrich*, son (b. 5 May 1582)

18 Jul 1628	*Eberhard III*, son (b. 16 Aug 1614
2 Jul 1674	*Wilhelm Ludwig*, son (b. 7 Jan 1647)
23 Jun 1677	*Eberhard Ludwig*, son (b. 18 Sep 1676)
31 Oct 1733	*Karl Alexander*, cousin (b. 24 Jan 1684)
12 Mar 1737	*Karl Eugen*, son (b. 11 Feb 1728)
24 Oct 1793	*Ludwig Eugen*, brother (b. 6 Jan 1731)
20 May 1795	*Friedrich Eugen*, brother (b. 21 Jan 1732)
23 Dec 1797	*Friedrich II*, son (b. 6 Nov 1754) from 25 Feb 1803 Elector; from 1 Jan 1806: *King Friedrich I*

Kings

30 Oct 1816	*Wilhelm I*, son (b. 27 Sep 1781)
25 Jun 1864	*Karl*, son (b. 6 Mar 1823)
6 Oct 1891	*Wilhelm II*, great-grandson of Friedrich I (b. 25 Feb 1848; d. 2 Oct 1921)
Nov 1918	Republic

MEMBERS OF GOVERNMENT

President of the Privy Council

18 Nov 1817	*Hans Otto von der Lühe* (b. Copenhagen 2 May 1761; d. Stuttgart 14 Mar 1836)
29 Jul 1821	*Christian Friedrich von Otto* (b. Dettingen 26 Oct 1758; d. Stuttgart 8 Sep 1836)
15 Nov 1831 – Mar 1848	*Paul Friedrich Theodor Eugen, Baron Maucler* (b. Étupes 30 May 1783; d. Ludwigsburg 28 Jan 1859)

Foreign Affairs and Lord Chamberlain

8 Nov 1816	*Ferdinand Ludwig, Count Zeppelin* (b. Güstrow 28 Nov 1772; d. Vienna 21 Jan 1829)
17 May 1819	*Heinrich Levin, Count Wintzingerode* (b. 10 Oct 1778; d. Schloss Bodenstein 15 Sep 1856)
2 Oct 1823 – 6 Mar 1848	*Joseph, Count Beroldingen* (b. Ellwangen 27 Nov 1780; d. Stuttgart 24 Jan 1868)

Home Affairs and Public Worship

8 Nov 1816 – 3 Nov 1817	*Karl August, Count Wangenhaim* (b. Gotha 14 Mar 1773; d. Coburg 19 Jul 1850) Minister for Ecclesiastical and Scholastic Affairs

8 Nov 1816 – 26 Feb 1817	(acting head of the Department of Home Affairs:) *Karl Eberhard von Wächter-Spittler* (b. Ludwigsburg 17 Mar 1775; d. Stuttgart 12 Apr 1840)
10 Nov 1817	*Christian Friedrich von Otto* (see President of the Privy Council)
29 Jul 1821 – 28 Dec 1830	(acting until 1 Jul 1827:) *Christoph Friedrich von Schmidlin* (b. Stuttgart 25 Aug 1789; d. Stuttgart 28 Dec 1830)
3 Jan 1831	*Sixt Eberhard von Kapff* (b. Göppingen 4 Oct 1774; d. Stuttgart 31 Aug 1851)
3 Apr 1832	*Jakob Friedrich von Weishaar* (b. Horb 3 Mar 1775; d. Köngen 19 Sep 1834)
10 Aug 1832	(acting until 26 Sep 1839:) *Johannes von Schlayer* (b. Tübingen 11 Mar 1792; d. Stuttgart 3 Jan 1860)
6 – 9 Mar 1848	(Home Affairs only) *Joseph Baron Linden* (b. Wetzlar 7 Jun 1804; d. Freiburg i.B. 31 May 1895)

Justice

30 Apr 1809	*Hans Otto von der Lühe* (see President of the Privy Council)
10 – 27 Nov 1817	*Konstantin Franz von Neurath* (b. 28 Jul 1777; d. 27 Nov 1817)
8 Mar 1818	*Paul, Baron Maucler* (see President of the Privy Council)
15 Nov 1831	*Karl Heinrich von Schwab* (b. 20 Mar 1781; d. 23 Jan 1847)
26 Sep 1839 – 6/9 Mar 1848	*Henrich von Prieser* (b. 20 May 1797; d. 28 Jan 1870)

Finance

8 Nov 1816	*Christian Friedrich von Otto* (see President of the Privy Council)
10 Nov 1817 – 5 Nov 1818	*Karl August, Baron Malchus* (b. Mannheim 27 Sep 1770; d. Heidelberg 24 Oct 1840)
5 Sep 1818	(acting until 27 Jul 1821:) *Ferdinand Heinrich August von Weckherlin* (b. Schorndorf 23 Feb 1767; d. Bad Boll 27 Jul 1828)
29 Oct 1827 – 27 Apr 1832	*Karl Friedrich Eberhard, Baron Varnbüler* (b. Stuttgart 12 Aug 1776; d. Stuttgart 27 Apr 1832)
30 Apr – 20 Sep 1832	*Christoph Ludwig von Herzog* (b. Lauffen 12 Nov 1788; d. Stuttgart 20 Sep 1832)

23 Sep 1832 – 5 Aug 1844	(acting until 26 Sep 1839:) *Johann Christoph von Herdegen* (b. Lauffen 20 Mar 1787; d. Stuttgart 16 Mar 1861)
31 Aug 1844 – 6 Mar 1848	*K Christian Gottlob von Gärttner* (b. Bietigheim 14 Sep 1788; d. 18 Jul 1861)

War

9 Nov 1816	*Friedrich, Count Franquemont* (b. Ludwigsburg 5 Mar 1770; d. Stuttgart 2 Jan 1842)
10 Aug 1829	*Ernst Eugen, Baron Hügel* (b. Ludwigsburg 26 Mar 1774; d. Kirchheim 30 Mar 1849)
15 Sep 1842 – 24 Jun 1848	*Johann Georg, Count Sontheim* (b. 26 Apr 1790; d. 14 Dec 1860)

9 Mar 1848 – 28 Oct 1849: von Römer

Prime Minister	*Friedrich von Römer* (b. Erkenbrechtsweiler 4 Jun 1794; d. Stuttgart 11 Mar 1864)
Foreign Affairs	13 May 1848 – 28 Oct 1849: *Karl Ludwig Friedrich von Roser* (b. Vaihingen 20 Mar 1787; d. Stuttgart 27 Dec 1861)
Home Affairs	*Gustav Heinrich von Duvernoy* (b. Stuttgart 9 Jul 1802; d. Stuttgart 24 Dec 1890)
Justice	*Friedrich von Römer* (see above)
Finance	*Adolf von Goppelt* (b. Heilbronn 2 Jan 1800; d. Heilbronn 12 Oct 1875)
Public Worship	9 Mar 1848 – 14 Aug 1848: *Paul Achatius von Pfizer* (b. Stuttgart 12 Sep 1801; d. Tübingen 30 Jul 1867) 14 Aug 1848 – 16 Sep 1849: *Eduard von Schmidlin* (b. Schöntal 15 Apr 1804: d. Stuttgart 25 Jul 1869)
War	9 Mar – 24 Jun 1848: *Johann Georg, Count Sontheim* (see War) 24 Jun 1848 – 28 Oct 1849: *August, Baron Rüpplin* (b. Porto Ferrajo 28 Nov 1797; d. Tarasp 26 Aug 1867)

28 Oct 1849 – 2 Jul 1850: von Schlayer

Prime Minister	*Johannes von Schlayer* (see Home Affairs and Public Worship)
Foreign Affairs	*Karl (Ebherhard) Baron Wächter-Spittler* (b. Stuttgart 26 Apr 1798; d. Stuttgart 21 Sep 1874)
Home Affairs	*Johannes von Schlayer* (see Home Affairs and Public Worship)

663

| War | *Fidel Karl von Baur-Breitenfeld* (b. Rottweil 8 Apr 1805; d. Ludwigsburg 20 Mar 1882) |

2 Jul 1850 – 21 Sep 1864: Linden

Prime Minister	*Joseph, Baron Linden* (see Home Affairs and Public Worship)
Foreign Affairs	6 Jul 1850 – 8 May 1851: *Joseph, Baron Linden* (see Home Affairs and Public Worship)
	8 May 1851 – 14 Jul 1854: *Konstantin (Justus Franz), Baron Neurath* (b. Wetzlar 22 Apr 1807; d. Leinfelden 8 Sep 1876)
	14 Jul 1854 – 29 Oct 1855 (acting:) *Joseph, Baron Linden* (see Home Affairs and Public Worship)
	29 Oct 1855 – 21 Sep 1864: *Karl Eugen, Baron Hügel* (b. 24 May 1805; d. Stuttgart 29 May 1870)
Home Affairs	*Joseph, Baron Linden* (see Home Affairs and Public Worship)
Justice	2 Jul 1850 – 7 Apr 1856: *Wilhelm von Plessen* (b. Engelberg 23 Nov 1808; d. Stuttgart 16 Jul 1887)
	7 Apr 1856 – 4 Oct 1864: *Karl, Baron Wächter-Spittler* (see Schlayer)
Finance	2 Jul 1850 – 21 May 1861: *Christian von Knapp* (b. Hohenheim 4 Feb 1800; d. Stuttgart 21 May 1861)
	5 Jun 1861 – 2 Sep 1864: *Karl Friedrich von Sigel* (b. Schondorf 27 Aug 1808; d. Stuttgart 23 Apr 1872)
Public Worship	23 Sep 1850 – 7 Apr 1856: *Karl, Baron Wächter-Spittler* (see Schlayer)
	9 Apr 1856 – 5 Apr 1861: *Gustav von Rümelin* (b. Ravenburg 26 Mar 1815; d. Tübingen 28 Oct 1889)
	5 Apr 1861 – 21 Sep 1864: *Ludwig von Golther* (b. Ulm 11 Jan 1823; d. Stuttgart 17 Sep 1876)
War	*Moriz von Miller* (b. Stuttgart 10 Mar 1792; d. Stuttgart 8 Oct 1866)

21 Sep 1864 – 31 Aug 1870: Varnbüler

Prime Minister and Foreign Affairs	*Karl Friedrich Gottlob, Baron Varnbüler von und zu Hemmingen* (b. Hemmingen 13 May 1809; d. Berlin 26 Mar 1889)
Home Affairs	21 Sep 1864 – 23 Mar 1870: *Ernst von Gessler* (b. Ellwangen 27 Oct 1818; d. Stuttgart 12 Dec 1884)
	23 Mar – 31 Aug 1870: *Friedrich Karl von Scheurlen* (b. Tübingen 3 Sep 1824; d. Stuttgart 1 Apr 1872)

Justice	4 Oct 1864 – 27 Apr 1867: *Konstantin, Baron Neurath* (see Linden) 27 Apr 1867 – 31 Aug 1870: *Hermann* (from 1887: *Baron*) *von Mittnacht* (b. Stuttgart 17 Mar 1825; d. Friedrichshafen 2 May 1909)
Finance	*Andreas von Renner* (b. Ditzingen 28 Sep 1814; d. 1898)
Public Worship	21 Sep 1864 – 23 Mar 1870: *Ludwig von Golther* (see Linden) 3 May – 31 Aug 1870: *Theodor von Gessler* (b. Ellwangen 16 Aug 1864; d. Urach 27 Jul 1886)
War	21 Sep 1864 – 1 Sep 1865: *Moriz von Miller* (see Linden) 1 Sep 1865 – 5 May 1866: *Karl Friedrich Kuno, Baron Widerhold* (b. Stuttgart 31 Aug 1809; d. Ludwigsburg 14 Dec 1885) 5 May 1866 – 27 Apr 1867: *Oskar von Hardegg* (b. 19 Oct 1815; d. Stuttgart 25 Aug 1877) 27 Apr 1867 – 23 Mar 1870: *Rudolf, Baron Wagner-Frommenhausen* (b. Frommenhausen 19 Dec 1822; d. Stuttgart 9 Feb 1891) 23 Mar – 31 Aug 1870: *Albert von Sückow* (b. Ludwigsburg 13 Dec 1828; d. Baden-Baden 14 Apr 1893)

31 Aug 1870 – 10 Nov 1900: Wächter/Mittnacht

Prime Minister	1871 – 1 Jul 1876: *Johann August, Baron Wächter* (b. The Hague 3 April 1807; d. Lautenbach 3 Aug 1879) 31 Jul 1876 – 10 Nov 1900: *Hermann* (from 1887: *Baron*) *Mittnacht* (see Varnbüler)
Foreign Affairs	31 Aug 1870 – 9 Jan 1871: *Adolf, Count Taube* (b. Stuttgart 9 Jul 1810; d. Kreuth 14 Sep 1899) acting Prime Minister 9 Jan 1871 – 27 Aug 1876: *Johann August, Baron Wächter* (see above) 27 Aug 1873 – 10 Nov 1900: *Hermann, Baron Mittnacht* (see Varnbüler)
Home Affairs	31 Aug 1870 – 1 Apr 1872: *Friedrich Karl von Scheurlen* (see Varnbüler) 4 Apr – 16 May 1872: *Theodor von Gessler* (see Varnbüler) 16 May 1872 – 13 Oct 1881: *Christian Christlieb*

	Heinrich von Sick (b. Stuttgart 9 Mar 1822; d. Stuttgart 13 Oct 1881)
	18 Oct 1881 – 30 Aug 1887: *Julius von Hölder* (b. Stuttgart 24 Mar 1819; d. Stuttgart 30 Aug 1887)
	9 Sep 1887 – 6 Dec 1893: *Karl Joseph von Schmid* (b. Munderkingen 4 Mar 1832; d. Stuttgart 6 Dec 1893)
	14 Dec 1893 – 10 Nov 1900: *Johann von Pischek* (b. Frankfurt a.M. 15 Jan 1843; d. Stuttgart 23 Aug 1916)
Justice	31 Aug 1870 – Dec 1878: *Hermann von Mittnacht* (see Varnbüler)
	Dec 1878 – 16 Sep 1896: *Eduard von Faber* (b. Altenstadt 30 Dec 1822; d. Stuttgart 18 Jan 1907)
	16 Sep 1896 – 10 Nov 1900: *Wilhelm von Breitling* (b. Gaildorf 4 Jan 1835; d. Stuttgart 20 Apr 1914)
Finance	31 Aug 1870 – 13 Oct 1891: *Andreas von Renner* (see Varnbüler)
	13 Oct 1891 – 9 Mar 1898: *Karl Viktor von Riecke* (b. Stuttgart 27 Mar 1830; d. Stuttgart 9 Mar 1898)
	Mar 1898 – 10 Nov 1900: *Karl von Zeyer* (b. Esslingen 19 Sep 1838; d. Stuttgart 1 Apr 1900)
Public Worship	31 Aug 1870 – 28 Feb 1885: *Theodor von Gessler* (see Varnbüler)
	1 Mar 1885 – 1 Apr 1900: *Otto von Sarwey* (b. Tübingen 24 Sep 1825; d. Stuttgart 1 Apr 1900)
	Apr – 10 Nov 1900: *Karl, Baron Weizsäcker* (b. Stuttgart 25 Feb 1853; d. Stuttgart 2 Feb 1926)
War	31 Aug 1870 – 13 Sep 1874: *Albert von Sückow* (see Varnbüler)
	13 Sep 1874 – 22 Jul 1883: *Theodor von Wundt* (b. Stuttgart 14 Jul 1825; d. Schuls 22 Jul 1883)
	Jul 1883 – 10 May 1892: *Gustav von Steinheil* (b. Ludwigsburg 3 Mar 1832; d. Stuttgart 13 Mar 1908)
	10 May 1892 – 10 Nov 1900: *Max, Baron Schott von Schottenstein* (b. Ulm 22 Nov 1836; d. Schloss Schottenstein 10 Aug 1917)

10 Nov 1900 – 4 Dec 1906: Schott/Breitling

Prime Minister	10 Nov 1900 – 15 Apr 1901: *Max, Baron Schott von Schottenstein* (see Wächter/Mittnacht)
	15 Apr 1901 – 4 Dec 1906: *Wilhelm August von Breitling* (see Mittnacht)
Foreign Affairs	10 Nov 1900 – end Jun 1906: *Julius, Baron Soden* (b.

Ludwigsburg 5 Feb 1846; d. Tübingen 2 Feb 1921)
End Jun – 4 Dec 1906: *Karl, Baron Weizsäcker* (see Wächter/Mittnacht)

Home Affairs   *Johann von Pischek* (see Wächter/Mittnacht)

Justice   *Wilhelm von Breitling* (see Wächter/Mittnacht)

Finance   *Karl von Zeyer* (see Wächter/Mittnacht)

Public Worship   10 Dec 1900 – end Jun 1906: *Karl, Baron Weizsäcker* (see Wächter/Mittnacht)
End Jun – 4 Dec 1906: *Karl von Fleischhauer* (b. Stuttgart 5 Sep 1852; d. Stuttgart 17 Jul 1921)

War   10 Nov 1900 – 15 Apr 1901: *Max, Baron Schott von Schottenstein* (see Wächter/Mittnacht)
15 Apr 1901 – 11 Jun 1906: *Albert von Schürlen* (b. Tübingen 6 May 1843; d. Stuttgart 19 Feb 1926)
11 Jun – 4 Dec 1906: *Otto von Marchtaler* (b. Wiblingen 9 Jun 1854; d. Stuttgart 11 Jan 1920)

4 Dec 1906 – 6 Nov 1918: Weizsäcker

Prime Minister and Foreign Affairs   *Karl, Baron Weizsäcker* (see Wächter/Mittnacht)

Home Affairs   4 Dec 1906 – 20 Dec 1912: *Johann von Pischek* (see Wächter/Mittnacht)
21 Dec 1912 – 20 Mar 1918: *Karl von Fleischhauer* (see Schott Breitling)
20 Mar – 6 Nov 1918: *Ludwig von Köhler* (b. Elberfeld 20 Oct 1868; d. Ludwigsburg (?) 26 Sep 1953)

Justice   4 Dec 1906 – 3 Dec 1917; *Friedrich von Schmidlin* (b. Wangen 1 Sep 1847; d. Stuttgart 1 May 1932)
4 Dec 1917 – 6 Nov 1918: *Karl von Mandry* (b. Tübingen 10 Mar 1866; d. Heilbronn 25 Nov 1926)

Finance   4 Dec 1906 – 1908: *Karl von Zeyer* (see Wächter/Mittnacht)
1908 – 15 Apr 1914: *Wilhelm von Gessler* (b. Stuttgart 11 Oct 1852; d. Stuttgart 12 Jan 1924)
15 Apr 1914 – 6 Nov 1918: *Theodor von Pistorius* (b. Tübingen 12 Nov 1861; d. Stuttgart 31 Jan 1939)

Public Worship   4 Dec 1906 – 20 Dec 1912: *Karl von Fleischhauer* (see Schott/Breitling)
21 Dec 1912 – 21 Mar 1918: *Hermann von Habermaas* (b. Stuttgart 5 Mar 1856; d. Stuttgart 1 Apr 1938)
21 Mar – 6 Nov 1918: *Karl von Fleischhauer* (see Schott/Breitling)

War   *Otto von Marchtaler* (see Schott/ Breitling)

6 – 9 Nov 1918: Liesching

Prime Minister and   *Theodor Liesching* (b. Stuttgart 14 Jul 1865; d.
   Foreign Affairs   Boblingen 25 Jul 1922)
Home Affairs   *Ludwig von Köhler* (see Weizsäcker)
Justice   *Theodor Liesching* (see above)
Finance   *Theodor von Pistorius* (see Weizsäcker)
Public Worship   *Johannes von Hieber* (b. Waldhausen 25 Jun 1862; d.
                              Uhingen 7 Nov 1951)
War   Post not filled
Labour   *Karl Hugo Lindemann* (b. Jaguerão, Brazil, 9 Aug
                              1867; d. after 1947)
Transport   *Johann Baptist von Kiene* (b. Langenargen 22 Jan
                              1852; d. Wangen 24 Sep 1919)

Yemen

HEADS OF STATE

Imams of Sana

about 1592   *al-Qasim al-Mansur ibn Muhammad ibn Ali*, descen-
                  dant of Yusuf al-Mansur al-Dai, 10th-century Zaydi
                  Imam (b. 1560-61)
19 Feb 1620   *al-Muayyad Muhammad*, son
29 Sep 1644   *al-Mutawakkil Ismail*, brother (b. 1610/11)
14 Aug 1676   *al-Mahdi Ahmad ibn al-Hasan*, nephew (b. 1633/34)
29 Jun 1681   *al-Hadi Muhammad*, son of Ismail
27 Apr 1686   *al-Mahdi Muhammad*, son of Ahmad
1716   *Al-Mutawakkil al-Qasim ibn al-Husain*, grandson of
                  Ahmad
1726/27   *al-Mansur al-Husain* (for 1st time) son
1726/27   *al-Hadi al-Majid Muhammad*, grandson of al-Husain
                  (?)
1727/28   *al-Mansur al-Husain* (for 2nd time)
1747   *al-Mahdi al-Abbas*, grandson of al-Qasim (?)
1776   *al-Mansur Ali*

1806/07	*al-Mahdi Ahmad*, son of al-Husain (?)
(?)	*al-Mansur Ali* (?)
1841	*al-Mahdi al-Qasim*
1845	*Muhammad Yahya*, deposed and executed
1872	under direct Turkish rule
1890/91	*Yahya Hamid ad-Din*
1904 – 17 Feb 1948	*Yahya Muhammad ibn Muhammad*, grandson (from 1918: *King*)

Yugoslavia

1 Dec 1918	Kingdom of the Serbs, Croats and Slovenes
From 3 Oct 1929	Kingdom of Yugoslavia

HEADS OF STATE

Kings

1 Dec 1918	*Peter I* (Karageorgević) (b. 11 Jul 1844) from 15 Jun 1903: *King of Serbia*
16 Aug 1921 – 9 Oct 1934	*Alexander II*, son (b. 16 Dec 1888; d. Marseilles 9 Oct 1934)

MEMBERS OF GOVERNMENT

Prime Ministers

30 Nov 1918	*Nikola Pašić* (for 1st time; for 9th time for Serbia) (b. 1 Jan 1846; d. 10 Dec 1926)
20 Dec 1918	*Stojan Protić* (for 1st time) (b. Kruševac 28 Jan 1857; d. Belgrade 28 Oct 1923)
19 Aug 1919	*Ljubomir Davidović* (for 1st time) (b. Vlaško Polje, 1863; d. Belgrade 1940)
18 Feb 1920	*Stojan Protić* (for 2nd time)
17 May 1920	*Milenko Vesnić* (b. Dunišić 25 Feb 1862; d. Paris 15 May 1921)
1 Jan 1921	*Nikola Pašić* (for 2nd time)

24 Dec 1921 – 4 Dec 1922	*Nikola Pašić* (for 3rd time)
16 Dec 1922	*Nikola Pašić* (for 4th time)
1 May 1923	*Nikola Pašić* (for 5th time)
27 Mar 1924	*Nikola Pašić* (for 6th time)
21 May 1924	*Nikola Pašić* (for 7th time)
27 Jul – 15 Oct 1924	*Ljubomir Davidović* (for 2nd time)
6 Nov 1924	*Nikola Pašić* (for 8th time)
29 Apr 1925 – 5 Apr 1926	*Nikola Pašić* (for 9th time)
8 Apr 1926	*Nikola Uzunović* (for 1st time) (b. Nish 1873; d. Belgrade (?) 20 Sep 1954)
29 Apr – 15 May 1926	*Nikola Uzunović* (for 2nd time)
17 May – 13 Oct 1926	*Nikola Uzunović* (for 3rd time)
13 Oct – 7 Dec 1926	*Nikola Uzunović* (for 4th time)
25 Dec 1926	*Nikola Uzunović* (for 5th time)
30 Jan 1927	*Nikola Uzunović* (for 6th time)
16 Apr 1927 – 8 Feb 1928	*Velja Vukićević* (for 1st time) (b. 23 Jul 1871; d. 27 Nov 1930)
23 Feb – 4 Jul 1928	*Velja Vukićević* (for 2nd time)

Foreign Ministers

29 Dec 1918 – 23 Nov 1920	*Ante Trumbić* (b. Split 17 May 1864; d. Zagreb 17 Nov 1938)
23 Nov – 14 Dec 1920	*Milenko Vesnić* (see Prime Ministers)
30 Dec 1920 – 24 Dec 1921	*Nikola Pašić* (see Prime Ministers)
5 Jan 1922 – Jul 1924	*Momčilo Ninčić* (for 1st time) (b. Jagodina 10 Jun 1876; d. Lausanne 21 Dec 1949)
28 Jul – 15 Oct 1924	*Vojislav Marinković* (for 1st time) (b. Belgrade 13 May 1876; d. 18 Sep 1935)
6 Nov 1924 – 6 Dec 1926	*Momčilo Ninčić* (for 2nd time)
24 Dec 1926 – 16 Apr 1927	*Ninko Perić* (b. 1886)
17 Apr 1927 – 29 Jun 1932	*Vojislav Marinković* (for 2nd time)

Zanzibar

1503	Conquered by Portugal
1652	Under the suzerainty of the imams, later saiyids, of Oman (q.v.)

HEADS OF STATE

Sultans

1856	*Majid bin Said*, son of Said bin Sultan, saiyid of Oman and Zanzibar, *de facto;* confirmed as sultan Apr 1861
7 Oct 1870	*Barghash bin Said*, brother (b. 1837)
27 Mar 1888	*Khalifa bin Barghash*, son (b. 1854)
13 Feb 1890*	*Ali bin Said*, uncle
15 Mar 1893	*Hamid bin Thuwaini*, nephew (b. 1857)
27 Aug 1896	*Hammud bin Mohammed*, nephew of Khalifa bin Barghash
18 Aug 1902	*Ali bin Hammud*, son (b. 7 Jun 1884)
9 Dec 1911 – 9 Oct 1960	*Khalifa bin Kharrub*, nephew of Hamid bin Thuwaini (b. 26 Aug 1879)

*From 1890 until 1963, Zanzibar was a British protectorate.

Index

Majnoni d'Intignano, L. 328, 329
Majorana, A. 328 [2]
Makar, V. P., *see* Nogin, V. P.
Makarov, A. A. 549, 550, 551
Maklakov, N. A. 549 [2]
Makov, L. A. 540
Makowski, W. 414, 420
Malakoff, A. J. J. Pélissier, Duc de 5
[2]
Malan, C. W. M. 487, 488
Malan, D. F. 486, 487 [4], 488
Malan, F. S. 483 [2], 484, 485 [2], 486
[2]
Malcampo y Monge, J., *see* San Rafael,
Marquis of
Malchus, K. A., Baron 662
Malcolm, J. 125
Malesherbes, C. G. de L. de 166
Malinov, A. 95 [2]
Mallarino, M.M. 133
Malmesbury, J. H. Harris, 3rd Earl
of 594, 597, 600, 603
Malou, J. 77, 79, 80 [4], 81
Maltzahn, H., Baron 247
Maltzan, M., Count 434
Malvy, L. 219, 220 [2], 221, 222 [2], 229
Malyantovich, —— 554
Malypetr, J. 142
Mamia Guriel 239 [3]
Mamiani della Rovere, T. 403 [2]
Manasein, N. A. 542
Manceron, F. 516
Mancini, P. S. 315, 319 [2], 321 [3]
Mandry, K. von 667
Manikovski, A. A. 552
Manin, D. 659 [4]
Manin, L. 658
Manion, R. J. 119, 123 [4]
Maniu, I. 455
Mann, E. (K. A. K.) von 248
Mannerheim, K. G. E., Baron 158
Manners, C., *see* Rutland, 4th Duke of
Manners, J. J., Lord (7th Duke of
Rutland) 595, 598, 601, 603, 605, 608
Manning, D. 645
Mansfeld, J. G. von, *see* Johann
Gebhard I

Mansfeld-Heldrungen, P. E.,
Count 364
Mansfield, W. Murray, 1st Earl of 569,
573
Mansfield, D. Murray, 2nd Earl of
(Viscount Stormont) 573, 576, 577,
578
Mansolas, D. 266 [2]
al-Mansur ibn Muhammad ibn Ali, al-
Qasim 668
Mantere, O. 159
Manteuffel, K. (O.), Baron 443
Manteuffel, O. T., Baron 432, 435, 436,
443
Mantha Thourath 342
Manu, G. 454
Manu, S. 455
Manuel II 424
Manuilov, A. A. 552 [2]
Manz, G. W. von 70
Mar, J. Erskine, 1st Earl of 473
Marcellus II 400
Marcère, É. L. G. D. de 198, 200 [3]
Marchet, G. 40
Marchtaler, O. von 667, 668
Marcy, W. L. 637, 639
Mardefeld, A. von 431
Marees von Swinderen, R. de 383
Marek, K. 43 [2], 44
Maret, H. B., *see* Bassano, Duc de
Marex Oyens, J. C. de 382
Margaret 363
Margaret of Parma 363
Marghiloman, A. 455, 457
Mari, D. M. 235
Mari, G. 235
Mari, L. 236
Mari, S. 235
Maria I 423
Maria II 423 [2]
Maria Christina (Spain,
1832–1840) 489
Maria Christina (Spain,
1885–1902) 490
Maria Luisa, Duchess of Parma 348
Maria Theresa 18, 89, 282, 406
Mariani, L. 403

Wilhelm II (Hesse-Cassel,
1821-1847) 278
Wilhelm II (Wurtemberg) 661
Wilhelm IV (Bavaria) 65
Wilhelm IV (Hesse-Cassel) 278
Wilhelm V (Bavaria) 65
Wilhelm V (Hesse-Cassel) 278
Wilhelm VI 278
Wilhelm VII 278
Wilhelm VIII 278
Wilhelm IX 278, see also Wilhelm I,
Elector
Wilhelm Ludwig 661
Wilhelmina 363
Wilkins, W. 636
William 274, see also William IV
(United Kingdom)
William I (Frederick Henry), Prince of
Wied 2
William I (Germany, Prussia) 242,
430
William I (Luxembourg; Netherlands,
1815-1840) 348, 363
William I (Netherlands, 1572-1585)
362
William II (Germany, Prussia) 242,
430
William II (Luxembourg; Netherlands,
1840-1848) 348, 363
William II (Netherlands, 1647-1650)
362
William III (Luxembourg; Netherlands,
1849-1890) 348, 363
William III (Netherlands, 1672-1702;
Scotland, United Kingdom) 362,
474, 558
William IV (Luxembourg) 348
William IV (Netherlands) 362 [2]
William IV, Count van den Bergh
362_
William IV (United Kingdom) 558,
see also William
William V 362
William of Austria, Archduke 23, 24
William Frederick, Prince of Nassau-
Diez 362
William Louis of Nassau-Diez 362

William (Nicholas) of Wurtemberg,
Duke 91
William the Younger 273
Williams, G. H. 643
Williman, G. 655
Willingdon, F. Freeman-Thomas, 1st
Viscount (1st Earl of Willingdon and
1st Marquis Willingdon) 100
Wilmington, S. Compton, 1st Earl
of 565 [2], 566
Wilmot, R. D. 107
Wilsdorf, V. von 472 [2]
Wilson, H. 642
Wilson, J. 649, 650
Wilson, J. R. 120
Wilson, T. W. 629, 650
Wilson, W. B. 651
Wilson, W. L. 647
Wimmer, F., Baron 46 [2]
Winchilsea, D. Finch, 7th Earl of (2nd
Earl of Nottingham) 561
Winchilsea, D. Finch, 8th Earl of (3rd
Earl of Nottingham) 566, 567 [2],
569, 572
Windebank, Sir F. 563
Windham, W. 578, 580
Windisch-Grätz, A. (A.), Prince 35
Windisch-Grätz, A. C. F., Prince
of 20
Windischgrätz, L., Prince 296, 297
Windom, W. H. 644, 646
Windsor, R. G. Windsor-Clive, 14th
Baron (1st Earl of Plymouth) 613
Windsor-Clive, R. G., see Windsor,
14th Baron
Wingate, Sir (F.) R. 153
Winter, G. L. 59 [2]
Winter, L. 138, 139, 140, 142, 143 [2]
Wintgens, W. 374
Wintzingerode, H. L., Count 661
Winzor, A. (Baron Winsor) 92
Wirschinger, —— von 67, 68
Wirt, W. 633, 634
Wirth, J. (K.) 252 [2], 253 [5], 260
Wissell, R. 249, 250, 251, 259
Witos, W. 417, 419, 420
Witt, A. de 365